ECONOMICS

N. GREGORY MANKIW
AND MARK P. TAYLOR

D1341103

FOURTH EDITION

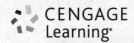
CENGAGE
Learning®

Economics, 4th Edition
N. Gregory Mankiw and Mark P. Taylor

Publisher: Annabel Ainscow
Commissioning Editor: Abbie Coppin
Content Project Manager: Sue Povey
Manufacturing Manager: Eyvett Davis
Marketing Manager: Vicky Pavlicic
Typesetter: diacriTech
Cover design: Simon Levy Associates

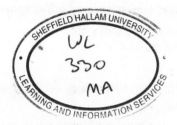

While the publisher has taken all reasonable care in the preparation of this book, the publisher makes no representation, express or implied, with regard to the accuracy of the information contained in this book and cannot accept any legal responsibility or liability for any errors or omissions from the book or the consequences thereof.

Products and services that are referred to in this book may be either trademarks and/or registered trademarks of their respective owners. The publishers and author/s make no claim to these trademarks. The publisher does not endorse, and accepts no responsibility or liability for, incorrect or defamatory content contained in hyperlinked material.

All the URLs in this book are correct at the time of going to press; however the Publisher accepts no responsibility for the content and continued availability of third party websites.

For product information and technology assistance,
contact **emea.info@cengage.com**

For permission to use material from this text or product,
and for permission queries,
email **emea.permissions@cengage.com**

British Library Cataloguing-in-Publication Data
A catalogue record for this book is available from the British Library.

ISBN: 978-1-4737-2533-1

Cengage Learning EMEA
Cheriton House, North Way, Andover, Hampshire SP10 5BE
United Kingdom

Cengage Learning products are represented in Canada by Nelson Education Ltd.

For your lifelong learning solutions, visit
www.cengage.co.uk

Purchase your next print book, e-book or e-chapter at
www.cengagebrain.com

Printed in China by RR Donnelley
Print Number 01 Print Year 2017

BRIEF CONTENTS

CONTENTS

PART 8
INEQUALITY 357

PART 9
TRADE 379

MACROECONOMICS
PROLOGUE 409

PART 10
THE DATA OF
MACROECONOMICS 415

PART 11
THE REAL ECONOMY IN
THE LONG RUN 451

ABOUT THE AUTHORS

AUTHORS

N. GREGORY MANKIW is the Robert M. Beren Professor of Economics at Harvard University. As a student, he studied economics at Princeton University and the Massachusetts Institute of Technology. As a teacher he has taught macroeconomics, microeconomics, statistics and principles of economics. Professor Mankiw is a prolific writer and a regular participant in academic and policy debates. In addition to his teaching, research and writing, Professor Mankiw has been a research associate of the National Bureau of Economic Research, and an advisor to the Federal Reserve Banks of Boston and New York and the Congressional Budget Office. From 2003 to 2005, he served as chairman of the US President's Council of Economic Advisors and was an advisor to Presidential candidate Mitt Romney during the 2012 US presidential election.

MARK P. TAYLOR is Dean of John M Olin Business School at Washington University, US, and was previously Dean of Warwick Business School at the University of Warwick, UK. He obtained his first degree in philosophy, politics and economics from Oxford University and his Master's degree in economics from London University, from where he also holds a doctorate in economics and international finance. Professor Taylor has taught economics and finance at various universities (including Oxford, Warwick and New York) and at various levels (including principles courses, advanced undergraduate and advanced postgraduate courses). He has also worked as a senior economist at the International Monetary Fund and at the Bank of England and, before becoming Dean of Warwick Business School, was a managing director at BlackRock, the world's largest financial asset manager, where he worked on international asset allocation based on macroeconomic analysis. His research has been extensively published in scholarly journals and he is today one of the most highly cited economists in the world. He has also been a member of the Academic Advisory Group of the Bank of England Fair and Effective Markets Review.

CONTRIBUTING AUTHOR

ANDREW ASHWIN has over 20 years' experience as a teacher of economics. He has an MBA from the University of Hull and a PhD in assessment and the notion of threshold concepts in economics from the University of Leicester. Andrew is an experienced author, writing a number of texts for students at different levels, and journal publications related to his PhD research. Andrew was Chair of Examiners for a major awarding body for business and economics in England and is a subject specialist consultant in Economics for the UK regulator, Ofqual. Andrew has a keen interest in assessment and learning in economics and has received accreditation as a Chartered Assessor with the Chartered Institute of Educational Assessors. He has also edited the journal of the Economics, Business and Enterprise Association.

PREFACE

This fourth edition of *Economics* reflects the way in which the discipline is evolving. Economics has and is undergoing a degree of soul-searching after heavy criticism following the Financial Crisis. Academics across the UK and Europe are engaged in a lively debate about the future direction of the subject both in the way it is taught at undergraduate level and how research into developing new knowledge should be conducted. This new edition seeks to reflect some of this debate whilst retaining a familiar look and structure. Readers should note that this edition adapts Greg Mankiw's best-selling US undergraduate *Economics* text to reflect the needs of students and instructors in the UK and European market. As each new edition is written, the adaptation evolves and develops an identity distinct from the original US edition on which it is based. Comments and feedback on this edition should be addressed to the editorial team at Cengage EMEA for passing on to the authors via EMEAMankiw@cengage.com

We have aimed to retain the lively, engaging writing style and to continue to have the novice economics student in mind. The use of examples and the Case Studies and In the News articles help to provide some context to the theory and discussion throughout the text. A complementary book, *Maths for Mankiw & Taylor Economics* has been produced alongside and seeks to develop further some of the mathematical elements of the text. MindTap provides a wealth of resources and support for the teaching and learning of Economics at undergraduate level and includes assignable assessment tasks, videos, case studies and more, to provide everything needed for undergraduate study in one place. Welcome to the wonderful world of economics – learn to think like an economist and a whole new world will open up to you.

ACKNOWLEDGEMENTS

Michael Barrow, *University of Sussex, UK*

Brian Bell, *London School of Economics, UK*

Keith Bender, *The University of Aberdeen, UK*

Thomas Braeuninger, *University of Mannheim, Germany*

Klaas De Brucker, *Vlekho Business School, Belgium*

Eleanor Denny, *Trinity College Dublin, Ireland*

Anna Maria Fiori, *IESEG School of Management, France*

Darragh Flannery, *University of Limerick, Ireland*

Gaia Garino, *University of Leicester, UK*

Chris Grammenos, *American College of Thessaloniki, Greece*

Getinet Haile, *University of Nottingham, UK*

Luc Hens, *Vrije University, Belgium*

Giancarlo Ianulardo, *University of Exeter, UK*

William Jackson, *University of York, UK*

Colin Jennings, *King's College London, UK*

Sarah Louise Jewell, *University of Reading, UK*

Arie Kroon, *Utrecht Hogeschool, The Netherlands*

Jassodra Maharaj, *University of East London, UK*

Paul Melessen, *Hogeschool van Amsterdam, The Netherlands*

Jørn Rattsø, *Norwegian University of Science & Technology, Norway*

Frédéric Robert-Nicoud, *University of Geneva, Switzerland*

Jack Rogers, *University of Exeter, UK*

Erich Ruppert, *Hochschule Aschaffenburg, Germany*

Noel Russell, *University of Manchester, UK*

Munacinga Simatele, *University of Hertfordshire, UK*

Robert Simmons, *University of Lancaster, UK*

Alison Sinclair, *University of Nottingham, UK*

Reto Schleiniger, *Zürich University of Applied Sciences, Switzerland*

The publisher also wishes to thank Neil Reaich and Brian Henry (INSEAD, France) for their contributions to the online resources.

PART 1
INTRODUCTION TO ECONOMICS

1 WHAT IS ECONOMICS?

THE ECONOMY AND ECONOMIC SYSTEMS

Every day billions of people around the world make decisions. They make decisions about providing for the fundamentals in life such as food, clothing and shelter and how they use non-work time for leisure and domestic tasks. Making these decisions involves interaction with other people and with governments and business organizations. At any time individuals could be mothers, fathers, sons, daughters, carers, employers, employees, houseworkers, producers, consumers, savers, taxpayers or benefit recipients. Many, but not all, of these interactions are related to some sort of exchange normally with the use of a medium of exchange such as money and sometimes a direct exchange of services. Individuals purchase final goods and services for final consumption and also provide the inputs into production – land labour and capital. We refer to these individuals collectively as households. The organizations which buy these factors and use them to produce goods and services are referred to collectively as firms.

The amount of interaction between households and firms – the amount of buying and selling which takes place – represents the level of **economic activity**. The more buying and selling there is the higher the level of economic activity. Households and firms in a particular geographic region are together referred to as the **economy**.

Economics studies the interactions between households and firms in relation to an exchange. It also covers situations where some output is produced but not in relation to the receipt of an income, such as the work done by unpaid carers and housewives and househusbands. It explores how people make a living; how resources are allocated amongst the many different uses they could be put to; and the way in which our activities influence not only our own well-being but that of others and the environment.

> **economic activity** how much buying and selling goes on in the economy over a period of time
> **economy** all the production and exchange activities that take place

1

The Economic Problem

There are three questions that any economy has to face:

- What goods and services should be produced?
- How should these goods and services be produced?
- Who should get the goods and services that have been produced?

To satisfy these questions, economies have resources at their disposal which are classified as land, labour and capital.

- **Land** – all the natural resources of the earth. This includes mineral deposits such as iron ore, coal, gold and copper; oil and gas; fish in the sea; and all the food and raw materials produced from the land.
- **Labour** – the human effort both mental and physical that goes into production. A worker in a factory producing precision tools, an investment banker, an unpaid carer, a road sweeper, a teacher – these are all forms of labour.
- **Capital** – the equipment and structures used to produce goods and services. Capital goods include machinery in factories, buildings, tractors, computers, cooking ovens – anything where the good is not used for its own sake but for the contribution it makes to production.

> **land** all the natural resources of the earth
> **labour** the human effort both mental and physical that goes in to production
> **capital** the equipment and structures used to produce goods and services

Scarcity and Choice

It is often assumed that these resources are ultimately scarce in relation to the demand for them. As members of households, we invariably do not have the ability to meet all our wants and needs. Our needs are the necessities of life which enable us to survive – food and water, clothing, shelter and proper health care – and our wants are the things which we believe make for a more comfortable and enjoyable life – holidays, different styles of clothes, smartphones, leisure activities, the furniture and items we have in our houses and so on. Our demand for these wants and needs is generally greater than our ability to satisfy them. **Scarcity** means that society has limited resources and therefore cannot produce all the goods and services people wish to have. Just as a household cannot give every member everything he or she wants, a society cannot give every individual the highest standard of living to which he or she might aspire. Because of the tension between our wants and needs and scarcity, decisions have to be made by households and firms about how to allocate our incomes and resources to meet our wants and needs.

> **scarcity** the limited nature of society's resources

Economics investigates the issues arising as a result of the decisions that households and firms make as a result of this tension. A typical textbook definition of **economics** is that it is the study of how society makes choices in managing its scarce resources and the consequences of this decision-making. This definition can, however, mask the complexity and extent of reach of economics. We might characterize households as having unlimited wants but not everyone in society is materialistic which the idea of unlimited wants can imply. Some people are more content with the simple things in life and their choices are based on what they see as being important. These choices are no less valid or important but a different reflection of the complexity of the subject. Some people choose to maintain their standard of living through crime. A decision to resort to crime has reasons and consequences and these may be of as much interest to an economist as the reasons why firms choose to advertise their products or why central banks make decisions on monetary policy.

> **economics** the study of how society manages its scarce resources

Some might point out that the very idea of scarcity should be questioned in some instances. In Greece, Spain and some other European countries, there are millions of people who want to work but who cannot find a job. It could be argued that labour is not scarce in this situation but job vacancies certainly are and economists will be interested in how such a situation arises and what might be done to alleviate the issues that arise as a result of high levels of unemployment.

The study of economics, therefore, has many facets but there are some central ideas which help define the field even though economics draws on related disciplines such as psychology, sociology, law, anthropology, geography, statistics and maths, amongst others. These central ideas provide themes around which this book is based and which form the basis of many first-year undergraduate degree courses.

HOW PEOPLE MAKE DECISIONS

Because the behaviour of an economy reflects the behaviour of the individuals who make up the economy, we can explore issues that arise when individuals are making decisions.

People Face Trade-offs

Households and firms are faced with making choices and in doing so have to consider the benefits gained from choosing one course of action. To get one thing that we like, we usually have to give up another thing that we might also like. Making decisions requires trading off the benefits of one action against those of another.

Consider an economics undergraduate student who must decide how to allocate their time. They can spend all of their time studying which will bring benefits such as a better class of degree; they can spend all their time enjoying leisure activities which yield different benefits; or they can divide their time between the two. For every hour they study, they give up the benefits of an hour they could have devoted to spending time in the gym, riding a bicycle, watching TV, sleeping or working at a part-time job for some extra spending money.

A firm might be faced with the decision on whether to invest in a new product or a new accounting system. Both bring benefits – the new product might result in improved revenues and profits in the future and the accounting system may make it more effective in controlling its costs and thus helping its profits. If scarce investment funds are put into the accounting system, the firm has to trade-off the benefits that the new product investment would have brought.

When people are grouped into societies, they face different kinds of trade-offs which can highlight the interaction of individuals and firms within society in general. An example is the trade-off between a clean environment and a high level of income. Laws that require firms to reduce pollution raise the cost of producing goods and services. Because of the higher costs, these firms can end up earning smaller profits, paying lower wages, charging higher prices, or some combination of these three. Thus, while pollution regulations give us the benefit of a cleaner environment and the improved levels of health that come with it, they can have the cost of reducing the incomes of the firms' owners, workers and customers.

An important principle in economics is efficiency, which deals with ways in which society gets the most it can (depending how this is defined) from its scarce resources. An outcome can be identified as being efficient by some measure, but not necessarily desirable. It is argued by some economists that there is a trade-off between efficiency and equity. **Equity** looks at the extent to which the benefits of outcomes are distributed fairly among society's members. In other words, efficiency refers to the size of the economic cake, and equity refers to how the cake is divided. Often, when government policies are being designed, these two goals conflict. Because equity is about 'fairness' it inevitably involves value judgements and differences in opinion lead to disagreements amongst policymakers and economists. Indeed, there are some economists who dismiss the idea of a trade-off between equity and efficiency as a myth in some contexts and point to the origin of the idea having been generalized to all situations. The historical context and origins of many economic ideas is important to understand. The origins of the equity and efficiency trade-off come from Arthur Okun in the 1970s. There are some economists who argue that improving equality can lead to improvements in efficiency – in effect that it is possible to have a bigger cake and to eat it.

equity the property of distributing economic prosperity fairly among the members of society

Policies aimed at achieving a more equal distribution of economic well-being, such as the social security system, involve a trade-off between the effects of a benefits system versus the effects on the efficiency of the tax system that pays for it. A government decision to raise the top rate of income tax on what it considers 'the very rich' but to abolish income tax for those earning the minimum wage is effectively a redistribution of income from the rich to the poor. It provides incentive effects for some in society to seek work but may reduce the reward for working hard and mean some in society choose to work less or even move to another country where the tax system is less onerous. Whether the trade-off is a 'good' thing is dependent on the philosophy, belief sets and opinions of the decision makers. Recognizing that people face trade-offs does not by itself tell us what decisions they will or should make. Acknowledging and understanding the consequences of trade-offs is important because people are likely to make more informed decisions if they understand the options that they have available.

> **SELF TEST** You will often hear the adage 'there is no such thing as a free lunch'. Does this simply refer to the fact that someone has to have paid for the lunch to be provided and served? Or does the recipient of the 'free lunch' also incur a cost?

Opportunity Cost

Because people face trade-offs, making decisions requires comparing the costs and benefits of alternative courses of action. In many cases, however, the costs of an action are not as obvious as might first appear.

Consider, for example, the decision whether to go to university. The benefits are intellectual enrichment and a lifetime of better job opportunities. In considering the costs, you might be tempted to add up the money you spend on tuition fees, books, and room and board over the period of the degree. This approach is intuitive and might be a way in which non-economists would approach the decision. An economist would point out that even if you decided to leave full-time education, you would still need a place to sleep and food to eat and so these costs would be incurred in any event. Room and board become a cost of higher education only if they were more expensive at university than elsewhere. It is possible that the cost of room and board at university is less than those you would pay living on your own. In this case, the savings on room and board are actually a benefit of going to university.

The second problem with this calculation of costs is that it ignores the largest cost of a university education – your time. For most students, the wages given up to attend university are the largest single cost of their higher education. When making decisions it is not always helpful to measure the cost in money terms but in terms of what other options have had to be sacrificed. **Opportunity cost** is the measure of the options sacrificed in making a decision. The opportunity cost of going to university is the wages from full-time work that you have had to sacrifice.

 opportunity cost whatever must be given up to obtain some item; the value of the benefits foregone (sacrificed)

Thinking at the Margin

Decisions in life are rarely straightforward and usually involve weighing up costs and benefits. Having a framework or principle on which to base decision-making can help if we want to maximize or minimize costs and benefits. Thinking at the margin is one such framework that economists adopt in thinking about decision-making. **Marginal changes** describe small incremental adjustments to an existing plan of action. Marginal analysis is based around an assumption that **economic agents** (an individual, firm or organization that has an impact in some way on an economy) are seeking to maximize or minimize outcomes when making decisions. Consumers may be assumed to seek to maximize the satisfaction they gain from their incomes, and firms to maximize profits and minimize costs. Maximizing and minimizing behaviour is based on a further assumption that economic agents behave rationally. Thinking at the margin means that decision makers choose a course of action such that the marginal cost is equal to the marginal benefit. If a decision results in greater marginal benefits than marginal costs it is worth making that decision and continuing up to the point where the marginal cost of the decision is equal to the marginal benefit.

> **marginal changes** small incremental adjustments to a plan of action
> **economic agents** an individual, firm or organization that has an impact in some way on an economy

The assumption of rational behaviour provides a framework around which decisions can be analyzed and has been a basic tenet of economics since the 1870s with thinkers such as William Stanley Jevons and Carl Menger building on work by David Ricardo and Jeremy Bentham, which became part of the so-called 'marginalist school'. The assumptions of rational economic behaviour have a number of implications which have been subject to criticism. In studying economic models which rely on the assumption of rational behaviour it is important to remember that if these assumptions are relaxed, outcomes might be very different. We will cover a number of economic models which are based on this assumption because it provides a view into the way in which economic analysis has developed historically and how it is subject to evolution and change but also because it provides a way of thinking about issues which can be contrasted with other ways of thinking when different assumptions are held.

People Respond to Incentives

If we assume the principle of rational behaviour and that people make decisions by comparing costs and benefits, it is logical to assume that their behaviour may change when the costs or benefits change. That is, people respond to incentives. The threat of a fine and the removal of a driving license is designed to regulate the way in which people drive and park their cars: putting a price on the provision of plastic bags in supermarkets aims to encourage people to re-use bags and reduce the total number used.

There has been an increase in the amount of research conducted on incentives because the intentions of policymakers do not always lead to the outcomes expected or desired. A fine imposed on parents who are late picking up their children from day-care centres might be expected to reduce the number of late pickups but one study in Israel showed that far from reducing the number of late pickups, parents were willing to pay the fine and the number arriving late actually increased. Such consequences are referred to as 'unintended consequences'.

> **SELF TEST** Many people across the EU are without work and claiming benefits. Governments throughout the EU are trying to cut spending but find themselves having to spend more on welfare benefits for the unemployed. What sort of incentives might governments put in place to encourage workers off welfare and into work? What might be the unintended consequences of the incentives you identify?

HOW PEOPLE INTERACT

Decision-making not only affects ourselves but other economic agents as well. We will now explore some issues which arise when economic agents interact with others.

Trade Can Make Everyone Better Off

America and China are competitors to Europe in the world economy because American and Chinese firms produce many of the same goods as European firms. It might be thought that if China increases its share of world trade at the expense of Europe this might be bad news for people in Europe. This might not be the case, however.

Trade between Europe and the United States and China is not like a sports contest, where one side wins and the other side loses (a zero-sum game). In some circumstances trade between economies can make all better off. Households, firms and countries have different resource endowments; individuals have talents and skills that allow them to produce some things more efficiently than others; some firms have experience and expertize in production of goods and services; and some countries, like Spain, are blessed by plenty of sunshine which allow their farmers to grow high quality soft fruit. Trade allows individuals, firms and countries to specialize in the activities they do best. With the income that they receive from specializing they can trade with others who are also specializing and can improve their standard of living as a result.

However, whilst trade can provide benefits and winners, there are also likely to be costs and losers. The economic development of some countries in the last 50 years has meant that many people have access to cheap, good quality goods and services as a result of the export of these goods and services. For workers and employers in these industries in developed economies, the competition from these developing countries might mean that they find themselves without work or have to close their businesses. In some situations it is difficult for these people to find alternative work and whole communities can be greatly affected by the changes being experienced. These people may not agree that 'trade can benefit everyone'.

Markets Can be a Good Way to Organize Economic Activity

The economic problem highlights three questions that any society has to answer. What goods and services should be produced, how are they to be produced and who will get what is produced is determined by the economic system. An **economic system** is the way in which resources are organized and allocated to provide for the needs of an economy's citizens. In many countries of the world, a capitalist economic system, based on markets, is the primary way in which the three questions are addressed. A **capitalist economic system** incorporates the principles of the private ownership of factors of production to produce goods and services which are exchanged through a price mechanism and where production is operated primarily for profit. Capitalist economic systems have proved capable of raising the standard of living of millions of people over the last two hundred years. We can measure the standard of living in terms of the income that people earn which allows them to purchase the goods and services they need to survive and enjoy life. Whilst capitalist systems have increased living standards for many it is not the case that everyone in society benefits equally. Capitalism has meant that some people and countries become very rich but others remain poor. The existence of the profit motive provides an incentive for entrepreneurs to take risks to organize factors of production and this dynamism in capitalist systems leads to developments in technology and capital efficiency which help generate profits for the individuals and firms concerned but also increase knowledge and information in society as a whole which further contributes to economic development.

> **economic system** the way in which resources are organized and allocated to provide for the needs of an economy's citizens
> **capitalist economic system** a system which relies on the private ownership of factors of production to produce goods and services which are exchanged through a price mechanism and where production is operated primarily for profit

Critics of capitalist systems argue that they are inherently unstable and lurch from boom-to-bust. In addition, capitalist systems favour those who have acquired ownership of factor inputs and are able to exploit workers as a result and wield considerable economic and political power which distorts resource allocation. Karl Marx spent a considerable amount of his life seeking to understand and analyze the capitalist system and develop theories to explain why it exploited workers and was unstable.

The role of markets in capitalist economic systems is central. In a **market economy** the three key questions of the economic problem are addressed through the decentralized decisions of many firms and households as they interact in markets for goods and services. Firms decide whom to hire and what to make. Households decide which firms to work for and what to buy with their incomes. These firms and households interact in the marketplace, where prices and, it is assumed, self-interest guide their decisions.

> **market economy** an economy that addresses the three key questions of the economic problem by allocating resources through the decentralized decisions of many firms and households as they interact in markets for goods and services

In a pure market economy (one without any government intervention) no one is considering the economic well-being of society as a whole. Free markets contain many buyers and sellers of numerous goods and services, and all of them are interested, primarily, in their own well-being. Yet, despite decentralized decision-making and self-interested decision makers, market economies have proven remarkably successful in organizing economic activity in a way that can promote overall economic well-being for millions of people even though it is recognized that there are inequalities that will arise.

The inequitable distribution of wealth in capitalist societies which was witnessed in the countries which benefitted from the Industrial Revolution in the 1700s and 1800s, led to the development of other economic systems most notably **planned economic systems** sometimes referred to as communist systems or *command economies*. Communist countries worked on the premise that central planners could guide economic activity and answer the three key questions of the economic problem. The theory behind central planning was that the government could organize economic activity in a way that promoted economic well-being for the country as a whole and led to a more equitable outcome.

planned economic systems economic activity organized by central planners who decided on the answers to the fundamental economic questions

Today, most countries that once had centrally planned economies such as Russia, Poland, Angola, Mozambique and the Democratic Republic of Congo have abandoned this system and are developing more market-based economies.

FYI

Adam Smith and the Invisible Hand

Adam Smith published *An Inquiry into the Nature and Causes of the Wealth of Nations* in 1776 and is a landmark in economics. Smith's work reflected a point of view that was typical of so-called 'enlightenment' writers at the end of the 18th century – that individuals are usually best left to their own devices, without government guiding their actions. This political philosophy provides the intellectual basis for the market economy.

Here is Adam Smith's description of how people interact in a market economy:

Man has almost constant occasion for the help of his brethren, and it is vain for him to expect it from their benevolence only. He will be more likely to prevail if he can interest their self-love in his favour, and show them that it is for their own advantage to do for him what he requires of them. … It is not from the benevolence of the butcher, the brewer, or the baker that we expect our dinner, but from their regard to their own interest. …

Every individual … neither intends to promote the public interest, nor knows how much he is promoting it. … He intends only his own gain, and he is in this, as in many other cases, led by an invisible hand to promote an end which was no part of his intention. Nor is it always the worse for the society that it was no part of it. By pursuing his own interest he frequently promotes that of the society more effectually than when he really intends to promote it.

Smith suggested that participants in the economy are motivated by self-interest and that the 'invisible hand' of the marketplace guides this self-interest into promoting general economic well-being. The term 'invisible hand' is widely used in economics to describe the way market economies allocate scarce resources but interestingly, Adam Smith only used the phrase once in *The Wealth of Nations*. The phrase was also used in an earlier book, *The Theory of Moral Sentiments*. In both instances, Smith outlined the idea that self-interested individuals' actions could produce socially desirable results. In the *Theory of Moral Sentiments*, the phrase is used to show how human desire for luxury can have the effect of providing employment for others and in *The Wealth of Nations* the phrase is used in relation to investment choices. There are similarities in sentiment in both uses but in the former case, Smith, it seems, was seeking to explore the political philosophy of the economic system he was writing about; a system which was very different in many respects to that which we witness today.

Governments Can Sometimes Improve Market Outcomes

An economy can allocate some goods and services through the price mechanism but markets do not always lead to efficient or equitable outcomes. In some cases, goods and services would not be provided by a market system because it is not practicable to do so and in other cases market-based allocations might be deemed undesirable with either too few or too many goods and services consumed. The capitalist system and markets relies on laws and regulations to ensure that property rights are enforced. Governments provide goods and services which might not be provided in sufficient quantities in a market system and set the legal and regulatory framework within which firms and households can operate. Government intervention in markets may aim to promote efficiency *and* equity. That is, most policies aim either to enlarge the economic cake or change the way in which the cake is divided or even try to achieve both. Market systems do not always ensure that everyone has sufficient food, decent clothing and adequate health care. Many public policies, such as income tax and the social security system, are designed to achieve a more equitable distribution of economic well-being.

When markets do allocate resources the resulting outcomes might still be deemed inefficient. Economists use the term **market failure** to refer to a situation in which the market on its own fails to produce an efficient allocation of resources. One possible cause of market failure is an **externality**, which is the uncompensated impact of one person's actions on the well-being of a bystander (a third party). For instance, the classic example of an external cost is pollution. Another possible cause of market failure is **market power**, which refers to the ability of a single person or business (or group of businesses) to unduly influence market prices or output. In the presence of market failure, well-designed public policy can enhance economic efficiency.

> **market failure** a situation where scarce resources are not allocated to their most efficient use
> **externality** the cost or benefit of one person's decision on the well-being of a bystander (a third party) which the decision maker does not take into account in making the decision
> **market power** the ability of a single economic agent (or small group of agents) to have a substantial influence on market prices or output

To say that the government *can* improve on market outcomes at times does not mean that it always *will*. Public policy is made by a political process that is also imperfect. Sometimes policies are designed simply to reward the politically powerful. Sometimes they are made by well-intentioned leaders who are not fully informed. One goal of the study of economics is to help you judge when a government policy is justifiable to promote efficiency or equity, and when it is not.

HOW THE ECONOMY AS A WHOLE WORKS

We started by discussing how individuals make decisions and then looked at how people interact with one another. We will now look at issues arising that concern the workings of the economy as a whole.

Microeconomics and Macroeconomics

Since roughly the 1930s, the field of economics has been divided into two broad subfields. **Microeconomics** is the study of how households and firms make decisions and how they interact in specific markets. **Macroeconomics** is the study of economy-wide phenomena. The Nobel Prize winning economist Ragnar Frisch is credited with being the first to use the two terms (along with the term 'econometrics' incidentally) and the Cambridge economist Joan Robinson an associate of Keynes was one of the first to define macroeconomics referring to it as 'the theory of output as a whole'.

> **microeconomics** the study of how households and firms make decisions and how they interact in markets
> **macroeconomics** the study of economy-wide phenomena, including inflation, unemployment and economic growth

Microeconomics might involve the study of the effects of a congestion tax on the use of cars in a city centre, the impact of foreign competition on the European car industry or the effects of attending university on a person's lifetime earnings. A macroeconomist might study the effects of borrowing by national governments, the changes over time in an economy's rate of unemployment or alternative policies to raise growth in national living standards.

Microeconomics and macroeconomics are closely intertwined. Because changes in the overall economy arise from the decisions of millions of individuals, it is impossible to understand macroeconomic developments without considering the associated microeconomic decisions. For example, a macroeconomist might study the effect of a cut in income tax on the overall production of goods and services in an economy. To analyze this issue, they must consider how the tax cut affects the decisions of households concerning how much to spend on goods and services.

Despite the inherent link between microeconomics and macroeconomics, the two fields are distinct. Because microeconomics and macroeconomics address different questions, they sometimes take quite different approaches and are often taught in separate courses.

An Economy's Standard of Living is Related to its Ability to Produce Goods and Services

A key concept in macroeconomics is **economic growth** – the percentage increase in the number of goods and services produced in an economy over a period of time, usually expressed over a quarter and annually. One measure of the economic well-being of a nation is given by **gross domestic product (GDP) per capita** (per head) of the population which can be seen as being the average income per head of the population. If you look at GDP per capita figures it becomes clear that many advanced economies have a relatively high income per capita whereas in countries in sub-Saharan Africa, average incomes are much lower and in some cases significantly lower. For example, in 2013, the GDP per capita of Benin in West Africa was reported by the World Bank as being $805. In comparison, the GDP per capita of Germany was $46 251. Put another way average incomes in Benin are around 1.74 per cent of those in Germany.

> **economic growth** the increase in the amount of goods and services in an economy over a period of time
> **gross domestic product per capita** the market value of all goods and services produced within a country in a given period of time divided by the population of a country to give a per capita figure

Not surprisingly, this large variation in average income is reflected in various other measures of the quality of life and **standard of living**. Citizens of high-income countries typically have better nutrition, better health care and longer life expectancy than citizens of low-income countries, as well as more TV sets, more gadgets and more cars.

> **standard of living** refers to the amount of goods and services that can be purchased by the population of a country. Usually measured by the inflation-adjusted (real) income per head of the population

Changes in the standard of living over time are also large. Between 2011 and 2015, economic growth, measured as the percentage growth rate of GDP, in Bangladesh averaged at around 4.8 per cent per year and in China at about 6.8 per cent a year but in Iraq the economy has shrunk by around 9.2 per cent over the same time period (Source: World Bank).

Variation in living standards is attributable to differences in countries' **productivity** – that is, the amount of goods and services produced by a worker (or other factor of production) per time period. In nations where workers can produce a large quantity of goods and services per unit of time, most people enjoy a high standard of living; in nations where workers are less productive, people endure a more meagre existence. Similarly, the growth rate of a nation's productivity determines the growth rate of its average income.

> **productivity** the quantity of goods and services produced from each hour of a worker or factor of production's time

The relationship between productivity and living standards also has profound implications for public policy. When thinking about how any policy will affect living standards, the key question is how it will affect our ability to produce goods and services. To boost living standards, policymakers need to raise productivity by ensuring that workers are well educated, have the tools needed to produce goods and services, and have access to the best available technology.

The standard of living is not the only measure of well-being. In the UK, for example, the Office for National Statistics (ONS) publishes data on well-being through 41 different measures which attempts to incorporate how people feel about their lives, whether they see what they do as worthwhile, their satisfaction with family life, how satisfied they are with their job and their health, where people live and how safe they feel, their involvement in sport, culture and volunteer work and the extent to which they access the natural environment.

Prices Rise When the Government Prints Too Much Money

In Zimbabwe in March 2007 inflation was reported to be running at 2200 per cent. That meant that a good priced at the equivalent of Z$2.99 in March 2006 would be priced at Z$65.78 just a year later. In February 2008, inflation was estimated at 165 000 per cent. Five months later it was reported as 2 200 000 per cent. In July 2008 the government issued a Z$100 billion note. At that time it was just about enough to buy a loaf of bread. Estimates for inflation in Zimbabwe in July 2008 put the rate of growth of prices at 231 000 000 per cent. In January 2009, the government issued Z$10, 20, 50 and 100 trillion dollar notes – 100 trillion is 100 followed by 12 zeros. This episode is one of history's most spectacular examples of **inflation**, an increase in the overall level of prices in the economy.

inflation an increase in the overall level of prices in the economy

High inflation is a problem because it imposes various costs on society; keeping inflation at a low level is a goal of economic policymakers around the world. In almost all cases of high or persistent inflation, a causal factor is the growth in the quantity of money. When a government creates large quantities of the nation's money, the value of the money falls. As outlined above, the Zimbabwean government was issuing money at ever higher denominations. It is generally accepted that there is a relationship between the growth in the quantity of money and the rate of growth of prices.

Society Faces a Short-run Trade-off Between Inflation and Unemployment

When the government increases the amount of money in the economy, one result is inflation. Another result, at least in the short run, is a lower level of unemployment. The curve that illustrates this short-run trade-off between inflation and unemployment is called the **Phillips curve**, after the economist who examined this relationship while working at the London School of Economics.

Phillips curve a curve that shows the short run trade-off between inflation and unemployment

The Phillips curve remains a controversial topic among economists, but the idea that society faces a short-run trade-off between inflation and unemployment is accepted amongst many. This simply means that, over a period of a year or two, many economic policies push inflation and unemployment in opposite directions. Policymakers face this trade-off regardless of whether inflation and unemployment both start out at high levels at low levels or somewhere in-between.

The trade-off between inflation and unemployment is only temporary, but it can last for several years. The Phillips curve is, therefore, crucial for understanding many developments in the economy. In particular, it is important for understanding the **business cycle** – the irregular and largely unpredictable fluctuations in economic activity, as measured by the number of people employed or the production of goods and services.

> **business cycle** fluctuations in economic activity such as employment and production

Policymakers in governments and central banks can exploit the short-run trade-off between inflation and unemployment using various policy instruments. By changing the amount that the government spends, the amount it taxes and the amount of money it prints, policymakers can influence the combination of inflation and unemployment that the economy experiences. Because these instruments of monetary and fiscal policy are potentially so powerful, how policymakers should use these instruments to control the economy, if at all, is a subject of continuing debate.

> **SELF TEST** What is the difference between microeconomics and macroeconomics? Write down three questions that the study of microeconomics might be concerned with and three questions that might be involved in the study of macroeconomics.

IN THE NEWS

Incentives

Intuition might tell us that people respond to incentives. Economics deals with human beings and what might seem to be a common sense statement reveals more complex relationships which make outcomes different to those expected.

Research by Gneezy, Meier, and Ray-Biel (2011), highlight some of these complexities. Their research suggested that incentives may work better in certain circumstances than in others and policymakers need to consider a wide variety of issues when deciding on putting incentives in place.

First of all, they have to consider the type of behaviour to be changed. For example, society might want to encourage what Gneezy et al. call 'prosocial' behaviour such as donating blood, sperm or organs, increasing the amount of waste put out for recycling, attending school, college or university, working harder in education to improve grades, improving the environment such as installing insulation or solar panels in homes to reduce energy waste, or finding ways of encouraging people to stop smoking.

Policymakers then have to consider the parties involved. This can be expressed as a principal-agent issue. The principal is a person or group for whom another person or group, the agent, is performing some act. In encouraging people to stop smoking, the smoker is the agent and society is the principal. Next, the type of incentive offered to bring about desired behaviours has to be considered – often this will be monetary. Gneezy et al. note that monetary incentives have a direct price effect and a psychological effect. Finally, policymakers have to think about how the incentive is framed.

Providing a monetary incentive to bring about a desired change in behaviour might seem an obvious policy choice such as offering a monetary incentive to go to school, donate blood or install solar panels. Gneezy et al. point to a number of reasons why the outcome might not be as obvious as first hoped. They suggest that in some cases, offering monetary incentives can 'crowd out' the desired behaviour. Offering a monetary incentive can change the perceptions of agents. People have intrinsic motivations – personal reasons for particular behaviours. Others have perceptions about the behaviour of others, for example someone who donates blood might be seen by others as being 'nice'. Social norms may also be affected, for example attitudes to the recycling of waste or smoking.

Gneezy et al. suggest that monetizing behaviour changes the psychology and the psychology effect can be greater than the direct price effect. The price effect would suggest that if you pay someone to donate more blood, you should get more people donating blood. People who donate blood, however, might do so out of a personal conviction – they have intrinsic motivations. By offering monetary incentives, the perception of the donor and others might change so that they are not seen as being 'nice' any more but as being 'mercenary' and not motivated intrinsically but by extrinsic reward – greed, in other words. If the psychological effect outweighs the direct money effect the result could be a reduction in the number of donors.

(*Continued*)

Incentives are a powerful influence in economics. The incentives are not always immediately obvious.

In the case of cutting smoking, the size of the money effect might be a factor. This chapter has raised the idea of rational people thinking at the margin. With smoking, the marginal decision to have one more cigarette imposes costs and benefits on the smoker – the benefit is the pleasure people get from smoking an additional cigarette, and the cost the (estimated) 11 minutes of their life that is cut as a result. The problem is that the marginal cost is not tangible and is likely to be outweighed by the marginal benefit (not to mention the addictive qualities of tobacco products). Over time, however, the total benefit of stopping smoking becomes much greater than the total cost. The incentive offered, therefore, has to be such that it takes into account these marginal decisions and it might be difficult to estimate the size of the incentive needed.

Other issues relating to incentives involve the trust between the principal and agent. If an incentive is provided, for example, this sends a message that the desired behaviour is not taking place and that there may be a reason for this. This might be that the desired behaviour is not attractive and/or is difficult to carry out. Incentives also send out a message that the principal does not trust the agent's intrinsic motivation, for example, that people will not voluntarily give blood or recycle waste effectively. Some incentives may work to achieve the desired behaviour in the short-term but will this lead to the desired behaviour continuing in the long-term when the incentive is removed?

Incentives might be affected by the way they are framed – how the wording or the benefits of the incentive is presented to the agent by the principal. Gneezy et al. use a very interesting example of this. Imagine a situation, they say, where you meet a person and develop a relationship. You want to provide that person with the incentive to have sex. The effect of the way the incentive is framed might have a considerable effect on the outcome. If, for example, you framed your 'offer' by saying 'I would like to make love to you and to incentivize you to do so I will offer you €50,' you might get a very different response to that if you framed it by saying: 'I would like to make love to you – I have bought you a bunch of red roses' (the roses just happened to cost €50).

Finally, the cost effectiveness of incentives has to be considered. Health authorities spend millions of euros across Europe on drugs to reduce blood pressure and cholesterol. Getting people to take more exercise can also help achieve the same result. What would be more cost-effective and a more efficient allocation of resources? Providing incentives (assuming they work) to encourage people to exercise more by, for example, paying for gym membership, or spending that same money on drugs but not dealing with some of the underlying causes?

Questions

1 Why should people need incentives to do 'good' things like donating blood or putting out more rubbish for recycling?
2 What is meant by the 'principal–agent' issue?
3 What might be the price and psychological effect if students were given a monetary incentive to attain top grades in their university exams?
4 Why might the size of a monetary incentive be an important factor in encouraging desired behaviour and what side-effects might arise if the size of an incentive was increased?
5 What is 'framing' and why might it be important in the way in which an incentive works? Refer to the need to increase the number of organ donors in your answer to this question.

SUMMARY

- Key issues arising in individual decision-making are that people face trade-offs among alternative goals, that the cost of any action is measured in terms of foregone opportunities, that rational people make decisions by comparing marginal costs and marginal benefits, and that people change their behaviour in response to the incentives they face.

- When economic agents interact with each other, the resulting trade can be mutually beneficial. In capitalist economic systems, the market mechanism is the primary way in which the questions of what to produce, how much to produce and who should get the resulting output are answered. Markets do not always result in outcomes that are efficient or equitable and in such circumstances governments can potentially improve market outcomes.

- The field of economics is divided into two subfields: microeconomics and macroeconomics. Microeconomists study decision-making by households and firms and the interaction among households and firms in the marketplace. Macroeconomists study the forces and trends that affect the economy as a whole.

- The fundamental lessons about the economy as a whole are that productivity is the ultimate source of living standards, that money growth is the ultimate source of inflation, and that society faces a short-run trade-off between inflation and unemployment.

QUESTIONS FOR REVIEW

1 What are the three questions which any society has to answer?

2 Describe the main features of a capitalist economic system.

3 Give three examples of important trade-offs that you face in your life.

4 What is the opportunity cost of going to a restaurant for a meal?

5 Water is necessary for life. Is the marginal benefit of a glass of water large or small?

6 Why should policymakers think about incentives?

7 Why can specialization and trade help improve standards of living?

8 Explain the two main causes of market failure and give an example of each.

9 Why is productivity important?

10 How are inflation and unemployment related in the short run?

PROBLEMS AND APPLICATIONS

1 Describe some of the trade-offs faced by each of the following:

   a. A family deciding whether to buy a new car.
   b. A government deciding whether to build a high-speed rail link between two major cities in the north of the country.
   c. A company chief executive officer deciding whether to recommend the acquisition of a smaller firm.
   d. A university lecturer deciding how much time to devote to preparing for their weekly lecture.

2 In early 2015, the number of unemployed people in Spain was around 4.3 million. Does this mean that labour is not a scarce resource in Spain?

3 You are trying to decide whether to take a holiday. Most of the costs of the holiday (airfare, hotel, foregone wages) are measured in euros, but the benefits of the holiday are psychological. How can you compare the benefits to the costs?

4 Many of the countries which had planned economic systems have transitioned to a more market-based economic system in the face of numerous problems. What do you think are the disadvantages of planned economic systems? How do market economies solve these problems? Can market systems solve all problems?

5 You win €10 000 on the EuroMillions lottery draw. You have a choice between spending the money now or putting it away for a year in a bank account that pays 5 per cent interest. What is the opportunity cost of spending the €10 000 now?

6 Three managers of the van Heerven Coach Company are discussing a possible increase in production. Each suggests a way to make this decision.

FIRST MANAGER: We need to decide how many additional coaches to produce. Personally, I think we should examine whether our company's productivity – number of coaches produced per worker per hour – would rise or fall if we increased output.

SECOND MANAGER: We should examine whether our average cost per worker – would rise or fall.

THIRD MANAGER: We should examine whether the extra revenue from selling the additional coaches would be greater or smaller than the extra costs.

Who do you think is right? Why?

7   Assume a social security system in a country provides income for people over the age of 65. If a recipient decides to work and earn some income, the amount he or she receives in social security benefits is typically reduced.

   a. How does the provision of this grant affect people's incentive to save while working?

   b. How does the reduction in benefits associated with higher earnings affect people's incentive to work past the age of 65?

8   Your flatmate is a better cook than you are, but you can clean more quickly than your flatmate can. If your flatmate did all of the cooking and you did all of the cleaning, would your household chores take you more or less time than if you divided each task evenly? Give a similar example of how specialization and trade can make two countries both better off.

9   Explain whether each of the following government activities is motivated by a concern about equity or a concern about efficiency. In the case of efficiency, discuss the type of market failure involved.

   a. Regulating water prices.

   b. Regulating electricity prices.

   c. Providing some poor people with vouchers that can be used to buy food.

   d. Prohibiting smoking in public places.

   e. Imposing higher personal income tax rates on people with higher incomes.

   f.   Instituting laws against driving whilst using a mobile phone.

10 In what ways is your standard of living different from that of your parents or grandparents when they were your age? Why do you think these changes occurred?

2 THINKING LIKE AN ECONOMIST

INTRODUCTION

In the spring of 2015, the UK went to the polls to elect a new government. In the debates that preceded the election, one of the political parties included a promise to increase spending on the National Health Service (NHS) by £2.5 billion a year and said that the funds for this additional investment would come from the levy of a tax on housing worth over £2 million, a windfall tax on tobacco companies and a tightening up of rules on tax avoidance.

How would an economist think about this promise? An economist would want to know what the additional investment would be spent on, whether the additional spending would result in a more efficient health service, and crucially, would want to know how 'efficient' was being defined in this context. Regardless of whether the economist has a personal view about whether the means of raising the funds are 'right', they would think about whether the amount of money raised through these measures would be sufficient and whether a tax on the houses of the wealthy or tightening rules on tax avoidance would have consequences on the behaviour of economic actors who would be affected, which political parties might not foresee and could compromise the intended outcome. The economist might want to investigate the effects of a windfall tax on tobacco companies – would it raise a sufficient amount of revenue? What effect would it have on the companies concerned? Would it result in the closure of some factories or workers being made redundant, and if so how many and what consequences would that have for the individuals and local areas concerned?

Ultimately, the economist would want to investigate the costs and benefits of such a decision, try to quantify those costs and benefits and offer an informed view of the consequences of the policy. It would not simply be a case of looking at the obvious costs and benefits but also the hidden costs and benefits which might lead to an outcome or outcomes that are very different to those the policy was designed to achieve.

Economics, like most other fields of study, has its own language, its own processes, its methods of discovery and its own way of thinking. As you embark on your study of economics you will have to learn lots of new terms and concepts. Many of the concepts you will come across in this book are abstract. Abstract concepts are ones which are not concrete or real – they have no tangible qualities. We will talk about markets, efficiency, comparative advantage and equilibrium, for example, but it is not possible to physically see these concepts.

As you work through your modules you will find that it is not always easy to think like an economist and there will be times when you are confused, and find some of the ideas and concepts being presented to you running contrary to common sense (i.e. they are counter-intuitive). What you will be experiencing is perfectly normal and a part of the learning journey.

Economic Methodology

This chapter discusses the field's methodology. There is considerable debate about this methodology. Different methodologies have their own assumptions and belief systems which influence the way issues are looked at and the outcomes and policy implications which arise as a result. Perhaps the dominant methodology is the *neo-classical* approach which is also referred to as 'mainstream economics'. The neo-classical approach takes the view that the market is a central feature in generating well-being and in answering the three questions all societies have to face, which we looked at in Chapter 1. In analyzing markets and outcomes, the neo-classical approach assumes that decisions are based on rationality, and that economic agents act out of self-interest and are autonomous. In making decisions based on these assumptions, the well-being of society as a whole can be improved through the guiding power of the 'invisible hand'.

Critics of this approach argue that the assumptions are flawed and that what is observed about human behaviour does not conform to the neo-classical view. They argue that such is the power of the neo-classical hold on economics, that other views, so called heterodox economics (where the term heterodox means views at odds with the mainstream), find it hard to gain any ground. These differing views include feminist economics, Marxist economics and the Austrian school.

Feminist Economics Feminist economics questions many of the assumptions of the neo-classical school. Economic well-being, they argue, is not simply provided through market exchange but also includes unpaid work carried out in the home. This housework, by both males and females, needs to have the recognition its significance to well-being deserves. Economic activity, therefore, needs to include a valuation of this unpaid work. Feminist economists also research into other areas where there are gender and social inequalities and would argue that it is not possible to have value-free analysis and research into economic issues. For example, the idea that humans face a trade-off between work and leisure is misleading in that 'leisure' is associated with pleasurable activities which people choose to take part in. For many women, non-'work' activity, i.e. that which is not paid, is not leisure at all and involves considerable work in caring for the home and family. To only assume that 'work' is valuable betrays a value judgement which relegates analysis of unpaid work below that of paid work.

Marxist Economics In later chapters, we will look at the working of markets and firms in more detail. Much of the analysis will be derived from the neo-classical approach but there are other explanations for how markets and firms work. Marxist economics presents different explanations for essentially the same phenomena and has developed from the work of Karl Marx in the 19th century. Marx sought to analyze and understand the capitalist system and explain how and why production takes place and the circumstances under which different groups in society have economic power. Marxist economics views firms and markets not as entities but as collections of humans and it is these humans who make decisions. Some humans have control over the means of production and are able to exploit that power in ways which lead to different outcomes and which drive dynamism in economies. This dynamism can be self-destructive, however, and the competition between capitalists to attempt to retain control over the means of production is partly what generates booms and busts in capitalist economies. Neo-classical economists would propose different explanations for the swings in the business cycle.

The Austrian School The Austrian school originated in work carried out at the University of Vienna in the latter part of the 19th century. Academics at Vienna were of the belief that economic well-being is maximized when markets are allowed to do their work and that the government should have a minimal role in the economy (referred to as 'laissez-faire' roughly translated as 'to leave' or 'let it be'). Individual liberty is a fundamental principle in Austrian school economics.

The Austrian school is now not based in Vienna but has adherents in different parts of the world. Key figures in the Austrian school include Carl Menger, Eugen Böhm-Bawerk, Friedrich Weiser, Ludwig von Mises and Friedrich August von Hayek. Other influential economists such as the 1991 Nobel Prize winner in Economics, Ronald Coase, were said to have been influenced by the Austrian school (Coase was at the London School of Economics when Hayek was on the faculty and acknowledged the impact he made). Austrian school economists would look at the explanation for business cycles in the supply side of the economy rather than focusing on demand. Excess supply is what drives the economy into recession and this, in turn, can be caused by interest rates being too low leading to too much investment and the availability of cheap money. It is this which triggers inflation. For Austrian economists therefore, inflation is not the main problem or focus of policy; inflation is a symptom of imbalances in the financial sector of the economy. Economists from the Austrian school had been warning of too-low interest rates and too high debt levels for many years in the early part of the 21st century and there are those who argue that it was these economists who correctly predicted the Financial Crisis of 2007–9 and not mainstream economists. Critics of the Austrian school argue that it relies on narrative analysis rather than mathematical, statistical and empirical analysis and as such, their claims cannot be tested and verified.

THE ECONOMIST AS SCIENTIST

The idea that economic issues, ideas and policies can be tested and analyzed derives from the neo-classical tradition. Economics has sought to borrow techniques from the physical sciences which have been a key part of the development of the subject over the last 150 years. Not everyone believes that economics can be a science but the tradition is well entrenched and as a result, needs to be reviewed and understood.

The example given at the start of this chapter gives a little bit of insight into one way in which economics can pursue questions through science. For example, the claim that a tax on the homes of the wealthy would raise £1.3 billion in three years and affect around 100 000 property owners is something which could be tested to see if there is any truth to it. After investigation, the economist might counter that such a tax would only raise £500 million in that same time period or would take up to eight years to raise the desired £1.3 billion. Note that the economist is not making a judgement as to whether the policy is right or wrong just whether the evidence actually bears out the claims being made. Like scientists in other fields, the economist is claiming to be seeking 'truth' – to see whether facts can be gathered to support or refute claims about how the world works. This is not to say that the motivations as to why the economist may have chosen to look into the issue in the first place, is because they thought the policy was morally wrong or right and wanted to prove or disprove a political point.

The scientific method involves devising theories, collecting data and then analyzing these data in an attempt to verify or refute theories. This is important because a theory has the characteristic that it is predictive. If we want to make predictions of the future on which decision-making is based, then it is vital that the theory being used is sound.

There is much debate about whether economics can ever be a science – principally because it is dealing with human behaviour. In addition, it has been proposed that there will always be an element of bias in any research, something which the financier George Soros calls the *Principle of Fallibility*. The essence of any science, however, is *scientific method* – the development and testing of theories about how the world works.

Empiricism

To make the statement 'prices rise when the government prints too much money' is to make a prediction. If predictions are to be made there has to be some evidence that the outcomes are realistic and replicable, i.e. that when governments print too much money, prices will indeed rise. This evidence is gathered through empirical study. Empirical means that information or data has been gathered either by observation, experience or experiment of an event or phenomena (such as a period of rising prices), the formulation of a hypothesis (that prices rise when government prints too much money) and models developed designed to replicate the data collected and the testing of the hypothesis. A hypothesis is an assumption; the word is derived from the Greek (*hypotithenai*) meaning 'to suppose'. A hypothesis can be developed through observation or experience of phenomena or through what we might call 'idle reasoning'. The economist might use scientific method to see whether the hypothesis can be supported, rejected or there might be no evidence to support the hypothesis either way. If the hypothesis can be supported, this allows conclusions to be drawn and predictions to be made.

Let us take the theory that prices rise when the government prints too much money. How might this theory have arisen? An economist observing rapid increases in prices in a country might also note that this has been accompanied by a rapid growth in the money supply. The data might be subject to some statistical test to see if there is any correlation between the two and whether there is any evidence of a cause and effect relationship. From this investigation, a theory of inflation might be developed which asserts that high inflation arises when the government prints too much money. To test this theory, the economist could collect and analyze data on prices and money from many different countries. If the correlation between the growth in the quantity of money and the rate at which prices are rising was not replicated in many other countries being studied, the economist would start to doubt the validity of their theory of inflation. If money growth and inflation were strongly correlated in international data, the economist would become more confident in the theory.

Although economists use theory and observation like other scientists, they do face an obstacle that makes their task especially challenging. Physicists, for example, can set up controlled experiments such as the Large Hadron Collider, which is seeking to re-create conditions that existed milli-seconds after the Big Bang. The experiments being conducted are designed to help confirm existing theories and/or develop new ones to explain forces and matter and how the universe began. By contrast, economists studying inflation are not allowed to manipulate a nation's monetary policy simply to generate useful data.

To find a substitute for laboratory experiments, economists pay close attention to the natural experiments offered by history. When political instability interrupts the flow of crude oil, for instance, oil prices rise around the world. For consumers of oil and oil products, such an event depresses living standards. For economic policymakers, it poses a difficult choice about how best to respond. For economists, it provides an opportunity to study the effects of a key natural resource on the world's economies, and this opportunity persists long after the increase in oil prices is over. Throughout this book, therefore, we consider many historical episodes. These episodes are valuable to study because they give us insight into the economy of the past and, more importantly, because they allow us to illustrate and evaluate economic theories of the present.

Inductive and Deductive Reasoning Inductive reasoning refers to the process of observation to form patterns which might provide evidence for a hypothesis, and lead to a theory. In contrast, deductive reasoning begins with a theory from which a hypothesis is drawn. The hypothesis is then subject to observation and either confirmation or rejection. One is not any better than the other – they are different ways of approaching research and may be closely linked. What is important is that any research is treated with a degree of critical awareness – we don't just simply accept the conclusions drawn from the research but question them and subject them to further testing. Through this circular process, refinements and improvements to theories and explanations can be developed which in turn allow us to develop understanding and make more informed decisions.

A classic example of the relationship between inductive and deductive reasoning can be seen in the case of observing swans. The researcher observes a river with swans swimming past. Every swan observed is white. At the end of the observation period the researcher draws a conclusion that 'all swans are white'. The evidence gathered does support the hypothesis that 'all swans are white'. A theory about why swans are always white might be developed to explain this phenomenon. Subsequent testing of the hypothesis might confirm that, based on the evidence, all swans are white and this might be the accepted hypothesis for many years until, one day, someone sees a black swan. At which point the hypothesis is rejected and the theory will have to be modified. This may lead the researcher to begin asking questions about why the majority of swans appear to be white and what reasons there might be for some swans being black, which can again be the subject of empirical research.

Theories Theories can be used to explain something and to make predictions. The theory of indifference curves and budget lines can be used to explain consumer behaviour. The value of the theory is how reliable it is in predicting consumer behaviour. If we observe the way consumers behave and the outcomes do not conform to the theory, it may be that new research has to be conducted to offer refinements to the theory or even consigning the theory to history.

Theorizing on its own can be said to be a tradition in neo-classical economics. Here, the economist uses logic, reason and induction to arrive at conclusions. Much of the logic might be based on assumptions which may not be subject to any supporting data. For example, the theory of consumer behaviour makes assumptions that consumers act rationally, prefer more to less, and make purchasing decisions based on pure self-interest.

Empiricist economics starts with observations and data to derive models which reflect the data. These models are used to arrive at conclusions and make predictions. Observations of consumer behaviour, for example, suggest that humans do not always act rationally when making purchasing decisions. Models can be developed which represent the data – how humans *do* behave as consumers – and these models used to generate theories which help make predictions about consumer behaviour in different situations. As these new models or theories come to the fore, the 'old' theories may be rejected because they do not explain what is observed or have any predictive value. In science, theories can be subject to the principle of **falsifiability** whereby it is possible to refute or reject the theory in the event that data becomes available to support such a rejection. The theory that 'all swans are white' can be falsified once a swan is observed which is not white. Economics has come under criticism for claiming to be a science but conveniently side-stepping falsifiability when data is generated which rejects long-held or cherished theories. This may be because economists question the data which appears to reject the theory or because the necessity of finding a new theory to explain what the data is telling us is difficult.

> **falsifiability** the possibility of a theory being rejected as a result of the new observations or new data

Even if the hypothesis is supported by the evidence this is not a reason for the economist to sit back and relax, happy in the knowledge they have found 'the truth'. Things change, new information, experience or observations may be made which render the original hypothesis redundant and subject to revision or refinement; there is a process which is never ending.

Empiricism or Rationalism?

Rationalism refers to the methodology where 'truths' are established through reason and intellectual deduction rather than appealing to emotions or the senses. If a consumer expresses a preference for good A over good B and prefers good B to good C, intuition and reason mean it can be concluded that they will always prefer good A to good C. This is an example of deductive logic and provided the premise (that A is preferred to B) is correct then it is *impossible* for the conclusion to be anything other than correct. Some ideas in economics may seem intuitive and have led to truths, 'laws' or beliefs that are widely held, and in some cases entrenched. For example, intuition tells us that if the price of a good rises, people will buy less of that good. Rationally, this would also make sense and logic would tell us that if the price of a good is higher, it changes the way people view that good, whether they can now afford it and how they view the good in relation to others that they could buy that are similar. Putting all these things together the conclusion must be that when prices rise, the amount purchased will fall. We have a theory which is generalizable (i.e. applicable across other goods) and which can be used to predict what happens to demand when prices change.

Empiricism asserts that knowledge is gained by real-world experience. A set of data can be used to create a model to represent these data and which provide conclusions about what exists and allow us to make predictions. Data is used to test theories and draw conclusions about the extent to which the theory matches the experience. For example, there are people who subscribe to the view that a large proportion of those who claim welfare benefits are 'scroungers' or that an increase in immigration will take jobs away from the indigenous population. Empirical research into these issues takes the data available to test these 'theories' and the outcome of this research might reveal different truths. Empirical evidence derived from observation of data does have to be interpreted and this can lead to different conclusions being drawn.

Cause and Effect One problem facing economists is separating out cause and effect. Is a rise in the price level caused by an increase in the money supply or does an increase in the money supply cause a rise in the price level? Observation and experience can lead to the identification of phenomena occurring which intuition would seem to suggest are related in some way. Empirical research can lead to a conclusion which provides an answer, for example, that a rise in the money supply is the cause of a rise in the price level. The question which has to be asked is 'how do we know this "answer" is correct?' Is a rise in the price level *always* caused by a rise in the money supply or are there other factors that can also influence the price level? How significant is the role of the money supply in determining the price level? How did those who researched the relationship establish the facts of the case and what premise and assumptions did they use in building the model? Can these facts and assumptions be accepted as an accurate representation of the 'truth' or are there interpretations of both which might impact on the conclusions drawn? If facts and assumptions are accepted, then we have to presume that those who collected them did so in an unbiased and unprejudiced way and that they were professionally competent and had sufficient expertize to be able to do so in a way in which we can trust. An inductive argument leads to the statement that it is *improbable* that a conclusion is incorrect if we accept the premise, assumptions and facts used in the model. Separating out cause and effect can be informed by statistical tests but is also subject to interpretation. It is not always easy to establish cause and effect particularly when controlled experiments are not possible, and this characterises much of economics.

Models can be developed, predictions made and conclusions drawn but there are then human values to take into consideration. Many economists, for example, will agree that there is sufficient evidence to suggest that government stimulus in a period of economic downturn can help reduce the number of people unemployed. What might be the subject of more disagreement is the significance of the effect or the value of the associated costs and benefits of such a policy. Models of climate change may suggest that the increase in human-generated carbon emissions will contribute to a change in the global climate and there may be few people who would disagree with this basic conclusion, partly because the 'facts' which form the basis for the model might be subject to debate. The model derived might lead to a policy suggestion that significant measures might have to be put in place to cut carbon emissions in the next 10 years to prevent the costs which our children and grandchildren will have to bear. There are likely to be many more people who disagree on whether the current sacrifices required are outweighed by the value of the benefits that will occur between 50 and 100 years into the future.

The debate about how economists come to know things and present theories and models which claim to be predictive is one which continues to pervade the discipline. The Cambridge economist, Joan Robinson, perhaps captured the debate very well when she wrote economics 'limps along with one foot in untested hypotheses and the other in untestable slogans … our task is to sort out as best we may, this mixture of ideology and science' (Robinson, J. (1968) *Economic Philosophy*. Pelican).

The Role of Assumptions

If you ask a physicist how long it would take for a cannonball to fall from the top of the Leaning Tower of Pisa, they will probably answer the question by assuming that the cannonball falls in a vacuum. Of course, this assumption is false. In fact, the building is surrounded by air, which exerts friction on the falling cannonball and slows it down. Yet the physicist will correctly point out that friction on the cannonball is so small in relation to its weight that its effect is negligible. Assuming the cannonball falls in a vacuum greatly simplifies the problem without substantially affecting the answer.

Economists make assumptions for the same reason: assumptions can simplify the complex world and make it easier to understand. To study the effects of international trade, for example, we may assume that the world consists of only two countries and that each country produces only two goods. Of course, the real world consists of dozens of countries, each of which produces thousands of different types of goods, but by assuming two countries and two goods, we can focus our thinking. Once we understand international trade in an imaginary world with two countries and two goods, we are in a better position to understand international trade in the more complex world in which we live.

The art in scientific thinking is deciding which assumptions to make. Suppose, for instance, that we were dropping a beach ball rather than a cannonball from the top of the building. Our physicist would realize that the assumption of no friction is far less accurate in this case: friction exerts a greater force on a beach ball than on a cannonball because a beach ball is much larger and, moreover, the effects of air friction may not be negligible relative to the weight of the ball because it is so light. The assumption that gravity works in a vacuum may, therefore, be reasonable for studying a falling cannonball but not for studying a falling beach ball.

Similarly, economists use different assumptions to answer different questions. Most economic issues will be affected by a number of different factors. If we try to model the issue taking into account all these factors, the complexity might lead to outcomes which do not help in developing understanding of economic phenomena. As a result, economists will often use a principle called *ceteris paribus*, which is Latin for 'other things being equal'. In researching a phenomenon, economists will look at what happens when one factor changes but all other factors assumed to have an effect are held constant. This is a core feature of neo-classical economic methodology. It might be assumed that the amount consumers wish to purchase is affected by the price of the good concerned, income, tastes and the prices of other related goods. Our understanding of consumer behaviour is simplified if we look at the effect on demand of a change in income and hold other factors constant. This can be repeated with the other factors to generate some general principles about the demand for goods and services.

Assumptions have to be tested to see the extent to which they are accurate and reasonable in the same way that it is deemed reasonable by the physicist to drop the assumption of friction when considering the effect of dropping a cannonball from the Leaning Tower of Pisa.

Experiments in Economics

Because economics is a science which is centred on human behaviour, it is not always possible to conduct experiments in the way in which physical sciences like biology, chemistry and physics do. However, there are two major fields of experimentation in economics that are worthy of note. Experiments in economics can be conducted in a 'laboratory' where data can be collected via observations on individual or group behaviour, through questionnaires and surveys, interviews and so on, or through the collection and analysis of data that exists such as wages, prices, stock prices and volumes of trades, unemployment levels, inflation and so on. The data can be analyzed in relation to a research question and conclusions drawn which help develop new understanding or refine and improve existing understanding. The conclusions drawn from such experiments may be generalizable; in other words, the findings of the experiment can be extended outside the 'laboratory' to explain behaviour or economic phenomena and provide the basis for prediction.

One example of how such laboratory experiments can help change understanding is the work of people such as Daniel Kahneman, Amos Tversky, Richard Thaler and Cass Sunstein, whose research has helped to provide insights into judgement and decision-making and has offered a different perspective on the assumptions of rational decision-making. Thaler, for example, conducted a number of experiments to explore how individuals respond when faced with different questions on losses and gains in relation to a reference point. He found that prior ownership of a good, for example a ticket to see a football game, altered people's willingness to sell, even at prices significantly higher than that which they had paid. Thaler's observations on the consistency of this behaviour across a number of experiments led him to coin the term *endowment effect* to explain the behaviour and it is now widely accepted that the endowment effect does exist and that it runs counter to the assumptions of rational behaviour in economics. We will look at this in more detail in Chapter 5. Thaler worked with Kahneman and Tversky and extended the theory to distinguish between goods which are held for trade and those which are held for use. The endowment effect, they suggested, was not universal; it was more powerful when goods were held for use.

A second type of experiment in economics is *natural experiments*. A natural experiment is one where the study of phenomena is determined by natural conditions which are not in the control of the experimenter. Natural experiments can be exploited when some change occurs which allows observation to be carried out on the effects of this change in one population and comparisons made with another population who are not affected. Examples of natural experiments include observing the effects of bans on smoking in public places on the number of people smoking or the possible health benefits; how far a change in the way in which education is financed affects standards; the effect of the years spent in education on income; the effects of a rise in a tax on property on the market for housing and the effects on the female labour market of changes in fertility treatment and availability.

Typically, natural experiments make use of the statistical tools of correlation and regression to determine whether there is any relationship between two or more variables, if any such relationship exists and if it does, what the nature and strength of the relationship is. From such analysis, a model can be developed which can be used to predict. At the heart of such analysis is the extent to which a relationship between two or more variables can be linked to cause and effect. As we have seen, just because two variables appear to have some relationship does not necessarily imply cause and effect. For example, a researcher might find that an observation of graduates in the workforce shows that their incomes are generally higher than those of non-graduates; can the researcher conclude that having a degree will lead to higher income? Possibly, but not necessarily. There might be other factors that have an effect on income apart from having a degree and trying to build a model which takes into account these different factors is an important part of the value of natural experiments.

Models in Economics

The use of models in economics is widespread and we will consider a number of them in this book. A model is a representation of reality used as a means of helping understand the real world and for making informed decisions and judgements. You may have used anatomical models in school biology classes or seen architects' models of new building developments. These models are not meant to replicate every detail of the reality they are representing but to aid in the visualization and understanding of the reality they represent. Economic models have two principle uses: one is for predicting or forecasting what might happen in the future as a consequence of a decision or policy and two, for simulating an event and providing a comparison to what would have happened if the decision, policy or change had not happened (the counterfactual). Economists' models are most often composed of diagrams and equations. By feeding in data, economists can use models to generate outcomes which provide some insight and form the basis of decision-making. The UK Treasury, for example, uses a model of the economy to provide predictions on what will happen to key indicators such as growth, inflation and unemployment of changes in taxes and government spending. The Institute for Fiscal Studies (IFS) in the UK is an independent research organization which provides analysis and insight into how policies affect individuals, businesses, families and government finances. It used models which provided an analysis of the manifesto commitments of some of the main political parties in the UK prior to the election in 2015.

As we use models to examine various economic issues throughout this book, you will see that all the models are built with assumptions. It is possible, for example, that the outcomes of analysis on the impact of a rise in value added tax (VAT) on economic growth and inflation will be different depending on the model used and the assumptions made. This is why the predictions made by Treasury economists, the Bank of England's economists, the IFS, the Office for Budget Responsibility and independent research economists might offer predictions and outcome that are all different even if some of the general principles are accepted and agreed.

Models will contain a number of variables. Some of these variables are determined by the model and some are generated within the model. For example, take the market model where the quantity demanded (Q_d) is dependent on the price (P). Q_d is said to be the dependent variable. Its value will be dependent on the functional relationships in the model (the factors that affect demand) such as incomes, tastes and the prices of other goods. Q_d can be described as an **endogenous variable**. Price, on the other hand, is the independent variable – it affects the model (the quantity demanded) but is not affected by it. The price is not determined by, or dependent on, the quantity demanded. Price would be referred to as an **exogenous variable**.

endogenous variable a variable whose value is determined within the model
exogenous variable a variable whose value is determined outside the model

Understanding the difference between endogenous and exogenous variables is important because it helps us to separate out cause and effect. Does a change in price, for example, cause a change in quantity demanded or does quantity demanded affect price?

There has been much criticism of economic models in recent years, particularly in the wake of the Financial Crisis. Part of the criticism is that some economic models are based on assumptions that are 'false' or at least are not typically representative of human behaviour to produce predictions which are accurate and of value. The data which is fed into a model also has to be the 'right' data. If data inputs are not representative of the behaviour or system being modelled, then the outcome will be irrelevant and of limited use. In addition, the behaviour that models attempt to convey can change as a result of the way in which humans understand, believe and interpret the model itself. This is referred to by George Soros as the *principle of reflexivity*. For example, if investors accept a model of markets which assumes they are efficient, then their behaviour will change based on that belief and this will have an effect on the market and on the model itself. After a period of time, the model may not offer a satisfactory explanation of behaviour any longer. This is a fundamental difference between economics as a social science and the physical sciences. Our understanding of the model of gravity in physics does not mean that gravity will subsequently change because of our understanding and our behaviour.

Models are also inherently unstable the longer the time period being considered and forecast. Shocks occur which are impossible to factor into the building of models which have not only short-term impacts but which also change longer term dynamics. For example, the attacks on the World Trade Centre on 11 September 2001 has had a fundamental impact on the ways governments think and behave that could not be envisaged before the event. One of the reasons why models of climate change are subject to debate and disagreement is that over time the internal dynamics of models change in ways which render future predictions inherently unstable. The so-called 'butterfly wing' effect as described in chaos theory highlights the complexity surrounding modelling in meteorology. The butterfly effect notes that a butterfly flapping its wings at a particular point in time and space creates small changes in conditions which can lead to significant changes in faraway places such that a flap of a butterfly's wings in New Mexico could be traced as the initial causal factor of a hurricane in China some time in the future. Chaos theory further tells us that minor errors in measurements or assumptions can be amplified to such an extent that any predictions made by the model are rendered useless and that the further into the future we are attempting to make forecasts and predictions, the more unstable our models are.

THE ECONOMIST AS POLICY ADVISOR

Often economists are asked to explain the causes of economic events and recommend policies to improve economic outcomes. Why, for example, is unemployment higher for teenagers than older workers and given this situation, what should the government do to improve the economic well-being of teenagers? These two roles lead to important distinctions in the way in which we need to view statements and analysis. To answer the first question, the economist might use scientific method to offer an explanation but the second involves a value judgement. This highlights the distinction between what is termed positive and normative economics.

Positive Versus Normative Analysis

Suppose that two people are discussing minimum wage laws.

Pascale: Minimum wage laws cause unemployment

Sophie: The government should raise the minimum wage

There is a fundamental difference in these two statements. Pascale's statement is making a claim about how the world works. Sophie, on the other hand is making a value judgement about a change she would like to see implemented.

Pascale's statement is referred to as a positive statement. **Positive statements** have the property that the claims in them can be tested and confirmed, refuted or shown to not be provable either way. It would be possible to conduct research to show whether there is any correlation between the imposition of minimum wage laws and a rise in unemployment. A positive statement does not have to be true – it is possible that the research might conclude that there is no link between minimum wages and unemployment.

positive statements claims that attempt to describe the world as it is

Sophie's, is said to be normative. **Normative statements** have the property that they include opinion and make a claim about how the world ought to be; it is not possible to test opinions and confirm or reject them.

normative statements claims that attempt to prescribe how the world should be

Positive analysis incorporates the use of scientific methodology to arrive at conclusions which can be tested. Normative analysis is the process of making recommendations about particular policies or courses of action. It is perfectly possible to conduct both positive and normative analysis. For example, the statement: *the government should reduce the deficit as this will benefit the economy*, contains a normative statement – an opinion that the government ought to reduce the deficit. It also includes a positive statement: *A reduction in the government deficit will benefit the economy*, which is capable of being tested.

A key difference between positive and normative statements, therefore, is how we judge their validity. Deciding what is good or bad policy is not merely a matter of science; it also involves our views on ethics, religion and political philosophy.

Of course, positive and normative statements may be related. Our positive views about how the world works affect our normative views about what policies are desirable. Pascale's claim that the minimum wage causes unemployment, if true, might lead us to reject Sophie's conclusion that the government should raise the minimum wage.

WHY ECONOMISTS DISAGREE

If economics is classed as a science and adheres to scientific methods, why does there appear to be considerable disagreement amongst economists surrounding many different policy initiatives? There are two basic reasons:

● Economists may disagree about the validity of alternative positive theories about how the world works.
● Economists may have different values and, therefore, different normative views about what policy should try to accomplish.

Let's discuss each of these reasons.

Differences in Scientific Judgements

History shows us that there have always been disagreements between scientists about 'truth' and reality. In 1964, for example, Peter Higgs at the University of Edinburgh had his original paper on the theoretical model predicting what came to be known as the Higgs Boson, rejected by the journal *Physics Lectures,* which saw the theory as having 'little relevance to physics'. In 2012, the experiments at Cern in Switzerland confirmed the existence of the Higgs Boson and in 2013, Professor Higgs was jointly awarded the Nobel Prize for Physics. Science is a search for understanding about the world around us. It is not surprising that as the search continues, scientists can disagree about the direction in which truth lies.

Economists often disagree for the same reason. Economics is a young science, and there is still much to be learned. Indeed, there are some who argue that economics can never be a true 'science' because processes that are considered appropriate and necessary in natural sciences cannot be applied to economics because it deals with human behaviour. Humans cannot be subjected to the same controls and comparisons that can be used in physics, for example.

Economists sometimes disagree because they have different beliefs about the validity of alternative theories or about the size of important parameters. For example, economists disagree about whether the government should levy taxes based on a household's income or based on its consumption (spending). Advocates of a switch from an income tax to a consumption tax believe that the change would encourage households to save more, because income that is saved would not be taxed. Higher saving, in turn, would lead to more rapid growth in productivity and living standards. Advocates of an income tax system believe that household saving would not respond much to a change in the tax laws. These two groups of economists hold different normative views about the tax system because they have different positive views about the responsiveness of saving to tax incentives.

Differences in Values

Anneka and Henrik both take water from the town well. To pay for maintaining the well, the town imposes a property tax on its residents. Anneka lives in a large house worth €2 million and pays a property tax of €10 000 a year. Henrik owns a small cottage worth €20 000 and pays a property tax of €1000 a year.

Is this policy fair? If not, who pays too much and who pays too little? Would it be better to replace the tax based on the value of the property with a tax that was just a single payment from everyone living in the town (a poll tax) in return for using the well – say, €1000 a year? After all, Anneka lives on her own and actually uses much less water than Henrik and the other four members of his family who live with him, and use more water as a result. Would that be a fairer policy?

This raises two interesting questions in economics – how do we define words like 'fair' and 'unfair', and who holds the power to influence and make decisions? If the power is in the hands of certain groups in government or powerful businesses, policies may be adopted even if they are widely perceived as being 'unfair'.

What about replacing the property tax not with a poll tax but with an income tax? Anneka has an income of €100 000 a year so that a 5 per cent income tax would present her with a tax bill of €5000. Henrik, on the other hand, has an income of only €10 000 a year and so would pay only €500 a year in tax and the members of his family who do not work don't pay any income tax. Does it matter whether Henrik's low income is due to his decision not to go to university and take a low paid job? Would it matter if it were due to a physical disability? Does it matter whether Anneka's high income is due to a large inheritance from her family? What if it were due to her willingness to work long hours at a dreary job?

These are difficult questions on which people are likely to disagree. If the town hired two experts to study how the town should tax its residents to pay for the well, we should not be surprised if they offered conflicting advice.

This simple example shows why economists sometimes disagree about public policy. As we learned earlier in our discussion of normative and positive analysis, policies cannot be judged on scientific grounds alone. Economists give conflicting advice sometimes because they have different values.

> **SELF TEST** Why might economic advisors to the government disagree about a question of policy such as reducing a budget deficit?

Unravelling the Positive from the Normative

Negotiations between 12 nations over creating a Trans-Pacific Partnership (TPP) have been ongoing since 2005. The 12 countries are Australia, Brunei, Canada, Chile, Japan, Malaysia, Mexico, New Zealand, Peru, Singapore, the United States and Vietnam. An agreement would effectively lead to an increase in free trade across partner countries. In April 2015, Professor Mankiw wrote an article in the *New York Times* which had as its headline 'Economists actually agree on this: The wisdom of free trade'. Professor Mankiw noted in the article that there is 'near unanimity' amongst economists on the issue of the benefits of free trade. Three days after the article was published, Jim Naureckas, the editor of the magazine *Extra!*, a print publication of a media watch group Fairness and Accuracy in Reporting (FAIR), wrote a stinging rebuke of the *New York Times* which suggested Professor Mankiw had ignored the fact that there is 'no consensus in the economics field that free trade necessarily benefits most people'. Professor Mankiw's article, he argued, had implied that 'all economists are for TPP because it is a free trade bill' and went on to suggest that 'many economists in fact oppose TPP' and that there are 'economists who reject the characterization of TPP … as a "free trade" bill'. Naureckas goes on to suggest that Professor Mankiw ignores economists such as Paul Krugman and Joseph Stiglitz (who Naureckas notes are both Nobel Prize winners in Economics) and that in so doing highlights an insecurity of argument; 'if you pretend there is no serious disagreement to your point of view, is an implication that your point of view can't stand up to disagreement', he notes.

This 'spat' is typical of the sort of controversies which surround economics. As a student of the subject, part of your training will be in unravelling the fact from the fiction, the positive from the normative; but it is rarely a simple process. In the respective articles above, there are crucial words and phrases used like *'near unanimity'*, *'many'* and *'serious disagreement'*. As a student of economics you might reasonably ask for more specific definitions of these words. *'Near unanimity'* does not mean 'all'. What evidence is there for Professor Mankiw to make this claim in any event and what is the validity of that evidence, assuming it exists? If there are *'many'* economists who do not believe that free trade necessarily brings benefits to most (and what does 'most' mean here?), what sort of numbers and types of economists are we talking about? Perhaps the most pertinent advice that can be given is 'never believe everything you read' and be critical in analyzing articles and opposing views so that at the very least you have some understanding of where proponents of different views are coming from and why they may have arrived at different perspectives on key issues such as free trade.

Discussions over the relative costs and benefits of the TPP highlight the distinction between positive and normative economics.

Sources: http://www.nytimes.com/2015/04/26/upshot/economists-actually-agree-on-this-point-the-wisdom-of-free-trade.html?_r=0; http://fair.org/home/nyt-lets-economic-pundit-disappear-tpps-economist-critics/

Economists as Decision-Makers

It could be said that economics is the science of decision-making. The way that economists go about making or recommending decisions involves, firstly identifying the problem or issue: for example, will measures to cut greenhouse gas emissions be efficient? The next stage is to look at the costs and benefits involved in the decision. These costs and benefits are not just the private costs and benefits to the individual concerned, they will also include the costs and benefits to third parties who are not directly involved in the actual decision. For example, cutting greenhouse gas emissions means that resources will have to be diverted to new ways of production or different ways of producing energy. The private costs will be those borne by the businesses that will have to implement measures to adhere to the limits placed upon them. The social costs might include the impact on local people of the construction of wind farms or new nuclear power stations.

Having identified the costs and benefits, the economist then seeks to place a value on them in order to get some idea of the relationship between the costs and benefits of making the decision. In some cases, valuing costs and benefits can be easy but many are much more challenging. The loss of visual amenity for a resident living near a wind turbine or the value of the possible loss of life from a nuclear catastrophe at a power plant may be very difficult to value. Economists have attempted to devise ways in which these values can be estimated but they are not perfect.

Once the sum of the costs and benefits are calculated, the decision then becomes clearer. If the cost outweighs the benefit then making the decision may be unwise, but if the costs are less than the benefits then it may mean the decision can be supported. Policymakers may want to look at the *extent* to which the costs outweigh the benefit or the benefit outweighs the costs. Every day millions of decisions are made by individuals, businesses and governments. Whilst not every one of these decisions will be made using the exact processes outlined above, and we certainly do not stop to think about how we rationalize our decisions, nevertheless our brains do engage in computational processes as we make decisions, but they are mostly subconscious. Economists and psychologists are increasingly finding out more about how humans make decisions, which is helping improve our understanding of the models which we use to analyze consumer behaviour.

IN THE NEWS

Austerity Plans

One of the major economic problems in the UK is the size of the deficit. The deficit is the difference between the amount the government receives each year through taxation and other revenues and the amount it spends on providing goods and services. When government spends more than it receives there is a deficit which has to be funded by borrowing. In the year to March 2015, the deficit was around £87 billion in the UK. That was down by around £11 billion on the year before but still relatively high. A key debate in the General Election in 2015 was how different parties would reduce the deficit and when they planned to 'balance the books'. To achieve deficit reduction over a five-year period of government, it is widely accepted that either taxes have to be raised or government spending cut or a combination of both; alongside a buoyant economy these would help boost tax revenues and reduce government spending on things like welfare and unemployment benefits.

The IFS is an independent research organization based in the UK which conducts analyzes of public policy and it looked at the various claims made by the main political parties in the run up to the election. It concluded that the electorate was 'left somewhat in the dark' by all parties with regard to the extent to which cuts in government spending and increases in taxes would be needed to meet their respective targets. The IFS provided data on what each party might need to do in order to meet their pre-election promises – data which the parties themselves might not have wanted to publicize. For example, the IFS noted that the Conservatives would have to introduce cuts in government spending of around £40 billion alongside its tax policies. The Labour Party would have to increase some taxes but if it could tighten up tax avoidance measures as it said it wanted to do, then the cuts to government spending on unprotected departments could be much lower at £1 billion. The Liberal Democrats would have to cut £12 billion from government spending in unprotected departments and made 'optimistic claims' that it could achieve cuts in social security spending by reducing fraud and error and encouraging benefit recipients back into work. The IFS also noted that its plans to reduce tax avoidance and evasion were 'highly uncertain'.

The IFS is a respected research organization which takes its role as an independent analyst very seriously, employing highly qualified and respected economists to carry out its research.

(*Continued*)

Questions

1 Why do you think that political parties might not wish to publicize the size of the tax increases and spending cuts which may be needed to achieve deficit reduction plans?

2 Several parties identified tightening up tax avoidance and tax evasion as being important elements of policy to increase tax revenue without having to increase tax rates. Why might the amount of tax revenue received from such a policy be 'highly uncertain'?

3 The effectiveness of policies to reduce the deficit will be dependent on a variety of factors. How does the principle of *ceteris paribus* help in the analysis of the outcomes of these policies?

4 The IFS will use models in its analysis. Why is an awareness and understanding of the assumptions made in the creation of these models important in judging the reliability of the resulting analysis?

5 Research into policy outcomes such as that conducted by the IFS is based on the aim of being objective and scientific. To what extent do you think that it is ever possible to be 'scientific' in the study of economic phenomena?

Understanding the implications of austerity policies requires some objective analysis.

SUMMARY

- Economics is characterized by different methodologies and approaches including neo-classical, feminist, Marxist and Austrian.

- Economists make assumptions and build simplified models in order to understand the world around them. Economists use empirical methods to develop and test hypotheses.

- Research can be conducted through using inductive and deductive reasoning – no one way is the 'right way'.

- Economists develop theories which can be used to explain phenomena and make predictions. In developing theories and models, economists have to make assumptions.

- Using theory and observation is part of scientific method but economists always have to remember that they are studying human beings and humans do not always behave in consistent or rational ways.

- A positive statement is an assertion about how the world *is*. A normative statement is an assertion about how the world *ought to be*.

- Economists who advise policymakers offer conflicting advice either because of differences in scientific judgements or because of differences in values. At other times, economists are united in the advice they offer, but policymakers may choose to ignore it.

QUESTIONS FOR REVIEW

1 How is economics like a science?

2 Why do economists make assumptions?

3 Should an economic model describe reality exactly?

4 What is meant by empirical study in economics?

5 Using an example, explain the difference between inductive and deductive reasoning.

6 Should economic theories be developed as a result of observation or before observation? Explain.

7 What is the difference between a positive and a normative statement? Give an example of each.

8 Why do differences in values lead to disagreements amongst economists?

9 Using an example, explain the difference between an endogenous and an exogenous variable.

10 Why do economists sometimes offer conflicting advice to policymakers?

PROBLEMS AND APPLICATIONS

1 Terms like Investment, Capital, Interest, Price and Cost have different meanings in economics than they do in normal everyday usage. Find out what the differences are and explain why economists might have developed these different meanings.

2 One common assumption in economics is that the products of different firms in the same industry are indistinguishable. For each of the following industries, discuss whether this is a reasonable assumption.

   a. steel
   b. novels
   c. wheat
   d. fast food
   e. mobile phones (think carefully about this one)
   f. hairdressers.

3 A researcher in a university notices that the price of flights to holiday destinations tends to be much higher outside semester dates. They formulate a theory to explain this phenomenon. Has the researcher arrived at the theory by induction or deduction? What steps might the researcher take to apply scientific method to test their theory?

4 A politician makes a speech in which they criticize the government's immigration policy, saying that it is too loose and encourages too many people to enter the country and take jobs away from local people. How might an economist go about assessing the validity of the politician's comments?

5 If models are not capable of representing the real world in any detail and rely too much on assumptions, then what value can they be? In the wake of the Financial Crisis, there has been much criticism of economists' models. Does this suggest that economists need to rethink the way they go about seeking to understand and represent the world?

6 Does the fact that there are different schools of thought in economics reduce its validity as an academic discipline?

7 Rival political groups argue about the value and effectiveness of speed cameras as a means of influencing driver behaviour and improving safety on the roads. An economist is asked to conduct research into the costs and benefits of speed cameras to help decision-making. What sort of factors will the economist have to take into consideration in such research and what might be the challenges in identifying and quantifying the full range of costs and benefits?

8 If you were prime minister, would you be more interested in your economic advisors' positive views or their normative views? Why?

9 Would you expect economists to disagree less about public policy as time goes on? Why or why not? Can their differences be completely eliminated? Why or why not?

10 Consider a theory which states that an increase in interest rates will lead to an increase in savings. How would the principle of *ceteris paribus* be important in investigating the predictive power of this theory?

PART 2
SUPPLY AND DEMAND: HOW MARKETS WORK

3

THE MARKET FORCES OF SUPPLY AND DEMAND

In Chapter 2 we introduced the idea of models as a way of representing reality. The first model we are going to explore is the model of supply and demand. Recall that one of the purposes of a model is to make predictions.

HGCA is the cereals and oilseeds division of the Agriculture and Horticulture Development Board in the UK. It provides market and research information to farmers. Information provided by HGCA showed that the price of rape seed oil in July 2009 was around £250 (€350) per tonne but rose to around £425 (€595) per tonne in early 2011 then hovered between this price and £350 (€490) per tonne until July 2013 before falling back to around £250 (€350) per tonne in early 2015. Market predictions put the price of rape seed oil at around £253 (€354) per tonne in August 2016. Part of the service HGCA provides to farmers is information about the supply and demand of arable products. Using information gathered from around the world about rape seed oil, it is able to make a prediction about future prices. The accuracy of these predictions is important to farmers as many will base decisions on whether to grow rape seed oil or another arable crop and how much land to devote to the crop. Farmers can use this information to estimate the likely returns they will get from producing rape seed oil in comparison to other crops such as wheat. Rape seed oil is used in the cooking and food processing industries as vegetable oil. Buyers of rape seed oil make up the demand for the product.

This chapter introduces the theory of supply and demand. It considers how buyers and sellers behave and how they interact with one another. It shows how prices act as a signal to both buyers and sellers to help them make decisions which in turn contributes to the allocation of the economy's scarce resources. The model of the market based on supply and demand, like any other model, is based on a series of assumptions. These assumptions have been the subject of criticism that they are not reflective of reality and as a result the predictive power of the model is limited. Others have argued that the model is sufficiently representative to have value and provides a useful benchmark for comparison with how many markets behave. At the very least, the model provides a framework to help shape thinking about how economic agents interact. Many undergraduate principles of economics modules will include the model of supply and demand as a central part of the microeconomics course and this chapter will cover this area. As we progress through the chapter and the analysis it is important to bear in mind the assumptions of the model.

THE ASSUMPTIONS OF THE MARKET MODEL

The terms *supply* and *demand* refer to the behaviour of people as they interact with one another in markets. A **market** is a group of buyers and sellers of a particular good or service. The buyers as a group determine the demand for the product, and the sellers as a group determine the supply of the product.

> **market** a group of buyers and sellers of a particular good or service

The market model represents a neoclassical view of how resources are allocated. This view arose from analysis developed in the 19th century and follows on from the work of Adam Smith and the invisible hand. One of the fundamental principles of the market model is if the assumptions hold, the resulting allocation of resources will be 'efficient'. What this means is that the price buyers pay for goods in the market is a reflection of the value or utility they get from acquiring the goods and that the price producers receive is a reflection of the cost of production including an element of profit which is sufficient to keep them in that line of production. If consumers and producers are both maximizing benefits and minimizing costs, it is assumed that society as a whole must be maximizing welfare because the goods and services produced are those which are most desirable and in demand.

The model of supply and demand which leads to this 'efficient' outcome is based on the following assumptions:

1. There are many buyers and sellers in the market.
2. Each buyer and seller has perfect information.
3. No individual buyer and seller is big enough or has the power to be able to influence price (both are said to be '*price takers*').
4. There is freedom of entry and exit to and from the market.
5. Goods produced are homogenous (identical).
6. Buyers and sellers act independently and only consider their own position in making decisions.
7. There are clearly defined property rights which mean that producers and consumers both take into account all costs and benefits when making decisions.

You will find that there are economists who believe that markets are the most effective way we have yet discovered to allocate scarce resources. This further implies that government intervention in markets should be kept to a minimum. There are others who say that the model is so flawed that there is a much bigger role for government to play in the economy. The diversity of opinion amongst economists is part of what makes the subject so fascinating. Awareness of the difference between positive and normative economics is important in distinguishing the belief systems on which particular views are based and whether the outcomes claimed are testable. Part of thinking as an economist is in teasing out the subtle (and sometimes not so subtle) belief systems and value judgements underlying statements, and being prepared to subject such statements to critique and analysis. The market model has been criticized for just this point because it is based on a number of value judgements. Consumers attempting to maximize utility includes an assumption that more is preferred to less and that this is desirable. Producers seeking to maximize profit will attempt to produce an output that minimizes cost and reduces waste to a minimum and that this is also desirable. Whether these are desirable are subject to considerable debate and are essentially normative value judgements.

Competitive Markets

Competition exists when two or more firms are rivals for customers. In economics, however, in a **competitive market** (the terms '*perfectly competitive market*' or '*perfect competition*' are synonymous with '*competitive market*') the assumptions outlined above hold which leads to some important conclusions. Because there

> **competitive market** a market in which there are many buyers and sellers so that each has a negligible impact on the market price

are many buyers and sellers in a perfectly competitive market, neither has any power to influence price – they must accept the price the market determines, they are said to be *price takers*. Each seller has no control over the price because other sellers are offering identical products and each seller only supplies a very small amount in relation to the total supply of the market. Because products are homogenous a seller has little reason to charge less than the going price, and if they charge more, buyers will make their purchases elsewhere. Similarly, no single buyer can influence the price because each buyer purchases only a small amount relative to the size of the market. Buyers make their decisions based on the utility or satisfaction they gain from consumption and in doing so are independent of the decisions of suppliers. Both buyers and sellers have perfect knowledge and so are able to make decisions independently. This implies that there is no need for advertising or branding and that both producers and consumers take into account all costs and benefits, including the costs and benefits which may affect a third party, when making decisions. For example, producers will take into account the costs to society of the pollution they create in production.

There are some markets in which the assumption of perfect competition applies to a degree. At the start of this chapter we referred to the market for rape seed oil which is part of the market for agricultural products. Production of rape seed oil across the European Union (EU) was around 24 million tonnes in 2015. Rape seed is part of a global oil seed market which includes the production of soya beans, which account for around 70 per cent of total oil seed production. In the EU agriculture market, there are about 14 million farmers who sell cereals, fruit, milk, beef, lamb and so on; because no single seller can influence the price of agricultural products, each takes the market price as given and can sell all their output at the market price (remember that the total output of individual sellers represents only a small fraction of total output). The products produced in agricultural markets are broadly similar – milk produced by one farmer is not that much different to that produced by another although it is important to remember that even in markets where products might be perceived as being homogenous, there are differences in quality and use. For example, wheat can be produced at different qualities with some going for animal feed and some for bread making.

The characteristics of agricultural markets make them useful for using as examples in describing competitive markets. As we proceed to look in more depth at the market model, let's keep in mind a particular good, milk, to help focus our thinking. The market for milk fulfils many of the characteristics of a perfectly competitive market; milk is fairly homogenous, there are about half a million dairy farms and there are millions of buyers of milk across the EU.

> **SELF TEST** What constitutes a market? List the main characteristics of a competitive market.

DEMAND

We begin our study of markets by examining the behaviour of buyers. Buyers or consumers represent the demand for goods and services.

The Demand Curve: The Relationship Between Price and Quantity Demanded

The **quantity demanded** of any good is the amount of the good that buyers are willing and able to purchase at different prices. Many things determine the quantity demanded of any good, but one determinant plays a central role – the price of the good. If the price of milk rose from €0.25 per litre to €0.35 per litre, less milk would be bought. If the price of milk fell to €0.20 per litre more milk would be bought. Because the quantity demanded falls as the price rises and rises as the price falls, we say that the quantity demanded is *negatively or inversely related* to the price. This relationship between price and quantity demanded is true for most goods in the economy and, in fact, is so pervasive that economists call it the **law of demand**.

> **quantity demanded** the amount of a good that buyers are willing and able to purchase at different prices
>
> **law of demand** the claim that, other things equal (*ceteris paribus*) the quantity demanded of a good falls when the price of the good rises

We can represent the relationship between the price and quantity demanded in a table such as the one shown in Figure 3.1. The table shows how many litres of milk Rachel is willing and able to buy each month at different prices for milk. This shows Rachel's willingness to pay for the product holding other factors, such as her income, tastes and the prices of other goods, constant. This willingness to pay is related to the utility or level of satisfaction Rachel gets from consuming milk. If milk has a zero price, Rachel would be willing to buy 20 litres per time period. At €0.10 per litre, Rachel would be willing to buy 18 litres. As the price rises further, she is willing to buy fewer and fewer litres. When the price reaches €1, Rachel would not be prepared to buy any milk at all. This table is a **demand schedule**, a table that shows the relationship between the price of a good and the quantity demanded, holding constant everything else that influences how much consumers of the good want to buy.

demand schedule a table that shows the relationship between the price of a good and the quantity demanded

The graph in Figure 3.1 uses the numbers from the table to illustrate the law of demand. By convention, price is on the vertical axis, and the quantity demanded is on the horizontal axis. The downwards sloping line relating price and quantity demanded is called the **demand curve**.

demand curve a graph of the relationship between the price of a good and the quantity demanded

---

FIGURE 3.1

Rachel's Demand Schedule and Demand Curve

The demand schedule shows the quantity demanded at each price. The demand curve, which graphs the demand schedule, shows how the quantity demanded of the good changes as its price varies. Because a lower price increases the quantity demanded, the demand curve slopes downwards.

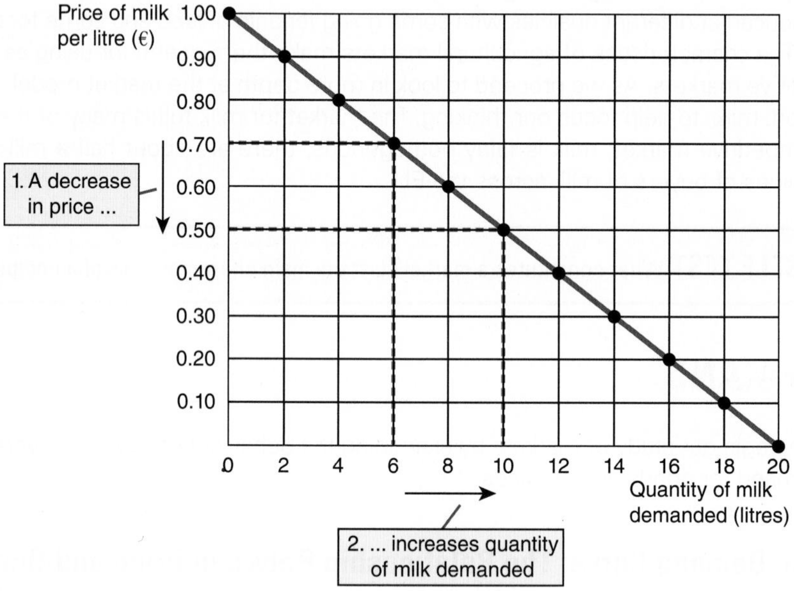

Price of milk per litre (€)	Quantity of milk demanded (litres per month)
0.00	20
0.10	18
0.20	16
0.30	14
0.40	12
0.50	10
0.60	8
0.70	6
0.80	4
0.90	2
1.00	0

Market Demand Versus Individual Demand

The demand curve in Figure 3.1 shows an individual's demand for a product. The *market demand* is the sum of all the individual demands for a particular good or service.

The table in Figure 3.2 shows the demand schedules for milk of two individuals – Rachel and Lars. Assuming Rachel and Lars are the only two people in the market, the market demand at each price is the sum of the two individual demands.

FIGURE 3.2

Market Demand as the Sum of Individual Demands
*The quantity demanded in a market is the sum of the quantities demanded by all buyers at each price. The market demand curve is found by adding horizontally the individual demand curves. At a price of €0.50, Rachel would like to buy 10 litres of milk but Lars would only be prepared to buy 5 litres at that price. The quantity demanded **in the market** at this price, therefore, is 15 litres.*

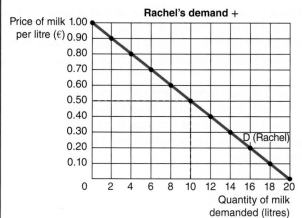

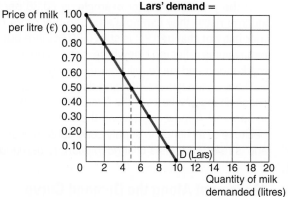

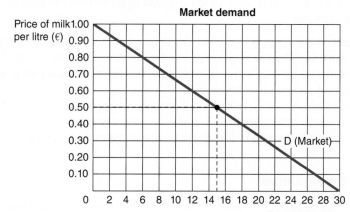

Price of milk per litre (€)	Rachel +	Lars =	Market
0.00	20	10	30
0.10	18	9	27
0.20	16	8	24
0.30	14	7	21
0.40	12	6	18
0.50	10	5	15
0.60	8	4	12
0.70	6	3	9
0.80	4	2	6
0.90	2	1	3
1.00	0	0	0

Figure 3.2 shows the demand curves that correspond to these demand schedules. To find the total quantity demanded at any price, we add the individual quantities found on the horizontal axis of the individual demand curves. The market demand curve shows how the total quantity demanded of a good varies as the price of the good varies, while all the other factors are held constant.

SHIFTS VERSUS MOVEMENTS ALONG THE DEMAND CURVE

The individual and market demand curves above were drawn under the assumption of *ceteris paribus* – other things being equal. We assumed that the other factors affecting demand were held constant so that we can analyze the effect of a change in price on demand. The willingness to pay determines the position of the demand curve. If any of the factors affecting demand *other than a change in price* change this will cause a shift in the position of the demand curve.

If the price of milk, for example, is €0.30 per litre a family might buy 5 litres of milk a week. If their income rises, they can now afford to buy more milk and so might now buy 7 litres a week. The price of milk has not changed – it is still €0.30 per litre but the amount of milk the family buys has increased. If this behaviour is reflected elsewhere in the economy by other families whose incomes have changed, then the market demand curve will shift to the right.

If any of the factors affecting demand other than price change then the amount consumers wish to purchase changes whatever the price. The shift in the demand curve is referred to as an *increase or decrease in demand.* A movement along the demand curve occurs when there is a change in price. This may occur because of a change in supply conditions. A change in price leads to a movement along the demand curve and is referred to as a *change in quantity demanded.*

Movement Along the Demand Curve

Let us assume that the price of milk falls which will lead to an increase in quantity demanded. There are two reasons for this increase:

1. **The income effect.** If we assume that incomes remain constant then a fall in the price of milk means that consumers can now afford to buy more with their income. In other words, their real income, what a given amount of money can buy at any point in time, has increased and part of the increase in quantity demanded can be put down to this effect.
2. **The substitution effect.** Now that milk is lower in price compared to other products such as fruit juice, some consumers will choose to substitute the more expensive drinks with the now cheaper milk. This switch accounts for the remaining part of the increase in quantity demanded.

A Shift in the Demand Curve

If one or more of the factors influencing demand other than price changes, the demand curve shifts. For example, suppose a top European medical school published research findings that suggested people who regularly drink milk live longer, healthier lives. The discovery would raise the demand for milk because consumers' tastes will change in favour of drinking more milk. At any given price, buyers would now want to purchase a larger quantity of milk and the demand curve for milk would shift.

Figure 3.3 illustrates shifts in demand. Any change that increases the quantity demanded at every price, such as our imaginary research report, shifts the demand curve to the right and is called *an increase in demand.* Any change that reduces the quantity demanded at every price shifts the demand curve to the left and is called *a decrease in demand.*

FIGURE 3.3

Shifts in the Demand Curve
Any change that raises the quantity that buyers wish to purchase at a given price shifts the demand curve to the right. Any change that lowers the quantity that buyers wish to purchase at a given price shifts the demand curve to the left.

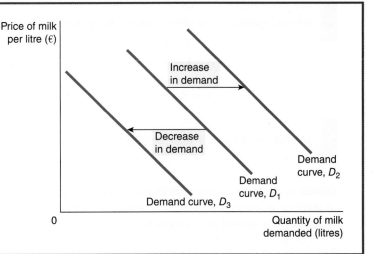

The following is a short summary of the main factors affecting demand, changes in which cause a shift of the demand curve.

Prices of Other (Related) Goods Suppose that the price of milk falls. The law of demand says that you will buy more milk. At the same time, you will probably buy less fruit juice. Because milk and fruit juice are both refreshing drinks, they satisfy similar desires. When a fall in the price of one good reduces the demand for another good, the two goods are called **substitutes**. Substitutes are often pairs of goods that are used in place of each other, such as butter and margarine, pullovers and sweatshirts, and cinema tickets and movie streaming. The more closely related substitute products are the more effect we might see on demand if the price of one of the substitutes changes.

> **substitutes** two goods for which an increase in the price of one leads to an increase in the demand for the other (and vice versa)

Now suppose that the price of breakfast cereals falls. According to the law of demand, more packets of breakfast cereals will be bought. When this happens we might expect to see the demand for milk increase as well, because breakfast cereals and milk are used together. When a fall in the price of one good raises the demand for another good, the two goods are called **complements**. Complements are often pairs of goods that are used together, such as petrol and cars, computers and software, bread and cheese, strawberries and cream, and bacon and eggs.

> **complements** two goods for which an increase in the price of one leads to a decrease in the demand for the other

Income Changes in incomes affect demand. A lower income means less to spend in total, so you would have to spend less on some – and probably most – goods. Equally, if income rises then it is likely that demand for many goods will also rise. If the demand for a good falls when income falls or rises as income rises, the good is called a **normal good**.

normal good a good for which, *ceteris paribus*, an increase in income leads to an increase in demand (and vice versa)

If the demand for a good rises when income falls, the good is called an **inferior good**. An example of an inferior good might be bus rides. If your income falls, you are less likely to buy a car or take a taxi and more likely to take the bus. As income falls, therefore, demand for bus rides tends to increase.

inferior good a good for which, *ceteris paribus*, an increase in income leads to a decrease in demand (and vice versa)

Tastes A key determinant of demand is tastes. If you like milk, you buy more of it. Understanding the role of tastes in consumer behaviour is taking on more importance as research in the fields of psychology and neurology are applied to economics.

Population Because market demand is derived from individual demands, it follows that the more buyers there are the higher the demand is likely to be. The size of the population, therefore, is a determinant of demand. A larger population, *ceteris paribus*, will mean a higher demand for all goods and services. Changes in the way the population is structured also influences demand. Many countries have an ageing population and this leads to a change in demand. If there is an increasing proportion of the population aged 65 and over, the demand for goods and services used by the elderly, such as the demand for retirement homes, insurance policies suitable for older people, the demand for smaller cars and for health care services, etc. is likely to increase in demand as a result.

Advertising Firms advertise their products in many different ways and it is likely that if a firm embarks on an advertising campaign then the demand for that product will increase.

Expectations of Consumers Expectations about the future may affect the demand for a good or service today. For example, if it was announced that the price of milk was expected to rise next month consumers may be more willing to buy milk at today's price.

> **SELF TEST** Make up an example of a demand schedule for pizza and graph the demand curve. Give an example of something that would cause the demand curve for pizza to shift to the right and to the left.

SUPPLY

We now turn to the other side of the market and examine the behaviour of sellers. Once again, to focus our thinking, we will continue to consider the market for milk.

The Supply Curve: The Relationship Between Price and Quantity Supplied

The **quantity supplied** of any good or service is the amount that sellers are willing and able to sell at different prices. When the price of milk is high, selling milk is profitable, and so sellers are willing to supply more. Sellers of milk work longer hours, buy more dairy cows and hire extra workers in order to increase supply to the market. By contrast, when the price of milk is low, the business is less profitable, and so sellers are willing to produce less milk. At a low price, some sellers may even choose to shut down, and their quantity supplied falls to zero. Because the quantity supplied rises as the price rises and falls as the price falls, we say that the quantity supplied is *positively related* to the price of the good. This relationship between price and quantity supplied is called the **law of supply**.

> **quantity supplied** the amount of a good that sellers are willing and able to sell at different prices
> **law of supply** the claim that, ceteris paribus, the quantity supplied of a good rises when the price of a good rises

The table in Figure 3.4 shows the quantity, Richard, a milk producer, is willing to supply, at various prices. At a price below €0.10 per litre, Richard does not supply any milk at all. As the price rises, he is willing to supply a greater and greater quantity. This is the **supply schedule**, a table that shows the relationship between the price of a good and the quantity supplied, holding constant everything else that influences how much producers of the good want to sell.

> **supply schedule** a table that shows the relationship between the price of a good and the quantity supplied

The graph in Figure 3.4 uses the numbers from the table to illustrate the law of supply. The curve relating price and quantity supplied is called the **supply curve**. The supply curve slopes upwards because, other things equal, a higher price means a greater quantity supplied.

> **supply curve** a graph of the relationship between the price of a good and the quantity supplied

FIGURE 3.4

Richard's Supply Schedule and Supply Curve

The supply schedule shows the quantity supplied at each price. This supply curve, which graphs the supply schedule, shows how the quantity supplied of the good changes as its price varies. Because a higher price increases the quantity supplied, the supply curve slopes upwards.

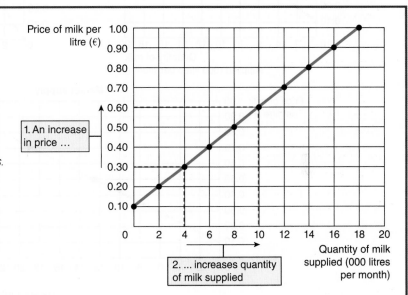

Price of milk per litre (€)	Quantity of milk supplied (000 litres per month)
0.00	0
0.10	0
0.20	2
0.30	4
0.40	6
0.50	8
0.60	10
0.70	12
0.80	14
0.90	16
1.00	18

Market Supply Versus Individual Supply

Just as market demand is the sum of the demands of all buyers, market supply is the sum of the supplies of all sellers. The table in Figure 3.5 shows the supply schedules for two milk producers – Richard and Megan. At any price, Richard's supply schedule tells us the quantity of milk Richard is willing to supply, and Megan's supply schedule tells us the quantity of milk Megan is willing to supply. The market supply is the sum of the two individual supplies (assuming Richard and Megan are the only suppliers in the market).

FIGURE 3.5

Market Supply as the Sum of Individual Supplies

The quantity supplied in a market is the sum of the quantities supplied by all the sellers at each price. Thus, the market supply curve is found by adding horizontally the individual supply curves. At a price of €0.50, Richard is willing to supply 8000 litres of milk per month, and Megan is willing to supply 5000 litres per month. The quantity supplied in the market at this price is 13 000 litres per month.

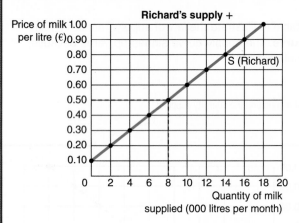

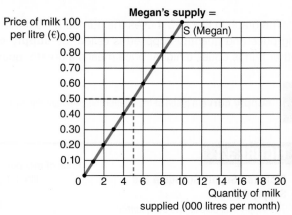

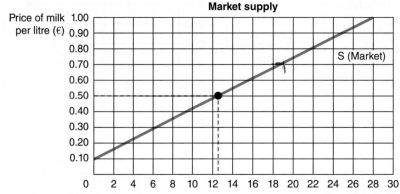

Price of milk per litre (€)	Richard +	Megan =	Market
	Quantity Supplied (000s litres per month)		
0.00	0	0	0
0.10	0	1	1
0.20	2	2	4
0.30	4	3	7
0.40	6	4	10
0.50	8	5	13
0.60	10	6	16
0.70	12	7	19
0.80	14	8	22
0.90	16	9	25
1.00	18	10	28

The graph in Figure 3.5 shows the supply curves that correspond to the supply schedules. As with demand curves, we find the total quantity supplied at any price by adding the individual quantities found on the horizontal axis of the individual supply curves. The market supply curve shows how the total quantity supplied varies as the price of the good varies.

Shifts in the Supply Curve

The supply curve for milk shows how much milk producers are willing to offer for sale at any given price, holding constant all the other factors beyond price that influence producers' decisions about how much to sell. This relationship can change over time, which is represented by a shift in the supply curve. For example, suppose the price of animal feed falls. Because animal feed is an input into producing milk, the fall in the price of animal feed makes selling milk more profitable. This raises the supply of milk: at any given price, sellers are now willing to produce a larger quantity. Thus, the supply curve for milk shifts to the right.

Figure 3.6 illustrates shifts in supply. Any change that raises quantity supplied at every price shifts the supply curve to the right and is called *an increase in supply*. Similarly, any change that reduces the quantity supplied at every price shifts the supply curve to the left and is called *a decrease in supply*.

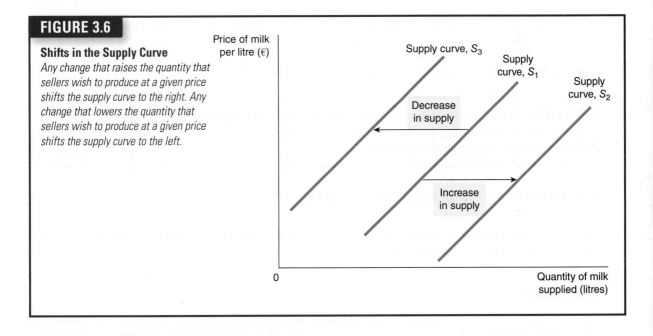

FIGURE 3.6

Shifts in the Supply Curve
Any change that raises the quantity that sellers wish to produce at a given price shifts the supply curve to the right. Any change that lowers the quantity that sellers wish to produce at a given price shifts the supply curve to the left.

A shift in the supply curve will be caused by one or more of the factors affecting supply *other than price*. The following provides a brief outline of these factors.

Profitability of Other Goods in Production and Prices of Goods in Joint Supply Firms have some flexibility in the supply of products and in some cases can switch production to other goods. For example, dairy farmers may decide to use some of their land to produce arable crops if the price of those crops rises in relation to the price of milk. If one crop becomes more profitable then it may be that the firm switches to the more profitable product. In other cases, firms may find that products are in joint supply; an increase in the supply of lamb, for example, might also lead to an increase in the supply of wool.

Technology Advances in technology increase productivity allowing more to be produced using fewer factor inputs. As a result costs, both total and unit, may fall and supply increases. The development of fertilizers and more efficient milking parlours, for example, have increased milk yields per cow and helped reduce costs as a result. By reducing firms' costs, the advance in technology increases the supply of milk.

Natural/Social Factors There are often many natural or social factors that affect supply. These include such things as the weather affecting crops, natural disasters, pestilence and disease, changing attitudes and social expectations (for example over the production of organic food, the disposal of waste, reducing carbon emissions, ethical supply sourcing and so on) all of which can have an influence on production decisions. Some or all of these may have an influence on the cost of inputs into production.

Input Prices – the Prices of Factors of Production To produce any output, sellers use various inputs including land, labour and capital. Dairy farmers, for example, will use fertilizer, feed, silage, farm buildings, veterinary services and the labour of workers. When the price of one or more of these inputs rises, producing milk is less profitable and firms supply less milk. If input prices rise substantially, a firm might shut down and supply no milk at all. If input prices fall for some reason, then production may be more profitable and there is an incentive to supply more at each price. Thus, the supply of a good is negatively related to the price of the inputs used to make the good.

Expectations of Producers Output levels can vary according to the expectations of producers about the future state of the market. The amount of milk a farm supplies today, for example, may depend on its expectations of the future. If it expects the price of milk to rise in the future, the firm might invest in more productive capacity or increase the size of the herd.

Number of Sellers If there are more sellers in the market then it makes sense that the supply would increase. Equally, if a number of dairy farms closed down then it is likely that the amount of milk supplied would also fall. The number of sellers in a market will be determined by the profitability of the product in question and the ease of entry and exit into and from the market.

SELF TEST Make up an example of a supply schedule for pizza and graph the implied supply curve. Give an example of something that would shift this supply curve. Would a change in price shift the supply curve?

SUPPLY AND DEMAND TOGETHER

Having analyzed supply and demand separately, we now combine them to see how they determine the quantity of a good sold in a market and its price.

Equilibrium

Figure 3.7 shows the market supply curve and market demand curve together. Equilibrium is defined as a state of rest, a point where there is no force acting for change. Economists refer to supply and demand as being *market forces.* In any market, the relationship between supply and demand exerts force on price. If supply is greater than demand or vice versa, then there is pressure on price to change. Market equilibrium occurs when the amount consumers wish to buy at a particular price is the same as the amount sellers are willing to offer for sale at that price. The price at this intersection is called the **equilibrium or market price**, and the quantity is called the **equilibrium quantity**. In Figure 3.7 the equilibrium price is 0.40 per litre, and the equilibrium quantity is 7000 litres of milk bought and sold per day.

> **equilibrium or market price** the price where the quantity demanded is the same as the quantity supplied
> **equilibrium quantity** the quantity bought and sold at the equilibrium price

At the equilibrium price, the quantity of the good that buyers are willing and able to buy exactly balances the quantity that sellers are willing and able to sell. The equilibrium price is sometimes called the *market-clearing price* because, *at this price*, everyone in the market has been satisfied: buyers have bought all they want to buy, and sellers have sold all they want to sell; there is no shortage in the market where demand is greater than supply and neither is there any surplus where supply is greater than demand.

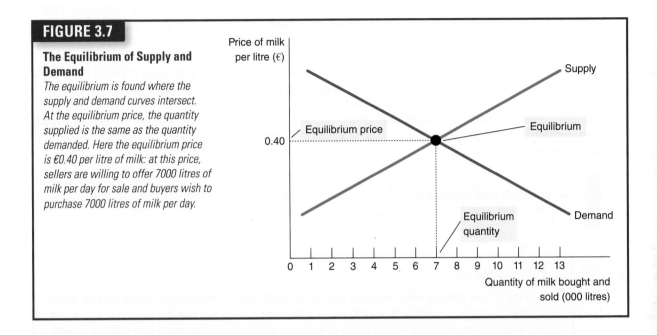

FIGURE 3.7

The Equilibrium of Supply and Demand
The equilibrium is found where the supply and demand curves intersect. At the equilibrium price, the quantity supplied is the same as the quantity demanded. Here the equilibrium price is €0.40 per litre of milk: at this price, sellers are willing to offer 7000 litres of milk per day for sale and buyers wish to purchase 7000 litres of milk per day.

The market will remain in equilibrium until something causes either a shift in the demand curve or a shift in the supply curve (or both). If one or both curves shift, at the existing equilibrium price, there will now be either a **surplus** or a **shortage**. The market mechanism takes time to adjust – sometimes it can be very quick (which tends to happen in highly organized markets like stock and commodity markets) and sometimes it is much slower to react. When the market is in disequilibrium and a shortage or surplus exists, the behaviour of buyers and sellers act as forces on price.

> **surplus** a situation in which the quantity supplied is greater than the quantity demanded at the going market price
> **shortage** a situation in which quantity demanded is greater than quantity supplied at the going market price

When there is a *surplus* or *excess supply* of a good, for example milk, suppliers are unable to sell all they want at the going price. Sellers find stocks of milk increasing so they respond to the surplus by cutting their prices. As the price falls, some consumers are persuaded to buy more milk and so there is a movement along the demand curve. Equally, some sellers in the market respond to the falling price by reducing the amount they are willing to offer for sale (a movement along the supply curve). Prices continue to fall until the market reaches a new equilibrium. The effect on price and the amount bought and sold depends on whether the demand curve or supply curve shifted in the first place (or whether both shifted). This is why analysis of markets is referred to as **comparative statics** because we are comparing one initial static equilibrium with another once market forces have worked their way through.

> **comparative statics** the comparison of one initial static equilibrium with another

If the shift in demand or supply that causes the equilibrium to be disturbed creates a shortage in the market, buyers' and sellers' behaviour again 'forces' price to change to bring the market back into equilibrium. A *shortage* or situation of *excess demand* occurs where the quantity of the good demanded exceeds the quantity supplied at the going price; buyers are unable to buy all they want at that price. With too many buyers chasing too few goods, sellers can respond to the shortage by raising their prices without losing sales. As the price rises, some buyers will drop out of the market and quantity demanded falls (a movement along the demand curve). Rising prices encourage some farmers to offer more milk for sale as it is now more profitable for them to do so and the quantity supplied rises. Once again this process will continue until the market moves towards equilibrium.

The activities of the many buyers and sellers 'automatically' push the market price towards the equilibrium price. Individual buyers and sellers don't consciously realize they are acting as forces for change in the market when they make their decisions but the collective act of all the many buyers and sellers tends to push markets towards equilibrium. This phenomenon is so pervasive that it is called the **law of supply and demand**: the price of any good adjusts to bring the quantity supplied and quantity demanded for that good into balance.

> **law of supply and demand** the claim that the price of any good adjusts to bring the quantity supplied and the quantity demanded for that good into balance

---

CASE STUDY   **Wheat Prices**

Across the EU and in many other countries around the world, data on the amount of land used for wheat production is readily available which makes it possible to be able to estimate the likely supply of wheat during a typical growing cycle. Farmers have to notify the authorities of how much land they are committing to growing wheat and also how much wheat is held in stock. The supply of wheat is determined by the amount of land used to grow wheat, the expected yield of wheat per acre, which in turn is affected by soil quality, weather conditions and other natural factors such as pests and diseases, the amount of wheat imported into the country and existing stocks of wheat. The demand for wheat comes from buyers using wheat for animal feed, for making fuel and for making food products including bread, cakes, pasta, biscuits and pastry products. Changes in these sectors will affect the demand for wheat so if there is an increase in the demand for biofuels, then the demand for wheat used in the production of biofuel will increase. How far this will affect the overall price for wheat will depend on the demand in other sectors; if the demand for animal feed falls, possibly because of favourable weather conditions which allow farmers to graze animals outside rather than having to feed them inside, then this might counterbalance the increase in the demand for wheat for biofuels and leave overall demand unchanged.

When all these factors are put together, the price farmers receive for wheat is determined. If demand for wheat is much higher than available supply then wheat prices will be likely to rise; if supply is greater than demand, wheat prices will be likely to fall and if demand and supply are relatively equal, the price of wheat will remain stable. Farmers face challenges in deciding how to use their land because the time taken to grow wheat has to be taken into account. Winter wheat is sown in the autumn in the UK and harvested in August. The price of wheat in September when soil preparation begins, is not necessarily any guide to the price the farmer will get on harvesting their crop. Farmers will use the data available and reports on supply, demand and prices to not only plan what to grow and how much but also to monitor changing market conditions throughout the growing period. The price which exists at the time of harvest is the price which farmers have to accept and the price received multiplied by the amount sold will determine the farmer's total revenue from wheat production.

Figure 3.8 shows the changing price of breadmaking wheat in the UK between January 2015 and March 2016. The figure shows that prices, overall, fell from around £176 per tonne to just over £105 per tonne. This fall in price could be significant for farmers. The figure also highlights the volatility of prices at different times during the period. Farmers selling wheat at the end of April 2015 would have

(Continued)

secured a price of just over £148 per tonne; just two weeks later, the price had dropped to around £135 per tonne. Most farmers will have a reasonably clear idea of the costs of production associated with growing wheat but changes in prices over which they have no control will affect the profit they make and make it harder to be able to estimate the likely profit they will generate in the future and hence how they can plan for the future. Having a model which quantifies demand and supply accurately and can give a reasonable prediction of future price, therefore, is important to farmers and buyers in planning and managing their businesses.

FIGURE 3.8

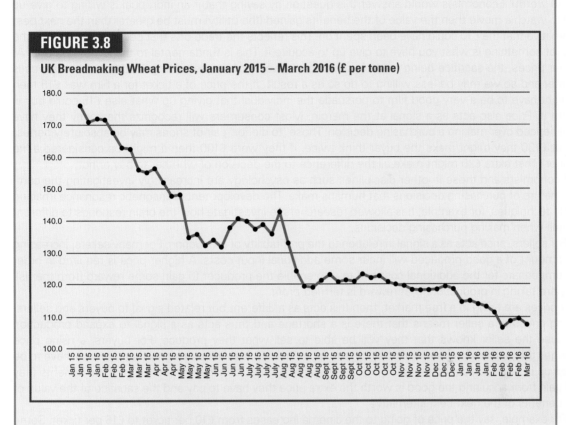

UK Breadmaking Wheat Prices, January 2015 – March 2016 (£ per tonne)

The market for wheat has a number of characteristics of a perfect market with supply and demand determining the price of wheat.

Prices as Signals

The main function of price in a competitive market is to act as a signal to both buyers and sellers. For buyers, price tells them something about what they have to give up (usually an amount of money) to acquire the benefits that having the good will confer on them. These benefits are referred to as the utility or satisfaction derived from consumption and reflects the willingness to pay. If an individual is willing to pay €10 to go and watch a movie, then economists will assume that the value of the benefits gained from watching the movie is worth that amount of money to the individual. But what does this mean? How much is €10 worth? Economists would answer this question by saying that if an individual is willing to give up €10 to watch a movie then the value of the benefits gained (the utility) must be greater than the next best alternative that the €10 could have been spent on. This reflects the trade-offs that people face and that the cost of something is what you have to give up to acquire it. This is fundamental to the law of demand. At higher prices, the sacrifice being made in terms of the value of the benefits gained from alternatives is greater and so we may be less willing to do so as a result. If the price of a ticket for a film was €15 then it might have to be a very good film to persuade the individual that giving up what else €15 could buy is worth it. Price also acts as a signal at the margin. Most consumers will recognize the agony they have experienced over making a purchasing decision. Those 'to die for' pair of shoes may be absolutely perfect but at €120 they might make the buyer think twice. If they were €100 then it might be considered a 'no brainer'. That extra €20 might make all the difference to the decision of whether to buy or not.

Economists and those in other disciplines such as psychology are increasingly investigating the complex nature of purchasing decisions that humans make. The development of magnetic resonance imaging (MRI) techniques, for example, has allowed researchers to investigate how the brain responds to different stimuli when making purchasing decisions.

For sellers, price acts as a signal in relation to the profitability of production. For many sellers, increasing the amount of a good produced will incur some additional input costs. A higher price is required in order to compensate for the additional cost and to also enable the producer to gain some reward from the risk they are taking in production. That reward is termed *profit*.

If prices are rising in a free market, then this acts as a different but related signal to buyers and sellers. Rising prices to a seller means that there is a shortage and thus acts as a signal to expand production because the seller knows that they will be able to sell what they produce. For buyers, a rising price changes the nature of the trade-off they have to face. Rising prices act as a signal that more will have to be given up in order to acquire the good and they will have to decide whether the value of the benefits they will gain from acquiring the good is worth the extra price they have to pay and the sacrifice of the value of the benefits of the next best alternative.

For example, say the price of going to the cinema increases from €10 per ticket to €15 per ticket. Some cinema goers will happily pay the extra because they really enjoy a night out at the cinema but some people might start to think that €15 is a bit expensive. They might think that they could have a night out at a restaurant with friends and have a meal and a few drinks for €15 and that would represent more value to them than going to the cinema. Some of these people would, therefore, stop going to the cinema and go to a restaurant instead – the price signal to these people has changed.

What we do know is that for both buyers and sellers, there are many complex processes that occur in decision-making. Whilst we do not fully understand all these processes yet, economists are constantly searching for new insights that might help them understand the workings of markets more fully. All of us go through these complex processes every time we make a purchasing decision – we may not realize it but we do! Having some appreciation of these processes is fundamental to thinking like an economist.

Three Steps to Analyzing Changes in Equilibrium

So far we have seen how supply and demand together determine a market's equilibrium, which in turn determines the price of the good and the amount of the good that buyers purchase and sellers produce. Of course, the equilibrium price and quantity depend on the position of the supply and demand curves. We use comparative static analysis to look at what happens when some event shifts one of these curves and causes the equilibrium in the market to change.

To do this we proceed in three steps:

1. We decide whether the event in question shifts the supply curve, the demand curve or, in some cases, both.
2. We decide whether the curve shifts to the right or to the left.
3. We use the supply and demand diagram to compare the initial and the new equilibrium, which shows how the shift affects the equilibrium price and quantity bought and sold.

To see how these three steps work in analyzing market changes, let's consider various events that might affect the market for milk. We begin the analysis by assuming that the market for milk is in equilibrium with the price of milk at €0.50 per litre and 13 000 litres are bought and sold per day and then follow our three-step approach.

Example: A Change in Demand Suppose that one summer, the weather is very hot. How does this event affect the market for milk? To answer this question, let's follow our three steps:

1. The hot weather affects the demand curve by changing people's taste for milk. That is, the weather changes the amount of milk that people want to buy at any given price.
2. Because hot weather makes people want to drink more milk, make refreshing milk shakes, or producers of ice cream buy more milk to make ice cream, the demand curve shifts to the right. Figure 3.9 shows this increase in demand as the shift in the demand curve from D_1 to D_2. (What you have to remember now is that demand curve D_1 does not exist anymore and so we have shown it as a dashed line.) This shift indicates that the quantity of milk demanded is higher at every price. At the existing market price of €0.50 buyers now want to buy 19 000 litres of milk but sellers are only offering 13 000 litres per day for sale at this price. The shift in demand has led to a shortage of milk in the market of 6000 litres per day represented by the bracket.
3. The shortage encourages producers to increase the output of milk (a movement along the supply curve). There is an *increase in quantity supplied*. But, the additional production incurs extra costs and so a higher price is required to compensate sellers. As sellers increase the amount of milk offered for sale as price rises, consumers behave differently. Some consumers who were willing to buy milk at €0.50 are not willing to pay more and so drop out of the market. As price creeps up, therefore, there is a movement along the demand curve representing those consumers who drop out of the market. The market forces of supply and demand continue to work through until a new equilibrium is reached. The new equilibrium price is now €0.60 per litre and the equilibrium quantity bought and sold is now 16 000

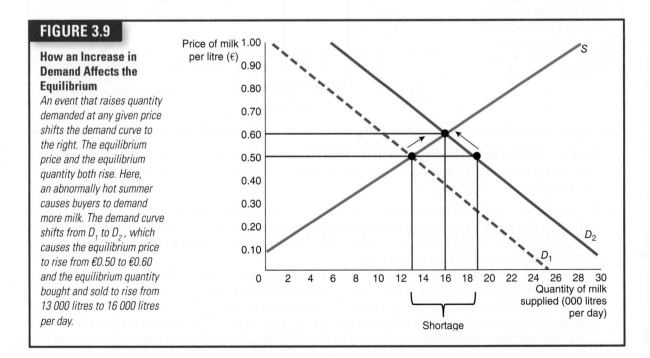

FIGURE 3.9

How an Increase in Demand Affects the Equilibrium
An event that raises quantity demanded at any given price shifts the demand curve to the right. The equilibrium price and the equilibrium quantity both rise. Here, an abnormally hot summer causes buyers to demand more milk. The demand curve shifts from D_1 to D_2, which causes the equilibrium price to rise from €0.50 to €0.60 and the equilibrium quantity bought and sold to rise from 13 000 litres to 16 000 litres per day.

litres per day. To compare our starting and finishing positions, the hot weather which caused the shift in the demand curve has led to an increase in the price of milk and the quantity of milk bought and sold.

Example: A Change in Supply Suppose that, during another summer, a drought drives up the price of animal feed for dairy cattle. How does this event affect the market for milk? Once again, to answer this question, we follow our three steps:

1. The change in the price of animal feed, an input into producing milk, affects the supply curve. By raising the costs of production, it reduces the amount of milk that firms produce and sell at any given price. Some farmers may send cattle for slaughter because they cannot afford to feed them anymore and some farmers may simply decide to sell up and get out of farming altogether. The demand curve does not change because the higher cost of inputs does not directly affect the amount of milk consumers wish to buy.

2. The supply curve shifts to the left because, at every price, the total amount that farmers are willing and able to sell is reduced. Figure 3.10 illustrates this decrease in supply as a shift in the supply curve from S_1 to S_2. At a price of €0.50 sellers are now only able to offer 2000 litres of milk for sale per day but demand is still 13 000 litres per day. The shift in supply to the left has created a shortage in the market of 11 000 litres per day. Once again, the shortage will create pressure on price to rise as buyers look to purchase milk.

3. As Figure 3.10 shows, the shortage raises the equilibrium price from €0.50 to €0.70 per litre and lowers the equilibrium quantity bought and sold from 13 000 to 8000 litres per day. As a result of the animal feed price increase, the price of milk rises, and the quantity of milk bought and sold falls.

FIGURE 3.10

How a Decrease in Supply Affects the Equilibrium

An event that reduces quantity supplied at any given price shifts the supply curve to the left. The equilibrium price rises, and the equilibrium quantity falls. Here, an increase in the price of animal feed (an input) causes sellers to supply less milk. The supply curve shifts from S_1 to S_2, which causes the equilibrium price of milk to rise from €0.50 to €0.70 and the equilibrium quantity to fall from 13 000 litres to 8000 litres per day.

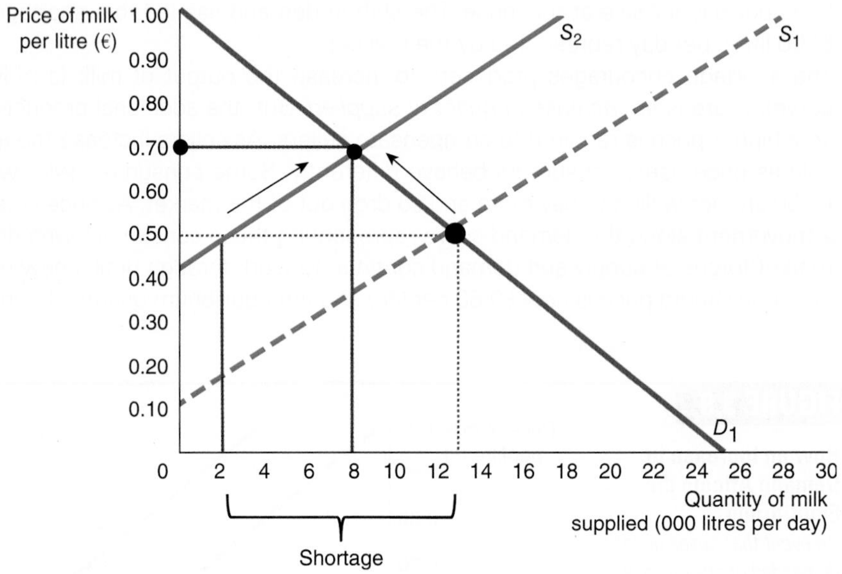

Example: A Change in Both Supply and Demand (i) Now suppose that the hot weather and the rise in animal feed occur during the same time period. To analyze this combination of events, we again follow our three steps:

1. We determine that both curves must shift. The hot weather affects the demand curve for milk because it alters the amount that consumers want to buy at any given price. At the same time, when the rise in animal feed drives up input prices, it alters the supply curve for milk because it changes the amount that firms want to sell at any given price.

2. The curves shift in the same directions as they did in our previous analysis: the demand curve shifts to the right, and the supply curve shifts to the left. Figure 3.11 illustrates these shifts.

3. As Figure 3.11 shows, there are two possible outcomes that might result, depending on the relative size of the demand and supply shifts. In both cases, the equilibrium price rises. In panel (a), where demand increases substantially while supply falls just a little, the equilibrium quantity bought and sold

also rises. By contrast, in panel (b), where supply falls substantially while demand rises just a little, the equilibrium quantity bought and sold falls. Thus, these events certainly raise the price of milk, but their impact on the amount of milk bought and sold is ambiguous (that is, it could go either way).

FIGURE 3.11

A Shift in Both Supply and Demand (i)

Here we observe a simultaneous increase in demand and decrease in supply. Two outcomes are possible. In panel (a), the equilibrium price rises from P_1 to P_2 and the equilibrium quantity rises from Q_1 to Q_2. In panel (b), the equilibrium price again rises from P_1 to P_2, but the equilibrium quantity falls from Q_1 to Q_2.

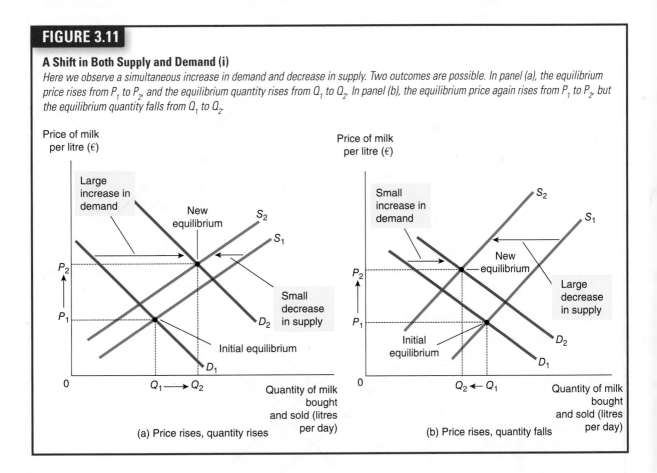

(a) Price rises, quantity rises

(b) Price rises, quantity falls

Example: A Change in Both Supply and Demand (ii) We are now going to look at a slightly different scenario but with both supply and demand changing together. Assume that forecasters have predicted a heatwave for some weeks. We know that the hot weather is likely to increase demand for milk and so the demand curve will shift to the right. However, sellers' expectations that sales of milk will increase as a result of the forecasts mean that they take steps to expand production of milk. This would lead to a shift of the supply curve to the right – more milk is now offered for sale at every price. To analyze this particular combination of events, we again follow our three steps:

1. We determine that both curves must shift. The hot weather affects the demand curve because it alters the amount of milk that consumers want to buy at any given price. At the same time, the expectations of producers alter the supply curve for milk because they change the amount that firms want to sell at any given price.
2. Both demand and supply curves shift to the right: Figure 3.12 illustrates these shifts.
3. As Figure 3.12 shows, there are three possible outcomes that might result, depending on the relative size of the demand and supply shifts. In panel (a), where demand increases substantially while supply rises just a little, the equilibrium price and quantity rises. By contrast, in panel (b), where supply rises substantially while demand rises just a little, the equilibrium price falls but the equilibrium quantity rises. In panel (c) the increases in demand and supply are identical and so equilibrium price does not change. Equilibrium quantity will increase, however. Thus, these events have different effects on the price of milk although the amount bought and sold in each case is higher. In this instance the effect on price is ambiguous.

FIGURE 3.12

A Shift in Both Supply and Demand (ii)

Here, again, we observe a simultaneous increase in demand and supply. Here, three outcomes are possible. In panel (a) the equilibrium price rises from P_1 to P_2 and the equilibrium quantity rises from Q_1 to Q_2. In panel (b), the equilibrium price falls from P_1 to P_2 but the equilibrium quantity rises from Q_1 to Q_2. In panel (c), there is no change to the equilibrium price but the equilibrium quantity rises from Q_1 to Q_2.

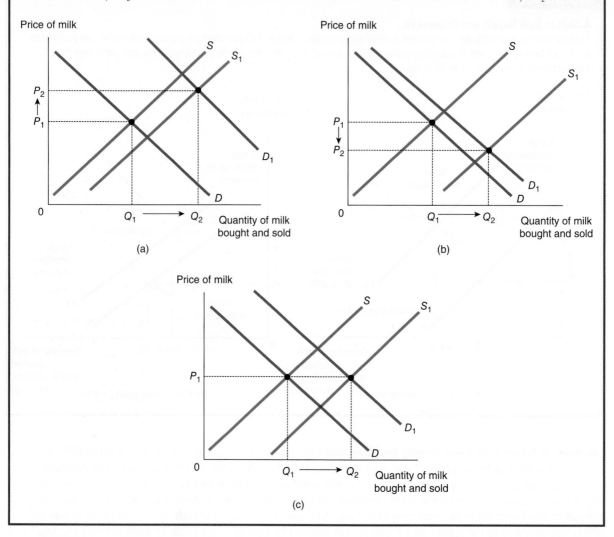

(a)

(b)

(c)

Summary We have just seen four examples of how to use demand and supply curves to analyze a change in equilibrium. Whenever an event shifts the demand curve, the supply curve, or perhaps both curves, you can use these tools to predict how the event will alter the amount bought and sold in equilibrium and the price at which the good is bought and sold. Table 3.1 shows the predicted outcome for any combination of shifts in the two curves. To make sure you understand how to use the tools of supply and demand, pick a few entries in this table and make sure you can explain to yourself why the table contains the prediction it does.

CONCLUSION: HOW PRICES ALLOCATE RESOURCES

This chapter has analyzed demand and supply in a single market. Although our discussion has centred on the market for milk, the lessons learned here apply in other markets as well. What must be remembered is that we have to take into account the assumptions that were outlined in this model. In many markets,

TABLE 3.1	What Happens to Price and Quantity When Demand or Supply Shifts?

As a test, make sure you can explain each of the entries in this table using a supply and demand diagram.

	No change in supply	An increase in supply	A decrease in supply
No change in demand	P same Q same	P down Q up	P up Q down
An increase in demand	P up Q up	P ambiguous Q up	P up Q ambiguous
A decrease in demand	P down Q down	P down Q ambiguous	P ambiguous Q down

some of the assumptions may not hold in which case the outcomes may be different to those predicted. What is consistent in the model is that whenever you go to a shop to buy something, you are contributing to the demand for that item. Whenever you look for a job, you are contributing to the supply of labour services. Because demand and supply are such pervasive economic phenomena, the model of demand and supply can be a powerful tool for analysis providing we take into account its assumptions. In Chapter 1 we noted that markets can be a good way to organize economic activity. It is still too early to judge whether market outcomes are good or bad but in this chapter we have begun to see how markets work. In any economic system, scarce resources have to be allocated among competing uses. Market economies harness the forces of demand and supply to serve that end. Demand and supply together determine the prices of the economy's many different goods and services; prices in turn are the signals that guide the allocation of resources.

For example, consider the allocation of property on the beach. Because the amount of this property is limited, not everyone can enjoy the luxury of living by the beach. Who gets this resource? The answer is: whoever is willing and able to pay the price. The price of seafront property adjusts until the quantity of property demanded exactly balances the quantity supplied. Thus, in market economies, prices are the mechanism for rationing scarce resources. Of course, this particular outcome may not be considered 'fair' by everyone – individuals who have money are in a more powerful position to occupy these desirable seafront properties and the market outcome in economies may be skewed to benefit those who have wealth and power at the expense of those who do not. This consideration of power is an important one which economists are also concerned with but, as noted in Chapter 2, involves assessing value judgements and a consideration of what is 'fair'. These are challenging questions which we should not shy away from and it is useful to have them in mind as we develop the analysis of market systems in subsequent chapters.

IN THE NEWS

Markets in Action

We have seen how we can use supply and demand analysis to begin to understand markets. The real world has examples of markets in action every day. This article highlights an example of markets in action.

The Market for Data Scientists

The market for labour includes an element of demand and supply. The demand for labour is driven by firms and organizations wanting to hire workers to produce an output and the supply of labour is dependent on the number of people willing and able to offer their services in different occupations. The price of labour is the wage rate. Data scientists use statistics, maths and skills in computer science to analyze business data, interpret what it means, identify patterns, and communicate information to business managers and leaders to help meet challenges and make decisions more effectively which will help improve the business' prospects. Many data scientists will have a post graduate degree and often a PhD. The supply of data scientists is therefore relatively limited because of the qualifications and skills needed to become one.

On the demand side, many firms face an increasingly challenging and complex business environment and have to manage data

The demand for data scientists is pushing up the wages rates of those who have the skills for such a job.

from many different sources. Making sense of all this data and what it means for the business is becoming more significant as firms seek to gain advantages over their rivals. The demand for data scientists, therefore, is growing. Surveys conducted by the Massachusetts Institute of Technology (MIT) Sloan Management School, SAS (a business analytics software and services company), and Burtch Works Study in the United States suggested that base salaries increased by 8 per cent in 2014 with salaries ranging from about €80 000 for a junior level to over €220 000 for more experienced data scientist managers. Those who change jobs can see their salaries increasing by around 16 per cent.

Questions

1 To what extent would you say that the market for data scientists is highly competitive? Explain.
2 Draw a demand and supply diagram for the market for data scientists with the wage rate (the price of labour) on the vertical axis and the quantity of data scientists on the horizontal axis. Show the equilibrium wage rate for data scientists and the equilibrium number of data scientists employed.
   a. Assume that the demand for data scientists increases. What would you predict will happen to the wage rate and the number of data scientists employed? What does your answer depend upon?
   b. Now assume that in the longer run, the supply of data scientists also increases. What would you predict will happen to the wage rate and the number employed and what does the outcome you predict depend upon?
3 The surveys conducted suggest that the demand for data scientists will continue to increase and that the wage rate will rise as a result (other things being equal). What signal do you think that the rise in the wage rate sends to both buyers and sellers in the market for data scientists?
4 The principle of *ceteris paribus* is important in the market model. In analyzing the market for data scientists and using the model to make predictions, what do you think will need to be assumed to be held constant? Is this a reasonable assumption to make in this instance? Explain.
5 How quickly do you think the market for data scientists can respond to changes in both demand and supply factors? Justify your answer.

Sources: http://www.forbes.com/sites/gilpress/2015/04/30/the-supply-and-demand-of-data-scientists-what-the-surveys-say/#2f4daf5d205e; http://www.burtchworks.com/files/2014/07/Burtch-Works-Study_DS_final.pdf

SUMMARY

- Economists use the model of supply and demand to analyze competitive markets. In a competitive market, there are many buyers and sellers, each of whom has little or no influence on the market price.

- The demand curve shows how the quantity of a good demanded depends on the price. According to the law of demand, as the price of a good falls, the quantity demanded rises. Therefore, the demand curve slopes downwards.

- In addition to price, other determinants of how much consumers want to buy include income, the prices of substitutes and complements, tastes, expectations, the size and structure of the population and advertising. If one of these factors changes, the demand curve shifts.

- The supply curve shows how the quantity of a good supplied depends on the price. According to the law of supply, as the price of a good rises the quantity supplied rises. Therefore, the supply curve slopes upwards.

- In addition to price, other determinants of how much producers want to sell include the price and profitability of goods in production and joint supply, input prices, technology, expectations, the number of sellers and natural and social factors. If one of these factors changes, the supply curve shifts.

- The intersection of the supply and demand curves determines the market equilibrium. At the equilibrium price, the quantity demanded equals the quantity supplied.

- The behaviour of buyers and sellers drives markets towards their equilibrium. When the market price is above the equilibrium price, there is a surplus of the good, which causes the market price to fall. When the market price is below the equilibrium price, there is a shortage, which causes the market price to rise.

- To analyze how any event influences a market, we use the supply and demand diagram to examine how the event affects the equilibrium price and quantity. To do this we follow three steps. First, we decide whether the event shifts the supply curve or the demand curve (or both). Second, we decide which direction the curve (or curves) shifts. Third, we compare the new equilibrium with the initial equilibrium.

- In market economies, prices are the signals that guide economic decisions and thereby allocate scarce resources. For every good in the economy, the price ensures that supply and demand are in balance. The equilibrium price then determines how much of the good buyers choose to purchase and how much sellers choose to produce.

QUESTIONS FOR REVIEW

1 What is a competitive market? Briefly describe the types of markets other than perfectly competitive markets.

2 What determines the quantity of a good that buyers demand?

3 What are the demand schedule and the demand curve, and how are they related? Why does the demand curve slope downwards?

4 Does a change in consumers' tastes lead to a movement along the demand curve or a shift in the demand curve? Does a change in price lead to a movement along the demand curve or a shift in the demand curve?

5 Francine's income declines and, as a result, she buys more cabbage. Are cabbages an inferior or a normal good? What happens to Francine's demand curve for cabbages?

6 What determines the quantity of a good that sellers supply?

7 What are the supply schedule and the supply curve, and how are they related? Why does the supply curve slope upwards?

8 Does a change in producers' technology lead to a movement along the supply curve or a shift in the supply curve? Does a change in price lead to a movement along the supply curve or a shift in the supply curve?

9 Define the equilibrium of a market. Describe the forces that move a market toward its equilibrium.

10 Describe the role of prices in market economies.

PROBLEMS AND APPLICATIONS

1 Explain each of the following statements using supply and demand diagrams.
   a. When there is a drought in southern Europe, the price of soft fruit rises in supermarkets throughout Europe.
   b. When a report is published linking a product with an increased risk of cancer, the price of the product concerned tends to fall.
   c. When conflict breaks out in the Middle East, the price of petrol in Europe rises and the price of a used Mercedes falls.

2 'An increase in the demand for mozzarella cheese raises the quantity of mozzarella demanded, but not the quantity supplied.' Is this statement true or false? Explain.

3 Technological advances have reduced the cost of producing mobile phones. How do you think this affected the market for mobile phones? For software used on mobile phones? For landlines?

4 Using supply and demand diagrams, show the effect of the following events on the market for sweatshirts.
   a. A drought in Egypt damages the cotton crop.
   b. The price of leather jackets falls.
   c. All universities require students to attend morning exercise classes in appropriate attire.
   d. New knitting machines are invented.

5 Suppose that in the year 2005 the number of births is temporarily high. How might this baby boom affect the price of babysitting services in 2010 and 2020? (Hint: 5-year-olds need babysitters, whereas 15-year-olds can be babysitters.)

6 Think about the market for cigars.
   a. Are cigars substitutes or complements for cigarettes?
   b. Using a supply and demand diagram, show what happens in the markets for cigars if the tax on cigarettes is increased.
   c. If policymakers wanted to reduce total tobacco consumption, what policies could they combine with the cigarette tax?

7 The market for pizza has the following demand and supply schedules:

Price (€)	Quantity demanded	Quantity supplied
4	135	26
5	104	53
6	81	81
7	68	98
8	53	110
9	39	121

Graph the demand and supply curves. What is the equilibrium price and quantity in this market? If the actual price in this market were above the equilibrium price, what would drive the market towards the equilibrium? If the actual price in this market were below the equilibrium price, what would drive the market towards the equilibrium?

8 Consider the following events: Scientists reveal that eating oranges decreases the risk of diabetes, and at the same time, farmers in Spain use a new fertilizer which increases the yield of oranges per tree. Illustrate and explain what effect these changes have on the equilibrium price and quantity of oranges.

9 Suppose that the price of tickets to see your local football team play at home is determined by market forces. Currently, the demand and supply schedules are as follows:

Price (€)	Quantity demanded	Quantity supplied
10	50 000	30 000
20	40 000	30 000
30	30 000	30 000
40	20 000	30 000
50	10 000	30 000

a. Draw the demand and supply curves. What is unusual about this supply curve? Why might this be true?

b. What are the equilibrium price and quantity of tickets?

c. Your team plans to increase total capacity in its stadium by 5000 seats next season. What admission price should it charge?

10 Market research has revealed the following information about the market for chocolate bars: $Qd = 1600 - 300P$, and the supply schedule is $Qs = 1400 + 700P$. Calculate the equilibrium price and quantity in the market for chocolate bars.

4 ELASTICITY AND ITS APPLICATIONS

The price a firm charges for its products is a vital part of its product positioning – what the product offering is in relation to competitors. We have seen in Chapter 3 how markets are dynamic and that price acts as a signal to both sellers and buyers; when prices change, the signal is altered and producer and consumer behaviour changes.

We know from Chapter 3 that the law of demand states that when price rises, demand falls and supply rises. What we did not discuss in the chapter was *how far* demand and supply change in response to changes in price – in other words, how sensitive supply and demand is to a change in price. When studying how some event or policy affects a market, we discuss not only the direction of the effects but their magnitude as well. **Elasticity** is a measure of how much buyers and sellers respond to changes in market conditions and knowledge of this concept allows us to analyze supply and demand with greater precision.

 elasticity a measure of the responsiveness of quantity demanded or quantity supplied to one of its determinants

THE PRICE ELASTICITY OF DEMAND

Businesses cannot directly control demand. They can seek to influence demand (and do) by utilizing a variety of strategies and tactics but ultimately the consumer invariably decides whether to buy a product or not. One important way in which consumer behaviour can be influenced is through a firm changing the prices of its goods. Many firms do have some control over the price they can charge although as we have seen, in perfectly competitive markets this is not the case as the firm is a price taker. An understanding of the price elasticity of demand is important in anticipating and analyzing the likely effects of changes in price on demand.

The Price Elasticity of Demand and its Determinants

The law of demand states that a fall in the price of a good raises the quantity demanded. The **price elasticity of demand** measures how much the quantity demanded responds to a change in price. Demand for a good is said to be *elastic* or price sensitive if the quantity demanded responds substantially to changes in price. Demand is said to be *inelastic or* price insensitive if the quantity demanded responds only slightly to changes in price.

price elasticity of demand a measure of how much the quantity demanded of a good responds to a change in the price of that good, computed as the percentage change in quantity demanded divided by the percentage change in price

The price elasticity of demand for any good measures how willing consumers are to move away from the good as its price rises. Thus, the elasticity reflects the many economic, social and psychological forces that influence consumer tastes. Based on experience, however, we can state some general rules about what determines the price elasticity of demand.

Availability of Close Substitutes Goods with close substitutes tend to have more elastic demand because it is easier for consumers to switch from that good to others. For example, butter and spreads are easily substitutable. A relatively small increase in the price of butter, assuming the price of spread is held fixed, causes the quantity of butter sold to fall by a relatively large amount. As a general rule, the closer the substitute the more price elastic the good is because it is easier for consumers to switch from one to the other. By contrast, because eggs are a food without a close substitute, the demand for eggs is less price elastic than the demand for butter.

Necessities versus Luxuries Necessities tend to have relatively inelastic demands, whereas luxuries have relatively elastic demands. People use gas and electricity to heat their homes and cook their food. If the price of gas and electricity rose together, people would not demand dramatically less of them. They might try and be more energy-efficient and reduce their demand a little, but they would still need hot food and warm homes. By contrast, when the price of sailing dinghies rises, the quantity of sailing dinghies demanded falls substantially. The reason is that most people view hot food and warm homes as necessities and a sailing dinghy as a luxury. Of course, whether a good is a necessity or a luxury depends not on the intrinsic properties of the good but on the preferences of the buyer. For an avid sailor with little concern over health issues, sailing dinghies might be a necessity with inelastic demand, and hot food and a warm place to sleep less of a necessity having a more elastic demand as a result.

Definition of the Market The elasticity of demand in any market depends on how we draw the boundaries of the market. Narrowly defined markets tend to be associated with a more price elastic demand than broadly defined markets, because it is easier to find close substitutes for narrowly defined goods. For example, food, a broad category, has a fairly price inelastic demand because there are no good substitutes for food. Ice cream, a narrower category, has a more price elastic demand because it is easy to substitute other desserts for ice cream. Vanilla ice cream, a very narrow category, has a very price elastic demand because other flavours of ice cream are very close substitutes for vanilla.

Proportion of Income Devoted to the Product Some products have a relatively high price and take a larger proportion of income than others. Buying a new suite of furniture for a lounge, for example, tends to take up a large amount of income whereas buying an ice cream might account for only a tiny proportion of income. If the price of a three-piece suite rises by 10 per cent, therefore, this is likely to have a greater effect on demand for this furniture than a 10 per cent increase in the price of an ice cream. The higher the proportion of income devoted to the product the greater the price elasticity is likely to be.

Time Horizon Goods tend to have more price elastic demand over longer time horizons. When the price of petrol rises, the quantity of petrol demanded falls only slightly in the first few months. Over time, however, people buy more fuel-efficient cars, switch to public transport and move closer to where they work. Within several years, the quantity of petrol demanded falls more substantially. Similarly, if the price of a unit of electricity rises much above an equivalent energy unit of gas, demand may fall only slightly in the short run because many people already have electric cookers or electric heating appliances installed in their homes and cannot easily switch. If the price difference persists over several years, however, people may find it worth their while to replace their old electric heating and cooking appliances with new gas appliances and the demand for electricity will fall.

Computing the Price Elasticity of Demand

Economists compute the price elasticity of demand as the percentage change in the quantity demanded divided by the percentage change in the price. That is:

$$\text{Price elasticity of demand} = \frac{\text{Percentage change in quantity demanded}}{\text{Percentage change in price}}$$

For example, suppose that a 10 per cent increase in the price of a packet of breakfast cereal causes the amount bought to fall by 20 per cent. Because the quantity demanded of a good is negatively related to its price, the percentage change in quantity will always have the opposite sign to the percentage change in price. In this example, the percentage change in price is a *positive* 10 per cent (reflecting an increase), and the percentage change in quantity demanded is a *negative* 20 per cent (reflecting a decrease). For this reason, price elasticities of demand are sometimes reported as negative numbers. In this book we follow the common practice of dropping the minus sign and reporting all price elasticities as positive numbers. (Mathematicians call this the *absolute value*.) With this convention, a larger price elasticity implies a greater responsiveness of quantity demanded to price.

In our example, the price elasticity of demand is calculated as:

$$\text{Price elasticity of demand} = \frac{20\%}{10\%} = 2$$

A price elasticity of demand of 2 reflects the fact that the change in the quantity demanded is proportionately twice as large as the change in the price.

Elasticity can have a value which lies between 0 and infinity. Between 0 and 1, elasticity is said to be inelastic, that is the percentage change in quantity demanded is less than the percentage change in price. If elasticity is greater than 1 it said to be elastic – the percentage change in quantity demanded is greater than the percentage change in price. If the percentage change in quantity demanded is the same as the percentage change in price then the elasticity is equal to 1 and is called unit or unitary elasticity.

We have and will use the term 'relatively' elastic or inelastic throughout our analysis. The use of this term is important. We can look at goods, for example, both of which are classed as 'inelastic' but where one is more inelastic than the other. If we are comparing good *x*, which has a price elasticity of 0.2, and good *y*, which has an elasticity of 0.5, then both are price inelastic but good *y* is more price elastic in comparison. As with so much of economics, careful use of terminology is important in conveying a clear understanding.

You will probably find that the institution you are studying in covers a more detailed method of calculating elasticity. In this next section we will describe two such methods, the midpoint or arc elasticity of demand, and point elasticity of demand. Some institutions may focus on only one of these methods in which case you can (if you wish) skip the method below which your institution does not cover.

Using the Midpoint (Arc Elasticity of Demand) Method

If you try calculating the price elasticity of demand between two points on a demand curve, you will notice that the elasticity from point A to point B seems different from the elasticity from point B to point A. For example, consider these numbers:

Point A: Price = €4 Quantity = 120

Point B: Price = €6 Quantity = 80

The standard way to compute a percentage change is to divide the change by the initial level and multiply by 100. Going from point A to point B, the price rises by 50 per cent, and the quantity falls by 33 per cent, indicating that the price elasticity of demand is 33/50 or 0.66. By contrast, going from point B to point A, the price falls by 33 per cent, and the quantity rises by 50 per cent, indicating that the price elasticity of demand is 50/33 or 1.5.

The midpoint method overcomes this problem by computing a percentage change by dividing the change by the midpoint (or average) of the initial and final levels. We can express the midpoint method with the following formula for the price elasticity of demand between two points, denoted (Q_1, P_1) and (Q_2, P_2):

$$\text{Price elasticity of demand} = \frac{(Q_2 - Q_1)/[(Q_2 + Q_1)/2]}{(P_2 - P_1)/[(P_2 + P_1)/2]}$$

The numerator is the proportionate change in quantity computed using the midpoint method, and the denominator is the proportionate change in price computed using the midpoint method.

Using the example above, €5 is the midpoint of €4 and €6. Therefore, according to the midpoint method, a change from €4 to €6 is considered a 40 per cent rise, because $(6 - 4)/5 \times 100 = 40$. Similarly, a change from €6 to €4 is considered a 40 per cent fall.

Because the midpoint method gives the same answer regardless of the direction of change, it is often used when calculating the price elasticity of demand between two points. In our example, when going from point A to point B, the price rises by 40 per cent, and the quantity falls by 40 per cent. Similarly, when going from point B to point A, the price falls by 40 per cent, and the quantity rises by 40 per cent. In both directions, the price elasticity of demand equals 1.

Using the Point Elasticity of Demand Method

Rather than measuring elasticity between two points on the demand curve, point elasticity of demand measures elasticity at a particular point on the demand curve. Let us take our general formula for price elasticity given by:

$$Price\ elasticity\ of\ demand = \frac{\%\Delta Qd}{\%\Delta P}$$

Where the Greek letter delta (Δ) means 'change'. To calculate the percentage change in quantity demanded and the percentage change in price we use the following formulas:

$$Percentage\ change\ in\ quantity\ demanded = \frac{\Delta Qd}{Qd} \times 100$$

And

$$Percentage\ change\ in\ price = \frac{\Delta P}{P} \times 100$$

We can substitute these two formulas into our elasticity formula to get:

$$Price\ elasticity\ of\ demand = \frac{\Delta Qd}{Qd} / \frac{\Delta P}{P}$$

This can be re-arranged to give:

$$Price\ elasticity\ of\ demand = \frac{P}{Qd} \times \frac{\Delta Qd}{\Delta P} \tag{1}$$

The slope of the demand curve is given by:

$$Slope = \frac{\Delta P}{\Delta Qd}$$

The ratio $\frac{Qd}{P}$ is the reciprocal of the slope of the demand curve. So the formula for the price elasticity of demand can also be written as:

$$Price\ elasticity\ of\ demand = \frac{P}{Qd} \times \frac{1}{\frac{\Delta P}{\Delta Qd}} \tag{2}$$

Using either equation 1 or equation 2 will lead to the same answer (the difference will be taking into account the negative sign, which as we have seen can be dropped when we are using absolute numbers).
   Using calculus the formula is:

$$Price\ elasticity\ of\ demand = \frac{P}{Qd} \times \frac{dQd}{dP}$$

This considers the change in quantity and the change in price as the ratio tends to the limit, in other words how quantity demanded responds to an infinitesimally small change in price.

The Variety of Demand Curves

Because the price elasticity of demand measures how much quantity demanded responds to changes in the price, it is closely related to the slope of the demand curve. The following heuristic (rule of thumb), is a useful guide *when the scales of the axes are the same*: the flatter the demand curve that passes through a given point, the greater the price elasticity of demand. The steeper the demand curve that passes through a given point, the smaller the price elasticity of demand.

Figure 4.1 shows five cases, each of which uses the same scale on each axis. This is an important point to remember because simply looking at a graph and the shape of the curve without recognizing the scale

---

FIGURE 4.1

The Price Elasticity of Demand

The steepness of the demand curve indicates the price elasticity of demand (assuming the scale used on the axes are the same). Note that all percentage changes are calculated using the midpoint method and rounded.

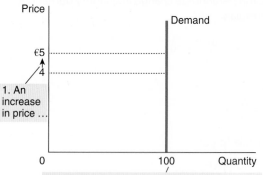

(a) Perfectly inelastic demand: Elasticity equals 0

1. An increase in price ...

2.... leaves the quantity demanded unchanged.

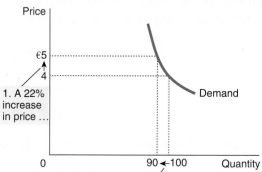

(b) Inelastic demand: Elasticity is less than 1

1. A 22% increase in price ...

2.... leads to an 11% decrease in quantity demanded.

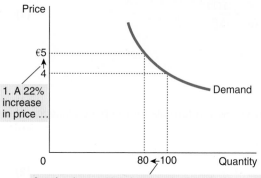

(c) Unit elastic demand: Elasticity equals 1

1. A 22% increase in price ...

2.... leads to a 22% decrease in quantity demanded.

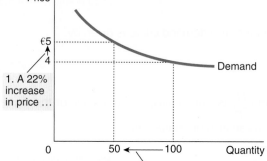

(d) Elastic demand: Elasticity is greater than 1

1. A 22% increase in price ...

2.... leads to a 67% decrease in quantity demanded.

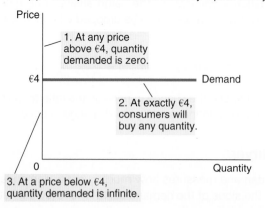

(e) Perfectly elastic demand: Elasticity equals infinity

1. At any price above €4, quantity demanded is zero.

2. At exactly €4, consumers will buy any quantity.

3. At a price below €4, quantity demanded is infinite.

can result in incorrect conclusions about elasticity. In the extreme case of a zero elasticity shown in panel (a), demand is *perfectly inelastic*, and the demand curve is vertical. In this case, regardless of the price, the quantity demanded stays the same. Panels (b), (c) and (d) present demand curves that are flatter and flatter, and represent greater degrees of elasticity. At the opposite extreme shown in panel (e), demand is *perfectly elastic*. This occurs as the price elasticity of demand approaches infinity and the demand curve becomes horizontal, reflecting the fact that very small changes in the price lead to huge changes in the quantity demanded.

Total Expenditure, Total Revenue and the Price Elasticity of Demand

When studying changes in demand in a market, we are interested in the amount paid by buyers of the good which will in turn represent the total revenue that sellers receive. **Total expenditure** is given by the total amount bought multiplied by the price paid. We can show total expenditure graphically, as in Figure 4.2. The height of the box under the demand curve is P and the width is Q. The area of this box, $P \times Q$, equals the total expenditure in this market. In Figure 4.2, where $P = €4$ and $Q = 100$, total expenditure is $€4 \times 100$ or $€400$.

> **total expenditure** the amount paid by buyers, computed as the price of the good times the quantity purchased

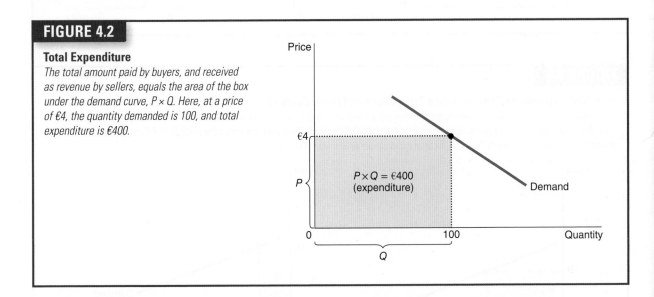

FIGURE 4.2

Total Expenditure
The total amount paid by buyers, and received as revenue by sellers, equals the area of the box under the demand curve, $P \times Q$. Here, at a price of €4, the quantity demanded is 100, and total expenditure is €400.

For businesses who are not price takers, having some understanding of the price elasticity of demand is important in decision-making. If a firm is thinking of changing price how will the demand for its product react? The firm knows that there is an inverse relationship between price and demand but the effect on its revenue will be dependent on the price elasticity of demand. It is entirely possible that a firm could reduce its price and increase total revenue. Equally, a firm could raise price and find its total revenue falling. At first glance this might sound counter-intuitive but it all depends on the price elasticity of demand for the product.

If demand is price inelastic, as in Figure 4.3, then an increase in the price causes an increase in total expenditure. Here an increase in price from €1 to €3 causes the quantity demanded to fall from 100 to 80, and so total expenditure rises from €100 to €240. An increase in price raises $P \times Q$ because the fall in Q is proportionately smaller than the rise in P.

If demand is price elastic an increase in the price causes a decrease in total expenditure. In Figure 4.4, for instance, when the price rises from €4 to €5, the quantity demanded falls from 50 to 20, and so total expenditure falls from €200 to €100. Because demand is price elastic, the reduction in the quantity demanded more than offsets the increase in the price. That is, an increase in price reduces $P \times Q$ because the fall in Q is proportionately greater than the rise in P.

FIGURE 4.3

How Total Expenditure Changes When Price Changes: Inelastic Demand

With a price inelastic demand curve, an increase in the price leads to a decrease in quantity demanded that is proportionately smaller. Therefore, total expenditure (the product of price and quantity) increases. Here, an increase in the price from €1 to €3 causes the quantity demanded to fall from 100 to 80, and total expenditure rises from €100 to €240.

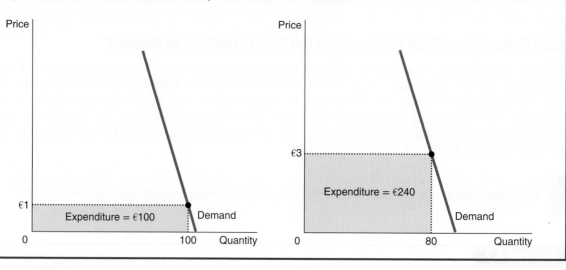

FIGURE 4.4

How Total Expenditure Changes When Price Changes: Elastic Demand

With a price elastic demand curve, an increase in the price leads to a decrease in quantity demanded that is proportionately larger. Therefore, total expenditure (the product of price and quantity) decreases. Here, an increase in the price from €4 to €5 causes the quantity demanded to fall from 50 to 20, so total expenditure falls from €200 to €100.

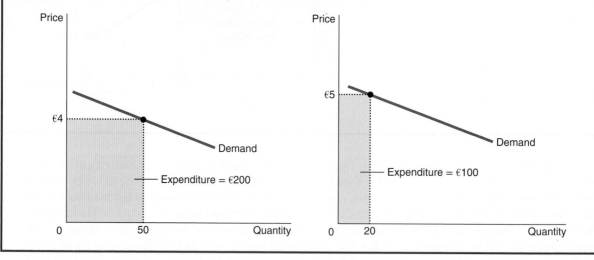

Although the examples in these two figures are extreme, they illustrate a general rule:

- When demand is price inelastic (a price elasticity less than 1), price and total expenditure move in the same direction
- When demand is price elastic (a price elasticity greater than 1), price and total expenditure move in opposite directions
- If demand is unit price elastic (a price elasticity exactly equal to 1), total expenditure remains constant when the price changes

Economists have attempted to place some estimates on the price elasticity of demand for certain goods – these do vary depending on which source you are looking at and the methods used by the researcher but Table 4.1 provides a summary of some of these estimates.

TABLE 4.1   Estimates of the Price Elasticity of Demand for a Selection of Goods

Product	Price Elasticity of Demand
Bread	0.25
Milk	0.3
Tobacco	0.4
Fuel	0.4
Wine	0.6
Shoes	0.7
Movies	0.9
Entertainment	1.4
Cars	1.9
Furniture	3.04
Particular brand of car	4.0

Elasticity and Total Expenditure along a Linear Demand Curve

Demand curves can be linear (straight) or curvilinear (curved). The elasticity at any point along a demand curve will depend on the shape of the demand curve. A linear demand curve has a constant slope. Slope is defined as 'rise-over-run', which here is the ratio of the change in price ('rise') to the change in quantity ('run'). The slope of the demand curve in Figure 4.5 is constant because each €1 increase in price causes the same 2-unit decrease in the quantity demanded.

FIGURE 4.5

Elasticity of a Linear Demand Curve
The slope of a linear demand curve is constant, but its elasticity is not. The demand schedule in the table was used to calculate the price elasticity of demand by the midpoint method. At points with a low price and high quantity, the demand curve is inelastic. At points with a high price and low quantity, the demand curve is elastic.

Price	Quantity	Total revenue (Price × Quantity)	Per cent change in price	Per cent change in quantity	Price elasticity	Quantity description
€7	0	€0	15	200	13.0	Elastic
6	2	12	18	67	3.7	Elastic
5	4	20	22	40	1.8	Elastic
4	6	24	29	29	1.0	Unit elastic
3	8	24	40	22	0.6	Inelastic
2	10	20	67	18	0.3	Inelastic
1	12	12	200	15	0.1	Inelastic
0	14	0				

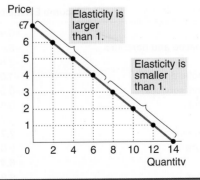

Even though the slope of a linear demand curve is constant, the elasticity is not. The reason is that the slope is the ratio of *changes* in the two variables, whereas the elasticity is the ratio of *percentage changes* in the two variables. The table in Figure 4.5 shows the demand schedule for the linear demand curve in the graph. The table uses the midpoint method to calculate the price elasticity of demand. At points with a low price and high quantity, the demand curve is price inelastic. At points with a high price and low quantity, the demand curve is price elastic.

The table also presents total expenditure at each point on the demand curve. These numbers illustrate the relationship between total expenditure and price elasticity. When the price is €1, for instance, demand is inelastic and a price increase to €2 raises total expenditure. When the price is €5, demand is elastic, and a price increase to €6 reduces total expenditure. Between €3 and €4, demand is exactly unit price elastic and total expenditure is the same at these two prices.

OTHER DEMAND ELASTICITIES

In addition to the price elasticity of demand, economists also use other elasticities to describe the behaviour of buyers in a market.

The Income Elasticity of Demand

The **income elasticity of demand** measures how quantity demanded changes as consumer income changes. It is calculated as the percentage change in quantity demanded divided by the percentage change in income. That is:

$$\text{Income elasticity of demand} = \frac{\text{Percentage change in quantity demanded}}{\text{Percentage change in income}}$$

> **income elasticity of demand** a measure of how much quantity demanded of a good responds to a change in consumers' income, computed as the percentage change in quantity demanded divided by the percentage change in income

Many goods are *normal goods*: higher income raises quantity demanded. Because quantity demanded and income change in the same direction, normal goods have positive income elasticities. *Inferior goods*, where higher income lowers the quantity demanded, sees quantity demanded and income move in opposite directions; inferior goods have negative income elasticities.

Even among normal goods, income elasticities vary substantially in size. Necessities, such as food and clothing, tend to have small income elasticities because consumers, regardless of how low their incomes, choose to buy some of these goods. Luxuries, such as caviar and diamonds, tend to have high income elasticities because consumers feel that they can do without these goods altogether if their income is too low. Table 4.2 provides some crude estimates of the income elasticity of demand

TABLE 4.2 **Estimates of the Income Elasticity of Demand for a Selection of Goods and Services**

Good/Service	Income Elasticity of Demand
Education	−6.9
Alcoholic drinks, tobacco and narcotics	−6.6
Transport	−2.8
Food and non-alcoholic drinks	−1.0
Household goods and services	−0.5
Restaurants and hotels	0.4
Health	1.7
Housing, fuel and power	2.7
Recreation and culture	5.0
Communication	6.4
Clothing and footwear	9.8

for groups of products or services calculated as the percentage change in average weekly household spending on these goods and services between 2001–2 and 2014, divided by the change in gross weekly income over the same period in pounds. The data is drawn from The Family Spending Survey 2014, published by the ONS.

The Cross-Price Elasticity of Demand

The **cross-price elasticity of demand** measures how the quantity demanded of one good changes as the price of another good changes. It is calculated as the percentage change in quantity demanded of good 1 divided by the percentage change in the price of good 2. That is:

$$\text{Cross-price elasticity of demand} = \frac{\textit{Percentage change in quantity demanded of good 1}}{\textit{Percentage change in the price of good 2}}$$

> **cross-price elasticity of demand** a measure of how much the quantity demanded of one good responds to a change in the price of another good, computed as the percentage change in quantity demanded of the first good divided by the percentage change in the price of the second good

Whether the cross-price elasticity is a positive or negative number depends on whether the two goods are substitutes or complements. Substitutes are goods that are typically used in place of one another, such as Pepsi and Coca-Cola. An increase in the price of Pepsi induces people to switch to Coca-Cola instead. Because the price of Pepsi and the quantity of Coca-Cola demanded move in the same direction, the cross-price elasticity is positive. Conversely, complements are goods that are typically used together, such as smartphones and payment plans. In this case, the cross-price elasticity is negative, indicating that an increase in the price of smartphones reduces the quantity of payment plans demanded. As with price elasticity of demand, cross-price elasticity may increase over time: a change in the price of electricity will have little effect on demand for gas in the short run but much stronger effects over several years.

> **SELF TEST** Define the price elasticity of demand. Explain the relationship between total expenditure and the price elasticity of demand.

PRICE ELASTICITY OF SUPPLY

The law of supply states that higher prices raise the quantity supplied. The **price elasticity of supply** measures how much the quantity supplied responds to changes in the price. Supply of a good is said to be *elastic* (or price sensitive) if the quantity supplied responds substantially to changes in the price. Supply is said to be *inelastic* (or price insensitive) if the quantity supplied responds only slightly to changes in the price.

> **price elasticity of supply** a measure of how much the quantity supplied of a good responds to a change in the price of that good, computed as the percentage change in quantity supplied divided by the percentage change in price

The Price Elasticity of Supply and its Determinants

The price elasticity of supply depends on the flexibility of sellers to change the amount of the good they produce in response to changes in price. For example, seafront property has a price inelastic supply because it is almost impossible to produce more of it quickly – supply is not very sensitive to changes in price. By contrast, manufactured goods, such as books, cars and television sets, have relatively price elastic supplies because the firms that produce them can run their factories longer in response to a higher price – supply is sensitive to changes in price.

Elasticity can take any value greater than or equal to 0. The closer to 0 the more price inelastic, and the closer to infinity the more price elastic.

The Time Period In most markets, a key determinant of the price elasticity of supply is the time period being considered. Supply is usually more elastic in the long run than in the short run. Over very short periods of time, firms may find it impossible to respond to a change in price by changing output. In the short run firms cannot easily change the size of their factories or productive capacity to make more or less of a good but may have some flexibility. For example, it might take a month to employ new labour and access more supplies of raw materials and after that time some increase in output can be accommodated. By contrast, over longer periods, firms can build new factories or close old ones, hire new staff, and buy in more capital and equipment. In addition, new firms can enter a market and old firms can shut down. Thus, in the long run, the quantity supplied can respond substantially to price changes.

Productive Capacity Most businesses, in the short run, will have a finite capacity – an upper limit to the amount that they can produce at any one time determined by the amount of factor inputs they possess. How far they are using this capacity depends, in turn, on the state of the economy. In periods of strong economic growth, firms may be operating at or near full capacity. If demand is rising for the product they produce and prices are rising, it may be difficult for the firm to expand output to meet this new demand and so supply may be price inelastic.

When the economy is growing slowly or is contracting, some firms may find they have to cut back output and may only be operating at 60 per cent of full capacity, for example. In this situation, if demand later increased and prices started to rise, it may be much easier for the firm to expand output relatively quickly and so supply would be more elastic.

The Size of the Firm/Industry It is possible that as a general rule, supply may be more elastic in smaller firms or industries than in larger ones. For example, consider a small independent furniture manufacturer. Demand for its products may rise and in response the firm may be able to buy in raw materials (wood, for example), to meet this increase in demand. Whilst the firm will incur a cost in buying in this timber, it is unlikely that the unit cost for the material will increase substantially. Compare this to a situation where a steel manufacturer increases its purchase of raw materials (iron ore, for example). Buying large quantities of iron ore on global commodity markets can drive up unit price and, by association, unit costs.

The response of supply to changes in price in large firms/industries, therefore, may be less elastic than in smaller firms/industries. This is also related to the number of firms in the industry – the more firms there are in the industry the easier it is to increase supply, *ceteris paribus*.

The Mobility of Factors of Production Consider a farmer whose land is currently devoted to producing wheat. A sharp rise in the price of rape seed might encourage the farmer to switch use of land from wheat to rape seed in the next planting cycle. The mobility of the factor of production land, in this case, is relatively high and so the supply of rape seed may be relatively price elastic.

A number of multinational firms that have plants in different parts of the world now build each plant to be identical. What this means is that if there is disruption to one plant the firm can more easily transfer operations to another plant elsewhere and continue production 'seamlessly' and equally can expand supply by utilising these plants more swiftly. Car manufacturers provide an example of this interchangeability of parts and operations. The chassis, for example, may be identical across a range of branded car models. This is the case with some Audi, Volkswagen, Seat and Skoda models. This means that supply may be more price elastic as a result.

Compare this to the supply of highly skilled oncology consultants. An increase in the wages of oncology consultants (suggesting a shortage exists) will not mean that a renal consultant or other doctors can suddenly switch to take advantage of the higher wages and increase the supply of oncology consultants. In this example, the mobility of labour to switch between different uses is limited and so the supply of these specialist consultants is likely to be relatively inelastic.

Ease of Storing Stock/Inventory In some firms, stocks can be built up to enable the firm to respond more flexibly to changes in prices. In industries where inventory build-up is relatively easy and cheap, supply is more price elastic than in industries where it is much harder to do this. Consider the fresh fruit industry, for example. Storing fresh fruit is not easy because it is perishable and so the price elasticity of supply in this industry may be more inelastic.

Table 4.3 presents some estimates of the price elasticity of supply.

TABLE 4.3	**Estimates of Price Elasticity of Supply**	
	Good	**Price Elasticity of Supply Estimate**
	Public transport in Sweden	0.44 to 0.64
	Recycled aluminium	0.5
	Natural gas (short-run)	0.5
	Labour in South Africa	0.35 to 1.75
	Beef	
	• Zimbabwe	2.0
	• Brazil	0.11 to 0.56
	• Argentina	0.67 to 0.96
	Corn (short run in US)	0.96
	Housing, long-run in selected US cities	Dallas: 38.6
		San Francisco: 2.4
		New Orleans: 0.9
		St Louis: 8.1
	Uranium	2.3 to 3.3
	Oysters	1.64 to 2.00
	Retail store space	3.2

Computing the Price Elasticity of Supply

Computing the price elasticity of supply is similar to the process we adopted for calculating the price elasticity of demand and the two methods of calculating price elasticity of demand, the midpoint or arc method and the point elasticity method, also applies to supply.

The price elasticity of supply is the percentage change in the quantity supplied divided by the percentage change in the price. That is:

$$Price\ elasticity\ of\ supply = \frac{Percentage\ change\ in\ quantity\ supplied}{Percentage\ change\ in\ price}$$

For example, suppose that a 10 per cent increase in the price of bicycles causes the amount of bicycles supplied to the market to rise by 15 per cent. We calculate the elasticity of supply as:

$$Price\ elasticity\ of\ supply = \frac{15}{10}$$

$$Price\ elasticity\ of\ supply = 1.5$$

In this example, the elasticity of 1.5 reflects the fact that the quantity supplied moves proportionately one and a half times as much as the price.

The Midpoint (Arc) Method of Calculating the Elasticity of Supply

As with the price elasticity of demand, the midpoint method for the price elasticity of supply between two points, denoted (Q_1, P_1) and (Q_2, P_2) has the following formula:

$$Price\ elasticity\ of\ supply = \frac{(Q_2 - Q_1)/[(Q_2 + Q_1)/2]}{(P_2 - P_1)/[(P_2 + P_1)/2]}$$

The numerator is the percentage change in quantity supplied computed using the midpoint method, and the denominator is the percentage change in price computed using the midpoint method.

For example, suppose that an increase in the price of premium orange juice from €2.85 to €3.15 a litre raises the amount that juice producers offer for sale from 90 000 to 110 000 litres per month. Using the midpoint method, we calculate the percentage change in price as:

$$Percentage\ change\ in\ price = (3.15 - 2.85)/3.00 \times 100 = 10\ per\ cent$$

Similarly, we calculate the percentage change in quantity supplied as:

$$Percentage\ change\ in\ quantity\ supplied = (110\ 000 - 90\ 000) / 100\ 000 \times 100 = 20\ per\ cent$$

In this case, the price elasticity of supply is:

$$Price\ elasticity\ of\ supply = \frac{20\%}{10\%} = 2$$

In this example, the elasticity of 2 reflects the fact that the quantity supplied moves proportionately twice as much as the price.

Point Elasticity of Supply Method

As with point elasticity of demand, point elasticity of supply measures elasticity at a particular point on the supply curve. Exactly the same principles apply as with point elasticity of demand so the formula for point elasticity of supply is given by:

$$Price\ elasticity\ of\ supply = \frac{P}{Qs} \times \frac{1}{\frac{\Delta P}{\Delta Qs}}$$

Using calculus the formula is:

$$Price\ elasticity\ of\ supply = \frac{P}{Qs} \times \frac{dQs}{dP}$$

The Variety of Supply Curves

Because the price elasticity of supply measures the responsiveness of quantity supplied to changes in price, it is reflected in the appearance of the supply curve (again, assuming we are using the same scales on the axes of diagrams being used). Figure 4.6 shows five cases. In the extreme case of a zero elasticity, as shown in panel (a), supply is *perfectly inelastic* and the supply curve is vertical. In this case, the quantity supplied is the same regardless of the price. In panels (b), (c) and (d) the supply curves are increasingly flatter associated with increasing price elasticity, which shows that the quantity supplied responds more to changes in the price. At the opposite extreme, shown in panel (e), supply is *perfectly elastic*. This occurs as the price elasticity of supply approaches infinity and the supply curve becomes horizontal, meaning that very small changes in the price lead to very large changes in the quantity supplied.

In some markets, the elasticity of supply is not constant but varies over the supply curve. Figure 4.7 shows a typical case for an industry in which firms have factories with a limited capacity for production. For low levels of quantity supplied, the elasticity of supply is high, indicating that firms respond substantially to changes in the price. In this region, firms have capacity for production that is not being used, such as buildings and machinery sitting idle for all or part of the day. Small increases in price make it profitable for firms to begin using this idle capacity. As the quantity supplied rises, firms begin to reach capacity. Once capacity is fully used, increasing production further requires the construction of new factories. To induce firms to incur this extra expense, the price must rise substantially, so supply becomes less elastic.

FIGURE 4.6

The Price Elasticity of Supply
The price elasticity of supply determines whether the supply curve is steep or flat (assuming that the scale used for the axes is the same). Note that all percentage changes are calculated using the midpoint method and rounded.

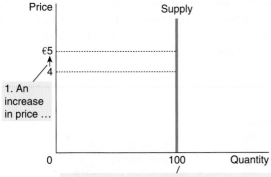

(a) Perfectly inelastic supply: Elasticity equals 0

Price
Supply
€5
4
1. An increase in price …
0   100   Quantity
2. … leaves the quantity supplied unchanged.

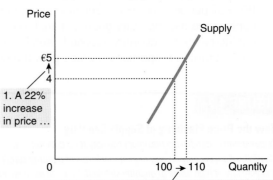

(b) Inelastic supply: Elasticity is less than 1

Price
Supply
€5
4
1. A 22% increase in price …
0   100 → 110   Quantity
2. … leads to a 10% increase in quantity supplied.

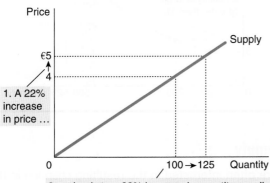

(c) Unit elastic supply: Elasticity equals 1

Price
Supply
€5
4
1. A 22% increase in price …
0   100 → 125   Quantity
2. … leads to a 22% increase in quantity supplied.

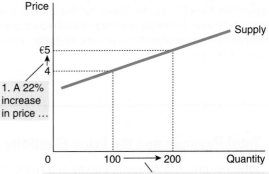

(d) Elastic supply: Elasticity is greater than 1

Price
Supply
€5
4
1. A 22% increase in price …
0   100 ——→ 200   Quantity
2. … leads to a 67% increase in quantity supplied.

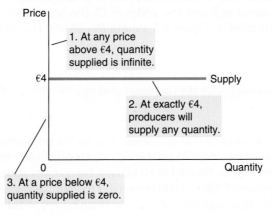

(e) Perfectly elastic supply: Elasticity equals infinity

Price
1. At any price above €4, quantity supplied is infinite.
€4   Supply
2. At exactly €4, producers will supply any quantity.
0   Quantity
3. At a price below €4, quantity supplied is zero.

SELF TEST Define the price elasticity of supply. Explain why the price elasticity of supply might be different in the long run from in the short run.

Figure 4.7 presents a numerical example of this phenomenon. In each case below we have used the midpoint method and the numbers have been rounded for convenience. When the price rises from €3 to €4 (a 29 per cent increase, according to the midpoint method), the quantity supplied rises from 100 to 200 (a 67 per cent increase). Because quantity supplied moves proportionately more than the price, the supply curve has elasticity greater than 1. By contrast, when the price rises from €12 to €15 (a 22 per cent increase), the quantity supplied rises from 500 to 525 (a 5 per cent increase). In this case, quantity supplied moves proportionately less than the price, so the elasticity is less than 1.

FIGURE 4.7

How the Price Elasticity of Supply Can Vary

Because firms often have a maximum capacity for production, the elasticity of supply may be very high at low levels of quantity supplied and very low at high levels of quantity supplied. Here, an increase in price from €3 to €4 increases the quantity supplied from 100 to 200. Because the increase in quantity supplied of 67 per cent (computed using the midpoint method) is larger than the increase in price of 29 per cent, the supply curve is elastic in this range. By contrast, when the price rises from €12 to €15, the quantity supplied rises only from 500 to 525. Because the increase in quantity supplied of 5 per cent is smaller than the increase in price of 22 per cent, the supply curve is inelastic in this range.

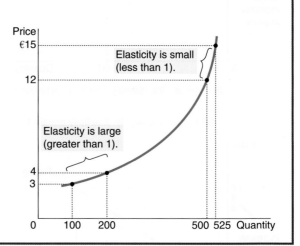

Total Revenue and the Price Elasticity of Supply

When studying changes in supply in a market we are often interested in the resulting changes in the **total revenue** received by producers. In any market, total revenue received by sellers is $P \times Q$, the price of the good times the quantity of the good sold. This is highlighted in Figure 4.8, which shows an upward sloping supply curve with an assumed price of €5 and a supply of 100 units. The height of the box under the demand curve is P and the width is Q. The area of this box, $P \times Q$, equals the total revenue received in this market. In Figure 4.8, where $P =$ €5 and $Q = 100$, total expenditure is €5 × 100 or €500.

---

total revenue the amount received by sellers of a good, computed as the price of the good times the quantity sold

---

Total revenue will change as price changes depending on the price elasticity of supply. If supply is inelastic, as in Figure 4.9, then an increase in price which is proportionately larger causes an increase in total revenue. Here, an increase in price from €4 to €5 causes the quantity supplied to rise only from 80 to 100, and so total revenue rises from €320 to €500 (assuming the firm sells the additional supply).

If supply is price elastic then a similar increase in price brings about a much larger than proportionate increase in supply. In Figure 4.10, we assume a price of €4 and a supply of 80 with total revenue of €320. Now a price increase from €4 to €5 leads to a much greater than proportionate increase in supply from 80 to 150 with total revenue rising to €750 – again, assuming the firm sells the additional supply.

FIGURE 4.8

The Supply Curve and Total Revenue
The total amount received by sellers equals the area of the box under the demand curve, P × Q. Here, at a price of €5, the quantity supplied is 100 and the total revenue is €500.

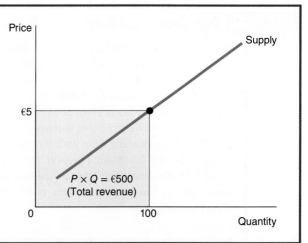

FIGURE 4.9

How Total Revenue Changes When Price Changes: Inelastic Supply
With an inelastic supply curve, an increase in price leads to an increase in quantity supplied that is proportionally smaller. Therefore, total revenue (the product of price and quantity) increases. Here, an increase in price from €4 to €5 causes the quantity supplied to rise from 80 to 100, and total revenue rises from €320 to €500.

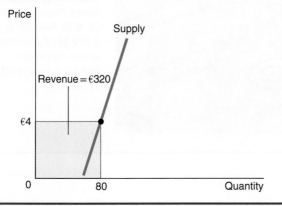
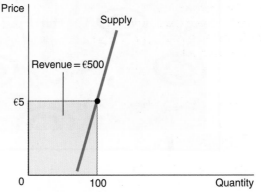

FIGURE 4.10

How Total Revenue Changes When Price Changes: Elastic Supply
With a price elastic supply curve, an increase in price leads to an increase in quantity supplied that is proportionally larger. Therefore, total revenue (the product of price and quantity) increases. Here, an increase in the price from €4 to €5 causes the quantity supplied to rise from 80 to 150, and total revenue rises from €320 to €750.

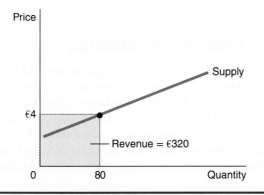
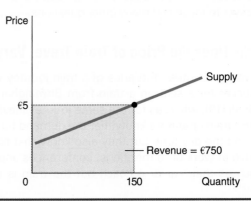

Developments in technology have made piracy and infringement of copyright and intellectual property a major problem for the media industry. Where such infringement occurs, the authorities can intervene to cut the supply of illegal or pirated products. Research by Luis Aguiar, Jörg Claussen and Christian Peukert for the Institute for Prospective Technological Studies in 2015, looked at the impact of supply-side intervention to prevent piracy in the movie industry. The study looked at what happened when an unlicensed movie streaming website, kino.to, in Germany was shut down. In the short term, the use of unlicensed streaming from websites fell, not only for kino.to but also other unlicensed sites. Four weeks after the shutdown, however, the use of unlicensed sites increased again. The researchers found that consumers find other unlicensed sites to use and that new entrants into the market provide more options. The research pointed to a high elasticity of supply in response to the closing down of illegal and unlicensed sites.

Copyright piracy is big business and preventing it is increasingly difficult.

Sources: Aguiar, Luis and Claussen, Jörg and Peukert, Christian, Online Copyright Enforcement, Consumer Behavior, and Market Structure (March 30, 2015). Available at SSRN: http://ssrn.com/abstract=2604197 or http://dx.doi.org/10.2139/ssrn.2604197

APPLICATIONS OF SUPPLY AND DEMAND ELASTICITY

Why is it the case that travel on the trains at some times during the day is a different price than at other times? Why, despite the increase in productivity in agriculture, have farmers' incomes gone down, on average, over recent years? At first, these questions might seem to have little in common. Yet both questions are about markets and the forces of supply and demand. An understanding of elasticity is a key part of the answer to these and many other questions.

Why Does the Price of Train Travel Vary at Different Times of the Day?

In many countries the price of a train journey varies at different times during the day and the week. A ticket for a seat on a train from Birmingham to London between 6.00am and 9.00am is around £85 (€119), whereas for the same journey leaving at midday the price is between £6 and £32 (€8 and €45). Train operators know that the demand for rail travel between 6.00am and 9.00pm is higher than during the day time but they also know that few commuters have choices about when they have to arrive at work or to meetings, conferences and so on. An individual can use other forms of transport such as their car or a coach but the train is often very convenient, so the amount of substitutes is considered low. The price elasticity of demand for train travel early in the morning, therefore, is relatively low compared to at midday. In the morning, train operators know that seats on trains will be mostly taken and there will be very few left empty, whereas during the day it is much more likely that trains will be running with empty seats. Knowing that there is a different price elasticity of demand means that train operators can maximize revenue at these different times by charging different prices.

Figure 4.11 shows the situation in the market for train travel. Panel (a) shows the demand and supply for tickets between Birmingham and London between 6.00am and 9.00am. The demand curve D_i is relatively steep indicating that the price elasticity of demand is relatively low. At a price of £80, 1000 tickets are bought and as a result the total revenue for the train operator is £80 000.

Panel (b) shows a demand curve D_e with a similar supply curve. *Ceteris paribus*, the train operator has the same number of trains available at all times during the day but notice that the supply curve is relatively steep and therefore inelastic because although the operator has some flexibility to increase the number of trains available and thus seats for passengers, there is a limit as to how far the capacity can be varied throughout the day.

If the train operator charged a price of £80 after 9.00am, the demand for tickets would be relatively low at 100. Total revenue, therefore would be £8000 and there would be many seats left empty. This is because the train operator effectively faces a different market during the day. Those who travel by train at this time may have a choice – they might be travelling for leisure or to see friends and they do not *need* to travel by train unlike those in the morning who have to get to work at a certain time. These passengers are price sensitive – charge too high a price and they will not choose to travel by train, but offer a price that these passengers see as being attractive and which to them represents value for money and they may choose to buy a train ticket.

FIGURE 4.11

Price Sensitivity in the Passenger Train Market

Panel (a) represents the market for train travel between 6.00am and 9.00am between two major cities. The demand for train travel at this time is relatively price inelastic – passengers are insensitive to price at this time because they have few alternatives and have to get into work and to meetings. The train operators generate revenue of £80 000 by selling 1000 tickets at £80 each.

Panel (b) shows the market after 9.00am. Train operators face a different demand curve at this time and passengers are more price sensitive. If the train operator continued to charge £80, demand would be just 100 and revenue would be £8000. If the train operator reduces the price to £40, demand would be 800 and the total revenue would be £32 000.

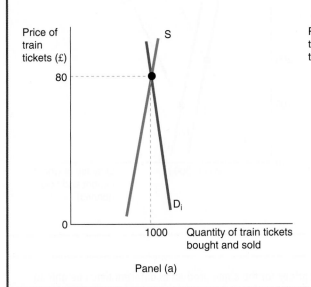

Panel (a)

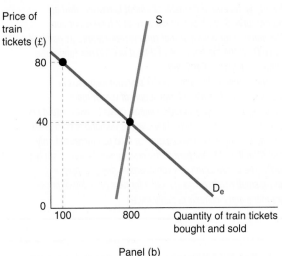

Panel (b)

If the train operator, therefore, set the price for train tickets after 9.00am at £40 the demand for train tickets would be 800 and total revenue would be £32 000. If we assume that train operators are acting rationally then they would prefer to generate revenue of £32 000 rather than £8000 and so it would be more sensible for them to charge a lower price to capture these more price sensitive passengers.

Why Have Farmers' Incomes Fallen Despite Increases in Productivity?

In many developed countries, agricultural production has increased over the last 50 years. One of the reasons is that farmers are able to use more machinery, and advances in science and technology have meant that productivity, the amount of output per acre of land, has increased. Assume a farmer has 1000 acres of land and grows wheat and that 20 years ago each acre of land yielded an average of 2 tonnes of wheat. We say 'an average' because output can be dependent on factors outside the farmer's control such as the weather, pests, diseases and so on. Assume that the price of wheat is €200 per tonne. Twenty years ago the average income for our farmer would be 2000 tonnes × €200 = €400 000.

Ceteris paribus, if productivity increases meant that average output per acre was now 3 tonnes per acre, income would rise to €600 000.

However, this assumes other things are equal. Research suggests that the demand for food is relatively price inelastic and also income inelastic. Over the 20-year period we are assuming in our analysis, the demand for wheat may only have risen by a relatively small amount and also is price and income inelastic. People may earn more money now than they did 20 years ago but evidence suggests that as people's incomes increase, they spend a smaller proportion of income on food. This is called 'Engel's law'.

Figure 4.12 shows a representation of this situation. In the first time period the supply curve, representing output per acre of 2 tonnes, intersects the demand curve D_1 at a price of €200 per tonne giving the farmer an income of €400 000.

Twenty years later, the productivity improvements at the farm see the supply curve shifting to S_2 representing an average output per acre of 3 tonnes. However, over the 20-year period, demand has increased but only by a small amount as people spend a smaller proportion of their income on food as they get richer. The fact that food is relatively price inelastic is indicated by the relatively steep demand curve and the result is that the market price has fallen to €100 per tonne with the farmer now selling 3000 tonnes. The farmer's income has fallen to €300 000.

FIGURE 4.12

The Effect of Increases in Demand and Supply of Wheat on Farm Incomes

Twenty years ago, the supply of wheat is represented as supply curve S_1 with output per acre at 2 tonnes per acre. The demand for wheat at that time is represented as demand curve D_1. If the market price of wheat is €200 per tonne, the farmer's income is €400 000.

The output of wheat per acre rises with increases in productivity and as a result the supply of wheat today increases and is represented by supply curve S_2 with output per acre now 3 tonnes per acre. However, as demand is both price and income inelastic, the demand for food has increased only slightly in that 20-year period; the new demand curve is shown as D_2. The combination of a considerable rise in supply and only a small rise in demand means farmers get a lower price per tonne and income is actually lower.

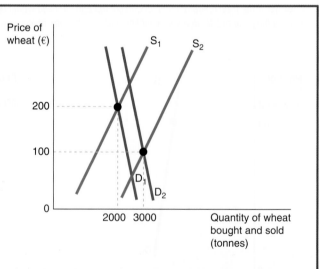

SELF TEST What must firms who charge different prices for the same product at different times be able to do for the pricing tactic to work? (Hint: can you use off-peak tickets for a train journey during peak hours?)

IN THE NEWS

Price Elasticity

Charities invariably rely on public donations to survive. Public policy provides incentives for people to give to worthy causes but how does the type of incentive affect the amount people are prepared to donate?

The Price Elasticity of Charitable Donations

Giving to charities is something that many people do. Governments often put in place incentives in the form of tax relief on charitable giving to incentivize people to donate. These incentives can include ways of claiming back income tax on charitable giving (a rebate method) and charities getting tax relief on donations received (so-called 'matched method'). These methods affect the price of giving to charities but which method influences the responsiveness of donations the most? The IFS in the UK conducted some research to find out if particular methods of tax relief were more effective in raising donations than others; in other words, it looked at the tax-price elasticity of donations.

In the UK, one of the main public policy incentives for charitable donations is called 'Gift Aid'. An individual can decide to give a certain amount to a chosen charity which in turn is the charity's income. The Charity can then claim tax relief of around 25p on every £1 donated. The sums involved are not insignificant; the IFS notes that Gift Aid donations amount to over £4.3 billion with the associated tax relief amounting to some £1.27 billion.

The IFS study suggested that the elasticity of match methods of donations was around -1.1, and around -0.2 for rebate methods. If governments want to improve the efficiency of donations to charities, the implications of this research is that match methods are much more effective in increasing donations than rebate methods given that individuals respond far more to a change in match methods than rebate methods.

Tax relief is one way of providing incentives to encourage people to give to charities.

Questions

1 Why is an understanding of price elasticity important to governments in understanding consumer behaviour in formulating public policy?
2 If the price elasticity of the match method is -1.1 and the rebate method -0.2, what would a 'price reduction' to donation givers of 10 per cent mean to the amount charities would receive (in percentage terms) in each case?
3 An important principle in economics is that people respond to incentives. Why do you think that people respond more to the matched method than the rebate method?
4 People earn different levels of income and in many countries those on higher incomes pay higher rates of tax on their income above certain levels. What relevance do you think this has for the design of tax benefits of donation giving?
5 Given the difference in the elasticities of the different methods, do you think that it would be advisable for governments to move only to a matched method rather than a rebate method? Justify your answer.

Source: http://www.ifs.org.uk/wps/wp1007.pdf

SUMMARY

- The price elasticity of demand measures how much the quantity demanded responds to changes in the price. Demand tends to be more price elastic if close substitutes are available, if the good is a luxury rather than a necessity, if the market is narrowly defined or if buyers have substantial time to react to a price change.

- The price elasticity of demand is calculated as the percentage change in quantity demanded divided by the percentage change in price. If the price elasticity is less than 1, so that quantity demanded moves proportionately less than the price, demand is said to be price inelastic. If the elasticity is greater than 1, so that quantity demanded moves proportionately more than the price, demand is said to be price elastic.

- The price elasticity of supply measures how much the quantity supplied responds to changes in the price. This elasticity often depends on the time horizon under consideration. In most markets, supply is more price elastic in the long run than in the short run.

- The price elasticity of supply is calculated as the percentage change in quantity supplied divided by the percentage change in price. If price elasticity is less than 1, so that quantity supplied moves proportionately less than the price, supply is said to be price inelastic. If the elasticity is greater than 1, so that quantity supplied moves proportionately more than the price, supply is said to be price elastic.

- Total revenue, the total amount received by sellers for a good, equals the price of the good times the quantity sold. For price inelastic demand curves, total revenue rises as price rises. For price elastic demand curves, total revenue falls as price rises.

- The income elasticity of demand measures how much the quantity demanded responds to changes in consumers' income. The cross-price elasticity of demand measures how much the quantity demanded of one good responds to changes in the price of another good.

QUESTIONS FOR REVIEW

1 Define the price elasticity of demand and the income elasticity of demand.

2 List and explain some of the determinants of the price elasticity of demand. Think of some examples to use to illustrate the factors you cover.

3 If the price elasticity is greater than 1, is demand elastic or inelastic? If the price elasticity equals 0, is demand perfectly elastic or perfectly inelastic?

4 How is the price elasticity of supply calculated? Explain what this measures.

5 Is the price elasticity of supply usually larger in the short run or in the long run? Why?

6 What are the main factors that affect the price elasticity of supply? Think of some examples to use to illustrate the factors you cover.

7 A business person reads that the price elasticity of demand for the product they sell is 1.25. If the person wishes to increase revenue should they increase or reduce price? Explain.

8 In the very short run, the price elasticity of demand for tobacco products is very low but over the medium term is less so. Explain.

9 What do we call a good whose income elasticity is less than 1?

10 What factors might affect the price elasticity of supply for a commodity such as rubber in the short run and the long run? Explain.

PROBLEMS AND APPLICATIONS

1 Seafront properties along the south coast of France have a price inelastic supply, and cars have a price elastic supply. Suppose that a rise in population doubles the demand for both products (that is, the quantity demanded at each price is twice what it was).

a. What happens to the equilibrium price and quantity in each market?

b. Which product experiences a larger change in price?

c. Which product experiences a larger change in quantity?

d. What happens to total consumer spending on each product?

2 Because better weather makes farmland more productive, farmland in regions with good weather conditions is more expensive than farmland in regions with bad weather conditions. Over time, however, as advances in technology have made all farmland more productive, the price of farmland (adjusted for overall inflation) has fallen. Use the concept of elasticity to explain why productivity and farmland prices are positively related across space but negatively related over time.

3 For each of the following pairs of goods, which good would you expect to have more price elastic demand and why?

a. Textbooks recommended by lecturers or mystery novels.

b. Downloads of tracks by Jay-Z or downloads of hip-hop music in general.

c. Heating oil during the next six months or heating oil during the next five years.

d. Lemonade or water.

4 Suppose that business travellers and holidaymakers have the following demand for airline tickets from Munich to Naples:

a. As the price of tickets rises from €200 to €250, what is the price elasticity of demand for (i) business travellers and (ii) holidaymakers? (Use either the midpoint or point method in your calculations.)

b. Why might holidaymakers have a different price elasticity to business travellers?

Price (€)	Quantity demanded (business travellers)	Quantity demanded (holidaymakers)
150	2100	1000
200	2000	800
250	1900	600
300	1800	400

5 Suppose that your demand schedule (per year) for streamed films is as follows:

Price (€)	Quantity demanded (income = €10 000)	Quantity demanded (income = €12 000)
8	40	50
10	32	45
12	24	30
14	16	20
16	8	12

a. Use the midpoint or point method to calculate your price elasticity of demand as the price of streaming increases from €8 to €10 per film if (i) your income is €10 000, and (ii) your income is €12 000.

b. Calculate your income elasticity of demand as your income increases from €10 000 to €12 000 if (i) the price is €12 per film, and (ii) the price is €16 per film.

6 Karen receives an energy bill and on looking through it notes that she is charged a different rate for gas and electricity during the day compared to the night time. Explain to Karen the likely reason for this difference in tariff.

7 Consider public policy aimed at smoking.

a. Studies indicate that the price elasticity of demand for cigarettes is about 0.4. If a packet of cigarettes is currently priced at €6 and the government wants to reduce smoking by 20 per cent, by how much should it increase the price through levying a tax?

b. If the government permanently increases the price of cigarettes, will the policy have a larger effect on smoking one year from now or five years from now? Explain.

c. Studies also find that teenagers have a higher price elasticity of demand for cigarettes than do adults. Why might this be true?

8 Many governments impose a duty (tax) on petrol. Why do you think governments choose to tax petrol?

9 Suppose that there is severe flooding in a region in which there is a high concentration of wheat farmers.

   a. Farmers whose crops were destroyed by the floods were much worse off, but farmers whose crops were not destroyed benefited from the floods. Why?

   b. What information would you need about the market for wheat to assess whether farmers as a group were hurt or helped by the floods?

10 Explain why the following might be true: a drought around the world raises the total revenue that farmers receive from the sale of grain, but a drought only in France reduces the total revenue that French farmers receive.

5 BACKGROUND TO DEMAND: CONSUMER CHOICES

In this chapter we look in more detail at the behaviour of consumers. The standard theory of consumer choice is based on a series of assumptions about how humans behave. As with other theories, it provides some predictions about the outcomes of behaviour which enables us to derive the demand curve and analyze the role of price and other factors in both the position and shifts in the demand curve.

The standard theory has been the subject of criticism that its assumptions are unrealistic and not reflective of the way in which humans make choices. Research, originally by psychologists, has highlighted a number of different approaches to looking at consumer behaviour. We will begin by looking at the standard theory of consumer choice.

THE STANDARD ECONOMIC MODEL

When you walk into a shop or look to make a purchase online, you are confronted with a range of goods that you might buy. Of course, because your financial resources are limited, you cannot buy everything that you want. The assumption is that you consider the prices of the various goods being offered for sale and buy a bundle of goods that, given your resources, best suits your needs and desires. In economic terminology, you are seeking to maximize your utility subject to the constraint of a limited income.

This model is called the classical theory of consumer behaviour or the *standard economic model (SEM)* and is fundamentally based on an assumption that humans behave rationally when making consumption choices.

The standard economic model provides a theory of consumer choice which provides a more complete understanding of demand. It examines the trade-offs that people face in their role as consumers. When a consumer buys more of one good, they can afford less of other goods. When they spend more time enjoying leisure and less time working, they have lower income and can afford less consumption. When they spend more of their income in the present and thus save less, they must accept a lower level of consumption in the future. The theory of consumer choice examines how consumers facing these trade-offs make decisions and how they respond to changes in their environment. These trade-offs involve a consideration of opportunity cost. When making a consumption choice with the constraint of limited incomes, consumers make sacrifices and in doing so this can provide information about the relative value which consumers put on their choices. If a consumer chooses good (I) above good (II), it suggests that good (I) provides more utility than the next best alternative sacrificed.

When making trade-offs, there are a number of assumptions that are made about consumers. These include:

- Buyers (or economic agents) are rational (they do the best they can given their circumstances)
- More is preferred to less
- Buyers seek to maximize their utility
- Consumers act in self-interest and do not consider the utility of others.

Value

A key concept in consumer behaviour and across many other areas of economics is value. Value is a subjective term – what one individual thinks represents value is often different to that of another individual. Value can be seen as the worth to an individual of owning an item represented by the satisfaction derived from its consumption and their willingness to pay to own it. In broad terms, consumption in this case does not just mean the final consumer. Value can be related to the purchase of a product which is a gift or something used by a business for production.

What makes a good valuable? Do companies mine for gold because it is valuable or is the value of gold determined by the work done by mining companies in extracting and refining gold? This type of question occupied the minds of early classical economists and is encapsulated in the so called water–diamond paradox. Adam Smith noted that water is an extremely important product but the price of water is relatively low whereas diamonds have little practical worth but command very high prices in comparison. Smith distinguished between value in use, reflecting the situation with water which is vital to life, and value in exchange, linked to diamonds which have limited value in use but have a high exchange value. Smith ascribed the value of a product to the labour which went into producing it. The value of gold, for example, is therefore determined by the factor inputs in production.

Around 100 years later, William Stanley Jevons proposed that products like gold have value because of the utility that gold gives to buyers. Classical economists used the term **utility** to refer to the satisfaction derived from consumption.

> **utility** the satisfaction derived from the consumption of a certain quantity of a product

This implies that companies will mine for gold because of this value. Jevons developed a theory of marginal utility which was capable of providing an answer to the water–diamonds paradox.

Utility is an ordinal concept; what this means is that it can be used as a means of ranking consumer choices but cannot have any meaningful arithmetic operations performed on it. For example, if a group of five people were asked to rank different films in order of preference using a 10-point scale (with each point referred to as a util) we might be able to conclude that film 5 was the most popular, followed by film 3 and film 8. If, however, person 1 ranked film 5 at 10 utils, whilst person 2 ranked the same film as 5 utils, we cannot say that person 1 values film 5 twice as much as person 2, only that they place it higher in their preferences. Value can be measured, therefore, by ranking but there are limitations to such ranking.

One way in which we can overcome this limitation is to look at value in terms of the amount consumers are prepared to pay to secure the benefits of consuming the product. This is called the *willingness to pay principle*. How much of our limited income we are prepared to pay is a reflection of the value we put on acquiring a good. It might not tell us much about the satisfaction from actually consuming the good (the buyer, as we have seen, might not be the final consumer) but it does give some idea of value.

For example, two friends, Alexa and Monique are in a store looking at a pair of shoes. Alexa picks up a pair of leopard print, high-heeled shoes priced at €75. Monique looks at her friend and frowns – why on earth is she thinking of buying those? No way would Monique pay that sort of money for such an awful pair of shoes. A discussion ensues about the shoes; clearly there is a difference of opinion on them. It is here we can distinguish between 'price' and 'value'. If Alexa buys the shoes, they must have some value to her. We could surmise that this value must be at least €75 because that is what she has to give up in money terms in order to acquire them. We also have to consider the opportunity cost of the purchase in that Alexa has also given up the opportunity of buying whatever else €75 would buy. We could make a reasonable assumption that Alexa's friend, Monique, believed there was a way in which she could allocate €75 to get more value – in other words, the alternative that €75 could buy (whatever that might be) represented greater value than purchasing those shoes.

It is possible that Alexa would have been prepared to pay much more for the shoes, in which case she is getting some additional benefit which she is not paying for. Economists call this consumer surplus and we will look in more detail at this later in the book. Alexa sticks to her guns and buys the shoes; Monique leaves the store baffled at her friend's purchasing decision. Monique clearly feels that giving up €75 to buy those shoes was a 'waste of money'. Monique's willingness to pay for this particular pair of shoes is much less than her friend and might even be zero.

The amount buyers are prepared to pay for a good, therefore, tells us something about the value they place on it.

THE BUDGET CONSTRAINT: WHAT THE CONSUMER CAN AFFORD

One of the assumptions the SEM makes is that more is preferred to less. Most people would like to increase the quantity or quality of the goods they consume – to take longer holidays, drive fancier cars or buy a bigger house. People consume less than they desire because their spending is *constrained*, or limited, by their income.

We will use a simple model which examines the decisions facing a consumer who buys only two goods, cola and pizza, in order to derive some insights about consumer choice in the SEM. Assume that the consumer has an income of €1000 per month and that they spend the entire income each month on cola and pizza. The price of a litre of cola is €2 and the price of a pizza is €10.

The table in Figure 5.1 shows some of the many combinations of cola and pizza that the consumer can buy with their income. The first row in the table shows that if the consumer spends all their income on pizza, they can eat 100 pizzas during the month, but would not be able to buy any cola at all. The second row shows another possible consumption bundle: 90 pizzas and 50 litres of cola. And so on. Each consumption bundle in the table uses up the consumer's income – exactly €1000.

The graph of this data is given in Figure 5.1. The line connecting points A to B is called the **budget constraint** and shows the consumption bundles that the consumer can afford given a specified income. Five points are marked on this figure. At point A, the consumer buys no cola and consumes 100 pizzas. At point B, the consumer buys no pizza and consumes 500 litres of cola. At point C, the consumer buys 50 pizzas and 250 litres of cola. At point C, the consumer spends an equal amount (€500) on cola and pizza.

> **budget constraint** the limit on the consumption bundles that a consumer can afford

---

FIGURE 5.1

The Consumer's Budget Constraint

The budget constraint shows the various bundles of goods that the consumer can afford for a given income. Here the consumer buys bundles of cola and pizza. The table and graph show what the consumer can afford if their income is €1000, the price of cola is €2 and the price of pizza is €10.

Litres of cola	Spending on cola (€)	Number of pizzas	Spending on pizza (€)	Total spending (€)
0	0	100	1000	1000
50	100	90	900	1000
100	200	80	800	1000
150	300	70	700	1000
200	400	60	600	1000
250	500	50	500	1000
300	600	40	400	1000
350	700	30	300	1000
400	800	20	200	1000
450	900	10	100	1000
500	1000	0	0	1000

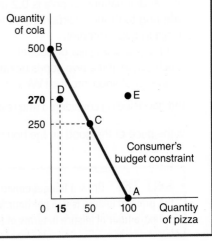

Point D is inside the budget constraint. The consumer can afford to buy any combination inside the budget constraint. In this example, point D shows a combination of 270 litres of cola and 15 pizzas; and if the consumer chose to purchase this combination they would not be using all their income, only spending €690 on this combination. The assumption of the SEM is that the consumer would wish to maximize their utility and could do so by spending all their income.

Point E is outside the budget constraint. No points outside the budget constraint are possible – the consumer does not have the income to be able to afford any combination of pizza and cola to the right of the budget constraint. Of course, these are only four of the many combinations of cola and pizza that the consumer can choose given a specified income. All the points on and inside the line from A to B are possible. In this case, it shows the trade-off between cola and pizza that the consumer faces.

For example, assume the consumer is at point A, consuming 100 pizzas and zero cola. If the consumer wants to purchase a drink to go with their pizza they must give up some pizza in order to buy some cola – they have to trade-off the benefits of consuming cola against the benefits foregone of reducing consumption of pizza. We can quantify this trade-off. If the consumer moves to point C then they have to forego the benefits that 50 pizzas would provide to gain the benefits that 250 litres of cola would bring. The consumer would have to make a decision about whether it is worth giving up those 50 pizzas to get the benefits of the cola. In making these decision, the consumer has to consider opportunity cost. The opportunity cost is the slope of the budget constraint measuring the rate at which the consumer can trade one good for the other. Remember, the slope between two points is calculated as the change in the vertical distance divided by the change in the horizontal distance ('rise over run'). From point A to point B, the vertical distance is 500 litres, and the horizontal distance is 100 pizzas. Because the budget constraint slopes downwards, the slope is a negative number – this reflects the fact that to get one extra pizza, the consumer has to *reduce* their consumption of cola by five litres. In fact, the slope of the budget constraint (ignoring the minus sign) equals the *relative price* of the two goods – the price of one good compared to the price of the other. A pizza costs five times as much as a litre of cola, so the opportunity cost of a pizza is 5 litres of cola. The budget constraint's slope of 5 reflects the trade-off the market is offering the consumer: 1 pizza for 5 litres of cola. It is useful to use a rule of thumb (a heuristic) here; the opportunity cost of a good on the horizontal axis (pizza in our example) is the slope of the budget constraint (5 in this example). What is the opportunity cost of 1 extra litre of cola in our example? The opportunity cost of the good on the vertical axis is the inverse of the slope of the budget constraint which in this case is $\frac{1}{5}$ or 0.2. To acquire 1 extra litre of cola the consumer has to sacrifice one-fifth of a pizza.

It is also useful to think of opportunity cost by using the following formula:

$$\text{Opportunity cost of cola} = \frac{\text{Sacrifice of pizza}}{\text{Gain in cola}}$$

In moving from point A to point C, the consumer would have to sacrifice 50 pizzas to gain 250 units of cola. The opportunity cost of additional units of cola consumed is the amount of pizza sacrificed. Substituting the figures into the formula, the opportunity cost is 0.2 which indicates that the opportunity cost of 1 additional unit of cola is 0.2 units of pizza sacrificed. Notice that throughout this analysis we are not referring to money costs here – the cost is expressed in terms of the sacrifice of the next best alternative (pizza in this example).

In some examples of budget constraints, you might find the opportunity cost calculation does not make much sense. If the two goods being considered were cola and tins of soup you could not ask the shop to chop up the tin of soup into five! What is important to remember is that the slope is related to the ratio of prices of the goods being considered (the relative prices), $\frac{P_x}{P_y}$ where P_y is the price of the good on the vertical axis and P_x is the price of the good on the horizontal axis. In our example the ratio of the prices is $\frac{10}{2}$ which is equal to 5.

SELF TEST Draw a budget constraint for a person with income of €5000 if the price of food is €10 per unit and the price of leisure is €15 per hour. What is the slope of this budget constraint? What is the opportunity cost of an extra hour of leisure in terms of food?

A Change in Income

Over time people's incomes change – sometimes they earn more but sometimes they earn less, such as if they are made redundant, for example. If our consumer gets a pay rise and now earns €1500 per month, they can now afford to buy more of both pizza and cola assuming the prices of these two goods do not change. The effect on the budget constraint is to cause it to shift to the right, as shown in Figure 5.2. If the consumer devoted all of their income to buying cola they could now buy 750 litres of cola compared to 500 litres when their income was €1000 per month. If the consumer devoted all their income to buying pizza they could not afford to buy 150 pizzas a month. Any point along the new budget constraint shows that the consumer can now buy more of both goods. If the consumer's income was to fall to €500 per month because they lost their job, for example, then the budget constraint would shift to the left, indicating that the consumer could now afford to buy less of both goods with their income.

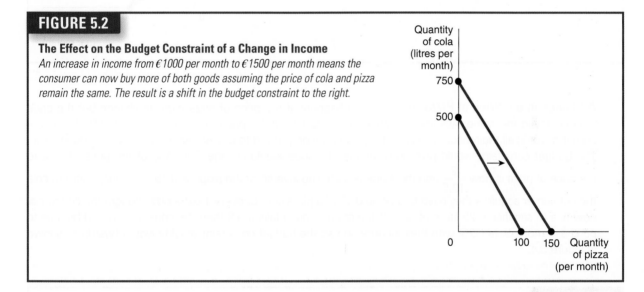

FIGURE 5.2

The Effect on the Budget Constraint of a Change in Income
An increase in income from €1000 per month to €1500 per month means the consumer can now buy more of both goods assuming the price of cola and pizza remain the same. The result is a shift in the budget constraint to the right.

Notice, however, that whilst the budget constraint in Figure 5.2 has shifted to the right, the slope is still the same. This is because the prices of the two goods have not changed. What happens to the budget constraint if one or more of the prices of cola and pizza changes?

A Change in Prices

A Change in the Price of Cola Assume the consumer's income is €1000 per month, the price of cola is €2 per litre and the price of pizza is €10. The budget constraint would look like that shown in Figure 5.1. Now assume that the price of cola rises to €5 per litre. The consumer would now only be able to afford to buy 200 litres of cola if they devoted all their income to cola. The budget constraint would, therefore, pivot inwards as shown in Figure 5.3.

The slope of the budget constraint has now changed. The ratio of the price of cola to the price of pizza is now $\frac{5}{10}$ so the slope of the budget constraint is –2. For every 1 litre of cola the consumer acquires they have to give up half a pizza and for every 1 extra pizza bought the consumer now has to sacrifice 2 litres of cola. Notice that as the price of cola has risen the consumer now has to sacrifice fewer litres of cola to purchase every additional pizza, but if the consumer is switching from cola to pizza they have to give up more pizza to buy an additional litre of cola.

If the price of cola were to fall but the price of pizza stayed the same, the budget constraint would pivot outwards as shown in Figure 5.3. If the price of cola fell to €1.60 the consumer will now be able to afford to buy more cola with their income. If all income was devoted to buying cola the consumer would now be able to purchase 625 litres of cola.

FIGURE 5.3

A Change in the Price of Cola
If the price of cola rises from €2 per litre to €5 per litre, the consumer can now afford to buy less cola with their income. The budget constraint pivots inwards and if the consumer devoted all their income to cola they would only be able to buy 200 litres compared to 500 litres before the price changed. If the price of cola falls from €2 per litre to €1.60 per litre, the consumer can afford to buy more cola with their income and the budget constraint pivots outwards.

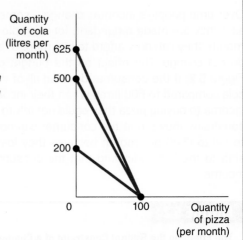

A Change in the Price of Pizza The opposite happens if the price of pizza were to change but the price of cola stayed the same. Assume the price of cola is €2 but the price of pizza rises to €12.50. If the consumer devotes all their income to pizza they can now only afford to buy 80 pizzas with their €1000 income. The budget constraint would pivot inwards and its slope would change. The ratio of the price of cola to the price of pizza is now $\frac{2}{12.5}$ and the slope is 6.25. The inverse of the slope is 0.16. For every 1 litre of cola the consumer acquires they have to give up 0.16 of a pizza and for every 1 extra pizza bought the consumer now has to sacrifice 6.25 litres of cola. If the price of pizza falls to €8 then the consumer would be able to purchase more pizza (125) with their income and so the budget constraint would pivot outwards as shown in Figure 5.4.

FIGURE 5.4

A Change in the Price of Pizza
A change in the price of pizza, ceteris paribus, would cause a pivot in the budget constraint. If the price of pizza fell then the budget constraint would pivot outwards and if the price of pizza rose the budget constraint would pivot inwards.

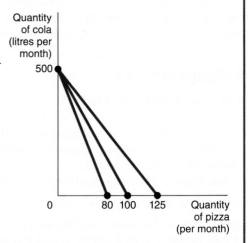

A change in the Price of Both Goods If the price of both goods changes then the shape of the budget constraint would depend on the relative change in the prices of the two goods. The slope would still be the ratio of the price of cola to the price of pizza. Figure 5.5 shows a rise in the price of cola from €2 to €4 and a fall in the price of pizza from €10 to €8. If the consumer devoted all their €1000 per month income to cola they could now afford to buy 250 litres of cola and if they devoted all their income to pizza they could now buy 125 pizzas per month. The ratio of the price of cola to the price of pizza would be $\frac{4}{8}$ and so the slope of the budget constraint would now be 2.

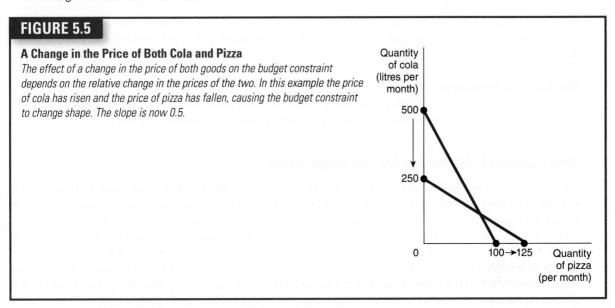

FIGURE 5.5

A Change in the Price of Both Cola and Pizza
The effect of a change in the price of both goods on the budget constraint depends on the relative change in the prices of the two. In this example the price of cola has risen and the price of pizza has fallen, causing the budget constraint to change shape. The slope is now 0.5.

PREFERENCES: WHAT THE CONSUMER WANTS

The budget constraint shows what combination of goods the consumer can afford given their income and the prices of the goods but a consumer's choices also depend on their preferences. We will continue our analysis using cola and pizza as the consumer's **choice set** – the set of alternatives available to the consumer.

> **choice set** the set of alternatives available to the consumer

Representing Preferences with Indifference Curves

The consumer's preferences allow them to choose among different bundles of cola and pizza. The SEM assumes that consumers behave rationally and that, if you offer two different bundles, they chose the bundle that best suits their tastes. Remember, we measure the level of satisfaction in terms of the utility it yields. We can represent consumer preferences in relation to the utility that different bundles of goods provide. If a consumer prefers one bundle of goods to another, the assumption of the SEM is that the first provides more utility than the second. If two bundles yield the same utility then the consumer is said to be *indifferent* between them. We can represent these preferences as indifference curves. An **indifference curve** shows the bundles of consumption that yield the same utility, i.e. makes the consumer equally happy. You can think of an indifference curve as an 'equal-utility' curve.

> **indifference curve** a curve that shows consumption bundles that give the consumer the same level of satisfaction

In our example we are going to use indifference curves that show the combination of cola and pizza with which the consumer is equally satisfied.

This model of preferences includes particular assumptions based on two axioms (points of reference or starting points).

The Axiom of Comparison Given any two bundles of goods, A and B, representing consumption choices, a consumer can compare these bundles such that A is preferred to B, B is preferred to A or the consumer is indifferent between A and B.

The Axiom of Transitivity Given any three bundles of goods, A, B and C, if the consumer prefers A to B and prefers B to C then they must prefer A to C. Equally, if the consumer is indifferent between A and B and is also indifferent between B and C then they must be indifferent between A and C.

Representing Indifference Curves Graphically

We can represent indifference curves graphically. The quantity of cola is on the vertical axis and the quantity of pizza is on the horizontal axis. The graph is sometimes called an indifference map. The map contains an infinite number of indifference curves. Figure 5.6 shows two of the consumer's many indifference curves.

The points A, B and C on indifference curve I_1 in Figure 5.6 all represent different combinations of cola and pizza. The consumer is indifferent between these combinations. However, indifference curve I_2 is further to the right than curve I_1 and given the assumption that more is preferred to less, the consumer would prefer to be on the highest indifference curve possible. Any point on I_2, therefore, is preferred to any point on I_1 because any combination of goods on I_2 give higher utility than any point on I_1.

FIGURE 5.6

The Consumer's Preferences

The consumer's preferences are represented with indifference curves, which show the combinations of cola and pizza that make the consumer equally satisfied. Because of the assumption that more is preferred to less, points on a higher indifference curve (I_2 here) are preferred to points on a lower indifference curve (I_1). A point along an indifference curve such as point B on indifference curve I_1, represents a bundle or combination of goods, cola and pizza in this case. The consumer is indifferent between any point along an indifference curve such as A, B or C along indifference curve I_1. Points D and E on indifference curve I_2 also represent combinations of goods between which the consumer is indifferent but any point on indifference curve I_2 is preferred to any point on indifference curve I_1.

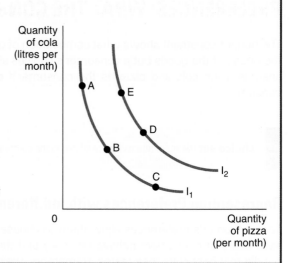

We can use indifference curves to rank any two bundles of goods. For example, the indifference curves tell us that point D is preferred to point B because point D is on a higher indifference curve than point B. This conclusion may be obvious, given that point D offers the consumer both more pizza and more cola. However, point D is also preferred to point A because even though point D has less cola than point A, it has more than enough extra pizza to make the consumer prefer it. By seeing which point is on the higher indifference curve, we can use the set of indifference curves to rank any combinations of cola and pizza.

Four Properties of Indifference Curves

Because indifference curves represent a consumer's preferences, they have certain properties that reflect those preferences.

Property 1: Higher indifference curves (further to the upper right) are preferred to lower ones. This is because of the assumption that consumers prefer more of something to less of it. Higher indifference curves represent larger quantities of goods than lower indifference curves. Thus, the consumer prefers being on higher indifference curves.

Property 2: Indifference curves are downwards sloping. The slope of an indifference curve reflects the rate at which the consumer is willing to substitute one good for the other. In most cases, the consumer likes both goods. Therefore, if the quantity of one good is reduced, the quantity of the other good must increase in order for the consumer to be equally happy. For this reason, most indifference curves slope downwards.

Property 3: Indifference curves do not cross. To see why this is true, suppose that two indifference curves did cross, as in Figure 5.7. Notice that point A is on the same indifference curve as point B, the two points would make the consumer equally happy. In addition, because point B is on the same indifference curve as point C, these two points would make the consumer equally happy. But these conclusions imply that points A and C would also make the consumer equally happy, even though point C has more of both goods. This contradicts the *axiom of transitivity* and, thus, indifference curves cannot cross.

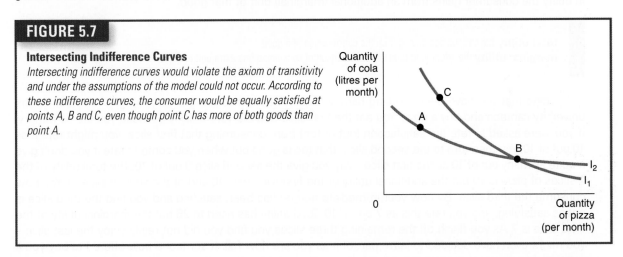

FIGURE 5.7

Intersecting Indifference Curves
Intersecting indifference curves would violate the axiom of transitivity and under the assumptions of the model could not occur. According to these indifference curves, the consumer would be equally satisfied at points A, B and C, even though point C has more of both goods than point A.

Property 4: Indifference curves are bowed inward. The slope of an indifference curve is the marginal rate of substitution (MRS) which we will cover in more detail later. The marginal rate of substitution usually depends on the amount of each good the consumer is currently consuming. In particular, because people are more willing to trade away goods that they have in abundance and less willing to trade away goods of which they have little, the indifference curves are bowed inward. As an example, consider Figure 5.8.

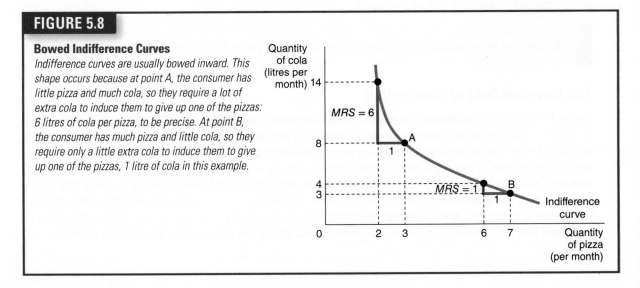

FIGURE 5.8

Bowed Indifference Curves
Indifference curves are usually bowed inward. This shape occurs because at point A, the consumer has little pizza and much cola, so they require a lot of extra cola to induce them to give up one of the pizzas: 6 litres of cola per pizza, to be precise. At point B, the consumer has much pizza and little cola, so they require only a little extra cola to induce them to give up one of the pizzas, 1 litre of cola in this example.

At point A, because the consumer has a lot of cola and only a little pizza, they are very hungry but not very thirsty. To induce the consumer to give up 1 pizza, the consumer has to be given 6 litres of cola: the marginal rate of substitution is 6 litres per pizza. By contrast, at point B, the consumer has little cola and a lot of pizza, so they are very thirsty but not very hungry. At this point, they would be willing to give up 1 pizza to get 1 litre of cola: the marginal rate of substitution is 1 litre per pizza. Thus, the bowed shape of the indifference curve reflects the consumer's greater willingness to give up a good that they already have in large quantity.

Total and Marginal Utility

Remember, we assume that consumers prefer more to less. This does not mean that if a consumer eats more and more pizza or drinks more and more cola, that the utility on an additional unit consumed is always the same. We need to distinguish between total utility and marginal utility. **Total utility** is the satisfaction consumers' gain from consuming a product. The **marginal utility** of consumption is the increase in utility the consumer gains from an additional (marginal) unit of that good.

total utility the satisfaction gained from the consumption of a good
marginal utility the addition to total utility as a result of consuming one extra unit of a good

Imagine that you have been working hard and now realize that you are very hungry. You head to the university canteen and buy a pizza. You eat the first slice of pizza very quickly because you are so hungry. If you were asked to rate the satisfaction (out of ten) from consuming that first slice, you might rate it as 10 out of 10. You then turn to the second slice, that too is good but when you come to rate it you don't give it quite as many out of 10 as the first slice – say you give the second slice 9 out of 10. The total utility of the 2 slices of pizza is 19 but the additional utility of the first slice was 10 and of the second slice, 9. You now consume the third slice. By now your immediate hunger has been satisfied and you find the third slice is not as satisfying, and you rate this as 7 out of 10. Total utility has risen to 26 but the marginal utility of the third slice is 7. As you finish off the remaining three slices you find you did not really enjoy the last slice – you might even have decided to leave part of it as you are now full. If someone now offered to buy you a second pizza you might refuse – eating one extra slice might just result in you being sick – and in this case you might even rate this next slice as having negative utility.

The tendency for the total utility from consumption to rise but at a slower rate with additional units of consumption is called diminishing marginal utility. **Diminishing marginal utility** refers to the tendency for the additional satisfaction from consuming extra units of a good to fall. Most goods are assumed to exhibit diminishing marginal utility; the more of the good the consumer already has, the lower the marginal utility provided by an extra unit of that good.

diminishing marginal utility the tendency for the additional satisfaction from consuming extra units of a good to fall

The Marginal Rate of Substitution

Figure 5.9 shows an indifference curve and three combinations of cola and pizza represented by points A, B and C. We know that the consumer is indifferent between these combinations. Assume the consumer starts at the combination of cola and pizza represented by point A with a combination of 20 pizzas and 5 litres of cola. If the consumer's consumption of pizza is reduced from point A to point B, the consumer is willing to give up 10 pizzas to increase consumption of cola from 5 litres to 12 litres. We know, however, that the additional consumption of cola will be subject to diminishing marginal utility. Moving from point B to point C, the consumer is willing to give up only 5 pizzas to gain an additional 8 litres of cola such that the bundle 5 pizzas and 20 litres of cola yields the same utility as at points B and A.

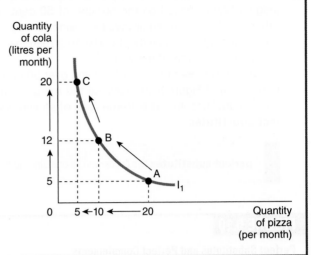

FIGURE 5.9

The Marginal Rate of Substitution
The slope of an indifference curve is not constant throughout its length but changes at every point. The marginal rate of substitution measures that rate at which a consumer is prepared to substitute one good for another.

In our example, the consumer starts off with a relatively large amount of pizza and a relatively small amount of cola. It is logical to assume that the consumer would be willing to give up relatively large amounts of pizza to acquire some additional cola. However, moving from point B to point C is a slightly different matter. The situation is almost reversed – to gain additional litres of cola the consumer is now willing to sacrifice fewer pizzas.

The rate at which consumers are willing to substitute one good for another is called the marginal rate of substitution. The slope at any point on an indifference curve equals the rate at which the consumer is willing to substitute one good for the other. The **marginal rate of substitution** (MRS) between two goods depends on their marginal utilities. In this case, the marginal rate of substitution measures how much cola the consumer requires in order to be compensated for a one-unit reduction in pizza consumption. For example, if the marginal utility of cola is twice the marginal utility of pizza, then a person would need 2 units of pizza to compensate for losing 1 unit of cola, and the marginal rate of substitution equals −2. More generally, the marginal rate of substitution (and thus the negative of the slope of the indifference curve) equals the marginal utility of one good divided by the marginal utility of the other good $\left(\dfrac{MUx}{MUy}\right)$.

---

marginal rate of substitution the rate at which a consumer is willing to trade one good for another

---

Notice that because the indifference curves are not straight lines, the marginal rate of substitution is not the same at all points on a given indifference curve.

Two Extreme Examples of Indifference Curves

The shape of an indifference curve tells us about the consumer's willingness to trade one good for the other. When the goods are easy to substitute for each other, the indifference curves are less bowed; when the goods are hard to substitute, the indifference curves are very bowed. To see why this is true, let's consider the extreme cases.

Perfect Substitutes Suppose that someone offered you bundles of 50 cent coins and 10 cent coins. How would you rank the different bundles?

Most probably, you would care only about the total monetary value of each bundle. If so, you would judge a bundle based on the number of 50 cent coins plus five times the number of 10 cent coins. In other words, you would always be willing to trade one 50 cent coin for five 10 cent coins, regardless of the number of coins in either bundle. Your marginal rate of substitution between 10 cent coins and 50 cent coins would be a fixed number: 5.

We can represent your preferences over 50 cent coins and 10 cent coins with the indifference curves in panel (a) of Figure 5.10. Because the marginal rate of substitution is constant, the indifference curves are straight lines. In this extreme case of straight indifference curves, we say that the two goods are **perfect substitutes**.

 perfect substitutes two goods with straight line indifference curves

---

FIGURE 5.10

Perfect Substitutes and Perfect Complements
When two goods are easily substitutable, such as 50 cent and 10 cent coins, the indifference curves are straight lines, as shown in panel (a). When two goods are strongly complementary, such as left shoes and right shoes, the indifference curves are right angles, as shown in panel (b).

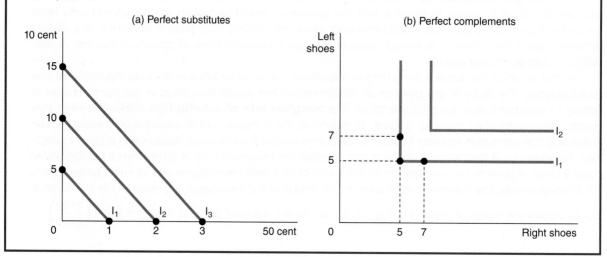

Perfect Complements Suppose now that someone offered you bundles of shoes. Some of the shoes fit your left foot, others your right foot. How would you rank these different bundles?

In this case, you might care only about the number of pairs of shoes. In other words, you would judge a bundle based on the number of pairs you could assemble from it. A bundle of 5 left shoes and 7 right shoes yields only 5 pairs. Getting 1 more right shoe has no value if there is no left shoe to go with it.

We can represent your preferences for right and left shoes with the indifference curves in panel (b) of Figure 5.10. In this case, a bundle with 5 left shoes and 5 right shoes is just as good as a bundle with 5 left shoes and 7 right shoes. It is also just as good as a bundle with 7 left shoes and 5 right shoes. The indifference curves, therefore, are right angles. In this extreme case of right-angle indifference curves, we say that the two goods are **perfect complements**.

 perfect complements two goods with right-angle indifference curves

In the real world, of course, most goods are neither perfect substitutes nor perfect complements. More typically, the indifference curves are bowed inward, but not so bowed as to become right angles.

SELF TEST Why is the amount of a good a person is consuming at a given point in time an important factor in determining the marginal rate of substitution? What happens to the total and marginal utility of two goods, *x* and *y*, if a consumer has a large quantity of good *x* but hardly any of good *y* and then opts to consume more of good *x*?

OPTIMIZATION: WHAT THE CONSUMER CHOOSES

One of the working assumptions of the SEM is that the consumer will seek to maximize utility subject to the constraint of a limited income. This is an example of a constrained optimization problem. How is this constrained optimization problem solved?

The Consumer's Optimal Choices

Using our cola and pizza example, taking into account the constraint of income as shown by the budget constraint, the consumer would like to end up with a combination of cola and pizza on the highest possible indifference curve.

Figure 5.11 shows the consumer's budget constraint (BC_1) and four of their many indifference curves. The highest indifference curve that the consumer can reach (I_3 in the figure) is the one that just barely touches the budget constraint. The point at which this indifference curve and the budget constraint touch is called the *optimum*. The consumer would prefer point A, but they cannot afford that point because it lies above their budget constraint. The consumer can afford point B, but that point is on a lower indifference curve and, therefore, provides the consumer less satisfaction. Taking into account the assumptions of the model, there is an alternative consumption choice, given their income, which would be preferable. The combination of cola and pizza at point C is affordable, being just on the budget constraint, but the consumer is not in equilibrium because there is an incentive for them to change their consumption choice and reach a higher indifference curve. What this means is that the consumer can reallocate their spending decisions and get more utility from their limited income. There is an incentive for them to reduce consumption of pizza and increase consumption of cola at point D on indifference curve I_2. By doing this the consumer is getting more utility from an additional euro spent on more cola compared to the marginal utility spent on another pizza. This is entirely logical. If you could spend one euro on more cola and get an extra 7 utils of utility compared to an extra 5 utils you would get from more pizza with the same euro, it makes sense to buy more cola (assuming rational behaviour).

FIGURE 5.11

The Consumer's Optimum
The consumer chooses the point on their budget constraint that lies on the highest achievable indifference curve. At this point, called the optimum, the marginal rate of substitution equals the relative price of the two goods. Here the highest indifference curve the consumer can reach is I_3.

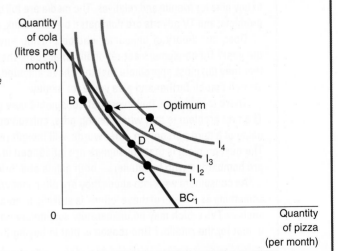

However, this is still not the optimum because the consumer can continue to reallocate their spending decisions reaching ever higher indifference curves (remember there are an infinite amount on the map) until the marginal utility of the last euro spent on cola is equal to the marginal utility of the last euro spent on pizza. The optimum represents the best combination of consumption of cola and pizza available to the consumer given their income and the assumptions of consumer behaviour in the model.

At the point of consumer equilibrium (the optimum), the slope of the indifference curve equals the slope of the budget constraint. We say that the indifference curve is *tangential* to the budget constraint. The slope of the indifference curve is the marginal rate of substitution between cola and pizza, and the slope of the budget constraint is the relative price of cola and pizza. Thus, the consumer chooses consumption of the two goods at the optimum so that the marginal rate of substitution equals the relative price.

That is:

$$MRS = \frac{P_x}{P_y}$$

Because the marginal rate of substitution equals the ratio of marginal utilities, we can write this condition for optimization as:

$$\frac{MU_x}{MU_y} = \frac{P_x}{P_y}$$

This expression can be rearranged to become:

$$\frac{MU_x}{P_x} = \frac{MU_y}{P_y}$$

At the optimum, the marginal utility per euro spent on good *x* equals the marginal utility per euro spent on good *y*. At any other point, the consumer is not in equilibrium. Why? As we saw above, this is because the consumer could increase utility by changing behaviour, switching spending from the good that provided lower marginal utility per euro to the good that provided higher marginal utility per euro.

At the consumer's optimum, the consumer's valuation of the two goods (as measured by the marginal rate of substitution) equals the market's valuation (as measured by the relative price). As a result of this consumer optimization, market prices of different goods reflect the value that consumers place on those goods.

CASE STUDY   **Christmas and the Rational Consumer**

Over the Christmas period, millions of people throughout Europe either travel to shopping centres or go online to buy gifts for friends and relatives. The media are full of adverts trying to persuade people to buy particular products, and TV adverts are dominated by food, drink, chocolate, perfumes, toys and electrical goods.

Does our theory of consumer choice provide any insights into consumer behaviour at this time of the year? Do consumers act rationally to allocate their limited income? Many people would like to think that they do; most appreciate that they have a limited income and there is an incentive to make budgets stretch that bit further and give value for money.

There is evidence, however, that consumers may not behave as rationally as they might like to think. The first problem is that when buying gifts, consumers are not the end user and so are anticipating the utility of a third person – in other words, will the gift receiver actually like the present when they open it? The next problem is that consumers are influenced in their consumption choices by the information they are bombarded with by retailers – both online and 'bricks and mortar'.

As consumers walk into shops they are often met with 'offers' – the number of people who stop and buy something as a result of these 'offers' is striking. In some cases they might be for so-called 'big ticket items' such as TVs which may be deliberately sold below cost to encourage purchase. Where is the rationality in that for the retailer? One reason is that in buying the TV the consumer invariably then also purchases

(Continued)

other accessories which they need – cables, stands, wall mounting brackets, maybe even a games console or some DVDs to complement the wonderful new TV – and before you know it the amount spent is far above any savings gained from purchasing the TV. We might also ask whether the consumer actually needed the TV in the first place – is this what they set out to buy? In some cases, of course, it is, but in others it is an impulse purchase and can that, by definition, be rational?

The supermarket may tell you that you have 'saved money' but is this really the case?

Doing the Christmas grocery shopping might be another case where rationality is compromised. Many stores provide information on their receipt or online order form telling consumers how much they have 'saved' as a result of their purchase decisions. The consumer might have decided to buy a six-pack of wine for €48 which will 'save' them €6. Did they intend to buy a six-pack in the first place? If not, then they may end up spending a great deal more than they originally intended. The consumer may feel it doesn't matter because 'it will all get drunk at some point so I might as well buy it'! Is that a rational statement?

The 'savings' list might sound impressive but the store does not offset the savings they tell you about by allocating the overheads of shopping – the time spent queuing, the cost of the fuel and vehicle depreciation used to get to the store, the parking fee, what the shopper could have been doing if they were not walking round a supermarket or sitting in front of their computer making their consumption choice and so on.

Then there is the cheerful retail operative who proudly announces to you that as a result of buying the two-for-one shirt offer you have 'saved €30'. The answer? No, I haven't, I have spent €30! I didn't need two shirts (I probably did not *need* one shirt) and if I was being asked to hand over €60 for the item regardless of how many shirts, I may not have made the decision to spend that much money. If I was never going to spend it then it is not a saving. Many consumers, however, do tell their friends that they 'saved' lots as a result of their trip, despite these facts. Psychologists call it *confirmation bias*.

There is also research which shows that far from being rational in our decision-making when shopping, we can be deeply irrational. Our brains react differently to information we see when we are shopping and retailers know this. Psychologists have shown that when humans are given information which creates an association they are more likely to behave in ways which confirm the association. If the brain is primed to look for bargains or offers we are more likely to make a purchase decision when confronted with information which seems to represent a 'bargain'. If prices are lower *than anticipated* then the decision-making part of the brain registers this and we are more likely to make the purchase as a result. Equally, if prices are much higher than anticipated a different part of the brain associated with registering pain is activated and we avoid the purchase.

Overall, therefore, whilst our model of consumer behaviour provides some insights, as with any model it is a representation of reality and not reality itself. There is now a great deal of research being conducted which is shedding more light on consumer behaviour which casts doubt on just how rational we are capable of being.

How Changes in Income Affect the Consumer's Choices

When income increases there is a parallel shift of the budget constraint with the same slope as the initial budget constraint because the relative price of the two goods has not changed. The increase in income means there is an incentive for the consumer to reallocate their spending decisions to increase utility and choose a better combination of cola and pizza. The consumer reallocates income until they reach a new optimum labelled 'new optimum' on a higher indifference curve as shown in Figure 5.12.

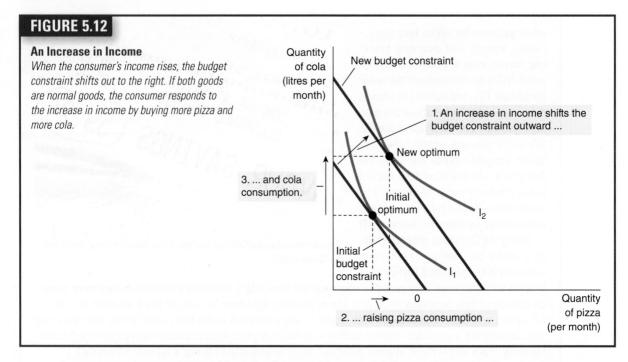

FIGURE 5.12

An Increase in Income

When the consumer's income rises, the budget constraint shifts out to the right. If both goods are normal goods, the consumer responds to the increase in income by buying more pizza and more cola.

Notice that in Figure 5.12 the consumer chooses to consume more cola and more pizza although the logic of the model does not require increased consumption of both goods in response to increased income. Remember, if a consumer wants more of a good when their income rises, economists call it a normal good. The indifference curves in Figure 5.12 are drawn under the assumption that both cola and pizza are normal goods.

Figure 5.13 shows an example in which an increase in income induces the consumer to buy more pizza but less cola.

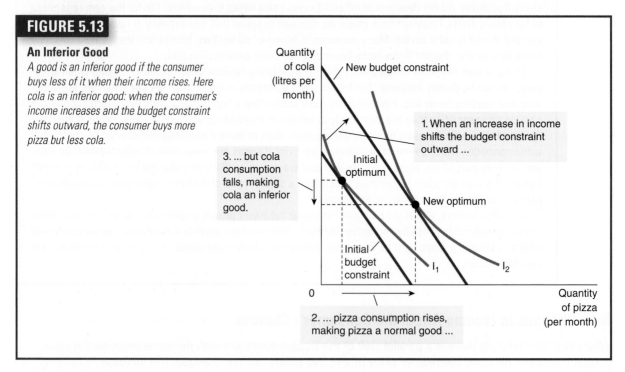

FIGURE 5.13

An Inferior Good

A good is an inferior good if the consumer buys less of it when their income rises. Here cola is an inferior good: when the consumer's income increases and the budget constraint shifts outward, the consumer buys more pizza but less cola.

If a consumer buys less of a good when their income rises, economists call it an inferior good. Figure 5.13 is drawn under the assumption that pizza is a normal good and cola is an inferior good. One example of an inferior good is bus rides. High-income consumers are more likely to own cars and less likely to ride the bus than low-income consumers. Bus rides, therefore, are an inferior good. When low-income consumers experience a rise in income they are more likely to acquire a car and use the bus less.

How Changes in Prices Affect the Consumer's Choices

Suppose that the price of cola falls from €2 to €1 a litre. We have seen how a change in the price of any good causes the budget constraint to pivot. With their available income of €1000 the consumer can now buy twice as many litres of cola than before but the same amount of pizza. Figure 5.14 shows that point A stays the same (100 pizzas). Yet if the consumer spends their entire income of €1000 on cola, they can now buy 1000 rather than only 500 litres. Thus, the end point of the budget constraint pivots outwards from point B to point C.

The pivoting of the budget constraint changes its slope. Because the price of cola has fallen to €1 from €2, while the price of pizza has remained €10, the consumer can now trade a pizza for 10 rather than 5 litres of cola. As a result, the new budget constraint is more steeply sloped. How such a change in the budget constraint alters the consumption of both goods depends on the consumer's preferences. For the indifference curves drawn in Figure 5.14, the consumer buys more cola and less pizza.

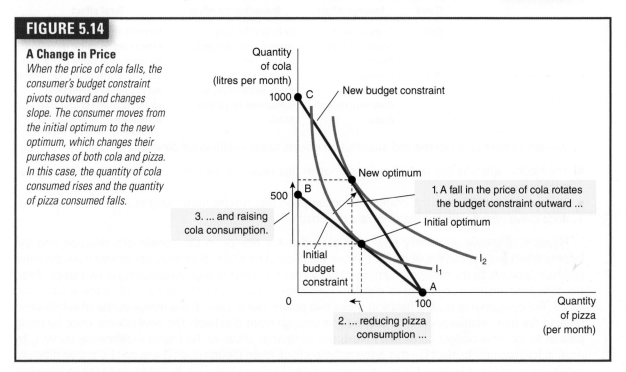

FIGURE 5.14

A Change in Price
When the price of cola falls, the consumer's budget constraint pivots outward and changes slope. The consumer moves from the initial optimum to the new optimum, which changes their purchases of both cola and pizza. In this case, the quantity of cola consumed rises and the quantity of pizza consumed falls.

Income and Substitution Effects

In Chapter 3 we took a brief look at the **income effect** and the **substitution effect** as reasons why a fall in price leads to a rise in quantity demanded.

> **income effect** the change in consumption that results when a price change moves the consumer to a higher or lower indifference curve
> **substitution effect** the change in consumption that results when a price change moves the consumer along a given indifference curve to a point with a new marginal rate of substitution

Consider this thought experiment: If the price of cola falls you are now able to purchase more cola with your income – you are *in effect* richer and can buy both more cola and more pizza. For example, assume your income is €1000 and the initial price of cola is €2 and pizza is €10. You currently buy 250 litres of cola and 50 pizzas. If the price of cola falls to €1 per litre you can adjust your spending and now buy 300 litres of cola (spending €300) and use the remaining €700 to buy more pizza than before (70 pizzas). This is the income effect.

Second, note that now that the price of cola has fallen, you get more litres of cola for every pizza that you give up. Because pizza is now *relatively* more expensive, you might decide to buy less pizza and more cola. This is the substitution effect.

Both of these effects occur when prices change. The decrease in the price of cola makes the consumer better off. If cola and pizza are both normal goods, the consumer will want to spread this improvement in their purchasing power over both goods. This income effect tends to make the consumer buy more pizza and more cola. Yet, at the same time, consumption of cola has become less expensive relative to consumption of pizza. This substitution effect tends to make the consumer choose more cola and less pizza.

The end result of these two effects is that the consumer certainly buys more cola, because the income and substitution effects both act to raise purchases of cola. But it is ambiguous whether the consumer buys more pizza, because the income and substitution effects work in opposite directions. This conclusion is summarized in Table 5.1.

TABLE 5.1 Income and Substitution Effects When the Price of Cola Falls

Good	Income effect	Substitution effect	Total effect
Cola	Consumer is richer, so they buy more cola.	Cola is relatively cheaper, so consumer buys more cola.	Income and substitution effects act in same direction, so consumer buys more cola.
Pizza	Consumer is richer, so they buy more pizza.	Pizza is relatively more expensive, so consumer buys less pizza.	Income and substitution effects act in opposite directions, so the total effect on pizza consumption is ambiguous.

We can interpret the income and substitution effects using indifference curves:

● The income effect is the change in consumption that results from the movement to a higher indifference curve.
● The substitution effect is the change in consumption that results from being at a point on an indifference curve with a different marginal rate of substitution.

Figure 5.15 shows graphically how to decompose the change in the consumer's decision into the income effect and the substitution effect. When the price of cola falls, the consumer moves from the initial optimum, point A, to the new optimum, point C. We can view this change as occurring in two steps. First, the consumer moves *along* the initial indifference curve I_1 from point A to point B – this is the substitution effect. The consumer is equally happy at these two points, but at point B the marginal rate of substitution reflects the new relative price. (The dashed line through point B reflects the new relative price by being parallel to the new budget constraint.) Next, the consumer *shifts* to the higher indifference curve I_2 by moving from point B to point C – this is the income effect. Even though point B and point C are on different indifference curves, they have the same marginal rate of substitution. That is, the slope of the indifference curve I_1 at point B equals the slope of the indifference curve I_2 at point C.

Although the consumer never actually chooses point B, this hypothetical point is useful to clarify the two effects that determine the consumer's decision. Notice that the change from point A to point B represents a pure change in the marginal rate of substitution without any change in the consumer's welfare. Similarly, the change from point B to point C represents a pure change in welfare without any change in the marginal rate of substitution. Thus, the movement from A to B shows the substitution effect, and the movement from B to C shows the income effect.

Income and Substitution Effects – a Numerical Example In the March 2016 Budget, the UK Chancellor of the Exchequer introduced a tax on sugary drinks. The tax added around 24p on a litre of these drinks and we can use this to estimate the income and substitution effect of the change in price. Assume that the individual demand function for sugary drinks is given by:

$$D_1 = 10 + \frac{Y}{10(P_x)}$$

FIGURE 5.15

Income and Substitution Effects
The effect of a change in price can be broken down into an income effect and a substitution effect. The substitution effect – the movement along an indifference curve to a point with a different marginal rate of substitution – is shown here as the change from point A to point B along indifference curve I_1. The income effect – the shift to a higher indifference curve – is shown here as the change from point B on indifference curve I_1 to point C on indifference curve I_2

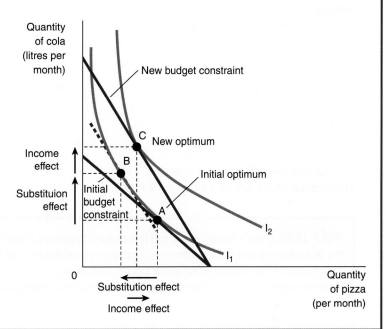

Further assume that the individual's income is £500 per week and the initial price of sugary drinks per litre is £3. Substituting these figures into the demand function gives:

$$D_1 = 10 + \frac{500}{10(3)}$$

$$D_1 = 10 + \frac{500}{30}$$

$$D_1 = 10 + 16.7$$

$$D_1 = 26.67 \; litres \; per \; week.$$

Now assume that the after-tax price of sugary drinks rises to £3.25 per litre but income stays the same at £500 per week. The new demand for sugary drinks will now be:

$$D_2 = 10 + \frac{500}{10(3.25)}$$

$$D_2 = 10 + \frac{500}{32.5}$$

$$D_2 = 25.38 \; litres \; per \; week.$$

The overall effect of the tax is to reduce the demand for sugary drinks by this individual by 1.29 litres per week.

To find how much of this reduction in demand was due to the income effect and how much to the substitution effect we have to find what demand would be if income was adjusted to keep purchasing power constant. Taking D_1 and multiplying it by the difference in the price as a result of the tax gives us 26.67(3.25 − 3.00) = 6.67. To keep purchasing power constant, therefore, income would need to be £506.67.

We can find the substitution effect by substituting the equivalized income and new price in to the demand function:

$$D_3 = 10 + \frac{506.67}{10(3.25)}$$

$$D_3 = 10 + \frac{506.67}{32.5}$$

$$D_3 = 25.6$$

The substitution effect is 25.6 − 26.67 = −1.07
The income effect will be 1.29 − 1.07 = 0.22

SELF TEST Draw a budget constraint line and indifference curves for cola and pizza. Show what happens to the budget constraint and the consumer's optimum when the price of pizza rises. In your diagram, decompose the change into an income effect and a substitution effect.

Deriving the Demand Curve Using the logic we have developed so far, we can now look at how the demand curve is derived. The demand curve shows the quantity demanded of a good for any given price. We can view a consumer's demand curve as a summary of the optimal decisions that arise from their budget constraint and indifference curves.

Figure 5.16 considers the demand for pizza. Assume the price of pizza is €10 indicated by the budget constraint BC_1 and a consumer optimum with indifference curve I_1 giving a quantity of pizza bought as Q_1. A series of other budget constraints labelled BC_2 to BC_5 indicate successive lower prices of pizza and the different consumer optimums indicated by the varying quantities of pizza purchased. The consumer optimums associated with each price of pizza are shown as the **price–consumption curve**. The price–consumption curve shows the consumer optimum for two goods as the price of one of the goods changes *ceteris paribus*.

> **price–consumption curve** a line showing the consumer optimum for two goods as the price of one of the goods changes, assuming incomes and the price of the good are held constant

Figure 5.16 represents the relationship between the change in the price of pizza and the quantity demanded. The price–quantity relationship is plotted on the lower graph to give the familiar demand curve. As the price of pizza falls the quantity demanded rises – the reasons being partly due to the income effect and partly to the substitution effect. The theory of consumer choice, therefore, provides the theoretical foundation for the consumer's demand curve, which we first introduced in Chapter 3.

Do All Demand Curves Slope Downwards?

The *law of demand* implies that when the price of a good rises, people buy less of it. This law is reflected in the downwards slope of the demand curve. As a matter of economic theory, however, demand curves can sometimes slope upwards violating the law of demand where consumers buy *more* of a good when the price rises. To see how this can happen, consider Figure 5.17. In this example, the consumer buys two goods – meat and potatoes. Initially, the consumer's budget constraint is the line from point A to point B. The optimum is point C. When the price of potatoes rises, the budget constraint shifts inwards and is now the line from point A to point D. The optimum is now point E. Notice that a rise in the price of potatoes has led the consumer to buy a larger quantity of potatoes.

FIGURE 5.16

Deriving the Demand Curve
The upper graph shows that when the price of pizza falls the consumer's optimum changes and these changes are shown as the price–consumption curve. The demand curve in the lower graph reflects the relationship between the price of pizza and the quantity demanded.

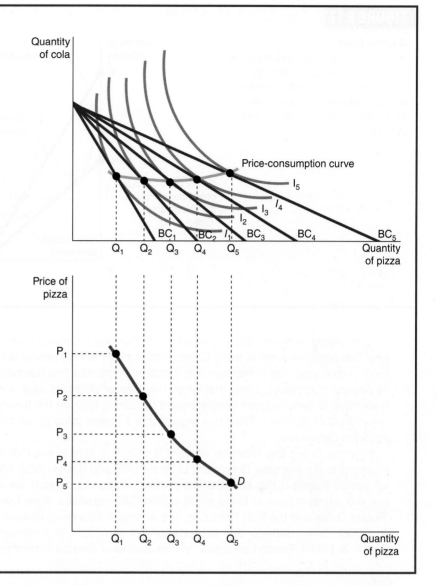

The consumer might respond in this seemingly perverse way if the good in question, potatoes in this example, are a strongly inferior good. When the price of potatoes rises, the consumer is poorer. The income effect makes the consumer want to buy less meat and more potatoes. At the same time, because the potatoes have become more expensive relative to meat, the substitution effect makes the consumer want to buy more meat and less potatoes. In this particular case, however, the income effect is so strong that it exceeds the substitution effect. In the end, the consumer responds to the higher price of potatoes by buying less meat and more potatoes.

Economists use the term **Giffen good** to describe a good that violates the law of demand. (The term is named after the British economist Robert Giffen, who first noted this possibility.) In our example, potatoes are a Giffen good. Giffen goods are inferior goods for which the income effect dominates the substitution effect. Therefore, they have demand curves that slope upward.

Giffen good a good for which an increase in the price raises the quantity demanded

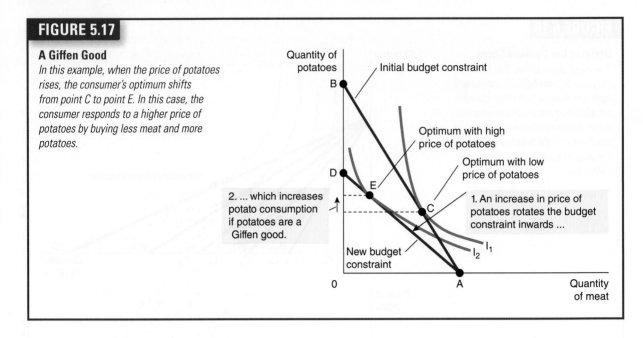

FIGURE 5.17

A Giffen Good
In this example, when the price of potatoes rises, the consumer's optimum shifts from point C to point E. In this case, the consumer responds to a higher price of potatoes by buying less meat and more potatoes.

Economists disagree about whether any Giffen good has ever been discovered. Some historians suggest that potatoes were in fact a Giffen good during the Irish potato famine of the 19th century. Potatoes were such a large part of people's diet (historians estimate that the average working man might eat up to 14 pounds of potatoes a day) that when the price of potatoes rose, it had a large income effect. People responded to their reduced living standard by cutting back on the luxury of meat and buying more of the staple food of potatoes. Thus, it is argued that a higher price of potatoes actually raised the quantity of potatoes demanded.

Whether or not this historical account is true, it is safe to say that Giffen goods are very rare. Some economists (for example, Dwyer and Lindsey, 1984 and Rosen, 1999) have claimed that a legend has built up around Robert Giffen and that the evidence does not support his idea. Others have suggested that rice and wheat in parts of China might exhibit Giffen qualities. (See: Dwyer, G.P. and Lindsay, C.M. (1984) 'Robert Giffen and the Irish Potato'. In *The American Economic Review*, **74:**188–92; Jensen, R and Miller, N. (2008) 'Giffen Behavior and Subsistence Consumption'. In *American Economic Review*, **97:**1553–77; Rosen, S. (1999) 'Potato Paradoxes'. In *The Journal of Political Economy*, **107:**294–13).

The Income Expansion Path

Having looked at conclusions that can be drawn from assuming a change in price (holding all other things constant) we now turn our attention to what happens if we change income (*ceteris paribus*).

How does the rational consumer respond to a change in income? In Chapter 3 we noted that, for a normal good, a rise in income is associated with a rise in demand but, for an inferior good, a rise in income means a fall in demand. We now have the analytical tools to understand why this is the case.

Normal Goods Figure 5.18 shows a series of increases in income represented by three budget constraints BC_1, BC_2 and BC_3 for cola and pizza. The consumer optimums in each case are indicated by points A, B and C.

If we connect these points we get the income expansion path which reflects the response of a rational consumer to a change in income. In this example, the increase in income has led to an increase in the consumption of both pizza and cola, and as a result we can conclude that both goods are normal goods. In both goods, the income effect outweighs the substitution effect.

Where Pizza is an Inferior Good Figure 5.19 shows a situation where as a result of the increase in income, represented by a shift of the budget constraint from BC_1 to BC_2, there is a change in the consumer optimum from point A to point B. The income expansion path indicates that as income rises, demand for cola increases (it is a normal good) but the demand for pizza has decreased indicating that it is an inferior good. In this case the substitution effect on pizza of the rise in income has outweighed the income effect.

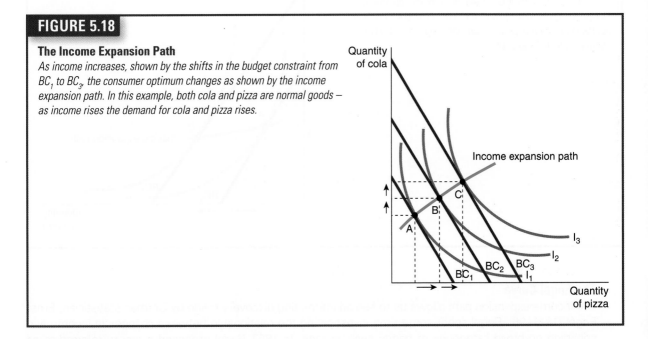

FIGURE 5.18

The Income Expansion Path
As income increases, shown by the shifts in the budget constraint from BC_1 to BC_3, the consumer optimum changes as shown by the income expansion path. In this example, both cola and pizza are normal goods – as income rises the demand for cola and pizza rises.

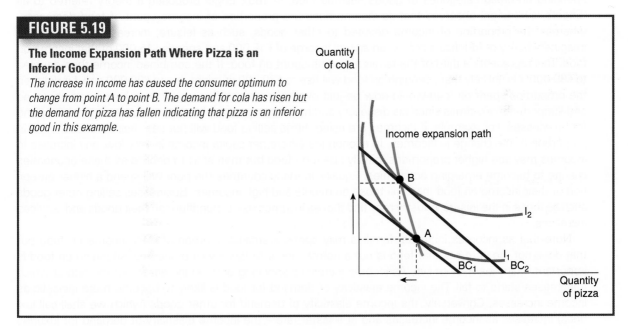

FIGURE 5.19

The Income Expansion Path Where Pizza is an Inferior Good
The increase in income has caused the consumer optimum to change from point A to point B. The demand for cola has risen but the demand for pizza has fallen indicating that pizza is an inferior good in this example.

Where Cola is an Inferior Good Figure 5.20 shows a situation again where, as a result of the increase in income, the budget constraint shifts from BC_1 to BC_2, and the consumer optimum is represented by points A and B. In this case the income expansion path shows that as income rises, demand for cola decreases, showing that it is an inferior good. The demand for pizza has increased as a result of the increase in income indicating that it is a normal good. In this case the substitution effect of the rise in income on cola is greater than the income effect.

FIGURE 5.20

The Income Expansion Path Where Cola is an Inferior Good

The increase in income has caused the consumer optimum to change from point A to point B. The demand for cola has fallen but the demand for pizza has risen indicating that cola is an inferior good in this example.

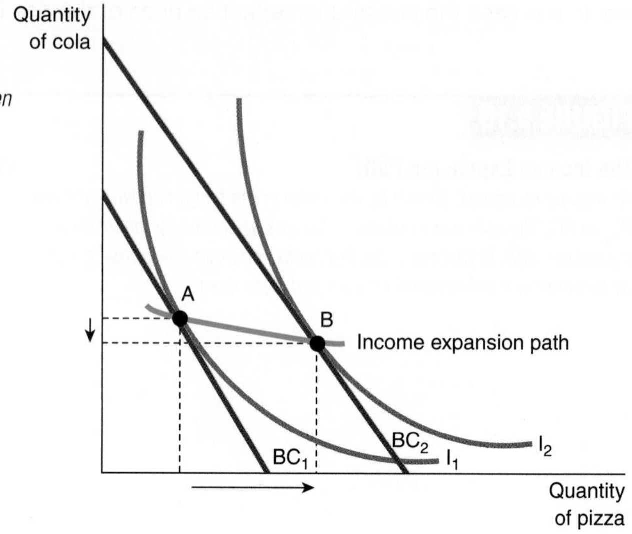

The Engel Curve

The income expansion path allows us to see an interesting discovery made by German statistician, Ernst Engel (1821–96). Engel spent some time investigating the relationship between changes in income and spending on broad categories of goods such as food. In 1857, Engel proposed a theory referred to as 'Engel's law'. Engel observed that as income rises the proportion of income spent of food decreases, whereas the proportion of income devoted to other goods, such as leisure, increases. For example, imagine a family of four has a combined annual income of €45 000 and spends €15 000 of that income on food. This represents a third of the family's income spent on food. If the combined income then doubled to €90 000 it is unlikely that spending on food will rise to €30 000; it might rise to €20 000 and if it did then the proportion spent on food would now be just over 22 per cent. Engel's findings have been observed and supported many times since his discovery and have important implications for government policy and for businesses. For example, if incomes are rising, firms selling food will not see their revenues rising in proportion to the change in incomes. In economies where per capita income is very low, any increase in incomes may see higher proportions initially spent on food but then start to decline as these economies change to become emerging economies. Equally, in many countries the poor will spend a higher proportion of their income on food than will those on middle and high incomes. Businesses selling other goods such as those in the leisure industry may find that as incomes rise expenditure on their goods and services increases.

Note that as incomes increase, families may spend a small proportion of their income on food but that does not mean to say that food is not a normal good. At low levels of income, spending on food is important – families have to live. As income increases spending on food increases but the rate at which it increases starts to fall. The income elasticity of demand for food is likely to become more inelastic as income increases. Conversely, the income elasticity of demand for other goods (which we shall call luxuries) increases as income increases and at a faster rate – the income elasticity of demand for luxuries becomes more elastic as income rises.

The upper graph in Figure 5.21 shows two goods: food on the vertical axis and luxuries on the horizontal axis. As income increases, as shown by the three budget constraints BC_1 to BC_3, the change in consumer optimum is shown by the three points A, B and C. As income increases, the demand for food and luxuries both increase – both are normal goods. However, the amount of food demanded is increasing at a diminishing rate whereas the increase in demand for luxuries is greater as income increases. The implication, therefore, is that the demand for food is income inelastic whereas the demand for luxuries is income elastic.

FIGURE 5.21

The Engel Curve
The upper graph shows the income–consumption curve for two goods, food and luxuries, which are both normal goods. The lower graph plots the change in demand for luxuries against changes in income.

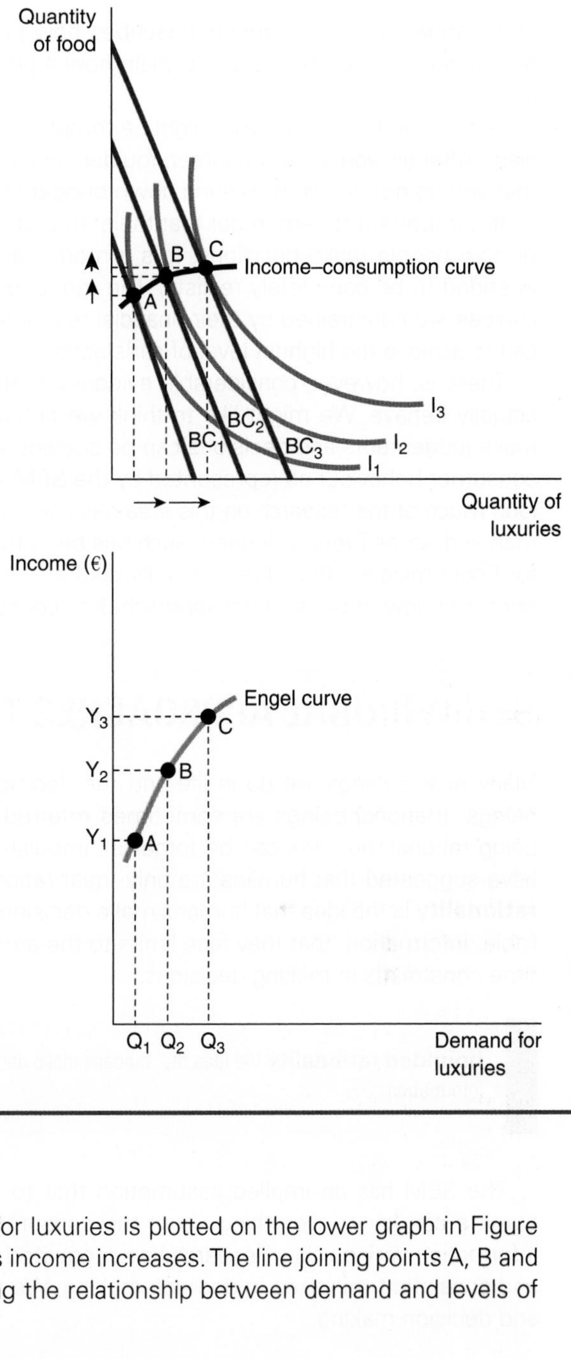

The relationship between income and the demand for luxuries is plotted on the lower graph in Figure 5.21 showing how the demand for luxuries increases as income increases. The line joining points A, B and C is the **Engel curve**. The Engel curve is a line showing the relationship between demand and levels of income.

Engel curve a line showing the relationship between demand and levels of income

In this example the increase in demand for luxuries is greater between income levels Y_2 and Y_3 than it was between Y_1 and Y_2 suggesting that the income elasticity of demand is getting greater as income rises. However, we can see that the proportionate increase in quantity demanded of luxuries between Y_1 and Y_2 is less than the proportionate increase in income, which suggests that the demand for luxuries is income inelastic between these income levels.

SUMMARY: DO PEOPLE REALLY BEHAVE THIS WAY?

The standard economic model describes how people make decisions based on certain assumptions. It has broad applicability and can explain how a person chooses between cola and pizza, food and leisure, and so on.

At this point, however, you might be tempted to treat the theory of consumer choice with some scepticism. After all, you are a consumer. You decide what to buy every time you walk into a shop. And you know that you do not decide by writing down budget constraints and indifference curves.

It is important to remember that the standard economic model does not try to present a literal account of how people make decisions. It is a model, and, as we first discussed in Chapter 2, models are not intended to be completely realistic. The model does have some merits; consumers are aware that their choices are constrained by their financial resources. Many, given those constraints, will do the best they can to achieve the highest level of satisfaction.

There is, however, considerable evidence that the SEM has limitations in explaining how consumers actually behave. We might like to think we behave rationally but research has shown that our ability to make judgements and decisions can be subject to systematic and consistent flaws – biases – that mean consumer behaviour as represented by the SEM is, at the very best, a limited model of consumer behaviour. Much of the research on this area has been inspired by the work of two psychologists, Daniel Kahneman and Amos Tversky. Indeed, such has been their impact that Kahneman was awarded the Nobel Prize for Economics in 2002 (Tversky sadly died at the relatively young age of 59 in 1996). We now present a brief overview of behavioural approaches to consumer behaviour.

BEHAVIOURAL APPROACHES TO CONSUMER BEHAVIOUR

Many of the things we do in life and the decisions we make cannot be explained as those of rational beings. (Rational beings are sometimes referred to by economists as *homo economicus*). Rather than being rational, humans can be forgetful, impulsive, confused, emotional and short-sighted. Economists have suggested that humans are only 'near rational' or that they exhibit 'bounded rationality'. **Bounded rationality** is the idea that humans make decisions under the constraints of limited, and sometimes unreliable, information, that they face limits to the amount of information they can process and that they face time constraints in making decisions.

> **bounded rationality** the idea that humans make decisions under the constraints of limited, and sometimes unreliable, information

The SEM has an implied assumption that to make a rational decision which maximizes utility, consumers can know everything about the consumption decision that they make and can process all this information very quickly. Research has suggested that this is far from the case. Humans make systematic and consistent mistakes in decision-making. We will now outline some of the main errors in judgement and decision-making.

People are Overconfident

Imagine that you were asked some numerical questions, such as the number of African countries in the United Nations, the height of the tallest mountain in Europe and so on. Instead of being asked for a single estimate, however, you were asked to give a 90 per cent confidence interval – a range such that you were 90 per cent confident the true number falls within it. When psychologists run experiments like this, they find that most people give ranges that are too small: the true number falls within their intervals far less than 90 per cent of the time. That is, most people are too sure of their own abilities.

People Give Too Much Weight to a Small Number of Vivid Observations

Imagine that you are thinking about buying a new smartphone from company X. To learn about its reliability, you read *Consumer Reports*, which has surveyed 1000 owners of the particular smartphone that you are looking at. Then you run into a friend who owns such a phone and she tells you that she is really unhappy with it. How do you treat your friend's observation? If you think rationally, you will realize that she has only increased your sample size from 1000 to 1001, which does not provide much new information. In addition, a process called the *reticular activation system* (RAS) works to bring your attention to instances of this smartphone – you will suddenly start to notice more of them. The RAS is an automatic mechanism in the brain that brings relevant information to our attention. Both these effects – your friend's story and noticing more of these smartphones around – mean that you may be tempted to attach a disproportionate weight to them in decision-making.

People are Reluctant to Change Their Minds

People tend to interpret evidence to confirm beliefs they already hold. In one study, subjects were asked to read and evaluate a research report on whether capital punishment deters crime. After reading the report, those who initially favoured the death penalty said they were surer in their view, and those who initially opposed the death penalty also said they were surer in their view. The two groups interpreted the same evidence in exactly opposite ways.

People Have a Natural Tendency to Look for Examples Which Confirm Their Existing View or Hypothesis

People identify, select or observe past instances and quote them as evidence for a viewpoint or hypothesis. Nassim Nicholas Taleb, author of the book *The Black Swan*, calls this 'naïve empiricism'. For example, every extreme weather event that is reported is selected as evidence of climate change, or a rise in the price of petrol of 10 per cent is symptomatic of a broader increase in prices of all goods.

People Use Rules of Thumb – Heuristics

The standard economic model implies that to act rationally buyers will consider all available information in making purchasing decisions and weigh up this information to arrive at a decision which maximizes utility subject to the budget constraint. In reality it is likely that many consumers will: (a) not have access to sufficient information to be able to make a fully rational choice; and (b), even if they did they would not be able to process this information fully partly due to a lack of mental facility (not everyone can do arithmetic quickly in their head nor make statistical calculations on which to base their choices). Instead when making decisions many people will use short cuts that help simplify the decision-making process. These short cuts are referred to as **heuristics** or *rules of thumb*. Some of these heuristics can be deep-seated and firms can take advantage of them to influence consumer behaviour.

 heuristics short cuts or rules of thumb that people use in decision-making

There are a number of different types of heuristics.

Anchoring This refers to the tendency for people to start with something they are familiar with or know and make decisions or adjustments based on this anchor. For example, a consumer may base the price they expect to pay for a restaurant meal on the last two prices they paid when eating out. If the price at the next restaurant is higher than this anchor price it may be that the consumer thinks the restaurant is 'expensive' or 'not good value for money' and may choose not to go again, whereas if the price they pay is lower than the anchor price they might see the restaurant as being good value for money and choose to return again. Often these anchors are biased and so the adjustment or decision is flawed in some way.

The Availability Heuristic Cases where decisions are made based on an assessment of the risks of the likelihood of something happening are referred to as availability heuristics. If examples readily come to mind as a result of excessive media coverage for example, decisions may be taken with a skewed assessment of the risks. If a consumer brings to mind the idea that the last couple of winters have been particularly bad then they might be more likely to buy equipment to help them combat adverse weather for the next winter. Consumers who use commuter trains are more likely to give negative feedback about the service they have received if their recent experience has been of some delays or cancellations even if the overall level of punctuality of the train operator has been very high.

The Representativeness Heuristic In this instance people tend to make judgements by comparing how representative something is to an image or stereotype that they hold. For example, people may be more prepared to pay money to buy a lottery ticket if a close friend has just won a reasonable amount of money on the lottery or make an association that if Bose headphones, for example, are good quality then its home theatre systems are also going to be good quality.

Persuasion Heuristics These are linked to various attributes that a consumer attaches to a product or a brand. For example, it has been shown that size does matter to consumers and so marketers can exploit this by making more exaggerated claims in adverts or using facts and figures to make the product more compelling in the mind of the consumer. The more that the marketers can highlight the positive attributes of their product (and the negative ones of their rivals) the more likely consumers are to make choices in favour of their product. In addition, consumers are also persuaded by people they like and respect. This may be utilized by firms through the people they use in adverts and celebrity endorsements but may also be important in terms of the people a firm employs to represent them in a sales or marketing capacity. It may also be relevant in cases where friends or colleagues talk about products and is one of the reasons why firms are keen to build a better understanding of how social media like Facebook and Twitter can be exploited.

Persuasion heuristics can also manifest themselves in the 'bandwagon' effect – if a large number of people go and see a film and rave about it then there is even more incentive for others to go and see it as well. Firms may look to try and create a bandwagon effect to utilize this persuasion heuristic in their marketing.

Simulation Heuristics These occur where people use mental processes to establish the likely outcome of something. The easier it is to simulate or visualize that outcome the more likely the individual is to make decisions based on it. For example, if it is easy to imagine a product which makes you look good then you are more likely to buy it. Pharmaceutical firms know that consumers are more likely to buy and take medicines that deal with known and experienced symptoms (things like headaches, strained muscles, sore throats and runny noses) than for something like high cholesterol – because it is hard to build a mental process for the effects of high cholesterol.

Expected Utility Theory and Framing Effects

In our analysis of the SEM we noted that indifference curves implied that consumers can rank preferences from best to worst (or vice versa). This is referred to as **expected utility theory**.

 expected utility theory the idea that preferences can and will be ranked by buyers

Expected utility theory is important because consumers have to make decisions based on ranking preferences on a regular basis. Imagine you are faced the choice between two types of surgery in a hospital. The surgeon is discussing your treatment with you and presents you with the following:
    Surgery type 1: 90 per cent of patients survive the surgery and live more than one year.
    Surgery type 2: 10 per cent of patients die within the first year.
    Which surgery type would you choose?

Expected utility theory says that consumers can rank the preference between these two options. Work done by Kahneman and Tversky suggest that the majority of people would choose surgery type 1 but the two surgery types offer essentially the same chance of a successful outcome. Expected utility theory implies that a rational economic agent would be indifferent between the two surgery types but Kahneman and Tversky's work suggests that the way in which such choices are presented can affect our judgements and the rational decision is violated.

Firms are careful to frame the way they present products and information to consumers to try to influence purchasing decisions and exploit these differences in perception. This is referred to as the **framing effect** whereby people respond to choices in differing ways dependent on how such choices are presented to them. For example, firms selling insurance know that people make judgements about the extent to which they are exposed to risk in deciding whether to take out insurance and how much cover they need. Adverts and marketing, therefore, may be framed to give the impression to consumers that they face increased risk.

> **framing effect** the differing response to choices dependent on the way in which choices are presented

IN THE NEWS

Neuroscience and Economics

Whilst economists can defend the use of models such as those used in this chapter, they are also aware that new information can also shed light on consumer decision-making. The development of magnetic resonance imaging (MRI) is one example of how economists are able to gain further insights into human behaviour and how links with other disciplines, notably psychology, is further extending the frontiers of our understanding.

The Brain and Consumer Choice: Neuroeconomics

Two pieces of research show how the work of psychologists and neuroscientists can help to increase our understanding of the processes involved in decision-making in consumption. In one piece of research, investigators looked at the role played by different areas of the brain in making decisions about investing in financial assets. The research was investigating how humans balance out anticipation of the gains and losses that we might get from purchases and whether there was any part of the brain that was associated with being stimulated when faced with the likely gains and losses of a prospective purchase.

The principle behind this investigation was based on the anticipatory effects that occur when faced with a purchasing decision. It is not difficult to conceptualize on a personal level. Think about when you go into a shop or a store and see something you really like. It might be an expensive purchase and you might know that you should not really be thinking of buying it but the item has really caught your attention and you are debating whether to buy it or not.

On the one hand, you know that the price that is being asked represents a loss – the money you will have to give up is an opportunity cost and means you will have to sacrifice other things that it could also buy you. Equally, you also know that owning this item will provide you with some form of gain – utility. When making the purchasing decision, therefore, you are balancing out these competing forces. The brain plays a role in this; there seem to be two main parts of the brain that are involved in such decisions – the *nucleus accumbens* and the *anterior insular*. The *nucleus accumbens* emits two neuro transmitters – dopamine and serotonin. The former is associated with desire and the latter with inhibition. The *anterior insula* is a part of the brain that has some association with emotional experience and conscious feelings. This will include feelings of pain, happiness, disgust, fear and anger.

(*Continued*)

The research was relatively complex but the main results from the investigations are given below:

- When making decisions on financial instruments, investors tend not to act rationally. These can be called 'risk-seeking mistakes' and 'risk-aversion mistakes'.
- Activity in the *nucleus accumbens* has an association with risk-seeking mistakes and risky choices.
- Activity in the *anterior insula* is associated with risk-aversion mistakes and riskless choices.
- Distinct neural circuits associated with anticipatory affect lead to different types of choices.
- *Nucleus accumbens* activation represents gain prediction.
- *Anterior insula* activation represents loss prediction.
- Activation of these brain regions can predict decisions to purchase.

The research suggests that expectations we might have about a purchase might trigger behavioural or affective (to do with emotions) responses which might influence what we eventually end up buying. There is a suggestion, for example, that the perceived risk associated with buying goods and services through credit cards is different to that of cash and that we are 'anaesthetized' against the effects of paying. As a result there may be a tendency to overspend when purchasing with credit cards compared to cash.

The second piece of research involves the effect on human behaviour of different emotional states and the effect that hormones play in influencing the brain and human behaviour. In a paper presented to a British Psychological Society (BPS) meeting in April 2009, Professor Karen Pine of the University of Hertfordshire outlined her research findings from a study looking at the link between the menstrual cycle in women and purchasing decisions. Professor Pine's study involved 443 women aged 18 to 50. It appeared to show a link between the stage of the menstrual cycle and purchasing decisions. Of the women in the sample, 153 were in the later stages of their menstrual cycle, known as the luteal phase. Of this group, over 60 per cent said that they had indulged in overspending and had bought items on impulse. The spending, in a small number of cases, was way over normal budgets – some women saying that they had overspent by as much as £250. In many cases, the women said that their purchasing decisions at this time were accompanied by feelings of remorse afterwards.

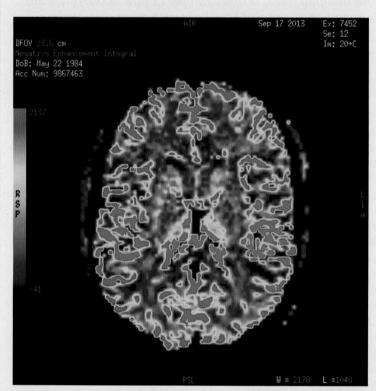

Improvements in technology enable firms to develop a greater understanding of consumer behaviour.

Professor Pine commented, 'The spending behaviour tends to be a reaction to intense emotions. They are feeling stressed or depressed and are more likely to go shopping to cheer themselves up and using it to regulate their emotions.' The study also found that those women with severe pre-menstrual tension (PMT) displayed more extreme examples of this behaviour.

Part of the explanation for this behaviour is that hormonal changes in women at certain times of the menstrual cycle are associated with changes to the part of the brain that is linked to inhibitions and emotions. It has also been suggested that purchasing decisions may be linked to a desire of women to make themselves look more attractive. There has been other research which suggested that part of female behaviour is driven by the need to demonstrate their fertility – a throwback to very early days when survival of the species depended in part on the ability to reproduce successfully. Around 14 days before the start of ovulation is a time which sees

(Continued)

women increase their spending on items that enhance their attractiveness. These items include make-up, high-heeled shoes and jewellery. Professor Pine has said that her findings are supported by other research which shows a so-called 'ornamental effect' linked to stages in the menstrual cycle.

Questions

1 To what extent should we assume that consumers can accurately estimate the potential gains and losses of a purchase decision (i.e. the utility)? How does your answer to this question affect your view of the SEM?
2 Think of a purchase you have made in recent months after which you experienced guilt. Explain why you felt guilty and whether such feelings can be accounted for in the SEM.
3 If research suggests that consumer behaviour is far more complex than the SEM suggests, does that mean the SEM is of no value and study of it ought to be discarded from undergraduate economics courses? Explain.
4 Explain the role that emotion might play in consumer decision-making. (You should think about the range of emotions that have been alluded to in the article.)
5 Some economists have suggested that human brains have not evolved to cope with the rapid changes in our lifestyles – that our brains are still hard-wired to cope with the need to survive, characteristic of early humans. Using the second piece of research outlined in the article, explain how such a theory might affect our understanding of consumer behaviour.

Source: https://uhra.herts.ac.uk/bitstream/handle/2299/4921/904314.pdf?sequence=1

SUMMARY

● The analysis of consumer choice looks at how consumers make decisions. There are a number of assumptions underpinning the model which include that people behave rationally to maximize utility from their given resources.

● A consumer's budget constraint shows the possible combinations of different goods they can buy given their income and the prices of goods. The slope of the budget constraint equals the relative price of the goods.

● The consumer's indifference curves represents their preferences. An indifference curve shows the various bundles of goods that make the consumer equally happy. Points on higher indifference curves are preferred to points on lower indifference curves. The slope of an indifference curve at any point is the consumer's marginal rate of substitution – the rate at which the consumer is willing to trade one good for the other.

● The consumer optimizes by choosing the point on their budget constraint that lies on the highest indifference curve. At this point, the slope of the indifference curve (the marginal rate of substitution between the goods) equals the slope of the budget constraint (the relative price of the goods).

● When the price of a good falls, the impact on the consumer's choices can be broken down into an income effect and a substitution effect. The income effect is the change in consumption that arises because a lower price makes the consumer better off. The substitution effect is the change in consumption that arises because a price change encourages greater consumption of the good that has become relatively cheaper. The income effect is reflected in the movement from a lower to a higher indifference curve, whereas the substitution effect is reflected by a movement along an indifference curve to a point with a different slope.

● The theory of consumer choice can be applied in many situations. It can explain why demand curves can potentially slope upward, why higher wages could either increase or decrease the quantity of labour supplied, and why higher interest rates could either increase or decrease saving.

QUESTIONS FOR REVIEW

1 What are the main assumptions of the standard economic model?
2 A consumer has income of €3000. Wine is priced at €3 a glass and cheese is priced at €6 a kilo. Draw the consumer's budget constraint. What is the slope of this budget constraint?

3 Draw a consumer's indifference curves for wine and cheese. Describe and explain four properties of these indifference curves.

4 Pick a point on an indifference curve for wine and cheese and show the marginal rate of substitution. What does the marginal rate of substitution tell us?

5 Show a consumer's budget constraint and indifference curves for wine and cheese. Show the optimal consumption choice. If the price of wine is €3 a glass and the price of cheese is €6 a kilo, what is the marginal rate of substitution at this optimum?

6 A person who consumes wine and cheese gets a rise, so their income increases from €3000 to €4000. Use diagrams to show what happens if both wine and cheese are normal goods. Now show what happens if cheese is an inferior good.

7 The price of cheese rises from €6 to €10 a kilo, while the price of wine remains at €3 a glass. For a consumer with a constant income of €3000, show what happens to consumption of wine and cheese. Decompose the change into income and substitution effects.

8 Can an increase in the price of cheese possibly induce a consumer to buy more cheese? Explain.

9 Explain why the assumptions of the standard economic model might not hold.

10 What are heuristics and how might they affect consumer decision-making?

PROBLEMS AND APPLICATIONS

1 Jacqueline divides her income between coffee and croissants (both of which are normal goods). An early frost in Brazil causes a large increase in the price of coffee in France.

  a. Show how this early frost might affect Jacqueline's budget constraint.

  b. Show how this early frost might affect Jacqueline's optimal consumption bundle, assuming that the substitution effect outweighs the income effect for croissants.

  c. Show how this early frost might affect Jacqueline's optimal consumption bundle, assuming that the income effect outweighs the substitution effect for croissants.

2 Compare the following two pairs of goods:

  a. Coke and Pepsi

  b. skis and ski bindings.

  In which case do you expect the indifference curves to be fairly straight, and in which case do you expect the indifference curves to be very bowed? In which case will the consumer respond more to a change in the relative price of the two goods?

3 Surette buys only orange juice and yoghurt.

  a. In 2017, Surette earns €20 000, orange juice is priced at €2 a carton and yoghurt is priced at €4 a tub. Draw Surette's budget constraint.

  b. Now suppose that all prices increase by 10 per cent in 2018 and that Surette's salary increases by 10 per cent as well. Draw Surette's new budget constraint. How would Surette's optimal combination of orange juice and yoghurt in 2018 compare to her optimal combination in 2017?

4 Economist George Stigler once wrote that, according to consumer theory, 'if consumers do not buy less of a commodity when their incomes rise, they will surely buy less when the price of the commodity rises'. Explain this statement using the concepts of income and substitution effects.

5 A consumer has an income of €30 000 a year and divides this income between buying food and spending on leisure. The average price of a unit of food is €15 and the average price of a unit of leisure is €10. Draw the consumer's budget constraint and draw an indifference curve to show the consumer's optimum.

Assume that the price of food rises in three stages over the year in €10 increments but that the price of leisure stays the same. Draw the consumer's new budget constraints, identify the new optimum and show the price–consumption path. Use the price–consumption path to derive the demand curve for food.

6 Indifference curves are convex to the origin (i.e. bow inwards). Using your knowledge of the properties of indifference curves, explain why indifference curves cannot be concave to the origin (i.e. bow outwards).

7 Using an example, explain why the consumer optimum occurs where the ratio of the prices of two goods is equal to the marginal rate of substitution.

8 Sketch a diagram to show the effect on demand of a change in income on a good which has an income elastic demand.

9 Choose three products you purchased recently. Think about the reasons that you made the particular purchase decision in each case. To what extent do you think you made the purchase decision in each case in line with the assumptions of the SEM? If you deviated from the SEM, think about why you did so.

10 Look at the following two statements:

  a. Which would you prefer: a 50 per cent chance of winning €150 or a 50 per cent chance of winning €100?
  b. Would you prefer a decision that guarantees a €100 loss or would you rather take a gamble where the chance of winning €50 was rated at 50 per cent but the chance of losing €200 rated also at 50 per cent?
  What would your choice be in a?
  What would your choice be in b?
  What is the difference between these two sets of statements and how do they illustrate the concept of framing?

BACKGROUND TO SUPPLY: FIRMS IN COMPETITIVE MARKETS

In the UK there are around 2.3 million businesses, and of that figure around 2 million employ fewer than nine people. While small firms form the majority of business enterprises, it is the very large firms which are more familiar to many people. In this chapter we will examine the behaviour of firms based on the assumptions of the competitive market where each buyer and seller is small compared to the size of the market and, therefore, has little ability to influence market prices. Under the assumptions of a competitive market, a firm's various costs – fixed, variable, average and marginal – all play important and interrelated roles. We will be using the term 'firm' as representative of the economic actor making up the supply side of the market. However, it is important to keep in mind that firms are made up of people and that the behaviour of people who make up these firms can lead to outcomes which are different to those we analyze in this section. The analysis in this chapter forms the basis for further discussion in later chapters about market structures and how the behaviour of firms invariably differs from that described under the assumptions of a competitive market.

THE COSTS OF PRODUCTION

All firms, regardless of size, incur costs as they make the goods and services that they sell. Costs are incurred because a firm uses factor inputs in production and these have to be paid for.

To provide some context we will use a fictional example of Paolo's Pizza Factory. Paolo, the owner of the firm, buys flour, tomatoes, mozzarella cheese, salami and other pizza ingredients. He also buys capital equipment in the form of mixers and ovens, and hires workers to help produce the final output. He then sells the resulting pizzas to consumers.

Costs as Opportunity Costs

Recall that the *opportunity cost* of an item refers to all those things that must be forgone to acquire that item. When economists speak of a firm's cost of production, they include the opportunity costs of making its output of goods and services. A firm's opportunity costs of production are sometimes obvious and sometimes less so. When Paolo pays €1000 for flour, Paolo can no longer use that €1000 to buy something else; he has to sacrifice what else that €1000 could have purchased.

When Paolo hires labour, the wages he pays are part of the firm's costs. The cost of ingredients and labour require that the firm pay out some money and such costs are referred to as **explicit costs**. By contrast, some of a firm's opportunity costs, called **implicit costs**, do not require a cash outlay. Imagine that Paolo is skilled with computers and could earn €100 per hour working as a programmer. For every hour Paolo works in his factory, he gives up €100 in income, and this forgone income is also classed as part of his costs by an economist.

> **explicit costs** input costs that require an outlay of money by the firm
> **implicit costs** input costs that do not require an outlay of money by the firm

This distinction between explicit and implicit costs highlights an important difference between how economists and accountants analyze a business. Economists are interested in studying firms' behaviour in making production and pricing decisions and include both explicit and implicit costs. By contrast, accountants have the job of keeping track of the money that flows into and out of firms. As a result, they measure the explicit costs but often ignore the implicit costs.

The difference between economists and accountants is easy to see in the case of Paolo. When Paolo gives up the opportunity to earn money as a computer programmer, his accountant will not count this as a cost of his pizza business. Because no money flows out of the business to pay for this cost, it never shows up on the accountant's financial statements. An economist, however, will count the foregone income as a cost because it will may influence the decisions that Paolo makes in his pizza business. For example, if the wage of computer programmers rose from €100 to €500 per hour, the opportunity cost to Paolo of running his pizza business might now change his decision-making. Paolo might decide he could earn more by closing his business and switching to working as a computer programmer.

The Cost of Capital as an Opportunity Cost

Assume that Paolo uses €300 000 of his savings to buy the pizza factory from the previous owner. If Paolo had instead left this money deposited in a savings account that pays an interest rate of 5 per cent, he would have earned €15 000 per year (assuming simple interest). To own his pizza factory, therefore, Paolo has given up the implicit opportunity cost of €15 000 a year in interest income. An economist views the €15 000 in interest income that Paolo gives up every year as a cost of his business, even though it is an implicit cost. Paolo's accountant, however, will not show this €15 000 as a cost because no money flows out of the business to pay for it.

To explore further the difference between economists and accountants, let's change the example slightly. Suppose now that Paolo did not have the entire €300 000 to buy the factory but, instead, used €100 000 of his own savings and borrowed €200 000 from a bank at an interest rate of 5 per cent. Paolo's accountant, who only measures explicit costs, will now count the €10 000 (simple) interest paid on the bank loan every year as a cost because this amount of money now flows out of the firm. By contrast, according to an economist, the opportunity cost of owning the business is still €15 000. The opportunity cost equals the interest on the bank loan (an explicit cost of €10 000) plus the forgone interest on savings (an implicit cost of €5000).

> **SELF TEST** Richard Collishaw is a farmer who is also a skilled metal worker. He makes unique garden sculptures that could earn him €40 an hour. One day, he spends 10 hours planting €500 worth of seeds on his farm. What opportunity cost has he incurred? What cost would his accountant measure? If these seeds will yield €1000 worth of crops, does Richard earn an accounting profit? Does he earn an economic profit? Would you advise Richard to continue as a farmer or switch to metal working?

PRODUCTION AND COSTS

Firms incur costs when they buy inputs to produce the goods and services that they plan to sell. In the analysis that follows, we make an important simplifying assumption: we assume that the size of Paolo's factory is fixed so that Paolo can vary the quantity of pizzas produced only by changing the number of workers. This assumption is realistic in the **short run**, but not in the **long run**. That is, Paolo cannot build a larger factory overnight, but he may be able to within a year or so. This initial analysis, therefore, should be viewed as describing the production decisions that Paolo faces in the short run.

short run the period of time in which some factors of production cannot be changed
long run the period of time in which all factors of production can be altered

The Production Function

Table 6.1 shows how the quantity of pizzas Paolo's factory produces per hour depends on the number of workers assuming other factors are fixed. In the first two columns, if there are no workers in the factory Paolo produces no pizzas. When there is 1 worker he produces 50 pizzas. When there are 2 workers he produces 90 pizzas, and so on.

TABLE 6.1	A Production Function and Total Cost: Paolo's Pizza Factory				
Number of workers	Output (quantity of pizzas produced per hour) or total product	Marginal product of labour	Cost of factory (€)	Cost of workers (€)	Total cost of inputs (cost of factory + cost of workers) (€)
0	0		30	0	30
		50			
1	50		30	10	40
		40			
2	90		30	20	50
		30			
3	120		30	30	60
		20			
4	140		30	40	70
		10			
5	150		30	50	80

The production function can be represented as a mathematical function where output (Q) is dependent on the factor inputs capital (K) and labour (L):

$$Q = f(K, L)$$

The third column in Table 6.1 gives the marginal product of a worker. This is presented midway between the increase in output to demonstrate that it is the addition to total output from the employment of an extra worker. The **marginal product** of any factor input (MP_F) in the production process is the increase in the quantity of output obtained from one additional unit of that factor input represented as:

$$MP_F = \frac{change\ in\ total\ product}{change\ in\ quantity\ of\ the\ factor}$$

The marginal product of labour, therefore, would be represented as:

$$MP_L = \frac{\Delta Q}{\Delta L}$$

where the Greek letter delta (Δ) means 'change in'.

marginal product the increase in output that arises from an additional unit of input

Panel (a) of Figure 6.1 presents a graph of the number of workers hired on the horizontal axis and the quantity of pizzas produced per hour on the vertical axis. This relationship between the quantity of inputs (workers) and quantity of output (pizzas) is called the **production function**.

production function the relationship between the quantity of inputs used to make a good and the quantity of output of that good

FIGURE 6.1

Paolo's Production Function

The production function in panel (a) shows the relationship between the number of workers hired and the quantity of output produced. Here the number of workers hired (on the horizontal axis) is from the first column in Table 6.1, and the quantity of output produced (on the vertical axis) is from the second column. The production function (total product) gets flatter as the number of workers increases, which reflects diminishing marginal product. The total cost curve in panel (b) shows the relationship between the quantity of output produced and total cost of production. Here the quantity of output produced (on the horizontal axis) is from the second column in Table 6.1, and the total cost (on the vertical axis) is from the sixth column. The total cost curve gets steeper as the quantity of output increases because of diminishing marginal product.

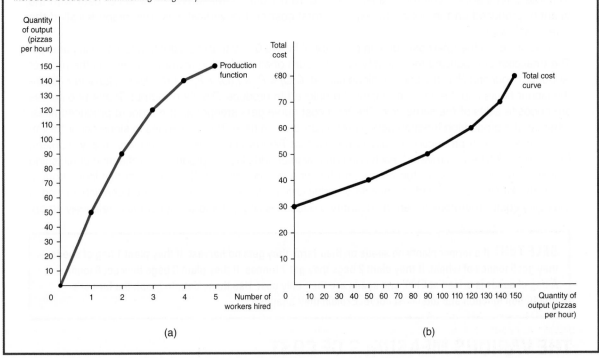

Hiring the first worker increases output by 50 units per hour. Hiring the second worker increases output from 50 to 90, so the marginal product of the second worker is 40 pizzas. The third worker hired increases total product from 90 to 120, so the marginal product of the third worker is 30 pizzas.

Notice that as the number of workers increases when we assume other factors are fixed, the marginal product (MP) declines. This property of the production function is called **diminishing marginal product**. Why does this happen? At first, when only a few workers are hired, they have easy access to Paolo's kitchen equipment. As the number of workers increases, additional workers have to share equipment and work in more crowded conditions, and if the number of workers continued to be increased the workers would start to get in each other's way and efficiency would be significantly impaired. Hence, as more and more workers are hired, each additional worker contributes less to the production of pizzas.

> **diminishing marginal product** the property whereby the marginal product of an input declines as the quantity of the input increases

Diminishing marginal product can be discerned from panel (a) of Figure 6.1. The production function's slope ('rise over run') tells us the change in Paolo's output of pizzas ('rise') for each additional input of labour ('run'). That is, the slope of the production function measures the marginal product of a worker. As the number of workers increases, the marginal product declines, and the production function becomes flatter.

From the Production Function to the Total Cost Curve

The last column of Table 6.1 is reproduced as a graph in panel (b) of Figure 6.1 to show Paolo's cost of producing pizzas. In this example, the cost of operating the factory is €30 per hour, which remains fixed; we assume labour is the only factor of production which can be varied in the short run, and the cost of a worker is €10 per hour. If Paolo hires 1 worker, his total cost is €40. If he hires 2 workers, his total cost is €50 and so on. With this information, the table now shows how the number of workers Paolo hires is related to the quantity of pizzas he produces and to his total cost of production.

An important relationship in Table 6.1 is between quantity produced (in the second column) and total costs (in the sixth column). Panel (b) of Figure 6.1 graphs these two columns of data with the quantity produced on the horizontal axis and total cost on the vertical axis. This graph is called the *total cost curve*.

Now compare the total cost curve in panel (b) of Figure 6.1 with the production function in panel (a). The total cost of producing the quantity Q is the sum of all production factors where P_L is the price of labour per hour and P_K is the price of hiring capital. $C(Q) = P_L \times L(Q) + P_K \times K(Q)$. Here $L(Q)$ and $K(Q)$ are the labour hours and the amount of capital employed to produce Q units of output. These two curves are opposite sides of the same coin. The total cost curve gets steeper as the amount produced rises, whereas the production function gets flatter as production rises. These changes in slope occur for the same reason. High production of pizzas means that Paolo's kitchen is crowded with many workers. Because the kitchen is crowded, each additional worker adds less to production, reflecting diminishing marginal product. Therefore, the production function is relatively flat. But now turn this logic around: when the kitchen is crowded, producing an additional pizza has used a lot of additional labour and is thus very costly. Therefore, when the quantity produced is large, the total cost curve is relatively steep.

SELF TEST If a farmer plants no seeds on their farm, they gets no harvest. If they plant 1 bag of seeds they get 5 tonnes of wheat. If they plant 2 bags they get 7 tonnes. If they plant 3 bags they get 8 tonnes. A bag of seeds is priced at €100, and seeds are their only cost. Use these data to graph the farmer's production function and total cost curve. Explain their shapes.

THE VARIOUS MEASURES OF COST

Our analysis of Paolo's Pizza Factory demonstrates how a firm's total cost reflects its production function. From data on a firm's total cost we can derive several related measures of cost to help in analyzing production and pricing decisions. Consider the example in Table 6.2. This table presents cost data on Paolo's neighbour: Luciano's Lemonade Stand.

The first column of the table shows the number of glasses of lemonade that Luciano might produce, ranging from 0 to 10 glasses per hour. The second column shows Luciano's total cost of producing glasses of lemonade. Figure 6.2 plots Luciano's total cost curve. The quantity of lemonade (from the first column) is on the horizontal axis, and total cost (from the second column) is on the vertical axis. Luciano's total cost curve has a shape similar to Paolo's. In particular, it becomes steeper as the quantity produced rises, which (as we have discussed) reflects diminishing marginal product.

Fixed and Variable Costs

Luciano's total cost can be divided into two types. Some costs, called **fixed costs**, are not determined by the amount of output produced; they can change but not as a result of changes in the amount produced. Luciano's fixed costs include any rent he pays because this cost has to be paid regardless of how much lemonade Luciano produces. Similarly, if Luciano needs to hire a bar person to serve the drinks, regardless of the quantity of lemonade sold, the bar person's salary is a fixed cost. The third column in Table 6.2 shows Luciano's fixed cost (FC), which, in this example, is €3.00.

fixed costs costs that are not determined by the quantity of output produced

TABLE 6.2   The Various Measures of Cost: Luciano's Lemonade Stand

Quantity of lemonade glasses (per hour)	Total cost (€)	Fixed cost (€)	Variable cost (€)	Average fixed cost (€)	Average Variable cost (€)	Average total cost (€)	Marginal cost (€)
0	3.00	3.00	0.00	-	-	-	
							0.30
1	3.30	3.00	0.30	3.00	0.30	3.30	
							0.50
2	3.80	3.00	0.80	1.50	0.40	1.90	
							0.70
3	4.50	3.00	1.50	1.00	0.50	1.50	
							0.90
4	5.40	3.00	2.40	0.75	0.60	1.35	
							1.10
5	6.50	3.00	3.50	0.60	0.70	1.30	
							1.30
6	7.80	3.00	4.80	0.50	0.80	1.30	
							1.50
7	9.30	3.00	6.30	0.43	0.90	1.33	
							1.70
8	11.00	3.00	8.00	0.38	1.00	1.38	
							1.90
9	12.90	3.00	9.90	0.33	1.10	1.43	
							2.10
10	15.00	3.00	12.00	0.30	1.20	1.50	

FIGURE 6.2

Here the quantity of output produced (on the horizontal axis) is from the first column in Table 6.2, and the total cost (on the vertical axis) is from the second column. As in Figure 6.2, the total cost curve gets steeper as the quantity of output increases because of diminishing marginal product.

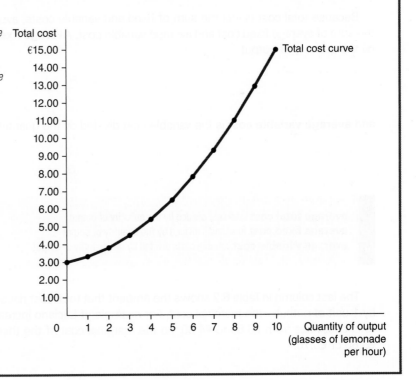

Variable costs change as the firm alters the quantity of output produced. Luciano's variable costs include the cost of lemons, sugar, glasses and straws: the more lemonade Luciano makes, the more of these items he needs to buy. Similarly, if Luciano pays his workers overtime to make more lemonade, the wages of these workers are variable costs. The fourth column of the table shows Luciano's variable cost. The variable cost is 0 if he produces nothing, €0.30 if he produces 1 glass of lemonade, €0.80 if he produces 2 glasses and so on.

> **variable costs** costs that are dependent on the quantity of output produced

A firm's total cost is the sum of fixed and variable costs. In Table 6.2 total cost in the second column equals fixed cost in the third column plus variable cost in the fourth column.

$$TC(Q) = VC(Q) + FC$$

Average and Marginal Cost

As the owner of his firm, Luciano has to decide how much lemonade to produce. A key part of this decision is how his costs will vary as he changes the level of production. In making this decision, Luciano might ask two questions about the cost of producing lemonade:

- How much does it cost to make the typical glass of lemonade?
- How much does it cost to increase production of lemonade by 1 glass?

To find the cost of the typical unit produced, we divide the firm's total costs by the quantity of output it produces. For example, if Luciano produces 2 glasses per hour, his total cost is €3.80, and the cost of the typical glass is €3.80/2, or €1.90. Total cost divided by the quantity of output is called **average total cost** (ATC).

$$ATC = \frac{TC}{Q}$$

Because total cost is just the sum of fixed and variable costs, average total cost can be expressed as the sum of average fixed cost and average variable cost. **Average fixed cost** is the fixed costs (FC) divided by the quantity of output:

$$AFC = \frac{FC}{Q}$$

and **average variable cost** is the variable cost divided by the quantity of output:

$$AVC = \frac{VC}{Q}$$

> **average total cost** total cost divided by the quantity of output
> **average fixed cost** fixed costs divided by the quantity of output
> **average variable cost** variable costs divided by the quantity of output

The last column in Table 6.2 shows the amount that total cost rises when the firm increases production by 1 unit of output – the marginal cost. For example, if Luciano increases production from 2 to 3 glasses, total cost rises from €3.80 to €4.50, so the marginal cost of the third glass of lemonade is €4.50 minus €3.80 or €0.70.

$$MC = \frac{\Delta TC}{\Delta Q}$$

Using calculus:

$$MC = \frac{dTC}{dQ}$$

> **marginal cost** the increase in total cost that arises from an extra unit of production

We can derive various average cost measures and marginal cost from the total cost function of the type $TC = f(Q)$.

For example, if the total cost function is given as $TC = 7Q^2 + 5Q + 1500$ we can see that the fixed costs are 1500. If $Q = 0$, then TC would be 1500. The terms $7Q^2 + 5Q$ are the variable costs.

AC would be $\dfrac{7Q^2 + 5Q + 1500}{Q}$, AVC would be $\dfrac{7Q^2 + 5Q}{Q}$ and AFC would be $\dfrac{1500}{Q}$ Marginal cost would be $\dfrac{dTC}{dQ} = 14Q + 5$.

Cost Curves and their Shapes

Graphs of average and marginal cost are useful when analyzing the behaviour of firms. Figure 6.3 graphs Luciano's costs using the data from Table 6.2. The horizontal axis measures the quantity the firm produces, and the vertical axis measures marginal and average costs. The graph shows four curves: average total cost (ATC), average fixed cost (AFC), average variable cost (AVC) and marginal cost (MC).

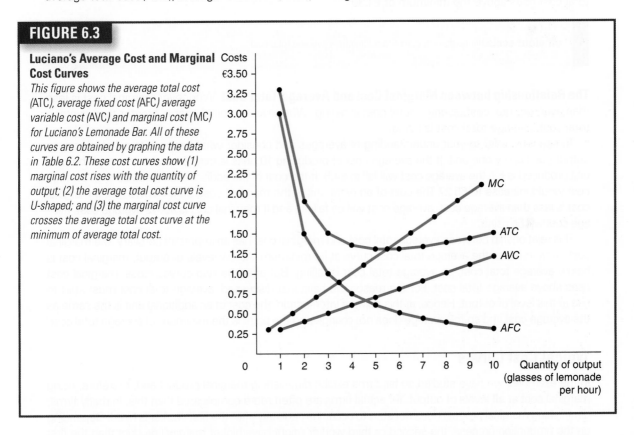

FIGURE 6.3

Luciano's Average Cost and Marginal Cost Curves

This figure shows the average total cost (ATC), average fixed cost (AFC) average variable cost (AVC) and marginal cost (MC) for Luciano's Lemonade Bar. All of these curves are obtained by graphing the data in Table 6.2. These cost curves show (1) marginal cost rises with the quantity of output; (2) the average total cost curve is U-shaped; and (3) the marginal cost curve crosses the average total cost curve at the minimum of average total cost.

The cost curves shown here for Luciano's Lemonade Bar have three particular features we will examine: the shape of marginal cost, the shape of average total cost, and the relationship between marginal and average total cost.

Rising Marginal Cost Luciano's marginal cost rises with the quantity of output produced. This reflects the property of diminishing marginal product. When Luciano is producing a small quantity of lemonade he has spare capacity and can easily put these idle resources to use, the marginal product of an extra worker is large, and the marginal cost of an extra glass of lemonade is small. By contrast, when Luciano employs a larger number of workers and is producing a large quantity of lemonade, his stand is crowded with workers and most of his equipment is fully utilized. In this situation, the marginal product of an extra worker is low, and the marginal cost of an extra glass of lemonade is large.

U-Shaped Average Total Cost Luciano's average total cost curve takes on a U-shape. To understand why this is so, remember that average total cost is the sum of average fixed cost and average variable cost. Average fixed cost always declines as output rises because the fixed cost does not change as output rises and so gets spread over a larger number of units. Average variable cost typically rises as output increases because of diminishing marginal product. Average total cost reflects the shapes of both average fixed cost and average variable cost. As shown in Figure 6.3, at very low levels of output, such as 1 or 2 glasses per hour, average total cost is high because the fixed cost is spread over only a few units. Average total cost then declines as output increases until the firm's output reaches 5 glasses of lemonade per hour, when average total cost falls to €1.30 per glass. When Luciano produces more than 6 glasses, average total cost starts rising again because average variable cost rises substantially. If further units of output were produced the average total cost curve would continue to slope upwards giving the typical U-shape referred to.

The bottom of the U-shape occurs at the quantity that minimizes average total cost. This quantity is sometimes called the **efficient scale** of the firm or *minimum efficient scale*. For Luciano, the efficient scale is 5 or 6 glasses of lemonade. If he produces more or less than this amount, his average total cost rises above the minimum of €1.30.

> **efficient scale** the quantity of output that minimizes average total cost

The Relationship between Marginal Cost and Average Total Cost Whenever marginal cost is less than average total cost, average total cost is falling. Whenever marginal cost is greater than average total cost, average total cost is rising.

To see why, refer to your understanding of averages and consider what happens to average cost as output goes up by one unit. If the average cost of producing 10 units is (say) €5 and the cost of the next unit produced is €3, the average cost will fall to €4.8. If the cost of the additional unit was €8 then average cost would increase to €5.27. The cost of an extra unit is the marginal cost, so it follows that if marginal cost is less than average cost, average cost will be falling; and if marginal cost is above average cost, average cost will be rising.

This relationship between average total cost and marginal cost has an important corollary: the marginal cost curve crosses the average total cost curve at its minimum. At low levels of output, marginal cost is below average total cost, so average total cost is falling. But after the two curves cross, marginal cost rises above average total cost. For the reason we have just discussed, average total cost must start to rise at this level of output. Hence, at this point of intersection, the cost of an additional unit is the same as the average cost and so the average does not change and the point is the minimum of average total cost.

Typical Cost Curves

In the examples we have studied so far, firms exhibit diminishing marginal product and, therefore, rising marginal cost at **all** levels of output. Yet actual firms are often more complicated than this. In many firms, diminishing marginal product does not start to occur immediately after the first worker is hired. Depending on the production process, the second or third worker might have higher marginal product than the first because a team of workers can divide tasks and work more productively than a single worker. Such firms would first experience increasing marginal product for a while before diminishing marginal product sets in.

The table in Figure 6.4 shows the cost data for such a firm, called Bella's Bagels. These data are used in the graphs. Panel (a) shows how total cost (*TC*) depends on the quantity produced, and panel (b) shows average total cost (*ATC*), average fixed cost (*AFC*), average variable cost (*AVC*) and marginal cost (*MC*). In the range of output from 0 to 4 bagels per hour, the firm experiences increasing marginal product, and the marginal cost curve falls. After 5 bagels per hour, the firm starts to experience diminishing marginal product, and the marginal cost curve starts to rise. This combination of increasing then diminishing marginal product also makes the average variable cost curve U-shaped.

FIGURE 6.4

Bella's Cost Curves

Many firms, like Bella's Bagels, experience increasing marginal product before diminishing marginal product and, therefore, have cost curves shaped like those in this figure. Panel (a) shows how total cost (TC) depends on the quantity produced. Panel (b) shows how average total cost (ATC), average fixed cost (AFC), average variable cost (AVC) and marginal cost (MC) depend on the quantity produced. These curves are derived by graphing the data from the table. Notice that marginal cost and average variable cost fall for a while before starting to rise.

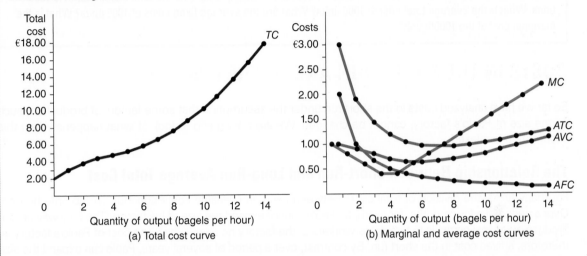

(a) Total cost curve

(b) Marginal and average cost curves

Quantity of bagels (per hour) Q	Total cost (€) TC = FC + VC	Fixed cost (€) FC	Variable cost (€) VC	Average fixed cost (€) AFC = FC/Q	Average Variable cost (€) AVC = VC/Q	Average Total cost (€) ATC = TC/Q	Marginal cost (€) MC = ΔTC/ΔQ
0	2.00	2.00	0.00	-	-	-	
							1.00
1	3.00	2.00	1.00	2.00	1.00	3.00	
							0.80
2	3.80	2.00	1.80	1.00	0.90	1.90	
							0.60
3	4.40	2.00	2.40	0.67	0.80	1.47	
							0.40
4	4.80	2.00	2.80	0.50	0.70	1.20	
							0.40
5	5.20	2.00	3.20	0.40	0.64	1.04	
							0.60
6	5.80	2.00	3.80	0.33	0.63	0.96	
							0.80
7	6.60	2.00	4.60	0.29	0.66	0.95	
							1.00
8	7.60	2.00	5.60	0.25	0.70	0.95	
							1.20
9	8.80	2.00	6.80	0.22	0.76	0.98	
							1.40
10	10.20	2.00	8.20	0.20	0.82	1.02	
							1.60
11	11.80	2.00	9.80	0.18	0.89	1.07	
							1.80
12	13.60	2.00	11.60	0.17	0.97	1.14	
							2.00
13	15.60	2.00	13.60	0.15	1.05	1.20	
							2.20
14	17.80	2.00	15.80	0.14	1.13	1.27	

Despite these differences from our previous example, Bella's cost curves share the three properties that are most important to remember:

● Marginal cost eventually rises with the quantity of output.
● The average total cost curve is U-shaped.
● The marginal cost curve crosses the average total cost curve at the minimum of average total cost.

SELF TEST A firm's total cost function is $TC = 0.000002q^3 - 0.006q^2 + 8q$. Find the total cost if output is 1000 units. What is the average total cost at 1000 units? What are the average fixed costs of 1000 units? What is the marginal cost of the 1000th unit?

COSTS IN THE SHORT RUN AND IN THE LONG RUN

So far we have analyzed costs in the short run under the assumption that some factors of production, such as the size of Paolo's factory, cannot be changed. We are now going to look at what happens when this assumption is relaxed.

The Relationship Between Short-Run and Long-Run Average Total Cost

For many firms, the division of total costs between fixed and variable costs depends on the time horizon. Over a period of a few months, for example, Paolo cannot expand the size of his factory. The only way he can produce additional pizzas is to hire more workers at the factory he already has. The cost of Paolo's factory is, therefore, a fixed cost in the short run. By contrast, over a period of several years, Paolo can expand the size of his factory, build or buy new factories. Thus, the cost of Paolo's factories is a variable cost in the long run.

Because many decisions are fixed in the short run but variable in the long run, a firm's long-run cost curves differ from its short-run cost curves. Figure 6.5 shows an example.

FIGURE 6.5

Average Total Cost in the Short and Long Runs
Because fixed costs are variable in the long run, the average total cost curve in the short run differs from the average total cost curve in the long run.

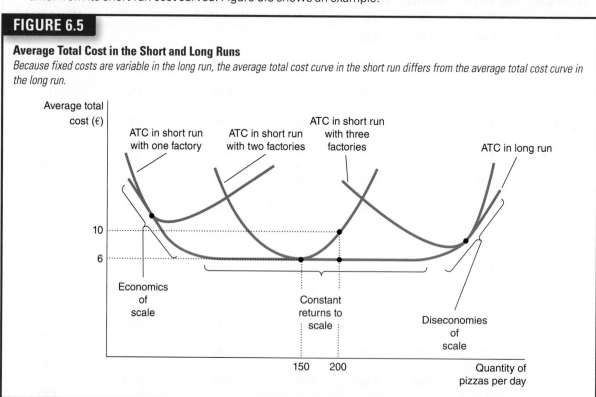

The figure presents three short-run average total cost curves representing the cost structures for three factories. It also presents the long-run average total cost curve. As Paolo adjusts the size of his capacity to the quantity of production, he moves along the long-run curve, and he adjusts capacity to the quantity of production.

This graph shows how short-run and long-run costs are related. The long-run average total cost curve is a much flatter U-shape than the short-run average total cost curve. In addition, all the short-run curves lie on or above the long-run curve. These properties arise because firms have greater flexibility in the long run. In essence, in the long run, the firm chooses which short-run curve it wants to use. But in the short run, it has to use whatever short-run curve it chose in the past.

The figure shows an example of how a change in production alters costs over different time horizons. When Paolo wants to increase production from 150 to 200 pizzas per day, he has no choice in the short run but to hire more workers with only two factories. Because of diminishing marginal product, average total cost rises from €6 to €10 per pizza. In the long run, however, Paolo can expand both his capacity and his workforce by building or acquiring a third factory, and average total cost returns to €6 per pizza.

How long does it take for a firm to get to the long run? The answer depends on the firm. It can take several years for a major manufacturing firm, such as a car company, to build a larger factory. By contrast, Paolo might be able to find new premises and expand sales in a matter of months. There is, therefore, no single answer about how long it takes a firm to adjust its production facilities.

Why is the long-run average total cost curve often U-shaped? At low levels of production, the firm benefits from increased size because it can take advantage of certain benefits such as greater specialization. Being larger it might suffer from coordination problems but these may not yet be acute. By contrast, at high levels of production, the benefits of specialization have already been realized, and coordination problems become more severe as the firm grows larger. Thus, long-run average total cost is falling at low levels of production because of increasing specialization and rising at high levels of production because of increasing coordination problems.

SELF TEST Why is the short run average cost curve U-shaped? Why is the long run average cost curve also U-shaped?

SUMMARY

To help summarize the important points we have raised so far in this chapter, Table 6.3 summarizes some of the definitions we have encountered.

TABLE 6.3   **The Many Types of Cost: A Summary**

Term	Definition	Mathematical description
Explicit costs	Costs that require an outlay of money by the firm	–
Implicit costs	Costs that do not require an outlay of money by the firm	–
Fixed costs	Costs that do not vary with the quantity of output produced	FC
Variable costs	Costs that vary with the quantity of output produced	VC
Total cost	The market value of all the inputs that a firm uses in production	$TC = FC + VC$
Average fixed cost	Fixed costs divided by the quantity of output	$AFC = FC/Q$
Average variable cost	Variable costs divided by the quantity of output	$AVC = VC/Q$
Average total cost	Total cost divided by the quantity of output	$ATC = TC/Q$
Marginal cost	The increase in total cost that arises from an extra unit of production	$MC = \Delta TC/\Delta Q$

RETURNS TO SCALE

Our analysis has shown that in the short run the firm has some options for increasing output by varying some factors of production. In the long run, the firm is able to increase all factors of production and change capacity.

Assume that business has been good for our pizza factory owner. Paolo has utilized his existing resources efficiently but finds that he is not able to supply the market with all that he could because of the constraints of the capacity of the factory. He knows that increasing the number of worker hours and machine hours will generate increased output up to a point, but that diminishing marginal productivity is a likelihood if factory space is held constant.

In the long run, the firm can expand all the factors of production. Our factory owner could search for a new site on which to build a new factory or could purchase an existing factory and equip it to produce pizzas. If all the factors of production are changed then the firm will be able to operate at a different scale.

Economies and Diseconomies of Scale

When a firm increases the scale of production there are three outcomes that can occur as highlighted in Figure 6.5. Assume our pizza factory owner currently employs 50 workers and 10 machines in a factory with a floor space of 1000m² and currently produces 2000 pizzas per day. The total cost of producing these 2000 pizzas per day is €4000. The average cost of each pizza is, therefore, €4000 / 2000 = €2 each.

Paolo doubles the input of all the factors of production and as a result now employs 100 workers, 20 machines and has 2000m² of capacity. The cost of expanding the scale of production is clearly going to be higher but what happens to the average cost depends on how far total cost increases in relation to the increase in output. If the total cost of production doubled to €8000 and output also doubled to 4000, the average cost of each pizza would still be €2. The firm is said to be experiencing **constant returns to scale**. This occurs when long-run average total cost does not vary with the level of output. If, however, the total cost of production at the new scale of production increased to €6000 and output doubled to 4000, the average cost of each pizza would now fall to €1.50 each. The firm will experience increasing returns to scale because the proportionate increase in output is greater than the proportionate increase in total cost. This is also referred to as **economies of scale,** which occur when long-run average total cost declines as output increases.

> **constant returns to scale** the property whereby long-run average total cost stays the same as the quantity of output changes
> **economies of scale** the property whereby long-run average total cost falls as the quantity of output increases

If the doubling of factor inputs (to 100 workers and 20 machines) leads to an increase in total costs (to €10 000, for example) that is greater than the increase in output (assume this is 4000), the firm is said to experience decreasing returns to scale and the average cost per pizza would now be €2.50 each. When long-run average total cost rises as output increases, there are said to be **diseconomies of scale**.

> **diseconomies of scale** the property whereby long-run average total cost rises as the quantity of output increases

Note that when we talk about economies of scale we are referring to *unit costs* (or average costs); clearly if a firm increases its capacity by building a new factory and then hiring more capital and labour to work in the factory, total costs are going to rise but if the relative increase in output is greater than the relative increase in total costs as a result, then the unit or average cost will fall. We are referring to the concept of scale as the proportionate increase of all factor inputs and the resultant relative increase in output. Consideration has to be taken of the price of factor inputs. In our example, the price of labour is €60 per unit and the price of capital €100 per unit. If these prices remain constant, then a 50 per cent increase in all factor inputs would increase total cost by 50 per cent. If this 50 per cent increase in inputs leads to a 75 per cent increase in output then average costs will fall.

Returns to scale can be found by using the formula:

$$Returns\ to\ scale = \frac{\%\Delta\ in\ quantity\ of\ output}{\%\Delta\ in\ quantity\ of\ all\ factor\ inputs}$$

Causes of Economies and Diseconomies of Scale

What might cause economies or diseconomies of scale? Economies of scale often arise because higher production levels allow *specialization* among workers and increase the possibility that technology can be used, which permits each worker to become better at his or her assigned tasks. For instance, modern assembly line production for furniture may require fewer workers in relation to the technology used but still produce more furniture. If a furniture manufacturer was producing only a small quantity of output, it could not take advantage of this approach and would have higher average total cost.

In addition to reasons of more effective use of technology, firms operating at larger scale can also gain advantages by being in a position to negotiate more favourable borrowing rates or can secure lower supply costs because they are buying in larger quantities and can agree discounts from suppliers.

There are also advantages to larger firms from external sources which are to do with the growth of the industry as a whole rather than the increase in the scale of operation. For example, infrastructure and transport systems may have been built to help service a distribution hub industry. Some firms are located in areas where there is a supply of skilled labour or which has a reputation which can benefit the firm, for example, banking and finance industries located in London or hi-tech workers along the so-called 'silicon corridor' around the M4 in the South of England. The development of local infrastructure may also give the firm advantages which all lead to lower unit costs. Diseconomies of scale can arise because of coordination and communication problems that are inherent in any large organization. The bigger the business organization, the more stretched the management team becomes, the more likely it is that communication and decision-making become dysfunctional and the less effective the managers become at keeping costs down.

The Implications of Economies of Scale

Economies of scale are the advantages of large-scale production that result in lower average or unit costs. Imagine a firm which makes bricks. The current plant has a maximum capacity of 100 000 bricks per week and the total costs are €200 000 per week. The average cost for each brick, therefore, is €2. The firm charges a price of €2.20 per brick giving it a profit margin of €0.20 per brick.

Now imagine that, in the long run, the firm expands. It doubles the size of its plant. The total costs, obviously, increase, however, a doubling of capacity will not lead to a doubling of the cost. Assume that after the expansion which doubles capacity to 200 000 bricks per week, TC is now €350 000 per week. The percentage increase in the total costs is less than the percentage increase in output. Total costs have risen by €150 000 or 75 per cent and total output by 100 per cent, which means that the average cost per brick is now €1.75.

This has implications for the firm outlined in the two following scenarios. In Scenario 1, the firm could maintain its price at €2.20 and increase its profit margin on each brick sold from €0.20 to €0.45. Assuming it sells all the bricks it produces, its revenue would increase to €440 000 per week.

In Scenario 2, the firm might choose to reduce its price to improve its competitiveness against its rivals. It could maintain its former profit margin of €0.20 and reduce the price to €1.95. In this case, if it sells all it produces its revenue would be €390 000 per week.

What the firm chooses to do would be dependent on its competitive position. If it played a dominant role in the market it might be able to increase its price and still sell all it produces. If it was in a more competitive market it might not have sold all its capacity in the first place so being able to reduce its price might mean that it can now increase sales against its rivals and increase its total revenue as a result.

CASE STUDY Economies of Scale in Shipping

Over the years, cargo ships have got bigger and bigger and one of the reasons is that bigger ships yield economies of scale. The reason is due to something called the *principle of increased multiples*. Assume a ship with the cargo capacity given by the dimensions 137m x 17m x 9m (which was typical of container ship capacity in the 1950s). This ship has a total carrying capacity of 20 961m^3. Assume the total cost of shipping the cargo from port A to port B is €100 000. This means each cubic metre carried has an average cost of €4.77. Now assume that the dimensions of the ship are increased to 400m x 59m x 15.5m, which is the sort of size of container ships being built after 2013. The total carrying capacity of this ship is now 365 800m^3. That is over 17 times the carrying capacity of the smaller ship. The cost of building and operating this larger ship will clearly be higher but it is unlikely that the cost will be 17 times higher. Assume that total costs for the journey are now €900 000. The average cost of each unit carried is now €2.46 per unit.

The economies of scale of building bigger ships in this example is clear. However, if this is the case, why not continue to build ever bigger ships to exploit economies of scale further? In some respects, this is what has been happening since the 1950s with container ships becoming ever bigger as shipping firms seek to drive down average costs and become more competitive. Lower shipping costs have resulting benefits on the supply chain in that it gets goods to market in a global economy much cheaper and therefore prices to consumers can be lowered.

Studies by shipping consultants Drewry Ltd, has shown that it may be getting to the stage where the economies of scale of larger ships are starting to run out and diseconomies of scale are beginning to set in. There may still be economies of scale to exploit in the actual transfer of goods across the seas but any scale benefits can be eroded once the ship reaches port. As ships become bigger, the ability and capacity of freight terminals to handle the size of ship and extent of the cargo is becoming strained, and as a result unit costs are beginning to increase – diseconomies of scale. Investment is likely to be needed in order to ensure that terminals are equipped to handle the size of ship coming into port if productivity improvements are to be maintained. This investment is likely to be considerable and careful analysis would have to be conducted to ensure that there are indeed economies of scale to be exploited and that diseconomies do not outweigh the average cost benefits of ever larger vessels.

As the size and carrying capacity of cargo ships gets ever bigger, diseconomies of scale may set in if ports cannot invest quickly enough to manage the capacity.

Source: http://www.drewry.co.uk/news.php?id=457

SELF TEST If Airbus produces nine jets per month, its long-run total cost is €9.0 million per month. If it produces ten jets per month, its long-run total cost is €9.5 million per month. Does Airbus exhibit economies or diseconomies of scale?

WHAT IS A COMPETITIVE MARKET?

Having looked at a firm's costs we now turn our attention to a firm's revenue. In Chapter 3 we looked at the assumptions of the competitive market.

An example of a market which does have some of the characteristics which approximate to a perfect market is the market for milk. No single seller of milk can influence the price of milk because each supplies a small amount of an essentially homogenous product (although even in this market firms try and make their product appear different by offering skimmed milk, semi-skimmed milk, full cream milk, flavoured milk and so on) relative to the size of the market. Anyone can decide to start a dairy farm, and if any existing dairy farmer decides to leave the dairy business then they can. Information about the milk industry is widespread and so both consumers and producers are able to make informed decisions. There are many individual buyers of milk – consumers buying milk for everyday use from supermarkets, the supermarkets themselves, food processors buying milk to make into dairy products such as cheese, yoghurts and so on. One exception to the assumption of a competitive market however is that in the UK there are a relatively small number of large firms who buy milk and who can, as a result, have some market control over price. Nevertheless, for the purposes of our continuing analysis of the competitive firm, we will assume that the market for milk fulfils a sufficient number of the assumptions to be of value.

The Revenue of a Competitive Firm

To keep matters concrete, we will consider a specific firm: the Grundy Family Dairy Farm. The Grundy Farm produces a quantity of milk Q and sells each unit at the market price P. The farm's total revenue is $P \times Q$. For example, if a litre of milk sells for €0.40 and the farm sells 10 000 litres per day, its total revenue is €4000 per day.

Because the Grundy Farm is small compared with the world market for milk, it takes the price as given by market conditions. This means, in particular, that the price of milk does not depend on the quantity of output that the Grundy Farm produces and sells. If the Grundys double the amount of milk they produce, the price of milk remains the same and their total revenue doubles. As a result, total revenue is proportional to the amount of output.

Table 6.4 shows the revenue for the Grundy Family Dairy Farm. The first two columns show the amount of output the farm produces and the price at which it sells its output. The third column is the farm's total revenue. The table assumes that the price of milk is €0.40 a litre, so total revenue is simply €0.40 times the number of litres.

TABLE 6.4	Total, Average and Marginal Revenue for a Competitive Firm			
Quantity (Q) Litres	Price (€) (P)	Total revenue (€) (TR =P × Q)	Average revenue (€) (AR =TR/Q)	Marginal revenue (€) (MR =ΔTR/ΔQ)
1000	0.40	400	0.40	
				0.40
2000	0.40	800	0.40	
				0.40
3000	0.40	1200	0.40	
				0.40
4000	0.40	1600	0.40	
				0.40
5000	0.40	2000	0.40	
				0.40
6000	0.40	2400	0.40	
				0.40
7000	0.40	2800	0.40	
				0.40
8000	0.40	3200	0.40	

As we did when looking at a firm's costs, consider these two questions:

● How much revenue does the farm receive for the typical litre of milk?
● How much additional revenue does the farm receive if it increases production of milk by 1 litre?

The last two columns in Table 6.4 answer these questions.

The fourth column in the table shows average revenue, which is total revenue (from the third column) divided by the amount of output (from the first column).

$$AR = \frac{TR}{Q}$$

Average revenue tells us how much revenue a firm receives for the typical unit sold. In Table 6.4, you can see that average revenue equals €0.40, the price of a litre of milk. This illustrates a general lesson that applies not only to competitive firms but to other firms as well. Total revenue is the price times the quantity ($P \times Q$), and average revenue is total revenue ($P \times Q$) divided by the quantity (Q). Therefore, *for all firms, average revenue equals the price of the good.*

average revenue total revenue divided by the quantity sold

The fifth column shows marginal revenue, which is the change in total revenue from the sale of each additional unit of output.

$$MR = \frac{\Delta TR}{\Delta Q}$$

marginal revenue the change in total revenue from an additional unit sold

The sale of one more litre of milk adds €0.40 to total revenue, therefore the marginal revenue is also €0.40. In Table 6.4, marginal revenue equals €0.40, the price of a litre of milk. This result illustrates a lesson that applies only to competitive firms. Total revenue is $P \times Q$, and P is fixed for a competitive firm. Therefore, when Q rises by one unit, total revenue rises by P euros. For competitive firms, marginal revenue equals the price of the good.

SELF TEST When a competitive firm doubles the amount it sells, what happens to the price of its output and its total revenue?

Total Revenue, Total Cost and Profit

It is conceivable that Paolo or the Grundy family started in business because of a desire to provide the world with pizza or milk or, perhaps, out of love for the pizza business or farming. Most firms, however, also have to make a profit. Economists often use the assumption that the goal of a firm is to maximize profit. Whilst the extent to which this assumption holds in the real world has been questioned, it is a useful starting point for our analysis.

What is a firm's profit? Profit is the difference between total revenue and total cost.

Profit = Total revenue − Total cost

We can express this in the formula:

$$\pi = TR - TC$$

where π represents profit.

Economic Profit versus Accounting Profit

We have seen that economists and accountants measure costs differently and they also measure profit differently. An economist measures a firm's **economic profit** as the firm's total revenue minus all the opportunity costs (explicit and implicit) of producing the goods and services sold. An accountant measures the firm's **accounting profit** as the firm's total revenue minus only the firm's explicit costs.

> **economic profit** total revenue minus total cost, including both explicit and implicit costs
> **accounting profit** total revenue minus total explicit cost

Figure 6.6 summarizes this difference. Notice that because the accountant ignores the implicit costs, accounting profit is usually larger than economic profit. For a business to be profitable from an economist's standpoint, total revenue must cover all the opportunity costs, both explicit and implicit.

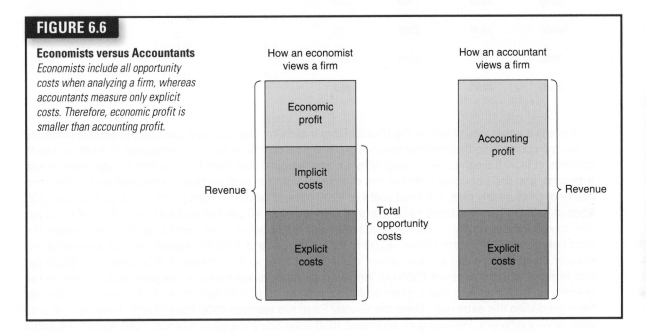

FIGURE 6.6

Economists versus Accountants
Economists include all opportunity costs when analyzing a firm, whereas accountants measure only explicit costs. Therefore, economic profit is smaller than accounting profit.

PROFIT MAXIMIZATION AND THE COMPETITIVE FIRM'S SUPPLY CURVE

A Simple Example of Profit Maximization

Let's begin our analysis of the firm's supply decision with the example in Table 6.5 using the Grundy Family Dairy Farm. In the first column of the table is the number of litres of milk the farm produces. The second column shows the farm's total revenue, which is €0.40 times the number of litres. The third column shows the farm's total cost. Total cost includes fixed costs, which are €200 in this example, and variable costs, which depend on the quantity produced.

The fourth column shows the farm's profit, which is computed by subtracting total cost from total revenue. If the farm produces nothing, it has a loss of €200. If it produces 1000 litres, it has a profit of €100. If it produces 2000 litres, it has a profit of €300 and so on. To maximize profit, the Grundy Farm chooses the quantity that makes profit as large as possible. In this example, profit is maximized when the farm produces 3000 or 4000 litres of milk, when the profit is €400.

| TABLE 6.5 | Profit Maximization: A Numerical Example | | | | | |

Quantity (Q) Litres	Total revenue (€) (TR)	Total cost (€) (TC)	Profit (€) (TR −TC)	Marginal revenue (€) (MR = ΔTR/ΔQ)	Marginal cost (€) (MC = ΔTC/ΔQ)	Change in profit (€) (MR − MC)
0	0	200	−200			
				0.4	0.1	0.3
1000	400	300	100			
				0.4	0.2	0.2
2000	800	500	300			
				0.4	0.3	0.1
3000	1200	800	400			
				0.4	0.4	0
4000	1600	1200	400			
				0.4	0.5	−0.1
5000	2000	1700	300			
				0.4	0.6	−0.2
6000	2400	2300	100			
				0.4	0.7	−0.3
7000	2800	3000	−200			
				0.4	0.8	−0.4
8000	3200	3800	−600			

There is another way to look at the Grundy Farm's decision: the Grundy's can find the profit-maximizing quantity by comparing the marginal revenue and marginal cost from each unit produced. The fifth and sixth columns in Table 6.5 compute marginal revenue and marginal cost from the changes in total revenue and total cost, and the last column shows the change in profit for each additional litre produced. If the farm does not produce any milk, the fixed costs of €200 have to be paid and so profit is −€200. The first 1000 litres of milk the farm produces has a marginal revenue of €0.40 per litre and a marginal cost of €0.10 per litre; hence, producing the additional 1000 litres adds €0.30 per litre produced to profit which means the farm now earns €100 in profit (from −€200 to €100). The second 1000 litres produced has a marginal revenue of €0.40 per litre and a marginal cost of €0.20 per litre, so this additional 1000 litres adds €0.20 per litre to profit which now totals €300. As long as marginal revenue exceeds marginal cost, increasing the quantity produced adds to profit. Since additional production of milk adds to profit it is worth the Grundy Farm producing this extra milk. Once the Grundy Farm has reached 4000 litres of milk, however, the situation is very different. Producing an additional 1000 litres has a marginal revenue of €0.40 per litre and a marginal cost of €0.50 per litre, so producing it would reduce profit by €100 (from €400 to €300). It does not make sense for the Grundy Farm to produce this additional 1000 litres and so, as a result, there is little incentive for the Grundy's to produce beyond 4000 litres.

This is another example of thinking at the margin. If marginal revenue is greater than marginal cost it is worth the Grundy's increasing the production of milk. If marginal revenue is less than marginal cost, the Grundy's should decrease production. If the Grundy's think at the margin and make incremental adjustments to the level of production, they are led to produce the profit-maximizing quantity. The profit maximizing output occurs, therefore, at the output where MR = MC.

Normal and Abnormal Profit

In the analysis that follows we make an important assumption related to our earlier discussion of the meaning of economic profit. We know that profit equals total revenue minus total cost, and that total cost includes the opportunity cost of the time and money that the firm owners devote to the business. A firm's revenue must compensate the owners for the time and money that they expend to keep their business going, which is sometimes referred to as normal profit or zero-profit equilibrium.

Consider an example. Suppose that a farmer had to invest €1 million to open their farm, which otherwise they could have deposited in a bank to earn €50 000 a year in interest. In addition, they had to give up another job that would have paid them €30 000 a year. Then the farmer's opportunity cost of farming includes both the interest they could have earned and the forgone wages – a total of €80 000. This sum must be calculated as part of the farmer's total costs referred to as **normal profit** – the minimum amount required to keep factor inputs in their current use. Even if profit is driven to zero, their revenue from farming compensates them for these opportunity costs.

 normal profit the minimum amount required to keep factors of production in their current use

Because of the different way accountants and economists measure profit, at the zero-profit equilibrium, economic profit is zero, but accounting profit is positive. Our farmer's accountant, for instance, would conclude that the farmer earned an accounting profit of €80 000, which is enough to keep the farmer in business. In the short run, as we shall see, profit can be above zero or normal profit, which is referred to as **abnormal profit**.

 abnormal profit the profit over and above normal profit

If firms are making abnormal profit then there is an incentive for other firms to enter the market to take advantage of the profits that exist and this creates a dynamic which moves the market to equilibrium.

The Marginal Cost Curve and the Firm's Supply Decision

To extend this analysis of profit maximization, consider the cost curves in Figure 6.7.

The figure shows a horizontal line at the market price (P). The price line is horizontal because the firm is a price taker: the price received is the same, regardless of the quantity that the firm decides to produce. Keep in mind that, for a competitive firm, the firm's price equals both its average revenue (AR) and its marginal revenue (MR).

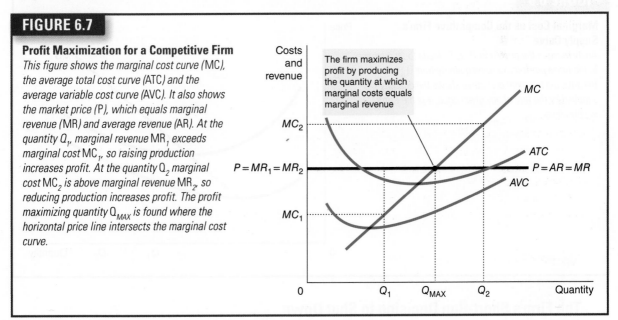

FIGURE 6.7

Profit Maximization for a Competitive Firm
This figure shows the marginal cost curve (MC), the average total cost curve (ATC) and the average variable cost curve (AVC). It also shows the market price (P), which equals marginal revenue (MR) and average revenue (AR). At the quantity Q_1, marginal revenue MR_1 exceeds marginal cost MC_1, so raising production increases profit. At the quantity Q_2 marginal cost MC_2 is above marginal revenue MR_2 so reducing production increases profit. The profit maximizing quantity Q_{MAX} is found where the horizontal price line intersects the marginal cost curve.

The firm maximizes profit by producing the quantity at which marginal costs equals marginal revenue

We can use Figure 6.7 to find the quantity of output that maximizes profit. Imagine that the firm is producing at Q_1. At this level of output, marginal revenue is greater than marginal cost. That is, if the firm raised its level of production and sales by 1 unit, the additional revenue (MR_1) would exceed the additional costs (MC_1). Profit, which equals total revenue minus total cost, would increase. Hence, if marginal revenue is greater than marginal cost, as it is at Q_1, it is worth the firm producing this output because it can increase profit.

When output is at Q_2, marginal cost is greater than marginal revenue. If the firm reduced production by 1 unit, the costs saved (MC_2) would exceed the revenue lost (MR_2). Therefore, if marginal revenue is less than marginal cost, as it is at Q_2, it is worth the firm cutting back production because the firm can increase profit.

Where do these marginal adjustments to level of production end? Regardless of whether the firm begins with production at a low level (such as Q_1) or at a high level (such as Q_2), there is an incentive for the firm to adjust its output decisions until the quantity produced reaches Q_{MAX}. At any other output level, there is an incentive for the firm to either increase or cut back output and increase profit. This analysis shows a general rule for profit maximization: at the profit-maximizing level of output, marginal revenue and marginal cost are exactly equal.

We can now see how the supply curve is derived. Because a competitive firm is a price taker, its marginal revenue equals the market price. For any given price, the competitive firm's profit-maximizing quantity of output is found by looking at the intersection of the price with the marginal cost curve. In Figure 6.7, that quantity of output is Q_{MAX}.

Figure 6.8 shows how a competitive firm responds to an increase in the price which may have been caused by a change in global market conditions. Remember that competitive firms are price takers and have to accept the market price for their product. Prices of commodities such as grain, metals, sugar, cotton, coffee, pork bellies, and so on are set by organized international markets and so the individual firm has no power to influence price. When the price is P_1, the firm produces quantity Q_1, the quantity that equates marginal cost to the price. Assume that an outbreak of bovine spongiform encephalopathy (BSE) results in the need to slaughter a large proportion of dairy cattle and as a result there is a shortage of milk on the market. When the price rises to P_2, the firm finds that marginal revenue is now higher than marginal cost at the previous level of output, so existing farmers look to increase production. The new profit-maximizing quantity is Q_2, at which marginal cost equals the new higher price. In essence, because the firm's marginal cost curve determines the quantity of the good the firm is willing to supply at any price – it is the competitive firm's supply curve.

FIGURE 6.8

Marginal Cost as the Competitive Firm's Supply Curve

An increase in the price from P_1 to P_2 leads to an increase in the firm's profit-maximizing quantity from Q_1 to Q_2. Because the marginal cost curve shows the quantity supplied by the firm at any given price, it is the firm's supply curve.

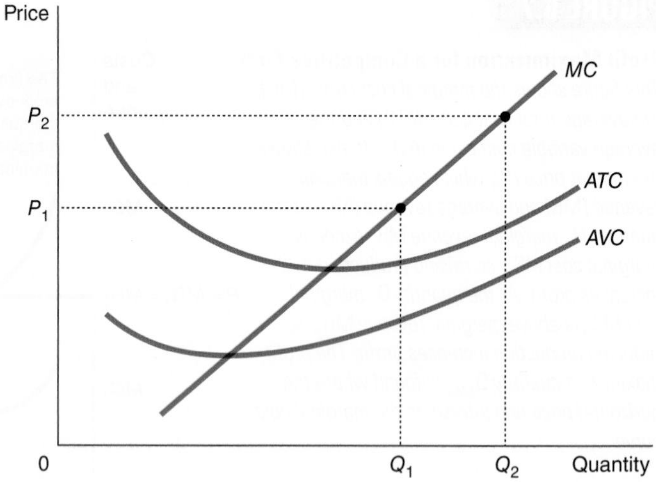

The Firm's Short-Run Decision to Shut Down

So far we have been analyzing the question of how much a competitive firm will produce. In some circumstances, however, the firm will decide to shut down and not produce anything at all.

Here we should distinguish between a temporary shutdown of a firm and the permanent exit of a firm from the market. A shutdown refers to a short-run decision not to produce anything during a specific period of time because of current market conditions. Exit refers to a long-run decision to leave the market. The short-run and long-run decisions differ because most firms cannot avoid their fixed costs in the short run but can do so in the long run. That is, a firm that shuts down temporarily still has to pay its fixed costs, whereas a firm that exits the market saves both its fixed and its variable costs.

For example, consider the production decision that a farmer faces. The cost of a milking parlour is one of the farmer's fixed costs. If the farmer decides not to milk their herd for some period of time, the parlour still represents a cost they cannot recover. When making the short-run decision whether to shut down for this period, the fixed cost of the parlour is said to be a sunk cost. By contrast, if the farmer decides to leave dairy farming altogether, he can sell the parlour along with the rest of the farm. When making the long-run decision whether to exit the market, the cost of the parlour is not sunk. (We return to the issue of sunk costs shortly.)

Now let's consider what determines a firm's shutdown decision. If the firm shuts down, it loses all revenue from the sale of its product. At the same time, it saves the variable costs of making its product (but must still pay the fixed costs). Thus, the firm shuts down if the revenue that it would get from producing is less than its variable costs of production; it is simply not worth producing a product which costs more to produce than the revenue generated by its sale. Doing so would reduce profit or make any existing losses even greater.

A little bit of mathematics can make this shutdown criterion more useful. If *TR* stands for total revenue and *VC* stands for variable costs, then the firm's decision can be written as:

$$\text{Shut down if } TR < VC$$

The firm shuts down if total revenue is less than variable cost. By dividing both sides of this inequality by the quantity *Q*, we can write it as:

$$\text{Shut down if } \frac{TR}{Q} < \frac{VC}{Q}$$

Notice that this can be further simplified. $\frac{TR}{Q}$ is average revenue. As we discussed previously, average revenue for any firm is simply the good's price *P*. Similarly, $\frac{VC}{Q}$ is average variable cost *AVC*. Therefore, the firm's shutdown criterion is:

$$\text{Shut down if } P < AVC$$

That is, a firm chooses to shut down if the price of the good is less than the average variable cost of production. This criterion is intuitive: when choosing to produce, the firm compares the price it receives for the typical unit to the average variable cost that it must incur to produce the typical unit. If the price doesn't cover the average variable cost, the firm is better off stopping production altogether. The firm can re-open in the future if conditions change so that price exceeds average variable cost.

We now have a full description of a competitive firm's profit-maximizing strategy. If the firm produces anything, it produces the quantity at which marginal cost equals the price of the good. Yet if the price is less than average variable cost at that quantity, the firm is better off shutting down and not producing anything. These results are illustrated in Figure 6.9. The competitive firm's short-run supply curve is the portion of its marginal cost curve that lies above average variable cost.

Sunk Costs

Economists say that a cost is a **sunk cost** when it has already been committed and cannot be recovered. In a sense, a sunk cost is the opposite of an opportunity cost: an opportunity cost is what you have to give up if you choose to do one thing instead of another, whereas a sunk cost cannot be avoided, regardless of the choices you make. Because nothing can be done about sunk costs, you can ignore them when making decisions about various aspects of life, including business strategy.

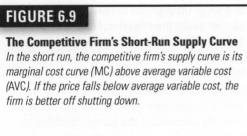

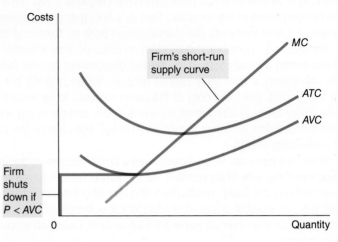

The Competitive Firm's Short-Run Supply Curve
In the short run, the competitive firm's supply curve is its marginal cost curve (MC) above average variable cost (AVC). If the price falls below average variable cost, the firm is better off shutting down.

---

sunk cost a cost that has already been committed and cannot be recovered

---

Our analysis of the firm's shutdown decision is one example of the importance of recognizing sunk costs. We assume that the firm cannot recover its fixed costs by temporarily stopping production. As a result, the firm's fixed costs are sunk in the short run, and the firm can safely ignore these costs when deciding how much to produce. The firm's short-run supply curve is the part of the marginal cost curve that lies above average variable cost, and the size of the fixed cost does not matter for this supply decision.

The Firm's Long-Run Decision to Exit or Enter a Market

The firm's long-run decision to exit the market is similar to its shutdown decision. If the firm exits, it again will lose all revenue from the sale of its product, but now it saves on both fixed and variable costs of production. Thus, the firm exits the market if the revenue it would get from producing is less than its total costs.

We can again make this criterion more useful by writing it mathematically. The firm's criterion can be written as:

$$Exit\ if\ TR < TC$$

The firm exits if total revenue is less than total cost. By dividing both sides of this inequality by quantity Q, we can write it as:

$$Exit\ if\ \frac{TR}{Q} < \frac{TC}{Q}$$

We can simplify this further by noting that $\frac{TR}{Q}$ is average revenue, which equals the price P, and that $\frac{TC}{Q}$ is average total cost ATC. Therefore, the firm's exit criterion is:

$$Exit\ if\ P < ATC$$

That is, a firm chooses to exit if the price of the good is less than the average total cost of production.

A parallel analysis applies to an entrepreneur who is considering starting a firm. The firm will enter the market if such an action would be profitable, which occurs if the price of the good exceeds the average total cost of production. The entry criterion is:

Enter if P > ATC

The criterion for entry is exactly the opposite of the criterion for exit.

We can now describe a competitive firm's long-run profit-maximizing strategy. If the firm is in the market, it produces the quantity at which marginal cost equals the price of the good. Yet if the price is less than average total cost at that quantity, the firm chooses to exit (or not enter) the market. These results are illustrated in Figure 6.10. The competitive firm's long-run supply curve is the portion of its marginal cost curve that lies above average total cost.

FIGURE 6.10

The Competitive Firm's Long-Run Supply Curve
In the long run, the competitive firm's supply curve is its marginal cost curve (MC) above average total cost (ATC). If the price falls below average total cost, the firm is better off exiting the market.

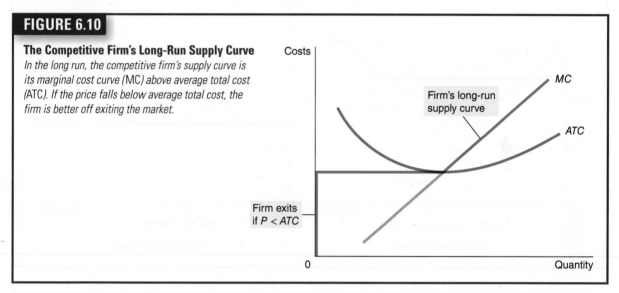

Measuring Profit in Our Graph for the Competitive Firm

As we analyze exit and entry, it is useful to be able to analyze the firm's profit in more detail. Recall that profit equals total revenue (*TR*) minus total cost (*TC*):

$$Profit = TR - TC$$

We can rewrite this definition by multiplying and dividing the right-hand side by *Q*:

$$Profit = \left(\frac{TR}{Q} - \frac{TC}{Q}\right) \times Q$$

But note that $\frac{TR}{Q}$ is average revenue, which is the price P, and $\frac{TC}{Q}$ is average total cost *ATC*. Therefore:

$$Profit = (P - ATC) \times Q$$

This way of expressing the firm's profit allows us to measure profit in our graphs.

Panel (a) of Figure 6.11 shows a firm earning abnormal profit. As we have already discussed, the firm maximizes profit by producing the quantity at which price equals marginal cost. The height of the shaded rectangle is $P - ATC$, the difference between price and average total cost. The width of the rectangle is *Q*, the quantity produced. Therefore, the area of the rectangle is $(P - ATC) \times Q$, which is the firm's profit.

Similarly, panel (b) of this figure shows a firm with losses (negative profit). In this case, maximizing profit means minimizing losses, a task accomplished once again by producing the quantity at which price equals marginal cost. Now consider the shaded rectangle. The height of the rectangle is $ATC - P$, and the width is Q. The area is $(ATC - P) \times Q$, which is the firm's loss. Because a firm in this situation is not making enough revenue to cover its average total cost, the firm would choose to exit the market.

FIGURE 6.11

Profit as the Area between Price and Average Total Cost

The area of the shaded box between price and average total cost represents the firm's profit. The height of this box is price minus average total cost (P − ATC), and the width of the box is the quantity of output (Q). In panel (a), price is above average total cost, so the firm has positive profit. In panel (b), price is less than average total cost, so the firm has losses.

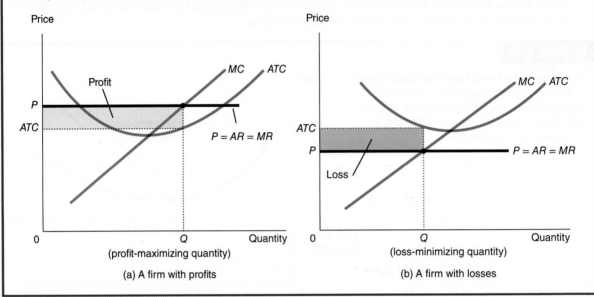

(a) A firm with profits

(b) A firm with losses

SELF TEST How does the price faced by a profit-maximizing competitive firm compare to its marginal cost? Explain.
When does a profit-maximizing competitive firm decide to shut down? When does a profit-maximizing competitive firm decide to exit a market?

THE SUPPLY CURVE IN A COMPETITIVE MARKET

Now that we have examined the supply decision of a single firm, we can discuss the supply curve for a market. There are two cases to consider. First, we examine a market with a fixed number of firms. Second, we examine a market in which the number of firms can change as old firms exit the market and new firms enter. Both cases are important, for each applies over a specific time horizon. Over short periods of time it is often difficult for firms to enter and exit, so the assumption of a fixed number of firms is appropriate. But over long periods of time, the number of firms can adjust to changing market conditions.

The Short Run: Market Supply with a Fixed Number of Firms

Consider first a market with 1000 identical firms. For any given price, each firm supplies a quantity of output so that its marginal cost equals the price, as shown in panel (a) of Figure 6.12. That is, as long as price is above average variable cost, each firm's marginal cost curve is its supply curve. The quantity of output supplied to the market equals the sum of the quantities supplied by each of the 1000 individual firms. Thus, to derive the market supply curve, we add the quantity supplied by each firm in the market. As panel (b) of Figure 6.12 shows, because the firms are identical, the quantity supplied to the market is 1000 times the quantity supplied by each firm.

FIGURE 6.12

Market Supply with a Fixed Number of Firms

When the number of firms in the market is fixed, the market supply curve, shown in panel (b), reflects the individual firms' marginal cost curves, shown in panel (a). Here, in a market of 1000 firms, the quantity of output supplied to the market is 1000 times the quantity supplied by each firm.

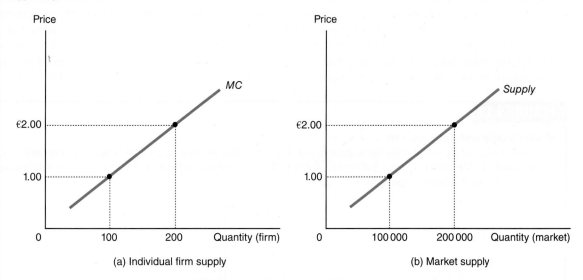

(a) Individual firm supply

(b) Market supply

The Long Run: Market Supply with Entry and Exit

Now consider what happens if firms are able to enter or exit the market. Let's suppose that everyone has access to the same technology for producing the good and access to the same markets to buy the inputs for production. Therefore, all firms and all potential firms have the same cost curves.

Decisions about entry and exit in a market of this type depend on the incentives facing the owners of existing firms and the entrepreneurs who could start new firms. If firms already in the market are making abnormal profit, then new firms will have an incentive to enter the market. This entry will expand the number of firms, increase the quantity of the good supplied, and drive down prices and profits back to a point where firms are making normal profit. Conversely, if firms in the market are making losses (subnormal profit), then some existing firms will exit the market. Their exit will reduce the number of firms, decrease the quantity of the good supplied, and drive up prices back to a point where normal profit is made. At the end of this process of entry and exit, firms that remain in the market must be at the level of production that is making zero economic or normal profit. Recall that we can write a firm's profits as:

$$Profit = (P - ATC) \times Q$$

This equation shows that an operating firm has zero profit if, and only if, the price of the good equals the average total cost of producing that good. If price is above average total cost, profit is positive, which encourages new firms to enter. If price is less than average total cost, profit is negative, which encourages some firms to exit. The process of entry and exit ends only when price and average total cost are driven to equality.

This analysis has a surprising implication. We noted earlier in the chapter that competitive firms produce so that price equals marginal cost. We just noted that free entry and exit forces price to equal average total cost. But if price is to equal both marginal cost and average total cost, these two measures of cost must equal each other. Marginal cost and average total cost are equal, however, only when the firm is operating at the minimum of average total cost. Recall from earlier in this chapter that the level of production with lowest average total cost is called the firm's efficient scale. Therefore, the long-run equilibrium of a competitive market with free entry and exit must have firms operating at their efficient scale.

Panel (a) of Figure 6.13 shows a firm in such a long-run equilibrium. In this figure, price P equals marginal cost MC, so the firm is profit-maximizing. Price also equals average total cost ATC, so profits are zero or normal. New firms have no incentive to enter the market, and existing firms have no incentive to leave the market.

From this analysis of firm behaviour, we can determine the long-run supply curve for the market. In a market with free entry and exit, there is only one price consistent with zero profit – the minimum of average total cost. As a result, the long-run market supply curve must be horizontal at this price, as in panel (b) of Figure 6.13. Any price above this level would generate profit, leading to entry and an increase in the total quantity supplied. Any price below this level would generate losses, leading to exit and a decrease in the total quantity supplied. Eventually, the number of firms in the market adjusts so that price equals the minimum of average total cost, and there are enough firms to satisfy all the demand at this price.

FIGURE 6.13

Market Supply with Entry and Exit
Firms will enter or exit the market until profit is driven to zero. Thus, in the long run, price equals the minimum of average total cost, as shown in panel (a). The number of firms adjusts to ensure that all demand is satisfied at this price. The long-run market supply curve is horizontal at this price, as shown in panel (b).

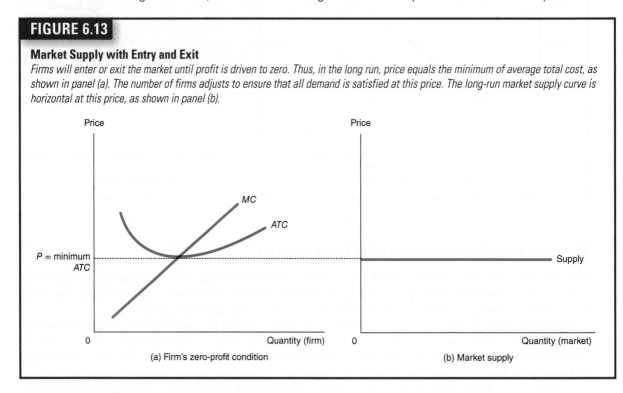

(a) Firm's zero-profit condition (b) Market supply

A Shift in Demand in the Short Run and Long Run

Because firms can enter and exit a market in the long run but not in the short run, the response of a market to a change in demand depends on the time horizon. To see this, let's trace the effects of a shift in demand. This analysis will show how a market responds over time, and it will show how entry and exit drive a market to its long-run equilibrium.

Suppose the market for milk begins in long-run equilibrium. Firms are earning zero profit, so price equals the minimum of average total cost. Panel (a) of Figure 6.14 shows the situation. The long-run equilibrium in the market shown by the graph on the right of the panel is point A, the quantity sold in the market is Q_1 and the price is P_1.

Now suppose scientists discover that milk has significant health benefits. As a result, the demand curve for milk shifts outward from D_1 to D_2, as in panel (b). The short-run equilibrium moves from point A to point B; as a result, the quantity rises from Q_1 to Q_2 and the price rises from P_1 to P_2. All of the existing firms respond to the higher price by raising the amount produced. Because each firm's supply curve reflects its marginal cost curve, how much they each increase production is determined by the marginal cost curve. In the new short-run equilibrium, the price of milk exceeds average total cost, so the firms are making positive or abnormal profit.

FIGURE 6.14

An Increase in Demand in the Short Run and Long Run

The market starts in a long-run equilibrium, shown as point A in panel (a). In this equilibrium, each firm makes zero profit, and the price equals the minimum average total cost. Panel (b) shows what happens in the short run when demand rises from D_1 to D_2. The equilibrium goes from point A to point B, price rises from P_1 to P_2, and the quantity sold in the market rises from Q_1 to Q_2. Because price now exceeds average total cost, firms make abnormal profits, which over time encourage new firms to enter the market. This entry shifts the short-run supply curve to the right from S_1 to S_2 as shown in panel (c). In the new long-run equilibrium, point C, price has returned to P_1 but the quantity sold has increased to Q_3. Profits are again zero, price is back to the minimum of average total cost, but the market has more firms to satisfy the greater demand.

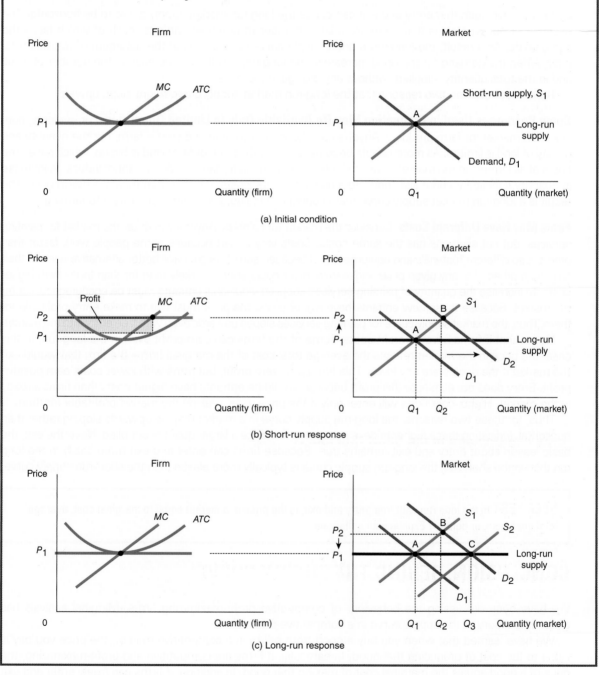

The abnormal profit in this market encourages new firms to enter. Some farmers may switch to milk from other farm products, for example. As the number of firms grow, the short-run supply curve shifts to the right from S_1 to S_2, as in panel (c), and this shift causes the price of milk to fall. Eventually, the price is driven back down to the minimum of average total cost, profits are zero and firms stop entering. Thus, the market reaches a new long-run equilibrium, point C. The price of milk has returned to P_1, but the quantity produced has risen to Q_3. Each firm is again producing at its efficient scale, but, because more firms are in the dairy business, the quantity of milk produced and sold is greater.

Why the Long-Run Supply Curve Might Slope Upwards

So far we have seen that entry and exit can cause the long-run market supply curve to be horizontal. The essence of our analysis is that there are a large number of potential entrants, each of which faces the same costs. As a result, the long-run market supply curve is horizontal at the minimum of average total cost. When the demand for the good increases, the long-run result is an increase in the number of firms and in the total quantity supplied, without any change in the price.

There are, however, two reasons that the long-run market supply curve might slope upward.

Some Resources Used in Production May Be Available Only in Limited Quantities For example, consider the market for farm products. Anyone can choose to buy land and start a farm, but the quantity and quality of land is limited. As more people become farmers, the price of farm land is bid up, which raises the costs of all farmers in the market. Thus, an increase in demand for farm products cannot induce an increase in quantity supplied without also inducing a rise in farmers' costs, which in turn means a rise in price. The result is a long-run market supply curve that is upwards sloping, even with free entry into farming.

Firms May Have Different Costs Consider the market for painters. Anyone can enter the market for painting services, but not everyone has the same costs. Costs vary in part because some people work faster than others, use different materials and equipment and because some people have better alternative uses of their time than others. For any given price, those with lower costs are more likely to enter than those with higher costs. To increase the quantity of painting services supplied, additional entrants must be encouraged to enter the market. Because these new entrants have higher costs, the price must rise to make entry profitable for them. Thus, the market supply curve for painting services slopes upwards even with free entry into the market.

Notice that if firms have different costs, some of the firms can earn profit even in the long run. In this case, the price in the market reflects the average total cost of the marginal firm – the firm that would exit the market if the price were any lower. This firm earns zero profit, but firms with lower costs earn positive profit. Entry does not eliminate this profit because would-be entrants have higher costs than firms already in the market. Higher-cost firms will enter only if the price rises, making the market profitable for them.

Thus, for these two reasons, the long-run supply curve in a market may be upwards sloping rather than horizontal, indicating that a higher price is necessary to induce a larger quantity supplied. Nevertheless, the basic lesson about entry and exit remains true. Because firms can enter and exit more easily in the long run than in the short run, the long-run supply curve is typically more elastic than the short-run supply curve.

SELF TEST In the long run with free entry and exit, is the price in a market equal to marginal cost, average total cost, both, or neither? Explain with a diagram.

CONCLUSION: BEHIND THE SUPPLY CURVE

We have been discussing the behaviour of competitive profit-maximizing firms. Marginal analysis has given us a theory of the supply curve in a competitive market.

We have learned that when you buy a good from a firm in a competitive market, the price you pay is close to the cost of producing that good. In particular, if firms are competitive and profit-maximizing, the price of a good equals the marginal cost of making that good. In addition, if firms can freely enter and exit the market, the price also equals the lowest possible average total cost of production.

In later chapters we will examine the behaviour of firms with market power. Marginal analysis will again be useful in analyzing these firms, but it will have quite different implications.

IN THE NEWS

Perfectly Competitive Markets

There has been criticism that the model of perfectly competitive markets rests on assumptions which do not exist in the real world and as a result the predictive power of the model is limited. This In the News looks at the world of peer-to-peer file sharing and a claim by one entrepreneur that the market is close to being perfectly competitive.

Peer-to-peer file sharing

With the developments in technology, sharing large files such as music and video files over the Internet has become more common. The language used to communicate between computers over the Internet is referred to as a protocol. BitTorrent is a protocol used in peer-to-peer file sharing. Sharing files requires an uploader and a downloader. Typically there might be a small number of uploaders but a large number of downloaders and as a result bandwidth can be limited. A torrent is a file containing information about content, for example an audio file, and is used to help locate uploaders and downloaders to connect them in an efficient way. This efficiency helps improve internet speeds for all users. Uploaders use BitTorrent to make a file available, referred to as a seed, and those downloading are referred to as leechers. To utilize the BitTorrent protocol, a computer programme is required called a client. One

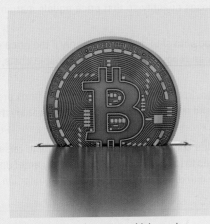

Will Bitcoin ever become a widely used currency?

such client is JoyStream, a company founded by Dr Bedeho Mender. JoyStream's business model is based on a payment network called bitcoin which allows seeders and leechers to receive and pay money for services such as files or bandwidth over the Internet. Buying bandwidth may enable the user to stream movies or audio more efficiently. JoyStream allows seeders to receive very small payments from leechers in bitcoin.

This means that seeders who own high value or rare content can charge prices above the marginal cost of provision. Other users can see that this content is of value and can prepare their own torrent files to share such content. Mender believes that this 'entry into the market' will mean that supply will increase and the competition will force prices down to a level where they equal marginal cost of supplying content or bandwidth – which will be very low. Mender has been quoted in Bitcoin Magazine as saying that 'the seeding market is very close to a perfectly competitive market'.

Questions

1 To what extent do you think the seeding market has the characteristics of a perfectly competitive market?
2 Assume that a seeder with access to high value premium content makes that content available. Use the short-run and long-run analysis to show what you would expect to happen to the profits made by seeders.
3 What might some of the implicit and explicit costs be for seeders which may influence their behaviour?
4 Given the context of the article, do you think the supply curve in this market is horizontal or upward sloping? Explain.
5 To what extent do you agree with the view of JoyStream's founder, Bedeho Mender, that 'the seeding market is very close to a perfectly competitive market'?

Source: https://bitcoinmagazine.com/articles/joystream-bittorrent-client-incentivizes-seeders-bitcoin-1434587555

SUMMARY

- When analyzing a firm's behaviour, it is important to include all the opportunity costs of production. Some, such as the wages a firm pays its workers, are explicit. Others, such as the wages the firm owner gives up by working in the firm rather than taking another job, are implicit.

- A firm's costs reflect its production process. A typical firm's production function gets flatter as the quantity of an input increases, displaying the property of diminishing marginal product. As a result, a firm's total cost curve gets steeper as the quantity produced rises.

- A firm's total costs can be divided between fixed costs and variable costs. Fixed costs are costs that are not determined by the quantity of output produced. Variable costs are costs that directly relate to the amount produced and so change when the firm alters the quantity of output produced.

- Average total cost is total cost divided by the quantity of output. Marginal cost is the amount by which total cost changes if output increases (or decreases) by one unit.

- For a typical firm, marginal cost rises with the quantity of output. Average total cost first falls as output increases and then rises as output increases further. The marginal cost curve always crosses the average total cost curve at the minimum of average total cost

- Many costs are fixed in the short run but variable in the long run. As a result, when the firm changes its level of production, average total cost may rise more in the short run than in the long run.

- Because a competitive firm is a price taker, its revenue is proportional to the amount of output it produces. The price of the good equals both the firm's average revenue and its marginal revenue.

- One goal of firms is to maximize profit, which equals total revenue minus total cost.

- To maximize profit, a firm chooses a quantity of output such that marginal revenue equals marginal cost. Because marginal revenue for a competitive firm equals the market price, the firm chooses quantity so that price equals marginal cost. Thus, the firm's marginal cost curve is its supply curve.

- In the short run when a firm cannot recover its fixed costs, the firm will choose to shut down temporarily if the price of the good is less than average variable cost. In the long run when the firm can recover both fixed and variable costs, it will choose to exit if the price is less than average total cost.

- In a market with free entry and exit, profits are driven to zero in the long run. In this long-run equilibrium, all firms produce at the efficient scale, price equals the minimum of average total cost, and the number of firms adjusts to satisfy the quantity demanded at this price.

- Changes in demand have different effects over different time horizons. In the short run, an increase in demand raises prices and leads to profits, and a decrease in demand lowers prices and leads to losses. But if firms can freely enter and exit the market, then in the long run the number of firms adjusts to drive the market back to the zero-profit equilibrium.

QUESTIONS FOR REVIEW

1 What is marginal product, and what does it mean if it is diminishing?

2 Draw a production function that exhibits diminishing marginal product of labour. Draw the associated total cost curve. (In both cases, be sure to label the axes.) Explain the shapes of the two curves you have drawn.

3 Give an example of an opportunity cost that an accountant might not count as a cost. Why would the accountant ignore this cost?

4 Define *economies of scale* and *diseconomies of scale* and explain why they might arise.

5 Draw the marginal cost and average total cost curves for a typical firm. Explain why the curves have the shapes that they do and why they cross where they do.

6 Under what conditions will a firm shut down temporarily? Under what conditions will a firm exit a market? Explain each.

7 Why is the point of profit maximization where marginal cost equals marginal revenue?

8 Does a firm's price equal marginal cost and the minimum of average total cost in the short run, in the long run, or both? Explain.

9 Explain the difference between increasing, constant and decreasing returns to scale.

10 Are market supply curves typically more elastic in the short run or in the long run? Explain.

PROBLEMS AND APPLICATIONS

1 Manton Bakery is a company that bakes bread. Here is the relationship between the number of workers at the bakery and Manton's output in a given day:

Workers	Output of loaves	Marginal product	Total cost	Average total cost	Marginal cost
0	0				
1	20				
2	50				
3	90				
4	120				
5	140				
6	150				
7	155				

a. Fill in the column of marginal product. What pattern do you see? How might you explain it?

b. A skilled baker costs €100 a day, and the firm has fixed costs of €200. Use this information to fill in the column for total cost.

c. Fill in the column for average total cost. (Recall that $ATC = \dfrac{TC}{Q}$.) What pattern do you see?

d. Now fill in the column for marginal cost. (Recall that $MC = \dfrac{\Delta TC}{\Delta Q}$.) What pattern do you see?

e. Compare the column for marginal product and the column for marginal cost. Explain the relationship.

f. Compare the column for average total cost and the column for marginal cost. Explain the relationship.

2 Your aunt announces that she is thinking about opening a restaurant. She estimates that it would cost €500 000 per year to rent the premises, buy a licence to serve alcohol and to buy in food. In addition, she would have to leave her €50 000 per year job as an accountant.

a. Define opportunity cost.

b. What is your aunt's opportunity cost of running the restaurant for a year? If your aunt thought she could sell €510 000 worth of food in a year, should she open the restaurant? Explain.

3 Your cousin Mark owns a painting company with fixed costs of €200 and the following schedule for variable costs:

Quantity of houses painted per month	1	2	3	4	5	6	7
Variable costs	€10	€20	€40	€80	€160	€320	€640

Calculate average fixed cost, average variable cost and average total cost for each quantity. What is the efficient scale of Mark's company?

4 What are the characteristics of a competitive market? Which of the following drinks do you think is best described by these characteristics? Why aren't the others?

a. tap water

b. bottled water

c. cola

d. beer.

5 A commercial fisherman charts the following relationship between hours spent and the quantity of fish caught per trip.

Hours	Quantity of fish caught (Kilos)
0	0
1	20
2	36
3	48
4	56
5	60

a. What is the marginal product of each hour spent fishing?
b. Using these data, graph the fisherman's production function. Explain the shape of the production function.
c. Assume the fisherman has a fixed cost of €500 for their boat and the opportunity cost of their time is €10 per hour. Graph the fisherman's total-cost curve and explain its shape.

6 You go out to the best restaurant in town and order a steak dinner for €40. After eating half of the steak, you realize that you are quite full. Your date wants you to finish your dinner, because you can't take it home and because 'you've already paid for it'. What should you do? Relate your answer to the material in this chapter.

7 Alejandro's lawn-mowing service is a profit-maximizing, competitive firm. Alejandro mows lawns for €27 each. His total cost each day is €280, of which €30 is a fixed cost. He mows 10 lawns a day. What can you say about Alejandro's short-run decision regarding shutdown and his long-run decision regarding exit?

8 Consider total cost and total revenue given in the table below:

Quantity	0	1	2	3	4	5	6	7
Total cost	€8	9	10	11	13	19	27	37
Total revenue	€0	8	16	24	32	40	48	56

a. Calculate profit for each quantity. How much should the firm produce to maximize profit?
b. Calculate marginal revenue and marginal cost for each quantity. Graph them. (Hint: put the points between whole numbers. For example, the marginal cost between 2 and 3 should be graphed at 2½). At what quantity do these curves cross? How does this relate to your answer to part (a)?
c. Can you tell whether this firm is in a competitive industry? If so, can you tell whether the industry is in long-run equilibrium?

9 A profit maximizing firm in a competitive market is currently producing 100 units of output. It has average revenue of €10, average total cost of €8 and fixed costs of €200. What is the firm's:

a. profit?
b. marginal cost?
c. average variable-cost

Is the efficient scale of the firm more than, less than or exactly 100 units?

10 Suppose the book-printing industry is competitive and begins in long-run equilibrium.

a. Draw a diagram describing the typical firm in the industry.
b. Hi-Tech Printing Company invents a new process that sharply reduces the cost of printing books. What happens to Hi-Tech's profits and the price of books in the short run when Hi-Tech's patent prevents other firms from using the new technology?
c. What happens in the long run when the patent expires and other firms are free to use the technology?

PART 3
MARKETS, EFFICIENCY AND WELFARE

7 CONSUMERS, PRODUCERS AND THE EFFICIENCY OF MARKETS

Market systems help address the three questions all economies have to answer – what is to be produced, how goods and services are produced and who gets what is produced. Having described the way markets allocate scarce resources we now need to address the question of whether these market allocations are desirable. We know that the price of a good adjusts to ensure that the quantity of a good supplied equals the quantity demanded. But, at this equilibrium, is the quantity of the good produced and consumed too small, too large or just right? In this chapter we take up the topic of **welfare economics**, the study of how the allocation of resources affects economic well-being. Economists use the term well-being a good deal and have taken steps to define the term. A UK Treasury Economic Working Paper published in 2008 (Lepper, L. and McAndrew, S. (2008) *Developments in the Economics of Well-being.* Treasury Working Paper Number 4) highlighted two main definitions of economic well-being – subjective and objective well-being. **Subjective well-being** refers to the way in which people evaluate their own happiness. This includes how they feel about work, leisure and their response to the events which occur in their lives. **Objective well-being** refers to measures of the quality of life and uses indicators such as educational attainment, measures of the standard of living, life expectancy and so on. Welfare economics uses some of the microeconomic techniques we have already looked at to estimate **allocative efficiency** – a measure of the utility (satisfaction) derived from the allocation of resources. We have seen how buyers place a value on consumption in Chapter 5, reflected in their willingness to pay. Allocative efficiency occurs when the value of the output that firms produce (the benefits to sellers) matches the value placed on that output by consumers (the benefit to buyers). Of course, this analysis is also based on the assumptions that buyers prefer more to less and that they can rank their preferences. The model assumes that consumers' well-being is improved if they have more goods and their total utility increases.

This chapter will look at how market systems allocate resources such that the resulting outcomes are 'efficient'. This will provide the basis against which we introduce the notion of equity in later chapters. In other words, an outcome may be 'efficient' but to what extent is it fair?

> **welfare economics** the study of how the allocation of resources affects economic well-being
> **subjective well-being** the way in which people evaluate their own happiness
> **objective well-being** measures of the quality of life using specified indicators.
> **allocative efficiency** a resource allocation where the value of the output by sellers matches the value placed on that output by buyers

We begin this chapter by examining the benefits that buyers and sellers receive from taking part in a market. We then examine how society can make these benefits as large as possible. This analysis leads to the conclusion, accepting the assumptions which underlie the model of the market, that the equilibrium of supply and demand maximizes the total benefits received by buyers and sellers.

CONSUMER SURPLUS

We begin our study of welfare economics by looking at the benefits buyers receive from participating in a market.

Willingness to Pay

Imagine that you own an extremely rare, signed vintage electric guitar which you decide to sell. One way to do so is to hold an auction.

Four guitar collectors show up for your auction: Lisa, Paul, Claire and Leon. Each of them would like to own the guitar, but there is a limit to the amount that each is willing to pay for it. Table 7.1 shows the maximum price that each of the four possible buyers would pay. Each buyer's maximum is called their **willingness to pay**, and it measures how much that buyer values the good. Each buyer has their own value assigned to the guitar, which is expressed as the price they are willing to pay to own it. Each will have some upper limit above which they will not be prepared to pay (possibly because they don't feel the guitar is worth it above that upper limit or because they know they cannot afford to pay any more). If the price were below this upper limit then each would be eager to buy the guitar.

> **willingness to pay** the maximum amount that a buyer will pay for a good

TABLE 7.1 **Four Possible Buyers' Willingness to Pay**

Buyer	Willingness to pay (€)
Lisa	1000
Paul	800
Claire	700
Leon	500

To sell your guitar, you begin the bidding at a low price, say €100. Because all four buyers are willing to pay much more, the price rises quickly. The bidding stops when Lisa bids €801. At this point, Paul, Claire and Leon have dropped out of the bidding because they are unwilling to bid any more than €800. Lisa pays you €801 and gets the guitar. Note that the guitar has gone to the buyer who values it most highly.

What benefit does Lisa receive from buying the guitar? Lisa might argue that she has 'found a real bargain': she was willing to pay €1000 for the guitar but paid only €801 for it. Lisa valued the benefits from owning the guitar more highly than the money she has had to give up to own it. One way to express the value of these benefits is in monetary terms. We say that Lisa receives *consumer surplus*.

Consumer surplus is the amount a buyer is willing to pay for a good minus the amount the buyer actually pays for it. We refer to 'getting a bargain' regularly in everyday language. In economics, a bargain means paying much less for something than we expected or anticipated and as a result we get a greater degree of consumer surplus than we expected.

> **consumer surplus** a buyer's willingness to pay minus the amount the buyer actually pays

Consumer surplus measures the benefit to buyers of participating in a market. In this example, Lisa receives a €199 benefit from participating in the auction because she pays only €801 for a good she values at €1000. Paul, Claire and Leon get no consumer surplus from participating in the auction because they left without the guitar and without paying anything.

Now consider a different example. Suppose that you had two identical guitars to sell. Again, you auction them off to the four possible buyers. To keep things simple, we assume that both guitars are to be sold for the same price and that no buyer is interested in buying more than one guitar. Therefore, the price rises until two buyers are left.

In this case, the bidding stops when Lisa and Paul bid €701. At this price, Lisa and Paul are each happy to buy a guitar and Claire and Leon are not willing to bid any higher. Lisa and Paul each receive consumer surplus equal to their willingness to pay minus the price. Lisa's consumer surplus is €299 and Paul's is €99. Lisa's consumer surplus is higher now than it was previously, because she gets the same guitar but pays less for it. The total consumer surplus in the market is €398.

Using the Demand Curve to Measure Consumer Surplus

Consumer surplus is closely related to the demand curve for a product. To see how they are related, let's continue our example and consider the demand curve for guitars.

We begin by using the willingness to pay of the four possible buyers to find the demand schedule for the guitar. The graph in Figure 7.1 shows the demand schedule that corresponds to Table 7.1. If the price is above €1000, the quantity demanded in the market is 0, because no buyer is willing to pay that much. If the price is between €801 and €1000, the quantity demanded is 1, because only Lisa is willing to pay

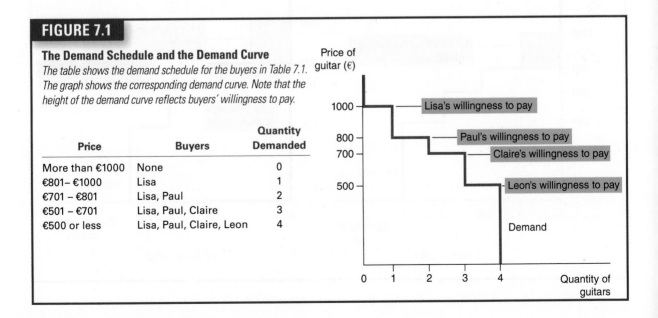

FIGURE 7.1

The Demand Schedule and the Demand Curve
The table shows the demand schedule for the buyers in Table 7.1. The graph shows the corresponding demand curve. Note that the height of the demand curve reflects buyers' willingness to pay.

Price	Buyers	Quantity Demanded
More than €1000	None	0
€801– €1000	Lisa	1
€701 – €801	Lisa, Paul	2
€501 – €701	Lisa, Paul, Claire	3
€500 or less	Lisa, Paul, Claire, Leon	4

such a high price. If the price is between €701 and €801, the quantity demanded is 2, because both Lisa and Paul are willing to pay the price. We can continue this analysis for other prices as well. In this way, the demand schedule is derived from the willingness to pay of the four possible buyers.

The graph in Figure 7.1 shows the demand curve that corresponds to this demand schedule. Note the relationship between the height of the demand curve and the buyers' willingness to pay. At any quantity, the price given by the demand curve shows the willingness to pay of the *marginal buyer*, the buyer who would leave the market first if the price were any higher. At a quantity of 4 guitars, for instance, the demand curve has a height of €500, the price that Leon (the marginal buyer) is willing to pay for a guitar. At a quantity of 3 guitars, the demand curve has a height of €700, the price that Claire (who is now the marginal buyer) is willing to pay.

Because the demand curve reflects buyers' willingness to pay, we can also use it to measure consumer surplus. Figure 7.2 uses the demand curve to compute consumer surplus in our example. In panel (a), the price is €801 and the quantity demanded is 1. Note that the area above the price and below the demand curve equals €199 (€1000 − 801 × 1). This amount is exactly the consumer surplus we computed earlier when only 1 guitar was sold.

Panel (b) of Figure 7.2 shows consumer surplus when the price is €701. In this case, the area above the price and below the demand curve equals the total area of the two rectangles: Lisa's consumer surplus at this price is €299 and Paul's is €99. This area equals a total of €398. Once again, this amount is the consumer surplus we computed earlier.

The area below the demand curve and above the price measures the consumer surplus in a market. The height of the demand curve multiplied by the quantity measures the value buyers place on the good, as represented by their willingness to pay for it. The difference between this willingness to pay and the market price is each buyer's consumer surplus. Thus, the total area below the demand curve and above the price is the sum of the consumer surplus of all buyers in the market for a good or service.

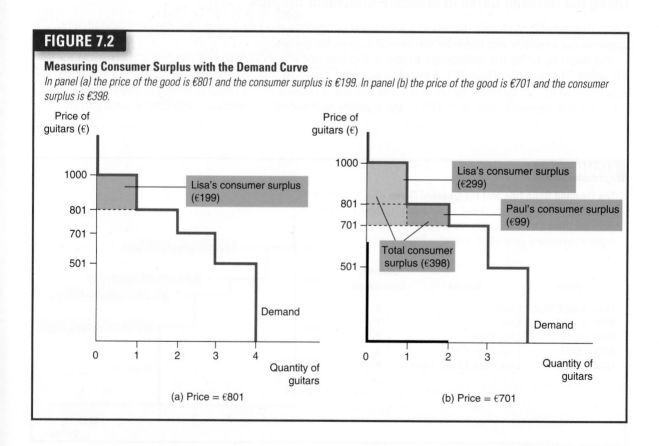

FIGURE 7.2

Measuring Consumer Surplus with the Demand Curve
In panel (a) the price of the good is €801 and the consumer surplus is €199. In panel (b) the price of the good is €701 and the consumer surplus is €398.

How a Lower Price Raises Consumer Surplus

The model we are using assumes buyers always want to pay less for the goods they buy and that a lower price makes them better off and improves their well-being. Figure 7.3 shows a typical downwards sloping demand curve. Although this demand curve appears somewhat different in shape from the step-like demand curves in our previous two figures, the ideas we have just developed apply nevertheless: consumer surplus is the area above the price and below the demand curve. In panel (a), consumer surplus at a price of P_1 is the area of triangle ABC.

FIGURE 7.3

How the Price Affects Consumer Surplus

In panel (a) the price is P_1, the quantity demanded is Q_1 and consumer surplus equals the area of the triangle ABC. When the price falls from P_1 to P_2 as in panel (b), the quantity demanded rises from Q_1 to Q_2 and the consumer surplus rises to the area of the triangle ADF. The increase in consumer surplus (area BCFD) occurs in part because existing consumers now pay less (area BCED) and in part because new consumers enter the market at the lower price (area CEF).

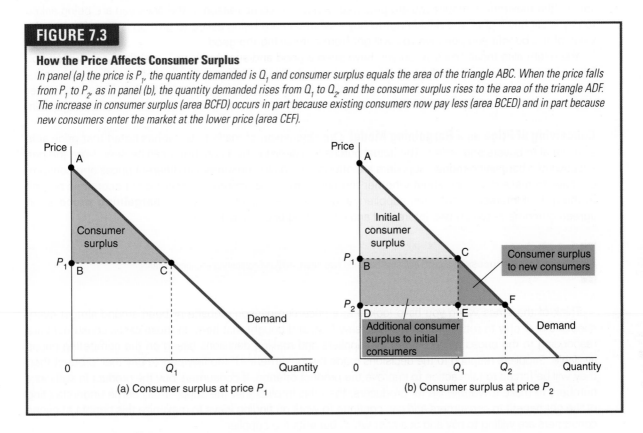

(a) Consumer surplus at price P_1 (b) Consumer surplus at price P_2

Now suppose that the price falls from P_1 to P_2, as shown in panel (b). The consumer surplus now equals area ADF. The increase in consumer surplus attributable to the lower price is the area BCFD.

This increase in consumer surplus is composed of two parts. First, those buyers who were already buying Q_1 of the good at the higher price P_1 are better off because they now pay less. The increase in consumer surplus of existing buyers is the reduction in the amount they pay; it equals the area of the rectangle BCED. Second, some new buyers enter the market because they are now willing to buy the good at the lower price. As a result, the quantity demanded in the market increases from Q_1 to Q_2. The consumer surplus these newcomers receive is the area of the triangle CEF.

What Does Consumer Surplus Measure?

Our goal in developing the concept of consumer surplus is to make normative judgements about the desirability of market outcomes. Imagine that you are a policymaker trying to design a good economic system. Given the assumptions made in our model, consumer surplus would be important to consider as it measures the net economic benefit in terms of surplus value that buyers receive from a good *as the buyers themselves perceive it*. The demand curve is a representation of the value of the economic benefit consumers get from consumption as measured by the price they have to pay to acquire the good;

it assumes that they can accurately determine their preferences themselves, the opportunity cost of the price they have to pay, and that their well-being is improved by more consumption. We assume that consumers (mostly unconsciously) weigh up the value to them of buying a good. Psychologists have shown that there are lots of different things going on when we make such choices apart from simply a rational weighing up of the costs and benefits as we saw in our discussion of heuristics in Chapter 5. As a consumer yourself, you will almost certainly be able to bring to mind instances where you have agonized over whether to buy something and if you were asked at that moment to describe your thinking you would no doubt be weighing up a variety of factors. If you are agonizing then you are operating right at this marginal value – the maximum amount you are prepared to pay. For some reason, if the price you are being asked to pay is slightly higher you decide not to buy – what you are being asked to give up is not offset by the value of the benefit you perceive you will get from purchasing the good.

You might also recall times when you have seen a good and snapped it up – you think to yourself you have a bargain. You now have the tools to understand why you experience that feeling of getting a bargain – it is because of the amount of consumer surplus you have gained from the purchase. Thus, consumer surplus provides one way in which we can measure the value of the benefits to consumers of consumption.

Conceiving of Price as a Bargaining Model Our discussion of markets so far has noted that price acts as a signal to buyers and sellers. The actual purchasing decision by a consumer can be seen from the perspective of a bargaining model. Suppliers are offering goods to consumers at different prices and consumers have to make decisions about whether the prices they are offered represent a net economic benefit to them. This interaction between suppliers and consumers can be seen as a **bargaining process**, an agreed outcome between two interested and competing economic agents.

> **bargaining process** an agreed outcome between two interested and competing economic agents

Think of the times when you have looked at a price comparison website or been around almost every shop in a mall only to return to the item you saw first, and bought that item. In these cases consumers are responding to the prices being offered by suppliers and making decisions based on the competing prices available. Suppliers respond to the decisions made by consumers – if too few people buy their product then they will be forced to take action to improve the product offering. If consumers buy the product in sufficient numbers to make it worthwhile for producers, then this implies that the supplier has some understanding of the net benefit to consumers and can continue to work on finding ways to maximize this benefit at prices consumers are willing to pay and at a cost which benefits the supplier.

Is Consumer Surplus Always a Good Measure of Economic Well-Being?

In some circumstances, policymakers might choose not to care about consumer surplus because they do not respect the preferences that drive buyer behaviour. For example, drug addicts are willing to pay a high price for heroin. Yet we would not say that addicts get a large benefit from being able to buy heroin at a low price (even though addicts might say they do). From the standpoint of society, willingness to pay, in this instance, is not a good measure of the buyers' benefit, and consumer surplus is not a good measure of economic well-being, because addicts are not looking after their long-term welfare.

The use of the word 'good' to describe products has not just arisen as a result of chance. A product described as a 'good' implies that consumption of it confers positive benefits on consumers. Products like non-medicinal drugs, tobacco and alcohol might be better described as 'bads' rather than 'goods' because they confer negative benefits to the consumer such as a deterioration in long-term physical and mental health – even though many consumers of these goods would claim that they enjoy and therefore benefit from consuming them.

In many markets, however, consumer surplus does reflect economic well-being. The underlying assumption to this is that we are presuming that buyers are rational when they make decisions and that their preferences should be respected. In this case, consumers are the best judges of how much benefit they receive from the goods they buy. As we have seen, this assumption is open to some debate. In addition it must be noted that an assumption made in the analysis so far is that one person's value of an extra unit of a euro is the same as someone else's. For example, if the price of a guitar in an auction rose by €1 from €750 to €751, do Paul and Lisa place the same value on that extra euro? In this analysis we are assuming they are but in reality this may not be the case; an additional euro to a very wealthy person may not be valued the same as an additional euro to a very poor person.

As with many things in economics, we are attempting to introduce some basic principles of the subject but, as you progress through your studies to intermediate and advanced levels, you will find that the simplified assumptions that are made can be challenged and new, more sophisticated understandings begin to emerge.

SELF TEST Think about an occasion when you have used an auction website such as eBay. If you won the auction, how much consumer surplus did you gain? If you dropped out of an auction, what were the factors which determined your decision? If you just missed out on a bid, would you have been prepared to pay a little more in hindsight? What does this tell you about your willingness to pay?

CASE STUDY **Consumer Surplus**

There is a very high chance that if you are reading this, you possess a smartphone and use it to access a variety of apps and internet services. If you do indeed own a smartphone, how valuable is it to you? Looking around the typical everyday environment, an onlooker might be tempted to say that smartphones are extremely valuable to users given the number of people who walk around focused on whatever their smartphone is communicating to them. Many smartphone owners are likely to have paid a relatively low price for the device itself and in many cases, the device comes at no price at all on agreeing a contract with a network provider. If asked to pay for the smartphone or pay a higher price for a new version of a device, many users look elsewhere – in other words, the willingness to pay for the device is relatively low and it might be concluded from this that the consumer surplus of a smartphone itself is also relatively low. This seems to be a counter-intuitive conclusion given the ubiquitous nature of the smartphone (it is estimated that there are some 2 billion smartphone owners across the world).

One reason may be because there are a relatively large number of substitutes in the market which tends to increase the price elasticity of demand for smartphones. The main reason may be because the device itself is simply a means of accessing what is really valuable, i.e. the services it enables the user to access. Communicating with friends through a wide range of social media applications, streaming, downloading files, sharing images and accessing the Internet may all be the 'product' that is really of value and provides considerable consumer surplus. Many people will think of these services as being 'free' – the use of Facebook, Twitter, Instagram and Spotify for example, do not require payment of any subscription or fee. If the amount of time spent using these services is a measure of value put on them by consumers, it can be concluded that consumer surplus from the use of internet services is relatively high. Indeed, two economists, Austan Goolsbee and Peter Klenow, have looked at this issue and estimate that it could be as high as two per cent of full income (defined as income from wages and the value placed on leisure time).

What are the real benefits of using smartphones?

PRODUCER SURPLUS

We now consider the benefits sellers receive from participating in a market. As you will see, our analysis of sellers' welfare is similar to our analysis of buyers' welfare.

Cost and the Willingness to Sell

Imagine that you own a house and need to get it painted externally. Four sellers of house painting services, Millie, Georgia, Julie and Nana are each willing to do the work for you if the price is right. You decide to take bids from the four painters and auction off the job to the painter who will do the work for the lowest price (assuming the quality each painter provides is the same).

Each painter is willing to take the job if the price she would receive exceeds her **cost** of doing the work. Here the term cost should be interpreted as the painter's opportunity cost: it includes the painter's out-of-pocket expenses (for paint, brushes and so on) as well as the value that the painter places on her own time. Table 7.2 shows each painter's cost. Because a painter's cost is the lowest price she would accept for her work, cost is a measure of her willingness to sell her services. Each painter would be eager to sell her services at a price greater than her cost, would refuse to sell her services at a price less than her cost, and would be indifferent about selling her services at a price exactly equal to her cost.

cost the value of everything a seller must give up to produce a good

TABLE 7.2   **The Costs of Four Possible Sellers**

Seller	Cost (€)
Millie	900
Julie	800
Georgia	600
Nana	500

When you take bids from the painters, the price might start off high, but it quickly falls as the painters compete for the job. Once Nana has bid slightly less than €600, she is the sole remaining bidder. Nana is willing to do the job for this price, because her cost is only €500. Millie, Georgia and Julie are unwilling to do the job for less than €600. What benefit does Nana receive from getting the job? Because she is willing to do the work for €500 but gets €599.99 for doing it, we say that she receives *producer surplus* of €99.99. **Producer surplus** is the amount a seller is paid minus the cost of production. Producer surplus measures the benefit to sellers of participating in a market.

producer surplus the amount a seller is paid for a good minus the seller's cost

Now suppose that you have two houses that need painting. Again, you auction off the jobs to the four painters. To keep things simple, let's assume that no painter is able to paint both houses and that you will pay the same amount to paint each house. Therefore, the price falls until two painters are left.

In this case, the bidding stops when Georgia and Nana each offer to do the job for a price slightly less than €800 (€799.99). At this price, Georgia and Nana are willing to do the work, and Millie and Julie are not willing to bid a lower price. At a price of €799.99, Nana receives producer surplus of €299.99, and Georgia receives producer surplus of €199.99. The total producer surplus in the market is €499.98.

Using the Supply Curve to Measure Producer Surplus

We begin by using the costs of the four painters to find the supply schedule for painting services. The table in Figure 7.4 shows the supply schedule that corresponds to the costs in Table 7.2. If the price is below €500, none of the four painters is willing to do the job, so the quantity supplied is zero. If the price is between €500 and €599.99, only Nana is willing to do the job, so the quantity supplied is 1. If the price is between €600 and €799.99, Nana and Georgia are willing to do the job, so the quantity supplied is 2, and so on. Thus, the supply schedule is derived from the costs of the four painters.

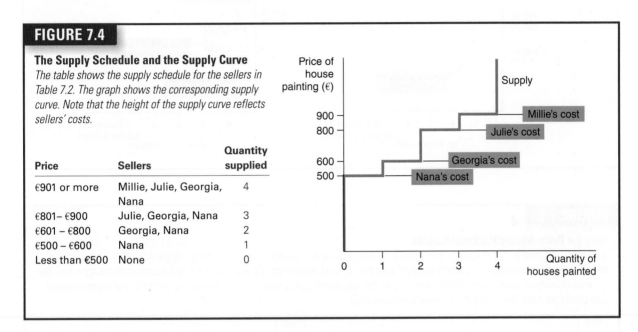

FIGURE 7.4

The Supply Schedule and the Supply Curve
The table shows the supply schedule for the sellers in Table 7.2. The graph shows the corresponding supply curve. Note that the height of the supply curve reflects sellers' costs.

Price	Sellers	Quantity supplied
€901 or more	Millie, Julie, Georgia, Nana	4
€801– €900	Julie, Georgia, Nana	3
€601 – €800	Georgia, Nana	2
€500 – €600	Nana	1
Less than €500	None	0

The graph in Figure 7.4 shows the supply curve that corresponds to this supply schedule. Note that the height of the supply curve is related to the sellers' costs. At any quantity, the price given by the supply curve shows the cost of the *marginal seller,* the seller who would leave the market first if the price were any lower. At a quantity of 4 houses, for instance, the supply curve has a height of €900, the cost that Millie (the marginal seller) incurs to provide her painting services. At a quantity of 3 houses, the supply curve has a height of €800, the cost that Julie (who is now the marginal seller) incurs.

Because the supply curve reflects sellers' costs, we can use it to measure producer surplus. Figure 7.5 uses the supply curve to compute producer surplus in our example. In panel (a) we assume that the price is €599.99. In this case, the quantity supplied is 1. Note that the area below the price and above the supply curve equals €99.99. This is Nana's producer surplus.

Panel (b) of Figure 7.5 shows producer surplus at a price of €799.99. In this case, the area below the price and above the supply curve equals the total area of the two rectangles. This area equals €499.98, the producer surplus we computed earlier for Georgia and Nana when two houses needed painting.

The lesson from this example applies to all supply curves: the area below the price and above the supply curve measures the producer surplus in a market. The logic is straightforward: the height of the supply curve measures sellers' costs, and the difference between the price and the cost of production is each seller's producer surplus. When multiplied by the quantity, the total area is the sum of the producer surplus of all sellers.

How a Higher Price Raises Producer Surplus

The concept of producer surplus offers an insight to the increase in well-being of a producer in response to a higher price.

Figure 7.6 shows a typical upwards sloping supply curve. Even though this supply curve differs in shape from the step-like supply curves in the previous figure, we measure producer surplus in the same way:

FIGURE 7.5

Measuring Producer Surplus with the Supply Curve

In panel (a) the price of the good is €599.99 and the producer surplus is €99.99. In panel (b) the price of the good is €799.99 and the producer surplus is €499.99.

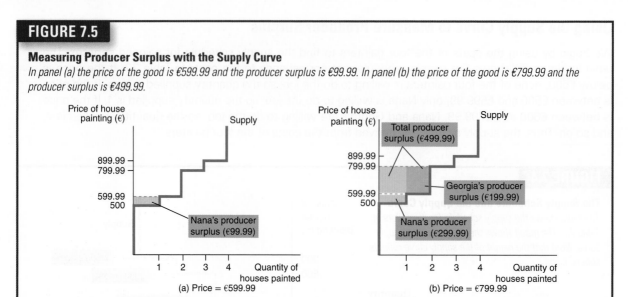

(a) Price = €599.99

(b) Price = €799.99

FIGURE 7.6

How the Price Affects Producer Surplus

In panel (a) the price is P_1, the quantity demanded is Q_1 and producer surplus equals the area of the triangle ABC. When the price rises from P_1 to P_2 as in panel (b), the quantity supplied rises from Q_1 to Q_2 and the producer surplus rises to the area of the triangle ADF. The increase in producer surplus (area BCFD) occurs in part because existing producers now receive more (area BCED) and in part because new producers enter the market at the higher price (area CEF).

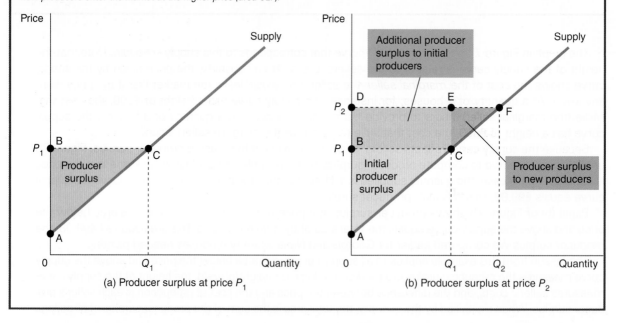

(a) Producer surplus at price P_1

(b) Producer surplus at price P_2

producer surplus is the area below the price and above the supply curve. In panel (a), the price is P_1 and producer surplus is the area of triangle ABC.

Panel (b) shows what happens when the price rises from P_1 to P_2. Producer surplus now equals area ADF. This increase in producer surplus has two parts. First, those sellers who were already selling Q_1 of the good at the lower price P_1 are better off because they now get more producer surplus for what they sell. The increase in producer surplus for existing sellers equals the area of the rectangle BCED. Second, some new sellers enter the market because they are now willing to produce the good at the higher price, resulting in an increase in the quantity supplied from Q_1 to Q_2. The producer surplus of these newcomers is the area of the triangle CEF.

SELF TEST Is producer surplus the same as profit? Explain.

MARKET EFFICIENCY

In economies throughout the world, there are trades made every day – millions of them. As part of our analysis of free markets we make many assumptions. For example, we assume that if an individual gives up €25 to buy a pair of jeans, the value of the economic benefit that individual gains is at the very least equal to the price paid but may include some consumer surplus if they were prepared to pay more than €25 to buy those jeans. Equally, we are assuming that the seller must value the sale to the consumer at the very least at €25 or they would not have sold the jeans and indeed may be getting some producer surplus from the sale.

Can we conclude, therefore, that the allocative outcome in a free market is efficient? To do this we have to define efficiency in this context.

Consumer and producer surplus provide a way in which we can measure the benefits to consumers and producers of trading. Recall that in Chapter 5, the consumer optimum was defined as the point where the marginal rate of substitution of an extra euro spent equalled the marginal utility of that extra euro. In Chapter 6, the optimum for a profit-maximizing producer was defined as the point where the marginal cost of an extra unit produced equalled the marginal revenue of an extra unit. In both cases we have noted that there will be incentives for firms and consumers to change their behaviour if they are at any point other than their respective equilibriums.

We have also noted that Adam Smith's theory of the invisible hand suggests that millions of independent decision makers, both consumers and producers, all go about their business but market forces lead to a degree of coherence between these decisions. In theory, free market economies will not tend to have instances where there are vast shortages and surpluses for long periods of time because there will be incentives for producers and consumers to change their behaviour which moves the market to equilibrium.

This analysis is the basis for what is called general equilibrium. General equilibrium is the notion that the decisions and choices of economic agents are coordinated across markets. General equilibrium encapsulates the idea that the market mechanism leads to outcomes that are efficient. Consumers are maximizing utility and producers are maximizing profits and producing at minimum average cost.

We are going to look at the notion of economic efficiency in relation to the analysis of consumer and producer surplus presented so far.

Economic Efficiency and Waste

If we were to look at efficiency as a general concept we would be likely to introduce the word 'waste'; if something is inefficient it is wasteful. To the consumer, spending money on a good which does not provide value can be considered a waste. Equally, if a producer spends money on producing a good which consumers do not want to buy, or could reorganize a combination of factors differently to reduce costs, then that also represents waste.

We can ask the question, therefore, are free markets wasteful? If waste existed then there would be a way to reallocate resources to reduce that waste – consumers would adjust their buying habits and producers their production methods. Consumer surplus is the benefit that buyers receive from participating in a market, and producer surplus is the benefit that sellers receive. At any point on the demand curve, therefore, the price represents the value placed on the good by consumers on the last unit consumed, whereas any point on the supply curve represents the additional cost to a producer in the market of producing one more unit. At any point we can also measure the consumer and producer surplus that exists. If at this particular price the quantity demanded is higher than the quantity supplied it tells us that the value placed on the additional unit by consumers is higher than the additional cost to the producer. In market equilibrium, therefore, the value of the additional unit to buyers is the same as the additional cost to producers. We can look at the consumer and producer surplus at equilibrium and add these together to get a measure of the **total surplus**. If the consumer surplus is a measure of the consumer's well-being and producer surplus is a measure of the seller's well-being, then total surplus can be used as a measure of society's economic well-being. We can summarize this as:

Total surplus = Value to buyers − Cost to sellers

total surplus the total value to buyers of the goods, as measured by their willingness to pay, minus the cost to sellers of providing those goods

If an allocation of resources maximizes total surplus, we say that the allocation exhibits **efficiency**. If an allocation is not efficient, then some of the gains from trade among buyers and sellers are not being realized. For example, an allocation is inefficient if a good is not being produced by the sellers with lowest cost. In this case, moving production from a high-cost producer to a low-cost producer will lower the total cost to sellers and raise total surplus. Similarly, an allocation is inefficient if a good is not being consumed by the buyers who value it most highly. In this case, moving consumption of the good from a buyer with a low valuation to a buyer with a high valuation will raise total surplus. In Chapter 1, we defined *efficiency* as 'the property of society getting the most it can from its scarce resources'. Now that we have the concept of total surplus, we can be more precise about what we mean by 'getting the most it can'. In this context, society will be getting the most it can from its scarce resources if it allocates them so as to maximize total surplus.

efficiency the property of a resource allocation of maximizing the total surplus received by all members of society

Figure 7.7 shows consumer and producer surplus when a market reaches the equilibrium of supply and demand. Recall that consumer surplus equals the area above the price and under the demand curve and producer surplus equals the area below the price and above the supply curve. Thus, the total area between the supply and demand curves up to the point of equilibrium represents the total surplus in this market.

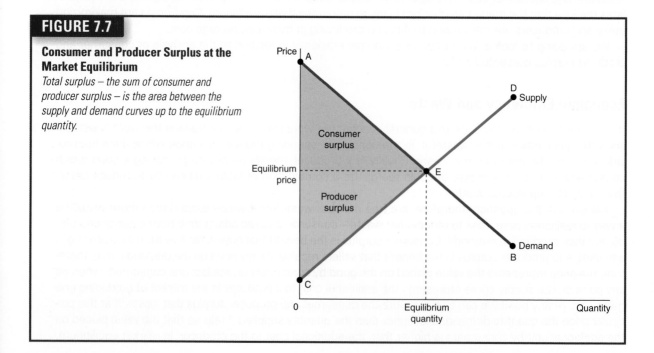

FIGURE 7.7

Consumer and Producer Surplus at the Market Equilibrium

Total surplus – the sum of consumer and producer surplus – is the area between the supply and demand curves up to the equilibrium quantity.

Pareto Efficiency At this point we introduce the concept of Pareto efficiency. The idea was developed by an Italian economist, Wilfredo Pareto (1848–1923). Pareto efficiency occurs if it is not possible to reallocate resources in such a way as to make one person better off without making anyone else worse off. Markets are all about trading and, as we have seen, the demand curve tells us something about the benefit consumers receive from allocating their income in a particular way, and the supply curve tells us something about the benefit to suppliers of offering goods for sale. When trades take place, the consumer gains some benefit and so does the producer and this is referred to as a **Pareto improvement**. A Pareto improvement occurs when an action makes at least one economic agent better off without harming another economic agent. Consumers and producers, therefore, will continue to readjust their decision-making with the resulting reallocation of resources until there are no further Pareto improvements. We can view economic efficiency, therefore, in terms of the point where all possible Pareto improvements have been exhausted.

Pareto improvement when an action makes at least one economic agent better off without harming another economic agent

Evaluating the Market Equilibrium

We have noted that total surplus is maximized at the point where the market is in equilibrium – an allocation of resources where consumers are maximizing utility and producers maximizing profits and producing at minimum average cost. Is it possible to reallocate resources in any other way to increase the well-being of consumers and producers, in other words, are there Pareto improvements that would result from any such resource allocations?

The price determines which buyers and sellers participate in the market. Those buyers who value the good more than the price (represented by the segment AE on the demand curve in Figure 7.7) choose to buy the good; those buyers who value it less than the price (represented by the segment EB) do not. Similarly, those sellers whose costs are less than the price (represented by the segment CE on the supply curve) choose to produce and sell the good; those sellers whose costs are greater than the price (represented by the segment ED) do not.

These observations lead to two insights about market outcomes based on the assumptions of the model:

1. Free markets allocate the supply of goods to the buyers who value them most highly, as measured by their willingness to pay
2. Free markets allocate the demand for goods to the sellers who can produce them at least cost

Thus, given the quantity produced and sold in market equilibrium, economic well-being cannot be increased by consumers or producers changing their respective allocations.

We can also identify a third insight about market outcomes:

3. Free markets produce the quantity of goods that maximizes the sum of consumer and producer surplus

To see why this is true, consider Figure 7.8. Recall that the demand curve reflects the value to buyers and that the supply curve reflects the cost to sellers. At quantities below the equilibrium level, the value to buyers exceeds the cost to sellers. In this region, increasing the quantity raises total surplus, and it continues to do so until the quantity reaches the equilibrium level. Beyond the equilibrium quantity, however, the value to buyers is less than the cost to sellers. Producing more than the equilibrium quantity would, therefore, lower total surplus.

These three insights about market outcomes tell us that the equilibrium outcome is an efficient allocation of resources given the assumptions of the model. This conclusion explains why some economists advocate free markets as a preferred way to organize economic activity.

SELF TEST Look back at the section on consumer optimum from Chapter 5 and on producer equilibrium from Chapter 6. How might you explain the relationship between these equilibrium points and market equilibrium in terms of economic efficiency?

FIGURE 7.8

The Efficiency of the Equilibrium Quantity
At quantities less than the equilibrium quantity, the value to buyers exceeds the cost to sellers. At quantities greater than the equilibrium quantity, the cost to sellers exceeds the value to buyers. Therefore, the market equilibrium maximizes the sum of producer and consumer surplus.

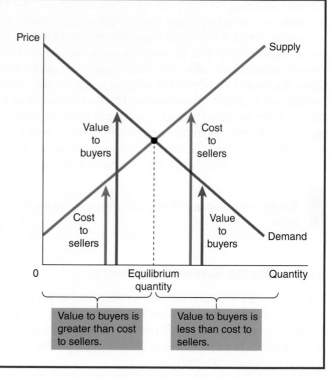

Efficiency and Equity

Much of this chapter has focused on efficiency. It is not surprising that there is a great deal of focus on efficiency in economics because it is something that can be measured and is quantifiable. Efficiency is a positive concept in that it can be stated *what is* an efficient allocation. This does not, however, tell us anything about whether the efficient allocation is desirable or not.

We also have to consider whether an allocation is fair and this is a normative concept. One way of looking at fairness in economic allocations is to consider equity – the property of distributing economic prosperity fairly among the members of society. In essence, the gains from trade in a market are like a cake to be distributed among the market participants. The question of efficiency is whether the cake is as big as possible. The question of equity is whether the cake is divided fairly and, as noted in Chapter 1, can involve trade-offs in decision-making. Evaluating the equity of a market outcome is more difficult than evaluating the efficiency. Whereas efficiency is an objective goal that can be judged on strictly positive grounds, equity involves normative judgements that go beyond economics and enter into the realm of political philosophy.

One of the problems with the analysis we have presented is an assumption that economic agents are all similar – that consumers and producers are a heterogeneous group. Clearly this is not the case. One of the most important things economists have to consider is the different way that people with different income endowments and economic power behave. The marginal utility gained from spending an extra unit of income for a very poor person is likely to be very different to that of a rich person, for example. Looking at well-being simply from the perspective of adding up the consumer and producer surpluses masks more complex issues.

Some economists point to the collective utility of society which is reflected by consumer and producer surplus in terms of a **social welfare function**. Social welfare functions attempt to take into account the fact that the marginal utilities of individual households are not all the same and indeed that their preferences are also different. This is based on the assumption that welfare is an ordinal function, i.e. that consumers can rank preferences. However, it is also assumed that households operate with imperfect knowledge. Decisions in the market may be made by those who have some power which can distort market outcomes. For example, the spending power of the rich or those with political influence can mean that market outcomes are disproportionately skewed. The outcome may be efficient but it is not necessarily fair.

> **social welfare function** the collective utility of society which is reflected by consumer and producer surplus

We must take into account, therefore, that different stakeholders will have different perspectives based on personal and shared belief systems on what is 'good' for society as a whole. One example of these different perspectives, which are referred to as social states, is in relation to income – would you rather have a society that focused on raising total income regardless of how it was distributed, i.e. that a small number of people owned a considerable portion of this income, or a social state where income was more evenly distributed among its citizens?

In the next chapters we begin to look at how these issues take on more relevance when governments get involved in free markets by affecting market outcomes to improve them. Clearly, if a government says it is adopting policies to try and improve market outcomes we are in the realm of normative economics and looking at *what should* be a market outcome rather than *what is*.

This chapter has introduced the basic tools of welfare economics – consumer and producer surplus – and used them to evaluate the meaning of efficiency in the free market model based on all its assumptions. We showed that in this model, market equilibrium maximizes the total benefits to buyers and sellers. A market outcome may be identified as efficient but it does not follow that this particular outcome is fair.

IN THE NEWS

Well-Being

Welfare economics has been a sub-topic in the discipline since the 19th century but exactly how we measure well-being is something that has been repeatedly visited and refined over the years. In the UK, the ONS established the Measuring National Well-being programme in 2010 and in 2015 published the third annual report on Life in the UK (see http://www.ons.gov. uk/ons/dcp171766_398059.pdf).

Measuring National Well-being: Life in the UK, 2015

The Financial Crisis of 2007–9 and subsequent recession hit many businesses and individuals in the UK. Real wages had been falling for some years and unemployment had risen as the economy shrank. By 2015, however, there were signs that the economy was recovering and real wages began to increase, unemployment fell and economic growth was stronger. The 2015 report on annual well-being in the UK continued to look at measures of well-being –which included health, where people live, what they do, and their relationships – and to report on how these measures have changed over time. In total 43 measures were reviewed including such things as how we use our leisure time and how safe we feel walking alone after dark.

The 2015 publication noted that compared to the last report, 14 of these measures had improved, 18 had shown no overall change, two had got worse and nine were not subject to assessment for the 2015 report. Over a three-year period, 12 measures had improved, ten showed no change, eight had got worse and 13 were not assessed. Measures not assessed may be because there was insufficient data to make a comparison or where there was no clarity on the direction of change.

One of the important findings in the report was that the overall economic 'cake' has increased but that the disposable income generated was not increasing in the same way. Despite this, more people reported feeling positive about life compared to 2012, which given the improvement in the economy is perhaps not surprising. Life expectancy

(Continued)

Healthy lifestyle choices can improve overall well-being but low income families may face significant disadvantages in making appropriate choices.

is increasing but almost a third of people in the survey expressed concerns about health with almost 20 per cent reporting a long-term illness or disability which affected their lives. Those on higher incomes tend to make better lifestyle choices such as not smoking, eating a healthier diet and taking exercise. Overall, however, over half of those surveyed (almost 52 per cent) did not engage in 'moderate intensity sport' for 30 minutes or more on a regular basis. The number of people living in relative poverty (defined where household income is less than 60 per cent of median income after housing costs) has not changed since 2010.

Questions

1 Consumer surplus and producer surplus can be used as a measure of well-being but given the article, how comprehensive and valuable a measure do you think this is?

2 Consumer and producer surplus provide measures which are positive; the measures reported by the ONS are gathered through a survey and in some cases reports people's self-perceptions with regard to some of the measures used. Which do you think an economist should place more reliance on and why?

3 What explanations might there be for the observation by the report that overall production in the UK has risen but disposable incomes have not increased in the same way?

4 Consider the ONS' approach of asking people to respond to questions through a scale, from 'completely satisfied' to 'completely dissatisfied'. What sort of scale is this and why might it present problems in interpreting people's responses?

5 Do you think economists should focus on measuring efficiency, which is a positive concept, and pay less attention to equity, which is a normative concept? How might research like the ONS 'Life in the UK, 2015' survey help in the analysis of well-being?

Source: http://webarchive.nationalarchives.gov.uk/20160105160709/http://www.ons.gov.uk/ons/dcp171766_398059.pdf

SUMMARY

- Consumer surplus equals buyers' willingness to pay for a good minus the amount they actually pay for it, and it measures the benefit buyers get from participating in a market. Consumer surplus can be computed by finding the area below the demand curve and above the price.

- Producer surplus equals the amount sellers receive for their goods minus their costs of production, and it measures the benefit sellers get from participating in a market. Producer surplus can be computed by finding the area below the price and above the supply curve.

- An allocation of resources that maximizes the sum of consumer and producer surplus is said to be efficient. Policymakers are often concerned with the efficiency, as well as the equity, of economic outcomes.

- The equilibrium of supply and demand maximizes the sum of consumer and producer surplus. That is, the invisible hand of the marketplace leads buyers and sellers to allocate resources efficiently.

QUESTIONS FOR REVIEW

1 What is meant by the term 'allocative efficiency'?

2 What is welfare economics?

3 Explain how buyers' willingness to pay, consumer surplus and the demand curve are related.

4 Explain how sellers' costs, producer surplus and the supply curve are related.

5 Prepare a supply-and-demand diagram, showing producer and consumer surplus at the market equilibrium.

6 What is efficiency and how might we measure it?

7 Using the supply-and-demand diagram you drew for Question 5, assume that the demand shifts to the right as a result of an increase in incomes. On the diagram, show how consumer surplus and producer surplus changes as a result of the shift in demand. Is total surplus increased, decreased or does it stay the same? What would the outcome depend on?

8 What is meant by a Pareto efficient outcome?

9 Why are issues relating to efficiency classed as positive? What are the normative issues we might want to be concerned with?

10 When the tickets for the Glastonbury Festival go on sale, the demand exceeds supply by a considerable margin. Many people who are willing to pay the price for tickets are excluded from the market. Explain how charging a higher price for tickets for the Glastonbury Festival would lead to a more efficient market allocation. Would this also be an equitable market allocation? Explain.

PROBLEMS AND APPLICATIONS

1 How would you define the concept of *welfare*? If well-being is about happiness and satisfaction with life, how would you, as an economist, go about trying to define and quantify happiness and satisfaction with life? Is it possible to do so?

2 An early freeze in Normandy ruins half of the apple harvest. What happens to consumer surplus in the market for apples? What happens to consumer surplus in the market for cider? Illustrate your answers with diagrams.

3 Suppose the demand for French bread rises. What happens to producer surplus in the market for French bread? What happens to producer surplus in the market for flour? Illustrate your answers with diagrams.

4 It is a hot day, and Günter is thirsty. Here is the value, in money terms, he places on a bottle of water:

Value of first bottle	€7
Value of second bottle	€5
Value of third bottle	€3
Value of fourth bottle	€1

a. From this information, derive Günter's demand schedule. Graph his demand curve for bottled water.

b. If the price of a bottle of water is €4, how many bottles does Günter buy? How much consumer surplus does Günter get from his purchases? Show Günter's consumer surplus on your graph.

c. If the price falls to €2, how does quantity demanded change? How does Günter's consumer surplus change? Show these changes on your graph.

5 Maria owns a water pump. Because pumping large amounts of water is harder than pumping small amounts, the cost of producing a bottle of water rises as she pumps more. Here is the cost she incurs to produce each bottle of water:

Cost of first bottle	€1
Cost of second bottle	€3
Cost of third bottle	€5
Cost of fourth bottle	€7

a. From this information, derive Maria's supply schedule. Graph her supply curve for bottled water.

b. If the price of a bottle of water is €4, how many bottles does Maria produce and sell? How much producer surplus does Maria get from these sales? Show Maria's producer surplus on your graph.

c. If the price rises to €6, how does quantity supplied change? How does Maria's producer surplus change? Show these changes in your graph.

6 Consider a market in which Günter from Problem 4 is the buyer and Maria from Problem 5 is the seller.

a. Use Maria's supply schedule and Günter's demand schedule to find the quantity supplied and quantity demanded at prices of €2, €4 and €6. Which of these prices brings supply and demand into equilibrium?
b. What are consumer surplus, producer surplus and total surplus in this equilibrium?
c. If Maria produced and Günter consumed one fewer bottle of water, what would happen to total surplus?
d. If Maria produced and Günter consumed one additional bottle of water, what would happen to total surplus?

7 Why might we want to think about market price as the outcome of a bargaining model?

8 The cost of producing smartphones has fallen over the past few years

a. Use a supply-and-demand diagram to show the effect of falling production costs on the price and quantity of smartphones sold.
b. In your diagram, show what happens to consumer surplus and producer surplus.
c. Suppose the supply of smartphones is very price elastic. Who benefits most from falling production costs – consumers or producers of smartphones?

9 Four consumers are willing to pay the following amounts for haircuts:

Hans:	Juan:	Peter:	Marcel:
€7	€2	€8	€5

There are four haircutting businesses with the following costs:

Firm A:	Firm B:	Firm C:	Firm D:
€3	€6	€4	€2

Each firm has the capacity to produce only one haircut. For efficiency, how many haircuts should be given? Which businesses should cut hair, and which consumers should have their hair cut? How large is the maximum possible total surplus?

10 Suppose a technological advance reduces the cost of making tablet devices.

a. Use a supply and demand diagram to show what happens to price, quantity, consumer surplus and producer surplus in the market for tablet devices.
b. Tablet devices and laptops are substitutes. Use a supply-and-demand diagram to show what happens to price, quantity, consumer surplus and producer surplus in the market for laptops. Should laptop producers be happy or sad about the technological advance in tablet devices?
c. Tablet devices and apps are complements. Use a supply-and-demand diagram to show what happens to price, quantity, consumer surplus and producer surplus in the market for apps. Should app producers be happy or sad about the technological advance in tablet devices?

8 SUPPLY, DEMAND AND GOVERNMENT POLICIES

We have seen that, under certain assumptions, markets can generate outcomes which are efficient. In the last chapter we introduced the idea that whilst market outcomes can be efficient they are not always fair. For this reason, and based on political belief systems and political influence, governments will seek to influence market outcomes.

We begin by considering policies that directly control prices which are usually enacted when policymakers believe that the market price of a good or service is unfair to buyers or sellers. We will then consider the impact of taxes and subsidies. Policymakers use taxes and subsidies to influence market outcomes and, in the case of taxes, to raise revenue for public purposes.

CONTROLS ON PRICES

We will look at two policies to control prices – price ceilings and price floors. These policies may be introduced by a government or a regulatory body but in some cases might also be set by a business. For example, prices are often set by sports and entertainment bodies which have similar results to legal price controls.

A **price ceiling** or a price cap is a legal maximum on the price at which a good can be sold. A **price floor** is the exact opposite – a minimum price that producers can charge for a good; producers are not allowed to charge a price any lower than this legal minimum.

> **price ceiling** a legal maximum on the price at which a good can be sold
> **price floor** a legal minimum on the price at which a good can be sold

To see how price controls affect market outcomes, we will look at an example which has interested economists for many years – rent control. If rental space for residential occupation (we will define this in terms of square metres) is sold in a competitive market free of government regulation, it is assumed that the price of housing adjusts to balance supply and demand: at the equilibrium price, the quantity of housing that buyers want to buy exactly equals the quantity that sellers want to sell.

To be concrete, suppose the equilibrium price is €30 per m². Not everyone may be happy with the outcome of this free market process. People looking for homes might complain that the €30 per m² is too expensive. Landlords, on the other hand, might complain that €30 per m² is too low and is depressing their incomes. House seekers and landlords lobby the government to pass laws that alter the market outcome by directly controlling the price of rental accommodation. If those seeking rental accommodation are successful in their lobbying, the government imposes a legal maximum on the price at which rental accommodation can be sold. Our model of the market allows us to make some predictions about what the effects of such a policy might be.

How Price Ceilings Affect Market Outcomes

When a price ceiling is imposed, two outcomes are possible. In panel (a) of Figure 8.1, the government imposes a price ceiling of €40 per m². In this case, because the price that balances supply and demand (€30 per m²) is below the ceiling, the price ceiling is *not binding*. The price in the market will level out at the equilibrium price of €30 per m², and the price ceiling has no long term effect on the price or the quantity sold.

FIGURE 8.1

A Market with a Price Ceiling

In panel (a), the government imposes a price ceiling of €40 per m². Because the price ceiling is above the equilibrium price of €30 per m², the price ceiling has no effect, and the market can reach the equilibrium of supply and demand. In this equilibrium, quantity supplied and quantity demanded both equal 5 million square feet. In panel (b), the government imposes a price ceiling of €20 per m². Because the price ceiling is below the equilibrium price of €30 per m², the market price equals €20 per m². At this price, 6 million square feet is demanded and only 4 million square feet is supplied, so there is a shortage of 2 million square feet.

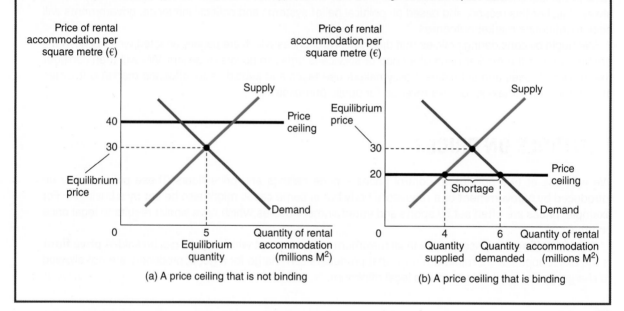

(a) A price ceiling that is not binding

(b) A price ceiling that is binding

In panel (b) of Figure 8.1, the government imposes a price ceiling of €20 per m². Because the equilibrium price of €30 per m² is above the price ceiling, the ceiling is a *binding constraint* on the market. Given this binding limit on price, incentives change. Some landlords will not find it profitable to rent out property at this price and remove the property from the market. For buyers, the lower price of rental accommodation means the sacrifice they have to make is less in terms of alternatives foregone and so the demand for rental accommodation increases at the binding price. At €20 per m², the quantity of rental accommodation demanded (6 million square metres in Figure 8.1) exceeds the quantity supplied (4 million square metres). There is a shortage of rental accommodation, so some people who want to rent accommodation at the going price are unable to.

When a shortage of rental accommodation develops because of this price ceiling, some mechanism for rationing accommodation will develop. The mechanism could simply be long queues or it is possible that an underground economy (sometimes referred to as a black market) can develop where those that are prepared to pay above the price ceiling rent, find a way of securing accommodation. This outcome is possible but also illegal, although there are often ways to 'dress up' a black market solution to make it harder for the authorities to catch and prosecute those taking part in the practice. Sellers could decide to ration accommodation according to their own personal biases, selling it only to friends, relatives, or members of their own racial or ethnic group.

The imposition of a price ceiling may have been motivated by a desire to help those seeking to rent homes but the predicted outcome means not all buyers benefit from the policy. Those who secure accommodation do get to pay a lower price but other buyers cannot get any accommodation at all.

The price ceiling will also affect sellers and some may not feel it is worth their while continuing in the market and leave, thus depressing market supply. Because the revenue landlords receive is lower, there may also be less work carried out on maintenance and repair and as a result the quality of rental accommodation might fall. Workers involved with repair and maintenance of rental property, and letting agents, may find their services are no longer required and they may be made redundant or go out of business. To society as a whole there is an opportunity cost of these redundant factor inputs.

This example in the market for rental accommodation allows us to make a general prediction: when the government imposes a binding price ceiling on a competitive market, a shortage of the good arises, and sellers must ration the scarce goods among the large number of potential buyers. The desirability of such an outcome will depend on the relative value of the costs and benefits incurred but also on the belief systems of the policymakers. Whether the outcome in a market with a price ceiling is 'better' than that in a free market is a normative issue. In using our model, we can present the contrasting outcomes and attempt to quantify the relative costs and benefits as a means of aiding decision-making but ultimately, the decision is likely to be one influenced by political considerations.

How Price Floors Affect Market Outcomes

To examine the effects of another kind of government price control, let's look at the market for alcohol. Governments in both England and Scotland have discussed the possibility of introducing minimum prices for alcohol to try and curb the damaging effects of excess alcohol consumption on both their citizens' health and on social behaviour. If a government imposes a price floor on the market for alcohol, we can use our model to predict two possible outcomes. If the government imposes a price floor of €0.25 per unit when the equilibrium price is €0.35, we obtain the outcome in panel (a) of Figure 8.2. In this case, because the equilibrium price is above the floor, the price floor is not binding. Market forces move the economy to the equilibrium, and the price floor has no effect.

FIGURE 8.2

A Market with a Price Floor

In panel (a), the government imposes a price floor of €0.25 per unit. Because this is below the equilibrium price of €0.35 per unit, the price floor has no effect. The market price adjusts to balance supply and demand. At the equilibrium, quantity supplied and quantity demanded both equal 5 million units. In panel (b), the government imposes a price floor of €0.45 per unit, which is above the equilibrium price of €0.35 per unit. Therefore, the market price equals €0.45 per unit. Because 6 million units are supplied at this price and only 3 million are demanded, there is a surplus of 3 million units.

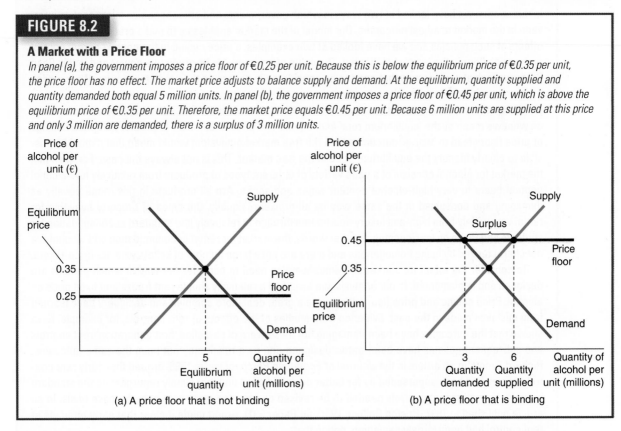

(a) A price floor that is not binding

(b) A price floor that is binding

Panel (b) of Figure 8.2 shows what happens when the government imposes a price floor of €0.45 per unit. In this case, because the equilibrium price of €0.35 per unit is below the floor, the price floor is a binding constraint on the market. At this floor, the quantity of alcohol supplied, 6 million units, exceeds the quantity demanded (3 million units), thus, a binding price floor causes a surplus. Notice, however, that the price floor has reduced the quantity demanded by 2 million units, from the original equilibrium quantity demanded of 5 million units to 3 million units, thus achieving the goal of the policy.

It has been argued that people on low incomes might be disproportionately affected by such a policy because they pay a higher price for alcohol which represents a higher proportion of their income; meanwhile, those people who would see themselves as responsible drinkers have to pay a higher price because of the proportion of drinkers who do abuse alcohol in some way and impose costs on society.

Summary

Price controls are used when governments or other agencies believe that the market is not allocating resources equitably (even if it is allocating resources efficiently). Just as there is an argument that an efficient allocation of resources is not an equitable one, there are costs and benefits of imposing price controls and there is considerable debate as to whether price controls are desirable or not.

There are other options available to governments for achieving what might be seen as being equitable outcomes and we shall look at these in more detail in the next section when we look at taxes and subsidies.

SELF TEST How might price ceilings like rent controls lead to those who the policy is designed to help being negatively affected? What might be the costs to individuals of price floors?

CASE STUDY   The Accuracy of Predictions

In this section we have looked at two ways in which governments and other agencies might seek to intervene in the market to adjust outcomes. Our model of the market enables us to make predictions about the effects of such policies and we have looked at two examples, a price ceiling in the context of rent control and a price floor in the context of alcohol. The value of any model is its predictive power and in this Case Study we look at some issues that need to be considered in assessing the predictive power of our model.

In comparing outcomes with and without any government intervention, we are assuming that the competitive market model is a useful approximation to the real word. In the first instance, we need to be clear on what we mean by the 'equilibrium rent' and 'equilibrium price of alcohol'. To predict that price ceilings or price floors lead to 'worse' outcomes than the free market equivalent would mean that it must be possible to clearly identify the equilibrium price in the free market. This is not always the case. For example, the market for alcohol consists of a wide variety of different types of products from relatively low-alcohol content beers to very high-alcohol content wines and spirits. Are all products in this range equally as damaging and consumed in the same way by all drinkers? Equally, the types of property available for rental vary widely from high-end luxury apartments through to relatively low standard accommodation for students and those on low incomes. In other words, the market for rental accommodation and alcohol are not characterized by being homogenous and there are not a large number of sellers who are price-takers.

To consider the effect on market outcomes we also need to consider the way in which policies are designed and implemented. In our analysis, we assumed a relatively simple rent freeze and fixed price on alcohol. Price ceiling and price floor policies are a great deal more complex and designers have learned from mistakes made in the past. Evidence from studies of the effects of rent controls, for example, have shown that the outcomes have been damaging but these were of so-called 'first generation' rent controls and subsequent policies have been better designed and as a result may not have the same outcomes. Richard Arnott, in an article in the *Journal of Economic Perspectives* in 1995, argued that early rent control policies had been superseded by far better designed ones and that simply regurgitating the standard arguments against rent controls needed to be revised and treated more on a case-by-case basis. In an article published in 1997 (Boston College Working Paper 391), Arnott made it clear that early attempts at rent control had been largely damaging, noting that:

(Continued)

'…the cumulative evidence – both quantitative and qualitative – strongly supports the predictions of the textbook model in virtually all respects. The decay and shrinkage of the rental housing markets in Britain and Israel caused by long-term rent control are persuasively documented in Coleman (1988) and Werczberger (1988), respectively; Friedrich v. Hayek (Fraser Institute, 1975) provides evidence of the harmful effects of hard rent controls in interwar Vienna, including their adverse effects on labour mobility; and Bertrand de Jouvenel (Fraser Institute, 1975) and Milton Friedman and George Stigler (Fraser Institute, 1975) argue strongly that the retention of controls immediately after World War II adversely affected the Paris and U.S. housing markets, respectively.' (Arnott, 1997, p8)

Just because a policy has negative outcomes does not mean it is a bad policy *per se* but can provide the basis for improvement in design. Looking at the market in more detail, understanding the limitations of policies as well as on the various factors that influence the decisions of buyers and sellers in the market can lead to beneficial market outcomes as Arnott (1995, p108) notes: 'a *well-designed* rent control program can improve on the unrestricted equilibrium of an imperfect market'.

Source: https://www.aeaweb.org/articles.php?doi=10.1257/jep.9.1.99

The design of policies in towns and cities can lead to different outcomes.

TAXES

Most governments, whether national or local, impose taxes to raise revenue and influence behaviour in some way. There are many different taxes in most countries but we can generally divide them into two categories: taxes on income and taxes on spending. Taxes on income are called **direct taxes** because the individual is ultimately responsible for paying the correct amount of tax.

> **direct taxes** a tax levied on income and wealth

For many people, an amount is subtracted from the gross income and passed to the tax authorities. If an individual owns shares and sells the shares making a profit, they are liable to pay income tax on the surplus. Companies making a profit have to pay income tax (but the name of the tax might be corporation or corporate tax); it is a tax on a company's income.

Taxes on expenditure are referred to as indirect taxes. An **indirect tax** might be levied on a business that is responsible to the tax authorities to pay the tax, but the business might pass on the tax to the consumer in the form of a higher price. Hence, the individual shares the burden of the tax and so contributes indirectly to the tax.

> **indirect tax** a tax levied on the sale of goods and services

We can further identify two types of tax on expenditure – a specific tax and an *ad valorem* tax. A **specific tax** is a set amount per unit of expenditure, for example, €0.75 per litre of petrol or €2.50 on a bottle of whisky. An **_ad valorem_ tax** is expressed as a percentage, for example a 10 per cent tax or a 20 per cent tax. There is a difference in the way in which these types of taxes affect market outcomes. In analyzing these outcomes we will look at who taxes initially affect and how the burden of the tax is shared – in other words, who actually pays the tax? Economists use the term **tax incidence** to refer to the distribution of a tax burden.

> **specific tax** a fixed rate tax levied on goods and services expressed as a sum per unit
> **_ad valorem_ tax** a tax levied as a percentage of the price of a good
> **tax incidence** the manner in which the burden of a tax is shared among participants in a market

How Taxes on Sellers Affect Market Outcomes

We are first going to analyze the market outcomes of a government imposing a specific tax and an *ad valorem* tax on sellers.

A Specific Tax Suppose the government imposes a tax on sellers of petrol of €0.50 for each litre of fuel they sell. We analyze the effects of this tax by applying our three steps approach.

Step One In this case, the immediate impact of the tax is on the sellers of petrol. The quantity of petrol demanded at any given price is the same; thus, the demand curve does not change. By contrast, the tax on sellers makes the petrol business less profitable at any given price – whatever the seller receives per litre, they now have to give €0.50 to the government. The seller is effectively facing an increase in the cost of production of €0.50 per litre.

Step Two Because the tax on sellers raises the cost of producing and selling petrol, it reduces the quantity supplied at every price. The supply curve shifts to the left (or, equivalently, upwards) and the shift is parallel to the original supply curve. The shift in the supply curve is a parallel one because regardless of the quantity supplied the seller has to pay the same amount per litre and so at every price the distance between the original and the new supply curve is the amount of the tax – €0.50.

For any market price of petrol, the effective price to sellers – the amount they get to keep after paying the tax – is €0.50 lower. For example, if the market price of petrol happened to be €2.00 per litre, the effective price received by sellers would be €1.50. Whatever the market price, sellers will supply a quantity of petrol as if the price were €0.50 lower than it is. Put differently, to induce sellers to supply any given quantity, the market price must now be €0.50 higher to compensate for the effect of the tax. Thus, as shown in Figure 8.3, the supply curve shifts *upward* from S_1 to S_2 by exactly the size of the tax (€0.50).

Step Three Having determined how the supply curve shifts, we can now compare the initial and the new equilibrium. Figure 8.3 shows that the equilibrium price of petrol rises from €1.00 to €1.30, and the equilibrium quantity falls from 100 to 90 million litres per time period. The tax reduces the size of the petrol market and buyers and sellers share the burden of the tax. Because the market price rises, buyers pay €0.30 more for each litre of petrol than they did before the tax was imposed. Sellers receive a higher price than they did without the tax, but the effective price (after paying the tax) falls from €1.00 to €0.80 per litre.

The total amount of tax paid by buyers and sellers can also be determined from Figure 8.3. Buyers pay an additional €0.30 per litre times the amount of petrol purchased (90 million litres) and so the total tax paid by buyers is €27 million. The burden of the tax on sellers is €0.20 per litre and they sell 90 million litres, so sellers contribute €18 million to the tax authorities. The total tax revenue is the vertical distance between the two supply curves multiplied by the amount bought and sold. In this example, the total tax raised is €0.50 × 90 million = €45 million.

FIGURE 8.3

A Specific Tax on Sellers

When a tax of €0.50 is levied on sellers, the supply curve shifts to the left by €0.50 at every price from S_1 to S_2. The equilibrium quantity falls from 100 to 90 million litres. The price that buyers pay rises from €1.00 to €1.30 per litre. The price that sellers receive (after paying the tax) falls from €1.00 to €0.80. Even though the tax is levied on sellers, buyers and sellers share the burden of the tax.

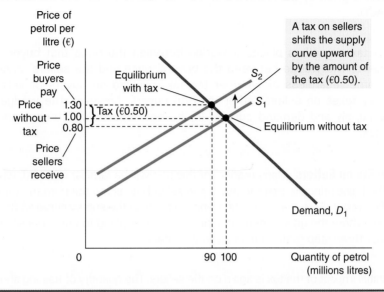

This illustrates a general principle highlighted in Figure 8.4. The original equilibrium price before the tax is *Pe* and the original equilibrium quantity is *Qe*. The levying of a tax (in this case a specific tax) shifts

FIGURE 8.4

Determining the Incidence (Burden) of Taxation

A specific tax of AC per unit shifts the supply curve from S to S + tax. Consumers now pay a higher price given by Pe_1 and buy Qe_1. The tax burden on the consumer is shown by the value of the shaded area Pe_1ABPe. Sellers now receive the amount D for each unit sold compared to Pe before the tax was levied. The burden of the tax on sellers, therefore, is given by the value of the shaded area PeBCD. The total tax revenue raised and due to the authorities is the area Pe_1ACD.

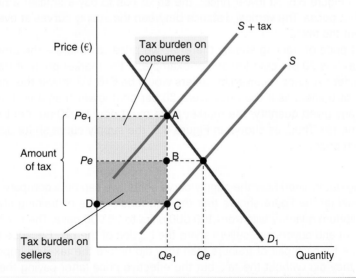

the supply curve to the left to S + tax. The new equilibrium price is Pe_1 and the new equilibrium quantity is Qe_1. The amount of the tax is the vertical distance between the two supply curves at the new equilibrium (AC). Buyers now pay a price of Pe_1 compared to Pe and so pay $Pe_1Pe \times Qe_1$ in tax, shown by the shaded rectangle Pe_1ABPe. Sellers now receive D whereas they received Pe before the tax was levied. As a result the burden of the tax for sellers is the amount $DPe \times Qe_1$. The total amount paid by sellers, therefore, is given by the shaded area $PeBCD$. The total tax revenue due to the tax authorities is the area Pe_1ACD.

Implications A tax on sellers places a wedge between the price that buyers pay and the price that sellers receive. The wedge between the buyers' price and the sellers' price is the same, and would be the same regardless of whether the tax is levied on buyers or sellers. In reality most governments levy taxes on sellers rather than on buyers, however. The wedge shifts the relative position of the supply and demand curves. In the new equilibrium, buyers and sellers share the burden of the tax.

An *Ad Valorem* Tax on Sellers Many readers of this text will be familiar with VAT, which is a tax levied as a percentage. The basic principle that the buyer and seller both share the burden of the tax is the same as that for a specific tax but there is a subtle difference in the way the supply curve shifts. Imagine the market for training shoes where the government announces that it is going to impose a sales tax of 20 per cent. Again, we use our three-step method to analyze the effect.

Step One The initial impact of the tax is again on the sellers. The quantity of training shoes demanded at any given price is the same; thus, the demand curve does not change. The seller again faces an increase in the cost of production but this time the effective increase in cost varies at each price. If the tax was 20 per cent and training shoes cost €20 to produce, the seller would have to give €4 to the government in tax (20 per cent of €20); if training shoes cost €50 to produce, the seller would have to give €10 to the government; and if training shoes cost €75 to produce the seller would have to give €15 to the government. The supply curve shifts to the left but it is not a parallel shift.

Step Two The tax on sellers raises the cost of producing and selling trainers as for a specific tax, but the amount that sellers have to give to the government is lower at low prices than at high prices because 20 per cent of a small amount is a different value than 20 per cent of a higher amount. The supply curve shifts to the left (or, equivalently, upwards) and the curve pivots upwards and to the left of the original supply curve as shown in Figure 8.6. At lower prices the seller has to pay a smaller amount of tax per pair of shoes than at higher prices. The vertical distance between the supply curves at every price is 20 per cent of the price without the tax.

For any market price of training shoes, the effective price to sellers – the amount they get to keep after paying the tax – is 20 per cent lower. For example, if the market price of trainers happened to be €20 per pair, the effective price received by sellers would be €16. Whatever the market price, sellers will supply a quantity of trainers as if the price were 20 per cent lower than it is. Put differently, to induce sellers to supply any given quantity, the market price must now be 20 per cent higher to compensate for the effect of the tax. Thus, as shown in Figure 8.5, the supply curve shifts *upward* from S_1 to S_2 by 20 per cent at each price.

Step Three Having determined how the supply curve shifts, we can now compare the initial and the new equilibrium. In panel (a) the figure shows that the equilibrium price of training shoes rises from €20 to €23, and the equilibrium quantity falls from 100 000 pairs to 85 000 pairs. The tax reduces the size of the training shoe market and buyers and sellers share the burden of the tax. Because the market price rises, buyers pay €3 more for each pair of trainers than they did before the tax was imposed. Sellers receive a higher price than they did without the tax, but the effective price (after paying the tax) falls from €20 to €19 per pair.

FIGURE 8.5

An Ad Valorem Tax on Sellers

When a tax of 20 per cent is levied on sellers, the supply curve shifts to the left from S_1 to S_2. At low prices, the amount of the tax paid is relatively low but 20 per cent of higher prices means the seller has to give more to the government. The shift in the supply curve is, therefore, not parallel. The market outcome will vary depending on the demand for trainers and the original market price. If market price were €20, as shown in panel (a), the equilibrium quantity falls from 100 000 to 85 000 pairs. The price that buyers pay rises from €20 to €23 per pair. The price that sellers receive (after paying the tax) falls from €20 to €19. Even though the tax is levied on sellers, buyers and sellers share the burden of the tax. In panel (b) the equilibrium price before the tax is €50 per pair and the equilibrium quantity bought and sold is 150 000 pairs of trainers. The tax of 20 per cent means that the vertical distance between the two supply curves is now €10 which is how much the supplier has to give to the tax authorities for every pair sold. The buyer now faces a price of €55 per pair and the price the seller receives (after paying the tax) falls from €50 to €45.

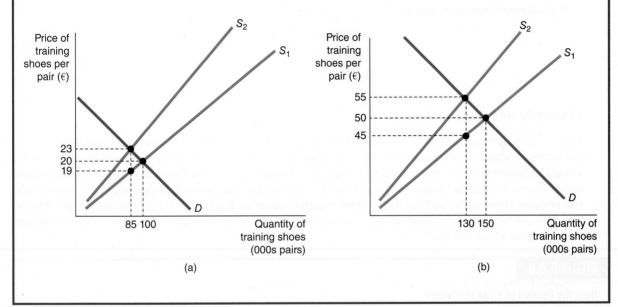

(a)   (b)

In panel (b) the initial equilibrium price before the tax is €50 and the amount of training shoes bought and sold is 150 000 pairs. A 20 per cent tax will mean that sellers have to pay the tax authorities €10 on each pair sold. The figure shows the equilibrium price has risen to €55 so buyers have to pay €5 more per pair of trainers and the price that sellers actually receive falls from €50 before the tax to €45 afterwards. In this example, the burden of the tax is shared equally between the buyer and seller.

The Algebra of a Specific Tax Assume that the demand function is given by the equation:

$$P = 30 - 1.5Q_D$$

and the supply equation by:

$$P = 6 + 0.5Q_S$$

A specific tax levied on the seller of t would make the supply function:

$$P = 6 + 0.5Q_S + t$$

In equilibrium, therefore:

$$6 + 0.5Q_S + t = 30 - 1.5Q_D$$
$$0.5Q_S + 1.5Q_D = 30 - 6 - t$$
$$2Q = 24 - t$$
$$Q = 12 - 0.5t$$

If no tax was levied then the quantity would be 12. If the tax t was levied at a rate of €6 per unit then the quantity would be nine and if the tax was levied at a rate of €8 per unit, the quantity would be eight. We can also substitute $Q = 12 - 0.5t$ into the demand equation and determine the effect on price of the tax. The demand equation would thus be:

$$P = 30 - 1.5(12 - 0.5t)$$

If $t = 5$ then the price would be:

$$P = 30 - 1.5(12 - 0.5(5))$$
$$P = 30 - 14.25$$
$$P = 15.75$$

If $t = 8$ then the price would be:

$$P = 30 - 1.5(12 - 4)$$
$$P = 30 - 12$$
$$P = 18$$

Elasticity and Tax Incidence

When a good is taxed, buyers and sellers of the good share the burden of the tax. But how exactly is the tax burden divided? Only rarely will it be shared equally. To see how the burden is divided, consider the impact of taxation in the two markets in Figure 8.6. In both cases, the figure shows the initial demand curve, the initial supply curve, and a tax that drives a wedge between the amount paid by buyers and the amount received by sellers. (Not drawn in either panel of the figure is the new supply or demand curve – which curve shifts depends on whether the tax is levied on buyers or sellers. This is irrelevant for the incidence of the tax.)

FIGURE 8.6

How the Burden of a Tax Is Divided
In panel (a), the supply curve is relatively elastic and the demand curve is relatively inelastic. In this case, the price received by sellers falls only slightly, while the price paid by buyers rises substantially. Thus, buyers bear most of the burden of the tax. In panel (b) the supply curve is relatively inelastic and the demand curve is relatively elastic. In this case, the price received by sellers falls substantially, while the price paid by buyers rises only slightly. Thus, sellers bear most of the burden of the tax.

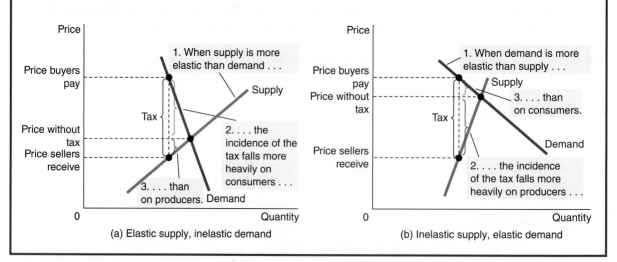

Panel (a) of Figure 8.6 shows a tax levied in a market with very elastic supply and relatively inelastic demand. That is, sellers are very responsive to changes in the price of the good (so the supply curve is relatively flat), whereas buyers are not very responsive (so the demand curve is relatively steep). When a tax is imposed on a market with these price elasticities, the price received by sellers does not fall much, so sellers bear only a small burden. By contrast, the price paid by buyers rises substantially, indicating that buyers bear most of the burden of the tax. Our analysis of elasticity in Chapter 4 should make this something that is not at all surprising. If the price elasticity of demand is low then demand will fall proportionately less in response to a rise in price – buyers are not very price sensitive. The seller can shift the burden of the tax onto the buyer safe in the knowledge that demand will only fall by a relatively small amount.

Panel (b) of Figure 8.6 shows a tax in a market with relatively inelastic supply and relatively price elastic demand. In this case, sellers are not very responsive to changes in the price, while buyers are very responsive. The figure shows that when a tax is imposed, the price paid by buyers does not rise much, while the price received by sellers falls substantially. Thus, sellers bear most of the burden of the tax. In this case, sellers know that if they try to pass on the tax to buyers that demand will fall by a relatively large amount.

The two panels of Figure 8.6 show a general lesson about how the burden of a tax is divided: a tax burden falls more heavily on the side of the market that is less elastic. Why is this true? In essence, the elasticity measures the willingness of buyers or sellers to leave the market when conditions become unfavourable. A small elasticity of demand means that buyers do not have good alternatives to consuming this particular good. A low elasticity of supply means that sellers do not have many alternatives to producing this particular good. When the good is taxed, the side of the market with fewer alternatives cannot easily leave the market and must, therefore, bear more of the burden of the tax.

SELF TEST In some countries governments levy both a specific tax (such as duties) and a sales tax such as VAT on products. Show the market outcome for cars if the government imposes a specific tax of €500 per car and VAT at a rate of 15 per cent.

SUBSIDIES

A subsidy is the opposite of a tax. A **subsidy** is a payment to buyers and sellers to supplement income or reduce costs of production to provide an advantage to the recipient of the subsidy. Subsidies are levied when governments want to encourage the consumption of a 'good' which they deem is currently under-produced. Taxes, on the other hand, may be levied on a 'bad' which the government believes is over-consumed. Subsidies are generally given to sellers and have the effect of reducing the cost of production as opposed to a tax which increases the cost of production. Subsidies exist in a variety of different areas including education, transport, agriculture, regional development, housing and employment.

> **subsidy** payment to buyers and sellers to supplement income or lower costs and which thus encourages consumption or provides an advantage to the recipient

How Subsidies Affect Market Outcomes

Many European countries provide subsidies for transport systems and the Common Agricultural Policy oversees subsidies to farmers amounting to around €60 billion a year. In Switzerland some €2.5 billion is spent on subsidies for rail transport, in Germany the figure is nearer to €9 billion, in France €6.8 billion, and in the UK around €3 billion.

Figure 8.7 shows how a subsidy works using the rail system as an example and utilizing our three steps approach. In the absence of a subsidy the equilibrium number of journeys bought and sold is Q_e and the equilibrium price for the average train ticket for each journey is €75.

FIGURE 8.7

A Subsidy on Rail Transport

When a subsidy of €30 per ticket is given to sellers, the supply curve shifts to the right from S to S + subsidy. The equilibrium quantity rises from Q_e to Q_1 journeys per year. The price that buyers pay for a journey falls from €75 to €60. The subsidy results in lower prices for passengers and an increased number of journeys available. Even though the subsidy is given to sellers, buyers and sellers share the benefits of the subsidy.

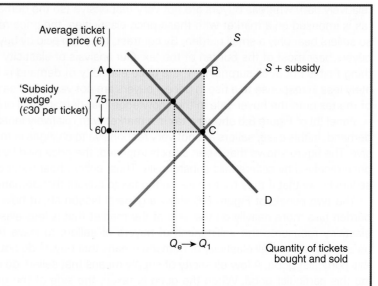

Step One If the government gives a subsidy of €30 per (average) ticket to train operators, it is the supply curve for journeys which is affected; the demand curve is not affected because the number of train journeys demanded at each price stays the same. The subsidy to train operators reduces the cost of providing a train journey by €30 and so the supply curve will shift.

Step Two Because the subsidy reduces the cost to the train operators, the supply curve shifts to the right by the amount of the subsidy from S to S + subsidy. To provide the number of train journeys shown by Q_1, the actual cost to operators is A but they get a subsidy shown by the distance BC which is €30 per ticket sold.

Step Three Comparing the initial and the new equilibrium we can see that the equilibrium price of each train journey is now lower at €60 and the equilibrium number of journeys travelled increases to Q_1.

The total cost of providing the subsidy is the amount of the subsidy (€30 per ticket in this case) multiplied by the number of tickets bought and sold (Q_e) shown by the shaded area A,B,C,60.

Implications There is a considerable debate surrounding the value of subsidies. We have seen from the example how price and quantity can be affected following the imposition of a subsidy. In the case of transport, it may have the effect of altering the incentives for people to travel on the train rather than on the roads and so have the benefit of reducing congestion on the roads as well as reducing possible pollution that is associated with road use. There are also costs associated with subsidies; for one thing, someone has to finance the subsidy and it is often the taxpayer. Subsidies may also encourage firms to overproduce, which has a wider effect on the market. Subsidies on commodities such as cotton, bananas and sugar distort the workings of the market and change global comparative advantage. Overproduction leads to excess supply on world markets and drives down prices as well as diverting trade to rich countries who can support producers through subsidies at the expense of poor countries whose producers cannot compete because prices are lower than the free market price.

CONCLUSION

In this chapter we have looked at how governments interact with the market mechanism in the form of price controls, taxes and subsidies.

In the next chapter we shall examine the effects of taxation and subsidies more fully, and we shall consider a broader range of policies.

IN THE NEWS

Price Floors

In the 2011 Budget speech, the UK government announced plans for a carbon price floor which came into operation in April 2013.

A Carbon Price Floor

The continued concern over carbon emissions and the effect increased carbon emissions might be having on the long-term climate, prompted the UK government to introduce a carbon price floor (CPF) in April 2013. The carbon price floor is designed to influence the price of carbon in the UK electricity generation market. Companies using fossil fuels to generate electricity are required to pay a tax in the form of a climate change levy (CCL) for gas, solid fossil fuel and a fuel duty for fuel oil and gas oil, called the carbon price support (CPS). When power generators using fossil fuels produce electricity, they also produce carbon emissions which are deemed polluting. The CPF aims to make generators pay for this pollution by imposing a minimum price to pollute.

Originally, the carbon price floor was set at £16 (€22.60) per tonne with a planned rise each year to reach £70 (€99) per tonne by 2030. By comparison, the rate set in the rest of Europe is £5.60 (€8) per tonne but might rise to a maximum of £9.70 (€13.70).

Key to the success of the policy is the level at which it is set. If the floor is set too low then firms might absorb any increased costs that result and see the increased price as a tax and not look for other low-carbon options. If it is set too high, firms will complain that in the difficult economic environment in which they are operating this will merely make them less competitive, especially if the levels set in the rest of Europe are much lower. In May 2015, for example, an announcement was made that one of the UK's biggest power stations at Ferrybridge in North Yorkshire would close seven years earlier than planned. One of the reasons cited was that it was now uneconomic to produce electricity at the plant because of the carbon price floor. In the 2014 budget, the UK government announced that it would be introducing a freeze on the price floor at £18 (€25) per tonne of carbon dioxide until at least 2019. The government reiterated its policy aim of providing an incentive for investment in low-carbon power generation and the reason for the freeze was that carbon prices across Europe were much lower than expected. The government did not want to see prices diverging too wildly between the UK and Europe.

Proponents of reductions in carbon emissions have argued that the freeze sends the wrong message to power generators and effectively makes polluting cheaper. Those on the other side of the argument suggest that even at the frozen price, power stations are struggling to compete and risk closure, as in Ferrybridge, which will reduce capacity and risk the UK not being able to meet power demand in future. The lead time to bring new power stations online, such as the proposed nuclear plant at Hinkley in Somerset, is very long and it is feared that plant closures before new ones come on line could seriously impact on generating capacity.

(Continued)

Questions

1 For the carbon price floor to be effective, what market conditions must exist?

2 Using supply and demand diagrams, explain how a carbon price floor is meant to reduce carbon emissions.

3 Consider the factors which might contribute to the success of the carbon price floor in achieving its goal.

4 What might be the possible costs of imposing a carbon price floor?

5 Do you think that the decision to freeze the price floor means that power generation firms will have less incentive to invest in cleaner technology? Justify your answer.

Source: http://sse.com/newsandviews/allarticles/2015/05/sse-announces-closure-of-ferrybridge-power-station/

Coal-fired power stations like Ferrybridge in North Yorkshire are closing as the focus shifts to low-carbon energy production.

SUMMARY

- A price ceiling is a legal maximum on the price of a good or service. An example is rent control. If the price ceiling is below the equilibrium price, the quantity demanded exceeds the quantity supplied. Because of the resulting shortage, sellers must in some way ration the good or service among buyers.

- A price floor is a legal minimum on the price of a good or service. If the price floor is above the equilibrium price, the quantity supplied exceeds the quantity demanded. Because of the resulting surplus, buyers' demands for the good or service must in some way be rationed among sellers.

- When the government levies a tax on a good, the equilibrium quantity of the good falls. That is, a tax on a market shrinks the size of the market.

- A tax on a good places a wedge between the price paid by buyers and the price received by sellers. When the market moves to the new equilibrium, buyers pay more for the good and sellers receive less for it. In this sense, buyers and sellers share the tax burden. The incidence of a tax (that is, the division of the tax burden) does not depend on whether the tax is levied on buyers or sellers.

- A subsidy given to sellers lowers the cost of production and encourages firms to expand output. Buyers benefit from lower prices.

- The incidence of a tax or subsidy depends on the price elasticities of supply and demand. The burden tends to fall on the side of the market that is less elastic because that side of the market can respond less easily to the tax (and more easily to the subsidy) by changing the quantity bought or sold.

QUESTIONS FOR REVIEW

1 Give an example of a price ceiling and an example of a price floor.

2 Which causes a shortage of a good – a price ceiling or a price floor? Which causes a surplus?

3 Under what circumstances is a price ceiling and a price floor referred to as binding?

4 What potential costs and benefits might a government have to consider in deciding whether to impose a price floor or a price ceiling?

5 What mechanisms allocate resources when the price of a good is not allowed to bring supply and demand into equilibrium?

6 Explain why there has been criticism of rent controls and whether this criticism needs revision in the light of new research.

7 How does a tax imposed on a good with a high price elasticity of demand affect the market equilibrium? Who bears most of the burden of the tax in this instance?

8 How does a subsidy on a good affect the price paid by buyers, the price received by sellers and the quantity bought and sold?

9 What determines how the burden of a tax or a subsidy is divided between buyers and sellers? Why?

10 How might an economist decide whether the benefits of a subsidy outweigh the cost?

PROBLEMS AND APPLICATIONS

1 Lovers of opera persuade the government to impose a price ceiling of €50 per ticket at the country's national opera house. Does this policy get more or fewer people to attend? What does the market outcome depend on?

2 The government has decided that the free market price of tobacco is too low.

   a. Suppose the government imposes a binding price floor in the tobacco market. Use a supply and demand diagram to show the effect of this policy on the price of tobacco and the quantity of tobacco sold. Is there a shortage or surplus of tobacco? What does the market outcome depend on?

   b. Tobacco producers complain that the price floor has reduced their total revenue. Is this possible? Explain.

   c. In response to producers' complaints, the government agrees to purchase all of the surplus tobacco at the price floor. Compared to the basic price floor, who benefits from this new policy? Who loses?

3 A recent study found that the demand and supply schedules for frisbees are as follows:

Price per frisbee (€)	Quantity demanded of frisbees (millions)	Quantity supplied of frisbees (millions)
11	1	15
10	2	12
9	4	9
8	6	6
7	8	3
6	10	1

What are the equilibrium price and quantity of frisbees?

   a. Frisbee manufacturers persuade the government that frisbee production improves scientists' understanding of aerodynamics and thus is important for national security. The government decides to impose a price floor €2 above the equilibrium price. What is the new market price? How many frisbees are sold?

   b. Irate university students march on the government and demand a reduction in the price of frisbees. The government decides to repeal the price floor and impose a price ceiling €1 below the former price floor. What is the new market price? How many frisbees are sold?

4 Suppose that, in the absence of any tax whatsoever, the equilibrium price of a flat is €150 000. Now suppose that the government requires buyers in the housing market to pay a tax of €5000 on every flat purchased.

   a. Draw a supply and demand diagram of the market for flats without the tax. Show the price paid by consumers, the price received by producers and the quantity of flats bought and sold. What is the difference between the price paid by consumers and the price received by producers?

   b. Now draw a supply and demand diagram for the market for flats with the tax. Show the price paid by consumers, the price received by producers and the quantity of flats bought and sold. What is the difference between the price paid by consumers and the price received by producers? Has the quantity of flats bought and sold increased or decreased?

5 A country's finance minister wants to raise tax revenue to help reduce government borrowing. Advise the minister what type of goods they should consider levying a tax to accomplish the minister's goal.

6 A government wants to reduce the incidence of anti-social behaviour which can result from excess alcohol consumption by young people aged between 18 and 25. Which do you think leads to a fairer market outcome: a specific tax on every

unit of alcohol sold or an *ad valorem* tax on the price of alcohol equal to 25 per cent of the price per unit? Use diagrams to help support your answer to the question.

7 If the government places a €1000 tax on luxury cars, will the price paid by consumers rise by more than €1000, less than €1000 or exactly €1000. Explain.

8 The government decides to reduce air pollution by reducing the consumption of petrol. It imposes €0.50 tax for each litre of petrol sold.

   a. Should it impose this tax on petrol companies or motorists? Explain carefully, using a supply and demand diagram.

   b. If the demand for petrol were more price elastic, would this tax be more effective or less effective in reducing the quantity of petrol consumed? Explain with both words and a diagram.

   c. Are consumers of petrol helped or hurt by this tax? Why?

   d. Are workers in the oil industry helped or hurt by this tax? Why?

9 Unemployment amongst young people across a number of European countries is very high. Imagine that European Union ministers proposed a youth employment subsidy designed to help increase the number of young people between the ages of 18 and 29 in work by making it easier for employers to take on extra workers. Assume that estimates of the cost of the subsidy would be €2500 per job and would create up to 175 000 new jobs. Use diagrams to show how the subsidy is designed to work and what its success might depend upon.

10 There is a debate in a country about the higher education system. Some political parties want to promote the value of university education and give as many young people the chance to attend university as possible. This party believe that the state should provide grants for young people to help them go to university. An opposing party also agrees that a university education is a good thing but believes that the benefits that a university education provides should be paid for by those who go to university and not by the state. They advocate students paying the tuition fees for their university at the start of each academic year.

Present an argument for and against both policies, and state which you think is the most efficient and equitable market outcome. Use diagrams to help support your answer where appropriate.

PART 4
THE ECONOMICS OF THE PUBLIC SECTOR

9 THE TAX SYSTEM

Taxes have been around a long time. In the Bible, for example, we can read how Jesus' parents had to return to Nazareth to be taxed and how, later, Jesus converted a prominent tax collector to become one of his disciples. In the Koran, there are references to *jizya*, which can be translated as the word 'tax'. In the Ottoman Empire *jizya* was a per-capita tax levied on non-Muslim, able-bodied resident males of military age. Since taxes, by definition, are a means of legally extracting money from individuals or organizations, it is not surprising that they have often been a source of heated political debate throughout history.

In Chapter 8 we looked at taxes and subsidies and the incidence of taxation. In this chapter we are going to explore some of the theory behind the design of tax systems and consider the fundamental principles of taxation. We will use the tools developed in Chapter 7 to analyze the welfare effects of taxation.

TAXES AND EFFICIENCY

Most governments levy taxes for two main reasons. One is to raise revenue to help pay for the various services that government provides. The second reason is to influence behaviour and achieve market outcomes that are deemed desirable. For example, governments might choose to levy high taxes on tobacco and alcohol to curb consumption; and taxes on certain types of energy production, such as solar panels for domestic houses, could be reduced or even made zero to try and encourage a switch from consumption of energy which is deemed damaging to the environment (or which will ultimately become scarcer and so subject to rising prices) to energy generation and consumption which is renewable and 'green'. There are many ways to achieve these different aims but in designing a tax system, policymakers have two major considerations: efficiency and equity.

One tax system is more efficient than another if it raises the same amount of revenue at a smaller cost to taxpayers and the government. The tax payment itself, the transfer of money from the taxpayer to the government, is an inevitable feature of any tax system and is an obvious cost. Yet taxes also impose two other costs; deadweight losses and administrative burdens. Taxes affect consumer and producer behaviour and produce different market outcomes compared to free market outcomes. We can attempt to measure the welfare effects of these different market outcomes by looking at the changes to consumer and producer surplus that result. Any reduction in total surplus in the market outcome when taxes are levied compared to a free market outcome is called the **deadweight loss**.

> **deadweight loss** the fall in total surplus that results from a market distortion, such as a tax

The second cost we need to be aware of is the administrative burdens that taxpayers bear as they comply with the tax laws. An efficient tax system is one that imposes small deadweight losses and small administrative burdens.

THE DEADWEIGHT LOSS OF TAXATION

Taxes have the effect of changing people's behaviour because incentives are changed. If the government taxes tea, some people will drink less tea and drink more coffee. If the government taxes housing worth more than a certain value, some people will look to live in smaller houses and spend more of their income on other things. If the government taxes earnings from labour, some people will not see additional work as having the same reward and may decide to work less and enjoy more leisure.

The effects of taxes on welfare might at first seem obvious. If the government imposes taxes in order to raise revenue, that revenue must come out of someone's pocket. When a good is taxed, buyers pay more and sellers receive less. To understand fully how taxes affect economic well-being, we must compare the reduced welfare of buyers and sellers to the amount of revenue the government raises and what that revenue is spent on.

The deadweight loss involved in taxation can be an inefficiency if people allocate resources according to the tax incentive rather than to the true costs and benefits of the goods and services that they buy and sell. In Chapter 8 we looked at the effect of a tax levied on a seller. The same result would be gained, however, if we had analyzed the effect of a tax on a buyer. When a tax is levied on buyers, the demand curve shifts downwards by the size of the tax; when it is levied on sellers, the supply curve shifts upwards by that amount. In either case, when the tax is imposed, the price paid by buyers rises, and the price received by sellers falls. In the end, buyers and sellers share the burden of the tax, regardless of how it is levied.

How a Tax Affects Market Participants

When using welfare economics to measure the gains and losses from a tax on a good, we take into account how the tax affects buyers, sellers and the government. The benefit to buyers and sellers can be measured by looking at the changes in consumer and producer surplus. What about the third interested party, the government? If T is the size of the tax and Q is the quantity of the good sold, then the government gets total tax revenue of $T \times Q$. It can use this tax revenue to provide services, such as roads, police and education, or to help people on low incomes or vulnerable members of society in need of support. Therefore, to analyze how taxes affect economic well-being, we use tax revenue to measure the government's benefit from the tax. Keep in mind, however, that this benefit actually accrues not to government but to those on whom the revenue is spent. To simplify our discussion in this chapter, we will not show a shift in either the supply or demand curve in the relevant figures, although one curve must shift. Which curve shifts depends on whether the tax is levied on sellers (the supply curve shifts) or buyers (the demand curve shifts). In this chapter, we can simplify the graphs by not bothering to show the shift. The key result for our purposes is that the tax places a wedge between the price buyers pay and the price sellers receive. Because of this tax wedge, the quantity sold falls below the level that would be sold without a tax. In other words, a tax on a good causes the size of the market for the good to shrink. These results should be familiar from our analysis in Chapter 8.

Figure 9.1 shows that the government's tax revenue is represented by the rectangle between the supply and demand curves. The height of this rectangle is the size of the tax, *T*, and the width of the rectangle is the quantity of the good sold, *Q*. Because a rectangle's area is its height times its width, this rectangle's area is $T \times Q$, which equals the tax revenue.

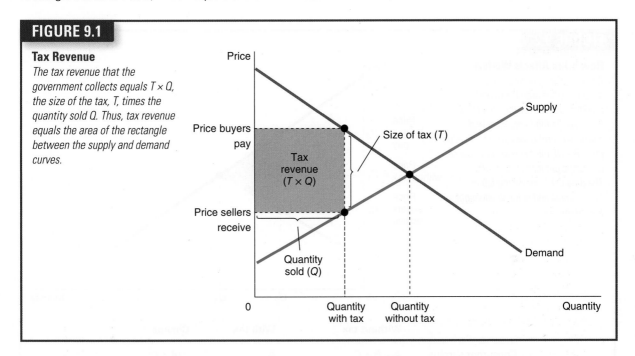

FIGURE 9.1

Tax Revenue
The tax revenue that the government collects equals $T \times Q$, the size of the tax, T, times the quantity sold Q. Thus, tax revenue equals the area of the rectangle between the supply and demand curves.

Welfare Without a Tax To see how a tax affects welfare, we begin by considering welfare before the government has imposed a tax. Figure 9.2 shows the supply and demand diagram and marks the key areas with the letters A to F.

Without a tax, the price and quantity are found at the intersection of the supply and demand curves. The price is P_1, and the quantity sold is Q_1. Because the demand curve reflects buyers' willingness to pay, consumer surplus is the area between the demand curve and the price, A + B + C. Similarly, because the supply curve reflects sellers' costs, producer surplus is the area between the supply curve and the price, D + E + F. In this case, because there is no tax, tax revenue equals zero.

Total surplus – the sum of consumer and producer surplus – equals the area A + B + C + D + E + F. In other words, total surplus is the area between the supply and demand curves up to the equilibrium quantity. The first column of the table in Figure 9.2 summarizes these conclusions.

Welfare With a Tax Now consider welfare after the tax is imposed. The price paid by buyers rises from P_1 to P_B, so consumer surplus now equals only area A (the area below the demand curve and above the buyer's price). The price received by sellers falls from P_1 to P_S, so producer surplus now equals only area F (the area above the supply curve and below the seller's price). The quantity sold falls from Q_1 to Q_2, and the government collects tax revenue equal to the area B + D.

To compute total surplus with the tax, we add consumer surplus, producer surplus and tax revenue. Thus, we find that total surplus is area A + B + D + F. The second column of the table provides a summary.

Changes in Welfare We can now see the effects of the tax by comparing welfare before and after the tax is imposed. The third column in the table in Figure 9.2 shows the changes. The tax causes consumer surplus to fall by the area B + C and producer surplus to fall by the area D + E. Tax revenue rises by the area B + D.

The change in total welfare includes the change in consumer surplus (which is negative), the change in producer surplus (which is also negative), and the change in tax revenue (which is positive). When we add these three pieces together, we find that total surplus in the market falls by the area C + E. Thus, the losses to buyers and sellers from a tax exceed the revenue raised by the government. The fall in total surplus that results when a tax (or some other policy) distorts a market outcome is the deadweight loss. The area C + E measures the size of the deadweight loss.

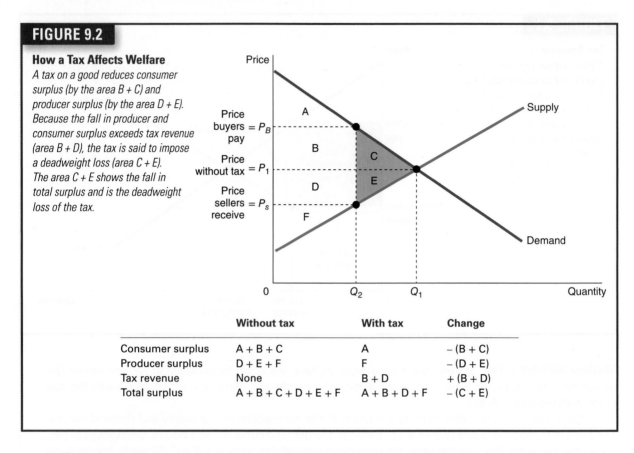

FIGURE 9.2

How a Tax Affects Welfare
A tax on a good reduces consumer surplus (by the area B + C) and producer surplus (by the area D + E). Because the fall in producer and consumer surplus exceeds tax revenue (area B + D), the tax is said to impose a deadweight loss (area C + E). The area C + E shows the fall in total surplus and is the deadweight loss of the tax.

	Without tax	With tax	Change
Consumer surplus	A + B + C	A	– (B + C)
Producer surplus	D + E + F	F	– (D + E)
Tax revenue	None	B + D	+ (B + D)
Total surplus	A + B + C + D + E + F	A + B + D + F	– (C + E)

To understand why taxes impose deadweight losses, recall that people respond to incentives. We have assumed that the equilibrium of supply and demand maximizes the total surplus of buyers and sellers in a market. When a tax raises the price to buyers and lowers the price to sellers, however, it gives buyers an incentive to consume less and sellers an incentive to produce less than they otherwise would. As buyers and sellers respond to these incentives, the size of the market shrinks below its optimum. Thus, because taxes distort incentives, they cause markets to allocate resources inefficiently.

Deadweight Losses and the Gains from Trade

To gain some intuition for why taxes result in deadweight losses, consider an example. Imagine that Carsten cleans Annika's house each week for €100. The opportunity cost of Carsten's time is €80, and the value of a clean house to Annika is €120. Thus, Carsten and Annika each receive a €20 benefit from their deal. The total surplus of €40 measures the gains from trade in this particular transaction.

Now suppose that the government levies a €50 tax on the providers of cleaning services. There is now no price that Annika can pay Carsten that will leave both of them better off after paying the tax. The most Annika would be willing to pay is €120, but then Carsten would be left with only €70 after paying the tax, which is less than his €80 opportunity cost. Conversely, for Carsten to receive his opportunity cost of €80, Annika would need to pay €130, which is above the €120 value she places on a clean house. As a result, Annika and Carsten cancel their arrangement. Carsten goes without the income, and Annika lives in a dirtier house.

The tax has made Carsten and Annika worse off by a total of €40, because they have lost this amount of surplus. At the same time, the government collects no revenue from Carsten and Annika because they decide to cancel their arrangement. The €40 is pure deadweight loss: it is a loss to buyers and sellers in a market not offset by an increase in government revenue. From this example, we can see the ultimate source of deadweight losses: taxes can cause deadweight losses if they prevent buyers and sellers from realizing some of the gains from trade.

The area of the triangle between the supply and demand curves (area C + E in Figure 9.2) measures these losses. This loss can be seen most easily in Figure 9.3 by recalling that the demand curve reflects the value of the good or the benefit to consumers and that the supply curve reflects the costs of producers. When the tax raises the price to buyers to P_B and lowers the price to sellers to P_S, the marginal buyers and sellers leave the market, so the quantity sold falls from Q_1 to Q_2. Yet, as the figure shows, the value of the good to these buyers still exceeds the cost to these sellers. As in our example with Carsten and Annika, the gains from trade – the difference between buyers' value and sellers' cost – is less than the tax. Thus, these trades do not get made once the tax is imposed. The deadweight loss is the surplus lost because the tax discourages these mutually advantageous trades.

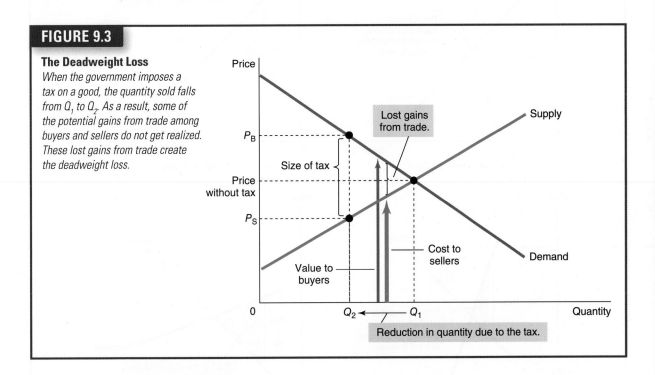

FIGURE 9.3

The Deadweight Loss
When the government imposes a tax on a good, the quantity sold falls from Q_1 to Q_2. As a result, some of the potential gains from trade among buyers and sellers do not get realized. These lost gains from trade create the deadweight loss.

SELF TEST Draw the supply and demand curve for parking on business premises in city centres. If the government imposes a tax on parking spaces, show what happens to the quantity sold, the price paid by buyers and the price paid by sellers. In your diagram, show the deadweight loss from the tax. Explain the meaning of the deadweight loss. Why might the government have imposed this tax? Do you think this was because of efficiency or equity reasons?

The Determinants of the Deadweight Loss

The size of the deadweight loss from a tax is determined by the price elasticities of supply and demand.

In the top two panels of Figure 9.4, the demand curve and the size of the tax are the same. The only difference in these figures is the elasticity of the supply curve. In panel (a) the supply curve is relatively inelastic: quantity supplied responds only slightly to changes in the price. In panel (b) the supply curve is relatively elastic: quantity supplied responds substantially to changes in the price. Notice that the deadweight loss, the area of the triangle between the supply and demand curves, is larger when the supply curve is more elastic.

FIGURE 9.4

Tax Distortions and Elasticities

In panels (a) and (b) the demand curve and the size of the tax are the same, but the price elasticity of supply is different. The more elastic the supply curve, the larger the deadweight loss of the tax. In panels (c) and (d) the supply curve and the size of the tax are the same, but the price elasticity of demand is different. The more price elastic the demand curve, the larger the deadweight loss of the tax.

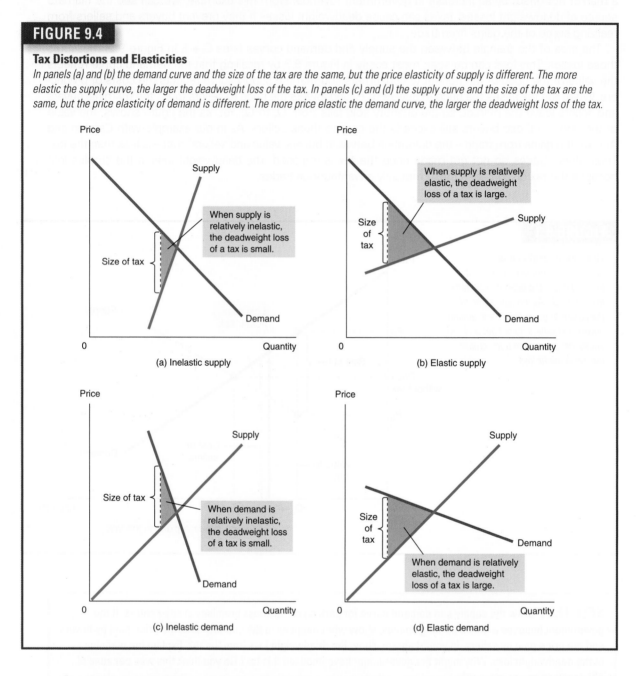

Panels (c) and (d) of Figure 9.4 show the supply curve and the size of the tax held constant. In panel (c) the demand curve is relatively price inelastic, and the deadweight loss is small. In panel (d) the demand curve is more price elastic, and the deadweight loss from the tax is larger.

The lesson from Figure 9.4 is explained because a tax induces buyers and sellers to change their behaviour. The tax raises the price paid by buyers, so they consume less. At the same time, the tax lowers the price received by sellers, so they produce less. Because of these changes in behaviour, the size of the market shrinks below the optimum. The elasticities of supply and demand measure how much sellers and buyers respond to the changes in the price and, therefore, determine how much the tax distorts the market outcome. Hence, the greater the elasticities of supply and demand, the greater the deadweight loss of a tax.

> **SELF TEST** The demand for beer is more price elastic than the demand for milk. Would a tax on beer or a tax on milk have larger deadweight loss?

Deadweight Loss and Tax Revenue as Taxes Vary

Here we consider what happens to the deadweight loss and tax revenue when the size of a tax changes.

Figure 9.5 shows the effects of a small, medium and large tax, holding constant the market's supply and demand curves. The deadweight loss equals the area of the triangle between the supply and demand curves. For the small tax in panel (a), the area of the deadweight loss triangle is quite small. But as the size of a tax rises in panels (b) and (c), the deadweight loss grows larger and larger.

FIGURE 9.5

Deadweight Loss and Tax Revenue from Three Taxes of Different Size

The deadweight loss is the reduction in total surplus due to the tax. Tax revenue is the amount of the tax times the amount of the good sold. In panel (a) a small tax has a small deadweight loss and raises a small amount of revenue. In panel (b) a somewhat larger tax has a larger deadweight loss and raises a larger amount of revenue. In panel (c) a very large tax has a very large deadweight loss, but because it has reduced the size of the market so much, the tax raises only a small amount of revenue.

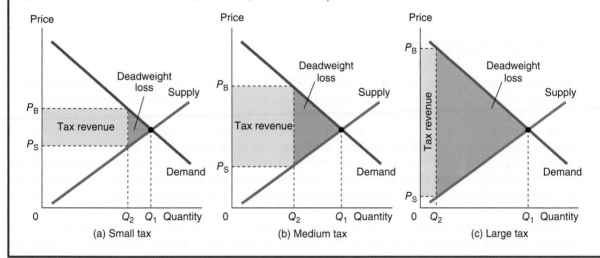

Indeed, the deadweight loss of a tax rises even more rapidly than the size of the tax. The reason is that the deadweight loss is an area of a triangle, and an area of a triangle depends on the *square* of its size. If we double the size of a tax, for instance, the base and height of the triangle double, so the deadweight loss rises by a factor of four. If we triple the size of a tax, the base and height triple, so the deadweight loss rises by a factor of nine.

The government's tax revenue is the size of the tax times the amount of the good sold. As Figure 9.5 shows, tax revenue equals the area of the rectangle between the supply and demand curves. For the small tax in panel (a), tax revenue is small. As the size of a tax rises from panel (a) to panel (b), tax revenue grows. But as the size of the tax rises further from panel (b) to panel (c), tax revenue falls because the higher tax drastically reduces the size of the market (Figure 9.6). It is likely that when taxes are very high, behaviour changes such that tax revenue would be very small.

> **SELF TEST** If the government doubles the tax on petrol, can you be sure that revenue from the petrol tax will rise? Can you be sure that the deadweight loss from the petrol tax will rise? Explain.

FIGURE 9.6

How Deadweight Loss and Tax Revenue Vary with the Size of a Tax

Panel (a) shows that, as the size of a tax grows larger, the deadweight loss grows larger. Panel (b) shows that tax revenue first rises, then falls. This relationship is sometimes called the Laffer curve.

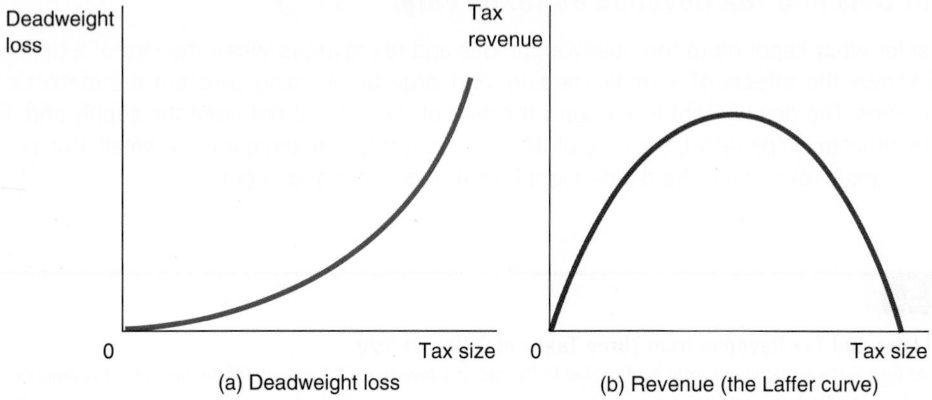

(a) Deadweight loss

(b) Revenue (the Laffer curve)

ADMINISTRATIVE BURDEN

The second cost that a tax imposes is administrative burden and a well-designed tax system seeks to reduce this to a minimum. In many countries, individuals and businesses are required to alert the tax authorities of their incomes and business activities so that the correct tax can be collected. These forms can often be long and complex and for businesses, in particular, this can be a time-consuming and stressful operation. If you ask someone who does this work, their opinion about the tax system is unlikely to be favourable. The administrative burden of any tax system is part of the inefficiency it creates. This burden includes not only the time spent filling out forms but also the time spent throughout the year keeping records for tax purposes and the resources the government has to use to enforce the tax laws.

Many taxpayers hire accountants or tax lawyers to help them with their taxes. These experts in the complex tax laws fill out the tax forms for their clients and help clients arrange their affairs in a way that minimizes the amount of taxes owed. This behaviour is referred to as tax avoidance (optimizing your affairs so that you pay as little tax as possible without breaking the law), and is perfectly legal. This is different from tax evasion, which involves lying about your affairs in order to reduce the amount of tax paid, and is illegal.

Critics of the tax system say that these advisors help their clients avoid taxes by abusing some of the detailed provisions of the tax system (or, as it is sometimes termed, the tax code). These detailed provisions are often dubbed 'loopholes'. In some cases, loopholes are government mistakes: they arise from ambiguities or omissions in the tax laws. On other case, they arise because the government has chosen to give special treatment to specific types of behaviour. For example, the UK tax system allows money spent on a personal pension plan to be exempt from income tax, up to a certain limit. This is because the government wants to encourage people to save for their retirement.

The resources devoted to complying with the tax laws are a type of deadweight loss. The government gets only the amount of taxes paid. By contrast, the taxpayer loses not only this amount but also the time and money spent documenting, computing and avoiding taxes.

The administrative burden of the tax system could be reduced by simplifying the tax laws. Yet simplification is often politically difficult. Most people are ready to simplify the tax code by eliminating the loopholes that benefit others, yet few are eager to give up the loopholes that they use. In the end, the complexity of tax law results from the political process as various taxpayers with their own special interests lobby for their causes. This process is called 'rent seeking' and is part of a branch of economics called public choice theory. Public choice theory is about the analysis of governmental behaviour, and the behaviour of individuals who interact with government. We will look at this in more detail in Chapter 11.

THE DESIGN OF THE TAX SYSTEM

There are a number of key factors in the design of a good tax system. Many economists would agree that there are some fundamental principles that characterize a good tax system but the reality is that most countries have very complex tax systems which might compromise both the efficiency of the system and the desire to be equitable. We are going to look at some of these principles in the next section.

Adam Smith's Four Canons of Taxation

The 18th century economist Adam Smith suggested that any good tax system should adhere to four basic principles or canons. These four principles are:

- **Equality** – each person should pay taxes according to their ability to pay, so that the rich should pay more in taxes than the poor.
- **Certainty** – tax payers need to know what taxes they are liable for and be able to plan ahead on this basis and at the same time governments should be able to have some certainty in how much they are able to collect in taxes.
- **Convenience** – paying taxes should be made as easy as possible and tax systems should be designed to be as simple as possible in order to help maximize tax revenue.
- **Economic** – any tax system must ensure that the cost of collecting and administering taxes is less than the amount collected.

Whilst these principles provide some guidance in the design of a good tax system they raise many questions. For example, if we agree on the principle that the rich should pay more in taxes than the poor, how much more should they pay? How do we define 'rich'? Is it fair that someone who has worked hard should pay far more in taxes than someone who is inherently lazy? At what point will this principle lead people to begin to seek ways to avoid tax and possibly exit the tax system altogether because of high tax rates?

We will look in more detail at some of the issues surrounding the design of a good tax system later in this section but we are now going to introduce some key concepts in any tax system.

Marginal Tax Rates Versus Average Tax Rates

When discussing the efficiency and equity of income or direct taxes, economists distinguish between two notions of the tax rate: the average and the marginal. The **average tax rate** (ATR) is total taxes paid divided by total income and can be expressed by the formula:

$$ATR = \frac{Tax\ liability}{Taxable\ income}$$

Where tax liability is the amount that the individual is liable to pay in tax to the tax authorities – the total tax paid.

The **marginal tax rate** (MTR) is the extra taxes paid on an additional unit of income expressed by the formula:

$$MTR = \frac{Change\ in\ tax\ liability}{Change\ in\ taxable\ income}$$

For example, suppose that the government taxes 20 per cent of the first €50 000 of income and 50 per cent of all income above €50 000. Under this tax, a person who earns €60 000 pays tax of €15 000: 20 per cent of the first €50 000 (0.20 × €50 000 = €10 000) plus 50 per cent of the next €10 000 (0.50 × €10 000 = €5000). For this person, the average tax rate is €15 000/€60 000, or 25 per cent. But the marginal tax rate is 50 per cent. If the taxpayer earned an additional euro of income, that euro would be subject to the 50 per cent tax rate, so the amount the taxpayer would owe to the government would rise by €0.50.

> **average tax rate** total taxes paid divided by total income
> **marginal tax rate** the extra taxes paid on an additional unit of income

The marginal and average tax rates each contain a useful piece of information. If we are trying to gauge the sacrifice made by a taxpayer, the average tax rate is more appropriate because it measures the fraction of income paid in taxes. By contrast, if we are trying to gauge how much the tax system distorts incentives, the marginal tax rate is more meaningful. The marginal tax rate measures how much the tax system discourages people from working. If you are thinking of working an extra few hours, the marginal tax rate determines how much the government takes of your additional earnings. It is the marginal tax rate, therefore, that determines the deadweight loss of an income tax.

Lump-Sum Taxes

Suppose the government imposes a tax of €4000 on everyone. That is, everyone owes the same amount, regardless of earnings or any actions that a person might take. Such a tax is called a **lump-sum tax**.

> **lump-sum tax** a tax that is the same amount for every person

A lump-sum tax shows clearly the difference between average and marginal tax rates. For a taxpayer with income of €20 000, the average tax rate of a €4000 lump-sum tax is 20 per cent; for a taxpayer with income of €40 000, the average tax rate is 10 per cent. For both taxpayers, the marginal tax rate is zero because no tax is owed on an additional unit of income.

A lump-sum tax is the most efficient tax possible. Because a person's decisions do not alter the amount owed, the tax does not distort incentives and, therefore, does not cause deadweight losses. Because everyone can easily compute the amount owed and because there is no benefit to hiring tax lawyers and accountants, the lump-sum tax imposes a minimal administrative burden on taxpayers. If lump-sum taxes are so efficient, why do we rarely observe them in the real world? The reason is that efficiency is only one goal of the tax system. A lump sum tax would take the same amount from the poor and the rich, an outcome most people would view as unfair and contrary to Smith's first canon. In the next section we consider the issue of equity.

SELF TEST What is meant by the efficiency of a tax system? What can make a tax system inefficient?

The Deadweight Loss Debate

The ideas covered so far in this chapter go to the heart of a profound political question: how big should the government sector be? The debate hinges on these concepts because the larger the deadweight loss of taxation, the larger the welfare cost of any government expenditure programme such as providing public health services or national defence. If taxation entails large deadweight losses, then these losses are a strong argument for a leaner government that does less and taxes less. But if taxes impose small deadweight losses, then government programmes are less costly than they otherwise might be.

So how big are the deadweight losses of taxation? This is a question about which economists disagree. To see the nature of this disagreement, consider one of the most important taxes in most advanced economies – the tax on labour. In the UK, for example, National Insurance contributions and, to a large extent, income tax, are taxes on labour. A labour tax places a wedge between the wage that firms pay and the wage that workers receive. If we add both forms of labour taxes together, the *marginal tax rate* on labour income – the tax on the last pound of earnings – is around 33 per cent for most UK manual workers. In some European countries – particularly Scandinavian countries – the marginal rate is even higher.

Although the size of the labour tax is easy to determine, the deadweight loss of this tax is less straightforward. Economists disagree about whether this 33 per cent labour tax has a small or a large deadweight loss. This disagreement arises because economists hold different views about the elasticity of labour supply.

Economists who argue that labour taxes are not very distorting believe that labour supply is fairly inelastic. Most people, they claim, would work full-time regardless of the wage. If so, the labour supply curve is almost vertical, and a tax on labour has a small deadweight loss.

Economists who argue that labour taxes are highly distorting believe that labour supply is more elastic. They admit that some groups of workers may supply their labour inelastically but claim that many other groups respond more to incentives. Here are some examples:
- Many workers can adjust the number of hours they work – for instance, by working overtime. The higher the wage, the more hours they choose to work.
- Some families have second earners with some discretion over whether to do unpaid work at home or paid work in the marketplace. When deciding whether to take a job, these second earners compare the benefits of being at home (including savings on the cost of childcare) with the wages they could earn.
- Many people can choose when to retire, and their decisions are partly based on the wage. Once they are retired, the wage determines their incentive to work part-time.
- Some people consider engaging in illegal economic activity, such as the drug trade, or working at jobs that pay 'under the table' to evade taxes. In deciding whether to work in the underground economy or at a legitimate job, these potential criminals compare what they can earn by breaking the law, with the wage they can earn legally.

In each of these cases, the quantity of labour supplied responds to the wage (the price of labour). Thus, the decisions of these workers are distorted when their labour earnings are taxed. Labour taxes encourage workers to work fewer hours, second earners to stay at home, the elderly to retire early and the unscrupulous to enter the underground economy.

These two views of labour taxation persist to this day. Indeed, whenever you see two political candidates debating whether the government should provide more services or reduce the tax burden, keep in mind that part of the disagreement may rest on different views about the elasticity of labour supply and the deadweight loss of taxation.

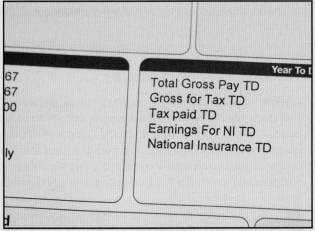

Taxes on income can lead to distorting effects on the labour market which result in deadweight losses.

TAXES AND EQUITY

In any country, tax policy always generates some of the most heated political debates. The heat is rarely fuelled by questions of efficiency. Instead, it usually arises from disagreements over how the tax burden should be distributed. Of course, if we are to rely on the government to provide some of the goods and services we want, taxes must fall on someone. How should the burden of taxes be divided among the population? How do we evaluate whether a tax system is fair? Everyone agrees that the tax system should be equitable, but there is much disagreement about what equity means and how the equity of a tax system can be judged.

The Benefits Principle

One principle of taxation, called the **benefits principle**, states that people should pay taxes based on the benefits they receive from government services. Just as a person who often goes to the cinema pays more in total for cinema tickets than a person who rarely goes, a person who gets great benefit from a good provided by the state should pay more for it than a person who gets little benefit.

 benefits principle the idea that people should pay taxes based on the benefits they receive from government services

The duty on petrol, for instance, is sometimes justified using the benefits principle, since in some countries, revenues from the tax on petrol are used to build and maintain roads. Because those who buy petrol are the same people who use the roads, this tax might be viewed as a fair way to pay for this government service.

The benefits principle can also be used to argue for Smith's first canon – that wealthy citizens should pay higher taxes than poorer ones. Why? Simply because the wealthy benefit more from public services. Consider, for example, the benefits of police protection from theft. Citizens with much to protect, it could be argued, get greater benefit from the police than those with less to protect. Therefore, according to the benefits principle, the wealthy should contribute more than the poor to the cost of maintaining the police force. The same argument can be used for many other public services, such as fire protection, national defence and the criminal justice system.

It is even possible to use the benefits principle to argue for anti-poverty programmes funded by taxes on the wealthy. If we assume that people prefer living in a society without poverty, this suggests that anti-poverty programmes are a desirable policy objective. If the wealthy place a greater value on this objective than other members of society, perhaps just because the wealthy have more to spend, then, according to the benefits principle, they should be taxed more heavily to pay for these programmes.

The Ability-to-Pay Principle

Another way to evaluate the equity of a tax system is called the **ability-to-pay principle**, which states that taxes should be levied on a person according to how well that person can shoulder the burden. This principle is sometimes justified by the claim that all citizens should make an 'equal sacrifice' to support the government. The magnitude of a person's sacrifice, however, depends not only on the size of their tax payment but also on their income and other circumstances. A €1000 tax paid by a poor person may require a larger sacrifice than a €10 000 tax paid by a rich person.

ability-to-pay principle the idea that taxes should be levied on a person according to how well that person can shoulder the burden

The ability-to-pay principle leads to two corollary notions of equity: vertical equity and horizontal equity. **Vertical equity** states that taxpayers with a greater ability to pay taxes should contribute a larger amount. **Horizontal equity** states that taxpayers with similar abilities to pay should contribute the same amount.

> **vertical equity** the idea that taxpayers with a greater ability to pay taxes should pay larger amounts
> **horizontal equity** the idea that taxpayers with similar abilities to pay taxes should pay the same amount

Although these notions of equity are widely accepted, applying them to evaluate a tax system is rarely straightforward.

Vertical Equity If taxes are based on ability to pay, then richer taxpayers should pay more than poorer taxpayers. But how much more should the rich pay? Much of the debate over tax policy concerns this question.

Consider the three tax systems in Table 9.1. In each case, taxpayers with higher incomes pay more. Yet the systems differ in how quickly taxes rise with income. The first system is called a **proportional tax** or sometimes a **flat tax** because all taxpayers pay the same fraction of income. The second system is called **regressive** because high-income taxpayers pay a smaller fraction of their income, even though they pay a larger amount. The third system is called **progressive** because high-income taxpayers pay a larger fraction of their income.

> **proportional tax** (or **flat tax**) a tax for which high-income and low-income taxpayers pay the same fraction of income
> **regressive tax** a tax for which high-income taxpayers pay a smaller fraction of their income than do low-income taxpayers
> **progressive tax** a tax for which high-income taxpayers pay a larger fraction of their income than do low-income taxpayers

Which of these three tax systems is most fair? Sometimes it is argued that a progressive tax system is fairer because richer people pay more tax and they can afford to do so because they are richer. But richer people will also pay more tax than poorer people under a flat tax system or even under a regressive tax system. In fact, there is no obvious answer, and economic theory does not offer any help in trying to find one. Equity, like beauty, is in the eye of the beholder.

TABLE 9.1 Three Tax Systems

Income (€)	Proportional or flat tax		Regressive tax		Progressive tax	
	Amount of tax (€)	Percentage of income (%)	Amount of tax (€)	Percentage of income (%)	Amount of tax (€)	Percentage of income (%)
50 000	12 500	25	15 000	30	10 000	20
100 000	25 000	25	25 000	25	25 000	25
200 000	50 000	25	40 000	20	60 000	30

Horizontal Equity If taxes are based on ability to pay, then similar taxpayers should pay similar amounts of taxes. But what determines if two taxpayers are similar? Individuals' circumstances can differ in many ways. To evaluate whether a tax system is horizontally equitable, one must determine which differences are relevant for a person's ability to pay and which differences are not.

Suppose Mr Smith and Ms Jones each have an income of €50 000 a year. Mr Smith is unmarried and has no children, but he has an illness that means that he has to employ someone to be with him while he is at work and getting to and from his place of business. This costs him €20 000 a year. Ms Jones is in good health and is a lone parent with a child aged three. Ms Jones has to pay €15 000 a year for childcare while she is at work. Would it be fair for Mr Smith and Ms Jones to pay the same tax because they have the same income? Would it be fairer to give Mr Smith a tax break to help him offset the costs of a caring assistant? Would it be fairer to give Ms Jones a tax break to compensate her for the cost of childcare?

There are no easy answers to these questions.

Tax Incidence and Tax Equity

Tax incidence – the study of who bears the burden of taxes – is central to evaluating tax equity. We know from Chapter 8 that the person who bears the burden of a tax is not always the person who gets the tax bill from the government. Because taxes alter supply and demand, they alter equilibrium prices. As a result, they affect people beyond those who, according to statute, actually pay the tax. When evaluating the vertical and horizontal equity of any tax, it is important to take account of these indirect effects.

Many discussions of tax equity ignore the indirect effects of taxes and are based on what economists mockingly call the 'flypaper theory of tax incidence'. According to this theory, the burden of a tax, like a fly on flypaper, sticks wherever it first lands.

A person not trained in economics might argue that a tax on expensive diamond rings is vertically equitable because most buyers of such products are wealthy. Yet if these buyers can easily substitute other luxuries for rings, then a tax on diamond rings might only reduce the sale of rings. In the end, the burden of the tax may fall more on those who make and sell diamond rings (in terms of lost income) than on those who buy them. Many workers who make diamond rings will not be wealthy; the equity of a ring tax could be quite different from what the flypaper theory indicates.

Corporate taxes – taxes levied on the profits that businesses make – provides a good example of the importance of tax incidence for tax policy. Corporate taxes are popular among voters. After all, corporations are not people. Voters are always eager to have their taxes reduced and have some impersonal business corporation pick up the tab. In a sense, corporation tax appears to be a tax that is imposed on nobody. But before deciding that corporation tax is a good way for the government to raise revenue, we should consider who bears the burden of corporation tax. This is a difficult question on which economists disagree, but one thing is certain: *people pay all taxes*. When the government levies a tax on a corporation, the corporation is more like a tax collector than a taxpayer. The burden of the tax ultimately falls on people – the owners, customers or workers of the corporation.

Some economists believe that workers and customers bear much of the burden of corporation tax. To see why, consider an example. Suppose that the government decides to raise the tax on the income earned by car companies. At first, this tax hurts the owners of the car companies who receive less profit. Over time, these owners will respond to the tax. Because producing cars is less profitable, they invest less in building new car factories. Instead, they invest their wealth in other ways – for example, by buying larger houses or by building factories in other industries or other countries. With fewer car factories, the supply of cars declines, as does the demand for car workers. Thus, a tax on corporations making cars causes the price of cars to rise and the wages of car workers to fall.

Corporation tax shows how dangerous the flypaper theory of tax incidence can be. Corporation tax is popular in part because it appears to be paid by rich corporations. Yet those who bear the ultimate burden of the tax – the customers and workers of corporations – are often not rich. If the true incidence of corporation tax were more widely known, this tax might be less popular among voters – and policymakers.

SELF TEST Explain the benefits principle and the ability-to-pay principle. What are vertical equity and horizontal equity? Why is studying tax incidence important for determining the equity of a tax system?

CONCLUSION

Oliver Wendell Holmes, an American jurist in a speech in 1904, is reputed to have said 'Taxes are the price we pay for a civilized society'. Indeed, our society cannot exist without some form of taxes. We all expect the government to provide us with certain services, such as roads, parks, police and national defence. These public services require tax revenue. This chapter has shed some light on how high the price of civilized society can be. Taxes do have costs not only because taxes transfer resources from one group of economic agents to another but also because they alter incentives and change market outcomes. Throughout this chapter we have assumed that the benefit to the government, or more accurately, the third party who receives the benefit of the tax spending, is equal to the tax revenue given by $T \times Q$. This may not always be the case. To get a more accurate analysis of the size of deadweight losses arising from taxes, we may have to find a way to place a value on the benefits of the tax spending. For example, if taxes are spent on improving the road infrastructure there is a benefit to car drivers and the overall economy through more efficient transport networks, which may be greater than the tax spending. Calculating the value of these benefits is not easy but has to be carried out to get a more accurate picture of the change in welfare. How the government chooses to spend tax revenue is also a factor to consider. A paper on the subject (Gupta, S. Verhoeven, M. and Tiongson, E.R. (2004) 'Public Spending on Health Care and the Poor'. In Gupta, S. Clements, B., Inchauste, G. (eds), *Helping Countries Develop: The Role of Fiscal Policy*, Washington, DC: IMF) concluded that in 70 developing and transition economies there was evidence to suggest that the impact of public spending on healthcare for the poor could be substantial in comparison with spending on the non-poor. A one per cent increase in public spending on health, for example, reduces child mortality by twice as many deaths among the poor as the non-poor and infant mortality rates are similarly affected. This highlights that there are many other factors that may have to be taken into consideration when analyzing changes in welfare as a result of taxes.

In the second half of this chapter we looked at equity and efficiency under different tax systems. Often, these two goals conflict. Many proposed changes to the tax laws increase efficiency while reducing equity, or they increase equity whilst reducing efficiency. People disagree about tax policy often because they attach different weights to these two goals.

Economics alone cannot determine the best way to balance the goals of efficiency and equity. This issue involves political philosophy as well as economics. But economists do have an important role in the political debate over tax policy: they can shed light on the trade-offs that society faces and can help us avoid policies that sacrifice efficiency without any benefit in terms of equity.

IN THE NEWS

Taxes and Happiness

Since 2012, the Sustainable Development Solutions Network (SDSN) have published a regular survey on the state of global happiness. The survey reports on measures of well-being based on the assumption that 'happiness' should be a focus of public policy.

Scandinavian Happiness and High Taxes

In the three reports published by the SDSN since 2012, one feature has been that Scandinavian countries are in the top five when countries are ranked for their happiness. The Danes in particular have scored well on the happiness index, enjoying the mantle of 'happiest people' on the planet. In the most recent report published in 2015, Denmark was ranked third and Norway fourth behind Iceland and Switzerland. The ranking relates to happiness as explained by different criteria including GDP per capita, social support, life expectancy, freedom to make life choices, generosity and perceptions of corruption.

Tax revenue and tax rates in Denmark and Norway are relatively high in comparison to other developed economies. Tax revenue as a percentage of GDP in Denmark is around 48 per cent and in Norway around 43 per cent. This compares with around 36 per cent, 35 per cent and 25 per cent in Germany the UK and the USA respectively. The top marginal tax rates in Denmark, Norway and Sweden are around 60–70 per cent compared to around 43 per cent in the USA. Intuition might suggest that higher taxes should not equate with higher levels of happiness.

One explanation for the regular appearance of Denmark and Norway in the top five of the world Happiness Report is that the quality of healthcare, education, infrastructure and social security support in these countries, paid for by tax revenue, is high and these contribute considerably to feelings of happiness and security. The support given

(Continued)

Scandinavian countries often top happiness surveys.

by governments to those in society who are least able to help themselves can translate into reductions in crime, teenage pregnancy, obesity, suicide and better healthcare which might mean people are able to live not just longer lives but also healthier, longer lives. People may value these aspects of society far more than they value the physical items that they are able to buy with higher levels of disposable income. After all, it might be one thing to have a high income which is taxed at a low level but be fearful of the danger of having what you have worked hard for stolen because society has a high crime rate, which may in turn be influenced by individuals turning to crime to feed drug habits brought on by the feeling of helplessness or inability to partake in society. Happiness may also be influenced by the fact that high tax rates mean the incentive to work is reduced. British journalist and author, Michael Booth, has noted that Danes have a relatively high leisure to work ratio which is partly explained by the fact that tax rates are so high. Many Danes, he notes, finish work relatively early each day and around 20 per cent 'do no work at all'.

There are, however, views which question the extent to which the Danes and Norwegians really are 'happy'. Happiness may be a function of expectation – if your expectations are relatively low then your reporting of happiness may be relatively high. People in Denmark and Norway might express pride at the fact that their education, welfare and health systems are comparatively well-funded and that they feel a great deal of security in knowing that they want for little in comparison to other countries in these areas. It might be argued that this sort of security makes for a boring life. Michael Booth, in his book, '*The Almost Nearly Perfect People: Behind the Myth of the Scandinavian Utopia*' presents a view from Copenhagen Business School economist, Ove Kaj Pederson: 'Every day I conclude the best place to live is Denmark, but for me this kind of social cohesion, these middle-class-oriented societies, do not present the kind of challenges I am looking for. I want to be in the best places, and you don't find the best places in Denmark when it comes to elite research and education. And why the hell can't you go down to the bookstore in the morning and buy *The New York Times* for five dollars? Or get a good cup of coffee for a cheap price?'

Questions

1 Tax revenues can be used to pay for healthcare which is free at the point of use and a strong healthcare system may contribute to happiness. Why do you think that many countries use tax revenues to pay for healthcare services for the population?

2 To what extent would you argue that the tax system in countries like Denmark and Norway are efficient and equitable? Explain your reasoning.

3 High taxes reduce the willingness to work but this also means more people have a better work–life balance. To what extent do you agree with this statement? Justify your answer.

4 Consumption taxes in Denmark and Norway are around 31 per cent and 26 per cent respectively whilst in the United States they are around 18 per cent. How far do consumption taxes satisfy Smith' canons of taxation and what type of tax system would you say consumption taxes are (i.e., are they progressive, proportional or regressive)? Explain.

5 In the case of countries like Denmark and Norway, can it be argued that the value of the benefits to society of high tax rates (indicated by the reports of happiness) outweigh the deadweight loss imposed by such a tax system? Explain.

SUMMARY

- The efficiency of a tax system refers to the costs that it imposes on taxpayers. There are two costs of taxes beyond the transfer of resources from the taxpayer to the government. The first is the distortion in the allocation of resources that arises as taxes alter incentives and behaviour. The second is the administrative burden of complying with the tax laws.

- A tax on a good reduces the welfare of buyers and sellers of the good, and the reduction in consumer and producer surplus usually exceeds the revenue raised by the government. The fall in total surplus – the sum of consumer surplus, producer surplus and tax revenue – is called the deadweight loss of the tax.

- Taxes have deadweight losses because they cause buyers to consume less and sellers to produce less, and this change in behaviour shrinks the size of the market below the level that maximizes total surplus. Because the elasticities of supply and demand measure how much market participants respond to market conditions, larger elasticities imply larger deadweight losses.

- As a tax grows larger, it distorts incentives more, and its deadweight loss grows larger. Tax revenue first rises with the size of a tax. Eventually, however, a larger tax reduces tax revenue because it reduces the size of the market.

- The equity of a tax system concerns whether the tax burden is distributed fairly among the population. According to the benefits principle, it is fair for people to pay taxes based on the benefits they receive from the government. According to the ability-to-pay principle, it is fair for people to pay taxes based on their capability to handle the financial burden. When evaluating the equity of a tax system, it is important to remember a lesson from the study of tax incidence: the distribution of tax burdens is not the same as the distribution of tax bills.

- When considering changes in the tax laws, policymakers often face a trade-off between efficiency and equity. Much of the debate over tax policy arises because people give different weights to these two goals.

QUESTIONS FOR REVIEW

1 What are the two main reasons that governments levy taxes?

2 What happens to consumer and producer surplus when the sale of a good is taxed? How does the change in consumer and producer surplus compare to the tax revenue? Explain.

3 Draw a supply and demand diagram with a tax on the sale of the good. Show the deadweight loss. Show the tax revenue.

4 How do the elasticities of supply and demand affect the deadweight loss of a tax? Why do they have this effect?

5 What happens to the deadweight loss and tax revenue when a tax is increased?

6 What are the four canons of taxation?

7 Explain how corporate profits are taxed twice.

8 Why is the burden of a tax to taxpayers greater than the revenue received by the government?

9 Give two arguments why wealthy taxpayers should pay more taxes than poor taxpayers.

10 What is the concept of horizontal equity, and why is it hard to apply?

PROBLEMS AND APPLICATIONS

1 The market for pizza is characterized by a downwards sloping demand curve and an upwards sloping supply curve.

a. Draw the competitive market equilibrium. Label the price, quantity, consumer surplus and producer surplus. Is there any deadweight loss? Explain.

b. Suppose that the government forces each pizzeria to pay a €11 tax on each pizza sold. Illustrate the effect of this tax on the pizza market, being sure to label the consumer surplus, producer surplus, government revenue and deadweight loss. How does each area compare to the pre-tax case?

c. If the tax was removed, pizza eaters and sellers would be better off, but the government would lose tax revenue. Suppose that consumers and producers voluntarily transferred some of their gains to the government. Could all parties (including the government) be better off than they were with a tax? Explain using the labelled areas in your graph.

2 Evaluate the following two statements. Do you agree? Why or why not?

a. 'If the government taxes land, wealthy landowners will pass the tax on to their poorer renters.'
b. 'If the government taxes blocks of flats, wealthy landlords will pass the tax on to their poorer renters.'

3 Evaluate the following two statements. Do you agree? Why or why not?

a. 'A tax that has no deadweight loss cannot raise any revenue for the government.'
b. 'A tax that raises no revenue for the government cannot have any deadweight loss.'

4 A government is considering increasing consumption and income taxes in order to raise revenue which will be earmarked for investment into improved transport and technology infrastructure. What might the short term and long term effects of this decision be? Do you think such a decision is justified? Explain.

5 Suppose that the government imposes a tax on heating oil.

a. Would the deadweight loss from this tax likely be greater in the first year after it is imposed or in the fifth year? Explain.
b. Would the revenue collected from this tax likely be greater in the first year after it is imposed or in the fifth year? Explain.

6 This chapter analyzed the welfare effects of a tax on a good. Consider now the opposite policy. Suppose that the government subsidizes a good: for each unit of the good sold, the government pays €2 to the buyer. How does the subsidy affect consumer surplus, producer surplus, tax revenue and total surplus? Does a subsidy lead to a deadweight loss? Explain.

7 A sales tax of 20 per cent is levied on clothing for adults but not on children's clothing. Discuss the merits of this distinction, considering both efficiency and equity.

8 Suppose that the tax system had the following features. Explain how individuals' behaviour is affected.

a. Contributions to charity are tax-deductible.
b. Sales of beer are taxed.
c. Realized capital gains are taxed, but accrued gains are not. (When someone owns a share of stock that rises in value, she has an 'accrued' capital gain. If she sells the share, she has a 'realized' gain.)

9 Suppose that a market is described by the following supply and demand equations:

$$Q_S = 2P$$
$$Q_D = 300 - P$$

a. Solve for the equilibrium price and the equilibrium quantity.
b. Suppose that a tax of T is placed on buyers, so the new demand equation is:

$$Q_D = 300 - (P + T):$$

Solve for the new equilibrium. What happens to the price received by sellers, the price paid by buyers and the quantity sold?
c. Tax revenue is $T \times Q$. Use your answer to part (b) to solve for tax revenue as a function of T. Graph this relationship for T between 0 and 300.
d. The deadweight loss of a tax is the area of the triangle between the supply and demand curves. Recalling that the area of a triangle is $1/2 \times$ base $\times$ height, solve for deadweight loss as a function of T. Graph this relationship for T between 0 and 300. (Hint: looking sideways, the base of the deadweight loss triangle is T, and the height is the difference between the quantity sold with the tax and the quantity sold without the tax.)
e. The government now levies a tax on this good of €200 per unit. Is this a good policy? Why or why not? Can you propose a better policy?

10 The tax on cigarettes and other smoking products is very high in many countries (in the UK it is over 80 per cent of the selling price) and has been rising over time. Discuss the merits of this policy, considering the principles of equity and efficiency.

PART 5
INEFFICIENT MARKET ALLOCATIONS

10 PUBLIC GOODS, COMMON RESOURCES AND MERIT GOODS

In all the chapters so far we have talked about the market providing goods and services. Demand reflects the benefit and value buyers put on goods, shown by their willingness to pay, and supply reflects the cost to producers. Price acts as a signal to buyers and sellers and allocates scarce resources among competing uses. Based on this understanding, how much would you, individually, be prepared to pay for national defence, justice or a police service? Would you be prepared to pay for street lighting, local playgrounds and parks? Have you ever thought about who owns things such as rivers, mountains, beaches, lakes and oceans? Many people enjoy the benefit of these goods but do not pay directly for them. These goods and services come under special categories in economic analysis. When goods are available but users do not have to pay directly, market forces that allocate resources in an economy are absent.

These types of goods would either not be produced under a market system or not produced in quantities deemed appropriate to satisfy needs. When this happens, the market fails to allocate scarce resources efficiently (because needs are not being met). The fact that some goods and services cannot be provided through a market system, or not provided in sufficient quantities, is referred to as an example of *market failure*. Goods and services which the market fails to provide are invariably provided by governments for the benefit of all, through taxation.

The **public sector** refers to the provision of goods and services which are funded and organized by the state on behalf of the population as a whole. This contrasts with the **private sector** where goods and services are funded and organized by private firms, usually, but not exclusively, with a view to making a profit. Some people would add to this categorization, a 'third' or 'voluntary sector', which consists of firms or organizations including charities, community groups and not-for-profit firms.

> **public sector** that part of the economy where business activity is owned, financed and controlled by the state, and goods and services are provided by the state on behalf of the population as a whole
> **private sector** that part of the economy where business activity is owned, financed and controlled by private individuals

THE DIFFERENT KINDS OF GOODS

In thinking about the various goods in the economy, it is useful to group them according to two characteristics:

- Is the good **excludable**? Can people who do not pay for the use of a good be prevented from using the good?
- Is the good **rival**? Does one person's use of the good diminish another person's ability to use it?

> **excludable** the property of a good whereby a person can be prevented from using it when they do not pay for it
> **rival** the property of a good whereby one person's use diminishes other people's use

Using these two characteristics, we can divide goods into four categories:

1. **Private goods** are both excludable and rival. Consider a chocolate bar, for example. A chocolate bar is excludable because it is possible to prevent someone from eating the bar – you just don't give it to them. A chocolate bar is rival because if one person eats the bar, another person cannot eat the same bar. Most goods in the economy are private goods like chocolate bars. To acquire a chocolate bar you invariably have to pay for it to gain the benefits. Our analysis of supply and demand so far has been based on the implicit assumption that goods were both excludable and rival.
2. **Public goods** are neither excludable nor rival. People cannot be prevented from using a public good, and one person's use of a public good does not reduce another person's ability to use it. For example, a country's national defence system: it protects all of the country's citizens equally and the fact that one person is being defended does not affect whether or not another citizen is defended. Once one citizen is defended it does not reduce the benefit to anyone else and so is not rival in consumption.
3. **Common resources** are rival but not excludable in consumption. When one person catches fish, there are fewer fish for the next person to catch. Yet these fish are not an excludable good because, given the vast size of an ocean, it is difficult to stop fishermen from taking fish out of it when, for example, they have not paid for a licence to do so.
4. **Club goods** are excludable but not rival in consumption. Consider fire protection in a small town. It is easy to exclude people from using this good if people chose not to pay: the fire service can just let their house burn down. Yet fire protection is not rival in consumption. Fire fighters spend much of their time waiting for a fire, so protecting an extra house is unlikely to reduce the protection available to others. In other words, once a town has paid for the fire service, the additional cost of protecting one more house is small. Club goods are a type of natural monopoly which we deal with in more detail in Chapter 14.

> **private goods** goods that are both excludable and rival
> **public goods** goods that are neither excludable nor rival
> **common resources** goods that are rival but not excludable
> **club goods** goods that are excludable but non-rival in consumption

For both public goods and common resources, a cost or benefit arises because something of value has no price attached to it. If one person were to provide a public good, such as a national defence system, other people would be better off, and yet they could not be charged for this benefit. Similarly, when one person uses a common resource, such as the fish in the ocean, other people are worse off, and yet they are not compensated for this loss. These are referred to as external effects or *externalities* and we will look at externalities in more detail in Chapter 11. Because of these external effects, private decisions about consumption and production can lead to an inefficient allocation of resources, and government intervention can potentially raise economic well-being.

> **SELF TEST** Explain why you might be unwilling to pay for a street light outside your house and how this highlights how a pure market system might fail to provide a good which yields benefits to consumers.

PUBLIC GOODS

To understand how public goods differ from other goods and what problems they present for society, let's consider an example: a fireworks display. This good is not excludable because it is impossible to prevent someone from seeing fireworks, and it is not rival because one person's enjoyment of fireworks does not reduce anyone else's enjoyment of them.

The Free Rider Problem

The citizens of a small Spanish town, Hereza, like seeing fireworks on 6 January when Spain celebrates Epiphany. Each of the town's 500 residents places a €10 value on the experience. The cost of putting on a fireworks display is €1000. Because the €5000 of benefits exceed the €1000 of costs, it is efficient for Hereza residents to have a fireworks display on 6 January.

Would the private market produce the efficient outcome? Probably not. Imagine that Conchita, a Hereza entrepreneur, decided to put on a fireworks display. Conchita may have trouble selling tickets to the event because her potential customers would quickly figure out that they could see the fireworks even without a ticket (unless Conchita could figure out a way in which she could keep the display 'private' somehow). Because fireworks are not excludable, people have an incentive to be free riders. A **free rider** is a person who receives the benefit of a good but avoids paying for it.

> **free rider** a person who receives the benefit of a good but avoids paying for it

One way to view this market failure is that it arises because of an externality. If Conchita did put on the fireworks display, she would confer an external benefit on those who saw the display without paying for it. When deciding whether to put on the display, Conchita ignores these external benefits. Even though a fireworks display is socially desirable, it is not privately profitable. As a result, Conchita makes the socially inefficient decision not to put on the display.

Although the private market fails to supply the fireworks display demanded by Hereza residents, the solution to Hereza's problem could be given by the local government sponsoring a Twelfth Night celebration. The town council raises revenue by levying taxes on property in the area (in Spain these local property taxes are known as *Impuesto sobre Bienes Inmuebles* (IBI)). Suppose that the council uses this mechanism so as to raise on average an extra €2 a year from every resident of Hereza and then uses the resulting revenue to hire Conchita to produce the fireworks. Everyone in Hereza is better off by €8 – the €10 in value from the fireworks minus the €2 tax bill.

The story of Hereza is simplified, but it is also realistic. In fact, many local councils in Spain do pay for fireworks for festivals, as do local councils in the United Kingdom on 5 November; local governments in France pay for fireworks on 14 July (Bastille Day) and many local governments in the USA pay for fireworks on 4 July (Independence Day). Moreover, the story shows a general lesson about public goods: because public goods are not excludable, the free rider problem prevents the private market from supplying them. The government, however, can potentially remedy the problem. If the government decides that the total benefits exceed the costs, it can provide the public good and pay for it with tax revenue, making everyone better off.

Some Important Public Goods

There are many examples of public goods. Here we consider three of the most important.

National Defence The defence of the country from foreign aggressors is a classic example of a public good. Once the country is defended, it is impossible to prevent any single person from enjoying the benefit of this defence. Moreover, when one person enjoys the benefit of national defence, they do not reduce the benefit to anyone else. Thus, national defence is neither excludable nor rival.

Basic Research The creation of knowledge is a public good. If a mathematician proves a new theorem, the theorem enters the general pool of knowledge that anyone can use without charge. Because knowledge is a public good, profit-seeking firms tend to free ride on the knowledge created by others and, as a result, devote too few resources to creating new knowledge.

In evaluating the appropriate policy towards knowledge creation, it is important to distinguish general knowledge from specific, technological knowledge. Specific, technological knowledge, such as the invention of a better battery, can be patented. The inventor thus obtains much of the benefit of their invention, although certainly not all of it. By contrast, a mathematician cannot patent a theorem; such general knowledge is freely available to everyone. In other words, the patent system makes specific, technological knowledge excludable, whereas general knowledge is not excludable.

Fighting Poverty Many government expenditure programmes are aimed at helping the poor. These anti-poverty programmes are financed by taxes on families that are financially more successful. Economists disagree among themselves about what role the government should play in fighting poverty. Here we note one important argument: advocates of anti-poverty programmes claim that fighting poverty is a public good.

Suppose that everyone prefers to live in a society without poverty. Even if this preference is strong and widespread, fighting poverty is not a 'good' that the private market can provide. No single individual can eliminate poverty because the problem is so large. Moreover, private charity is hard pressed to solve the problem: people who do not donate to charity can free ride on the generosity of others. In this case, taxing the wealthy to raise the living standards of the poor can make everyone better off. The poor are better off because they now enjoy a higher standard of living, and those paying the taxes are better off because they enjoy living in a society with less poverty and the associated problems that can arise because of poverty – crime, drug abuse, mental illness and so on.

The Difficult Job of Cost-benefit Analysis

So far we have seen that the government provides public goods because the private market on its own will not produce an efficient quantity. Yet deciding that the government must play a role is only the first step. The government must then determine what kinds of public goods to provide and in what quantities.

Suppose that the government is considering a public project, such as building a new motorway or autobahn. To judge whether to build the motorway, it must compare the total benefits of all those who would use it to the costs of building and maintaining it. To make this decision, the government might hire a team of economists and engineers to conduct a study, called a **cost-benefit analysis**, the goal of which is to estimate the total costs and benefits of the project to society as a whole.

> **cost-benefit analysis** a study that compares the costs and benefits to society of providing a public good

Cost-benefit analysis might be used when considering major infrastructure projects such as building dams, bridges, new railway lines, opening up canals and waterways for freight (and leisure) traffic, developing new port facilities, introducing or extending speed cameras on the road network, developing new water treatment and distribution networks, public transport networks such as subways and tram systems, investing in networks to improve internet access for both businesses and private consumers, extending or constructing new airports and so on.

Cost-benefit analysts have a tough job. Because a motorway will be available to everyone free of charge (unless it is specifically built as a private sector project as a toll road), there is no price with which to judge the value of the motorway. Simply asking people how much they would value the motorway is not reliable: quantifying benefits is difficult using the results from a questionnaire, and respondents have little incentive to tell the truth. Those who would use the motorway have an incentive to exaggerate the benefit they receive to get the motorway built. Those who would be harmed by the motorway have an incentive to exaggerate the costs to them to prevent the motorway from being built.

The efficient provision of public goods is intrinsically more difficult than the efficient provision of private goods. Buyers of a private good reveal the value they place on it by the prices they are willing to pay when they purchase and thus use a good (this is referred to as *revealed preference*). Sellers reveal their costs by the prices they are willing to accept. By contrast, cost-benefit analysts do not observe any price signals when evaluating whether the government should provide a public good. Their findings on the costs and benefits of public projects are, therefore, rough approximations at best.

Contingent Valuation Methods (CVM) To overcome some of the problems associated with cost-benefit analysis, contingent valuation can be used. This method is a survey-based approach which aims to place a monetary value on a good through getting respondents to state a preference and a willingness to pay. The difference between revealed preference as outlined above and stated preference is that the latter allows a valuation based on non-use, that is, the value that individuals place on a good even if they do not use them. Questions in surveys provide respondents with options which attempt to discover their preferences in both how much they are prepared to give up to secure the benefit (for example, reduced pollution), termed willingness-to-pay (WTP) and how much they would need to be paid to put up with a cost (for example, a certain level of pollution) termed willingness to accept (WTA). For example, CVM might be used when seeking to find out what value individuals place on having improved water and sewage treatment services.

In preparing the survey, care needs to be taken to ensure that the good itself and the proposed changes to the good are clearly defined so that respondents can more easily understand what they are being asked to value. The data collected allow researchers to be able to link WTP and WTA responses to changes in utility measured in monetary units. However, CVM presents difficulties in that respondents may not be familiar with the scenarios and the choices they are being asked to make. In addition, it is not always clear how seriously respondents treat the questions or think about their responses because there is no cost associated to them in doing so. As a result the reliability of the surveys can be questioned.

SELF TEST What is the free rider problem? Why does the free rider problem induce the government to provide public goods? How should the government decide whether to provide a public good?

The Optimal Provision of a Public Good

Governments provide public goods because they provide a benefit to society as a whole. We can assume that governments might continue to provide a public good up to a point where the marginal benefit gained from an extra unit provided is equal to the marginal cost of providing that extra unit. When considering the marginal cost of providing public goods we also have to consider the opportunity cost of the resources used in the provision of public goods. The marginal benefit of an extra unit of provision of a public good will be shared by a large number of consumers because of the fact that public goods are non-rival. To find the total benefit of the provision of public goods we have to add up all the marginal benefits that users gain.

This is represented in Figure 10.1. On the vertical axis is price in euros and on the horizontal axis the quantity of the public good provided. In reality there are large numbers of people who benefit from public goods, but in Figure 10.1 we assume there are just two consumers denoted by the demand curves D_1 and D_2. We could extend the number of demand curves to match the number of people in society but providing the simplification of representing society with just two people illustrates the principle just as well.

The demand curve D_1 represents the first consumer's demand for the public good and demand curve D_2 the second consumer's demand for the public good. Demand curve D_1 shows that consumer 1 places a value on the 20th unit of the public good provided of €31.25 and demand curve D_2 shows that consumer 2 places a value on the 20th unit of the public good provided of €93.75. Because the good is non-rival, both gain benefits from using the public good and so the sum of the benefits of the two consumers of the 20th unit provided is the vertical summation of these two values (€125). We can sum the benefits of both consumers at quantities of the public good from 0 to 80 units and we get the marginal social benefit (MSB) curve - a kinked demand curve shown as ABC which is the vertical summation of the two individual consumer demand curves.

The optimum provision of this public good would be where the marginal cost of providing the public good intersects the MSB curve. If the marginal cost of providing this public good were €100 per unit then the optimum provision would be 30 units of the public good. If the government provided more of this public good (say 40 units), the marginal cost of providing this amount would exceed the MSB which at 40 units is €75. It would also not be efficient to produce anything less than 30 units (20 for example), because the MSB at 20 units (€125) is greater than the marginal cost of provision (€100) so it would be appropriate to expand provision of this public good.

FIGURE 10.1

The Optimum Provision of a Public Good

Society's collective benefit from the provision of a public good is given by the two demand curves D₁ and D₂. The sum of the benefits of these two consumers is the vertical summation of the value each places on the marginal unit of the public good supplied. The kinked demand curve, ABC, is the marginal social benefit (MSB) curve. The optimum provision of this public good is the intersection of the marginal cost of providing this public good with the MSB curve when 30 units are provided and the MSB at this level of provision is equal to the marginal cost at €100.

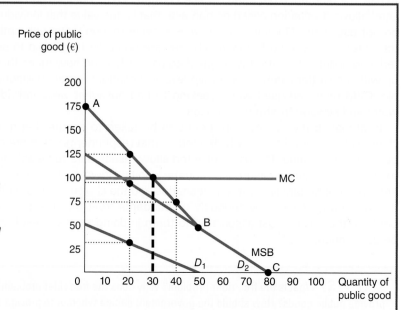

As we have noted many times so far, this is a model to illustrate a point. In this case the point is that in deciding on an appropriate allocation of resources for the provision of public goods, some consideration has to be given to the costs of providing that good and the benefit accruing to society as a whole of the provision. Economists will try to quantify the costs and benefits and whilst it will never be possible to fully quantify such costs and benefits, an attempt to do so enables a more informed decision to be made which might better meet society's needs and use scarce resources more effectively.

COMMON RESOURCES

Common resources, like public goods, are not excludable: they are available free of charge to anyone who wants to use them. Common resources are, however, rival: one person's use of the common resource reduces other people's ability to use it. Thus, common resources give rise to a new problem. Once the good is provided, users and policymakers need to be concerned about how much it is used. This problem is best understood from the classic parable called the **Tragedy of the Commons**, a term used by Garrett Hardin in an essay published in 1968.

> **Tragedy of the Commons** a parable that illustrates why common resources get used more than is desirable from the standpoint of society as a whole

The Tragedy of the Commons

Consider life in a small town and the many economic activities that take place in the town. One of these activities is raising sheep. Many of the town's families own flocks of sheep and support themselves by selling the sheep's wool, which is used to make clothing.

As our story begins, the sheep spend much of their time grazing on the land surrounding the town, called the Town Common. No family owns the land. Instead, the town residents own the land collectively, and all the residents are allowed to graze their sheep on it. Collective ownership works well because land is plentiful. As long as everyone can get all the good grazing land they want, the Town Common is not a rival good, and allowing residents' sheep to graze for free causes no problems. Everyone in town is happy.

As the years pass, the population of the town grows, and so does the number of sheep grazing on the Town Common. With a growing number of sheep and a fixed amount of land, the land starts to lose its ability to replenish itself. Eventually, the land is grazed so heavily that it becomes barren. With no grass left on the Town Common, raising sheep is impossible, and the town's once prosperous wool industry disappears and many families lose their source of livelihood.

The 'tragedy' occurs because social and private incentives differ. Avoiding the destruction of the grazing land depends on the collective action of the shepherds. If the shepherds acted together, they could reduce the sheep population to a size that the Town Common could support. Yet no single family has an incentive to reduce the size of its own flock because each flock represents only a small part of the problem.

In essence, the Tragedy of the Commons arises because of an externality. When one family's flock grazes on the common land, it reduces the quality of the land available for other families. This is a social cost. Because people neglect the social cost when deciding how many sheep to own, the result is an excessive number of sheep.

If the tragedy had been foreseen, the town could have solved the problem in various ways. It could have regulated the number of sheep in each family's flock, taken account of the social cost by taxing sheep, or auctioned off a limited number of sheep-grazing permits.

In the case of land, however, there is a simpler solution. The town can divide up the land among town families. Each family can enclose its allotment of land with a fence and then protect it from excessive grazing. In this way, the land becomes a private good rather than a common resource. This outcome occurred during the enclosure movement in England in the 17th century.

The Tragedy of the Commons is a story with a general lesson: when one person uses a common resource, they diminish other people's enjoyment of it. Because of this negative externality, common resources tend to be used excessively. The government can solve the problem by reducing use of the common resource through regulation or taxes. Alternatively, the government can sometimes turn the common resource into a private good.

This lesson has been known for thousands of years. The ancient Greek philosopher Aristotle pointed out the problem with common resources: 'What is common to many is taken least care of, for all men have greater regard for what is their own than for what they possess in common with others.'

Some Important Common Resources

There are many examples of common resources. In many cases private decision makers use the common resource too much. Governments often regulate behaviour or impose fees to mitigate the problem of overuse.

Clean Air and Water Markets do not adequately protect the environment. Pollution is a social cost that can be remedied with regulations or with taxes on polluting activities (as we shall see in more detail in Chapter 11). One can view this market failure as an example of a common-resource problem. Clean air and clean water are common resources like open grazing land, and excessive pollution is like excessive grazing. Environmental degradation is a modern Tragedy of the Commons.

Congested Roads Roads can be either public goods or common resources. If a road is not congested, then one person's use does not affect anyone else. In this case, use is not rival, and the road is a public good. Yet if a road is congested, then use of that road yields a social cost. When one person drives on the road, it becomes more crowded, and other people must drive more slowly. In this case, the road is a common resource.

One way for the government to address the problem of road congestion is to charge drivers a toll. A toll is, in essence, a tax on the social cost of congestion. Often, as in the case of local roads, tolls are not a practical solution because the cost of collecting them is too high. Nevertheless, tolls are often charged on stretches of motorways in continental Europe and the USA, and occasionally in the UK (on the M6, for example).

Sometimes congestion is a problem only at certain times of day. If a bridge is heavily travelled only during rush hour, for instance, the congestion social cost is larger during this time than during other times of day. The efficient way to deal with these social costs is to charge higher tolls during rush hour. This toll would provide an incentive for drivers to alter their schedules to reduce traffic when congestion is greatest.

Another policy that responds to the problem of road congestion is a tax on petrol. Petrol is a complementary good to driving: an increase in the price of petrol tends to reduce the quantity of driving demanded. Therefore, a petrol tax reduces road congestion. A petrol tax, however, is an imperfect solution to road congestion. The problem is that the petrol tax affects other decisions besides the amount of driving on congested roads. For example, the petrol tax discourages driving on non-congested roads, even though there is no congestion social cost for these roads.

Fish, Whales and Other Wildlife Many species of animals are common resources. Fish and whales, for instance, have commercial value, and anyone can go to the ocean and catch whatever is available. Each person has little incentive to maintain the species for the next year. Just as excessive grazing can destroy the Town Common, excessive fishing and whaling can destroy valuable marine populations.

The ocean remains one of the least regulated common resources. Two problems prevent an easy solution. First, many countries have access to the oceans, so any solution would require international cooperation among countries that hold different values. Second, because the oceans are so vast, enforcing any agreement is difficult. As a result, fishing rights have been a frequent source of international tension among normally friendly countries.

Within the United Kingdom and European countries, various laws aim to protect fish and other wildlife. For example, the government charges for fishing and hunting licences, and it restricts the lengths of the fishing and hunting seasons. Fishermen are often required to throw back small fish, and hunters can kill only a limited number of animals or shoot certain wild birds such as pheasant or grouse during specified periods of the year. All these laws reduce the use of a common resource and help maintain animal populations.

SELF TEST Why do governments try to limit the use of common resources?

CASE STUDY   **Do Common Resources Always Equate to Tragedy?**

In the discussion on the Tragedy of the Commons, there are a number of assumptions made in the analysis which may seem very plausible but, as with many things in economics, it pays to look closely at the assumptions of any model and question them. A number of people have done just that and arrive at different conclusions about common resources than Garrett Hardin did in his 1968 essay. Hardin's analysis suggests that where communities shared common resources, the inevitable result was the destruction of those resources. This is based on the assumption that each individual acts 'rationally' by seeking to exploit the resources for their own benefit and pays no attention to the impact of their decision on other users. The only solution is government intervention to regulate and legislate.

Critics of Hardin's analysis point to the fact that in some communities, collective self-regulation can be successful in preventing the 'tragedy' and inevitability of destruction of collective resources. In Germany there has been history of local communities supervising the use of arable and meadowland and in England voluntary associations existed to manage common land through granting rights to graze a certain number of animals called 'stints' or 'gaits'. Humans do not exist in isolation and are fundamentally social creatures. Hardin's assumption that each herdsperson was a rational, self-interested non-social being can be questioned, and in some cases it is just as likely that there will be some collective recognition of the problem of over-use of common resources and agreed solutions put in place which benefit the social group. What may be necessary is some form of incentive to prevent individuals from seeking to renege on the social agreement and as we shall see in Chapter 16, game theory can tell us much about human behaviour and how incentives can be designed to enforce the collective will.

Common land doesn't always result in tragedy!
Source: http://www.garretthardinsociety.org/articles/art_tragedy_of_the_commons.html

MERIT GOODS

Some goods can be provided by the market mechanism but if left purely to the market they may be under-consumed. These types of goods are termed **merit goods**. Merit goods arise because consumers may have imperfect information about the benefits of these goods and are not able to value them appropriately as a result. If the market signal does not fully convey the value of the benefits to consumers then they are likely to under-invest in these goods. The benefits to consumers may occur sometime in the future but the price the consumer is being asked to pay occurs in the present. Merit goods are an example of an **intertemporal choice** problem in economics – the term intertemporal relates to decision-making over time when current decisions affect choices made in the future.

> **merit goods** goods which can be provided by the market but may be under-consumed as a result of imperfect information about the benefits
>
> **intertemporal choice** where decisions made today can affect choices facing individuals in the future

Examples of merit goods include education, health care, pensions and insurance. In each of these cases the market can provide these goods. There are plenty of examples of private firms providing education (schools and universities run by private firms on the basis of students paying fees to attend). Private healthcare may be provided by profit or non-profit organizations such as BUPA, Spire, BMI Healthcare – and Capio in Sweden; but access to services is through payment at the point of use, unlike publicly provided health care services which are primarily free at the point of use and financed by the state through taxpayers. Equally, there are plenty of firms providing a range of insurance and pension services who are part of the private sector.

Education as a Merit Good

If you are reading this then there is a very good chance that you are at university. You will have made a decision to invest in your future by pursuing an undergraduate degree. In so doing you are sacrificing earnings that you could have generated and may also be incurring a considerable debt burden which you will have to pay off at some point in the future. One of the reasons why you have chosen to study is likely to be that you hope getting a degree will enable you to get a job which you will enjoy and which will also give you a higher salary. The lifetime earnings of those with a degree are higher than those without.

However, what you do not know at this point in time is the precise nature of the future benefits you will gain or how your degree will enable you to make different choices in the future, choices which may bring you considerable benefits which you simply cannot calculate at this point in time. Because of this imperfect information, some people may choose not to go to university. But there are not only private benefits to the individual of going to university, there are also social benefits. A better educated workforce is more likely to be more productive and if society's stock of human capital is more productive then standards of living overall tend to be higher. If you get a better job then you will pay more taxes and so government will be able to provide more services and this also benefits society. When looking at issues surrounding the commons we noted that there were social costs associated with consumption, costs that affect people other than the decision maker. In the case of a merit good, e.g. education, the problem is that there are social benefits which are not considered by the individual in their decision-making.

When looking at school education the issue is a little more complicated. The decision to send a child to school is invariably the parents, but the beneficiary is the child. This is a classic principal–agent problem. The principal (the parent) is acting on behalf of the agent (the child) and if schooling was left to the market there might be a conflict of interest. If the parent has to pay for education but is not getting the benefit then there is an incentive for the parent to not send their child to school, which leads to under-consumption of education.

Training of workers is another aspect of education that is under-consumed. Firms often complain that the mainstream education system does not adequately prepare young people for the world of work. When an employee gets a job firms invariably have to spend money training them, but the amount spent on training is likely to be far less than would be the socially optimum level. Spending on training would yield some private benefit to the firm in the form of improved productivity but there would also be some social benefit of this improved productivity as noted above. The worker would be in a stronger position to access new employment if they were made redundant because of their increased productivity, thus reducing the potential costs to the state of having to provide benefits.

The firm may not invest the full amount on training despite the private benefit because it fears that it might not receive the full benefit of the investment. Workers might be better skilled as a result and they may find work with rival firms who gain the benefit of the investment in training that the original firm made.

It is for these reasons that across Europe the state provides education and training for people, and subsidizes education and training in the workplace.

Health Care, Insurance and Pensions as Merit Goods

Few people are in a position to be able to judge when and if they need health care and insurance. For many young people, the prospect of saving today to fund a pension in 30–40 years' time is a decision they do not feel in a position to make – the benefits are too far in the future to be meaningful. If individuals had to pay for their own health care, insurance and pension provision then there would be an incentive to under-consume.

Many young people, for example, feel healthy and are in work and find it hard to conceive of what it might be like to be ill or what income they might need when they retire. The price of acquiring sufficient health care cover or pension provision is likely to be seen as too high and so some would not spend money on this necessary provision.

Some people look at insurance in the same way. Paying for life assurance and insuring home and contents is a gamble – we all know that our lives will end at some point but we don't know when, and when it does happen it will not be us that get the benefit of life cover, it will be someone else. We all know that there is a risk that our homes could be burgled or damaged by fire or some other disaster but it might never happen throughout our lives. There is an incentive, therefore, to put off taking out life cover or insurance on our homes. When we do die we might be leaving our loved ones with little or no income and/or the possible need to pay off mortgages or other debt, which could prove catastrophic. If our homes are subject to some disaster or crime then the cost of putting our property back to a state it was in before the incident could be significant. The problem is that, in each case, individuals do not have the information to make informed (rational) decisions on the relative costs and benefits and so these goods are under-consumed as a result.

The state can intervene in these cases to force firms and individuals to contribute to a pension scheme, to provide health care free at the point of use via taxes and to force people to take out insurance (most countries make taking out vehicle insurance, for example, a legal requirement of owning a vehicle). In these cases, it can be argued that individuals are not in the best place to be able to judge the benefits of consumption (both private and social) and so the state intervenes to ensure that goods which have merit are provided.

De-merit Goods

We have made reference to the distinction between 'goods' and 'bads'. Not all products which are consumed are good for us. **De-merit goods** have the characteristic of being over-consumed if left to the market. This is because consumption of these goods imposes private and social costs and, in making a consumption decision, the individual does not have the information to fully understand these costs. Tobacco, alcohol, pornography and non-medicinal drugs are examples of de-merit goods.

> **de-merit goods** goods that are over-consumed if left to the market mechanism and which generate both private and social costs which are not taken into account by the decision maker

When individuals consume goods like tobacco and alcohol, even though they are legal in many countries, there are private costs to the individual of the consumption. The damage to health that both of these goods generate may be partly known by the consumer but the full extent of the damage they are causing themselves is unknown. In addition, consumption of these goods might be associated with addiction and as a result it becomes harder for the individual to break the habit of smoking and drinking.

In addition to the private costs there are also social costs. The cost to the health care system of treating patients with tobacco and alcohol-related illness and disease is extensive and the resources spent on this care could be used to treat other patients and conditions – in other words, the decision of smokers and drinkers diverts resources from what might be argued to be more socially efficient allocations. In addition, alcohol consumption is cited as a cause of anti-social behaviour and the resources needed to deal with these problems represent a cost to society as a whole and again diverts resources away from other uses. The police, for example, could be dealing with other types of crime but if they have to devote resources to policing town and city centres into the night to deal with drunken groups of people, and the violence and crime that can arise as a result of excessive alcohol consumption, they cannot deal with other types of crime.

There is a case, therefore, for the state to intervene to regulate or legislate these markets, to tax products deemed to have private and social costs to reduce consumption.

CONCLUSION

In this chapter, we have seen there are some 'goods' that the market does not provide adequately. Markets do not ensure that the air we breathe is clean or that our country is defended from foreign aggressors. Instead, societies rely on the government to help provide goods that if left to the market would be either under or over-consumed.

There is considerable debate over the extent to which the state should get involved in the provision of public and merit goods and whether such intervention represents both a more efficient and equitable allocation of scarce resources. These debates are at the heart of issues which are not only influenced by economic understanding but also politics. Politics is about power and it may be that different groups in society have the power to influence decision-making more extensively than others and so resource allocation can be further distorted. The issues which have been touched upon in this chapter will be revisited on numerous occasions during the course of your studies and we have attempted to introduce some of the basic principles that underpin these issues.

IN THE NEWS

Common Resources

Fish in the sea are an example of a common resource. For centuries, coastal communities have relied on fishing as a key part of the local economy but as commercial fishing became more sophisticated, concerns that overfishing would deplete stocks and lead to the extinction of some species has led to governments and the European Union regulating and legislating to protect fish stocks.

The Common Fisheries Policy

The Common Fisheries Policy (CFP) was originally introduced as a means of managing fishing fleets and fish stocks in the 1970s. The policy aims to promote a sustainable fishing industry across Europe; it takes a long term view of the management of common resources and attempts to manage a delicate balance between supporting the livelihoods of those in the fishing industry and maintaining fish stocks for the future.

The policy has caused a great deal of conflict in the years it has been in existence seemingly satisfying few of the stakeholders in the industry. In January 2014, a new set of regulations came into force following lengthy discussions in the previous few years. The background to the reforms was that three out of four fish stocks were overfished, fishing fleets were catching smaller and smaller fish which commanded lower prices, and the establishment of fish quotas had led to unintended consequences whereby large numbers of fish caught had to be thrown back into the sea – most of them dead.

The new policy establishes what is called a 'maximum sustainable yield' (MSY), a level of fishing which can be exploited over time and maintains the fish population at a size which maximizes productivity. The MSY replaces the annual bargaining over quotas. By fishing to this level, it is hoped that stocks and catches will increase, profit margins and return on investment for the fishing industry would all rise and lead to an increase in the gross value added for the industry of some €2.7 billion in the next ten years. In addition, fishermen will be required to land all their catch and improve the technology and equipment used for monitoring catches to help phase out the practice of discarding unwanted fish. The policy hopes that there will be an incentive for fisherman to invest in better technology to reduce discards.

The European Maritime and Fisheries Fund (EMFF) will be given a budget of €6.7 billion to help fund the industry up to 2020 and provide support for small-scale fishing fleets. Fishing will be restricted to a 12 nautical mile zone from the coast and larger fleets would be able to trade their shares of catches to others. The new policy also aims to transfer decision-making powers locally rather than a top-down EU approach.

Reform of fisheries policies may help reduce waste and improve fish stocks for the future.

Questions

1   Are fish in the sea rival, excludable, both or neither? Explain.

2   Do you think that a body like the European Union is the most appropriate to regulate and legislate to manage a common resource like fish? Justify your answer.

3   Refer back to the Case Study in this Chapter. Do the actions of fishermen support the conclusions Hardin arrived at in his essay on the Tragedy of the Commons?

4   If the MSY works, how will fishermen see increased catches, profit margins and returns on investment but fish stocks recover at the same time?

5   Will the policy of forcing fishermen to land all their catch lead to the practice of discards being eliminated? Explain.

Source: http://europa.eu/rapid/press-release_MEMO-11-503_en.htm?locale=en

SUMMARY

- Goods differ in whether they are excludable and whether they are rival. A good is excludable if it is possible to prevent someone from using it. A good is rival if one person's use of the good reduces other people's ability to use the same unit of the good. It can be argued that markets work best for private goods, which are both excludable and rival. Markets do not work as well for other types of goods.

- Public goods are neither rival nor excludable. Examples of public goods include fireworks displays, national defence and the creation of fundamental knowledge. Because people are not charged for their use of a public good, they have an incentive to free ride if the good was provided privately. Therefore, governments provide public goods, making their decision about the quantity based on cost-benefit analysis.

- Common resources are rival but not excludable. Examples include common grazing land, clean air and congested roads. Because people are not charged for their use of common resources, they tend to use them excessively. Therefore, governments try to limit the use of common resources.

- Merit goods such as education and health might be under-consumed if left to the market and so the state can step in to help provide services which provide social as well as private benefits.

- De-merit goods are goods which are over-consumed and which confer both private and social costs. Governments might intervene in the market to reduce consumption in some way either through the price mechanism (levying taxes on these goods, for example), or through regulation and legislation.

QUESTIONS FOR REVIEW

1 What is the difference between the public sector and the private sector? Give an example of goods and services provided by each.

2 Explain what is meant by a good being 'excludable'. Give three examples of goods which exhibit the characteristics of being excludable.

3 Explain what is meant by a good being 'rival'. Give three examples of goods which exhibit the characteristics of being rival in consumption.

4 Define and give an example of a public good. Can the private market provide this good on its own? Explain.

5 Explain how public goods might also lead to the free-rider problem. Give an example to support your answer.

6 What is cost-benefit analysis of public goods? Why is it important? Why is it hard to quantify the full costs and benefits of the provision of public goods?

7 Define and give an example of a common resource. Without government intervention, will people use this good too much or too little? Why?

8 What is the marginal social benefit curve? How can the optimum provision of a public good be calculated?

9 Why are merit goods under-consumed?

10 How might governments prevent over-consumption of de-merit goods?

PROBLEMS AND APPLICATIONS

1 The text says that both public goods and common resources involve social effects.
   a. Are the social effects associated with public goods generally positive or negative? Use examples in your answer. Is the free market quantity of public goods generally greater or less than the efficient quantity?
   b. Are the social effects associated with common resources generally positive or negative? Use examples in your answer. Is the free market use of common resources generally greater or less than the efficient use?

2 Think about the goods and services provided by your local government.
   a. Explain what category each of the following goods falls into:
   - police protection
   - road gritting
   - street lighting

- education
- radio broadcasts
- rural roads
- city streets.

b. Why do you think the government provides items that are not public goods?

3 In the UK owners of TV sets are required by law to buy a licence. Alex is a student at university and loves watching live sport on TV. He uses digital access to watch live sport, but he has not bought a TV licence.

a. What name do economists have for Alex?

b. How can the government solve the problem caused by people like Alex?

c. Can you think of ways the private market can solve this problem?

4 The text states that private firms will not undertake the efficient amount of basic scientific research.

a. Explain why this is so. In your answer, classify basic research into one of the types of goods covered at the start of the chapter.

b. What sort of policy has the United Kingdom adopted in response to this problem?

c. It is often argued that this policy increases the technological capability of British producers relative to that of foreign firms. Is this argument consistent with your classification of basic research in part (a)? (Hint: can excludability apply to some potential beneficiaries of a public good and not others?)

5 Why is there litter along most major roads but rarely in people's gardens?

6 An *Economist* article (19 March 1994) states: 'In the past decade, most of the rich world's fisheries have been exploited to the point of near-exhaustion.' The article continues with an analysis of the problem and a discussion of possible private and government solutions.

a. 'Do not blame fishermen for overfishing. They are behaving rationally, as they have always done.' In what sense is 'overfishing' rational for fishermen?

b. 'A community, held together by ties of obligation and mutual self-interest, can manage a common resource on its own.' Explain how such management can work in principle, and what obstacles it faces in the real world.

c. 'Until 1976 most world fish stocks were open to all comers, making conservation almost impossible. Then an international agreement extended some aspects of [national] jurisdiction from 12 to 200 miles offshore.' Discuss how and why this agreement reduces the scope of the problem.

d. The *Economist* article notes that many governments come to the aid of suffering fishermen in ways that encourage increased fishing. How do such policies encourage a vicious cycle of overfishing?

e. 'Only when fishermen believe they are assured a long-term and exclusive right to a fishery are they likely to manage it in the same far-sighted way as good farmers manage their land.' Defend this statement.

f. What other policies to reduce overfishing might be considered?

7 The demand curve for a public park for two consumers who represent society is given by:
$$P = 150 - Q_{D1} \text{ and } P = 250 - Q_{D2}$$

Graph the two demand curves and show the marginal social benefit curve for this public park. If the marginal cost of providing the park was €240, what would the optimum provision of this park be? Explain why any quantity above or below this amount would represent a less than efficient allocation.

8 In a market economy, information about the quality or function of goods and services is a valuable good in its own right. How does the private market provide this information? Can you think of any way in which the government plays a role in providing this information?

9 Do you think the Internet is a public good? Why or why not?

10 High-income people are willing to pay more than lower income people to avoid the risk of death. For example, they are more likely to pay for safety features on cars. Do you think cost-benefit analysts should take this fact into account when evaluating public projects? Consider, for instance, a rich town and a poor town, both of which are considering the installation of traffic lights. Should the rich town use a higher monetary value for a human life in making this decision? Why or why not?

11 MARKET FAILURE AND EXTERNALITIES

MARKET FAILURE

In Chapter 10 we looked at some examples where markets fail to allocate resources efficiently because of the nature of the goods. In previous chapters we have presented the model of the market mechanism and in Chapter 1 noted that markets can be a good way of allocating scarce resources dependent on certain assumptions. Two of these assumptions are perfect information and rational behaviour and if these break down, the market model begins to lose its value in allowing predictions to be made. In addition, firms and individuals have different levels of power within markets which means they can influence outcomes. All these factors mean that the market may fail to allocate scarce resources in a way predicted by the model. Chapters 11 and 12 will explore some of these market failures starting first with an analysis of problems which arise largely as a result of imperfect information on the part of decision makers which come under the collective heading of externalities.

EXTERNALITIES

Belief Systems

Market systems are subject to a number of imperfections not least of which is the different degrees of power which different economic agents hold and mean that economic outcomes may be different to those predicted by our model of the market system. We will deal with this in later chapters. Even if we take the outcomes of the market model as remotely accurate, we still have to be aware of the belief systems economic agents hold and which will impact on their judgement of the desirability of outcomes and the basis for answering the key questions economies have to answer.

Proponents of market systems often point to Adam Smith's principle of the 'invisible hand'. We saw in Chapter 1 that the intellectual basis for the market system is individuals being left to their own devices without government interference motivated by self-interest. If individuals go about their business aiming to satisfy their own needs the 'invisible hand' of the market place guides this self-interest into promoting general well-being. However, critics of this belief system argue that individuals make decisions without fully understanding the costs and benefits and lead to inefficiencies which the market system on its own does not solve.

For example, firms that make and sell paper also create, as a by-product of the manufacturing process, a chemical called dioxin. Scientists believe that once dioxin enters the environment it raises the population's risk of cancer, birth defects and other health problems. The production of dioxin imposes costs on people which firms making paper do not have to pay. These are referred to as externalities.

An **externality** arises when a person engages in an activity that influences the well-being of a bystander (a third party) who neither pays nor receives any compensation for that effect. If the impact on the bystander is adverse, it is called a **negative externality**; if it is beneficial, it is called a **positive externality**. Negative and positive externalities are linked to the social costs and social benefits that exist when a decision is made. Many individuals and firms make decisions based on the private costs and benefits they incur but do not always consider the social costs and benefits of their decision. As a result the price mechanism does not reflect the true cost and benefit of a decision and this can lead to a market outcome where the quantity might be privately efficient but socially inefficient, and as a result the market allocation might be too high or too low. Price does not act as a true signal to consumers and producers to enable them to make informed decisions.

> **externality** the cost or benefit of one person's decision on the well-being of a bystander (a third party) which the decision maker does not take into account when making the decision
> **negative externality** the costs imposed on a third party of a decision
> **positive externality** the benefits to a third party of a decision

The Social Costs and Social Benefits of Decision-Making

We have seen how the operation of markets is based on millions of decisions being made by individuals and groups. In making these decisions there will be private costs and private benefits. In making a car journey, for example, a person incurs various private costs such as the fuel used in the journey, the wear and tear (depreciation) on the car, the contribution of any vehicle tax, and the insurance costs that the individual has to pay.

In using their car the individual also gains a number of private benefits: convenience, warmth, the pleasure of driving, listening to music, not to mention getting to a destination relatively quickly. However, in deciding to make the journey the individual may not take into consideration the cost (or benefit) *to society* that is imposed as a result of their decision to drive. An extra car on the road contributes to congestion, road wear and tear, emissions that the car gives off, the noise pollution and the increased risk of accident which may cause injury or even death to a third party. There may also be some social benefits of the decision; using a car means that there is an extra seat available for someone else to use on public transport, for example.

These social costs and benefits are not taken into consideration by the individual as they get into their car. There are costs which have to be borne by a third party. The cost of repairing damaged roads, the cost of dealing with accident and injury, delays caused as a result of congestion, the effects and costs of dealing with pollution and so on, all have to be borne by others – often the taxpayer. Equally, any social benefits arising from the decision are gained by those not party to the initial decision without them having to pay for the benefit derived.

In the presence of externalities, society's interest in a market outcome extends beyond the well-being of buyers and sellers who participate in the market; it also includes the well-being of bystanders who are affected indirectly. Because buyers and sellers neglect the external effects of their actions when deciding how much to demand or supply, the market equilibrium is not efficient when there are externalities. That is, the equilibrium fails to maximize the total benefit to society as a whole.

Types of Externalities Externalities come in many forms, as do the policy responses that try to deal with the market failure. Here are some examples:

- The exhaust from cars is a negative externality because it creates smog that other people have to breathe. Drivers do not take into consideration this externality and so tend to drive too much, thus increasing pollution. The government attempts to solve this problem by setting emission standards for cars. It may also tax petrol and vehicle ownership in order to reduce the amount that people drive.
- Restored historic buildings convey a positive externality because people who walk or drive by them can enjoy their beauty and the sense of history that these buildings provide. Building owners do not get the full benefit of restoration and, therefore, tend to discard older buildings too quickly. Many national governments respond to this problem by regulating the destruction of historic buildings and by providing tax incentives to owners who restore them.
- Barking dogs create a negative externality because neighbours are disturbed by the noise. Dog owners do not bear the full cost of the noise and, therefore, tend to take too few precautions to prevent their dogs from barking. The government may address this problem by making it illegal to 'disturb the peace'.

- Research into new technologies provides a positive externality because it creates knowledge that other people can use. Because inventors cannot capture the full benefits of their inventions, they tend to devote too few resources to research. The government addresses this problem partially through the patent system, which gives inventors an exclusive use over their inventions for a period of time.
- A programme of vaccination against a flu virus or any other communicable disease protects those who receive it from the risk of contracting the virus. Those who are not vaccinated, however, may receive some benefit too because the prevalence of the virus is lower and so there is a reduced risk that they will contract the illness. Health services also benefit because they do not have to devote resources to treating those with illnesses. Governments encourage vaccinations because there are positive benefits to society as a whole.

In each of these cases, some decision makers fail to take account of the external effects of their behaviour. Governments may step in to influence this behaviour to protect the interests of bystanders.

EXTERNALITIES AND MARKET INEFFICIENCY

In this section we use the concepts of consumer and producer surplus and deadweight loss to examine how externalities affect economic well-being. The analysis shows precisely why externalities cause markets to allocate resources inefficiently.

Welfare Economics: A Recap

To make our analysis concrete, we will consider a specific market – the market for aluminium. Figure 11.1 shows the supply and demand curves in the market for aluminium.

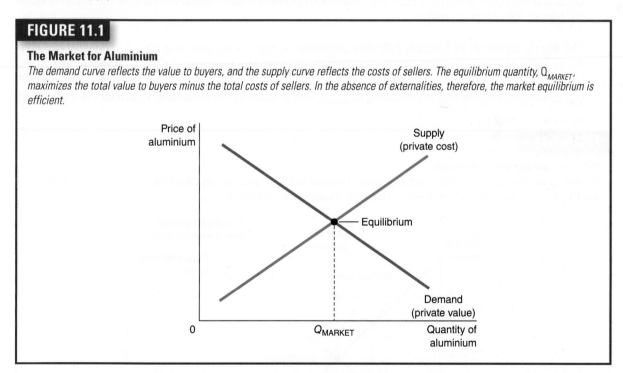

FIGURE 11.1

The Market for Aluminium
The demand curve reflects the value to buyers, and the supply curve reflects the costs of sellers. The equilibrium quantity, Q_{MARKET}, maximizes the total value to buyers minus the total costs of sellers. In the absence of externalities, therefore, the market equilibrium is efficient.

The supply and demand curves contain important information about costs and benefits. The demand curve for aluminium reflects the value of the benefits of aluminium to consumers, as measured by the prices they are willing to pay. At any given quantity, the height of the demand curve shows the willingness to pay of the marginal buyer. In other words, it shows the value to the consumer of the last unit of aluminium bought. Similarly, the supply curve reflects the costs of producing aluminium. At any given quantity, the height of the supply curve shows the cost of the marginal seller – the cost to the producer of the last unit of aluminium sold. The demand and supply curves, therefore, reflect the private benefit to consumers and the private cost to suppliers.

The quantity produced and consumed at the market equilibrium, shown as Q_{MARKET} in Figure 11.1, is efficient in the sense that the market allocates resources in a way that maximizes the total value to the consumers who buy and use aluminium minus the total costs to the producers who make and sell aluminium. At the equilibrium price, the value placed on the last unit of aluminium consumed by buyers is the same as the cost incurred by sellers of supplying that last unit.

Negative Externalities

Now let's suppose that for each unit of aluminium produced, a certain amount of a pollutant enters the atmosphere. This pollutant may pose a health risk for those who breathe the air, it is a negative externality. There is a cost involved in dealing with the effects of the pollutant which may be the health care that those affected have to receive. This cost is not taken into consideration by producers of aluminium who only consider the private costs of production. How does this externality affect the efficiency of the market outcome?

Because of the externality, the cost to *society* of producing aluminium is larger than the cost to the aluminium producers. For each unit of aluminium produced, the *social* (or *external*) *cost* includes the private costs of the aluminium producers plus the costs to those bystanders affected adversely by the pollution. Figure 11.2 shows the social cost of producing aluminium. The social cost curve is above the supply curve because it takes into account the external costs imposed on society by aluminium producers. At every price the social cost, measured by the vertical distance between the social cost curve and the private cost curve, is higher than the private cost, so we can say that the social cost curve is the sum of the private costs and the social or external cost. The difference between these two curves reflects the social or external cost of the pollution emitted.

The Social Optimum or Socially Efficient Outcome At the market outcome (Q_{MARKET}) consumers value the benefits of consuming this quantity of aluminium at OP. The true cost of Q_{MARKET} is higher at P_1 – the marginal consumer values aluminium at less than the social cost of producing it. The vertical distance $P P_1$ represents the welfare loss of producing Q_{MARKET}. This is equal to the social cost of producing that output.

FIGURE 11.2

Pollution and the Social Optimum

In the presence of a negative externality, such as pollution, the social cost of the good exceeds the private cost. The optimal quantity or socially efficient outcome, $Q_{OPTIMUM}$, is therefore smaller than the equilibrium quantity, Q_{MARKET}.

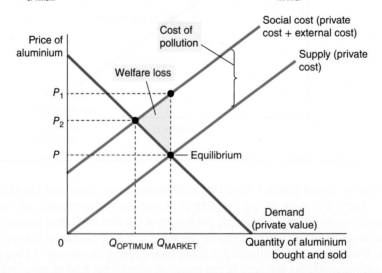

The optimal amount of aluminium produced would be where the demand curve intersects the social cost curve at $Q_{OPTIMUM}$ at a price of P_2. This is also referred to as the *socially efficient outcome*. This is the optimal amount of aluminium from the standpoint of society as a whole. At P_2 consumers value the benefits of consuming aluminium at the same level as the private cost to suppliers and the cost to society as a whole. The socially efficient quantity is, therefore, lower than the private market outcome and the socially efficient price is higher reflecting the true value to society of the socially efficient market outcome.

The equilibrium quantity of aluminium (Q_{MARKET}) is larger than the socially optimal quantity, $Q_{OPTIMUM}$. The reason for this inefficiency is that the market equilibrium reflects only the private costs of production. Reducing aluminium production and consumption below the market equilibrium level raises total economic well-being. We can measure changes in well-being by the welfare loss associated with different market outcomes. We can measure this welfare loss through summing the distance between the value placed on the consumption of aluminium and the social cost of production between the market outcome, Q_{MARKET} and the optimum outcome $Q_{OPTIMUM}$. The total amount is shown by the shaded triangle in Figure 11.2. This triangle is referred to as a *welfare triangle*.

To rectify the inefficiency, some way of forcing the decision maker to take into consideration some or all of the social costs has to be put in place. In our example, one way to do this would be to tax aluminium producers for each tonne of aluminium sold. The tax would shift the supply curve for aluminium upward by the size of the tax. If the tax accurately reflected the social cost of the pollution released into the atmosphere, the new supply curve would coincide with the social cost curve. In the new market equilibrium, aluminium producers would produce the socially optimal quantity of aluminium.

The use of such a tax is called **internalizing an externality** because it gives buyers and sellers in the market an incentive to take account of the external effects of their actions. By having to include the tax into their decision-making, the government is able to intervene with the intention of making the price signal more accurate. Aluminium producers would, in essence, take the costs of pollution into account when deciding how much aluminium to supply because the tax would provide an incentive to make them pay for these external costs.

internalizing an externality altering incentives so that people take account of the external effects of their actions

Positive Externalities

Although some activities impose costs on third parties, others yield benefits. For example, consider education. Education yields positive externalities because a more educated population leads to improved productivity and increases the potential for economic growth, which can benefit everyone. Notice that the productivity benefit of education is not necessarily an externality: the consumer of education reaps most of the benefit in the form of higher wages and greater job mobility. If some of the productivity benefits of education spill over and benefit other people, as is the case if economic growth is stimulated, then this effect would count as a positive externality as well.

The analysis of positive externalities is similar to the analysis of negative externalities. As Figure 11.3 shows, the demand curve does not reflect the value to society of the good. The value placed on an activity such as education is valued less by consumers than the total value to society. At the equilibrium market allocation of Q_{MARKET} the value of the private benefits to individuals of education is P but the value to society as a whole is P_1. The vertical distance between P and P_1 is the value of the social benefits to society. Because the social value (or external benefit) is greater than the private value, the social value curve, or marginal social benefit (MSB) curve, lies above the demand curve. The MSB is the private value plus the external benefit to society at each price. At every price the benefit to society is greater than the private benefit, hence the social value curve lies to the right of the private benefit curve. The optimal quantity is found where the social value curve and the supply curve (which represents costs) intersect at a price of P_2. Hence, the socially optimal quantity is greater than the quantity determined by the private market and the price is higher than the private equilibrium price. This implies that the value of education is underpriced at market equilibrium. The welfare loss associated with the private market outcome at Q_{MARKET} is shown by the shaded triangle.

FIGURE 11.3

Education and the Social Optimum

In the presence of a positive externality, the social value of the good exceeds the private value. The optimal quantity, $Q_{OPTIMUM}$, is therefore larger than the equilibrium quantity, Q_{MARKET}.

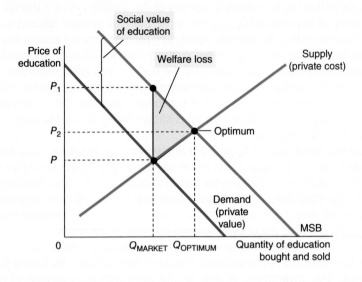

> The market failure can be corrected by inducing market participants to internalize the externality. To move the market equilibrium closer to the social optimum, a subsidy could be introduced. In fact, that is exactly the policy many governments follow by heavily subsidizing education.

SELF TEST Give an example of a negative externality and a positive externality. Explain why market outcomes are inefficient in the presence of externalities.

Positional Externalities

Positional goods have the characteristic that the utility from consumption of a good is dependent on how it compares with others in the same class. For example, some cars are considered to be better quality or confer higher esteem than others. Purchases or decisions which alter the context of the evaluation by an individual of the positional good can generate a **positional externality**.

> **positional externality** purchases or decisions which alter the context of the evaluation by an individual of the positional good

Positional externalities arise because people have a propensity to compare relative positions. If you were presented with the following, which option would you choose?

- **Option A.** Your income = €60 000 per annum; all others' income = €150 000
- **Option B.** Your income = €50 000 per annum; all others' income = €40 000

If we assume rational behaviour, the logical option would be to choose Option A because the absolute quantity of goods you could purchase with €60 000 is higher than that which could be purchased with €50 000. Studies have shown, however, that many people would choose Option B because of the difference in the relative earnings of the two groups. In Option A, the relative difference is far greater and people opt for B because they believe their relative position is better. Such 'irrational' choices have been put forward to partly explain why, despite increases in average incomes and house sizes over the last 50 years, measures of happiness are relatively stable.

The implications of positional externalities can be significant. For example, if a professional squash player wants to improve their performance, they might hire a sports psychologist to advise them on getting the extra edge that might make a difference to their performance and win percentage. As a result of the squash player making this decision, other squash players' performances are affected negatively. The improvement in performance of the squash player who hires the sports psychologist in terms of the payoff they receive (i.e. winning) will of necessity worsen their rivals' payoffs (i.e. they will now not win). The incentive for all other professional squash players is to also hire a sports psychologist and see if they can make up that competitive gap and possibly improve it. If all squash players do this, however, the overall effect is likely to be neutral and so the overall benefit of professional squash players as a collective is zero despite the additional costs incurred. Such an outcome, therefore is inefficient.

Positional externalities also exist in the world of education and business. To get to university, individuals require certain grades in examinations taken at the end of secondary education. Universities demand ever higher grades in an effort to select the highest performing students and those with the most academic potential. As a result, individual schools and colleges might try to find ways to help their students improve their grades relative to other schools and colleges.

However, the result is that every school and college invests scarce resources into extra revision classes, sending teachers onto courses to better understand the examination systems and other measures to try and gain an advantage for their students. What universities are faced with is ever increasing numbers of students applying with similar qualifications thus making differentiation more difficult.

Firms looking to recruit the best workers might request particular skills and qualifications. This may be the requirement for applicants to have a Master's degree, to have had internships at relevant businesses or to have developed people and communication skills. Individual applicants have an incentive to invest time and resources in gaining these qualifications and skills to try and put themselves ahead of rival applicants. The overall effect is that all applicants present themselves with Master's degrees and any amount of experience and skills, so the outcome is of limited benefit to the recruiting firm and considerable cost for the applicants.

The existence of positional externalities which leads to individuals investing in a series of measures designed to gain them an advantage but which simply offset each other is referred to as **positional arms races**.

 positional arms race a situation where individuals invest in a series of measures designed to gain them an advantage but which simply offset each other

PRIVATE SOLUTIONS TO EXTERNALITIES

In practice, both private actors and public policymakers respond to externalities in various ways. All of the remedies share the goal of moving the allocation of resources closer to the social optimum. In this section we examine private solutions.

The Types of Private Solution

In many cases, governments will intervene in markets to correct perceived market failures. However, this is not always the case and in some circumstances, private solutions can go some way to correcting market failure.

Social Norms of Moral Behaviour Sometimes the problem of externalities is solved with moral codes and social sanctions. Consider, for instance, why most people do not litter. Although there are laws against littering, these laws are not vigorously enforced. Most people do not litter just because they believe it is the wrong thing to do. Advertising and parental guidance help us to distinguish what society accepts as a norm for behaviour. This moral injunction tells us to take account of how our actions affect other people. In economic terms, it tells us to internalize externalities.

Charities Many charities are established to deal with externalities. For example, Greenpeace, whose goal is to protect the environment, is a non-profit organization funded with private donations; universities (which are charities) sometimes receive gifts from alumni, corporations and foundations, in part because education has positive externalities for society.

Self-interest The private market can often solve the problem of externalities by relying on the self-interest of the relevant parties. Sometimes the solution takes the form of integrating different types of business. For example, consider an apple grower and a beekeeper who are located next to each other. Each business confers a positive externality on the other: by pollinating the flowers on the trees, the bees help the orchard produce apples. At the same time, the bees use the nectar they get from the apple trees to produce honey. Nevertheless, when the apple grower is deciding how many trees to plant and the beekeeper is deciding how many bees to keep, they neglect the positive externality. As a result, the apple grower plants too few trees and the beekeeper keeps too few bees. These externalities could be internalized if the beekeeper bought the apple orchard or if the apple grower bought the beehives: both activities would then take place within the same firm, and this single firm could choose the optimal number of trees and bees. Internalizing externalities is one reason that some firms are involved in related types of business.

Social Contracts Another way for the private market to deal with external effects is for the interested parties to enter into a contract. In the foregoing example, a contract between the apple grower and the beekeeper can solve the problem of too few trees and too few bees. The contract can specify the number of trees, the number of bees and perhaps a payment from one party to the other. By setting the right number of trees and bees, the contract can solve the inefficiency that normally arises from these externalities and make both parties better off. Joint ventures and partnering are good examples of where such contracts can generate positive externalities and improve efficiency.

The Coase Theorem

How effective is the private market in dealing with externalities? A famous result, called the **Coase theorem**, after British economist Ronald Coase, suggests that it can be very effective in some circumstances. According to the Coase theorem, if private parties can bargain *without cost* over the allocation of resources, then the private market can solve the problem of externalities and allocate resources efficiently.

> **Coase theorem** the proposition that if private parties can bargain without cost over the allocation of resources, they can solve the problem of externalities on their own

To see how the Coase theorem works, consider an example. Suppose that Sofie owns a dog named Brandy. Brandy barks and disturbs Lucas, Sofie's neighbour. Sofie gets a benefit from owning the dog, but the dog confers a negative externality on Lucas.

The socially efficient outcome might consist of two options. One is to compare the benefit that Sofie gets from the dog to the cost that Lucas bears from the barking. If the benefit exceeds the cost, it is efficient for Sofie to keep the dog and for Lucas to live with the barking. The second option is that if the cost to Lucas exceeds the benefit to Sofie, then she should get rid of the dog. The problem arises in valuing the respective costs and benefits.

According to the Coase theorem, the private market can reach the efficient outcome on its own by Lucas offering to pay Sofie to get rid of the dog. Sofie will accept the deal if the amount of money Lucas offers is greater than the benefit to her of keeping the dog.

By bargaining over the price, Sofie and Lucas can reach an efficient outcome. For instance, suppose that Sofie gets a €500 benefit from the dog and Lucas bears an €800 cost from the barking. In this case, Lucas can offer Sofie €600 to get rid of the dog, and Sofie will gladly accept. Both parties are better off than they were before, and an efficient outcome is reached.

It is possible, of course, that Lucas would not be willing to offer any price that Sofie would accept. For instance, suppose that Sofie gets a €1000 benefit from the dog and Lucas bears an €800 cost from the barking. In this case, Sofie would turn down any offer below €1000, while Lucas would not offer any amount above €800. Therefore, Sofie ends up keeping the dog. Given these costs and benefits, however, this outcome is efficient.

So far, we have assumed that Sofie has the legal right to keep a barking dog. In other words, we have assumed that Sofie can keep Brandy unless Lucas pays her enough to induce her to give up the dog voluntarily. How different would the outcome be, on the other hand, if Lucas had the legal right to peace and quiet?

According to the Coase theorem, the initial distribution of rights does not matter for the market's ability to reach the efficient outcome. For instance, suppose that Lucas can legally compel Sofie to get rid of the dog. Although having this right works to Lucas's advantage, it probably will not change the outcome. In this case, Sofie can offer to pay Lucas to allow her to keep the dog. If the benefit of the dog to Sofie exceeds the cost of the barking to Lucas, then Sofie and Lucas will strike a bargain in which Sofie keeps the dog.

Although Sofie and Lucas can reach the efficient outcome regardless of how rights are initially distributed, the distribution of rights is not irrelevant: it determines the distribution of economic well-being. Whether Sofie has the right to a barking dog or Lucas the right to peace and quiet determines who pays whom in the final bargain. In either case, the two parties can bargain with each other and solve the externality problem. Sofie will end up keeping the dog only if the benefit exceeds the cost.

Why Private Solutions Do Not Always Work

Despite the appealing logic of the Coase theorem, it applies only when the interested parties have no trouble reaching and enforcing an agreement. In the world, however, bargaining does not always work, even when a mutually beneficial agreement is possible.

Transaction Costs Sometimes the interested parties fail to solve an externality problem because of **transaction costs**, the costs that parties incur in the process of agreeing to and following through on a bargain, for example, the cost incurred of employing lawyers to draft and enforce contracts.

 transactions costs the costs that parties incur in the process of agreeing and following through on a bargain

Bargaining Problems At other times bargaining simply breaks down. The recurrence of wars and labour strikes shows that reaching agreement can be difficult and that failing to reach agreement can be costly. The problem is often that each party tries to hold out for a better deal. For example, suppose that Sofie gets a €500 benefit from the dog, and Lucas bears an €800 cost from the barking. Although it is efficient for Lucas to pay Sofie to get rid of the dog, there are many prices that could lead to this outcome. Sofie might demand €750, and Lucas might offer only €550. As they haggle over the price, the inefficient outcome with the barking dog persists.

Coordinating Interested Parties Reaching an efficient bargain is especially difficult when the number of interested parties is large because coordinating everyone is costly. For example, consider a factory that pollutes the water of a nearby lake. The pollution confers a negative externality on local fishermen. According to the Coase theorem, if the pollution is inefficient, then the factory and the fishermen could reach a bargain in which the fishermen pay the factory not to pollute. If there are many fishermen, however, trying to coordinate them all to bargain with the factory may be almost impossible.

Asymmetric Information and the Assumption of Rational Behaviour There are two other key reasons why reaching an efficient bargain may not arise: asymmetric information and the assumption of rational behaviour. An example of the former is that Sofie and Lucas may not have perfect knowledge of the costs and benefits to each other of the barking dog. In such situations it becomes very difficult to negotiate an efficient outcome. Both parties have imperfect information about the situation of the other and so incentives may be distorted. Lucas, for example, might exaggerate the cost to him of the barking dog whilst Sofie does the same with regard to the benefits she gets from keeping her dog. The situation is further complicated by the existence of *free riders*. Lucas may not be the only person in the neighbourhood suffering from the barking dog but others may not live directly next to Sofie. These other 'victims' can benefit from any agreement that Sofie and Lucas arrive at but do not pay any of the costs of solving the problem. If Lucas is aware of this then why should he pay the full amount to solve the problem when others will also benefit but not contribute? If all victims think the same way then the problem will remain unsolved and there will be an inefficient outcome.

As regards the assumption of rational behaviour, we assumed that an efficient outcome could be found if Lucas offered €600 for Sofie to get rid of the dog. If Sofie were able to put a price on the value of the dog to her and this was €500, then it would be irrational for her not to accept the money to get rid of the dog. The money could be used to secure something which gave greater value to her than the ownership of the dog. Of course, in real life such rational behaviour may be clouded by all sorts of behavioural and psychological influences that Sofie may not be able to value: the guilt she may feel in getting rid of the dog, the reactions of her friends and family, the sentimental value of the dog to her and so on. In addition, the assumption is that humans always value things based on some monetary value which represents other goods which could be purchased. This is not always the case.

When private bargaining does not work, the government can sometimes play a role. The government is an institution designed for collective action. In the polluting factory example above, the government can act on behalf of the fishermen, even when it is impractical for the fishermen to act for themselves. In the next section, we examine how the government can try to remedy the problem of externalities.

SELF TEST Give an example of a private solution to an externality. What is the Coase theorem? Why are private economic actors sometimes unable to solve the problems caused by an externality?

PUBLIC POLICIES TOWARDS EXTERNALITIES

Public policies refer to instances where governments step in to seek to correct a perceived market failure. Governments tend to respond in one of two ways. *Command-and-control policies* regulate behaviour directly. *Market-based policies* provide incentives so that private decision makers will choose to solve the problem on their own through manipulation of the price signal.

Command and Control Policies: Regulation

The government can remedy an externality by making certain behaviours either required or forbidden. For example, it is a crime in any European country to dump poisonous chemicals into the water supply. In this case, the external costs to society far exceed the benefits to the polluter. Governments institute a command-and-control policy that prohibits this act altogether.

In most cases of pollution, however, the situation is not this simple. Despite the stated goals of some environmentalists, it would be impossible to prohibit all polluting activity. For example, virtually all forms of transport – even the horse – produce some undesirable polluting by-products but it would not be sensible for the government to ban all transport. Instead of trying to eradicate pollution altogether, society has to weigh the costs and benefits to decide the kinds and quantities of pollution it will allow.

Environmental regulations can take many forms. Sometimes a government may dictate a maximum level of pollution that a factory may emit. Other times a government requires that firms adopt a particular technology to reduce emissions. In all cases, to design good rules, government regulators need to know the details about specific industries and about the alternative technologies that those industries could adopt. This information is often difficult for government regulators to obtain.

Market-based Policy: Corrective Taxes and Subsidies

Instead of regulating behaviour in response to an externality, the government can use market-based policies to align private incentives with social efficiency. A government can internalize an externality by taxing activities that have negative externalities and subsidizing activities that have positive externalities. Taxes enacted to correct the effects of negative externalities are called **Pigovian taxes**, after the English economist Arthur Pigou (1877–1959), an early advocate of their use.

> **Pigovian tax** a tax enacted to correct the effects of a negative externality

It is argued that Pigovian taxes can reduce pollution at a lower cost to society. To see why this might be the case, let us consider an example.

Suppose that two factories – a paper mill and a steel mill – are each dumping 500 tonnes of effluent into a river each year. The government decides that it wants to reduce the amount of pollution. It considers two solutions:

- *Regulation.* The government could tell each factory to reduce its pollution to 300 tonnes of effluent per year.
- *Pigovian tax.* The government could levy a tax on each factory of €50 000 for each tonne of effluent it emits.

The regulation would dictate a level of pollution, whereas the tax would give factory owners an economic incentive to reduce pollution. The intention of the tax would be to encourage firms to reduce pollution up to the point where the marginal abatement cost is equal to the tax rate imposed. The **marginal abatement cost** is the cost expressed in terms of the last unit of pollution not emitted (abated).

> **marginal abatement cost** the cost expressed in terms of the last unit of pollution not emitted (abated)

Some economists argue that a tax is just as effective as a regulation in reducing the overall level of pollution. The government can achieve whatever level of pollution it wants by setting the tax at the appropriate level. The higher the tax, the larger the reduction in pollution. Indeed, if the tax is high enough, the factories will close down altogether, reducing pollution to zero.

However, regulation requires each factory to reduce pollution by the same amount, but an equal reduction is not necessarily the least expensive way to clean up the water. It is possible that the paper mill can reduce pollution at lower cost than the steel mill. If so, the paper mill would respond to the tax by reducing pollution substantially to avoid the tax, whereas the steel mill would respond by reducing pollution less and paying the tax.

In essence, the Pigovian tax places a price on the right to pollute. Just as markets allocate goods to those buyers who value them most highly, a Pigovian tax allocates pollution to those factories that face the highest cost of reducing it. Whatever the level of pollution the government chooses, it can achieve this goal at the lowest total cost using a tax.

Some economists also argue that Pigovian taxes are better for the environment. Under the command-and-control policy of regulation, the factories have no reason to reduce emissions further once they have reached the target of 300 tonnes of effluent. By contrast, the tax gives the factories an incentive to develop cleaner technologies, because a cleaner technology would reduce the amount of tax the factory has to pay.

Pigovian taxes are designed to use incentives in the presence of externalities, to move the allocation of resources closer to the social optimum. Pigovian taxes raise revenue for the government, and can also enhance economic efficiency.

Despite the logic of Pigovian taxes, examples of pollution taxes are scarce. Some economists point out that what constitutes a pollution tax depends on how environmental tax systems are defined. There are, however, some problems associated with such taxes, not least identifying the appropriate rate to levy. In addition there are political problems associated with levying Pigovian taxes. The cost of levying and administering these taxes might be higher compared to regulation.

Tradable Pollution Permits

Returning to our example of the paper mill and the steel mill, let us suppose that the government decides to adopt regulation and requires each factory to reduce its pollution to 300 tonnes of effluent per year. Then one day, after the regulation is in place and both mills have complied, the two firms go to the government with a proposal. The steel mill wants to increase its emission of effluent by 100 tonnes per year. The paper mill has agreed to reduce its emission by the same amount if the steel mill pays it €5 million.

From the standpoint of economic efficiency, allowing the deal is good policy. The deal must make the owners of the two factories better off, because they are voluntarily agreeing to it. Moreover, the deal does not have any external effects because the total amount of pollution remains the same. Thus, social welfare is enhanced by allowing the paper mill to sell its right to pollute to the steel mill.

The same logic applies to any voluntary transfer of the right to pollute from one firm to another. If firms are permitted to make these deals, a new scarce resource is created: pollution permits. A market to trade these permits can develop, governed by the forces of supply and demand with the price signal allocating the right to pollute. The firms that can reduce pollution only at high cost will be willing to pay the most for the pollution permits. The firms that can reduce pollution at low cost will prefer to sell whatever permits they have.

One advantage of allowing a market for pollution permits is that the initial allocation of pollution permits among firms does not matter from the standpoint of economic efficiency. The logic behind this conclusion is similar to that behind the Coase theorem. Those firms that can reduce pollution most easily would be willing to sell whatever permits they get, and those firms that can reduce pollution only at high cost would be willing to buy whatever permits they need. As long as there is a free market for the pollution rights, the final allocation will be efficient whatever the initial allocation.

Although reducing pollution using pollution permits may seem quite different from using Pigovian taxes, in fact the two policies have much in common. In both cases, firms pay for their pollution. With Pigovian taxes, polluting firms must pay a tax to the government. With pollution permits, polluting firms must pay to buy the permit. (Even firms that already own permits must pay to pollute: the opportunity cost of polluting is what they could have received by selling their permits on the open market.) Both Pigovian taxes and pollution permits internalize the externality of pollution by making it costly for firms to pollute.

The similarity of the two policies can be seen by considering the market for pollution. Both panels in Figure 11.4 show the demand curve for the right to pollute. This curve shows that the lower the price of polluting, the more firms will choose to pollute. In panel (a) the government uses a Pigovian tax to set a price for pollution. In this case, the supply curve for pollution rights is perfectly elastic (because firms can pollute as much as they want by paying the tax), and the position of the demand curve determines the quantity of pollution. In panel (b) the government sets a quantity of pollution by issuing pollution permits. The level at which this quantity is set is crucial. In this case, the supply curve for pollution rights is perfectly inelastic (because the quantity of pollution is fixed by the number of permits), and the position of the demand curve determines the price of pollution. Hence, for any given demand curve for pollution, the government can achieve any point on the demand curve either by setting a price with a Pigovian tax or by setting a quantity with pollution permits.

In some circumstances, however, selling pollution permits may be better than levying a Pigovian tax. Suppose the government wants no more than 600 tonnes of effluent to be dumped into the river. Because the government does not know the demand curve for pollution, it is not sure what size tax would achieve that goal. In this case, it can simply auction off 600 pollution permits. The auction price would yield the appropriate size of the Pigovian tax.

A number of governments around the world have introduced markets in pollution permits as a way to control pollution. In 2002, European Union environment ministers unanimously agreed to set up a market to trade pollution permits for carbon dioxide (CO_2), the main so-called greenhouse gas of concern. Pollution permits, like Pigovian taxes, are increasingly being viewed as a cost-effective way to keep the environment clean.

FIGURE 11.4

The Equivalence of Pigovian Taxes and Pollution Permits
In panel (a) the government sets a price on pollution by levying a Pigovian tax, and the demand curve determines the quantity of pollution. In panel (b) the government limits the quantity of pollution by limiting the number of pollution permits, and the demand curve determines the price of pollution. The price and quantity of pollution are the same in both cases.

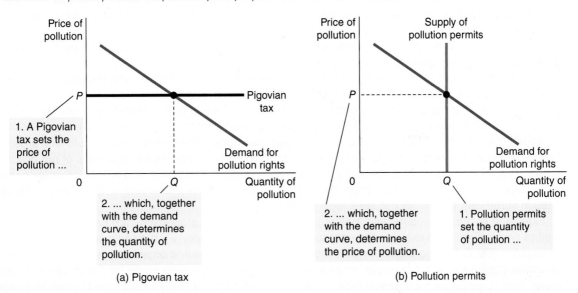

(a) Pigovian tax   (b) Pollution permits

PUBLIC/PRIVATE POLICIES TOWARDS EXTERNALITIES

Property Rights

In some cases, private solutions to externalities can occur but need some form of legal back-up to be able to work. One such example is the establishment of **property rights**. Property rights refer to the exclusive right of an individual, group or organization to determine how a resource is used. The existence of well-established property rights, enshrined in law, allows the owners of that property to be able to use it as they see fit and to have some protection in law if their rights are infringed.

> **property rights** the exclusive right of an individual, group or organization to determine how a resource is used

To see how this works, let us take a simple example. Lothar is the legally recognized owner of a Mercedes Benz car. Max is on his way home from a night out with his friends and as a prank lets down the tyres on Lothar's car. Close circuit TV cameras capture Max in the act and he is arrested for criminal damage. Lothar has the right to prosecute Max for the damage caused to his property and can expect to receive some money from Max to pay for the damage caused. The damage might not only be valued in terms of the cost of re-inflating the tyres but also for the estimated cost (decided by the courts) to Lothar of him having to miss a meeting early the next morning because he could not use his car.

It could be argued that in some cases, the market fails to allocate resources efficiently because property rights are not well established. That is, some item of value does not have an owner with the legal authority to control it. For example, although few would doubt that the 'good' of clean air or national defence is valuable, no one has the right to attach a price to it and profit from its use. A factory pollutes the air too much because no one owns the air which is polluted and can charge the factory for the pollution it emits. The market does not provide for national defence because no one can charge those who are defended for the benefit they receive.

Government Solutions to the Absence of Property Rights When the absence of property rights causes a market failure, the government can potentially solve the problem. Sometimes, as in the sale of pollution permits, the solution is for the government to help define property rights and thereby unleash market forces. In some countries, common resources such as rivers, are put under the ownership of an agency established by the government. The agency is given the right to ownership of rivers, for example, and so can take action against those that cause damage to the river in some way. Other times, as in the restriction on hunting seasons, the solution is for the government to regulate private behaviour. Still other times, as in the provision of national defence, the solution is for the government to supply a good that the market fails to supply. In all cases, if the policy is well planned and well run, it can make the allocation of resources more efficient and thus raise economic well-being.

In order for any economy to work efficiently, a system of property rights has to be established and understood. This is not as easy as it sounds, however.

With things such as rivers, streams, land and air it is less easy to establish who the legal owners are. If a system can be devised whereby the ownership of property is established then those that cause damage to that property can be brought to book. Extending property rights, therefore, might be one area where externalities can be internalized. For example, if property rights over the air that we breathe can be extended, then any firm polluting that air (in whatever way, noise, smell, smoke, etc.) could face prosecution for doing so. The threat of prosecution is sufficient to act as an incentive to find ways of not polluting the air. This might mean that a notional property zone is established above and around privately owned properties where the owner of the property also 'owns' the air above and around it. If that air is then polluted in some way, the owner can seek legal redress.

Extension of property rights also means that the owner of the property (which can be intellectual as well as physical) can also exercise the right to sell or share that property if they so wish at some mutually agreeable price. Extending property rights allows individuals, groups and organizations to be able to arrive at efficient solutions. If, for example, an individual was assigned property rights for the air one kilometre above their property, then if a nearby factory wanted to pollute that air they would have to enter into negotiations with the house owner to do so at some mutually agreeable price. The resulting right to pollute could also be sold to another party. A more developed system of property rights can improve well-being and it has been identified as playing a crucial role in good governance, particularly relevant for developing countries to be able to attract the sort of inward investment that will help their economies to grow.

Difficulties in Establishing Property Rights There are problems with extending property rights, however. How do we apportion rights to such things as air, the seas, rivers and land? The cost of establishing property rights and getting international agreement on what they entail is considerable and may counteract the social benefits they might provide. If property rights were extended to the volume of air one kiolmetre above a person's property, imagine the complexity of the negotiations that would have to be carried out with any business nearby, or airlines and the military for the right to share that air! Property owners may also have insufficient knowledge about their rights and exactly what they mean; it is also not a costless exercise to prove that property rights have been violated.

In the music industry the complexities of property rights have been the subject of debate and countless lawsuits in recent years. It not only relates to the issues of file sharing, pirating, copying CDs for personal use and downloading, but also to the artists themselves and the rights to the music that they have written and performed. Intellectual property law is an incredibly complex area and different countries interpret property rights in different ways making any international agreement even more difficult.

Despite the complexities, there have been efforts to extend property rights to help bring social benefits. In many parts of Europe, property rights over public spaces such as national parks, rivers and seas have meant that environmental laws can be established and enforced and this has led to an improvement in well-being for millions who are able to use these spaces, enjoy cleaner rivers and exploit the resources of the sea.

Control of Positional Arms Races

To reduce the instances of positional arms races, an incentive must exist to prevent the investment in attempts to gain some benefit which is ultimately mutually offsetting. This could take place through legislation to ban particular types of performance enhancing drug in sport, for example, or through some form of informal agreement between participants or through the establishment of a social norm on behaviour which becomes accepted by most participants.

In other cases some form of legally binding arbitration agreement might be made where participants agree to an external body overseeing a dispute and where all parties agree to abide by the decision made by this body.

Carbon Trading Permits

The European Union has prided itself on being a leader in setting up carbon trading through the European Trading Scheme (ETS). By 2015, ten years of the scheme's operation proved a time to reflect on its successes or otherwise. The scheme sets limits on the amount of carbon certain large industries like steel, cement and power generation are allowed to emit over a period of time. Permits are issued to these industries and they have to work to meet their allowance. If they manage to reduce their carbon emissions below their permitted levels, then they can sell the excess permits to others who may have had more difficulty meeting their targets.

Whilst such methods are, in theory, possible solutions to this type of pollution, the practice has seen different outcomes. The EU was accused of reducing the effectiveness of the system by *giving* permits to industry rather than auctioning them off. As a result, there was a surplus of permits on the market and their price dropped. The effectiveness of the emissions trading scheme in reducing carbon emissions, and acting as an incentive to producers to find more socially efficient ways of operating, was called into question. The end of 2007 brought in the next phase of the scheme and it was hoped that the EU would learn the lessons from its mistakes.

New limits covering the period between 2008 and 2012 planned to tighten the amount of carbon pollution that could be emitted, to reduce emissions by nine per cent between 2008 and 2012. There were also a larger number of permits that had to be bought by industry rather than being given to them. In 2007 emissions of carbon were up by one per cent but the amount of carbon emitted was below targets set by the EU: 1.88 billion tonnes, as against a target of 1.90 billion tonnes. It seems that France and Germany had been successful in getting emissions below target levels whilst the UK, Spain and Italy were producing above their target levels. The overall figures, however, implied that tougher limits might be required and that there would be a surplus of permits on the market, driving down prices.

The new targets initially had some effect. The price of permits on the market began to rise. Since the beginning of 2008, when the new targets came into operation, permits were trading above €20 per tonne and analysts were expecting the price to rise further as the year progressed.

However, the recession in 2008 changed things. The global downturn led to a reduction in output and so firms were better able to meet their carbon emission limits. This also meant they were able to sell their permits and so the market saw a significant rise in the supply of permits which pushed down prices from a high of €30 to around €12 per permit. The Climate Change Summit, held in December 2009 in Copenhagen, was supposed to deliver a global agreement on carbon emissions and analysts were anticipating the market for carbon permits to rise significantly as a result of an announcement cutting carbon emissions. The failure to reach any binding agreement at the summit kept the market depressed and by early February 2010, prices were hovering at around €13 per permit.

At this level, the price of a permit does not present a sufficient incentive for firms to invest in technology to reduce carbon emissions. For firms to be prepared to incur the costs of investing in new technologies, the price of carbon permits must be high enough to give an incentive to divert resources to developing more efficient production methods and other technologies such as carbon capture and storage. If the cost of such investment is above the level a firm has to pay for a permit, then there is

The pressure to reduce carbon emissions has led to developments in new energies and in carbon trading permits.
Source: http://www.corporateleadersgroup.com/resources/ publications/10-years-of-carbon-pricing-in-europe-2013-a-business- perspective

(Continued)

no incentive to invest. Analysts have suggested that prices of permits need to be between €30 and €50 each to begin to have any effect on such investment; at these levels the opportunity cost of buying more permits to emit carbon starts to become too high.

In 2015, a report, commissioned by The Prince of Wales's Corporate Leaders Group which includes a number of major businesses such as 3M, Shell, EDF Energy, Philips, Kingfisher, Sky and Glaxo Smith Kline (GSK), and published by the University of Cambridge Institute for Sustainability and Leadership (CISL), aimed to review the first ten years of the scheme from a business perspective. The report noted that the leadership and vision of the chief executive officer was crucial in companies successfully implementing carbon reduction policies. In embracing policies to reduce carbon emissions, companies can increase efficiency, which in turn yields more carbon efficiencies. The report acknowledged that recession had forced carbon prices lower but suggested that carbon reduction would continue as firms seek further efficiencies. Jos Delbeke, the Director General of Climate Action for the European Commission, is quoted in the report as saying: 'Since 1990 economic growth [in the EU] is up 45 per cent and emissions are down 19 per cent – that has been a very important achievement...the ETS has been responsible for a big chunk in delivery.' Interviews with business leaders in the group suggest a largely positive view on the ETS although its weaknesses are acknowledged. Matt Wilson, Head of the Global Environmental Sustainability Centre of Excellence for GSK noted: 'I am in favour of the ETS... Europe has been able to create a market that is working more or less... with limitations and weaknesses, but I think we are positive and it's supported our investment policies...Possibly we were over-allocated, but we've also done a huge amount in this space, and we've been motivated to do something in the space because it makes really good financial sense to do it.' Karl Buttiens, Director of Investment and CO_2 Strategy for AncelorMittal, a steel company, commented that ETS has been a good policy for the energy generation sector but he is not convinced that it is right – in its current format – for the steel sector, as they cannot pass on the additional cost of a carbon price. They are competing in a world market and do not yet have the technology to decarbonise. He further stated that the Company 'fully accept' that it should pay for inefficiency but that 'internalizing the externalities' of carbon emissions is a cost that should fall on the consumer.

Objections to the Economic Analysis of Pollution

Some environmentalists argue that it is in some sense morally wrong to allow anyone to pollute the environment in return for paying a fee. Clean air and clean water, they argue, are fundamental human rights that should not be debased by considering them in economic terms.

The response to this view acknowledges the importance of trade-offs. Clean air and clean water have value but this must be compared to their opportunity cost – that is, to what one must give up to obtain them. Eliminating all pollution would reverse many of the technological advances that allow us to enjoy a high standard of living. Few people might be willing to accept poor nutrition, inadequate medical care or shoddy housing to make the environment as clean as possible.

A clean environment is a good like other goods. Like all normal goods, it has a positive income elasticity: rich countries can afford a cleaner environment than poor ones and, therefore, usually have more rigorous environmental protection. In addition, like most other goods, clean air and water obey the law of demand: the lower the price of environmental protection, the more the public will want. The economic approach of using pollution permits and Pigovian taxes reduces the cost of environmental protection and can, therefore, increase the public's demand for a clean environment.

SELF TEST A glue factory and a steel mill emit smoke containing a chemical that is harmful if inhaled in large amounts. Describe three policy responses to this externality. What are the pros and cons of each of your solutions?

GOVERNMENT FAILURE

In this chapter we have looked at ways in which market failure can be corrected and in so doing, it is invariably governments that implement policies to correct such market failures. In order to improve market outcomes decision-making has to be based on high quality information and positive, rather than normative, analysis of problems and solutions. The reality is that government decision-making may itself be flawed and not based on perfect information or rational, positive analysis.

The Importance of Power

Governments are made up of humans invested with power to make decisions. What we may assume to be economic decisions being taken by government inevitably become political decisions. Politics is about power – who wields that power and how power is brought to bear on individuals and groups within government will affect decision-making in ways which may not always amount to efficient nor equitable outcomes despite what politicians may claim. In considering these outcomes we look at the benefits to people of government decision-making in relation to the costs. If the benefits are greater than the costs it can be argued that government decisions can be deemed 'efficient'. However, there might be instances where the benefits of government decision-making accrue to a small number of people but the costs are spread across large sections of the population. In those circumstances it can be argued that the market outcome is inefficient. When governments make decisions that conflict with economic efficiency it is termed **government failure**. No government decision can be taken at face value without considering the politics behind it in the same way that market decisions have to be viewed in the light of belief systems. In the final section of this chapter we will look at some aspects of government failure.

> **government failure** a situation where political power and incentives distort decision-making so that decisions are made which conflict with economic efficiency

Public Choice Theory

Governments are urged to step in to help improve market outcomes or solve perceived problems in many different areas: gun crime, drugs, prisons, poverty, housing, health, education, obesity, ultra-thin models in the fashion industry, binge-drinking, racism, military intervention, terrorism, famine and so on. Ostensibly, government intervenes to act in the public interest to improve market outcomes. The **public interest** can be defined as a principle based on making decisions to maximize the benefits gained from decisions to the largest number of people at minimum cost.

> **public interest** making decisions based on a principle where the maximum benefit is gained by the largest number of people at minimum cost

The circumstances under which governments intervene in markets might not be one based on rational analysis of the choices available but as a reaction to public pressure or moral panic spread by news organizations. Moral panic can lead to excessive pressure being put on governments and in such situations decisions can be made not on the basis of rationality and efficiency but on placating some individual or group self-interest. There are three key actors in public choice theory: voters, law-makers or politicians, and bureaucrats.

Decision-making under these circumstances comes under the heading of public choice theory. **Public choice theory** is about the analysis of governmental behaviour, and the behaviour of individuals who interact with government.

> **public choice theory** the analysis of governmental behaviour, and the behaviour of individuals who interact with government

The theory developed when economists looked at some apparent contradictions in human behaviour. Any decision will involve some sort of cost, so there will be some people that will be affected adversely by those decisions (the 'losers'). If those people are in the minority and the benefits to the majority (the 'winners') outweigh those costs, a decision might then be regarded as acting in the public interest. However, if the winners are in the minority and the costs are borne by the majority losers, then government failure might exist.

An Example: Road Congestion One solution for road congestion is to make people pay for the use of the roads. If this results in a reduction in road usage, or a more efficient use of the roads, there will not only be widespread benefits for road users, but also for the environment as a whole. However, if there is a vocal group that are very much against road pricing which have political power and influence (they might be backed by an influential newspaper, for example), this group might be able to use their political power to get the policy of road pricing abandoned. They may have decided to champion the cause of the road user, going so far as to provide car stickers showing support for the abandonment of road pricing. Would this be an efficient outcome?

The Invisible Hand versus Public Interest

Public choice theory developed out of an economics tradition that stems from Adam Smith's invisible hand. However, despite this seemingly clear support for self-interest, Smith did spend time discussing government in *The Wealth of Nations*. That discussion was based around the understanding of a moral concern with public interest. The basis of public choice theory, therefore, centres on the behaviour of people as individuals in comparison to the behaviour of those individuals when they become political animals. Can an individual put aside their personal feelings and preferences and become transformed to understand and appreciate the broader public perspective when they are in government?

Public choice theory tries to look at the economic analysis of human behaviour as individuals and transfers this analysis to political science. What public choice theory looks at are cases where that individual interest leads to decisions and the allocation of resources which may not be the most efficient allocation.

Voter Incentives

Voters are asked to make choices in a democratic political system and to choose politicians to represent their views in government. It is assumed that voters will make their choices based on self-interest – the party or politician who offers the promise of the most benefits at the least cost to the voter. However, voters also know that their individual vote counts for little in the grand scheme of things (it is unlikely to make the difference between a government getting into power or not) and as a result they have little incentive to gather information on which to make an informed decision. This is called the **rational ignorance effect**.

> **rational ignorance effect** the tendency of a voter to not seek out information to make an informed choice in elections

What information the voter does rely on to make their decision comes either from their parents (there is some evidence that voting follows such patterns), from TV coverage, and from leaflets supplied by political parties. Such information is likely to be heavily biased and lacking in detail on the huge range of political decisions which any government has to make. As a result, the rational ignorance effect is reinforced. The effect also helps to explain why fewer people in some countries are taking the time to vote in elections; they simply do not see that their vote makes any difference and so there is little incentive for them to do so.

Politician Incentives

Politicians might claim that they have entered politics to fulfil a burning desire to act in the public interest. The more cynical might suggest that the actions and decisions made by politicians are motivated by attracting votes; after all, without votes politicians are not in a position to do anything even if they are genuinely motivated by the public interest.

It is in the interest of politicians to reflect the interests of the local communities they are seeking to serve because if they do they are more likely to attract votes and as a result get elected and re-elected. Some politicians can rely on the rational ignorance effect and the fact that the communities they represent have a large amount of voter inertia – in other words, voters are aligned to a political party so no matter what the politician does (within reason of course) it is highly unlikely they will not get re-elected.

Bureaucrat Incentives

Governments cannot survive without bureaucrats to administer government, provide advice and carry out the legislative programme. Civil servants, especially those in senior positions, are able to wield extensive power as a result and it is highly likely that they will seek to represent the interests of the particular agency or government department they happen to be working for. Those interests might involve protecting or securing larger departmental budgets but might also involve seeking career progression or recognition for the work they are doing. These interests are not necessarily aligned to economic efficiency; voters, for example, might want to see overseas aid or funding for the arts cut in times of domestic economic difficulty and the resources diverted to helping those in need in the domestic economy. Such a policy might have some economic merit but for the particular departments such a policy would be highly damaging to the politicians and bureaucrats involved and so there might exist a conflict of interest which might not lead to an efficient economic outcome.

The Special-Interest Effect

How might government failure manifest itself? Public choice theory likens politicians to a business. Imagine that a business produces a good which does not meet customer needs. It is very likely to fail. Politicians are like products: if they do not meet the customer's (voters) needs, they fail – they are not re-elected at the next election. The obvious behaviour, therefore, is to do what the consumer (the electorate) wants. What the electorate wants is not always clear. What is clear is that those who make the most noise and are the most organized are likely to be the ones that attract the most media attention or have access to the political decision makers whether they are politicians or bureaucrats, and these may be the people who politicians listen to.

Individuals have specific knowledge about certain issues that are closely related to them. As a result of this information, special-interest groups that represent these views tend to develop and can exercise power through lobbying or cultivating close relationships. Politicians who are able to influence decision-making may be more inclined to listen to these groups and base their decisions on what these groups are saying. The **special-interest effect** may lead to minorities gaining significant benefits but the cost is borne by the population as a whole; the benefits to the winners are massively outweighed by the cost borne by the losers. If the value of the benefits to the special-interest group is less than the costs to the population as a whole, then this is an example of inefficiency.

> **special-interest effect** where benefits to a minority special-interest group are outweighed by the costs imposed on the majority

In many cases it might be relatively easy for politicians to align themselves to a special-interest group, especially if that group does exercise political power by having connections with key media organizations or lobby groups. The incentives to align might not only be publicity but also the possibility of accessing funds to help support future election campaigns and as a result the incentive to support these organized groups is considerably stronger than the incentive to align with disorganized rationally ignorant voters.

Logrolling is a term used to describe vote trading in government. Logrolling is an aspect of government failure that helps reinforce the special-interest effect. A voting member of the government (it could be the House of Commons in the UK, a member of the European Parliament or any other legislative chamber) will vote for something which they do not really support or believe in on the understanding that another member will vote in support of something that they do feel passionate about and want to support.

> **logrolling** the agreement between politicians to exchange support on an issue

The argument for logrolling is that decisions or laws that affect relatively small groups of people to a significant extent can be secured, when, as a general rule, such laws would not be passed as it might not have a wide enough effect on society as a whole. The benefits to the group might still be more significant than the costs of implementing the policy or law. Without logrolling, those benefits would not be gained.

The problem with logrolling comes when the benefits to the winners are negligible in comparison to the costs to the losers. In a complex web of agreements and deals over voting, it is quite possible that the net gain to society is less than the costs imposed in achieving those net gains. In other words, resources are allocated inefficiently and the public interest is not maximized. One excellent example of where this might occur in reality is the whole issue of agricultural support – subsidies. The vast majority of the public know that subsidies exist but do not really understand the complexities of the issue or the effect it has on them.

For farmers, the issue is a very real one and there are plenty of lobbying groups that have particular self-interests – be it in dairy farming, arable farming, livestock and so on. The net effect of this web of agricultural support mechanisms in place throughout the world on society as a whole, represents a significant misallocation of resources.

Rent Seeking

'Rent' in this context refers to the income some individual or group receives from an activity. The rents concerned do not always have positive social benefits; in fact, they are likely to have a negative social impact. **Rent seeking** refers to cases where resources are allocated to provide rents for individuals or groups and where those rents have negative social value.

> **rent seeking** where individuals or groups take actions to redirect resources to generate income (rents) for themselves or the group

For example, in the US in 2003, President Bush announced tariffs would be imposed on steel imports to the US. The announcement was warmly welcomed by a steel industry that was struggling to compete with imports. The benefits of the tariffs to this group might be extensive, not least in the jobs that might be saved as a result. However, when balanced out against the wider effects, these benefits might pale into insignificance. There were threats of retaliation by other nations affected by the tariffs. This led to a reduction in demand for US-manufactured goods – along with potential job losses across a wide range of industries that might have used steel but also those who had nothing to do with the steel industry. In addition, the tariffs meant that steel prices to US users rose – either through having to pay the tariff price for imported steel, or the switch to more expensive US producers. The ultimate effect was that the rents to the steel industry in the US could ultimately be argued to have had a negative social value.

Rent seeking amounts to a particular group being able to influence policy to the extent that they are able to gain favours. This can transfer wealth from others to themselves. Whether this wealth transfer is economically efficient or not is of no concern to the group. Indeed it can also be argued that if rent seeking is successful, these groups will divert more resources to such an activity rather than either solving the problems they are experiencing (such as the US steel industry being uncompetitive) or being more productive.

Short-Termism

Most political systems allow for governments to be in power for relatively short periods of time. The consequence of this is that there is always an incentive for politicians to respond more to projects that yield short-term benefits and maximize their re-election potential rather than long-term projects that might be economically more efficient but where the benefits might not be realized for some time.

The fallout of the Financial Crisis of 2007–9 has highlighted just how many governments across Europe relied on debt financing for government expenditure programmes. The current benefits to countries of these programmes (jobs in public sector activity, spending on the provision of major sporting events such as the Olympics, the World Cup and European Championships, for example) have provided short-term benefits to the population in those countries, but the longer-term necessity to finance this debt by having to increase taxation and impose austerity programmes to help reduce the debt, imposes a significant cost on society as a whole. Once again the value of the benefits is massively outweighed by the costs imposed and represents an economically inefficient allocation.

Public Sector Inefficiency

In the 1980s many governments across the developed world put in place a programme of transferring publicly owned assets to the private sector – so called **privatization**.

 privatization the transfer of publicly owned assets to private sector ownership

One of the reasons for this programme was a belief-system which argued that the public sector cannot run certain types of activity as efficiently as the private sector. This, it is argued, is because the existence of the profit motive in the private sector is a powerful motivator to improve productivity, reduce costs and seek efficiency in production. In the public sector, incentives are different. Managers in public sector operations know that ultimately the taxpayer can bail them out and so the risk inherent in decision-making is not the same as that in the private sector where individuals risk their own wealth. In addition, decision makers in the public sector do not gain the same individual benefits and returns that is the case in the private sector if efficiency or productivity is increased and costs cut, and as a result it is more likely that inefficiency will exist. How far these points are 'fact' is difficult to judge and ultimately, such policies may be driven by a belief-system.

Cronyism

We have assumed that markets allocate resources on the basis of the interaction between supply and demand and the price mechanism. When government intervenes in the price mechanism through levying taxes and subsidies, regulating business and passing laws which affect the ability of a business to carry out its activities, the market mechanism is distorted and there is the potential for resource allocation to be determined by political rather than economic forces. Where these political forces are influenced by political favours, the term **cronyism** is used.

> **cronyism** a situation where the allocation of resources in the market is determined in part by political decision-making and favours rather than by economic forces

Cronyism can mean that governments pass laws, institute regulations, levy taxes and impose subsidies which are a response to influence from powerful lobby or special interest groups in return for favours to increase the welfare of the individual politician or the government as a whole. Such favours might be in the form of a news organization pledging its support for the government, financial donations to the party, personal gifts to politicians or promises of senior posts in management when the individual's political career is over.

Inefficiency in the Tax System

Taxes are a reality in most people's lives. We saw in Chapter 9 that firms and individuals can seek to avoid paying taxes and in some cases, illegally evade taxes. The cost to society of the combined activities of tax avoidance and tax evasion is substantial. Because of the very nature of the two, estimates vary on the size of the underground economy but some suggest it could be around 15 per cent of the total tax receipts of some governments. The opportunity cost of such figures is substantial. There are plenty of people who argue that benefit fraud is wrong, but equally there are plenty of people who do not see it as wrong. There are few individuals in society who have not contributed to the underground economy in some way. Most would not see themselves as criminals.

One of the reasons for the existence of tax avoidance and tax evasion might be the design of the tax system. No system is going to be perfect but if people perceive that the system is unfair, there is a greater incentive to find ways around the system or live outside it. In such circumstances, there is a clear case of government failure.

CONCLUSION

The assumptions underlying the market mechanism point to an economic outcome which is efficient from the standpoint of society as a whole. The assumptions, however, do not take account of externalities, such as pollution, and as a result, evaluating a market outcome requires taking into account the well-being of third parties as well. In this case, the market may fail to allocate resources efficiently.

In some cases, people can solve the problem of externalities on their own. The Coase theorem suggests that the interested parties can bargain among themselves and agree on an efficient solution. Sometimes, however, an efficient outcome cannot be reached, perhaps because the large number of interested parties makes bargaining difficult.

When people cannot solve the problem of externalities privately, the government often steps in. The government can address the problem by utilising the market to require decision makers to bear the full costs of their actions. Pigovian taxes on emissions and pollution permits, for instance, are designed to internalize the externality of pollution. Increasingly, they are being seen as effective policies for those interested in protecting the environment. Market forces, properly redirected, can be an effective remedy for market failure.

However, even though government might intervene to correct market failure we also have to account for government failure. Political influence and the incentives of voters, politicians and bureaucrats can often lead to a conflict of interest and as a result the benefits to a small number of people are grossly outweighed by the costs imposed on the majority. In such cases, the attempts to improve market outcomes might lead to further distortions which mean allocations are inefficient.

IN THE NEWS

Fracking

Hydraulic fracturing or fracking, is a technique for extracting gas and oil from shale deposits underground. The technique has been widely adopted in the United States and has led to the country increasing its output of oil and gas and partly contributing to the fall in global fuel prices witnessed in 2014. Whilst fracking has led to an increase in supply of oil and gas, the technique is controversial and attempts to secure licenses to apply the technique in the UK have met with resistance. The fracking debate in the UK is a good example of the issues covered in this chapter.

Fracking: An externality too far?

Some 30 000 fracking wells have been sunk in the United States between 2011 and 2014 but at the time of writing, the prospects for the exploitation of oil and gas reserves in shale deposits in the UK might not be realized for some years despite permission being given for some exploratory wells in Yorkshire in May 2016 to a company called Third Energy.

Proponents of fracking point to the benefit for millions of cheaper fuel prices and thousands of new jobs, and the need for the UK to focus on satisfying its energy needs in the future in the face of estimated shortages caused as a result of decades of under-investment. Those against fracking argue that the negative externalities are extensive. They include the possibilities of increased risk of earthquakes, pollution of drinking water supplies, emission of toxic chemical waste and reductions in the value of homes and properties in surrounding areas. They also argue that society should not be investing in more energy supplies based on fossil fuels which add to global warming, and that investment in fracking diverts resources from renewable sources of energy.

That there is risk with fracking is not denied even by the industry itself but it does claim that the risks are known about, can be mitigated and are no worse nor any better than those in any other major investment in energy. What is important, it is argued, is that the government put in place strict regulation to control the industry and to manage the risks at an acceptable level. Opponents are not convinced and the anti-fracking lobby is becoming well organized and vocal. Professor Mike Bradshaw at Warwick Business School has suggested that a more detached and rational approach to fracking may be necessary to weigh up the costs and benefits. He is reported to have said: 'This is an industrial activity just like any industrial activity, and like all sources of energy it has environmental impacts. Whether those environmental impacts are greater than other industrial activity is a case for planners and industry.'

Questions

1 What might the positive and negative externalities be that arise from fracking?
2 Given your answer to Question 1, in a market economy with no government involvement, what might the market outcome be and how might this compare to the socially efficient outcome? Explain your reasoning.
3 In the case of fracking, what do you think the most efficient solution would be to the externalities that arise from the technique (remember to consider both the positive and negative externalities).
4 In the UK, opponents of fracking seem to have been successful in stalling or preventing the technique from being used. Do you think public choice theory has anything to offer in explaining this success? Justify your answer.
5 To what extent do you agree with the view expressed by Mike Bradshaw in resolving the fracking issue?

Source: http://www.theguardian.com/commentisfree/2015/aug/19/ why-is-fracking-bad-google-answer

Fracking remains a highly controversial technique with strong arguments for and against the process.

SUMMARY

- When a transaction between a buyer and seller directly affects a third party, the effect is called an externality. Negative externalities, such as pollution, cause the socially optimal quantity in a market to be less than the equilibrium quantity. Positive externalities, such as technology spillovers, cause the socially optimal quantity to be greater than the equilibrium quantity.

- Those affected by externalities can sometimes solve the problem privately. For instance, when one business confers an externality on another business, the two businesses can internalize the externality by merging. Alternatively, the interested parties can solve the problem by negotiating a contract. According to the Coase theorem, if people can bargain without cost, then they can reach an agreement in which resources are allocated efficiently. In many cases, however, reaching a bargain among the many interested parties is difficult, so the Coase theorem does not apply.

- When private parties cannot adequately deal with external effects, such as pollution, the government often steps in. Sometimes the government prevents socially inefficient activity by regulating behaviour. At other times it internalizes an externality using Pigovian taxes. Another public policy is to issue permits. For instance, the government could protect the environment by issuing a limited number of pollution permits. The end result of this policy is largely the same as imposing Pigovian taxes on polluters.

- Government intervention to correct market failure might be subject to its own failures. This is because minority groups are able to exercise political power to influence decision-making of politicians and bureaucrats to gain benefits which might be outweighed by the costs imposed on the majority.

QUESTIONS FOR REVIEW

1 Using examples, explain three sources of market failure.

2 Give an example of a negative externality and an example of a positive externality.

3 Using an appropriate example, explain the difference between private and social costs, and private and social benefits.

4 Use a supply and demand diagram to explain the effect of a negative externality in production.

5 List some of the ways that the problems caused by externalities can be solved without government intervention.

6 Using a demand and supply diagram, represent the market for road use. What is the private market outcome and what is likely to be the socially efficient outcome? Explain and refer to your diagram to help support your answer.

7 Imagine that you are a non-smoker sharing a room with a smoker. According to the Coase theorem, what determines whether your room-mate smokes in the room? Is this outcome efficient? How do you and your room-mate reach this solution?

8 Use an example to explain the idea of a positional externality.

9 How would an extension of property rights help reduce the instances of market failure?

10 Explain how government intervention in markets might not improve market outcomes.

PROBLEMS AND APPLICATIONS

1 Do you agree with the following statements? Why or why not?

a. 'The benefits of Pigovian taxes as a way to reduce pollution have to be weighed against the deadweight losses that these taxes cause.'

b. 'When deciding whether to levy a Pigovian tax on consumers or producers, the government should be careful to levy the tax on the side of the market generating the externality.'

2 Consider the market for fire extinguishers.

a. Why might fire extinguishers exhibit positive externalities?

b. Draw a graph of the market for fire extinguishers, labelling the demand curve, the social value curve, the supply curve and the social cost curve.

c. Indicate the market equilibrium level of output and the efficient level of output. Give an intuitive explanation for why these quantities differ.

d. If the external benefit is €10 per extinguisher, describe a government policy that would result in the efficient outcome.

3 In many countries, contributions to charitable organizations are deductible from income tax. In what way does this government policy encourage private solutions to externalities?

4 It is rumoured that the Swiss government subsidizes cattle farming, and that the subsidy is larger in areas with more tourist attractions. Can you think of a reason why this policy might be efficient?

5 Consider the market for train travel. At certain times of the day, trains are extremely crowded going to major towns and cities but at other times of the day carriages are virtually empty.

  a. Is this an example of market failure?
  b. What externalities exist on the train system if the situation described persists?
  c. Can you think of a way in which the government might step in to make the market outcome more efficient?

6 Greater consumption of alcohol leads to more motor vehicle accidents and, thus, imposes costs on people who do not drink and drive.

  a. Illustrate the market for alcohol, labelling the demand curve, the social value curve, the supply curve, the social cost curve, the market equilibrium level of output and the efficient level of output.
  b. On your graph, shade the area corresponding to the deadweight loss of the market equilibrium. (Hint: the deadweight loss occurs because some units of alcohol are consumed for which the social cost exceeds the social value.) Explain.

7 Many observers believe that the levels of pollution in society are too high.

  a. If society wishes to reduce overall pollution by a certain amount, why is it efficient to have different amounts of reduction at different firms?
  b. Command-and-control approaches often rely on uniform reductions among firms. Why are these approaches generally unable to target the firms that should undertake bigger reductions?
  c. Some economists argue that appropriate Pigovian taxes or tradable pollution rights will result in efficient pollution reduction. How do these approaches target the firms that should undertake bigger reductions?

8 The Pristine River has two polluting firms on its banks. European Industrial and Creative Chemicals each dump 100 tonnes of effluent into the river each year. The cost of reducing effluent emissions per tonne equals €10 for European Industrial and €100 for Creative. The government wants to reduce overall pollution from 200 tonnes to 50 tonnes per year.

  a. If the government knew the cost of reduction for each firm, what reductions would it impose to reach its overall goal? What would be the cost to each firm and the total cost to the firms together?
  b. In a more typical situation, the government would not know the cost of pollution reduction at each firm. If the government decided to reach its overall goal by imposing uniform reductions on the firms, calculate the reduction made by each firm, the cost to each firm and the total cost to the firms together.
  c. Compare the total cost of pollution reduction in parts (a) and (b). If the government does not know the cost of reduction for each firm, is there still some way for it to reduce pollution to 50 tonnes at the total cost you calculated in part (a)? Explain.
  d. Assume that the chief executive officers of European Industrial and Creative Chemicals have considerable influence with politicians and civil servants from the country's Department of Industry. How might market outcomes be changed as a consequence?

9 Suppose that the government decides to issue tradable permits for a certain form of pollution.

  a. Does it matter for economic efficiency whether the government distributes or auctions the permits? Does it matter in any other ways?
  b. If the government chooses to distribute the permits, does the allocation of permits among firms matter for efficiency? Does it matter in any other ways?

10 Some people argue that the primary cause of global warming is carbon dioxide, which enters the atmosphere in varying amounts from different countries but is distributed equally around the globe within a year. In order to solve this problem, some economists have argued that carbon dioxide emissions should be reduced in countries where the costs are least, with the countries that bear that burden being compensated by the rest of the world.

  a. Why is international cooperation necessary to reach an efficient outcome?
  b. Is it possible to devise a compensation scheme such that all countries would be better off than under a system of uniform emission reductions? Explain.
  c. Explain how the concepts of rent seeking and cronyism might be used by critics of climate change theory to argue for different approaches to public policy.

12 INFORMATION AND BEHAVIOURAL ECONOMICS

Economics is a study of the choices that people make and the resulting interactions they have with one another. Perhaps one of the major developments in economics in recent years has been the influence of academics from other disciplines offering explanations for the interactions humans have with one another. Two key people in this respect have been Daniel Kahneman and Amos Tversky, both psychologists. Kahneman became the first psychologist to win the Nobel Prize for Economics, a prize Kahneman insists would have been shared with his friend and fellow researcher, Amos Tversky, had Tversky not died at the relatively young age of 59 in 1996.

The insights from psychology into the study of economic issues has come to be referred to as *behavioural economics*. It offers a view of human behaviour and interactions that is more subtle and complex than that found in conventional economic theory, but may also be more accurate in explaining how humans make choices when compared to the standard economic model. In this chapter we will look at some of the insights into informational and behavioural economics which has pushed the boundaries of understanding and opened up new and interesting avenues of research.

PRINCIPAL AND AGENT

To begin we look at the principal–agent problem. The two parties to an economic decision can be referred to as principal and agent. A **principal** is a person or organization for whom another person (called the agent) is performing some act – they can be seen as the client. An **agent** is a person or organization who is performing an act or acting on behalf of another person or organization (the principal) – they can be seen as an advisor. The agent invariably has some information which is not known to the principal. In most cases, the principal is using the agent to act for them and to bring about a desired exchange.

> **principal** a person for whom another person, called the agent, is performing some act
> **agent** a person who is performing an act for another person, called the principal

The relationship between principal and agent is a key one and has been of increasing interest in recent years following the Financial Crisis of 2007–8. It is often referred to as the *principal–agent problem*; why is the relationship a problem?

To explain, consider this example. You want to go on holiday and decide to visit a travel agent, that will be performing the act of supplying you with a suitable holiday. You have to rely on the information given to you in making your decision on a holiday. If the travel agent tells you that hotel *x* is excellent, has superb views, is quiet, peaceful and romantic with excellent food and service, and is valued highly by other customers, how do you know that this is really the case? You might have suspicions that the hotel may be in the middle of a building site, be overrun by noisy children, have less than average food, poor service and poor quality rooms. You could check the accuracy of the information given by the travel agent by going away and looking at a review site on the Internet or checking a satellite image of the area in order to verify the information given. Such actions involve additional cost. You might presume that the agent must be giving you accurate information because if they did not they would lose your custom and you could share your experience on other review sites on the Web. The wish to get repeat custom and the profit motive might be a sufficient monitoring device to ensure that the travel agent is acting in your best interest in the advice they are giving, but there may be other motivations that you are unaware of which are driving their advice. Quite simply, you cannot be sure that the interests of the agent are sufficiently aligned with your interests as the principal. At the heart of the principal–agent problem is asymmetric information.

ASYMMETRIC INFORMATION

Many times in life, one individual, a business or an organization, knows more about something than another. In economics, the different access to information of buyers and sellers or any two people is called **asymmetric information**. (Something which is symmetric is identical on both sides – when it is asymmetric, one side is different to another.)

> **asymmetric information** where two parties have access to different information

Examples abound. A worker knows more than their employer about how much effort they put into their job. A seller of a used car knows more than the buyer about the car's condition. The first is an example of a *hidden action*, whereas the second is an example of a *hidden characteristic*. In each case, the party in the dark (the employer, the car buyer) would like to know the relevant information, but the informed party (the worker, the car seller) may have an incentive to conceal it. This is another aspect of the principal–agent problem where invariably the agent has access to information which may not be shared with the principal. It can, however, also be the case that the principal has an incentive to hide information from the agent.

Because asymmetric information is so prevalent, economists have devoted much effort in recent decades to studying its effects. The 2001 Nobel Prize in economics was awarded to three economists (George Akerlof, Michael Spence and Joseph Stiglitz) for their pioneering work on this topic. Let's discuss some of the insights that this research has revealed.

Hidden Actions and Moral Hazard

Moral Hazard **Moral hazard** is a problem that arises when the agent is performing some task on behalf of the principal. In many cases the principal is not able to monitor the behaviour of the agent. This might be because the agent has specific expertize and the principal does not have the knowledge to monitor the agent's behaviour, and even if the agent explained it is not certain the principal could be sure that what they were being told was accurate. In the example of the travel agent above, it is possible to do some research to check the information given by the agent as a means of monitoring the agent's behaviour (at additional cost to the principal), but this is not always possible. If the principal cannot perfectly monitor the agent's behaviour, the agent might have an incentive to undertake less effort than the principal considers desirable and as a result the agent may not be fully responsible for the consequences of their actions. The phrase *moral hazard* refers to the risk, or 'hazard', of inappropriate or otherwise 'immoral' behaviour by the agent.

> **moral hazard** the tendency of a person who is imperfectly monitored to engage in dishonest or otherwise undesirable behaviour

The employment relationship is an example where moral hazard occurs. In this situation the employer is the principal and the worker is the agent. The moral hazard problem is the temptation of imperfectly monitored workers to shirk their responsibilities. Employers can respond to this problem in various ways:

- *Better monitoring.* Parents hiring nannies or au pairs have been known to plant hidden video cameras in their homes to record the individual's behaviour when the parents are away. The aim is record any instances of irresponsible behaviour.
- *High wages.* Some employers may choose to pay their workers a wage above the level that equilibrates supply and demand in the labour market. A worker who earns an above-equilibrium wage is less likely to shirk, because if they are caught and lose their job, they might not be able to find another high-paying job. Paying higher wages than equilibrium is called *efficiency wages.*
- *Delayed payment.* Firms can delay part of a worker's compensation, so if the worker is caught shirking and loses their job they suffer a larger penalty. One example of delayed compensation is the year-end bonus. Similarly, a firm may choose to pay its workers more, later in their lives. Thus, the wage rises that workers get as they age, may reflect not just the benefits of experience but also a response to moral hazard.

These various mechanisms to reduce the problem of moral hazard need not be used alone. Employers can use a combination of them.

Beyond the workplace there are many other examples of moral hazard. Individuals with insurance cover, be it fire, motor vehicle or medical insurance, may behave differently as a result of having that cover. A motorist, for example, might drive more recklessly in the knowledge that in the event of an accident the cost will be met primarily by the insurance company. Similarly, families choosing to live near a river may benefit from the scenic views but the increased risk of flooding imposes a cost to the insurance company and the government in the event of a serious flood.

Moral hazard has also been much discussed in the wake of the Financial Crisis with regard to the behaviour of individuals in the investment banking arms of banks. The risks that were being taken by some dealers were seen as being too great. As the problems came to light the potential for a number of banks to collapse was considerable and the effect on the wider economy meant that governments and international institutions stepped in to rescue banks. The phrase 'too big to fail' was widely used and it can be argued that many in the banking industry knew this. As a result, dealers and their managers were more willing to take risks that might be considered reckless, even immoral, because they knew that they would not have to face the full consequences of their decision-making and actions.

Adverse Selection Moral hazard can lead to **adverse selection**. This means that the market process may end up with 'bad' outcomes because of asymmetric information. Adverse selection occurs when the buyer (principal) knows more about their situation than the seller (agent). The seller knows this and would rather avoid having to do business with these buyers and so might be tempted to charge a higher price as a result. Other buyers, who sellers don't want to avoid, might be put off buying the good because it is too high a price – the very people who the seller would rather do business with.

> **adverse selection** where a principal knows more about their situation than the agent, leading to the agent preferring not to do business with the principal

Adverse selection is a feature of banking, finance and insurance industries. A bank, for example, may set rules and regulations for its accounts which may lead to some customers, who are not very profitable to the bank, adversely selecting the bank – customers the bank would rather not have. In insurance, the person seeking insurance cover has more information about his or her situation than the insurer. A person who knows they are high risk will look to buy insurance but not necessarily divulge the extent of the risk they pose to the insurance company. The insurance company would prefer not to have to take on these high-risk buyers. It may be difficult for the insurance company to distinguish between its high-risk and low-risk customers; many insurance companies use sophisticated statistical devices to try and do this. The insurance company would rather take on the low-risk customers than the high-risk ones but high-risk customers may be more likely to seek out policies from an insurance company. Because of this, all seekers of insurance may have to pay higher premiums.

In the wake of the financial crisis, it became clear that some investment banks were putting very risky assets into financial products, and clients buying these products did not know the full extent of the risk they were buying. In this case clients (the principals) were dealing with suppliers (agents) who they would have been better off not dealing with.

Many regulations are aimed at addressing the problem: an insurance company may require homeowners to buy smoke detectors and burglar alarms, or pay higher premiums if there is a history of reckless driving (or even refuse to provide insurance cover to the individual); and the government may prohibit building homes on land with a high risk of flooding or impose new regulations to curb the behaviour of banks. But the insurance company does not have perfect information about how cautious homeowners are, the government does not have perfect information about the risk that families undertake when choosing where to live, and regulators do not know fully the risks that bankers take in investment decisions. As a result, the problem of moral hazard persists.

Hidden Characteristics: Adverse Selection and the Lemons Problem

The Market for Used Cars
The classic example of adverse selection is the market for used cars. Sellers of used cars know their vehicles' defects while buyers often do not. Because owners of the worst cars are more likely to sell them than are the owners of the best cars, buyers are apprehensive about getting a poor car. If you are unlucky enough to buy a poor car, then we might say that you have bought a 'lemon'. This was the term used by Nobel Prize-winner George Akerlof in his much cited research article, 'The Market for Lemons' (see Akerlof, G. (1970) 'The Market for Lemons: Quality, Uncertainty and the Market Mechanism'. *Quarterly Journal of Economics*, 84:488–500). His co-prize winners in 2001, Joseph Stiglitz and Michael Spence, also used the term in the context of asymmetric information; it comes from the old-fashioned fruit or gambling machines where three wheels spin and come to rest indicating a picture of a fruit that determines the payout; traditionally, a lemon was bad luck, paying out nothing.

Akerlof used the market for used cars as the basis for his explanation. In this market, the seller has information about the car that the buyer does not have. The seller might know the history of the car and details about how it was driven, whether it has been involved in any accidents and so on. The buyer only has the word of the seller on which to base their decision. Few car buyers have the expertize to be able to conduct a thorough check of a vehicle and be able to verify the seller's claims. This is a clear case of asymmetric information.

Akerlof suggested that there would be two types of cars in the market: good cars, which we will refer to as oranges, and bad cars, which he called 'lemons'. If you go to buy a second-hand car from a dealer, you do not know whether the dealer is selling you an orange or a lemon. You might be willing to pay a reasonable price to buy an orange but clearly not willing to pay that same price to buy a lemon. The seller, however, knows whether the car they are trying to sell you is a lemon or an orange. If the seller presents you with a vehicle which they claim is a good quality car, as a buyer, you have to consider whether it is an orange or a lemon. In effect, there is a probability of 0.5 that it will be one or the other.

Given that you have imperfect information, you simply do not know whether the car you are buying is an orange or a lemon. To get an orange, you might have to pay €10 000. The seller on the other hand, who has a lemon for sale, will be prepared to accept almost anything to get rid of it. Let's say that they are willing to accept €4000 for it. If you offer the seller €4000 for the car they are trying to sell and it is a sure-fire orange, they will laugh you out of the showroom. As the buyer, however, you are not sure whether you want to offer €10 000 for the possibility of buying a lemon.

Akerlof also raised the issue about why anyone would want to sell a good car in the first place. If an individual owns a good car, it is highly unlikely that they would get the true value of the car paid to them. Logic would suggest that the only reason they would want to sell their existing car and buy another is because they were looking to replace a sub-standard vehicle with a better quality one. If everyone does this would the market exist at all?

The result is that the market tends to be dominated by lemons. The seller is not willing to sell oranges for less than €10 000 but the buyer is unwilling to pay that much because of the possibility of being sold a lemon. The conclusion that Akerlof came to was that the market in this type of scenario would only see low quality goods traded.

As a result of this information asymmetry, many people avoid buying vehicles in the used car market. This lemons problem can explain why a used car only a few weeks old sells for thousands of euros less than a new car of the same type. A buyer of the used car might surmise that the seller is getting rid of the car quickly because the seller knows something about it that the buyer does not.

The Labour Market A second example of adverse selection occurs in the labour market. According to efficiency wage theory, workers vary in their abilities, and they may know their own abilities better than do the firms that hire them. When a firm cuts the wage it pays, the more talented workers are more likely to quit, knowing they are better able to find other employment. Conversely, a firm may choose to pay an above-equilibrium wage to attract a better mix of workers.

Suppose that a firm is not doing so well and needs to cut the wage bill. It can do this either by reducing wages or by keeping wages where they are and laying off workers at random for a few weeks. If it cuts wages, the very best workers may quit, because they surmise they will be able to find a better job elsewhere. Of course, the better workers who are randomly selected when the firm chooses instead to impose layoffs may also choose to quit and find a steadier job elsewhere. In this case only *some* of the best workers quit (since not all of them are laid off because workers were chosen randomly) while if the firms cuts wages *all* (or most probably, a great number) of the best workers will quit.

The Insurance Market A third example of adverse selection occurs in markets for insurance. For example, buyers of health insurance know more about their own health problems than do insurance companies. Because people with greater hidden health problems are more likely to buy health insurance than are other people, the price of health insurance reflects the costs of a sicker-than-average person. As a result, people in average health may be discouraged from buying health insurance by the high price.

When markets suffer from adverse selection, the invisible hand does not necessarily work its magic. In the used car market, owners of good cars may choose to keep them rather than sell them at the low price that sceptical buyers are willing to pay. In the labour market, wages may be stuck above the level that balances supply and demand, resulting in unemployment. In insurance markets, buyers with low risk may choose to remain uninsured, because the policies they are offered fail to reflect their true characteristics. Advocates of government-provided health insurance sometimes point to the problem of adverse selection as one reason not to trust the private market to provide the right amount of health insurance on its own.

Signalling to Convey Private Information Although asymmetric information is sometimes a motivation for public policy, it also motivates some individual behaviour that otherwise might be hard to explain. Markets respond to problems of asymmetric information in many ways. One of them is **signalling**, which refers to actions taken by an informed party for the sole purpose of credibly revealing private information.

 signalling an action taken by an informed party to reveal private information to an uninformed party

Firms may spend money on advertising to signal to potential customers that they have high-quality products. Students may study for university degrees in order to signal to potential employers that they are high-ability individuals. The signalling theory of education asserts that education increases a person's productivity, rather than merely conveying information about innate talent. These two examples of signalling (advertising and education) may seem very different, but below the surface they are much the same: in both cases, the informed party (the firm, the student) is using a signal to convince the uninformed party (the customer, the employer) that the informed party is offering something of high quality.

What does it take for an action to be an effective signal? Obviously, it must be costly. If a signal were free, everyone would use it, and it would convey no information. For the same reason, there is another requirement: the signal must be less costly, or more beneficial, to the person with the higher-quality product. Otherwise, everyone would have the same incentive to use the signal, and the signal would reveal nothing.

Consider again our two examples. In the advertising case, a firm with a good product reaps a larger benefit from advertising because customers who try the product once are more likely to become repeat customers. Thus, it is rational for the firm with the good product to pay for the cost of the signal (advertising), and it is rational for the customer to use the signal as a piece of information about the product's quality. In the education case, a talented person can get through university more easily than a less talented one. Thus, it is rational for the talented person to pay for the cost of the signal (education), and it is rational for the employer to use the signal as a piece of information about the person's talent.

The world is replete with instances of signalling. Magazine advertisements sometimes include the phrase 'as seen on TV'. Why does a firm selling a product in a magazine choose to stress this fact? One possibility is that the firm is trying to convey its willingness to pay for an expensive signal (a spot on television) in the hope that you will infer that its product is of high quality. For the same reason, graduates of elite universities are always sure to put that fact on their CVs.

Screening to Induce Information Revelation

When an uninformed party takes actions to induce the informed party to reveal private information, the phenomenon is called **screening**.

> **screening** an action taken by an uninformed party to induce an informed party to reveal information

Some screening is common sense. A person buying a used car may ask that it be checked by a car mechanic before the sale. A seller who refuses this request reveals their private information that the car is a lemon. The buyer may decide to offer a lower price or to look for another car.

Other examples of screening are more subtle. For example, consider a firm that sells car insurance. The firm would like to charge a low premium to safe drivers and a high premium to risky drivers. But how can it tell them apart? Drivers know whether they are safe or risky but the risky ones won't admit to it. A driver's history is one piece of information (which insurance companies in fact use) but, because of the intrinsic randomness of some car accidents, history is an imperfect indicator of future risks.

The insurance company might be able to sort out the two kinds of drivers by offering different insurance policies that would induce them to separate themselves. One policy would have a high premium and cover the full cost of any accidents that occur. Another policy would have low premiums but would have, say, a €1000 excess (that is, the driver would be responsible for the first €1000 of damage, and the insurance company would cover the remaining risk). Notice that the excess is more of a burden for risky drivers because they are more likely to have an accident. Thus, with a large enough excess, the low-premium policy with an excess would attract the safe drivers, while the high-premium policy without an excess would attract the risky drivers. Faced with these two policies, the two kinds of drivers would reveal their private information by choosing different insurance policies.

Asymmetric Information and Public Policy

We have examined two kinds of asymmetric information – moral hazard and adverse selection – and we have seen how individuals may respond to the problem with signalling or screening. Now let's consider what the study of asymmetric information suggests about the proper scope of public policy.

The tension between market success and market failure is central in microeconomics. We have learned that the equilibrium of supply and demand is efficient, given certain assumptions, in the sense that it maximizes the total surplus that society can obtain in a market. This conclusion is tempered by the problem of public goods and externalities. We will see more examples of market failure when we look in more detail at firms' behaviour when the assumption of perfect competition is dropped.

The study of asymmetric information gives us new reason to be wary of markets. When some people know more than others, the market may fail to put resources to their best use. People with high-quality used cars may have trouble selling them because buyers will be afraid of getting a lemon. People with few health problems may have trouble getting low-cost health insurance because insurance companies lump them together with those who have significant (but hidden) health problems.

Although asymmetric information may imply government action, three facts complicate the issue. First, as we have seen, the private market can sometimes deal with information asymmetries on its own using a combination of signalling and screening. Second, the government may not have any more information than the private parties. Even if the market's allocation of resources is not first-best, it may be second-best. That is, when there are information asymmetries, policymakers may find it hard to improve upon the market's admittedly imperfect outcome. Third, the government is itself an imperfect institution, as we have seen in our analysis of government failure.

CASE STUDY   The Deadweight Loss of Christmas

For millions of people around the world, 25 December is a day for exchanging gifts. Using the standard economic model to explain gift-giving presents problems because the assumption of the self-interest of the purchaser is distorted by the fact that the purchaser is buying something not to satisfy their own preferences but anticipating the preferences of the recipient. Joel Waldfogel reviewed this issue in a 1993 paper (Waldfogel, J. (1993) 'The Deadweight Loss of Christmas'. In *The American Economic Review*, December, 83:5:1328–36). Waldfogel began with the premise that the optimal outcome for a gift-giver would be to replicate the choices the recipient would have made if they had spent the same amount of money the gift-giver spent. The difference between the two would be the deadweight loss of gift-giving.

Waldfogel's research suggested that the size of the deadweight loss could be between a tenth and a third of the value of the gift. Gift-giving can be inefficient when the utility of the recipient could have been higher if they had spent the same amount of money that the gift-giver spent themselves. The size of the deadweight loss is dependent on the extent to which the gift-giver can replicate the preferences of the recipient – and this obviously depends on the extent of the information asymmetry between them. If the gift-giver knows the recipient extremely well (i.e. has perfect information about the recipient's preferences) then they can replicate that person's preferences and the gift will yield value above its cost. However, the existence of information asymmetry is likely to mean that there will be some deadweight loss associated with gift-giving.

What is the best sort of gift to give? The gift-giver has to estimate the utility the recipient will receive from the gift. If they give cash, the recipient can use that cash to maximize their preferences but any other gift may not match the utility the recipient could have achieved if they had spent the money themselves. The more ignorant the gift-giver is of the preferences of the recipient the greater the deadweight loss. It can be argued, therefore, that giving cash is always the best gift to give, unless the giver knows the preferences of the recipient extremely well.

This brings us to the type of giver; is one type of giver likely to have more knowledge about the preferences of the recipient than another? Waldfogel's research suggested that aunts/uncles and grandparents' gifts are most likely to be associated with higher deadweight losses, whereas those from friends and significant others have the lowest.

Giving gifts can create anxiety not only in the gift receiver but also the gift giver.

SELF TEST A person who buys a life insurance policy pays a certain amount per year and receives for their family a much larger payment in the event of their death. Would you expect buyers of life insurance to have higher or lower death rates than the average person? How might this be an example of moral hazard, and of adverse selection? How might a life insurance company deal with these problems?

DEVIATIONS FROM THE STANDARD ECONOMIC MODEL

Economics is a study of human behaviour, but it is not the only field that can make that claim. The social science of psychology also sheds light on the choices that people make in their lives. The fields of economics and psychology usually proceed independently, in part because they address a different range of questions. Behavioural economics makes use of basic psychological insights to explain human behaviour, especially when faced with making decisions and when faced with choices.

In Chapter 5 we introduced the standard economic model and looked at some behavioural approaches to explaining consumer behaviour, which cast doubt on the assumption that people always behave rationally.

People Aren't Always Rational

Economic theory is populated by a particular species, sometimes called *Homoeconomicus*. Two prominent behavioural economists from the University of Chicago, Richard Thaler and Cass Sunstein, refer to them as '*econs*'. Members of this species are always rational. As managers of firms, they maximize profits. As consumers, they maximize utility. Given the constraints they face, they rationally weigh all the costs and benefits and choose the best possible course of action.

Real people, however, are *Homo sapiens*. Although in many ways they resemble the rational, calculating people assumed in economic theory, they are far more complex. They can be forgetful, impulsive, confused, emotional and short-sighted. These imperfections of human reasoning are the bread-and-butter of psychologists.

Herbert Simon, one of the first social scientists to work at the boundary of economics and psychology, suggested that humans should be viewed not as rational maximizers but as **satisficers**. Rather than always choosing the best course of action, they make decisions that are merely 'good enough', in other words, decisions may be made based on securing a satisfactory rather than optimal outcome.

satisficers those who make decisions based on securing a satisfactory rather than optimal outcome

We saw in chapter 5 how humans might be considered as only 'near rational' or that they exhibit *bounded rationality*. We also saw how humans make systematic mistakes or errors in decision-making under different conditions. What follows are some further findings which have an effect on consumer decision-making.

Mental Accounting You may know some people who steadily collect money in tins so as to have money to pay a bill when it arrives – electricity, gas, holidays and so on. This is an example of how people have a tendency to separate money into different accounts based on different criteria. Having these accounts might provide the individual with some comfort but they might also be completely irrational. For example, if an individual diverts some portion of their income into a savings account each month to save for a holiday, whilst at the same time only paying off the minimum amount on their credit card, this would be deemed highly irrational. The diverted money would be better spent on reducing the debt, which is also accruing interest over time – the longer the debt is deferred, the larger the debt will be. The fact that people do not do this suggests that they attach a subjective value to each 'account' which is not a logical and rational allocation of their funds.

Similarly, when people receive funds from unexpected sources, such as a tax rebate or a bonus payment from work, they tend to view it and spend it differently to their 'normal income'. This is also an example of irrational behaviour; regardless of the origin of the money, it is still money and can be allocated in exactly the same way to satisfy preferences.

Herd Mentality There are occasions when people make decisions which follow those of a much larger group – sometimes this group may not be tangible but for some reason individuals are persuaded by the apparent power of the group. For example, in periods where house or stock prices are rising there may be a tendency for individuals to make decisions on the purchase of these assets which are at odds with their 'true value'. Indeed, this is how asset price bubbles arise. Individuals may make decisions based on herd behaviour because of reasons of social conformity (humans have a tendency to want to 'belong' to a group and to reflect the behaviour of the group), and because there may be a sense of 'if so many people are making these decisions they can't all be wrong', and feelings that other people may be more informed.

Prospect Theory Imagine that someone offered you the prospect of winning €200 but then a day later losing €100, or, of winning €100. Which would you choose? Research suggests that more people would choose the second option. Closer inspection of the choices offered reveal that they are both the same in terms of the net gain to individuals – the net gain in each case is €100. So why do more people choose the second option if the net gain is the same?

Kahneman and Tversky suggested the reason was because people do not value gains and losses in the same way. Losses appear to be attached with more emotion than do gains. **Prospect theory** suggests that when presented with different prospects (outcomes) from a transaction or an exchange, people will value the losses and gains differently even if the value of each is the same. This helps explain, for example, why some people are willing to drive 25km to save €10 on a €50 item but would not be willing to drive the same distance to save the same amount of money (€10) on a €500 item even though the nominal saving is the same.

> **prospect theory** a theory that suggests people attach different values to gains and losses and do so in relation to some reference point

This insight has important implications for financial decisions where the risk of making losses in relation to the gains that could be made are important. In such situations, decision makers might exhibit risk aversion to the potential for making losses but undervalue the potential gains that could be made. This is partly because humans attach reference points to decision-making which mean we place values on changes rather than on absolute magnitudes. For example, if we are in a room which is heated to 35 degrees Celsius and then walk into a room which is heated to 25 degrees Celsius we would suggest that the room is 'cold', whereas at other times most people consider 25 degrees Celsius to be 'warm'.

When evaluating gains and losses from decision-making, therefore, we react to some reference point. This is possibly why humans place such a value on a loss rather than a gain; gains provide a different reference point compared to losses. This also helps explain why the owner of something tends to place a higher value on it than anyone else – the **endowment effect**.

> **endowment effect** where the value placed on something owned is greater than on an identical item not owned

If we are putting up a house for sale, for example, not only are we pricing the asset value of the house in terms of the bricks and mortar components but there will also be a considerable emotional investment in it, and the value of that emotional investment will be priced into the sale – it is the value we place on losing all those emotional experiences. For the buyer who has not got these emotional ties to the property, the value will be far less. Similar experiences exist when people access tickets for key sporting or musical events. Once the ticket is 'owned' it tends to be valued far more highly because the owner can now begin to articulate in their mind the value of the loss they will experience if they give up the ticket.

The way losses and gains are presented, therefore, can have an effect on the way in which we make choices and decisions and the way in which businesses can exploit human psychology. This is linked to the section on framing outlined in chapter 5.

People Care about Fairness

Another insight about human behaviour is best illustrated with an experiment called the *ultimatum game.* The game works like this: two volunteers (who are otherwise strangers to each other) are told that they are going to play a game and could win a total of €100. Before they play, they learn the rules. The game begins with a flip of a coin, which is used to assign the volunteers to the roles of player A and player B. Player A's job is to propose a division of the €100 prize (in whole euros) between themselves and the other player. After player A makes their proposal, player B decides whether to accept or reject it. If they accept it, both players are paid according to the proposal. If player B rejects the proposal, both players walk away with nothing. In either case, the game then ends.

Before proceeding, stop and think about what you would do in this situation. If you were player A, what division of the €100 would you propose? If you were player B, what proposals would you accept?

Conventional economic theory assumes in this situation that people are rational wealth-maximizers. This assumption leads to a simple prediction: player A should propose that they get €99 and player B gets €1, and player B should accept the proposal. After all, once the proposal is made, player B is better off accepting it as long as they get something out of it (remember, people are assumed to act at the margin – a €1 euro gain is better than nothing). Moreover, because player A knows that accepting the proposal is in player B's interest, player A has no reason to offer them more than €1.

Yet when experimental economists ask real people to play the ultimatum game, the results are very different from this prediction. People in the role of player B usually reject proposals that give them only €1 or a similarly small amount. Knowing this, people in the role of player A usually propose giving player B much more than €1. Some people will offer a 50 – 50 split, but it is more common for player A to propose giving player B an amount such as €30 or €40, keeping the larger share for themselves. In this case, player B usually accepts the proposal.

What's going on here? The natural interpretation is that people are driven in part by some innate sense of fairness. A 99–1 split seems so wildly unfair to many people that they reject it, even to their own detriment. By contrast, a 70–30 split is still unfair, but it is not so unfair that it induces people to abandon their normal self-interest.

Throughout our study of household and firm behaviour, the innate sense of fairness has not played any role. But the results of the ultimatum game suggest that perhaps it should. We will see in later chapters that wages are determined by labour supply and labour demand. Some economists have suggested that the perceived fairness of what a firm pays its workers should also enter the picture. Thus, when a firm has an especially profitable year, workers (like player B) may expect to be paid a fair share of the prize, even if standard equilibrium does not dictate it. The firm (like player A) might well decide to give workers more than the equilibrium wage for fear that the workers might otherwise try to punish the firm with reduced effort, strikes or even vandalism.

To return to the ultimatum game, do you think that a sense of fairness may have its price? If the players were given, say, €1000 to divide to the nearest hundred, and player A proposed a split of €900 to themselves and €100 to player B, do you think that player B would be just as likely to reject the proposal as before? What if the prize money were raised to €1 million, to be divided to the nearest €100 000? The answer may depend on framing – behaviour and decision-making will be dependent on the way decision problems or choices are framed.

People Are Inconsistent over Time

Imagine some dreary task, such as doing your laundry or tidying your room. Now consider the following questions:

1. Would you prefer (A), to spend 50 minutes doing the task immediately or (B), to spend 60 minutes doing the task tomorrow?
2. Would you prefer (A), to spend 50 minutes doing the task in 90 days or (B), to spend 60 minutes doing the task in 91 days?

When asked questions like these, many people choose B to question 1 and A to question 2. When looking ahead to the future (as in question 2), they minimize the amount of time spent on the dreary task. Faced with the prospect of doing the task immediately (as in question 1), they choose to put it off

In some ways, this behaviour is not surprising: everyone procrastinates from time to time but from the standpoint of the theory of rational humans, it is puzzling. Suppose that, in response to question 2, a person chooses to spend 50 minutes in 90 days. Then, when the ninetieth day arrives, we allow them to change their mind. In effect, they then face question 1, so they opt for doing the task the next day. Why should the mere passage of time affect the choices they make?

Many times in life, people make plans for themselves but then they fail to follow them through. A smoker promises themselves that they will quit, but within a few hours of smoking their last cigarette, they crave another and break their promise. A person trying to lose weight promises that they will stop eating chocolate bars but when they get to the checkout at the supermarket and see the tempting array of confectionery next to the cash register, the promise is forgotten. In both cases, the desire for instant gratification induces the decision maker to abandon their own past plans.

Some economists believe that the consumption-saving decision is an important instance where people exhibit this inconsistency over time. For many people, spending provides a type of instant gratification. Saving, like passing up the cigarette or the dessert, requires a sacrifice in the present for a reward in the distant future. And just as many smokers wish they could quit and many overweight individuals wish they ate less, many consumers wish they saved more.

An implication of this inconsistency over time is that people should try to find ways to commit their future selves to following through on their plans. A smoker trying to quit may throw away their cigarettes, and a person on a diet may put a lock on the refrigerator and ask someone else to do the shopping. What can a person who saves too little do? They should find some way to lock up their money before they spend it. Some personal pension plans do exactly that. A worker can agree to have some money taken out of their salary payment before they ever see it. The money is placed in an account and invested on their behalf by the pension company. When they retire they can use the money to fund a pension, but the money can only be used before retirement with a penalty. This is one reason why people take out pension plans: they protect people from their own desires for instant gratification.

SELF TEST Describe at least three ways in which human decision-making differs from that of the rational individual of conventional economic theory.

CONCLUSION

This chapter has examined some of the issues in behavioural explanations of human decision-making – behavioural economics. You may have noticed that we have sketched out ideas rather than fully developing them. This is no accident. One reason is that you might study these topics in more detail in advanced courses. Another reason is that these topics remain active areas of research and, therefore, are still being fleshed out.

To see how these topics fit into the broader picture, recall the ideas that markets can be a good way to organize economic activity and that governments can sometimes improve market outcomes. As you study economics, you can more fully appreciate the benefits and limitations of these ideas. The study of asymmetric information facilitates a more critical awareness of the claims made in favour of both market-based outcomes and of the suggestion that any market failure can be improved by involving government. If there is a unifying theme to these topics, it is that life is messy. Information is imperfect, government is imperfect and people are imperfect.

IN THE NEWS

Behavioural Economics

The developments in understanding human behaviour which have come under the umbrella term 'behavioural economics' has garnered interest at major levels of public policy making. Not everyone, however, is convinced that behavioural economics offers the answers to society's problems.

Does behavioural economics have all the answers?

The Behavioural Insights Team (BIT) lays claim to have 'started life inside 10 Downing Street as the world's first government institution dedicated to the application of behavioural sciences. Our objectives remain the same as they always have been:

- making public services more cost-effective and easier for citizens to use;
- improving outcomes by introducing a more realistic model of human behaviour to policy; and wherever possible,
- enabling people to make "better choices for themselves".'

The very fact that the UK government has invested in joint ownership of the BIT, alongside a charity and its employees, is testament to how far this branch of economics has come. It is almost fashionable to debunk traditional economics as being 'broken' and based on outmoded ways of thinking and suspect empirical techniques and assumptions.

The BIT is charged with looking at ways in which understanding of human behaviour can be utilized to improve outcomes which may include encouraging people to invest in pensions for their retirement, recycle waste more efficiently and donate organs amongst other things. Of course, now we know that humans don't behave rationally, it makes sense to get rid of old-fashioned economic ideas and replace them with shiny new behavioural economics ones. Doesn't it?

Behavioural economics may, however, have more in common with traditional economics than meets the eye. Reading some of the papers produced by leading figures in the movement reveal a considerable reliance on the use of mathematical models to reveal understanding. What Kahneman and his colleagues have done is to largely model human behaviour based on different assumptions than those in the standard economic model but they produce models to predict human behaviour nonetheless and this could be argued to be an extension of neoclassical economic principles of explaining behaviour.

Kahneman and Thaler would both argue that there is some merit in traditional economic theory which should be weaved in with new insights. Some academics who have been put into the behavioural economics camp have argued that the insights research brings can be hijacked by politicians seeking to give the impression that policy is well thought out and based on sound research. For example, claims that 'nudge' techniques can be the 'best way' to improve energy efficiency by, for example, making people aware of the amount of electricity they are using through having devices in the home whir-

ring away and ringing up the cash being 'spent', or by revealing more clearly what other 'energy efficient' people are spending. Would a policy based on this behavioural technique be as effective as increasing the price of electricity through a tax? We know that if prices rise, then demand falls – a 'law' of economics. Which policy would be more effective in increasing energy efficiency and what would the consequences be in each case?

Behavioural economics may be at a critical point in its development. Few doubt that it can reveal important insights into human behaviour but as is often the case with such developments, those who have immersed themselves in the research associated with the field are often the most aware of its potential limitations.

Behavioural economics might provide answers to incentives to improve things like recycling.

(*Continued*)

Questions

1 To what extent do you think behavioural economics offers a more 'realistic model of human behaviour'?

2 Does the market mechanism allow people to 'make better decisions for themselves' or is it always the case that people need a 'nudge' to help them make better decisions?

3 Behavioural economics has been used as a means of trying to encourage people to donate organs by a 'nudge' which presents people with a scenario where they ask themselves whether they would have an organ transplant if they needed it and if so, this should be an incentive for them to help others. What are the assumptions behind such a policy and to what extent do you think it will be successful in increasing organ donations?

4 Do you think that making people aware of their spending on electricity and gas is a more effective way of improving energy efficiency or would a tax on gas and electricity raising its price be more effective? Justify your reasoning.

5 To what extent do you think that the models used by behavioural economists and organizations like the BIT are, to all intents and purposes, the same as those used in what might be classed as 'traditional' economics?

Source: http://www.behaviouralinsights.co.uk/

SUMMARY

- In many economic transactions, information is asymmetric. When there are hidden actions, principals may be concerned that agents suffer from the problem of moral hazard.

- When there are hidden characteristics, buyers may be concerned about the problem of adverse selection among the sellers. Private markets sometimes deal with asymmetric information with signalling and screening.

- The study of psychology and economics reveals that human decision-making is more complex than is assumed in conventional economic theory.

- Human beings make errors in decision-making that reflect biases and can also be influenced by the way information is framed and how they value outcomes.

- People are not always rational; they care about the fairness of economic outcomes (even to their own detriment), and they can be inconsistent over time.

QUESTIONS FOR REVIEW

1 Explain, using examples, the difference between a 'principal' and an 'agent'.

2 Why does the existence of asymmetric information mean that economic decisions do not conform to the assumptions of the standard economic model?

3 What is the difference between a 'hidden action' and a 'hidden characteristic'?

4 What is moral hazard? List three things an employer might do to reduce the severity of this problem.

5 What is adverse selection? Give an example of a market in which adverse selection might be a problem.

6 Define *signalling* and *screening*, and give an example of each.

7 Why can mental accounting lead to irrational decision-making?

8 Why might herd mentality lead to asset prices rising faster than the fundamental value of the assets?

9 Use an example to explain prospect theory.

10 Describe the ultimatum game. What outcome from this game would conventional economic theory predict? Do experiments confirm this prediction? Explain.

PROBLEMS AND APPLICATIONS

1 In each of the following cases, who is the principal and who is the agent and explain why there might be asymmetry of information.

   a. A suspicious wife hires a private detective to report on the movements of her husband.
   b. A car leasing company providing a holidaymaker with a rental vehicle.
   c. A homeowner seeking insurance for her home against flooding.
   d. An individual making a routine visit to the dentist for a check-up.

2 In the situations in Question 1 above, identify the hidden actions and the hidden characteristic(s).

3 Each of the following situations involves moral hazard. In each case, identify the principal and the agent, and explain why there is asymmetric information. How does the action described reduce the problem of moral hazard?

   a. Landlords require tenants to pay security deposits.
   b. Firms compensate top executives with options to buy company shares at a given price in the future.
   c. Car insurance companies offer discounts to customers who install anti-theft devices in their cars.

4 Suppose that Live-Long-and-Prosper Health Insurance Ltd charges €5000 annually for a family insurance policy. The company's president suggests that the company raise the annual price to €6000 in order to increase its profits. If the firm followed this suggestion, what economic problem might arise? Would the firm's pool of customers tend to become more or less healthy on average? Would the company's profits necessarily increase?

5 A boyfriend can signal to a girlfriend that he loves her by giving an appropriate gift. Do you think saying 'I love you' can also serve as a signal? Why or why not?

6 Some AIDS activists believe that health insurance companies should not be allowed to ask applicants if they are infected with the HIV virus that causes AIDS. Would this rule help or hurt those who are HIV positive? Would it exacerbate or mitigate the problem of adverse selection in the market for health insurance? Do you think it would increase or decrease the number of people without health insurance? In your opinion, would this be a good policy?

7 The government is considering two ways to help the needy: giving them cash, or giving them free meals at soup kitchens. Provide an argument for giving cash. Present an argument, based on asymmetric information, for why the soup kitchen may be better than the cash handout.

8 Michael turns up to an interview in a brand new designer suit. What do you think Michael is trying to do? How might the employer find out if Michael represents a good investment as a prospective employee?

9 Imagine that you are in charge of health policy in your country. A mutation of the swine flu virus leads to a rapid increase in the number of people contracting the virus with the expectation that 1200 people will die as a result. There are medications and inoculation programmes that will help save some lives but it is inevitable that some people will die. Your problem is presenting the news to the population. Your officials present you with the following wordings as part of your speech on the policy:

   a. Our inoculation programme will save the lives of 400 people.
   b. We are going to offer a programme to all the population that will have a one-third chance that 1200 people will live.
   c. Unfortunately, despite the best efforts of this government, our inoculation programme will not be enough to save everyone and so I have to tell you that even with the programme, 400 people will die.
   d. Our inoculation programme will help but I have to be honest with you and tell you that the programme has a one-third chance that no-one will die but a two-thirds chance that 1200 people will die.

   Which option would you choose? Does it matter which one you chose? Why? Why not? How does this highlight prospect theory and the idea of framing?

10 Two ice-cream stands are deciding where to locate along a one-kilometre beach. Each person sitting on the beach buys exactly one ice-cream cone per day from the stand nearest to them. Each ice cream seller wants the maximum number of customers. Where along the beach will the two stands locate?

PART 6
FIRM BEHAVIOUR AND MARKET STRUCTURES

13 FIRMS' PRODUCTION DECISIONS

In this chapter we are going to look in more detail at a firm's production decisions and then move on in subsequent chapters to see how firms' behaviour changes when the assumptions of perfect competition are dropped.

ISOQUANTS AND ISOCOSTS

One of the issues facing businesses in considering production decisions is to attempt to maximize output or minimize costs but with a constraint of limited factor inputs. This is a further example of a constrained optimization problem. Different firms have different ratios of factor inputs – land, labour and capital – in the production process. This can vary not only between industries but also within industries. For example, some farms are highly land-intensive whereas others may be far more capital- or labour-intensive. Arable farms tend to have a very high proportion of land in comparison to a pig farm and be classed as land-intensive.

Businesses can utilize their factors of production in different ways to produce any given output so an important question that firms need to address is how to organize its factor inputs to maximize output at minimum cost. The use of isocost and isoquant lines provides a model to help conceptualize the process. The principles are very similar to the model of consumer behaviour we introduced in Chapter 5, which made use of indifference curves and budget constraints. In this model the firm is faced with different combinations of factors which yield the same amount of output (isoquants) and has a given budget available to pay for those factors of production (isocosts).

Production Isoquants

A **production isoquant** is a function which represents all the possible combinations of factor inputs that can be used to produce a given level of output. For simplicity we are going to assume just two factor inputs: labour and capital. To further focus our thinking, let us assume that the capital in question is a machine that coats pizzas with a tomato base, adds the filling and then bakes the pizzas. The number of hours the machine is in operation varies with the amount of pizzas produced. The labour input will be the number of person hours needed to mix and produce the dough for the pizza base, feed the machine and then package the finished pizzas.

> **production isoquant** a function representing all possible combinations of factor inputs that can be used to produce a given level of output

Figure 13.1 shows a graphical representation of the production isoquants that relate to the combinations of labour and capital that can be used to produce pizzas. An output level of $Q = 600$ could be produced using 5 hours of labour and 1 hour of the machine indicated by point A, or 2 hours of labour and 2 hours of the machine shown by point B. The isoquant line $Q = 600$ connects all the possible combinations of capital and labour which could produce an output of 600 pizzas. Given the level of capital and labour inputs for the pizza factory, a series of isoquants can be drawn for different levels of output. Figure 13.1 shows the isoquants for output levels of $Q = 600$, $Q = 750$, $Q = 900$ and $Q = 1050$. In theory, the whole of the graphical space could be covered with isoquants all relating to the different levels of possible output.

It is unlikely that any business would sit down and draw out isoquants in the way we have done here – remember, this is a model. The reality is, however, that firms have to make decisions about factor combinations in deciding output. Firms will often look at the option of substituting capital for labour by making staff redundant and investing instead in new equipment, for example. Firms may also look at replacing existing machinery for new ones or look for outsourcing opportunities, both of which would have an effect on the shape and position of the isoquants.

FIGURE 13.1

Production Isoquants for a Pizza Factory

Given the possibility of employing different amounts of capital and labour, the isoquant map connects together combinations of capital and labour which could be employed to produce different levels of output of pizzas. For an output level Q = 600, the machine operating for 5 hours and 1 hour of labour time could produce 600 pizzas per day but so could the combination 2 hours for the machine and 2 hours of labour time. Five hours of the machine and 5 hours of labour could produce an output level Q = 900 (shown by point C); a combination of 2 hours of the machine and 10 hours of labour could also produce 900 pizzas indicated by point D.

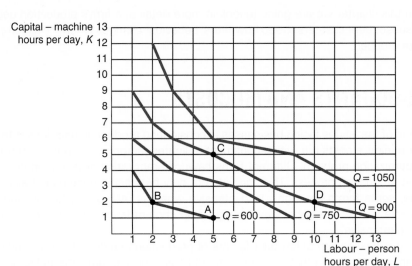

Substituting one factor for another will incur costs. It may not be easy to be able to substitute one factor for another; machinery may be highly specialized and workers may have skills that machines simply cannot replicate (the ability to make clients feel confident and at ease, for example). The slope of the isoquant represents the **marginal rate of technical substitution** (MRTS). This is the rate at which one factor input can be substituted for another at a given level of output. Referring to Figure 13.1, take the output level, $Q = 1050$ and a combination of labour and capital at 5 and 6 hours respectively. If the owner of the pizza factory considered reducing labour hours by 2, they would have to increase the amount of hours the machine was used by 3 to 9 hours in order to maintain output at 1050. The MRTS would be given by the ratio of the change in capital to the change in labour, $\dfrac{\Delta K}{\Delta L}$. The change in capital is from 6 to 9 units and the change in labour is from 5 to 3. The $MRTS = \dfrac{3}{2}$, or 1.5. This tells us that the owner has to increase the amount of hours of capital by 1.5 for every 1 hour of labour reduced to maintain production at $Q = 1050$.

> **marginal rate of technical substitution** the rate at which one factor input can be substituted for another at a given level of output

The way we have drawn the isoquants in Figure 13.1 would suggest a different MRTS at different points because the slope of each isoquant is different. It is common to see isoquants drawn as smooth curves, as shown in Figure 13.2.

FIGURE 13.2

Production Isoquants
It is common to represent production isoquants as a series of smooth curves representing the different combinations of capital and labour which would be used to produce different levels of output represented in this figure as $Q = x$, $Q = x_1$, $Q = x_2$, etc.

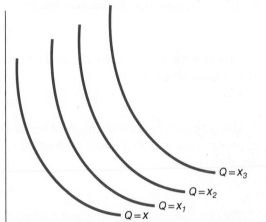

When a firm reduces one unit of a factor and substitutes it for another, unless the factors are perfect substitutes, it is likely that the addition to total output of each successive unit of the factor employed will diminish according to the law of diminishing marginal productivity. At the same time, as less of the other factor is used its marginal product will be higher. This helps explain why isoquants are convex to the origin. If a firm employs a large amount of capital and not much labour, in substituting one unit of capital for a unit of labour, the marginal product of that extra unit of labour is likely to be relatively high (and the slope of the isoquant relatively steep) but as additional units of labour are substituted the marginal product diminishes and so the slope of the isoquant gradually gets less steep. The MRTS is the ratio of the marginal products of labour and capital:

$$MRTS = \frac{MP_L}{MP_K}$$

Where the $\quad MP_L = \dfrac{change\ in\ the\ quantity\ of\ output\,(\Delta Q)}{change\ in\ the\ quantity\ of\ labour\,(\Delta L)}$ and

$$MP_K = \frac{change\ in\ the\ quantity\ of\ output\,(\Delta Q)}{change\ in\ the\ quantity\ of\ capital\,(\Delta K)}$$

Isocost Lines

Our analysis so far has looked at different combinations of factor inputs to produce given outputs. A business has to take into consideration that factor inputs cost money. Labour has to be paid wages, and energy to power machines has to be purchased in addition to the cost of the machines themselves. Firms do not have unlimited funds to purchase factor inputs and so face constraints. Many firms will set budgets for purchasing factor inputs which have to be adhered to. Isocost lines take the cost of factor inputs into consideration. An **isocost line** shows the different combination of factor inputs which can be purchased with a given budget.

 isocost line a line showing the different combination of factor inputs which can be purchased with a given budget

Assume that the price of an hour's operation of the pizza machine is P_K then the cost of capital would be $P_K K$ (the price of capital multiplied by the amount of capital hours used), and the cost of labour is given by $P_L L$ (the price of labour multiplied by the amount of labour hours). Given a budget constraint represented by TC_{KL} we can express the relationship as:

$$P_K K + P_L L = TC_{KL}$$

Now assume that the price of capital to make pizzas is €10 per hour and the price of labour, €6 per hour. Our formula would look like this:

$$10K + 6L = TC_{KL}$$

Using 3 capital hours and 9 hours of labour would cost 10(3) + 6(9) = €84. Are there other combinations of capital and labour that would produce pizzas at a cost of €84? We can find this out by rearranging the equation to give:

$$€84 = 10K + 6L$$

We can now find values for K and L which satisfy this equation. For example, dividing both sides by 10 and solving for K we get:

$$K = \frac{84}{10} - \frac{6L}{10}$$
$$K = 8.4 - 0.6L$$

Table 13.1 shows the combinations of capital and labour that satisfy this equation. For example, if six units of labour were used then $K = 8.4 - 0.6(6)$.

$$K = 8.4 - 3.6$$
$$K = 4.8$$

The information in Table 13.1 can be graphed as in Figure 13.3 with the number of capital hours on the vertical axis and the number of labour hours on the horizontal axis, given the price of capital at €10 per hour and the price of labour is €6 per hour. The isocost line $TC_{KL} = 84$ connects all the combinations of labour and capital to make pizzas which cost €84. At point C, 5.4 hours of capital and 5 hours of labour will have a total cost of €84 but so will the combination of 1.2 hours of capital and 12 hours of labour at point D.

Other isocost lines could be drawn connecting combinations of capital and labour at different levels of total cost. For each of these isocost lines, the vertical intercept shows how many units of capital the factory owner could buy with their budget constraint if they used zero hours of labour. The horizontal intercept shows how many hours of labour the factory owner could buy if zero hours of capital were purchased. The isocost line shows the combinations of capital and labour that could be purchased given the budget constraint.

TABLE 13.1 Factor Combinations to Satisfy the Equation $K = 8.4 - 0.6L$

K	L
8.4	0
7.8	1
7.2	2
6.6	3
6.0	4
5.4	5
4.8	6
4.2	7
3.6	8
3.0	9
2.4	10
1.8	11
1.2	12
0.6	13
0	14

FIGURE 13.3

Isocost Lines

Isocost lines connect combinations of capital and labour that a business can afford to buy given a budget constraint. The isocost line shown relates to a budget constraint of €84. With this budget constraint the factory owner could spend all the money on 8.4 hours of capital if capital was priced at €10 per hour but would not be able to afford any workers. This gives the vertical intercept at point A. If the business chose to spend the budget entirely on labour then it would be able to purchase 14 hours of labour per day if labour was priced at €6 per hour but not be able to use any machines. This gives the horizontal intercept at point B. Any point on the isocost line between these two extremes connects together combinations of capital and labour that could be purchased with the available budget. At point C, the factory owner could afford to buy 5.4 hours of capital and 5 hours of labour at the given prices of capital and labour; at point D, they could afford to buy 1.2 hours of capital and 12 hours of labour.

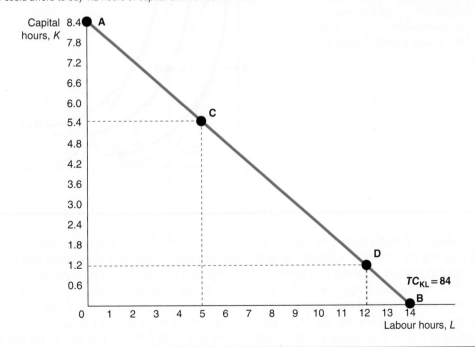

The slope of the isocost line is the ratio of the price of capital to labour. As the isocost line is a straight line the slope is constant throughout. In this example, the slope is 0.6. This tells us that in order not to increase cost, for every one additional hour of labour employed they have to reduce the amount of capital by 0.6 hours. The inverse of this is that for every additional hour of capital employed they must reduce labour by 1.6 hours.

SELF TEST What factors could cause the slope of the isoquant and isocost curves to change?

THE LEAST-COST INPUT COMBINATION

We now know the combination of factor inputs needed to produce given quantities of output (pizzas in our case) given by the isoquant curves and the cost of using different factor combinations given by the isocost lines. We can put these together to find the least cost input combination.

Figure 13.4 shows different isoquants relating to three different output levels $Q = x$, $Q = x_1$, $Q = x_2$, and three isocost lines relating to three different cost levels for capital and labour giving the budget constraints TC_{KL1}, TC_{KL2} and TC_{KL3}.

Any point where the isocost line cuts the isoquant line is a possible combination of factors that could be used. The more resources a business has at its disposal the higher the output it can produce and this is determined by the amount of resources it can afford and hence by the prices of capital and labour.

FIGURE 13.4

The Least-Cost Input Combination

Three isoquants representing different output levels, $Q = x$, $Q = x_1$ and $Q = x_2$, and are shown along with three different isocost lines representing three different cost levels and budget constraints for the firm. The least-cost input combination is where the isoquant is tangential to the given budget constraint. Given a budget constraint of TC_{KL2}, the least-cost combination of capital and labour is given as point C where the firm employs K hours of capital and L hours of labour.

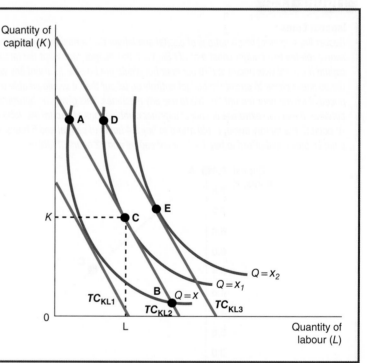

Let us assume that the factory owner has a budget constraint of TC_{KL2}. They could produce output $Q = x$, and employ the combination of factors of production at point A. Similarly they could use fewer hours of capital and more hours of labour and produce the same output at point B. However, we could reasonably assume that if there was a way in which a business could use its existing budget and resources to produce more output then it would do so. It may make such a decision if it thought that it could sell more output.

Starting at point A, therefore, the factory owner could reduce the amount of capital used and increase the amount of labour to produce a higher output level $Q = x_1$ at point C. The owner cannot produce the output $Q = x_1$ using the combination of factors given by point D, because the owner does not have the funds to be able to afford this combination as it falls on a different isocost line, TC_{KL3}. They can afford to employ capital and labour in the combination given at point C. At point C the isoquant curve $Q = x_1$, is tangential to the isocost line TC_{KL2}. This is the least-cost input combination given the desired output level for the factory owner. At this point there is no incentive for them to change the combination of factors of production employed because to do so would mean that those resources would not be producing at maximum efficiency at minimum cost.

The owner might want to produce an output level given by $Q = x_2$ at point E, but given their budget constraint they cannot afford to produce this level of output. The optimum point, therefore, given existing productivity levels and the price of factor inputs, is C.

At this point of tangency, the point of least-cost input occurs where the marginal rate of technical substitution is equal to the ratio of the prices of factors. This is represented by the equation:

$$\frac{MP_L}{MP_K} = \frac{P_L}{P_K}$$

This is also sometimes written as:

$$\frac{MP_L}{P_K} = \frac{MP_K}{P_L}$$

SELF TEST Using Figure 13.4, explain what would happen if the price of labour hours fell but the price of capital hours remained the same. What would happen to the least-cost input combination?

Summary

Let us summarize this section by thinking through this logically. If you were the factory owner faced with a budget constraint, you would want to ensure that you use your money in the best way possible to produce the maximum amount possible. Taking a factor input combination such as that at A, if there was a way in which you could reorganize those factor inputs so that they did not cost you any more but you could produce more pizzas, it would make sense to do so.

Cutting back on the use of capital and increasing labour means the additional output produced is greater but does not cost any more. Provided the benefit of doing this is greater than the cost incurred, it makes sense to make such a decision. If there is still a way to continue cutting capital use and increasing labour which would bring about increased production of pizzas, then it is clearly sensible to continue doing so until you reach a point where there is no benefit in shifting resources any further.

The least-cost input combination can change if either the price of labour or capital changes (in which case the slope of the isocost line would change), or if both prices changed equally then the isocost line would shift either inwards or outwards depending on the direction of the price change. The shape of the isoquant curve might also change if the marginal productivity of either capital or labour changed.

Remember that early in this analysis we mentioned that this approach was a way of conceptualizing how businesses behave. The assumption is that firms want to maximize output at minimum cost. Firms will have some idea of the productivity of factor inputs and also of the cost of buying in factors. They will continually be looking to find ways to reorganize factors of production they employ to increase output but keep costs under control. The use of this model helps us to understand the logic behind business restructuring, outsourcing, seeking out cheaper suppliers, using different raw materials in different ways, spending money on training workers to be more effective in their jobs (and other ways of influencing productivity), and it helps explain why businesses are dynamic and constantly changing and evolving organizations.

The Productivity Puzzle

Productivity, measured as output per factor input per time period, is important not only to firms but also to the economy as a whole. Increasing productivity implies getting more from each factor input even if the cost of employing that factor stays the same or rises by a smaller proportion than the increase in output. For example, assume a factory worker produces pizzas and is paid €10 per hour. The worker produces 20 pizzas per hour and as a result the unit cost of each pizza would be €0.50 (assuming the only cost was labour). If some way of increasing output per hour can be found which increases the worker's output to 25 per hour, then the unit cost would fall to €0.40. Simple enough concept in theory but more difficult to achieve in practice.

Since the Financial Crisis in 2007, productivity has declined in the UK and even though economic growth has been relatively strong since 2013, productivity has been poor such that output per hour is around 15 per cent lower than it would have been if pre-crisis levels of productivity had been maintained. Why productivity should be so sluggish in a period of relatively strong growth has been dubbed the 'productivity puzzle'.

Reasons put forward for this 'puzzle' include the reluctance of firms to shed labour during the recession which has left many overstaffed, firms looking to cut costs by bringing in workers on low pay who may not be as productive but are cheaper, and a lack of investment in capital due to difficulties in securing loans.

For many businesses, looking at their internal processes is one way of improving productivity. Finding better ways to do things, reducing time spent on wasteful activities like finding the right equipment or waiting for resources to be delivered, reducing the time it takes to make decisions and allowing workers at lower levels who may have far more experience and knowledge of the processes they work with every day to make their own decisions, are all possibilities which can improve productivity at limited additional cost. In terms of the model we have looked at in this chapter, such changes would improve the marginal productivity of capital and labour and thus change the shape of the isoquant curve.

How do businesses utilize resources effectively to improve productivity?

CONCLUSION

In this chapter we have introduced a simplified technical analysis of how a firm might make production decisions based on it having two variable factors of production in the short run. The price of the factors of production and the budget of the firm determines the amount of factors that can be purchased and the factors can be used in different combinations to produce given amounts of output. Firms will constantly review the factor combinations they use in response to changing prices of factors and changes in the productivity of factors – to try and produce the maximum output at minimum cost. The least-cost input model allows us to conceptualize the changes that firms can make in response to changing factor market conditions.

IN THE NEWS

Efficiency

Efficiency can be defined in different ways – it can be extracting maximum output from minimum factor input or maximizing output at minimum cost. Individual firms may not be large enough to take advantage of efficiencies themselves but collective organization can bring these efficiencies to a far wider range of firms.

The Green Growth Service

The Green Growth Service (GGS) is an independent organization funded through the European Regional Development Fund and the UK Regional Growth Fund. It provides support and advice to businesses with the aim of reducing their environmental impact and generating efficiencies as a result. GGS has been working with businesses in the Greater Manchester area in England through the Business Growth Hub which was set up in 2011 to provide support to businesses seeking to grow and create new jobs. Figures released in August 2015 show that around £100 million of savings have been secured by businesses in the region as a result of the collaboration between businesses, the GGS and the Business Growth Hub. The focus on savings in energy, water use and materials allow firms to improve productivity by more efficient use of factor inputs. The savings include reducing 25 million tonnes of materials from production processes, diverting over 370 000 tonnes of waste from landfill, saving over 550 gigawatt hours of energy every day and reducing water usage by 5 million cubic tonnes. One firm in Oldham, Greater Manchester, has recorded savings of almost £150 000 since 2012. Quantum Profile Systems Ltd makes rigid and flexible PVC components. The savings are not cost free but the company estimates that some of the changes it introduces will generate sufficient savings to repay the investment in less than 2 years.

Questions

1 Consider how investment in energy efficient systems, such as those outlined in the article, might affect the isoquant curve in the model of firm's production decisions.
2 Why might firms like Quantum Profile Systems need to utilize the services of organizations like the GGS and The Business Growth Hub?
3 Explain how investment in reducing waste would affect a firm's productivity levels.
4 Using the model of production decision making outlined in this chapter, how would the measures to improve energy efficiency and materials use impact on the least-cost input combination? Explain your reasoning.
5 What is meant by the phrase 'The savings are not cost free'?

Source: http://www.businessgrowthhub.com/ green-growth

Regional support can help to improve efficiency and reduce environmental impacts of business activity.

SUMMARY

- The use of isoquants and isocosts helps to conceptualize the reasons why firms make decisions to change factor combinations used in production and how the prices of factor combinations can also influence those decisions.

- The least-cost input combination occurs where the isoquant curve is tangential to the isocost line. At this point, the producer cannot reorganize existing resources, given their budget constraint, to increase output any further.

- Changes in productivity of factors will alter the shape of the isoquant curve and changes in factor prices can alter the shape of the isocost curve.

QUESTIONS FOR REVIEW

1 What is the constrained optimization problem facing firms?

2 Explain the difference between capital-, labour- and land-intensive production and give an example of a firm in each case to illustrate the principle.

3 What is a production isoquant?

4 What is the marginal rate of technical substitution?

5 What is an isocost line?

6 What determines the slope of an isocost line?

7 Given the TC function $P_K K + P_L L = TC_{KL}$ where the price of capital is 50 and the price of labour is 10, what would be the total cost of 12 units of capital and 8 units of labour ?

8 What is the least-cost input combination?

9 What determines the slope of the isoquant curve?

10 If capital and labour were perfect substitutes, what would be the shape of an isoquant? Explain.

PROBLEMS AND APPLICATIONS

1 Isoquants are drawn as convex to the origin. Referring to the marginal rate of technical substitution, why do you think that isoquants are convex to the origin?

2 Look at the table of quantities below and sketch the isoquants implied by the data for the output levels $Q = 110$, $Q = 150$ and $Q = 180$

Capital (Machine hours per day)	Labour (person hours per day)				
	1	2	3	4	5
1	40	80	110	130	150
2	80	120	150	170	210
3	110	150	180	200	220
4	130	170	200	220	230
5	150	180	210	230	240

On your graph, put capital on the vertical axis and labour on the horizontal axis.

3 Using the graph you have constructed for Question 2, calculate the marginal rate of technical substitution for the output level $Q = 110$ when the firm moves from a combination of 3 machine hours of capital and 1 person hour of labour, to 1 machine hour of capital and 3 person hours of labour.

4 Look at the sketch of three production isoquants in the figure below. What do the shape of these isoquants tell you about the relationship between capital and labour in this particular instance?

Capital (K)

$Q=x_1$ $Q=x_2$ $Q=x_3$

0

Labour (L)

5 Given the total cost function $50K + 12L = TC_{KL}$, calculate the total cost for a firm if it used the following combinations of capital and labour:

a. 5 units of capital and 8 units of labour
b. 10 units of labour and 3 units of capital
c. 7 units of capital and 12 units of labour.

6 Given the total cost function $50K + 12L = TC_{KL}$, at the following total cost levels, solve for K and find the factor combinations that satisfy the equation from $K = 1$ to $K = 5$.

a. $TC = 170$
b. $TC = 510$
c. $TC = 850$

7 If a firm faced the following situation:

$$\frac{MP_L}{P_K} > \frac{MP_K}{P_L}$$

What would be the incentives for the firm to change its production decisions? At what point would the firm stop changing its production decisions? Explain.

8 Sketch a diagram to show a firm's least-cost input combination. On your diagram show what would happen to the firm's optimum position if:

a. the price of capital increased but the price of labour stayed the same
b. the price of both labour and capital increased by the same amount
c. the price of labour and capital both increase but the price of capital increases by a greater amount than the price of labour.

9 A haulage firm uses containers to carry products for clients which currently measure 10m long by 2m wide by 4m high. The owner of the firm has decided to invest in new containers which double their length, width and height. Why might the owner have made this decision and what is likely to happen to:

a. the total costs for the firm; and
b. the average costs.
Explain your reasoning.

10 Draw a diagram to show a firm operating at a least-cost input combination. Now assume that the input price of one factor increases whilst the other remains constant. How would this change the firm's production decisions and its optimum position? Explain.

14 MARKET STRUCTURES I: MONOPOLY

IMPERFECT COMPETITION

So far in our analysis of firms we have assumed that conditions of perfect competition exist. In the vast majority of cases, these assumptions cannot hold entirely; firms have some control over price, they deliberately set out to seek ways to differentiate their products from their rivals, some firms have more power than others to influence the market in some way, and information is imperfect. When the assumptions of perfect competition do not hold, we say that firms are operating under imperfect competition. A firm operating under **imperfect competition** has the characteristic that it can differentiate its product in some way and so has some influence over the price it can charge for its product.

> **imperfect competition** exists where firms are able to differentiate their product in some way and so can have some influence over price

There are different degrees of imperfect competition and we begin our analysis of firm behaviour under imperfect competition by looking at the opposite end of the competitive spectrum: monopoly. Strictly, a monopoly is a market structure with only one firm; however, in reality firms can exercise monopoly power by being the dominant firm in the market. Indeed, in many countries, firms might be investigated by regulators if they account for over 25 per cent of market share, with **market share** being the proportion of total sales in a market accounted for by a particular firm. The larger the market share a firm has the more market power it has. A firm can exercise market power when it is in a position to raise the price of its product and retain some sales – in other words, it is the opposite of the situation of a firm who is a *price taker*; it is a *price maker*.

> **market share** the proportion of total sales in a market accounted for by a particular firm

Perhaps the most obvious example of how one firm can dominate a market is that of the Microsoft Corporation in the personal computer market. Microsoft produces its operating systems, Windows, which, in August 2016, was reported to account for around 86 per cent of the market (which now includes operating systems for desktop PCs, laptops and mobile devices). There are other firms who also provide operating systems across devices such as such as Apple's iOS mobile device operating system, the open source Linux and Android, but Microsoft's Windows operating systems dominate the market. Even though Windows is still a dominant player in the market, it is not immune to competitive pressure and the development of mobile devices has seen its market share falling in recent years.

If a person or business wants to buy a copy of Windows, they have little choice but to give Microsoft the price that the firm has decided to charge for its product. Because of its ability to control the market for operating systems, Microsoft is said to have a monopoly in the market. Microsoft has been able to develop its business and secure market power which leads to behaviour that is different to that we studied when looking at a perfectly competitive firm.

In this chapter we examine the implications of this market power. We will see that market power alters the relationship between a firm's costs and the price at which it sells its product to the market. A competitive firm takes the price of its output as given by the market and then chooses the quantity it will supply so that price equals marginal cost. By contrast, the price charged by a monopoly exceeds marginal cost. This result is clearly true in the case of Microsoft's Windows. The marginal cost of Windows – the extra cost that Microsoft would incur by supplying a license to download the system – is only a few euros. The market price of Windows is many times marginal cost.

It is perhaps not surprising that monopolies charge relatively high prices for their products. Customers of monopolies might seem to have little choice but to pay whatever the monopoly charges. This might imply that monopolies can charge whatever price they choose because the customer has no choice but of course, if Microsoft set the price of Windows too high, fewer people would buy the product. People would buy fewer computers, switch to other operating systems or make illegal copies. Monopolies cannot achieve any level of profit they want because high prices reduce the amount that their customers buy. Although monopolies can control the prices of their goods, their profits are not unlimited.

As we examine the production and pricing decisions of monopolies, we also consider the implications of monopoly for society as a whole. We will make an assumption that monopoly firms, like competitive firms, aim to maximize profit. This goal has very different ramifications for competitive and monopoly firms.

WHY MONOPOLIES ARISE

A firm is a **monopoly** if it is the sole seller of its product and if its product does not have close substitutes. Whilst this is the strict definition of a monopoly, as we have seen, firms are said to have monopoly power if they are a dominant seller in the market and are able to exert some control over the market as a result. In the analysis that follows, however, the assumption is that there is only one seller.

monopoly a firm that is the sole seller of a product without close substitutes

The fundamental cause of monopoly is **barriers to entry**: a barrier to entry exists where there is something that prevents a firm from entering an industry. Remember, when we analyzed firm behaviour in perfect competition we assumed there was free entry and exit to the market. The stronger the barriers to entry the more difficult it is for a firm to enter a market and the more market power a firm in the industry can exert.

barriers to entry anything which prevents a firm from entering a market or industry

A monopoly can remain the only seller in its market because other firms cannot enter the market and compete with it. Barriers to entry, in turn, have four main sources:

- A key resource is owned by a single firm.
- The government gives a single firm the exclusive right to produce some good or service.
- The costs of production make a single producer more efficient than a large number of producers.
- A firm is able to gain control of other firms in the market and thus grow in size.

Let's briefly discuss each of these.

Monopoly Resources

The simplest way for a monopoly to arise is for a single firm to own a key resource. For example, consider the market for water in a small town on a remote island not served by the water company from the mainland. If there is only one well in town and it is impossible to get water from anywhere else, then the owner of the well has a monopoly on water. Not surprisingly, the monopolist has much greater market power than any single firm in a competitive market. In the case of a necessity like water, the monopolist could command quite a high price, even if the marginal cost is low.

Although exclusive ownership of a key resource is a potential cause of monopoly, in practice monopolies rarely arise for this reason. Actual economies are large, and resources are owned by many people. Indeed, because many goods are traded internationally, the natural scope of their markets is often worldwide. There are, therefore, few examples of firms that own a resource for which there are no close substitutes.

Government-Created Monopolies

In many cases, monopolies arise because the government has given one firm the exclusive right to sell some good or service. Sometimes the monopoly arises from the sheer political clout of the would-be monopolist. European kings, for example, once granted exclusive business licences to their friends and allies in order to raise money – a highly prized monopoly being the exclusive right to sell and distribute salt in a particular region of Europe. Even today, governments sometimes grant a monopoly (perhaps even to themselves) because doing so is viewed to be in the public interest. In Sweden, for example, the retailing of alcoholic beverages is carried out under a state-owned monopoly known as the Systembolaget. The Swedish government deems it to be in the interest of public health to be able to directly control the sale of alcohol. As a member of the EU, questions have been raised about this policy but Sweden is keen to maintain its control of alcohol sales.

In a study commissioned by the Swedish National Institute for Public Health in 2007, researchers concluded that if retail alcohol sales were privatized, the net effects on the country would be negative with an increase in alcohol-related illness and deaths, fatal accidents, suicides and homicides, and a large increase in the number of working days lost to sickness. (See Holder, H. (Ed.) (2007) *If Retail Alcohol Sales in Sweden were Privatized, What Would be the Potential Consequences?*)

The patent and copyright laws are two important examples of how the government creates a monopoly to serve the public interest. When a pharmaceutical company discovers a new drug, it can apply to the government for a patent. If the government deems the drug to be truly original, it approves the **patent**, which gives the company the exclusive right to manufacture and sell the drug for a fixed number of years – often 20 years. A patent, therefore, is a means of establishing and enforcing property rights.

> **patent** the right conferred on the owner to prevent anyone else making or using an invention or manufacturing process without permission

Similarly, when a novelist finishes a book, they can **copyright** it. The copyright is a government guarantee that no one can print and sell the work without the author's permission and thus conveys rights to the owner to control how their work is used. Copyright relates to the expression of ideas where some judgement or skill is used to create the work. It covers the creation of literary works, music, the arts, sound recordings, broadcasts, films and typographical arrangements of published material. The copyright makes the novelist a monopolist in the sale of their novel and is a means of establishing intellectual property rights.

> **copyright** the right of an individual or organization to own things they create in the same way as a physical object, to prevent others from copying or reproducing the creation

The effects of patent and copyright laws are easy to see. Because these laws give one producer a monopoly, they lead to higher prices than would occur under competition. By allowing these monopoly producers to charge higher prices and earn higher profits, the laws also encourage some desirable behaviour. Drug companies are allowed to be monopolists in the drugs they discover in order to encourage research. Authors are allowed to be monopolists in the sale of their books to encourage them to write more and better books.

The laws governing patents and copyrights have benefits and costs. The benefits of the patent and copyright laws are the increased incentive for creative activity. These benefits are offset, to some extent, by the costs of monopoly pricing, which we examine fully later in this chapter.

Natural Monopolies

In Chapter 10, reference was made to *club goods* which were defined as goods that are excludable but not rival in consumption. Club goods are a type of natural monopoly. An industry is a **natural monopoly** when a single firm can supply a good or service to an entire market at a lower cost than could two or more firms. A natural monopoly arises when there are economies of scale over the relevant range of output. Figure 14.1 shows the average total costs of a firm with economies of scale. In this case, a single firm can produce any amount of output at least cost. That is, for any given amount of output, a larger number of firms leads to less output per firm and higher average total cost.

> **natural monopoly** a monopoly that arises because a single firm can supply a good or service to an entire market at a smaller cost than could two or more firms

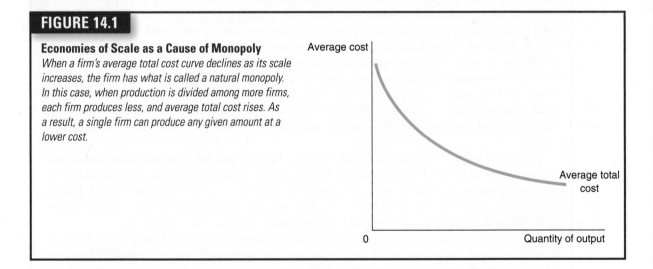

FIGURE 14.1

Economies of Scale as a Cause of Monopoly
When a firm's average total cost curve declines as its scale increases, the firm has what is called a natural monopoly. In this case, when production is divided among more firms, each firm produces less, and average total cost rises. As a result, a single firm can produce any given amount at a lower cost.

An example of a natural monopoly is the distribution of water. To provide water to residents of a town, a firm must build a network of pipes throughout the town. If two or more firms were to compete in the provision of this service, each firm would have to pay the fixed cost of building a network. Thus, the average total cost of water is lowest if a single firm serves the entire market.

Some goods in the economy are excludable but not rival as noted in Chapter 10. An example is a bridge used so infrequently that it is never congested. The bridge is excludable because a toll collector can prevent someone from using it. The bridge is not rival because use of the bridge by one person does not diminish the ability of others to use it. Because there is a fixed cost of building the bridge and a negligible marginal cost of additional users, the average total cost of a trip across the bridge (the total cost divided by the number of trips) falls as the number of trips rises. Hence, the bridge is a natural monopoly.

When a firm is a natural monopoly, it is less concerned about new entrants eroding its monopoly power. Normally, a firm has trouble maintaining a monopoly position without ownership of a key resource or protection from the government. However, the monopolist's profit attracts entrants into the market, and these entrants make the market more competitive. By contrast, entering a market in which another firm has a natural monopoly is unattractive. Would-be entrants know that they cannot achieve the same low costs that the monopolist enjoys because, after entry, each firm would have a smaller piece of the market.

In some cases, the size of the market is one determinant of whether an industry is a natural monopoly. Again, consider a bridge across a river. When the population is small, the bridge may be a natural monopoly. A single bridge can satisfy the entire demand for trips across the river at lowest cost. Yet as the population grows and the bridge becomes congested, satisfying the entire demand may require two or more bridges across the same river. Thus, as a market expands, a natural monopoly can evolve into a competitive market.

CASE STUDY   **Mergers, Acquisitions and Monopoly**

People in the UK and Europe will be familiar with the stationery and office supplies firms, Staples and Office Depot. Both are US firms but have a global reach; both are very large firms. In March 2016, the share price quoted on NASDAQ put the market capitalization of Office Depot at $3.5 billion (€3.1bn/£2.42bn) and the company has annual revenues of around $16 billion (€14.2bn/£11.05bn). Staples' market capitalization is around $6.6 billion (€5.9bn/£4.6bn), with annual revenues of around $22.5 billion (€20bn/£15.5bn).

The two firms put in an application to merge in a $6.3 billion deal. On the face of it the two firms would be likely to increase monopoly power in the market and this could potentially be damaging to competition. One question might be where does this other competition come from? In reality, it is unlikely that too many new firms are going to enter this market – the economies of scale of being large is crucial to the ability of firms in the market to provide competitive prices to consumers. Existing firms, could, however, enter this market; Amazon is one firm which may provide competition to a merged company. Would Amazon's ability to compete be impeded by the merger of Office Depot and Staples?

The other element is those who buy from Office Depot and Staples. Thousands of firms, large and small across the globe, acquire supplies from Office Depot and Staples. These firms sell to customers such as supermarkets (like the Walmart group, which owns the UK supermarket Asda) and firms who negotiate global contracts with Office Depot and Staples for the supply of their offices throughout the world.

The merger has been approved in the EU, Australia, New Zealand and China, subject to certain conditions, but the US Federal Trade Commission (FTC) blocked the proposed merger on the grounds that the monopoly power of the merged group would be too great and that competition would be impeded. The FTC has said that it wants to ensure that the US' top 100 companies are protected but has accepted that the vast majority of commercial customers will not be any worse off as a result of the merger.

The view of the FTC has been criticised by the two companies concerned and some commentators. It is widely accepted that the merger will create a firm with monopoly power but critics of the FTC's decision argue that the effects of this monopoly power will be moderated by the nature of the way the industry runs. It is argued, for example, that the suggestion that top US firms will be somehow competitively disadvantaged by having to negotiate with a merged Office Depot and Staples is ridiculous. Walmart's market capitalization, for example, is around $216 billion (€192bn/£149.3bn) and CVS Health, which sells a lot of stationery in its retail stores, has a market capitalization of $111 billion (€98.5bn/£76.7bn). The idea that these firms could be held to ransom by the combined power of the merged firms is unrealistic.

(continued)

Equally, the idea that a firm like Amazon, with a market capitalization of $263 billion (€233.4bn/£181.7bn), would be unable to compete effectively is also unrealistic. The FTC are also, it is argued, ignoring the effect of online retailers, even smaller ones, who may be able to provide products at lower prices but would also exploit other advantages like quality or speed and convenience of service (including delivery by drone!). It is not that a merged firm has monopoly power, therefore, that should be a criterion for deciding whether to approve a merger but how effective the resulting monopoly power is in restricting competition. In this case, it is argued that the merger would not impede competition to any great extent.

Would the merger of Staples and Office Depot have a negative impact on consumers?

External Growth

Many of the largest firms in the world have grown partly through acquisition, merger or takeover of other firms. As they do so, the industry becomes more concentrated; there are fewer firms in the industry. One effect of this is that a firm might be able to develop monopoly power over its rivals and erect barriers to entry to make it harder for new firms to enter. It is for this reason that governments monitor such acquisitions to see if there are implications for competition.

> **SELF TEST** What are the four reasons that a market might have a monopoly? Give three examples of monopolies, and explain the reason for each.

HOW MONOPOLIES MAKE PRODUCTION AND PRICING DECISIONS

Now that we know how monopolies arise, we can consider how a monopoly firm decides how much of its product to make and what price to charge for it. The analysis of monopoly behaviour in this section is the starting point for evaluating whether monopolies are desirable and what policies the government might pursue in monopoly markets.

Monopoly Versus Competition

The key difference between a competitive firm and a monopoly is the monopoly's ability to influence the price of its output. A competitive firm is small relative to the market in which it operates and, therefore, takes the price of its output as given by market conditions. By contrast, because a monopoly is the sole producer in its market, it can alter the price of its good by adjusting the quantity it supplies to the market.

One way to view this difference between a competitive firm and a monopoly is to consider the demand curve that each firm faces. When we analyzed profit maximization by competitive firms, we drew the market price as a horizontal line. Because a competitive firm can sell as much or as little as it wants at this price, the competitive firm faces a horizontal demand curve, as in panel (a) of Figure 14.2. If it charged any price above this price, however, it would lose all of its sales to its rivals. In effect, because the competitive firm sells a product with many perfect substitutes (the identical products of all the other firms in its market), the demand curve that any one firm faces is perfectly elastic.

By contrast, because a monopoly is the sole producer in its market, its demand curve is the market demand curve. Thus, the monopolist's demand curve slopes downwards for all the usual reasons, as in panel (b) of Figure 14.2. If the monopolist raises the price of its good, consumers buy less of it. Looked at another way, if the monopolist reduces the quantity of output it sells, the price of its output increases.

FIGURE 14.2

Demand Curves for Competitive and Monopoly Firms
Because competitive firms are price-takers, they in effect face horizontal demand curves, as in panel (a). In such a situation the firm is a price-taker and has no market power. Because a monopoly firm is the sole producer in its market, it faces the downward sloping market demand curve, as in panel (b). As a result, the monopoly has to accept a lower price if it wants to sell more output.

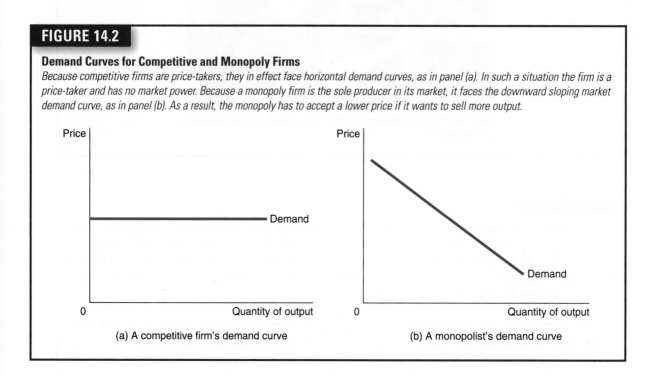

(a) A competitive firm's demand curve

(b) A monopolist's demand curve

The market demand curve provides a constraint on a monopoly's ability to profit from its market power. A monopolist would prefer, if it were possible, to charge a high price and sell a large quantity at that high price. The market demand curve makes that outcome impossible. In particular, the market demand curve describes the combinations of price and quantity that are available to a monopoly firm. By adjusting the quantity produced (or, equivalently, the price charged), the monopolist can choose any point on the demand curve, but it cannot choose a point off the demand curve.

A Monopoly's Revenue

Consider a town with a single producer of water. Table 14.1 shows how the monopoly's revenue might depend on the amount of water produced.

The first two columns show the monopolist's demand schedule. If the monopolist produces just 1 litre of water, it can sell that litre for €1. If it produces 2 litres, it must lower the price to €0.90 in order to sell both litres. And if it produces 3 litres, it must lower the price to €0.80 and so on. If you graphed these two columns you would get a typical downwards sloping demand curve.

The third column of the table presents the monopolist's *total revenue.* It equals the quantity sold (from the first column) times the price (from the second column). The fourth column computes the firm's *average revenue,* the amount of revenue the firm receives per unit sold which equates to price.

The last column of Table 14.1 computes the firm's *marginal revenue*, the amount of revenue that the firm receives for each additional unit of output.

TABLE 14.1 **A Monopoly's Total, Average and Marginal Revenue**

Quantity of water (Q)	Price (P)	Total revenue (TR = P × Q)	Average revenue (AR = TR/Q)	Marginal revenue (MR = ΔTR/ ΔQ)
0 litres	€1.1	€0	–	
				€1
1	1.0	1.0	€1	
				0.8
2	0.9	1.8	0.9	
				0.6
3	0.8	2.4	0.8	
				0.4
4	0.7	2.8	0.7	
				0.2
5	0.6	3.0	0.6	
				0
6	0.5	3.0	0.5	
				−0.2
7	0.4	2.8	0.4	
				−0.4
8	0.3	2.4	0.3	

Table 14.1 shows a result that is important for understanding monopoly behaviour: a monopolist's marginal revenue is always less than the price of its good. For example, if the firm raises production of water from 3 to 4 litres, it will increase total revenue by only €0.40, even though it will be able to sell each litre for €0.70. For a monopoly, marginal revenue is lower than price because a monopoly faces a downwards sloping demand curve. To increase the amount sold, a monopoly firm must lower the price of its good. Hence, to sell the fourth litre of water, the monopolist must get less revenue for each of the first 3 litres.

Marginal revenue for monopolies is very different from marginal revenue for competitive firms. When a monopoly increases the amount it sells, it has two effects on total revenue:

● *The output effect.* More output is sold, so *Q* is higher, which tends to increase total revenue.
● *The price effect.* The price falls, so *P* is lower, which tends to decrease total revenue.

Because a competitive firm can sell all it wants at the market price, there is no price effect. When it increases production by 1 unit, it receives the market price for that unit, and it does not receive any less for the units it was already selling. That is, because the competitive firm is a price-taker, its marginal revenue equals the price of its good. By contrast, when a monopoly increases production by 1 unit, it must reduce the price it charges for every unit it sells, and this cut in price reduces revenue on the units it was already selling. As a result, a monopoly's marginal revenue is less than its price.

Figure 14.3 graphs the demand curve and the marginal revenue curve for a monopoly firm. (Because the firm's price equals its average revenue, the demand curve is also the average-revenue curve.) These two curves always start at the same point on the vertical axis because the marginal revenue of the first unit sold equals the price of the good. But thereafter, for the reason we just discussed, the monopolist's marginal revenue is less than the price of the good. Thus, a monopoly's marginal revenue curve lies below its demand curve.

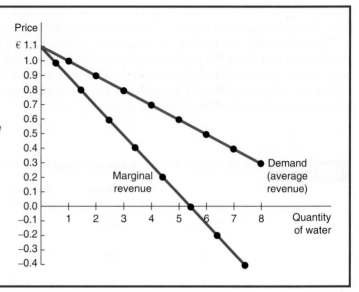

FIGURE 14.3

Demand and Marginal Revenue Curves for a Monopoly
The demand curve shows how the quantity affects the price of the good. The marginal revenue curve shows how the firm's revenue changes when the quantity increases by 1 unit. Because the price on all units sold must fall if the monopoly increases production, marginal revenue is always less than the price.

Table 14.1 and Figure 14.3 show that marginal revenue can become negative. Marginal revenue is negative when the price effect on revenue is greater than the output effect. In this case, when the firm produces an extra unit of output, the price falls by enough to cause the firm's total revenue to decline, even though the firm is selling more units.

Profit Maximization

Now that we have considered the revenue of a monopoly firm, we are ready to examine how such a firm maximizes profit.

Figure 14.4 graphs the demand curve, the marginal revenue curve and the cost curves for a monopoly firm. These curves contain all the information we need to determine the level of output that a profit-maximizing monopolist will choose.

Suppose, first, that the firm is producing at a low level of output, such as Q_1. In this case, marginal cost is less than marginal revenue. If the firm increased production by 1 unit, the additional revenue would exceed the additional costs, and profit would rise. Thus, when marginal cost is less than marginal revenue, the firm can increase profit by producing more units.

A similar argument applies at high levels of output, such as Q_2. In this case, marginal cost is greater than marginal revenue. If the firm reduced production by one unit, the costs saved would exceed the revenue lost. Thus, if marginal cost is greater than marginal revenue, the firm can raise profit by reducing production.

In the end, the firm adjusts its level of production until the quantity reaches Q_{MAX}, at which marginal revenue equals marginal cost. Thus, the monopolist's profit-maximizing quantity of output is determined by the intersection of the marginal revenue curve and the marginal cost curve. In Figure 14.4, this intersection occurs at point A.

Remember that competitive firms maximize profit at the quantity of output at which marginal revenue equals marginal cost. In following this rule for profit maximization, competitive firms and monopolies are alike. But there is also an important difference between these types of firm: the marginal revenue of a competitive firm equals its price, whereas the marginal revenue of a monopoly is less than its price. That is:

For a competitive firm: $P = MR = MC$.

For a monopoly firm: $P > MR = MC$.

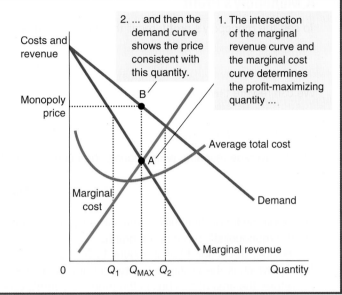

FIGURE 14.4

Profit Maximization for a Monopoly

A monopoly maximizes profit by choosing the quantity at which marginal revenue equals marginal cost (point A). It then uses the demand curve to find the price that will induce consumers to buy that quantity (point B).

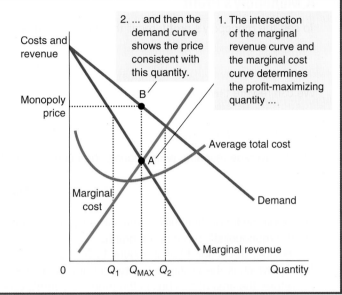

The equality of marginal revenue and marginal cost at the profit-maximizing quantity is the same for both types of firm. What differs is the relationship of the price to marginal revenue and marginal cost.

The monopoly finds the profit-maximizing price for its product through the demand curve. The demand curve relates the amount that customers are willing to pay to the quantity sold. Thus, after the monopoly firm chooses the quantity of output that equates marginal revenue and marginal cost, it uses the demand curve to find the price consistent with that quantity. In Figure 14.4, the profit-maximizing price is found at point B.

We can now see a key difference between markets with competitive firms and markets with a monopoly firm: in competitive markets, price equals marginal cost. In monopolized markets, price exceeds marginal cost. As we will see, this finding is crucial to understanding the social cost of monopoly.

FYI

Why a Monopoly Does Not Have a Supply Curve

You may have noticed that we have analyzed the price in a monopoly market using the market demand curve and the firm's cost curves. We have not made any mention of the market supply curve.

What happened to the supply curve? Although monopoly firms make decisions about what quantity to supply (in the way described in this chapter), a monopoly does not have a supply curve. A supply curve tells us the quantity that firms choose to supply at any given price. This concept makes sense when we are analyzing competitive firms, which are price takers. But a monopoly firm is a price-maker, not a price-taker. It is not meaningful to ask what such a firm would produce at any price because the firm sets the price at the same time it chooses the quantity to supply.

Indeed, the monopolist's decision about how much to supply is impossible to separate from the demand curve it faces. The shape of the demand curve determines the shape of the marginal revenue curve, which in turn determines the monopolist's profit-maximizing quantity. In a competitive market, supply decisions can be analyzed without knowing the demand curve, but that is not true in a monopoly market. Therefore, we never talk about a monopoly's supply curve.

A Monopoly's Profit

To see the monopoly's profit, recall that profit (π) equals total revenue (TR) minus total costs (TC):

$$\pi = TR - TC$$

We can rewrite this as:

$$\pi = (TR/Q - TC/Q) \times Q$$

TR/Q is average revenue, which equals the price P, and TC/Q is average total cost ATC. Therefore:

$$\pi = (P - ATC) \times Q$$

This equation for profit (which is the same as the profit equation for competitive firms) allows us to measure the monopolist's profit in our graph.

Consider the shaded box in Figure 14.5. The height of the box (BC) is price minus average total cost, $P-ATC$, which is the profit on the typical unit sold. The width of the box (DC) is the quantity sold Q_{MAX}. Therefore, the area of this box is the monopoly firm's total profit.

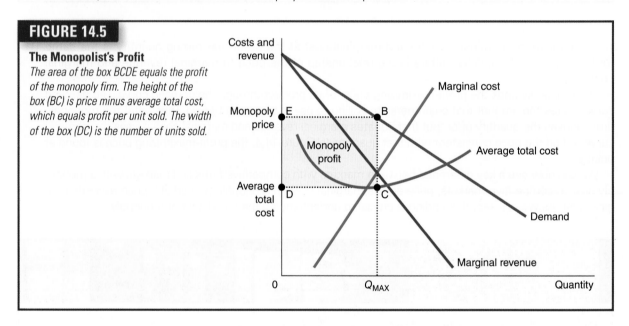

FIGURE 14.5

The Monopolist's Profit
The area of the box BCDE equals the profit of the monopoly firm. The height of the box (BC) is price minus average total cost, which equals profit per unit sold. The width of the box (DC) is the number of units sold.

SELF TEST Can a monopolist determine both the price it chooses to charge and the amount it sells? Why? Why not?

THE WELFARE COST OF MONOPOLY

Is monopoly a good way to organize a market? We have seen that a monopoly, in contrast to a competitive firm, charges a price above marginal cost. From the standpoint of consumers, this high price makes monopoly undesirable. At the same time, however, the monopoly is earning profit from charging this high price. From the standpoint of the owners of the firm, the high price makes monopoly very desirable. Is it possible that the benefits to the firm's owners exceed the costs imposed on consumers, making monopoly desirable from the standpoint of society as a whole?

We can answer this question using total surplus as our measure of economic well-being. Recall that total surplus is the sum of consumer surplus and producer surplus. In this case, there is a single producer – the monopolist.

We have noted that the equilibrium of supply and demand in a competitive market maximizes total surplus. Because a monopoly leads to an allocation of resources different from that in a competitive market, the outcome must, in some way, fail to maximize total economic well-being.

The Deadweight Loss

The fact that the market outcome under monopoly is different to that under conditions of perfect competition means there is a deadweight loss associated with monopoly. Total surplus equals the value of the good to consumers minus the costs of making the good incurred by the monopoly producer. In Figure 14.6 the demand curve reflects the value of the good to consumers, as measured by their willingness to pay for it. The marginal cost curve reflects the costs of the monopolist. Thus, the socially efficient quantity is found where the demand curve and the marginal cost curve intersect. Below this quantity, the value to consumers exceeds the marginal cost of providing the good, so increasing output would raise total surplus. Above this quantity, the marginal cost exceeds the value to consumers, so decreasing output would raise total surplus.

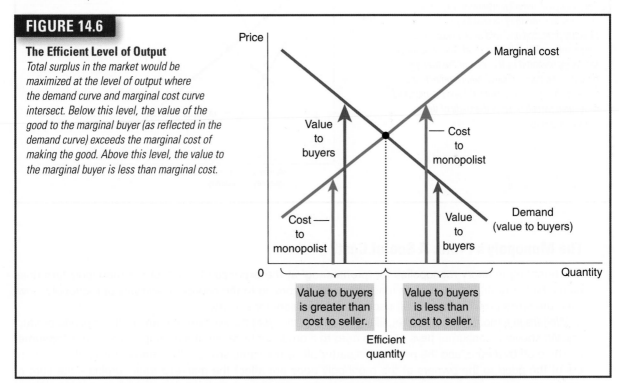

FIGURE 14.6

The Efficient Level of Output
Total surplus in the market would be maximized at the level of output where the demand curve and marginal cost curve intersect. Below this level, the value of the good to the marginal buyer (as reflected in the demand curve) exceeds the marginal cost of making the good. Above this level, the value to the marginal buyer is less than marginal cost.

The efficient outcome would be where the demand curve intersects the marginal cost curve where $P = MC$. Because this price would give consumers an accurate signal about the cost of producing the good, consumers would buy the efficient quantity. The monopolist chooses the profit maximizing output where the marginal revenue and marginal cost curves intersect but this is not the same as the socially efficient output where the demand and marginal cost curves intersect. Figure 14.7 shows the comparison. The monopolist produces less than the socially efficient quantity of output.

We can also view the inefficiency of monopoly in terms of the monopolist's price. Because the market demand curve describes a negative relationship between the price and quantity of the good, a quantity that is inefficiently low is equivalent to a price that is inefficiently high. When a monopolist charges a price above marginal cost, some potential consumers value the good at more than its marginal cost but less than the monopolist's price. These consumers do not end up buying the good. Because the value these consumers place on the good is greater than the cost of providing it to them, this result is inefficient. Thus, monopoly pricing prevents some mutually beneficial trades from taking place.

Figure 14.7 shows the deadweight loss. Recall that the demand curve reflects the value to consumers and the marginal cost curve reflects the costs to the monopoly producer. Thus, the area of the deadweight loss triangle between the demand curve and the marginal cost curve equals the total surplus lost because of monopoly pricing.

The deadweight loss caused by monopoly is similar to the deadweight loss caused by a tax. A tax on a good, remember, places a wedge between consumers' willingness to pay (as reflected in the demand curve) and producers' costs (as reflected in the supply curve). Because a monopoly exerts its market power by charging a price above marginal cost, it places a similar wedge. In both cases, the wedge causes the quantity sold to fall short of the social optimum. The difference between the two cases is that the government gets the revenue from a tax, whereas a private firm gets the monopoly profit.

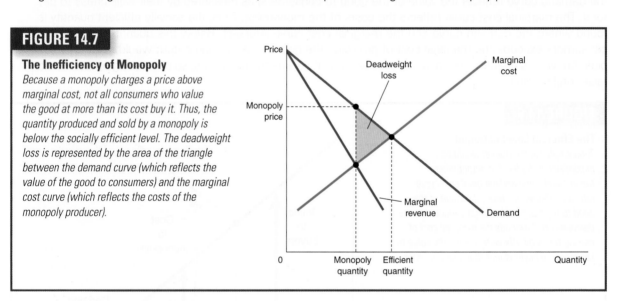

FIGURE 14.7

The Inefficiency of Monopoly
Because a monopoly charges a price above marginal cost, not all consumers who value the good at more than its cost buy it. Thus, the quantity produced and sold by a monopoly is below the socially efficient level. The deadweight loss is represented by the area of the triangle between the demand curve (which reflects the value of the good to consumers) and the marginal cost curve (which reflects the costs of the monopoly producer).

The Monopoly's Profit: A Social Cost?

It is tempting to decry monopolies for 'profiteering' at the expense of the public; a monopoly firm does earn a higher profit by virtue of its market power. According to the economic analysis of monopoly, however, the firm's profit is not in itself necessarily a problem for society.

Welfare in a monopolized market, like all markets, includes the welfare of both consumers and producers. Whenever a consumer pays an extra euro to a producer because of a monopoly price, the consumer is worse off by a euro, and the producer is better off by the same amount. This transfer from the consumers of the good to the owners of the monopoly does not affect the market's total surplus – the sum of consumer and producer surplus. In other words, the monopoly profit itself does not represent a shrinkage in the size of the economic pie; it merely represents a bigger slice for producers and a smaller slice for consumers. Whether consumers are more deserving than producers requires a judgement on the part of policymakers.

The problem in a monopolized market arises because the firm produces and sells a quantity of output below the level that maximizes total surplus. The deadweight loss measures how much the economic pie shrinks as a result. This inefficiency is connected to the monopoly's high price: consumers buy fewer units when the firm raises its price above marginal cost. But keep in mind that the profit earned on the units that continue to be sold is not the problem. The problem stems from the inefficiently low quantity of output. Put differently, if the high monopoly price did not discourage some consumers from buying the good, it would raise producer surplus by exactly the amount it reduced consumer surplus, leaving total surplus unchanged from the socially efficient outcome.

There is, however, a possible exception to this conclusion. Suppose that a monopoly firm has to incur additional costs to maintain its monopoly position. For example, a firm with a government-created monopoly might need to hire lobbyists to convince lawmakers to continue its monopoly. In this case, the monopoly may use up some of its monopoly profits paying for these additional costs. If so, the social loss from monopoly includes both these costs and the deadweight loss resulting from a price above marginal cost.

> **SELF TEST** Without conferring monopoly power through barriers to entry such as patents, would any competitive firm produce goods which have wider social benefits such as pharmaceutical drugs? Does this sort of consideration have to be taken into account when looking at the welfare loss associated with monopolies?

PRICE DISCRIMINATION

So far we have been assuming that the monopoly firm charges the same price to all customers. Yet in many cases firms try to sell the same good to different customers for different prices, even though the costs of producing for the two customers are the same. This practice is called **price discrimination**. For a firm to price discriminate, it must have some market power.

> **price discrimination** the business practice of selling the same good at different prices to different customers

A Parable about Pricing

To understand why a monopolist would want to price discriminate, let's consider an example. Imagine that you are the chief executive officer (CEO) of Readalot Publishing Company. Readalot's best-selling author has just written their latest novel. To keep things simple, let's imagine that you pay the author a flat €2 million for the exclusive rights to publish the book. Let's also assume – for simplicity – that the cost of printing the book is zero. Readalot's profit, therefore, is the revenue it gets from selling the book minus the €2 million it has paid to the author. Given these assumptions, how would you, as Readalot's CEO, decide what price to charge for the book?

Your first step in setting the price is to estimate what the demand for the book is likely to be. Readalot's marketing department tells you that the book will attract two types of readers. The book will appeal to the author's 100 000 die-hard fans. These fans will be willing to pay as much as €30 for the book. In addition, the book will appeal to about 400 000 less enthusiastic readers who will be willing to pay up to €5 for the book.

What price maximizes Readalot's profit? There are two natural prices to consider: €30 is the highest price Readalot can charge and still get the 100 000 diehard fans, and €5 is the highest price it can charge and still get the entire market of 500 000 potential readers. At a price of €30, Readalot sells 100 000 copies, has revenue of €3 million, and makes profit of €1 million. At a price of €5, it sells 500 000 copies, has revenue of €2.5 million, and makes a profit of €500 000. Thus, Readalot maximizes profit by charging €30 and forgoing the opportunity to sell to the 400 000 less enthusiastic readers.

Notice that Readalot's decision causes a deadweight loss. There are 400 000 readers willing to pay €5 for the book, and the marginal cost of providing it to them is zero. Thus, €2 million of total surplus is lost when Readalot charges the higher price. This deadweight loss is the usual inefficiency that arises whenever a monopolist charges a price above marginal cost.

Now suppose that Readalot's marketing department makes an important discovery: these two groups of readers are in separate markets. All the die-hard fans live in Switzerland and all the other readers live in

Turkey. Moreover, it is difficult for readers in one country to buy books in the other. How does this discovery affect Readalot's marketing strategy?

In this case, the company can make even more profit. To the 100 000 Swiss readers, it can charge €30 for the book. To the 400 000 Turkish readers, it can charge €5 for the book (or the Turkish lira equivalent). In this case, revenue is €3 million in Switzerland and €2 million in Turkey, for a total of €5 million. Profit is then €3 million, which is substantially greater than the €1 million the company could earn charging the same €30 price to all customers. Not surprisingly, Readalot chooses to follow this strategy of price discrimination.

Although the story of Readalot Publishing is hypothetical, it describes accurately the business practice of many publishing companies. Textbooks, for example, have been sold at different prices in Europe from those charged in the United States. Even more important is the price differential between hardcover books and paperbacks. When a publisher has a new novel, it initially releases an expensive hardcover edition and later releases a cheaper paperback edition. The difference in price between these two editions far exceeds the difference in printing costs. The publisher's goal is just as in our example. By selling the hardcover to die-hard fans (and libraries) who must have the book as soon as it is published, and the paperback to less enthusiastic readers who don't mind waiting, the publisher price discriminates and raises its profit.

The Moral of the Story

Like any parable, the story of Readalot Publishing is stylized. Yet, also like any parable, it teaches some important and general lessons. In this case, there are three lessons to be learned about price discrimination.

The first and most obvious lesson is that price discrimination is a rational strategy for a profit-maximizing monopolist. In other words, by charging different prices to different customers, a monopolist can increase its profit. In essence, a price-discriminating monopolist charges each customer a price closer to his or her willingness to pay than is possible with a single price.

The second lesson is that price discrimination requires the ability to separate customers according to their willingness to pay. In our example, customers were separated geographically. But sometimes monopolists choose other differences, such as age or income, to distinguish among customers. Energy companies are able to discriminate through setting different prices at different times of the day with off-peak usage priced lower than peak time. Similarly, rail companies charge different prices to passengers at certain times of the day with peak travel attracting a much higher price than off-peak travel. Where there is a difference in the price elasticity of demand the monopolist can exploit this and practice price discrimination. Between the hours of 6.00am and 9.30am on weekday mornings, for example, the price elasticity of demand for rail travel is relatively low whereas between 9.30am and 4.00pm it tends to be relatively high. A higher price can be charged at the peak time but during the off-peak period, the firm may benefit from charging a lower price and encouraging more passengers to travel; the cost of running the train is largely fixed and the marginal cost of carrying an additional passenger is almost zero. Lowering the price, therefore, is a way of utilizing the capacity on the train and adding to profit.

A corollary to this second lesson is that certain market forces can prevent firms from price discriminating. In particular, one such force is **arbitrage**, the process of buying a good in one market at a low price and selling it in another market at a higher price in order to profit from the price difference.

> **arbitrage** the process of buying a good in one market at a low price and selling it in another market at a higher price in order to profit from the price difference

In our example, suppose that Swiss bookshops could buy the book in Turkey for €5 and resell it to Swiss readers at a price well below €30. This arbitrage would prevent Readalot from price discriminating because no Swiss resident would buy the book at the higher price. In fact, the increased use of the Internet for buying books and other goods through companies like Amazon is likely to affect the ability of companies to price discriminate internationally. Where firms can enforce the division of the market, as in the case of rail fares, it can practice price discrimination. A passenger buying a ticket at off-peak rates is not allowed to travel on a train running during peak periods, and hence arbitrage is circumvented.

The third lesson from our parable is perhaps the most surprising: price discrimination can raise economic welfare. Recall that a deadweight loss arises when Readalot charges a single €30 price, because the 400 000 less enthusiastic readers do not end up with the book, even though they value it at more than its marginal cost of production. By contrast, when Readalot price discriminates, all readers end up with the book, and the outcome is efficient. Thus, price discrimination can eliminate the inefficiency inherent in monopoly pricing.

Note that the increase in welfare from price discrimination shows up as higher producer surplus rather than higher consumer surplus. In our example, consumers are no better off for having bought the book: the price they pay exactly equals the value they place on the book, so they receive no consumer surplus. The entire increase in total surplus from price discrimination accrues to Readalot Publishing in the form of higher profit.

The Analytics of Price Discrimination

Let us consider a little more formally how price discrimination affects economic welfare. We begin by assuming that the monopolist can price discriminate perfectly. **Perfect price discrimination** describes a situation in which the monopolist knows exactly the willingness to pay of each customer and can charge each customer a different price. In this case, the monopolist charges each customer exactly their willingness to pay, and the monopolist gets the entire surplus in every transaction.

> **perfect price discrimination** a situation in which the monopolist knows exactly the willingness to pay of each customer and can charge each customer a different price

Figure 14.8 shows producer and consumer surplus with and without price discrimination. Without price discrimination, the firm charges a single price above marginal cost, as shown in panel (a). Because some potential customers who value the good at more than marginal cost do not buy it at this high price, the monopoly causes a deadweight loss. Yet when a firm can perfectly price discriminate, as shown in panel (b), each customer who values the good at more than marginal cost buys the good and is charged their willingness to pay. All mutually beneficial trades take place, there is no deadweight loss, and the entire surplus derived from the market goes to the monopoly producer in the form of profit.

FIGURE 14.8

Welfare With and Without Price Discrimination
Panel (a) shows a monopolist that charges the same price to all customers. Total surplus in this market equals the sum of profit (producer surplus) and consumer surplus. Panel (b) shows a monopolist that can perfectly price discriminate. Because consumer surplus equals zero, total surplus now equals the firm's profit. Comparing these two panels, you can see that perfect price discrimination raises profit, raises total surplus and lowers consumer surplus.

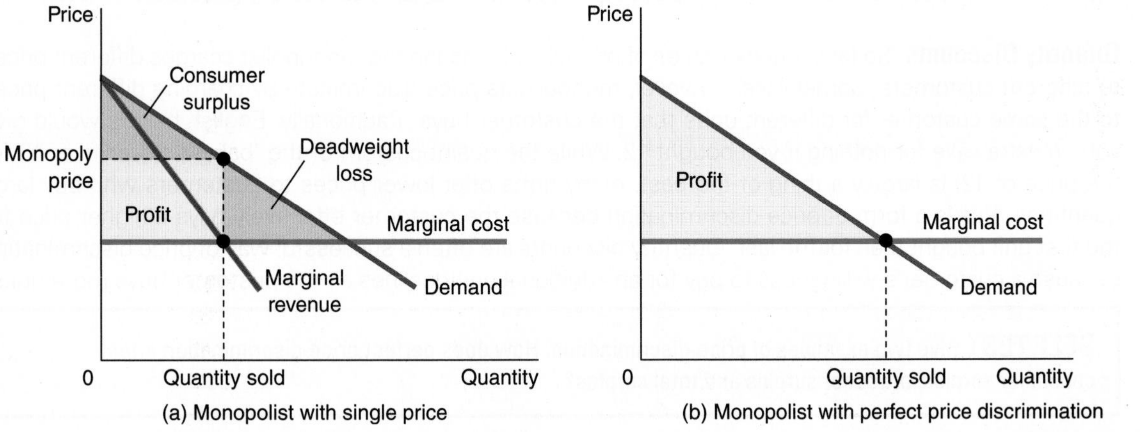

(a) Monopolist with single price

(b) Monopolist with perfect price discrimination

In reality, of course, price discrimination is not perfect. Customers do not walk into shops with signs displaying their willingness to pay. Instead, firms price discriminate by dividing customers into groups: young versus old, weekday versus weekend shoppers, Germans versus British and so on. Unlike those in our parable of Readalot Publishing, customers within each group differ in their willingness to pay for the product, making perfect price discrimination impossible.

How does this imperfect price discrimination affect welfare? The analysis of these pricing schemes is quite complicated, and it turns out that there is no general answer to this question. Compared to the monopoly outcome with a single price, imperfect price discrimination can raise, lower or leave unchanged total surplus in a market. The only certain conclusion is that price discrimination raises the monopoly's profit – otherwise the firm would choose to charge all customers the same price.

Examples of Price Discrimination

Firms use various business strategies aimed at charging different prices to different customers. Let's consider some examples.

Cinema Tickets Many cinemas charge a lower price for children and senior citizens than for other patrons. This fact is hard to explain in a competitive market. In a competitive market, price equals marginal cost, and the marginal cost of providing a seat for a child or senior citizen is the same as the marginal cost of providing a seat for anyone else. Yet this fact is easily explained if cinemas have some local monopoly power and if children and senior citizens have a lower willingness to pay for a ticket. In this case, cinemas raise their profit by price discriminating.

Airline Prices Seats on aeroplanes are sold at many different prices. Most airlines charge a lower price for a round-trip ticket between two cities if the traveller stays over a Saturday night. At first this seems odd. Why should it matter to the airline whether a passenger stays over a Saturday night? The reason is that this rule provides a way to separate business travellers and personal travellers. A passenger on a business trip has a high willingness to pay and, most likely, does not want to stay over a Saturday night. By contrast, a passenger travelling for personal reasons has a lower willingness to pay and is more likely to be willing to stay over a Saturday night. Thus, the airlines can successfully price discriminate by charging a lower price for passengers who stay over a Saturday night.

Discount Coupons Many companies offer discount coupons to the public in newspapers and magazines. A buyer simply has to cut out the coupon in order to get €0.50 off their next purchase. Why do companies offer these coupons? Why don't they just cut the price of the product by €0.50?

The answer is that coupons allow companies to price discriminate. Companies know that not all customers are willing to spend the time to cut out coupons. Moreover, the willingness to clip coupons is related to the customer's willingness to pay for the good. A rich and busy executive is unlikely to spend their time cutting discount coupons out of the newspaper, and they are probably willing to pay a higher price for many goods. A person who is unemployed is more likely to clip coupons and has a lower willingness to pay. Thus, by charging a lower price only to those customers who cut out coupons, firms can successfully price discriminate.

Quantity Discounts So far in our examples of price discrimination the monopolist charges different prices to different customers. Sometimes, however, monopolists price discriminate by charging different prices to the same customer for different units that the customer buys. Traditionally, English bakers would give you an extra cake for nothing if you bought 12. While the quaint custom of the 'baker's dozen' (i.e. 13 for the price of 12) is largely a thing of the past, many firms offer lower prices to customers who buy large quantities. This is a form of price discrimination because the customer effectively pays a higher price for the first unit bought than for the last. Quantity discounts are often a successful way of price discriminating because a customer's willingness to pay for an additional unit declines as the customer buys more units.

SELF TEST Give two examples of price discrimination. How does perfect price discrimination affect consumer surplus, producer surplus and total surplus?

PUBLIC POLICY TOWARDS MONOPOLIES

We have seen that monopolies produce less than the socially desirable quantity of output and, as a result, charge prices above marginal cost. Policymakers in the government can respond to the problem of monopoly in one of four ways, by:

- trying to make monopolized industries more competitive.
- regulating the behaviour of the monopolies.
- turning some private monopolies into public enterprises.
- doing nothing at all.

All industrialized countries have some sort of process for legally prohibiting mergers or activity by firms with market power that are against the public interest. This is variously referred to as anti-trust law and anti-trust policy and also as competition law and competition policy, depending on where in the world you are.

In Europe, each country has a competition authority. In the UK it is the Competition Commission; in Germany it is the Federal Cartel Office (*Bundeskartellamt*); in 2009 the French Competition Authority began discharging its regulatory powers following reform of competition regulation; and in Italy the Anti-trust Authority (*Autorità garante della concorrenza e del mercato*) oversees competition issues. National competition authorities such as these cooperate with each other and with the European Union Competition Commission (the competition authority for the EU) through the European Competition Network (ECN). The aim of the network is to coordinate activities and share information to help enforce EU competition law in member states where the opportunities for cross-border business have increased as the EU has developed and expanded.

Whilst each national country can enforce its own competition legislation, these laws have to be in line with overall EU competition legislation. In the UK, for example, the Competition Act 1998 and the Enterprise Act 2002 both deal with competition issues within the UK but cross-border competition cases will, until the UK's post-Brexit negotiations have been concluded, be dealt with under EU law. There are well-defined criteria for deciding whether a proposed merger of companies belonging to more than one EU country is subject to reference exclusively to the European Commission rather than to national authorities, such as the size of the worldwide or European turnover of the companies in question.

Competition legislation covers three main areas:

- Acting against cartels and cases where businesses engage in restrictive business practices which prevent free trade.
- Banning pricing strategies which are anti-competitive such as price fixing, predatory pricing, price gouging and so on; as well as through behaviour which might lead to a restriction in competition such as the sharing of information or carving up markets between different firms, rigging bids in tender processes or deliberately restricting production to reduce competition.
- Monitoring and supervising acquisitions and joint ventures.

The legislation allows competition authorities the right to fine firms who are found guilty of restricting competition, ordering firms to change behaviour and banning proposed acquisitions. The investigation will consider whether the acquisition, regardless of what size company it produces, is in the public interest. This is in recognition of the fact that companies sometimes merge not to reduce competition but to lower costs through more efficient joint production. These benefits from mergers are often called **synergies**, where the perceived benefits of the combined operations are greater than those which would arise if the firms stayed separate.

synergies where the perceived benefits of the combined operations of a merged organization are greater than those which would arise if the firms stayed separate

Clearly, competition authorities must be able to determine which mergers are desirable and which are not. That is, they must be able to measure and compare the social benefit from synergies to the social costs of reduced competition. In the UK, the Competition and Markets Authority (CMA), an independent, non-ministerial body with members from private industry as well as some academic economists, investigates mergers and competition issues, enforces competition law and is able to bring criminal proceedings against breaches of the law.

Regulation

Another way in which the government deals with the problem of monopoly is by regulating the behaviour of monopolists. This solution is common in the case of natural monopolies, such as utility companies providing water, gas and electricity. These companies are not allowed to charge any price they want. Instead, government agencies regulate their prices.

What price should the government set for a natural monopoly? This question is not as easy as it might at first appear. One might conclude that the price should equal the monopolist's marginal cost. If price equals marginal cost, customers will buy the quantity of the monopolist's output that maximizes total surplus, and the allocation of resources will be efficient.

There are, however, two practical problems with marginal-cost pricing as a regulatory system. The first is illustrated in Figure 14.9. Natural monopolies, by definition, have declining average total cost. When average total cost is declining, marginal cost is less than average total cost. If regulators are to set price equal to marginal cost, that price will be less than the firm's average total cost, and the firm will lose money. Instead of charging such a low price, the monopoly firm would just exit the industry.

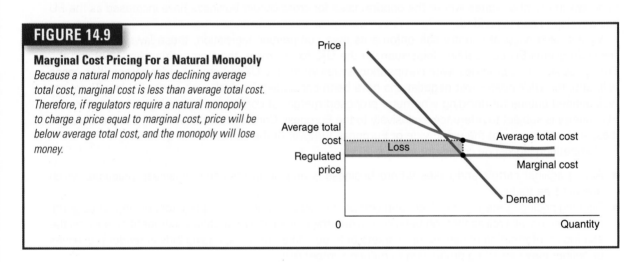

FIGURE 14.9

Marginal Cost Pricing For a Natural Monopoly
Because a natural monopoly has declining average total cost, marginal cost is less than average total cost. Therefore, if regulators require a natural monopoly to charge a price equal to marginal cost, price will be below average total cost, and the monopoly will lose money.

Regulators can respond to this problem in various ways, none of which is perfect. One way is to subsidize the monopolist. In essence, the government picks up the losses inherent in marginal-cost pricing. Yet to pay for the subsidy, the government needs to raise money through taxation, which involves its own deadweight losses. Alternatively, the regulators can allow the monopolist to charge a price higher than marginal cost. If the regulated price equals average total cost, the monopolist earns exactly zero economic profit. Yet average-cost pricing leads to deadweight losses, because the monopolist's price no longer reflects the marginal cost of producing the good. In essence, average-cost pricing is like a tax on the good the monopolist is selling.

The second problem with marginal-cost pricing as a regulatory system (and with average-cost pricing as well) is that it gives the monopolist no incentive to reduce costs. Each firm in a competitive market tries to reduce its costs because lower costs mean higher profits. If a monopolist knows that regulators will reduce prices whenever costs fall, the monopolist will not benefit from lower costs. In practice, regulators deal with this problem by allowing monopolists to keep some of the benefits from lower costs in the form of higher profit, a practice that requires some departure from marginal-cost pricing.

For example, in the UK, utility companies have often been subject to price caps whereby the regulator determines that the real price of the company's product – a kilowatt hour of electricity, for example – should fall by a given number of percentage points each year, reflecting productivity rises. Say, for example, this is 2 per cent. The company would then be allowed to raise its prices each year by the inflation rate *minus* 2 per cent. If the company increases its productivity by, say 4 per cent each year, however (in other words it can produce the same amount of output with 4 per cent less inputs), then in real terms its profits will go up each year. In this way, the system of price caps aims to give natural monopolies the motivation to improve efficiency and productivity.

Public Ownership

The third policy used by the government to deal with monopoly is public ownership. That is, rather than regulating a natural monopoly that is run by a private firm, the government can run the monopoly itself. An industry owned by the government is called a nationalized industry. This solution is common in many European countries, where the government owns and operates utilities such as the telephone, water and electric companies.

The key issue in the debate over public versus private ownership is how the ownership of the firm affects the costs of production. Private owners have an incentive to minimize costs as long as they reap part of the benefit in the form of higher profit. If the firm's managers are doing a bad job of keeping costs down, the firm's owners will fire them. By contrast, if the government bureaucrats who run a monopoly do a bad job, the losers are the customers and taxpayers, whose only recourse is the political system. The bureaucrats may become a special interest group and attempt to block cost-reducing reforms. Put simply, as a way of ensuring that firms are well run, the voting booth could be argued to be less reliable than the profit motive.

Doing Nothing

Each of the foregoing policies aimed at reducing the problem of monopoly has drawbacks. As a result, some economists argue that it is often best for the government not to try to remedy the inefficiencies of monopoly pricing. Here is the assessment of economist George Stigler, who won the Nobel Prize for his work in industrial organization, writing in the *Fortune Encyclopaedia of Economics*:

> A famous theorem in economics states that a competitive enterprise economy will produce the largest possible income from a given stock of resources. No real economy meets the exact conditions of the theorem, and all real economies will fall short of the ideal economy – a difference called 'market failure'. In my view, however, the degree of 'market failure' for the American economy is much smaller than the 'political failure' arising from the imperfections of economic policies found in real political systems.

As this quotation makes clear, determining the proper role of the government in the economy requires judgements about politics as well as economics and the issues we discussed in the section on government failure in Chapter 11 have to be taken into account.

SELF TEST Describe the ways policymakers can respond to the inefficiencies caused by monopolies. List a potential problem with each of these policy responses.

CONCLUSION: THE PREVALENCE OF MONOPOLY

This chapter has discussed the behaviour of firms that have control over the prices they charge. We have seen that these firms behave differently from firms in competitive markets. Table 14.2 summarizes some of the key similarities and differences between competitive and monopoly markets.

From the standpoint of public policy, a crucial result is that monopolists produce less than the socially efficient quantity and charge prices above marginal cost. As a result, they cause deadweight losses. In some cases, these inefficiencies can be mitigated through price discrimination by the monopolist, but at other times they call for policymakers to take an active role.

How prevalent are the problems of monopoly? There are two answers to this question. In one sense, monopolies are common. Most firms have some control over the prices they charge. They are not forced to charge the market price for their goods, because their goods are not exactly the same as those offered by other firms. A Honda Accord is not the same as a Volkswagen Passat. Ben and Jerry's ice cream is not the same as Wall's. Each of these goods has a downwards sloping demand curve, which gives each producer some degree of monopoly power.

Yet firms with substantial monopoly power are quite rare. Few goods are truly unique. Most have substitutes that, even if not exactly the same are very similar. Ben and Jerry can raise the price of their ice cream a little without losing all their sales, but if they raise it very much sales will fall substantially.

In the end, monopoly power is a matter of degree. It is true that many firms have some monopoly power. It is also true that their monopoly power is usually limited.

TABLE 14.2   **Competition versus Monopoly: A Summary Comparison**

	Competition	Monopoly
Similarities		
Goal of firms	Maximize profits	Maximize profits
Rule for maximizing	MR = MC	MR = MC
Can earn economic profits in the short run?	Yes	Yes
Differences		
Number of firms	Many	One
Marginal revenue	MR = P	MR < P
Price	P = MC	P > MC
Produces welfare-maximizing level of output?	Yes	No
Entry in long run?	Yes	No
Can earn economic profits in long run?	No	Yes
Price discrimination possible?	No	Yes

IN THE NEWS

Monopoly and Barriers to Entry

Barriers to entry can be erected to prevent entry into an industry and to maintain the market power of a firm or firms in an industry. Can barriers to entry be maintained indefinitely?

The Nigerian Telecommunications Market

Nigeria has a population of around 178 million, around 2.5 per cent of the total population of the Earth. Over three-quarters of the population subscribe to telecommunications systems including mobile and internet services. Nigerian Telecommunications (NITEL) was a public telecoms provider with monopoly power. NITEL had been accused of erecting barriers to entry into the industry and even of withholding information to the government in order to protect its monopoly position and prevent the market from being opened up to competition. With the development of mobile phones, NITEL developed part of its business under the name Mtel. The Nigerian government attempted to sell off NITEL and Mtel in 2002 but nothing came of the plans and the business remained a public monopoly.

However, the size of the market and the accusations that NITEL and Mtel were not investing sufficiently in developing the business encouraged some firms to seek to enter the market; not perhaps the recognisable global names but smaller firms who saw opportunities to develop. In 2001, for example, MTN Nigeria paid around €250 million to secure licenses to offer mobile communication services. Other firms followed suit including Etisalat from the United Arab Emirates (UAE), Indian firm Bharti Airtel, and a local Nigerian business, Globalcom. In the face of such competition, NITEL and Mtel struggled. Investment in infrastructure has brought down prices to consumers and it has been estimated that telecoms now account for around 8.5 per cent of Nigerian gross domestic product, up from just over 1 per cent in 2003.

In April 2015, the government sold NITEL and Mtel to a consortium named NATCOM Development and Investment Limited, for around €225 million. Whether the new business can survive is open to doubt. Industry watchers have noted that the company's infrastructure is poor and lacked investment, and competition in the market may mean the new business will struggle to be able to compete effectively.

Questions

1 What are barriers to entry and why might **NITEL** have sought to erect strong barriers to entry in the Nigerian telecommunications market?
2 The fate of **NATCOM** is not clear. Why do you think **NITEL** and Mtel failed to invest in developing the infrastructure of the business during its years of having monopoly power?
3 Why do you think larger more well-known global telecommunications businesses did not seek to enter the Nigerian market given its size and potential?
4 What disadvantages may new entrants like MTN have faced in seeking to compete with NITEL and Mtel?
5 Does the story of NITEL and Mtel support the view that monopolies are essentially 'bad' and need to be controlled through legislation and regulation? Explain your reasoning.

Barriers to entry in the Nigerian telecomms market may be preventing competition, which would otherwise improve the service to customers.

SUMMARY

● A monopoly is a firm that is the sole seller in its market. A monopoly arises when a single firm owns a key resource, when the government gives a firm the exclusive right to produce a good, or when a single firm can supply the entire market at a smaller cost than many firms could.

● Because a monopoly is the sole producer in its market, it faces a downwards sloping demand curve for its product. When a monopoly increases production by 1 unit, it causes the price of its good to fall, which reduces the amount of revenue earned on all units produced. As a result, a monopoly's marginal revenue is always below the price of its good.

- Like a competitive firm, a monopoly firm maximizes profit by producing the quantity at which marginal revenue equals marginal cost. The monopoly then chooses the price at which that quantity is demanded. Unlike a competitive firm, a monopoly firm's price exceeds its marginal revenue, so its price exceeds marginal cost.

- A monopolist's profit-maximizing level of output is below the level that maximizes the sum of consumer and producer surplus. That is, when the monopoly charges a price above marginal cost, some consumers who value the good more than its cost of production do not buy it. As a result, monopoly causes deadweight losses similar to the deadweight losses caused by taxes.

- Policymakers can respond to the inefficiency of monopoly behaviour in four ways. They can use competition law to try to make the industry more competitive. They can regulate the prices that the monopoly charges. They can turn the monopolist into a government-run enterprise. Or, if the market failure is deemed small compared to the inevitable imperfections of policies, they can do nothing at all.

- Monopolists can often raise their profits by charging different prices for the same good based on a buyer's willingness to pay. This practice of price discrimination can raise economic welfare by getting the good to some consumers who otherwise would not buy it. In the extreme case of perfect price discrimination, the deadweight losses of monopoly are completely eliminated. More generally, when price discrimination is imperfect, it can either raise or lower welfare compared to the outcome with a single monopoly price.

QUESTIONS FOR REVIEW

1 What are barriers to entry? What are the main barriers to entry?

2 What are the main sources of monopoly power?

3 Give an example of a government-created monopoly. Is creating this monopoly necessarily bad public policy? Explain.

4 Define natural monopoly. What does the size of a market have to do with whether an industry is a natural monopoly?

5 Why is a monopolist's marginal revenue less than the price of its good? Can marginal revenue ever be negative? Explain.

6 Draw the demand, marginal revenue and marginal cost curves for a monopolist. Show the profit-maximizing level of output. Show the profit-maximizing price.

7 In your diagram from the previous question, show the level of output that maximizes total surplus. Show the deadweight loss from the monopoly. Explain your answer.

8 What gives the government the power to regulate mergers between firms? From the standpoint of the welfare of society, give a good reason and a bad reason that two firms might want to merge.

9 Describe the two problems that arise when regulators tell a natural monopoly that it must set a price equal to marginal cost.

10 Give two examples of price discrimination. In each case, explain why the monopolist chooses to follow this business strategy.

PROBLEMS AND APPLICATIONS

1 A publisher faces the following demand schedule for the next novel of one of its popular authors:

Price (€)	Quantity demanded
100	0
90	100 000
80	200 000
70	300 000
60	400 000
50	500 000
40	600 000
30	700 000
20	800 000
10	900 000
0	1 000 000

The author is paid €2 million to write the book, and the marginal cost of publishing the book is a constant €10 per book.

a. Compute total revenue, total cost and profit at each quantity. What quantity would a profit-maximizing publisher choose? What price would it charge?
b. Compute marginal revenue. (Recall that $MR = \Delta TR/\Delta Q$.) How does marginal revenue compare to the price? Explain.
c. Graph the marginal revenue, marginal cost and demand curves. At what quantity do the marginal revenue and marginal cost curves cross? What does this signify?
d. In your graph, shade in the deadweight loss. Explain in words what this means.
e. If the author were paid €3 million instead of €2 million to write the book, how would this affect the publisher's decision regarding the price to charge? Explain.
f. Suppose the publisher was not profit-maximizing but was concerned with maximizing economic efficiency. What price would it charge for the book? How much profit would it make at this price?

2 Consider the delivery of mail. In general, what is the shape of the average total cost curve? How might the shape differ between isolated rural areas and densely populated urban areas? How might the shape have changed over time? Explain.

3 Suppose the Eau de Jeunesse Water Company has a monopoly on bottled water sales in France. If the price of tap water increases, what is the change in Eau de Jeunesse's profit-maximizing levels of output, price and profit? Explain in words and with a graph.

4 A small town is served by many competing supermarkets, which have constant marginal cost.

a. Using a diagram of the market for groceries, show the consumer surplus, producer surplus and total surplus.
b. Now suppose that the independent supermarkets combine into one chain. Using a new diagram, show the new consumer surplus, producer surplus and total surplus. Relative to the competitive market, what is the transfer from consumers to producers? What is the deadweight loss?

5 A company is considering building a bridge across a river. The bridge would cost €2 million to build and nothing to maintain. The following table shows the company's anticipated demand over the lifetime of the bridge:

Price per crossing (€)	Number of crossings (in thousands)
8	0
7	100
6	200
5	300
4	400
3	500
2	600
1	700
0	800

a. If the company was to build the bridge, what would be its profit-maximizing price? Would that be the efficient level of output? Why or why not?
b. If the company is interested in maximizing profit, should it build the bridge? What would be its profit or loss?
c. If the government were to build the bridge, what price should it charge for passengers and vehicles to use the bridge? Explain your answer.
d. Should the government build the bridge? Explain.

6 The Placebo Drug Company holds a patent on one of its discoveries.

a. Assuming that the production of the drug involves rising marginal cost, draw a diagram to illustrate Placebo's profit-maximizing price and quantity. Also show Placebo's profits.
b. Now suppose that the government imposes a tax on each bottle of the drug produced. On a new diagram, illustrate Placebo's new price and quantity. How does each compare to your answer in part (a)?
c. Although it is not easy to see in your diagrams, the tax reduces Placebo's profit. Explain why this must be true.
d. Instead of the tax per bottle, suppose that the government imposes a tax on Placebo of €110 000 regardless of how many bottles are produced. How does this tax affect Placebo's price, quantity and profits? Explain.

7 Pablo, Dirk and Franz run the only bar in town. Pablo wants to sell as many drinks as possible without losing money. Dirk wants the bar to bring in as much revenue as possible. Franz wants to make the largest possible profits. Using a single diagram of the bar's demand curve and its cost curves, show the price and quantity combinations favoured by each of the three partners. Explain.

8 The Best Computer Company just developed a new computer chip, on which it immediately acquires a patent.

a. Draw a diagram that shows the consumer surplus, producer surplus and total surplus in the market for this new chip.

b. What happens to these three measures of surplus if the firm can perfectly price discriminate? What is the change in deadweight loss? What transfers occur?

9 Explain why a monopolist will always produce a quantity at which the demand curve is price elastic. (Hint: if demand is price inelastic and the firm raises its price, what happens to total revenue and total costs?)

10 Many schemes for price discriminating involve some cost. For example, discount coupons take up time and resources from both the buyer and the seller. This question considers the implications of costly price discrimination. To keep things simple, let's assume that our monopolist's production costs are simply proportional to output, so that average total cost and marginal cost are constant and equal to each other.

a. Draw the cost, demand and marginal revenue curves for the monopolist. Show the price the monopolist would charge without price discrimination.

b. On your diagram, mark the area equal to the monopolist's profit and call it X. Mark the area equal to consumer surplus and call it Y. Mark the area equal to the deadweight loss and call it Z.

c. Now suppose that the monopolist can perfectly price discriminate. What is the monopolist's profit? (Give your answer in terms of X, Y and Z.)

d. What is the change in the monopolist's profit from price discrimination? What is the change in total surplus from price discrimination? Which change is larger? Explain. (Give your answer in terms of X, Y and Z.)

e. Now suppose that there is some cost of price discrimination. To model this cost, let's assume that the monopolist has to pay a fixed cost C in order to price discriminate. How would a monopolist make the decision whether to pay this fixed cost? (Give your answer in terms of X, Y, Z and C.)

15 MARKET STRUCTURES II: MONOPOLISTIC COMPETITION

You arrive at university and set off into the town for a taste of the night life. The town has eight night clubs all in walking distance of the main transport hub. Each one has music, bars, light snacks, places to talk, different prices for food and drink, different entry prices, rules and closing times. When you are choosing between these different night clubs what kind of market are you participating in?

On the one hand, the market for night clubs seems competitive. In most towns and cities there are plenty of clubs vying for your attention. A buyer in this overall market has many competing products from which to choose.

However, the market for night clubs has some elements of monopoly power because each club is able to present itself in a unique way and as a result, night club owners have some latitude in choosing what price to charge. The sellers in this market are price-makers rather than price-takers. The price of entry into a night club greatly exceeds the marginal cost of one extra person entering.

In this chapter we examine imperfect markets that have some features of competition and some features of monopoly. This market structure is called **monopolistic competition**, another example of imperfect competition. Monopolistic competition describes a market with the following attributes:

- *Many sellers.* There are many firms competing for the same group of customers.
- *Product differentiation.* Each firm produces a product that is at least slightly different from those of other firms, whether physically different or whether perceived as being different by consumers. The firm has some control over the extent to which it can differentiate its product from its rivals, thus reducing the degree of substitutability and garnering an element of customer or brand loyalty. Therefore, rather than being a price-taker, each firm faces a downwards sloping demand curve.
- *Free entry.* Firms can enter (or exit) the market without restriction. Thus, the number of firms in the market adjusts until economic profits are driven to zero.

monopolistic competition a market structure in which many firms sell products that are similar but not identical

Table 15.1 lists some other examples of the types of market with these attributes, in addition to the example of night clubs we have opened this chapter with. Monopolistic competition is a market structure that lies between the extreme cases of competition and monopoly.

TABLE 15.1	Examples of Markets which have Characteristics of Monopolistic Competition

Computer games	Vets
Restaurants	Hotel accommodation
Conference organizers	Air conditioning systems
Wedding planners	Pest control
Plumbing	Removal services
Coach hire	Beauty consultants
Funeral directors	Shop fitters
Fabric manufacturers	Waste disposal
Tailors	Dentists
Music teachers	Children's entertainers
Books	Gas engineers
CDs/DVDs	Steel fabricators
Landscape architects	Driving schools
Environmental consultants	Opticians
Furniture manufacturers	Chimney sweeps

COMPETITION WITH DIFFERENTIATED PRODUCTS

To understand monopolistically competitive markets, we first consider the decisions facing an individual firm. We then examine what happens in the long run as firms enter and exit the industry. Next, we compare the equilibrium under monopolistic competition to the equilibrium under perfect competition. Finally, we consider whether the outcome in a monopolistically competitive market is desirable from the standpoint of society as a whole.

The Monopolistically Competitive Firm in the Short Run

Each firm in a monopolistically competitive market is, in many ways, like a monopoly. Why? Because its product is different from those offered by other firms it faces the same downward sloping demand curve. Thus, it can follow the monopolist's rule for profit maximization: choose the quantity of production where marginal revenue equals marginal cost, and then use its demand curve to find the price consistent with that quantity.

Figure 15.1 shows the cost, demand and marginal revenue curves for two typical firms, each in a different monopolistically competitive industry. In both panels of this figure, the profit-maximizing quantity is found at the intersection of the marginal revenue and marginal cost curves, but there are different outcomes for the two firms' profits. In panel (a), price exceeds average total cost, so the firm makes a profit. In panel (b), price is below average total cost. In this case, the firm is unable to make a positive profit, so the best the firm can do is to minimize its losses.

All this should seem familiar. A monopolistically competitive firm chooses its quantity and price just as a monopoly does. In the short run, these two types of market structure are similar.

The Long-Run Equilibrium

The situations depicted in Figure 15.1 do not last long. When demand seems to be strong and firms are making profits, as in panel (a), new firms have an incentive to enter the market (remember that there is free entry and exit into the market). This entry means that more firms are now offering products for sale in the industry. For example, the popularity of night clubs has led to more people wanting to set up new night clubs to take advantage of the demand and the profits that can be made. The increase in supply means customers have more choice and causes the price received by all firms in the industry to fall. If an existing firm wishes to sell more then it must reduce its price. There are now more substitutes available in the market and so the effect for an individual firm already in the market is that the demand curve for its product shifts to the left as the number of products from which customers can now choose increases.

FIGURE 15.1

A Monopolistic Competitor in the Short Run

Monopolistic competitors, like monopolists, maximize profit by producing the quantity at which marginal revenue equals marginal cost. The firm in panel (a) makes a profit because, at this quantity, price is above average total cost. The firm in panel (b) makes losses because, at this quantity, price is less than average total cost.

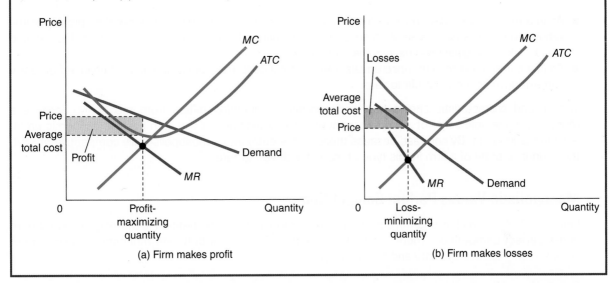

Profit encourages entry, and entry shifts the demand curves faced by firms to the left. As the demand for firms' products falls, these firms experience declining profit.

Some firms in the industry will have just been surviving, but as new firms enter and their demand curve shifts to the left they may find themselves making sub-normal profits and as a result might decide to leave the industry. When firms are making losses, as in panel (b), firms in the market have an incentive to exit. As firms exit, the supply will fall and price will rise. There are now fewer substitutes, and so customers have fewer products from which to choose. This decrease in the number of firms effectively expands the demand faced by those firms that stay in the market. In other words, losses encourage exit, and exit has the effect of shifting the demand curves of the remaining firms to the right. As the demand for the remaining firms' products rises, these firms experience rising profit (that is, declining losses).

This process of entry and exit continues until the firms in the market are making exactly zero economic profit (normal profit). Figure 15.2 depicts the long-run equilibrium. Once the market reaches this equilibrium, new firms have no incentive to enter, and existing firms have no incentive to exit.

FIGURE 15.2

A Monopolistic Competitor in the Long Run

In a monopolistically competitive market, if firms are making profit, new firms enter and the demand curves for the incumbent firms shift to the left. Similarly, if firms are making losses, old firms exit and the demand curves of the remaining firms shift to the right. Because of these shifts in demand, a monopolistically competitive firm eventually finds itself in the long-run equilibrium shown here. In this long-run equilibrium, price equals average total cost, and the firm earns zero profit.

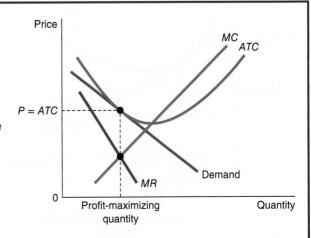

Notice that the demand curve in this figure is tangential to the average total cost curve. These two curves must be tangential once entry and exit have driven profit to zero. Because profit per unit sold is the difference between price (found on the demand curve) and average total cost, the maximum profit is zero only if these two curves touch each other without crossing.

To sum up, two characteristics describe the long-run equilibrium in a monopolistically competitive market:

- As in a monopoly market, price exceeds marginal cost. This conclusion arises because profit maximization requires marginal revenue to equal marginal cost and because the downwards sloping demand curve makes marginal revenue less than the price.
- As in a competitive market, price equals average total cost. This conclusion arises because free entry and exit drive economic profit to zero.

The second characteristic shows how monopolistic competition differs from monopoly. Because a monopoly is the sole seller of a product without close substitutes, it can earn positive economic profit, even in the long run. By contrast, because there is free entry into a monopolistically competitive market, the economic profit of a firm in this type of market is driven to zero.

Monopolistic Versus Perfect Competition

Figure 15.3 compares the long-run equilibrium under monopolistic competition to the long-run equilibrium under perfect competition. There are two noteworthy differences between monopolistic and perfect competition – excess capacity and the mark-up.

Excess Capacity The assumption of free entry and exit drive each firm in a monopolistically competitive market to a point of tangency between its demand and average total cost curves. Panel (a) of Figure 15.3 shows that the quantity of output at this point is smaller than the quantity that minimizes average total cost.

FIGURE 15.3

Monopolistic Versus Perfect Competition
Panel (a) shows the long-run equilibrium in a monopolistically competitive market, and panel (b) shows the long-run equilibrium in a perfectly competitive market. Two differences are notable. (1) The perfectly competitive firm produces at the efficient scale, where average total cost is minimized. By contrast, the monopolistically competitive firm produces at less than the efficient scale. (2) Price equals marginal cost under perfect competition, but price is above marginal cost under monopolistic competition.

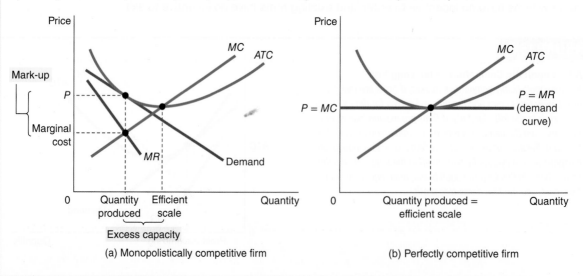

(a) Monopolistically competitive firm

(b) Perfectly competitive firm

Thus, under monopolistic competition, firms produce on the downwards sloping portion of their average total cost curves. In this way, monopolistic competition contrasts starkly with perfect competition. As panel (b) of Figure 15.3 shows, free entry in competitive markets drives firms to produce at the minimum of average total cost.

In the long run, perfectly competitive firms produce at the efficient scale, whereas monopolistically competitive firms produce below this level. Firms are said to have *excess capacity* under monopolistic competition. In other words, a monopolistically competitive firm, unlike a perfectly competitive firm, could increase the quantity it produces and lower the average total cost of production.

Mark-Up over Marginal Cost A second difference between perfect competition and monopolistic competition is the relationship between price and marginal cost. For a competitive firm, such as that shown in panel (b) of Figure 15.3, price equals marginal cost. For a monopolistically competitive firm, such as that shown in panel (a), price exceeds marginal cost, because the firm always has some market power.

How is this mark-up over marginal cost consistent with free entry and zero profit? The zero-profit condition ensures only that price equals average total cost. It does *not* ensure that price equals marginal cost. Indeed, in the long-run equilibrium, monopolistically competitive firms operate on the declining portion of their average total cost curves, so marginal cost is below average total cost. Thus, for price to equal average total cost, price must be above marginal cost.

In this relationship between price and marginal cost, we see a key behavioural difference between perfect competitors and monopolistic competitors. Imagine that you were to ask a firm the following question: 'Would you like to see another customer come through your door ready to buy from you at your current price?' A perfectly competitive firm would be ambivalent. Because price exactly equals marginal cost, the profit from an extra unit sold is zero. By contrast, a monopolistically competitive firm is always eager to get another customer. Because its price exceeds marginal cost, an extra unit sold at the posted price means more profit. According to an old quip, monopolistically competitive markets are those in which sellers send greetings cards to the buyers.

Monopolistic Competition and the Welfare of Society

Is the outcome in a monopolistically competitive market desirable from the standpoint of society as a whole? Can policymakers improve on the market outcome? There are no simple answers to these questions.

One source of inefficiency is the mark-up of price over marginal cost. Because of the mark-up, some consumers who value the good at more than the marginal cost of production (but less than the price) will be deterred from buying it. Thus, a monopolistically competitive market has the normal deadweight loss of monopoly pricing.

Although this outcome is clearly undesirable compared to the first-best outcome of price equal to marginal cost, there is no easy way for policymakers to fix the problem. To enforce marginal-cost pricing, policymakers would need to regulate all firms that produce differentiated products. Because such products are so common in the economy, the administrative burden of such regulation would be overwhelming.

Moreover, regulating monopolistic competitors would entail all the problems of regulating natural monopolies. In particular, because monopolistic competitors are making zero profits already, requiring them to lower their prices to equal marginal cost would cause them to make losses. To keep these firms in business, the government would need to help them cover these losses. Rather than raising taxes to pay for these subsidies, policymakers may decide it is better to live with the inefficiency of monopolistic pricing.

Another way in which monopolistic competition may be socially inefficient is that the number of firms in the market may not be the 'ideal' one. That is, there may be too much or too little entry. One way to think about this problem is in terms of the externalities associated with entry. Whenever a new firm considers entering the market with a new product, it considers only the profit it would make. Yet its entry would also have two external effects:

- *The product-variety externality.* Because consumers get some consumer surplus from the introduction of a new product, entry of a new firm conveys a positive externality on consumers.
- *The business-stealing externality.* Because other firms lose customers and profits from the entry of a new competitor, entry of a new firm imposes a negative externality on existing firms.

Thus, in a monopolistically competitive market, there are both positive and negative externalities associated with the entry of new firms. Depending on which externality is larger, a monopolistically competitive market could have either too few or too many products.

Both of these externalities are closely related to the conditions for monopolistic competition. The product-variety externality arises because a new firm would offer a product different from those of the existing firms. The business-stealing externality arises because firms post a price above marginal cost and, therefore, are always eager to sell additional units. Conversely, because perfectly competitive firms produce identical goods and charge a price equal to marginal cost, neither of these externalities exists under perfect competition.

In the end, we can conclude only that monopolistically competitive markets do not have all the welfare properties of perfectly competitive markets. That is, total surplus is not maximized under monopolistic competition. Yet because the inefficiencies are subtle, hard to measure and hard to fix, there is no easy way for public policy to improve the market outcome.

SELF TEST List the three key attributes of monopolistic competition. Draw and explain a diagram to show the long-run equilibrium in a monopolistically competitive market. How does this equilibrium differ from that in a perfectly competitive market?

ADVERTISING AND BRANDING

It is nearly impossible to go through a typical day in a modern economy without being bombarded with advertising, or to ignore the existence of brand names. Whether you are reading a newspaper, watching television or travelling, some firm will try to convince you to buy its product or put its brand in front of you. Such behaviour is a natural feature of monopolistic competition. When firms sell differentiated products and charge prices above marginal cost, each firm has an incentive to advertise or develop brands in order to attract more buyers to its particular product or develop loyalty.

The amount of advertising varies substantially across products. Firms that sell highly differentiated consumer goods, such as over-the-counter drugs, perfumes, soft drinks, razor blades, breakfast cereals and dog food, typically spend between 10 and 20 per cent of revenue for advertising. Firms that sell industrial products, such as drill presses and communications satellites, typically spend very little on advertising. And firms that sell homogeneous products, such as wheat, peanuts or crude oil, spend nothing at all. Estimates from Neilsen suggest that firms such as Procter and Gamble and British Sky Broadcasting (BskyB) spent over £10 million (€12.3 million) on advertising in the UK alone and eMarketer reported that total global media advertising spend in 2015 was around €535 billion. Advertising takes many forms: newspapers, magazines, TV, radio and via the Internet.

The Debate over Advertising

Is society wasting the resources it devotes to advertising? Or does advertising serve a valuable purpose? Assessing the social value of advertising is difficult and often generates heated argument among economists. Let's consider both sides of the debate.

The Critique of Advertising Critics of advertising argue that firms advertise in order to manipulate people's tastes. Much advertising is psychological rather than informational. Consider, for example, the typical television advert for some brand of soft drink. The advert probably does not tell the viewer about the product's price or quality. Instead, it might show a group of happy people at a party on a beach on a beautiful sunny day. In their hands are cans of the soft drink. The goal of the advert is to convey a subconscious (if not subtle) message: 'You too can have many friends and be happy and beautiful, if only you drink our product.' Critics of advertising argue that such an advert creates a desire that otherwise might not exist.

Critics also argue that advertising impedes competition. Advertising often tries to convince consumers that products are more different than they truly are. By increasing the perception of product differentiation and fostering brand loyalty, advertising makes buyers less concerned with price differences among similar goods. With a less elastic demand curve, each firm charges a larger mark-up over marginal cost.

The Defence of Advertising Defenders of advertising argue that firms use advertising to provide information to customers. Advertising conveys the prices of the goods being offered for sale, the key features and qualities of a good or service, the existence of new products and the locations of retail outlets. This information allows customers to make better choices about what to buy and, thus, enhances the ability of markets to allocate resources efficiently.

Defenders also argue that advertising fosters competition. Because advertising allows customers to be more fully informed about all the firms in the market, customers can more easily take advantage of price differences. Thus, each firm has less market power. In addition, advertising allows new firms to enter more easily, because it gives entrants a means to attract customers from existing firms.

Advertising as a Signal of Quality

Many types of advertising contain little apparent information about the product being advertised. Consider a firm introducing a new breakfast cereal. A typical advertisement might have some highly paid actor eating the cereal and telling the audience how wonderful it tastes. How much information does the advertisement really provide?

Defenders of advertising argue that even advertising that appears to contain little hard information may in fact tell consumers something about product quality. The willingness of the firm to spend a large amount of money on advertising can itself be a *signal* to consumers about the quality of the product being offered.

Consider a hypothetical problem facing Nestlé and Kellogg. Each company has just come up with a recipe for a new breakfast cereal, which it would sell for €3 a box. To keep things simple, let's assume that the marginal cost of making cereal is zero, so the €3 is all profit. Each company knows that if it spends €10 million on advertising, it will get 1 million consumers to try its new cereal. And each company knows that if consumers like the cereal, they will buy it not once but many times.

First, consider Kellogg's decision. Based on market research, Kellogg knows that its cereal is only mediocre. Although advertising would sell one box to each of 1 million consumers, the consumers would quickly learn that the cereal is not very good and stop buying it. Kellogg decides it is not worth paying €10 million in advertising to earn only €3 million in sales. So it does not bother to advertise. It sends its cooks back to the drawing board to find another recipe.

Nestlé, on the other hand, knows that its cereal is great. Each person who tries it will buy a box a month for the next year. Thus, Nestlé sell 1 million boxes per month over the year and the €10 million in advertising will bring in €36 million in sales. Advertising is profitable here because Nestlé has a good product that consumers will buy repeatedly. Thus, Nestlé chooses to advertise.

Now that we have considered the behaviour of the two firms, let's consider the behaviour of consumers. We began by asserting that consumers are inclined to try a new cereal that they see advertised. Is this behaviour rational? Should a consumer try a new cereal just because the seller has chosen to advertise it?

In fact, it may be completely rational for consumers to try new products that they see advertised. In our story, consumers decide to try Nestlé's new cereal because Nestlé advertises. Nestlé chooses to advertise because it knows that its cereal is quite good, while Kellogg chooses not to advertise because it knows that its cereal is only mediocre. By its willingness to spend money on advertising, Nestlé signals to consumers the quality of its cereal. Each consumer thinks, quite sensibly (if subconsciously), 'If the Nestlé Company is willing to spend so much money advertising this new cereal, it must be really good.'

What is most surprising about this theory of advertising is that the content of the advertisement is irrelevant. Nestlé signals the quality of its product by its willingness to spend money on advertising. (This example is used for illustrative purposes only and is not meant to infer that Kellogg deliberately produces inferior products!)

What the advertisements say is not as important as the fact that consumers know ads are expensive. By contrast, cheap advertising doesn't signal quality to consumers. In our example, if an advertising campaign cost less than €3 million, for example, both Nestlé and Kellogg would use it to market their new cereals. Because both good and mediocre cereals would be advertised, consumers could not infer the quality of a new cereal from the fact that it is advertised. Over time, consumers would learn to ignore such cheap advertising.

This theory can explain why firms pay celebrities large amounts of money to make advertisements that, on the surface, appear to convey no information at all. The information is not in the advertisement's content, but simply in its existence and expense.

CASE STUDY   Advertising – What Does it Really Do?

Ask many people the question 'why do firms advertise?' and they are likely to tell you that it is an attempt by firms to try and increase demand for their products or services. If you consider this view intuitively it might make sense but then ask yourself the question, 'How many times have you seen an advert on the TV and then rushed out to buy the product advertised?' The chances are that this has not (consciously) happened very often at all. If adverts do not make us rush out to buy products what do they do?

Sutherland and Sylvester (2000) argue that it is largely a myth that adverts are designed to persuade us to buy products or services. They point out the following:

> *Advertising influences the order in which we evoke or notice the alternatives we consider. This does not feel like persuasion and it is not. It is nevertheless effective. Instead of persuasion and other major effects we should look for 'feathers', or minor effects. These can tip the balance when alternative brands are otherwise equal and, through repetition, can grow imperceptibly by small increments over time.*

They liken the effect of advertising to that of watching someone grow up. You know that they are growing but the day-to-day changes in the individual are imperceptible. If you have not seen someone for some time, however, you do tend to notice the difference in their height, shape, features and so on. So it is with many advertising campaigns. The primary aim, they argue, is to generate a series of small effects, which ultimately influence our behaviour and may cause us to view differently the products or the brands that we choose, especially in a crowded marketplace with a large amount of competition.

Exactly how adverts work, therefore, is not easy to quantify. Sutherland and Sylvester suggest that many involved in the advertising industry do not really understand why some adverts seem to work and others don't work anything like as well. It has long been recognized that psychology has a lot to do with advertising. Our understanding of the way the brain works has been revolutionized by the developments afforded by magnetic resonance imaging (MRI) scans. The advertising industry has not been slow in looking at this technology and its potential for improving the focus and efficiency of advertising.

In essence, this technique looks at the response of the brain to different images and messages. Using MRI techniques, the areas of the brain that respond to different stimuli can be identified. The field developed as a result of work carried out by a neuroscientist called Read Montague. Montague is Professor at the VTC Research Institute at Virginia Tech in the United States. Whilst in a previous position at Baylor College of Medicine in Texas, he presided over a challenge to see if people preferred different brands of cola. His initial studies suggested that people preferred Pepsi but their buying behaviour tended to favour Coke. In a repeat of the experiment in 2004 using MRI technology, Montague and his colleagues gave a group of individuals two colas, Pepsi and Coke, to taste and asked them to state which they preferred. The respondents did not know that the two colas were in fact Pepsi and Coke. The subjects stated preferences were almost 50:50 although activity in a part of the brain associated with processing feelings of reward showed a higher response for Pepsi.

However, when the experiment was repeated and the respondents were told what they were drinking, around 75 per cent stated that they preferred Coke. Montague found that brain activity in the lateral pre-frontal cortex showed signs of enhanced activity during the exercise. This area of the brain is associated with higher level thinking. Montague posited that the brain was now using memories and making an association with the images and messages associated with commercials for Coke that respondents had witnessed over the years. He also suggested that such activity might lead to consumers preferring one product to another, even if there was other evidence to suggest that under normal circumstances, they would not have chosen that product.

Advertising is all around us but how far are we affected by it?

Sources: Sutherland, M. and Sylvester, A.K. (2000) *Advertising and the Mind of the Consumer: What Works, What Doesn't, and Why.* St Leonards, New South Wales: Allen and Unwin.

Branding and Brand Names

Advertising is closely related to **branding**. In many markets, there are two types of firms. Some firms sell products with widely recognized brand names, while other firms sell generic substitutes. For example, in a typical supermarket, you can find Pepsi next to less familiar colas, or Kellogg's cornflakes next to the supermarket's own brand of cornflakes, made for it by an unknown firm. Most often, the firm with the famous brand name spends more on advertising and charges a higher price for its product.

 branding the means by which a business creates an identity for itself and highlights the way in which it differs from its rivals

Just as there is disagreement about the economics of advertising, there is disagreement about the economics of brand names and branding. Let's consider both sides of the debate.

Critics argue that branding causes consumers to perceive differences that do not really exist. In many cases, the generic good is almost indistinguishable from the brand-name good. Consumers' willingness to pay more for the brand-name good, these critics assert, is a form of irrationality fostered by advertising. Economist Edward Chamberlin, one of the early developers of the theory of monopolistic competition, concluded from this argument that brand names were bad for the economy. He proposed that the government discourage their use by refusing to enforce the exclusive trademarks that companies use to identify their products.

More recently, economists have defended brand names as a useful way for consumers to ensure that the goods they buy are of high quality. There are two related arguments. First, brand names provide consumers with *information* which cannot be easily judged in advance of purchase. Second, brand names give firms an *incentive* to meet the needs of consumers, because firms have a financial stake in maintaining the reputation of their brand names. Note that branding does not always equate to high quality. Branding is primarily a means by which the firm creates an association in the consumer and because that association becomes familiar, the consumer is more likely to retain some loyalty to the firm and thus repeat purchase. Some firms, for example, will happily admit their goods are 'cheap and cheerful' but the key association in consumers' minds is one of value for money. Firms such as Lidl, Netto, Poundstretcher and Poundland are as much interested in developing their brand names as are Armani and Ralph Lauren.

To see how these arguments work in practice, consider a famous brand name: Ibis hotels. Imagine that you are driving through an unfamiliar town and you need somewhere to stay for the night. You see a Hotel Ibis and a local hotel next door to it. Which do you choose? The local hotel may in fact offer better accommodation at lower prices, but you have no way of knowing that. In contrast, Hotel Ibis offers a consistent product across many European cities. Its brand name is useful to you as a way of judging the quality of what you are about to buy.

The Ibis brand name also ensures that the company has an incentive to maintain quality. (In reality, hotel chains such as Ibis provide the opportunity for private firms to operate a hotel under the Ibis brand name, and reap the benefits of the brand name if they are committed to meeting its associated standards.) For example, if some customers were to become very ill from bad food served at breakfast at an Ibis hotel, the news would be disastrous for the company. Ibis would lose much of the valuable reputation that it has built up over the years and, as a result, it would lose sales and profit not just in the hotel that served the bad food but in its many hotels across Europe. Hence, Ibis has an incentive to ensure that its breakfast food is safe and that standards are maintained in all the hotels bearing its brand.

The debate over brand names thus centres on the question of whether consumers are rational in preferring brand names over generic substitutes. Critics argue that brand names are the result of an irrational consumer response to advertising. Defenders of brand names argue that consumers have good reason to pay more for brand-name products because they can be more confident in the quality of these products.

CONTESTABLE MARKETS

The theory of contestable markets was developed by William J. Baumol, John Panzar and Robert Willig in 1982. The key characteristic of a perfectly contestable market (the benchmark to explain firms' behaviours) is that firms are influenced by the threat of new entrants into a market. The more highly contestable a market is, the lower the barriers to entry. We have seen how, in monopolistically competitive markets, despite the fact that each firm has some monopoly control over its product, the ease of entry and exit means that in the long run profits can be competed away as new firms enter the market. This threat of new entrants may make firms behave in a way that departs from what was assumed to be the traditional goal of firms – to maximize profits. The suggestion by Baumol and colleagues was that firms may deliberately limit profits made to discourage new entrants. Profits might be limited by what is termed **entry limit pricing**. This refers to a situation where a firm will keep prices lower than they could be in order to deter new entrants. Similarly, firms may also practise **predatory or destroyer pricing** whereby the price is held below average cost for a period to try and force out competitors or prevent new firms from entering the market. Incumbent firms may be in a position to do this because they may have been able to gain some advantages of economies of scale which new entrants may not be able to exploit.

> **entry limit pricing** a situation where a firm will keep prices lower than they could be in order to deter new entrants
>
> **predatory or destroyer pricing** a situation where firms hold price below average cost for a period to try and force out competitors or prevent new firms from entering the market

In a contestable market firms may also erect other artificial barriers to prevent entry into the industry by new firms. Such barriers might include operating at over-capacity, which provides the opportunity to flood the market and drive down price in the event of a threat of entry. Firms will also carry out aggressive marketing and branding strategies to 'tighten' up the market or find ways of reducing costs and increasing efficiency to gain competitive advantage. Searching out sources of competitive advantage is a topic written on extensively by Michael Porter, who defined **competitive advantage** as being the advantages firms can gain over another which are both distinctive and defensible. These sources are not simply to be found in terms of new product development but through close investigation and analysis of the supply chain, where little changes might make a difference to the cost base of a firm which it can then exploit to its advantage.

> **competitive advantage** the advantages firms can gain over another which have the characteristics of being both distinctive and defensible

Hit-and-run tactics might be evident in a contestable market where firms enter the industry, take the profit and get out quickly (possible because of the freedom of entry and exit). In other cases firms may indulge in what is termed **cream-skimming** – identifying parts of the market that are high in value added and exploiting those markets.

> **cream-skimming** a situation where a firm identifies parts of a market that are high in value added and seeks to exploit those markets

The theory of contestable markets has been widely adopted as a beneficial addition to the theory of the firm and there has been extensive research into its application.

There are numerous examples of markets exhibiting contestability characteristics including financial services; airlines, especially flights on domestic routes; the IT industry and in particular internet service providers (ISPs), software and web developers; energy supplies; and the postal service. The key to analyzing market structures, therefore, could be argued to be the focus on the degree of freedom of entry and exit. If policymakers can keep barriers to entry as low as possible, i.e. try to ensure a high degree of contestability, then there is more likelihood that market outcomes will be efficient.

SELF TEST How might advertising make markets less competitive? How might it make markets more competitive? Give the arguments for and against brand names.

CONCLUSION

Monopolistic competition is true to its name: it is a hybrid of monopoly and competition. Like a monopoly, each monopolistic competitor faces a downwards sloping demand curve and, as a result, charges a price above marginal cost. As in a perfectly competitive market, there are many firms, and entry and exit drive the profit of each monopolistic competitor toward zero. Table 15.2 summarizes these lessons.

Because monopolistically competitive firms produce differentiated products, each firm advertises in order to attract customers to its own brand. To some extent, advertising manipulates consumers' tastes, promotes irrational brand loyalty and impedes competition. Equally, advertising can provide information, establish brand names of reliable quality and foster competition.

The theory of monopolistic competition seems to describe many markets in the economy but the theory does not yield simple and compelling advice for public policy. From the standpoint of the economic theorist, the allocation of resources in monopolistically competitive markets is not perfect. Yet, from the standpoint of a practical policymaker, there may be little that can be done to improve it.

TABLE 15.2   **Monopolistic Competition: Between Perfect Competition and Monopoly Market structure**

	Market structure		
	Perfect competition	**Monopolistic competition**	**Monopoly**
Features that all three market structures share			
Goal of firms	Maximize profits	Maximize profits	Maximize profits
Rule for maximizing	$MR = MC$	$MR = MC$	$MR = MC$
Can earn economic profits in the short run?	Yes	Yes	Yes
Features that monopoly and monopolistic competition share			
Price-taker?	Yes	No	No
Price	$P = MC$	$P > MC$	$P > MC$
Produces welfare-maximizing level of output?	Yes	No	No
Features that perfect competition and monopolistic competition share			
Number of firms	Many	Many	One
Entry in long run?	Yes	Yes	No
Can earn economic profits in long run?	No	No	Yes

IN THE NEWS

Advertising and Branding

As markets become more competitive, firms have to find ways to differentiate their products. This In the News shows how one firm in the fast-food industry has attempted to do just that.

Noodles and Company

The fast food market has a large number of firms each offering differentiated products with a similar customer focus – to provide food quickly at a reasonable price. Noodles and Company is one such firm in a busy market for fast food. Starting in 1995, the firm entered the United States fast food market with the aim of 'providing fresh food fast'. Of course, the vast majority of fast food restaurants would also make claims that they provide fresh food fast so the

(Continued)

competitive edge has to be focused on something different. After all, few fast food firms are going to tell customers that their food is not fresh!

As the market becomes increasingly crowded, the importance of differentiating your product offering becomes more important. Noodles and Company recognized this and made attempts to do just this in October 2015 by announcing a brand positioning campaign. The firm emphasised 'real' in its offering – 'real food, real cooking and real flavours' – by removing artificial colourings, sweeteners and preservatives from many of its core ingredients; including menu items which recognized customers with food allergies; and targeting customers in the 25 – 35 age range, some of whom are unattached and free to spend but increasingly becoming parents with young children (marketers refer to this segment as 'millennials').

The focus on fresh food and ingredients does not come without a cost, however. Sourcing fresh ingredients can be more expensive. For example, Noodles is exploring sourcing chickens from suppliers which are anti-biotic and hormone-free and has used pork products from animals which have been 'naturally raised'. It is possible to access these supplies but they cost more to produce and as a result Noodles has to consider whether to pass on the increased cost to its target market in the form of higher prices, which would amount to an increase of around a fifth. Will millennials be affluent enough to afford to pay the higher prices and more importantly, will they be willing to pay higher prices to get food which have 'green' and organic credentials?

Questions

1 To what extent would you agree that the fast food market is monopolistically competitive?
2 If firms like Noodles and Company make abnormal profits in the short run as a result of innovation and differentiation, what would you expect to happen in the long run?
3 In seeking to develop a new advertising and branding campaign which focuses on 'real' food, what signals are Noodles and Company hoping to give to the market?
4 To what extent do you think the market for fast food exhibits characteristics of being contestable?
5 What are the challenges facing firms in the fast food industry in capturing market share and growth given the market structure?

The fast food company Noodles and Company are seeking to differentiate themselves from the competition.

SUMMARY

● A monopolistically competitive market is characterized by three attributes: many firms, differentiated products and free entry.

● The equilibrium in a monopolistically competitive market differs from that in a perfectly competitive market in two related ways. First, each firm in a monopolistically competitive market has excess capacity. That is, it operates on the downwards sloping portion of the average total cost curve. Second, each firm charges a price above marginal cost.

● Monopolistic competition has the standard deadweight loss of monopoly caused by the mark-up of price over marginal cost. In addition, the number of firms (and thus the variety of products) can be too large or too small. In practice, the ability of policymakers to correct these inefficiencies is limited.

● The product differentiation inherent in monopolistic competition leads to the use of advertising and brand names. Critics of advertising and brand names argue that firms use them to take advantage of consumer irrationality and to reduce competition. Defenders of advertising and brand names argue that firms use them to inform consumers and to compete more vigorously on price and product quality.

● The theory of contestable markets suggests that firm behaviour may be directed at pricing strategies designed to prevent new entrants or to exploit the value in markets. Public policy, therefore, might be more directed at focusing on keeping barriers to entry as low as possible so that prices are driven down towards average cost. Low barriers to entry provide a constraint on firms seeking to adopt strategies to prevent competition.

QUESTIONS FOR REVIEW

1 Describe the three attributes of monopolistic competition. How is monopolistic competition like monopoly? How is it like perfect competition?

2 Identify five ways a firm in a monopolistically competitive market might seek to differentiate its products from its rivals?

3 Draw a diagram depicting a firm in a monopolistically competitive market that is making profits. Now show what happens to this firm as new firms enter the industry.

4 Draw a diagram of the long-run equilibrium in a monopolistically competitive market. How is price related to average total cost? How is price related to marginal cost?

5 Does a monopolistic competitor produce too much or too little output compared to the most efficient level? What practical considerations make it difficult for policymakers to solve this problem?

6 Is the purpose of advertising simply to shift the demand curve for a product to the right?

7 How might advertising reduce economic well-being? How might advertising increase economic well-being?

8 How might advertising with no apparent informational content in fact convey information to consumers?

9 Explain two benefits that might arise from the existence of brand names.

10 In what ways does the theory of contestable markets suggest that firm behaviour might be affected by the degree of freedom of entry and exit into a market?

PROBLEMS AND APPLICATIONS

1 Classify the following markets as perfectly competitive, monopolistic or monopolistically competitive, and explain your answers:
   a. wooden HB pencils
   b. bottled water
   c. copper
   d. strawberry jam
   e. lipstick.

2 What feature of the product being sold distinguishes a monopolistically competitive firm from a monopoly firm?

3 The chapter states that monopolistically competitive firms could increase the quantity they produce and lower the average total cost of production. Why don't they do so?

4 Sparkle is one firm of many in the market for toothpaste, which is in long-run equilibrium.

   a. Draw a diagram showing Sparkle's demand curve, marginal revenue curve, average total cost curve and marginal cost curve. Label Sparkle's profit-maximizing output and price.
   b. What is Sparkle's profit? Explain.
   c. On your diagram, show the consumer surplus derived from the purchase of Sparkle toothpaste. Also show the deadweight loss relative to the efficient level of output.
   d. If the government forced Sparkle to produce the efficient level of output, what would happen to the firm? What would happen to Sparkle's customers?

5 Do monopolistically competitive markets typically have the optimal number of products? Explain.

6 Consider a monopolistically competitive market with N firms. Each firm's business opportunities are described by the following equations:

Demand: $Q = \dfrac{100}{N} - P$

Marginal Revenue: $MR = \dfrac{MR}{N} - 2Q$

Total Cost: $TC = 50 + Q^2$

Marginal Cost: $MC = 2Q$

  a. How does *N*, the number of firms in the industry, affect each firm's demand curve? Why?

  b. How many units does each firm produce? (The answers to this and the next two questions depend on *N*.)

  c. What price does each firm charge?

  d. How much profit does each firm make?

  e. In the long run, how many firms will exist in this market?

7 If you were thinking of entering the ice cream business, would you try to make ice cream that is just like one of the existing (successful) brands? Explain your decision using the ideas of this chapter.

8 Describe three adverts that you have seen on TV. In what ways, if any, were each of these adverts socially useful? In what ways were they socially wasteful? Did the adverts affect the likelihood of your buying the product? Why or why not?

9 For each of the following pairs of firms, explain which firm would be more likely to engage in advertising:

  a. A family-owned farm or a family-owned restaurant.

  b. A manufacturer of forklift trucks or a manufacturer of cars.

  c. A company that invented a very reliable watch or a company that invented a less reliable watch that costs the same amount to make.

10 The makers of *Panadol* pain reliever do a lot of advertising and have very loyal customers. In contrast, the makers of generic paracetamol do no advertising, and their customers shop only for the lowest price. Assume that the marginal costs of Panadol and generic paracetamol are the same and constant.

  a. Draw a diagram showing *Panadol's* demand, marginal revenue and marginal cost curves. Label *Panadol's* price and mark-up over marginal cost.

  b. Repeat part (a) for a producer of generic paracetamol. How do the diagrams differ?

  c. Which company has the bigger mark-up? Explain.

  d. Which company has the bigger incentive for careful quality control? Why?

  e. How might barriers to entry influence the behaviour of the makers of *Panadol*?

  f. What factors would affect the extent to which the makers of *Panadol* could engage in predatory or destroyer pricing to force out competitors in this market.

16 MARKET STRUCTURES III: OLIGOPOLY

The Europeans love chocolate. The average German eats about 180, 62-gram bars of chocolate a year. The Belgians are not far behind at 177 bars, the Swiss around 173 and the British eat around 164 bars per year. There are many firms producing chocolate in Europe including Anthon Berg in Denmark, Camille Bloch, Lindt and Favarger in Switzerland, Guylian and Godiva in Belgium, and Hachez in Germany. However, Europeans are liable to find that what they are eating is likely to be made by one of three companies: Cadbury (owned by the US firm Kraft), Mars or Nestlé. These firms dominate the chocolate industry in the European Union. Being so large and dominant they are able to influence the quantity of chocolate bars produced and, given the market demand curve, the price at which chocolate bars are sold.

The European market for chocolate bars is a further example of imperfect competition but in this case the market is dominated by a relatively small number of very large firms. This type of imperfect competition is referred to as **oligopoly** – competition amongst the few. In oligopolistic markets, there might be many thousands of firms in the industry but sales are dominated by a small number of firms. The market is said to be concentrated in the hands of a few firms. The **concentration ratio** refers to the proportion of total market share accounted for by a particular number of firms. A two-firm concentration ratio of 90 per cent, for example, means that 90 per cent of all sales in the market are accounted for by just two firms. A five-firm concentration ratio of 75 per cent means that three-quarters of all sales in the market are accounted for by five firms. The small number of dominant sellers makes rigorous competition less likely, and it makes strategic interactions among them vitally important. As a result, the actions of any one seller in the market can have a large impact on the profits of all the other sellers. That is, oligopolistic firms are interdependent in a way that competitive firms are not. Our goal in this chapter is to see how this interdependence shapes the firms' behaviour and what problems it raises for public policy.

> **oligopoly** competition amongst the few – a market structure in which only a few sellers offer similar or identical products and dominate the market
>
> **concentration ratio** the proportion of total market share accounted for by a particular number of firms

CHARACTERISTICS OF OLIGOPOLY

The main characteristic of oligopolistic markets is that there are a relatively small number of dominant firms in the market. Each firm may offer a product similar or identical to the others. One example is the market for chocolate bars. Other examples include the world market for crude oil – a few countries in the Middle East control much of the world's oil reserves – and supermarkets in parts of Europe. In the UK, for example, there are many thousands of firms selling groceries but the industry is dominated by four very large firms: Tesco, Sainsbury's, Morrisons and Asda. There are approximately a dozen companies that now sell cars in Europe so whether this can be described as an oligopoly is open to debate. There are thousands of small independent breweries across Europe but sales are dominated by a relatively small number of firms, A-BInBev, Heineken, Carlsberg and SABMiller.

SELF TEST Look at the following markets. Which do you think can be classed as being oligopolistic market structures in the country where you live and what is the approximate concentration ratio in each case? Banking, mobile phone networks, insurance, the chemical industry, electrical goods, detergents and entertainment.

Differentiation

Firms in oligopolistic market structures do sell products that are similar but may seek to differentiate themselves in some way. One lager, for example, is not that dissimilar to many others but somehow brewing firms have to try and convince customers that their particular lager is different. This may be done through making the alcohol content higher or lower (or even zero alcohol), having a beer that is light in calories, in the way the product is packaged, how the beer stays fizzy and so on.

Firms such as Procter & Gamble produce household care products including Daz, Ariel, Bold and Fairy washing products. These are essentially all products to wash clothes but Procter & Gamble find ways to differentiate this product portfolio and even within a particular brand, produce different versions of each such as washing powders, tablets and liquids, with or without fabric softener and/or stain remover. Procter & Gamble is trying to differentiate its products to meet different customer needs and market segments and also to capture market share from its rivals. **Market segments** refer to the way in which firms break down customers into groups with similar buying habits or characteristics such as age, culture, gender, income, location, aspiration, interest, background and so on.

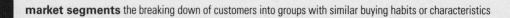

market segments the breaking down of customers into groups with similar buying habits or characteristics

Interdependence

Because oligopolistic markets are dominated by a few large firms, they are said to be interdependent. This means that what one firm does has some influence on the others and each firm may or may not react to the decisions of others. Each firm in the industry will be considering its own actions but its behaviour will be influenced by what it thinks the action and reaction of its rivals will be.

A result of this interdependence is that tension can arise between firms of whether to cooperate or act purely in self-interest. The group of oligopolists is best off cooperating and acting like a monopolist – producing a small quantity of output and charging a price above marginal cost. Yet because each oligopolist cares about only its own profit, there are powerful incentives at work that hinder a group of firms from maintaining the monopoly outcome.

A Duopoly Example

To understand the behaviour of oligopolies, let's consider an oligopoly with only two members, called a *duopoly*. Duopoly is the simplest type of oligopoly. Oligopolies with three or more members face the same problems as oligopolies with only two members, so we do not lose much by analyzing the case of duopoly.

Imagine a town in which only two residents – Jacques and Joelle – own wells that produce water safe for drinking. Each Saturday, Jacques and Joelle decide how many litres of water to pump, bring the water to town, and sell it for whatever price the market will bear. To keep things simple, suppose that Jacques and Joelle can pump as much water as they want without cost. That is, the marginal cost of water equals zero.

Table 16.1 shows the town's demand schedule for water. The first column shows the total quantity demanded, and the second column shows the price. If the two well owners sell a total of 10 litres of water, water sells for €110 a litre. If they sell a total of 20 litres, the price falls to €100 a litre, and so on. Graphing these two columns of numbers gives the standard downwards sloping demand curve.

The last column in Table 16.1 shows the total revenue from the sale of water. It equals the quantity sold times the price. Because there is no cost to pumping water, the total revenue of the two producers equals their total profit.

TABLE 16.1   Total Revenue from the Sale of Water

Quantity (in litres)	Price (€)	Total revenue (and total profit €)
0	120	0
10	110	1100
20	100	2000
30	90	2700
40	80	3200
50	70	3500
60	60	3600
70	50	3500
80	40	3200
90	30	2700
100	20	2000
110	10	1100
120	0	0

Let's now consider how the organization of the town's water industry affects the price of water and the quantity of water sold.

Competition, Monopolies and Cartels

Table 16.1 shows that total profit is maximized at a quantity of 60 litres and a price of €60 a litre. A profit-maximizing monopolist, therefore, would produce this quantity and charge this price which would exceed marginal cost. The result would be inefficient, for the quantity of water produced and consumed would fall short of the socially efficient level of 120 litres.

What outcome should we expect from our duopolists? The tension between self-interest and cooperation exists because of the characteristic of interdependence and so one possibility is that Jacques and Joelle get together and agree on the quantity of water to produce and the price to charge for it. Such an agreement among firms over production and price is called **collusion**, and the group of firms acting in unison is called a **cartel**. Once a cartel is formed, the market is in effect served by a monopoly, and we can apply analysis assuming monopoly. That is, if Jacques and Joelle were to collude, they would agree on the monopoly outcome because that outcome maximizes the total profit that the producers can get from the market. Our two producers would produce a total of 60 litres, which would be sold at a price of €60 a litre. Once again, price exceeds marginal cost, and the outcome is socially inefficient.

> **collusion** an agreement among firms in a market about quantities to produce or prices to charge
> **cartel** a group of firms acting in unison

A cartel must agree not only on the total level of production but also on the amount produced by each member. In our case, Jacques and Joelle must agree how to split between themselves the monopoly production of 60 litres. Each member of the cartel will want a larger share of the market because a larger market share means larger profit. If Jacques and Joelle agreed to split the market equally, each would produce 30 litres, the price would be €60 a litre and each would get a profit of €1800.

The Equilibrium for an Oligopoly

Although oligopolists would like to form cartels and earn monopoly profits, often that is not possible. Competition laws prohibit explicit agreements among oligopolists as a matter of public policy. In addition, squabbling among cartel members over how to divide the profit in the market sometimes makes agreement among them impossible. Let's therefore consider what happens if Jacques and Joelle decide separately how much water to produce.

At first one might expect Jacques and Joelle to reach the monopoly outcome on their own, for this outcome maximizes their joint profit. In the absence of a binding agreement, however, the monopoly outcome is unlikely. To see why, imagine that Jacques expects Joelle to produce only 30 litres (half of the monopoly quantity). Jacques would reason as follows:

I could produce 30 litres as well. In this case, a total of 60 litres of water would be sold at a price of €60 a litre. My profit would be €1800 (30 litres × €60 a litre). Alternatively, I could produce 40 litres. In this case, a total of 70 litres of water would be sold at a price of €50 a litre. My profit would be €2000 (40 litres × €50 a litre). Even though total profit in the market would fall, my profit would be higher, because I would have a larger share of the market.

Because of the interdependence between the two firms, Joelle might reason the same way. If so, Jacques and Joelle would each bring 40 litres to town. Total sales would be 80 litres, and the price would fall to €40. Thus, if the duopolists individually pursue their own self-interest when deciding how much to produce, they produce a total quantity greater than the monopoly quantity, charge a price lower than the monopoly price and earn total profit less than the monopoly profit.

Although the logic of self-interest increases the duopoly's output above the monopoly level, it does not push the duopolists to reach the competitive allocation. Consider what happens when each duopolist is producing 40 litres. The price is €40, and each duopolist makes a profit of €1600. In this case, Jacques's self-interested logic leads to a different conclusion:

My profit is €1600. Suppose I increase my production to 50 litres. In this case, a total of 90 litres of water would be sold, and the price would be €30 a litre. Then my profit would be only €1500. Rather than increasing production and driving down the price, I am better off keeping my production at 40 litres.

The outcome in which Jacques and Joelle each produce 40 litres looks like some sort of equilibrium. In fact, this outcome is called a **Nash equilibrium** (named after mathematician, John Nash). A Nash equilibrium is a situation in which economic actors interacting with one another each choose their best strategy given the strategies the others have chosen. In this case, given that Joelle is producing 40 litres, the best strategy for Jacques is to produce 40 litres. Similarly, given that Jacques is producing 40 litres, the best strategy for Joelle is to produce 40 litres. Once they reach this Nash equilibrium, neither Jacques nor Joelle has an incentive to make a different decision.

> **Nash equilibrium** a situation in which economic actors interacting with one another each choose their best strategy given the strategies that all the other actors have chosen

Oligopolists would be better off cooperating and reaching the monopoly outcome. Yet because they pursue their own self-interest, they do not end up reaching the monopoly outcome and maximizing their joint profit. Each oligopolist is tempted to raise production and capture a larger share of the market. As each of them tries to do this, total production rises and the price falls.

At the same time, self-interest does not drive the market all the way to the competitive outcome. Like monopolists, oligopolists are aware that increases in the amount they produce reduce the price of their product. Therefore, they stop short of following the competitive firm's rule of producing up to the point where price equals marginal cost.

In summary, when firms in an oligopoly individually choose production to maximize profit, they produce a quantity of output greater than the level produced by monopoly and less than the level produced by competition. The oligopoly price is less than the monopoly price but greater than the competitive price (which equals marginal cost).

How the Size of an Oligopoly Affects the Market Outcome

We can use the insights from this analysis of duopoly to discuss how the size of an oligopoly is likely to affect the outcome in a market. Suppose, for instance, that Monika and Liesel suddenly discover water sources on their property and join Jacques and Joelle in the water oligopoly. The demand schedule in Table 16.1 remains the same, but now more producers are available to satisfy this demand. How would an increase in the number of sellers from two to four affect the price and quantity of water in the town?

If the sellers of water could form a cartel, they would once again try to maximize total profit by producing the monopoly quantity and charging the monopoly price. Just as when there were only two sellers, the members of the cartel would need to agree on production levels for each member and find some way to enforce the agreement. As the cartel grows larger, however, this outcome is less likely. Reaching and enforcing an agreement becomes more difficult as the size of the group increases.

If the oligopolists do not form a cartel – perhaps because competition laws prohibit it – they must each decide on their own how much water to produce. To see how the increase in the number of sellers affects the outcome, consider the decision facing each seller. At any time, each well owner has the option to raise production by 1 litre. In making this decision, the well owner weighs two effects:

- *The output effect.* Because price is above marginal cost, selling one more litre of water at the going price will raise profit.
- *The price effect.* Raising production will increase the total amount sold, which will lower the price of water and lower the profit on all the other litres sold.

If the output effect is larger than the price effect, the well owner will increase production. If the price effect is larger than the output effect, the owner will not raise production. (In fact, in this case, it is profitable to reduce production.) Each oligopolist continues to increase production until these two marginal effects exactly balance, taking the other firms' production as given.

Now consider how the number of firms in the industry affects the marginal analysis of each oligopolist. The larger the number of sellers, the less concerned each seller is about its own impact on the market price. That is, as the oligopoly grows in size, the magnitude of the price effect falls. When the oligopoly grows very large, the price effect disappears altogether, leaving only the output effect. In this extreme case, each firm in the oligopoly increases production as long as price is above marginal cost.

We can now see that a large oligopoly is essentially a group of competitive firms. A competitive firm considers only the output effect when deciding how much to produce: because a competitive firm is a price-taker, the price effect is absent. Thus, as the number of sellers in an oligopoly grows larger, an oligopolistic market looks more and more like a competitive market. The price approaches marginal cost and the quantity produced approaches the socially efficient level.

The Effects of International Trade Imagine that Toyota and Honda are the only car manufacturers in Japan, Volkswagen and BMW are the only car manufacturers in Germany, and Citroën and Peugeot are the only car manufacturers in France. If these nations prohibited international trade in cars, each would have a motorcar oligopoly with only two members, and the market outcome would likely depart substantially from the competitive equilibrium. With international trade, however, the car market is a world market and the oligopoly in this example has six members. Allowing free trade increases the number of producers from which each consumer can choose, and this increased competition keeps prices closer to marginal cost. Thus, the theory of oligopoly provides a reason why all countries can benefit from free trade.

SELF TEST If the members of an oligopoly could agree on a total quantity to produce, what quantity would they choose? If the oligopolists do not act together but instead make production decisions individually, do they produce a total quantity more or less than in your answer to the previous question? Why?

Oligopolies and Kinked Demand Curves

Interdependence can have other consequences which can be seen in the existence of so-called price rigidities or price stickiness in oligopolistic markets. This is the observation that in oligopolistic market structures, prices do not change greatly over time and, given the changes in demand and supply in such markets, this might seem surprising. There is a logic to the idea of price rigidities if we assume particular conditions; these are that the products being produced are homogenous and that if a firm raises its price its rivals will not follow suit but if a firm lowers its price its rivals will follow suit and all reduce their prices.

Assume that our duopolists, Jacques and Joelle, are currently charging a price of €40 per litre. Jacques is thinking about increasing price to €50 per litre but knows that if he does Joelle will keep her price at €40 per litre. In that situation, because the product is homogenous (i.e. undifferentiated) Jacques risks customers switching to Joelle and losing sales. The demand curve facing Jacques is therefore highly price elastic at a price higher than €40 per litre.

Alternatively, Jacques might consider a strategy of reducing price from €40 to try and capture market share from Joelle. However, he knows that if he does reduce price to (say) €30 per litre, Joelle will follow suit and very quickly he will not gain any benefit from the lower price. Jacques faces a highly price inelastic demand curve at a price below €40. Our duopolists effectively face two demand curves as shown in Figure 16.1: one demand curve which is relatively price elastic, D_e, and another which is relatively price inelastic, D_i. If Jacques increases his price to €50, Joelle does not change her price and demand falls from Q_0 to Q_1. The proportionate change in demand is greater than the increase in price and Jacques sees his total revenue fall. Equally, if Jacques reduces his price to €30, Joelle follows suit and so demand only rises by a small proportion to Q_2 from Q_0. The proportionate increase in demand is less than the reduction in price and, again, Jacques sees his revenue fall.

FIGURE 16.1

The Oligopolists Kinked Demand Curve
Jacques faces two demand curves with different average elasticities. Demand curve D$_e$ is relatively elastic and demand curve D$_i$ is relatively inelastic. If Jacques increases or decreases price the response of Joelle means that his total revenue would fall in each case. There is no incentive for Jacques or Joelle to change price and the duopolists face a kinked demand curve.

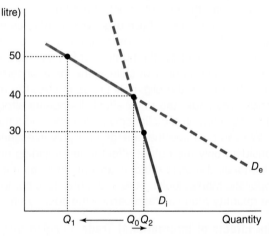

If we assume that Jacques and Joelle both behave in the same way then there is no incentive for them to change price. Neither will want to put price up if they think the other will not follow suit and if either decides to reduce price the other will, and so neither will benefit. The duopolists effectively face a kinked demand curve. At any price above €40 they face the price elastic part of the demand curve D_e and at any price below €40 they face the demand curve D_i.

If the assumptions we have made above hold, then the focus of competitive behaviour of firms in an oligopoly might be on finding ways to differentiate their products rather than attempting to compete on price – so called **non-price competition**. Types of non-price competition may include a focus on quality, service, delivery, style, design, location, convenience, packaging, advertising and promotion, branding and so on.

> **non-price competition** a situation where two or more firms seek to increase demand and market share by methods other than through changing price

There are limitations to the kinked demand curve theory which call into question the assumptions that underpin it. Empirical evidence to support the theory is limited and prices are not as sticky in oligopolies as the model assumes. Firms may engage in collusion to set price or output. There is some evidence that if one firm increases its price others may follow suit but how the firm finds the exact point of the kink in the demand curve is not clear.

GAME THEORY AND THE ECONOMICS OF COOPERATION

As we have seen, oligopolies would like to reach the monopoly outcome, but doing so requires cooperation, which at times is difficult to maintain. In this section we look more closely at the problems people face when cooperation is desirable but difficult. To analyze the economics of cooperation, we need to learn a little about game theory.

Game theory is the study of how people behave in strategic situations. By 'strategic' we mean a situation in which each person, when deciding what actions to take, must consider how others might respond to that action. Because the number of firms in an oligopolistic market is small, each firm must act strategically. Each firm knows that its profit depends not only on how much it produces but also on how much the other firms produce. In making its production decision, each firm in an oligopoly should consider how its decision might affect the production decisions of all the other firms.

> **game theory** the study of how people behave in strategic situations

Game theory is extremely useful for understanding the behaviour of oligopolies. In the following section we present some of the principles of game theory which have been applied to firms in oligopolistic markets. In any game there are players or actors (which might be firms) who face various options in decision-making which are called strategies. In making a decision (choosing a strategy) there are outcomes or payoffs that arise as a result of the decision. Each player is assumed to know their own mind and to be able to identify the payoff of the strategy they choose. However, each player knows that their opponent or rival also faces the same decisions and strategies and that these will also have associated payoffs. This has been referred to as the 'I think they think that I think that they think that I think …' scenario. Each player, therefore, has to put themselves into the position of the other player(s) before deciding on a strategy. The choices are represented as a **payoff matrix** which is a table showing the possible combination of outcomes (payoffs) depending on the strategy chosen by each player.

> **payoff matrix** a table showing the possible combination of outcomes (payoffs) depending on the strategy chosen by each player

For example, look at the payoff matrix represented by Figure 16.2.

FIGURE 16.2

Payoff Matrix
The matrix shows two players, Firm X and Firm Y and the decisions they can take with regard to keeping or breaking their agreement. The triangles show the payoff associated with their respective decisions.

Imagine that the two players are firms *X* and *Y*, who enter into an agreement to fix the price in a market. The payoff to each firm is the profit they make as a result of the agreement. Firm *X* is represented on the vertical plane of the matrix. It has two strategies – keep the agreement or break the agreement. The payoffs it faces are represented in the beige triangles of the matrix. Firm *Y* is represented on the horizontal plane of the matrix and it also faces the same strategies. Its payoffs are represented in the blue triangles of the matrix.

Assume that both Firm *X* and Firm *Y* make the decision to keep to the agreement. The payoff to both is given by looking at the top left-hand quadrant and the payoff is that both firms take a profit of €100. If Firm *X* keeps to the agreement but Firm *Y* opts to break the agreement then the payoffs are given by the top right-hand quadrant. In this case, Firm *X* will gain a profit of €50 but Firm *Y* gets a profit of €200. If Firm *Y* keeps the agreement but Firm *X* breaks the agreement the payoffs are given by the bottom left quadrant – Firm *X* gains a profit of €200 and Firm *Y* of €50. If both firms break the agreement the outcome is the bottom right quadrant and both earn a profit of €25.

The Prisoners' Dilemma

The **prisoners' dilemma** is a game which provides insight into the difficulty of maintaining cooperation. Many times in life, people fail to cooperate with one another even when cooperation would make them all better off. An oligopoly is just one example.

> **prisoners' dilemma** a particular 'game' between two captured prisoners that illustrates why cooperation is difficult to maintain even when it is mutually beneficial

The prisoners' dilemma is a story about two criminals who have been captured by the police. Let's call them Mr Green and Mr Blue. The police have enough evidence to convict Mr Green and Mr Blue of a crime, illegal distribution of cannabis, so that each would spend a year in jail given existing sentencing rules. The police also suspect that the two criminals have committed a jewellery robbery together in which a victim was badly injured, but they lack hard evidence to convict them of this major crime. The police question Mr Green and Mr Blue in separate rooms, and offer each of them the following deal:

> *With the evidence we have on the drug possession we can lock you up for 1 year. If you confess to the jewellery robbery and implicate your partner, however, we'll give you immunity and you can go free. Your partner will get 20 years in jail. But if you both confess to the crime, we won't need your testimony and we can avoid the cost of a trial, so you will each get an intermediate sentence of 8 years.*

The possible outcomes, 1 year in prison, go free, etc. are the payoffs. If Mr Green and Mr Blue care only about their own sentences, what would you expect them to do? Would they confess or remain silent? Figure 16.3 shows their choices.

FIGURE 16.3

The Prisoners' Dilemma

In this game between two criminals suspected of committing a crime, the sentence that each receives depends both on their decision whether to confess or remain silent and on the decision made by the other.

Mr Blue's decision \ Mr Green's decision	Confess	Remain silent
Confess	Mr Green gets 8 years Mr Blue gets 8 years	Mr Green gets 20 years Mr Blue goes free
Remain silent	Mr Green goes free Mr Blue gets 20 years	Mr Green gets 1 year Mr Blue gets 1 year

Each prisoner has two strategies: confess or remain silent. The sentence each prisoner gets depends on the strategy they choose and the strategy chosen by their partner in crime.

Consider first Mr Green's decision. He reasons as follows:

What is Mr Blue is going to do? If he remains silent, my best strategy is to confess, since then I'll go free rather than spending a year in jail. If he confesses, my best strategy is still to confess, since then I'll spend 8 years in jail rather than 20. So, regardless of what Mr Blue does, I am better off confessing.

In the language of game theory, a strategy is called a **dominant strategy** if it is the best strategy for a player to follow regardless of the strategies pursued by other players. In this case, confessing is a dominant strategy for Mr Green. He spends less time in jail if he confesses, regardless of whether Mr Blue confesses or remains silent.

dominant strategy a strategy that is best for a player in a game regardless of the strategies chosen by the other players

Mr Blue faces exactly the same choices as Mr Green, and he reasons in much the same way. Regardless of what Mr Green does, confessing is also a dominant strategy for Mr Blue.

In the end, both Mr Green and Mr Blue confess, and both spend 8 years in jail. Yet, from their standpoint, this is a terrible outcome. If they had *both* remained silent, both of them would have been better off, spending only 1 year in jail on the drugs charge. By each pursuing his own interests, the two prisoners together reach an outcome that is worse for each of them.

To see how difficult it is to maintain cooperation, imagine that before the police captured Mr Green and Mr Blue, the two criminals had made a pact not to confess. Clearly, this agreement would make them both better off *if* they both live up to it, because they would each spend only 1 year in jail. The temptation of both individuals, however, would be to renege on their pact. Mr Blue, for example, might reason that if Mr Green does remain silent, he can go free by confessing. Mr Green applies the same logic and self-interest takes over and leads them to confess. Cooperation between the two prisoners is difficult to maintain, because cooperation is individually irrational.

Oligopolies as a Prisoners' Dilemma

The tension between self-interest and cooperation exemplified in the prisoners' dilemma is very similar to the tensions that exist between firms in imperfect competition and particularly between oligopolistic firms. Game theory has been applied extensively to the analysis of oligopolies as a result.

Consider an oligopoly with two countries: Iran and Saudi Arabia. Both countries sell crude oil. After prolonged negotiation, the countries agree to keep oil production low in order to keep the world price of oil high. After they agree on production levels, each country must decide whether to cooperate and live up to this agreement or to ignore it and produce at a higher level. Figure 16.4 shows the payoff matrix and how the profits of the two countries depend on the strategies they choose.

If both countries stick to their agreement they would earn $50 billion in profit (the bottom right-hand quadrant). Suppose, however, you are the leader of Saudi Arabia. You might reason as follows:

I could keep production low as we agreed, or I could raise my production and sell more oil on world markets. If Iran lives up to the agreement and keeps its production low, then my country earns profit of $60 billion (oil is priced in US dollars) with high production compared to $50 billion if I stick to our agreement and maintain low production. In this case, my country is better off with high production.

If, however, Iran fails to live up to the agreement and produces at a high level, then my country earns $40 billion with high production and $30 billion with low production. Once again, my country is better off with high production. Regardless of what Iran chooses to do, my country is better off reneging on our agreement; producing at a high level is thus my dominant strategy.

Of course, Iran reasons in exactly the same way, and so both countries pursue their dominant strategy and produce at a high level. The result is the inferior outcome (from Iran and Saudi Arabia's standpoint) with each country earning $40 billion in profits instead of the $50 billion they could have earned if they had both stuck to their agreement.

FIGURE 16.4

An Oligopoly Game

In this game between members of an oligopoly, the profit that each earns depends on both its production decision and the production decision of the other oligopolist.

	Saudi Arabia's decision	
	High production	**Low production**
Iran's decision — **High production**	Saudi Arabia gets $40 billion / Iran gets $40 billion	Saudi Arabia gets $30 billion / Iran gets $60 billion
Low production	Saudi Arabia gets $60 billion / Iran gets $30 billion	Saudi Arabia gets $50 billion / Iran gets $50 billion

This example illustrates why oligopolies have trouble maintaining monopoly profits. The monopoly outcome is jointly rational for the oligopoly, but each oligopolist has an incentive to cheat. Just as self-interest drives the prisoners in the prisoners' dilemma to confess, self-interest makes it difficult for the oligopoly to maintain the cooperative outcome with low production, high prices and monopoly profits.

Other Examples of the Prisoners' Dilemma

Advertising When two firms advertise to attract the same customers, they face a problem similar to the prisoners' dilemma. For example, consider the decisions facing two chemical companies, BASF and Evonik. If neither company advertises, the two companies split the market and earn €4 million in profit. If both advertise, they again split the market, but profits are lower at 3 million each, since each company must bear the cost of advertising. If one company advertises while the other does not, the one that advertises attracts customers from the other.

FIGURE 16.5

An Advertising Game

In this game between firms selling similar products, the profit that each earns depends on both its own advertising decision and the advertising decision of the other firm.

	Evonik's decision	
	Advertise	**Don't advertise**
BASF's decision — **Advertise**	Evonik gets €3 million profit / BASF gets €3 million profit	Evonik gets €2 million profit / BASF gets €5 million profit
Don't advertise	Evonik gets €5 million profit / BASF gets €2 million profit	Evonik gets €4 million profit / BASF gets €4 million profit

Figure 16.5 shows how the profits of the two companies depend on their actions. You can see that advertising is a dominant strategy for each firm. Thus, both firms choose to advertise, even though both firms would be better off if neither firm advertised.

Common Resources Imagine that two oil companies – Shell and BP – own adjacent oil fields. Under the fields is a common pool of oil worth €12 million. Drilling a well to recover the oil costs €1 million. If each company drills one well, each will get half of the oil and earn a €5 million profit (€6 million in revenue minus €1 million in costs).

Suppose that either company could drill a second well. If one company has two of the three wells, that company gets two-thirds of the oil, which yields a profit of €6 million (two-thirds of €12 million = €8 million minus €2 million in costs to drill two wells). The other company gets the remaining one-third of the oil, for a profit of €3 million (€4 million minus €1 million in drilling costs). If each company drills a second well, the two companies again split the oil. In this case, each bears the cost of a second well, so profit is only €4 million for each company.

Figure 16.6 shows the game. Drilling two wells is a dominant strategy for each company. Once again, the self-interest of the two players leads them to an inferior outcome.

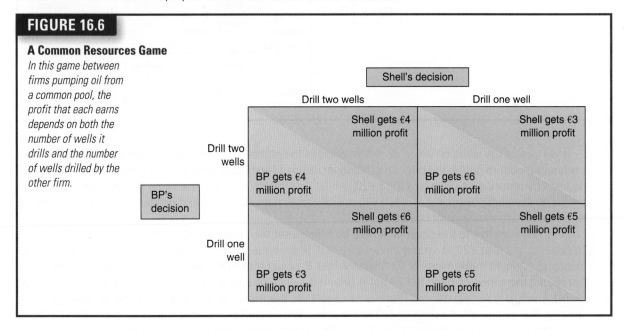

FIGURE 16.6

A Common Resources Game
In this game between firms pumping oil from a common pool, the profit that each earns depends on both the number of wells it drills and the number of wells drilled by the other firm.

Shell's decision

	Drill two wells	Drill one well
Drill two wells	Shell gets €4 million profit / BP gets €4 million profit	Shell gets €3 million profit / BP gets €6 million profit
Drill one well	Shell gets €6 million profit / BP gets €3 million profit	Shell gets €5 million profit / BP gets €5 million profit

BP's decision

Nash Equilibrium

In our analysis of Jacques and Joelle (our economic actors), we mentioned that they reach an equilibrium which meant that neither has an incentive to choose any different strategy given the strategy that the other adopted. This was referred to as a Nash equilibrium.

The story of John Nash was dramatized in the film *A Beautiful Mind*, based on a book of the same name by Sylvia Nasar. Nash entered the world of game theory in the late 1940s and 1950s and gained the Nobel Prize for Economics in 1994 for his contribution to the field. His work has had an impact on a number of economic and political situations. At the heart of Nash's ideas was the mix of both cooperative and non-cooperative games. In the former, there are enforceable agreements between players (which may be in the form of legislation or the threat of fines from a regulator or similar) whilst in the latter there are not. The key thing in both cases is that the players in the game know that they cannot predict with any certainty what the other is going to do (exactly the situation facing firms in an oligopolistic market). Equally, they know what *they* want but are aware that all the other players think as they do.

The solutions that Nash derived were based around this thinking, where each player had to try to put him or herself in the position of others. The 'equilibrium' position would be where each player makes a decision which represents the best outcome in response to what other players' decisions are. The definition of a Nash equilibrium is a point where no player can improve their position by selecting any other available strategy whilst others are also playing their best option and not changing their strategies. One of the implications of Nash's work is that cooperation may well be the best option in the long term.

Let us take an example. Assume there are two firms competing with each other for profits in a market. The two firms have three decisions to make with regard to their pricing strategies. They can choose to set their price at either €10, €20 or €30. The payoff matrix showing the profits made at these different prices is shown in Figure 16.7.

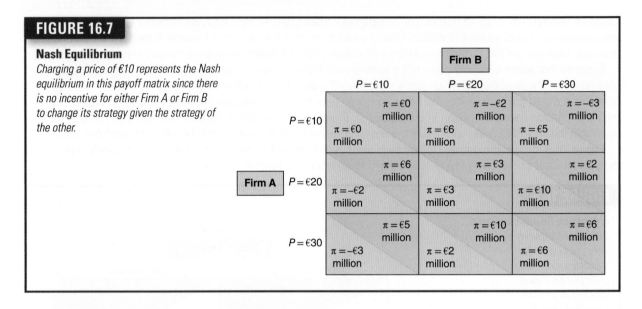

FIGURE 16.7

Nash Equilibrium
Charging a price of €10 represents the Nash equilibrium in this payoff matrix since there is no incentive for either Firm A or Firm B to change its strategy given the strategy of the other.

If we look at the situation when each firm decides to set their price at €30, they both make a profit of €6 million (the bottom right-hand box). This, however, is not a Nash equilibrium, since Firm A could improve its position by reducing its price by €10 to €20, whilst A's strategy remains the same (setting price at €30). In this case, A would now gain a profit of €10 million rather than €6 million and B would be making €2 million as shown in the middle right box of the matrix.

Let's compare this to the situation where both firms set their price at €10. In this case, if Firm A decided to raise its price to €20, it would be worse off if B continued the strategy of charging €10. In such an instance, A would make a loss of €2 million whilst B would make €6 million. The same position applies to firm B; if it increased its price to €20 but A retained a price of €10, B would now make a loss of €2 million whilst A would make €6 million. There is no incentive, therefore, for either firm to change their position; the payoff of zero profit at a price of €10 represents a Nash equilibrium. Any other pricing decision by either firm would lead to one having an incentive to change its price to gain some advantage.

The price of €10, however, is not the best outcome for either firm. If they both agreed to charge a price of €30 they would both generate profits of €6 million.

Cooperative and Non-cooperative Games Two questions arise from this: can any such agreement be enforced, and what happens if the game is repeated many times over? These were questions asked by two other Nobel Prize winning economists, Thomas C. Schelling and Robert J. Aumann, who won the Prize in 2005. Schelling looked at non-cooperative and cooperative games. Cooperative game theory assumes that there is a set of outcomes or agreements that is known to each player and that each player has preferences over these outcomes. Non-cooperative game theory assumes players have a series of strategies they could use to gain an outcome and that each player has a preference over their desired outcome. The behaviour of firms or individuals might be affected by bargaining which entails some form of conflict of interest but in essence each player will be looking to maximize their returns, whilst knowing at the same time that some agreement is preferable to no agreement at all. In this scenario, how does a player manage to influence the negotiations in order to move towards their preferred outcome without upsetting the other players and thus failing to secure any agreement – an outcome which would be disadvantageous to all concerned, including the player?

Schelling proposed that it might be in the interests of the player to worsen their own options in order to gain some sort of concession from another player. Where difficulties arise is if both parties to a conflict make commitments that are seen as being irreversible and incompatible. The result could be stalemate and potential serious conflict.

In most 'game' situations, the protagonists know something about the position of the other – but not everything. However, if there is any perceived chink in the armour of the other player and this is detected by the other, then there is a potential benefit to follow the hard route. This is why this sort of game is referred to as 'chicken' or 'hawk/dove'. Schelling included other complications to the analysis by looking at how the strategies of each player would change in light of threats and action. Schelling noted that parties will need to recognize that the costs to them of cheating or reneging and gaining some short-term benefit is far outweighed by the costs to them in the longer term of the destruction of the trust that results from cheating or reneging. The relationships between players will need to be assessed in the context of repeated playing of the game over a period of time.

This is the area that Aumann worked on – the field of long-term cooperation around game theory. We have already seen how, in the prisoners' dilemma, the dominant strategy for Mr Green and Mr Blue was to confess. Aumann asked the question about what the equilibrium outcome would be if the game were repeated over and over again, with each prisoner trying to maximize the *average* payoff from each game.

In such a situation, Aumann showed that the equilibrium outcome was to cooperate because any cheating on the agreement in the short term would be punishable by a refusal to cooperate at some point in the future – and both players would know this. Any short-term gains, therefore, are outweighed by longer-term losses. Aumann expressed this through what he referred to as a 'supergame' – that is, looking at the collection of repeated games as a whole game in itself. Aumann's work was extended to look at how groups of players might react in such situations. In an agreement between oligopolists, for example, there is always the tendency or incentive for one firm to break the agreement to seek to gain some advantage in the market. Aumann's work suggested that long-term cooperation could be 'enforced' by the many, against the few who might be seeking to defect.

The work was extended in subsequent research to try to take into account the strategies players might adopt in repeated games with incomplete information. This provides an incentive to players to hide, or seek to conceal, information from their rivals. Firms are very keen to keep their costs to themselves. If one player does manage to access information about their rivals and has some form of strategic advantage, therefore, what is the best way to utilize this knowledge? If this situation arose, would playing your hand to gain short-term benefit reveal that you did actually know more than you were letting on? For the player who does not have the information they would like, could they discover anything about the other player's position by reviewing the strategies and decisions made by that player in the past?

Such scenarios are relevant to the world of financial markets where the issue of how to manage people who have access to privileged information, such as information about market moves, potential mergers or takeovers, announcements about key corporate decisions or product launches, business plans and strategies and so on, which they can use for personal (or corporate) gain.

The Prisoners' Dilemma and the Welfare of Society

The prisoners' dilemma describes many of life's situations, and it shows that cooperation can be difficult to maintain, even when cooperation would make both players in the game better off. Clearly, this lack of cooperation is a problem for those involved in these situations. But is lack of cooperation a problem from the standpoint of society as a whole? The answer depends on the circumstances.

In some cases, the non-cooperative equilibrium is bad for society as well as the players. In the common resources game in Figure 16.6, the extra wells dug by Shell and BP are pure waste. In both cases, society would be better off if the two players could reach the cooperative outcome. By contrast, in the case of oligopolists trying to maintain monopoly profits, lack of cooperation is desirable from the standpoint of society as a whole. The monopoly outcome is good for the oligopolists, but it is bad for the consumers of the product.

Why People Sometimes Cooperate

Cartels sometimes do manage to maintain collusive arrangements, despite the incentive for individual members to defect. Very often, the reason that players can solve the prisoners' dilemma is that they play the game not once but many times.

Let's return to our duopolists, Jacques and Joelle who would like to maintain the monopoly outcome in which each produces 30 litres, but self-interest drives them to an equilibrium in which each produces 40 litres. Figure 16.8 shows the game they play. Producing 40 litres is a dominant strategy for each player in this game.

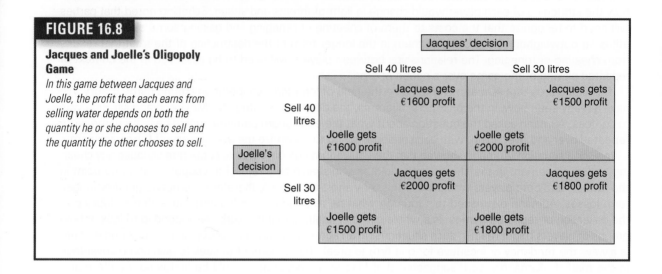

FIGURE 16.8

Jacques and Joelle's Oligopoly Game

In this game between Jacques and Joelle, the profit that each earns from selling water depends on both the quantity he or she chooses to sell and the quantity the other chooses to sell.

Jacques' decision

	Sell 40 litres	Sell 30 litres
Joelle's decision Sell 40 litres	Jacques gets €1600 profit / Joelle gets €1600 profit	Jacques gets €1500 profit / Joelle gets €2000 profit
Sell 30 litres	Jacques gets €2000 profit / Joelle gets €1500 profit	Jacques gets €1800 profit / Joelle gets €1800 profit

Imagine that Jacques and Joelle try to form a cartel. To maximize total profit they would agree to the cooperative outcome in which each produces 30 litres. Yet, if Jacques and Joelle are to play this game only once, neither has any incentive to live up to this agreement. Self-interest drives each of them to renege and produce 40 litres. If Jacques takes the decision to renege on the agreement and produce 40 litres he stands to earn €2000 in profit. Joelle thinks exactly the same way and so they both end up producing 40 litres and earning €1600 in profit.

Now suppose that Jacques and Joelle know that they will play the same game every week. When they make their initial agreement to keep production low, they can also specify what happens if one party reneges. They might agree, for instance, that once one of them reneges and produces 40 litres, both of them will produce 40 litres forever after. This penalty is easy to enforce, for if one party is producing at a high level, the other has every reason to do the same.

The threat of this penalty may be all that is needed to maintain cooperation. Each person knows that defecting would raise his or her profit from €1800 to €2000 but this benefit would last for only one week. Thereafter, profit would fall to €1600 and stay there. As long as the players care enough about future profits, they will choose to forgo the one-time gain from defection. Thus, in a game of repeated prisoners' dilemma, the two players may well be able to reach the cooperative outcome.

Tacit Collusion A repeated games scenario might also lead to a market outcome in which some form of collusion is suspected but in fact has arisen out of firms recognizing that they are interdependent. When firm behaviour results in a market outcome that appears to be anti-competitive, but has arisen because firms acknowledge that they are interdependent, this is referred to as **tacit collusion**. An example can be seen in typical out-of-town shopping malls where several firms have outlets all selling similar goods – carpets, electrical goods, furniture and so on. Shopping around these stores, customers might have their suspicions aroused by the fact that regardless of the store, the prices are all very similar and in some cases identical. Even the promotional material promising to refund the difference if the customer can find the same good elsewhere cheaper looks to be an empty promise given the price similarity.

tacit collusion when firm behaviour results in a market outcome that appears to be anti-competitive but has arisen because firms acknowledge that they are interdependent

Is this an example of collusion? Have all the firms got together and fixed prices? Not necessarily. This may be a case of tacit collusion. A firm selling LED TVs in one part of the shopping mall is likely to be aware that if it charges a price higher than its rivals, it will lose sales but equally it knows that if it competes aggressively on price its rivals are likely to follow suit. Each retailer thinks the same way and so prices tend to be very similar across the mall. In some cases, retailers will attempt to signal to their rivals that they will respond in kind by offering price guarantees such as the offer of refunds (which effectively means the store is saying to its rivals, 'if you charge a lower price we will match it') and confidently predicting that customers will not find the product at a lower price anywhere else (within reason of course). These sorts of messages might be thought of as being targeted at the customer but they can also be seen as being targeted just as much at rivals, hence the suggestion that collusion is taking place albeit the collusion is tacit.

CASE STUDY   **The Prisoners' Dilemma Tournament**

Political scientist, Robert Axelrod, held a tournament which invited people to send in computer programs designed to play repeated prisoners' dilemma games. Each program played the game against other programmes and the winner was the programme that received the fewest total years in prison. The winner turned out to be a simple strategy called *tit-for-tat*. In such a strategy, a player begins by cooperating and then does whatever the other player did last time. A tit-for-tat player cooperates until the other player defects so then carries on defecting until the other player cooperates again. The strategy starts out friendly, penalizes unfriendly players, and forgives them if warranted. Axelrod found that this simple strategy did better than other more complicated strategies people had sent in. The strategy is based around the idea that penalties must be imposed for non-cooperation but that the option of returning to a cooperative outcome is possible and even preferable. In the example of Jacques and Joelle above, the threat to produce 40 litres forever after one of them reneges is referred to as a *grim trigger strategy* since it leads to an end of cooperation forever following the first defection. In contrast, tit-for-tat is referred to as a *softer trigger strategy* which allows for forgiveness and a return to cooperation.

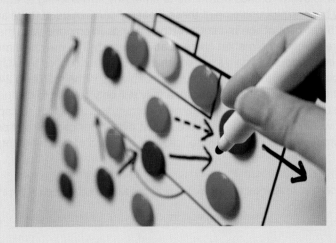

Game theory provides an insight into understanding strategic decision-making.

SELF TEST Tell the story of the prisoners' dilemma. Write down a table showing the prisoners' choices and explain what outcome is likely. What does the prisoners' dilemma teach us about oligopolies?

ENTRY BARRIERS IN OLIGOPOLY

Oligopolistic firms have the characteristic that they act strategically. We have looked at game theory as a way of explaining the interdependence of firms in oligopolies and how this can affect their behaviour. In addition, oligopolistic firms might benefit from the fact that there are barriers to entry to the industry which limits new competitors from entering the market. Where firms in an oligopoly are large, they may benefit from economies of scale which mean that firms operate at a lower point on the long-run average cost curve. New potential entrants will find it difficult to enter because they will not have the same economies of scale and as a result will have higher unit costs and have to charge higher prices. This limits their ability to compete.

In addition it is also likely that new entrants will face high set-up costs to enter an industry dominated by a relatively small number of firms. High set-up costs may mean that it will be some years before a new entrant begins to generate profits and implies that they must have the financial resources to be able to survive making losses whilst they become established. Invariably, set-up costs may be sunk costs which cannot be recovered if the potential new entrant were to exit the market having not been successful in competing. Oligopolistic firms might make this situation worse by advertising. Existing firms may have large budgets devoted to advertising not simply to inform customers but as a means of erecting a barrier to entry. If a new entrant is seeking to compete in such a market, they may also have to advertise heavily to make consumers aware of them in an attempt to attract business away from the established firms. The high costs of advertising simply increase the set-up costs and act as a further deterrent to entry.

The existence of patents is an obvious barrier to entry. For firms in oligopolistic markets, a patent not only provides the means by which the firm can recover the cost of developing new products by charging higher prices whilst competition is limited but also gives it time to be able invest in research and development (R&D) to bring more new products to market. Firms seeking to enter these markets must be able to finance R&D, which again requires significant financial reserves and other resources, not least highly skilled labour.

An investigation into some of the major oligopolistic markets such as alcohol, beauty and household care reveals that firms have relatively large numbers of brands. Procter and Gamble, for example, have Ariel, Daz, Dreft, Lenor, Bold 2in1 and Fairy, all of which are brands in the market for washing clothes. It may be that these brands are designed to cater for different market segments but they might also act as a barrier to entry, because they give little space for a new market entrant. Other firms in the clothes washing market might each have multiple brands and as a result the market may be characterised by **brand proliferation**. Oligopolistic firms might reason that some consumers will be very loyal to a particular brand but that there will always be some consumers who switch brands from time to time. Any firm seeking to enter a market to capture profits which exist may hope to pick up some of these 'floating' consumers. If there are only four firms and only four brands and 25 per cent of the market switches brands in any one year then the new entrant may be able to pick up a relatively large market share relatively quickly. The new firm might expect to attract a quarter of the floating consumers and gain a market share of 6.25 per cent as a result. However, if each of the four firms have six brands each then the total number of brands in the market is 24, and it will be much harder for a new entrant to build market share because they will only be able to capture a smaller slice of the brand switching consumer. In this example, the new entrant would expect to capture 1/24th of the floating consumers which would give it a market share of just over 1 per cent. Brand proliferation, therefore, may be a worthwhile strategy for an oligopolist to follow as a means of deterring entry.

brand proliferation a strategy designed to deter entry to a market by producing a number of products within a product line as different brands

PUBLIC POLICY TOWARD OLIGOPOLIES

Cooperation among oligopolists is seen as undesirable from the standpoint of society as a whole, because it leads to production that is too low and prices that are too high. To prevent this, policymakers may attempt to induce firms in an oligopoly to compete rather than cooperate.

Restraint of Trade and Competition Law

One way that policy discourages cooperation is through the common law. Normally, freedom of contract is an essential part of a market economy. Businesses and households use contracts to arrange mutually advantageous trades. In doing this, they rely on the court system to enforce contracts. Yet, for many centuries, courts in Europe and North America have deemed agreements among competitors to reduce quantities and raise prices to be contrary to the public interest. They have therefore refused to enforce such agreements.

Given the long experience of many European countries in tackling abuses of market power, it is perhaps not surprising that competition law is one of the few areas in which the European Union has been able to agree on a common policy. The European Commission can refer directly to the Treaty of Rome to prohibit price-fixing and other restrictive practices such as production limitation, and is especially likely to do so where a restrictive practice affects trade between EU member countries. The EU Competition Commission sets out its role as follows:

The antitrust area covers two prohibition rules set out in the Treaty on the Functioning of the European Union.

- *First, agreements between two or more firms which restrict competition are prohibited by Article 101 of the Treaty, subject to some limited exceptions. This provision covers a wide variety of behaviours. The most obvious example of illegal conduct infringing [the Article] is a cartel between competitors (which may involve price-fixing or market sharing).*
- *Second, firms in a dominant position may not abuse that position (Article 102 of the Treaty). This is, for example, the case for predatory pricing aiming at eliminating competitors from the market.*

The Commission is empowered by the Treaty to apply these prohibition rules and enjoys a number of investigative powers to that end (e.g. inspection in business and non-business premises, written requests for information, etc.). It may also impose fines on undertakings that violate EU antitrust rules. Since 1 May 2004, all national competition authorities are also empowered to apply fully the provisions of the Treaty in order to ensure that competition is not distorted or restricted. National courts may also apply these prohibitions so as to protect the individual rights conferred to citizens by the Treaty.

Controversies over Competition Policy

Over time, much controversy has centred on the question of what kinds of behaviour competition law should prohibit. Most commentators agree that price-fixing agreements among competing firms should be illegal. Yet competition law has been used to condemn some business practices whose effects are not obvious. Here we consider three examples.

Resale Price Maintenance One example of a controversial business practice is *resale price maintenance,* also called *fair trade.* Imagine that RS Electronics sells Blu-ray players to retail stores for €50. If RS requires the retailers to charge customers €75, it is said to engage in resale price maintenance. Any retailer that charged less than €75 would have violated its contract with RS.

At first, resale price maintenance might seem anti-competitive and, therefore, detrimental to society. Like an agreement among members of a cartel, it prevents the retailers from competing on price. For this reason, the courts have often viewed resale price maintenance as a violation of competition law.

Yet some economists defend resale price maintenance on two grounds. First, they deny that it is aimed at reducing competition. To the extent that RS Electronics has any market power, it can exert that power through the wholesale price, rather than through resale price maintenance. Moreover, RS has no incentive to discourage competition among its retailers. Indeed, because a cartel of retailers sells less than a group of competitive retailers, RS would be worse off if its retailers were a cartel.

Second, economists believe that resale price maintenance has a legitimate goal. RS may want its retailers to provide customers with a pleasant showroom and a knowledgeable sales force. Yet, without resale price maintenance, some customers would take advantage of one store's service to learn about the Blu-ray player's special features and then buy the item at a discount retailer that does not provide this service. To some extent, good service is a public good among the retailers that sell RS' products. When one person provides a public good, others are able to enjoy it without paying for it. In this case, discount retailers would free ride on the service provided by other retailers, leading to less service than is desirable. Resale price maintenance is one way for RS to solve this free-rider problem.

The example of resale price maintenance illustrates an important principle: business practices that appear to reduce competition may in fact have legitimate purposes. This principle makes the application of competition law all the more difficult. The competition authorities in each EU nation under the European Competition Network are in charge of enforcing these laws and must determine what kinds of behaviour public policy should prohibit as impeding competition and reducing economic well-being. Often that job is not easy.

Predatory Pricing Firms with market power normally use that power to raise prices above the competitive level. But should policymakers ever be concerned that firms with market power might charge prices that are too low? This question is at the heart of a second debate over competition policy.

Imagine that a large airline, call it Eurovia Airlines, has a monopoly on some route. Then Euro Express enters and takes 20 per cent of the market, leaving Eurovia with 80 per cent. In response to this competition, Eurovia starts slashing its fares. Some anti-trust analysts argue that Eurovia's move could be anti-competitive: the price cuts may be intended to drive Euro Express out of the market so Eurovia can recapture its monopoly and raise prices again. Such behaviour is called *predatory pricing*.

Although it is common for companies to complain to the relevant authorities that a competitor is pursuing predatory pricing, some economists are sceptical of this argument and believe that predatory pricing is rarely, and perhaps never, a profitable business strategy. Why? For a price war to drive out a rival, prices have to be driven below cost. Yet if Eurovia starts selling cheap tickets at a loss, it is likely that it will have to fly more planes, because low fares will attract more customers. Euro Express, meanwhile, can respond to Eurovia's predatory move by cutting back on flights. As a result, Eurovia ends up bearing more than 80 per cent of the losses, putting Euro Express in a good position to survive the price war.

Economists continue to debate whether predatory pricing should be a concern for competition policymakers. Various questions remain unresolved. Is predatory pricing ever a profitable business strategy? If so, when? Are the authorities capable of telling which price cuts are competitive and thus good for consumers and which are predatory? There are no simple answers.

Tying A third example of a controversial business practice is *tying*. Suppose that Makemoney Movies produces two new films – *Spiderman* and *Hamlet*. If Makemoney offers cinemas the two films together at a single price, rather than separately, the studio is said to be tying its two products.

Some economists have argued that the practice of tying should be banned. Their reasoning is as follows: imagine that *Spiderman* is a blockbuster, whereas *Hamlet* is an unprofitable art film. Then the studio could use the high demand for *Spiderman* to force cinemas to buy *Hamlet*. It seems that the studio could use tying as a mechanism for expanding its market power.

Other economists are sceptical of this argument. Imagine that cinemas are willing to pay €20 000 for *Spiderman* and nothing for *Hamlet*. Then the most that a cinema would pay for the two films together is €20 000 – the same as it would pay for *Spiderman* by itself. Forcing the cinema to accept a worthless film as part of the deal does not increase the cinema's willingness to pay. Makemoney cannot increase its market power simply by bundling the two films together.

Why, then, does tying exist? One possibility is that it is a form of price discrimination. Suppose there are two cinemas. City Cinema is willing to pay €15 000 for *Spiderman* and €5000 for *Hamlet*. Country Cinema is just the opposite: it is willing to pay €5000 for *Spiderman* and €15 000 for *Hamlet*. If Makemoney charges separate prices for the two films, its best strategy is to charge €15 000 for each film, and each cinema chooses to show only one film. Yet if Makemoney offers the two films as a bundle, it can charge each cinema €20 000 for the films. Thus, if different cinemas value the films differently, tying may allow the studio to increase profit by charging a combined price closer to the buyers' total willingness to pay.

Tying remains a controversial business practice. Microsoft has been investigated for 'tying' its internet browser and other software like its Windows Media Player with its Windows operating system. The argument that tying allows a firm to extend its market power to other goods is not well founded, at least in its simplest form. Yet economists have proposed more elaborate theories for how tying can impede competition. Given our current economic knowledge, it is unclear whether tying has adverse effects for society as a whole.

All the analysis is based on an assumption that rivals may have sufficient information to be able to make a decision and that the decision will be a rational one. In reality firms do not have perfect information and do not behave rationally. Most firms in oligopolistic markets work very hard to protect sensitive information and only give out what they have to by law. Some information may be given to deliberately obfuscate the situation and hide what their true motives/strategies/tactics are. Economists have tried to include these imperfections into theories. Behavioural economics has become more popular in recent years because of the fact that it offers some greater insights into the *observed* behaviour of the real world which often does not conform to the assumptions of rationality.

SELF TEST What kind of agreement is illegal for businesses to make? Why is competition law controversial?

CONCLUSION

Oligopolies would like to act like monopolies, but self-interest drives them closer to competition. Thus, oligopolies can end up looking either more like monopolies or more like competitive markets, depending on the number of firms in the oligopoly and how cooperative the firms are. The story of the prisoners' dilemma shows why oligopolies can fail to maintain cooperation, even when cooperation is in their best interest.

Policymakers regulate the behaviour of oligopolists through competition law. The proper scope of these laws is the subject of ongoing controversy. Although price fixing among competing firms clearly reduces economic welfare and is declared as being illegal in many countries, some business practices that appear to reduce competition may have legitimate if subtle purposes. As a result, policymakers need to be careful when they use the substantial powers of competition law to place limits on firm behaviour.

IN THE NEWS

Oligopolies

Some oligopolistic markets become more concentrated over time as firms merge or get taken over. Does this increased concentration mean firms need to advertise less?

Market Concentration and Advertising

The market for alcohol is oligopolistic. It is dominated by four large firms and in recent years has become more concentrated as rival firms merge. In 2008, InBev and Anheuser-Busch merged to form AB InBev and in 2015, AB InBev made several offers to take over SAB Miller culminating in an almost $70 billion (€61.4bn) agreement in October 2015. SAB Miller itself had grown as a result of merger; in 2008 Miller and Coors merged. Ambarish Chandra of the University of Toronto and Matthew Weinberg of Drexel University looked at the relationship between market structure and advertising and their research suggested that greater market concentration actually leads to increased advertising spending per capita.

Their findings were counter to one of the early theories of advertising which predicted that advertising was primarily a means of competition and as markets became more concentrated, advertising spending would fall. Chandra and Weinberg's findings were more similar to theories of advertising put forward by Lester G. Telser of the University of Chicago in 1964, which suggested that advertising can help a firm with market power to increase that power by creating barriers to entry and hence reducing the potential of losing market share. Other theories, such as Dorfman and Steiner in 1954, hypothesized that when markets become more concentrated, there are cost savings for firms which free up resources for more advertising. Chandra and Weinberg found little evidence to support this idea. Instead, they argue that lower distribution costs experienced by Miller and Coors went to finance price reductions instead of increased advertising.

(*Continued*)

Chandra and Weinberg sought to explain the increased advertising by Miller and Coors in terms of spill-over effects. If one brewer advertises its brands heavily then this not only raises awareness of the brands to consumers but also raises awareness of other brands from other brewers. As a market becomes more concentrated, firms recognize the spill-over benefits of advertising as a positive externality affecting awareness and demand for its wider range of brands secured through merger and takeover. Firms being aware of these spill-over effects make the strategic decision to increase spending on advertising not simply because they are seeking to inform or attract customers and thus provide a benefit to the customer but because there are wider benefits to the firm itself.

The Austrian school look at advertising, not from the lens of whether it is wasteful and more or less likely in competitive or concentrated market structures but as a factor of production which entrepreneurs will purchase to enable them to sell products at prices higher than costs of production. Economists of the Austrian school such as Mises and Menger argue that looking at a model of the firm based on perfect competition as a starting point and introducing increasing degrees of imperfection to look at how firm behaviour changes is largely meaningless. Perfect knowledge, they argue, does not exist. In the model of perfect competition, of course, firms are price-takers and goods are homogenous so there is no need to advertise. Economists in the Austrian school argue that the cost of advertising is no different to any other cost of production. It is, as a result, no more or no less the cause of higher prices nor a waste of resources than spending on any other factor of production. If a firm spends money on advertising and it does not have the ultimate effect of increasing sales and revenues then the only resources that have been wasted is the firm's itself; these are not society's resources.

Questions

1 Explain the logic that the more competitive a market the higher the likely advertising spend.

2 Are firms in an oligopoly more or less likely to spend on advertising if the products they are selling are homogenous?

3 When firms in an oligopolistic market structure merge and the resulting entity has an increased number of brands, why might it be strategically beneficial for the new entity to expand advertising?

4 To what extent do you agree with the view that firms in an oligopoly can use advertising as a barrier to entry? Justify your argument.

5 Consider the view of the Austrian school that advertising is not wasteful and that the cost of advertising is no different to any other cost of production.

The brewing industry is highly concentrated, dominated by a small number of very large firms.

Sources: Chandra, Ambarish and Weinberg, Matthew, 'How Does Advertising Depend on Competition?' Evidence from U.S. Brewing (June 22, 2015). Rotman School of Management Working Paper No. 2621899. Available at SSRN: http://ssrn.com/abstract=2621899 or http://dx.doi.org/10.2139/ssrn.2621899; 'Advertising and Competition', Lester G. Telser, *Journal of Political Economy*, Vol. 72, No. 6 (Dec., 1964), pp. 537–62; 'Optimal Advertising and Optimal Quality', Robert Dorfman and Peter O. Steiner, *The American Economic Review*, Vol. 44, No. 5 (Dec., 1954), pp. 826–36

SUMMARY

● Oligopolists maximize their total profits by forming a cartel and acting like a monopolist. Yet, if oligopolists make decisions about production levels individually, the result is a greater quantity and a lower price than under the monopoly outcome. The larger the number of firms in the oligopoly, the closer the quantity and price will be to the levels that would prevail under competition.

- The prisoners' dilemma shows that self-interest can prevent people from maintaining cooperation, even when cooperation is in their mutual interest. The logic of the prisoners' dilemma applies in many situations, including advertising, common-resource problems and oligopolies.

- Policymakers use competition law to prevent oligopolies from engaging in behaviour that reduces competition. The application of these laws can be controversial, because some behaviour that may seem to reduce competition may in fact have legitimate business purposes.

QUESTIONS FOR REVIEW

1 What is meant by the term concentration ratio?

2 What are the main characteristics of an oligopolistic market structure?

3 If a group of sellers could form a cartel, what quantity and price would they try to set?

4 Compare the quantity and price of an oligopoly with those of a monopoly and a competitive market.

5 How does the number of firms in an oligopoly affect the outcome in its market?

6 What is the kinked demand curve and why might it be a feature of an oligopolistic market?

7 What is the prisoners' dilemma, and what does it have to do with oligopoly?

8 What effect might repeated playing of the prisoners' dilemma have on the equilibrium of an oligopoly?

9 What ways might oligopolists use to restrict entry to an industry?

10 What kinds of behaviour do the competition laws prohibit?

PROBLEMS AND APPLICATIONS

1 A large share of the world supply of diamonds comes from Russia and South Africa. Suppose that the marginal cost of mining diamonds is constant at €1000 per diamond, and the demand for diamonds is described by the following schedule:

Price (€)	Quantity
8 000	5 000
7 000	6 000
6 000	7 000
5 000	8 000
4 000	9 000
3 000	10 000
2 000	11 000
1 000	12 000

a. If there were many suppliers of diamonds, what would be the price and quantity?

b. If there was only one supplier of diamonds, what would be the price and quantity?

c. If Russia and South Africa formed a cartel, what would be the price and quantity? If the countries split the market evenly, what would be South Africa's production and profit? What would happen to South Africa's profit if it increased its production by 1000 while Russia stuck to the cartel agreement?

d. Use your answer to part (c) to explain why cartel agreements are often not successful.

2 This chapter discusses companies that are oligopolists in the market for the goods they sell. Many of the same ideas apply to companies that are oligopolists in the market for the inputs they buy. If sellers who are oligopolists try to increase the price of goods they sell, what is the goal of buyers who are oligopolists?

3 Describe several activities in your life in which game theory could be useful. What is the common link among these activities?

4 Suppose that you and a fellow student are assigned a project on which you will receive one combined grade. You each want to receive a good grade (which means you have to work), but you also want to do as little work as possible (which means you shirk). In particular, here is the situation:

- If both of you work hard, you both get an A, which gives each of you 40 units of happiness.
- If only one of you works hard, you both get a B, which gives each of you 30 units of happiness.
- If neither of you works hard, you both get a D, which gives each of you 10 units of happiness.

a. Fill in the payoffs in the following matrix:

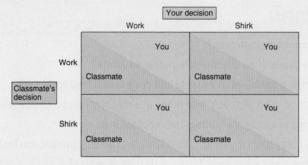

b. What is the likely outcome? Explain your answer.

c. If you get this person as your partner on a series of projects throughout the year, rather than only once, how might that change the outcome you predicted in part b?

d. Another person on your course cares more about good grades. They get 50 units of happiness for a B and 80 units of happiness for an A. If this person was your partner (but your preferences were unchanged), how would your answers to parts a. and b. change? Which of the two partners would you prefer? Would they also want you as a partner?

5 Synergy and Dynaco are the only two firms in a specific hi-tech industry. They face the following payoff matrix as they decide upon the size of their research budget.

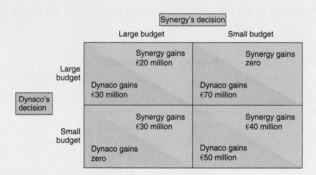

a. Does Synergy have a dominant strategy? Explain.

b. Does Dynaco have a dominant strategy? Explain.

c. Is there a Nash equilibrium for this scenario? Explain.

6 In the 1970s, concern over the health effects of tobacco led to many countries banning tobacco advertising on television.

a. Why might tobacco companies have not fought too hard against the ban?

b. In the wake of the ban, the profits of tobacco companies rose. Why might this scenario have occurred?

c. Could the ban still be good public policy even though tobacco company profits grew? Explain your answer.

7 Assume that two airline companies decide to engage in collusive behaviour.

Let's analyze the game between two such companies. Suppose that each company can charge either a high price for tickets or a low price. If one company charges €100, it earns low profits if the other company charges €100 also, and high profits if the other company charges €200. On the other hand, if the company charges €200, it earns very low profits if the other company charges €100, and medium profits if the other company charges €200 also.

a. Draw the payoff matrix for this game.

b. What is the Nash equilibrium in this game? Explain.

c. Is there an outcome that would be better than the Nash equilibrium for both airlines? How could it be achieved? Who would lose if it were achieved?

8 Farmer Wild and Farmer Scott graze their cattle on the same field. If there are 20 cows grazing in the field, each cow produces €4000 of milk over its lifetime. If there are more cows in the field, then each cow can eat less grass, and its milk production falls. With 30 cows on the field, each produces €3000 of milk; with 40 cows, each produces €2000 of milk. Cows cost €1000 apiece.

a. Assume that Farmer Wild and Farmer Scott can each purchase either 10 or 20 cows, but that neither knows how many the other is buying when they make their purchase. Calculate the payoffs of each outcome.

b. What is the likely outcome of this game? What would be the best outcome? Explain.

c. There used to be more common fields than there are today. Why?

9 Little Kona is a small coffee company that is considering entering a market dominated by Big Brew. Each company's profit depends on whether Little Kona enters and whether Big Brew sets a high price or a low price:

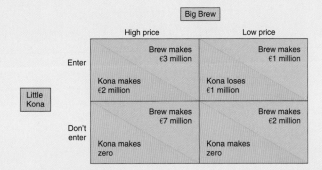

Big Brew threatens Little Kona by saying, 'If you enter, we're going to set a low price, so you had better stay out.' Do you think Little Kona should believe the threat? Why or why not? What do you think Little Kona should do?

10 Consider an oligopoly with four firms who decide to engage in a price war. Can there be any winners in this war?

PART 7
FACTOR MARKETS

17 THE ECONOMICS OF FACTOR MARKETS

The labour market consists of people who are willing to offer their skills and services and those who wish to buy these services. People earn income in various ways. Wages, salaries and fringe benefits such as pension provision, health insurance and bonuses, form the majority of income for labour in most economies but income can also be earned from self-employment.

Labour markets present a fascinating insight into the many debates which take place within economics and other disciplines on fundamental aspects of our lives. The vast majority of people will have to work to support their living. The income they get in return for this work can be explained in terms of the basic principles of the model of supply and demand. There are, however, many imperfections in labour markets (as there are in most other markets) and there are different theories as to why wages differ and indeed, what we should include when looking at labour markets. This chapter will explore some of these different approaches to labour markets.

THE MARGINAL PRODUCT THEORY OF DISTRIBUTION

We are going to begin by looking at the marginal product theory of distribution. This theory is based on the demand and supply of factors of production (in this case labour) and makes assumptions that employers and workers operate in a perfectly competitive market. The model assumes that labour is free to enter and exit the market, and firms are equally free to employ and shed labour at will – in other words, people can move into and out of work easily and employers can 'hire and fire' workers when they need to. The theory was developed by US economist, John Bates Clark in the 1880s, a time when marginal analysis was a feature of economic thinking. Clark applied the principles of marginal product to all factors of production. Here, we will look at its application to labour.

THE DEMAND FOR LABOUR

The demand for labour comes from employers. Labour is not desired for its own sake but for what it adds to output. The demand for a factor of production, as a result, is referred to as a **derived demand**. That is, a firm's demand for a factor of production is derived (determined) from its decision to supply a good in another market. The demand for computer programmers is inextricably tied to the supply of computer software, and the demand for petrol station attendants is inextricably tied to the supply of petrol.

 derived demand a situation where demand is determined by the supply in another market

Firms, thus, hire workers because of what they contribute to production and the payment to workers (the wage) is the price that employers have to pay to hire those labour services.

The Competitive Profit-Maximizing Firm

To help our analysis, we will use the example of an apple producer. The firm owns an apple orchard and during the harvesting period must decide how many apple pickers to hire to pick the crop. After the firm makes its hiring decision, the workers pick apples, the firm then sells the apples, pays the workers, and keeps what is left as profit. We assume that our firm is *competitive* both in the market for apples (where it is a seller) and in the market for apple pickers (where it is a buyer). Because there are many other firms selling apples and hiring apple pickers, a single firm takes the price and the wage as given by market conditions. It only has to decide how many workers to hire and how many apples to sell. We also assume that the firm is *profit-maximizing* and does not directly care about the number of workers it has or the number of apples it produces. The firm's supply of apples and its demand for workers are derived from its primary goal of maximizing profit.

The Production Function and the Marginal Product of Labour

In hiring labour, the firm considers how the number of apple pickers affects the quantity of apples it can harvest and sell. Table 17.1 gives a numerical example. In the first column is the number of workers. In the second column is the quantity of apples the workers harvest each week. These two columns of numbers describe the firm's ability to produce a quantity of output as a result of labour inputs holding all other factors constant, such as technology, the number of trees, quality of the land, transport and so on. This firm's production function based on Table 17.1, is graphed in Figure 17.1. It shows that if the firm hires one worker, that worker will pick 1000 kilos of apples per week. If the firm hires two workers, the two workers together will pick 1800 kilos per week, and so on.

The third column in Table 17.1 gives the **marginal product of labour**, the increase in the amount of output from an additional unit of labour. When the firm increases the number of workers from 1 to 2, for example, the amount of apples produced rises from 1000 to 1800 kilos. Therefore, the marginal product of the second worker is 800 kilos.

TABLE 17.1 **How the Competitive Firm Decides How Much Labour to Hire**

Labour	Output	Marginal product of labour	Value of the marginal product of labour	Wage	Marginal profit
L (number of workers)	Q (kilos per week)	$MP_L = \Delta Q / \Delta L$ (kilos per week)	$VMP_L = P \times MP_L$ (€)	W (€)	$\Delta Profit = VMP_L - W$ (€)
0	0				
		1000	1000	500	500
1	1000				
		800	800	500	300
2	1800				
		600	600	500	100
3	2400				
		400	400	500	−100
4	2800				
		200	200	500	−300
5	3000				

marginal product of labour the increase in the amount of output from an additional unit of labour

As the number of workers increases and because other factors are fixed, the marginal product of labour declines. When only a few workers are hired, they pick apples from the best trees in the orchard. As the number of workers increases, additional workers have to pick from the trees with fewer apples. Hence, as more and more workers are hired, each additional worker contributes less to the production of apples which explains why the production function in Figure 17.1 becomes flatter as the number of workers rises.

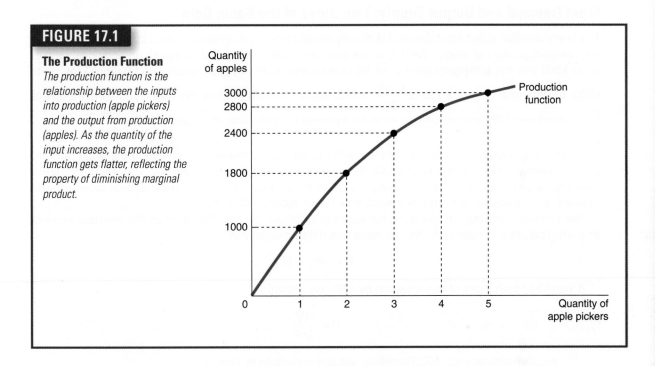

FIGURE 17.1

The Production Function
The production function is the relationship between the inputs into production (apple pickers) and the output from production (apples). As the quantity of the input increases, the production function gets flatter, reflecting the property of diminishing marginal product.

The Value of the Marginal Product and the Demand for Labour

Our profit-maximizing firm considers how much profit each worker would bring in. The profit from an additional worker is the worker's contribution to revenue minus the worker's wage.

The worker's contribution to revenue is found by taking the price of apples and multiplying this by the amount of apples the worker produces. If a kilo of apples sells for €1 and an additional worker produces 800 kilos of apples, then the worker produces €800 of revenue for the firm.

The **value of the marginal product** of any input is the marginal product of that input multiplied by the market price of the output. You might also see this referred to as the *marginal physical product* (MPP). The fourth column in Table 17.1 shows the value of the marginal product of labour in our example, assuming the price of apples is €1 per kilo. Because the market price is constant for a competitive firm, the value of the marginal product diminishes as the number of workers rises. Economists sometimes call this column of numbers the firm's **marginal revenue product**: it is the extra revenue the firm gets from hiring an additional unit of a factor of production.

value of the marginal product the marginal product of an input times the price of the output
marginal revenue product the extra revenue a firm gets from hiring an additional unit of a factor of production

Suppose that the market wage for apple pickers is €500 per week, Table 17.1 shows that the first worker the firm hires yields €1000 in revenue, or €500 in profit. The second worker yields €800 in additional revenue, or €300 in profit. The third worker produces €600 in additional revenue, or €100 in profit. After the third worker, however, hiring workers is unprofitable. The fourth worker would yield only €400 of additional revenue. Because the worker's wage is €500, hiring the fourth worker would mean a €100 reduction in profit. Thus, the firm hires only three workers. A competitive, profit-maximizing firm hires workers up to the point where the value of the marginal product of labour equals the wage. The firm's labour demand curve is the value of marginal product curve and tells us the quantity of labour that a firm demands at any given wage.

Input Demand and Output Supply: Two Sides of the Same Coin

The firm's decision about input demand is closely linked to its decision about output supply. Consider how the marginal product of labour (MP_L) and marginal cost (MC) are related. Suppose an additional worker costs €500 and has a marginal product of 50 kilos of apples. In this case, producing 50 more kilos costs €500; the marginal cost of a kilo is $\frac{€500}{50} = €10$. More generally, if W is the wage, and an extra unit of labour produces MP_L units of output, then the marginal cost of a unit of output is $MC = \frac{W}{MP_L}$

Diminishing marginal product is closely related to increasing marginal cost. When our apple orchard grows crowded with workers, each additional worker adds less to the production of apples (MP_L falls). Similarly, when the apple firm is producing a large quantity of apples, the orchard is already crowded with workers, so it is costlier to produce an additional kilo of apples (MC rises).

The profit-maximizing firm chooses the quantity of labour so that the value of the marginal product ($P \times MP_L$) equals the wage (W). We can write this mathematically as:

$$P \times MP_L = W$$

If we divide both sides of this equation by MP_L, we obtain:

$$P = \frac{W}{MP_L}$$

$\frac{W}{MP_L}$ equals marginal cost, MC. Therefore, we can substitute to obtain:

$$P = MC$$

The price of the firm's output is equal to the marginal cost of producing a unit of output. *Thus, when a competitive firm hires labour up to the point at which the value of the marginal product equals the wage, it also produces up to the point at which the price equals marginal cost.*

What Causes the Labour Demand Curve to Shift?

The labour demand curve reflects the value of the marginal product of labour. The labour demand curve will shift in the following circumstances:

The Output Price If the output price changes, the value of the marginal product changes, and the labour demand curve shifts. An increase in the price of apples, for instance, raises the value of the marginal product of each worker who picks apples and, therefore, increases labour demand from the firms that supply apples. Conversely, a decrease in the price of apples reduces the value of the marginal product and decreases labour demand.

Technological Change Technological advances raises the marginal product of labour through increasing productivity which is defined as the amount produced per time period per worker. This in turn increases the demand for labour. Such technological advances can explain persistently rising employment in the face of rising wages.

The Supply of Other Factors The quantity available of one factor of production can affect the marginal product of other factors. A fall in the supply of ladders, for instance, will reduce the marginal product of apple pickers and thus the demand for apple pickers.

SELF TEST Define *marginal product of labour* and *value of the marginal product of labour*. Describe how a competitive, profit-maximizing firm decides how many workers to hire.

THE SUPPLY OF LABOUR

Individuals offer their labour services in return for payment (wages and salaries) and represent the supply of labour.

The Trade-Off between Work and Leisure

When considering how much labour to supply, it is assumed that people face a trade-off between work and leisure. The more hours you spend working, the fewer hours you have to watch TV, socialize with friends or pursue your favourite hobby. In considering this trade-off, individuals have to consider the opportunity cost of leisure.

If your wage is €15 per hour, the opportunity cost of an hour of leisure is €15. If you get a pay rise to €20 per hour, the opportunity cost of enjoying leisure goes up.

The labour supply curve reflects how workers' decisions about the labour–leisure trade-off respond to a change in that opportunity cost. An upward sloping labour supply curve means that an increase in the wage induces workers to increase the quantity of labour they supply. Because time is limited, more hours of work mean that workers are enjoying less leisure. That is, workers respond to the increase in the opportunity cost of leisure by taking less of it.

How Do Wages Affect Labour Supply?

We can analyze how a person decides to allocate their time between work and leisure by using the concepts of income and substitution effects.

Cristina is a freelance software designer. Cristina is awake for 100 hours per week. She spends some of this time going out with friends, watching television, going to the cinema and night clubs, and so on, and the rest of her time developing software on her computer. For every hour she spends developing software, she earns €50, which she spends on consumption goods. Thus, her wage (€50) reflects the trade-off Cristina faces between leisure and consumption. For every hour of leisure she gives up, she works one more hour and gets €50 to spend on consumption.

Figure 17.2 shows Cristina's budget constraint. If she spends all 100 hours enjoying leisure, she has no consumption. If she spends all 100 hours working, she earns a weekly consumption of €5000 but has no time for leisure. If she works a normal 40-hour week, she enjoys 60 hours of leisure and has weekly consumption of €2000.

Figure 17.2 uses indifference curves to represent Cristina's preferences for consumption and leisure. If it is assumed that Cristina always prefers more leisure and more consumption, she prefers points on higher indifference curves to points on lower ones. At a wage of €50 per hour, Cristina could work 80 hours a week, enjoy 20 hours of leisure and earn €4000 as shown by point A on indifference curve I_1. However, her optimum is a combination of consumption and leisure represented by the point labelled B where she enjoys 60 hours of leisure and earns €2000. This is the point on the budget constraint that is on the highest possible indifference curve, which is curve I_2.

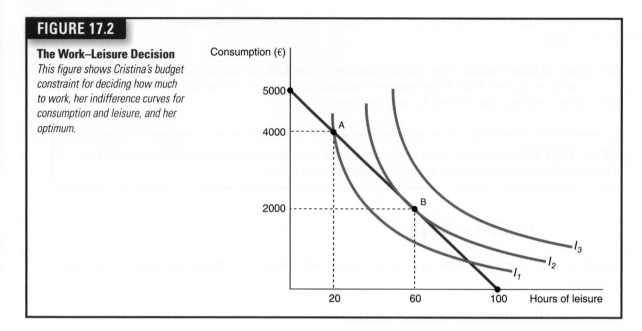

FIGURE 17.2

The Work–Leisure Decision
This figure shows Cristina's budget constraint for deciding how much to work, her indifference curves for consumption and leisure, and her optimum.

Figure 17.3 shows two possible outcomes if Cristina's wage increases from €50 to €60 per hour. In each case, the budget constraint, shown in the left-hand graph, pivots outward from BC_1 to BC_2 and becomes steeper, reflecting that at the higher wage, Cristina can get more consumption for every hour of leisure she gives up.

In both panels, consumption rises. Yet the response of leisure to the change in the wage is different in the two cases. In panel (a), Cristina responds to the higher wage by enjoying less leisure. In panel (b), Cristina responds by enjoying more leisure.

In each panel, the right-hand graph in Figure 17.3 shows the labour supply curve implied by Cristina's decision between leisure and consumption and thus her supply of labour. In panel (a), a higher wage induces Cristina to enjoy less leisure and work more, so the labour supply curve slopes upward. In panel (b), a higher wage induces Cristina to enjoy more leisure and work less, so the labour supply curve slopes 'backwards'.

The reason for this backward bending supply curve comes from considering the income and substitution effects of a higher wage.

When Cristina's wage rises, leisure becomes more costly relative to consumption, and this encourages Cristina to substitute consumption for leisure and work more hours; this is the substitution effect. As Cristina's wage rises, however, she moves to a higher indifference curve. She is now better off than she was. As long as consumption and leisure are both normal goods, she tends to want to use this increase in well-being to enjoy both higher consumption and greater leisure. At a higher wage rate, she could work fewer hours and still be better off and this effect tends to make the labour supply curve slope backwards. This is the result of the income effect.

In the end, economic theory does not give a clear prediction about whether an increase in the wage induces Cristina to work more or less. If the substitution effect is greater than the income effect for Cristina, she works more. If the income effect is greater than the substitution effect, she works less. The labour supply curve, therefore, could be either upwards or backwards sloping.

This concept has an important application to debates over the effect of tax cuts on work. Some economists argue that cutting taxes encourages people to work more hours because the reward is greater. Such an argument is also used as the basis for supporting an entrepreneurial culture – keep taxes low and this encourages entrepreneurs. Others point out that lower taxes do increase disposable income but workers may now use this higher income to enjoy more leisure and not work additional hours. Having some idea of the relative strength of the income and substitution effects is important in analyzing and assessing such policy initiatives.

FIGURE 17.3

An Increase in the Wage

The two panels of this figure show how a person might respond to an increase in the wage. The graphs on the left show the consumer's initial budget constraint BC_1 and new budget constraint BC_2, as well as the consumer's optimal choices over consumption and leisure. The graphs on the right show the resulting labour supply curve. Because hours worked equal total hours available minus hours of leisure, any change in leisure implies an opposite change in the quantity of labour supplied. In panel (a), when the wage rises, consumption rises and leisure falls, resulting in a labour supply curve that slopes upwards. In panel (b), when the wage rises, both consumption and leisure rise, resulting in a labour supply curve that slopes backwards.

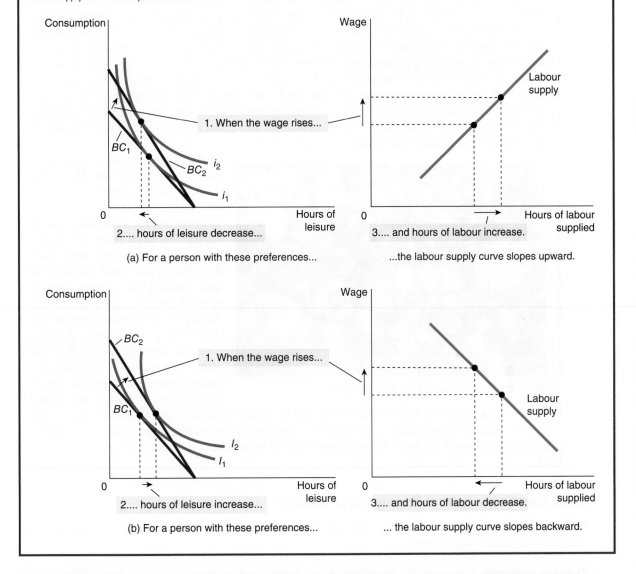

(a) For a person with these preferences...

...the labour supply curve slopes upward.

(b) For a person with these preferences...

... the labour supply curve slopes backward.

CASE STUDY **Income Effects on Labour Supply: Historical Trends, Lottery Winners and the Carnegie Conjecture**

The idea of a backwards sloping labour supply curve might at first seem like a mere theoretical curiosity, but in fact it is not. Evidence indicates that the labour supply curve, considered over long periods of time, does in fact slope backwards. A hundred years ago many people in Europe and North America worked six days a week. Today five-day working weeks are the norm. At the same time that

(*Continued*)

the length of the working week has been falling, the wage of the typical worker (adjusted for inflation) has been rising.

Here is how economists explain this historical pattern: over time, advances in technology raise workers' productivity and, thereby, the demand for labour. The increase in labour demand raises equilibrium wages. As wages rise, so does the reward for working. Yet rather than responding to this increased incentive by working more, many workers choose to take part of their greater prosperity in the form of more leisure. In other words, the income effect of higher wages dominates the substitution effect.

Further evidence that the income effect on labour supply is strong comes from a very different kind of data: winners of lotteries. Winners of large prizes in the lottery see large increases in their incomes and, as a result, large outward shifts in their budget constraints. Because the winners' wages have not changed, however, the *slopes* of their budget constraints remain the same. There is, therefore, no substitution effect. By examining the behaviour of lottery winners, we can isolate the income effect on labour supply. Nearly all the research on the effects of winning the lottery on labour supply has so far been done in the USA, but the results are striking. Of those winners who win more than $50 000, almost 25 per cent quit working within a year, and another 9 per cent reduce the number of hours they work. Of those winners who win more than $1 million, almost 40 per cent stop working. The income effect on labour supply of winning such a large prize is substantial.

Would you continue to work if you won the lottery?

Similar results were found in a study, published in the May 1993 issue of the *Quarterly Journal of Economics*, of how receiving a bequest affects a person's labour supply. The study found that a single person who inherits more than $150 000 is four times as likely to stop working as a single person who inherits less than $25 000. This finding would not have surprised the 19th-century industrialist Andrew Carnegie. Carnegie warned that 'the parent who leaves his son enormous wealth generally deadens the talents and energies of the son, and tempts him to lead a less useful and less worthy life than he otherwise would'. That is, Carnegie viewed the income effect on labour supply to be substantial and, from his paternalistic perspective, regrettable. During his life and at his death, Carnegie gave much of his vast fortune to charity.

What Causes the Labour Supply Curve to Shift?

The labour supply curve shifts whenever people change the amount they want to work at a given wage. This could be due to the following.

Changes in Norms A generation or two ago, it was the norm for women to stay at home while raising children. Today, family sizes are smaller and more mothers choose to work. The result is an increase in the supply of labour.

Changes in Alternative Opportunities The supply of labour in any one labour market depends on the opportunities available in other labour markets. If the wage earned by pear pickers suddenly rises, some apple pickers may choose to switch occupations. As a result the supply of apple pickers falls.

Immigration Movement of workers from region to region, or country to country, is an obvious and often important source of shifts in labour supply. When immigrants move from one European country to another, the supply of labour increases and contracts in the respective countries concerned. In fact, much of the policy debate about immigration centres on its effect on labour supply and, thereby, equilibrium in the labour market.

> **SELF TEST** Who has a greater opportunity cost of enjoying leisure – a shelf stacker in a supermarket or a leading cancer surgeon? Explain. Can this help explain why doctors work such long hours?

EQUILIBRIUM IN THE LABOUR MARKET

Under the assumptions of a competitive market, two points can be noted:

- The wage adjusts to balance the supply and demand for labour.
- The wage equals the value of the marginal product of labour.

Figure 17.4 shows the labour market in equilibrium where the wage and the quantity of labour have adjusted to balance supply and demand.

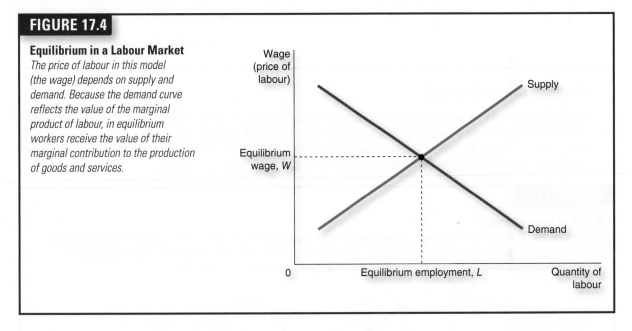

FIGURE 17.4

Equilibrium in a Labour Market
The price of labour in this model (the wage) depends on supply and demand. Because the demand curve reflects the value of the marginal product of labour, in equilibrium workers receive the value of their marginal contribution to the production of goods and services.

Profit maximizing firms have hired workers until the value of the marginal product equals the wage. Hence, the wage must equal the value of the marginal product of labour once it has brought supply and demand into equilibrium. Any event that changes the supply or demand for labour must change the equilibrium wage and the value of the marginal product by the same amount, because these must always be equal. To see how this works, let's consider some events that shift these curves.

Shifts in Labour Supply

Suppose that immigration increases the number of workers willing to pick apples. As Figure 17.5 shows, the supply of labour shifts to the right from S_1 to S_2. At the initial wage W_1, the quantity of labour supplied now exceeds the quantity demanded. This surplus of labour puts downward pressure on the wage of apple pickers, and the fall in the wage from W_1 to W_2 in turn makes it profitable for firms to hire more workers. As the number of workers employed in each apple orchard rises, the marginal product of a worker falls, and so does the value of the marginal product. In the new equilibrium, both the wage and the value of the marginal product of labour are lower than they were before the influx of new workers.

FIGURE 17.5

A Shift in Labour Supply
When labour supply increases from S₁ to S₂, perhaps because of immigration of new workers, the equilibrium wage falls from W₁ to W₂. At this lower wage, firms hire more labour, so employment rises from L₁ to L₂. The change in the wage reflects a change in the value of the marginal product of labour: with more workers, the added output from an extra worker is smaller.

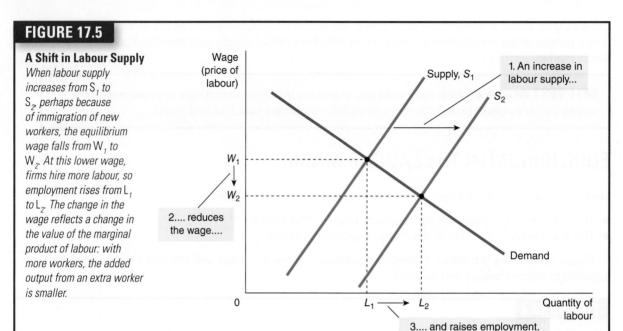

Shifts in Labour Demand

Now suppose that an increase in the popularity of apples causes their price to rise. This price increase raises the *value* of the marginal product. With a higher price of apples, hiring more apple pickers is now profitable. As Figure 17.6 shows, when the demand for labour shifts to the right from D_1 to D_2, the equilibrium wage rises from W_1 to W_2, and equilibrium employment rises from L_1 to L_2.

FIGURE 17.6

A Shift in Labour Demand
When labour demand increases from D₁ to D₂, perhaps because of an increase in the price of the firms' output, the equilibrium wage rises from W₁ to W₂ and employment rises from L₁ to L₂. The change in the wage reflects a change in the value of the marginal product of labour: with a higher output price, the added output from an extra worker is more valuable.

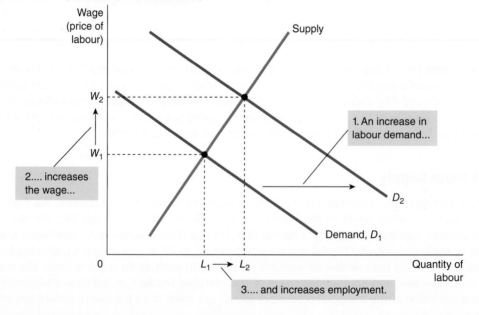

Under the assumptions of competitive labour markets, therefore, labour supply and labour demand together determine the equilibrium wage, and shifts in the supply or demand curve for labour cause the equilibrium wage to change. At the same time, profit maximization by the firms that demand labour will lead to an equilibrium wage which equals the value of the marginal product of labour.

SELF TEST How does emigration of workers from a country affect labour supply, labour demand, the marginal product of labour and the equilibrium wage?

OTHER THEORIES OF THE LABOUR MARKET

The model of the labour market we have looked at so far in this chapter is based on assumptions that labour is free to move from one job to another and that profit maximizing firms will employ workers up to the point where the wage rate is equal to the value of the marginal product the additional workers adds. This neoclassical theory is one of several which seek to explain the labour market. We are now going to look at a Marxist interpretation of the labour market.

MARXIST LABOUR THEORY

In Chapter 5 we referred to the distinction made between value in use and value in exchange. Adam Smith argued that the labour which went into production helped determine the value in exchange. It has to be remembered that theories of the labour market were being developed at a time when agricultural production dominated most economies in which economists were working. David Ricardo observed that the factor inputs of labour and land and the resulting output, was not just dependent on labour but the quality and thus productivity of the land being used. More productive land required less labour to produce a given output and so landowners could charge higher rent for more productive land. The rent for land is determined by the demand for and supply of land with the more productive land generating rent which the landlord, effectively, does nothing to earn and which represents surplus value. The relevance of Ricardo's insight into rent is that it highlighted the fact that returns to factor inputs other than labour could be explained at least in part by the idea of surplus value.

Marx looked at the labour theory of value, and in particular the idea of surplus value. According to Marx, goods have a use value which relates to the fact that most goods have some use in consumption and are purchased because they have some value to the consumer. Goods also have an exchange value which is the ratio of exchange between different goods, for example, one economics textbook might be exchanged for twenty bottles of beer. The overall value of any good is determined by the labour which goes into producing them which is referred to as the *socially necessary time*. The **socially necessary time** is the average labour contribution workers make to production. If workers, on average, could produce 10 units of a good but one worker took twice as long to produce 10 units, it would not mean the price of the good in which labour takes longer should be double. Marx saw labour as no different to any other commodity in a capitalist economy where the price of a product was related to its value. The value of a good combines what Marx called *dead labour* and *living labour*. **Dead labour** refers to all the labour which has been used in the past to produce the capital goods and raw materials used in the production of a good. **Living labour** is the labour utilized in the production of the good itself. Any good produced has a value which is given by the labour expended in production, both dead and living. In a competitive capitalist economy, therefore, the wage that labour receives should reflect its value.

---

socially necessary time the quantity of labour necessary under average conditions of labour productivity to produce a given commodity
dead labour labour used in the past to produce capital goods and raw materials used in the production of a good
living labour labour utilised in the production of the good itself

In a subsistence economy, labour produces just enough to survive and if all people were surviving in a subsistence economy there would be no social division – everyone would be the same. Once productivity increases beyond subsistence, there will be a surplus – people will produce more than they need to survive (necessary labour) and be able to use this surplus labour for exchange. Marx suggested that this surplus labour is taken by the ruling classes, those who do not need to work simply for subsistence. Surplus value in a capitalist society is the revenue of the bourgeois class, provided by workers (the proletariat), without the latter receiving any value in exchange. The commodities produced by the worker, however, do have value in exchange in a capitalist society which is based on specialisation and the division of labour. This implies that commodities are not being produced for consumption by producers but for exchange. The labour time that goes into making commodities as a cost of production has implications for the relative prices between goods. If one good takes twice the time to produce, it is likely to have a price which is around twice that of the other good. Over history, Marx argued, the production and exchange of commodities becomes generalized and based on accounting systems denominated in worker hours. This is the origin of the labour theory of value explored by Adam Smith, Ricardo and others and developed by the marginalist school of which James Bates Clark was one.

Not all workers have the same skills and abilities – in order to reward time spent training and honing skills, wages need to be higher. When markets changed in early capitalist society with one good becoming less important and another becoming more important (for example, the transition from transport based on the horse to that of the automobile), the labour hours expended on transport based on the horse was less socially necessary than labour hours in the automobile industry. The productivity of workers in the horse transport industry may not have changed in actual terms but the value of that productivity in terms of the ability of the entrepreneur to exchange the output becomes worth less. Profits fall. In the automobile industry, the workers' output is worth more and as a result profits rise. If entrepreneurs can raise productivity above the average it generates additional surplus. In so doing, of course, the average productivity also rises until surplus profit disappears. In a capitalist system the entrepreneur can hire workers at a price which is less than the total value of the output produced; workers do not need all of the value of what they produce to live and so the entrepreneur is able to use this surplus value for their own benefit. The wage of a worker is thus a fraction of the day's labour they provide.

Entrepreneurs/employers would not hire workers if this difference did not exist because buying labour would generate no benefit to the employer. If we look at the price of any commodity we can say that the price is made up of the cost of the factors of production which went into making it –land, labour, capital and enterprise. Land, in itself, is of no value unless labour is applied to it and capital is generated by labour so ultimately it can be argued that labour is the source of all value.

Marx's theory was a theory of the historical development of class struggles which culminates in the struggle between the working class and employers in a capitalist system, the latter being in a position to exploit surplus value through being invested in different powers, such as those given by property rights. Workers in a capitalist system do not have any power over their own production; the output of their production is not used for themselves as was the case in subsistence economies, but by the employer. Where employers were large firms with elements of monopoly power, workers had even less power and were more likely to be exploited by being paid lower wages.

FEMINIST ECONOMICS AND THE LABOUR MARKET

In discussions of the labour market, labour is invariably presented as a generic term which does not specify the gender of labour being referred to. In the neo-classical model, the assumptions relating to the determination of the wage rate through the interaction of the supply and demand for labour, treat all labour as if it were the same and that the 'labour market' consists only of those willing and able to work at the going wage rate and sell their services for a monetary exchange. The output of workers employed is considered 'productive' and contributes to well-being as defined by gross domestic product.

Feminist economists suggest that far from being treated homogenously, women are routinely discriminated against in the labour market which is dominated by males. The neo-classical model stresses the trade-off between work and leisure. Workers are free to make choices between work and leisure and this implies that non-work activities (i.e. leisure) are somehow pleasurable. This trade-off helps determine the supply of labour. Feminist economists argue that far from making a choice between work and leisure, many women work in the home bringing up children and looking after the household which is not classed as 'productive' work in the neo-classical model but which contributes considerably to well-being and welfare. This 'work' is ignored in the neo-classical model. This approach to analyzing the labour market, it is argued, is too narrow and does not adequately reflect the supply of labour.

Feminist economics analyzes the social norms which exist in the labour market. Later in this chapter we will look at discrimination more widely but in respect to women, feminist economics points not to differences due to the supply and demand of women in the labour market and their different abilities and skills but the way in which women are perceived. For example, there are stereotypes and social constraints often related to perceptions of women's role in society as being primarily based on bringing up children and being part of a non-wage economy in the household. The existence of these social norms combined with the dominance of males in decision-making positions of power mean that women's job choices are inappropriately narrow and wage rates are lower than is typical of their male counterparts.

The tools of economic analysis, the use of econometrics and the fundamental assumptions that underlie models in economics, such as the theory of wage determination, attempt to explain why wages differ for women. According to feminist economists, these tools and models fail to explore and question fundamental aspects of the differences which exist between men and women. Many of the 'traditional' economic models assume rational behaviour, the pursuit of self-interest and autonomy in decision-making and feminist economists (amongst others) argue that these assumptions are subject to question, especially when it comes to gender. For example, if social and political institutions drive women down the road of the caring professions as a career choice, the idea of autonomy in decision-making breaks down.

One area of research of feminist economics has been the reasons for occupational segregation. Why are women often 'encouraged' down the road of the caring professions as a career rather than other occupational routes? Part of the explanation they offer is that social, political and institutional structures are inherently discriminating between males and females. In part these social and political structures focus on the role of women in the home. For women who do stay at home (not always by choice) and raise children and look after the family, there is a considerable amount of labour expended in this role but it is unpaid. If this were a 'normal' labour market based on the exchange of labour services, what sort of wage would women get? The answers to this question has important consequences for policy making and for wage determination in occupations which mirror the work done by women in the household. For example, for those women who are working in the caring professions, does the wage they get paid equate with estimations of similar work done in the household if quantitative studies were carried out to arrive at such figures? Would such estimations highlight even further than many feminist economists already suspect, that wages in these caring professions is held artificially low by discrimination?

Market power within the labour market gives rise to different outcomes than that predicted by a model based on the assumptions of perfect competition. In our analysis of the supply and demand of labour at the start of this chapter, for example, labour as a factor input in a market was assumed to be a mutually beneficial exchange between the employer (the owner of the apple orchard) and the workers (apple pickers). In many labour markets the existence of power in the hands of employers may mean that the exchange is more beneficial to them than to workers and to women in particular.

That power might help to explain why women get paid less than men in many cases and why women face barriers to progression in some jobs. These are not reasons which form part of the assumptions of the neo-classical theory of the labour market where workers are free to enter and exit the labour market, and where there are no barriers to them progressing if they have the right skills and abilities which reflect the value of marginal product.

MONOPSONY

The role of power in the labour market can also be seen in the case of **monopsony**, a market in which there is a single (or dominant) buyer. Imagine the labour market in a small town dominated by a single large employer. That employer can use its market power to exert an influence on the going wage and conditions of workers.

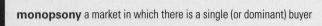

> **monopsony** a market in which there is a single (or dominant) buyer

A monopsony is in many ways similar to a monopoly. A monopsony firm in a labour market hires fewer workers than would a competitive firm: by reducing the number of jobs available, the monopsony firm moves along the labour supply curve, reducing the wage it pays and raising its profits. The existence of monopsonists reduce economic activity in a market below the socially optimal level, distorts outcomes and causes deadweight losses.

Figure 17.7 illustrates the situation. In a competitive market the employer would hire L_1 workers at a wage rate of W_1 where the demand curve for labour intersects the supply curve for labour. In a situation where an employer has monopsony power, the employer will take into account that fact that the supply curve for labour represents the average cost of labour. At the competitive wage W_1, the number of people employed is L_1 and so the total cost of employing L_1 workers is the wage rate multiplied by the number of workers ($W_1 \times L_1$). The average cost of employing labour is thus the total cost divided by the number of workers, which is the wage rate W_1.

FIGURE 17.7

The Wage Rate and Employment Level in a Monopsony
An employer with monopsony power will set the number of workers employed where the marginal cost of labour equals the marginal product. The monopsonist will employ a lower number of workers than the competitive market outcome and at a lower wage rate.

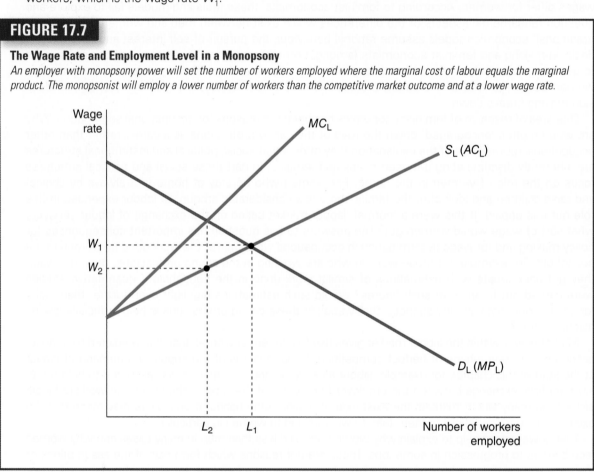

A monopsonist will look to equate the marginal cost of labour with the marginal product. The MC of labour will be higher than the average cost of labour if the average cost of labour is rising. Each additional unit of labour employed must be higher than the average to keep the average rising. The MC of labour is shown by the curve MC_L. If the monopsonist sets the employment level where the MC of labour equals the MP of labour, the number of workers employed will be L_2, lower than the competitive number of workers employed. If the employer wishes to employ L_2 amount of labour then the wage rate workers will accept will be given by the supply curve of labour at W_2. The wage rate in a monopsony situation will therefore be lower than the competitive wage rate.

Monopsonies are likely to be relatively rare although on a small scale, a number of towns in parts of Europe may be highly dependent on a major employer – a motor vehicle manufacturer, a steel works or chocolate manufacturer, for example. In such situations, the analysis may have to be amended to take into consideration the effect that monopoly power of the employer has on the local labour market.

WAGE DIFFERENTIALS

In most economies there are significant differences in the earnings of workers. To understand the wide variation in earnings that we observe, we must go beyond the general framework of the model of the labour market and examine more precisely what determines the supply and demand for different types of labour and the role of power and social norms.

Compensating Differentials

When a worker is deciding whether to take a job, there are a number of non-monetary characteristics which are taken into account. Individuals are not simply motivated by self-interest and rationality but also by altruism, compassion, duty, relationships, a belief in community and a sense of fairness. Those choosing jobs in the caring professions, for example, might be motivated far more by a desire to care and the satisfaction gained in helping vulnerable people than by the wage. Equally, some jobs require few skills and carry limited responsibilities and these might be important to workers; others might require considerable skill and experience, some of which may be very dull whilst others can be very dangerous. The way individuals judge these non-monetary characteristics determines how many people are willing (and able) to do the job at any given wage. The supply of labour for jobs requiring limited skills, little experience and which carry few responsibilities may be greater than the supply of labour for highly skilled and dangerous jobs. As a result, these types of jobs tend to have lower equilibrium wages than those which require high skill levels and experience.

Economists use the term **compensating differential** to refer to a difference in wages that arises from non-monetary characteristics of different jobs. Compensating differentials are prevalent in the economy. Here are some examples:

> **compensating differential** a difference in wages that arises to offset the non-monetary characteristics of different jobs

- Workers who maintain and repair major roads, such as motorways, are paid more than other public sector workers who repair roads in towns and cities. This is because the danger level of working on major roads is much higher, not to mention the fact that they often have to work unsociable hours (when drivers are not using the motorways).
- Workers who work night shifts at factories and in other forms of employment such as 24-hour retail outlets are paid more than similar workers who work day shifts. The higher wage compensates them for having to work at night and sleep during the day, a lifestyle that most people find undesirable (and disorientating!).
- University lecturers and professors are on average paid less than lawyers and doctors, who have similar levels of education. Lecturers' lower wages are offset by the intellectual and personal satisfaction that their jobs offer.
- Heterodox economists (those who adopt methodologies and approaches which are considered outside the mainstream of economics) argue that far from adopting a positive approach to estimating compensating differentials, there is much normative judgement in considering compensating differentials which can lead to distortions in the labour market and differences in wages as a result. Feminist economists, for example, argue that some societal norms are based on judgements about the innate abilities of men and women and their capabilities, and have an impact on wage rates and opportunity.

The view that women are not as physically capable as men to do certain jobs or that women are more adept in the caring professions is a normative judgement and affects policy decisions and reinforces stereotypes. The result is that women tend to be funnelled towards low-paid and low-status jobs that have little to do with compensating differentials.

Human Capital

Human capital is the accumulation of investments in people. The most important type of human capital is education. Like all forms of capital, education represents an expenditure of resources at one point in time to raise productivity in the future. But, unlike an investment in other forms of capital, an investment in education is tied to a specific person, and this linkage is what makes it human capital.

> **human capital** the accumulation of investments in people, such as education and on-the-job training

It is argued that workers with more human capital will earn more than those with less human capital. University graduates in Europe and North America, for example, earn almost twice as much over their working life as those workers who end their education after secondary school. This large difference tends to be even larger in less developed countries, where educated workers are in scarce supply.

The human capital argument suggests that firms are willing to pay more for the highly educated because they have higher marginal products. Workers are willing to pay the cost of becoming educated only if there is a reward for doing so. In essence, the difference in wages between highly educated workers and less educated workers may be considered a compensating differential for the cost of becoming educated.

Human capital theory presents a causal relationship between education and training, increases in productivity and as a result, wages. The theory implies that the reason why women earn less than men can be explained, in part, by differences in human capital endowment. Feminist economists argue that the neo-classical model assumes that women choose to not invest as much in education or have less experience or training opportunities compared to men due to having to take time off their careers to raise families. Because of their other non-work responsibilities, women may choose to enter into lower paid jobs which provide more flexibility in managing their work and family lives. These explanations, it is argued, are underpinned by an assumption that female earnings supplement male earnings in the family household. Feminist economists argue that these assumptions lead to policy decisions on training and legislation on the flexibility of labour markets that are inappropriate because they do not fundamentally address the discrimination of women in the workplace nor change the societal norms under which decisions are made.

Ability, Effort and Chance

Football players in the top European leagues such as the English Premiership or the Spanish *La Liga* get paid more than those in the minor leagues partly because they have greater natural ability. Natural ability is important for workers in all occupations. Because of heredity and upbringing, people differ in their physical and mental attributes. Some people have physical and mental strength, whereas others have less of both. Some people are able to solve complex problems, others less so. Some people are outgoing, others awkward in social situations. These and many other personal characteristics determine how productive workers are and, therefore, play a role in determining the wages they earn.

Closely related to ability is effort. Some people are prepared to put long hours and considerable effort into their work whereas others are content to do what they are required to do and no more. Firms may be prepared to reward workers directly by paying people on the basis of what they produce and those who put in more effort may be more productive. Salespeople, for instance, are often paid based on a percentage of the sales they make. At other times, greater effort is rewarded less directly in the form of a higher annual salary or a bonus.

Chance also plays a role in determining wages. If a person attended college to learn how to repair analogue devices and then found this skill made obsolete by the developments in digital technology, he or she would end up earning a low wage compared to others with similar years of training. The low wage of this worker is due to chance.

An Alternative View of Education: Signalling

Some economists have proposed an alternative theory to human capital theory, which emphasizes that firms use educational attainment as a way of sorting between high-ability and low-ability workers. According to this view, when people earn a university degree, for instance, they do not become more productive, but they do *signal* their high ability to prospective employers. It is rational, therefore, for firms to interpret a degree as a signal of ability.

In the signalling theory of education, schooling has no real productivity benefit, but the worker signals their innate productivity to employers by their willingness to spend years at school. The action is being taken not for its intrinsic benefit but because the willingness to take that action conveys private information to someone observing it.

The Superstar Phenomenon

Although most actors earn little and often take other jobs to support themselves, some earns millions of pounds for taking part in a production. Similarly, while most people who play tennis do it for free as a hobby, some earn millions on the professional circuit. These individuals are superstars in their fields, and often their great public appeal is reflected in astronomical incomes.

To understand the tremendous incomes of some individuals, we must examine the special features of the markets in which they sell their services. Superstars arise in markets that have two characteristics:

- Every customer in the market wants to enjoy the good supplied by the best producer.
- The good is produced with a technology that makes it possible for the best producer to supply every customer at low cost.

If Daniel Craig, for example, is the best actor around, then everyone will want to see his next film; seeing twice as many films by an actor half as good is not a valued substitute. Moreover, it is *possible* for everyone to enjoy Daniel Craig's acting skills. Because it is easy to make multiple copies of a film, Daniel Craig can provide his service to millions of people simultaneously. According to Box Office Mojo, Daniel Craig's lifetime gross total box office takings amount to $1 358 414 547, an average of $59 061 502 per film (and that was before the release of the 2015 James Bond film, 'Spectre'); that's a considerable value of marginal product to film producers! Similarly, because sport is broadcast on television, millions of fans can enjoy the athletic skills of footballers, rugby players, athletes, basketball players and so on.

Above-Equilibrium Wages: Minimum Wage Laws, Unions and Efficiency Wages

For some workers, wages are set above the level that brings supply and demand into equilibrium. We are going to look at three possible reasons for this.

Minimum Wage Laws Minimum wage laws are an example of a price floor. **Minimum wage** laws dictate the lowest price for labour that any employer may pay. Panel (a) of Figure 17.8 shows the labour market with the wage adjusting to balance labour supply and labour demand.

> **minimum wage** the lowest price an employer may legally pay to a worker

Panel (b) of Figure 17.8 shows the labour market with a minimum wage. If the minimum wage is above the equilibrium level, the quantity of labour supplied exceeds the quantity demanded. The result is unemployment. Thus, the minimum wage raises the incomes of those workers who have jobs, but it lowers the incomes of those workers who cannot find jobs.

To understand fully the minimum wage, keep in mind that the economy contains not a single labour market, but many labour markets for different types of workers. The impact of the minimum wage depends, in part, on the skill and experience of the worker.

FIGURE 17.8

How the Minimum Wage Affects the Labour Market

Panel (a) shows a labour market in which the wage adjusts to balance labour supply and demand. Panel (b) shows the impact of a binding minimum wage. Because the minimum wage is a price floor, it causes a surplus: the quantity of labour supplied exceeds the quantity demanded. The result is unemployment. Panel (c) shows that the more elastic labour demand is, the higher will be ensuing unemployment. In panel (d), because the minimum wage is binding across the whole industry, firms are able to pass a higher proportion of the wage costs on to higher prices without a drastic fall in demand for output, and so the labour demand curve for an individual firm actually shifts to the right at or above the minimum wage, so that the impact on employment is much less.

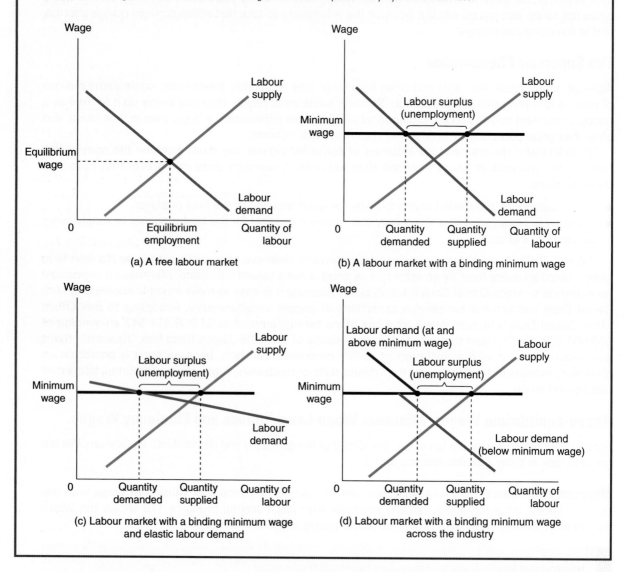

(a) A free labour market

(b) A labour market with a binding minimum wage

(c) Labour market with a binding minimum wage and elastic labour demand

(d) Labour market with a binding minimum wage across the industry

Workers with high skills and much experience are not affected, because their equilibrium wages are well above the minimum. For these workers, the minimum wage is not binding. One would therefore expect a diagram such as that in panel (b) of Figure 17.8, where the minimum wage is above the equilibrium wage and unemployment results, to apply primarily to the market for low-skilled and teenage labour. Note, however, that the *extent* of the unemployment that results depends upon the elasticities of the supply and demand for labour. In panel (c) of Figure 17.8 we have redrawn the diagram with a more elastic demand curve for labour and we can see that this results in a higher level of unemployment. It is often argued that the demand for unskilled labour is in fact likely to be highly elastic with respect to the price of labour because employers of unskilled labour, such as fast food restaurants, usually face highly price-elastic demand curves for their own product and so cannot easily pass on wage rises in the form of higher prices without seeing their revenue fall.

This is only true, however, if one firm raises its price while others do not. If all fast food companies are forced to raise prices slightly in order to pay the minimum wage to their staff, this may result in a much smaller fall in the demand for the output of any one firm. If this is the case, then the imposition of a statutory minimum wage may actually lead to a rightward shift in the segment of the labour demand curve at or above the statutory minimum wage: a firm is able to pay the higher wage without drastically reducing its labour demand because it can pass on the higher wage costs by charging a higher price for its product, safe in the knowledge that other firms in the industry will have to do the same and hence that it will not suffer a dramatic fall in demand for its output. In this case – as in panel (d) of Figure 17.8 – although there is an increase in unemployment relative to the case with no minimum wage, this is mainly because the supply of labour is higher with the minimum wage imposed. This is because some workers will be attracted by the higher wage to enter the labour market – second earners, for example, or young people who otherwise would have stayed in full-time education.

Advocates of minimum wage laws view the policy as one way to raise the income of the working poor. They point out that workers who earn the minimum wage can still afford only a relatively meagre standard of living. They argue that although a minimum wage can have some adverse effects, these effects are small and the benefits to workers are greater than the costs.

Opponents of the minimum wage contend that it is not the best way to combat poverty since it affects only the income of those in employment and may raise unemployment. They also note that not all minimum wage workers are heads of households trying to help their families escape poverty – some may be second earners or even third earners in relatively well-off households.

An alternative to the minimum wage is the concept of the **living wage**. The living wage is calculated by the Centre for Research in Social Policy (CRSP), based at Loughborough University in the UK, for the Living Wage Foundation. The CRSP calculates the living wage based on an estimation of minimum household needs which provide an 'acceptable' standard of living in the UK. The result is published in November each year and is invariably higher than the minimum wage legislated by the UK government. For example, in November 2015, the minimum wage was set at £6.70 (€9.56) per hour for people over 21 whereas the Living Wage was £8.25 (€11.77) per hour. The Living Wage Foundation argues that paying a living wage is not only a moral responsibility of firms but is also beneficial in that a higher wage results in lower absenteeism, improves productivity and is beneficial to recruitment and retention. Payment of the Living Wage is voluntary.

> **living wage** an hourly rate set independently, based on an estimation of minimum household needs which provide an 'acceptable' standard of living in the UK

In July 2015, the UK Chancellor of the Exchequer, announced that the government would be introducing a legally binding National Living Wage (NLW) from April 2016 initially set at £7.20 for over-25s with a target to ensure that the NLW reaches 60 per cent of median earnings by 2020. Median earnings are calculated by arranging all wages from the highest to the lowest and choosing the middle value. The introduction of the NLW is in conjunction with steps to reduce benefits payments and is designed to shift incentives from welfare to work. The reductions in benefits will, argued the Chancellor, be compensated for by the NLW. The NLW is not the same as the Living Wage – the latter is calculated based on the cost of living and not median wages.

Monopsony and Minimum Wages We have seen how wage rates and the number of people employed could be lower than the competitive equilibrium when an employer has some market power. An employer with monopsony power will set the number of workers employed where the marginal cost of labour equals the marginal product which was highlighted in Figure 17.7. If the minimum wage is set above the wage rate being paid by a monopsonist, the effect could actually be to increase employment rather than lead to unemployment. Refering back to Figure 17.7, if the minimum wage is set at the equilibrium wage rate of W_1 then the number of workers employed would rise from L_2 to L_1. The labour market outcome of a minimum wage, therefore, may depend on the extent to which the market is competitive; if employers have market power then a minimum wage might result in a net social benefit.

The Market Power of Labour Unions A second reason that wages might rise above their equilibrium level is the market power of labour unions. A **union** is a worker association that bargains with employers over wages and working conditions. Unions often raise wages above the level that would prevail without a union, perhaps because they can threaten to withhold labour from the firm by calling a **strike**. Studies suggest that union workers earn about 10 to 20 per cent more than similar non-union workers.

> **union** a worker association that bargains with employers over wages and working conditions
> **strike** the organized withdrawal of labour from a firm by a union

Efficiency Wages A third reason for above-equilibrium wages is suggested by the theory of **efficiency wages**. This theory holds that a firm can find it profitable to pay high wages because doing so increases the productivity of its workers. In particular, high wages may reduce worker turnover (hiring and training new workers is an expensive business), increase worker effort, and raise the quality of workers who apply for jobs at the firm. In addition, a firm may feel it has to offer high wages in order to attract and keep the best people – this has been an argument put forward by the banking sector in response to plans by governments in Europe to tax bankers' earnings in the wake of the Financial Crisis. If this theory is correct, then some firms may choose to pay their workers more than they would normally earn.

> **efficiency wages** above-equilibrium wages paid by firms in order to increase worker productivity

> **SELF TEST** Define *compensating differential* and give an example. Give two reasons why more educated workers earn more than less educated workers.

THE ECONOMICS OF DISCRIMINATION

The previous discussion hinted at the possibilities of discrimination, in particular based on gender, in the labour market. **Discrimination** occurs when the marketplace offers different opportunities to similar individuals who differ only by race, ethnic group, gender, age or other personal characteristics. Discrimination reflects some people's prejudice against certain groups in society and also may reflect institutional or societal biases and norms which reinforce discrimination.

> **discrimination** the offering of different opportunities to similar individuals who differ only by race, ethnic group, gender, age or other personal characteristics

Measuring Labour Market Discrimination

Assessing the extent to which discrimination in labour markets affect the earnings of different groups of workers is not easy. Data from the Organisation for Economic Cooperation and Development (OECD) show that income inequalities in the UK are higher than those for France and Germany where the average income of the richest 10 per cent is around 7 times as large as for the poorest 10 per cent. In the UK it is around 10 times, with the OECD average being around 9.5. A report published in 2010 by the National Equality Panel (Hills, J. *et al.* (2010) *An Anatomy of Economic Inequality in the UK*) showed that women, earn 21 per cent less in terms of median hourly pay for all employees and 13 per cent less than men for those working full time. The report also found that Pakistani and Bangladeshi Muslim men and Black African Christian men earn between 13 and 21 per cent less than White British Christian men. Chinese men are one of the highest paid groups in Britain but they are paid 11 per cent less than would be expected given their qualifications. In the EU, the average pay gap, defined as the difference in average gross hourly earnings of women and men, was estimated at 16.4 per cent in 2012.

Taken at face value, these differentials look like evidence that UK and European employers discriminate against those from ethnic minorities and women. Simply observing differences in wages among broad groups – whites and blacks, men and women – however, does not prove that employers discriminate.

Consider, for example, the role of human capital. Whether an individual has a degree, along with the type of degree, can account for some of these differences. Those with a degree in sciences may earn more than those who have degrees from the humanities and arts. Human capital may also be more important in explaining wage differentials than measures of years of schooling suggest. The quality of education might affect the quality of human capital. The quality of education both in schools and at higher education can also be measured by expenditure, class size, ratio of teachers to pupils and so on. If we could measure the quality as well as the quantity of education, the differences in human capital among these groups would seem even larger.

The Federal Bureau of Statistics in Germany points out that gender pay differences in Germany may be due to a number of factors. These include differences in educational attainment, the type of employment (with many of the jobs women enter tending to be low-skill, low-paid jobs), and a high proportion of women working in part-time occupations. Only 41 per cent of women aged between 25 and 59 were in full-time employment compared to the EU average of 48 per cent, according to figures published by the German Federal Institute for Population Research in 2013.

Human capital acquired in the form of job experience can also help explain wage differences. In particular, women tend to have less job experience on average than men. One reason is that female labour force participation has increased in industrialized economies over the past several decades. Because of this historic change, in both Europe and North America, the average female worker today is younger than the average male worker. In addition, women are more likely to interrupt their careers to raise children. For both reasons, the experience of the average female worker is less than the experience of the average male worker.

Men and women do not always choose the same type of work, and this fact may help explain some of the earnings differential between men and women. For example, women are more likely to be personal assistants or receptionists and be in the caring professions, and men are more likely to be lorry drivers. The relative wages of personal assistants, receptionists and lorry drivers depend in part on the working conditions of each job. Because these non-monetary aspects are hard to measure, it is difficult to gauge the practical importance of compensating differentials in explaining the wage differences that we observe. Again, feminist economists argue that these are often due to the institutional and societal norms that exist in many economies and that there exists, as a result, institutional and societal discrimination which depresses women's pay in comparison to men. It is not a case of sex discrimination but gender discrimination. Sex, it is argued, relates to the biological differences between men and women whereas gender bias refers to the social and cultural construction of roles, rules and expectations attached to women and men in society, and which can distort outcomes.

Discrimination by Employers

If one group in society receives a lower wage than another group, after controlling for human capital and job characteristics, who is to blame for this differential? The answer is not obvious. It might seem natural to blame employers for discriminatory wage differences. After all, employers make the hiring decisions that determine labour demand and wages. If some groups of workers earn lower wages than they should, then it seems that employers are responsible. Yet some economists are sceptical of this answer. They believe that competitive market economies provide a natural antidote, in the form of the profit motive, to employer discrimination.

Imagine an economy in which workers, both male and female, are differentiated by their hair colour. Blondes and brunettes have the same skills, experience and work ethic. Yet, because of discrimination, employers prefer not to hire workers with blonde hair. Thus, the demand for blondes is lower than it otherwise would be. As a result, blondes earn a lower wage than brunettes.

How long can this wage differential persist? In the neo-classical model, it will be assumed that a firm could hire blonde workers and pay lower wages and thus have lower costs than firms that hire brunettes. Over time, more and more 'blonde' firms enter the market to take advantage of this cost advantage. The existing 'brunette' firms have higher costs and, therefore, begin to lose money when faced with the new competitors. These losses induce some brunette firms to go out of business. Eventually, the entry of blonde firms and the exit of brunette firms cause the demand for blonde workers to rise and the demand for brunette workers to fall. This process continues until the wage differential disappears.

Put simply, business owners who care only about making money (and employ people of whatever colour hair) are at an advantage when competing against those who are discriminating and only employ brunettes. As a result, firms that do not discriminate tend to replace those that do. In this way, it is argued, competitive markets have a natural remedy for employer discrimination. Of course, this analysis is highly dependent on the assumptions made for a competitive market and presumes a number of societal norms and values, such as the importance of the profit motive, as a reason for conducting business.

Discrimination by Customers and Governments

Customer Preferences In some instances, a firm may discriminate on the basis that it perceives its customers have particular preferences. For example, security firms might seek to employ male only workers on the assumption that customers would not feel confident if female workers were employed; firms with call centres may avoid employing workers with different regional or country-specific accents which it thinks its customer will either not understand or find difficult to listen to; or customer-facing firms may not employ disabled workers, those with particular religions, and those with visible external practices like the wearing of the hijab and niqab by Muslim women.

Government Policy Another way for discrimination to persist in competitive markets is for the government to mandate discriminatory practices. If, for instance, the government passed a law stating that women were not allowed to take front-line combat roles in its armed forces or work down coal mines, or only people above a certain height or set of physical characteristics could work in the emergency services, then a wage differential could persist in a competitive market.

Becker's 'Employer Taste' Model

One important piece of research into the economics of discrimination is from Nobel Prize winner Gary Becker from the University of Chicago, who in 1971 revised his earlier 1957 work on this area. The basis of the employer taste model is that (for whatever reason) some employees will resist working with other employees, possibly because of gender, sexual orientation or race. People may, therefore, have a 'taste' for only working with certain groups of people. Those outside this accepted group may end up being disadvantaged as a result.

Assume that a UK firm, which grows asparagus, hires workers to cut the spears. It has a choice of employing locals or migrant workers. Local people have a prejudice against migrant workers for some reason. Our analysis of a competitive firm assumes that workers will be employed up to the point at which the wage equals the marginal revenue product of labour. Assume that both local and migrant workers have the same level of productivity. If the firm has to employ workers at a going wage (which is above the minimum wage) then it may choose not to employ workers from the disadvantaged group because of the preferences of its core workforce. If, however, the firm is able to pay workers from the disadvantaged group lower wages then it faces a trade-off. There is an incentive for it to increase profits by employing these 'disadvantaged' workers – the migrant workers from Europe. If migrant workers were prepared to work for the minimum wage then the firm could lower its costs and increase profit as a result.

A discriminatory firm might employ migrant workers but would pay them a lower wage to avoid upsetting their local workers. This is the 'employer taste' model – discrimination will exist because employers do not employ labour from certain genders, race, etc. unless the workers are prepared to accept lower wages. This discrimination may continue whilst there is some limit to the competition in the labour market – in this case it might be that all firms are prepared to act in the same way.

However, if there were other asparagus farms in the area who were not discriminatory then one of these firms might choose to hire all workers at the minimum wage which would increase its overall profits. Such a firm would also employ more workers (remember that the lower the wage rate the more workers a firm is willing to employ). There could be an influx of migrant workers to the area who are willing to take advantage of the jobs available. These non-discriminatory firms could not only produce more output but at a lower wage cost per unit and so make more profit, possibly driving out the discriminatory firm from the industry.

In the UK, such a situation has manifested itself in recent years. The extension of membership of the EU in 2004 led to an increase in the number of migrant workers from countries such as Poland, Lithuania and the Czech Republic coming to Britain to find work. Many of these workers appeared willing to take jobs that paid relatively low wages, such as cutting asparagus spears. In Cambridgeshire, in the southeast of England, a large number found work on farms in the region, picking and packing fruit and vegetables. In the town of Wisbech, for example, there are tensions between 'local' and migrant workers from Eastern Europe with local workers claiming that migrant workers are taking jobs because they are prepared to accept lower pay.

The sensitivity of the situation in Wisbech is difficult. Some employers have been accused of exploiting migrant labour by paying them low wages but some counter that they are paying at least the minimum wage and that they find migrant workers not only willing to work for lower pay but that their productivity levels are relatively high compared with some 'local' labour. In this case not only are migrant workers prepared to work for lower wages but their marginal product is higher at each price (wage). Some farmers claim that 'local' workers are not prepared to do the sort of work that is available and believe that it is too low paid.

SELF TEST Why is it hard to establish whether a group of workers is being discriminated against? Explain how profit-maximizing firms tend to eliminate discriminatory wage differentials. How might a discriminatory wage differential persist?

THE OTHER FACTORS OF PRODUCTION: LAND AND CAPITAL

Firms need to hire other factor inputs to production apart from labour. For example, our apple-producing firm might have to choose the size of its apple orchard (land) and the number of ladders to make available to its apple pickers, the baskets that are used to collect the picked apples, plus the trucks used to transport the apples, the buildings used to store them and even the trees themselves.

Equilibrium in the Markets for Land and Capital

What determines how much the owners of land and capital earn for their contribution to the production process? Before answering this question, we need to distinguish between two prices: the purchase price and the rental price. The *purchase price* of land or capital is the price a person pays to own that factor of production indefinitely. The *rental price* is the price a person pays to use that factor for a limited period of time. It is important to keep this distinction in mind because, as we will see, these prices are determined by somewhat different economic forces.

Having defined these terms, we can now apply the theory developed for the labour market to the markets for land and capital. Much of what we have learned about wage determination applies also to the rental prices of land and capital. As Figure 17.9 illustrates, the rental price of land, shown in panel (a), and the rental price of capital, shown in panel (b), are determined by supply and demand. Moreover, the demand for land and capital is determined just like the demand for labour. For both land and capital, the firm increases the quantity hired until the value of the factor's marginal product equals the factor's price. Thus, the demand curve for each factor reflects the marginal productivity of that factor.

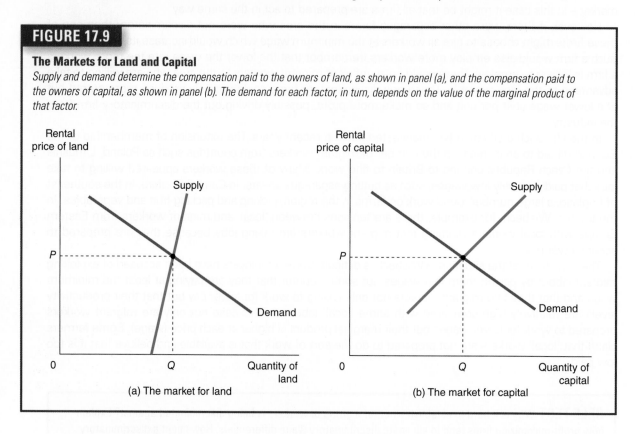

FIGURE 17.9

The Markets for Land and Capital
Supply and demand determine the compensation paid to the owners of land, as shown in panel (a), and the compensation paid to the owners of capital, as shown in panel (b). The demand for each factor, in turn, depends on the value of the marginal product of that factor.

(a) The market for land

(b) The market for capital

We can now explain how much income goes to labour, how much goes to landowners and how much goes to the owners of capital. Assuming that the factors of production are competitive and profit-maximizing, each factor's rental price must equal the value of the marginal product for that factor: labour, land and capital each earn the value of their marginal contribution to the production process.

Now consider the purchase price of land and capital. The rental price and the purchase price are related: buyers are willing to pay more for a piece of land or capital if it produces a valuable stream of rental income. As we have just seen, the equilibrium rental income at any point in time equals the value of that factor's marginal product. Therefore, the equilibrium purchase price of a piece of land or capital depends on both the current value of the marginal product and the value of the marginal product expected to prevail in the future.

Linkages Among the Factors of Production

We have seen that the price paid to any factor of production – labour, land or capital – equals the value of the marginal product of that factor. The marginal product of any factor, in turn, depends on the quantity of that factor that is available. Because of diminishing marginal product, a factor in abundant supply has a low marginal product and thus a low price, and a factor in scarce supply has a high marginal product and a high price. As a result, when the supply of a factor falls, its equilibrium factor price rises.

When the supply of any factor changes, however, the effects are not limited to the market for that factor. In most situations, factors of production are used together in a way that makes the productivity of each factor dependent on the quantities of the other factors available to be used in the production process. As a result, a change in the supply of any one factor alters the earnings of all the factors.

For example, suppose one night lightning strikes the storehouse in which are kept the ladders that the apple pickers use to pick apples from the orchards, and many of the ladders are destroyed in the ensuing fire. What happens to the earnings of the various factors of production? Most obviously, the supply of ladders falls and, therefore, the equilibrium rental price of ladders rises. Those owners who were lucky enough to avoid damage to their ladders now earn a higher return when they rent out their ladders to the firms that produce apples.

Yet the effects of this event do not stop at the ladder market. Because there are fewer ladders with which to work, the workers who pick apples have a smaller marginal product. Thus, the reduction in the supply of ladders reduces the demand for the labour of apple pickers, and this causes the equilibrium wage to fall.

This story shows a general lesson: an event that changes the supply of any factor of production can alter the earnings of all the factors. The change in earnings of any factor can be found by analyzing the impact of the event on the value of the marginal product of that factor.

FYI

What is Capital Income?

Labour income is an easy concept to understand: it is the wages and salaries that workers get from their employers. The income earned by capital, however, is less obvious.

In our analysis, we have been implicitly assuming that households own the economy's stock of capital – equipment, machinery, computers, warehouses and so forth – and rent it to firms that use it. Capital income, in this case, is the rent that households receive for the use of their capital. This assumption simplified our analysis of how capital owners are compensated, but it is not entirely realistic. In fact, firms usually own the capital they use and, therefore, they receive the earnings from this capital.

These earnings from capital, however, eventually get paid to households. Some of the earnings are paid in the form of interest to those households who have lent money to firms (anyone who has savings in a financial institution, who pays into a pension fund or an insurance policy is indirectly actually lending money to businesses). Bondholders and bank depositors are two examples of recipients of interest. Thus, when you receive interest on your bank account, that income is part of the economy's capital income.

In addition, some of the earnings from capital are paid to households in the form of dividends. Dividends are payments by a firm to the firm's shareholders. A shareholder is a person who has bought a share in the ownership of the firm and, therefore, is entitled to share in the firm's profits. (This is usually called an equity or, quite simply, a share.)

A firm does not have to pay out all of its earnings to households in the form of interest and dividends. Instead, it can retain some earnings within the firm and use these earnings to buy additional capital. Although these retained earnings do not get paid to the firm's shareholders, the shareholders benefit from them nonetheless. Because retained earnings increase the amount of capital the firm owns, they tend to increase future earnings and, thereby, the value of the firm's equities.

Under the assumptions of a competitive model, capital is paid according to the value of its marginal product and gets transmitted to households in the form of interest or dividends or whether it is kept within the firms as retained earnings.

SELF TEST What determines the income of the owners of land and capital? How would an increase in the quantity of capital affect the incomes of those who already own capital? How would it affect the incomes of workers?

ECONOMIC RENT

Consider a professional footballer in a top European league. Some players in these leagues earn tens of thousands of euros a week. Assume a player earns €100 000 per week; if that player's wages were cut to €50 000, would he still be a professional footballer? What if his wages were cut to €20 000 a week, or €5000 a week? (€5000 a week is still €260 000 a year). At what point would the player make the decision to stop being a professional footballer and switch to doing something else instead?

Now consider a plot of land and a series of machines used by a business for manufacturing CDs. The demand for CDs is falling but the business could use the machines and factory to produce Blu-ray DVDs. At what point does the falling earnings from CDs lead to the business switching from CD production to Blu-ray DVD production? If the earnings from CD or Blu-ray production fall, at what point does the firm decide to switch the use of the land and capital away from that particular use and to another use altogether?

This is the subject of what is called economic rent. **Economic rent** is the amount a factor of production earns over and above its transfer earnings. **Transfer earnings** are, in turn, the minimum payment required to keep a factor of production in its current use. The transfer earnings of a factor, therefore, represents the opportunity cost of the factor being employed in its current use.

> **economic rent** the amount a factor of production earns over and above its transfer earnings
> **transfer earnings** the minimum payment required to keep a factor of production in its current use

Let us go back to our professional football example. Assume that a player is currently earning €200 000 per year. The player also happens to be a qualified chartered surveyor and assume that the average annual income for those in this profession is €88 400. Provided the player earns in excess of the amount he could earn as a surveyor, it is rational for the player to continue as a professional footballer. If the player's wages were cut to €100 000 a year then there would still be an incentive for the player to stay as a footballer. However, if the player's wages were cut to €85 000 then he could earn more from being a surveyor and it would be rational for him to transfer to that occupation.

The difference between the amount the factor earns and the transfer earnings is termed the economic rent. If the player earns €200 000 then the economic rent, in our example, is €111 600. This is the amount by which the player's earnings could fall before there was an incentive to transfer to alternative employment.

We can see the size of the economic rent in Figure 17.10. The wage rate is given by the intersection of the demand and supply curve at W_1. If the wage rate was W_2, the number of people willing to work in this industry would be zero (the vertical intercept of the supply curve). At wage rates higher than W_2, for example, W_3, L_2 workers would be willing to offer their services. For the L_2 worker, the wage rate of W_3 is just sufficient to encourage them into that employment but for all the other workers up to L_2 the wage rate is higher than the amount they would be willing to earn to offer their services. A wage of W_3, therefore, will yield some economic rent for these workers.

When L_1 workers are employed, the total economic rent is given by the area above the supply curve, W_1, A, W_2. The area under the supply curve, shown by 0, W_2, A, L_1 is the value of the transfer earnings.

The principle of economic rent can be applied to all factors of production. It is important when thinking of land that you do not confuse the general use of the term *rent* with the economic definition. Economic rent has applications across a range of economic situations. In particular, it has been discussed with reference to taxation. If economic rent exists for any factor of production, the government could, in theory, tax a portion of that rent without affecting the employment of that factor in a particular use. A government might, therefore, debate how much of a banker's bonus to tax if there is an assumption that a large part of the earnings of bankers represents economic rent. Governments might consider taxing land and providing the tax does not push earnings below the transfer earnings then the land will continue to be used in its current form.

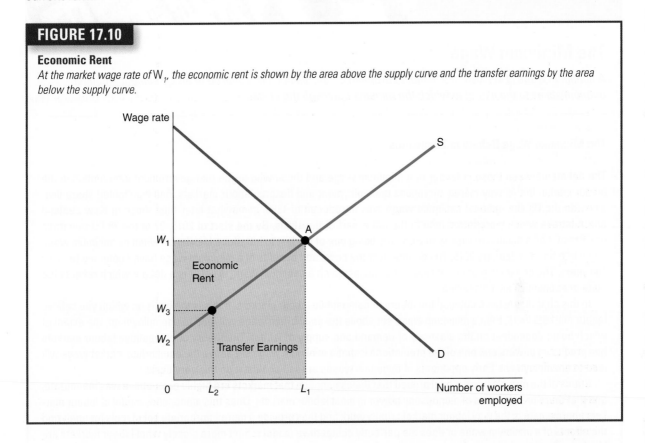

FIGURE 17.10

Economic Rent

At the market wage rate of W$_1$, the economic rent is shown by the area above the supply curve and the transfer earnings by the area below the supply curve.

CONCLUSION

The main theory developed in this chapter is called the *neoclassical theory of distribution*. According to the neoclassical theory, the amount paid to each factor of production depends on the supply and demand for that factor. The demand, in turn, depends on that particular factor's marginal productivity. In equilibrium, each factor of production earns the value of its marginal contribution to the production of goods and services.

The theory explains why some workers are paid more than others. It is because some workers can produce a good of greater market value than can others and so the wages of workers reflect the market prices of the goods they produce. In competitive markets, workers earn a wage equal to the value of their marginal contribution to the production of goods and services. There are, however, many things that affect the value of the marginal product. Firms pay more for workers who are more talented, more diligent, more experienced and more educated because these workers are more productive. Firms pay less to those workers against whom customers discriminate because these workers contribute less to revenue.

We have also looked at some different interpretations of the labour market by exploring the basics behind Marxist thinking on labour and the critique offered by feminist economists which present different perspectives on how wages are determined and the importance and role of societal norms in understanding wage rates and wage differences.

IN THE NEWS

The Minimum Wage

A minimum wage is in existence in most European countries but it is a source of disagreement amongst economists as to the extent to which the benefits outweigh the costs.

The Minimum Wage Debate in Economics

The debate between those in favour of a minimum wage and those who argue that government intervention in the labour market in this way merely increases unemployment and distorts labour markets, has highlighted sharp divisions. In the UK the national minimum wage was introduced in 1999, somewhat later than those in New Zealand and Australia which were introduced in the latter part of the 1800s. By the start of 2015, 22 of the 28 EU countries pre-Brexit, had a minimum wage with Germany being one of the last to introduce legislation when its minimum wage came into force in January 2015. The debate over the costs and benefits of a minimum wage have continued for over 100 years. The debate is more than simply the rate at which a minimum wage is set, it is a debate which reflects the state of economics as a discipline.

In this chapter we have outlined the theory of competitive labour markets. If this is the basis on which you believe labour markets work, then a minimum wage set above the equilibrium wage will lead to unemployment, the extent of which being dependent on the elasticity of demand and supply of labour. The theory of competitive labour markets has predictive powers and one of the predictions is that a minimum wage set above the equilibrium market wage will lead to unemployment. Early opponents of minimum wages argued against it on this very basis.

Critics of the neo-classical model argued that the assumption that markets are highly competitive was inaccurate, and that there are elements of monopsony power in most labour markets. Does this monopsony model of labour markets approximate to the way labour markets really work and thus provide a more appropriate set of tools for analyzing the effects of a minimum wage or does the perfectly competitive model reflect more closely what labour markets are like in reality? A study by Card and Krueger in 1995 in the US suggested that in some contexts (their work focused on the fast food industry), a minimum wage might have a positive effect on employment. This outcome would not be predicted by the competitive model.

What this highlights is a fundamental methodological debate in economics. If the predictions of the competitive model of the labour market are inaccurate then it brings into question whether such a model is of value. If the model is of limited value, then it raises the question whether it should be taught as the basis of the theory of the labour market to undergraduate students. Many economists align themselves with neo-classical principles and if the fundamental assumptions on which they base their research and views was found to be wanting, then this brings into question their whole reason for being.

Economics is not simply about adherents to the neo-classical model and those opposing it. There are other schools of thought including the so-called 'institutionalists'. Institutional economics places some emphasis on the role of institutions in shaping the goals, rules and social norms which influence economic activity. Institutions include the laws that governments pass, the customs that evolve over time and are accepted as norms in society, the codes of conduct

Are the benefits provided by minimum wages greater than the costs?

(*Continued*)

that firms and households adopt, the way in which rules and norms are enforced and the political power that rests with different social groups. Institutionalists might argue that the neo-classical theory of the labour market ignores where people and firms in society are in terms of their wealth (i.e. are people in an economy 'rich' or 'poor' on average) and are citizens essentially satisfied with their situation or very dissatisfied? These are important considerations in the analysis of minimum wages, they argue, because if society as a whole believes that wages for the low paid are too low and that there is considerable unfairness in labour markets with the low paid having little power, then their behaviour in response to the imposition of a minimum wage may be very different to the self-interested, rational being who is free to negotiate the sale of their labour and move from job to job as assumed by the neo-classical model.

The debate over the appropriate level of the minimum wage and indeed whether there should be a minimum wage at all will continue. It could be argued that the actual level of the minimum wage is almost irrelevant – what is at stake is the very basis of the underpinning philosophy and methodology in economics.

Questions

1 To what extent do you think that the assumptions of the neo-classical model of the labour market allow predictions to be made about the minimum wage which are both negative and significant? Explain your reasoning.
2 Minimum wage laws are set with the intention of helping the low paid. In low paid jobs, what powers might employers have which might imply some element of monopsony exist in this market?
3 How might the existence of laws, rules, customs and social norms affect the predictions of the neo-classical model of the labour market in response to minimum wages, which institutionalists would argue render the outcome inaccurate and unpredictable?
4 Why might a minimum wage in low paid jobs such as the fast food industry actually increase employment?
5 In this chapter, we have looked at the Living Wage. Is the fact that, according to the Living Wage Foundation, 'thousands of employers are signed up and proudly displaying the Living Wage Employer Mark' testament to the fact that institutionalist explanations of the labour market are not without foundation?

Source: http://davidcard.berkeley.edu/papers/njmin-aer.pdf

SUMMARY

- The demand for labour is a derived demand that comes from firms that use factors to produce goods and services. Competitive, profit-maximizing firms hire each factor up to the point at which the value of the marginal product of the factor equals its price.

- The supply of labour arises from individuals' trade-off between work and leisure. An upwards sloping labour supply curve means that people respond to an increase in the wage by enjoying less leisure and working more hours.

- The price paid to each factor adjusts to balance the supply and demand for that factor. Because factor demand reflects the value of the marginal product of that factor, in equilibrium each factor is compensated according to its marginal contribution to the production of goods and services.

- Because factors of production are used together, the marginal product of any one factor depends on the quantities of all factors that are available. As a result, a change in the supply of one factor alters the equilibrium earnings of all the factors.

- Marxist theory of the labour market stresses the importance of surplus value which is exploited by owners of factors of production and means that labour does not earn the full value of the work that they provide.

- Feminist economists criticise the neo-classical theory of the labour market, suggesting that it is primarily male-oriented, does to recognise the value of non-market labour activity and that societal norms and approaches to research by 'mainstream' economics lead to outcomes and policies which mean opportunities for women in the labour market, as well as the wages they earn, are likely to be less than those available to males.

- Workers earn different wages for many reasons. To some extent, wage differentials compensate workers for job attributes. Other things equal, workers in hard, unpleasant jobs get paid more than workers in easy, pleasant jobs.

● Workers with more human capital get paid more than workers with less human capital. There are criticisms of the human capital approach which are based on the societal norms which underlie the theory.

● Although years of education, experience and job characteristics affect earnings as neo-classical theory predicts, there is much variation in earnings that cannot be explained by things that economists can measure. Some unexplained variation in earnings can be attributed to natural ability, effort and chance and some to inherent biases and norms which exist in society.

● Some economists have suggested that more educated workers earn higher wages not because education raises productivity but because workers with high natural ability use education as a way to signal their high ability to employers. If this signalling theory is correct, then increasing the educational attainment of all workers would not raise the overall level of wages.

● Wages are sometimes pushed above the level that brings supply and demand into balance. Three reasons for above-equilibrium wages are minimum wage laws, unions and efficiency wages.

● Some differences in earnings are attributable to discrimination on the basis of race, gender or other factors. Measuring the amount of discrimination is difficult, however, because one must correct for differences in human capital and job characteristics.

● In theory, competitive markets can limit the impact of discrimination on wages. If the wages of a group of workers are lower than those of another group for reasons not related to marginal productivity, then non-discriminatory firms will be more profitable than discriminatory firms. Profit maximizing behaviour, therefore, can reduce discriminatory wage differentials.

QUESTIONS FOR REVIEW

1 Explain how a firm's production function is related to its marginal product of labour, how a firm's marginal product of labour is related to the value of its marginal product and how a firm's value of marginal product is related to its demand for labour.

2 Give two examples of events that could shift the demand for labour and two that could shift the supply of labour.

3 Explain how the wage can adjust to balance the supply and demand for labour while simultaneously equalling the value of the marginal product of labour.

4 If the population of Norway suddenly grew because of a large immigration, what would you expect to happen to wages? What would happen to the rents earned by the owners of land and capital?

5 Why do deep-sea divers assessing oil rigs in the North Sea get paid more than other workers with similar amounts of education?

6 Explain the idea of surplus value and why its existence means that workers do not get paid the full value of their labour, contrary to neo-classical explanations of wage rates.

7 What are the criticisms levelled against 'mainstream' theory of the labour market by feminist economists?

8 Give three reasons why a worker's wage might be above the level that balances supply and demand.

9 What difficulties arise in deciding whether a group of workers has a lower wage because of discrimination?

10 Give an example of how discrimination might persist in a competitive market.

PROBLEMS AND APPLICATIONS

1 Suppose that the government proposes a new law aimed at reducing heath care costs: all citizens are to be required to eat one apple daily.

   a. How would this apple-a-day law affect the demand and equilibrium price of apples?
   b. How would the law affect the marginal product and the value of the marginal product of apple pickers?
   c. How would the law affect the demand and equilibrium wage for apple pickers?

2 Show the effect of each of the following events on the market for labour in the computer tablet manufacturing industry.

   a. The government buys tablets for all university students.
   b. More university students graduate in engineering and computer science.
   c. Computer firms build new manufacturing factories.

3 Your enterprising uncle opens a sandwich shop that employs seven people. The employees are paid €6 per hour and a sandwich sells for €13. If your uncle is maximizing his profit, what is the value of the marginal product of the last worker he hired? What is that worker's marginal product?

4 Imagine a firm that hires two types of workers – some with computer skills and some without. If technology advances so that computers become more useful to the firm, what happens to the marginal product of the two types? What happens to equilibrium wages? Explain, using appropriate diagrams.

5 Assume that the value of a good is determined by the amount of labour time a worker puts into production. How does Marx explain why a worker who is inefficient and takes twice the time of the average worker to produce the good is not more valuable?

6 a. To what extent should any model of the labour market take into consideration non-market labour employed in the home such as raising children and housework?
   b. Do social norms and the approaches taken by economists in researching labour markets mean that women are routinely discriminated against?
   c. Can the existence of lower wages in caring professions be purely explained by conventional economic theory of the labour market?

7 This chapter has assumed that labour is supplied by individual workers acting competitively. In some markets, however, the supply of labour is determined by a union of workers.

   a. Explain why the situation faced by a labour union may resemble the situation faced by a monopoly firm.
   b. The goal of a monopoly firm is to maximize profits. Is there an analogous goal for labour unions?
   c. Now extend the analogy between monopoly firms and unions. How do you suppose that the wage set by a union compares to the wage in a competitive market? How do you suppose employment differs in the two cases?
   d. What other goals might unions have that make unions different from monopoly firms?

8 University students sometimes work as summer interns for private firms or the government. Many of these positions pay little or nothing.

   a. What is the opportunity cost of taking such a job?
   b. Explain why students are willing to take these jobs.
   c. If you were to compare the earnings later in life of workers who had worked as interns and those who had taken summer jobs that paid more, what would you expect to find?

9 a. Explain the difference between a 'minimum wage' and a 'living wage'. What should governments use to base calculations of wage rates for the lower paid?
   b. Proponents of the living wage argue that firms have a moral duty to pay but that there are also benefits to firms of higher productivity and lower absenteeism as well as improved recruitment and retention. Critics argue that holding the wage rate above market equilibrium causes unemployment. What side of the argument do you agree with most? Explain your reasoning.

10 Consider three different policies which governments could use to tackle discrimination in the workplace. Comment on the likely success of these policies in reducing discrimination in the labour market.

PART 8
INEQUALITY

18 INCOME INEQUALITY AND POVERTY

In much of our studies so far, we have looked at market outcomes and discussed welfare in terms of total surplus. In the last chapter, we touched on the fact that people earn different incomes, and some of the reasons why, including Marxist and feminist interpretations whose theories are not considered part of the mainstream neo-classical approach to economics.

In almost every economy in the world, there are wide differences in the way in which incomes are distributed amongst the population. In some economies, these gaps are very wide with a relatively small number of people being very rich and a relatively large number of people being poor.

In this chapter we discuss this distribution of income – a topic that raises some fundamental questions about the role of economic policy. We have noted that governments can sometimes improve market outcomes. This possibility is particularly important when considering the distribution of income. The market system may, if conditions are right, allocate resources efficiently, or at least as efficiently as any system yet devised, but it does not necessarily ensure that resources are allocated fairly, i.e. equitably.

There is a debate, therefore, about whether governments and international bodies should redistribute income to achieve greater equality both nationally and globally and if they do, what the most effective way of achieving this goal is. Advocates of market systems argue that if governments do get involved in such actions, the problem of trade-offs arises between equity and efficiency; their policies to make the distribution of income more equitable, distort incentives, alter behaviour and make the allocation of resources less efficient.

Critics of this approach dismiss the idea of a trade-off between equity and efficiency and argue that well-designed policies can improve inequality without any significant impact on efficiency. In addition, they also argue that inequality is responsible for misery, hunger, far lower life expectancies, and that there is a moral duty for seeking to improve equality that goes beyond the neo-classical assertions about efficiency and total surplus.

THE MEASUREMENT OF INEQUALITY

We begin our study of the distribution of income by addressing four questions of measurement:

- How much inequality is there in our society?
- How many people live in poverty?
- What problems arise in measuring the amount of inequality?
- How often do people move among income classes?

Income Inequality

Imagine that you lined up all the families in the economy according to their annual income. Then you divided the families into groups: the bottom 10 per cent, the next 10 per cent and so on up to the top 10 per cent. This would be dividing the population by deciles. If you divided the families into the bottom 20 per cent, the next 20 per cent and so on, this would be dividing the population by quintile. We could then look at how incomes fall in these different groupings to get some indication of the income distribution. This is highlighted in Figure 18.1. Here we have depicted the population split into deciles. Panel A represents country X. Here, the top 10 per cent of the population earns a total of €1m per year whereas the bottom 10 per cent earns just €5000 per year. In panel B, representing country Y, the top 10 per cent earns €250 000 per year and the bottom 10 per cent earns €60 000 a year. Looking at the total incomes earnt, Country X is clearly richer with a total income of €2 040 000 compared to the total income of country Y which is €1 350 000. However, if we take the top 20 per cent of the population of country X, these people earn 73.5 per cent of the total wealth of the country whereas in country Y, the top 20 per cent earn 35 per cent of the total income of the country. Which country would you prefer to live in?

FIGURE 18.1

Income Inequality – an Example
*The panels depict two countries'
populations divided into deciles and the
total income earnt per year by each decile.
Panel A depicts country X where the top
10 per cent of the population earn €1m per
year and the bottom 10 per cent, €5000.
Panel B. depicts country Y where the top
10 per cent of the population earn a total
of €250 000 per year and the bottom 10 per
cent, €60 000 per year.*

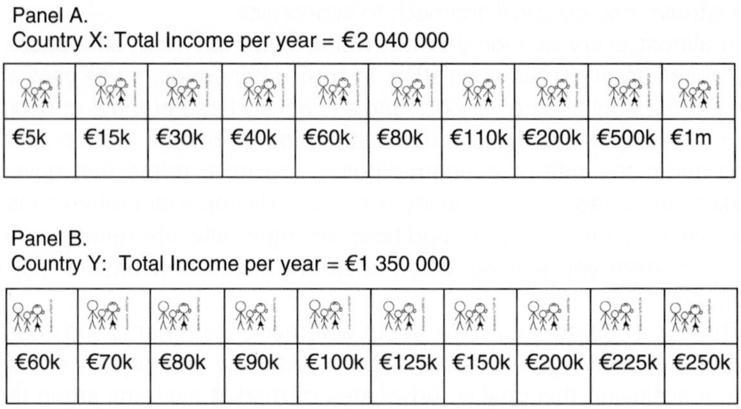

Panel A.
Country X: Total Income per year = €2 040 000

€5k	€15k	€30k	€40k	€60k	€80k	€110k	€200k	€500k	€1m

Panel B.
Country Y: Total Income per year = €1 350 000

€60k	€70k	€80k	€90k	€100k	€125k	€150k	€200k	€225k	€250k

This example shows that the distribution of income in country X is more unequal than in country Y. If you are one of the top 20 per cent of the population in country X you might be perfectly happy living in that country but many people would prefer to live in country Y because the distribution of income seems 'fairer'. There have been a number of studies which seem to suggest that people have an innate sense of fairness which often overrides rational self-interest.

In country Y, the differences in incomes between the lower decile or quintile groups are quite similar to those of the top decile or quintile groups but in country X the figures are skewed to one end of the scale, i.e. the richest 10 per cent or 20 per cent of the population account for a far higher proportion of income than the lower groups.

According to data from the IFS published in 2014, the distribution of income in the UK is highly skewed, although since the Financial Crisis inequality has reduced slightly. The IFS suggest that the reason for this is that real earnings fell but benefit levels were stable According to provisional estimates by the ONS, the median income in the UK in 2014–15 was calculated at £492 per week (€702), and 10.6 million individuals (16.8 per cent of the population) live in poverty, defined as having an income below 60 per cent of median income. Across Europe there are similar income inequalities. About 40 per cent of the total income is earned by the top quintile (Source of data, Eurostat).

There are two common measures of income inequality which we will now look at, the Lorenz curve and the Gini coefficient.

The Lorenz Curve

We noted above that the population (or households) can be grouped in different ways. The **Lorenz curve** shows the relationship between the cumulative percentage of households and the cumulative percentage of income. Figure 18.2 shows the relationship in graphical form. If income is distributed evenly, then each proportion of households account for the same percentage of income, and the resulting line connecting all these points is a 45-degree line of perfect equality. For example, if total income in the country was €100 million then the bottom 10 per cent would account for €10 million, the next 10 per cent, €10 million and so on. However, we know that such equality is highly unlikely so it what it called a Lorenz curve (rather than a single straight line) portrays the degree of inequality in a country.

> **Lorenz curve** the relationship between the cumulative percentage of households and the cumulative percentage of income

FIGURE 18.2

The Lorenz Curve
If each decile accounted for the same percentage of cumulative income the line of perfect equality would be a 45-degree line. The Lorenz curve shows the degree of inequality in a country – the more bowed the curve the greater the degree of inequality.

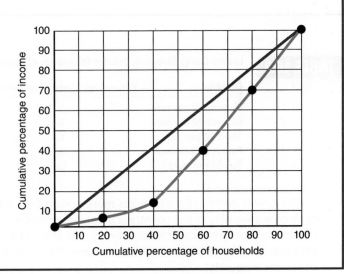

Assume that the share of income in a country is that given in Table 18.1 measured in quintiles. The bottom 20 per cent (quintile) has a share of total income of 5 per cent, the second quintile, 10 per cent, the third, 25 per cent, the fourth 30 per cent and the top quintile 30 per cent. The share of income must add up to 100 per cent and when we express the share as the cumulative share of income we get the figures in the third column. We then plot the data from the third column onto our graph to get the Lorenz curve shown in Figure 18.2.

Compare the Lorenz curve in Figure 18.2 with that in Figure 18.3. The cumulative share in income in Figure 18.3 is taken from Table 18.2.

TABLE 18.1 **The Lorenz Curve**

Quintile	Percentage share of income (%)	Cumulative share of income (%)
Bottom 20 per cent	5	5
Second 20 per cent	10	15
Third 20 per cent	25	40
Fourth 20 per cent	30	70
Top 20 per cent	30	100

FIGURE 18.3

Lorenz Curve Showing Greater Inequality of Income

The Lorenz curve shown in the figure in comparison to the one in Figure 18.2 is more bowed, reflecting the greater degree of income inequality in this country. In this example, income is heavily concentrated in the hands of the top 20 per cent of households.

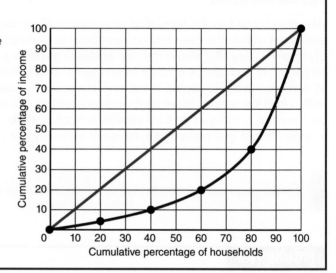

TABLE 18.2 **Lorenz Curve Showing Greater Inequality of Income**

Quintile	Percentage share of income (%)	Cumulative share of income (%)
Bottom 20 per cent	5	5
Second 20 per cent	5	10
Third 20 per cent	10	20
Fourth 20 per cent	20	40
Top 20 per cent	60	100

The Lorenz curve in Figure 18.3 is more bowed than that in Figure 18.2. The reason is that the degree of income inequality in this country is greater than that in the country depicted in Figure 18.2. In this country, the bottom 40 per cent of households only account for 10 per cent of income whereas the top 20 per cent accounts for 60 per cent of total income. The more bowed the Lorenz curve the greater the degree of income inequality.

The Gini Coefficient

We have seen that the more bowed the Lorenz curve the greater the degree of income inequality. The Gini coefficient was developed by an Italian statistician, Corrado Gini (1884–1965) in 1912. The **Gini coefficient** measures the ratio of the area between the 45 degree line of perfect income equality (a benchmark of absolute equality) and the Lorenz curve, to the entire area under the 45 degree line of perfect income equality.

$$Gini\ coefficient = \frac{Area\ between\ the\ line\ of\ perfect\ income\ equality\ and\ Lorenz\ curve}{Area\ under\ the\ line\ of\ perfect\ income\ equality}$$

> **Gini coefficient** a measure of the degree of inequality of income in a country

Comparing the Gini coefficient between different countries allows us to observe different income distributions. The Gini coefficient tells us nothing about *how* income is distributed between different countries, merely that one country has a more unequal distribution than another.

The Gini coefficient is a number between 0 and 1. A Gini coefficient of 0 means that income equality is perfect, in other words there is no difference between the line of perfect income equality and the actual Lorenz curve. At the other extreme if all income was in the hands of just one household then the area between the line of perfect income equality and the actual Lorenz curve would be equal to 1. It follows, therefore, that the higher the Gini coefficient the greater the degree of income inequality.

The principle of the Gini coefficient is shown in Figure 18.4. In panel (a) the area between the line of perfect income inequality and the actual Lorenz curve is the orange shaded area A, and the total area under the 45-degree line of perfect income inequality is the triangle 0, X, 100 (area A plus the blue shaded area, B). Calculating the area A, and dividing that by the total area A + B, gives the Gini coefficient. Calculating the area between the 45-degree line and the actual Lorenz curve is done through the use of integral calculus and is described in in the maths supplement to this book. Panel (b) shows a situation where the area A is much smaller than that shown for the country in panel (a) and in this case the income inequality would be much less reflected by a lower Gini coefficient.

FIGURE 18.4

The Gini Coefficient

The Gini coefficient is found by dividing the area A by the total area under the 45-degree line of perfect income equality (the area A + B).

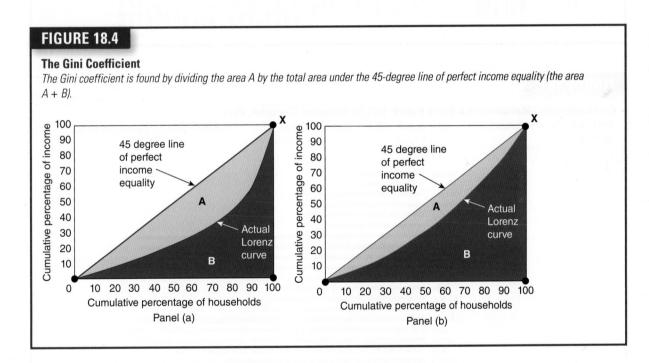

Gini Coefficients in the UK and Europe Figure 18.5 shows the change in the Gini coefficient for Great Britain between 1961 and 2012–13. It can be seen that the degree of income inequality has risen quite markedly over the last 50 years from around 0.25 in the 1960s to over 0.4 in the later part of the first decade of the 21st century, falling back to around 0.38 in 2012–13 (Source: Institute for Fiscal Studies).

The Gini coefficient for the 28 countries of the EU pre-Brexit, expressed on a scale from 0–100, was 31in 2014, a slight increase from 30.5 in 2013 and up from 30.4 in 2010. Norway is one of the countries with the lowest Gini coefficient, at 23.5 in 2014, whereas Cyprus is one of the highest at 34.8.

FIGURE 18.5

Gini Coefficient in Great Britain between 1961 and 2012–13

Over the last 50 years the Gini coefficient in Great Britain has increased, suggesting that the inequality of income has increased in the country.

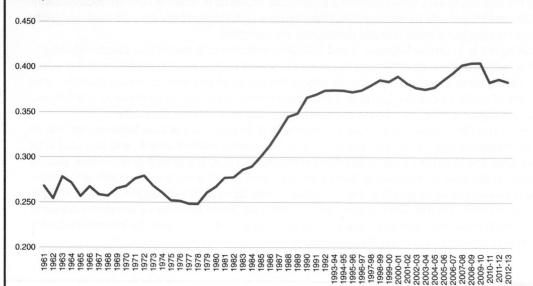

FIGURE 18.6

Gini Coefficient (Measured on a Scale from 0–100) for European Countries, 2014

The Gini coefficients as measured on a scale from 0–100 for European countries, 2014. Note: data for Estonia, Iceland and Ireland is for 2013.

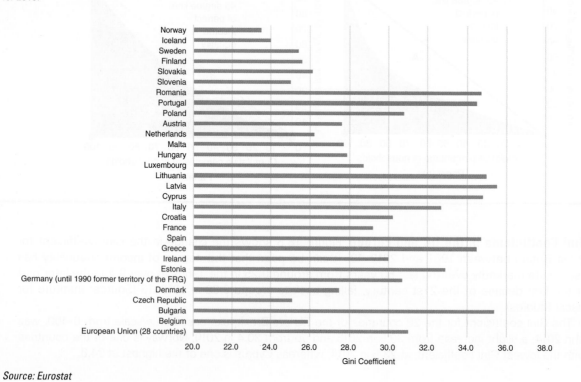

Source: Eurostat

CASE STUDY Gini coefficients Around the World

Having looked at the Gini coefficients in Europe, how do these compare with those across the rest of the world? Figure 18.7 shows some selected Gini coefficients from around the world for 2013 (data sourced from The World Bank). Collecting data on income inequality is not easy because not every country has advanced statistical services that can collect and publish such data.

FIGURE 18.7

Gini Coefficients from Around the World
The figure shows Gini coefficients from selected countries around the world arranged in descending order of inequality.

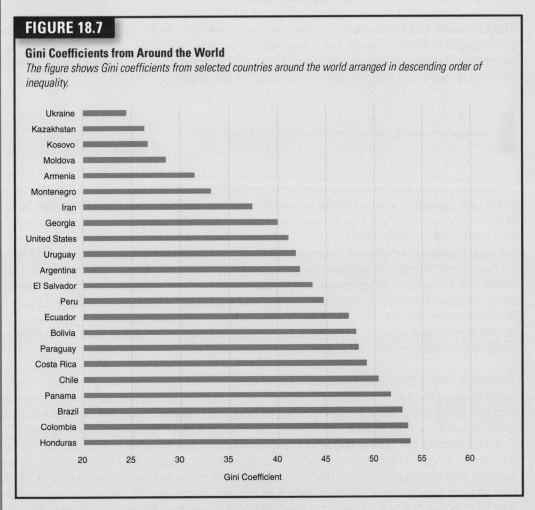

There are relatively high Gini coefficients in South American countries. Brazil is termed an emerging economy, one of the so called BRIC nations (Brazil, Russia, India and China), but whilst economic growth in Brazil has been relatively strong, the degree of inequality in the country is relatively high. In a highly developed country like the United States, income inequality is relatively high; whereas in the countries that used to be part of the former Union of Soviet Socialist Republics (USSR) and the Balkan countries which were allied to the USSR, income inequality is relatively low.

Inequality remains high in countries like Brazil despite rapid economic growth.

Problems in Measuring Inequality

Although data on income distribution give us some idea about the degree of inequality in society, interpreting these data is not as straightforward as it might first appear. The data are based on households' annual incomes. What people care about, however, is not their incomes but their ability to maintain a good standard of living. For various reasons, data on income distribution give an incomplete picture of inequality in living standards. We examine these reasons below.

The Economic Life Cycle Incomes vary predictably over people's lives. A young worker, especially one still engaged in full-time study, has a low income. Income then rises as the worker gains maturity and experience, peaking at around age 50, and then falls sharply when the worker retires at around age 65. This regular pattern of income variation is called the **life cycle**.

> **life cycle** the regular pattern of income variation over a person's life

Because people can borrow and save to smooth out life cycle changes in income, their standard of living in any year depends more on lifetime income than on that year's income. The young often borrow, perhaps to go to university or to buy a house, and then repay these loans later when their incomes rise. People have their highest saving rates when they are middle-aged. Because people can save in anticipation of retirement, the large declines in incomes at retirement need not lead to similar declines in standards of living.

This normal life cycle pattern causes inequality in the distribution of annual income, but it does not represent true inequality in living standards. To gauge the inequality of living standards in our society, the distribution of lifetime incomes is more relevant than the distribution of annual incomes. Unfortunately, data on lifetime incomes are not readily available. When looking at any data on inequality, however, it is important to bear in mind that a person's lifetime income smoothes out the highs and lows of the life cycle and as a result lifetime incomes tend to be more equally distributed across the population than are annual incomes.

Transitory versus Permanent Income Incomes also vary over people's lives because of random and transitory forces. One year a frost kills off the Normandy apple crop and Normandy apple growers see their incomes fall temporarily. At the same time, the Normandy frost drives up the price of apples and English apple growers see their incomes temporarily rise. The next year the reverse might happen.

Just as people can borrow and lend to smooth out life cycle variation in income, they can also borrow and lend to smooth out transitory variation in income. When workers are in employment, they might save some of their earnings 'for a rainy day'. Similarly, workers made redundant may use some of their savings, or borrow to maintain their lifestyle while they source another job. To the extent that families save and borrow to buffer themselves from transitory changes in income, changes in earnings do not affect their standards of living. A family's ability to buy goods and services depends largely on its **permanent income**, which is its normal, or average, income. To gauge inequality of living standards, the distribution of permanent income is more relevant than the distribution of annual income. Although permanent income is hard to measure, it is an important concept. Because permanent income excludes transitory changes in income, permanent income is more equally distributed than is current income.

> **permanent income** a person's normal income

Economic Mobility

'The rich' and 'the poor' are not groups consisting of the same families year after year. **Economic mobility**, the movement of people among income classes, is possible in many economies. Movements up the income ladder can be due to good luck or hard work, and movements down the ladder can be due to bad luck or laziness. Some of this mobility reflects transitory variation in income, while some reflects more persistent changes in income.

> **economic mobility** the movement of people among income classes

Economic mobility can mean that poverty is not always a long-term problem for families. There are, however, families in developed countries that remain below the poverty line almost all their lives. Equally, families in less developed economies face lives of hardship along with lower life expectancy. Because it is likely that the temporarily poor and the persistently poor face different problems, policies that aim to combat poverty need to distinguish between these groups.

The Poverty Rate

A commonly used gauge of the distribution of income is the poverty rate. The **poverty rate** is the percentage of the population whose family income falls below an absolute level called the **poverty line**. Poverty is a relative concept – one person's measure of poverty is what another person might call wealthy. A millionaire is wealthy compared to someone earning €50 000 a year but is poor compared to a billionaire! For this reason, economists distinguish between absolute and relative poverty. **Absolute poverty** is when individuals do not have access to the basic requirements of life – food, shelter and clothing. **Relative poverty** occurs when individuals are excluded from being able to take part in what are considered the normal, acceptable standards of living in a society.

> **poverty rate** the percentage of the population whose family income falls below an absolute level called the poverty line
> **poverty line** an absolute level of income set by the government below which a family is deemed to be in poverty. In the UK and Europe this is measured by earnings less than 60 per cent of median income
> **absolute poverty** a level of poverty where an individual does not have access to the basics of life – food, clothing and shelter
> **relative poverty** a situation where an individual is not able to access what would be considered acceptable standards of living in society

To get some idea of levels of poverty across different countries, therefore, similar measures have to be used. In Europe the measure for defining the poverty line is set at 60 per cent of the median income. If measuring across Europe, this income has to be equivalized and is called the *equivalized household income* and takes into account differences in the cost of living across the EU. If the median income is €20 000 then any family earning less than €12 000 a year would be classed as living in poverty. The median income in different European countries varies.

The EU statistics service, Eurostat, publishes data showing at-risk-of-poverty rates for persons falling under at least one of three criteria: at risk of poverty after social transfers (income poverty), severely materially deprived, and living in households with very low work intensity. It is clear from Figure 18.8 that these vary considerably across Europe. Around 24.5 per cent of the population of the EU is at risk of poverty (equivalent to almost 120 million people). This figure is slightly lower compared to 24.8 per cent in 2012 but higher than 2008 when the figure was recorded at 23.8 per cent of the population.

The highest risk countries tend to be those that were part of the former Soviet Union which have been undergoing considerable economic restructuring from command economies to market economies. In Bulgaria, for example, 48 per cent of the population is at risk of poverty, in Romania it is just over 40 per cent, and in Hungary 33.5 per cent. In Greece the percentage of the population at risk of poverty has increased from 28.1 per cent in 2008 to 35.7 per cent in 2013, largely due to the economic problems the country has faced after the Financial Crisis.

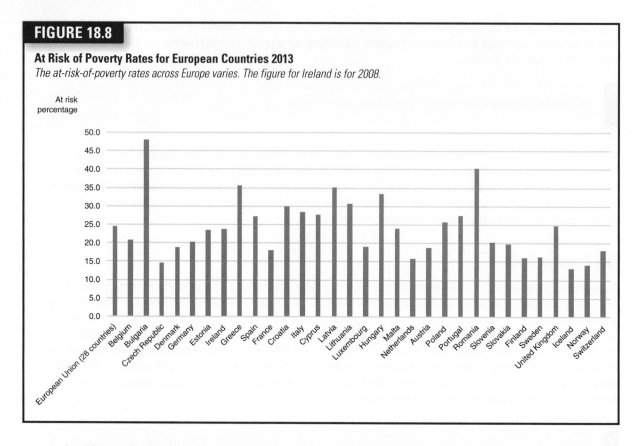

FIGURE 18.8

At Risk of Poverty Rates for European Countries 2013
The at-risk-of-poverty rates across Europe varies. The figure for Ireland is for 2008.

Looking at the poverty rate in addition to other data on inequality is important. We might observe that average incomes have risen over time but not everyone is able to share in the increased prosperity that has occurred. Understanding why some people get left behind is crucial to developing support policies to help people gain a better standard of living.

THE POLITICAL PHILOSOPHY OF REDISTRIBUTING INCOME

That the world's economies have varying degrees of inequality, however it is measured, is not in doubt. What, and indeed whether to do anything about inequality involves considerable differences of opinion. There are those who believe in the power of markets who would point to the market mechanism as the most effective way of alleviating poverty and inequality. There are those who feel the market is a flawed system which merely exacerbates poverty and inequality, in many cases because economic power lies in the hands of the wealthy and those who own factor inputs. These people look to governments and other bodies to implement policies to reduce poverty and inequality.

In looking at such policies, there are inevitably normative issues involved. Different policy options can be the subject of research which will provide some indication of the relative costs and benefits but ultimately, any policy decision is going to be driven by opinion on what is 'right' and what is 'right' may be influenced in turn by preferences and what is called relative position.

The idea of **relative position** is that humans view their own position against a reference point which provides us with a means of comparison on our feelings of well-being. What we have, what we own, the country in which we live, the facilities we have and our standard of living are not independent of any reference point. If, for example, a government cuts tax allowances which leaves middle income earners €2000 a year better off, we might assume that this would make those people happy that their well-being has improved given they can now afford to buy more goods and services with their increased income. However, if government also cut tax allowances for higher income earners which left this group €10 000 a year better off, the middle income earners might feel they have been treated unfairly. The relative position of middle income earners seems to have got worse even though they are €2000 a year better off. Relative position has been offered as a reason why, despite the fact that many developed economies have experienced relatively large growth rates over the last 50 years, surveys of populations of these countries do not show that happiness has increased at the same rate.

> **relative position** the idea that humans view their own position against a reference point which provides a means of comparison on feelings of well-being

Human beings make decisions and in doing so they are influenced by moral and political standpoints and their own belief systems. These belief systems are, to a large extent, a matter of political philosophy and we will look at some of the main schools of thought in this area.

Utilitarianism

A prominent school of thought in political philosophy is **utilitarianism**. The founders of utilitarianism were the British philosophers Jeremy Bentham (1748–1832) and John Stuart Mill (1806–73). To a large extent, the goal of utilitarians is to apply the logic of individual decision-making to questions concerning morality and public policy. The starting point of utilitarianism is the notion of utility, which you might recall is the level of happiness or satisfaction that a person receives from consumption or their individual circumstances. Utility is a measure of well-being and, according to utilitarians, is the ultimate objective of all public and private actions. The proper goal of the government, they claim, is to maximize the sum of utility of everyone in society.

> **utilitarianism** the political philosophy according to which the government should choose policies to maximize the total utility of everyone in society

The utilitarian case for redistributing income is based on the assumption of *diminishing marginal utility*. It seems reasonable that an extra euro of income to a poor person provides that person with more additional utility than does an extra euro to a rich person. In other words, as a person's income rises, the extra well-being derived from an additional euro of income falls. Imagine that Dieter and Ernst are the same, except that Dieter earns €80 000 per year and Ernst earns €20 000 per year. In this case, taking a euro from Dieter to pay Ernst will reduce Dieter's utility and raise Ernst's utility. But, because of diminishing marginal utility, Dieter's utility falls by less than Ernst's utility rises. Thus, this redistribution of income raises total utility, which is the utilitarian's objective. This assumption, together with the utilitarian goal of maximizing total utility, implies that the government should try to achieve a more equal distribution of income.

At first, this utilitarian argument might seem to imply that the government should continue to redistribute income until everyone in society has exactly the same income. Indeed, that would be the case if the total amount of income – €100 000 in our example – were fixed. But, in fact, it is not. Utilitarians reject complete equalization of incomes because they accept the idea that people respond to incentives.

To take from Dieter to pay Ernst, the government must pursue policies that redistribute income, such as the income tax and welfare systems that operate in all industrialized countries. Under these policies, people with high incomes pay high taxes, and people with low incomes receive income transfers. We have noted, however, the argument that taxes distort incentives and cause deadweight losses. If the government uses income taxes or reduced transfers to deduct from additional income people earn, both Dieter and Ernst have less incentive to work hard. As they work less, society's income falls, and so does total utility. The utilitarian government has to balance the gains from greater equality against the losses from distorted incentives. To maximize total utility, therefore, the government stops short of making society fully egalitarian.

This reflects the idea of the equity-efficiency trade-off. However, there are those who argue that this is a fallacy and that reducing inequality in society through tax and welfare policies does not have to mean that economic growth is sacrificed and even if it is, the overall well-being of individuals who are helped and supported by such policies is more important than a measure of economic growth. Nobel Prize winning economist, Gunnar Myrdal, for example, argued that policies to reduce inequality could actually lead to more stable and improved economic growth because health, life expectancy and access to society through increased education and opportunities could lead to greater productivity and future growth. Countries like Denmark and Sweden have received praise for their investment in welfare systems and both countries appear near the top of lowest inequality measures and high up in surveys of 'happiness'.

Supporters of the idea of redistribution of income argue that this shows the equity–efficiency trade-off is a myth although there are those who counter that there are many reasons, not always positive, why Denmark and Sweden come near the top of happiness surveys, and not always because the populations of each country are actually 'happy' but partly because of social norms which make it shameful to report feeling unhappy or uncontended.

Liberalism

A second way of thinking about inequality might be called **liberalism**. Philosopher John Rawls develops this view in his book *A Theory of Justice*. This book was first published in 1971, and it quickly became a classic in political philosophy.

> **liberalism** the political philosophy according to which the government should choose policies deemed to be just, as evaluated by an impartial observer behind a 'veil of ignorance'

Rawls begins with the premise that a society's institutions, laws and policies should be just. He then takes up the natural question: how can we, the members of society, ever agree on what justice means? It might seem that every person's point of view is inevitably based on his or her particular circumstances – whether he or she is talented or less talented, diligent or lazy, educated or less educated, born to a wealthy family or a poor one. Could we ever *objectively* determine what a just society would be?

To answer this question, Rawls proposes the following thought experiment. Imagine that before any of us is born, we all get together for a meeting to design the rules that govern society. At this point, we are all ignorant about the station in life each of us will end up filling. In Rawls's words, we are sitting in an 'original position' behind a 'veil of ignorance'. In this original position, Rawls argues, we can choose a just set of rules for society because we must consider how those rules will affect every person. As Rawls puts it, 'Since all are similarly situated and no one is able to design principles to favour his particular conditions, the principles of justice are the result of fair agreement or bargain.' Designing public policies and institutions in this way allows us to be objective about what policies are just.

Rawls then considers what public policy designed behind this veil of ignorance would try to achieve. In particular, he considers what income distribution a person would consider fair if that person did not know whether he or she would end up at the top, bottom or middle of the distribution. Rawls argues that a person in the original position would be especially concerned about the possibility of being at the *bottom* of the income distribution. In designing public policies, therefore, we should aim to raise the welfare of the worst-off person in society. That is, rather than maximizing the sum of everyone's utility, as a utilitarian would do, Rawls would maximize the minimum utility. Rawls's rule is called the **maximin criterion**.

> **maximin criterion** the claim that the government should aim to maximize the well-being of the worst-off person in society

Because the maximin criterion emphasizes the least fortunate person in society, it justifies public policies aimed at equalizing the distribution of income. By transferring income from the rich to the poor, society raises the well-being of the least fortunate. The maximin criterion would not, however, lead to a completely egalitarian society. If the government promised to equalize incomes completely, people would have less incentive to work hard, society's total income might fall and the least fortunate person might be worse off as a result. The maximin criterion still allows disparities in income, because these could improve incentives and thereby raise society's ability to help the poor. Nonetheless, because Rawls's philosophy puts weight on only the least fortunate members of society, it calls for more income redistribution than does utilitarianism.

Rawls's views are controversial, but the thought experiment he proposes allows us to consider the redistribution of income as a form of *social insurance*. That is, from the perspective of the original position behind the veil of ignorance, income redistribution is like an insurance policy. Homeowners buy fire insurance to protect themselves from the risk of their housing burning down. Similarly, when we as a society choose policies that tax the rich to supplement the incomes of the poor, we are all insuring ourselves against the possibility that we might have been a member of a poor family. Because people dislike risk, we might regard ourselves as being fortunate to have been born into a society that provides us this insurance.

It is not at all clear, however, that rational people behind the veil of ignorance would truly be *so* averse to risk as to follow the maximin criterion. Indeed, because a person in the original position might end up anywhere in the distribution of outcomes, he or she might treat all possible outcomes equally when designing public policies. In this case, the best policy behind the veil of ignorance would be to maximize the average utility of members of society, and the resulting notion of justice would be more utilitarian than Rawlsian.

Libertarianism

A third view of inequality is called **libertarianism**. The two views we have considered so far – utilitarianism and liberalism – both view the total income of society as a shared resource that a 'social planner' can freely redistribute to achieve some social goal. By contrast, libertarians argue that society itself earns no income – only individual members of society earn income. According to libertarians, the government should not take from some individuals and give to others in order to achieve any particular distribution of income.

> **libertarianism** the political philosophy according to which the government should punish crimes and enforce voluntary agreements but not redistribute income

For instance, philosopher Robert Nozick writes the following in his famous 1974 book *Anarchy, State, and Utopia*:

> *We are not in the position of children who have been given portions of pie by someone who now makes last minute adjustments to rectify careless cutting. There is no central distribution, no person or group entitled to control all the resources, jointly deciding how they are to be doled out. What each person gets, he gets from others who give to him in exchange for something, or as a gift. In a free society, diverse persons control different resources, and new holdings arise out of the voluntary exchanges and actions of persons.*

Whereas utilitarians and liberals try to judge what amount of inequality is desirable in a society, Nozick denies the validity of this very question. The libertarian alternative to evaluating economic *outcomes* is to evaluate the *process* by which these outcomes arise. When the distribution of income is achieved unfairly – for instance, when one person steals from another – the government has the right and duty to remedy the problem. As long as the process determining the distribution of income is just, the resulting distribution can be deemed fair, no matter how unequal.

Nozick criticizes Rawls's liberalism by drawing an analogy between the distribution of income in society and the distribution of marks awarded to students taking a course of study. Suppose you were asked to judge the fairness of the marks awarded in the economics course you are now taking. Would you imagine yourself behind a veil of ignorance and choose a marks distribution without knowing the talents and efforts of each student? Or would you ensure that the process of assigning marks to students is fair without regard for whether the resulting distribution is equal or unequal?

Libertarians conclude that equality of opportunities is more important than equality of incomes. They believe that the government should enforce individual rights to ensure that everyone has the same opportunity to use their talents and achieve success. Once these rules of the game are established, the government has no reason to alter the resulting distribution of income.

Libertarian Paternalism

Finally, we introduce a relatively new concept linked to these philosophies put forward by University of Chicago economists, Richard H. Thaler and Cass R. Sunstein (see Thaler, R.H. and Sunstein C.R. (2009) *Nudge: Improving decisions about health, wealth and happiness*. London: Penguin). Libertarian paternalism recognizes that people should be free to choose but that 'choice architects' (the government in the case of making decisions about rectifying inequality) have a legitimate role in trying to influence people's behaviour in order to make their lives longer, healthier and better – improving their utility. Thaler and Sunstein question whether specific policy moves are the best way of changing behaviour to improve utility and whether 'nudges' could achieve the end result whilst retaining the freedom of people to make choices. 'Nudges' relate to details that might often seem insignificant but when paid attention to, can influence the choices people make to 'nudge' them in the direction of improving their own and society's welfare. Their work covers diverse areas but includes savings for pensions and social security systems, both of which have an impact on inequality in society.

SELF TEST Franz earns more than Paloma. Someone proposes taxing Franz in order to supplement Paloma's income. How would a utilitarian, a liberal and a libertarian evaluate this proposal?

POLICIES TO REDUCE POVERTY

Poverty is one of the most difficult problems that policymakers face. Poor families are more likely than the overall population to experience homelessness, drug dependency, domestic violence, health problems, teenage pregnancy, illiteracy, unemployment, low educational attainment and have lower life expectancy. In the UK, the ONS has reported that people living in wealthy areas of Southern England have life expectancies which are around 10 years longer than those who live in poor areas of Glasgow in Scotland. Within Scotland itself, the life expectancy of people in the least deprived areas is around 12.5 years longer than those in the most deprived areas. Even within Glasgow, a distance of a few miles can make a difference. According to the Glasgow Indicators Project developed by the Glasgow Centre for Population Health published in 2014, men in the richer neighbourhoods in Glasgow live 15 years, on average, longer than those from the poorest areas of the city. Members of poor families are both more likely to commit crimes and more likely to be victims of crimes. Although it is hard to separate the causes of poverty from the effects, there is no doubt that poverty is associated with various economic and social ills and with lower life expectancy.

Here we consider some of the policy options which could and have been implemented to help alleviate poverty and inequality.

Minimum Wage Laws

As we saw in Chapter 17, advocates of a minimum wage view it as a way of helping the working poor without any cost to the government. Critics view it as hurting those it is intended to help. Given the assumptions of competitive labour markets, for jobs with low levels of skill and experience, a high minimum wage forces the wage above the level that balances supply and demand. It therefore raises the cost of labour to firms and reduces the quantity of labour that those firms demand. The result is higher unemployment among those groups of workers affected by the minimum wage. Although those workers who remain employed benefit from a higher wage, those who might have been employed at a lower wage are worse off.

The magnitude of these effects, we know, depends on the elasticity of demand. Advocates of a high minimum wage argue that the demand for unskilled labour is relatively inelastic, so that a high minimum wage depresses employment only slightly. Critics of the minimum wage argue that labour demand is more elastic, especially in the long run when firms can adjust employment and production more fully. They also note that many minimum wage workers are teenagers from middle-income families, so that a high minimum wage is imperfectly targeted as a policy for helping the poor.

The effects are also dependent on the degree of substitutability between workers in different industries – the ease with which workers can transfer from one industry to another. Minimum wage laws affect industries in different ways; some industries are not affected greatly by minimum wage laws because they already pay in excess of the minimum wage and so the labour market equilibrium is not affected in that particular market. In low-paid industries, such as cleaning, hotel and catering and restaurants, however, all employers are affected in the same way if they have to increase pay to meet minimum wage laws. As a result, minimum wage laws prevent one employer gaining any advantage over another by paying workers lower wages and thus having lower costs. Whilst minimum wage laws are a contentious issue, it is also a highly complex one requiring detailed analysis and an understanding that the labour market is not simply an amorphous 'one'; it consists of many smaller markets each of which has a varying influence on other markets.

Social Security

One way to raise the living standards of the poor is for the government of a country to supplement their incomes. The primary way in which the government does this is through **social security**. This is a broad term that generally encompasses government benefits which cover lone parents and carers, those incapable of work, or else disabled, payments made to those in work and with families but who receive low incomes and have to care for children, to unemployed people who are able and willing to work but temporarily cannot find a job.

> **social security** government benefits that supplement the incomes of the needy

A common criticism of the social security system is that it may create bad incentives where people become too reliant on the benefits system or believe that it is an entitlement rather than a support mechanism. However, governments may introduce other mechanisms to create good incentives, for example making work more attractive than living off benefits by providing income top-ups – these act like a negative income tax, if an individual is in work but on low pay.

It is very difficult to tell the size and significance of the different incentive effects, both positive and negative. Proponents of the benefit system point out that being a poor, single mother is not easy, and they are sceptical that many people are encouraged to pursue such a life if it were not thrust upon them. Moreover, if it can be proved that a person is incapable of work or is disabled, it seems cruel and ridiculous to argue that this is because of the benefits they are receiving. It is often easy, however, for the popular press to portray examples of those who abuse the system; it is important that, as a budding economist, you ask appropriate questions and try to distinguish between fact and opinion in such cases.

Negative Income Tax

Whenever the government chooses a system to collect taxes, it affects the distribution of income. This is clearly true in the case of a progressive income tax, whereby high-income families pay a larger percentage of their income in taxes than do low-income families. Many economists have advocated supplementing the income of the poor using a **negative income tax**. According to this policy, every family would report its income to the government. High-income families would pay a tax based on their incomes. Low-income families would receive a subsidy. In other words, they would 'pay' a 'negative tax'.

negative income tax a tax system that collects revenue from high-income households and gives transfers to low-income households

For example, suppose the government used the following formula to compute a family's tax liability:
Taxes due = (1/3 of income) − €10 000

In this case, a family that earned €60 000 would pay €10 000 in taxes, and a family that earned €90 000 would pay €20 000 in taxes. A family that earned €30 000 would owe nothing and a family that earned €15 000 would 'owe' − €5000. In other words, the government would send this family a cheque for €5000.

Under a negative income tax, poor families would receive financial assistance without having to demonstrate need. The only qualification required to receive assistance would be a low income.

In-Kind Transfers

In-kind transfers are designed to provide the poor directly with some of the goods and services they need to raise living standards. For example, charities provide the needy with food, shelter and toys at Christmas. Governments in some countries give poor families vouchers that can be used to buy food or clothing in shops; the shops then redeem the vouchers for money. In the UK, families on low incomes may qualify for free school meals for their children and medical benefits such as free prescriptions, dental treatment and eyesight tests.

in-kind transfers transfers to the poor given in the form of goods and services rather than cash

Advocates of in-kind transfers argue that such transfers ensure the poor get what they need most. Among the poorest members of society, alcohol and drug addiction is more common than it is in society as a whole. By providing the poor with food and shelter rather than cash, society can be more confident that it is not helping to support such addictions.

Advocates of cash payments, on the other hand, argue that in-kind transfers are inefficient and disrespectful. The government does not know, they say, what goods and services the poor need most. Many of the poor are ordinary people down on their luck. Despite their misfortune, they are in the best position to decide how to raise their own living standards. Rather than giving the poor in-kind transfers of goods and services that they may not want, it may be better to give them cash and allow them to buy what they think they need most.

Anti-Poverty Policies and Work Incentives

Many policies aimed at helping the poor can have unintended consequences. Suppose it is estimated that a family needs an income of €15 000 a year to maintain a reasonable standard of living and the government promises to guarantee every family that income. Whatever a family earns, the government makes up the difference between that income and €15 000.

The incentive effects of this policy might mean that any person who earns under €15 000 by working, has less incentive to find and keep a job. For every euro that the person would earn, the government would reduce their income supplement by one euro. In effect, the government taxes 100 per cent of their additional earnings to give an effective marginal tax rate of 100 per cent. The adverse effects of this high effective tax rate can persist over time. A person who is discouraged from working loses the on-the-job training, skills and experience that a job might offer them. In addition, his or her children miss the lessons learned by observing a parent with a full-time job, and this may adversely affect their own ability to find and hold a job.

Although the anti-poverty policy we have been discussing is hypothetical, it is not as unrealistic as it might first appear. In the UK, for example, some benefits aimed at helping the poor are tied to family income. As a family's income rises, the family becomes ineligible for these benefits. When all benefits being received are taken together, it is common for families to face effective marginal tax rates that are very high. Sometimes the effective marginal tax rates even exceed 100 per cent, so that poor families are worse off when they earn more: they are caught in a 'poverty trap'. In addition, by taking work, some families face additional costs such as childcare which can exacerbate the problem. The unintended consequence of such a policy is to discourage families from working. According to critics of anti-poverty policies, these social security benefits alter work attitudes and create a 'culture of poverty'.

One proposed solution to this problem is to reduce benefits to poor families more gradually as their incomes rise. For example, if a poor family loses €0.30 of benefits for every extra €1 it earns, then it faces an effective marginal tax rate of 30 per cent. Although this effective tax reduces work effort to some extent, it does not eliminate the incentive to work completely. The problem with this solution is that it greatly increases the cost of the social security system. The more gradual the phase-out, the more families are eligible for some level of benefits – and the more the social security system costs. Thus, policymakers face a trade-off between burdening the poor with high, effective marginal tax rates and burdening taxpayers with a costly anti-poverty programme affecting the government's finances.

There are various other ways to try to reduce the work disincentive of anti-poverty programmes, such as stopping or reducing benefits to people who have not found a job within a reasonable period of time or who have turned down job offers for no good reason. In the UK, this kind of reasoning underpins the structure of the benefits paid to the unemployed, called Jobseeker's Allowance. To receive the allowance, the claimant must be capable of starting work immediately and of actively taking steps to find a job such as attending interviews, writing applications, improving their skills or seeking job information. They must also have a current 'jobseeker's agreement' with the Employment Service, which includes such information as their hours available for work, their desired job and any steps that the claimant is willing to take to find work (such as moving to a different town). They must be prepared to work up to 40 hours a week and have a reasonable prospect of finding work (i.e. not place too many restrictions on the type of work they are willing to undertake). If a claimant refuses to take up a job offer without good reason, they may be denied further payments of Jobseeker's Allowance.

> **SELF TEST** List three policies aimed at helping the poor, and discuss the pros and cons of each.

CONCLUSION

People have long reflected on the distribution of income in society. Plato, the ancient Greek philosopher, concluded that in an ideal society the income of the richest person would be no more than four times the income of the poorest person. Although the measurement of inequality is difficult, it is clear that many economies have much more inequality than Plato recommended.

The issue of poverty and inequality arouses passions and generates considerable debate but much of this is driven by different belief systems and as a result, getting consensus on the best and most effective way of dealing with the problem is challenging. Philosophers, economists and policymakers do not agree on how much income inequality is desirable, or even whether public policy should aim to alter the distribution of income. Much of public debate reflects this disagreement. Whenever taxes are raised, for instance, politicians argue over how much of the tax hike should fall on the rich, people from the middle-income group, and the poor.

If the trade-off between equity and efficiency is not a fallacy, as some claim, then consideration has to be given to the extent to which any policy penalizes those who are prepared to work hard and be successful (however that is measured) and reward the workshy, lazy and unsuccessful. The use of such terminology as 'workshy', 'lazy', 'hardworking' and 'successful' are emotive terms which betray a belief system about what is important and valued in society. If economics has a contribution, it has to take into account these different value systems in researching policies targeted at alleviating poverty and inequality.

IN THE NEWS

Making Work 'Work'

In 2015, the UK Chancellor of the Exchequer announced changes to the welfare system that highlights the difficulties and divisiveness associated with policies designed to tackle poverty and inequality whilst attempting to reduce the burden on government finances.

Tax Credits and the Living Wage

The July 2015 budget, the first for the Conservative government elected in May of that year, saw the Government announce plans to reduce some benefits and increase the minimum wage in an attempt to incentivise work over benefits but also to reduce the government's expenditure on welfare as part of its deficit reduction plans.

Tax credits include Working Tax Credit, applied to those in work, and Child Tax Credit for families with children. The aim of these benefits is to encourage people to work by redistributing income through payment of money to people and families on low incomes. Some 4.5 million people claim tax credits and estimates on the cost to the government (and, by implication, the tax payer) are around £30 billion a year (€42.5bn). This represents around 14 per cent of the £217 billion (€280bn) welfare budget.

Claimants of tax credits are not homogenous. They can be single people, single mothers, and they can be families with one or both parents working, one or both working part-time and with different numbers of children and of different ages. In the 2015 Budget, the Chancellor announced that tax credits would be cut so that people earning over £3850 a year (€5500) would see their benefits reduced whereas before the proposed changes, the threshold was £6420 (€9100). Similarly, the income threshold for those claiming child tax credit would fall from £16 105 to £12 125 (€22 800 to €17 184). Balancing this out would be the proposed introduction of the National Living Wage (NLW), which the government argue, would increase the earnings of workers, alongside changes to support for childcare. The Chancellor noted that this change in priorities would not only make work more attractive but also reduce the government's expenditure by around £12 billion (€17bn) a year.

The effects of the changes aroused considerable division and disagreement not only between the right and left of the political divide but within the Conservative party itself. Part of the reason is that it is feared many people will be adversely affected by the proposed changes and end up being worse off, but also because the Prime Minister, David Cameron, did seem to 'promise' that child tax credits would not be cut in his pre-election speeches.

The IFS produced an analysis of the impact of the proposed changes in 2019/20, and concluded that deciles two, three and four of the household income distribution would face average losses of £1349, £980 and £690 per year respectively (€1910, €1388 and €977). The increase in the NLW would mean that each group would gain £90, £120 and £160 per year respectively (€127, €170 and €227). The IFS also noted that the change in the NLW might have an effect on the number of hours worked (in theory,

A key thrust of policy from the UK Chancellor of the Exchequer has been to encourage those on welfare to get into work.

an increase in wages would increase the number of hours worked), make employment more attractive and have an overall impact on GDP – but that there was disagreement on the extent of these effects or indeed, whether the NLW would negatively impact GDP and employment. Overall, of the 8.4 million working-age households affected by the changes, the IFS estimates they will be on average £550 per year (€779) worse off as a result of the welfare and benefits proposals.

(*Continued*)

In the 'Comprehensive Spending Review' in November 2015, in which the Chancellor sets out the government's spending plans for the next five years, then Chancellor, George Osborne, announced that following the feedback on the plans and as a result of better than expected tax receipts over the lifetime of the Parliament, the plans for reducing tax credits would be cancelled. However, the introduction of a Universal Credits system designed to bring together tax and welfare benefits to simplify the system, would still mean that families on benefits would experience cuts in their incomes in the long run.

Questions

1 To what extent do governments have a responsibility to reduce inequality and poverty in a country?
2 A policy such as the tax credits system in the UK is designed to redistribute income. In effect it takes the taxes paid by working people and gives it to those less fortunate. Should taxpayers 'subsidize' the poor in this way? Explain your reasoning.
3 Some analysts have suggested that the NLW will negatively impact employment and GDP. Explain why this might be so.
4 The UK Government have argued that increases in the tax thresholds and support for childcare have to be taken into consideration alongside the increase in the NLW in assessing the overall impact of the changes to the welfare and benefits system. Outline the economic arguments which might affect the extent and significance of the proposed changes.
5 If the IFS' analysis is correct and working age households will end up being worse off as a result of the changes, is the reduction in the government's overall spending on welfare and the impact on the deficit more important to the nation as a whole than the effect on a small proportion of the overall population? Justify your argument.

Source: https://fullfact.org/economy/welfare-budget/

SUMMARY

- Data on the distribution of income show wide disparity in industrialized economies.
- Because in-kind transfers, the economic life cycle, transitory income and economic mobility are so important for understanding variation in income, it is difficult to gauge the degree of inequality in our society using data on the distribution of income in a single year. When these other factors are taken into account, they tend to suggest that economic well-being is more equally distributed than is annual income.
- Political philosophers differ in their views about the role of government in altering the distribution of income. Utilitarians would choose the distribution of income to maximize the sum of utility of everyone in society. Liberals would determine the distribution of income as if we were behind a 'veil of ignorance' that prevented us from knowing our own stations in life. Libertarians would have the government enforce individual rights to ensure a fair process but then not be concerned about inequality in the resulting distribution of income. Libertarian paternalism advocates 'nudging' people in directions which improve both their own and society's overall welfare.
- Various policies aim to help the poor – minimum wage laws, social security, negative income taxes and in-kind transfers. Although each of these policies helps some families escape poverty, they also have unintended side effects. Because financial assistance declines as income rises, the poor often face effective marginal tax rates that are very high. Such high effective tax rates discourage poor families from escaping poverty on their own.

QUESTIONS FOR REVIEW

1 What is meant by the terms 'income inequality' and 'income distribution'?
2 Explain the Lorenz curve and what it measures.
3 How is the Gini coefficient calculated and what does it show?
4 How does the extent of income inequality in your country compare to that of other nations around the world?

5 Poverty is described as a relative concept – what does this mean?

6 Distinguish between absolute and relative poverty.

7 When gauging the amount of inequality, why do transitory and life cycle variations in income cause difficulties?

8 How would a utilitarian, a liberal and a libertarian determine how much income inequality is permissible?

9 What are the pros and cons of in-kind (rather than cash) transfers to the poor?

10 Describe how anti-poverty programmes can discourage the poor from working. How might you reduce this disincentive? What are the disadvantages with your proposed policy?

PROBLEMS AND APPLICATIONS

1 What factors might account for the levels of income inequality that exist in a country? Use the country you are studying in as a case study to help illustrate your answer.

2 The Gini coefficient in Portugal, measured on a scale from 0–100, was 34.5 in 2014 whereas the Gini coefficient in Norway was 23.5. Does this mean that the bottom 20 per cent of the population in Portugal must be poorer than the equivalent quintile in Norway? Explain.

3 Economists often view life cycle variation in income as one form of transitory variation in income around people's lifetime, or permanent, income. In this sense, how does your current income compare to your permanent income? Do you think your current income accurately reflects your standard of living?

4 The chapter discusses the importance of economic mobility.

   a. What policies might the government pursue to increase economic mobility within a generation?
   b. What policies might the government pursue to increase economic mobility across generations?
   c. Do you think we should reduce spending on social security benefits in order to increase spending on government programmes that enhance economic mobility? What are some of the advantages and disadvantages of doing so?

5 Consider two communities. In one community, ten families have incomes of €100 each and ten families have incomes of €20 each. In the other community, ten families have incomes of €200 each and ten families have incomes of €22 each.

   a. In which community is the distribution of income more unequal? In which community is the problem of poverty likely to be worse?
   b. Which distribution of income would Rawls prefer? Explain.
   c. Which distribution of income do you prefer? Explain.

6 Suppose there are two possible income distributions in a society of ten people. In the first distribution, nine people would have incomes of €30 000 and one person would have an income of €10 000. In the second distribution, all ten people would have incomes of €25 000.

   a. If the society had the first income distribution, what would be the utilitarian argument for redistributing income?
   b. Which income distribution would Rawls consider more equitable? Explain.
   c. Which income distribution would Nozick consider more equitable? Explain.

7 Suppose that a family's tax liability equalled its income multiplied by one-half, minus €10 000. Under this system, some families would pay taxes to the government, and some families would receive money from the government through a 'negative income tax'.

   a. Consider families with pre-tax incomes of €0, €10 000, €20 000, €30 000 and €40 000. Make a table showing pre-tax income, taxes paid to the government or money received from the government, and after-tax income for each family.
   b. What is the marginal tax rate in this system (i.e. out of every €1 of extra income, how much is paid in tax)? What is the maximum amount of income at which a family receives money from the government?
   c. Now suppose that the tax schedule is changed, so that a family's tax liability equals its income multiplied by one-quarter, minus €10 000. What is the marginal tax rate in this new system? What is the maximum amount of income at which a family receives money from the government?
   d. What is the main advantage of each of the tax schedules discussed here?

8 John and Carlos are utilitarians. John believes that labour supply is highly elastic, whereas Carlos believes that labour supply is quite inelastic. How do you suppose their views about income redistribution differ?

9 Why is an understanding of belief systems important in assessing approaches to dealing with poverty and inequality?

10 Do you agree or disagree with each of the following statements? What do your views imply for public policies, such as taxes on inheritance?

a. 'Every parent has the right to work hard and save in order to give his or her children a better life.'
b. 'No child should be disadvantaged by the sloth or bad luck of his or her parents.'

8. John and Carlos are utilitarians. John believes that labour supply is highly elastic, whereas Carlos believes that labour supply is quite inelastic. How do you suppose their views about income redistribution differ?

9. Why is an understanding of belief systems important in assessing approaches to dealing with poverty and inequality?

10. Do you agree or disagree with each of the following statements? What do you see as likely for public policies, such as taxes on inheritance?

a. 'Every parent has the right to work hard and save in order to give his or her children a better life.'
b. 'No child should be disadvantaged by the good or bad luck of his or her parents.'

PART 9
TRADE

19 INTERDEPENDENCE AND THE GAINS FROM TRADE

onsider this typical day. You wake up in the morning and make some coffee from beans grown in Kenya, or tea from leaves grown in Sri Lanka. Over breakfast, you listen to a radio programme on a device made in China. You get dressed in clothes manufactured in Thailand. You drive to the university in a car made of parts manufactured in more than a dozen countries around the world. Then you open up your economics textbook published by a company located in Hampshire in the UK, printed on paper made from trees grown in Finland and written by authors from the US and England.

Every day you rely on many people from around the world, most of whom you do not know, to provide you with the goods and services that you enjoy. Such interdependence is possible because people trade with one another. One of the early insights from economists like Adam Smith and David Ricardo was that trade can be beneficial and this insight is something that many economists still hold dear. In this chapter we will look at the benefits to trade and also at arguments which cast doubt on the extent to which trade benefits everyone.

THE PRODUCTION POSSIBILITIES FRONTIER

We begin our analysis by looking at a model of the economy where no trade takes place and simplified to the production of goods in two categories, capital goods and consumer goods. The country has a certain amount of resources of land, labour and capital available to allocate between the production of these goods which can be shown using a production possibilities frontier (PPF). (You might also see this referred to as a production possibilities boundary or production possibilities curve – they are the same thing.) The **production possibilities frontier** is a graph that shows the various combinations of output – in this case, capital goods and consumer goods – that the economy can produce given the available factors of production and technology that firms can use to turn these factors into output.

> **production possibilities frontier** a graph that shows the combinations of output that the economy can possibly produce given the available factors of production and technology

Figure19.1 is an example of a PPF. In this economy, if all resources were devoted to the production of capital goods, the economy would produce 1 million units of capital goods and no consumption goods. If all resources were used to produce consumer goods, the economy would produce 3 million units and no capital goods. The two end points of the production possibilities frontier represent these extreme possibilities. If the economy were to divide its resources between the two goods, it could produce 700 000 capital goods and 2 million consumer goods, shown in the figure by point A. The outcome at point D is not possible because the economy does not have enough of the factors of production to support that level of output. In other words, the economy can produce at any point on or inside the production possibilities frontier, but it cannot produce at points outside the frontier.

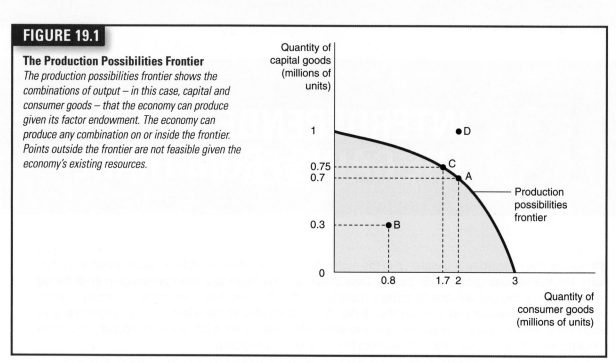

FIGURE 19.1

The Production Possibilities Frontier
The production possibilities frontier shows the combinations of output – in this case, capital and consumer goods – that the economy can produce given its factor endowment. The economy can produce any combination on or inside the frontier. Points outside the frontier are not feasible given the economy's existing resources.

An outcome is said to be *efficient* if the economy is getting all it can from the scarce resources it has available. Points on the PPF represent efficient levels of production. When the economy is producing at such a point, say point A, there is no way to produce more of one good without producing less of the other. Point B represents an *inefficient* outcome. For some reason, the economy is producing less than it could from the resources it has available and so some of its resources are lying idle (they are unemployed or underemployed). At point B, the country is producing only 300 000 units of capital goods and 800 000 consumer goods. If the source of the inefficiency were eliminated, the economy could move from point B to point A, increasing production of both capital goods (to 700 000) and consumer goods (to 2 million).

The production possibilities frontier illustrates the idea of a trade-off in that once a society has reached the efficient points on the frontier, the only way of getting more of one good is to get less of the other. When the economy moves from point A to point C, for instance, society produces more capital goods but at the expense of producing fewer consumer goods.

The production possibilities frontier can also be used to show opportunity cost. If some factors of production are reallocated from the consumer goods industry to the capital goods industry, moving the economy from point A to point C, for example, it gives up 300 000 consumer goods to get 50 000 additional capital goods. The opportunity cost of 300 000 consumer goods is 50 000 capital goods.

Calculating Opportunity Costs Remember that the opportunity cost is the cost expressed in terms of the next best alternative sacrificed – what has to be given up in order to acquire something. In the example the country had to give up 300 000 consumer goods to acquire 50 000 additional capital goods. The opportunity cost can be expressed in terms of either capital goods or consumer goods – they are the reciprocal of each other.

As a general principle we can express the opportunity cost as a ratio expressed as the sacrifice in one good in terms of the gain in the other:

$$Opportunity\ cost\ of\ good\ y = \frac{Sacrifice\ of\ good\ x}{Gain\ in\ good\ y}$$

Expressing the opportunity cost in terms of good *x* would give:

$$Opportunity\ cost\ of\ good\ x = \frac{Sacrifice\ of\ good\ y}{Gain\ in\ good\ x}$$

The opportunity cost of 1 additional unit of consumer goods or capital goods can be calculated by firstly writing out the known quantities:

The OC of 300 000 consumer goods is 50 000 capital goods

Divide both quantities by the number of consumer goods:

$$The\ OC\ of\ \frac{300\ 000}{300\ 000}\ consumer\ goods\ is\ \frac{50\ 000}{300\ 000}\ capital\ goods$$

Now complete the calculation to get the opportunity cost of 1 additional unit of consumer goods in terms of capital goods sacrificed:

The OC of 1 consumer good is 0.17 (2dp) capital goods

This tells us that for every 1 additional unit of consumer goods acquired, we have to give up 0.17 of a capital good.

To find the opportunity cost of capital goods in terms of consumer goods, follow the same process but in reverse.

The OC of 50 000 capital goods is 300 000 consumer goods

$$The\ OC\ of\ \frac{50\ 000}{50\ 000}\ capital\ goods\ is\ \frac{300\ 000}{50\ 000}\ consumer\ goods$$

The OC of 1 capital good is 6 consumer goods.

The Shape of the Production Possibilities Frontier

The production possibilities frontier in Figure 19.2 is bowed outward (concave to the origin). This is due to the fact that when economies move resources from one use to another, unless they are perfect substitutes (in which case the PPF would be a straight line), as the rate at which the increase in output of one good increases, the opportunity cost in terms of the other changes. For example, if the economy is using most of its resources to make consumer goods at point A in Figure 19.2, land, labour and capital is being used to make consumer goods even if these resources are not best suited to making these goods. If the country moves from point A to point B, the gain in capital goods is 250 000 units but the sacrifice in consumer goods is 200 000. The opportunity cost of 1 additional unit of capital goods will be 0.8 consumer goods sacrificed. Resources released from producing consumer goods are now able to produce capital goods, a use to which they may be more appropriately suited. If the economy moves from point B to point C, the gain in capital goods is a further 200 000 units but the sacrifice in terms of consumer goods is now 700 000. The opportunity cost of 1 additional unit of capital goods now is 3.5 consumer goods sacrificed.

If the country continues to shift resources to capital goods from consumer goods the ease of substitutability of factors becomes weaker and the sacrifice in consumer goods becomes greater. Moving from point C to point D yields an additional 250 000 capital goods but at a cost of 1.1 million units of consumer goods. The opportunity cost of 1 additional unit of capital goods is now 4.4 units of consumer goods. The reason that the opportunity cost in terms of consumer goods is rising is that the resources being put to use producing more capital goods are now less suited to the purpose and so the sacrifice in consumer goods increases.

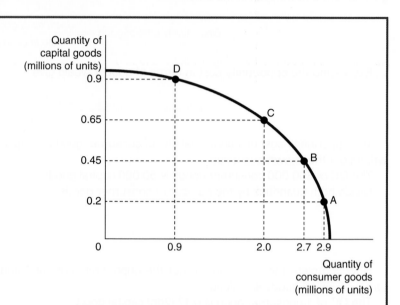

FIGURE 19.2

The Shape of the Production Possibilities Frontier

The PPF is concave to the origin. The shape of the PPF reflects the opportunity cost of producing different quantities of capital goods and consumer goods. If the country switches resources from consumer goods to capital goods, the opportunity cost in terms of the increase in consumer goods sacrificed for every additional unit of capital goods rises as the output combination moves from point A to point D.

The PPF illustrates two of the key questions any economy has to answer: what is to be produced and how will the output be produced? Most economies could use the resources it has at its disposal in a variety of ways. For example, it is possible that the UK could allocate resources to the production of oranges. Large amounts of land could be set aside for the construction of glasshouses in which the climate, water and nutrition needs of orange trees is controlled by computer technology. In Spain the same amount of oranges could be produced using far fewer resources simply because the climate is more conducive to growing oranges. The opportunity cost of using resources in this way in the UK is likely to be high, therefore.

A Shift in the Production Possibilities Frontier

The production possibilities frontier shows the trade-off between the production of different goods at a given time, but the trade-off can change over time. For example, technological advances can mean that factors of production are considerably more productive in terms of output per unit per time period. Countries might also be in a position to recover or make use of more natural resources or the effects of education in the country means the labour force becomes more productive. Over time, therefore, opportunity cost ratios of production change and this can affect the shape and position of the production possibilities frontier.

Figure 19.3 shows three possible outcomes. In panel (a) the PPF has shifted outwards showing that it is now possible to produce more of both capital goods and consumer goods as indicated by the move to point B. If all resources were devoted to capital goods, the economy could now produce 1.2 million units and if all resources were devoted to consumer goods the country could produce 3.6 million units. The relative opportunity cost ratios, however, remain the same because the PPF has shifted outwards, parallel at every point to the original curve. Because of this economic growth, society might move production from point A to point B, enjoying more consumer goods and more capital goods.

Panel (b) shows a shift in the PPF but this time the economic advances in the productivity of the capital goods industry is greater than that of the consumer goods industry. If all resources were now devoted to capital goods production, the country could produce 1.5 million units and if it devoted all output to consumer goods it could produce 3.2 million units. The opportunity cost ratio at all points on the new PPF will now be different to those on the original PPF.

Panel (c) shows the situation where the economic advances in productivity in the consumer goods industry is greater than in the capital goods industry. In this case, if all resources were devoted to producing consumer goods, the country could now produce 3.7 million units and if all resources were devoted to producing capital goods, 1.1 million units could be produced.

It may also be possible that productivity in one industry might actually reduce whilst that in the other rises in which case the PPF might take the look of that in panel (d) of Figure 19.3. In this case there has been an increase in productivity in the capital goods industry but a reduction in the consumer goods industry.

FIGURE 19.3

Shifts in the Production Possibilities Frontier
Panels (a) to (d) show different shifts in the PPF as a result of changes in the productivity of factors used in producing capital and consumer goods.

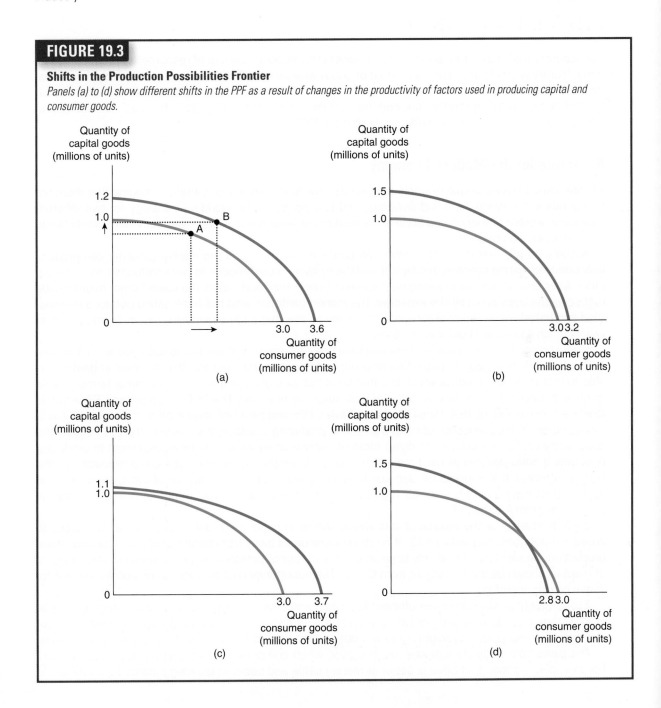

The production possibilities frontier simplifies a complex economy to highlight and clarify some basic ideas. We can now extend the analysis to look at how different factor endowments and factor productivity in different countries can lead to countries trading and gaining advantages.

SELF TEST Use the information in Figure 19.3 to calculate the opportunity cost ratios of both capital and consumer goods in each scenario presented in the different panels. Assume, in each case, that the country moves from devoting all its resources to capital goods and then switches to devoting all its resources to consumer goods.

INTERNATIONAL TRADE

Each country has its own PPF and in isolation faces choices about the use of resources to produce goods. If the country wants to increase the amount of goods available to all its citizens, then it can rely on increasing the number of factors it has at its disposal or the efficiency with which its resources are used to shift the PPF outwards. In addition to this, countries might also choose to engage in trade as a means of providing benefits to its citizens and effectively shift the PPF.

A Parable for the Modern Economy

We are going to use a simple example to illustrate how trade can lead to benefits. Imagine that there are two goods in the world, beef and potatoes, and two people in the world (our analogy for two different countries), a cattle farmer named Silvia and a market gardener named Johan, each of whom would like to eat both beef and potatoes.

Assume initially that the cattle farmer can produce only meat and the market gardener can produce only potatoes. In one scenario, the farmer and the gardener could choose to have nothing to do with each other. After several months of eating beef roasted, boiled, fried and grilled, the cattle farmer might decide that self-sufficiency is not all she expected. The market gardener, who has been eating potatoes mashed, fried and baked, would most likely agree. It is easy to see that trade would allow them to enjoy greater variety: each could have beef and potatoes.

Now assume that the farmer and the gardener are each capable of producing both goods. In this case each has a PPF analogous to two different countries. Suppose, for example, that the market gardener is able to rear cattle and produce meat, but that he is not very good at it and that the cattle farmer is able to grow potatoes, but her land is not very well suited to this crop. The PPF for Johan and Silvia would look like those in Figure 19.4. Panel (a) shows Silvia's PPF and panel (b) shows Johan's. Because Silvia is more efficient in the production of meat than she is producing potatoes, the shape of the PPF reflects the opportunity cost of any decision to divert more of her resources away from producing meat to producing potatoes. If Silvia devoted all her time and resources to producing potatoes she could produce Q_M, the vertical intercept. If she makes the decision to divert resources to the production of meat, the sacrifice in terms of lost meat output is relatively high compared to the gains in output of potatoes as shown by the move from point A to point B.

Johan's situation is the reverse of this and is shown in panel (b). If Johan allocates all resources to producing potatoes, he produces Q_P. If he diverts resources away from potato production towards meat production, he sacrifices a relatively large amount of output of potatoes to gain a relatively small amount of meat as shown by the movement from C to D. The opportunity cost of diverting resources to meat for Johan is high, therefore.

Economically, it would be more efficient for Johan and Silvia to cooperate with each other, specialize in what they both do best and benefit from trading with each other at some mutually agreeable rate of exchange. For example, they might agree to a rate of exchange of 1 kg of meat for every 5 kg of potatoes.

The gains from trade are less obvious, however, when one person is better at producing *every* good. For example, suppose that Silvia is better at rearing cattle *and* better at growing potatoes than Johan. In this case, should the farmer or gardener choose to remain self-sufficient, or is there still reason for them to trade with each other?

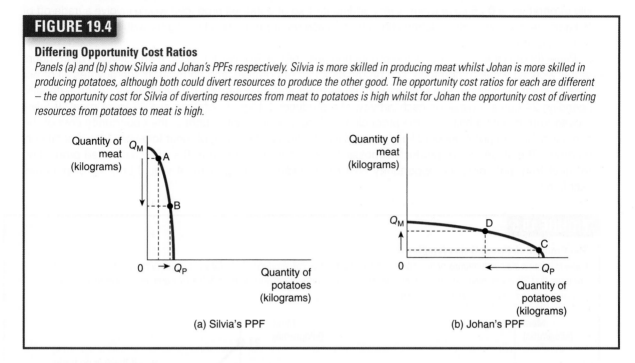

FIGURE 19.4

Differing Opportunity Cost Ratios

Panels (a) and (b) show Silvia and Johan's PPFs respectively. Silvia is more skilled in producing meat whilst Johan is more skilled in producing potatoes, although both could divert resources to produce the other good. The opportunity cost ratios for each are different – the opportunity cost for Silvia of diverting resources from meat to potatoes is high whilst for Johan the opportunity cost of diverting resources from potatoes to meat is high.

(a) Silvia's PPF

(b) Johan's PPF

Production Possibilities

Suppose that Johan and Silvia each work 8 hours a day 6 days a week (a working week of 48 hours) and take Sunday off. They can spend their time growing potatoes, rearing cattle, or a combination of the two. Table 19.1 shows the amount of time each person takes to produce 1 kg of each good. The gardener can produce 1 kg of meat in 6 hours and 1 kg of potatoes in an hour and a half. The farmer, who is more productive in both activities, can produce a kilogram of meat in 2 hours and a kilogram of potatoes in 1 hour. The last columns in Table 19.1 show the amounts of meat or potatoes the gardener and farmer can produce in a 48-hour working week, producing only that good.

TABLE 19.1 **The Production Opportunities of Johan the Gardener and Silvia the Farmer**

	Time needed to make 1 kg of:		Amount of meat or potatoes produced in 48 hours	
	Meat	Potatoes	Meat	Potatoes
Johan	6 hrs/kg	1.5 hrs/kg	8 kg	32 kg
Silvia	2 hrs/kg	1 hr/kg	24 kg	48 kg

Panel (a) of Figure 19.5 illustrates the amounts of meat and potatoes that Johan can produce. If he devotes all 48 hours of his time to potatoes, he produces 32 kg of potatoes (measured on the horizontal axis) and no meat. If he devotes all his time to meat, he produces 8 kg of meat (measured on the vertical axis) and no potatoes. If Johan divides his time equally between the two activities, spending 24 hours a week on each, he produces 16 kg of potatoes and 4 kg of meat. The figure shows these three possible outcomes and all others in between.

This graph is Johan's production possibilities frontier. Note that in this case, the PPF is a straight line indicating that the slope is constant and thus the opportunity cost to Johan of switching between potatoes and meat is constant. Johan faces a trade-off between producing meat and producing potatoes. If Johan devotes an extra hour to producing meat, he sacrifices potato production. Assume Johan starts at point

A producing 4 kg of meat and 16 kg of potatoes. If he then devoted all resources to producing potatoes, he would produce 32 kg of potatoes and sacrifice 4 kg of potatoes. The opportunity cost of 1 additional kilo of potatoes is 0.25 kg of meat. Every additional 1 kg of potatoes produced would involve a trade-off of ¼ kg of meat. Conversely, if Johan chose to increase meat production by 1 kg he would have to sacrifice 4 kg of potatoes.

Panel (b) of Figure 19.5 shows the production possibilities frontier for Silvia. If she devotes all 48 hours of her working week to potatoes, she produces 48 kg of potatoes and no meat. If she devotes all of her time to meat production, she produces 24 kg of meat and no potatoes. If Silvia divides her time equally, spending 24 hours a week on each activity, she produces 24 kg of potatoes and 12 kg of meat. If Silvia moved from devoting half her time producing each to producing all potatoes, the opportunity cost of the additional 24 kg of potatoes is 12 kg of meat. Silvia would sacrifice ½ kg of meat for every 1 kg of additional potatoes. The slope of this production possibilities frontier is, therefore, 0.5. If Silvia shifted production to meat from potatoes, the opportunity cost of an additional 1 kg of meat would be 2 kg of potatoes sacrificed.

FIGURE 19.5

The Production Possibilities Frontier

Panel (a) shows the combinations of meat and potatoes that Johan can produce. Panel (b) shows the combinations of meat and potatoes that Silvia can produce. Both production possibilities frontiers are derived from Table 19.1 and the assumption that the gardener and farmer each work 8 hours a day.

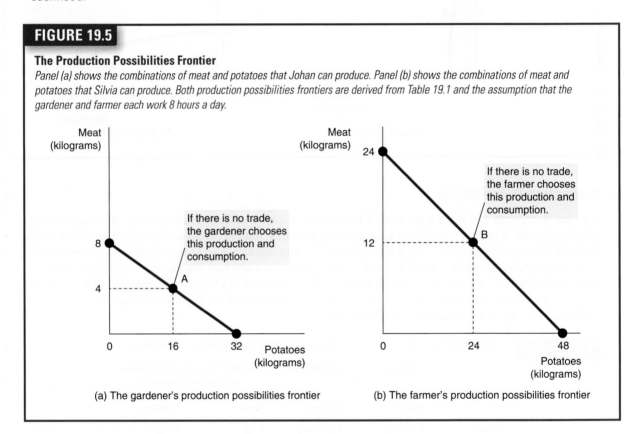

(a) The gardener's production possibilities frontier

(b) The farmer's production possibilities frontier

If the gardener and farmer choose to be self-sufficient, rather than trade with each other, then each consumes exactly what he or she produces. In this case, the production possibilities frontier is also the consumption possibilities frontier. That is, without trade, Figure 19.5 shows the possible combinations of meat and potatoes that Johan and Silvia can each consume.

Although these production possibilities frontiers are useful in showing the trade-offs that the gardener and farmer face, they do not tell us what Johan and Silvia will actually choose to do. To determine their choices, we need to know the tastes of the gardener and the farmer. Assume they choose the combinations identified by points A and B in Figure 19.5: Johan produces and consumes 16 kg of potatoes and 4 kg of meat, while Silvia produces and consumes 24 kg of potatoes and 12 kg of meat.

Specialization and Trade

After several years of feeding her family on combination B, Silvia gets an idea and she goes to talk to Johan:

SILVIA: Johan, I have a proposal to put to you. I know how to improve life for both of us. I think you should stop producing meat altogether and devote all your time to growing potatoes. According to my calculations, if you devote all of your working week to growing potatoes, you'll produce 32 kg of potatoes. If you give me 15 of those 32 kg, I'll give you 5 kg of meat in return. You will have 17 kg of potatoes left to enjoy and also 5 kg of meat every week, instead of the 16 kg of potatoes and 4 kg of meat you now make do with. If you go along with my plan, you'll have more of *both* foods. (To illustrate her point, Silvia shows Johan panel (a) of Figure 19.6.)

JOHAN: That seems like a good deal for me, Silvia, but how is it that we can both benefit?

SILVIA: Suppose I spend 12 hours a week growing potatoes and 36 hours rearing cattle. Then I can produce 12 kg of potatoes and 18 kg of meat. You will give me 15 kg of your potatoes in exchange for the 5 kg of my meat. This means I end up with 27 kg of potatoes and 13 kg of meat. So I will also be able to consume more of both foods than I do now. (She points out panel (b) of Figure 19.6.)

JOHAN: Hmm, sounds like a good idea, let me think about it.

SILVIA: To help, I've summarized my proposal for you in a simple table. (The farmer hands the gardener a copy of Table 19.2.)

FIGURE 19.6

How Trade Expands the Set of Consumption Opportunities
The proposed trade between the gardener and the farmer offers each of them a combination of meat and potatoes that would be impossible in the absence of trade. In panel (a), the gardener consumes at point A* rather than point A. In panel (b), the farmer consumes at point B* rather than point B. Trade allows each to consume more meat and more potatoes.

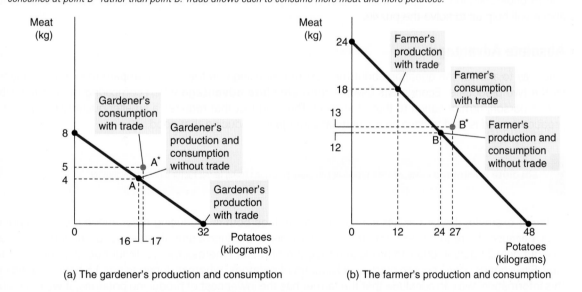

(a) The gardener's production and consumption

(b) The farmer's production and consumption

JOHAN: *(after pausing to study the table)* These calculations seem correct; so we can both be better off?

SILVIA: Yes, because trade allows each of us to specialize in doing what we do best. You will spend more time growing potatoes and less time rearing cattle. I will spend more time rearing cattle and less time growing potatoes. As a result of specialization and trade, each of us can consume more meat and more potatoes without working any more hours.

TABLE 19.2	The Gains from Trade: A Summary			

	Johan		Silvia	
	Meat	**Potatoes**	**Meat**	**Potatoes**
Without trade:				
Production and consumption	4 kg	16 kg	12 kg	24 kg
With trade:				
Production	0 kg	32 kg	18 kg	12 kg
With trade	Gets 5 kg	Gives 15 kg	Gives 5 kg	Gets 15 kg
Final consumption	5 kg	17 kg	13 kg	27 kg
Gains from trade:				
Increase in consumption	+1 kg	+1 kg	+1 kg	+3 kg

> **SELF TEST** Draw an example of a production possibilities frontier for Jan, who is stranded on an island after a shipwreck and spends his time gathering coconuts and catching fish. Does this frontier limit Jan's consumption of coconuts and fish if he lives by himself? Does he face the same limits if he can trade with natives on the island?

THE PRINCIPLE OF COMPARATIVE ADVANTAGE

The principle of *comparative advantage* helps explain why benefits from trade can arise even though Johan, the famer, is not as efficient in both rearing cattle and growing potatoes as Silvia the farmer.

As a first step in the explanation, consider the following question: in our example, who can produce potatoes at lower cost – the gardener or the farmer? There are two possible answers which provide the key to understanding the gains from trade. The slope of the production possibilities frontier discussed above will help us to solve the puzzle.

Absolute Advantage

One way to answer the question about the cost of producing potatoes is to compare the inputs required by the two producers. Economists use the term **absolute advantage** when comparing the productivity of one person, firm or nation to that of another. The producer that requires a smaller quantity of inputs to produce a good is said to have an absolute advantage in producing that good.

 absolute advantage exists where a producer can produce a good using fewer factor inputs than another

In our example, the farmer has an absolute advantage both in producing meat and in producing potatoes, because she requires less time than the gardener to produce a unit of either good. The farmer needs to input only 2 hours in order to produce a kilogram of meat, whereas the gardener needs 6 hours. Similarly, Silvia needs only 1 hour to produce a kilogram of potatoes, whereas Johan needs 1.5 hours. Based on this information, we can conclude that the farmer has the lower cost of producing potatoes, if we measure cost in terms of the quantity of inputs.

Opportunity Cost and Comparative Advantage

There is another way to look at the cost of producing potatoes. Rather than comparing inputs required, we can compare the opportunity costs. Let's first consider Silvia's opportunity cost in relation to the amount of hours she needs to work. According to Table 19.1, producing 1 kg of potatoes takes her 1 hour of work.

When Silvia spends that 1 hour producing potatoes, she spends 1 hour less producing meat. Because Silvia needs 2 hours to produce 1 kg of meat, 1 hour of work would yield ½ kg of meat. Hence, the farmer's opportunity cost of producing 1 kg of potatoes is ½ kg of meat.

Now consider Johan's opportunity cost. Producing 1 kg of potatoes takes him 1½ hours. Because he needs 6 hours to produce 1 kg of meat, 1½ hours of work would yield ¼ kg of meat. Hence, the gardener's opportunity cost of 1 kg of potatoes is ¼ kg of meat.

Table 19.3 shows the opportunity costs of meat and potatoes for the two producers. Remember that the opportunity cost of meat is the inverse of the opportunity cost of potatoes. Because 1 kg of potatoes costs the farmer ½ kg of meat, 1 kg of meat costs the farmer 2 kg of potatoes. Similarly, because 1 kg of potatoes costs the gardener ¼ kg of meat, 1 kg of meat costs the gardener 4 kg of potatoes.

TABLE 19.3   **The Opportunity Cost of Meat and Potatoes**

	Opportunity cost of:	
	1 kg of meat	**1 kg of potatoes**
Gardener	4 kg potatoes	0.25 kg meat
Farmer	2 kg potatoes	0.5 kg meat

Comparative advantage describes the opportunity cost of two producers; the producer who gives up less of other goods to produce good X has the smaller opportunity cost of producing good X and is said to have a comparative advantage in producing it. In our example, the gardener has a lower opportunity cost of producing potatoes than does the farmer: a kilogram of potatoes costs the gardener only ¼ kg of meat, while it costs the farmer ½ kg of meat. Conversely, Silvia has a lower opportunity cost of producing meat than does Johan: a kilogram of meat costs Silvia 2 kg of potatoes, while it costs Johan 4 kg of potatoes. Thus, the gardener has a comparative advantage in growing potatoes, and the farmer has a comparative advantage in producing meat.

> **comparative advantage** the comparison among producers of a good according to their opportunity cost. A producer is said to have a comparative advantage in the production of a good if the opportunity cost is lower than that of another producer

Although it is possible for one person to have an absolute advantage in both goods (as Silvia does in our example), it is impossible for one person to have a comparative advantage in both goods. Because the opportunity cost of one good is the inverse of the opportunity cost of the other, if a person's opportunity cost of one good is relatively high, their opportunity cost of the other good must be relatively low. Comparative advantage reflects the relative opportunity cost. Unless two people have exactly the same opportunity cost, one person will have a comparative advantage in one good, and the other will have a comparative advantage in the other good.

Comparative Advantage and Trade

In theory, differences in opportunity cost and comparative advantage create the gains from trade. The theory predicts that when each person specializes in producing the good for which he or she has a comparative advantage, total production in the economy rises, and this increase in the size of the economic cake can be used to make everyone better off.

Consider the proposed deal from the viewpoint of Johan. He gets 5 kg of meat in exchange for 15 kg of potatoes. In other words, Johan buys each kilogram of meat for a price of 3 kg of potatoes. This price of meat is lower than his opportunity cost for 1 kg of meat, which is 4 kg of potatoes. Thus, the gardener benefits from the deal because he gets to buy meat at a good price.

Now consider the deal from Silvia's viewpoint. The farmer buys 15 kg of potatoes for a price of 5 kg of meat. That is, the price of potatoes is ⅓ kg of meat. This price of potatoes is lower than her opportunity cost of 1 kg of potatoes, which is ½ kg of meat. The farmer benefits because she is able to buy potatoes at a good price.

These benefits arise because each person concentrates on the activity for which he or she has the lower opportunity cost: the gardener spends more time growing potatoes, and the farmer spends more time producing meat. As a result, the total production of potatoes and the total production of meat both rise. In our example, potato production rises from 40 to 44 kg, and meat production rises from 16 to 18 kg. The gardener and farmer share the benefits of this increased production.

FYI

The Legacy of Adam Smith and David Ricardo

Economists have long understood the principle of comparative advantage. Here is how Adam Smith put the argument:

It is the maxim of every prudent master of a family, never to attempt to make at home what it will cost him [sic] more to make than to buy. The tailor does not attempt to make his own shoes, but buys them off the shoemaker. The shoemaker does not attempt to make his own clothes but employs a tailor. The gardener attempts to make neither the one nor the other, but employs those different artificers. All of them find it for their interest to employ their whole industry in a way in which they have some advantage over their neighbours, and to purchase with a part of its produce, or what is the same thing, with the price of part of it, whatever else they have occasion for.

This quotation is from Smith's 1776 book, *An Inquiry into the Nature and Causes of the Wealth of Nations*, which was a landmark in the analysis of trade and economic interdependence.

Smith's book inspired David Ricardo to become an economist, having already made his fortune as a stockbroker in the City of London. In his 1817 book *Principles of Political Economy and Taxation*, Ricardo developed the principle of comparative advantage as we know it today. The Principle was originally put forward by Robert Torrens, a British Army officer and owner of the *Globe* newspaper in 1815. Ricardo's defence of free trade was not a mere academic exercise. Ricardo put his economic beliefs to work as a member of the British parliament, where he opposed the Corn Laws, which restricted the import of grain.

The conclusions of Adam Smith and David Ricardo form the basis of arguments in favour of free trade and against the imposition of tariffs or other restraints on trade. These arguments have had their critics, including the late Joan Robinson, a widely respected Cambridge economist, who noted that the theory Ricardo developed was largely based on an historical context of early 19th Century Britain and its trade with Portugal, and that economies had evolved over time. Some of the assumptions that Ricardo had made do not hold in modern economies in the same way (that all resources are employed and that prices are stable) and this means that the theory has to be reassessed in the light of the way economies have changed.

SELF TEST Jan can gather ten coconuts or catch one fish per hour. His friend, Marie, can gather 30 coconuts or catch two fish per hour. What is Jan's opportunity cost of catching one fish? What is Marie's? Who has an absolute advantage in catching fish? Who has a comparative advantage in catching fish?

Should Countries in Europe Trade with other Countries?

Our model of Johan and Silvia can be extended to represent whole countries. Many of the goods that Europeans enjoy are produced abroad, and many of the goods produced across Europe are sold abroad. Goods produced abroad and purchased for use in the domestic economy are called **imports**. An import leads to a flow of money from the country in payment. Goods produced domestically and sold abroad are called **exports**.

> **imports** goods produced abroad and purchased for use in the domestic economy leading to an outflow of funds from a country
>
> **exports** goods produced domestically and sold abroad leading to an inflow of funds into a country

To see how countries can benefit from trade, suppose there are two countries, Germany and the Netherlands, and two goods, machine tools and cut flowers. Imagine that the two countries produce cut flowers equally well: a German worker and a Dutch worker can each produce 1 tonne per month. By contrast, because Germany has more land suitable for manufacturing, it is better at producing machine tools: a German worker can produce 2 tonnes of machine tools per month, whereas a Dutch worker can produce only 1 tonne of machine tools per month.

The principle of comparative advantage states that each good should be produced by the country that has the smaller opportunity cost of producing that good. Because the opportunity cost of an additional 1 tonne of cut flowers is 2 tonnes of machine tools in Germany but only 1 tonne of machine tools in the Netherlands, the Dutch have a comparative advantage in producing cut flowers. The Netherlands should produce more cut flowers than it wants for its own use and export some of them to Germany. Similarly, because the opportunity cost of a tonne of cut flowers is 1 tonne of machine tools in the Netherlands but only ½ a tonne of machine tools in Germany, the Germans have a comparative advantage in producing machine tools. Germany should produce more machine tools than it wants to consume and export some of it to the Netherlands. Through specialization and trade, both countries can have more machine tools and more cut flowers.

In reality, of course, the issues involved in trade among nations are more complex than this simple example suggests, as we will see later. Most important among these issues is that each country has many citizens with different interests. International trade can make some individuals worse off, even as it makes the country as a whole better off. When Germany exports machine tools and imports cut flowers, the impact on a German worker is not the same as the impact on a German cut flower worker.

> **SELF TEST** Suppose that the world's fastest typist happens to be trained in brain surgery. Should they do their own typing or hire a personal assistant? Explain.

THE DETERMINANTS OF TRADE

Having seen that there are benefits to countries of trading, in this next section we look at the gains and losses of international trade. Consider the market for olive oil. The olive oil market is well suited to examining the gains and losses from international trade: olive oil is made in many countries around the world, and there is much world trade in olive oil. Moreover, the olive oil market is one in which policymakers often consider (and sometimes implement) trade restrictions to protect domestic olive oil producers from foreign competitors. We examine here the olive oil market in the imaginary country of Isoland.

The Equilibrium Without Trade

Assume that the Isolandian olive oil market is isolated from the rest of the world. By government decree, no one in Isoland is allowed to import or export olive oil, and the penalty for violating the decree is so large that no one dares try.

Because there is no international trade, the market for olive oil in Isoland consists solely of Isolandian buyers and sellers. As Figure 19.7 shows, the domestic price adjusts to balance the quantity supplied by domestic sellers and the quantity demanded by domestic buyers. The figure shows the consumer and producer surplus in the equilibrium without trade. The sum of consumer and producer surplus measures the total benefits that buyers and sellers receive from the olive oil market.

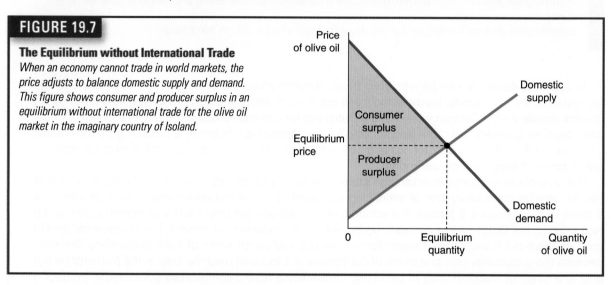

FIGURE 19.7

The Equilibrium without International Trade
When an economy cannot trade in world markets, the price adjusts to balance domestic supply and demand. This figure shows consumer and producer surplus in an equilibrium without international trade for the olive oil market in the imaginary country of Isoland.

Now suppose that Isoland elects a new president. The president campaigned on a platform of 'change' and promised the voters bold new ideas. Their first act is to assemble a team of economists to evaluate Isolandian trade policy. The president asks them to report back on three questions:

- If the government allowed Isolandians to import and export olive oil, what would happen to the price of olive oil and the quantity of olive oil sold in the domestic olive oil market?
- Who would gain from free trade in olive oil and who would lose, and would the gains exceed the losses?
- Should a tariff (a tax on olive oil imports) or an import quota (a limit on olive oil imports) be part of the new trade policy?

The World Price and Comparative Advantage

The first issue our economists take up is whether Isoland is likely to become an olive oil importer or an olive oil exporter. In other words, if free trade were allowed, would Isolandians end up buying or selling olive oil in world markets? To answer this question, the economists compare the current Isolandian price of olive oil with the price of olive oil in other countries. We call the price prevailing in world markets the **world price**. If the world price of olive oil is higher than the domestic price, then Isoland would become an exporter of olive oil once trade is permitted. Isolandian olive oil producers would be eager to receive the higher prices available abroad and would start selling their olive oil to buyers in other countries. Conversely, if the world price of olive oil is lower than the domestic price, then Isoland would become an importer of olive oil. Because foreign sellers offer a better price, Isolandian olive oil consumers would buy olive oil from other countries.

world price the price of a good that prevails in the world market for that good

In essence, comparing the world price and the domestic price before trade indicates whether Isoland has a comparative advantage in producing olive oil. The domestic price reflects the opportunity cost of olive oil: it tells us how much an Isolandian must give up to get one unit of olive oil. If the domestic price is low, the cost of producing olive oil in Isoland is low, suggesting that Isoland has a comparative advantage in producing olive oil relative to the rest of the world. If the domestic price is high, then the cost of producing olive oil in Isoland is high, suggesting that foreign countries have a comparative advantage in producing olive oil. By comparing the world price and the domestic price before trade, we can determine whether Isoland is better or worse at producing olive oil than the rest of the world.

THE WINNERS AND LOSERS FROM TRADE

To analyze the welfare effects of free trade, the Isolandian economists begin with the assumption that Isoland is a small economy compared with the rest of the world so that its actions have a negligible effect on world markets. The small economy assumption has a specific implication for analyzing the olive oil market: if Isoland is a small economy, then the change in Isoland's trade policy will not affect the world price of olive oil. The Isolandians are said to be *price-takers* in the world economy. They can sell olive oil at this price and be exporters, or buy olive oil at this price and be importers.

The Gains and Losses of an Exporting Country

Figure 19.8 shows the Isolandian olive oil market when the domestic equilibrium price before trade is below the world price. Once free trade is allowed, the domestic price rises to equal the world price. No seller of olive oil would accept less than the world price, and no buyer would pay more than the world price.

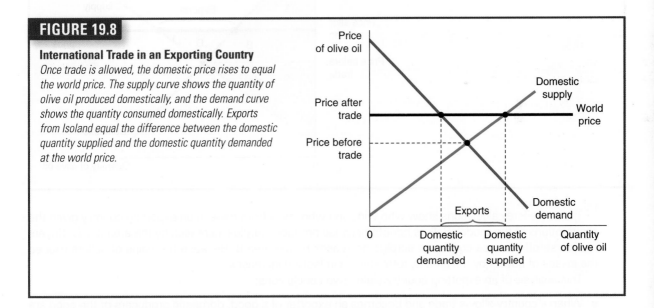

FIGURE 19.8

International Trade in an Exporting Country
Once trade is allowed, the domestic price rises to equal the world price. The supply curve shows the quantity of olive oil produced domestically, and the demand curve shows the quantity consumed domestically. Exports from Isoland equal the difference between the domestic quantity supplied and the domestic quantity demanded at the world price.

With the domestic price now equal to the world price, the domestic quantity supplied is greater than the domestic quantity demanded, Isoland sells olive oil to other countries. Thus, Isoland becomes an olive oil exporter. Although domestic quantity supplied and domestic quantity demanded differ, the olive oil market is still in equilibrium because there is now another participant in the market: the rest of the world. One can view the horizontal line at the world price as representing the demand for olive oil from the rest of the world. This demand curve is perfectly price elastic because Isoland, as a small economy, can sell as much olive oil as it wants at the world price.

Now consider the gains and losses from opening up trade. Clearly, not everyone benefits. Trade forces the domestic price to rise to the world price. Domestic producers of olive oil are better off because they can now sell olive oil at a higher price, but domestic consumers of olive oil are worse off because they have to buy olive oil at a higher price.

To measure these gains and losses, we look at the changes in consumer and producer surplus, which are shown in the graph and table in Figure 19.9. Before trade is allowed, the price of olive oil adjusts to balance domestic supply and domestic demand. Consumer surplus, the area between the demand curve and the before-trade price, is area A + B. Producer surplus, the area between the supply curve and the before-trade price, is area C. Total surplus before trade, the sum of consumer and producer surplus, is area A + B + C.

After trade is allowed, the domestic price rises to the world price. Consumer surplus is area A (the area between the demand curve and the world price). Producer surplus is area B + C + D (the area between the supply curve and the world price). Thus, total surplus with trade is area A + B + C + D.

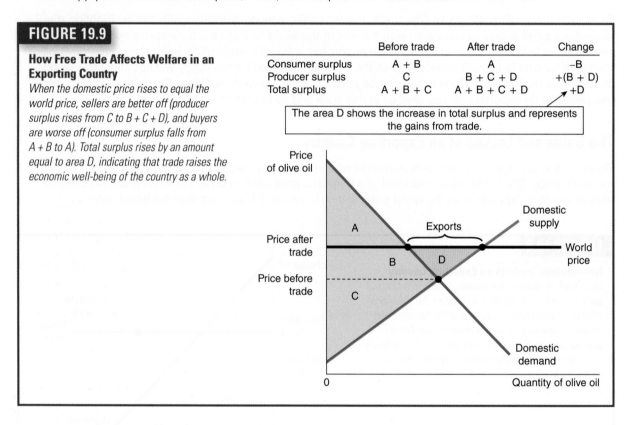

FIGURE 19.9

How Free Trade Affects Welfare in an Exporting Country

When the domestic price rises to equal the world price, sellers are better off (producer surplus rises from C to B + C + D), and buyers are worse off (consumer surplus falls from A + B to A). Total surplus rises by an amount equal to area D, indicating that trade raises the economic well-being of the country as a whole.

	Before trade	After trade	Change
Consumer surplus	A + B	A	−B
Producer surplus	C	B + C + D	+(B + D)
Total surplus	A + B + C	A + B + C + D	+D

The area D shows the increase in total surplus and represents the gains from trade.

These welfare calculations show who wins and who loses from trade in an exporting country given the assumptions of the model. Sellers benefit because producer surplus increases by the area B + D. Buyers are worse off because consumer surplus decreases by the area B. Because the gains of sellers exceed the losses of buyers by the area D, total surplus in Isoland increases.

This analysis of an exporting country yields two conclusions:

● When a country allows trade and becomes an exporter of a good, domestic producers of the good are better off and domestic consumers of the good are worse off.
● Trade raises the economic well-being of a nation in the sense that the gains of the winners exceed the losses of the losers.

The Gains and Losses of an Importing Country

Now suppose that the domestic price before trade is above the world price. Once again, after free trade is allowed, the domestic price must equal the world price. As Figure 19.10 shows, the domestic quantity supplied is less than the domestic quantity demanded. The difference between the domestic quantity demanded and the domestic quantity supplied is bought from other countries, and Isoland becomes an olive oil importer.

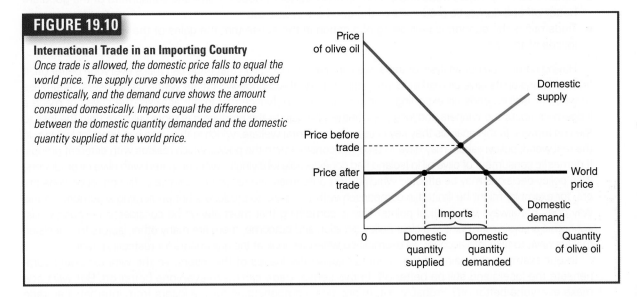

FIGURE 19.10

International Trade in an Importing Country
Once trade is allowed, the domestic price falls to equal the world price. The supply curve shows the amount produced domestically, and the demand curve shows the amount consumed domestically. Imports equal the difference between the domestic quantity demanded and the domestic quantity supplied at the world price.

In this case, the horizontal line at the world price represents the supply of the rest of the world. This supply curve is perfectly elastic because of the assumptions made that Isoland is a small economy and, therefore, can buy as much olive oil as it wants at the world price.

Now consider the gains and losses from trade. Once again, not everyone benefits. When trade forces the domestic price to fall, domestic consumers are better off (they can now buy olive oil at a lower price), and domestic producers are worse off (they now have to sell olive oil at a lower price). Changes in consumer and producer surplus measure the size of the gains and losses, as shown in the graph and table in Figure 19.11. Before trade, consumer surplus is area A, producer surplus is area B + C, and total surplus is area A + B + C. After trade is allowed, consumer surplus is area A + B + D, producer surplus is area C and total surplus is area A + B + C + D.

These welfare calculations show who wins and who loses from trade in an importing country given the assumptions of the model. Buyers benefit because consumer surplus increases by the area B + D. Sellers are worse off because producer surplus falls by the area B. The gains of buyers exceed the losses of sellers, and total surplus increases by the area D.

FIGURE 19.11

How Free Trade Affects Welfare in an Importing Country
When the domestic price falls to equal the world price, buyers are better off (consumer surplus rises from A to A + B + D), and sellers are worse off (producer surplus falls from B + C to C). Total surplus rises by an amount equal to area D, indicating that trade raises the economic well-being of the country as a whole.

	Before trade	After trade	Change
Consumer surplus	A	A + B + D	+(B + D)
Producer surplus	B + C	C	–B
Total surplus	A + B + C	A + B + C + D	+D

The area D shows the increase in total surplus and represents the gains from trade.

This analysis of an importing country yields two conclusions parallel to those for an exporting country:

● When a country allows trade and becomes an importer of goods, domestic consumers of the good are better off and domestic producers of the good are worse off.

● Trade raises the economic well-being of a nation in the sense that the gains of the winners exceed the losses of the losers.

Having completed our analysis of trade, we can draw a conclusion that trade can make everyone better off. If Isoland opens up its olive oil market to international trade the change will create winners and losers, regardless of whether Isoland ends up exporting or importing olive oil. Notice that in our analysis, we have not made a judgement about the winners and losers – whether the gain to the producers is more valuable than the loss to the consumers. In this analysis they key is the effect on total welfare, which in this case has risen for Isoland. In the real world, policymakers may have to take into consideration the power which resides with different groups. If domestic consumers of olive oil in Isoland had considerable lobbying power compared with olive oil producers, then policy decisions may be affected which distort outcomes and reduce total welfare. The effect on consumers, for example, might be limited in comparison with the gains to producers but presenting arguments in this way does not always win political points! This is something that must always be considered because whilst economic analysis may point to a clear policy decision and outcome, there are many other factors that decision makers have to take into account, as exemplified when we look at the arguments for restricting trade.

In our example, the gains of the winners exceed the losses of the losers, so the winners could compensate the losers and still be better off. In this sense, trade *can* make everyone better off. But *will* trade make everyone better off? Probably not. In practice, compensation for the losers from international trade is rare. Without such compensation, opening up to international trade is a policy that expands the size of the economic cake, whilst perhaps leaving some participants in the economy with a smaller slice.

We can now see why the debate over trade policy is so often contentious. Whenever a policy creates winners and losers, the stage is set for a political battle. Nations sometimes fail to enjoy the gains from trade simply because the losers from free trade have more political influence than the winners. The losers lobby for trade restrictions, such as tariffs and import quotas.

FYI

Other Benefits of International Trade

Our conclusions so far have been based on the standard analysis of international trade. There are several other economic benefits of trade beyond those emphasized in the standard analysis which can be taken into account. Here, in a nutshell, are some of these other benefits:

● *Increased variety of goods.* Goods produced in different countries are not exactly the same. German beer, for instance, is not the same as American beer. Free trade gives consumers in all countries greater variety from which to choose.

● *Lower unit costs through economies of scale.* Some goods can be produced at low unit or average cost only if they are produced in large quantities. A firm in a small country cannot take full advantage of economies of scale if it can sell only in a small domestic market. Free trade gives firms access to larger world markets and allows them to realize economies of scale more fully.

● *Increased competition.* A company shielded from foreign competitors is more likely to have market power, which in turn gives it the ability to raise prices above competitive levels. This is a type of market failure. Opening up trade fosters competition with the benefits that arise from more competitive markets.

● *Enhanced flow of ideas.* The transfer of technological advances around the world is often thought to be linked to international trade in the goods that embody those advances. The best way for a poor, agricultural nation to learn about the computer revolution, for instance, is to buy some computers from abroad, rather than trying to make them domestically.

● *Generates economic growth.* For poor countries, the increase in output can be a trigger to generating economic growth which may also bring an improvement in the standard of living for its citizens.

RESTRICTIONS ON TRADE

Despite the benefits that can arise from trade, the fact that there will always be winners and losers as we have seen means that arguments for restricting trade in some way are regularly promoted. We will look at three main methods of restricting trade, tariffs, quotas and non-tariff barriers, and then some of the arguments for trade.

The Effects of a Tariff

The Isolandian economists turn their attention to considering the effects of a **tariff** – a tax on imported goods. The tariff matters only if Isoland becomes an olive oil importer. Concentrating their attention on this case, the economists compare welfare with and without the tariff.

> **tariff** a tax on goods produced abroad and sold domestically

The graph in Figure 19.12 shows the Isolandian market for olive oil. Under free trade, the domestic price equals the world price. A tariff raises the price of imported olive oil above the world price by the amount of the tariff. Domestic suppliers of olive oil, who compete with suppliers of imported olive oil, can now sell their olive oil for the world price plus the amount of the tariff. Thus, the price of olive oil – both imported and domestic – rises by the amount of the tariff and is, therefore, closer to the price that would prevail without trade.

The change in price affects the behaviour of domestic buyers and sellers. Because the tariff raises the price of olive oil, it reduces the domestic quantity demanded from Q_1^D to Q_2^D and raises the domestic quantity supplied from Q_1^S to Q_2^S. Thus, the tariff reduces the quantity of imports and moves the domestic market closer to its equilibrium without trade.

Now consider the gains and losses from the tariff. Because the tariff raises the domestic price, domestic sellers are better off, and domestic buyers are worse off. In addition, the government raises revenue. To measure these gains and losses, we look at the changes in consumer surplus, producer surplus and government revenue. These changes are summarized in the table in Figure 19.12.

FIGURE 19.12

The Effects of a Tariff

A tariff reduces the quantity of imports and moves a market closer to the equilibrium that would exist without trade. Total surplus falls by an amount equal to area D + F. These two triangles represent the deadweight loss from the tariff.

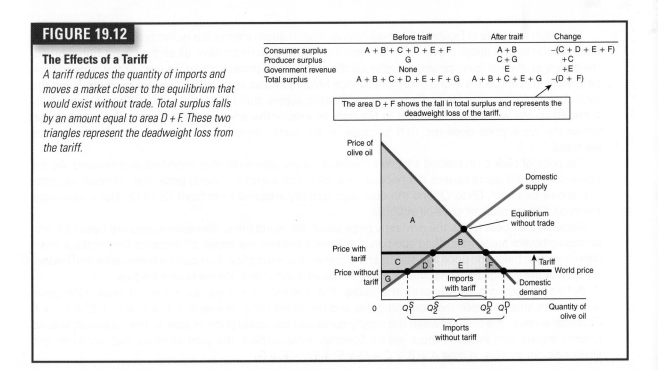

	Before traiff	After traiff	Change
Consumer surplus	A + B + C + D + E + F	A + B	–(C + D + E + F)
Producer surplus	G	C + G	+C
Government revenue	None	E	+E
Total surplus	A + B + C + D + E + F + G	A + B + C + E + G	–(D + F)

The area D + F shows the fall in total surplus and represents the deadweight loss of the tariff.

Before the tariff, the domestic price equals the world price. Consumer surplus, the area between the demand curve and the world price, is area A + B + C + D + E + F. Producer surplus, the area between the supply curve and the world price, is area G. Government revenue equals zero. Total surplus – the sum of consumer surplus, producer surplus and government revenue – is area A + B + C + D + E + F + G.

Once the government imposes a tariff, the domestic price exceeds the world price by the amount of the tariff. Consumer surplus is now area A + B. Producer surplus is area C + G. Government revenue, which is the quantity of after-tariff imports times the size of the tariff, is the area E. Thus, total surplus with the tariff is area A + B + C + E + G.

To determine the total welfare effects of the tariff, we add the change in consumer surplus (which is negative), the change in producer surplus (positive) and the change in government revenue (positive). We find that total surplus in the market decreases by the area D + F. This fall in total surplus is the *deadweight loss* of the tariff.

A tariff causes a deadweight loss simply because a tariff is a type of tax and can distort incentives and change the allocation of resources. In this case, we can identify two effects. First, the tariff on olive oil raises the price of olive oil that domestic producers can charge above the world price and, as a result, encourages them to increase production of olive oil (from Q_1^S to Q_2^S). Second, the tariff raises the price that domestic olive oil buyers have to pay and, therefore, encourages them to reduce consumption of olive oil (from Q_1^D to Q_2^D). Area D represents the deadweight loss from the overproduction of olive oil, and area F represents the deadweight loss from the under consumption. The total deadweight loss of the tariff is the sum of these two triangles.

The Effects of an Import Quota

The Isolandian economists next consider the effects of an **import quota** – a limit on the quantity of imports. In particular, imagine that the Isolandian government distributes a limited number of import licences. Each licence gives the licence holder the right to import 1 tonne of olive oil into Isoland from abroad. The Isolandian economists want to compare welfare under a policy of free trade and welfare with the addition of this import quota.

 import quota a limit on the quantity of a good that can be produced abroad and sold domestically

The graph and table in Figure 19.13 show how an import quota affects the Isolandian market for olive oil. Because the import quota prevents Isolandians from buying as much olive oil as they want from abroad, the supply of olive oil is no longer perfectly elastic at the world price. Instead, as long as the price of olive oil in Isoland is above the world price, the licence holders import as much as they are permitted, and the total supply of olive oil in Isoland equals the domestic supply plus the quota amount. That is, the supply curve above the world price is shifted to the right by exactly the amount of the quota. (The supply curve below the world price does not shift because, in this case, importing is not profitable for the licence holders.)

The price of olive oil in Isoland adjusts to balance supply (domestic plus imported) and demand. As the figure shows, the quota causes the price of olive oil to rise above the world price. The domestic quantity demanded falls from Q_1^D to Q_2^D and the domestic quantity supplied rises from Q_1^S to Q_2^S. Not surprisingly, the import quota reduces olive oil imports.

Because the quota raises the domestic price above the world price, domestic sellers are better off, and domestic buyers are worse off. In addition, the licence holders are better off because they make a profit from buying at the world price and selling at the higher domestic price. To measure these gains and losses, we look at the changes in consumer surplus, producer surplus and licence-holder surplus.

Before the government imposes the quota, the domestic price equals the world price. Consumer surplus, the area between the demand curve and the world price, is area A + B + C + D + E' + E" + F. Producer surplus, the area between the supply curve and the world price, is area G. The surplus of licence holders equals zero because there are no licences. Total surplus, the sum of consumer, producer and licence-holder surplus, is area A + B + C + D + E' + E" + F + G.

FIGURE 19.13

The Effects of an Import Quota

An import quota, like a tariff, reduces the quantity of imports and moves a market closer to the equilibrium that would exist without trade. Total surplus falls by an amount equal to area D + F. These two triangles represent the deadweight loss from the quota. In addition, the import quota transfers E' + E" to whoever holds the import licences.

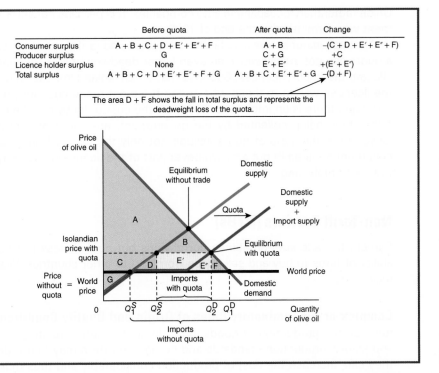

	Before quota	After quota	Change
Consumer surplus	A + B + C + D + E' + E" + F	A + B	–(C + D + E' + E" + F)
Producer surplus	G	C + G	+C
Licence holder surplus	None	E' + E"	+(E' + E")
Total surplus	A + B + C + D + E' + E" + F + G	A + B + C + E' + E" + G	–(D + F)

The area D + F shows the fall in total surplus and represents the deadweight loss of the quota.

After the government imposes the import quota and issues the licences, the domestic price exceeds the world price. Domestic consumers get surplus equal to area A + B, and domestic producers get surplus equal to area C + G. The licence holders make a profit on each unit imported equal to the difference between the Isolandian price of olive oil and the world price. Their surplus equals this price differential times the quantity of imports. Thus, it equals the area of the rectangle E' + E". Total surplus with the quota is the area A + B + C + E' + E" + G.

To see how total welfare changes with the imposition of the quota, we add the change in consumer surplus (which is negative), the change in producer surplus (positive) and the change in licence-holder surplus (positive). We find that total surplus in the market decreases by the area D + F. This area represents the deadweight loss of the import quota.

This analysis should seem somewhat familiar. Indeed, if you compare the analysis of import quotas in Figure 19.13 with the analysis of tariffs in Figure 19.12, you will see that they are essentially identical. Both tariffs and import quotas raise the domestic price of the good, reduce the welfare of domestic consumers, increase the welfare of domestic producers and cause deadweight losses. There is only one difference between these two types of trade restriction: a tariff raises revenue for the government (area E in Figure 19.12), whereas an import quota creates surplus for licence holders (area E' + E" in Figure 19.13).

Tariffs and import quotas can be made to look even more similar. Suppose that the government tries to capture the licence-holder surplus for itself by charging a fee for the licences. A licence to sell 1 tonne of olive oil is worth exactly the difference between the Isolandian price of olive oil and the world price, and the government can set the licence fee as high as this price differential. If the government does this, the licence fee for imports works exactly like a tariff: consumer surplus, producer surplus and government revenue are exactly the same under the two policies.

In practice, however, countries that restrict trade with import quotas rarely do so by selling the import licences. For example, in 1991 the European Union reached an agreement with Japan to 'voluntarily' limit the sale of Japanese cars in member countries of the EU. In this case, the Japanese government allocates the import licences to Japanese firms, and the surplus from these licences (area E' + E") accrues to those firms. This kind of import quota is, from the standpoint of the welfare of the European Union, strictly worse than an EU tariff on imported cars. Both a tariff and an import quota raise prices, restrict trade and cause deadweight losses, but at least the tariff produces revenue for the European

Union rather than for Japanese auto companies. It is perhaps not surprising, therefore, that this arrangement was terminated at the end of 1999.

Although in our analysis so far import quotas and tariffs appear to cause similar deadweight losses, a quota can potentially cause an even larger deadweight loss, depending on the mechanism used to allocate the import licences. Suppose that when Isoland imposes a quota, everyone understands that the licences will go to those who spend the most resources lobbying the Isolandian government. In this case, there is an implicit licence fee – the cost of lobbying. The revenues from this fee, however, rather than being collected by the government, are spent on lobbying expenses. The deadweight losses from this type of quota include not only the losses from overproduction (area D) and under consumption (area F) but also whatever part of the licence-holder surplus (area E' + E") is wasted on the cost of lobbying.

Non-Tariff Barriers (NTBs)

Barriers to trade are sometimes not obvious but nevertheless present significant restrictions on the ability of firms to buy and sell goods from and to other countries. We will briefly outline some of the main ones.

Complex or Discriminatory Rules of Origin and Quality Conditions Countries may impose strict rules on the production of goods in its domestic market relating to technical specifications, health and safety, production standards and so on. Exporters may find it difficult to meet these rules or if they can, increase the cost of production considerably and thus make the imports less competitive against domestically produced goods. In addition, firms may be required to give precise details as to where goods come from – something which is not easy given the widespread use of many different component parts from across the globe in many cases. The country establishing the NTB may only allow goods to be imported if they adhere to strict rules of origin which exporters might not be able to meet.

Sanitary or Phyto Sanitary Conditions Firms may be required to provide details of food and plant exports which again have to adhere to strict conditions. Phyto sanitary refers to the health of plants and exporting firms may have to show that plants are free from pest and disease, and that measures have been taken to ensure the conditions of growth adhere to the standards laid down by the country setting the NTB. In the case of food exports, a country may set very high food safety standards and regulations which exporters find difficult or costly to meet.

Administrative Regulations Some countries might set up administrative procedures that have to be met prior to any goods or services coming into the country. The paperwork or 'red tape' involved can be excessive and add to the costs of the exporter which again make the firm less competitive. Some countries might require excessive or unreasonable labelling or packaging regulations or set burdensome customs entry procedures including the necessity of providing valuations of goods at the point of entry which might be challenged (given value can be a subjective issue) or certification to prove authenticity, which again can lead to an increase in costs.

Currency Manipulation Some countries might implement measures to artificially influence the value of their currency, leading to exporters finding the price they face being higher than it would otherwise be, and as a result, reducing their competitiveness against domestic producers. We will see in the macroeconomics section of the book how exchange rates behave in response to government policies.

CASE STUDY   **Non-tariff Barriers for Indian Workers**

India is recognised for having many workers with expertize in technology. These workers are attractive to firms in other countries and as a result, some firms seek to employ Indian workers, sometimes on a temporary basis. In order to go abroad to work, these workers invariably require a visa for which a fee must be paid. In December 2015, a new law was signed in the US which increases the fees for visas for working in the US. The increase affects firms employing 50 or more workers in the US, and with more than half their staff coming from overseas. The doubling of the fees for one type of visa from around $2000 to $4000 and for another type from $2250 to $4500 was criticized by Indian government officials as a 'non-tariff barrier on people'. Given the rise in the fees, workers would be less likely to apply and this, in effect, represents a barrier to trade, according to the Indian Ministry for Commerce and Industry.

Indian workers face non-tariff barriers to enter the USA to deploy their skills.

The Lessons for Trade Policy

The team of Isolandian economists can now write to the new president:

Dear Madam President,

    You asked us three questions about opening up trade. These are our answers.

Question: If the government allowed Isolandians to import and export olive oil, what would happen to the price of olive oil and the quantity of olive oil sold in the domestic olive oil market?
Answer: Once trade is allowed, the Isolandian price of olive oil would be driven to equal the price prevailing around the world. If the world price is now higher than the Isolandian price, our price would rise. The higher price would reduce the amount of olive oil Isolandians consume and raise the amount of olive oil that Isolandians produce. Isoland would, therefore, become an olive oil exporter. This occurs because, in this case, Isoland would have a comparative advantage in producing olive oil.

Conversely, if the world price is now lower than the Isolandian price, our price would fall. The lower price would raise the amount of olive oil that Isolandians consume and lower the amount of olive oil that Isolandians produce. Isoland would, therefore, become an olive oil importer. This occurs because, in this case, other countries would have a comparative advantage in producing olive oil.

Question: Who would gain from free trade in olive oil and who would lose, and would the gains exceed the losses?
Answer: The answer depends on whether the price rises or falls when trade is allowed. If the price rises, producers of olive oil gain and consumers of olive oil lose. If the price falls, consumers gain and producers lose. In both cases, the gains are larger than the losses. Thus, free trade raises the total welfare of Isolandians.

Question: Should a tariff or an import quota be part of the new trade policy?
Answer: A tariff, like most taxes, has deadweight losses: the revenue raised would be smaller than the losses to the buyers and sellers. In this case, the deadweight losses occur because the tariff would move the economy closer to our current no-trade equilibrium. An import quota works much like a tariff and would cause similar deadweight losses. The best policy, from the standpoint of economic efficiency, would be to allow trade without a tariff or an import quota.

We hope you find these answers helpful as you decide on your new policy.

Your obedient servants,
Isolandian economics team

> **SELF TEST** Draw the supply and demand curve for wool suits in the country of Autarka. When trade is allowed, the price of a suit falls from 300 to 200 grams of gold. In your diagram, what is the change in consumer surplus, the change in producer surplus and the change in total surplus? How would a tariff on suit imports alter these effects?

The Arguments for Restricting Trade

The letter from the economics team persuades the new president of Isoland to consider opening up trade in olive oil. She notes that the domestic price is now high compared to the world price. Free trade would, therefore, cause the price of olive oil to fall and hurt domestic olive oil producers. Before implementing the new policy, she asks Isolandian olive oil companies to comment on the economists' advice.

Not surprisingly, the olive oil companies are opposed to free trade in olive oil. They believe that the government should protect the domestic olive oil industry from foreign competition. Let's consider some of the arguments they might give to support their position and how the economics team might respond.

The Jobs Argument Opponents of free trade often argue that trade with other countries destroys domestic jobs. In our example, free trade in olive oil would cause the price of olive oil to fall, reducing the quantity of olive oil produced in Isoland and thus reducing employment in the Isolandian olive oil industry. Some Isolandian olive oil workers would lose their jobs.

The counterargument to this is that trade can create jobs at the same time that it destroys them. When Isolandians buy olive oil from other countries, those countries obtain the resources to buy other goods from Isoland. Isolandian workers would move from the olive oil industry to those industries in which Isoland has a comparative advantage. This assumes that workers can move easily between different jobs, which of course, is possible but by no means cost-free. The movement of workers between industries does impose hardship in the short run but in the long run it can be argued that it allows Isolandians as a whole to enjoy a higher standard of living.

The National Security Argument When an industry is threatened with competition from other countries, opponents of free trade often argue that the industry is vital for national security. Free trade would allow Isoland to become dependent on foreign countries to supply vital resources. If a war later broke out, Isoland might be unable to produce enough to defend itself and remain self-sufficient.

Some economists acknowledge that protecting key industries may be appropriate when there are legitimate concerns over national security. It is also possible that this argument may be used too quickly by producers eager to gain at consumers' expense. Certainly, it is tempting for those in an industry to exaggerate their role in national defence to obtain protection from foreign competition.

The Infant Industry Argument New industries sometimes argue for temporary trade restrictions to help them get started. After a period of protection, the argument goes, these industries will mature and be able to compete with foreign competitors. Similarly, older industries sometimes argue that they need protection to help them adjust to new conditions. In 2002, for example, when US President George Bush imposed steep tariffs on the import of steel from the European Union, he argued that the industry needed protection in order to be able to afford to pay the pensions and healthcare costs of its retired workers and while it was going through a period of adjustment to make its production more efficient in order to be able to cope with intense foreign competition.

Some economists are sceptical about such claims. The primary reason is that the infant industry argument is difficult to implement in practice. To apply protection successfully, the government would need to decide which industries will eventually be profitable and decide whether the benefits of establishing these industries exceed the costs to consumers of protection. Yet 'picking winners' is extraordinarily difficult. It is made even more difficult by the political process, which often awards protection to those industries that are politically powerful. Once a powerful industry is protected from foreign competition, the 'temporary' policy is hard to remove.

In addition, some economists are sceptical about the infant industry argument even in principle. Suppose, for instance, that the Isolandian olive oil industry is young and unable to compete profitably against foreign rivals but there is reason to believe that the industry can be profitable in the long run. In this case, the owners of the firms should be willing to incur temporary losses to obtain the eventual profits. Protection is not necessary for an industry to grow. Firms in various industries – such as many internet firms today – incur temporary losses in the hope of growing and becoming profitable in the future. Many of them succeed, even without protection from foreign competition.

The Unfair Competition Argument A common argument is that free trade is desirable only if all countries play by the same rules. If firms in different countries are subject to different laws and regulations, then it is unfair (the argument goes) to expect the firms to compete in the international marketplace. For instance, suppose that the government of Neighbourland subsidizes its olive oil industry by giving olive oil companies large tax breaks. The Isolandian olive oil industry might argue that it should be protected from this foreign competition because Neighbourland is not competing fairly.

Would it, in fact, hurt Isoland to buy olive oil from another country at a subsidized price? Certainly, Isolandian olive oil producers would suffer, but Isolandian olive oil consumers would benefit from the low price. Moreover, the case for free trade is no different: the gains of the consumers from buying at the low price would exceed the losses of the producers. Neighbourland's subsidy to its olive oil industry may be a bad policy, but it is the taxpayers of Neighbourland who bear the burden. Isoland can benefit from the opportunity to buy olive oil at a subsidized price.

The Protection as a Bargaining Chip Argument Another argument for trade restrictions concerns the strategy of bargaining. Many policymakers claim to support free trade but, at the same time, argue that trade restrictions can be useful when we bargain with our trading partners. They claim that the threat of a trade restriction can help remove a trade restriction already imposed by a foreign government. For example, Isoland might threaten to impose a tariff on olive oil unless Neighbourland removes its tariff on wheat. If Neighbourland responds to this threat by removing its tariff, the result can be freer trade.

The problem with this bargaining strategy is that the threat may not work. If it doesn't work, the country has a difficult choice. It can carry out its threat and implement the trade restriction, which would reduce its own economic welfare. Or it can back down from its threat, which would cause it to lose prestige in international affairs. Faced with this choice, the country might wish that it had never made the threat in the first place.

CRITICISMS OF COMPARATIVE ADVANTAGE THEORY

The theory of comparative advantage has appeal and intuitively makes sense. In some surveys of economists, there seems to be a considerable number who agree that free trade is essentially a 'good' thing. The belief in free trade is based on the benefits espoused by the theory of comparative advantage. As noted earlier, there has been criticisms of the theory because of the context in which it was developed and that its assumptions are too simplistic to describe modern economies.

For example, countries with a large supply of unskilled labour and land might reasonably be expect to have a comparative advantage in the production of primary products and to trade the surplus of these with other more developed nations who may have a comparative advantage in the production of manufactured goods. In Africa, this scenario applies to many countries but these countries seem to have failed to reap the benefits of trade in the way that the theory suggests and remain extremely poor.

Other developing economies like India, China and South Korea, in contrast, have seen more rapid growth and improvement in their citizen's well-being. China's leaders have invested heavily in manufacturing industry, South Korea in large enterprises and India have a reputation in software and computer program development. Given that there are plenty of other countries in the world that had developed industries in these fields, it can be argued that India, China and South Korea were not exploiting comparative advantage. Rather, a conscious decision by the authorities to invest and build skills in industries where they did not have a comparative advantage has helped them to develop at a faster rate than many countries in Africa.

Rather than focus on comparative advantage, a more relevant point is that countries may make active decisions to specialise not in those industries in which it has the factor endowments that give them comparative advantage but in industries where the benefits to the population as a whole are likely to be greatest. For countries like China, South Korea and India, these decisions might be based on what is called the

Prebisch–Singer hypothesis. This hypothesis states that as incomes rise, spending on manufactured goods rises, whilst spending on primary products fall. For countries focusing on primary products like many in Africa, which have appropriate resource endowments, they are likely to become poorer over time compared to those which invest in manufactured goods production.

> **Prebisch–Singer hypothesis** a hypothesis suggesting that the rate at which primary products exchange for manufactured goods declines over time meaning that countries specialising in primary good production become poorer

Attempts to impose free trade on countries based on the theory of comparative advantage, therefore, could lead to countries not gaining the benefits the theory predicts. Joan Robinson noted that Ricardo's analysis focused on Britain and Portugal and used cloth and wine as the two goods concerned, with Britain having the comparative advantage in cloth production and Portugal in wine production. In specializing in wine production, the cloth industry in Portugal withered but the benefits from exporting wine were also limited because the global market for wine was not expanding quickly.

Empirical research into the Prebisch-Singer hypothesis, published in 2013 by Arezki, Hadri, Lougani and Rao for the International Monetary Fund, looked at 25 primary products since 1650 and found that results on the Prebisch-Singer hypothesis were mixed but that 'in the majority of cases, the Prebisch-Singer hypothesis is not rejected'. Critics of the theory of comparative advantage thus point to historical evidence that gains from trade can be garnered through investment in goods that have higher value in world trade markets rather than in goods where resource endowments suggest they have a comparative advantage.

CONCLUSION

The principle of comparative advantage shows that trade can make everyone better off. Despite these apparent benefits, there are fierce debates about trade policy. The theory of comparative advantage has been criticised as having assumptions which are too static and which do not reflect the way in which economies have developed since the original theory was developed in the early 19th century. Regardless of the benefits of free trade, most countries in the world have some sort of trade restrictions in place or group together to get the benefits of free trade between themselves whilst imposing trade restrictions on those countries outside the free trade 'club'.

IN THE NEWS

Winners and Losers?

In 2015, the Chinese President, Xi Jinping visited the UK amidst much pomp and ceremony. Mr Xi's visit coincided with a series of announcements on job losses in the UK steel industry with one of the reasons cited for the closures being the dumping of steel on the world market by China. The issue highlights the debates on free trade.

The UK Steel Industry

In October 2015, the coke ovens and blast furnace at the Redcar steelworks in North East England were turned off signalling the end of 98 years of steel making at the site. Around 2200 jobs at the steelworks were lost with more expected to follow as suppliers and local businesses feel the after-effects. In the same month, Tata Steel UK, part of the Indian conglomerate, announced that 1200 jobs would be lost at two plants in Scotland and in Scunthorpe in Lincolnshire. The press dubbed this a 'crisis in the steel industry' and unions called on the government to step in to help support the industry.

(Continued)

Tata and Sahaviriya Steel Industries UK (SSI), which owned the Redcar plant, cited global market conditions for the decisions. The price of steel had risen from just over $200 per tonne in September 2013 to around $480 per tonne in January 2015 but fell sharply to around $170 per tonne in early November 2015. The reasons for the price fall was said to be lower demand because of a general slowdown in economic activity but more importantly, a surplus of steel caused by supplies of steel being placed on the market by developing countries and in particular, China. Chinese steel exports rose by 28 per cent to 43.5 million tonnes in the first five months of 2015 and traders on metals markets claimed that China was selling steel at below cost in an attempt to reduce stocks. In addition to these global shocks, UK producers faced higher energy costs compared to some of its European counterparts and the strength of the UK pound also made UK steel uncompetitive.

The announcements about job losses came at the same time as the Chinese president Xi Jinping visited the UK on a state visit. The UK government were urged to raise the issue of cheap steel exports from China with Mr Xi. Unions and opposition members of parliament (MPs) called on the government to reduce energy prices to the steel industry, which the government said it could only do with the permission of the European Union. The government did announce that it was providing £80 million (€111m) to support workers in Redcar with the money to be used to help workers retrain and set themselves up in business and a further £9 million (€12.5m) to support workers in Scunthorpe. Some unions and opposition MPs also called for the government to take over the steel works at Redcar, arguing that steel was a strategically important industry for the UK. The government rejected this saying that given the global steel market, such a move would not represent good value for money for the UK taxpayer.

The closure of steel industry in Redcar on Teesside has been partly blamed on cheap Chinese exports of steel.

Questions

1 Use a supply and demand diagram to help explain the fall in steel prices between January and October 2015.

2 Does the theory of comparative advantage explain why China is able to produce steel more efficiently than the UK?

3 Chinese steel producers were accused of selling steel at prices below cost on global markets. If this was the case, to what extent do you think this was justified? (Hint: selling below cost might help keep plants in China open and jobs secured).

4 Why do you think that the UK government had to secure the permission of the European Union to provide subsidies to reduce energy costs to industries like steel?

5 The UK government sought to provide support for steel workers who lost their jobs. Does this imply that the assumption that 'losers' in global trade can simply move to other jobs in industries which are expanding, and in which the UK has a comparative advantage, is flawed?

SUMMARY

- Production possibilities frontiers provide a model to show potential output of goods and services in an economy and the opportunity cost ratios of diverting resources to different uses.

- The PPF can shift outwards if countries find ways of improving their factor productivity or exploit factor endowments more effectively.

- The shape and position of a PPF is dependent on the productivity of factor inputs and degree of specialization involved in the country in different industries.

- Each person consumes goods and services produced by many other people both in their country and around the world. Interdependence and trade are desirable because they allow people to enjoy a greater quantity and variety of goods and services.

- There are two ways to compare the ability of two people in producing a good. The person who can produce the good with the smaller quantity of inputs is said to have an *absolute advantage* in producing the good. The person who has the smaller opportunity cost of producing the good is said to have a *comparative advantage*. The gains from trade are based on comparative advantage, not absolute advantage.

- Trade can make everyone better off because it allows people to specialize in those activities in which they have a comparative advantage.

- The effects of free trade can be determined by comparing the domestic price without trade to the world price. A low domestic price indicates that the country has a comparative advantage in producing the good and that the country will become an exporter. A high domestic price indicates that the rest of the world has a comparative advantage in producing the good and that the country will become an importer.

- When a country allows trade and becomes an exporter of a good, producers of the good are better off, and consumers of the good are worse off. When a country allows trade and becomes an importer of a good, consumers are better off, and producers are worse off. In both cases, the gains from trade exceed the losses.

- A tariff – a tax on imports – moves a market closer to the equilibrium that would exist without trade and, therefore, reduces the gains from trade. Although domestic producers are better off and the government raises revenue, the losses to consumers exceed these gains.

- An import quota – a limit on imports – has effects that are similar to those of a tariff. Under a quota, however, the holders of the import licences receive the revenue that the government would collect with a tariff.

- There are various arguments for restricting trade: protecting jobs, defending national security, helping infant industries, preventing unfair competition and responding to foreign trade restrictions.

- Critics of the theory of comparative advantage argue that the assumptions of the theory do not hold in real life, that the development of the theory was based on a particular historical context which does not exist anymore, and that developing countries investing in higher value industries, rather than those in which they have the factor endowments which provide comparative advantage, have seen greater economic benefits.

QUESTIONS FOR REVIEW

1 Draw a PPF for a country producing only computers and wheat. What determines the shape and position of the PPF you have drawn? Use your diagram to show the opportunity cost of different output combinations.

2 What does the domestic price that prevails without international trade tell us about a nation's comparative advantage?

3 Explain how absolute advantage and comparative advantage differ.

4 Can two countries gain from trade if the opportunity cost ratios relating to production of goods they can both produce is the same? Explain.

5 When does a country become an exporter of a good? An importer?

6 Thousands of tourists visit European cities every year. Is tourism an import or an export to a country? Explain.

7 Draw the supply and demand diagram for an importing country. What is consumer surplus and producer surplus before trade is allowed? What is consumer surplus and producer surplus with free trade? What is the change in total surplus?

8 Describe what a tariff is, and its economic effects. What is an import quota? Compare its economic effects with those of a tariff.

9 List five arguments often given to support trade restrictions. How do economists respond to these arguments?

10 Have countries like South Korea, China and India experienced very rapid growth because they have a comparative advantage in the production of manufactured products? Explain.

PROBLEMS AND APPLICATIONS

1 Draw the PPF for a country which produces just oranges and cars. Assume that the country is better at producing oranges than cars.

   a. What can you say about the opportunity cost of the country diverting more resources into producing cars?

   b. The country discovers new resources which will mean that its ability to produce cars is significantly improved. What happens to the shape of the PPF as a result of this discovery?

   c. What can you say about the opportunity cost facing the country after this new discovery?

2 Look at the table below which shows the production possibilities for two products, pens and pencils.

Point	Pens	Pencils
A	10	0
B	5	10
C	2	25

   a. Calculate the opportunity cost of producing 1 additional pen between points A and B.

   b. Calculate the opportunity cost of producing 1 additional pencil between points A and B.

   c. Calculate the opportunity cost of producing 1 additional pen between points B and C. What conclusions can you come to about this opportunity cost compared to the calculation you made in a. above?

   d. Calculate the opportunity cost of producing 1 additional pencil between points B and C. What conclusions can you come to about this opportunity cost compared to the calculation you made in b. above?

3 European and Chinese workers can each produce 4 capital goods a year. A European worker can produce 10 tonnes of grain a year, whereas a Chinese worker can produce 5 tonnes of grain a year. To keep things simple, assume that Europe and China have 100 million workers each.

   a. For this situation, construct a table analogous to Table 19.1.

   b. Graph the production possibilities frontier of the European and Chinese economies.

   c. For Europe, what is the opportunity cost of a car? Of grain? For China, what is the opportunity cost of a car? Of grain? Put this information in a table analogous to Table 19.3.

   d. Which has an absolute advantage in producing capital goods? In producing grain?

   e. Which has a comparative advantage in producing capital goods? In producing grain?

   f. Without trade, half of Europe and China's workers produce capital goods and half produce grain. What quantities of capital goods and grain does Europe and China produce?

   g. Starting from a position without trade, give an example in which trade makes both Europe and China better off.

4 Morgan and Oliver share a flat. They spend most of their time studying (of course), but they leave some time for their favourite activities: cooking pizza and making homebrew beer. Oliver takes 4 hours to produce 1 barrel of homebrew and 2 hours to make a pizza. Morgan takes 6 hours to brew 1 barrel of beer and 4 hours to make a pizza.

   a. What is each flatmate's opportunity cost of making a pizza? Who has the absolute advantage in making pizza? Who has the comparative advantage in making pizza?

   b. If Oliver and Morgan trade foods with each other, who will trade away pizza in exchange for homebrew?

   c. The price of pizza can be expressed in terms of barrels of homebrew. What is the highest price at which pizza can be traded that would make both flatmates better off? What is the lowest price? Explain.

5 The UK and Poland both produce cakes and coats. Suppose that a British worker can produce 50 cakes per hour or 1 coat per hour. Suppose that a Polish worker can produce 40 cakes per hour or 2 coats per hour.

   a. Which country has the absolute advantage in the production of each good? Which country has the comparative advantage?

   b. If the UK and Poland decide to trade, which commodity will Poland trade to the UK? Explain.

   c. If a Polish worker could produce only 1 coat per hour, would Poland still gain from trade? Would the UK still gain from trade? Explain.

6 France represents a small part of the world apple market.

   a. Draw a diagram depicting the equilibrium in the French apple market without international trade. Identify the equilibrium price, equilibrium quantity, consumer surplus and producer surplus.

   b. Suppose that the world apple price is below the French price before trade, and that the French apple market is now opened to trade. Identify the new equilibrium price, quantity consumed, quantity produced domestically and quantity imported. Also show the change in the surplus of domestic consumers and producers. Has domestic total surplus increased or decreased?

7 The world price of wine is below the price that would prevail in France in the absence of trade.

    a. Assuming that French imports of wine are a small part of total world wine production, draw a graph for the French market for wine under free trade. Identify consumer surplus, producer surplus and total surplus in an appropriate table.

    b. Now suppose that an outbreak of phyloxera (a sap sucking insect which damages grape vines) in California and South America destroys much of the grape harvest there. What effect does this shock have on the world price of wine? Using your graph and table from part (a), show the effect on consumer surplus, producer surplus and total surplus in France. Who are the winners and losers? Is France better or worse off?

8 Suppose that European Union countries impose a common tariff on imported cars to protect the European car industry from foreign competition. Assuming that Europe is a price-taker in the world car market, show on a diagram: the change in the quantity of imports, the loss to European consumers, the gain to European car manufacturers, government revenue and the deadweight loss associated with the tariff. The loss to consumers can be decomposed into three pieces: a transfer to domestic producers, a transfer to the government and a deadweight loss. Use your diagram to identify these three pieces.

9 When the government of Tradeland decides to impose an import quota on foreign cars, three proposals are suggested:

- Sell the import licences in an auction.
- Distribute the licences randomly in a lottery.
- Let people wait in line and distribute the licences on a first-come, first-served basis.

Compare the effects of these policies. Which policy do you think has the largest deadweight losses? Which policy has the smallest deadweight losses? Why? (Hint: the government's other ways of raising tax revenue themselves all cause deadweight losses.)

10 Answer the questions on comparative advantage below.

    a. Explain how countries in Africa, which have an abundance of labour as a natural resource, can benefit from trade and allow countries to grow by specializing in the export of primary products.

    b. What factors might have caused countries in Africa to have not exploited their comparative advantage and as such have remained relatively poor in comparison to some of the more rapidly developed nations?

    c. Does the Prebisch–Singer hypothesis suggest that the theory of comparative advantage is of limited use in explaining modern trade between nations?

MACROECONOMICS PROLOGUE

There are a number of areas of controversy in macroeconomics. Some of the disagreements of economists stem from economic history and different schools of thought, which have shaped thinking over the last 250 years. It has to be remembered that some of the most revered economic thinkers were people of their day, describing, analyzing and thinking about problems which were highly relevant at particular points in history. Economies and the context in which they operate do not stand still, and what was relevant and prescient about the way an economic system was thought to have worked in one period of history does not necessarily mean that its mechanics and analysis can be transferred to other time periods. For example, the analysis of the causes of the Great Depression of the 1930s and the policy options which were appropriate to remedy some of the problems caused by the crisis, may have some similarities to the causes and consequences of the Financial Crisis of 2007–9. However, the world in 2007 was a very different place to that of 1929–30. Given the differences, to what extent are policy measures which derived from the analysis of the Great Depression relevant and applicable to post-Crisis economies?

To have some appreciation of the different and sometimes competing analyzes of macroeconomic issues, it is helpful to have some brief background to the history of economic thought and some of the key individuals that have pushed the boundaries of thinking in the discipline. This prologue is provided for that purpose.

A WORLD BEFORE MARKETS

Organizing economic activity through markets is a relatively new phenomenon given that it was around 1.8 million years ago that the hunter-gatherer species evolved. These species survived by living off food gathered from the wild – plants and animals. Around 10 000 years ago, humans became more domesticated and survived more through the development of agriculture and living in groups as opposed to roaming the land. As agricultural techniques developed, communities gradually developed early trade through barter, the exchange of goods. Trade is only possible with the existence of surpluses and the fertility of land in such circumstances becomes important. It is perhaps not surprising that land became important in tribes gaining power. Power relationships become an increasingly important feature of human society and the ownership and right to use land was the basis of the feudal society, which was typical across large parts of Europe dating as far back as the 5th century.

The feudal system was hierarchical based on the ownership or right to use land. In return for the varying rights for the use of land, groups pledged allegiance to their superior. The relationships were often based on the provision of service in return for the right to use land, with such service often being military in nature.

Feudal society was primarily a subsistence society with inhabitants using the land to provide for their needs. However, trade between groups and countries was steadily growing, mostly based on barter. Trade led to improvements in the standard of living and the developments of towns and cities, in many cases located near major ports and rivers, to facilitate the transport of goods. This signaled the growth in what was termed *mercantilism*, where nation states became the focus of economic wealth and power. At the heart of this wealth and power was gold, and to a lesser extent silver. Trade developed alongside the growth in some national identity and merchants who acted as brokers between producers and consumers became more wealthy and powerful as a result.

Whilst trade was seen as being mainly beneficial, nation states were not averse to imposing import restrictions if they felt that imports were damaging the national interest. In order to encourage trade, the development of monopoly power over the production of goods through craft guilds became more common. Craft guilds not only 'guaranteed' high quality goods but also reflected the importance of national power, wealth and prestige. In order to facilitate the trade of these goods, barter became less efficient and a monetary system, often based on gold, began to develop. Of course, transporting gold long distances to facilitate trade was dangerous and risky and as a result, early banking systems developed to guarantee exchange and facilitate the safe and secure movement of funds between traders.

CLASSICAL ECONOMICS

It was in the midst of the mercantilist era that Adam Smith was writing. Smith was looking to analyze and explain the increasingly complex economic system that had evolved. The idea of the importance of nation states can be seen in the background of Smith's idea of the invisible hand. Individuals can act to promote their own well-being but at the same time their actions also promote the well-being of society as a whole (or the nation state).

Smith and his contemporaries had identified the market system, which is the basis of so much of the teaching in undergraduate economics. The market system brings together buyers and sellers with price acting as a signal to both and influencing their respective behaviour. The basis of the market system was individuals acting in self-interest. Why individuals acted in the way they do, and the consequences of their decision-making, was subject to analysis. In order to understand the system and the behaviour of economic actors, some simplification had to be made and models were developed for this purpose. These models became more and more sophisticated as the techniques for analysis and the methodologies of research were developed and refined. The fundamentals of market analysis which forms a core of undergraduate first-year courses and beyond was developed in the period from the late 18th century to the end of the 19th century, and included the work of highly respected thinkers including Smith himself, David Ricardo, Thomas Malthus and John Stuart Mill. It is possible to summarize common beliefs and approaches of classical economics as follows:

- Humans are essentially self-interested and act to maximize their individual welfare.
- If left to the market, the interests of individuals and of societies can be maximized through the workings of markets. Prices act as signals to economic actors and markets ensure that resources are allocated to their most efficient uses through the 'invisible hand'.
- The role of government in the market system should be minimized to that which ensures that market systems can operate efficiently. This is primarily through enforcing laws and property rights, and the provision of defence and justice.

This summary is important because it contains the fundamental belief systems of those economists who subscribe to the market system as being the most efficient and effective way of allocating scarce resources. It not only helps to understand the basis of microeconomics but also of macroeconomics. Economists who believe in the power of free markets are more likely to be supportive of policy measures, which have their roots in market-based solutions, to both micro and macroeconomic issues.

Neo-classical Economics and Marginalism

The interest in economics and the methodology of analyzing economic issues developed through the application of mathematics to help understand, explain and predict. This was particularly prevalent in the development of marginal analysis, the understanding of the behaviour of economic actors at the margin. Maths was used as a means of providing a proof of behaviour but rested on a number of assumptions not least that economic actors behave rationally and seek to maximize or minimize subject to constraints. The development of constrained optimization techniques of economic analysis is associated with William Jeavons, Leon Walras, Karl Menger, Wilfredo Pareto and Knut Wicksell. These methods of analysis were being reflected by other noted economists including Alfred Marshall, who popularized the use of supply and demand models initially used by Antoine Augustin Cournot, and Francis Ysidro Edgeworth who, along with Walras, explored concepts in general equilibrium. General Equilibrium is a logical extension to neo-classical economic beliefs in that if the move to equilibrium was the natural state for an individual market then it was equally natural for all markets to ultimately move to equilibrium.

The neo-classical belief in the power of free markets and the application of mathematical and statistical methodologies to analyze and understand economics has dominated the discipline for many years. Critics argue that this dominance is perpetuated by the continued teaching of students of this basic philosophy and that alternative views of economic phenomena and methodologies has been subjugated as a result.

MARXIST ECONOMICS

Karl Marx's analysis of economics and economic systems is based on the idea that 'modern' human history is dominated by class struggles and the exploitation of one class by another. This exploitation is based on economic power, slaves and slave owners, feudal lords and peasants, and ultimately, under a capitalist economic system, the bourgeoisie, capital – owning class, and the proletariat. Marx had an explanation for the tendency of capitalism to experience repeated crises. At the heart of his argument is the labour theory of value which we encountered in Chapter 17. Marx suggested that over a business cycle, the rate of profit would decline. He saw equilibrium not in terms of market clearing but the tendency of rates of profit on capital to equalize to capitalists who are in constant competition with each other. This market competition prevents capitalists from taking all surplus value for themselves; some of it has to be reinvested in order to maintain the advantage over competitors. Some of this investment is in machinery which Marx referred to as 'constant capital'.

Improvements in technology mean that this investment increases the ratio of constant capital to variable capital (labour). If this ratio increases at a faster rate than the ratio of surplus value to variable capital, there will be a tendency for the rate of profit to fall. Ultimately this drive by capitalists to keep ahead of each other would drive some businesses out of the market, and unemployment (the reserve army of the unemployed) would increase as a result. Pressure on wages will cause wage rates to fall and hence the rate of profit would fall, and the process would begin over.

Ultimately, these crises would lead to workers taking to organizing themselves and take the means of production into their own hands, possibly through revolution. One of the features of socialism, the social ownership and greater democratic control of the means of production, was a greater focus on equity as opposed to efficiency. This was a recognition that the outcomes of classical economic theory might be 'efficient' but not necessarily 'fair'. Marx was writing at a time when the amount of labour working in factories was extensive; it is perhaps no surprise that their latent power was to be feared. It is easy to see why the owning class were wary of the development of trade unions and organized labour. Marx's critique challenged the neo-classical orthodoxy and represented a challenge to the fundamental basis of the 'organized, civilized' society of the late 19th century.

THE AUSTRIAN SCHOOL

We have already mentioned some of the economists associated with the Austrian School – Menger, Jeavons and Walras. Menger wrote *Principles of Economics,* published in 1871, and argued that analysis of economics, such as individual preferences and decisions at the margin, were universally applicable, much along the same lines that the classical economists had argued using the 'law of demand and supply'. Menger's view was not accepted by other economists in Germany at the time, notably, William Roscher, a professor at the University of Leipzig from 1848 until his death in 1894. It was, allegedly, some of Roscher's students who used the term 'Austrian school', as a means of insulting Menger and others on the faculty at the University of Vienna. Despite the insult, economists of the Austrian school have made significant contributions to economic thinking, although since the 1930s the Austrian school has been associated with universities other than Vienna, for example, Chicago. In particular, Ludwig von Mises, Friedrich Hayek (the Nobel Prize winner for Economics in 1974 who taught at the University of Chicago) and Friedrich von Wieser have been at the forefront of an intellectual tradition that is linked to the Austrian school.

The fundamental beliefs associated with the Austrian school is that of the power of free markets, private property, property rights and individual choice but tempered by an understanding of decision-making over time and under conditions of uncertainty. Austrian school economists recognize that ultimately individuals are the only ones that make choices but in so doing generate unintended consequences. In analyzing choices, a focus on the process and relationships of exchange and bargaining is important. This reflects the idea that understanding human sciences like economics is not a case of being able to predict but to understand. Recognition of the role of subjective views in economics, is thus important in analyzing issues such as utility and opportunity cost.

Thinkers in the Austrian school tradition have made numerous contributions to macroeconomics most notably in the field of monetary theory for which Hayek received his Nobel Prize. Austrian economists are noted for proposing free banking and the denationalization of money. Free banking would see the abolishment of central banks and a system where banks would compete in a free market, setting interest rates and issuing their own currency.

KEYNESIANISM

Keynesian economics is associated with the work of John Maynard Keynes (1883–1946). The very fact that a school of thought is named after him is perhaps a testament to the importance of Keynes. Keynes studied under Alfred Marshall and Arthur Pigou at Cambridge in the early 1900s, where he eventually ended up teaching. His most notable work, *The General Theory of Employment, Interest and Money*, published in 1936, has influenced subsequent generations of economists and presented a challenge to neo-classical and Austrian school assumptions that free markets, left to their own devices, clear. Keynes suggested that there was no reason that, for example, labour markets should clear, and that the persistence of unemployment over a period could be due to demand deficiencies in the economy. Demand deficiencies could be corrected by government intervention in the economy, by using tax and spending instruments to boost aggregate demand (or to reduce it when the economy was overheating). Keynes' ideas were developed by other notable economists including Joan Robinson, John Hicks, James Tobin, Arthur Okun, Robert Solow and Paul Samuelson.

Some of these developments were christened 'New-Keynesianism', in particular the work of Samuelson and Solow in developing the so-called 'neo-classical synthesis', which sought to explain the short-term failure of markets to clear because of sticky wages and prices. The attempt to explain Keynesian ideas in the context of neo-classical principles was coined 'bastard Keynesianism' by Joan Robinson.

A number of developed economies adopted Keynesian demand management policies after the Second World War and unemployment remained relatively low and growth stable up until the late 1960s when global pressures began to have wider economic impacts. The collapse of the Bretton Woods system of fixed exchange rates against gold, and the oil price shocks caused by the tensions between Arabs and Israelis in the early 1970s, began to reveal fault lines in economies. Some argued that demand management policies had led to complacency amongst firms and workers, who expected governments to always come to the rescue when economic times got hard. This, it is argued, led to a lack of competitiveness and over-reliance on the state. In the 1960s, research by economists into the role of money and monetary policy and the problems being experienced by a number of countries of accelerating inflation and rising unemployment (stagflation) led to the decline in the use of demand management policies and Keynesian ideas became eclipsed by monetarism. The Financial Crisis of 2007–9 and the subsequent global recession led to a resurgence of interest in Keynes' ideas.

MONETARISM

Monetarism has become associated with a number of things not least an assumption that all monetarists are advocates of free markets. This is not the case. Monetarism is essentially linked to a number of beliefs, most notably that in the long run increases in the money supply have no effect on real variables (so called monetary neutrality) but in the short run this neutrality may not exist. Monetary neutrality implies that an increase in the money supply will, over a period, lead to an increase in the price level but not in real variables such as output, consumption and relative prices. The idea that changes in the money supply would lead to changes in the price level was encapsulated in the Fisher equation of exchange.

One of the leading economists of the monetarist school was Milton Friedman, winner of the Nobel Prize for Economics in 1976. Friedman had challenged aspects of Keynes' ideas when he published *A Theory of the Consumption Function* in 1957, which developed the idea of the permanent income hypothesis. In other work he researched price determination in individual markets but his association with the revival of monetarism is perhaps what he will be remembered for. Friedman noted that 'inflation is almost and everywhere a monetary phenomenon'. The subjugation of Keynesian demand management policies in the 1970s as inflation accelerated alarmingly in a number of developed economies, and the acceptance of Friedman's analysis of the role of the money supply, led to a greater focus on attempting to control the money supply as a means of controlling inflation.

In the UK and US, the respective governments announced targets for the growth in the money supply throughout much of the 1980s but in the event, failed to achieve these targets and the policy was abandoned in favour of exchange rate targeting and later, inflation targeting.

FEMINIST ECONOMICS

In this prologue, you may have noticed that all the economists mentioned have been men. Indeed, of the 47 Nobel Prize winners in Economics since 1969, only one has been a woman (Elinor Olstrom in 2009 for her work on local commons). The Nobel Prize committee praised Olstrom for 'challenging the conventional wisdom' and in particular adopting different research methods from those typical in economic science. The challenging of conventional wisdoms, norms and ways of researching and discovery, is perhaps what encapsulates the essence of feminist economics.

By focusing on econometric and mathematical methods, and with the preponderance of neo-classically trained faculty in many universities, feminist economists ask if the right questions and right approaches are being used to analyze key economic issues. In addition, they suggest that the conclusions that arise from existing methods of research may ignore the role which women play in society, make assumptions that miss key features of society, and reinforce gender inequality and inefficiency.

A particular area where feminist economists have been active researchers is in the analysis of labour markets and the way in which a nation's wealth and well-being is calculated. By ignoring the role which women play in the home and the social and economic benefits that are derived from non-paid work (primarily carried out by women), the analysis of wealth creation and well-being, they argue, is incomplete and inaccurate. Gender inequality in the workplace is not simply as manifested by the fact that women are often paid different rates for the same job, despite legislation outlawing this in many countries, but in the under-representation of women in amongst all sections of society. This, it is argued, is not only something that is unfair and inequitable but it is also damaging to the potential growth of a country.

PART 10
THE DATA OF MACROECONOMICS

20 MEASURING A NATION'S WELL-BEING

Economics is divided into two branches: microeconomics and macroeconomics. Microeconomics is the study of how individual households and firms make decisions and how they interact with one another in markets. Macroeconomics is the study of the economy as a whole. The goal of macroeconomics is to explain the economic changes that affect many households, firms and markets simultaneously. Economists analyze the economy as a whole as it provides an indication of the overall well-being. In Chapter 7 we introduced two measures of well-being. Subjective well-being refers to the way in which people evaluate their own happiness and objective well-being refers to measures of the quality of life and uses indicators such as educational attainment, measures of the standard of living, life expectancy and so on. Many of the macroeconomic variables which economists study are inextricably linked with these definitions of well-being. Having a reasonable income means that people can afford to buy the necessitates and luxuries in life which contribute to subjective well-being and countries with higher national incomes can provide better quality education, more secure jobs, higher quality of housing, infrastructure and healthcare, amongst other things, which affect objective well-being.

This chapter considers ways in which well-being can be measured. One of the most common ways in which the well-being of an economy is measured is through *gross domestic product,* or simply GDP, which measures the total income of a nation. GDP is a widely reported macroeconomic statistic but it has its critics and the way the data is collected also has limitations. As with many things, what is considered a good measure of well-being depends on underlying belief systems and judgements. For example, GDP measures focus on incomes with the implication that higher national income equates to an increased ability to acquire more goods and services which in turn means increased well-being. This can be interpreted as being based on a consumerist value system which may not take adequate account of factors which can also contribute to subjective and objective well-being. Some economists have pointed out that despite considerable increases in GDP in the last 50 years in many developed countries, reports of subjective well-being have not risen by the same amount. There may be a number of reasons for this but it seems that what economists and politicians might use as a measure of the health and wealth of an economy are not perceived in the same way by the citizens of a country.

We will begin our investigation of measures of well-being by looking at national income. Given the caveats outlined above, this remains one of the most important ways in which well-being is reported and measured.

THE ECONOMY'S INCOME AND EXPENDITURE

Incomes are used as a measure of well-being because incomes can be used to purchase life's necessities and luxuries. Income is, therefore, equated with the standard of living. In Chapter 1, we defined the standard of living as the amount of goods and services that can be purchased by the population of a country. By this definition, those with higher incomes enjoy higher standards of living – better housing, better healthcare, fancier cars, more opulent vacations and so on. The same logic can be applied to a nation's overall economic well-being. To judge whether an economy is doing well or poorly, we can look at the total income that everyone in the economy is earning. This is the task of GDP.

GDP measures two things at once: the total income of everyone in the economy and the total expenditure on the economy's output of goods and services. These two things are really the same because every transaction has two parties: a buyer and a seller. Every euro of spending by some buyer is a euro of income for a seller. For example, if Michael pays Astrid €20 to clean the windows at his house, Astrid is a seller of a service and Michael is a buyer. Astrid earns an income of €20 and Michael spends €20. Thus, the transaction contributes equally to the economy's income and to its expenditure. GDP, whether measured as total income or total expenditure, rises by €20.

The equality of income and expenditure can be seen through the circular-flow diagram in Figure 20.1. This is a model which describes all the transactions between households and firms in a simple economy. In this economy, the market for goods and services is where households and firms interact through firms providing goods and services which are bought by households. The spending by households on these goods and services represents the revenue of firms. The two also interact in the market for factors of production. Firms use the money they receive from sale of goods and services to purchase the factors of production (land, labour, capital and enterprise) from households who provide these factor services. The factor incomes received by households (wages, rent, interest and profit) is used to pay for goods and services. In this economy, money flows from households to firms and then back to households.

Not all of the incomes households receive is spent in the market for goods and services. Some of this income is subject to tax which is paid to the government. Some income will be saved and the funds find their way into financial institutions in the form of pension saving, insurance and assurance, and saving in bank accounts. Some of the income spent on goods and services by households leaves the economy in the form of spending on imports. Similarly, some of the income received by firms is paid to the government in business taxes. Taxes (T), saving (S) and spending on imports (M) are called leakages to the circular flow.

Governments use tax revenue and borrowing from financial institutions to spend on government services and investment on infrastructure, education, health, defence and so on representing government spending (G) which goes back into the circular flow. Firms make use of the funds provided by savers in financial institutions through borrowing to finance investment spending on new plant, equipment and expansion. This investment (I) finds its way back into the market for goods and services. Firms will also sell some of the goods and services they produce abroad and so the revenue from exports (X) flows back into the system. Financial institutions also lend money overseas and firms overseas invest money into the country which is recorded as net capital outflow (NCO). Government spending (G), investment spending (I) and revenue from exports (X) are referred to as injections to the circular flow.

In theory, measuring GDP through income or expenditure will arrive at the same result. National income, national expenditure and GDP are invariably used synonymously. A common measure of showing GDP is to add up the sum of expenditures in the economy – consumer spending (C), investment spending (I), government spending (G), and the difference between the amount paid out on imports (M) and that received in exports (X) (net exports, ($X - M$) or NX). This provides a measure of GDP given by the following equation:

$$GDP(NY) = C + I + G + NX$$

FIGURE 20.1

The Circular-Flow Diagram

Households buy goods and services from firms, and firms use the revenue from sales to pay wages to workers, rent to landowners, interest on capital and profit to firm owners. GDP equals the total amount spent by households in the market for goods and services. It also equals the total wages, rent, interest and profit paid by firms in the markets for the factors of production. Leakages to the circular flow include taxes, savings and spending on imports whereas injections to the circular flow include government spending, investment, and revenue generated from exports.

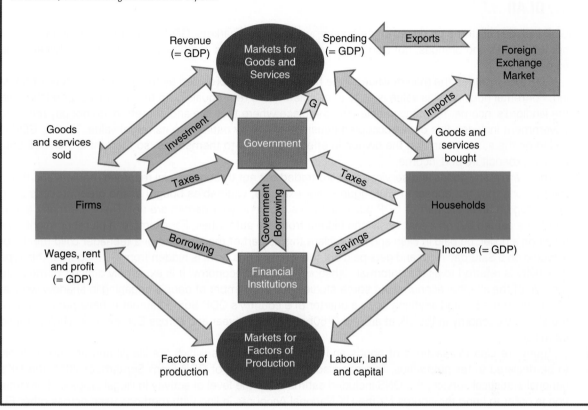

SELF TEST What two things are measured by gross domestic product? How can it measure two things at once?

THE MEASUREMENT OF GROSS DOMESTIC PRODUCT

Gross domestic product (GDP) is the market value of all final goods and services produced within a country in a given period of time.

> **gross domestic product (GDP)** the market value of all final goods and services produced within a country in a given period of time

Let's consider each phrase in this definition.

'GDP Is the Market Value ...'

GDP adds together many different kinds of products into a single measure of the value of economic activity. To do this, it uses market prices. Because market prices measure the amount people are willing to pay for different goods, they reflect the value of those goods. If the price of an apple is twice the price of an orange, then an apple contributes twice as much to GDP as does an orange.

'... Of All ...'

GDP includes all items produced in the economy and sold in markets. GDP measures the market value of not just apples and oranges, but also pears and grapefruit, books and films, haircuts and healthcare, and so on.

GDP also includes the market value of the housing services provided by the economy's stock of housing. For rental housing, this value is easy to calculate – the rent equals both the tenant's expenditure and the landlord's income. Yet many people own the place where they live and, therefore, do not pay rent. The government includes this owner-occupied housing in GDP by estimating its rental value. That is, GDP is based on the assumption that the owner, in effect, pays rent to themselves, so the rent is included both in their expenditure and income.

There are many goods and services that are traded but not through official recorded markets and these transactions may not appear in GDP figures. For example, vegetables bought at the greengrocer's shop or the supermarket are part of GDP but vegetables grown in your garden are not. There are many trades which are carried out on a cash basis and hidden from the authorities. For example, a plumber might do a repair on a boiler, be paid in cash and not declare this as part of their income or a teenager child minds for a couple on a Saturday night and gets paid but the value of this work is hidden from GDP figures. This type of activity is referred to as the 'informal', 'shadow' or 'black' economy. It is extremely difficult to measure the size of the shadow economy but some studies put the number of people engaging in shadow work at 30 million in the EU and anything up to a quarter of a country's GDP. Some estimates have put the size of the shadow economy in the UK at around £150bn (€213bn) a year and across Europe as a whole, around €2 trillion.

There are also transactions of goods and services in markets which are illegal and as such unlikely to be declared to tax authorities. This can also affect the value of GDP. From September 2014, the UK's national statistical service, the ONS included estimates of the level of activity in illegal drugs and prostitution in order to bring the figures for the UK National Accounts in line with methods used across other EU countries. The ONS estimated that the average impact on the UK economy by including illegal drugs and prostitution amounts to around £11 billion (€15.6 billion) per year.

A number of economists have noted that calculations of GDP do not take into account the value of work carried out by housewives and househusbands and neither is the value of childcare work carried out by grandparents, for example. Feminist economists, in particular, criticize the distinction between 'productive' work carried out in markets and 'unproductive work' which is not. The work done in supporting families in the home can contribute significantly to overall well-being and is the centre of most people's lives. This contribution is not considered in GDP calculations and as a result, not only undervalues the true measure of well-being in the economy but also the value of women's productive contribution to the economy.

'... Final ...'

When a paper company sells paper to a greetings card company, the paper is called an *intermediate good,* and the card is called a *final good.* GDP includes only the value of final goods. The reason is that the value of intermediate goods is already included in the prices of final goods. Adding the market value of the paper to the market value of the card would be double counting. That is, it would (incorrectly) count the paper twice.

An important exception to this principle arises when an intermediate good is produced and, rather than being used, is added to a firm's inventory of goods to be used or sold at a later date. In this case, the intermediate good is taken to be 'final' for the moment, and its value as inventory investment is added to GDP. When the inventory of the intermediate good is later used or sold, the firm's inventory investment is negative, and GDP for the later period is reduced accordingly.

'… Goods and Services …'

GDP includes both tangible goods (food, clothing, cars) and intangible services (haircuts, house cleaning, doctor's visits). When you (legally) download an album by your favourite band, you are buying a good, and the purchase price is part of GDP. When you pay to hear a concert by the same band, you are buying a service, and the ticket price is also part of GDP.

'… Produced …'

GDP includes goods and services currently produced. It does not include transactions involving items produced in the past. When you buy a new textbook for your economics course, the value of the textbook is included in the GDP of the country in which the publisher operates. When one person sells a used textbook to another person, the value of the used textbook is not included in GDP.

'… Within a Country …'

GDP measures the value of production within the geographic confines of a country. When an Australian citizen works temporarily in the United Kingdom, their production is part of UK GDP. When a UK citizen owns a factory in Bulgaria, the production at their factory is not part of UK GDP (it's part of Bulgaria's GDP). Thus, items are included in a nation's GDP if they are produced domestically, regardless of the nationality of the producer.

'… In a Given Period of Time'

GDP measures the value of production that takes place within a specific interval of time. Usually that interval is a year or a quarter of a year (three months). GDP measures the economy's flow of income and expenditure during that interval.

When the government reports the GDP for a quarter, it usually presents GDP 'at an annual rate'. This means that the figure reported for quarterly GDP is the amount of income and expenditure during the quarter multiplied by four. The government uses this convention so that quarterly and annual figures on GDP can be compared more easily.

In addition, when the government reports quarterly GDP, it presents the data after they have been modified by a statistical procedure called *seasonal adjustment*. The unadjusted data show clearly that the economy produces more goods and services during some times of year than during others (as you might guess, December's holiday shopping season is a high point in many countries whilst the period before Ramadan is a high point for many Muslim countries). When monitoring the condition of the economy, economists and policymakers often want to look beyond these regular seasonal changes. Therefore, government statisticians adjust the quarterly data to take out the seasonal cycle.

SELF TEST Which contributes more to GDP – the production of €1 of tin or the production of €1 of gold? Why?

Other Measures of Income

When the ONS or Eurostat computes the GDP every three months for the UK and the EU respectively, they also compute various other measures of income to arrive at a more complete picture of what's happening in the economy. These other measures differ from GDP by excluding or including certain categories of income. What follows is a brief description of five of these income measures, ordered from largest to smallest, based on the UK.

- *Gross national product* **(GNP)** is the total income earned by a nation's permanent residents (called nationals). It differs from GDP by including income that domestic citizens earn abroad and excluding income that foreigners earn in the domestic country, as we saw above. For most countries, domestic residents are responsible for most domestic production, so GDP and GNP are quite close.
- *Net national product* **(NNP)** is the total income of a nation's residents (GNP) minus losses from depreciation. *Depreciation* is the wear and tear on the economy's stock of equipment and structures, such as lorries rusting and computers becoming obsolete.
- *National income* **(NY)** is the total income earned by a nation's residents in the production of goods and services. It differs from net national product by excluding indirect business taxes (such as sales taxes) and including business subsidies. NNP and national income also differ because of a 'statistical discrepancy' that arises from problems in data collection.
- *Personal income* is the income that households and non-corporate businesses receive. Unlike national income, it excludes *retained earnings*, which is income that corporations have earned but have not paid out to their owners. It also subtracts corporate income taxes and contributions for social insurance. In addition, personal income includes the interest income that households receive from their holdings of government debt and the income that households receive from government transfer programmes, such as welfare and social security payments.
- *Disposable personal income* is the income that households and non-corporate businesses have left after satisfying all their obligations to the government. It equals personal income minus personal taxes and certain non-tax payments (such as parking tickets).

Although the various measures of income differ in detail, they almost always tell the same story about economic conditions. When GDP is growing rapidly, these other measures of income are usually growing rapidly; when GDP is falling, these other measures are usually falling as well.

THE COMPONENTS OF GDP

Spending in the economy takes many forms. At any moment, the Müller family may be having lunch in a Munich restaurant; Honda may be building a car factory on the banks of the Rhine; and the German army may be procuring weapons from German arms manufacturers. German GDP includes all of these various forms of spending on domestically produced goods and services. Similarly, each country in Europe will monitor the forms of spending and income to arrive at the GDP for that country.

Earlier we noted that national income could be described by the equation:

$$Y \equiv C + I + G + NX$$

Notice that we have used the three-bar, 'identically equals' symbol, '$\equiv$', in this equation. This is because the equation is an *identity* – an equation that must be true by the way the variables in the equation are defined. In this case, because each euro or pound of expenditure included in GDP is placed into one of the four components of GDP, the total of the four components must be equal to GDP. For the most part we'll follow normal practice in dealing with identities and use the usual equals sign, '='. Let's look at each of these four components more closely.

Consumption

Consumption is spending by households on goods and services. 'Goods' include household spending on durables, such as cars and appliances like washing machines and fridges, and non-durable goods, such as food and clothing.

 consumption spending by households on goods and services, with the exception of purchases of new housing

'Services' include such intangible items as haircuts, entertainment and medical care. Household spending on education is also included in consumption of services (although one might argue that it would fit better in the next component).

Investment

Investment is the purchase of buildings, equipment and machinery that will contribute to future productive output. It is the sum of purchases of capital equipment, inventories and structures. Investment in structures includes expenditure on new housing. By convention, the purchase of a new house is the one form of household spending categorized as investment rather than consumption.

 investment spending on capital equipment, inventories and structures, including household purchases of new housing

The treatment of inventory accumulation is noteworthy. When Sony produces a smartphone and, instead of selling it, adds it to its inventory, Sony is assumed to have 'purchased' the phone for itself. That is, the national income accountants treat the phone as part of Sony's investment spending. (If Sony later sells the phone out of inventory, Sony's inventory investment will then be negative, offsetting the positive expenditure of the buyer.) Inventories are treated this way because one aim of GDP is to measure the value of an economy's production, and goods added to inventory are part of that period's production.

Government Spending

Government spending includes spending on goods and services by local and national governments. It includes the salaries of government workers and spending on public works.

 government spending spending on goods and services by local and national governments

The meaning of 'government spending' requires a little clarification. When the government pays the salary of an army general, that salary is part of government spending. What happens when the government pays a social security benefit to one of the elderly? Such government spending is called a **transfer payment** because it is not made in exchange for a currently produced good or service. Transfer payments alter household income, but they do not reflect the economy's production (from a macroeconomic standpoint, transfer payments are like negative taxes). Because GDP is intended to measure income from, and expenditure on, the production of goods and services, transfer payments are not counted as part of government spending.

transfer payment a payment for which no good or service is exchanged

Net Exports

Net exports equal the purchases of domestically produced goods and services by foreigners (exports), which generates a flow of funds into a country, minus the domestic purchases of foreign goods (imports), which result in funds leaving a country. A domestic firm's sale to a buyer in another country, such as the sale of Sony phones to customers in the USA, increases Japanese net exports.

net exports spending on domestically produced goods and services by foreigners (exports) minus spending on foreign goods by domestic residents (imports)

The 'net' in 'net exports' refers to the fact that the value of imports is subtracted from the value of exports. This subtraction is made because imports of goods and services are included in other components of GDP. For example, suppose that a UK household buys a £30 000 car from Volvo, the Swedish car maker. That transaction increases consumption in the UK by £30 000 because car purchases are part of consumer spending in the UK. It also reduces net exports by £30 000 because the car is an import (note it represents an export for Sweden). In other words, net exports include goods and services produced abroad (with a minus sign) because these goods and services are included in consumption, investment and government purchases (with a plus sign). Thus, when a domestic household, firm or government buys a good or service from abroad, the purchase reduces net exports – but because it also raises consumption, investment or government purchases, it does not affect GDP. The above example shows the importance of making sure that we focus on a particular country when discussing imports and exports because of the potential for confusion to arise.

Once GDP figures are published they can be presented in different ways. One of the most common is GDP per head or per capita. GDP per capita is found by dividing the GDP of a country by the population of that country to express national income per head of the population. This measure is useful in comparing GDP across different countries.

CASE STUDY Revisions to GDP Figures

National or regional statistical services such as the ONS or Eurostat have very sophisticated systems for collecting and calculating national income data. The European system of national and regional accounts (known as ESA95) compiles data on the structure and developments of member state economies. It uses an agreed accounting framework which is recognized across the world to allow each economy to be described and to be able to draw accurate and reliable comparisons between different regions and economies or groups of economies. It is worth trying to imagine how challenging a task collecting all this data actually is. Just look around you whenever you are out at the amount of economic activity which is taking place – people buying and selling goods and services in shops, online transactions, people travelling on public transport, people using their cars for which they have bought insurance, fuel and paid for maintenance, road sweepers cleaning up litter, emptying bins and removing chewing gum off the pavements, police patrolling the streets and so on. Trying to collect all the data for the expenditures that are taking place is a massive task. Inevitably, any published GDP figure is provisional and statistical services continue to revise the data they receive and publish revised figures on a regular basis.

(Continued)

Providing accurate data is important because business, government and investment decisions are all made with the macroeconomic environment in mind. It is made very clear, therefore, that GDP data when published is subject to revision and these revisions can sometimes be significant. Initial figures for quarterly GDP are referred to as 'flash estimates' because they are based on a fraction of the total data used for final estimate. The ONS, for example, will provide at least two revisions to initial estimates and once all the data is in, initial estimates can be confirmed or revised up or down. Announcements on GDP data, therefore, need to be looked at with some caution – one quarter's figures may not necessarily be a reliable indicator of the pattern of GDP over time.

The complexity of business activity makes gathering accurate GDP data challenging.

SELF TEST List the four components of expenditure. Which of these do you think accounts for the largest proportion of GDP in a country? Why?

REAL VERSUS NOMINAL GDP

Changes in total expenditure on goods and services from one year to another can be looked at in two ways:

1. the economy is producing a larger output of goods and services (a real increase); or
2. goods and services are being sold at higher prices (a nominal increase).

When studying changes in the economy over time, these two effects are separated with the focus being on a measure of the total quantity of goods and services the economy is producing that is not affected by changes in the prices of those goods and services.

To do this, economists use a measure called **real GDP**. Real GDP answers a hypothetical question: what would be the value of the goods and services produced this year if we valued these goods and services at the prices that prevailed in some specific year in the past? By evaluating current production using prices that are fixed at past levels, real GDP shows how an economy's overall production of goods and services changes over time. The GDP figures produced using this method are called **GDP at constant prices**. GDP figures produced without taking into consideration the change in prices over time are called **GDP at current or market prices** and are calculated by taking the output of goods and services and multiplying by the price of those goods and services in the reporting year.

To see more precisely how real GDP is constructed, let's consider an example.

> **real GDP** the measure of the value of output in the economy which takes into account changes in prices over time
> **GDP at constant prices** gross domestic product calculated using prices that existed at a particular base year which takes into account changes in inflation over time
> **GDP at current or market prices** gross domestic product calculated by multiplying the output of goods and services by the price of those goods and services in the reporting year

A Numerical Example

Table 20.1 shows some data for an economy that produces only two goods – apples and potatoes. The table shows the quantities of the two goods produced and their prices in the years 2016, 2017 and 2018.

TABLE 20.1   **Real and Nominal GDP**

This table shows how to calculate real GDP, nominal GDP and the GDP deflator for a hypothetical economy that produces only apples and potatoes.

		Prices and quantities		
Year	Price of apples per kg (€)	Quantity of apples (kg)	Price of potatoes per kg (€)	Quantity of potatoes (kg)
2016	1	100	2	50
2017	2	150	3	100
2018	3	200	4	150

Year	Calculating nominal GDP
2016	(€1 per kg apples × 100 kg) + (€2 per kg potatoes × 50 kg) = €200
2017	(€2 per kg apples × 150 kg) + (€3 per kg potatoes × 100 kg) = €600
2018	(€3 per kg apples × 200 kg) + (€4 per kg potatoes × 150 kg) = €1200

Year	Calculating real GDP (base year 2016)
2016	(€1 per kg apples × 100 kg) + (€2 per kg potatoes × 50 kg) = €200
2017	(€1 per kg apples × 150 kg) + (€2 per kg potatoes × 100 kg) = €350
2018	(€1 per kg apples × 200 kg) + (€2 per kg potatoes × 150 kg) = €500

Year	Calculating the GDP deflator
2016	(€200/€200) × 100 = 100
2017	(€600/€350) × 100 = 171
2018	(€1200/€500) × 100 = 240

To compute total spending in this economy, we would multiply the quantities of apples and potatoes by their prices. In the year 2016, 100 kg of apples are sold at a price of €1 per kg, so expenditure on apples equals €100. In the same year, 50 kg of potatoes are sold for €2 per kg, so expenditure on potatoes also equals €100. Total expenditure in the economy – the sum of expenditure on apples and expenditure on potatoes – is €200. This amount, the production of goods and services valued at current or market prices (i.e. the price existing in the reporting year), is called **nominal GDP**.

> **nominal GDP** the production of goods and services valued at current prices

The table shows the calculation of nominal GDP for these three years. Total spending rises from €200 in 2016 to €600 in 2017 and then to €1200 in 2018. Part of this rise is attributable to the increase in the quantities of apples and potatoes produced, and part is attributable to the increase in the prices of apples and potatoes.

To obtain a measure of the amount produced that is not affected by changes in prices, we use real GDP, the production of goods and services valued at constant prices. Real GDP is calculated by first choosing one year as a *base year*. We then use the prices of apples and potatoes in the base year to compute the value of goods and services in all of the years. In other words, the prices in the base year provide the basis for comparing quantities in different years.

Suppose that we choose 2016 to be the base year in our example. We can then use the prices of apples and potatoes in 2016 to compute the value of goods and services produced in 2016, 2017 and 2018. Table 20.1 shows these calculations. To compute real GDP for 2016 we use the prices of apples and potatoes in 2016 (the base year) and the quantities of apples and potatoes produced in 2016. (For the base year, real GDP always equals nominal GDP.) To compute real GDP for 2017, we use the prices of apples and potatoes in 2016 (the base year) and the quantities of apples and potatoes produced in 2017. Similarly, to compute real GDP for 2018, we use the prices in 2016 and the quantities in 2018. When we find that real GDP has risen from €200 in 2016 to €350 in 2017 and then to €500 in 2018, we know that the increase is attributable to an increase in the *quantities produced*, because the prices are being held fixed at base-year levels.

The growth rate in real GDP takes the difference between GDP across the two time periods under consideration denoted by $GDP_t - GDP_{t-1}$, divided by GDP in year $_{t-1}$, minus one. Multiplying the result by 100 gives the percentage rate of growth in real GDP.

$$Growth\ rate\ of\ real\ GDP\ in\ year\ t = \frac{(GDP_t - GDP_{t-1})}{GDP_{t-1} - 1}$$

The GDP Deflator

Nominal GDP reflects both the prices of goods and services and the quantities of goods and services the economy is producing. In contrast, by holding prices constant at base-year levels, real GDP reflects only the quantities produced. From these two statistics we can compute a third, called the **GDP deflator**, sometimes also referred to as the *implicit price level*, which reflects the prices of goods and services but not the quantities produced.

> **GDP deflator** a measure of the price level calculated as the ratio of nominal GDP to real GDP times 100

The GDP deflator is calculated as follows:

$$GDP\ Deflator = \frac{Nominal\ GDP}{Real\ GDP} \times 100$$

Because nominal GDP and real GDP must be the same in the base year, the GDP deflator for the base year always equals 100. The GDP deflator for subsequent years measures the change in nominal GDP from the base year that cannot be attributable to a change in real GDP by measuring the current level of prices relative to the level of prices in the base year

Imagine that the quantities produced in the economy rise over time but prices remain the same. In this case, both nominal and real GDP rise together, so the GDP deflator is constant. Now suppose that prices rise over time but the quantities produced stay the same. In this second case, nominal GDP rises but real GDP remains the same, so the GDP deflator rises as well. Notice that, in both cases, the GDP deflator reflects what's happening to prices, not quantities.

Real GDP is found by taking the nominal GDP and dividing by the GDP deflator.

$$Real\ GDP = \frac{Nominal\ GDP}{GDP\ Deflator}$$

Let's now return to our numerical example in Table 20.1. The GDP deflator is computed at the bottom of the table. For 2016, the base year, nominal GDP is €200, and real GDP is €200, so the GDP deflator is 100. For the year 2017, nominal GDP is €600, and real GDP is €350, so the GDP deflator is 171. Because the GDP deflator rose in year 2017 from 100 to 171, we can say that the price level increased by 71 per cent.

The GDP deflator is one measure that economists use to monitor the average level of prices in the economy. We examine another – the consumer prices index – in the next chapter, where we also describe the differences between the two measures.

> **SELF TEST** Define real and nominal GDP. Which is a better measure of economic well-being? Why?

Chain Linking

We have looked at measuring GDP through income and expenditure methods and said that in theory they are the same. GDP can also be measured by looking at the output or production method. The price of a product represents the value of the inputs that went into production. At each stage of the production process the value of output can be recorded – the value added. The ONS defines **gross value added** (GVA) as the 'contribution to the economy of each individual producer, industry or sector'. GVA is used as the measure of the output and income approaches to measuring GDP. Statistics offices usually classify output according to industry types – construction, agriculture forestry and fisheries, mining, services and so on.

> **gross value added** the contribution of domestic producers, industries and sectors to an economy

The measure for GDP is a 'volume measure', measuring 'how much' has been produced. In the UK the ONS has to produce a single measure of GDP and does this by using the three approaches – income, expenditure and output – with the final figure reflecting the three measures. In theory these measures should all be the same but the process of collecting information from millions of transactions means that in reality they would never be exact.

Imagine a situation, for example, where someone has some work done on their house – say the plastering of a room. The total price for the work paid by the owner of the house might be £1500 – this should represent the sum of the resources used in the job. The plasterer may declare to Her Majesty's Revenue and Customs (HMRC), that is responsible for collecting UK taxes, that the work represented income of £1200 (to evade paying income tax – illegal, but nevertheless it happens), and the resources used might have included the plasterboard, plaster, electricity, buckets, nails, water, trowels and hawks, the vehicles to get to and from the builders' merchants, etc. It is easy to see how, even in such a simple example, it becomes incredibly difficult to keep track of every item involved!

The choice of which base year to use in calculating real GDP is also important. Up until early 2004, the ONS used a method referred to as 'fixed base aggregations'. For example, it might have compared the data using 1995 as the base year. However, as with any statistical data which use a base year in their compilation, this can lead to inconsistencies because circumstances change. Goods, for example, that were common in 1995 may not exist anymore and there might be some products that were not available at that time – DVDs, for example. In general, the more you can update the base year, the more accurate the statistics will be.

Fixed base aggregations in GDP statistics were used as follows. The growth of the different parts of the economy was given weights when trying to arrive at the final figure for GDP. This takes account of their relative importance in the economy and a base year of 1995 was used to help determine these weights. These base years were updated every five years.

The method known as '**annual chain linking**' helps to overcome these problems. Rather than updating the base year every five years, this method does it every year, calculating the prices in previous years' prices (PYPs). You will see GDP tables expressed as 'GDP (CVM)', where CVM means Chained Volume Measures, as opposed to 'GDP in constant prices'. The ONS and other statistical services are constantly looking to update their methods to provide more reliable and accurate data and this is one example of such a revision of methods.

> **annual chain-linking** a method of calculating GDP volume measures based on prices in the previous year

Table 20.2 shows an example of how the chain linking method works. We will use our previous example of an economy producing apples and potatoes in the years 2016 and 2017 with the following prices and quantities.

TABLE 20.2 **Chain Linking**

Year	Price of apples per kg (€)	Quantity of apples per kg	Price of potatoes per kg (€)	Quantity of potatoes
2016	1	100	2	50
2017	2	150	3	100

2016 nominal GDP = (100 x €1) + (50 x €2) = €200
2017 nominal GDP = (150 x €2) + (100 x €3) = €600
If 2016 is used as the base year, the value of 2016 and 2017 production at 2016 prices is as follows:
2016: Nominal GDP = Real GDP = €200
2017: Real GDP = (150 x €1) + (100 x €2) = €350
The percentage change in real GDP $= \left(\dfrac{(350 - 200)}{200}\right) \times 100 = 75\%$

Chain weighted real GDP uses average prices over the time period:

Average price of apples between 2016 and 2017 $= \dfrac{(€1 + €2)}{2} = €1.50$

Average price of potatoes between 2016 and 2017 $= \dfrac{(€2 + €3)}{2} = €2.50$

2016 GDP at average prices = (100 x €1.50) + (50 x €2.50) = €275
2017 GDP at average prices = (150 x €1.50) + (100 x €2.50) = €475
Percentage change in chain-weighted GDP $= \left(\dfrac{(€475 - €275)}{275}\right) \times 100 = 72.7\%$

Implicit GDP Deflator $= \dfrac{\text{Nominal GDP}}{\text{Real GDP}} \times 100$

In 2016, the implicit GDP deflator $= \dfrac{200}{200} \times 100 = 100$

In 2017, the implicit GDP deflator $= \dfrac{600}{350} \times 100 = 171.4$

The percentage change in the implicit GDP deflator = 71.4%
With chain-weighting, the base year is the mid-point between the two years.
The 2016 chain-weighted GDP deflator $= \dfrac{\text{Nominal GDP}_{2016}}{\text{Real GDP at 2016 average prices}} \times 100$

$$= \left(\dfrac{200}{275}\right) \times 100 = 72.7$$

$$\text{The 2017 chain-weighted GDP deflator} = \frac{\text{Nominal GDP}_{2017}}{\text{Real GDP at 2017 average prices}} \times 100$$

$$= \left(\frac{600}{475}\right) \times 100 = 126.3$$

$$\text{The percentage change in the chain-weighted GDP deflator} = \left(\frac{(126.3 - 72.7)}{72.7}\right) \times 100 = 73.7\%$$

In terms of analysis of the data it should make little difference, but recognizing it enables you to be more confident that the data are more likely to be accurate and reliable compared to the previous measures. The vast majority of official data is produced using chain-weighted measures.

THE LIMITATIONS OF GDP AS A MEASURE OF WELL-BEING

The use of GDP as a measure of well-being is well established. Yet some people dispute the validity of GDP as a measure of well-being. Critics of the use of GDP suggest that it is too focussed on material possessions and income. They argue that there are many things that are not measured by GDP but contribute to the quality of life and economic well-being, such as the health of a country's children, or the quality of their education, or even the beauty of the poetry making up their literary heritage.

To counter this, it can be argued that GDP might not measure these things, but nations with larger GDP can afford better healthcare, better educational systems, and can afford to teach more of their citizens to read and enjoy poetry. GDP does not take account of our intelligence, integrity, courage or wisdom, but all of these laudable attributes are easier to foster when people are less concerned about being able to afford the material necessities of life. In short, GDP does not directly measure those things that make life worthwhile, but it does measure our ability to obtain the inputs into a worthwhile life.

It is widely recognized, however, that GDP is not a perfect measure of well-being. Some things that contribute to a good life are left out of GDP.

- Leisure. Suppose, for instance, that everyone in the economy suddenly started working every day of the week, rather than enjoying leisure on weekends. More goods and services would be produced, and GDP would rise. Yet, despite the increase in GDP, we should not conclude that well-being had improved. The loss from reduced leisure would offset the gain from producing and consuming a greater quantity of goods and services.
- Work in the home and volunteer work. Because GDP uses market prices to value goods and services, it excludes the value of much activity that takes place outside of markets. In particular, GDP omits the value of goods and services produced at home. Volunteer work also contributes to the well-being of those in society but GDP does not reflect these contributions.
- The quality of the environment. Imagine that the government eliminated all environmental regulations. Firms could then produce goods and services without considering the pollution they create, and GDP might rise. Yet well-being would most likely fall. The deterioration in the quality of air and water would more than offset the gains from greater production.
- Distribution of incomes. In Chapter 18 we looked at the distribution of income. A society in which 100 people have annual incomes of €50 000 has GDP of €5 million and, not surprisingly, GDP per capita of €50 000; so does a society in which 10 people earn €500 000 and 90 suffer with nothing at all. Few people would look at those two situations and call them equivalent. GDP per person tells us what happens to the average person, but behind the average lies a large variety of personal experiences. GDP does not tell us much about income distributions.

The Economics of Happiness

It does appear that, despite the massive increase in wealth, incomes, and access to material goods and services for many people in developed countries over the last 50 years, our perception of happiness has not really changed that much. Increased wealth has not brought with it similar increases in happiness. Numerous surveys have highlighted relatively stable rates of 'happiness' in rich countries. Professor Richard Layard, one of a group of economists including Andrew Oswald, Stephen Nickell, Robert Skidelsky, Tim Besley, Will Hutton and those behavioural economists that we have met before in this book, have studied this apparent paradox. Layard states that in relation to Western societies: 'on average, people are no happier than they were fifty years ago', (Layard, R. (2005) *Happiness: Lessons from a New Science*. London: Penguin).

Psychologists and economists have found that links between how people see their own happiness and other things that might influence their judgement, are statistically strong. This also seems to apply across different countries. As a result, we might be able to conclude that there are a range of factors that can contribute to a definition of happiness; if you are fortunate enough to find yourself being able to boast having these characteristics, or in some cases managing to avoid them, then you are more likely to be happy.

Layard identified some key factors that may contribute to 'happiness'. He suggested that some of the factors associated with promoting happiness include sex, socializing, relaxing, praying, worshipping or meditating, eating, exercising, watching TV and shopping, among others. Other studies have suggested that an individual's level of education, health, whether they are married, single or divorced, the level of income enjoyed, whether they are working/unemployed/retired, their aspirations and whether they have experienced bereavement, can all be contributory factors.

From such characteristics, equations to statistically arrive at measures of well-being can be derived. These have been used by both economists and psychologists and have been found to be surprisingly reliable in statistical terms. One of the leading thinkers on the economics of happiness is Professor Andrew Oswald who is based at the University of Warwick. Oswald offers the following formula:

$$W_{it} = \alpha + \beta X_{it} + \varepsilon_{it}$$

In this formula, W_{it} is the reported well-being of an individual at a particular time period, X represents a collection of variables that are known to be characteristics affecting well-being at a particular time period: these could be economic, such as income, or demographic (such as gender). The final term is an error term, which is used to take into account unobserved factors that may have an impact on the final outcome.

One of the factors above that may be affecting happiness levels more than we might expect is aspirations. You are very likely, whatever your age, to have been regaled by your parents that things were different in their day and that 'people these days have so much more'. That is very true but what might also be the case is that different generations are starting to expect more. If your parents have managed to reach middle age and have a comfortable Jaguar to drive around in, you might start to expect such a vehicle to be the norm and would hope it might be your first car and so on.

Layard suggests that unhappiness results from society viewing how it is developing in terms of a zero-sum game. What he means by this is that we might increasingly view the scramble to gain money and status in terms of a competitive game that has a winner and a loser. If I get a high-ranking job with a large salary and lots of status, it means that you somehow lose out – either by not being able to get that same job, or in some sort of psychological way. Such a perception of life being a zero-sum game is a source of much unhappiness. This reflects the idea of *positional externalities* which we look at in Chapter 11.

If we know something of the factors that can contribute to making someone 'happy' and also that our current measure is not the best at reflecting this, then it makes sense to look elsewhere for a measure of well-being. One such idea is to use something called the Measure of Domestic Progress (MDP). The MDP looks at many of the factors that we might associate with economic growth but takes into consideration the relative effects of economic growth and other things that GDP calculations do not consider. For example, there is an attempt to place a value on the amount of unpaid domestic work that is carried out, which is taken as being a positive factor in contributing to well-being. It also assigns a negative effect to various social and environmental impacts of growth such as pollution, depletion of natural resources and costs of crime and family breakdown.

Other attempts to suggest more effective measures of improvements in well-being include such things as the Measure of Economic Welfare (MEW) developed by James Tobin and William Nordhaus, the Index of Sustainable Economic Welfare and the Genuine Progress Indicator.

Personal Well-Being Measures

To take into consideration some of the limitations of GDP and to make use of some of the research carried out on well-being, a number of national statistical offices now publish data which attempts to measure subjective and objective well-being. The ONS in the UK is one such body. It has published reports on personal well-being in the UK since 2012 using four 'high level' measures and 41 headline measures. The report is produced through a survey which asks around 165 000 people a series of questions. The four 'high level' measures are:

1. Overall, how satisfied are you with your life nowadays?
2. Overall, to what extent do you feel the things you do in your life are worthwhile?
3. Overall, how happy did you feel yesterday?
4. Overall, how anxious did you feel yesterday?

Answers are given on a scale of 0 to 10 with 10 being 'completely' and 0 being 'not at all'. The headline measures include areas such as personal health and finances, the environment, relationships, where people live, education and skills, the economy and governance. ONS hopes that the reports offer a further insight into national well-being which supplements other data such as GDP measures. Given the report has only been published since 2012, the ability to identify longer term trends is in its infancy but one key factor that has been noted is that there is a relationship between reported well-being and the state of the economy, with unemployment being a particular contributor to low levels of well-being.

Other statistical offices such as Eurostat and the OECD are also developing well-being statistics which reflect the recognition that GDP figures alone do not offer a full picture of well-being. Eurostat's Quality of Life indicators include similar categories to the ONS reports and include data on material living conditions, work, health, education, leisure and social interaction, economic and physical safety, governance and basic rights, the natural and living environment and the overall experience of life.

INTERNATIONAL DIFFERENCES IN GDP AND THE QUALITY OF LIFE

GDP data is used as a way of comparing well-being across different countries. Rich and poor countries have vastly different levels of GDP per person.

Table 20.3 shows 13 of the world's countries ranked in order of GDP per person.

TABLE 20.3 GDP, Life Expectancy and Literacy

The table shows GDP per person (measured in US dollars) and two measures of the quality of life for 13 countries.

Country	GDP per capita (Current US$) (2015)	Life expectancy at birth (males and females) total years (2013)	Literacy rate (% of people over 15), adult total (2013)
United States	54 629	79	99
Germany	47 627	81	99
United Kingdom	45 603	81	99
Russia	12 735	71	100
Mexico	10 230	77	94
Brazil	11 384	74	91
China	7594	75	94 (2010)
Indonesia	3492	71	93 (2011)
India	1595	66	69 (2011)
Pakistan	1334	67	57 (2012)
Bangladesh	1092	71	60
Mozambique	602	50	51 (2012)
Niger	427	58	15 (2012)

Source: World Bank and UNICEF

The table also shows life expectancy (the expected life span at birth) and literacy (the percentage of the adult population who can read). These data show a clear pattern. In rich countries, such as the United Kingdom, the United States and Germany, people can expect to live into their late 70s or early 80s, and almost all of the population can read. In poor countries, such as Niger, Mozambique, Bangladesh and Pakistan, people typically can expect to live much shorter lives and the proportion of the population which is literate is relatively low.

Although data on other aspects of the quality of life are less complete, they tell a similar story. Countries with low GDP per person tend to have more infants with low birth weight, higher rates of infant mortality, higher rates of maternal mortality, higher rates of child malnutrition and less common access to safe drinking water. In countries with low GDP per person, fewer school-age children are actually in school, and those who are in school must learn with fewer teachers per student. These countries also tend to have fewer televisions, fewer telephones, fewer paved roads and fewer households with electricity.

CONCLUSION

This chapter has discussed how economists measure well-being. Much of the study of macroeconomics we will look at in the rest of this book is aimed at revealing the long-run and short-run determinants of a nation's gross domestic product. Why, for example, do most economies experience fluctuations in economic activity? Why are key macroeconomic measures such as inflation, unemployment, interest rates and exchange rates important in determining economic well-being? What can governments do to promote more rapid growth in GDP? What can policymakers do to reduce the severity of fluctuations in GDP? These are the questions we will take up shortly.

Despite the focus on GDP as a measure of economic well-being, we must not forget the limitations of this measure and that overall economic well-being may include many factors other than income.

IN THE NEWS

Well-being

The ONS in the UK produces a report called 'Personal Well-being in the UK'. This In the News looks at some of the highlights from the report published in 2015, for the financial year 2014/15.

Personal Well-being in the UK

The ONS report showed that personal well-being has improved each year since the first report in 2012, a time when the UK was still suffering the effects of the Financial Crisis of 2007 – 08 and the subsequent recession. In particular, there has been an improvement in reports over levels of anxiety which may be due in part to the improvements in the economy. London and the South East are invariably seen as being the economic powerhouse of the UK with higher levels of income per capita than other parts of the country but the Well-being Report showed that people in London had lower average well-being measures than for the rest of the UK. Perhaps this highlights the criticism of the use of GDP as a sole measure of well-being in that high levels of income do not always equate with happiness.

Of the four high level measures, satisfaction with life was 7.6, feeling that what one does in life is worthwhile at 7.8 and happiness yesterday, 7.5. All these figures are out of 10 and the

There are many factors that affect well-being – strong family support is but one of these factors.

(*Continued*)

Report showed that all were up slightly on the previous year. Feeling anxious yesterday had a score of 2.9 out of 10, slightly down on the previous year.

The report offered some tentative reasons for the improvements in personal well-being, partly to do with the improvements in the economy since the recession and the reduction in unemployment but also noted that happiness levels can fall in periods of rapid change. The Financial Crisis could be interpreted as a period of rapid change.

There were geographical differences in well-being. In England, the North East, Yorkshire and The Humber were the only two regions which did not record significant improvements in low levels of well-being. The North West of England reported the highest average improvements in the first three high-level measures. In Wales there was no positive improvements across any of the high-level measures. The Report suggested that higher levels of unemployment in these regions might offer some explanation for the lack of improvement in well-being. In contrast, Northern Ireland had the highest average rating for life satisfaction for three of the four measures.

Questions

1 What do you think is the value of the Personal Well-Being report and why do you think the ONS produces it?
2 What do you think is a better measure of well-being, a self-report survey style measure such as the Personal Well-being Report or GDP?
3 Of the four high-level measures, would you expect that if the first three show increased reports of well-being that the fourth must always be falling? Explain.
4 What do you think is the explanation for the regional differences in reports of well-being across the UK?
5 How reliable do you think reports such as the Personal Well-being report are as a measure of well-being in the economy?

Source: Personal Well-being in the UK 2014/15. Office for National Statistics. http://www.ons.gov.uk/ons/dcp171778_417216.pdf. Accessed 29th November 2015.

SUMMARY

- Because every transaction has a buyer and a seller, the total expenditure in the economy must equal the total income in the economy.

- GDP measures an economy's total expenditure on newly produced goods and services and the total income earned from the production of these goods and services. More precisely, GDP is the market value of all final goods and services produced within a country in a given period of time.

- GDP is divided among four components of expenditure: consumption, investment, government purchases and net exports. Consumption includes spending on goods and services by households, with the exception of purchases of new housing. Investment includes spending on new equipment and structures, including households' purchases of new housing. Government spending includes spending on goods and services by local and central governments. Net exports equal the value of goods and services produced domestically and sold abroad (exports) minus the value of goods and services produced abroad and sold domestically (imports).

- Nominal GDP uses current prices to value the economy's production of goods and services. Real GDP uses constant base-year prices to value the economy's production of goods and services. The GDP deflator – calculated from the ratio of nominal to real GDP – measures the level of prices in the economy.

- GDP is one measure of economic well-being. It has limitations because it excludes many activities which occur illegally and does not take account of the benefits to well-being from work done outside markets such as looking after the home, rearing children, caring and volunteer work.

- Because of the limitations of using GDP, a number of governments are now supporting efforts to report on broader measures of well-being which include both subjective and objective reporting of how people feel about their lives and circumstances.

QUESTIONS FOR REVIEW

1 Explain why an economy's income must equal its expenditure.

2 What is meant by the term 'GDP per capita' and how is it measured?

3 Which contributes more to GDP – the production of an economy car or the production of a luxury car? Why?

4 A farmer sells wheat to a baker for €2. The baker uses the wheat to make bread, which is sold for €3. What is the total contribution of these transactions to GDP?

5 Many years ago, Jamanda paid €500 to put together a vinyl record collection. Today she sold her albums at a car boot sale for €100. How does this sale affect current GDP?

6 List the four components of GDP. Give an example of each.

7 Why do economists use real GDP rather than nominal GDP to gauge economic well-being?

8 In the year 2017, the economy produces 100 loaves of bread that sell for €2 each. In the year 2018, the economy produces 200 loaves of bread that sell for €3 each. Calculate nominal GDP, real GDP and the GDP deflator for each year (use 2017 as the base year). By what percentage does each of these three statistics rise from one year to the next?

9 What are the limitations of using GDP as a measure of well-being for a country?

10 What is the difference between subjective and objective reports of well-being and how do such reports seek to provide a more complete measure of well-being?

PROBLEMS AND APPLICATIONS

1 What components of GDP (if any) would each of the following transactions affect? Explain.

   a. A family buys a new refrigerator.
   b. Aunt Jane buys a new house.
   c. Aston Martin sells a DB7 from its inventory.
   d. You buy a pizza.
   e. The government builds a new motorway.
   f. You buy a bottle of Californian wine.
   g. Honda expands its factory in Derby, England.

2 The 'government purchases' component of GDP does not include spending on transfer payments such as social security. Thinking about the definition of GDP, explain why transfer payments are excluded.

3 Why do you think households' purchases of new housing are included in the investment component of GDP rather than the consumption component? Can you think of a reason why households' purchases of new cars should also be included in investment rather than in consumption? To what other consumption goods might this logic apply?

4 As the chapter states, GDP does not include the value of used goods that are resold. Why would including such transactions make GDP a less informative measure of economic well-being?

5 Below are some data from the land of milk and honey.

Year	Price of milk (€)	Quantity of milk (litres)	Price of honey (€)	Quantity of honey (jars)
2016	1	100	2	50
2017	1	200	2	100
2018	2	200	4	100

   a. Compute nominal GDP, real GDP and the GDP deflator for each year, using 2016 as the base year.
   b. Compute the percentage change in nominal GDP, real GDP and the GDP deflator in 2017 and 2018 from the preceding year. For each year, identify the variable that does not change. Explain in words why your answer makes sense.
   c. Did economic well-being rise more in 2017 or 2018? Explain.

6 If prices rise, people's income from selling goods increases. The growth of real GDP ignores this gain, however. Why, then, do economists prefer real GDP as a measure of economic well-being?

7 One day Boris the barber collects €400 for haircuts. Over this day, his equipment depreciates in value by €50. Of the remaining €350, Boris sends €30 to the government in sales taxes, takes home €220 in wages, and retains €100 in his business to add new equipment in the future. From the €220 that Boris takes home, he pays €70 in income taxes. Based on this information, compute Boris' contribution to the following measures of income:

a. gross domestic product
b. net national product
c. national income
d. personal income
e. disposable personal income.

8 Economists sometimes prefer to use GNP rather than GDP as a measure of economic well-being. Which measure should we prefer if we are analyzing the total income of domestic residents? Which measure should we prefer if we are analyzing the total amount of economic activity occurring in the economy?

9 Given the limitations of using GDP as a measure of well-being, should calculation of GDP be scrapped in favour of wider reporting of well-being such as objective and subjective well-being?

10 The participation of women in many European and North American economies has risen dramatically over the past three decades.

a. How do you think this rise affected GDP?
b. Now imagine a measure of well-being that includes time spent working in the home and taking leisure. How would the change in this measure of well-being compare to the change in GDP?
c. Can you think of other aspects of well-being that are associated with the rise in women's labour-force participation? Would it be practical to construct a measure of well-being that includes these aspects?

21 MEASURING THE COST OF LIVING

When people get their wages and buy the goods and services they need to live and enjoy life, the price of these goods and services determines how many goods and services can be bought. Over time, prices change and it can be difficult to make comparisons about how wages and prices compare over time. The **cost of living** refers to how much money people need to maintain certain standards of living in terms of the goods and services they can afford to buy. In the UK in 1900, for example, a copy of *The Times* newspaper was priced at 1.2p, a pint of beer and milk could be bought for less than 1p and a dozen fresh eggs was 6.9p. In 1930, the average house price in the UK was £590; a loaf of bread was around 3p (these prices are expressed in decimal currency equivalents). At the turn of the 21st century, the average level of prices was 66 times the level of 1900. Because prices were so much lower in the early 1900s than they are today, it is not clear whether people enjoyed a lower or higher standard of living given average wages in 1900 compared to average wages today.

> **cost of living** how much money people need to maintain standards of living in terms of the goods and services they can afford to buy

Taking a snapshot of prices of goods and services in an economy at a particular point in time gives the **price level**. Looking at how the price level changes over time is the rate of change of the price level. To see how the price level changes and, therefore, to provide a way of comparing the cost of living over time, we need to find some way of turning money figures into meaningful measures of purchasing power. That is exactly the job of a statistic called the *Consumer Prices Index* (CPI).

> **price level** a snapshot of the prices of goods and services in an economy at a particular period of time

The CPI is used to monitor changes in the cost of living over time. When the CPI rises, the typical family has to spend more money to maintain the same standard of living. Economists use the term *inflation* to describe a situation in which the economy's overall price level is rising and *deflation* when the overall price level is falling. The *inflation rate* is the percentage change in the price level from the previous period; if this is negative, the economy is experiencing deflation.

THE CONSUMER PRICES INDEX

The **Consumer Prices Index** (CPI) is a measure of the overall prices of the goods and services bought by a typical consumer. Each month, a government body (in the UK the Office for National Statistics (ONS) and in Europe, Eurostat) computes and reports the CPI.

> **Consumer Prices Index** a measure of the overall prices of the goods and services bought by a typical consumer

How the Consumer Prices Index Is Calculated

To see how these statistics are constructed, let's consider a simple economy in which consumers buy only two goods – salad and burgers. Table 21.1 shows the five steps that the ONS and Eurostat follow. (We will use the ONS as the base for the example here but the principle applies to the way price changes are measured in Europe as a whole.)

TABLE 21.1   **Calculating the Consumer Prices Index and the Inflation Rate: An Example**

This table shows how to calculate the CPI and the inflation rate for a hypothetical economy in which consumers buy only salad and burgers.

Step 1: Survey consumers to determine a fixed basket of goods

4 salads and 2 burgers.

Step 2: Find the price of each good in each year

Year	Price of salad (€)	Price of burgers (€)
2016	1	2
2017	2	3
2018	3	4

Step 3: Compute the cost of the basket of goods in each year

2016	(€1 per salad × 4 salads) + (€2 per burger × 2 burgers) = €8
2017	(€2 per salad × 4 salads) + (€3 per burger × 2 burgers) = €14
2018	(€3 per salad × 4 salads) + (€4 per burger × 2 burgers) = €20

Step 4: Choose one year as a base year (2016) and compute the CPI in each year

2016 $\left(\dfrac{€8}{€8}\right) \times 100 = 100$

2017 $\left(\dfrac{€14}{€8}\right) \times 100 = 175$

2018 $\left(\dfrac{€20}{€8}\right) \times 100 = 250$

Step 5: Use the CPI to compute the inflation rate from previous year

2017 $\left(\dfrac{(175 - 100)}{100}\right) \times 100 = 75\%$

2018 $\left(\dfrac{(250 - 175)}{175}\right) \times 100 = 43\%$

1. *Fix the basket.* The first step in computing the CPI is to determine which prices are most important to the typical consumer. If the typical consumer buys more salad than burgers, then the price of salad is more important than the price of burgers and, therefore, should be given greater weight in measuring the cost of living. The ONS sets these weights by surveying consumers and finding the basket of goods and services that the typical consumer buys. In the example in Table 21.1, the typical consumer buys a basket of 4 salads and 2 burgers.
2. *Find the prices.* The second step is to find the prices of each of the goods and services in the basket for each point in time. The table shows the prices of salad and burgers for three different years.
3. *Compute the basket's cost.* The third step is to use the data on prices to calculate the cost of the basket of goods and services at different times. The table shows this calculation for each of the three years. Notice that only the prices in this calculation change. By keeping the basket of goods the same (4 salads and 2 burgers), we are isolating the effects of price changes from the effect of any quantity changes that might be occurring at the same time.
4. *Choose a base year and compute the index.* The fourth step is to designate one year as the base year, which is the benchmark against which other years are compared. To calculate the index, the price of the

basket of goods and services in each year is divided by the price of the basket in the base year, and this ratio is then multiplied by 100. The resulting number is the CPI.

In the example in Table 21.1, the year 2016 is the base year. In this year, the basket of salad and burgers costs €8. Therefore, the price of the basket in all years is divided by €8 and multiplied by 100. The CPI is 100 in 2016. (The index is always 100 in the base year.) The CPI is 175 in 2017. This means that the price of the basket in 2017 is 175 per cent of its price in the base year. Put differently, a basket of goods that costs €100 in the base year costs €175 in 2017. Similarly, the CPI is 250 in 2018, indicating that the price level in 2018 is 250 per cent of the price level in the base year.

5. *Compute the inflation rate.* The fifth and final step is to use the CPI to calculate the **inflation rate**, which is the percentage change in the price index from the preceding period. That is, the inflation rate between two consecutive years is computed as follows:

$$\text{Inflation rate in year 2} = 100 \times \frac{(CPI \text{ in year 2} - CPI \text{ in year 1})}{CPI \text{ in year 1}}$$

In our example, the inflation rate is 75 per cent in 2017 and 43 per cent in 2018.

$$CPI_{year\ t} = \frac{\text{Cost of basket of goods in year } t \text{ prices}}{\text{Cost of basket of goods in base year prices}}$$

The inflation rate is given by:

$$Inflation_{year\ t} = \frac{\left(Price\ index_{year\ t}\right) - \left(Price\ index_{year\ t-1}\right)}{\left(Price\ index_{year\ t-1}\right)} \times 100$$

> **inflation rate** the percentage change in the price index from the preceding period

Although this example simplifies the real world by including only two goods, it shows how statistics offices compute the CPI and the inflation rate. The offices collect and processes data on the prices of thousands of goods and services every month and, by following the five foregoing steps, determines how quickly the cost of living for the typical consumer is rising. In addition to the CPI for the overall economy, statistics offices also calculate price indices for the sub-categories of 'goods' and of 'services' separately, as well as the **producer prices index** (PPI), which measures the prices of a basket of goods and services bought by firms rather than consumers. Because firms eventually pass on their costs to consumers in the form of higher consumer prices, changes in the PPI are often thought to be useful in predicting changes in the CPI.

> **producer prices index** a measure of the prices of a basket of goods and services bought by firms

Problems in Measuring the Cost of Living

The goal of the CPI is to measure changes in the cost of living – how much people have to pay to purchase goods and services. In other words, the CPI tries to gauge how much incomes must rise in order to maintain a constant standard of living. Assume that an individual in 2016 has an income of €120 per week and only buys burgers at €2 each. Their standard of living is 60 burgers a week. In 2017, burgers rise in price to €3 and so the standard of living, assuming income does not change, is now only 40 burgers a week. We would say that the individual's standard of living has fallen because they can now afford to consume fewer burgers. To keep their standard of living constant at 60 burgers, the person's income needs to rise from €120 per week to €180 per week. If the rise in incomes keeps pace with the rise in prices then the individual's standard of living will remain constant. If incomes rise by a lower percentage than the CPI, then standards of living are being eroded and, if incomes rise at a faster rate than the CPI, standards of living are improving and people are better off.

The CPI, however, is not a perfect measure of the cost of living. Three problems with the index are widely acknowledged but difficult to solve.

Substitution Bias The first problem is called *substitution bias*. When prices change from one year to the next, they do not all change proportionately: some prices rise more than others and some prices fall. Consumers respond to these differing price changes by buying less of the goods whose prices have risen by large amounts and by buying more of the goods whose prices have risen less or perhaps even have fallen (and, of course, different consumers will respond to price changes in different ways because of the price elasticity of demand). Consumers substitute towards goods that have become relatively less expensive. If a price index is computed assuming a fixed basket of goods, it ignores the possibility of consumer substitution and, therefore, overstates the increase in the cost of living from one year to the next.

Let's consider a simple example. Imagine that in the base year apples are cheaper than pears, and so consumers buy more apples than pears. When the statistics office constructs the basket of goods, apples will be weighted more heavily than pears. Suppose that next year pears are cheaper than apples. Consumers may respond to the price changes by buying more pears and fewer apples. Yet, when computing the CPI, the statistics office uses a fixed basket, which in essence assumes that consumers continue buying the now expensive apples in the same quantities as before. For this reason, the index will measure a much larger increase in the cost of living than consumers actually experience.

The Introduction of New Goods The second problem with the CPI is the *introduction of new goods*. When a new good is introduced, consumers have more variety from which to choose. Greater variety, in turn, makes each euro or pound more valuable, so consumers need fewer units of currency to maintain any given standard of living. Yet because the CPI is based on a fixed basket of goods and services, it does not reflect this change in purchasing power.

For example, when video players were introduced, consumers were able to watch their favourite films at home. Compared with going to the cinema, the convenience was greater and the cost was less. A perfect cost of living index would have reflected the introduction of the video player with a decrease in the cost of living. The CPI, however, did not decrease in response to the introduction of the video player. Eventually, the ONS did revise the basket of goods to include video players, and subsequently the index reflected changes in their prices. As time has passed the index had to be revised to take account of the decline in video and the rise of DVD, then Blu-ray DVD and, more recently, the increase in downloading and streaming of films.

Unmeasured Quality Change The third problem with the CPI is *unmeasured quality change*. If the quality of a good deteriorates from one year to the next, the effective value of a euro or pound falls, even if the price of the good stays the same. Similarly, if the quality rises from one year to the next, the effective value of a euro or pound rises. Statistics offices do their best to account for quality change. When the quality of a good in the basket changes – for example, when a car model has more horsepower or gets better fuel mileage from one year to the next – statistics offices adjust the price of the good to account for the quality change. They are, in essence, trying to compute the price of a basket of goods of constant quality.

To take another example, in 2004 the ONS introduced digital cameras into the CPI for the first time. As well as the problems associated with introducing a new good into the index that we discussed earlier, digital cameras are also subject to very rapid technological progress – features such as zoom and the number of megapixels keep on improving rapidly and the sale of digital cameras has now been impacted by the developments in camera technology which is incorporated in smartphones. Thus, while the average price of a digital camera or a smartphone might remain the same over a period, the average quality may have risen substantially. The ONS attempts to correct for this by a method known as *hedonic quality adjustment*. This involves working out the average characteristics (e.g. screen size, number of megapixels, zoom features, etc.) of the average digital camera and adjusting the price when one of these average characteristics increases. Despite these efforts, changes in quality remain a problem, because quality is so hard to measure.

Relevance of the CPI A final problem with the index is that people may not see the reported CPI measure of inflation as relevant to their particular situation. This is because their spending patterns are individual and might not be typical of the representative pattern on which the official figures are based. For example, if an individual spent a high proportion of their income on fuel and their mortgage, the effect of price rises in gas, electricity, petrol and a rise in mortgage rates would have a disproportionate effect on their experience of inflation. This different perception of inflation can have an effect on expectations, the importance of which we will see in later chapters.

Because of the different perceptions that people have about inflation and how it affects them, the ONS published a Personal Inflation Calculator (PIC) in 2007. The PIC allows users to be able to input their own details such as what their personal monthly expenditure is, how much they spend on food, meals out, alcohol, clothing and footwear, fuel for transport and so on. In addition, the calculator looks at what is spent on utilities such as water, council tax, vehicles, holidays and housing.

The ONS hopes that the PIC will help people to develop more of an interest in how inflation is calculated and be more aware of how the reality of price rises in their lives might differ to the officially published figures.

FYI

What is in the CPI's Basket?

When constructing the CPI, the UK ONS tries to include all the goods and services that the typical consumer buys. Moreover, it tries to weight these goods and services according to how much consumers buy of each item. Every month the ONS collects around 180 000 prices of 700 goods and services from around 150 areas throughout the UK that are supposed to be representative of the goods and services used on a regular basis. As buying habits change, the basket of goods and services has to change also. Each year the ONS announces a revision to the basket of goods and services that make up the basis of inflation figures in the UK. The ONS has to take into consideration not only how representative the sample of goods and services is but also any changes in importance in the typical household budget and whether the replacement brands that shops bring in are of comparable quality.

Table 21.2 shows the main groupings of the products included in the CPI in 2015.

Over time, food is not as important in the typical household budget, and similarly tobacco and alcohol are also less important. Housing, though, has become more important, perhaps reflecting the interest people have in their homes (there is a large proportion of the population in the UK who own their own homes unlike the situation in other parts of Europe where renting is more common). Over the last 30 years, there has been increased spending on leisure services, which includes spending on holidays, which has risen significantly in importance.

Some goods and services that are not as representative any more are removed from the basket. This is measured by the amount spent on these goods and services. If consumer expenditure on items exceeds £400 million annually then these are normally included in the basket but if expenditure falls below £100 million then there has to be a very good reason put forward to keep these goods in the basket. In recent years this has included microwave ovens, which first made an appearance in the index in the 1980s. They are still popular, say the ONS, but their reliability and falling prices means that the amount spent on them has reduced and as a result, they have been removed from the basket. Other items that have dropped out include film for 35 mm cameras (the cameras themselves dropped out in 2007), top 40 CD singles and television repair. As technology changes the way we live, the ONS says that people prefer to download music rather than buy singles, and households tend to replace TVs rather than get them repaired.

(Continued)

TABLE 21.2	CPI Division Level Weights, 2014 to 2015		
CPI Division	**2014 Weight (parts per thousand)**	**2015 Weight (parts per thousand)**	**Per cent change (%)**
Food and Non-alcoholic Beverages	112	110	-1.8
Alcoholic Beverages and Tobacco	45	43	-4.4
Clothing and Footwear	72	70	-2
Housing, Water, Electricity, Gas and Other Fuels	129	128	-0.8
Furniture, Household Equipment and Maintenance	60	59	-1.7
Health	24	25	4.2
Transport	152	149	-2.0
Communication	32	31	-3.1
Recreation and Culture	144	147	2.1
Education	22	26	18.2
Restaurants and Hotels	120	121	0.8
Miscellaneous Goods and Services	88	91	3.4
Total	1000	1000	

Source: ONS Consumer Price Inflation Basket of Goods and Services 2015 http://www.ons.gov.uk/ons/rel/cpi/cpi-rpi-basket/2015/index.html accessed 1 December 2015

The goods and services that came into the basket in 2015 include e-cigarette refills and liquid, craft beers, protein powder, games consoles, online subscriptions and music streaming subscription.

The CPI, the Harmonized Index of Consumer Prices and the Retail Prices Index

Before the end of 2003, it was more usual in the UK to measure prices using the Retail Prices Index (RPI). In December 2003, however, the UK Chancellor of the Exchequer announced that all policy announcements concerning inflation and prices would relate to the CPI rather than the RPI, so that movements in the CPI became the main measure of inflation and would come into line with the rest of Europe and many other countries around the world.

The RPI is constructed in the way described above, and differs from the CPI mainly in the goods and services included in the basket and in the coverage of households. In particular, the CPI excludes a number of items that are included in the RPI, mainly related to housing, such as council tax (a local government tax) and house mortgage interest payments. These items are excluded because if council taxes rise or mortgage payments rise because interest rates have risen, then the inflation rate as measured by the RPI will rise, even though underlying inflationary pressures in the economy may not have changed. Also, the CPI covers all private households, whereas the RPI excludes the top 4 per cent by income, and pensioner households who derive at least three-quarters of their income from state benefits. The CPI also includes the residents of institutional households such as student hostels, and foreign visitors to the UK. This means that it covers some items that are not in the RPI, such as stockbrokers' fees, university accommodation fees and foreign students' university tuition fees. The two indices also differ in some of the very fine details of the way in which prices are measured (such as allowance for quality adjustment).

What were the reasons for introducing the CPI? One reason is that some economists believe that it is closer to the concept of the overall price level employed in macroeconomic analysis – although others would argue that it may be misleading in the way in which it understates housing costs by excluding mortgage interest payments and council taxes. The main reason for its adoption, however, is that the construction of the CPI is identical to that used in the EU to construct price indices for other EU member countries. Because these price indices are harmonized in their construction across countries, they are known in Europe as harmonized indices of consumer prices, or HICPs. This allows direct comparison of inflation rates across EU member states. Such comparisons are not possible using national consumer prices indices due to differences in index coverage and construction. The CPI published by the UK Office for National Statistics is, in fact, the UK HICP.

Figure 21.1 shows inflation measured by the HICP in 2014 for each of the members of the European Union. Because we know that the price index has been constructed using the same conventions for each country, we can compare the figures directly.

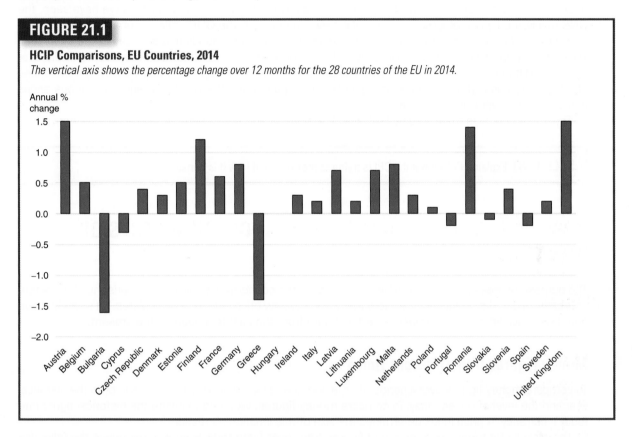

FIGURE 21.1

HCIP Comparisons, EU Countries, 2014
The vertical axis shows the percentage change over 12 months for the 28 countries of the EU in 2014.

The GDP Deflator versus the Consumer Prices Index

In the preceding chapter we examined another measure of the overall level of prices in the economy – the GDP deflator. The GDP deflator is the ratio of nominal GDP to real GDP. Because nominal GDP is current output valued at current prices and real GDP is current output valued at base-year prices, the GDP deflator reflects the current level of prices relative to the level of prices in the base year.

Economists and policymakers monitor both the GDP deflator and the CPI to gauge how quickly prices are rising. Usually, these two statistics tell a similar story. Yet there are two important differences that can cause them to diverge.

The first difference is that the GDP deflator reflects the prices of all goods and services *produced domestically*, whereas the CPI reflects the prices of all goods and services *bought by consumers*. For example, suppose that the price of an aeroplane produced by Dassault, a French aerospace firm, and sold to the French Air Force rises. Even though the aeroplane is part of GDP in France, it is not part of the basket of goods and services bought by a typical consumer. Thus, the price increase shows up in the GDP deflator for France but not in France's CPI.

As another example, suppose that Volvo raises the price of its cars. Because Volvos are made in Sweden, the car is not part of French GDP. But French consumers buy Volvos, and so the car is part of the typical consumer's basket of goods. Hence, a price increase in an imported consumption good, such as a Volvo, shows up in the CPI but not in the GDP deflator.

This first difference between the CPI and the GDP deflator is particularly important when the price of oil changes. Although the UK does produce some oil, as with many parts of Europe, much of the oil used in the UK is imported from the Middle East. As a result, oil and oil products such as petrol and heating oil comprise a much larger share of consumer spending than they do of GDP. When the price of oil changes, the CPI changes by much more than does the GDP deflator.

The second and subtler difference between the GDP deflator and the CPI concerns how various prices are weighted to yield a single number for the overall level of prices. The CPI compares the price of a *fixed* basket of goods and services with the price of the basket in the base year. Whilst, as we have seen, the ONS revise the basket of goods on a regular basis, in contrast, the GDP deflator compares the price of *currently produced* goods and services with the price of the same goods and services in the base year. Thus, the group of goods and services used to compute the GDP deflator changes automatically over time. This difference is not important when all prices are changing proportionately. However, if the prices of different goods and services are changing by varying amounts, the way we weight the various prices matters for the overall inflation rate.

The inflation rate as measured by both the GDP deflator and the CPI do tend to move together.

SELF TEST Explain briefly what the CPI is trying to measure and how it is constructed.

CORRECTING ECONOMIC VARIABLES FOR THE EFFECTS OF INFLATION

The purpose of measuring the overall level of prices in the economy is to permit comparisons of monetary figures from different points in time. Now that we know how price indices are calculated, let's see how we might use such an index to compare a certain figure from the past to a figure in the present.

Money Figures from Different Times

To compare money figures over a period of time, we need to know the level of prices in both the historical year and the level of prices today. To compare money figures, we need to inflate the historical figure into today's currency. A price index determines the size of this inflation correction.

The formula for turning euro or pound figures from *year T* into today's euro or pounds is the following (assuming the price level today and the price level in *year T* are measured against the same base year):

$$\text{Amount in today's currency} = \text{Amount in year T currency} \times \frac{\text{Price level today}}{\text{Price level in year T}}$$

A price index such as the CPI measures the price level and determines the size of the inflation correction. To illustrate, let us take an example of the salary for members of parliament in the UK. In 1947 this was £1000 per year according to the House of Commons Information Office. The ONS reports the RPI for 1947 at 28.9 and for 2015 1018.6. Substituting these figures into the formula gives:

$$\text{Salary in 2015£} = \text{Salary in 1947£} \times \frac{\text{RPI in 2015}}{\text{RPI in 1947}}$$

$$\text{Salary in 2015} = £1000 \times \left(\frac{1018.6}{28.9}\right)$$

$$\text{Salary in 2015} = £35\,230$$

We find that the salary paid to an MP in 1947 is equivalent to a salary today of £35 230. The basic annual salary of an MP in 2015 was £74 000. It seems that an MP in 2015 is considerably better off in terms of salary earned than their compatriots in 1947.

Indexation

As we have just seen, price indices are used to correct for the effects of inflation when comparing monetary figures from different times. This type of correction shows up in many places in the economy. When some money amount is automatically corrected for inflation by law or contract, the amount is said to be **indexed** for inflation. For example, many long-term contracts between firms and unions include partial or complete indexation of the wage to the CPI. Such a provision is called a *cost-of-living allowance*, or COLA. A COLA automatically raises the wage each year based on the CPI or other measure such as the RPI, at a particular point in time.

indexed the automatic correction of a money amount for the effects of inflation by law or contract

Income tax brackets – the income levels at which the tax rates change – are also often moved annually in line with inflation, although, in most countries, they are not formally indexed. Indeed, there are many ways in which the tax system is not indexed for inflation, even when perhaps it should be. We discuss these issues more fully when we discuss the costs of inflation later in this book.

 CASE STUDY Adjusting for Inflation

What was the most popular film of all time? The answer might surprise you. Film popularity is usually gauged by worldwide box office receipts. By that measure, as of the beginning of 2016, *Avatar* (released in 2009) was the number one film of all time grossing $2.79 billion, followed by *Titanic* (1993 – $2.19 billion). *Star Wars: The Force Awakens* (2015 - $2.01 billion) leapt into number three; *Jurassic World*, released in 2015, came in number four grossing $1.67 billion, followed by *Marvel's The Avengers* (2012) at $1.52 billion, *Furious 7* (2015) ($1.52 billion) then *Harry Potter and the Deathly Hallows, Part 2* (2011 – $1.34 billion) *Frozen* (2013) $1.28 billion; and coming in tenth was *Iron Man 3* (2013) at $1.21 billion. But this ranking ignores an obvious but important fact: prices, including those of cinema tickets, have been rising over time. When we correct box office receipts for the effects of inflation, the story is very different.

Table 21.4 shows the top ten films of all time ranked by inflation-adjusted worldwide box office receipts in US dollars. The original *Star Wars,* released in 1977, is at number two, while *The Sound of Music* takes the number three spot and the number one film of all time is the American Civil War drama, *Gone with the Wind* ($1.757 billion adjusted), which was released in 1939 and is well ahead of *Avatar* ($846 million adjusted), which doesn't even make the top ten (appearing at number 15). In the 1930s, before everyone had televisions in their homes, cinema attendance was about three or four times what it is today. But the films from that era rarely show up in popularity rankings because ticket prices were only a fraction of what they are today. Scarlett and Rhett, the main characters in *Gone with the Wind,* fare a lot better once we correct for the effects of inflation.

TABLE 21.4 The Most Popular Films of All Time, Inflation-Adjusted

Film	Year of release
Gone with the Wind	1939
Star Wars	1977
The Sound of Music	1965
E.T.	1982
Titanic	1997
The Ten Commandments	1956
Jaws	1975
Doctor Zhivago	1965
The Exorcist	1973
Snow White and the Seven Dwarfs	1937

(Source of data: http://www.boxofficemojo.com)

(Continued)

Gone with the Wind, the US Civil War drama, still leading the all time box office receipts – when adjusted for inflation.

Real and Nominal Interest Rates

Correcting economic variables for the effects of inflation is particularly important, and somewhat tricky, when we look at data on interest rates. Savings deposited in an interest bearing account provides a return based on the interest rate available. Conversely, when people borrow from a bank to fund purchases, such as a car, interest is payable on the loan. Interest represents a payment in the future for a transfer of money in the past. As a result, interest rates always involve comparing amounts of money at different points in time. To fully understand interest rates, we need to know how to correct for the effects of inflation.

Let's consider an example. Suppose that Carla deposits €1000 in a savings account that pays an annual interest rate of 10 per cent. After a year passes, Carla has accumulated €100 in interest. Carla then withdraws her €1100. Is Carla €100 richer than she was when she made the deposit a year earlier?

The answer depends on what we mean by 'richer'. Carla does have €100 more than she had before. In other words, the number of euros has risen by 10 per cent. If prices have risen at the same time, each euro now buys less than it did a year ago. Thus, her purchasing power has not risen by 10 per cent. If the inflation rate was 4 per cent, then the amount of goods she can buy has increased by only 6 per cent. If the inflation rate was 15 per cent, then the price of goods has increased proportionately more than the number of euros in her account. In that case, Carla's purchasing power has actually fallen by 5 per cent.

The interest rate that the savings account pays is called the **nominal interest rate**, and the interest rate corrected for inflation is called the **real interest rate**. We can write the relationship between the nominal interest rate, the real interest rate and inflation as follows:

$$r_t = i_t - \pi_t$$

The real interest rate in a particular time period (r_t) = Nominal interest rate in that time perod (i_t) – Inflation rate in the same time period (π_t).

The real interest rate is the difference between the nominal interest rate and the rate of inflation. The nominal interest rate tells you how fast the number of pounds or euros in your bank account rises over time. The real interest rate tells you how fast the purchasing power of your bank account rises over time.

nominal interest rate the interest rate as usually reported without a correction for the effects of inflation
real interest rate the interest rate corrected for the effects of inflation

Figure 21.2 shows the nominal interest rate (measured as the average annual rate of discount on three-month Treasury bills), the inflation rate (measured by the RPI) and the real interest rate (the difference between the two). You can see that real and nominal interest rates do not always move together. For example, in the late 1970s, nominal interest rates were high, but because inflation was higher, real interest rates were negative. Equally, since the Financial Crisis in 2008, real interest rates have also been negative even though inflation has been much lower than in the late 1970s. This means that inflation is eroding people's savings more quickly than nominal interest payments increased them. By contrast, in the 1990s, nominal interest rates hovered at around 5.0 per cent but inflation was relatively low, real interest rates were also relatively low.

FIGURE 21.2

Real and Nominal Interest Rates

This figure shows the inflation rate (RPI), nominal, and real interest rates using average annual changes since 1976. The nominal interest rate is the rate on a three-month Treasury bill. The real interest rate is the nominal interest rate minus the annual inflation rate as measured by the RPI.

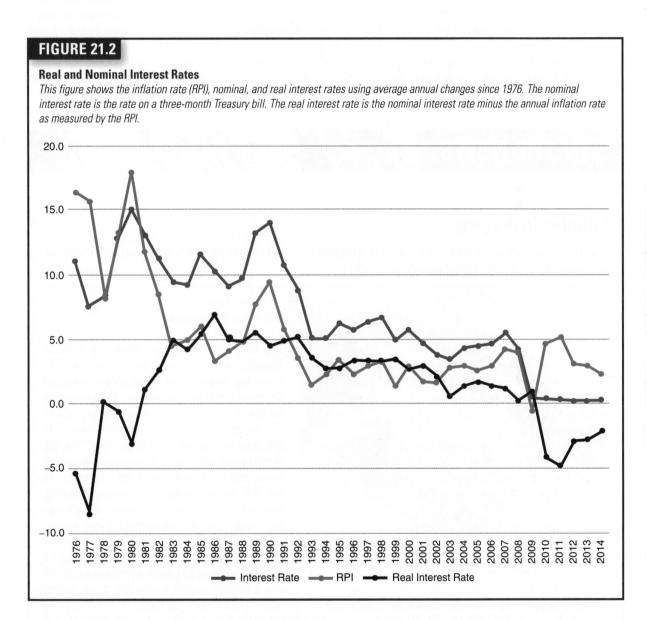

SELF TEST Why is it important to adjust for inflation when considering wage increases and the returns from any financial investment?

CONCLUSION

Throughout recent history, the real values behind the currencies of most major industrialized countries, such as the pound, euro and dollar, have not been stable. Persistent increases in the overall level of prices in advanced economies such as those of the UK, the other countries of Europe and of the USA have been the norm. When comparing figures in monetary or nominal terms from different times, it is important to keep in mind that a pound or euro today is not the same as a pound or euro ten years ago or, most likely, ten years from now.

This chapter has discussed how economists measure the overall level of prices in the economy and how they use price indices to correct economic variables for the effects of inflation. This analysis is only a starting point. We have not yet examined the causes and effects of inflation or how inflation interacts with other economic variables. To do that, we need to go beyond issues of measurement. Indeed, that is our next task. Having explained how economists measure macroeconomic quantities and prices in the past two chapters, we are now ready to develop the models that explain long-run and short-run movements in these variables.

IN THE NEWS

Inflation in Uruguay

Countries around the world face similar issues in managing inflation. In this In the News, we look at the experience of Uruguay whose CPI tipped into double digits in 2015.

Double-digit Uruguayan inflation can affect standards of living for people in the country.

Inflation in Uruguay

The Uruguayan statistical office, the Instituto Nacional de Estadistica (INE) publishes the Consumer Prices Index (Indice de Precios del Consumo (IPC)) for the country. The target rate for the IPC is 3–7 per cent but the annualised rate following publication of the November 2015 IPC showed inflation at 10.04 per cent. The INE reported that food and beverages price increases accounted for a large part of the overall rise in the IPC but garments and footwear, housing, construction, leisure and culture all showed increases in prices compared to the year before.

The tipping of the IPC into double digits is not good news for the government or indeed for workers. Uruguay has some strong trades unions and if inflation cannot be brought down, unions will push for pay rises to ensure workers' living standards are maintained and if such pay rises are met, that could cause further economic problems. The increase in the rate of inflation came despite a voluntary agreement reached earlier in 2015 between the government and retailers, including supermarkets, to freeze the prices of around 1600 goods for a three-month period.

The government was also reported to be looking at ways of cutting prices of power, communications, fuel, health-care and water prices, all of which are under the direct control of the government, in an attempt to bring inflation

(*Continued*)

back under double digits. External factors may compromise those attempts, however. The Uruguayan peso weakened against the US dollar meaning that import prices rose. This put pressure on the IPC. Uruguayan imports account for around one-fifth of its GDP so when import prices rise, it can have a significant effect on inflation.

Some of these upward effects on inflation might be offset by a slowdown in domestic demand. The country's neighbours, Brazil and Argentina, have experienced problems of their own and their economic fortunes influence Uruguay's economy. The difficult balance for the government is managing demand so that inflationary pressures reduce without adversely affecting the country's economic growth too much. The government had been predicting economic growth of 2.5 per cent in 2015, increasing to 3.0 per cent by 2019.

Questions

1 **Why might an inflation rate at double digits be considered problematic for a country such as Uruguay?**
2 **In what way can inflation erode workers' standards of living?**
3 **If unions are successful in negotiating wage rises which maintain standards of living, what effect do you think this will have on future inflation in Uruguay?**
4 **The agreement between retailers and the government to freeze prices for a period is designed to ease inflationary pressures. Why do you think that inflation accelerated despite this freeze?**
5 **Explain why a weakening of the Uruguayan peso causes inflationary pressures in the country.**

SUMMARY

- The CPI shows the changes in the prices of a basket of goods and services relative to the prices of the same basket in the base year. The index is used to measure the overall level of prices in the economy. The percentage change in the CPI measures the inflation rate.

- The CPI is an imperfect measure of the cost of living for three reasons. First, it does not take into account consumers' ability to substitute towards goods that become relatively cheaper over time. Second, it does not take into account increases in the purchasing power of money due to the introduction of new goods. Third, it is distorted by unmeasured changes in the quality of goods and services. Because of these measurement problems, the CPI overstates true inflation.

- Although the GDP deflator also measures the overall level of prices in the economy, it differs from the CPI because it includes goods and services produced rather than goods and services consumed. As a result, imported goods affect the CPI but not the GDP deflator. In addition, while the CPI uses a fixed basket of goods, the GDP deflator automatically changes the group of goods and services over time as the composition of GDP changes.

- Money figures (e.g. in euros) from different points in time do not represent a valid comparison of purchasing power. To compare a money figure from the past to a money figure today, the older figure should be inflated using a price index.

- Various laws and private contracts use price indices to correct for the effects of inflation.

- A correction for inflation is especially important when looking at data on interest rates. The nominal interest rate is the interest rate usually reported; it is the rate at which the amount of money in a savings account increases over time. In contrast, the real interest rate takes into account changes in the value of the money over time. The real interest rate equals the nominal interest rate minus the rate of inflation.

QUESTIONS FOR REVIEW

1 What are the five stages of constructing a prices index?
2 Why do statisticians use weighting in constructing price indices?
3 Which do you think has a greater effect on the CPI: a 10 per cent increase in the price of chicken or a 10 per cent increase in the price of caviar? Why?
4 Describe the three problems that make the CPI an imperfect measure of the cost of living.

5 Why do statisticians change the composition of the basket of goods used in constructing a prices index from time to time?

6 Assume that the price of a bottle of wine in 1990 was €3.50 and in 2017 it is €8.50. Further assume that the price index in 1990 was 95 and in 2017 was 160. Was wine cheaper in 1990 than in 2017? Explain.

7 If the price of a French Navy submarine rises, is the French CPI or the French GDP deflator affected more? Why?

8 Over a long period of time, the price of a box of chocolates rose from €1 to €6. Over the same period, the CPI rose from 150 to 300. Adjusted for overall inflation, how much did the price of the box of chocolates change?

9 Explain the meaning of nominal interest rate and real interest rate. How are they related?

10 Why is knowledge of real interest rates of importance to people who rely on their savings for their income?

PROBLEMS AND APPLICATIONS

1 Suppose that people consume only three goods, as shown in this table:

	Tennis balls	Tennis racquets	Cola
2016 price (€)	2	40	1
2016 quantity	100	10	200
2017 price (€)	2	60	2
2017 quantity	100	10	200

a. What is the percentage change in the price of each of the three goods? What is the percentage change in the overall price level?

b. Do tennis racquets become more or less expensive relative to cola? Does the well-being of some people change relative to that of others? Explain.

2 Suppose that the residents of Vegopia spend all of their income on cauliflower, broccoli and carrots. In 2017 they buy 100 heads of cauliflower for €200, 50 bunches of broccoli for €75 and 500 carrots for €50. In 2018 they buy 75 heads of cauliflower for €225, 80 bunches of broccoli for €120 and 500 carrots for €100. If the base year is 2017, what is the CPI in both years? What is the inflation rate in 2018?

3 Go to the website of the UK ONS (http://www.statistics.gov.uk) or Eurostat (http://ec.europa.eu/eurostat/web/main/home) and find data on the CPI. By how much has the index including all items risen over the past year for your country? For which categories of spending have prices risen the most? The least? Have any categories experienced price declines? Can you explain any of these facts?

4 Which of the problems in the construction of the CPI might be illustrated by each of the following situations? Explain.

a. the increase in streaming films

b. the introduction of air bags in cars

c. increased personal computer purchases in response to a decline in their price

d. increased use of digital cameras in smartphones

e. reduced use of fuel-efficient cars after petrol prices fall.

5 Suppose the government were to determine the level of the state retirement pension in the UK so that it increased each year in proportion to the increase in the CPI.

a. If the elderly consume the same market basket as other people, would such a policy provide the elderly with an improvement in their standard of living each year? Explain.

b. In fact, the elderly consume more health care than younger people, and healthcare costs tend to rise faster than overall inflation. What would you do to determine whether the elderly are actually better off from year to year?

6 How do you think the basket of goods and services you buy differs from the basket bought by the typical household? Do you think you face a higher or lower inflation rate than is indicated by the CPI? Why?

7 In some years in some countries, income tax brackets are not increased in line with inflation. Why do you think the government might do this? (Hint: this phenomenon is known as 'bracket creep'.)

8 When deciding how much of their income to save for retirement, should workers consider the real or the nominal interest rate that their savings will earn? Explain.

9 Suppose that a borrower and a lender agree on the nominal interest rate to be paid on a loan. Then inflation turns out to be higher than they both expected.

   Is the real interest rate on this loan higher or lower than expected?

   Does the lender gain or lose from this unexpectedly high inflation? Does the borrower gain or lose?

10 Assume that in 2016, the price of food increased by 2 per cent over the year. In 2017, the price of food rises by 1.9 per cent over the year. Further assume that food has a high weighting in the construction of the CPI. What do you think the effect on the 2017 CPI will be as a result of the change in the price of food?

PART 11
THE REAL ECONOMY IN THE LONG RUN

22 PRODUCTION AND GROWTH

We have spent the first two chapters in this macroeconomics section looking at how to measure growth and changes in the price level. These are important macroeconomic variables. We are now going to turn our attention on looking at what determines the level of economic growth. In Chapter 18, we looked at the disparities in incomes in countries and between countries. The average person in a rich country, such as the countries of Western Europe, has an income more than ten times as high as the average person in a poor country, such as India, Indonesia or Nigeria. The Nobel Prize winning economist, Robert E. Lucas, spent some time looking at different growth rates and levels of poverty and inequality between countries. Lucas asked why countries have different growth rates and exhibited such wide variations in living standards. The news and social media brings these variations in standards of living sharply into focus, in some respects making us more aware of the vast differences in living standards than perhaps ever before. Indeed, around 30 years ago Lucas wrote: 'The consequences for human welfare involved in questions like these are simply staggering: once one starts to think about them, it is hard to think about anything else.' It is worth dwelling on Lucas' words; there are millions of people around the world for whom life is a daily struggle. Simply finding enough food and water to maintain life is a challenge. Contrast this with the lifestyles of many people in the developed world and the moral implications of such a comparison is significant.

What explains these diverse experiences? How can the rich countries be sure to maintain their high standard of living? What policies should the poor countries pursue to promote more rapid growth in order to join the developed world? These are among the most important questions in macroeconomics. As we have seen, an economy's GDP measures both the total income earned in the economy and the total expenditure on the economy's output of goods and services. The level and growth of real GDP is one gauge of economic prosperity. Here we focus on the long-run determinants of the level and growth of real GDP. Later in this book we study the short-run fluctuations of real GDP around its long-run trend.

ECONOMIC GROWTH AROUND THE WORLD

It is typical for analysis of economic growth to use the level of GDP in relation to the population. In particular, we can identify two concepts, GDP per capita and GDP per worker. GDP per capita takes the level of real GDP at a point in time and divides it by the population to get a measure of income per head of the population. This serves as a useful basis for comparison across countries. It is typical to present such data in US dollars.

$$Real\ GDP\ per\ capita = \frac{Real\ GDP}{Total\ Population}$$

Similarly, we could look at real GDP in relation to the number of people employed in the population to give a measure of income per head of the working population.

$$Real\ GDP\ per\ worker = \frac{Real\ GDP}{Number\ of\ people\ in\ employment}$$

Table 22.1 shows real GDP per capita in a number of selected countries. The data in the table show that living standards vary widely from country to country and have changed at very different rates over the last 50 years. Income per person in Ireland in 2014, for instance, is about 33 times that in India even though India's per capita income has increased by 19 times since 1960. The poorest countries such as the Democratic Republic of the Congo and Niger have very low average levels of income which have barely changed over 50 years.

TABLE 22.1 Real GDP Per Capita, Current US$, Selected Countries

Country Name	1960	1970	1980	1990	2000	2010	2014
Afghanistan	60	157	276			570	659
Albania				639	1 193	4 094	4 619
Austria	935	2 054	10 843	21 629	24 517	46 593	51 127
Azerbaijan				1237	655	5 843	7 884
Bangladesh	89	138	223	295	407	760	1 093
Belgium	1 274	2 776	12 913	20 679	23 152	44 361	47 517
Burkina Faso	68	81	283	352	227	574	713
Central African Republic	75	103	350	490	245	447	371
China	89	112	193	316	955	4 515	7 594
Cyprus			4 232	9 642	14 307	30 439	27 194
Czech Republic				3 902	5 995	19 764	19 554
Democratic Republic of the Congo	220	244	546	267	397	311	440
Denmark	1 365	3 422	13 833	26 862	30 744	57 648	60 634
Egypt		221	528	765	1 461	2 668	3 199
Estonia					4 070	14 632	19 720
Finland	1 179	2 467	11 232	28 381	24 253	46 205	49 541
France	1 338	2 862	12 713	21 795	22 466	40 706	42 733
Germany		2 751	12 092	22 220	23 685	41 726	47 627
Greece	534	1 500	5 915	9 673	11 961	26 863	21 683
Iceland	1 415	2 606	14 991	25 675	31 820	41 696	52 111
India	84	115	272	375	452	1 388	1 596
Ireland	686	1 485	6 366	14 017	26 101	47 904	53 314
Italy	804	2 101	8 432	20 765	20 059	35 878	34 960
Luxembourg	2 242	4 479	17 226	34 872	48 827	102 863	
Netherlands	1 069	2 878	13 563	20 937	25 958	50 341	51 590
Niger	132	145	421	314	160	351	427
Nigeria	93	224	871	322	378	2 315	3 203
Norway	1 442	3 306	15 772	28 243	38 147	87 646	97 363
Poland				1 698	4 493	12 530	14 423
Portugal	360	934	3 369	7 885	11 502	22 540	22 081
Romania				1 651	1 662	8 139	9 997

(*Continued*)

TABLE 22.1 Real GDP Per Capita, Current US$, Selected Countries (*Continued*)

Country Name	1960	1970	1980	1990	2000	2010	2014
Russian Federation				3 485	1 772	10 675	12 736
Slovenia					10 228	23 418	23 963
South Africa	423	811	2 921	3 182	3 099	7 390	6 478
Spain	396	1 209	6 200	13 773	14 788	30 738	30 262
Sweden	1 983	4 669	16 857	30 162	29 283	52 076	58 887
Switzerland	1 787		18 785	38 332	37 813	74 277	
Turkey	508	491	1 567	2 791	4 215	10 112	10 530
United Arab Emirates			42 879	27 989	34 208	34 342	44 204
United Kingdom	1 380	2 348	10 032	19 095	26 296	38 362	45 603
Zambia	229	427	655	404	340	1 456	1 722
Zimbabwe	281	362	916	838	535	677	896

Source: World Bank

Table 22.2 shows that countries with a relatively high per capita GDP often have relatively low levels of annual growth. The UK, for example, has an average growth of around 2.8 per cent over the period shown, Germany and Norway around 3.1 per cent and France around 3.3 per cent. Other countries such as the United Arab Emirates and China have seen periods of rapid growth and China's average growth since 1970 has been around 9.6 per cent. China is now the world's second largest economy behind the United States although its people still have a relatively low per capita income. Many of the developed countries in Western Europe have been able to sustain long periods of growth and whilst the average is not spectacular, the per capita incomes of people in these countries is much higher than some of the countries that currently experience high annual growth rates. Rich countries won't always be richer, and poor countries won't always be poor.

TABLE 22.2 Annual Real GDP Growth (%)

Country Name	1961	1970	1980	1990	2000	2010	2014
Afghanistan						8.4	2.0
Albania				−9.6	7.3	3.7	1.9
Austria	5.5	9.3	1.7	4.3	3.4	1.9	0.3
Azerbaijan					11.1	4.9	2.0
Bangladesh	6.1	5.6	0.8	5.6	5.3	5.6	6.1
Belgium	5.0	7.4	4.4	3.1	3.6	2.5	1.1
Burkina Faso	4.0	0.1	0.8	−0.6	1.8	8.4	4.0
Central African Republic	5.0	2.3	−4.5	−2.1	−2.5	3.0	1.0
China	−27.3	19.4	7.8	3.9	8.4	10.6	7.4
Cyprus			5.8	7.4	5.7	1.4	−2.3
Czech Republic					4.3	2.3	2.0
Democratic Republic of the Congo	−10.9	−0.2	2.2	−6.6	−6.9	7.1	9.0
Denmark	6.4	3.5	−0.5	1.6	3.7	1.6	1.1
Egypt		5.6	10.0	5.7	5.4	5.1	2.2
Finland	7.6	7.0	5.4	0.7	5.6	3.0	−0.1
France	5.5	6.9	1.6	2.9	3.9	2.0	0.2
Germany			1.4	5.3	3.0	4.1	1.6
Greece	11.1	11.0	0.7	0.0	4.0	−5.4	0.8
Iceland	−0.1	10.6	5.7	1.2	4.7	−3.1	1.9
India	3.7	5.2	6.7	5.5	3.8	10.3	7.4
Ireland			3.1	8.5	9.5	−0.3	4.8
Italy	8.2	9.0	3.4	2.0	3.7	1.7	−0.4

(*Continued*)

TABLE 22.2	Annual Real GDP Growth (%) (*Continued*)						
Country Name	**1960**	**1970**	**1980**	**1990**	**2000**	**2010**	**2014**
Luxembourg	3.8	2.4	0.8	5.3	8.4	5.1	
Netherlands	0.3	13.6	1.3	4.2	4.4	1.1	0.9
Niger	4.5	3.1	−2.2	−1.3	−1.4	8.4	6.9
Nigeria	0.2	25.0	4.2	12.8	5.3	7.8	6.3
Norway	6.3	2.9	4.6	1.9	3.2	0.6	2.2
Poland					4.3	3.7	3.4
Portugal	5.5	16.5	4.6	4.0	3.8	1.9	0.9
Romania				−5.6	2.1	−0.9	1.8
Russian Federation				−3.0	10.0	4.5	0.6
Slovenia					4.2	1.2	2.6
South Africa	3.8	5.2	6.6	−0.3	4.2	3.0	1.5
Spain	11.8	6.2	2.2	3.8	5.3	0.0	1.4
Sweden	5.7	11.2	1.7	0.8	4.7	6.0	2.3
Switzerland				3.7	3.9	3.0	
Turkey	1.2	3.2	−2.4	9.3	6.8	9.2	2.9
United Arab Emirates			23.9	18.3	10.9	1.6	3.6
United Kingdom	2.6	10.4	−2.2	0.5	3.8	1.9	2.6
Zambia	1.4	4.8	3.0	−0.5	3.9	10.3	6.0
Zimbabwe	6.3	22.6	14.4	7.0	−3.1	11.4	3.2

Source: World Bank

What explains why, for example, there have been rapid improvements in the standard of living for many people in China and India, whereas countries like Niger, the Central African Republic and the Democratic Republic of the Congo have remained amongst the poorest countries on the planet? Why do some countries zoom ahead while others lag behind? These are precisely the questions that we take up next.

SELF TEST Look at Tables 2.1 and 2.2. Can you identify any patterns between per capita incomes and annual GDP growth rates in the countries shown? What might explain these patterns?

FYI

The Magic of Compounding and the Rule of 70

Suppose you observe that one country has an average growth rate of 1 per cent per year while another has an average growth rate of 3 per cent per year. At first, this might not seem like a big deal. What difference can 2 per cent make?

The answer is, a big difference. Even growth rates that seem small when written in percentage terms seem large after they are compounded for many years.

Consider an example. Suppose that two economics graduates – Milton and Janet – both take their first jobs at the age of 22 earning €20 000 a year. Milton lives in an economy where all incomes grow at 1 per cent per year, while Janet lives in one where incomes grow at 3 per cent per year. Calculations using the principle of compounding show what happens. For Milton, after the first year he earns an additional 1 per cent of €20 000 (€200). In year 2 he earns an additional 1 per cent of €20 200 (€22 402) and so on. To calculate compound figures over time we use the formula $M = P(1 + i)^n$ where M is the total value at the end of the period, P is the initial value, i is the rate of

(*Continued*)

interest (or rate of growth) and n the number of years. After 40 years, therefore, Milton earns $20\ 000\ (1 + 0.01)^{40}$ which equals €29 777 a year.

Janet, on the other hand, earns €$20\ 000\ (1 + 0.03)^{40}$ and earns €65 240, 40 years later. Because of that difference of 2 percentage points in the growth rate, Janet's salary is more than twice Milton's.

An old rule of thumb, called the *rule of 70*, is helpful in understanding growth rates and the effects of compounding. According to the rule of 70, if some variable grows at a rate of x per cent per year, then that variable doubles in approximately $\dfrac{70}{x}$ years. In Milton's economy, incomes grow at 1 per cent per year, so it takes about 70 years for incomes to double. In Janet's economy, incomes grow at 3 per cent per year, so it takes about, $\dfrac{70}{3}$ or a little over 23 years for incomes to double.

GROWTH THEORY

Over time, economic growth in most countries varies. Sometimes the economy experiences strong periods of growth and at other times growth is slower and sometimes the economy shrinks. Over a period of time, a trend can be established which is usually expressed as a growth rate in percentage terms. We saw in Chapter 20 that real GDP growth is given by:

$$\text{Growth rate of real GDP in year } t = \frac{(GDP_t - GDP_{t-1})}{GDP_{t-1} - 1}$$

Trend growth and actual growth are important factors when we look at business cycles later in the book. Different countries have different trend growth rates. In order for a country to experience considerable improvements in living standards, sustained growth over a period of time is necessary. The annual growth does not necessarily need to be high but it has to be consistent. What determines whether a country can maintain sustained growth over a period and why some countries can grow faster than others is a central feature of macroeconomics and research into growth theory has resulted in Nobel Prizes for Simon Kuznets in 1971, Robert Solow in 1987.

In 1956, Robert. M. Solow and Trevor Swan identified the rate of human and physical capital and population growth as being key determinants of economic growth. Over the years, economists have looked at other factors that may influence economic growth which include the following:

- the level of macroeconomic stability in an economy
- the type of trade policy that exists in a country (is the country outward looking or does it tend to be insular?)
- the nature and quality of institutions and governance (i.e. how effectively the rule of law operates and how well governments are able to control corruption) in the country concerned
- the extent to which violence, war and conflict exist in a country
- regional characteristics such as whether the country is part of Europe, North America, Asia or sub-Saharan Africa
- geographical factors such as physical resource endowments and climate
- the extent to which a country is competitive in international markets
- internal factors such as the amount of productive land available.

The next section will cover the role of productivity in growth which can be referred to as the *neoclassical theory of growth*. Initially, we will look at the nature of the term *productivity* which is central to neoclassical growth theory.

PRODUCTIVITY

Some of the concepts in this chapter revisit those covered in Chapter 6 when we looked at the production function and the concepts of marginal and diminishing marginal product. Your knowledge of these concepts will be useful in this section; the main difference is that we are now thinking on a macroeconomic level rather than a microeconomic one.

Why Productivity is So Important

Let's begin our study of productivity and economic growth by developing a simple model based on an individual who finds herself shipwrecked on a desert island, who we will call Annie. Because Annie lives alone, she catches her own fish, grows her own vegetables and makes her own clothes. We can think of Annie's activities – her production and consumption of fish, vegetables and clothing – as being a simple economy. What determines Annie's standard of living? If Annie is good at catching fish, growing vegetables and making clothes, she lives well. If she is bad at doing these things, she lives poorly. Because Annie can consume only what she produces, her living standard is tied to her productive ability.

Remember that *productivity* refers to the quantity of goods and services that a worker (or any factor of production) can produce in a specified time period. In the case of Annie's economy, productivity is the key determinant of her living standards and growth in productivity is the key determinant of the growth in living standards. The more fish Annie can catch per hour, the more she eats for dinner. If Annie finds a better place to catch fish, her productivity rises. This increase in productivity makes Annie better off: she could eat the extra fish, or she could spend less time fishing and devote more time to making other goods she enjoys.

The key role of productivity in determining living standards is as true for nations as it is for Annie. Recall that an economy's GDP measures three things at once: the total income earned by everyone in the economy, the total expenditure on the economy's output of goods and services and the value of the output produced.

Like Annie, a nation can enjoy a high standard of living if it can produce a large quantity of goods and services. Western Europeans live better than Malians because western European workers are more productive than Malian workers. Hence, to understand the large differences in living standards we observe across countries or over time, we focus on the production of goods and services.

How Productivity is Determined

To illustrate the determinants of productivity, we return to our example of Annie. Many factors will determine Annie's productivity. Annie will be better at catching fish, for instance, if she has more fishing rods, if she has been trained in the best fishing techniques, if her island has a plentiful fish supply, and if she invents a better fishing lure. Each of these determinants of Annie's productivity – which we can call *physical capital*, *human capital*, *natural resources* and *technological knowledge* – has a counterpart in more complex and realistic economies. Let's consider each of these factors in turn.

Physical Capital Workers can be more productive if the capital stock is high. The stock of equipment and structures that are used to produce goods and services is called physical capital, or just *capital*. For example, when carpenters make furniture, they use saws, lathes and drill presses. More and better quality tools such as electric circular saws and precision routers, allow work to be done more quickly and more accurately. A carpenter with only basic hand tools can make less furniture each week than a carpenter with sophisticated and specialized woodworking equipment.

An important feature of capital is that it is a *produced* factor of production. Capital is an input into the production process that in the past was an output from the production process. The carpenter uses a lathe to make the leg of a table. Earlier the lathe itself was the output of a firm that manufactures lathes. The lathe manufacturer in turn used other equipment to make its product. Thus, capital is a factor of production used to produce all kinds of goods and services, including more capital.

Human Capital A second determinant of productivity is human capital. Human capital is the economist's term for the knowledge and skills that workers acquire through education, training and experience. Human capital includes the skills accumulated in early childhood programmes, primary school, secondary school, university or college, and on-the-job training for adults in the labour force.

Although education, training and experience are less tangible than lathes, bulldozers and buildings, human capital is like physical capital in many ways. Like physical capital, human capital raises a nation's ability to produce goods and services. Also like physical capital, human capital is a produced factor of production. Producing human capital requires inputs in the form of teachers, lecturers, libraries and student time. Indeed, students can be viewed as 'workers' who have the important job of producing the human capital that will be used in future production.

Natural Resources A third determinant of productivity is **natural resources**. Natural resources are inputs into production that are provided by nature, such as land, rivers and mineral deposits. Natural resources take two forms: renewable and non-renewable. A forest is an example of a renewable resource. When one tree is cut down, a seedling can be planted in its place to be harvested in the future. Oil is an example of a non-renewable resource. Because oil is produced by nature over many thousands or even millions of years, there is only a limited supply. Once the supply of oil is depleted, it is impossible to create more (at least not for thousands of years).

> **natural resources** the inputs into the production of goods and services that are provided by nature, such as land, rivers and mineral deposits

Differences in natural resources are responsible for some of the differences in standards of living around the world. The historical success of the United States was driven in part by the large supply of land well suited for agriculture. Today, some countries in the Middle East, such as Kuwait and Saudi Arabia, are rich simply because they happen to be on top of some of the largest pools of oil in the world.

Although natural resources can be important, they are not necessary for an economy to be highly productive in producing goods and services. Japan, for instance, is one of the richest countries in the world, despite having few natural resources. International trade makes Japan's success possible. Japan imports many of the natural resources it needs, such as oil, and exports its manufactured goods to economies rich in natural resources.

Technological Knowledge One fourth determinant of productivity is **technological knowledge** – the understanding of the best ways to produce goods and services. One hundred and fifty years ago, most Europeans and North Americans worked on farms, because farm technology required a high input of labour in order to feed the entire population. Today, thanks to advances in the technology of farming, a small fraction of the populations of western Europe, the USA and Canada can produce enough food to feed their entire populations. This technological change made labour available to produce other goods and services.

> **technological knowledge** society's understanding of the best ways to produce goods and services

Technological knowledge takes many forms. Some technology is common knowledge – after it starts to be used by one person, everyone becomes aware of it. For example, once Henry Ford successfully introduced production in assembly lines in the USA, other car makers and industrial producers throughout the world quickly followed suit. Other technology is proprietary – it is known only by the company that discovers it. Only the Coca-Cola Company, for instance, knows the secret recipe for making its famous soft drink. Still other technology is proprietary for a short time. When a pharmaceutical company discovers a new drug, the patent system gives that company a temporary right to be its exclusive manufacturer. When the patent expires, however, other companies are allowed to make the drug. All these forms of technological knowledge are important for the economy's production of goods and services.

It is worthwhile to distinguish between technological knowledge and human capital. Although they are closely related, there is an important difference. Technological knowledge refers to *society's* understanding about how the world works. Human capital refers to the resources expended transmitting this understanding to the *labour force*. To use a relevant metaphor, knowledge is the quality of society's textbooks, whereas human capital is the amount of time that the population has devoted to reading them. Workers' productivity depends on both the quality of textbooks they have available and the amount of time they have spent studying them.

Technical progress means that the *quality* of physical and human capital is improved so for any given quantity of capital and labour, the average productivity of both is higher, meaning that a higher output can be produced from the economy's factors of production. In essence, technical progress can help to counterbalance the effects of diminishing marginal product. If additional factors are employed but the total productivity of those factors increases, then the economy can experience growth.

Given the aggregate production function $Y = A + f(K, L)$, where A is the rate of technological progress, if the capital/labour ratio is constant, factor productivity can rise if there is an increase in technological progress. For example, if technological progress increases by 0.5 per cent a year, then $A = (1 + 0.005)$. Average labour productivity can increase by 0.5 per cent even if the ratio of capital to labour stays constant. If this is the case, then the production function will actually shift upwards (or the production possibilities curve we studied in Chapter 19 will shift outwards), reflecting the ability of the economy to produce more of every good.

THE DETERMINANTS OF ECONOMIC GROWTH

The Solow and Swan growth theory (hereafter referred to simply as the Solow model or theory) establishes some key elements of the determinants of economic growth. The assumptions of the model are that there are constant returns to scale, a closed economy (so $Y = C+S$) and that increases in capital and labour are subject to diminishing marginal product.

Recall that the output level (GDP), denoted by the letter Y, is determined by the level of technology (A), and the quantities and productivity of labour and capital (K and L). The resulting aggregate production function can be represented as in Figure 22.1. GDP is on the vertical axis and the physical capital stock is on the horizontal axis. Assuming technology is given, an increasing physical capital stock is associated with a rising GDP, relatively quickly at first but then slows due to the law of diminishing marginal product. The level of investment in capital stock is shown by the line I. This investment is dependent on the savings ratio in the country and a higher savings rate will be associated with an increase in capital accumulation. Levels of physical capital stock are associated with levels of GDP. If the capital stock is K_1, for example, GDP will be Y_1. The distance between the level of GDP at K_1 and the investment level is consumption, and the remainder is investment.

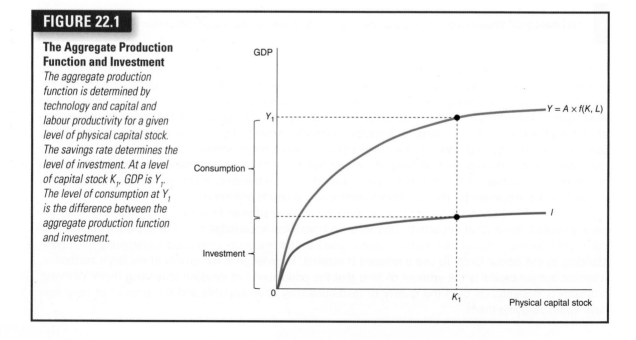

FIGURE 22.1

The Aggregate Production Function and Investment
The aggregate production function is determined by technology and capital and labour productivity for a given level of physical capital stock. The savings rate determines the level of investment. At a level of capital stock K_1, GDP is Y_1. The level of consumption at Y_1 is the difference between the aggregate production function and investment.

Long-run Equilibrium

For an economy with a given level of physical capital, the growth path will be dependent on the level of technology, the productivity of labour and capital and the savings rate which determines investment in physical capital. We have also seen that some investment is spent on replacing worn out and obsolete capital. If physical capital lasts for an average of 15 years, then the depreciation rate will be $\frac{1}{15}$ or 6.7 per cent. The depreciation rate is assumed to be relatively constant as a proportion of the amount of physical capital. These three elements of the growth model are represented in Figure 22.2. This time on the vertical axis is output per worker given by GDP (Y) divided by the number of workers, L, $\frac{Y}{L}$. The horizontal axis is the capital–output ratio or capital per worker given by the amount of physical capital, K, divided by the number of workers, L, $\frac{K}{L}$. The ratio of capital to labour is one aspect of how productive labour can be. One of the reasons put forward for the rapid growth in countries like Korea and Vietnam is that not only have they a supply of relatively cheap labour but both countries have invested in capital and as a result labour productivity is relatively high. In comparison, average incomes in many African countries remain very low, and the main difference is that in these African countries, investment in capital stock is low and as a result, labour productivity is also very low. In addition to the aggregate production function, $Y = A\,(K, L)$, and investment (I), which is determined by the savings rate, we have included the depreciation rate, δK. The depreciation rate is assumed to be a constant proportion of capital per worker.

Let us now look at what happens if a country finds itself with a capital per worker level of K_1 in Figure 22.2.

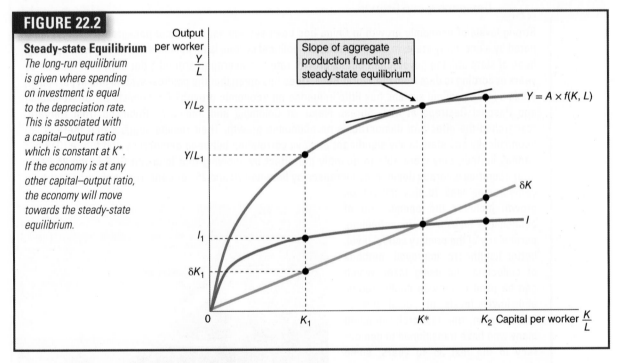

FIGURE 22.2

Steady-state Equilibrium
*The long-run equilibrium
is given where spending
on investment is equal
to the depreciation rate.
This is associated with
a capital–output ratio
which is constant at K^*.
If the economy is at any
other capital–output ratio,
the economy will move
towards the steady-state
equilibrium.*

At K_1, investment per worker is higher than depreciation per worker and so the capital–output ratio, or capital per worker rises. As capital per worker rises, output per worker increases from the initial level of $\frac{Y}{L_1}$. The economy will continue to grow until it reaches a capital–output ratio of K^*. At this ratio, investment spending is equal to the depreciation rate and the capital–output ratio will remain constant. Solow called this the **steady-state equilibrium**. This capital–output ratio gives an output per worker of $\frac{Y}{L_2}$. If the capital–output ratio was K_2, spending on depreciation would be higher than investment and the capital–output ratio would fall pushing the economy back towards the steady-state equilibrium at K^*. This steady-state equilibrium will be associated with a particular growth rate in the economy given by the slope of the aggregate production function shown by the tangential line in Figure 22.2.

> **steady-state equilibrium** the point in a growing economy where investment spending is the same as spending on depreciation and the capital–output ratio remains constant

The Solow model provides a means of understanding the transition of economies over time. Less developed economies will have lower capital–output ratios. Investment in capital will increase the capital per worker and lead to growth. In Figure 22.2, the growth rate at the capital–output level K_1, is higher than that at the steady-state equilibrium, K^* as indicated by the steeper slope of the aggregate production function at the output per worker level of $\frac{Y}{L_1}$. However, investment is determined by the savings ratio. In less developed countries this may be relatively low because incomes are low and for those on low incomes, the priority is likely to be more on feeding the family and surviving rather than saving. In addition, less developed countries may not have sufficiently developed financial institutions to funnel savings, and problems of governance and corruption can often mean these economies continue to remain poor and do not transition to more sustained growth associated with the steady-state equilibrium.

> **SELF TEST** List and describe four determinants of a country's productivity.

CASE STUDY   Democracy and Growth

Strong levels of economic growth in China has been set against a political background that is dominated by a one-party state. In Saudi Arabia, the political system is an absolute monarchy with the King, head of state and the government but its growth rate has averaged around 5 per cent over the last 35 years according to data from the World Bank. Does this mean that the political system and in particular, a democratic political system, has little influence on economic growth? Economists Daron Acemoglu and Pascual Restrepo at MIT, Suresh Naidu at Colombia and James A. Robinson from Harvard, researched the effects of democracies on economic growth. Their results suggest that there is 'an economically and statistically significant *positive* correlation between democracy and future GDP per capita'. Further, they were able to quantify the effect by showing that long-run GDP in the 25 years after countries embrace democracy increases by between 20 and 25 per cent. The explanation for how democracies lead to this impact on growth includes the opening up of economies, investment in schooling, particularly at the primary school level, better healthcare, improved methods of collecting and using taxes which can be used to provide public goods, and lower levels of social unrest. Countries in the research included many who have transitioned to democracy in the last 35–40 years, some examples being Albania, Argentina, Bhutan, the Czech Republic, Ghana, Honduras, Hungary, Liberia, Mali, Nicaragua, Niger, Pakistan, Poland, Sierra Leone, Slovenia, South Africa, Thailand, Turkey and Zambia.

Does the development of a democratic political system go hand-in-hand with improved economic prospects?

Source: Acemoglu, D., Naidu, S., Restrepo, P. and Robinson, J.A. (2015) Democracy Does Cause Growth. MIT.

CAUSES OF GROWTH

The Solow model provides a way of predicting that the capital–output ratio of economies will eventually converge to the steady state. The evidence does not fully support the predictions of the model and this is due in part to its assumptions. In particular, steady-state equilibrium will be dependent on an economy's particular characteristics – its population, the level of physical and human capital, the savings rate, the depreciation rate, the proportion of the labour force in work and the level of technology. Rather than using the model to compare economies with very different characteristics, it may be more valuable to understand growth by comparing groups of economies with similar characteristics. We can use the model developed so far to understand more complex interactions in economies which will influence growth.

Changes in the Savings Rate

An increase in the savings rate can increase investment and the capital–output ratio. If we assume the economy starts at the steady state equilibrium shown as K^* in Figure 22.3, investment will now be higher than spending on depreciation and this will increase the capital–output ratio moving the economy to a new steady-state equilibrium at K^{**}.

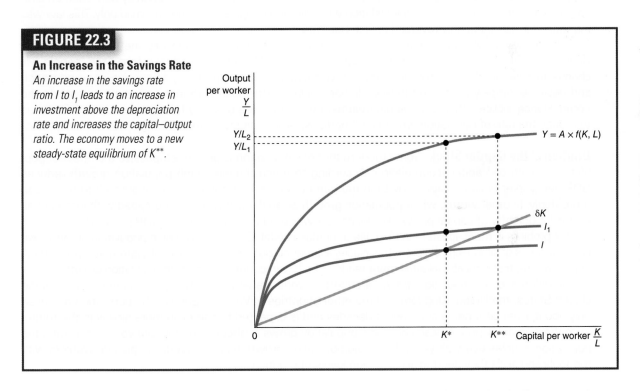

FIGURE 22.3

An Increase in the Savings Rate
An increase in the savings rate from I to I_1 leads to an increase in investment above the depreciation rate and increases the capital–output ratio. The economy moves to a new steady-state equilibrium of K^{**}.

An Increase in the Population

If the population grows at the same rate as income, then GDP per capita will remain constant. The reality is that population growth varies depending on the country. In many countries, the population is rising and the reasons can be complex. The **birth rate**, the number of people born per thousand of the population, can be rising *ceteris paribus*, or the **death rate**, the number of deaths per thousand of the population, could be falling *ceteris paribus*. Or there could be a mixture of the two. In the UK and many European countries, the death rate is falling; more people are living longer, and the birth rate is relatively constant meaning that the population is rising. A rising population, however, does not mean that the labour force is increasing. An ageing population could mean that the labour force is shrinking. In addition, the **migration rate**, the difference between the number of people entering a country from abroad and the number leaving, can also influence the overall level and make-up of the population. One argument put forward in support of immigration to the UK, for example, has been that those people coming into the country are bringing with them skills which help increase productivity. If this is the case, then the aggregate production function could shift upwards reflecting the improved productivity of labour given the level of technology and the amount of capital available. Research and analysis of this issue is an important macroeconomic topic, particularly given the migrant crisis which has affected many countries in Europe.

> **birth rate** the number of people born per thousand of the population
> **death rate** the number of deaths per thousand of the population
> **migration rate** the difference between the number of people entering a country from abroad and the number leaving

The Solow growth model shows that if the labour force is rising, then in order for the capital–output ratio to remain constant, investment must cover depreciation and provide more capital. If investment does not keep pace with the rise in the population, people will become poorer. In part, this helps to explain why many less developed countries experience continued high levels of poverty because their population rises but investment fails to keep pace. Policymakers have tried to curb population growth by education on birth control and in the case of China, by legislation which limited couples to having one child only. This law was introduced in 1979 and only reversed in October 2015.

Another way in which a country can influence population growth is to invoke the use of incentives. Bearing a child, like any decision, has an opportunity cost. When the opportunity cost rises, people will choose to have smaller families. In particular, women, with the opportunity to receive good education and desirable employment, tend to want fewer children than those with less opportunities outside the home. Hence, policies that foster equal treatment of women are one way for less developed economies to reduce the rate of population growth and, perhaps, raise their standards of living.

Dilution of the Capital Stock   Some modern theories of economic growth emphasize the effect of population growth on capital accumulation. According to these theories, high population growth reduces GDP per worker because rapid growth in the number of workers forces the capital stock to be spread more thinly. In other words, when population growth is rapid, each worker is equipped with less capital. A smaller quantity of capital per worker leads to lower productivity and lower GDP per worker.

This problem is most apparent in the case of human capital. Countries with high population growth have large numbers of school-age children. This places a larger burden on the educational system. It is not surprising, therefore, that educational attainment tends to be low in countries with high population growth.

The differences in population growth around the world are large. In developed countries, such as the United States, the United Kingdom and the other countries of Western Europe, the population has risen only about 1 per cent per year in recent decades and is expected to rise even more slowly in the future. In contrast, in many poor African countries, population grows at about 3 per cent per year. At this rate, the population doubles every 23 years. This rapid population growth makes it harder to provide workers with the tools and skills they need to achieve high levels of productivity.

Promoting Technological Progress   Although rapid population growth may depress economic prosperity by reducing the amount of capital each worker has, it may also have some benefits. Some economists have suggested that world population growth has been an engine of technological progress and economic prosperity. The mechanism is simple: if there are more people, there is a greater probability that some of those people will come up with new ideas that will lead to technological progress, which benefits everyone.

The economist Michael Kremer has provided some support for this hypothesis in an article titled 'Population Growth and Technological Change: One Million BC to 1990', which was published in the *Quarterly Journal of Economics* in 1993. Kremer begins by noting that over the broad span of human history, world growth rates have increased as world population has. For example, world growth was more rapid when the world population was 1 billion (which occurred around the year 1800) than it was when the population was only 100 million (around 500 BC). This fact is consistent with the hypothesis that having more people induces more technological progress.

Kremer's second piece of evidence comes from comparing regions of the world. The melting of the polar ice caps at the end of the ice age around 10 000 BC flooded the land bridges and separated the world into several distinct regions that could not communicate with one another for thousands of years. If technological progress is more rapid when there are more people to discover things, then larger regions should have experienced more rapid growth.

According to Kremer, that is exactly what happened. The most successful region of the world in 1500 (when Columbus re-established technological contact) comprised the 'Old World' civilizations of the large Eurasia-Africa region. Next in technological development were the Aztec and Mayan civilizations in the Americas, followed by the hunter-gatherers of Australia, and then the primitive people of Tasmania, who lacked even fire-making and most stone and bone tools.

The smallest isolated region was Flinders Island, a tiny island between Tasmania and Australia. With the smallest population, Flinders Island had the fewest opportunities for technological advance and, indeed, seemed to regress. Around 3000 BC, human society on Flinders Island died out completely. A large population, Kremer concludes, is a prerequisite for technological advance.

At first sight this conclusion does seem to be at odds with casual empirical observation of the modern world: as we previously noted, in many rich, developed countries population growth has been only about 1 per cent per year in recent decades, while in many poor countries, such as those of sub-Saharan Africa, population growth is much higher. So why doesn't this higher population growth help these poor countries to grow, if Kremer's argument is right? The point is that Kremer was really analyzing *world* economic growth, or rather, economic growth in isolated regions of the world. Nowadays, in a very poor country, it is unlikely that technological advances will be made that are not already known in developed countries; the problem is not lack of technological progress but difficulty in applying technology because of the scarcity of human capital and perhaps because of problems arising from political instability and corruption. Moreover, because many talented people from less developed countries tend to emigrate to richer, developed countries where they may work, for example, as scientists or entrepreneurs, population growth in less developed countries may actually enhance economic growth in developed countries.

An increase in Technology

Increases in technology can be a public good. Assuming the technology is not protected, and even if it is this tends to be for a limited time, it is freely available to everyone to exploit. The aggregate production function shows that even if capital and labour remain constant, an increase in technology will increase income because both capital and labour become more productive. This can be seen in the developments in computer technology over the last 20 years. In 1997, widespread availability of the Internet was in its infancy and the capacity and functionality of the mobile phone was very different. The computing power many people routinely carry around with them every day in 2017 is staggering. In 1965, Intel engineer Gordon Moore predicted that the processing power of computers would double every two years. Whilst the rate of change has slowed in recent years, the pace of change has been largely in line with Moore's prediction, such that it has been dubbed 'Moore's law'.

The application of technology to business has led to increases in productivity and different ways of doing things. Innovation often occurs because someone muses on problems and finds ways of resolving those problems and thus builds on existing knowledge. Not only does technology mean that the effects of diminishing marginal product can be offset but it leads to proportional increases in productive capacity. If labour and capital productivity is measured as an index and year X is 100, a 5 per cent increase over one year means productivity rises to 105. A further 5 per cent increase in year X+2 would see the productivity index rising to 110.25. Increases in technology can lead to exponential increases in productivity and GDP. In 1960, for example, the Office for National Statistics (ONS) reports that output per worker in the UK, using 2012 as the base year for the index, was 35.8. In 2014 the index stood at 101.6.

FYI

Thomas Malthus

Thomas Robert Malthus (1766–1834), an English minister and early economic thinker, is famous for his book entitled: *An Essay on the Principle of Population as It Affects the Future Improvement of Society*. In it, Malthus argued that an ever-increasing population would continually strain society's ability to provide for itself. As a result, mankind was doomed to forever live in poverty.

Malthus's logic began by noting that 'food is necessary to the existence of man' and that 'the passion between the sexes is necessary and will remain nearly in its present state'. He concluded that 'the power of population is infinitely greater than the power in the earth to produce subsistence for man'. According to Malthus, the only check on population growth was 'misery and vice'. Attempts by charities or governments to alleviate poverty were counterproductive, he argued, because they merely allowed the poor to have more children, placing even greater strains on society's productive capabilities.

Fortunately, Malthus's dire forecast was far off the mark. Although the world population has increased about six-fold over the past two centuries, living standards around the world are, on average, much higher. As a result of economic growth, chronic hunger and malnutrition are less common now than they were in Malthus's day. Famines occur from time to time, but they are more often the result of an unequal income distribution or political instability than an inadequate production of food.

Where did Malthus go wrong? He assumed – correctly – that world population would rise exponentially, since as more people are born and survive, more and more people are born as their children, and so on. He also assumed – incorrectly – that the amount of food produced could rise only linearly, by increasing the amount of land under cultivation with productivity remaining constant. Growth in mankind's ingenuity over the years has offset the effects of a larger population. Pesticides, fertilizers, mechanized farm equipment, new crop varieties and other technological advances that Malthus never imagined have allowed each farmer to feed ever greater numbers of people. Even with more mouths to feed, fewer farmers are necessary because each farmer is so much more productive than Malthus ever imagined.

Summary

Our look at the Solow growth model provides some insight into the causes of growth and provides some indications about where policymakers might direct their focus if increases in economic growth and growth per capita are considered desirable policy objectives. The aggregate production function provides a model for showing how income/output can grow when more inputs of capital and labour are used and how improvements in technology can make those factor inputs more productive. Key to growth is the accumulation of capital stock. A higher capital stock, *ceteris paribus*, will help generate higher output. Capital accumulation is made possible by investment from saving. If the savings rate leads to investment that is higher than spending on depreciation, the economy will move towards its steady state equilibrium. Increases in the savings rate in itself, does not generate increases in output per capita because of the diminishing marginal product of labour and capital. Improvements in technology can offset the effects of diminishing marginal product and generate both increased output and output per capita. The way in which the size and structure of the population changes is a factor that has to be taken into account in whether increases in output lead to an increase in GDP per capita.

The Solow growth model allows predictions to be made about how countries grow. The transition to steady-state equilibrium has been researched and a number of studies suggest that many countries do move towards a state where long-run growth rates are similar, most notably Barro and Sala-i-Martin (1992), Mankiw, Romer and Weil (1992) and Evans (1996)[1].

ENDOGENOUS GROWTH THEORY

The Solow growth model suggests that investment in capital alone cannot increase growth per capita because of diminishing marginal product and that capital accounts for only around a third of contribution to output. Long-run growth is generated by changes in technology. In the Solow model, technology is exogenous in that the level of technology is not affected by either capital accumulation or changes in the population. What the Solow model does not do is offer an explanation as to what determines the level of technology and technological changes. As noted above, and given our definition of technology, technology can be viewed as a public good which has the characteristic of being non-rival. As knowledge and ideas develop, these become publicly available and can be used by anyone; one person's use does not prevent anyone else from using that same knowledge or idea. If technology is a public good, then what incentive is there for anyone to innovate and come up with new ideas if they are not able to profit from them?

Paul Romer sought to investigate why improvements in technology occur and the resulting model he developed is referred to as endogenous growth theory. **Endogenous growth theory** is a theory of long-run economic growth which results from the creation of new knowledge and technology which impacts on everyone and makes them more productive as a result. The rate of economic growth in the long-run is determined by the rate of growth in total factor productivity and this total factor productivity is dependent on the rate at which technology progresses.

> **endogenous growth theory** a theory that the rate of economic growth in the long-run, is determined by the rate of growth in total factor productivity and this total factor productivity is dependent on the rate at which technology progresses

Earlier in the chapter we looked at how technology has changed at a rapid rate in the last 50 years. An important element of such exponential changes in technology is innovation and investment by firms into R&D. Much of this innovation and R&D might be carried out by firms in the expectation of gaining a competitive advantage. Competitive advantage as we saw in Chapter 15, can be defined as the advantages over rivals which are both distinctive (i.e, not easy to copy) and defensible (that the firm can prevent others from copying their ideas). It is assumed, therefore, that the incentives firms have to innovate and invest in R&D is driven by the profit motive. If technology does have the characteristic of being non-rival then this has policy implications in that policies have to be developed to encourage firms to innovate, perhaps through extending intellectual property rights and to provide wider social benefits through improvements in education.

In the Solow model, capital accumulation is generated through saving and improvements in human capital through education. Capital accumulation, however, is not simply a case of increasing capital at a constant rate. When firms invest in new equipment, there may be increases in the knowledge required to operate and utilize that new equipment effectively and efficiently, which in itself increases intellectual capital and offsets diminishing marginal product. For example, if a firm invests in a new accounting system, its workers have to be trained in its use, which increases their human capital. If they leave the firm, they take their knowledge and skills with them, which benefits other firms. In using the new system, some workers may identify ways in which the system can be tweaked to benefit the particular characteristics

---

[1] Barro, R.J. and Sala-i-Martin, X. (1992). 'Convergence'. *Journal of Political Economy* **100**, 223–51. Evans, P. 1996. 'Using cross-country variances to evaluate growth theories'. *Journal of Economic Dynamics and Control.* **20**, 1027–49. 1
Mankiw, N.G., Romer, D. and Weil, D.N. (1992). 'A contribution to the empirics of economic growth'. *Quarterly Journal of Economics.* **107**, 407–37.

of the business itself and this can be fed back to the developers of the system to incorporate in subsequent versions in addition to improving productivity in the firm itself. Intellectual capital, therefore, grows through innovation, which in turn affects productivity.

As innovation develops, new technologies replace old ones and new skills are needed which render existing skills obsolete. In 1942, Austrian economist Joseph Schumpeter developed the idea of **creative destruction** to describe this process. The implication of this process is that as technology changes over time, there will be winners and losers. Some firms will go out of business and workers may have to retrain to secure new skills and the process can be highly damaging to those involved. However, ultimately, if growth is to be secured, society will have to accept that R&D and innovation are both contributors to the rate at which creative destruction happens and are essential to increases in technology. Finding ways to encourage investment in R&D becomes a core focus of government policy.

> **creative destruction** the process where new technologies replace old ones and new skills are needed which render existing skills obsolete

ECONOMIC GROWTH AND PUBLIC POLICY

So far, we have determined that a society's standard of living depends, in part, on its ability to produce goods and services and that its productivity depends on physical capital, human capital, natural resources and technological knowledge. Let's now turn to the question faced by policymakers around the world: what can government policy do to raise productivity and living standards?

The Importance of Saving and Investment

We introduced the role of the savings ratio in relation to investment earlier in the chapter. Investment is necessary to sustain and increase the capital stock. Because capital is a produced factor of production, a society can change the amount of capital it has. If today the economy produces a large quantity of new capital goods, then tomorrow it will have a larger stock of capital and be able to produce more of all types of goods and services. Thus, one way to raise future productivity is to invest more current resources in the production of capital.

When considering the accumulation of capital, however, the notion of trade-offs has to be considered. Given that resources are scarce, devoting more resources to producing capital requires devoting fewer resources to producing goods and services for current consumption. That is, for society to invest more in capital, it must consume less and save more of its current income (the savings ratio must rise). The growth that arises from capital accumulation requires that society sacrifice consumption of goods and services in the present in order to enjoy higher consumption in the future.

In the 1930s, the rulers of Russia deliberately diverted resources to the production of capital goods in an attempt to try to catch up with the richer and more industrialized Western countries such as Germany, the United States and the United Kingdom. It managed to expand production in core industries such as coal and steel significantly, which in turn increased its capacity to produce other capital goods (and military equipment). The trade-off for the Russian people at the time was fewer consumer goods and a harsh life. It could be argued that whilst this represented significant short-term hardship for many of its people, the decision helped Russia to be in a position to fight off the Germans in the Second World War and emerge to be one of the planet's superpowers.

Research suggests that the correlation between growth and investment is strong. Countries that devote a large share of GDP to investment, such as China, Japan and Australia, also have a stronger average growth rate. Countries that devote a small share of GDP to investment, such as the Central African Republic, Zimbabwe and Bangladesh, tend to have low growth rates. Studies that examine a more comprehensive list of countries confirm this strong correlation between investment and growth. There is, however, a problem in interpreting these data. A correlation between two variables does not establish which variable is the cause and which is the effect. It is possible that high investment causes high growth, but it is also possible that high growth causes high investment. (Or, perhaps, high growth and high investment are both caused by a third variable that has been omitted from the analysis.) The data by themselves cannot tell us the direction of causation. Nevertheless, because capital accumulation affects productivity so clearly and directly, many economists interpret these data as showing that high investment leads to more rapid economic growth.

Diminishing Returns and the Catch-Up Effect

We have seen that increasing the savings rate will not lead to indefinite long-run growth because of diminishing returns; an increase in the saving rate leads to higher growth only for a while. As the higher saving rate allows more capital to be accumulated, the benefits from additional capital become smaller over time, and so growth slows down. In the long run, the higher saving rate leads to a higher level of productivity and income, but not to higher growth in these variables. Reaching this long run, however, can take quite a while. According to studies of international data on economic growth, increasing the saving rate can lead to substantially higher growth for a period of several decades.

The diminishing returns to capital has another important implication: other things equal, it is easier for a country to grow fast if it starts out relatively poor. This effect of initial conditions on subsequent growth is sometimes called the **catch-up effect**. In poor countries, workers can lack even the most rudimentary tools and, as a result, have low productivity. Small amounts of capital investment would substantially raise these workers' productivity. By contrast, workers in rich countries have large amounts of capital with which to work, and this partly explains their high productivity. Yet with the amount of capital per worker already so high, additional capital investment has a relatively small effect on productivity. Studies of international data on economic growth confirm this catch-up effect: controlling for other variables, such as the percentage of GDP devoted to investment, poor countries do tend to grow at a faster rate than rich countries.

catch-up effect the property whereby countries that start off poor tend to grow more rapidly than countries that start off rich

This catch-up effect can help explain variations in observations on average investment as a proportion of GDP and average growth rates over time. Over the past 40 years, Japan allocated around 10 per cent more to investment as a proportion of GDP compared to China, but China grew at an average rate 1.7 times the Japanese annual average growth rate. The explanation is the catch-up effect. In 1961 Japan had GDP per person about 15 times that of China, in part because investment in China up to the end of the 1960s had been so low. With a small initial capital stock, the benefits to capital accumulation were much greater in China, and this gave the country a higher subsequent growth rate.

Investment from Abroad

The Solow model assumes a closed economy. Saving by domestic residents is not the only way for a country to invest in new capital. The other way is investment by foreigners.

Investment from abroad takes several forms. BMW might build a car factory in Portugal. A capital investment that is owned and operated by a foreign entity is called **foreign direct investment**. Alternatively, a German might buy equity in a Portuguese corporation (that is, buy a share in the ownership of the corporation); and the Portuguese corporation can use the proceeds from the equity sale to build a new factory. An investment that is financed with foreign money but operated by domestic residents is called

foreign portfolio investment. In both cases, Germans provide the resources necessary to increase the stock of capital in Portugal. That is, German saving is being used to finance Portuguese investment.

> **foreign direct investment** capital investment that is owned and operated by a foreign entity
> **foreign portfolio investment** investment that is financed with foreign money but operated by domestic residents

When foreigners invest in a country, they do so because they expect to earn a return on their investment. BMW's car factory increases the Portuguese capital stock and, therefore, increases Portuguese productivity and Portuguese GDP. Yet BMW takes some of this additional income back to Germany in the form of profit. Similarly, when a German investor buys Portuguese equity, the investor has a right to a portion of the profit that the Portuguese corporation earns.

Investment from abroad, therefore, does not have the same effect on all measures of economic prosperity. Recall that GDP is the income earned within a country by both residents and non-residents, whereas GNP is the income earned by residents of a country both at home and abroad. When BMW opens its car factory in Portugal, some of the income the factory generates accrues to people who do not live in Portugal. As a result, foreign investment in Portugal raises the income of the Portuguese (measured by GNP) by less than it raises the production in Portugal (measured by GDP).

Nevertheless, investment from abroad is one way for a country to grow. Even though some of the benefits from this investment flow back to the foreign owners, this investment does increase the economy's stock of capital, leading to higher productivity and higher wages. Moreover, investment from abroad is one way for poorer countries to learn the state-of-the-art technologies developed and used in richer countries. For these reasons, many economists who advise governments in less developed economies advocate policies that encourage investment from abroad. Often this means removing restrictions that governments have imposed on foreign ownership of domestic capital.

An organization that tries to encourage the flow of capital to poor countries is the World Bank. This international organization obtains funds from the world's advanced industrialized countries, and uses these resources to make loans to less developed countries so that they can invest in roads, sewage systems, schools and other types of capital. It also offers the countries advice about how the funds might best be used. The World Bank, together with its sister organization, the International Monetary Fund (IMF), was set up after the Second World War. One lesson from the war was that economic distress often leads to political turmoil, international tensions and military conflict. Thus, every country has an interest in promoting economic prosperity around the world. The World Bank and the IMF were set up to achieve that common goal.

Education

Education – investment in human capital – is at least as important as investment in physical capital for a country's long-run economic success. In the developed economies of Western Europe and North America, each extra year of schooling raises a worker's income by about 10 per cent on average. In less developed countries, where human capital is especially scarce, the gap between the wages of educated and uneducated workers is even larger. Thus, one way in which government policy can enhance the standard of living is to provide good schools and to encourage the population to take advantage of them.

Investment in human capital, like investment in physical capital, has an opportunity cost. When students are in school, they forego the wages they could have earned. In less developed countries, children often drop out of school at an early age, even though the benefit of additional schooling is very high, simply because their labour is needed to help support the family.

Some economists have argued that human capital is particularly important for economic growth because human capital conveys positive externalities. An educated person, for instance, might generate new ideas about how best to produce goods and services. If these ideas enter society's pool of knowledge, so that everyone can use them, then the ideas are an external benefit of education. In this case, the return to schooling for society is even greater than the return for the individual. This argument would justify the large subsidies to human capital investment that we observe in the form of public education.

One problem facing some poor countries is the **brain drain** – the emigration of many of the most highly educated workers to rich countries where these workers can enjoy a higher standard of living. If human capital does have positive externalities, then this brain drain makes those people left behind poorer than they otherwise would be. This problem offers policymakers a dilemma. On the one hand, rich countries like those of western Europe and North America have the best systems of higher education, and it would seem natural for poor countries to send their best students abroad to earn higher degrees. On the other hand, those students who have spent time abroad may choose not to return home, and this brain drain will reduce the poor nation's stock of human capital even further.

 brain drain the emigration of many of the most highly educated workers to rich countries

Health and Nutrition

The term *human capital* usually refers to education, but it can also be used to describe another type of investment in people: expenditures that lead to a healthier population. Other things equal, healthier workers are more productive. The right investments in the health of the population provide one way for a nation to increase productivity and raise living standards.

Economic historian Robert Fogel, has suggested that a significant factor in long-run economic growth is improved health from better nutrition. He estimates that in Great Britain in 1780, about one in five people were so malnourished that they were incapable of manual labour. Among those who could work, insufficient intake of calories substantially reduced the work effort they could carry out. As nutrition improved so did workers' productivity.

Fogel studies these historical trends in part by looking at the height of the population. Short stature can be an indicator of malnutrition, especially during gestation and the early years of life. Fogel finds that as nations develop economically, people eat more and the population gets taller. From 1775 to 1975, the average caloric intake in Great Britain rose by 26 per cent and the height of the average man rose by 3.6 inches (around 10 cm). Similarly, during the spectacular economic growth in the Republic of Korea from 1962 to 1995, caloric consumption rose by 44 per cent and, average male height rose by 2 inches (5 cm). Of course, a person's height is determined by a combination of genetic predisposition and environment. Because the genetic make-up of a population is slow to change, such increases in average height are likely due to changes in the environment – nutrition being the obvious explanation.

Moreover, studies have found that height is an indicator of productivity. Looking at data on a large number of workers at a point in time, researchers have found that taller workers tend to earn more. Because wages reflect a worker's productivity, this finding suggests that taller workers tend to be more productive. The effect of height on wages is especially pronounced in poorer countries, where malnutrition is a bigger risk.

Fogel won the Nobel Prize in Economics in 1993 for his work in economic history, which includes not only his studies on nutrition but also work on American slavery and the role of the railroads in the development of the American economy. In the lecture he gave when awarded the Prize, he surveyed the evidence on health and economic growth. He concluded that 'improved gross nutrition accounts for roughly 30 per cent of the growth of per capita income in Britain between 1790 and 1980'.

Today malnutrition is fortunately rare in developed nations (obesity is a more widespread problem). For people in developing nations, poor health and inadequate nutrition remain obstacles to higher productivity and improved living standards. The United Nations estimates that almost a third of the population in sub-Saharan Africa is undernourished.

The causal link between health and wealth runs in both directions. Poor countries are poor, in part, because their populations are not healthy, and their populations are not healthy, in part, because they are poor and cannot afford adequate health care and nutrition. It is a vicious circle but opens the possibility of a virtuous circle. Policies that lead to more rapid economic growth would naturally improve health outcomes, which in turn would further promote economic growth.

Property Rights, Political Stability and Good Governance

Other ways in which policymakers can foster economic growth are by protecting property rights, promoting political stability and maintaining good governance. As noted when we discussed economic interdependence, production in market economies arises from the interactions of millions of individuals and firms. When you buy a car, for instance, you are buying the output of a car dealer, a car manufacturer, a steel company, an iron ore mining company and so on. This division of production among many firms allows the economy's factors of production to be used as effectively as possible. To achieve this outcome, the economy has to coordinate transactions among these firms, as well as between firms and consumers. Market prices are one way in which these transactions are coordinated.

An important prerequisite for the price system to work is an economy-wide respect for *property rights*. A mining company will not make the effort to mine iron ore if it expects the ore to be stolen. The company mines the ore only if it is confident that it will benefit from the ore's subsequent sale. For this reason, courts serve an important role in a market economy: they enforce property rights. Through the criminal justice system, the courts discourage direct theft. In addition, through the civil justice system, the courts ensure that buyers and sellers live up to their contracts.

Although people in developed countries tend to take property rights for granted, those living in less developed or emerging countries understand that lack of property rights can be a major problem. In many countries, the system of justice does not work well. Contracts are hard to enforce, and fraud often goes unpunished. In more extreme cases, the government not only fails to enforce property rights but actually infringes upon them. To do business in some countries, firms are expected to bribe powerful government officials. Such corruption impedes the coordinating power of markets. It also discourages domestic saving and investment from abroad. The problem of corruption and bribery is extensive. Transparency International is a pressure group that exists to advance the cause of anti-corruption. Each year it publishes an index showing perceptions of corruption across the world. Countries are scored on a scale of 0–100 with 0 being highly corrupt and 100 being highly clean. Around two-thirds of the 176 countries in the ranking fall below 50.

One threat to property rights is political instability. When revolutions and coups are common, there is doubt about whether property rights will be respected in the future. If a revolutionary government might confiscate the capital of some businesses, as was often true after communist revolutions, domestic residents have less incentive to save, invest and start new businesses. At the same time, foreigners have less incentive to invest in the country. Even the threat of revolution can act to depress a nation's standard of living. It is no coincidence that countries with a strong military power, who are subject to frequent coups, are ones that are at the bottom of any standard of living league table.

Thus, economic prosperity depends in part on political prosperity. A country with an efficient court system, honest government officials and a stable constitution will enjoy a higher economic standard of living than a country with a poor court system, corrupt officials and frequent revolutions and coups. These are the key features of good governance – the extent to which a country is ruled by sound democracies, where the rule of law, the authority of law, the absence of corruption and independent judicial processes are in existence. If these things are in place, then it is more likely that contracts and property rights can be enforced and free markets can operate effectively to allocate scarce resources. Without good governance, many economists believe that economic development will be compromised.

Free Trade

Some of the world's poorest countries have tried to achieve more rapid economic growth by pursuing *inward-oriented policies*. These policies are aimed at raising productivity and living standards within the country by avoiding interaction with the rest of the world. This approach gets support from some domestic firms, which claim that they need protection from foreign competition in order to compete and grow. This is called an infant-industry argument, and together with a general distrust of foreigners has at times led policymakers in less developed countries to impose tariffs and other trade restrictions.

Many economists would support the pursuit of *outward-oriented policies* that integrate these countries into the world economy. When we studied international trade earlier in the book, we showed how international trade can improve the economic well-being of a country's citizens. Trade is, in some ways, a type of technology. When a country exports wheat and imports steel, the country benefits in the same way as if it had invented a technology for turning wheat into steel. A country that eliminates trade restrictions will, therefore, experience the same kind of economic growth that would occur after a major technological advance.

The adverse impact of inward orientation becomes clear when one considers the small size of many less developed economies. The total GDP of Argentina, for instance, is about that of the southeast of England (if we include London). Imagine what would happen if the southeast were suddenly to declare that it was illegal to trade with anyone beyond the regional boundaries. Without being able to take advantage of the gains from trade, the southeast would need to produce all the goods it consumes. It would also have to produce all its own capital goods, rather than importing state-of-the-art equipment from other cities. Living standards in the southeast would fall, and the problem would probably only get worse over time. This is precisely what happened when Argentina pursued inward-oriented policies throughout much of the 20th century and can also partly explain the economic problems in North Korea which has effectively cut itself off from the rest of the world. By contrast, countries pursuing outward-oriented policies, such as the Republic of Korea, Singapore and Taiwan, have enjoyed high rates of economic growth.

The amount that a nation trades with others is determined not only by government policy but also by geography. Countries with good natural seaports find trade easier than countries without this resource. It is not a coincidence that many of the world's major cities, such as Paris, Boston, New York, Hong Kong and London, are located either next to oceans or on the banks of a major river giving easy access for seafaring trade vessels. Similarly, because landlocked countries find international trade more difficult, they tend to have lower levels of income than countries with easy access to the world's waterways.

Research and Development

As we have seen in our short look at endogenous growth theory, technological advance can come from private research by firms and individual inventors. Just as government has a role in providing a public good such as national defence, it also has a role in encouraging the research and development of new technologies. The governments in most advanced countries do this in a number of ways, for example through science research laboratories owned and funded by the government, or through a system of research grants offered to promising researchers. It may also offer tax breaks and concessions for firms engaging in research and development.

Yet another way in which government policy encourages research is through the patent system. When a person or firm invents a new product, such as a new drug, the inventor can apply for a patent. If the product is deemed truly original, the government awards the patent, which gives the inventor the exclusive right to make the product for a specified number of years. In essence, the patent gives the inventor a property right over the invention, turning their new idea from a public good into a private good. By allowing inventors to profit from their inventions – even if only temporarily – the patent system enhances the incentive for individuals and firms to engage in research.

Population Growth

Economists and other social scientists have long debated how population growth affects a society. The most direct effect is on the size of the labour force: a large population means more workers to produce goods and services. At the same time, it means more people to consume those goods and services. Beyond these obvious effects, population growth interacts with the other factors of production in ways that are less obvious and more open to debate.

SELF TEST Describe three ways in which a government policymaker can try to raise the growth in living standards in a society. Are there any drawbacks to these policies?

CONCLUSION: THE IMPORTANCE OF LONG-RUN GROWTH

In this chapter we have discussed theories of growth and how this relates to differences in the standard of living across nations and how policymakers can endeavour to raise the standard of living through policies that promote economic growth. Policymakers who want to encourage growth in standards of living must aim to increase their nation's productive ability by encouraging rapid accumulation of the factors of production and ensuring that these factors are employed as effectively as possible.

Economists differ in their views of the role of government in promoting economic growth. At the very least, government can lend support by maintaining property rights and political stability. More controversial is whether government should target and subsidize specific industries that might be especially important for technological progress. There is no doubt that these issues are among the most important in economics. The success of one generation's policymakers in learning and heeding the fundamental lessons about economic growth determines what kind of world the next generation will inherit.

IN THE NEWS

Economic Growth in China

One of the remarkable growth stories of the past 20 years has been China. In 2015, however, global financial markets began to slide and commodity prices slumped amidst reports that the growth miracle was coming to an end and with it, key drivers to the global economy.

Economic Growth in China: The End of a Miracle?

Between 1980 and 2010, the average growth rate of GDP in China was around 10 per cent. Between 2011 and 2014 it averaged 8 per cent. In October 2015, China reported a growth rate for the third quarter of 6.9 per cent, the first time that growth had been reported below 7 per cent since 2009. The report showed that investment had also slowed. Attempts to support the economy by the government included the approval of over 200 infrastructure projects in roads, energy, rail and sewerage projects, amongst others, costing more than €258 billion.

Even though the economy has slowed, the strong growth in China succeeded in lifting millions out of poverty in a relatively short period of time, perhaps more so than any single event in history. Professor Justin Yifu Lin, former Chief Economist and Senior Vice President of the World Bank, noted that in 1979 China had a per capita income of just $182 which was less than a third of the average of Sub-Saharan African countries. Over the last 30 years, economic growth has averaged over 9 per cent, 600 million people have been raised out of poverty. Lin referred to studies by economic historian, Angus Maddison (2001) which showed that average annual per capita income growth in the West was around 0.05 per cent prior to the 18th century, meaning it took 1400 years for European per capita income to double, rising to 1 per cent in the 19th century (taking 70 years for per capita income to double) and 2 per cent in the 20th century (35 years for per capita income to double). To emphasize the extent of the 'miracle' of Chinese growth, some estimates put the GDP per capita in China in the late 1970s similar to that in 17th century England. In 2015, GDP per capita is more akin to England in the 1960s. In around 30 years, the country has managed to develop as much as it took England 350 years to achieve.

One of the main ways that China achieved this growth was to invest massively in capital to complement its already extensive labour resources. Lin also argues that China has been able to take advantage of what he calls 'backwardness' – the ability to 'borrow' technology, innovation and institutions at relatively low risk and cost from advanced nations. The World Bank Commission noted this as the ability for developing countries to 'import what the rest of the world knew and export what it wanted'. This ability is one factor that can help a developing nation to secure sustained per-capita growth at high levels for a considerable period of time.

The slowdown in growth has prompted concern that China will not be able to sustain such high growth rates in the future and if this is the case, the effects will be felt across the global economy; such is the importance of China. In 2015, the country's stock markets experienced volatile swings, manufacturing profits fell and prices of manufacturing goods fell for the 43rd consecutive month indicating excess capacity. Concerns over high debt, weaker industrial production and over-production of housing are adding to some forecasts that the economic miracle is finally over. Indeed, the Solow growth model predicts that additional capital can only go so far in generating sustained growth.

(*Continued*)

Lin, however, believes that China can continue to grow at rates in excess of 8 per cent or more for the next 20 years. He bases this conclusion on the continued benefits the country can gain from 'backwardness' and the fact that there is still a massive gap to make up before China matches the per-capita income of country's like the United States. However, China will have to move to exploiting technological change rather than relying on its supply of cheap labour because this comparative advantage is already beginning to narrow as other low-wage economies develop. China will need to move from absorbing technology, therefore, to being an innovator.

Growth in China may have slowed but at over 6 per cent it is still impressive.

Questions

1 **China's population is in excess of 1 billion. Is this natural factor endowment a key reason why China has been able to generate such remarkable economic growth in the last 30 years? If so, why can't other countries with very large populations also grow at such rates?**

2 **Assume that over the last 35 years, China's economy has grown at an average rate of 9 per cent. Use the rule of 70 to estimate how long it takes for incomes in China to double. Does this help lend weight to the estimates on how far the Chinese economy has grown in comparison to England in the article?**

3 **Explain how the idea of 'backwardness' allows China to be able to generate rapid and sustained economic growth over a period.**

4 **One of the key ways China has succeeded in generating growth is through massive capital accumulation. Does the Solow growth model help explain why growth is now starting to slow?**

5 **To what extent does Lin's belief that the Chinese government has to pursue innovation a reflection of endogenous growth theory?**

SUMMARY

● Economic prosperity, as measured by GDP per person, varies substantially around the world. The average income in the world's richest countries is more than ten times that in the world's poorest countries. Because growth rates of real GDP also vary substantially, the relative positions of countries can change dramatically over time.

● The standard of living in an economy depends, in part, on the economy's ability to produce goods and services. Productivity, in turn, depends on the amounts of physical capital, human capital, natural resources and technological knowledge available to workers.

● The Solow growth model notes that the accumulation of capital is subject to diminishing returns: the more capital an economy has, the less additional output the economy gets from an extra unit of capital. Because of diminishing returns, higher saving leads to higher growth for a period of time, but growth eventually slows down as the economy approaches a higher level of capital, productivity and income. Also because of diminishing returns, the return to capital is especially high in poor countries. Other things equal, these countries can grow faster because of the catch-up effect.

● Endogenous growth theory focuses on the importance of explaining how technology can change and offset the effects of diminishing marginal productivity. Innovation and R&D are important ways in which technology growth can arise.

● Government policies can try to influence the economy's growth rate in many ways: by encouraging saving and investment, encouraging investment from abroad, fostering education, maintaining property rights and political stability, allowing free trade, promoting the research and development of new technologies, and controlling population growth.

QUESTIONS FOR REVIEW

1 What does the level of a nation's GDP measure? What does the growth rate of GDP measure? Would you rather live in a nation with a high level of GDP and a low growth rate, or in a nation with a low level of GDP and a high growth rate?

2 List and describe four determinants of productivity.

3 In what way is a university degree a form of capital?

4 Does a higher rate of saving lead to higher growth temporarily or indefinitely?

5 Assuming the population is stable, what effects will an increase in capital accumulation have on growth? Can a country generate sustained growth through rising capital investment?

6 What is the steady-state equilibrium?

7 Why is technological progress important in improving growth rates in any economy?

8 Why would removing a trade restriction, such as a tariff, lead to more rapid economic growth?

9 How does the rate of population growth influence the level of GDP per person?

10 Describe two ways in which the government can try to encourage advances in technological knowledge.

PROBLEMS AND APPLICATIONS

1 Most countries import substantial amounts of goods and services from other countries. Yet the chapter says that a nation can enjoy a high standard of living only if it can produce a large quantity of goods and services itself. Can you reconcile these two facts?

2 List the capital inputs necessary to produce each of the following:

 a. cars
 b. secondary education
 c. air travel
 d. fruit and vegetables.

3 UK income per person today is roughly four times what it was a century ago. Many other countries have also experienced significant growth over that period. What are some specific ways in which your standard of living is likely to differ from that of your great-grandparents?

4 The idea of creative destruction suggests that economic growth through changes in technology can have winners and losers. In the country in which you are studying, what firms or industries have declined or disappeared as a result of new technologies? How might governments manage the effects of creative destruction on those negatively affected by the process?

5 To what extent do you think that endogenous growth theory

 a. refutes the Solow model, or
 b. provides a further refinement to the Solow model?

6 Societies choose what share of their resources to devote to consumption and what share to devote to investment. Some of these decisions involve private spending; others involve government spending.

 a. Describe some forms of private spending that represent consumption, and some forms that represent investment.
 b. Describe some forms of government spending that represent consumption, and some forms that represent investment.

7 What is the opportunity cost of investing in capital? Do you think a country can 'over-invest' in capital? What is the opportunity cost of investing in human capital? Do you think a country can 'over-invest' in human capital? Explain.

8 In many developing nations, young women have lower enrolment rates in secondary schooling than do young men. Describe three ways in which greater educational opportunities for young women could lead to faster economic growth in these countries.

9 Using an appropriate data source, conduct some research into the economic and political characteristics of two contrasting countries – one with a relatively high GDP per capita and one with a relatively low GDP per capita. What factors affect these differences in GDP per capita? Is there any evidence that the country with the lower GDP per capita has experienced higher growth rates in the last 20 years? If so, why and if not, why not?

10 International data show a positive correlation between political stability and economic growth.

    a. Through what mechanism could political stability lead to strong economic growth?

    b. Through what mechanism could strong economic growth lead to political stability?

23 UNEMPLOYMENT

Losing a job can be the most distressing economic event in a person's life. Most people rely on their labour earnings to maintain their standard of living, and many people get from their work not only income but also a sense of personal accomplishment. A job loss means a lower living standard in the present, anxiety about the future and reduced self-esteem. It is not surprising, therefore, that politicians campaigning for office often speak about how their proposed policies will help create jobs. Indeed, the importance of unemployment in an economy is reflected in the attention given to it by politicians and there are a number of reasons for this. Unemployment affects standards of living, and from a macroeconomic perspective, people who would like to work but cannot find a job are not contributing to the economy's production of goods and services. Although some degree of unemployment is inevitable in a complex economy with thousands of firms and millions of workers, the amount of unemployment varies substantially over time and across countries. When a country keeps its workers as fully employed as possible, it achieves a higher level of GDP than it would if it left many of its workers standing idle.

This chapter begins our study of unemployment. The problem of unemployment is usefully divided into two categories – the long-run problem and the short-run problem. In this chapter we discuss the determinants of the long-run problem – an economy's *natural rate of unemployment*. As we will see, the designation *natural* does not imply that this rate of unemployment is desirable. Nor does it imply that it is constant over time or impervious to economic policy. It merely means that this unemployment does not go away on its own, even in the long run.

As we will see, long-run unemployment does not arise from a single problem that has a single solution. Instead, it reflects a variety of related problems. As a result, there is no easy way for policymakers to reduce the economy's natural rate of unemployment and, at the same time, to alleviate the hardships experienced by the unemployed.

IDENTIFYING UNEMPLOYMENT

We begin this chapter by examining more precisely what the term *unemployment* means. We consider how governments measure unemployment, what problems arise in interpreting the unemployment data, how long the typical spell of unemployment lasts and why there will always be some people unemployed.

What is Unemployment?

Intuition might suggest that unemployment simply means someone who does not have a job. This intuition hides a number of subtleties, however. If you are in full-time education, for example, you are studying and thus are not available for full-time paid employment. What if you were not a student but were suffering from some long-term illness that meant that you were unfit for work or if you were a parent who had made the choice of staying at home to look after children and raise a family? Again, in both these instances, although you would not have a job, we would not say that you were unemployed because you would not be available for work. These examples provide a guide that an unemployed person is not simply 'someone who does not have a job' but more accurately, 'someone who does not have a job and who is available for work'.

The notion of 'being available for work' requires further clarification. The wage rate for jobs that are unfilled is a factor in whether people choose to make themselves available for work. If too low, people may choose not to work. At another extreme, suppose you won so much money on the Euro Millions Lottery that you decided you would leave university and live off your winnings for the rest of your life. Would you be unemployed? No, because you would still be unavailable for work, no matter what wage rate you were offered. Thus, being unemployed also depends upon whether you are willing to work at going wage rates.

We are now in a position to give a more precise definition of what it means to be unemployed: the number unemployed in an economy is the number of people of working age who are able and available for work at current wage rates and who do not have a job.

How is Unemployment Measured?

There are two basic ways government agencies go about measuring the unemployment rate in the economy:

The Claimant Count One simple way is to count the number of people who, on any given day, are claiming unemployment benefit payments from the government – the so-called *claimant count*. Since a government agency is paying out the benefits, it will be relatively easy to gather data on the number of claimants. The government also has a good idea of the total labour force in employment, since it is receiving income tax payments from them. Adding to this the number of unemployment benefit claimants is a measure of the *total labour force*, and expressing the claimant count as a proportion of the labour force is a measure of the *unemployment rate*.

Unfortunately, there are a number of important drawbacks with the claimant count method. One obvious problem is that it is subject to changes in the rules the government applies for eligibility to unemployment benefit. Suppose the government gets tougher and changes the rules so that fewer people are now entitled to unemployment benefit. The claimant count will go down and so will the measured unemployment rate, even though there has been no change in the number of people with or without work. The opposite would happen if the government became more lenient and relaxed the rules so that more people became eligible.

In the UK, for example, there have been about 30 changes to the eligibility rules over the past 25 years, all but one of which have reduced the claimant count and so reduced the unemployment rate based on this measure. The following are examples of categories of people who are excluded from the UK claimant count: people over the age of 55 who are without a job; those on government training programmes (largely school-leavers who have not found a job); anyone looking for part-time work; and people who have left the workforce for a while and now wish to return to employment (for example, women who have raised a family). Many – if not all – of the people in these categories would be people who do not have a job, are of working age and are able and available for work at current wage rates; yet they would be excluded from measured unemployment in the UK using the claimant count method.

Labour Force Surveys The second, and probably more reliable, method of measuring unemployment is through the use of surveys – in other words, going out and asking people questions – based on an accepted definition of unemployment. Questions then arise as to whom to interview, how often (since surveys use up resources and are costly) and what definition of unemployment to use. Although the definition of unemployment that we developed earlier seems reasonable enough, the term 'available for work at current wage rates' may be too loose for this purpose. In the UK and many other countries, the government carries out Labour Force Surveys (LFS) based on the standardized definition of unemployment from the International Labour Office, or ILO. The ILO definition of an unemployed person is someone who is without a job and who is willing to start work within the next two weeks and either has been looking for work within the past four weeks or is waiting to start a job.

The Labour Force Survey is carried out quarterly throughout Europe. National statistical services collect the data which are then processed by Eurostat. The surveys are published in different languages but scrutinized by statisticians to ensure comparability between the surveys carried out in each member state.

In the UK, the survey is based on a sample of about 60 000 households, and across Europe as a whole the sample size is around 1.5 million. Based on the answers to survey questions, the government places each adult (aged 16 and older) in each surveyed household into one of three categories:

1. A person is considered employed if he or she spent some of the previous week working at a paid job.
2. A person is unemployed if he or she fits the ILO definition of an unemployed person.
3. A person who fits neither of the first two categories, such as a full-time student, homemaker or retiree, is not in the labour force (or, to use ILO terminology, is **economically inactive**).

economically inactive people who are not in employment or unemployed due to reasons such as being in full-time education, being full-time carers and raising families

Once the government has placed all the individuals covered by the survey in a category, it computes various statistics to summarize the state of the labour market. The **labour force** is defined as the sum of the employed and the unemployed:

labour force labour force the total number of workers, including both the employed and the unemployed

$$Labour\ force = Number\ of\ employed + Number\ of\ unemployed$$

Then the **unemployment rate** can be measured as the percentage of the labour force that is unemployed:

unemployment rate the percentage of the labour force that is unemployed:

$$Unemployment\ rate = \left(\frac{Number\ of\ unemployed}{Labour\ force}\right) \times 100$$

Unemployment rates are computed for the entire adult population and for more narrowly defined groups – men, women, youths and so on.

The same survey results are used to produce data on labour force participation. The **labour force participation rate** measures the percentage of the total adult population of the country that is in the labour force:

labour force participation rate (or economic activity rate) the percentage of the adult population that is in the labour force

$$Labour\ force\ participation\ rate = \left(\frac{Labour\ force}{Adult\ population}\right) \times 100$$

This statistic tells us the fraction of the population that has chosen to participate in the labour market. The labour force participation rate, like the unemployment rate, is computed both for the entire adult population and for more specific groups.

To see how these data are computed, consider the UK figures for February 2016. According to the *Labour Market Statistics* published by the ONS, 31.42 million people were in work and 1.69 million people were unemployed. The labour force was:

$$Labour\ force = 31.42 + 1.69 = 33.11\ million$$

The unemployment rate was:

$$Unemployment\ rate = \left(\frac{1.69}{33.11}\right) \times 100 = 5.1\%$$

There were 8.88 million people aged between 16 and 64 classed as economically inactive.

The total population of the UK was estimated by the ONS as being 64.6 million of which around 41.3 million were between 16 and 64 and classed as the adult population. The labour force participation rate, therefore, was:

$$Labour\ force\ participation\ rate = \left(\frac{33.11}{41.3}\right) \times 100 = 80.17\%$$

Table 23.1 shows the unemployment rate across the EU.

TABLE 23.1 **Unemployment Rates in the European Union (December 2015)**

Country	Unemployment rate (%)
Austria	5.8
Belgium	7.9
Bulgaria	8.8
Croatia	16.5
Cyprus	15.7
Czech Republic	4.5
Denmark	6.0
Estonia	6.5
Finland	9.5
France	10.2
Germany	4.5
Greece	24.5 (October 2015)
Hungary	6.3
Ireland	8.8
Italy	11.4
Latvia	10.2
Lithuania	8.5
Luxembourg	6.1
Malta	5.1
Netherlands	6.6
Poland	7.1
Portugal	11.8
Romania	6.7
Slovak Republic	10.6
Slovenia	8.8
Spain	20.8
Sweden	7.1

Source: EUROSTAT

THE CAUSES OF UNEMPLOYMENT

We have defined unemployment as a situation where people of working age are out of work but able and available for work at current wage rates. The basis of this definition rests on the model of the labour market we introduced in Chapter 17. In that model there is a demand for workers by employers, which is a derived demand, and a supply of labour willing and able to work at different wage rates. The equilibrium wage rate is that which brings together the number of workers willing and able to work at that wage rate with the demand for labour at that wage rate. If this model were replicated at the macro level, there would be an equilibrium wage rate which would mean all those seeking work at that wage rate would be employed. At equilibrium, therefore, there is no unemployment. Changes in the supply of and demand for labour would create surpluses and shortages in the labour market and the adjustment of the wage rate would ensure that all workers are always fully employed.

A look at statistics on the labour market, however, shows that in almost every country there are always some people who are unemployed, i.e. that labour markets do not clear instantaneously. The reasons for this unemployment include:

Frictional Unemployment

At any point in time in the economy there are people who are between jobs. They might have been made redundant or dismissed, are returning to work after a period of leave for travelling, seeking work after leaving university or school/college, looking for work after having time off to raise a family or wanting a career change. It takes time for workers to search for the jobs that are best suited for them. The unemployment that results from the process of matching workers and jobs is called **frictional unemployment**, and it is often thought to explain relatively short spells of unemployment.

> **frictional unemployment** unemployment that results because it takes time for workers to search for the jobs that best suit their tastes and skills

People who decide to change careers or leave one job without having another to go to immediately are making a conscious choice to become unemployed for a period. In many cases, they may have every intention of finding new work but there will be an interim period where they are unemployed. In some cases, people may see jobs available but feel it is not something that suits them, is not at a level they are looking for or where they feel the wage is too low. In some cases, people may choose to remain unemployed because state benefit levels are relatively generous or tax and benefit laws are such that taking a job would leave the individual worse off. **Voluntary unemployment** refers to a situation where people choose to remain unemployed rather than take jobs which are available. This is in contrast to **involuntary unemployment** which occurs when people want work at going market wage rates but cannot find employment. Involuntary unemployment may be caused by structural reasons.

> **voluntary unemployment** where people choose to remain unemployed rather than take jobs which are available
> **involuntary unemployment** where people want work at going market wage rates but cannot find employment

Structural Unemployment

When the quantity of labour supplied exceeds the quantity demanded and the number of jobs available may be insufficient to give a job to everyone who wants one, **structural unemployment** exists. Structural unemployment can explain longer spells of unemployment. There are a number of causes of structural unemployment and labour market theory implies that there are imperfections in the market which prevent wages adjusting to the changing demand and supply of labour. Some of these imperfections include:

> **structural unemployment** unemployment that results because the number of jobs available in some labour markets is insufficient to provide a job for everyone who wants one

Occupational and Geographic Immobility Workers who lose their jobs in one industry may find that jobs that are available require skills and experience they do not possess or are not in the immediate region where they live. To move from one occupation to another requires knowledge, skills and experience to be transferable and this is not always the case. In December 2015, for example, the last deep coal mine in the UK closed at Kellingley in Yorkshire. Four hundred and fifty workers lost their jobs. Many of these workers had extensive experience working in coal mining but their skills and expertize may not have been easily transferable to jobs available in the area which were in IT or distribution logistics, for example. Where workers are unable to easily move from one occupation to another, this is referred to as **occupational immobility**.

> **occupational immobility** where workers are unable to easily move from one occupation to another

Jobs that were available for these unemployed miners might be 30–50 miles away and it may not be possible for them to easily commute to take on these jobs and in addition, the cost of commuting might mean the job becomes unviable given the wage being offered. In some cases, if jobs are available in other parts of the country, there are other very practical reasons why it is not easy for workers to move to these jobs. Differences in house prices or family commitments might mean that even though jobs are available it is not practical for workers to take these jobs. Where people are unable to take work because of the difficulties associated with moving to different regions, this is termed **geographical immobility**.

> **geographical immobility** where people are unable to take work because of the difficulties associated with moving to different regions

Technological Change As we saw in Chapter 22, changes in technology are important drivers of long-run economic growth but such change has winners and losers. The losers are those whose knowledge, skills and experience are now redundant and as a result they have to seek new employment. The number of people working on production lines in vehicle manufacture, for example, is now substantially less than it was 30 years ago largely due to the development of machines which can do the work of humans far more efficiently and cheaper.

Structural Change in the Economy Over time structural changes affect the make-up of economies. In the UK, for example, the 18th and 19th Centuries saw a shift from a predominantly agrarian economy to industrial and manufacturing and this in turn has evolved into an economy which is dominated by service industries. Structural change can be caused by competition from abroad or by changes in technology and changes in societal norms and trends. The decline in the coal mining industry in the UK is partly due to the availability of cheaper coal imports from abroad, the increased cost of extracting coal in more marginal seams and also by commitments made to reduce the use of carbon emissions into the atmosphere which resulted in the closure of coal-fired power stations.

Labour Market Imperfections

We can use the model of the labour market to identify how unemployment can be caused by wages being above the market equilibrium. These are classed as imperfections in the labour market which prevent the wage rate from adjusting to equate the demand and supply of labour. An introduction to the three primary causes of wages being above market equilibrium was given in Chapter 17. It should be noted that the structural unemployment that arises from above-equilibrium wages is, in an important sense, different from the frictional unemployment that arises from the process of job search. The need for job search is not due to the failure of wages to balance labour supply and labour demand. When job search is the explanation for unemployment, workers are *searching* for the jobs that best suit their tastes and skills. By contrast, when the wage is above the equilibrium level, the quantity of labour supplied exceeds the quantity of labour demanded, and workers are unemployed because they are *waiting* for jobs to open up.

Minimum Wage Laws Minimum wage laws are a price floor applied to the labour market. Minimum wages can have an important effect on certain groups with particularly high unemployment rates. When a minimum wage law forces the wage to remain above the level that balances supply and demand, it raises the quantity of labour supplied and reduces the quantity of labour demanded compared to the equilibrium level. There is a surplus of labour. Because there are more workers willing to work than there are jobs, some workers are unemployed (Refer to Figure 17.8 to see a graphical representation of this explanation). It is important to note that most workers in many developed economies have wages well above the legal minimum. Minimum wage laws are binding most often for the least skilled and least experienced members of the labour force, such as teenagers. It is among these workers that minimum wage laws can offer an explanation for the existence of unemployment.

Unions and Collective Bargaining A union is a worker association that bargains with employers over wages and working conditions. **Union density** measures the proportion of the workforce that is unionized, excluding people who cannot, for legal or other reasons, be members of a union – for example, members of the armed forces. Broadly speaking, this amounts to expressing the number of union members as a proportion of civilian employees plus the unemployed. According to the OECD, union density in the UK in 2013, was 25.4 per cent, and has been steadily falling since 1995 when it stood at around 32.4 per cent and an even greater marked fall from the beginning of the 1980s, when it was over 50 per cent. In other European countries there is a similar trend of falling union density. In Germany density has fallen from 23.3 per cent in 1999 to 17.7 per cent in 2013, in the Netherlands the fall has been from 24.6 per cent to 17.6 per cent in 2013. However, there are exceptions with countries like Finland, Denmark, Iceland and Sweden having densities between 66 per cent and 82 per cent; however, even in these countries, the density is gradually falling.

union density a measure of the proportion of the workforce that is unionized

The Economics of Unions A union is a type of cartel. Like any cartel, a union is a group of sellers acting together in the hope of exerting their joint market power. Workers in a union act as a group when discussing their wages, benefits and working conditions with their employers. The process by which unions and firms agree on the terms of employment is called **collective bargaining**.

collective bargaining the process by which unions and firms agree on the terms of employment

When a union bargains with a firm, it asks for higher wages, better benefits and better working conditions than the firm would offer in the absence of a union. If the union and the firm do not reach agreement, the union can take various steps to put pressure on employers to come to an agreement including working to rule (doing only what is agreed in the contract of employment) and as a last resort organizing a withdrawal of labour from the firm, called a strike. Because a strike reduces production, sales and profit, a firm facing a strike threat is likely to agree to pay higher wages than it otherwise would. Economists who study the effects of unions typically find that union workers earn significantly more than similar workers who do not belong to unions.

When a union raises the wage above the equilibrium level, it raises the quantity of labour supplied and reduces the quantity of labour demanded, resulting in unemployment. Those workers who remain employed are better off, but those who were previously employed and are now unemployed are worse off.

The role of unions in the economy depends in part on the laws that govern union organization and collective bargaining. Normally, explicit agreements among members of a cartel are illegal. If firms that sell a common product were to agree to set a high price for that product, they would generally be held to be in breach of competition law and the government would prosecute these firms in the civil and criminal courts. In contrast, unions are given exemption from these laws in the belief that workers need greater market power as they bargain with employers.

Legislation affecting the market power of unions is a perennial topic of political debate. Members of parliaments sometimes debate *right-to-work laws*, which give workers in a unionized firm the right to choose whether to join the union. In the absence of such laws, unions can insist during collective bargaining that firms make union membership a requirement for employment.

Are Unions Good or Bad for the Economy? Economists disagree about whether unions are good or bad for the economy as a whole. Let's consider both sides of the debate.

Critics of unions argue that unions are merely a type of cartel. When unions raise wages above the level that would prevail in competitive markets, they reduce the quantity of labour demanded, cause some workers to be unemployed and reduce the wages in the rest of the economy. The resulting allocation of labour is, critics argue, both inefficient and inequitable. It is inefficient because high union wages reduce employment in unionized firms below the efficient, competitive level. It is inequitable because some workers benefit at the expense of other workers.

Advocates of unions contend that unions are a necessary antidote to the market power of the firms that hire workers. In some regions where one particular company is the dominant employer, if workers do not accept the wages and working conditions that the firm offers, they may have little choice but to move or stop working. In the absence of a union, therefore, the firm could use its market power to pay lower wages and offer worse working conditions than would prevail if it had to compete with other firms for the same workers. In this case, a union may balance the firm's market power and protect workers from being at the mercy of the firm owners.

Advocates also claim that unions are important for helping firms respond efficiently to workers' concerns. Whenever a worker takes a job, the worker and the firm must agree on many attributes of the job in addition to the wage: hours of work, overtime, holidays, sick leave, health benefits, promotion schedules, job security and so on. By representing workers' views on these issues, unions allow firms to provide the right mix of job attributes. In many countries unions have now taken on additional roles in supporting workers with respect to offering legal support in the event of an individual dispute at work, advice on pensions, financial services such as insurance, and support for those who have been injured or disabled at work and have to retire early. Even if unions have the adverse effect of pushing wages above the equilibrium level and causing unemployment, they have the benefit of helping firms keep a happy and productive workforce.

In the end, there is no consensus among economists about whether unions are good or bad for the economy. Like many institutions, their influence is probably beneficial in some circumstances and adverse in others.

> **SELF TEST** How does a union in the car industry affect wages and employment at Ford and Nissan plants in the UK? How might it affect wages and employment in other industries?

The Theory of Efficiency Wages The theory of efficiency wages suggests firms operate more efficiently if wages are above the equilibrium level. Therefore, it may be profitable for firms to keep wages high even in the presence of a surplus of labour. The decision to keep wages above equilibrium levels may seem odd at first given that wages are a large part of many firms' costs. Normally, we expect profit-maximizing firms to want to keep costs – and therefore wages – as low as possible. The novel insight of efficiency wage theory is that paying high wages might be profitable because they might raise the efficiency of a firm's workers.

There are several types of efficiency wage theory. Each type suggests a different explanation for why firms may want to pay high wages. Let's now consider four of these types.

Worker Health The first and simplest type of efficiency wage theory emphasizes the link between wages and worker health. Better paid workers eat a more nutritious diet, and workers who eat a better diet are healthier and more productive. A firm may find it more profitable to pay high wages and have healthy, productive workers than to pay lower wages and have less healthy, less productive workers.

This type of efficiency wage theory is of primary relevance for less developed countries where inadequate nutrition can be a common problem. Unemployment is high in the cities of many poor African countries, for example. In these countries, firms may fear that cutting wages would, in fact, adversely influence their workers' health and productivity. In other words, concern over nutrition may explain why firms do not cut wages despite a surplus of labour.

Worker Turnover A second type of efficiency wage theory emphasizes the link between wages and worker turnover. Workers quit jobs for many reasons – to take jobs in other firms, to move to other parts of the country, to leave the labour force and so on. The frequency with which they quit depends on the entire set of incentives they face, including the benefits of leaving and the benefits of staying. The more a firm pays its workers, the less often its workers will choose to leave. Thus, a firm can reduce turnover among its workers by paying them a high wage. Reducing turnover is important for firms because it is costly for firms to hire and train new workers. Even after they are trained, newly hired workers are not as productive as experienced workers. Firms with higher turnover, therefore, will tend to have higher production costs. Firms may find it profitable to pay wages above the equilibrium level in order to reduce worker turnover.

Worker Effort A third type of efficiency wage theory emphasizes the link between wages and worker effort. In many jobs, workers have some discretion over how hard to work. As a result, firms monitor the efforts of their workers, and workers caught shirking their responsibilities can be disciplined and possibly dismissed. Not all shirkers are caught immediately because monitoring workers is costly and imperfect. A firm can respond to this problem by paying wages above the equilibrium level. High wages, it is argued, make workers more eager to keep their jobs and provide an incentive to put forward their best effort.

In the *worker effort* variant of efficiency wage theory, if the wage were at the level that balanced supply and demand, workers would have less reason to work hard because if they were fired, they could quickly find new jobs at the same wage. Therefore, firms raise wages above the equilibrium level, causing unemployment and providing an incentive for workers not to shirk their responsibilities.

Worker Quality A fourth and final type of efficiency wage theory emphasizes the link between wages and worker quality. When a firm hires new workers, it cannot perfectly gauge the quality of the applicants. By paying a high wage, the firm attracts a better pool of workers to apply for its jobs.

To see how this might work, consider a simple example. Waterwell Company owns one well and needs one worker to pump water from the well. Two workers, X and Y, are interested in the job. X, a proficient worker, is willing to work for €10 per hour. Below that wage, they would rather start their own car-washing business. Y, a complete incompetent, is willing to work for anything above €2 per hour. Below that wage, they would rather sit on the beach. Economists say that X's *reservation wage* – the lowest wage they would accept – is €10 per hour, and Y's reservation wage is €2 per hour.

What wage should the firm set? If the firm was interested in minimizing labour costs, it would set the wage at €2 per hour. At this wage, the quantity of workers supplied (one) would balance the quantity demanded. Y would take the job, and X would not apply for it. Suppose Waterwell knows that only one of these two applicants is competent, but it does not know whether it is X or Y. If the firm hires the incompetent worker, they may damage the well, causing the firm huge losses. In this case, the firm has a better strategy than paying the equilibrium wage of €2 per hour and hiring Y. It can offer €10 per hour, inducing both X and Y to apply for the job. By choosing randomly between these two applicants and turning the other away, the firm has a 50:50 chance of hiring the competent one. By contrast, if the firm offers any lower wage, it is sure to hire the incompetent worker.

This story illustrates a general phenomenon. When a firm faces a surplus of workers, it might seem profitable to reduce the wage it is offering. However, by reducing the wage, the firm induces an adverse change in the mix of workers. In this case, at a wage of €10 per hour, Waterwell has two workers applying for one job; but if Waterwell responds to this labour surplus by reducing the wage, the competent worker (who has better alternative opportunities) will not apply. Thus, it is profitable for the firm to pay a wage above the level that balances supply and demand.

Demand Deficient Unemployment

In Chapter 31 we will introduce John Maynard Keynes whose ideas on unemployment changed the nature of economics. Up until the First World War, economists had largely assumed that the market mechanism would function such that unemployment would not persist and that wages would adjust to bring the demand and supply of labour into equilibrium. The post-war world began to experience significant economic shocks, the most notable of which was the Great Depression. The effects of the stock market crash in the United States in 1929 spread across the world and many countries experienced high and persistent unemployment. According to classical economics, this should not happen. Keynes argued that the principal cause of this unemployment was due to insufficient demand in the economy. This view ran counter to a prevailing orthodoxy, which is referred to as **Say's law** after Jean Baptiste Say (1767–1832), a French economist. Say's law is succinctly expressed as 'supply creates its own demand' and is a theory that overproduction in both the short run and the long run is not possible. It seems that Say was not the first to promote the idea; James Mill, the father of John Stuart Mill, and Adam Smith had both written about the idea. The theory rests on the identity of national income accounting. If output of goods and services increases and is sold, the income derived from the sale is used by recipients to purchase goods and services. Say noted: 'the mere circumstance of the creation of one product immediately opens a vent for other products'. Keynes rejected the short-run interpretation of Say's law and suggested that short-run shocks to the economy such as the stock market crash can reduce effective demand. By **effective demand**, Keynes meant the amount that people were not only willing to buy at different prices but what they can and do actually purchase. It was quite possible, Keynes argued, that demand could remain well below that sufficient to generate full employment and for unemployment to persist.

> **Say's law** an argument that production or supply is a source of demand, that supply creates its own demand
> **effective demand** the amount that people are not only willing to buy at different prices but what they can and do actually purchase

Summary

Since the 1930s there has been an ongoing debate in economics about the principal causes of unemployment and the extent to which these causes stem from the supply side of the economy or the demand side. This debate continues and has been brought into sharper focus with the rise in unemployment in many European countries as a result of the Financial Crisis of 2007–9. In essence, the debate centres on the extent to which unemployment is cyclical or structural – the latter accounting for the level of unemployment not due to changes in the economic cycle. As we build the theoretical building blocks of macroeconomics it must be remembered that policies to cut unemployment still deeply divide opinion in the economics profession.

> **SELF TEST** How is the unemployment rate measured? How might the unemployment rate overstate the amount of joblessness? How might it understate it?

THE NATURAL RATE OF UNEMPLOYMENT

Even when the overall economy is growing, the unemployment rate never falls to zero. Figure 23.1 shows the unemployment rate in the UK since 1971. The figure shows that the economy always has some unemployment and that the amount changes – often considerably – from year to year. In the figure, a trend line has been added which shows that the average unemployment rate over the last 40-plus years is around 7 per cent. The existence of unemployment regardless of the economic cycle is referred to as the

natural rate of unemployment (NRU) and the deviation of unemployment from its natural rate is called **cyclical unemployment**. The NRU can be viewed as the rate of unemployment the economy gravitates to given the number of people losing jobs over a period and the number finding work over that same period. Unemployment is a dynamic process. At any period of time, there are people losing jobs (called job separation) and people finding jobs. Suppose that every month, the rate at which people lose jobs (denoted by the Greek letter alpha, α) is 4.9 per cent, and the rate at which people find jobs (denoted by the Greek letter psi, ψ) is 65 per cent. The NRU is found by taking the job separation rate and dividing this by the sum of the job finding rate and the job separation rate:

$$NRU = \frac{\alpha}{(\psi + \alpha)} \times 100$$

In our example, the NRU is: $\left(\dfrac{4.9}{69.9}\right) \times 100 = 7\%$.

> **natural rate of unemployment** the normal rate of unemployment around which the unemployment rate fluctuates
>
> **cyclical unemployment** the deviation of unemployment from its natural rate

FIGURE 23.1

UK Unemployment Rate Since 1971

This graph uses annual data on the unemployment rate to show the fraction of the labour force without a job, calculated by the LFS definition. A trend line has been added to show the natural rate of unemployment, the normal level of unemployment around which the unemployment rate fluctuates.

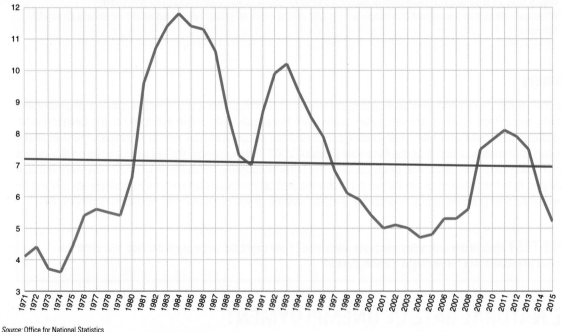

Source: Office for National Statistics

Later in this book we discuss short-run economic fluctuations, including the year-to-year fluctuations in unemployment. In this chapter, however, we focus on the long-run and examine why there is always some unemployment in market economies and whether the theory of NRU stands the test of time.

How Long Are the Unemployed without Work?

In judging how serious the problem of unemployment is, one question to consider is whether unemployment is typically a short-term or long-term condition. If unemployment is short term, one might conclude that it is not a big problem. Workers may require a few weeks between jobs to find the openings that best suit their tastes and skills. Yet if unemployment is long-term, one might conclude that it is a serious problem. Workers unemployed for many months are more likely to suffer economic and psychological hardship.

Because the duration of unemployment can affect our view about how big a problem it is, economists have devoted much energy to studying data on the duration of unemployment spells. In this work, they have uncovered a result that is important, subtle and seemingly contradictory: most spells of unemployment are short, and most unemployment observed at any given time is long-term.

To see how this statement can be true, consider an example. Suppose that you visited the government's unemployment office every week for a year to survey the unemployed. Each week you find that there are four unemployed workers. Three of these workers are the same individuals for the whole year, while the fourth person changes every week. Based on this experience, would you say that unemployment is typically short-term or long-term?

Some simple calculations help answer this question. In this example, you meet a total of 55 unemployed people: 52 of them are unemployed for one week, and three are unemployed for the full year. This means that 52/55, or 95 per cent, of unemployment spells end in one week. Thus, most spells of unemployment are short. Yet consider the total amount of unemployment. The three people unemployed for one year (52 weeks) make up a total of 156 weeks of unemployment. Together with the 52 people unemployed for one week, this makes 208 weeks of unemployment. In this example, 156/208, or 75 per cent, of unemployment is attributable to those individuals who are unemployed for a full year. Thus, most unemployment observed at any given time is long-term.

This subtle conclusion implies that economists and policymakers must be careful when interpreting data on unemployment and when designing policies to help the unemployed. Most people who become unemployed will soon find jobs. Yet most of the economy's unemployment problem is attributable to the relatively few workers who are jobless for long periods of time.

CASE STUDY **Long-Term Unemployment in the European Union**

A report published by the European Employment Observatory Review (see 'Long Term Unemployment 2012'. *European Employment Observatory Review,* September 2012) highlights some key trends in long-term unemployment in the EU. The report notes the significant costs both to the individual and to society of long-term unemployment which include loss of self-esteem, increasing difficulties of finding work because of the erosion of skills, damage to health, material deprivation, social exclusion and the cost of supporting the long-term unemployed.

Some 10 million people in the EU have been unemployed for longer than a year. Of these, 1.9 million have not had a job for over two years, 3 million have not had jobs for up to 17 months and 3.2 million have been out of work for between 24 and 47 months. The overall rate of long-term unemployment (LTU) in the EU sits at around 5.1 per cent in 2014 but some countries are faring better than others. In Spain the LTU rate has risen from 2 per cent in 2008 to 12.9 per cent in 2014 whereas in Germany the rate has decreased from 4.8 per cent in 2007 to 2.2 per cent in 2014.

The countries which have the lowest rates of LTU tend to be the more developed countries of northern Europe such as Norway, Sweden, Luxembourg, Austria and Denmark, all of whom had LTU rates under 2.0 per cent in 2014, whereas those countries hit hardest by the Financial Crisis such as Greece and Spain have very high rates (19.5 per cent and 12.9 per cent in 2014, respectively).

One of the dangers of long-term unemployment is that workers find it impossible to find work because the longer they are out of work the less likely it is that firms will see these people as being serious contenders for jobs. The result is what is called **hysteresis** – the lagging effects of past economic events on future ones. Those who are unemployed for long periods gradually adjust to a lower standard of living, they also find it increasingly harder to get work and so may lose interest in returning to the labour market.

hysteresis the lagging effects of past economic events on future ones

When looking at the breakdown of the LTU, it seems that older people are more likely to be victims of LTU but a worrying trend is the increasing number of young people across the EU who are falling into the LTU bracket. Prior to the Financial Crisis it was women who were more likely to be LTU but this has now shifted and more men are now LTU.

Long-term unemployment creates political tensions of which governments are acutely aware.

Job Search

One reason why economies always experience some unemployment is job search. **Job search** is the process of matching workers with appropriate jobs. If all workers and all jobs were the same, so that all workers were equally well suited for all jobs, job search would not be a problem. Laid-off workers would quickly find new jobs that were well suited for them. Workers, of course, differ in their tastes and skills, jobs differ in their attributes, and information about job candidates and job vacancies is disseminated slowly among the many firms and households in the economy.

 job search the process by which workers find appropriate jobs given their tastes and skills

Why Some Frictional Unemployment Is Inevitable

Frictional unemployment is often the result of changes in the demand for labour among different firms. When consumers decide that they prefer Brand X to Brand Y, the company producing Brand X increases employment, and the other firm lays off workers. The former Brand Y workers must now search for new jobs, and the Brand X producer must decide which new workers to hire for the various jobs that have opened up. The result of this transition is a period of unemployment.

Similarly, because different regions of the country produce different goods, employment can rise in one region while it falls in another. Consider, for instance, what happens when the world price of oil falls. Firms extracting oil from the fields below the North Sea, off the coast of Scotland, respond to the lower price by cutting back on production and employment. At the same time, cheaper petrol stimulates car sales, so car manufacturing firms in northern and central England raise production and employment. Changes in the composition of demand among industries or regions are called *sectoral shifts*. Because it takes time for workers to search for jobs in the new sectors, sectoral shifts temporarily cause unemployment.

Frictional unemployment is inevitable simply because the economy is always changing. Along the way, workers in declining industries find themselves out of work and searching for new jobs.

In addition to the effects of sectoral shifts on unemployment, workers will leave their jobs sometimes because they realize that the jobs are not a good match for their tastes and skills and they wish to look for a better job. Many of these workers, especially younger ones, find new jobs at higher wages, although given the vast improvements in information technology in recent years (especially the Internet) it is likely that many people search for new jobs without actually quitting their current job. Nevertheless, this churning of the labour force is normal in a well-functioning and dynamic market economy, and the result is some amount of frictional unemployment.

Public Policy and Job Search

Even if some frictional unemployment is inevitable, the precise amount is not. The faster information spreads about job openings and worker availability, the more rapidly the economy can match workers and firms. The Internet, for instance, may help facilitate job search and reduce frictional unemployment. In addition, public policy may play a role. If policy can reduce the time it takes unemployed workers to find new jobs, it can reduce the economy's natural rate of unemployment.

Government policies try to facilitate job search in various ways. One way is through government-run employment agencies or job centres, which give out information about job vacancies. Another way is through public training schemes, which aim to ease the transition of workers from declining to growing industries and to help disadvantaged groups escape poverty. Advocates of these policies believe that they make the economy operate more efficiently by keeping the labour force more fully employed, and that they reduce the inequities inherent in a constantly changing market economy.

Critics of these policies question whether the government should get involved with the process of job search. They argue that it is better to let the private market match workers and jobs. In fact, most job search in the economy takes place without intervention by the government. Newspaper advertisements, internet job sites, head-hunters and word of mouth all help spread information about job openings and job candidates. Similarly, much worker education is done privately, either through schools or through on-the-job training. These critics contend that the government is no better – and most likely worse – at disseminating the right information to the right workers and deciding what kinds of worker training would be most valuable. They claim that these decisions are best made privately by workers and employers.

Unemployment Insurance

One government policy that increases the amount of frictional unemployment, without intending to do so, is **unemployment insurance** (or, as it is called in the UK, national insurance). This policy is designed to offer workers partial protection against job loss. People who choose to quit their jobs, those that are fired for a just reason, or those who have just entered the labour force, are not eligible. Benefits are paid only to the unemployed who are laid off because their previous employers no longer needed their skills.

unemployment insurance a government programme that partially protects workers' incomes when they become unemployed

While unemployment insurance reduces the hardship of unemployment, it is argued that it can also increase the amount of unemployment. This explanation is based on incentives. Because unemployment benefits stop when a worker takes a new job, the unemployed, it is argued, devote less effort to job search and are more likely to turn down unattractive job offers. In addition, because unemployment insurance makes unemployment less onerous, workers are less likely to seek guarantees of job security when they negotiate with employers over the terms of employment. However, research on unemployment insurance in Europe gives a different perspective. In a paper by Konstantinos Tatsiramos (Tatsiramos, K. (2006) *Unemployment Insurance in Europe: Unemployment Duration and Subsequent Employment Stability*. Institute for the Study of Labor Discussion Paper no. 2280), the benefits to workers searching for jobs and receiving unemployment insurance is greater than the costs:

> This paper provides evidence on the effect of unemployment benefits on unemployment and employment duration in Europe, using individual data from the European Community Household Panel for

eight countries. Even if receiving benefits has a direct negative effect increasing the duration of unemployment spells, there is also a positive indirect effect of benefits on subsequent employment duration. This indirect effect is pronounced in countries with relatively generous benefit systems, and for recipients who have remained unemployed for at least six months. In terms of the magnitude of the effect, recipients remain employed on average two to four months longer than non-recipients. This represents a 10 to 20 per cent increase relative to the average employment duration, compensating for the additional time spent in unemployment.

The effect of unemployment insurance is likely to be related to the way the scheme is designed and operated. In one US study, when unemployed workers applied to collect unemployment insurance benefits, some of them were randomly selected and each offered a $500 bonus if they found new jobs within 11 weeks. This group was then compared with a control group not offered the incentive. The average spell of unemployment for the group offered the bonus was 7 per cent shorter than the average spell for the control group. This experiment suggests that the design of the unemployment insurance system influences the effort that the unemployed devote to job search.

Several other studies examined search effort by following a group of workers over time. Unemployment insurance benefits, rather than lasting forever, usually run out after six months or a year. These studies found that when the unemployed become ineligible for benefits, the probability of their finding a new job rises markedly. Thus, receiving unemployment insurance benefits does reduce the search effort of the unemployed.

Even though unemployment insurance reduces search effort and raises unemployment, we should not necessarily conclude that the policy is a bad one. The policy does achieve its primary goal of reducing the income uncertainty that workers face. In addition, when workers turn down unattractive job offers, they have the opportunity to look for jobs that better suit their tastes and skills. Some economists have argued that unemployment insurance improves the ability of the economy to match each worker with the most appropriate job.

The study of unemployment insurance shows that the unemployment rate is an imperfect measure of a nation's overall level of economic well-being. Some economists agree that eliminating unemployment insurance would reduce the amount of unemployment in the economy. Yet economists disagree on whether economic well-being would be enhanced or diminished by this change in policy.

SELF TEST How would an increase in the world price of oil affect the amount of frictional unemployment? Is this unemployment undesirable? What public policies might affect the amount of unemployment caused by this price change?

Criticisms of the Natural Rate Hypothesis

The work of John Maynard Keynes in the 1930s provided a number of challenges to the prevailing orthodoxy, specifically that the price mechanism was subject to fundamental flaws. These flaws meant that unemployment would not be short-term whilst markets adjusted but could be persistent and long-term. As Keynes' ideas were developed by economists, the apparent fundamental disagreement about how the macroeconomy works was 'resolved' through what came to be called the **neoclassical synthesis** (it is also called New Keynesian economics or Neo-Keynesianism). The term has been attributed to American Nobel Prize winning economist, Paul Samuelson. Samuelson referred to himself as a 'cafeteria Keynesian'. He was often seen as being a devotee of Keynesian ideas but saw himself picking the parts of Keynesian ideas which appealed to him and which he saw had benefit to macroeconomic analysis. The synthesis states that the reason why markets did not adjust quickly to imbalances of the supply and demand for labour was because of sticky prices and sticky wages. We will look at these ideas later in the book but at this stage it is sufficient to say that prices and wages do not move quickly to eliminate surpluses and shortages in the market. This can result in high unemployment persisting in the short run. Appropriate use of monetary and fiscal policy could, according to the synthesis, help markets to adjust more effectively and correct imbalances. Once prices and wages have had time to adjust, full employment can be reached once again. The underlying philosophy was still *laissez-faire* capitalism – the belief that markets are the most effective way of allocating scarce resources and where appropriate, should be left to do their work. What the synthesis did was to bring classical ideas into line with Keynes apparent rejection of the benefits of unfettered markets. The synthesis spawned the idea of the NRU and has become a mainstay of economics teaching and philosophy over the last 40 years.

> **neoclassical synthesis** the idea that markets can be slow to adjust in the short run due to sticky prices and sticky wages but revert to long-run classical principles which could be aided by appropriate use of fiscal and monetary policies

Over the last 40 years, there have been many refinements to the neoclassical synthesis. Much of Keynesian unemployment was 'involuntary' – even at prevailing wage rates, most people who are unemployed would prefer to be in work. The neoclassical synthesis explained this as a temporary situation which would eventually be resolved once prices and wages had time to adjust. It was suggested that people will not make decisions about their future economic situation (such as negotiating wage increases and considering the security of their jobs) in a vacuum and that firms and households would build in their expectations of inflation and the economy into their decision-making. This was called *rational expectations* and again, we will deal with this in more detail later in the book.

The prevailing view of the NRU came to be that unemployment would only differ from its natural rate if expected inflation was different to actual inflation. Over time the NRU would be relatively stable. Research by Roger Farmer, a Senior Fellow at the Bank of England and Professor at the University of California, Los Angeles (UCLA), casts doubt on this stability. Average unemployment in the United States in the 1950s was around 4.5 per cent, a little higher in the 1960s, jumped to around 6.3 per cent in the 1970s, 7.3 per cent in the 1980s, around 5.7 per cent in the 1990s and about 5.6 per cent in the 2000s. Farmer suggests that the data does not match the theory and that the NRU 'is false'. Farmer goes on to explore an alternative theory which is linked to an understanding of the trade-off between unemployment and inflation, which we will explore in later chapters.

Other economists suggest that the NRU can change over time and there might be different reasons for this. One is the idea of hysteresis. The concept is 'borrowed' from physics and refers to an object which fails to return to its original state after some external shock even when that shock subsides. Recessions, for example, can have significant impact on both employment and unemployment. People not only lose their jobs during a recession but those in work may come to have different views about their jobs and the degree of security they have in work. These views may persist even once the recession has gone in what Ball and Mankiw (2002), refer to as a 'permanent scar on the economy'. (Ball, L and Mankiw N.G (2002) The NAIRU in Theory and Practice. *Journal of Economic Perspectives*. 16. 4, pp 115–36). Other reasons for the changing NRU could be due to the changes in the structure of the labour force, the proportion of different age groups and their levels of experience, skills and productivity as a result, the developments in technologies which influence competitiveness and productivity, and the improvements in job matching – the way in which workers who are seeking employment are matched with the jobs which are available.

MARX AND THE RESERVE ARMY OF THE UNEMPLOYED

The idea of the NRU may have been developed after the Second World War but the idea that there are always some people who are unemployed has been around for much longer. Karl Marx believed that unemployment was a necessary condition for capitalism to survive. Marx referred to the unemployed as the 'reserve industrial army of labour'. This reserve army consisted of different groups of people including the long-term unemployed through to those who move in and out of the labour market at different times for different reasons. Some of the people who are chronically unemployed (i.e. the long term unemployed) may be almost unemployable for some employers. This may be because they have few skills, limited experience or a history of poor employment records and as such they are only employed if there is a considerable shortage in the labour market. Equally, women who look after families are classed as part of this reserve army because they can be brought in to the labour market in times of crisis, which was the case during the First and Second World Wars when many women were employed on the land and in factories.

Marx suggested that capitalism could not achieve full employment, a situation where those who want work can find jobs. Under capitalism, the labour market consists of those who are willing and able to work at different wage rates (the supply of labour) and the buyers of labour (employers) and both are free to either sell or buy labour. In this labour market, workers will be moving from one job to another and employers will at times shed labour as economic and technological conditions change. If full employment were a reality, those seeking work would be able to find a job quickly. This ability to move from job to job quickly would give suppliers of labour considerable power and force employers to compete with each other to hire workers which would push up the wage rate and the sort of conditions that workers demand. The effect would be to erode the surplus value that capitalists get from employing labour power.

In response, capitalist employers invest further in machinery, which represents a thinly veiled threat to workers that their power can be curtailed. If wage rates were pushed up because of worker power, employers would look to replace labour with machinery and thus make existing workers unemployed. The existence of this threat of unemployment is sufficient to prevent workers from exploiting their labour power and shifts the balance to employers. Having a reserve army of the unemployed is a fundamental reminder to workers that they too could join it if they push their power too far.

The existence of a reserve army of the unemployed is also of value to capitalists in exploiting growth in economic activity. It provides a ready-made pool of potential workers that can be dipped into when output needs to be increased quickly to meet demand. If full employment existed, there would be no surplus labour and hiring additional workers to cope with increases in demand would push up costs which would lead to lower profits and less incentive to expand. This would slow the overall growth in economic activity. A reserve army of unemployed provides a way in which capitalists can take on new workers, even those who are classed as 'unemployable' to help cope with increasing output demands but provides a means of paying these workers low wages to exploit surplus value from them.

THE COST OF UNEMPLOYMENT

We mentioned at the outset of this chapter that unemployment can be one of the most distressing things to happen to anyone in their lives. Unemployment imposes costs on the individual and their family and friends but there is also a wider cost of unemployment which affects government, the taxpayer and the economy as a whole.

The Costs of Unemployment to the Individual

Loss of Earnings One of the first and perhaps most obvious costs of unemployment to an individual is the loss of earnings that results from being unemployed. Many countries provide some form of unemployment insurance as we have seen but the sums given to the unemployed are relatively small and in most cases nowhere near the earnings that the individual would have earned in work. In some countries there might be other state benefits that an unemployed worker can claim which mean that in the case of workers in low-skilled, low-paid industries the incentive to take work can be reduced. In many other cases, however, unemployment means that individuals have to re-evaluate their household spending budgets. This might require households to cut back on certain luxuries like spending on leisure activities, going to the cinema, going out to eat and so on, but might also cut down on luxuries such as clothing, furniture, electrical goods, having extensions built on a house and so on. We will see shortly how this has an effect on society as a whole.

The unemployed and their families are more likely to be at risk of slipping into poverty. Remember, the definition of poverty is a household income less than 60 per cent below the median income. It is unlikely that welfare support from the state is ever going to be, on its own, sufficient to put families above this level so unless the unemployed have savings to draw upon it is more likely that they will fall into poverty. The Trades Union Congress (TUC) in the UK estimate that around 60 per cent of working age adults in families where there is unemployment are likely to be in poverty.

In addition, some families will find that unemployment means that they face problems in paying for rent or mortgages and this can result in the loss of homes. The unemployed are more likely to have to go into debt in order to pay bills and this can add to the problems highlighted in our next section.

Stress, Self-Esteem and Health Problems Being unemployed can lead to significant mental health problems. The process of becoming unemployed is stressful and can be a life-changing event for some people. Having to adjust to claiming benefits, applying for other jobs, possibly getting additional training and the chances of having repeated experiences of either not having any replies to applications or in the event of unsuccessful interviews, the feeling of rejection, is not only stressful in itself but can lead to feelings of guilt and a reduction in self-esteem. These experiences can bring on stress-related illnesses and the incidences of health problems in the unemployed can increase the longer that the unemployment continues.

Drug and Alcohol Abuse and Crime Closely linked to the self-esteem problems, the boredom that can result from being unemployed and the feeling of worthlessness that many unemployed people say they experience, is the increased potential to turn to alcohol and illegal drugs as a means of escape.

When people move from being employed and having an income to be able to afford a reasonable standard of living, to experiencing tight restrictions on incomes and spending, the feeling of social exclusion and deprivation can be acute and cause some to turn to crime as a means of maintaining what they see as a reasonable standard of living. Indeed, the correlation between crime rates and drug abuse is very high; once people get involved with a drug or alcohol habit it becomes expensive and one way of funding this habit is to turn to crime.

Family Breakdown Families who have an experience of unemployment are more prone to break-up. Divorce rates amongst the unemployed are higher as the stresses of coping with adjusting to new income levels, trying to find work and so on, take their toll.

De-Skilling The longer someone is out of work the more likely it is that they will lose touch with changes in the workplace and the labour market in general and the more likely it is that they might be viewed as being unemployable or not favourable candidates for employment. Changes in the workplace, in technology and in the skills needed for employment change rapidly. Those in work are able to take advantage of training – both off-the-job and on-the-job, to maintain their skill levels, but the unemployed may be excluded from being able to maintain or improve their skill levels and as a result find it even harder to find work. This can lead to the hysteresis effect.

The Costs of Unemployment to Society and the Economy

The Opportunity Cost of Unemployment An individual who is willing and able to work represents a unit of productive output. If that person is unemployed the opportunity cost to society is the value of the goods and services that the individual could have produced. This 'lost output' can be considerable and represents a lower standard of living for society as a whole. In Chapter 19 we looked at the production possibilities frontier (PPF). If there is unemployment in society which is not simply frictional unemployment then society will not be operating on the PPF but instead somewhere inside it, which represents an inefficient use of resources.

The Tax and Benefits Effect People who are unemployed have lower incomes and may rely solely on government welfare payments to support their standard of living. If people lose their jobs, then they do not pay as much in income taxes and if they also reduce spending they do not pay consumption taxes at the same level as if they were in employment. The higher the level of unemployment in a country the greater the impact on tax revenue for the government. Not only is government revenue adversely affected but government spending is also likely to be higher. The unemployed will claim additional benefits and governments may also incur costs in having to deal with the social problems caused by unemployment such as drug and alcohol abuse, family breakdown and the increase in crime.

If government income is reduced through lower tax receipts and there is also a requirement to increase spending because of higher welfare spending, the pressure on government budgets can increase and it is more likely that the government experience a budget deficit – a situation where its spending is higher than its revenue from taxation. If governments experience a budget deficit, then the deficit has to be funded by additional borrowing. Increased government borrowing can not only cause crowding out but also puts upward pressure on interest rates, which in turn might affect investment decisions by firms. The knock-on effects can have ripples throughout the economy as our next point highlights.

The Reverse Multiplier Effect

We have seen that when people experience unemployment they cut back their spending on luxuries and may also switch their spending to substitute goods which may be seen as inferior goods. Firms who produce these different goods may see a change in spending patterns which can have an effect on cash flows and ultimately profits.

Goods with a relatively high income elasticity of demand are likely to be affected more significantly. If sales fall, firms earn lower incomes and may have to adjust their business to manage cash flows. This might involve cutting back on orders from suppliers, building up stocks as goods remain unsold and in some cases firms may have to either lay-off workers or even make workers redundant or close down the business if it becomes insolvent. If workers are made redundant or lose their jobs in this way, this then means those workers receive lower incomes and so the process continues.

Not all firms will be affected in such an extreme way but it is the case that in periods of high unemployment, firms may see falling profit levels and this in turn means they pay lower corporate taxes which puts further pressure on government budgets. Some firms might see demand for their services actually increase in periods of high unemployment. If the unemployed switch spending to inferior goods, the producers of those goods might see demand rise. In the aftermath of the Financial Crisis and beyond, low-cost supermarkets across the UK and Europe reported seeing an increase in sales whilst traditional supermarkets reported reduced sales.

The effect of unemployment, if more than simply frictional unemployment, is to produce a multiplied impact on economic activity as a whole. If there are concentrated pockets of workers losing their jobs such as a major employer in an area, then the effect of this reverse multiplier effect can be considerable. Indeed, there are areas of the UK and Europe where the decline in industries concentrated in particular areas has led to considerable regional deprivation which has lasted for many years. Once an area is caught in the cycle of economic decline it is extremely hard to recover.

CONCLUSION

In this chapter we discussed the measurement of unemployment, the reasons why economies always experience some degree of unemployment and some of the costs of unemployment to society and the economy as a whole. We have seen how job search, minimum wage laws, unions, efficiency wages and structural and technological change can all help explain why some workers do not have jobs. We have also seen that there are questions about whether the NRU is still a useful concept for policymaking.

The analysis of this chapter yields an important lesson: although the economy will always have some unemployment, its natural rate is not immutable. Many events and policies can change the amount of unemployment the economy typically experiences. As the information revolution changes the process of job search, as governments adjust the minimum wage, as workers form or quit unions, and as firms alter their reliance on efficiency wages, the natural rate of unemployment evolves.

Unemployment is not a simple problem with a simple solution. The costs of unemployment are significant not only to individuals but also to the economy and society which is why so many governments around the world are highly sensitive to the problem and look to develop policies to deal with unemployment. It is worth noting that when high unemployment persists, the potential for social disorder and political upheaval is greater. It might not be surprising, therefore, that governments are keen to ensure that the problems which can arise from unemployment are given due consideration in policy formulation.

IN THE NEWS

The Natural Rate of Unemployment

In the aftermath of the Financial Crisis, economists are observing relationships between key macroeconomic variables in a number of countries which do not seem to be behaving in quite the same way as accepted models suggest.

Falling Unemployment Rates and Rising Employment in the UK

In February 2016, the ONS in the UK published figures for labour market. Compared to the previous quarter, employment rose by 205 000 meaning that 74.1 per cent of people aged between 16 and 64 were in work, the highest employment rate since 1971. The unemployment rate also fell, from 6.0 per cent in December 2014 to 5.1 per cent. Is this the Natural Rate of Unemployment? That depends on who you ask; the Office for Budget Responsibility puts the UK's NRU at around 5.4 per cent, the OECD estimates it at 6.9 per cent and Trevor Williams, Chief Economist at Lloyds Bank Commercial and member of the Institute of Economic Affairs, is quoted in a House of Lords Library Note as suggesting it is between 5.5 and 6.0 per cent. Whatever the NRU for the UK, an unemployment rate of 5.1 per cent was much lower than the 7.0 per cent 'threshold' which Mark Carney, the Governor of the Bank of England, had suggested would be the point at which consideration of interest rate rises would be triggered. In February 2016, interest rates were at their historic low of 0.5 per cent and the unemployment rate continued to fall. Why is the NRU such a crucial trigger point?

One reason is that when unemployment rates fall below what is considered a country's NRU, it is a sign that the labour market is becoming tighter. If the demand for labour begins to outstrip supply, wage rates start to be pushed up and firms' costs rise. The increase in firms' costs can be passed on in the form of higher prices and the rate of growth of prices starts to accelerate. If central banks believe that if real wages are starting to increase more rapidly, it may be a time to increase interest rates to help keep inflation from rising too rapidly.

In the UK, however, inflation remained at or near zero for most of 2015 and in January 2016 was reported at 0.3 per cent. Many economists could not see any chances of inflation speeding up in the foreseeable future. Martin Weale, one of the Bank of England's Monetary Policy Committee members in 2015, and a supposed 'hawk' (by which is meant he tends to look for increases in interest rate rises to curb potential inflation earlier rather than later) commented in an interview, that he was surprised that the downward pressure on prices had continued longer than he anticipated. Weale noted that the Committee would be looking at how the change in the unemployment rate would affect real wage growth and that it was not certain that wages would adjust to the fall in unemployment rate and the increase in employment.

Unemployment rates in the UK have fallen whereas in some European countries, unemployment remains stubbornly high.

Questions

1 Explain what you understand by the 'natural rate of unemployment'.

2 Why do you think there are different estimates of the NRU for a country like the UK?

3 Do you think that it is inevitable that once unemployment falls below the NRU that inflation will begin to accelerate? Justify your view.

4 Why might rising employment and falling unemployment rates not necessarily lead to increases in real wage rates (Marx's idea of the reserve army of the unemployed might have some relevance here)?

5 Why do you think policymakers are interested in real wages rather than nominal wages when assessing policy decisions?

SUMMARY

- The unemployment rate is the percentage of those who would like to work who do not have jobs. The government calculates this statistic monthly based on a survey of thousands of households.

- The unemployment rate is an imperfect measure of joblessness. Some people who call themselves unemployed may actually not want to work, and some people who would like to work have left the labour force after an unsuccessful search.

- In many advanced economies, most people who become unemployed find work within a short period of time. Nevertheless, most unemployment observed at any given time is attributable to the few people who are unemployed for long periods of time.

- One reason for unemployment is the time it takes for workers to search for jobs that best suit their tastes and skills. Unemployment insurance is a government policy that, while protecting workers' incomes, increases the amount of frictional unemployment.

- A second reason why an economy may always have some unemployment is if there is a minimum wage that exceeds the wage that would balance supply and demand for the workers who are eligible for the minimum wage. By raising the wage of unskilled and inexperienced workers above the equilibrium level, minimum wage laws raise the quantity of labour supplied and reduce the quantity demanded. The resulting surplus of labour represents unemployment.

- A third reason for unemployment is the market power of unions. When unions push the wages in unionized industries above the equilibrium level, they create a surplus of labour.

- A fourth reason for unemployment is suggested by the theory of efficiency wages. According to this theory, firms find it profitable to pay wages above the equilibrium level. High wages can improve worker health, lower worker turnover, increase worker effort and raise worker quality.

- Unemployment also occurs due to structural changes in the economy which result in firms and industries closing down whilst new firms and industries grow. Structural changes cause winners and losers and it is not always easy or practical for people to find new jobs.

- John Maynard Keynes suggested, contrary to the accepted view at the time, that unemployment could remain at high levels for extended periods and that governments should use fiscal policy to help alleviate unemployment by boosting government spending.

- The neoclassical synthesis reconciled the classical view and Keynes' ideas by arguing that in the short-run, markets might not adjust because of sticky prices and wages but in the long-run, classical principles hold.

- Marx argued that capitalism needed unemployment to regulate the power of workers.

- The costs of unemployment to individuals include lower incomes, loss of self-esteem, de-skilling, an increase in the possibility of mental health problems, family breakdown and crime.

- The costs of unemployment to society as a whole includes the opportunity cost of lost output which reduces potential growth, the impact on government income and expenditure, the social costs of dealing with unemployment and its effects, the underuse of resources and the reverse multiplier effect.

QUESTIONS FOR REVIEW

1 Why might a person who does not have a job not be unemployed?

2 How do national statistical offices compute the labour force, the unemployment rate and the labour force participation rate?

3 Is unemployment typically short-term or long-term? Explain.

4 Why is frictional unemployment inevitable? How might the government reduce the amount of frictional unemployment?

5 Why, according to Marx, does capitalism need a 'reserve army of the unemployed'?

6 What is the hysteresis effect?

7 What is the 'neoclassical synthesis'?

8 What claims do advocates of unions make to argue that unions are good for the economy?

9 Explain four ways in which a firm might increase its profits by raising the wages it pays.

10 Outline three costs of unemployment to (a) an individual and (b) to society.

PROBLEMS AND APPLICATIONS

1 Assume that in a country, of all adult people, 29 500 000 were employed, 1 120 000 were unemployed and 11 000 000 were not in the labour force. How big was the labour force? What was the labour force participation rate? What was the unemployment rate?

2 Go to the website of the UK Office for National Statistics (http://www.statistics.gov.uk) or Eurostat (http://ec.europa.eu/eurostat) or the statistics office for the country in which you are studying. What is the national unemployment rate right now? Find the unemployment rate for the demographic group that best fits a description of you (for example, based on age, sex and ethnic group). Is it higher or lower than the national average? Why do you think this is so?

3 According to a Labour Force Survey in a country, total employment increased by around 1.35 million workers between 2011 and 2017, but the number of unemployed workers increased by 350 000.

   a. How are these numbers consistent with each other?
   b. In some cases, there can be an increase in the number of people employed but the number of unemployed people declines by a smaller amount. Why might one expect a reduction in the number of people counted as unemployed to be smaller than the increase in the number of people employed?

4 Are the following workers more likely to experience short-term or long-term unemployment? Explain.

   a. A construction worker laid off because of bad weather.
   b. A manufacturing worker who loses their job at a plant in an isolated area.
   c. A bus industry worker laid off because of competition from the railway.
   d. A short-order cook (a specialist in making simple, quick meals in restaurants) who loses their job when a new restaurant opens across the street.
   e. An expert welder with little formal education who loses their job when the company installs automatic welding machinery.

5 Both Marx and Keynes criticised Say's law as being a fallacy. What do you think is the flaw in Say's argument?

6 To what extent do you think the reasons why some frictional unemployment will always exist confirms the idea of sticky wages and the neoclassical synthesis?

7 Consider an economy with two labour markets, neither of which is unionized. Now suppose a union is established in one market.

   a. Show the effect of the union on the market in which it is formed. In what sense is the quantity of labour employed in this market an inefficient quantity?
   b. Show the effect of the union on the non-unionized market. What happens to the equilibrium wage in this market?

8 Some workers in the economy are paid a flat salary and some are paid by commission. Which compensation scheme would require more monitoring by supervisors? In which case do firms have an incentive to pay more than the equilibrium level (as in the worker effort variant of efficiency wage theory)? What factors do you think determine the type of compensation firms choose?

9 Explain why changes to the structure of the population and policies to improve job matching might lead to changes in the NRU.

10 Statistics from the International Labour Organization in 2015, suggest that there are around 73.3 million young people (those aged between 16 and 23) unemployed worldwide. Young people are three times more likely to be unemployed than those in other age groups and each month out of work prior to age 23 increases the likelihood that they will experience longer periods of unemployment later in life.

   a. Why are such statistics of importance to policymakers?
   b. What specific costs might be associated with youth unemployment to young people and to society?
   c. Should policymakers devote more resources to dealing with youth unemployment compared to other groups in society? Justify your response.

PART 12
INTEREST RATES, MONEY AND PRICES IN THE LONG RUN

24 SAVING, INVESTMENT AND THE FINANCIAL SYSTEM

In order to carry out business of virtually any sort, firms have to have capital. This applies to very large firms such as BP right through to small one-person businesses. Start-up businesses might fund some capital expenditure from past savings but more likely, most entrepreneurs have to find money to invest from other sources.

There are various ways to finance capital investment. Funds can be borrowed from a bank or from a friend or relative. This type of borrowing involves a promise not only to return the money at a later date but also to pay interest for the use of the money. Alternatively, firms can convince someone to provide the money needed for the business in exchange for a share of future profits. In either case, investment in capital equipment is being financed by someone else's saving.

The **financial system** consists of those institutions in the economy that help to match one person's saving with another person's investment. As we seen, saving and investment are key ingredients to long-run economic growth: when a country saves a large portion of its GDP, more resources are available for investment in capital, and higher capital raises a country's productivity and living standard. We have also seen that there is a proportion of income that is not spent and which is saved. At the same time there are economic actors who want to borrow in order to finance investments in new and growing businesses.

This chapter examines how the financial system brings together savers and borrowers. First, we discuss the large variety of institutions that make up the financial system. Second, we discuss the relationship between the financial system and some key macroeconomic variables – notably saving and investment. Third, we develop a model of the supply and demand for funds in financial markets. In the model, the interest rate is the price that adjusts to balance supply and demand. The model shows how various government policies affect the interest rate and, thereby, society's allocation of scarce resources.

financial system the group of institutions in the economy that help to match one person's saving with another person's investment

FINANCIAL INSTITUTIONS IN THE ECONOMY

At the broadest level, the financial system moves the economy's scarce resources from savers (people who spend less than they earn) to borrowers (people who spend more than they earn). Savers save for various reasons – to help put a child through university in several years or to retire comfortably in several decades. Similarly, borrowers borrow for various reasons – to buy a house in which to live or to start a business with which to make a living. Many savers supply their money to the financial system with the expectation that they will get it back with interest at a later date. The expectation that the reward for saving will be the receipt of interest is not universal – Islamic finance has a very different approach but in this chapter we will be focusing on what might be called 'traditional' financial institutions. Borrowers demand money from the financial system with the knowledge that they will be required to pay it back with interest at a later date.

The financial system is made up of various financial institutions that help coordinate savers and borrowers. Financial institutions can be grouped into two categories – financial markets and financial intermediaries.

Financial Markets

Financial markets are the institutions through which a person who wants to save can directly supply funds to a person who wants to borrow. Two of the most important financial markets in advanced economies are the bond market and the stock market.

> **financial markets** financial institutions through which savers can directly provide funds to borrowers

The Bond Market When BP, the oil company, wants to borrow to finance a major new oil exploration project, it can borrow directly from the public. It does this by selling bonds. A **bond** is a certificate of indebtedness that specifies the obligations of the borrower to the holder of the bond. Put simply, a bond is an IOU. It identifies the time at which the loan will be repaid, called the *date of maturity*, and the rate of interest that will be paid periodically (called the *coupon*) until the loan matures. The buyer of a bond gives their money to BP in exchange for this promise of interest and eventual repayment of the amount borrowed (the *principal*). The buyer can hold the bond until maturity or can sell the bond at an earlier date to someone else.

> **bond** a certificate of indebtedness

There are literally millions of bonds traded in advanced economies. When large corporations or national and local governments need to borrow in order to finance the purchase of a new factory, a new jet fighter or a new school, they often do so by issuing bonds. If you look at the *Financial Times* or the business section of many national newspapers, you will find a listing of the prices and interest rates on some of the most important bond issues. Although these bonds differ in many ways, two characteristics of bonds are most important.

The first characteristic is a bond's *term* – the length of time until the bond matures. Some bonds have short terms, such as a few months, while others have terms as long as 30 years. (The British government has even issued a bond that never matures, called a *perpetuity*. This bond pays interest forever, but the principal is never repaid.) The interest rate on a bond depends, in part, on its term. Long-term bonds are riskier than short-term bonds because holders of long-term bonds have to wait longer for repayment of the principal. If a holder of a long-term bond needs their money earlier than the distant date of maturity, they have no choice but to sell the bond to someone else, perhaps at a reduced price. To compensate for this risk, long-term bonds usually (but not always) pay higher interest rates than short-term bonds.

The second important characteristic of a bond is its *credit risk* – the probability that the borrower will fail to pay some of the interest or principal. Such a failure to pay is called a *default*. Borrowers can (and sometimes do) default on their loans. When bond buyers perceive that the probability of default is high, they demand a higher interest rate to compensate them for this risk.

When national governments want to borrow money to finance public spending, they issue bonds. You will hear this referred to as *sovereign debt*. Some government bonds are considered a safe credit risk, such as those from Germany, for example, and tend to pay low interest rates. UK government bonds have come to be referred to as *gilt-edged* bonds, or more simply as *gilts*, reflecting that, in terms of credit risk, they are 'as good as gold' – (early bond certificates had a gold edge – hence the term 'gilt edged'). In contrast, financially shaky corporations raise money by issuing *junk bonds*, which pay very high interest rates; in recent years some countries' debt has been graded as 'junk'. Buyers of bonds can judge credit risk by checking with various private agencies, such as Standard & Poor's, which rate the credit risk of different bonds. Sometimes, these bonds are referred to euphemistically, but less graphically, as *below investment grade bonds*.

Bond Prices and Yield One important point to note is the relationship between a bond's price and its yield. Assume that a corporation issues a €1000 bond over a ten-year period with a coupon of 3.5 per cent. For the duration of the ten years, the corporation will pay the bond holder €35 a year in interest and when the bond matures the corporation will pay back the bond holder the €1000 principal. At any time during the ten-year period the bond holder can sell the bond on the bond market. The price they get will depend on the supply and demand of those bonds on the market. The yield of the bond (in simple terms) is given by the $\frac{coupon}{price} \times 100$. Price is quoted as a percentage of the principal.

Assume the bond holder needs to get access to cash (liquidity) quickly – they decide to sell their bond. The price of the bond on the market is €995. The yield on this bond, therefore, is $\frac{35}{995} \times 100 = 3.52\%$. If the seller was able to sell the bond for €1050, the yield would be $\frac{35}{1050} \times 100 = 3.33\%$. This illustrates an important point – there is an inverse relationship between price and yield. As bond prices rise, the yield falls and vice versa.

The reason why bond prices rise and fall on the markets is due to the demand and supply of bonds (the number of people wanting to buy bonds and the number of people wanting to sell bonds). Bond prices (and, therefore, yields) are affected by existing bonds in the market, the issue of new bonds, the likelihood of the bond issuer defaulting and interest rates on other securities. The issue of a new bond is also affected by these factors. If current interest rates are high, new issues have to have a coupon which will compete and vice versa.

The Stock Market One way for BP to raise funds for an oil exploration project is to sell stock in the company. **Stock** represents ownership in a firm and is, therefore, a claim to the future profits that the firm makes. For example, if BP sells a total of 1 000 000 shares of stock, then each share represents ownership of $\frac{1}{1\,000\,000}$ of the business. A stock is also commonly referred to as a *share* or as an *equity*. In this book, we'll use the terms 'share' and 'stock' (and 'stockholder' and 'shareholder') more or less interchangeably.

stock (or share or equity) a claim to partial ownership and the future profits in a firm

The sale of stock to raise money is called *equity finance,* whereas the sale of bonds is called *debt finance.* Although corporations use both equity and debt finance to raise money for new investments, stocks and bonds are very different. The owner of BP shares is a part owner of BP; the owner of a BP bond is a creditor of the corporation. If BP is very profitable, the shareholders enjoy the benefits of these profits, whereas the bondholders get only the interest on their bonds. If BP runs into financial difficulty, the bondholders are paid what they are due before shareholders receive anything at all. Compared to bonds, stocks offer the holder both higher risk and potentially higher return.

As we noted just now, stocks are also called shares or equities. In the UK, bonds are also, confusingly, referred to as 'stock'. This term for government bonds has been in use in England since the late 17th century and is well established. In order to avoid confusion, however, the term is often qualified as *government stock* or *gilt-edged stock*. In general, though, despite the confusing use of language, the term *stock* refers to ownership of a firm.

Corporations can issue stock by selling shares to the public through organized stock exchanges. These first time sales are referred to as the *primary market*. Shares that are subsequently traded among stockholders on stock exchanges is referred to as the *secondary market*. In these transactions, the corporation itself receives no money when its stock changes hands. Most of the world's countries have their own stock exchanges on which the shares of national companies trade.

The prices at which shares trade on stock exchanges are determined by the supply and demand for the stock in these companies. Because stock represents a claim to future profits in a corporation, the demand for a stock (and thus its price) reflects people's perception of the corporation's future profitability. When people become optimistic about a company's future, they raise their demand for its stock and thereby bid up the price of a share of stock. Conversely, when people come to expect a company to have little profit or even losses, the price of a share falls.

Various stock indices are available to monitor the overall level of stock prices for any particular stock market. A *stock index* is computed as an average of a group of share prices. The Dow Jones Industrial Average has been computed regularly for the New York Stock Exchange since 1896. It is now based on the prices of the shares of 30 major US companies. The Financial Times Stock Exchange (FTSE) 100 Index, is based on the top 100 companies (according to the total value of their shares) listed on the London Stock Exchange (LSE), while the FTSE All-Share Index is based on all companies listed on the LSE. Indices of prices on the Frankfurt stock market, based on 30 and 100 companies respectively, are the DAX 30 and DAX 100. The NIKKEI 225 (or just plain NIKKEI Index) is based on the largest 225 companies, in terms of market value of shares, traded on the Tokyo Stock Exchange.

Because share prices reflect expected profitability, stock indices are watched closely as possible indicators of future economic conditions.

Financial Intermediaries

Financial intermediaries are financial institutions through which savers can indirectly provide funds to borrowers. The term *intermediary* reflects the role of these institutions in standing between savers and borrowers. Here we consider two of the most important financial intermediaries – banks and investment funds.

financial intermediaries financial institutions through which savers can indirectly provide funds to borrowers

Banks If the owner of a small business wants to finance an expansion of their business, they probably take a strategy quite different from BP. Unlike BP, a small business person would find it difficult to raise funds in the bond and stock markets. Most buyers of stocks and bonds prefer to buy those issued by larger, more familiar companies. The small business person, therefore, most likely finances their business expansion with a loan from a bank

Banks are the financial intermediaries with which people are most familiar. A primary function of banks is to take in deposits from people who want to save and use these deposits to make loans to people who want to borrow. Banks pay depositors interest on their deposits and charge borrowers slightly higher interest on their loans. The difference between these rates of interest covers the banks' costs and returns some profit to the owners of the banks.

Besides being financial intermediaries, banks play a second important role in the economy: they facilitate purchases of goods and services by allowing people to draw against their deposits, or to use debit cards to transfer money electronically from their account to the account of the person or corporation they are buying something from. In other words, banks help create a special asset that people can use as a *medium of exchange.* A medium of exchange is an item that people can easily use to engage in transactions. A bank's role in providing a medium of exchange distinguishes it from many other financial institutions. Stocks and bonds, like bank deposits, are a possible *store of value* for the wealth that people have accumulated in past saving, but access to this wealth is not as easy, cheap and immediate as just swiping a debit card. For now, we ignore this second role of banks, but we will return to it when we discuss the monetary system later in the book.

Investment or mutual fund An **investment or mutual fund** is a vehicle that allows the public to invest in a selection, or *portfolio*, of various types of shares, bonds, or both shares and bonds. The shareholder of the fund accepts all the risk and return associated with the portfolio. If the value of the portfolio rises, the shareholder benefits; if the value of the portfolio falls, the shareholder suffers the loss.

> **investment or mutual fund** an institution that sells shares to the public and uses the proceeds to buy a portfolio of stocks and bonds

The primary advantage of these funds is that they allow people with small amounts of money to diversify. Buyers of shares and bonds are well advised to heed the adage, 'Don't put all your eggs in one basket.' Because the value of any single stock or bond is tied to the fortunes of one company, holding a single kind of stock or bond is very risky. By contrast, people who hold a diverse portfolio of shares and bonds face less risk because they have only a small stake in each company. Investment funds make this diversification easy. With only a few hundred euros, a person can buy shares in an investment fund and, indirectly, become the part owner or creditor of hundreds of major companies. For this service, the company operating the investment fund charges shareholders a fee, usually between 0.5 and 2.0 per cent of assets each year. Closely related to investment funds are unit trusts, the difference being that when people put money into a unit trust, more 'units' or shares are issued, whereas the only way to buy into an investment fund is to buy existing shares in the fund. For this reason, unit trusts are sometimes referred to as 'open-ended'.

FYI

Key Terms in Stock Markets

When following the stock of any company, there are three key numbers to note. These numbers are reported on the financial pages of some newspapers, and they can be easily obtained online.

- **Price**. The single most important piece of information about a stock is its price. There are invariably several prices reported. The *last* price is the price at which the stock more recently traded. The *previous close* is the price of the last transaction that occurred before the stock exchange closed in its previous day of trading. A news service may also give the *high* and *low* prices over the past day of trading and, sometimes, over the past year as well. It may also report the change from the previous day's closing price.
- **Dividend**. Corporations pay out some of their profits to their shareholders; this amount is called the dividend. (Profits not paid out are called retained earnings and are used by the corporation for additional investment.) News services often report the dividend paid over the previous year for each share of stock. They sometimes report the dividend yield, which is the dividend expressed as a percentage of the stock's price.
- **Price–earnings ratio**. A corporation's earnings, or accounting profit, is the amount of revenue it receives for the sale of its products minus its costs of production as measured by its accountants. *Earnings per share* is the company's total earnings divided by the number of shares of stock outstanding. The *price–earnings ratio*, often called the P/E, is the price of a corporation's stock divided by the amount the corporation earned per share over the past year. Historically, the typical price–earnings ratio is about 15. A higher P/E indicates that a corporation's stock is expensive relative to its recent earnings; this might indicate either that people expect earnings to rise in the future or that the stock is overvalued. Conversely, a lower P/E indicates that a corporation's stock is cheap relative to its recent earnings; this might indicate either that people expect earnings to fall or that the stock is undervalued.

> **SELF TEST** What is stock? What is a bond? How are they different? How are they similar?

Other Financial Instruments

The Financial Crisis of 2007–9 highlighted the role of the range of financial instruments traded in the financial system. These instruments play a role in the financial system but have become increasingly complex; indeed, there were some senior bankers who were accused of not fully understanding what they were trading! In this section we will look at some of these instruments.

Collateralized Debt Obligations (CDOs) CDOs are pools of asset-backed securities which are dependent on the value of the asset that backs them up and the stream of income that flows from these assets. Essentially, CDOs work in the following way. In setting up a CDO, a manager encourages investors to buy bonds, the funds of which are used to buy pools of debt – mortgage debt. This debt is split and rated according to its risk into tranches; low-risk tranches attract low interest rates whilst the riskier tranches attract higher interest rates.

Under '*normal*' circumstances (the relevance of the emphasis will become clear later) the payments by mortgage holders provide sufficient income each month to pay the interest to each of the tranche holders. There is a risk, of course, that some of the mortgage holders in the initial debt could default on payment but historical data enable investors to have some idea of what this risk will be. In the event of default, some of the riskier tranches may not get paid – that is the risk they take and why they get a higher interest rate.

The development of new approaches to risk management enable these structures to be extended further into second and third 'waves' of securitized debt. Asset managers could buy particular tranches of debt (backed, remember, by mortgages ultimately) and mix them with other types of debt and sell them on to other investors. Investors in these higher risk tranches are assured by the ratings on the investment. Calculation of default correlations during the latter part of the 1990s and into the first years of the 2000s was relatively low but when times were not '*normal*' the correlations could start to become far more unstable.

Problems for CDOs began when holders of sub-prime mortgages began to default on payments. The **sub-prime market** offered mortgage opportunities to those not traditionally seen as being part of the financial markets because of their high credit risk and was part of the way in which banks and other lenders sought to increase their lending. Individuals seen as being a relatively low credit risk for mortgage lending were known as the prime market; the term is said to have derived from analogy with the best cuts of meat from an animal. It followed that there was a sub-prime group for whom access to mortgages was altogether more difficult.

 sub-prime market individuals not traditionally seen as being part of the financial markets because of their high credit risk

Some of these people had credit histories that were very poor, some did not have jobs, but in the atmosphere of risk seeking and changed priorities, which typified the financial markets in the early part of the noughties, this group provided lenders with a market opportunity because they were willing to pay high rates of interest on their mortgages.

Initial defaults in the sub-prime market which began around 2005 might have been seen as being 'pin pricks' in the structure but as the defaults began to gather pace the payments to the first tranches began to reduce. Those at the top of the ratings list may have still got paid but the riskier lower tranches began to see their payments dry up. In turn, the asset-backed securities sold in the second and subsequent 'waves' began to see their payments cease and as the sub-prime problem became worse it became clear that it was likely that these subsequent 'waves' would not be paid back and were thus worthless. Holders of this debt (including banks, governments and local governments around the world) found that they had to write-off large assets. The term 'toxic assets' became familiar to many who may never have thought they were affected by high finance. These were mortgage-backed securities and other debt (such as bonds) that were not able to be repaid in many cases because the value of the assets against which they are secured have fallen significantly.

Credit Default Swaps (CDS)
A **credit default swap** is a means by which bondholders can insure themselves against the risk of default.

> **credit default swap** a means by which a bondholder can insure against the risk of default

Whenever a bond is sold there is an associated risk attached to it. In the case of bonds backed by a pool of mortgage debt, such as CDOs, the risk is that the mortgage payer defaults on the payment in some way. CDS are a means of insuring against the risk involved.

To see how this works let us take an example.

Assume a bank has bought a bond in an asset-backed security (in reality of course it might be many bonds) worth €5 million. The bond has a principal, therefore, of €5 million. The coupon payment (the interest on the bond) is 10 per cent. The bond is backed by the stream of cash flows being paid by mortgage holders – the underlying asset to the bond. The bondholder knows that there is a risk that some mortgage holders might default and as a result the bond return might also be in default – i.e. it does not pay the coupon or possibly the principal. If mortgage holders all meet their obligations and pay the money back (the principal) the bank will have earned interest for as long as it held the bond. If the bond was a ten-year bond with a coupon of 10 per cent then the bondholder would have earned a 10 per cent return on the bond for ten years (€500 000 per year for ten years).

The bondholder can go to an insurance company (which could also be another bank or a hedge fund) and take out a policy on the risk. The bank seeking to insure the risk is referred to as the *protection buyer* and the insurance company or other financial institution, the *protection seller*. The policy will agree to restore the bondholder to their original position should the bond default. The bondholder pays the insurance company premiums over the life of the policy, let us assume this is €500 000 a year over ten years, and in return the insurance company would agree to pay the bondholder €5 million if the bond defaults in some way during the period of the agreement.

What the bondholder has done is to swap the risk in the bond with the insurance company. In the event of the bond defaulting then the protection seller pays out to the protection buyer. These CDS could also be traded and in many cases the protection buyer might take out a number of such hedges against its risk. The price of a CDS is quoted in terms of basis points where a basis point is $\frac{1}{100}$ th (0.01) of 1 per cent. The price quoted reflects the cost of protecting debt for a period of time. For example, the price of a CDS for BP might be quoted at 255 bps, suggesting that the cost of protecting €10 million of BP debt for five years would be €255 000 a year.

If the bond was subject to default this would trigger a payment called a *credit event*. If a credit event occurs, there are two ways in which the contract could be closed. One is through a physical settlement. In this case the protection buyer would deliver the bond to the seller who would give the buyer the value of the bond, called par. The CDS market expanded rapidly throughout the 'noughties' leading to multiple trading. The holder of the CDS, therefore, might not actually own the bond in question and so this method of settlement clearly does not work. The growth in the market meant that the number of contracts far outweighed the number of bonds on which they were based. To settle the claims of contract holders through physical means would not be possible. As a consequence, protection sellers undertook to settle the contract claim through cash settlement where the positions were cleared by the transfer of cash.

The protection seller also has to put up some form of collateral to cover its exposure to the possible default as part of the CDS agreement. The size of the exposure in the example above would be €5 million. This would be part of the contract between the insurance seller and the buyer. The amount of the collateral required would depend on the market value of the bond and the credit rating of the protection seller. The market value of the bond can change because the bondholder can sell their bond.

If a bond associated with a mortgage pool is deemed a higher risk, it may become more difficult to sell it and the price would fall. At a lower price the risk involved for the protection buyer is higher and they can exercise a call (known as a *collateral call*) on the protection seller to increase the collateral supplied. If, for example, the price of the bond in the example above fell to 40 cents in the euro, the insurance company would have to find 0.60 × €5 000 000 in additional collateral (€3 million). Equally, if the rating of the protection seller is downgraded then the risk to the protection buyer also rises – the seller may be not be able to meet its obligations. Once again, the protection buyer can call the seller to ask for more collateral to be provided. The insurance company would then have to find more funds to top up the collateral it has to provide to reflect the lower value of the bond.

If the seller was unable to meet its obligations, the buyer would have some protection in the form of the collateral supplied by the seller. If the bond runs its course and matures without any credit event then the collateral is returned to the seller (who also, remember, receives premiums from the buyer).

CDS represent sound business principles when the risk of default is very low, which was the case when they were first developed in the late 1990s and when the bonds being insured were corporate bonds with a low risk attached to them. The expansion of CDS presented a different challenge to the financial markets when the housing market collapse occurred from around 2007.

Summing Up

An advanced economy contains a large variety of financial institutions. In addition to the bond market, the stock market, banks and investment funds, there are also pension funds, insurance companies and – notably in the UK and USA – even the local pawnbroker's shop: places where people who might be deemed bad credit risks can borrow money and leave some valuable item such as a watch or a piece of jewellery as security in case the loan is not repaid. Clearly, these institutions differ in many ways and the products they sell have become more complex in lots of cases. When analyzing the macroeconomic role of the financial system, however, it is more important to keep in mind the similarity of these institutions than the differences. These financial institutions all serve the same goal – directing the resources of savers into the hands of borrowers.

FYI

Dark Pools

Despite having a rather sinister sounding name, dark pools (or alternative trading systems (ATS)) are just an electronic network which puts buyers of shares in touch with sellers. However, the nature of dark pools has raised some concerns and in November 2015, the Securities and Exchange Commission (SEC) in the United States levied fines of up to $20 million (€18m) on ITG and UBS for misuse of information and other abuses.

How do dark pools work? Under normal circumstances, trades in shares are carried out via a number of exchanges such as the London and New York stock exchanges. Traders on those exchanges can see who is doing the buying and who is doing the selling. Any completed transaction can affect the market and traders will be able to amend their positions in the light of this information. Dark pools allow trades to be carried out anonymously so the trade can go through but no one knows – crucially at the time of the trade – who is doing the buying and selling. Dark pools tend to be used for trades where significant volumes of shares are transacted. The following is an outline of how it works.

Assume an institutional investor, such as a pension fund or insurance company, has $1 billion worth of shares in ExxonMobil that it wants to sell. It knows that if it attempts to trade this amount it is likely to affect the market. Typically, this sort of volume would have to be broken up and sold in chunks. If the price of ExxonMobil shares was currently $500 each, then as the sale progresses, the insurance company would end up with lower prices for the latter chunks of shares than the first lots. The average price it gains from the sale would, therefore, be less than $500 each.

The price would fall because the supply of ExxonMobil shares would be rising, traders would see the trades going through and adjust their positions accordingly. If the insurance company carries out the trade via a dark pool, it places the shares into an electronic exchange. In the pool there are buyers and sellers all looking for trades, but anonymously. The use of algorithms to improve the efficiency of the trades in dark pools is common. The algorithm is programmed to search for buyers who want to purchase $1 billion of ExxonMobil shares, for example, and matches the two together. At this point in the trade no-one knows who the traders are. Once the trade is completed then it is announced. The announcement may, or may not, have an effect on the market. The advantage for the pension fund or insurance company is that it completes the trade for the volume of shares it wants to deal and the use of dark pools prevents the market reacting to the sale at the time it is happening and thus affecting the price the seller gets.

(*Continued*)

There has been some criticism of dark pools. It is feared that dark pools may take too much trade away from traditional exchanges. As they develop, more trading will be conducted in secret and in some cases, even though the trades are announced, the identity of the trader is not revealed. Dark pools may discriminate against individual investors who can be affected by the price changes that result from the activity which they could not foresee because of the very nature of the anonymous transactions. In addition, the use of dark pools has expanded with the SEC in 2015 estimating that around 15 per cent of dollar volume stocks are traded on ATS. The original idea of dark pools being useful for trading large blocks of shares has been diluted and trade sizes have been falling.

The SEC is seeking to develop regulations to improve the transparency of dark pools. This might become even more important as dark pool technologies are extended beyond shares to the corporate bond market.

SAVING AND INVESTMENT IN THE NATIONAL INCOME ACCOUNTS

Events that occur within the financial system are central to understanding developments in the overall economy. The institutions that make up this system – the bond market, the stock market, banks and investment funds – have the role of coordinating the economy's saving and investment, which in turn are important determinants of long-run growth in GDP and living standards. As a result, macroeconomists need to understand how financial markets work and how various events and policies affect them.

As a starting point for an analysis of financial markets, we discuss in this section the key macroeconomic variables that measure activity in these markets. Our emphasis here is on accounting. *Accounting* refers to how various numbers are defined and added up. A personal accountant might help an individual add up their income and expenses. A national income accountant does the same thing for the economy as a whole. The national income accounts include, in particular, GDP and the many related statistics.

Some Important Identities

The rules of national income accounting include several important identities. Recall that GDP is both total income in an economy and the total expenditure on the economy's output of goods and services. GDP (denoted as Y) is divided into four components of expenditure: consumption (C), investment (I), government purchases (G) and net exports (NX).

$$Y = C + I + G + NX \qquad \textbf{(24.1)}$$

This equation is an identity because every euro of expenditure that shows up on the left-hand side also shows up in one of the four components on the right-hand side. Because of the way each of the variables is defined and measured, this equation must always hold. Sometimes we make this clear by using an identity sign, with three bars, instead of the usual equals sign with two bars:

$$Y \equiv C + I + G + NX \qquad \textbf{(24.2)}$$

In general, though, we can use the usual equality sign.

In this chapter, we simplify our analysis by assuming that the economy we are examining is closed. A *closed economy* is one that does not interact with other economies, does not engage in international trade in goods and services, and does not engage in international borrowing and lending. Of course, actual economies are *open economies* – that is, they interact with other economies around the world. Nevertheless, assuming a closed economy is a useful simplification with which we can learn some lessons that apply to all economies.

Because a closed economy does not engage in international trade, imports and exports are exactly zero. Therefore, net exports (NX) are also zero which leaves the identity:

$$Y = C + I + G \qquad \textbf{(24.3)}$$

This equation states that GDP is the sum of consumption, investment and government purchases. Each unit of output sold in a closed economy is consumed, invested or bought by the government.

To see what this identity can tell us about financial markets, if we take Y, on the left hand side of the equation, to be GDP, we can subtract from this things that are consumed (consumption spending and government spending). To retain the equation, we must also subtract C and G from the right hand side, which gives:

$$Y - C - G = (C - C) + I + (G - G) \tag{24.4}$$

$$Y - C - G = I \tag{24.5}$$

What remains after paying for consumption and government purchases is called **national saving**, or just saving, and is denoted S. Recall from the circular flow of income diagram in Chapter 20, that there are withdrawals and injections from the circular flow. Saving is one of the withdrawals from the circular flow but reappears in the economy in the form of investment when savings are channelled by financial institutions.

> **national saving (saving)** the total income in the economy that remains after paying for consumption and government purchases

Given $Y - C - G = S$ we can substitute this into equation 24.5 to get:

$$S = I \tag{24.6}$$

This equation states that saving equals investment.

To understand the meaning of national saving, it is helpful to manipulate the definition a bit more. Let T denote the amount that the government collects from households in taxes (a withdrawal from the circular flow) minus the amount it pays back to households in the form of transfer payments (such as social security payments). We can then write national saving in either of two ways:

$$S = Y - C - G \tag{24.7}$$

Or:

$$S = (Y - T - C) + (T - G) \tag{24.8}$$

Equations 24.7 and 24.8 are the same, because the two Ts in equation 24.8 cancel each other, but each reveals a different way of thinking about national saving. In particular, equation 24.8 separates national saving into two pieces: private saving $(Y - T - C)$ and public saving $(T - G)$.

Private saving is the amount of income that households have left after paying their taxes and paying for their consumption. In particular, because households receive income of Y, pay taxes of T and spend C on consumption, private saving is $Y - T - C$. **Public saving** is the amount of tax revenue that the government has left after paying for its spending. The government receives T in tax revenue and spends G on goods and services. If T exceeds G, the government runs a **budget surplus** because it receives more money than it spends. This surplus of $T - G$ represents public saving. If the government spends more than it receives in tax revenue, then G is larger than T. In this case, the government runs a **budget deficit**, and public saving $T - G$ is a negative number. In this case the government has to borrow money to fund spending by issuing sovereign debt in the form of bonds.

> **private saving** the income that households have left after paying for taxes and consumption
> **public saving** the tax revenue that the government has left after paying for its spending
> **budget surplus** where government tax revenue is greater than spending because it receives more money than it spends
> **budget deficit** where government tax revenue is less than spending and the government has to borrow to finance spending

Now consider how these accounting identities are related to financial markets. The equation $S = I$ reveals an important fact: for the economy as a whole, saving must be equal to investment. This fact raises some important questions: what mechanisms lie behind this identity? What coordinates those people who are deciding how much to save and those people who are deciding how much to invest? The answer is the financial system. The bond market, the stock market, banks, investment funds, and other financial markets and intermediaries, stand between the two sides of the $S = I$ equation. They take in the nation's saving and direct it to the nation's investment.

CASE STUDY   **Debt and Deficit**

The Financial Crisis brought the words 'debt' and 'deficit' into almost every household. Prior to the crisis, a number of governments across Europe had been spending more than they raised in taxes and had to borrow to finance the difference. Any borrowing has to be paid back and a vital part of any successful financial system is the trust between both lenders and borrowers. One of the problems which a number of European countries faced was the prospect that they would default on borrowings. If this happens and trust breaks down, the financial system comes under severe pressure.

It is important to distinguish between *government debt* and a *government deficit*. A **government deficit** refers to a situation where a government spends more than it generates in tax revenue over a period and has to borrow to fund spending. For example, if the UK government budgets to spend £750 billion in 2018–19 but only generates £700 billion in tax and other revenue, it will need to borrow £50 billion. The government's deficit for the year is £50 billion. This sum of money becomes part of the **national debt** which is the accumulation of the total debt the government owes. Both the debt and the deficit can be expressed as a percentage of GDP. For example, the UK government deficit was reported by the ONS to be £93.5 billion for the financial year ending in March 2015. This represented 5.1 per cent of GDP. The national debt, however, was reported at £1.6 trillion or 87.5 per cent of GDP. Whilst the deficit had shrunk by £9.6 billion compared to March 2014, the national debt rose by £79.3 billion.

A number of European countries have taken steps to try and reduce their deficits and have put in place austerity policies designed to cut government spending and increase revenue through higher or more widespread taxes or tightening tax loopholes to improve the efficiency of the tax system.

Understanding the difference between debt and deficit is important in appreciating the challenges facing governments.

Eurostat reported the EU28 government deficit in 2014 at €401.8 billion and combined national debt at over €12 trillion. Only Denmark, Germany, Estonia and Luxembourg recorded a budget surplus in 2014. Spain and Ireland both adopted severe austerity policies and both have managed to reduce their deficits; in Ireland's case, its deficit fell from €21.8bn in 2011 to €7.6bn in 2014 and in Spain, the deficit has fallen from €101.3bn to €61.4bn over the same period. The cost of reducing the deficits has not been lost on the populations of both countries.

government deficit a situation where a government spends more than it generates in tax revenue over a period
national debt the accumulation of the total debt owed by a government

The Meaning of Saving and Investment

The terms *saving* and *investment* can sometimes be confusing. Most people use these terms casually and sometimes interchangeably. In contrast, the macroeconomists who put together the national income accounts use these terms carefully and distinctly.

Consider an example. Suppose that Connah earns more than he spends and deposits his unspent income in a bank or uses it to buy a bond or some stock from a corporation. Because Connah's income exceeds his consumption, he adds to the nation's saving. Connah might think of himself as 'investing' his money, but a macroeconomist would call Connah's act saving rather than investment.

In the language of macroeconomics, investment refers to the purchase of new capital, such as equipment or buildings. When Orla borrows from the bank to build herself a new house, she adds to the nation's investment. Similarly, when the O'Connell Corporation issues some new shares and uses the proceeds to build a new brass fittings factory, it also adds to the nation's investment.

Although the accounting identity $S = I$ shows that saving and investment are equal for the economy as a whole, this does not have to be true for every individual household or firm. Connah's saving can be greater than his investment, and he can deposit the excess in a bank. Orla's saving can be less than her investment, and she can borrow the shortfall from a bank. Banks and other financial institutions make these individual differences between saving and investment possible by allowing one person's saving to finance another person's investment.

SELF TEST Define private saving, public saving, national saving and investment. How are they related?

THE MARKET FOR LOANABLE FUNDS

This section will present a model of financial markets which can explain how financial markets coordinate the economy's saving and investment. The model also gives us a tool with which we can analyze various government policies that influence saving and investment.

To keep things simple, we assume that the economy has only one financial market, called the **market for loanable funds**. All savers go to this market to deposit their saving, and all borrowers go to this market to get their loans. Thus, the term *loanable funds* refers to all income that people have chosen to save and lend out, rather than use for their own consumption. In the market for loanable funds, there is one interest rate, which is both the return for saving and the cost of borrowing.

> **market for loanable funds** the market in which those who want to save supply funds, and those who want to borrow to invest demand funds

The assumption of a single financial market, of course, is not literally true. As we have seen, the economy has many types of financial institutions. The purpose of this model is to provide a representative simplification which helps explain and predict.

Supply and Demand for Loanable Funds

The economy's market for loanable funds consists of the supply of and demand for loanable funds and the price in this market is the interest rate. The supply of loanable funds comes from those people who have some extra income they want to save and lend out. This lending can occur directly, such as when a household buys a bond from a firm, or it can occur indirectly, such as when a household makes a deposit in a bank, which in turn uses the funds to make loans. In both cases, saving is the source of the supply of loanable funds.

The demand for loanable funds comes from households and firms who wish to borrow to make investments. This demand includes families taking out mortgages to buy homes, borrowing to buy a new car and firms borrowing to buy new equipment or build factories. In each case, investment is the source of the demand for loanable funds.

The interest rate represents the amount that borrowers pay for loans and the amount that lenders receive on their saving. Because a high interest rate makes borrowing more expensive, the quantity of loanable funds demanded falls as the interest rate rises. Similarly, because a high interest rate makes saving more attractive, the quantity of loanable funds supplied rises as the interest rate rises. In other words, the demand curve for loanable funds slopes downwards, and the supply curve for loanable funds slopes upwards.

Figure 24.1 shows the interest rate that balances the supply and demand for loanable funds. In the equilibrium shown, the interest rate is 5 per cent, and the quantity of loanable funds demanded and the quantity of loanable funds supplied both equal €500 billion.

Shifts in the demand and supply of loanable funds bring about changes to the interest rate. If the interest rate was lower than the equilibrium level because of a shift in demand to the right or of supply to the left, the quantity of loanable funds supplied would be less than the quantity of loanable funds demanded. The resulting shortage of loanable funds would encourage lenders to raise the interest rate they charge. A higher interest rate would encourage saving (thereby increasing the quantity of loanable funds supplied – a movement along the supply curve) and discourage borrowing for investment (thereby decreasing the quantity of loanable funds demanded, a movement along the demand curve). Conversely, if the demand for loanable funds shifts to the left or the supply of loanable funds shifts to the right, the quantity supplied would exceed the quantity demanded. As lenders competed for the scarce borrowers, interest rates would be driven down. In this way, the interest rate approaches the equilibrium level at which the supply and demand for loanable funds balance.

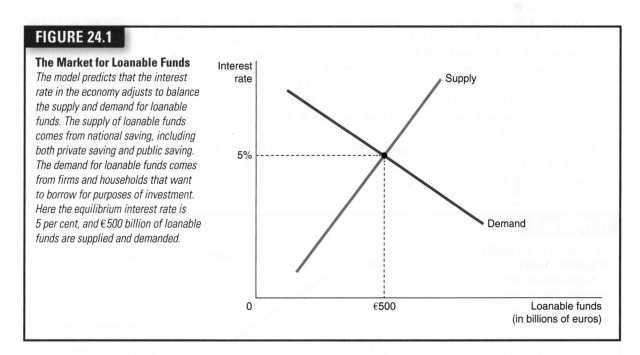

FIGURE 24.1

The Market for Loanable Funds
The model predicts that the interest rate in the economy adjusts to balance the supply and demand for loanable funds. The supply of loanable funds comes from national saving, including both private saving and public saving. The demand for loanable funds comes from firms and households that want to borrow for purposes of investment. Here the equilibrium interest rate is 5 per cent, and €500 billion of loanable funds are supplied and demanded.

Recall that the real interest rate is the difference between the nominal interest rate and the inflation rate $(r_t = i_t - \pi_t)$.

The nominal interest rate is the interest rate as usually reported – the monetary return to saving and cost of borrowing. Because inflation erodes the value of money over time, the real interest rate more accurately reflects the real return to saving and cost of borrowing. Therefore, the supply and demand for loanable funds depends on the real (rather than nominal) interest rate, and the equilibrium in Figure 24.1 should be interpreted as determining the real interest rate in the economy. For the rest of this chapter, when you see the term *interest rate*, you should remember that we are talking about the real interest rate.

This model of the supply and demand for loanable funds shows that financial markets work much like other markets in the economy. The model predicts that the interest rate adjusts to balance supply and demand in the market for loanable funds, it coordinates the behaviour of people who want to save (the suppliers of loanable funds) and the behaviour of people who want to invest (the demanders of loanable funds).

We can now use this model to examine various government policies that affect the economy's saving and investment.

Policy 1: Saving Incentives

We know from Chapter 22 that saving is an important long-run determinant of a nation's productivity. Hence if a country can raise its saving rate, the growth rate of GDP should increase (subject to diminishing marginal productivity) and, over time, the citizens of that country should enjoy a higher standard of living.

Many economists have used the principle that people respond to incentives to suggest that the savings rates in some countries are depressed because of tax laws that discourage saving. Governments collect revenue by taxing income, including interest and dividend income. To see the effects of this policy, consider a 25-year-old who saves €1000 and buys a 30-year bond that pays an interest rate of 9 per cent. In the absence of taxes, the €1000 grows to €13 268 when the individual reaches age 55. Yet if that interest is taxed at a rate of, say, 33 per cent, then the after-tax interest rate is only 6 per cent. In this case, the €1000 grows to only €5743 after 30 years. The tax on interest income substantially reduces the future pay-off from current saving and, as a result, reduces the incentive for people to save.

In response to this problem, many economists and some politicians have sometimes advocated replacing the current income tax with a consumption tax. Under a consumption tax, income that is saved would not be taxed until the saving is later spent; in essence, a consumption tax is like the VAT that European countries impose on many goods and services. VAT is an indirect tax, however, levied on a good or service at the time it is purchased by a final consumer, whereas a consumption tax could also be a direct tax levied on an individual by calculating how much consumer expenditure they carried out over the year and taxing them on that, perhaps at higher and higher rates as the level of consumer expenditure rises.

A more modest proposal is to expand eligibility for special savings accounts that allow people to shelter some of their saving from taxation. Let's consider the effect of such a saving incentive on the market for loanable funds, as illustrated in Figure 24.2.

FIGURE 24.2

An Increase in the Supply of Loanable Funds

A change in the tax laws to encourage more saving would shift the supply of loanable funds to the right from S_1 to S_2. As a result, the equilibrium interest rate would fall, and the lower interest rate would stimulate investment. Here the equilibrium interest rate falls from 5 per cent to 4 per cent, and the equilibrium quantity of loanable funds saved and invested rises from €500 billion to €600 billion.

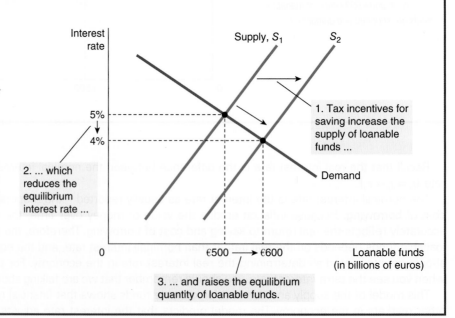

1. Tax incentives for saving increase the supply of loanable funds ...

2. ... which reduces the equilibrium interest rate ...

3. ... and raises the equilibrium quantity of loanable funds.

The tax change alters the incentive for households to save *at any given interest rate,* it would, therefore, affects the quantity of loanable funds supplied at each interest rate. The supply of loanable funds would shift. The demand for loanable funds would remain the same, because the tax change would not directly affect the amount that borrowers want to borrow at any given interest rate.

Because saving would be taxed less heavily, households would increase their saving by consuming a smaller fraction of their income. Households would use this additional saving to increase their deposits in banks or to buy more bonds. The supply of loanable funds would increase, and the supply curve would shift to the right from S_1 to S_2, as shown in Figure 24.2.

Finally, we compare the old and new equilibria. In the figure, the increased supply of loanable funds reduces the interest rate from 5 per cent to 4 per cent. The lower interest rate raises the quantity of loanable funds demanded from €500 billion to €600 billion. That is, the shift in the supply curve moves the market equilibrium along the demand curve. With a lower cost of borrowing, households and firms are motivated to borrow more to finance greater investment. Our model predicts that if a reform of the tax laws encouraged greater saving, the result would be lower interest rates and greater investment.

Although this analysis of the effects of increased saving is widely accepted among economists, there is less consensus about what kinds of tax changes should be enacted. Many economists endorse tax reform aimed at increasing saving in order to stimulate investment and growth. Yet others are sceptical that these tax changes would have much effect on national saving. Crucial to the outcome is the **interest elasticity of demand and supply** – the responsiveness of the demand and supply of loanable funds to changes in the interest rate. Sceptics also doubt the equity of the proposed reforms. They argue that, in many cases, the benefits of the tax changes would accrue primarily to the wealthy, who are least in need of tax relief.

interest elasticity of demand and supply the responsiveness of the demand and supply of loanable funds to changes in the interest rate

Policy 2: Investment Incentives

Suppose that the government passed a tax reform aimed at making investment more attractive. In essence, this is what governments do when they institute tax allowances on investment, sometimes referred to as *investment tax credits.* These allowances give tax advantages to any firm building a new factory or buying a new piece of equipment. Let's consider the effect of such a tax reform on the market for loanable funds, as illustrated in Figure 24.3.

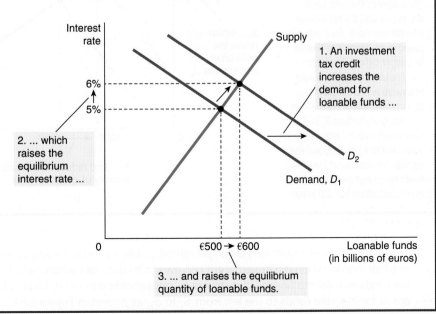

FIGURE 24.3

An Increase in the Demand for Loanable Funds

If the passage of an investment tax credit encouraged firms to invest more, the demand for loanable funds would increase. As a result, the equilibrium interest rate would rise, and the higher interest rate would stimulate saving. Here, when the demand curve shifts from D_1 to D_2, the equilibrium interest rate rises from 5 per cent to 6 per cent, and the equilibrium quantity of loanable funds saved and invested rises from €500 billion to €600 billion.

Interest rate

Supply

6%

5%

2. ... which raises the equilibrium interest rate ...

1. An investment tax credit increases the demand for loanable funds ...

D_2

Demand, D_1

0   €500 → €600   Loanable funds (in billions of euros)

3. ... and raises the equilibrium quantity of loanable funds.

Tax allowances on investment rewards firms that borrow and invest in new capital, it would alter investment at any given interest rate and, thereby, change the demand for loanable funds. By contrast, because the tax credit would not affect the amount that households save at any given interest rate, it would not affect the supply of loanable funds.

Because firms would have an incentive to increase investment at any interest rate, the quantity of loanable funds demanded would be higher at any given interest rate. Thus, the demand curve for loanable funds would move to the right, as shown by the shift from D_1 to D_2 in Figure 24.3.

The increased demand for loanable funds raises the interest rate from 5 per cent to 6 per cent, and the higher interest rate in turn increases the quantity of loanable funds supplied from €500 billion to €600 billion, as households respond by increasing the amount they save (a movement along the supply curve). Thus, if a reform of the tax system encouraged greater investment, the result would be higher interest rates and greater saving.

Policy 3: Government Budget Deficits and Surpluses

Recall that a *budget deficit* is an excess of government spending over tax revenue. Governments finance budget deficits by borrowing in the bond market, and the accumulation of past government borrowing is called the government or national debt. A *budget surplus,* an excess of tax revenue over government spending, can be used to repay some of the government debt. If government spending exactly equals tax revenue, the government is said to have a *balanced budget.*

Imagine that the government starts with a balanced budget and then, because of a tax cut or a spending increase, starts running a budget deficit. Figure 24.4 shows what our model predicts will happen.

National saving – the source of the supply of loanable funds – is composed of private saving and public saving. A change in the government budget balance represents a change in public saving and, thereby, in the supply of loanable funds. Because the budget deficit does not influence the amount that households and firms want to borrow to finance investment at any given interest rate, it does not alter the demand for loanable funds.

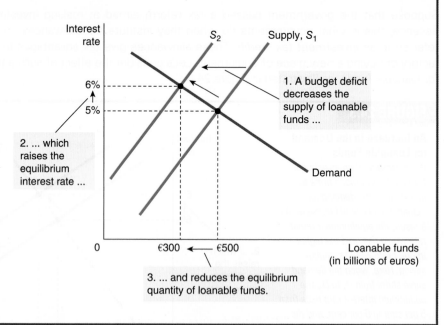

FIGURE 24.4

The Effect of a Government Budget Deficit

When the government spends more than it receives in tax revenue, the resulting budget deficit lowers national saving. The supply of loanable funds decreases, and the equilibrium interest rate rises. Thus, when the government borrows to finance its budget deficit, it 'crowds out' households and firms who otherwise would borrow to finance investment. Here, when the supply shifts from S_1 to S_2, the equilibrium interest rate rises from 5 per cent to 6 per cent, and the equilibrium quantity of loanable funds saved and invested falls from €500 billion to €300 billion.

1. A budget deficit decreases the supply of loanable funds ...

2. ... which raises the equilibrium interest rate ...

3. ... and reduces the equilibrium quantity of loanable funds.

When the government runs a budget deficit, public saving is negative, and this reduces national saving. In other words, when the government borrows to finance its budget deficit, it reduces the supply of loanable funds available to finance investment by households and firms. Thus, a budget deficit shifts the supply curve for loanable funds to the left from S_1 to S_2, as shown in Figure 24.4.

In the figure, when the budget deficit reduces the supply of loanable funds, the interest rate rises from 5 per cent to 6 per cent. This higher interest rate then alters the behaviour of the households and firms that participate in the loan market. In particular, many demanders of loanable funds are discouraged by the higher interest rate (a movement along the demand curve). Fewer families buy new homes, and fewer firms choose to build new factories. The fall in investment because of government borrowing is called **crowding out** and is represented in the figure by the movement along the demand curve from a quantity of €500 billion in loanable funds to a quantity of €300 billion. That is, when the government borrows to finance its budget deficit, it crowds out private borrowers who are trying to finance investment.

> **crowding out** a decrease in investment that results from government borrowing

Our model predicts that when the government reduces national saving by running a budget deficit, the interest rate rises and investment falls. Because investment is important for long-run economic growth, government budget deficits reduce the economy's growth rate. This analysis is the reason why many governments seek to reduce borrowing and is behind many of the austerity policies which have been instituted across countries in Europe since the Financial Crisis.

Government budget surpluses work the opposite way to budget deficits. When government collects more in tax revenue than it spends, its saves the difference by retiring some of the outstanding government debt. This budget surplus, or public saving, contributes to national saving. Thus, a budget surplus increases the supply of loanable funds, reduces the interest rate and stimulates investment. Higher investment, in turn, means greater capital accumulation and more rapid economic growth.

CONCLUSION

'Neither a borrower nor a lender be', Polonius advises his son in Shakespeare's *Hamlet*. If everyone followed this advice, this chapter would have been unnecessary.

Few economists would agree with Polonius. In our economy, people borrow and lend often, and usually for good reason. You may borrow one day to start your own business or to buy a home. People may lend to you in the hope that the interest you pay will allow them to enjoy a more prosperous retirement. The financial system has the job of coordinating all this borrowing and lending activity.

In many ways, financial markets are like other markets in the economy. The price of loanable funds – the interest rate – is governed by the forces of supply and demand, just as other prices in the economy are. In one way, however, financial markets are special. Financial markets, unlike most other markets, serve the important role of linking the present and the future. Those who supply loanable funds – savers – do so because they want to convert some of their current income into future purchasing power. A decision to save is a postponement of consumption in the present to consumption at some point in the future. The time element in these decisions is referred to as *intertemporal choice* and is a very important element in the research and analysis of financial markets. When interest rates change, economic actors respond by changing consumption in time period *t* and postponing consumption to time period *t + n*. This is called the **intertemporal substitution effect** and the rate at which economic actors respond to changes in the interest rate by changing consumption and savings decisions. Those who demand loanable funds – borrowers – do so because they want to invest today in order to have additional capital in the future to produce goods and services. Thus, well-functioning financial markets are important not only for current generations but also for future generations who will inherit many of the resulting benefits.

> **intertemporal substitution effect** the response of economic actors to changes in the interest rate by changing consumption and savings decisions

IN THE NEWS

Boosting Investment

When governments review their tax and spending plans, businesses often call for tax breaks to encourage investment. The UK is no exception as this article highlights.

Capital Allowances

In April 2016, the UK Treasury published plans for restructuring business taxes. Part of the reason was to try to provide a firm basis on which firms could plan for the future and in particular, planning their investment. The Confederation of British Industry (CBI), an organization representing some 190 000 businesses in the UK, said that the UK was lagging behind its key competitors in investment in physical capital such as plant, equipment, buildings, machinery and vehicles. The CBI noted that key competitors spend around 20 per cent of GDP on such investment whereas the UK only spends around 16 per cent.

Part of the reason for the weaker spending on investment by the UK, according to the CBI, is the less generous capital allowances in the UK compared to some of its competitors. The rules mean that firms have to finance investment in plant and machinery and cannot offset these costs against taxable profits. If capital allowances are broadened, the CBI says that it would provide an incentive for firms to boost investment and this would ultimately be a benefit to the UK economy. Not only does capital investment improve productivity but it also provides jobs for workers in industries making capital equipment. In addition, the CBI suggested that a more generous capital allowance regime would encourage foreign capital to the UK. In a report published by the CBI, it stated that if the UK capital allowances were brought in line more closely to other G7 countries, total investment could rise by £50 billion and reach around 17.4 per cent of GDP.

Road construction may be one way in which growth can be boosted and capital allowances may help in encouraging such investment.

Questions

1 Why do firms need to have certainty when planning investment?

2 Should the government be responsible for providing incentives to invest? Should businesses themselves not take the responsibility (and reward) from increasing investment?

3 If broader capital allowances were introduced, what effects might this have on the market for loanable funds? Try to consider different outcomes in your analysis and specify what factors determine the different outcomes.

4 Why do the CBI argue that investment is not only good for firms but it is also good for the UK?

5 Why is the financial system important in ensuring that firms who want to invest can do so?

SUMMARY

- The financial system of an advanced economy is made up of many types of financial institutions, such as the bond market, the stock market, banks and investment funds. All of these institutions act to direct the resources of households, who want to save some of their income, into the hands of households and firms who want to borrow.

- National income accounting identities reveal some important relationships among macroeconomic variables. In particular, for a closed economy, national saving must equal investment. Financial institutions are the mechanism through which the economy matches one person's saving with another person's investment.

- The interest rate is determined by the supply and demand for loanable funds. The supply of loanable funds comes from households who want to save some of their income and lend it out. The demand for loanable funds comes from households and firms who want to borrow for investment. To analyze how any policy or event affects the interest rate, one must consider how it affects the supply and demand for loanable funds.

- National saving equals private saving plus public saving. A government budget deficit represents negative public saving and, therefore, reduces national saving and the supply of loanable funds available to finance investment. When a government budget deficit crowds out investment, it reduces the growth of productivity and GDP.

QUESTIONS FOR REVIEW

1 What is the role of the financial system?

2 Name and describe two markets that are part of the financial system in the economy of the country in which you are studying.

3 What is a financial intermediary? Name and describe two financial intermediaries.

4 Why is it important for people who own stocks and bonds to diversify their holdings? What type of financial institution makes diversification easier?

5 What is national saving? What is private saving? What is public saving? How are these three variables related?

6 What is a collateralized debt obligation?

7 How do credit default swaps help reduce the risk involved in buying bonds?

8 What is investment? How is it related to national saving?

9 Describe a change in the tax system that might increase private saving. If this policy were implemented, how would it affect the market for loanable funds?

10 What is a government budget deficit? How does it affect interest rates, investment and economic growth?

PROBLEMS AND APPLICATIONS

1 For each of the following pairs, which bond would you expect to pay a higher interest rate? Explain.

   a. A bond of the UK government or a bond of an east European government.
   b. A bond that repays the principal in year 2020 or a bond that repays the principal in year 2035.
   c. A bond from BP or a bond from a software company operating from a business park on the outskirts of a large city.
   d. A bond issued by the national government or a bond issued by a local authority.

2 What is the difference between gambling at cards or in lotteries or on the race track, and gambling on the stock market? What social purpose do you think is served by the existence of the stock market?

3 Declines in share prices are sometimes viewed as harbingers of future declines in real GDP. Why do you suppose that might be true?

4 When the Greek government asked for support from the European Union to repay bonds that were coming up for maturity, interest rates rose on bonds issued by a number of other EU countries like Portugal, Spain and Ireland. Why do you suppose this happened? What can you predict happened to the price of bonds from these countries during this period?

5 What factors might affect the decisions of economic actors to save more today for consumption in the future? Why are the decisions of economic actors today important for the welfare of economic actors in the future?

6 Explain the difference between saving and investment as defined by a macroeconomist. Which of the following situations represent investment? Saving? Explain.

   a. Your family takes out a mortgage and buys a new house.
   b. You use your €500 wage payment to buy stock in BP.
   c. Your flatmate earns €200 and deposits it in her account at a bank.
   d. You borrow €5000 from a bank to buy a car to use in your pizza delivery business.

7 Suppose GDP is €2 trillion, taxes are €0.6 trillion, private saving is €0.2 trillion and public saving is €0.1 trillion. Assuming this economy is closed, calculate consumption, government purchases, national saving and investment.

8 Suppose that BP is considering exploring a new oil field.

   a. Assuming that BP needs to borrow money in the bond market to finance the purchase of new oil rigs and drilling machinery, why would an increase in interest rates affect BP's decision about whether to carry out the exploration?
   b. If BP has enough of its own funds to finance the development of the new oil field without borrowing, would an increase in interest rates still affect BP's decision about whether to undertake the new project? Explain.

9 Suppose the government borrows €5 billion more next year than this year.

   a. Use a supply-and-demand diagram to analyze this policy. Does the interest rate rise or fall?
   b. What happens to investment? To private saving? To public saving? To national saving? Compare the size of the changes to the €5 billion of extra government borrowing.
   c. How does the elasticity of supply of loanable funds affect the size of these changes?
   d. How does the elasticity of demand for loanable funds affect the size of these changes?
   e. Suppose households believe that greater government borrowing today implies higher taxes to pay off the government debt in the future. What does this belief do to private saving and the supply of loanable funds today? Does it increase or decrease the effects discussed in parts (a) and (b)?

10 This chapter explains that investment can be increased both by reducing taxes on private saving and by reducing the government budget deficit.

   a. Why is it difficult to implement both of these policies at the same time?
   b. What would you need to know about private saving in order to judge which of these two policies would be a more effective way to raise investment?

THE BASIC TOOLS OF FINANCE

This chapter introduces some tools that help understand the decisions that people make as they participate in financial markets. The field of **finance** – a sub-discipline of economics – develops these tools in great detail, and you may choose to take modules as part of your studies that focus on this topic. Because the financial system is so important to the functioning of the economy, many of the basic insights of finance are central to understanding how the economy works. The tools of finance may also help you think through some of the decisions that you will make in your own life.

> **finance** the field of economics that studies how people make decisions regarding the allocation of resources over time and the handling of risk

This chapter takes up three topics. First, we discuss how to compare sums of money at different points in time. Second, we discuss how to manage risk. Third, we build on our analysis of time and risk to examine what determines the value of an asset, such as a share of stock.

PRESENT VALUE: MEASURING THE TIME VALUE OF MONEY

Imagine that someone offered to give you €100 today or €100 in ten years. Which would you choose? The rational answer would be that getting €100 today is better, because you can always deposit the money in a bank, still have it in ten years and earn interest on the €100 along the way. The lesson: money today is more valuable than the same amount of money in the future.

Now consider a harder question: imagine that someone offered you €100 today or €200 in ten years. Which would you choose? To answer this question, you need some way to compare sums of money from different points in time. Economists do this with a concept called *present value*. The **present value** of any future sum of money is the amount today that would be needed, at current interest rates, to produce that future sum. Put another way, what sum of money would you need to put into an interest-bearing account at a particular interest rate to generate the future sum; what is that future sum worth in today's terms? The answer to this question allows comparison of sums of money over time. If the value of a future sum expressed in today's terms is greater than the initial sum, then it is worth accepting and vice versa.

> **present value** the amount of money today that would be needed to produce, using prevailing interest rates, a given future amount of money

To learn how to use the concept of present value, let's work through a couple of examples.

Question: If you put €100 in a bank account today, how much will it be worth in N years? That is, what will be the **future value** of this €100? Here we are looking at the future value as the amount of money in the future that an amount of money today will yield, given prevailing interest rates.

 future value the amount of money in the future that an amount of money today will yield, given prevailing interest rates

Answer: Let's use r to denote the interest rate expressed in decimal form (an interest rate of 5 per cent means $r = 0.05$). Suppose that interest is paid annually and that the interest paid remains in the bank account to earn more interest – a process called **compounding**. Then the €100 will become:

$(1 + r) \times €100$	*after one year*
$(1 + r) \times (1 + r) \times €100$	*after two years*
$(1 + r) \times (1 + r) \times (1 + r) \times €100$	*after three years*
$(1 + r)^N \times €100$	*after N years*

For example, if we are investing at an interest rate of 5 per cent for ten years, then the future value of the 100 will be $(1.05)^{10} \times €100$, which is €163 (rounded up to the nearest whole euro. Note: we will follow this rounding up for the remainder of the chapter).

 compounding the accumulation of a sum of money in, say, a bank account, where the interest earned remains in the account to earn additional interest in the future

Question: Now suppose you are going to be paid €200 in N years (guaranteed risk-free). What is the *present value* of this future payment at an interest rate of 5 per cent? That is, how much would you have to deposit in a bank right now at an interest rate of 5 per cent to yield €200 in N years?

Answer: To answer this question, turn the previous answer on its head. In the first question, we computed a future value from a present value by *multiplying* by the factor $(1 + r)^N$. To compute a present value from a future value, we *divide* by the factor $(1 + r)^N$. Thus, the present value of €200 in N years is $\frac{€200}{(1 + r)^N}$.

If we take the answer to this calculation and deposit it in a bank today, after N years it would become $(1 + r)^N \times \left[\frac{€200}{(1 + r)^N}\right]$, which is €200. For instance, if the interest rate is 5 per cent, the present value of €200 in ten years is $\frac{€200}{(1.05)^{10}} = €123$. If €123 deposited in a bank today, at an interest rate of 5% would become €200 in ten years' time.

This illustrates the general formula: if r is the interest rate, then an amount X to be received in N years has present value of $\frac{X}{(1 + r)^N}$.

Let's now return to our question: should you choose €100 today or €200 in ten years? Our calculation tells us that the present value of €200, at an interest rate of 5 per cent, is €123. This suggests that, given the interest rate and the absence of risk, you should prefer the €200 in ten years. The future €200 has a present value of €123, which is greater than €100. You are better off waiting for the future sum. Knowing the present value now allows us to pose the question in a slightly different way – would you prefer €100 today or €123 today? This, of course, is a much easier question to answer assuming you are being rational. The use of present values allows us to be able to rephrase questions on future value in this way to aid decision-making.

The answer to the question is dependent on the interest rate. If the interest rate were 8 per cent, then the present value of €200 in ten years would be $\dfrac{€200}{(1.08)^{10}} = €93$. In this case, you should take the €100 today (as above, if we turn the question round would you rather have €100 today or €93 today?). Why should the interest rate matter for your choice? The answer is that the higher the interest rate, the more you can earn by depositing your money at the bank, so the more attractive getting €100 today becomes.

Applying the Concept of Present Value

The concept of present value is useful in many applications, including the decisions that companies face when evaluating investment projects. For instance, imagine that Citroën is thinking about building a new car factory. Suppose that the factory will cost €100 million today and will yield the company €200 million in ten years. Should Citroën undertake the project? You can see that this decision is exactly like the one we have been studying. To make its decision, the company will compare the present value of the €200 million return to the €100 million cost.

The company's decision, therefore, will depend on the interest rate. If the interest rate is 5 per cent, then the present value of the €200 million return from the factory is €123 million, and the company will choose to pay the €100 million cost. By contrast, if the interest rate is 8 per cent, then the present value of the return is only €93 million, and the company might decide to forgo the project. Thus, the concept of present value helps explain why investment – and thus the quantity of loanable funds demanded – declines when the interest rate rises. We must remember that the decision will also have to take account of many other factors such as risk, changing interest rates and inflation and is thus far more complex but the use of present value aids decision-making.

Here is another application of present value: suppose you win the Euro Millions Lottery and you are given a choice between €20 000 a year for 50 years (totalling €1 000 000) or an immediate payment of €400 000. Which would you choose? To make the right choice, you need to calculate the present value of the stream of payments. After performing fifty calculations similar to those above (one calculation for each payment) and adding up the results, you would learn that the present value of this million-euro prize at a 7 per cent interest rate is €256 000. You are better off picking the immediate payment of €400 000. The million euros may seem like more money, but the future cash flows, once discounted to the present, are worth far less.

SELF TEST The interest rate is 7 per cent. What is the present value of €150 to be received in ten years? What is the present value if the interest rate is 2 per cent and 4 per cent?

MANAGING RISK

Decision-making will always involve some element of risk. In the examples on present value above, we ignored risk but seeking to understand and take account of risk is vital in any decision-making. **Risk** is the probability of something happening which results in a loss or some degree of hazard or damage. The rational response to risk is not necessarily to avoid it at any cost, but to take it into account in your decision-making. Let's consider how a person might do that.

risk the probability of something happening which results in a loss or some degree of hazard or damage

Risk Aversion

Research suggests that people tend to be **risk averse**. This means more than simply people dislike bad things happening to them. It means that they dislike bad things more than they like comparable good things. (This is also reflected in *loss aversion* – research suggests that losing something makes people twice as miserable as gaining something makes them happy!)

risk averse exhibiting a dislike of uncertainty

For example, suppose a friend offers you the following opportunity. They flip a coin. If it comes up heads, they will pay you €1000. If it comes up tails, you will have to pay them €1000. Would you accept the bargain? You wouldn't if you were risk averse, even though the probability of winning is the same as the probability of losing (50 per cent). For a risk-averse person, the pain from losing the €1000 would exceed the gain from winning €1000.

Economists have developed models of risk aversion using the concept of *utility*, which is a person's subjective measure of well-being or satisfaction. Every level of wealth provides a certain amount of utility, as shown by the utility function in Figure 25.1. The function exhibits the property of diminishing marginal utility: the more wealth a person has, the less utility they get from an additional euro. Thus, in the figure, the utility function gets flatter as wealth increases. Because of diminishing marginal utility, the utility gained from winning €1000 is less than from losing €1000. As a result, people are risk averse.

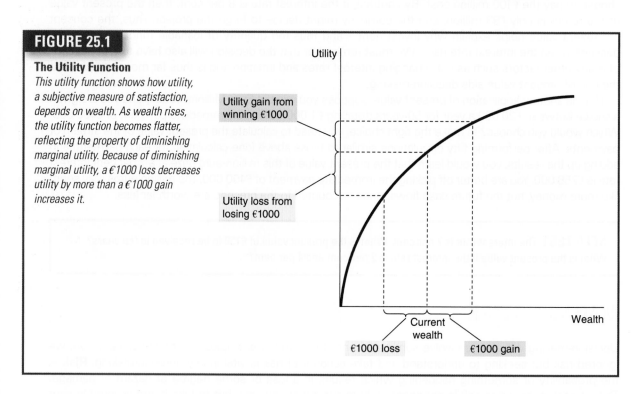

FIGURE 25.1

The Utility Function
This utility function shows how utility, a subjective measure of satisfaction, depends on wealth. As wealth rises, the utility function becomes flatter, reflecting the property of diminishing marginal utility. Because of diminishing marginal utility, a €1000 loss decreases utility by more than a €1000 gain increases it.

Risk aversion provides the starting point for explaining various things we observe in the economy. Let's consider three of them: insurance, diversification and the risk–return trade-off.

The Markets for Insurance

One way to deal with risk is to buy insurance. The general feature of insurance contracts is that a person facing a risk pays a fee to an insurance company, which in return agrees to accept all or part of the risk. There are many types of insurance. Car insurance covers the risk of your being in a car accident, fire insurance covers the risk that your house will burn down, and life assurance covers the risk that you will die and leave your family without income.

In a sense, every insurance contract is a gamble. It is possible that you will not be in a car accident or that your house will not burn down. In most years, you will pay the insurance company the premium and get nothing in return except peace of mind. Indeed, the insurance company is counting on the fact that most people will not make claims on their policies; otherwise it couldn't pay out the large claims to those few who are unlucky and still stay in business.

From the standpoint of the economy as a whole, the role of insurance is not to eliminate the risks inherent in life but to spread them around more efficiently. Consider fire insurance, for instance. Owning fire insurance does not reduce the risk of losing your home in a fire. If that unlucky event occurs, the insurance company compensates you. The risk, rather than being borne by you alone, is shared among the thousands of insurance company shareholders. Because people are risk averse, it is easier for 10 000 people to bear $\dfrac{1}{10\,000}$ of the risk than for one person to bear the entire risk themselves.

The markets for insurance suffer from two types of problems, *adverse selection* and *moral hazard* which we covered in Chapter 12. Insurance companies are aware of these problems, and the price of insurance reflects these risks that the insurance company will face after the insurance is bought. The high price of insurance is why some people, especially those who know themselves to be low risk, decide against buying insurance and, instead, endure some of life's uncertainty on their own.

FYI

Pricing Risk

We have seen how bond issues are a means by which firms can borrow money. The buyer has to have confidence that they will get their money back and also receive an appropriate reward for lending the money in the first place. There is a risk involved that the issuer will not be able to pay back the money and that risk is associated with a probability. If the issuer is very sound then the probability of default may be close to zero, but if the issuer is extremely weak then the probability is closer to 1. We saw in Chapter 24 how financial markets now deal in pools of debt (collections of different types of loans sold to an investor). As debt is pooled the outcomes become more varied. In any given pool of mortgage debt, for example, there will be some borrowers who will default and not be able to pay off their mortgages – possibly because of family bereavement or loss of their job. Other mortgage holders may look to pay off their mortgages early, some may move house and thus settle their mortgage, some will increase monthly payments or pay lump sums to help reduce the repayment period of their mortgage and so on. Assessing probabilities with such a wide range of outcomes becomes difficult.

The risk involved with such debt is therefore difficult to assess with any certainty. However, investors want to price risk as part of their decision-making so they can judge the value of an asset. If an asset is very risky then the expected returns will need to be higher and vice versa. In order to have an efficient market, that risk has to be priced and the information on which the risk is based has to be reliable, accurate – and understood.

Let's consider an example. In your class there may be a number of students that you associate with every day. Take any one individual and we can identify a number of 'risks' for that person. For example, there is a risk that the individual:

- fails their exams and has to leave the course
- will be involved in a car crash
- will travel on an aircraft more than five times a year
- may be mugged
- may get flu.

What are the chances of these events happening? The analysis of such outcomes is what actuaries in the insurance industry have to do. An estimate of the probability of such events happening can be derived from analysis of

(Continued)

data, specifically historical data. It is possible, therefore, to gather data on the average 19-year-old student coming from a particular area and with a particular background, and use this data to arrive at the probability of the event occurring. Historical data tell us, for example, that young people aged between 18 and 24 are more likely to be mugged than the elderly, despite popular perception. If we are able to identify these probabilities then they can be priced. Securities can be issued based on the chances of these things happening – the more likely the event to occur, the higher the price and vice versa.

Whilst it may be possible to identify probabilities for an individual it may be more problematic when looking at relationships between individuals. For example, if person X fails their exams what is the probability that you will also fail your exams? If that individual gets flu what are the chances that you also get flu? In both cases the probability might depend on your relationship with that person. If you spend a lot of time with that person then it may be that you share similar distractions – going out every night instead of studying, skipping lectures and so on. If this were the case then the probability of you also failing your exams and getting flu might be high, but if you have no relationship at all then the chance of you sharing bad habits which lead you to also failing your exams are lower. However, given that you share some time with that person in a lecture hall or seminar room, for example, might mean that the probability of also getting flu is relatively high.

Looking at such relationships involves the concept of correlation – the extent to which there is any statistical relationship between two variables. If person X is involved in a car crash (and you were not in the car with them) what is the chance of you also being involved in a car crash? The chances are the correlation is very low; the probability of you both getting mugged is higher regardless of the relationship between you and so there will be a stronger correlation in this instance. The correlation is likely to become more and more unstable the more variables are introduced (number of students in this example). In the case of pools of debt, the same problems arise and the efficiency of the information on which investors are basing their decision becomes ever more complex; probabilities become very difficult to assess and, therefore, to price.

Actuaries have been studying these types of correlations for some years. Issuing life assurance involves a risk. Life assurance means that the event covered – the death of an individual – will occur at some point in the future (unlike insurance where the event might never happen). The job of the actuary is to provide information to the insurer on the chances of death occurring under different situations. Where information becomes available which indicates risk factors change, actuaries have to incorporate this into models to help insurers price the risk adequately (i.e. set the premiums for the policy). In the 1980s much work was done on studying a phenomenon known as stress cardiomyopathy, a condition for which, in the wake of some exceptional emotional trauma, the human brain releases chemicals into the bloodstream that leads to a weakening of the heart and an increased chance of death. The condition has been referred to as a 'broken heart' because it seemed to manifest itself in particular where one partner dies soon after the death of the other. A study by Spreeuw, J. and Wang, X. (2008), *'Modelling the short-term dependence between two remaining lifetimes'*, showed that following the death of a female partner, a male was over six times more likely to die than than if their partner had not died, and women more than twice as likely. The conclusion for the insurance industry is to take such information and build it into the pricing of offering joint-life policies.

Diversification of Idiosyncratic Risk

The traditional wisdom of the adage: 'Don't put all your eggs in one basket.' Has been turned into a science. It goes by the name **diversification**.

 diversification the reduction of risk achieved by replacing a single risk with a large number of smaller unrelated risks

The market for insurance is one example of diversification. Imagine a town with 10 000 homeowners, each facing the risk of a house fire. If someone starts an insurance company and each person in town becomes both a shareholder and a policyholder of the company, they all reduce their risk through diversification. Each person now faces $\dfrac{1}{10\,000}$ of the risk of 10 000 possible fires, rather than the entire risk of a single fire in their own home. Unless the entire town catches fire at the same time, the downside that each person faces is much smaller.

When people use their savings to buy financial assets, they can also reduce risk through diversification. A person who buys stock in a company is placing a bet on the future profitability of that company. That bet is often quite risky because companies' fortunes are hard to predict. Microsoft evolved from a start-up by some geeky teenagers into one of the world's most valuable companies in only a few years; Enron, a former US energy company which became insolvent with the loss of millions to investors and the jobs of workers because of fraud, went from one of the world's most respected companies to an almost worthless one in only a few months. Fortunately, a shareholder need not tie their own fortune to that of any single company. Risk can be reduced by placing a large number of small bets, rather than a small number of large ones.

Figure 25.2 shows how the risk of a portfolio of shares depends on the number of shares in the portfolio. Risk is measured here with a statistic called *standard deviation*, which you may have learned about in a mathematics or statistics course. Standard deviation measures the volatility of a variable – that is, how much the variable is likely to fluctuate. The higher the standard deviation of a portfolio's return, the more volatile and riskier it is.

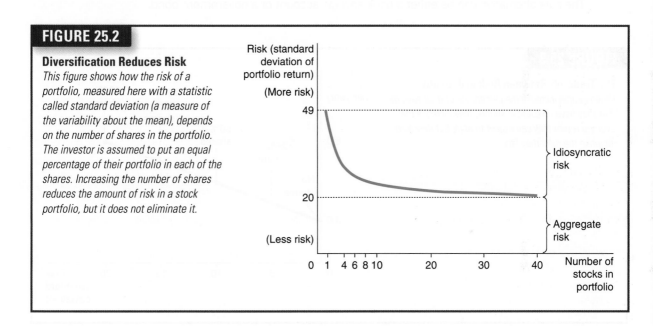

FIGURE 25.2

Diversification Reduces Risk

This figure shows how the risk of a portfolio, measured here with a statistic called standard deviation (a measure of the variability about the mean), depends on the number of shares in the portfolio. The investor is assumed to put an equal percentage of their portfolio in each of the shares. Increasing the number of shares reduces the amount of risk in a stock portfolio, but it does not eliminate it.

The figure shows that the risk of a stock portfolio reduces substantially as the number of shares increase. For a portfolio with a single share, the standard deviation is 49 per cent. Going from 1 share to 10 shares eliminates about half the risk. Going from 10 to 20 shares reduces the risk by another 13 per cent. As the number of shares continues to increase, risk continues to fall, although the reductions in risk after 20 or 30 shares are small.

Notice that it is impossible to eliminate all risk by increasing the number of stocks or shares in the portfolio. Diversification can eliminate **idiosyncratic risk** – the uncertainty associated with specific companies. But diversification cannot eliminate **aggregate risk** – the uncertainty associated with the entire economy, which affects all companies. For example, when the economy goes into a recession, many companies experience falling sales, reduced profit and low stock returns. Diversification reduces the risk of holding stocks, but it does not eliminate it.

idiosyncratic risk risk that affects only a single economic actor
aggregate risk risk that affects all economic actors at once

The Trade-Off Between Risk and Return

There is a trade-off between risk and return which is at the heart of understanding financial decisions. Risks are inherent in holding shares, even in a diversified portfolio. Risk-averse people are willing to accept this uncertainty because they are compensated for doing so. Historically, shares have offered much higher rates of return than alternative financial assets, such as bonds and bank savings accounts. Over the past two centuries, stocks have offered an average real return of about 8 per cent per year, while short-term government bonds paid a real return of only 3 per cent per year.

When deciding how to allocate their savings, people have to decide how much risk they are willing to undertake to earn the higher return. Figure 25.3 illustrates the risk-return trade-off for a person choosing to allocate their portfolio between two asset classes:

- The first asset class is a diversified group of risky stocks, with an average return of 8 per cent and a standard deviation of 20 per cent. (Note that a normal random variable stays within two standard deviations of its average about 95 per cent of the time. Thus, while actual returns are centred around 8 per cent, they typically vary from a gain of 48 per cent to a loss of 32 per cent.)
- The second asset class is a safe alternative. With a return of 3 per cent and a standard deviation of zero. The safe alternative can be either a bank savings account or a government bond.

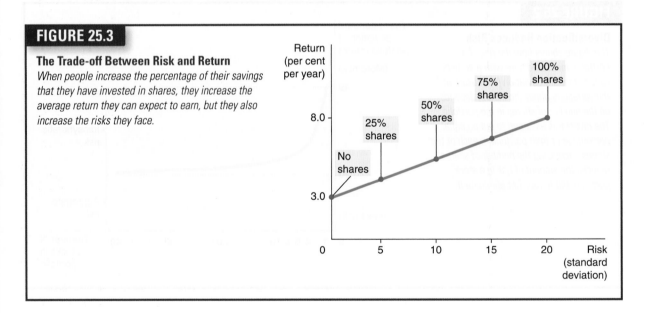

FIGURE 25.3

The Trade-off Between Risk and Return

When people increase the percentage of their savings that they have invested in shares, they increase the average return they can expect to earn, but they also increase the risks they face.

Each point in this figure represents a particular allocation of a portfolio between risky shares and the safe asset. The figure shows that the more a person puts into stock, the greater is both the risk and the return.

Acknowledging the risk–return trade-off does not, by itself, tell us what a person should do. The choice of a particular combination of risk and return depends on a person's risk aversion, which reflects a person's own preferences. But it is important for shareholders to realize that the higher average return that they enjoy comes at the price of higher risk.

SELF TEST Describe three ways that a risk-averse person might reduce the risk they face.

The Quants and Zero Risk

Many financial institutions have found highly skilled mathematicians and physicists extremely useful and are known as 'the quants'. One such 'quant' is David Li, a talented mathematician who worked on quantitative analysis at the Wall Street investment bank, J.P. Morgan Chase. In 2000 he published a paper in the *Journal of Fixed Income* entitled 'On Default Correlation: A Copula Function Approach'.

Li had some background in actuarial science as well as business and in his role within J.P. Morgan Chase, he was part of a growing number of highly qualified mathematical and statistical individuals being employed by financial institutions to identify risk and find ways of reducing it to a minimum – if not eliminating it totally. The basis behind this 'quantitative finance' was that the market could be beaten. What quantitative finance provided was the possibility of improved information that enabled decision-makers to invest with significantly reduced risk.

The basis of Li's paper in 2000 focused on the problems of probabilities and correlation of events. For example, a company in the southwest of England sources animal hide and processes it into a range of different quality leather for sale to manufacturers of leather products. It sources its hides from a company in Kenya. Analysis of data can give reasonably reliable estimates of the probability of both these businesses' chances of failure. The probability of the UK company failing might be 0.3 and the probability of the Kenyan company failing, 0.4. However, given the relationship between the two, if the Kenyan company did fail then there is a relatively high probability that the UK company might also fail if it cannot source the same high-quality hides elsewhere quickly. The correlation between the two companies failing, therefore, is relatively high.

What is the correlation between the chances of the UK company failing and an Icelandic tourism operator also failing? Intuition might suggest that the correlation would be weak given the fact that the two companies are operating in different markets and are not related. However, they may be related by the fact that they have both acquired loans from a bank based in Germany. If that bank suffered problems then the chance of the two companies failing would be relatively high. Li attempted to apply his skills to the effect of the default of one business on another. If this could be modelled, then it could help decision-makers to reduce the risk of investing.

The chances of two or more events occurring together can be modelled through the use of a statistical device called a copula, which produces a distribution. The specific distribution that Li used was a Gaussian Copula, which to many students is the familiar 'bell curve' given by a normal distribution. Li looked at the probability of any two or more elements in a pool of debt defaulting and his formula showed that this was equal to the normal distribution (the copula) times the probabilities of the time taken for the elements to default (referred to as survival times) multiplied by a correlation constant. The survival time aspect of the formula was derived from Li's knowledge of the work of actuaries in looking at survival rates of partners following the death of one of them. In this scenario, events (in this case death) tend to an average and there are also certainties – death will occur at some point in the future. With assets, the outcomes were not so clear cut and while Li's formula looked 'elegant' it was not able to take into account the range and randomness of events which were not so clear cut. Indeed, Li recognized (as any good scientist would claim to do) that his formula did have limitations. In 2005, he is quoted as saying 'Very few people understand the essence of the model.'

For those in the financial world, the model was useful in that it appeared to be able to reduce risk to a 'simple' number and thus help price that risk. It told decision-makers what effect the default of one company might have on another regardless of the knowledge of either company. Li's formula gained some currency in financial markets to the extent that ratings agencies such as Moody's and Standard & Poor's incorporated it into their methodology. In particular the formula was used to assess risk on collateralized debt obligations (CDOs).

Li's formula provided investors with new information which they could use to factor in when making decisions – it became part of the set of 'relevant generally available information'. The problem was that

(Continued)

those using it may not have fully understood the information which they were exploiting. The whole point of employing top-ranked mathematicians, statisticians and physicists in the world of finance since the latter part of the 1990s was that their skills were very special – it was simply not something that anybody else but these brilliant minds could do; if it had have been possible then others would have done it!

The information in these models is not only highly technical but based on various assumptions that are standard in science but which are recognized as 'provisional'; any theory or model is simply there to be taken apart and either destroyed or improved upon. The information we now have on the Financial Crisis, some of the causes of which were laid at the feet of these 'quants', is something that markets can now factor into decision-making. There are a great many things in economics that can be modelled and mathematics can be very useful in helping to provide the means to analyze and to predict, but ultimately economics is about human behaviour. Despite such rigorous analysis, the old adage about baskets and eggs still applies!

David Li was referred to by some media outlets as the man who was responsible for the credit crunch and subsequent recession.

ASSET VALUATION

This section considers a simple question: what determines the price of a share of stock? One part of the answer is supply and demand but that is not the end of the story. To understand share prices, we need to think more deeply about what determines a person's willingness to pay for a share of stock.

Fundamental Analysis

Let's imagine that you have decided to put 60 per cent of your savings into company shares and, to achieve diversification, you have decided to buy 20 different shares. How should you pick the 20 for your portfolio?

When you buy company shares, you are buying shares in a business. When deciding which businesses you want to own, it is natural to consider two things: the value of the business and the price at which the shares are being sold. If the price is less than the value, the stock is said to be *undervalued*. If the price is more than the value, the stock is said to be *overvalued*. If the price and the value are equal, the stock is said to be *fairly valued*. When choosing 20 stocks for your portfolio, you should prefer undervalued stocks. In these cases, you are getting a 'bargain' by paying less than the business is worth.

This is easier said than done. Learning the price is easy: you can just look it up in the newspaper or online or have it downloaded to an app on your mobile device. Determining the value of the business is the hard part. The term **fundamental analysis** refers to the detailed analysis of a company to determine its value. Many financial sector firms hire stock price analysts to conduct such fundamental analysis and offer advice about which stocks to buy.

fundamental analysis the study of a company's accounting statements and future prospects to determine its value

The value of a stock to a shareholder is what they get out of owning it, which includes the present value of the stream of dividend payments and the final sale price. Recall that *dividends* are the cash payments that a company makes to its shareholders. A company's ability to pay dividends, as well as the value of the stock when the shareholder sells their shares, depends on the company's ability to earn profits. Its profitability, in turn, depends on a large number of factors – the demand for its product, how much competition it faces, how much capital it has in place, whether its workers are unionized, how loyal its customers are, what kinds of government regulations and taxes it faces and so on. The job of fundamental analysts is to take all these factors into account to determine how much a share of stock in the company is worth.

If you want to rely on fundamental analysis to pick a stock portfolio, there are three ways to do it. One way is to do all the necessary research yourself, by reading through companies' annual reports and so forth. A second way is to rely on the advice of financial analysts. A third way is to buy into an investment fund, which has a manager (sometimes called a fund manager) who conducts fundamental analysis and makes the decision for you.

In the next chapter, we will explore financial markets in the wake of the Financial Crisis in further detail.

CONCLUSION

This chapter has developed some of the basic tools used in making financial decisions. The concept of present value reminds us that a pound or euro in the future is less valuable than a pound or euro today, and it gives us a way to compare sums of money at different points in time. The theory of risk management reminds us that the future is uncertain and that risk-averse people can take precautions to guard against this uncertainty. The study of asset valuation tells us that the stock price of any company should reflect its expected future profitability.

Although most of the tools of finance are well established, there is controversy about the validity of models on which asset pricing is based and whether stock prices are, in practice, rational estimates of a company's true worth. Rational or not, the large movements in stock prices that we observe have important macroeconomic implications. Stock market fluctuations often go hand in hand with fluctuations in the economy more broadly. We will look at the stock market again when we study economic fluctuations later in the book.

IN THE NEWS

The Value of Present Value

Following the Financial Crisis, one country seemed to be more severely affected than many others: Greece. In 2015 a third bailout was finally negotiated after lengthy discussions with the EU, the European Central Bank and the IMF (the 'troika'). A central focus of the negotiations on the extent to which Greece's creditors might lose some or all of the money they had lent.

Greek Debt and Present Value

Throughout much of 2015, Greece was locked in intense negotiations with the IMF and the European Union about its debt. The country faced repayments of parts of its debt and it seemed to be highly debatable whether Greece could honour its obligations. The political situation was a further complicating factor with the Greek government voted to power on an anti-austerity platform. As deadlines came and went, financial markets looked on trying to estimate what the outcome would be and whether Greece would be able to negotiate further financial support or whether it would be forced to leave the Eurozone and the European Union.

(Continued)

The negotiations in July 2015 led to a third bailout for the country in return for a number of economic reforms of the tax and pensions system but in many respects that was when the hard work really began for the Greek people and its politicians. One of the negotiation points was the subject of debt relief. What this means is that some debt (mostly bond debt) would be written off with the result that lenders would have to accept they would not get back some or all of what they had lent to Greece. Writing off debt in this way is not a palatable thing in financial markets because the trust between borrowers and lenders is eroded. However, in late 2015, the deputy governor of Greece's central bank, Ioannis Mourmouras, said that the average maturity of the loans was around 32 years and with interest rates very low, the net present value of the debt was low enough for Greece to be able to manage these debts. Mourmouras noted that future discussions on debt relief would be based on the net present value. If the Greek government borrowed €500 million via bonds with a principal of 1 per cent and 30 years to maturity, the value of the stream of payments Greece has to make on the bond can be discounted to reflect the net present value. Some finance experts say that valuing a bond using NPV is an accepted and fair way. For lenders, the 'true value' of the debt they are owed is not €500 million (plus the interest payments) because this has to be discounted over the period of the years to maturity. Doing so means that the amount Greece will have to find to pay these debts will be lower and thus more manageable.

Questions

1 Why do you think reform of the tax and pensions system was insisted upon by the so called 'troika' as part of any agreement for a bailout?
2 Much of the debt Greece owes is in the form of bonds. Why is trust such an important part of the smooth functioning of the sovereign bond market (i.e. bonds bought by national governments)?
3 What is the net present value of a €500 million bond, with an interest rate of 1 per cent and 30 years to maturity? What would the NPV be if the interest rate was 5 per cent?
4 Would you agree with the statement that the only fair way to value a bond is through its NPV?
5 How would you expect lenders to respond to the problem of sovereign debt such as those experienced by Greece in assessing the trade-off between risk and return?

Could present value calculations help the Greek economy manage its debt more effectively?

SUMMARY

- Because savings can earn interest, a sum of money today is more valuable than the same sum of money in the future. A person can compare sums from different times using the concept of present value. The present value of any future sum is the amount that would be needed today, given prevailing interest rates, to produce that future sum.
- Because of diminishing marginal utility, most people are risk averse. Economic agents can reduce risk using insurance, through diversification, and by choosing a portfolio with lower risk and lower return.
- The value of an asset, such as a share of stock, equals the present value of the cash flows the owner of the share will receive, including the stream of dividends and the final sale price. If financial markets process available information rationally, a stock price will equal the best estimate of the value of the underlying business.

QUESTIONS FOR REVIEW

1 Outline the concept of present value.

2 The interest rate is 7 per cent. Use the concept of present value to compare €200 to be received in ten years and €300 to be received in 20 years.

3 What benefit do people get from the market for insurance? What two problems impede the insurance company from working perfectly?

4 What is meant by the term 'fundamental analysis'?

5 What is diversification? Does a shareholder get more diversification going from 1 to ten stocks or going from 100 to 120 stocks?

6 Comparing company shares and government bonds, which has more risk? Which pays a higher average return?

7 What factors should a stock analyst think about in determining the value of a share of stock?

8 What is the trade-off between risk and return?

9 Why do you think that humans tend to value losing a sum of money more than they value gaining the same amount?

10 Why is knowledge of whether people are risk averse or risk seeking important in financial markets?

PROBLEMS AND APPLICATIONS

1 Assume the interest rate is 6 per cent. In each of the following three cases, state which you would rather receive and briefly explain why:
   a. €200 today or €480 in two years?
   b. €205 today or €240 in one year?
   c. €1000 in one year or €1220 in two years?

2 A company has an investment project that would cost €10 million today and yield a payoff of €15 million in four years.

   a. Should the firm undertake the project if the interest rate is 11 per cent? 10 per cent? 9 per cent? 8 per cent?
   b. Can you figure out the exact cut-off for the interest rate between profitability and non-profitability?

3 For each of the following kinds of insurance, give an example of behaviour that can be called *moral hazard* and another example of behaviour that can be called *adverse selection*:

   a. health insurance
   b. car insurance.

4 Imagine that you intend to buy a portfolio of ten shares with some of your savings. Should the shares be of companies in the same industry? Should the shares be of companies located in the same country? Explain.

5 For which kind of stock would you expect to pay the higher average return: stock in an industry that is very sensitive to economic conditions (such as a car manufacturer) or stock in an industry that is relatively insensitive to economic conditions (such as a water company)? Why?

6 A company faces two kinds of risk. An idiosyncratic risk is that a competitor might enter its market and take some of its customers. An aggregate risk is that the economy might enter a recession, reducing sales. Which of these two risks would more likely cause the company's shareholders to demand a higher return? Why?

7 Sam has a utility function $U = w^{0.5}$, where w is her wealth in millions of euros and U is the utility she obtains from that wealth. Sam has made it through to the final stage of a game show. The host offers Sam a choice between (i) €4 million for sure, or (ii) a gamble that pays €1 million with probability 0.6, and €9 million with probability 0.4.

   a. Graph Sam's utility function. Is she risk averse? Explain.
   b. Does (i) or (ii) offer Sam a higher expected prize? Explain your reasoning with appropriate calculations. (Hint: The expected value of a random variable is the weighted average of the possible outcomes, where the probabilities are the weights.)

c. Does (i) or (ii) offer Sam a higher expected utility? Again, show your calculations.

d. Should Sam pick (i) or (ii)? Why?

8 When company executives buy and sell stock based on private information they obtain as part of their jobs, they are engaged in *insider trading*.

a. Give an example of inside information that might be useful for buying or selling stock.

b. Insider trading is illegal. Why do you suppose that is?

9 Financial markets in the early years of the 21st century were heavily influenced by the work of quantitative analysts ('quants') who looked at ways to reassess the pricing of risk. Discuss some of the advantages and disadvantages of pricing risk using mathematics and mathematical models.

10 How might you go about pricing the risk on the following:

a. the price of a 10-year bond from the Portuguese government

b. the price of a 10-year bond from the German government

c. the construction of a new oil well off the South African coast.

26 ISSUES IN FINANCIAL MARKETS

The Financial Crisis from 2007–9 led to a widespread and deep global recession. Ten years later, the effects are still being felt. Many economists agree on the causes of the crisis but there is still much disagreement about the underlying theories and models which might explain what was witnessed and perhaps more importantly, whether these models and theories have any relevance for the future. In this chapter we will look at the causes of the crisis and then consider some of the debate which has surrounded the crisis and its aftermath.

THE CAUSES OF THE CRISIS

As we have noted, macroeconomics is a relatively new discipline. The events of the 1930s prompted a closer review of the economy as a whole. The Second World War, the post-war reconstruction and the collapse of the Bretton Woods system in 1971 (where governments committed to fix prices of domestic currencies against a specific amount of gold), the oil crisis of the 1970s and recession of the early 1980s were set against the background of demand management and subsequent debate about the role of the money supply in macroeconomic policy making. The boom of the late 1980s gave way to recession in the early 1990s and then to a period of reduced volatility. In 2004, US Federal Reserve (the Fed) governor, Ben Bernanke, a renowned student of the Great Depression of the 1930s, gave a speech to the Eastern Economic Association in Washington DC in which he noted the decline in macroeconomic volatility. The reasons Bernanke put forward included structural change, improved macroeconomic policies and 'good luck'. In 2007, the UK Chancellor, Gordon Brown, presented his eleventh budget and noted: '*my report to the country is of rising employment and rising investment; continuing low inflation, and low interest and mortgage rates; and this is a Budget... built on the foundation of the longest period of economic stability and sustained growth in our country's history... we will never return to the old boom and bust.*'

The benign economic conditions which had resulted in relatively low inflation, high employment, low unemployment and stable growth in many developed countries was termed **The Great Moderation** (in the UK, it is termed 'The Great Stability'). In 2005 few people were predicting the calamitous events which would take place over the next four years. Some commentators had warned that the rise in asset prices, specifically house prices both in the UK and the US, would at some point have to suffer a correction but arguments reigned about the relative size of that correction and the effects on the economy as a consequence. In hindsight, it is possible to identify some longer term trends which led to the crisis.

The Great Moderation the period of economic stability characterised by relatively low inflation, high employment, low unemployment and stable and persistent growth

533

Deregulation

In the UK and the US, deregulation began in the 1980s set against the belief that excessive regulation limited the ability of the supply side of the economy to operate efficiently. A series of legislation dramatically changed the banking and financial landscape. Rules and regulations surrounding the activities of banks and building societies were abolished or relaxed.

The pace of financial deregulation did not decline with the end of the 1980s. In both the UK and US, successive governments gradually picked away at regulation, allowing financial institutions to trade globally and giving more freedom for them to innovate than ever before. Progress in technology fuelled innovation and if one wanted to really get on in the financial centres of the world, an ability to manipulate statistics and be a mathematical wizard were the qualifications to have.

Deregulation allowed financial institutions to expand their role. A number of building societies used the new rules to become banks and existing commercial banks entered the mortgage market. For the average household, access to a mortgage now became easier. The increased demand for housing pushed prices up. As house prices rise the difference between the principal borrowed and the value of the house increases, referred to as **positive equity**. An individual may have a mortgage for £250 000 but a property worth £375 000 and thus positive equity of £125 000. Lenders were not shy in allowing borrowers to exploit this equity and with the security of a house in the background (and the expectation that prices would continue to rise) the ease with which people were able to build up their debt increased. Homeowners were able to borrow money to buy cars, holidays, finance weddings and other luxuries as well as carry out home improvements and extensions.

 positive equity the positive difference between the principal borrowed on a house and its value

For financial institutions, the expectations of continued economic growth partly explain how attention turned from what might be termed 'prudent' lending to riskier investments on the back of new financial instruments. Banks, many of whom had been former mutual societies run for the benefit of their members, now had the pressure of generating returns for shareholders and in the search for ever larger returns, lending protocols were stretched to the limit and sometimes broken.

In the US, shocks to the system in the form of the dot.com collapse and the terrorist attacks of 9/11 did lead to dips in economic activity. In each case the Fed responded by cutting interest rates and flooding the markets with cash to help maintain liquidity. Preparations for a predicted information technology (IT) disaster at the turn of the millennium (the 'Y2K threat') had meant that many large financial organizations had invested heavily in technology. Inadvertently, therefore, the Y2K threat possibly gave many financial organizations advantages which enabled them to improve productivity above what it would have been had the threat not occurred. Banks looked to widen the market segments that they were prepared to do business with in the search for new markets and opportunities to improve returns. The prevalence of relatively low rates of interest meant the prospect of high-yield returns became even more attractive especially given the fact that such returns were linked to bonuses for staff.

Pension funds were being hit by changes to the way in which many corporate businesses managed their pension provision. The suspension of expensive final salary pension schemes along with cuts in contributions from government and employees meant that pension fund managers became eager to find investments that offered increased yields. In the UK similar conditions enabled banks and mortgage lenders to compete for new custom through developing ever more attractive products including low-start mortgages, 2-year fixed rate deals, debt roll-up mortgages and mortgages based on an increasing proportion of the value of property and multiples of income.

Deregulation and global trading meant that capital movements across national boundaries was much easier. Funds could be borrowed from countries with low interest rates (particularly Japan who experienced negative interest rates at times in the early 2000s) and invested in assets in countries with higher yields. The growth of hedge funds looking to secure high returns on investments for the clients whom they represented, along with the developments in IT which enabled them to exploit very small price differentials between markets, all combined to provide the background for a more risk-seeking mentality to pervade the financial markets.

Asset Price Rises

Alan Greenspan, the former Chair of the Fed, commented in September 2009: 'That is the unquenchable capability of human beings when confronted with long periods of prosperity to presume that it will continue'. Greenspan was referring to the period when both credit and housing markets expanded in the latter part of the 1990s and into the new millennium. Total UK debt including credit cards and mortgages in 2006 was reported at being over £1.2 trillion (€1.55 trillion) and the Bank of England noted that outstanding balances on credit cards had risen by over 380 per cent since 1994. In the UK, the average house price rose from around £30 000 in 1983 (€38 800) to almost £200 000 (€258 794) in 2007. In the US, the S&P/Case-Schiller national home price index increased from 100 in 2000 to around 190 in 2006.

For the struggling first-time buyer, the existence of low interest rates offered some hope. Traditionally, lenders had used the value of the property and income levels as a base from which to calculate the amount they were prepared to lend. Loans above 75 per cent of the value of the property were rare. Typical multiples would be 2.5 times the main income and 1.5 times the second income. For a couple with the main 'breadwinner' earning £20 000 and the other earning £15 000 the amount which could be borrowed would be £72 500. With the average house price standing at around £90 000 in 2001 (and remember that is an average) the predicament facing people in this position is clear.

In the US, the situation was not that much different. What became clear was that there was a latent demand for mortgages. The demand was latent rather than effective because whilst there were plenty of people who might have been willing to enter the market they were not always able to do so because of an inability to access the mortgage market.

It is at this point in the story that the effects of deregulation, the existence of relatively low interest rates, apparently stable economic conditions and the increase in risk-seeking activity amongst financial institutions all come together. The rise in house prices in the UK and the US has been termed an 'asset bubble'. We will look in more detail at asset bubbles later in the chapter but essentially, an asset bubble is said to occur when prices begin to differ substantially from their fundamental values. Was the rise in house prices an example of an asset bubble or were the increases due to fundamental changes in supply and demand?

The demand for housing outstripped supply. As market price rose the desire to get on the housing ladder before the first rung was raised too high further fuelled demand. For those who had managed to buy a house in the early 1980s, the amount of positive equity in their property was such that it allowed them to borrow and in some cases, this borrowing was used to fund second homes. These second homes might be a retreat near the coast or in the countryside, an apartment in one of the many new developments in Spain or a property bought with the intention of letting it out and using the rent to help pay for the second mortgage. The purchase of second homes was seen as a way providing people with a 'pension' for their retirement. Constant rising house prices offered something more reliable than the traditional pension schemes, many of which seemed to be perpetually in trouble or subject to 'black holes' in the financing, and abandonment or cessation by companies and public sector organizations who had previously provided them.

The 'rules' under which a mortgage could be secured were relaxed by many lending institutions. Many offered mortgages at much more generous loan-to-value ratios. In the UK, Northern Rock offered a mortgage product that allowed borrowers up to 125 per cent of the value of the house or six times annual income. Whilst this new 'Together' loan (so-called because it allowed borrowers to tie up mortgage lending and pay off existing debt) was greeted with raised eyebrows by some, it allowed those who previously could not access the market to do so. It was seen as being one of the benefits of the strong and stable economic climate.

The Sub-prime Market

In the United States, extending mortgage opportunities to those not traditionally seen as being part of the market was also part of the way in which banks and other lenders sought to increase their lending. As we saw in Chapter 24, some of these people had credit histories that were very poor, some did not have jobs, but in an atmosphere of risk-seeking and changed priorities this group provided lenders with a market opportunity. The former Chair of the Federal Reserve, Ben Bernanke, notes that the mortgage market developed by extending mortgages beyond those who would be considered to have a sound credit rating, first to what he refers to as 'non-prime' and later to sub-prime. These mortgages often required limited paperwork before they were granted and significantly lower deposits. The Fed estimated that around 10 per cent of mortgages were 'non-prime' in 2003 but rose to over 30 per cent by 2006. A paper published by Mayer, Pence and Sherlund in the *Journal of Economic Perspectives* (23, Winter 2009) suggested that the percentage of mortgages offered in the US requiring low or no documentation rose from around 39 per cent in 2003 to 60 per cent by 2007.

Borrowers in the US may have been contacted in the first instance by a broker who outlined the possibilities for the borrower. These 'affordability products' sometimes included so-called 'teaser rates' which offered low (sometimes zero) interest rates for an initial period, often two years. Interest rates after the first two years could rise significantly and in some products, after subsequent years, the interest rate increased further. The attraction for many prospective house buyers was that the chance to get a mortgage and buy a house was being offered to them for the first time. If house prices kept rising, the homeowner would be able to generate positive equity in the property and eventually remortgage to a more 'mainstream' mortgage. Positive equity allowed homeowners to be able to manage rising interest rates on the mortgage. However, when house prices began to fall, the option of remortgaging disappeared and many homeowners found their monthly repayments rising beyond their ability to pay.

Typical of sub-prime loans were '2/28' or '3/27' loans. The 2 and 3 indicated the number of years of the teaser rate and the remainder, the period over which a variable rate would apply. Brokers would then look to sell the mortgage to a bank or other mortgage provider and received a commission for doing so. Under 'normal' circumstances the bank would not only have acquired a liability but also an asset (the payments received by the borrower on the mortgage). The mortgage would generate a stream of cash flows in the form of the payment of the mortgage principal and interest over a period of years. Such an asset could be valuable in the new deregulated banking environment.

The growth of sub-prime mortgages began to take an increasing share of the total mortgage market in the US and the risk involved in terms of the loan-to-value ratio also rose from around 50 per cent to over 80 per cent by 2005–6. Sub-prime loans accounted for around 35 per cent of all mortgages issued in 2004. It was not only the poor who were taking advantage of the sub-prime market, however. Existing homeowners took advantage of the positive equity in their properties to re-mortgage or buy second homes. Speculation in the housing market was not confined to just those in the financial markets that could benefit from new financial instruments that could be traded for profit. Some saw opportunities to enter the housing market, borrow funds to buy property and almost immediately put it back onto the market – a phenomenon known as 'flipping'. The hope was that rapidly rising house prices would mean that the property could be sold quickly and a profit realised.

The economic background to this was a sharp cut in interest rates by the Fed in response to the collapse of the dot.com boom and to 9/11. A low interest rate environment seemed to insulate sub-prime mortgage holders from the extent of the debt which they had taken on. From 2003 onwards, the official US interest rate (the Fed funds rate) stayed at 1 per cent and for 31 consecutive months the real or inflation-adjusted interest rate was effectively negative. Meanwhile the housing market price rise further contributed to economic growth as employment in housing related business expanded to meet the growth in activity. The housing market was responsible for creating over 788 000 jobs in the US between 2001 and 2005 – some 40 per cent of the total increase in employment.

There is some debate among economists as to whether the rise in house prices in the US and the UK during this period could be called a 'bubble'. Many would argue that it was, although some have noted that the rise in productivity and incomes during this time led to sharply rising prices as demand for housing naturally outstripped supply. However, while rising productivity may explain part of the housing price boom, many people buying houses were doing so simply in the expectation that the price would continue to rise, and many lenders were offering attractive mortgages to people with low credit ratings because they thought that the property on which the mortgage was secured would continue to rise in price. When people buy an asset not because of the flow of services it yields (a roof over one's head in the case of a house) but simply because they believe it is going to rise in price, we have one of the essential characteristics of a bubble.

Sub-prime Mortgages and Securitization

In Chapter 25, we outlined the principles of CDOs and credit default swaps (CDS). Packaging mortgage-backed securities into pools of debt and selling them on is known as **securitization.** This section provides more detail on how this was done and how the resulting risk could be 'insured' against.

 securitization the packaging of mortgage-backed securities into pools of debt and selling them on

Assume a bank has agreed to lend 10 000 individuals' mortgages for property with each individual borrowing $100 000 (we are using dollars since the sub-prime market was primarily in the US). The bank is known as the **originator**. These mortgages could be bundled up to form $1 billion worth of debt. Mathematicians analyze the debt and make an assessment that the debt has a (say) 1 per cent chance of default; of the 10 000 individuals associated with this debt, 100 are likely to default at some point over its lifetime. The bank presents the debt package to a credit rating agency and, given the limited risk involved as a result of the pooling of the debt, is able to access a favourable credit rating.

 originator a bank or financial institution that securitizes assets

Having secured an appropriate credit, the bank then sets up what is called a **Special Purpose Vehicle** or SPV. The establishment of an SPV allows the bank to separate its financial obligations. Rather than buyers of the debt having a claim on the bank as a whole in case of default, the setting up of an SPV means that the investor has a claim against the SPV. Equally the investor has the right to receive payments first by dealing with an SPV. The SPV buys the collection of debt and will sell it to investors which may be other banks and financial institutions. The funds raised by the SPV allow it to be able to buy the debt from the bank. The SPV will issue bonds for this purpose. For the prospective investor the bond is associated with the stream of cash flows from the package of loans which also have a high rate of interest attached to them. Given that the debt package has been given a high credit rating, the risk associated with the investment is considered relatively low. The investor is protected by the value of the underlying assets. Remember, if there is a default on any of the loans the bank has the option of seizing the properties which are the security for the original loan.

Special Purpose Vehicle an entity set up to issue bonds to investors to raise finance to buy collections of assets

The SPV issues bonds for a total value lower than the package of debt. The difference is the 'first-loss position' of the originator (the bank in this example). The aim is to ensure that the potential loss on the pool of debt is not greater than the difference between the total value of the pool and the value of the bonds issued to sell on the debt. In our example, the pool of debt (the collection of mortgages), is worth $1 billion. The SPV will receive the mortgage payments and uses the cash flows to pay the bond interest and the principal. The debt is sold by the SPV for $950 million – the difference, therefore, being $50 million. Analysis shows that the likely default losses on this package of debt would be no more than (say) $30 million. This means that the cash inflows from mortgage owners is sufficient to pay the investors their money back - $950 million. This represents a 3 per cent loss rate based on the total value of the debt package.

The SPV issues shares in itself and becomes a subsidiary company of the bank (or originator) with its own legal status. Shares may be bought by the originator and by other parties in the financial community. The attraction of doing so is that the SPV generates high returns based on the flow of cash of the underlying asset (the mortgage). The benefit of setting up an SPV for the bank is that it transfers liabilities to the SPV and therefore these do not appear on its balance sheet. As a result, the bank does not have to set aside reserves to cover these loans and this leaves it free to increase lending or engage in deals which further expand its earnings and profits. The setting up of an SPV also protects investors. If the bank (which originated the debt) fails, then creditors of the bank (those to whom the bank owes money) cannot make any claim against investors given that the SPV is a separate legal entity. Equally, if the SPV fails in some way then the investor does not have recourse to any claim against the bank or the originator. The bank can also earn commission on the sale of the debt to the SPV.

SELF TEST What is the benefit of a SPV to a bank in managing its balance sheet?

The issue of bonds by the SPV would be in bundles, called tranches, which reflect different levels of risk. The process of splitting up the bundles of debt into these different levels of risk is called **tranching**. Given these different levels of risk, different types of investors would be sought for each tranche, which might relate to the maturity date of the mortgages in the pool or be associated with a different rate of interest. Typically in sub-prime securitisation there were six tranches (known as '6-pack deals'). Each tranche can be sold separately. As we saw Chapter 25, institutions would further use CDS as a means of insuring themselves against the risk of default.

tranching the splitting up bundles of debt into different levels of risk

The Rise in Defaults

The expansion of the CDS market presented a different challenge to the financial markets when the housing market collapse came. It must be remembered that not only were these contracts taken out in relation to bonds linked to sub-prime loans but the trade of these contracts might mean that banks and other financial institutions might be buying the contract whilst not possessing the asset (the bond) or the underlying asset (the mortgages).

One of the problems associated with CDS is that the seller may have a number of deals relating to these bonds and indeed the buyer may have taken out a number of insurance contracts with different sellers. Add into the mix the possibility that these contracts could also be bought and sold globally as part of speculative deals and the web of financial interdependence grows – all based, remember, on a collection of sub-prime mortgages. Traders might, therefore, deliberately buy CDS on the expectation that the bond associated with it would fail. If it did, then the trader stands to gain a return in the form of the bond value which has been insured or the collateral which has been set aside. The market progressed from being one which insured bond holders against risk to one where accurate speculation could generate large returns for traders. Those buying these derivatives (so called because their value is derived from an underlying asset) may have little if any idea of the strength of the underlying assets associated with their trade.

The precise value of the CDS market is difficult to pinpoint because it consists of a private financial transaction between the two parties – a so called 'over the counter' transaction. In over the counter transactions, there is no official record of who has made a trade with whom and whether the seller can actually meet the obligations. The CDS market was estimated at between $45 and $60 trillion. To put this into some sort of perspective, $60 trillion is more than global GDP which was estimated at $54.3 trillion in 2006! A number of major banks had exposure to CDS including Lehman Bros, Icelandic banks, Barclays and RBS, and in addition insurance companies like AIG were also heavily committed.

In 2006–7, the prevailing concern amongst central banks was the development of inflationary pressure. The Bank of England had started to increase interest rates in June 2006 and in a series of quarter point rises, saw Base Rate increase to 5.75 per cent by July 2007. In the US, the Fed raised interest rates for 16 consecutive months to June 2006 and the Federal Funds Rate reached 5.25 per cent by the autumn of 2006. As interest rates rose, borrowers, especially those on sub-prime mortgages, began to feel the pressure and reports of the number of defaults on sub-prime loans began to rise.

Once mortgage defaults began to rise to alarming numbers the number of financial institutions affected and their exposure became clearer. The whole edifice was based on the expectation that the underlying assets would continue to generate the income stream over time – in other words, that the very large majority of mortgage holders would continue to pay their monthly mortgage repayments.

How did these mortgage defaults begin to happen? We have already seen how teaser rates tempted many to take on the burden of a mortgage but without necessarily fully understanding the financial commitments they were making. After the teaser rate period finished the mortgages had to be restructured based on a new rate of interest. The new rate of interest not only reflected the need to claw back some of the interest not paid in the initial teaser rate period but also the fact that these borrowers were higher risk.

As mortgage rates rose, borrowers found it increasingly difficult to meet their monthly payments. In some cases, the difference between initial monthly payments and restructured payments based on new interest rates was significant; many homeowners found their monthly mortgage payments more than doubling. The sub-prime market consisted of people least able to cope with such changes and in addition those who had taken out sub-prime mortgages for second homes and the buy-to-let market also found themselves stretched.

Faced with payments they could not afford, borrowers looked to sell their property or face the prospect of foreclosure – the point where the mortgage lender seizes the property. As the number of foreclosures increased, house prices fell. As house prices fell, more and more people were caught in negative equity, where the value of their property was less than the mortgage secured on it. Trying to sell the house was not an option for many; they would still be left with a large debt which they had no hope of paying off. The situation was particularly bad in certain areas of the US. The house price rise had been particularly acute in Las Vegas, Los Angeles and Miami. These were areas that were hit worst by the rise in foreclosures. As the number of foreclosures rose the supply of housing increased and, true to basic economic principles of supply and demand, the price of houses continued to fall.

Once mortgage payers defaulted on loans, banks who lent money to SPVs called in the debt. Banks found themselves having to take the assets of the SPV back onto their balance sheet. This limited their ability to lend because they had to put aside reserves to cover these liabilities which now appeared on their balance sheet. In some cases, they may have had to write down the value of the assets, further damaging their balance sheet and ability to lend.

Every day, banks have obligations to meet – loans they have taken out that need paying off, interest payments, CDS that mature, bonds that need to be paid, etc. They must have sufficient liquid funds to be able to meet these obligations. Many banks borrow the funds they need from the interbank market. As the sub-prime market collapsed, the exposure to bad debt started to become more obvious and a number of banks reported significant write-downs and losses. Confidence in the banking system, so important to its functioning, began to fall. Banks were not sure of their own exposure to these bad debts (referred to as toxic debt) and so were also unsure about the extent of other banks' exposure. Interbank lending began to become much tighter as banks were unwilling to lend to each other and they also faced the task of trying to shore up their own balance sheets. Accessing credit was, therefore, far more expensive and limited in nature, and the higher price of borrowing was passed onto the consumer – individuals and businesses. When business loans are less easy to obtain or more expensive, businesses find it difficult to manage their cash flow and insolvency can result.

Banking Crisis In August 2008, the problems facing banks began to mount. In March of that year the US investment bank Bear Stearns' exposure to sub-prime markets led it to seek support from the Fed. Other banks with a heavy exposure to sub-prime began to announce losses and write-downs only to have to issue worse revised figures a short time later. Bear Stearns was rescued by being acquired by JP Morgan

Chase. In the UK, Northern Rock suffered a run on its assets as account holders queued to get their money before the bank collapsed—the first run on a UK bank for more than 100 years.

In the US, it became obvious that two of the major players in the mortgage market, the Federal National Mortgage Association, commonly known as 'Fannie Mae', and the Federal Home Loan Mortgage Corporation, known as 'Freddie Mac', were facing deep financial problems. Fannie Mae was founded in 1938 and Freddie Mac in 1970. Their business involved buying mortgages from lenders and then selling on the debt to investors. They effectively guaranteed the borrowing for millions of mortgage owners and accounted for around half of the US mortgage market, which was worth $12 trillion. Such was their importance that the US authorities stepped in to support them. As in the UK with Northern Rock, the US government announced in early September 2008 that it was going to take temporary ownership of the two companies to save them from collapse. If the two had become insolvent, house prices in the US, which were falling at rates of around 15 per cent in some areas, would be likely to have fallen even further, increasing negative equity. It was estimated at the time that up to around 10 per cent of US homeowners were facing difficulties in meeting their mortgage payments, and risked having their homes repossessed.

The flood of bad news from banks made it clear that the problems were significant. The authorities were faced with the challenge of intervening to help prevent the collapse of banks. However, the prospect of saving banks led to the problem of moral hazard. If banks knew that they would be bailed out by the government, then they would have less of an incentive to pursue prudential lending practices. The idea of simply saving a bank, who many people saw as having forsaken the prudence that for so long characterized these institutions, was something that stuck in the throat of 'Main Street' America. Millions of ordinary Americans were facing significant hardship and the loss of their homes; businesses were finding it increasingly difficult to access the funds that they needed to survive in the face of a growing threat of recession. Nobody was stepping in to help them, they argued. Bankers who had caused the problems, it was said, seemed to be getting off lightly.

Banking Collapse The issue of moral hazard might be the reason why one of the most spectacular banking collapses in recent times occurred on 15 September 2008. The US investment bank Lehman Brothers, had been a bank at the forefront of the sub-prime and CDS market. It had built its business on leveraging – borrowing heavily to finance its activities. Over the weekend of 13 and 14 September 2008, last ditch talks were convened to try and find a way of rescuing Lehman Brothers in the same way that Bear Stearns and Merrill Lynch had been rescued. The debts at Lehman and the extent of their exposure to sub-prime and CDS were too great, however, and Lehman Brothers filed for Chapter 11 bankruptcy protection on 15 September.

When Lehman collapsed it led to billions of dollars of claims on Lehman CDS – payments which had to be made by those who sold the protection. As a means of settling these claims, Lehman's bonds were sold via auction in early October 2008. The value of the bonds was set by the auction at around 8 cents to the dollar. A $10 million bond would only be worth $800 000, meaning that protection sellers would have to make up the remaining $9 200 000 to meet the CDS obligation. With claims estimated at anything between $400 and $600 billion, this put a massive strain on the financial system and many banks who had sold CDS on Lehman were now exposed and in danger of failing themselves, which put further pressure on the system.

Basically, banks found that they had to meet payment obligations and did not have the funds available in reserves to do so. Banks who were struggling to meet their obligations attempted to raise funds in the interbank money markets which, as we have already seen, were almost at a standstill. Banks around the world found themselves in this difficult situation had to take more assets back onto their balance sheet. This meant they had to reinstate sufficient reserves to support these liabilities and this further reduced their willingness to lend. Instead the focus shifted to restoring balance sheets by taking in deposits but not lending. The collapse of Lehman was seen as a spectacular event because it showed that central banks were not prepared to step in to help any bank that got into trouble.

The Path to Global Recession

The problems in financial markets began to translate themselves to the real economy fairly quickly. Interest rates had been rising up to the middle of 2008 in an attempt to curb demand in the US, UK and Europe and those increases had started to feed through via the interest rate transmission mechanism.

For many people, however, the problems in the housing market led to job losses. As mortgages became harder to access, demand for homes fell and many involved in real estate were affected. The number of jobs created in the US that were linked to the house price boom began to be reversed. With house prices falling, homeowners feel less secure and perceive the equity in their homes to be falling. The incentive to borrow against the positive equity in property is reduced and homeowners may also feel a lack of confidence and decide to cut back on some of the luxuries they once enjoyed. These may be little things such as going to the cinema, taking weekend breaks, going to a pub or a restaurant. If restaurants suffer a fall in the number of weekly covers they take they may have to cut back on orders of ingredients, which begins to affect suppliers and so on down the supply chain. For the owners of these businesses the effect can be significant. In the UK, the British Beer & Pub Association, for example, published figures which showed that in the first half of 2009, an average of 52 pubs a week closed down – 33 per cent more than during the equivalent period in 2008. These pub closures pushed up the jobless numbers by around 24 000.

It was, however, the effect of the tight credit market that helped exacerbate the depth of the downturn in many countries. One by one, countries in the developed world saw economic growth falling. A major cause of the downturn was due to the problems businesses had in accessing funds from banks. Businesses, especially small businesses, rely on cash flow for their survival. Many need flexibility and understanding from their banks when faced with shocks to their cash flow and tight credit markets meant that many businesses found banks unwilling to lend and extend overdrafts. Even if the bank was prepared to lend, the interest rate attached to the loan was often prohibitive. Faced with cash flow problems and an inability to get the finance to support them, many smaller businesses began to close.

Larger businesses were not immune from the problems. The motor vehicle industry, in particular, suffered significant falls in sales. In January 2008, monthly production of vehicles in the US was 817 767; by February 2009 this had fallen to 388 267 – a fall of 52.2 per cent in just over a year. The fall in production affected component suppliers and the negative multiplier effect worked its way through the economy. As demand fell, businesses closed and unemployment rose. In the US, the unemployment rate rose from 6.2 per cent in August 2008 to 9.7 per cent a year later; the unemployment rate in the UK rose by 2.4 per cent over the same period and across the EU, unemployment was in excess of 10 per cent.

THE EFFICIENT MARKETS HYPOTHESIS

In Chapter 24, we looked at diversification of share portfolios. One way of doing this is to invest in a fund and let an 'expert' fund manager conduct the fundamental analysis required to maximize returns. There is another way, however, to choose shares for a portfolio: pick them randomly by, for instance, putting the stock pages of the *Financial Times* on a notice board and throwing darts at the page. This may sound crazy, but there is reason to believe that it won't lead you too far astray. That reason is called the **efficient markets hypothesis (EMH)** It is worth dwelling on the word 'hypothesis' and its meaning. As noted in Chapter 2, 'hypothesis' comes from the Greek *hypotithenai* meaning 'to suppose'. More generally it means an assumption made which is subject to empirical testing to validate the assumption or otherwise. We have dwelt on the meaning again because it is important to note that the EMH is not a universal truth or a religion but an assumption about how financial markets behave which is subject to testing.

> **efficient markets hypothesis (EMH)** the theory that asset prices reflect all publicly available information about the value of an asset

To understand this theory, the starting point is that stock markets contain a large number of buyers and sellers and that the market has sufficient liquidity to enable stock to be bought and sold at any time. Buyers and sellers in the market monitor news stories and conduct fundamental analysis to try to determine stock values. The second piece to the efficient markets hypothesis is that the equilibrium of supply and demand sets the market price. This means that, at the market price, the number of shares being offered for sale exactly equals the number of shares that people want to buy. In other words, at the market price, the number of people who think the share is overvalued exactly balances the number of people who think it's undervalued. As judged by the typical person in the market, all shares are fairly valued all the time.

According to this theory, the stock market is **informationally efficient**. It reflects all available information about the value of the asset. Share prices change when information changes. When good news about a company's prospects become public, the value and the stock price both rise. When a company's prospects deteriorate, the value and price both fall. At any moment in time, the market price is the best guess of the company's value based on available information.

> **informationally efficient** reflecting all available information in a rational way

One implication of the efficient markets hypothesis is that stock prices should follow a **random walk**. This means that changes in stock prices are impossible to predict from available information. If, based on publicly available information, a person could correctly predict that a stock price would rise by 10 per cent tomorrow, the stock market must be failing to incorporate that information today. According to this theory, the only thing that can move stock prices is news that changes the market's perception of the company's value. But news must be unpredictable – otherwise, it wouldn't really be news. For the same reason, changes in stock prices should be unpredictable.

> **random walk** the path of a variable whose changes are impossible to predict

If the efficient markets hypothesis is correct, then there is little point in spending many hours studying the business pages to decide which shares to add to your portfolio. If prices reflect all available information, no stock is a better buy than any other. The best you can do is buy a diversified portfolio.

Central to the EMH is the role of information. Information is necessary to enable the valuer to make judgements. This information could include data of different kinds. It might include statistical data based on historical records or on reliable forecasting techniques. Data can also be gained from official statements of a business, financial audits, from government or organizations like the IMF, World Bank and OECD, from other specialist market analysts such as Mintel and Experian, representatives of retail trades and so on. In valuing the price of an asset, therefore, the assumption is that the market is informationally efficient in that it reflects all available information about the value of that asset.

The extent to which this assumption can be accepted is open to question. Access to information and the speed at which information travels is now greater than ever before. Despite the growth in technology, information transfer is not instantaneous nor is it assimilated and understood by all at the same speed and with the same depth. There is, therefore, a time lag involved with information transfer. If individuals are able to exploit this time lag they can use this to their advantage to make profits; this is the basis of arbitrage.

Even if information is widely available and extensive it does not mean that it is always understood. Information may not only be misunderstood but also be partial; gathering information requires some investment in terms of research (information gathering and processing) on the part of decision makers; there are transactions costs associated with information gathering.

Efficient Markets Hypothesis: A Cause of the Financial Crisis?

The assumption of efficient markets and the belief that markets self-correct and revert to reflect true market value was the basis of the regulatory framework that underpinned the financial system in most major centres of the world prior to the Financial Crisis of 2007–9. New information becomes available all the time but to the extent that this information really is new, it is unpredictable. In hindsight it always seems that we could have foreseen events after they have arisen; a chain of causality can invariably be established.

The EMH implies there is no predictability in stock prices which means that no one investor can gain any benefit through exploiting predictability. There has been considerable research into the EMH following the Financial Crisis. Research suggests that there may be some predictability in stock prices depending on certain circumstances. Smaller companies quoted on stock markets may not have many buyers and sellers and price movements are more predictable for these types of companies. Secondly, the time period under consideration may also reveal some predictability. Comparing the return to a stock in any one week with that of the next appears to have a more significant relationship than comparisons between one particular week and a year hence. It has also been shown that if a stock is subject to rising prices in one period of time, this is followed by lower prices in the next period; how long this period of time is varies between stocks but is capable of being defined with careful analysis of historical data. There is also evidence that analysis of a company's earnings over time shows that they are less volatile than the change in the price of the stock over that same period of time. If markets were efficient, we might expect the relationship between the two to be much closer.

Other patterns which suggest markets are not efficient include the fact that returns on stocks tend to be higher in January on average than at other times of the year. In addition, the time of the day or week when purchasing shares can also affect returns. Research suggests that buying shares late in the day on Tuesday or on Thursday can result in higher than average returns than buying at other times during the week. Similarly, late on Wednesday and on Fridays seems to be the best time to sell shares and returns over the weekend tend to be lower than at other times during the week (possibly because the number of buyers and sellers in the market is lower at this time).

These patterns give rise to predictability which can be exploited by those in the market. However, it must be considered that if this information is freely available and widely known, then it will be built into decision-making. In so doing the opportunity for profiting from the predictability disappears or becomes so small as to not be worthwhile exploiting.

Herd Mentality Much of the reasoning behind the EMH is based on the assumption of rational behaviour. The question raised in the wake of the Financial Crisis was the extent to which 'bubbles' in asset prices represented rational behaviour as opposed to a herd mentality or mass psychology. If speculative bubbles do exist, it suggests that markets react to what Alan Greenspan, a former chair of the Fed, called 'irrational exuberance', and what Keynes referred to as 'animal spirits'. In speculative bubbles, asset prices rise because of an expectation of what others will think the asset will be worth in the future. This is referred to as herd mentality. Herd mentality is a central characteristic of behavioural finance, a relatively new branch of finance which seeks to incorporate understanding of behavioural and cognitive psychology with finance economics.

Rather than looking at information, analyzing it rationally and basing decisions on the data available, herd mentality can take over and people respond to others' behaviour. It can manifest itself when markets are rising as they were in the period before the Crisis. If house prices have been rising for 20 years, why shouldn't they continue to rise in the next 20 years? Participants in the market may not be expert analysts but ordinary households making decisions with imperfect knowledge. People taking on mortgages or buying second homes may not have looked at other relevant data such as the growth in credit and changes in real wages which may have an impact on longer term property prices. People jump into the market having heard of the returns that can be made and as more people join in, decision-making becomes further based on mimicking others' behaviour rather than on fundamental analysis.

Herd mentality is not a new phenomenon. In the 16th century, many people lost large sums of money in the tulip market. In the 18th century, similar losses were experienced by investors who had bought shares in the South Sea Company; the Great Depression of the 1930s was triggered in part by a speculative boom in shares and in the latter part of the 20th century, investors lost money in the so called 'dot com' bubble. What appears to be a common feature of these episodes is the spreading of news about 'easy money' which leads to more and more people wanting to be involved to take advantage. There is an old adage which says that if something sounds too good to be true, it probably is. There is a subtle difference between valuing an asset based on fundamental analysis – the present value of future dividends – and valuing it based on the emulation of others' behaviour and an assumption that prices will rise indefinitely. When the price gets detached from the fundamentals and starts to be contingent only on what everyone in the market expects everyone else will think, a bubble starts to form.

Keynes believed that, given the fact most investors would sell shares they own at some point in the future, it was not unreasonable to have some concern about others' valuation of that asset. Such views could lead to irrational waves of optimism and pessimism. The EMH is based on an assumption that there are a sufficient number of people in the market who act rationally to counter the few that do not.

Asset Price Bubbles

Bubbles exists when the market price of an asset exceeds its price based on fundamental analysis over a period (how long a period is debatable). This definition implies that prices will increase much higher than their fundamental value and when the bubble bursts, price falls will be similarly significant. There is much debate about whether asset price bubbles ever exist and if they do what should be done about them. Part of the debate arises because if bubbles do exist, they are driven by behavioural factors rather than rational analysis. The EMH would suggest that large swings in asset prices are the result of major changes in information about fundamentals. Proponents of the EMH view would argue that bubbles can only exist if driven by irrational behaviour or rigidities in the market, which prevents prices from adjusting quickly. These market rigidities might exist if the market is small, for example, as noted earlier.

The challenges for the authorities (central banks and government) is to be able to tell when a bubble is occurring and if it is, whether to take action and when. A decision to intervene and take policy action to 'burst' the bubble would have to be dependent on whether the authorities believed that the bubble was going to get out of hand and that it would have damaging effects on the wider economy when it does burst. It could be that the bubble will burst of its own accord and the market self corrects. Research into major bubbles suggests different levels of effect on the economy.

The potential danger is that bubbles affect the real economy through a wealth effect which fuels consumer spending and encourages firms to make decisions based on changes in their balance sheets as a result of changing asset values. The increase in house prices in the US and UK did fuel additional borrowing and further consumer spending and this led to an acceleration of inflation which prompted central banks to increase interest rates. If central banks intervene too early and attempt to burst the bubble, would the effect on the wider economy be more damaging than the aftermath of the bubble bursting of its own accord? These are unknowns and require judgement on behalf of central bankers.

This is highlighted by comments made by Fed chair, Ben Bernanke. In May 2007, for example, he had given a speech at a conference in Chicago and said:

'We believe the effect of the troubles in the sub-prime sector on the broader housing market will likely be limited, and we do not expect significant spillovers from the sub-prime market to the rest of the economy or to the financial system.'

(http://www.federalreserve.gov/newsevents/speech/bernanke20070517a.htm)

He reiterated this view a month later when he said:

'At this point, the troubles in the sub-prime sector seem unlikely to seriously spill over to the broader economy or the financial system.'

(http://www.federalreserve.gov/newsevents/speech/Bernanke20070605a.htm)

This illustrates the difficulties in assessing whether a bubble exists, the extent of it if it does exist, what its effects are likely to be and whether intervention is necessary. The challenges are made more difficult with globalization making it much easier for money to move between economic centres around the global economy.

Research into bubbles has identified some common characteristics which might provide indicators to policymakers. Bubbles tend to occur during periods of low inflation when interest rates are also likely to be relatively low. Market liquidity tends to be relatively fluid meaning that borrowers can access funds. As a result, borrowers become too aggressive in **leveraging** – borrowing funds for investment in the expectation of a return. These conditions see people coming into the market for a chance to make a profit based not on fundamentals but on the value they think other people will be prepared to pay at some point in the future. This is the point where animal instincts or herd mentality takes over. When this happens, economic actors under-price risk. For many sub-prime mortgage owners, it can be argued that few had a complete understanding of the risks they faced in taking on debt.

leveraging borrowing funds for investment in the expectation of a return

The person who developed the model of the EMH, Eugene Famer, has faced considerable criticism since the Crisis. However, in 2013, he was awarded the Nobel Prize for Economics for his work on capital asset pricing. In his Nobel Prize lecture, Famer addressed the issue of asset price bubbles. In his speech, he noted that proponents of bubbles argue that the bursting of bubbles represent a market correction of irrational price increases. He noted that evidence suggests major falls in stock prices are relatively quickly followed by price increases that more than correct the price fall. He poses the questions: is the initial price rise caused by 'irrational exuberance'; is the price fall caused by irrational pessimism or the subsequent price rise caused by further irrational exuberance?

On the difficulties of identifying bubbles, Fama argues that it is easy to highlight a few people who had predicted bubbles after the event, something he refers to as 'ex-post selection bias'. In his Nobel Prize speech, he cites two examples. One concerned Yale economist Robert J. Shiller, who claimed that he had warned then Fed chairman, Alan Greenspan, in 1996 of irrationally high stock prices. Fama presents an example of the Centre for Research in Security Prices (CRSP) Index of US stock market wealth. In December 1996, the index was 1518; in September 2000 it had reached 3191 but then fell. Was this a bubble? When the bubble burst did it result in a significant fall in prices? Did Shiller have information which was that much better than thousands of other people? Fama notes that the CRSP fell to a low of 1739 by March 2003, 15 per cent above its December 1996 level. He then poses the question were prices irrationally high when Shiller alerted Greenspan in 1996 or have they continued to be irrationally high?

The second example relates to house prices. In 2003, Karl E. Case and Shiller published a paper called 'Is there a bubble in the housing market?' Using the S&P/Case-Shiller 20-City Home Price Index, Fama notes that it rose from 142.99 in July 2003 to a peak of 206.52 in July 2006. If this represents a bubble and was predicted by Case and Shiller, prices would fall significantly and indeed the Index reflected this, reaching a low of 134.07 in March 2012. Fama points out that this price fall was 6.7 per cent in comparison to July 2003 and questions whether the value to homeowners from housing services in the nine years from 2003 to 2012 was less than 6.7 per cent? He then goes on to point out that the index in October 2013 was 165.91, 16 per cent above the July 2003 level. Were prices irrationally high in 2003 and were they also irrationally high in 2013?

Summary The debate over bubbles reflects that of the rationality and behavioural approaches and of economic methodology. Fama puts his faith in the development of models which are subject to testing against evidence. If found wanting, the model can either be an inappropriate one, which needs adjustment to better explain what is happening, or that markets are inefficient. If it is the latter, which the idea of bubbles implies, then other models need to be developed which offer a coherent alternative. Fama argues that to date, no such alternative has been put forward. Proponents of the behavioural approach argue that there is much evidence of 'animal spirits', 'irrational exuberance' or 'herd mentality', not least through the work of Kahneman and Tversky and others, which we outlined in Chapter 12. There is no reason to believe that the insights provided by this research applies any less to finance markets than any other walk of life.

Perhaps it is safe to conclude that there is much life in the debate and provides interesting avenues for further research.

CASE STUDY The South Sea Bubble

In 1720, Isaac Newton is quoted as saying 'I can calculate the motions of the heavenly bodies but not the madness of people.' Newton had made a profit of £7000 (about £800 000 or €1.03 million in today's values) selling shares of the South Sea Company in April of that year. Along with many other people, however, Newton believed that the value of the company would continue to rise and he purchased more shares. Newton ended up losing £20 000 (about £2.3 million or €3 million).

The South Sea Company was formed in 1711. It entered into an agreement to assume part of the debt of the government, which at the time was financing the War of Spanish Succession, in return for a monopoly on the trade to Spanish colonies in South America. The Treaty of Utrecht was signed in 1713 to end the war. Its terms were not favourable to the South Sea Company as it limited trade opportunities to the Spanish colonies. A further debt conversion was announced in 1719 where the South Sea Company became just one of three corporations, including the Bank of England, which owned around 36 per cent of the total national debt. Despite the fact that the company had no real evidence of trading success, the directors of the company continued to make claims to shareholders of the wealth and riches that trade promised, not least large quantities of gold and silver just waiting to be brought back to Europe.

In January 1720, the South Sea Company's share price was £128. The claims by the Company pushed up the share price and more dabbling in debt conversion with Parliament saw its price rise to £550 by the end of March. Newton sold his shares in April; by May the price had risen further. In June Parliament passed the Bubble Act which was introduced by the South Sea Company and required all joint-stock companies to acquire a royal charter. Part of the reason for the legislation was to help control the explosion of companies entering the market all making claims for their ventures which were sending prices rising causing mini-bubbles. Cynics would argue that the South Sea Company also used the legislation to manage the growing threat of competition it faced. Having received its royal charter, shareholders took this as being a sign that the company's claims were sound and demand for its shares continued to rise. By the end of June, the share price had risen to £1050.

For some reason (and this perhaps is where Newton's lament over the madness of people is most pertinent), some people began to sell their shares and the share price began to fall in July. For those that had come in near the top of the market (like Newton's second purchase) the imperative to sell became more urgent. The price continued to fall quickly and by September stood at around £175. The collapse affected thousands of people and a number of institutions. Subsequent investigations into the collapse revealed bribery and corruption practices and prosecutions of company officials and members of the government.

The South Sea Bubble was an example of how asset prices can rise way above their true market value. It seems that history can repeat itself and in many ways, the issues that existed then (a lack of knowledge by participants in the market) is similar to today. The complexities of how markets operate may be far greater and the technologies far more sophisticated, but the success of markets relies to a large extent on participants having good information on which to base their decisions. No matter how intelligent an individual is, it seems, if they do not have access to all available information then poor decisions can be made as Newton found out to his cost.

The South Sea Scheme – a caricature by William Hogarth, an 18th-century sociocritical English painter and graphic artist.

The Efficient Markets Hypothesis in Hindsight

It is easy to use hindsight and reflect that price rises in the housing market in the first half of the noughties was a classic example of an asset and credit bubble. We have noted that most financial institutions employed very smart people who searched for ways of analyzing and predicting the market to make profits. We have also seen that it is difficult to be clear if and when a bubble is occurring and if it is, what to do about it. If economic actors recognize that a bubble exists, then this will become part of known information and result in action in kind.

During a bubble it makes sense to sell when prices are high in the expectation and knowledge that prices are going to fall. One thing to note is that in market trades there will always be a winner and a loser. If one trader manages to exploit undervaluation, someone on the opposite side of the trade must have been overvaluing that same trade in order for the exchange to take place. At any one time, there may be people predicting a bubble and those scoffing at the idea; both cannot be right. Fama argues that the word 'bubble' has little meaning and that observations on whether markets are experiencing a bubble are right and wrong in equal measures.

Surely the Financial Crisis is evidence that there was little rational behaviour in financial markets? Fama counters that part of the sub-prime problem was down to US government policy to promote home ownership among all classes of society and that it was not just the collapse in sub-prime house prices that caused the Financial Crisis but a global fall in house prices which took place across most house price bands, not simply those linked to sub-prime.

This decline resulted in problems for the banking sector and a lack of availability of credit in markets. This could be argued to be an economic cause – a global downturn in economic activity which led to people in all walks of life being unable to meet their credit (and mortgage) commitments. There will always be a group of people who are at the margin – just able to afford their commitments provided things don't change – but when they do, these people are the first to default; they are literally living on the edge. Fama argues that the downturn in economic activity started to show itself before the financial crisis as a worldwide fall in house prices. There is still considerable debate amongst macroeconomists about what actually causes recessions and it can be argued that the financial markets were a victim of the recession and not the cause of it.

Supporters of the EMH argue that financial markets provide a conduit from those who wish to save to those who wish to borrow – including corporates – and that financial innovation of the type that generated CDOs and CDS have contributed much to the development of countries across the globe and to the welfare of millions of people over the last 30 years. If the EMH is about valuing stock prices using all available information, there is an assumption that markets will understand completely the models which they are working with and the information which they have available to price assets. It is highly unlikely that every economic actor knows everything about what they are working with and so there is always some element of unknown information. Those fund managers working with David Li's formula, for example, may not have fully understood the model but chose to use it anyway, and decisions are made with less than complete information.

Minsky's Financial Instability Hypothesis

Hyman Minsky (1919–96) was Professor of Economics at Washington University in St Louis in the US. Minsky began writing on financial instability in the 1950s. Despite his death in 1996, many of his ideas have been revived and have relevance to the Financial Crisis of 2007–9. Minsky was a keen student of business cycles. He rejected the classical assumption that the invisible hand would result in equilibrium but also rejected the Keynesian idea of demand management. Minsky saw capitalism as fundamentally flawed and that financial crises were a natural feature of such a system.

Minsky's hypothesis began with an assumption that a capitalist economy has capital assets and a sophisticated financial system. Firms in capitalist systems buy resources which represent future income streams or profit. Part of the spending on resources includes investment in capital. Much investment is purchased using borrowed money, which are liabilities on a firm's balance sheet. These liabilities are, in effect, a commitment undertaken by firms to pay streams of money at points in the future, including the eventual repayment of the principal. The facilitators of these exchanges are the institutions of the financial system, including banks. Depositors place their money into these financial institutions who use the money to lend to firms. At some future time, firms will repay the money (and will also pay interest) and this money effectively flows through banks back to depositors. In effect, depositors have a claim on future profits of firms. Expectations of the size of these profits is a key determinant in the flow of money from depositors to financial institutions and then to firms. Actual profits will validate the contracts made between depositors and financial institutions – in other words, in the case of a bond, whether the bond holder will get what they signed up for when they purchased the asset.

The financial system is complicated by the fact that households are able to access credit to buy consumer goods and invest in shares and other financial assets.

Governments are also heavily involved in the financial system, borrowing for their own use and, in some cases, stepping in to bailout financial institutions and firms. Many central banks are now independent of government but this does not mean they are not influenced by government policy. For example, the Bank of England is tasked with the responsibility of maintaining stable inflation as well as overseeing the security and efficiency of the financial system.

The emphasis on the way the capitalist system works is central to the instability hypothesis and in particular the link between expected profits and investment. The question Minsky proposed was what role debt has in this system? He accepted that financial institutions are profit-making bodies and that profits can be increased through innovation. Minsky referred to bankers as 'merchants of debt'. There are different ways in which financial institutions can operate. One way is to take in deposits, re-lend and hedge against the risk involved, specifically the risk of default. This might be viewed as 'traditional banking'.

A second way is through speculative financing. Here, the obligations an institution has are met by the income streams it receives although these income streams are insufficient to pay off the principal. In this case, new debt is issued to enable the institution to meet its principle obligations.

Finally, there are 'Ponzi' units. The term 'Ponzi' is named after an Italian, Charles Ponzi, who developed a money-making venture in America in the 1920s. He relied on attracting new investors to the scheme, whose money was used to pay existing investors and hence maintain the venture. Ponzi schemes are illegal across much of the developed world. Ponzi units share some of the characteristics of a Ponzi scheme in that the income streams from activities are insufficient to pay the principal and the interest due on debts. Ponzi units finance their obligations through further borrowing or selling assets. The risk to debt holders of such an approach is considerably higher than hedge financing.

If hedge financing is the main way in which financial institutions operate then the economy may be more like a self-equilibrating system. If, however, speculative and Ponzi finance begins to account for a larger proportion, then the economy will be more likely to be what Minsky called a 'deviation amplification system'. Where financial systems are strong, and appropriate regulation is in place, innovation may be limited and the economy will be experiencing a 'period of tranquillity'. This stability, however, encourages risk taking and innovation (for example, more speculative and Ponzi financing), pushing the economy towards instability and a speculative frenzy which we have seen termed 'irrational exuberance', 'herd mentality', 'animal spirits' and asset bubbles. The situation can be exacerbated by the authorities failing to intervene, partly because they are caught in the belief that the situation is under control and partly because of regulatory capture. **Regulatory capture** refers to a situation where regulatory agencies become unduly influenced and dominated by the industries they are supposed to be regulating.

> **regulatory capture** a situation where regulatory agencies become unduly influenced and dominated by the industries they are supposed to be regulating

In the Financial Crisis, the ratings agencies such as Moody's and Standard & Poors, could be argued to have been subject to regulatory capture given the potential for a conflict of interest to arise because banks paid fees to the agencies rather than to investors. The agencies had a vested interest in keeping their clients (the banks) happy because of their need for repeat business. Central banks may have been seduced by the *Great Moderation* into believing that the period of stable growth, low inflation and high employment could continue. If problems did arise (such as the dot.com boom), their response was to flood the market with liquidity and reduce interest rates. There is, therefore, a complacency which sets in and fails to guard against potential instability.

Minsky's hypothesis, therefore, has three main aspects:

1. Economies can have stable financing systems but also unstable ones.
2. During periods of relative stability and prosperity, the economy will transition to increasing instability as innovation and risk taking increase.
3. Business cycles are not caused by external shocks alone but are made worse by the internal dynamics of a capitalist system.

Minsky argues that financial markets create their own internal forces which generate periods of asset inflation and credit expansion. This will be followed by contractions in credit and asset deflation. Financial markets are not self-optimizing or stable, and far from allocating resources efficiently, the outcomes may be sub-optimal.

Minsky suggested that some of these internal forces relate to the lack of supply of assets which drive demand in those markets. For example, the lack of supply of housing drives demand for housing and forces prices upwards creating a bubble. Changing asset prices (such as houses) in turn act as a driver for demand for those assets. If house prices are rising quickly there is an incentive for buyers to want to get into the market quickly to avoid having to pay higher prices and also to benefit from rising prices once they have purchased. This simply fuels demand further in the face of limited supply and so drives price up higher.

The story of the Financial Crisis resonates remarkably closely with the Minsky hypothesis; it is not surprising, therefore, that his ideas were seen as being 'ahead of their time' and worth reviving and exploring.

SUMMARY

The Financial Crisis led to one of the most damaging economic episodes since the Great Depression. The causes of the Crisis have been well documented and the implications for economics widespread. Some of the fundamental approaches, methodologies and theories which have dominated the discipline have been called into doubt. There have been criticisms of the EMH and developments in behavioural economics applied to finance as economists search for new models and theories which better predict future events.

There are plenty of articles, books and comment on post-Crisis economics. There are many which proclaim that 'dead theories' are walking amongst us and that students are being disadvantaged by being taught these defunct theories. The Nobel Prize committee has also been criticized for awarding the Prize for Economic Sciences to Eugene Fama, and for focusing too much on orthodox approaches to economics. Econometric studies can provide (sometimes) weak support for certain models but users of such approaches argue that this is how empirical study works and simple observation or anecdote is insufficiently rigorous. If a model is to be cast aside, then it is argued, something else has to replace it which is capable of being tested.

There are, however, economists who are defending the orthodoxy and it is perhaps safe to say that the discipline faces an interesting period of development as research continues. This chapter seeks to briefly introduce some of the issues which the Financial Crisis has created. There is much more detail and complexity behind all of the issues covered here and as your studies develop, you may have the opportunity or interest to explore these further. As you read, you will need to exercise judgement in considering the claims and counterclaims of economists and commentators. It is not the intention of this chapter to promote any particular view or model but to outline some of the arguments which have surfaced in the discipline. As we progress through the rest of the book, you will do well to remember that economics is still a relatively young discipline which is still evolving. We will try and present a flavour of that evolution as we continue our journey through macroeconomics.

IN THE NEWS

Efficient Markets

The debate over efficient markets has been one of the central features of the post-Crisis landscape. In this article, we look at a decision by the US Federal Reserve to increase interest rates in December 2015.

The Response to an Increase in Interest Rates

On 15 and 16 December 2015, the US federal open market committee (FOMC) met to discuss the economic situation in the US and beyond, and took the decision to increase the federal funds rate (the rate of interest charged by the Fed on loans to the banking system which sets the interest rate structure across the financial system) to a range between 0.25 per cent and 0.5 per cent. This was seen as an historic decision as it was the first rate increase since 2006. Interest rates had been at historic lows since the Financial Crisis.

A rate rise had been expected for some time, many economists had been predicting that there would be a rise at the previous meeting of the FOMC in October 2015. It didn't happen then but signals from the Fed chair, Janet Yellen, led many to believe that a rise in December was a certainty. The attention quickly turned from the rate rise itself to the future prospects for further rate rises and the speed at which the Fed would increase rates further.

One interesting element of the whole episode was the comparisons drawn between the role of Janet Yellen and that of Mark Carney, the governor of the Bank of England. Carney had spoken of potential rate rises in the UK several times through 2014 and 2015, at one stage indicating that once unemployment fell to 7 per cent or lower, interest rates would be increased. Unemployment in the UK fell below this level but the Bank of England did not increase interest rates. Critics of Carney pointed to the clear signals that Yellen had been sending as opposed to the vacillation in those sent by the Bank.

The words of central bank heads are considered extremely important. It is often written that 'every word is being closely scrutinized by economists' to get some clues and insight into central bank policy and thinking. The clear signals sent by Yellen were liked by the financial markets because it provided an element of certainty, and markets like certainty. The interest rate rise was expected by the markets and had already been priced into deals long before the actual announcement was made on 16 December 2015. To the extent that the rate rise was not a shock and was expected, it becomes part of the available information, and markets can base decisions on this information accordingly. This is what the EMH would predict; markets process information efficiently. Tim Worstall, a Fellow at the Adam Smith Institute in London, and opinion writer for Forbes (amongst other magazines and news services) wrote the following:

'there's flavours of this theory [EMH] but just about all economists would sign up to the "weak" flavour... It would be very difficult indeed to find an economist out there who wouldn't be happy enough with that description. Sure, we could find someone who said that only 95 per cent of the effect is already in prices, others who might argue for 99 per cent. But the basic idea: something as well known as the Fed's interest rate rise is already in prices is agreed.'

Maybe the EMH is not dead after all?

The signals sent out by central banks such as The Bank of England are deemed vital to market information flows and decision-making.

(*Continued*)

Questions

1 One of the key conclusions of the EMH is that 'you can't beat the market'. Is the fact that financial institutions employed highly qualified maths, physics and statistics graduates to develop ways to exploit information asymmetries testament to the view that few working in financial markets believed in the EMH? Explain your reasoning.

2 What is meant by the phrase 'the markets would have already priced in the interest rate rise'?

3 Why is certainty important to financial markets?

4 Why do you think that interest rates in many developed countries have stayed very low since the Financial Crisis?

5 To what extent to do you agree with the view expressed by Tim Worstall? In considering his view, what sort of questions would you ask about him and his background to enable you to evaluate his comments objectively?

SUMMARY

- A period of relative economic stability across many developed economies was referred as The Great Moderation or Great Stability.

- Deregulation of financial markets had been a feature of policy in the US and UK which led to an increase in innovation and a build-up of debt and credit by households and governments.

- House prices had been rising for some time and the belief that they would continue to rise led to more people becoming mortgage holders including those who had poor credit ratings.

- As inflation began to accelerate, central banks began to increase interest rates and the number of people defaulting on mortgages began to rise.

- As the number of defaults increased, the complex web of financial interdependence began to unravel and a number of banks and financial institutions collapsed or had to be bailed out by governments.

- The Financial Crisis led to one of the worst economic downturns since the Great Depression. Many countries are still suffering the effects.

- A number of economic theories and approaches came under severe criticism following the Crisis. In particular, the EMH came under attack for ignoring behavioural effects which were seen as being at the heart of asset bubbles.

- Other approaches and theories saw a revival of interest including Keynesian demand management and Minsky's Financial Instability Hypothesis.

QUESTIONS FOR REVIEW

1 What were the main characteristics of The Great Moderation?

2 What is deregulation and what were the main features of the deregulation of the financial markets in the 1980s and 1990s?

3 What were the causes of the rise in house prices in the UK and the US between 1980 and 2005?

4 What is meant by the term 'sub-prime market'?

5 Describe the role of financial innovation in the lead up to the Financial Crisis.

6 Why did many countries experience a banking crisis in 2007–8?

7 What is meant by the term 'efficient markets hypothesis'?

8 What is meant by the term 'animal instincts'?

9 What are the main characteristics of asset bubbles?

10 Briefly outline the key features of Minsky's Financial Instability Hypothesis.

PROBLEMS AND APPLICATIONS

1 Explain how deregulation of the financial system may have affected the following:

 a. A newly married couple, aged 24, who have just secured their first job and want to buy a house.
 b. Joint homeowners with a house valued at £350 000 with a mortgage of £200 000 who want to celebrate their 25th wedding anniversary with a world cruise and who are looking to borrow money to do so.
 c. The market for newly constructed properties.

2 In the face of a financial crisis such as that created by the dot.com collapse and the 9/11 terrorist attacks in the United States, why would a central bank have responded by lowering interest rates and flooding the markets with liquidity?

3 The chapter refers to former head of the Federal Reserve Bank, Alan Greenspan's comment on 'the unquenchable capability of human beings when confronted with long periods of prosperity to presume that it will continue'. What do you think he meant by this?

4 As the Financial Crisis developed, newspapers often carried lurid headlines about the extent to which house prices were falling, for example, 'House Prices Fall 50 Per Cent'. Economists might view these headlines from a more critical perspective:

 a. What does *'House Prices Fall 50 Per Cent'* actually mean? (This might sound a strange question but think about it from a homeowner's perspective.)
 b. Is the price of a house and its value the same thing? Explain.
 c. Is the value of a house only relevant to those who are actually buying and selling a property? Explain.
 d. A homeowner bought a house in 2003 for €320 000 and in 2006 it was valued at €550 000. They had to sell the property at the height of the Financial Crisis due to a job relocation. The price they received was €380 000. How much did the homeowner lose (if anything)? Explain your answer.

5 Why did banks and other mortgage lenders believe that it was 'safe' to turn their attention to lending money for the purchase of property to people with very low, or non-existent credit ratings?

6 What is meant by the term 'efficient' in the efficient markets hypothesis?

7 Consider some of the implications of the assumption of rational behaviour in a market for an asset such as bonds. What might you expect to see happening in such a market in response to new information?

8 Consider Eugene Fama's comments in his Nobel Prize lecture on identifying asset bubbles.

 a. Do the examples he gives convince you that the concept of asset bubbles have 'little meaning'?
 b. If people are aware of herd mentality then should this imply that such behaviour will become part of the available information that people will factor into decision-making?

9 'I suspect that the end result will not be an abandonment of the belief of many in the profession that the stock market is remarkably efficient in its utilization of information. Periods such as 1999 where "bubbles" seem to have existed, at least in certain sectors of the market, are fortunately the exception rather than the rule. Moreover, whatever patterns or irrationalities in the pricing of individual stocks that have been discovered in a search of historical experience, are unlikely to persist and will not provide investors with a method to obtain extraordinary returns. If any $100 bills are lying around the stock exchanges of the world, they will not be there for long.' (Malkiel, B.G. (2003) *The Efficient Markets Hypothesis and its Critics*. CEPS Working Paper no 91). To what extent would you agree with this assessment of the value of the EMH?

10 Does Minsky's Financial Instability Hypothesis provide a more coherent explanation for the Financial Crisis? If so, what policy implications does the hypothesis suggest?

27 THE MONETARY SYSTEM

One of the key requirements of a capitalist system is the use of a medium of exchange or money. Paper and metals used as money have no intrinsic value, but their use in society is based on the trust that it will be accepted in exchange. The development of credit and debit cards and contactless payment systems are also widely used because it is accepted that money will be transferred more or less instantly from one bank account to another.

The social custom of using money for transactions is extraordinarily useful in a large, complex society. Prior to the development of capitalist societies, many people relied on **barter** – the exchange of one good or service for another – to obtain the things they needed. A capitalist economy would not function if it relied on barter primarily because trade would require the **double coincidence of wants** – a situation where parties to an exchange each have a good or service that the other wants.

> **barter** the exchange of one good or service for another
> **double coincidence of wants** a situation in exchange where two parties each have a good or service that the other wants and can thus enter into an exchange

The existence of money makes trade easier. As money flows from person to person in the economy, it facilitates production and trade, thereby allowing specialization. In this chapter we begin to examine the role of money in an economy. Because money is so important, we devote much effort in the rest of this book to learning how changes in the quantity of money affect various economic variables, including inflation, interest rates, production and employment. Consistent with our long-run focus in the previous three chapters, in the next chapter we will examine the long-run effects of changes in the quantity of money. The short-run effects of monetary changes are a more complex topic, which we will take up later in the book. This chapter provides the background for all of this further analysis.

THE MEANING OF MONEY

Money is the set of assets in the economy that people regularly use to buy goods and services from other people. Cash is money because it can be used to buy a meal at a restaurant or a ticket to a music festival. By contrast, if you happened to own part of Facebook, as Mark Zuckerberg does, you would be wealthy, but this asset is not considered a form of money. You could not buy a meal or a festival ticket with this wealth without first obtaining some cash. According to the economist's definition, money includes only those few types of wealth that are regularly accepted by sellers in exchange for goods and services.

> **money** the set of assets in an economy that people regularly use to buy goods and services from other people

The Functions of Money

Money has three functions in the economy: it is a medium of exchange; a unit of account; and a store of value. These three functions together distinguish money from other assets in the economy, such as stocks, bonds, residential property and works of art.

A Medium of Exchange When a buyer and seller enter into a transaction money acts as the **medium of exchange**, the item that buyers give to sellers when they purchase goods and services. This transfer of money from buyer to seller allows the transaction to take place. When you walk into a shop, you are confident that the shop will accept your money for the items it is selling because money is the commonly accepted medium of exchange.

medium of exchange an item that buyers give to sellers when they want to purchase goods and services

A Unit of Account In a market economy, buyers and sellers need a way in which they can measure and record transactions and draw comparisons. A **unit of account** is the yardstick people use to post prices and record debts. When you go shopping, you might observe that a pair of shoes is priced at €80 and a ham-and-cheese sandwich at €2. Even though it would be accurate to say that the price of a pair of shoes is 40 sandwiches and the price of a sandwich is $\frac{1}{40}$ of a pair of shoes, prices are never quoted in this way. Similarly, if you take out a loan in euros or pounds from a bank, the size of your future loan repayments will be measured in euros or pounds, not in a quantity of goods and services. When we want to measure and record economic value, we use money as the unit of account.

unit of account the yardstick people use to post prices and record debts

A Store of Value When a seller accepts money today in exchange for a good or service, that seller can hold the money and become a buyer of another good or service at another time. A **store of value** is an item that people can use to transfer purchasing power from the present to the future. Money is not the only store of value in the economy, for a person can also transfer purchasing power from the present to the future by holding other assets. The term **wealth** is used to refer to the total of all stores of value, including both money and non-monetary assets.

store of value an item that people can use to transfer purchasing power from the present to the future
wealth the total of all stores of value, including both money and non-monetary assets

Liquidity

Economists use the term **liquidity** to describe the ease with which an asset can be converted into the economy's medium of exchange. Because money is the economy's medium of exchange, it is the most liquid asset available. Other assets vary widely in their liquidity. Most stocks and bonds can be sold easily with small cost, so they are relatively liquid assets. By contrast, selling a car or a piece of art work requires more time and effort, so these assets are less liquid.

liquidity the ease with which an asset can be converted into the economy's medium of exchange

When people decide in what form to hold their wealth, they have to balance the liquidity of each possible asset against its usefulness as a store of value. Money may be the most liquid asset, but it is far from perfect as a store of value. When prices rise, the value of money falls. In other words, when goods and services become more expensive, each euro or pound in your pocket can buy less.

The Kinds of Money

When money takes the form of a commodity with intrinsic value, it is called **commodity money**. The term *intrinsic value* means that the item would have value even if it were not used as money. One example of commodity money is gold. Gold has intrinsic value because it is used in industry and in the making of jewellery. Although today we no longer use gold as money, historically gold has been a common form of money because it is relatively easy to carry, measure, and verify for impurities. When an economy uses gold as money (or uses paper money that is convertible into gold on demand), it is said to be operating under a **gold standard**.

> **commodity money** money that takes the form of a commodity with intrinsic value
> **gold standard** a system in which the currency is based on the value of gold and where the currency can be converted to gold on demand

Although gold has, historically, been the most common form of commodity money, other commodity monies have been used from time to time. For example, in the hyperinflation in Zimbabwe in the early 2000s the country's people began to lose faith in the Zimbabwean dollar; people began to trade goods and services with one another, using cigarettes as the store of value, unit of account and medium of exchange.

Money without intrinsic value is called **fiat money**. A fiat is simply an order or decree, and fiat money is established as money by government decree. For example paper euros are able to circulate as legal tender in 19 European countries because the governments of those countries have decreed that the euro be valid currency in each of their economies.

> **fiat money** money without intrinsic value that is used as money because of government decree

Although governments are central to establishing and regulating a system of fiat money (by having a monopoly in issuing notes and coins and prosecuting counterfeiters, for example), other factors are also required for the success of such a monetary system. To a large extent, the acceptance of fiat money depends as much on expectations and social convention as on government decree. Zimbabweans preferred to accept cigarettes (or American dollars) in exchange for goods and services, because they were more confident that these alternative monies would be accepted by others in the future.

Money in the Economy

As we will see, the quantity of money circulating in the economy, called the **money stock**, has a powerful influence on many economic variables.

> **money stock** the quantity of money circulating in the economy

In determining the money stock, the most obvious asset to include is **currency** – the paper notes and metal coins in the hands of the public. Currency is clearly the most widely accepted medium of exchange in a modern economy.

currency the paper banknotes and coins in the hands of the public

Yet currency is not the only asset that you can use to buy goods and services. Most businesses also accept payment by debit card, which allows money to be transferred electronically between bank accounts.

A debit card is not really money in itself; it is the bank account on which the debit card draws which contains the money. A debit card is just a *means* of transferring money between accounts. Credit cards are not really a method of payment but a method of *deferring* payment. When you buy a meal with a credit card, the bank that issued the card pays the restaurant what it is due – you have effectively borrowed from the bank. At a later date, you will have to repay the bank (perhaps with interest). When the time comes to pay your credit card bill, you will probably do so by direct transfer from your current account. The balance in this current account is part of the economy's stock of money. Notice that credit cards are very different from debit cards, which automatically withdraw funds from a bank account to pay for items bought. A restaurateur is willing to accept payment by credit card because they get money immediately by having their bank account credited for the price of the meal, even though you do not have to pay the credit card company back immediately. Again, however, it is the underlying movement in the restaurateur's bank balance that matters.

Thus, although a debit card and a credit card can each be used to settle the restaurant bill, none of them are money – they are each a method of transferring money between bank accounts. The true movement in money occurs when bank balances change.

Wealth held in current bank accounts, therefore, is almost as convenient for buying things as wealth held as cash. Measures of the money stock include **demand deposits** – balances in bank accounts that depositors can access *on demand* simply by using their debit card. It is not only balances in current accounts that are part of the money stock, there are a large variety of other accounts that people hold at banks and other financial institutions. Bank depositors usually cannot use their debit cards against the balances in their savings accounts, but they can (mostly) easily transfer funds from savings into current accounts. In addition, depositors in money market funds can often use debit cards against their balances. Thus, these other accounts should plausibly be counted as part of the money stock.

demand deposits balances in bank accounts that depositors can access on demand by using a debit card

In a complex economy, it is, in general, not easy to draw a line between assets that can be called 'money' and assets that cannot. The coins in your pocket are clearly part of the money stock, and your smart phone clearly is not, but there are many assets for which the choice is less clear. Therefore, various measures of the money stock are available for advanced economies. Panel (a) of Figure 27.1 shows the three most important measures for the euro area, in cumulative billions of euro in November 2015. M1 is a 'narrow' measure, M2, an 'intermediate' measure and M3 a 'broad' measure. Each of these measures uses a slightly different criterion for distinguishing between monetary and non-monetary assets. Panel (b) of Figure 27.1 shows a breakdown of the various components of the money stock.

In the UK, the most widely observed measures of the money stock are M0 (a narrower measure than the European M1, corresponding to notes and coins in circulation plus bankers' balances held with the Bank of England) and M4 (a broad measure, similar – but not identical – to the European M3).

For our purposes in this book, we need not dwell on the differences between the various measures of money. The important point is that the money stock for an advanced economy includes not just currency but also deposits in banks and other financial institutions that can be readily accessed and used to buy goods and services.

FIGURE 27.1

Three Measures of the Money Stock for the Euro Area (billions of euro), November 2015

Panel (a) shows the three measures of euro area money stock. M1 (a 'narrow' monetary aggregate that comprises currency in circulation and overnight deposits), M2 (an 'intermediate' monetary aggregate that comprises M1 plus deposits with an agreed maturity of up to two years and deposits redeemable at notice of up to three months) and M3 (a 'broad' monetary aggregate that comprises M2 plus repurchase agreements, money market fund shares and units as well as debt securities with a maturity of up to two years). Panel (b) shows the size of the different components of the money stock.

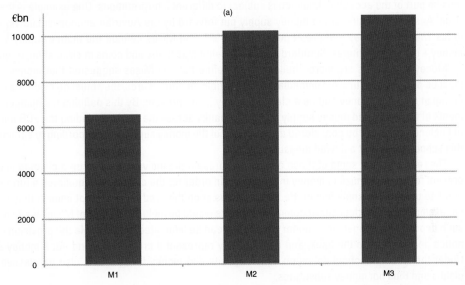

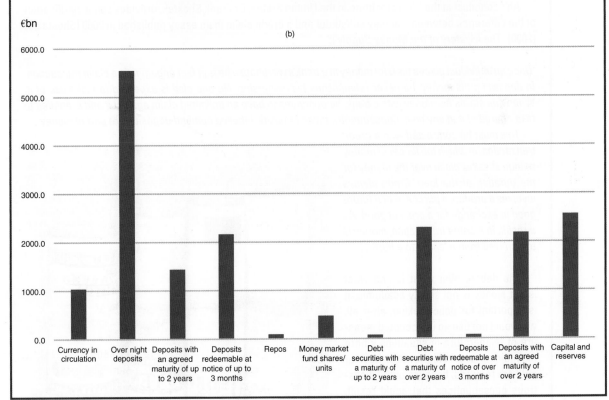

SELF TEST List and describe the three functions of money.

CASE STUDY   The 'True' Austrian Money Supply

As with many aspects of economics, definitions of the money supply are open to different interpretations. The role of the money supply is going to be central to much of the analysis in the rest of this book as noted but it is clear that if the measure of the money supply being used varies then it is likely that the analysis and the conclusions drawn will also vary. Fortunately, economists of almost every persuasion are in agreement that currency – notes and coins – are a part of the money supply. What else should count as money and thus be part of the accepted definition is subject to different interpretations. One example is the so-called 'True' Austrian definition of the money supply put forward by the Austrian economist Ludwig von Mises in his *Theory of Money and Credit* published in 1953. von Mises defined the money supply as standard money + money substitutes. Standard money he defined as notes and coins in circulation, or currency.

Money substitutes are more challenging to define but von Mises suggested that money substitutes must be perfectly secure and immediately convertible. In other words, they must be evidence of the ownership of standard money and be a claim to money in the present. By this definition, a number of the elements of the measured money supply by central banks across the world, including the ECB and the Bank of England, would not be considered as being part of the money supply and, according to economists from this school, represent a flawed measure.

The reason is that some of these elements represent the individual giving up a claim to money in the present for some promise of money in the future. In order for the claim to be liquidated a further transaction has to be made sometime in the future and as such the credit claim is not immediately convertible. For example, savings deposits at commercial banks would be included as part of M2 in many countries but such deposits have legal terms under which they can be liquidated, for example the provision of a 30-day notice period given to the bank, and as such they represent a credit claim and not a money substitute. Under the Austrian school definition, time deposits and money funds would also be classed as credit claims and thus not money substitutes.

An economist at the Mises Institute in the United States, Dr Frank Shostak, provides some clarification of the difference between a money substitute and a credit claim in an essay published in 2000 (Shostak, F. (2000) *'The Mystery of the Money Supply'*):

'Once an individual places his (sic) money in a bank's warehouse he is in fact engaging in a claim transaction. In depositing his money, he never relinquishes his ownership. No one else is expected to make use of it. When Joe stores his money with a bank, he continues to have an unlimited claim against it and is entitled to take charge of it at any time. Consequently, these deposits, labelled demand deposits, are part of money …

This must be contrasted with a credit transaction, in which the lender of money relinquishes his claim over the money for the duration of the loan. Credit always involves a creditor's purchase of a future good in exchange for a present good. As a result, in a credit transaction, money is transferred from a lender to a borrower.'

The debate over what is and what is not money is not simply academic, it is important for policymaking; after all, we would not use an unaccepted measure of temperature in situations where maintaining a specific level of heat or cold are required, because of the disastrous consequences that could result. If we use incorrect measures of the money supply it follows that the consequences could be equally serious.

What is the true measure of the money supply?

THE ROLE OF CENTRAL BANKS

Whenever an economy relies on a system of fiat money – as all modern advanced economies do – many (but not all) economists believe that some agency must be responsible for regulating the system. This agency is generally known as the **central bank** – an institution designed to regulate the quantity of money made available in the economy, called the **money supply**. Two of the most important central banks in Europe are the European Central Bank and the Bank of England. Other major central banks around the world include the US central bank – the Federal Reserve – the Bank of Japan and the People's Bank of China.

> **central bank** an institution designed to regulate the quantity of money in the economy
> **money supply** the quantity of money available in the economy

The Functions of Central Banks

Most central banks have two main functions; macroeconomic stability is the maintenance of stable growth and prices and the avoidance of excessive and damaging swings in economic activity. The second main function is the maintenance of stability in the financial system. To achieve the first function, central banks have the power to increase or decrease the amount of currency in that economy. The set of actions taken by the central bank in order to affect the money supply is known as **monetary policy**.

> **monetary policy** the set of actions taken by the central bank in order to affect the money supply

We discuss later in this chapter how the central bank actually changes the money supply, but it is worth noting here that an important tool the central bank can use is **open market operations** – the purchase and sale of non-monetary assets from and to the banking sector. For example, if the central bank decides to increase the money supply, it can do this by 'creating currency' through buying bonds in the bond market. After the purchase, the extra currency is in the hands of former bond holders (or more specifically, in their bank accounts). Thus, an open market purchase of bonds by the central bank increases the money supply. Conversely, if the central bank decides to decrease the money supply, it can do this by selling bonds from its portfolio. After the sale, the currency it receives for the bonds leads to a reduction in bank accounts. Thus, open market sale of bonds by the central bank decreases the money supply.

> **open market operations** the purchase and sale of non-monetary assets from and to the banking sector by the central bank

The central bank of an economy is an important institution because changes in the money supply can profoundly affect the economy. For reasons we discuss more fully in the coming chapters, the central bank's policy decisions have an important influence on the economy's rate of inflation in the long run and the economy's employment and production in the short run. In particular, because of the link between the amount of money in the economy and the inflation rate, the central bank is often tasked as the guardian of price stability in a modern economy charged with the duty to maintain inflation at or near an inflation target – a policy we'll discuss more fully in the coming chapters. To be precise, the central bank should perhaps be thought of as the guardian of inflation stability, rather than price stability, since even with a constant, low rate of inflation, prices are by definition rising. Still, if inflation is low and stable, prices might be said to be rising in a stable fashion – and, in any case, this usage is now well established, so we'll follow suit.

To maintain financial stability, central banks use their relationship with the rest of the banking system to supply liquidity, the cash needed to ensure transactions in the financial system are honoured. Banks have both long-term and short-term assets and also have deposits on demand which can be withdrawn at any time. At any time, therefore, banks can run short of the liquidity necessary to meet their obligations and the central bank steps in to provide the funds necessary to ensure that banks can continue to operate. This function is referred to as *lender of last resort*. In most cases, banks are not insolvent, they are simply short of funds at a particular time. The central bank can provide short-term loans to the banking system to ease the flow of funds in the system and ensure liquidity.

Many central banks are also tasked with the responsibility to monitor the banking system and supervise and regulate the system. Central banks assess banks' ability to meet different levels of financial stress and impose regulations to ensure that banks operate in a prudent manner.

THE EUROPEAN CENTRAL BANK AND THE EUROSYSTEM

The **European Central Bank (ECB)**, located in Frankfurt, Germany, was officially created on 1 June 1998 as a number of European countries had decided that they wished to enter European Monetary Union (EMU) and have the same currency – the euro – circulating among them. We'll discuss the pros and cons of monetary union in a later chapter. For now, though, we just note that if a group of countries has the same currency, then it makes sense for the countries in the group to have a common monetary policy, and the ECB was set up for precisely this purpose. There were originally 11 countries making up the euro area: Austria, Belgium, Finland, France, Germany, Ireland, Italy, Luxembourg, the Netherlands, Portugal and Spain. By 2010, there were 16 countries, the new additions being Cyprus, Greece, Malta, Slovakia and Slovenia. Estonia adopted the euro in 2011, Latvia in 2014 and Lithuania in 2015 to make the euro area, at the time of writing, consist of 19 countries.

> **European Central Bank** the overall central bank of the 19 countries comprising the European Monetary Union

The primary objective of the ECB is to promote price stability throughout the euro area and to design and implement monetary policy that is consistent with this objective. The ECB operates with the assistance of the national central banks in each of the euro area countries, such as the Banque de France, the Banca d'Italia, the Bank of Greece and the German Bundesbank. The network made up of the ECB together with the 19 euro area national central banks is termed the **Eurosystem**.

> **Eurosystem** the system made up of the ECB plus the national central banks of each of the 19 countries comprising the European Monetary Union

The implementation of monetary policy by the ECB is under the control of the Executive Board, which comprises the President and Vice-President of the ECB and four other people of high standing in the banking profession. While the Executive Board – as the name suggests – is responsible for *executing* monetary policy, the monetary policy of the ECB is actually designed by the Governing Council, which comprises the whole of the Executive Board plus the governors of the national central banks in the Euro system (25 people in total). The Governing Council, which meets twice a month in Frankfurt, is the most important decision-making body of the ECB and decides, for example, on the level of the ECB's key interest rate, the refinancing rate. The Governing Council also decides how to interpret its duty to achieve price stability. The official definition of the ECB's monetary policy strategy is:

> *'in the pursuit of price stability, it aims to maintain inflation rates below but close to 2 per cent over the medium term'.*

An important feature of the ECB and of the Euro system in general is its independence. When performing Euro system-related tasks, neither the ECB, nor a national central bank, nor any member of their decision-making bodies is allowed to seek or take instructions from any external body, including any member governments or any European Union institutions.

The President of the ECB and other members of the Executive Board are appointed for a minimum non-renewable term of office of eight years (although a system of staggered appointments was used for the first Executive Board for members other than the President in order to ensure continuity) and the governors of the 19 national central banks in the Euro system are appointed for a minimum renewable term of office of five years.

THE BANK OF ENGLAND

The Bank of England was founded in 1694, although it is not the oldest European central bank (the Swedish Riksbank was founded in 1668). Arguably the most significant event in the Bank of England's 300-year history was when the UK government granted it independence in the setting of interest rates in 1997, which was formalized in an Act of Parliament in 1998. The important body within the Bank that makes the decision on the level at which to set the Bank's key interest rate, the repo rate, is the Monetary Policy Committee (MPC). The MPC consists of the Governor and two Deputy Governors of the Bank of England, two other members appointed by the Bank after consultation with the Chancellor of the Exchequer (the UK finance minister) and four other members appointed by the Chancellor. The Governor and the two Deputy Governors serve five-year renewable terms of office, while other MPC members serve three-year renewable terms. The MPC meets monthly and its interest rate decision is announced immediately after the meeting.

The Bank of England's mission is to 'promote the good of the people of the United Kingdom by maintaining monetary and financial stability'. The definition of price stability for the UK is given by the UK government and, in particular, the Chancellor of the Exchequer. The 1998 Bank of England Act requires that the Chancellor write to the Governor of the Bank of England once a year to specify what price stability is to be defined as. Currently, the inflation target of 2 per cent is expressed in terms of an annual rate of inflation based on the CPI. If the target is missed by more than one percentage point on either side, i.e. if the annual rate of CPI inflation is more than 3 per cent or less than 1 per cent, the Governor of the Bank of England must write an open letter to the Chancellor explaining the reasons why inflation has increased or fallen to such an extent and what the Bank proposes to do to ensure inflation comes back to target.

In changes made to financial regulation in the UK in June 2010, the Chancellor of the Exchequer announced that the Bank of England would have new responsibilities focusing on monetary policy and financial stability, which have been confirmed in the Financial Services Bill, 2012. The new system led to the Bank of England getting additional responsibilities for financial stability, macro-prudential supervision and oversight of micro-prudential supervision. These regulatory functions are overseen by three main groups, the Prudential Regulatory Authority (PRA), which is responsible for day-to-day supervision of bank safety and soundness (micro-prudential policy), the Financial Policy Committee (FPC), charged with 'identifying, monitoring and addressing systemic risks to the UK financial system' and the Financial Conduct Authority (FCA) which manages protection of investors, market supervision and regulation, and the conduct of banks and financial services.

> **SELF TEST** If a central bank wants to increase the supply of money, how may it do so?

BANKS AND THE MONEY SUPPLY

Central banks play a crucial role in the monetary system. Most firms in the banking sector exist to make a profit. Whilst there are numerous differences between financial intermediaries which make up the banking sector, we will assume they all have in common the basic function of accepting deposits and making loans. Banks have to monitor their balance sheets which consist of assets and liabilities. Most banks will earn interest on assets and have to pay interest on liabilities. The difference between the average interest it earns on its assets and the average interest rate paid on its liabilities is termed the **spread** and is a primary determinant of the profit a bank makes. We say 'most banks' because banks operating under Islamic Shariah principles do not base operations on interest (Riba) but instead on the sharing of risk and reward between lenders and borrowers.

 spread the difference between the average interest banks earn on assets and the average interest rate paid on liabilities

A Bank's Balance Sheet

A bank's balance sheet consists of its assets and liabilities. A bank's assets might include reserves of cash, securities it holds, and loans. Its liabilities include demand deposits, savings deposits, borrowings from other banks in the interbank market and, if it is a public limited company, equity capital. Its assets must equal its liabilities plus equity capital.

Banks keep some money in its vault to cover possible withdrawals. Some of a bank's reserves are held at the central bank and the bank can instruct the central bank to transfer funds from its account to that of other banks in settling transactions. It is important to note that the amount of reserves do not, in themselves, act as a constraint to a bank in the amount it lends.

Broad measures of the money supply include bank deposits and currency. According to the Bank of England, bank deposits of various kinds account for around 97 per cent of broad money in the UK with currency making up the other 3 per cent. Banks do not sit around waiting for customers to walk through their doors and deposit money and then use this money to lend to other people and businesses. Banks actively find ways of making new loans. This might be in the form of granting a loan to a business for expansion or the purchase of new plant and equipment, a loan to an individual to buy a car or the granting of a mortgage to a couple seeking to buy a house. In granting a loan, the bank credits the account of the borrower with the funds. As far as the borrower is concerned, their bank statement now shows that they have 'money' to spend on whatever it is they arranged the loan for. At the point a new loan is agreed, new money is created and the money supply increases. These new loans represent assets to the bank (because the borrower will have to pay the loan plus interest to the bank) but at the same time increases liabilities by the same amount. The bank's balance sheet also expands.

The flip side of this is that when bank loans are repaid, the money supply contracts. For example, if an individual borrowed €10 000 to buy a new car, they will have to pay monthly instalments which consist of part of the capital sum (the €10 000) and some interest. If the monthly payment is €300, the borrower's outstanding loan shrinks by this amount effectively reducing the money supply.

It is not only consumers and businesses borrowing and paying back loans which impact on the money supply in this way. Banks buy and sell a range of assets including bonds. The purchase of government bonds is a way in which the banking system can hold assets which are relatively liquid as they can be sold to the central bank. Banks will also buy and sell bonds on the bond market. If a bond is purchased from a non-banking sector holder (i.e. not purchased from another bank), the funds are credited to the seller's account. This increases the money supply. Equally, if banks sell bonds to the non-banking sector, the buyer's account is debited with the sum paid and the money supply contracts.

Banks will also be involved with borrowing funds over much longer terms and with more restrictions. These loans may be highly illiquid in that they cannot easily be converted into cash. Banks can take this type of debt onto its balance sheet because it represents a form of funding which helps protect the bank from external shocks. As we saw in Chapter 26, a number of banks became heavily exposed to paying short-term obligations which pushed them to the brink of collapse. If too many of a bank's liabilities are short-term, they become more unstable in the event that borrowers demand their money. Having more long-term debt helps reduce the risk. Since the Financial Crisis a number of central banks have sought to regulate on the amount of long-term debt bank's hold as a way of improving security in the banking sector.

Constraints on Bank Lending Whilst banks create money by lending, there are a number of constraints on its ability to be able to do this at will. Crucial to the constraints are monetary policy and the interest rate set by the central bank. This rate sets the basis for the structure of interest rates throughout the economy because it is the rate at which the central bank will lend to the banking system. If the central bank increases lending rates to the banking system, banks have to increase the interest rate on lending to maintain spreads, and this leads to a reduction in the demand for loans. Similarly, a reduction in interest rates would be expected to stimulate the demand for loans. Exactly how much loans contract or increase in response to changes in interest rates depends on the interest elasticity of demand.

If bank lending is increasing and money growth is rising too fast, the central bank will look at the risk this poses in accelerating inflation over and above the target rate. If it is felt that the risk is too great, the central bank will increase its lending rate which is designed to slow down the rate of growth of money through reducing lending. The Financial Crisis led to a slowdown in economic growth and the threat from inflation began to subside. Central banks reduced interest rates in an attempt to encourage lending and expand the growth in money to help stimulate the economy. The fact that rates have stayed so low in so many countries is testament to the severity of the economic slowdown and the challenges in rebuilding confidence.

In addition, banks operate in a competitive market; in order to generate appropriate profits, banks must be mindful of the cost of seeking out and making loans against the returns they get. The profit they make is determined, as we have seen, by the spread and this in turn is influenced by central bank monetary policy. To attract new loans, banks may have to offer rates which are lower than competitors. This, in turn, affects the profitability of its operations. If a borrower banking with First European Bank takes out a loan of €15 000 to buy a car, the funds are transferred to the seller's bank, let us call it Second European Bank from First's reserves at the central bank. This results in a reduction in First's reserves and an increase in Second's. First now faces a situation in which it has fewer reserves and more loans in relation to its overall deposits. With fewer reserves it is in a more risky position if it needs to meet potential withdrawals or its payment obligations. Banks, therefore, cannot continue to lend indefinitely in this way. In addition, different institutions will have different cost structures, shareholder expectations of profit not to mention the response of the public to the bank's activities. Whether it can attract new loans will be dependent on market forces and its profit requirements. Taking on more long-term debt, as outlined above, helps provide a further constraint. Long-term debt may provide the bank with more security but attracting these funds requires a higher interest rate which in turn affects banks' spread. There is a trade-off between profitable lending and security which the bank needs to make a judgement on.

The Financial Crisis brought risk into sharp focus. Central banks have increased the amount of regulation of the banking system in continued efforts to prevent the risk of crises developing in the future. Banks themselves also have to be mindful of the risk they take in making loans that borrowers will default (termed a **credit risk**). This might mean them securing funding (referred to, inaccurately, as setting aside reserves) to absorb losses that might arise from default or wider bank sector problems, which might threaten their ability to function.

> **credit risk** the risk a bank faces in defaults on loans

Macroprudential policy One of the criticisms of central banks during the Financial Crisis was that they did not have sufficient powers to deal with systemic risk in the banking system. **Systemic risk** refers to the risk of failure across the whole of the financial sector rather than just to one or two institutions. The risk is increased because of the interconnectedness and interdependence of the financial system. Once problems begin to occur in one area of the banking system, it cascades down to others and results in a severe economic downturn.

> **systemic risk** the risk of failure across the whole of the financial sector

In the UK, the FPC has been set up to assess the risks inherent across the financial system along with powers to take action to prevent or reduce these risks. This is referred to as **macroprudential policy**.

> **macroprudential policy** policies designed to limit the risk across the financial sector by focusing on improving 'prudential' standards of operation that enhance stability and reduce risk

Banks accept deposits from many people often in the form of short-term deposits. Bank customers may want to take out loans over much longer durations and so banks 'transform' many short-term deposits into a smaller number of longer-term loans. A bank's assets are all the financial, physical and intangible assets they hold or are due to be paid at some point in the future. Financial assets include loans made to households and firms, mortgages, lending to other banks and the wholesale market (transactions between large financial institutions, for example merchant banks that might be arranging for the listing of a company on the stock exchange). Other assets include cash, holdings of bonds and reserves at the central bank. Physical assets include all the property the bank owns and intangible assets will include the brand value and reputation of the bank.

A bank's liabilities are what it owes to others. This includes all the deposits from households and firms, borrowings from other banks and wholesale markets, purchases of bonds from pension funds and insurance companies and its share capital. If a bank makes a loan it runs the risk that the loan will not be paid back – the borrower will default. If defaults reach high levels the bank's assets fall and its liabilities increase. The other risk a bank faces is that it will be unable to meet demand for withdrawals. If withdrawals increase substantially (for example, through a bank run), the bank may have to sell off assets to raise funds and in doing so depresses the price of those assets. This is termed a **liquidity risk**. The failure of one bank can have cascade effects onto other banks and across the financial system.

> **liquidity risk** the risk that a bank may not be able to fund demand for withdrawals

As noted above, banks face a trade-off between risk and reward. They want to lend more money to make higher profits but are constrained by the need to maintain liquidity to insulate themselves from the risk of insolvency. Banks have to have sufficient sources of funding to meet their obligations. This means that if there were a sudden increase in demand for withdrawals, the bank would be in a position to secure adequate funding to be able to meet that demand. Banks do not, therefore, have a large vault where funds are stored away to use in the event of a crisis but instead have to ensure that they are able to fund any such crisis event that occurs. This is the function of 'reserves'.

Banks have to structure their balance sheets to ensure they have a profile of assets and liabilities which enable them to respond to a rise in defaults and increased demand for withdrawals. Macroprudential regulation lays down minimum requirements banks must adhere to in structuring their balance sheets. Since share capital is the banks 'own money' rather than money it has 'borrowed' from depositors, capital is seen as being important in being able to provide a buffer against shocks. The regulation encourages banks to take account of the risks they face and that they themselves are capable of managing those risks rather than relying on the taxpayer to bail them out.

Another aspect of regulation is the so-called Basel Accord. This is a set of agreements by the Basel Committee on Bank Supervision, a group of central bank governors and heads of regulatory bodies, which meets around four times a year to review banking supervision. The group establishes ratios of capital in the form of shareholder's equity and irredeemable and non-cumulative preference shares. The ratio of this capital in relation to the rest of the bank's assets is seen as a measure of the financial strength of a bank. It effectively acts as a cushion against financial shocks.

The so-called Basel III negotiations between 27 countries set new reserve requirements in September 2010. The new rules came into force in 2013 and are to be phased in over a period of six years (although some relaxation to the requirements on the capital reserves needed to survive a 30-day crisis was agreed in 2013 and were phased in from 2015). The regulations mean that banks will have to have higher reserves to support lending; for every €50 of lending banks will have to have €3.50 of reserves compared to €1 prior to the Basel III agreement. This obviously more than triples the amount of reserves that banks will have to keep. If banks do not adhere to the new regulations, then they risk seeing the authorities placing restrictions on their activities including paying out dividends to shareholders and bonuses to staff.

THE CENTRAL BANK'S TOOLS OF MONETARY CONTROL

Central banks in many developed economies have a central function of maintaining economic stability and stable inflation. The principle way they seek to achieve these objectives is through influencing the price of money in the economy through setting interest rates. In general, a central bank has three main tools in its monetary toolbox: open market operations, the refinancing rate and reserve requirements.

Open Market Operations

If the central bank wants to increase the money supply, it will buy bonds in the bond market. After the purchase, the extra currency is in the hands of the public in the form of a rise in account balances in banks. Thus, an open market purchase of bonds by the central bank effectively increases broad money. If, on the other hand, the central bank wants to decrease broad money, it can sell bonds from its portfolio to the public. After the sale, the currency it receives for the bonds decreases account balances in banks. To be precise, the open market operations discussed in these simple examples are called **outright open market operations**, because they each involve an outright sale or purchase of non-monetary assets to or from the banking sector without a corresponding agreement to reverse the transaction at a later date.

> **outright open market operations** the outright sale or purchase of non-monetary assets to or from the banking sector by the central bank without a corresponding agreement to reverse the transaction at a later date

The Refinancing Rate

The central bank of an economy will set an interest rate at which it is willing to lend to commercial banks on a short-term basis. As we shall see, the name of this interest rate differs across central banks, although in general in this book we'll follow the practice of the European Central Bank and refer to it as the *refinancing rate*.

The way in which the central bank lends to the banking sector is through a special form of open market operations. Although outright open market operations have traditionally been used by central banks to regulate broad money, central banks more often use a slightly more sophisticated form of open market operations that involves buying bonds or other assets from banks and at the same time agreeing to sell them back later. When it does this, the central bank has effectively made a loan and taken the bonds or other assets as collateral or security on the loan. The central bank will have a list of eligible assets that it will accept as collateral – 'safe' assets such as government bonds or assets issued by large corporations, on which the risk of default by the issuer is negligible. The interest rate that the central bank charges on the loan is the refinancing rate. Because the central bank has bought the assets but the seller has agreed to buy them back later at an agreed price, this kind of open market operation is often called a **repurchase agreement** or 'repo' for short.

> **repurchase agreement** the sale of a non-monetary asset together with an agreement to repurchase it at a set price at a specified future date

Banks need to structure their balance sheets to ensure they can meet credit and liquidity risk. Because deposits and withdrawals at banks can fluctuate randomly, some banks may find that they have an excess of reserves one day while other banks may find that they are short of reserves. Therefore, the commercial banks in an economy will generally lend money to one another on a short-term basis – overnight to a couple of weeks – so that banks with excess reserves can lend them to banks that have inadequate reserves to cover their lending. This market for short-term reserves is called the **money market**. If there is a *general* shortage of liquidity in the money market (because the banks together have done a lot of lending), then the short-term interest rate at which they lend to one another will begin to rise, while it will begin to fall if there is excess liquidity among banks. The central bank closely monitors the money market and may intervene in it in order to affect the supply of liquidity to banks, which in turn affects their lending and hence, the money supply.

> **money market** the market in which the commercial banks lend money to one another on a short-term basis

Suppose, for example, that there is a shortage of liquidity in the market because the banks have been increasing their lending. A commercial bank may then attempt to obtain liquidity from the central bank by selling assets to the central bank and at the same time agreeing to purchase them back a short time later. As we said before, in this type of open market operation the central bank effectively lends money to the bank and takes the assets as collateral on the loan. Because the commercial bank is legally bound to repurchase the assets at a set price, this is called a *repurchase agreement* and the difference between the price the bank sells the assets to the central bank and the price at which it agrees to buy them back, expressed as an annualized percentage of the selling price, is called the repurchase or repo rate by the Bank of England and the refinancing rate by the European Central Bank. The ECB's **refinancing rate** is thus the rate at which it will lend to the banking sector of the euro area, while the **repo rate** is the rate at which the Bank of England lends short term to the UK banking sector.

> **refinancing rate** the interest rate at which the European Central Bank lends on a short-term basis to the euro area banking sector
> **repo rate** the interest rate at which the Bank of England lends on a short-term basis to the UK banking sector

In the example given, the central bank added liquidity to the banking system by lending reserves to banks. This would have the effect of increasing broad money. Because the loans made through open market operations are typically very short term, with a maturity of at most two weeks, the banks are constantly having to repay the loans and borrow again, or 'refinance' the loans. If the central bank wants to mop up liquidity it can simply decide not to renew some of the loans. In practice, however, the central bank will set a reference rate of interest – the Bank of England's repo rate or the ECB's refinancing rate – and will conduct open market operations, adding to or mopping up liquidity, close to this reference rate.

In the USA the interest rate at which the Federal Reserve lends to the banking sector (corresponding to the ECB's refinancing rate or the Bank of England's repo rate) is called the **discount rate** (also called the federal funds rate).

> **discount rate** the interest rate at which the Federal Reserve lends on a short-term basis to the US banking sector

Now we can see why the setting of the central bank's refinancing rate is the key instrument of monetary policy. If the central bank raises the refinancing rate, commercial banks will try and pull in their lending rather than borrow reserves from the central bank, and so the money supply will fall. If the central bank lowers the refinancing rate, banks will feel freer to lend, knowing that they will be able to borrow more cheaply from the central bank in order to meet their reserve requirements, and so the money supply will tend to rise.

Quantitative Easing

During the Financial Crisis of 2007–9, central banks adopted new tactics to try and support the economy, one of which was an asset purchasing facility (APF) or quantitative easing (QE). In the UK the Bank of

England cut interest rates to 0.5 per cent and in the US rates fell to a target of between 0 and 0.25 per cent. Having effectively exhausted the use of lowering the price of money in the economy, central banks looked at affecting the quantity of money as part of their armoury in triggering economic activity.

The process of QE involves the central bank buying assets from private sector institutions financed by the creation of broad money. Private sector institutions might include banks, pension funds and insurance companies. The type of assets purchased varies from bonds and gilt-edged stock to commercial paper (short-term promissory notes issued by companies with a maturity ranging up to 270 days but with an average of 30 days), equities and possibly toxic assets. In selling assets to the central bank, institutions will hold more money in relation to other assets and look to maintain their portfolios by using the money to buy bonds and shares of companies, which is in effect lending to firms.

An example may serve to help understand the process (we will use pounds in this example and assume the central bank is the Bank of England). Assume a pension fund has £1 billion worth of gilt-edged stock. It decides that it wants to sell £500 million worth. The Bank of England announces that it intends to purchase gilts at an auction and sets a specific date for the auction (normally a Monday and Wednesday each week for a specified period of time). The process takes place via what is called a 'reverse auction'. Rather than the buyer putting in bids for what they would be willing to pay for the item, the seller submits an electronic bid to the Bank stating what they would like to sell and at what price they would be willing to sell at. The Bank itself has a specified amount that it intends to buy at that time and the bids coming in from banks and other institutions may mean that the auction is oversubscribed (i.e. more bids to sell are received than the Bank intends to buy) and as a result the Bank is able to select which offers it will accept and at what price.

The pension fund in our example held government debt on its balance sheet but following the sale of the debt to the central bank, it now has £500 million. This credit appears in its bank account thus affecting the banking sector. The pension fund can use this £500 million to buy bonds and shares.

There will be further ripple effects in the bond market. Remember, companies use the bond market as a means of raising funds. Over a period of time these bonds will mature and firms may issue new bonds to replace them. These new bond issues may have different coupon rates to existing ones depending on current conditions in the bond market. Assume that a company has issued a 10-year bond with a coupon, on issue, of 5 per cent. The price at which the bond sells on the market will not necessarily be the same as its par value (what it was originally issued at). The ratio of the coupon to the price gives investors the yield $\left(Yield = \dfrac{Coupon}{Price} \right)$. For example, if the company issues a £100 bond, with a coupon of 5 per cent, the yield will also be 5 per cent. However, if demand for this bond rises then its price may rise (to £105 for example) and as a result the yield will fall:

$$\left(\frac{5\ percent}{105} = 4.76\ percent \right)$$

This is the inverse relationship between bond prices and yield we introduced in an earlier chapter.

If the central bank intervenes to buy bonds the supply of bonds will fall and bond prices will rise. As bond prices rise, yields fall. If our company now issues a new bond it can offer that bond at a lower coupon (there is no incentive not to buy it since buying existing bonds does not give any better return). Using the example above, if our company wanted to issue a new bond to replace the matured £100 bond, then it could offer the bond at a coupon of 4.76 per cent (or slightly higher) and have every chance of raising the finance. For the company it is now raising funds at 4.76 per cent rather than 5 per cent. This means that firms are now able to borrow at cheaper rates. This provides an impetus for generating increased economic activity.

QE, therefore, works in a variety of ways to influence incentives. The principle of QE is relatively simple; the acid test is whether it works or not. The central bank is in a position to monitor the effects of the process as it collects data about money flows in the economy, the effect on the money supply, credit flows in corporate markets, interest rates on different types of lending (for example on mortgages) and the amount and type of lending taking place.

IN THE NEWS

Open market Operations

Whilst it is difficult for central banks to control the money supply in precise ways, the use of open market operations can be a useful tool in managing relatively short-term interest rates.

China's Central Bank in Record Market Intervention

In February 2013, The People's Bank of China (PBOC), the country's central bank, created a record in its open market operations. The PBOC bought 450 billion yuan (€64 billion) worth of assets which represented the largest single day injection into the money markets beating the previous record of 395 billion yuan (€56 billion) in October 2012. The operation involved the purchase of 14-day reverse bond repurchase agreements. The PBOC purchased securities from the money markets with the agreement to sell them back at a higher price in 14 days (this is the opposite to a repo, and for money market institutions, selling the securities and buying them back in 14 days, it is a repo). In the first instance, therefore, the PBOC had injected funds into the money markets but sucked out more funds when it sold the securities back.

Since that time, the PBOC has continued its open market operations on and off as it deems appropriate. The end of December 2015, was one of the first occasions for six months that it did not use open market operations. Weakness in the Chinese economy had seen the PBOC injecting cash into the system to help reduce borrowing costs for firms and stimulate growth. On 22 and 24 December 2015, the PBOC had made 70 billion yuan (€9.9 bn) of seven-day reverse repurchase agreements available. On 31 December 2015, only 10 billion yuan (€1.4 bn) was offered for auction.

The seven-day repurchase rate fell to 2.32 per cent, reflecting a fall over the year in 2015 as a whole. If repo rates are falling, it is a sign that demand for money is lower than supply. Repo rates typically rise in the run up to holiday periods or when the month or quarter end approaches as lenders look to ensure that they have sufficient liquidity to meet regulatory requirements. The PBOC uses open market operations to manage interest rates. When the demand for money increases as during holiday periods, an injection of funds into the system helps reduce the pressure on interest rates to rise and when demand slows, the selling back of the securities reduces the supply of funds and thus maintains interest rates at a more stable level than without the operation.

Questions

1 What is meant by the term open-market operations?
2 What is a repurchase agreement and why was the action of the PBOC termed a 'reverse repurchase agreement'?
3 Assume no intervention in the money markets by the PBOC. Use a supply and demand diagram with interest rates on the vertical axis (the price of money) to show how increases in interest rates can occur in times when the demand for money rises.
4 If the PBOC refrains from using open market operations or scaling back the amounts it makes available, what does this tell you about liquidity in the system?
5 Again, using a supply and demand diagram, explain how the open market operations of the PBOC can help to stabilize interest rates.

The People's Bank of China in Beijing.

SUMMARY

- The term *money* refers to assets that people regularly use to buy goods and services.

- Money serves three functions. As a medium of exchange, it provides the item used to make transactions. As a unit of account, it provides the way in which prices and other economic values are recorded. As a store of value, it provides a way of transferring purchasing power from the present to the future.

- Commodity money, such as gold, is money that has intrinsic value: it would be valued even if it were not used as money. Fiat money, such as paper euros or pounds, is money without intrinsic value: it would be worthless if it were not used as money.

- In an advanced economy, money takes the form of currency and various types of bank deposits, such as current accounts.

- Central banks monitor economic and price stability. They have an important role in managing broad money through variations in the price of money (interest rates).

- The European Central Bank is the overall central bank for the 19 countries participating in European Monetary Union. The Euro system is made up of the European Central Bank plus the corresponding 19 national central banks.

- The UK central bank is the Bank of England. It was granted independence in the setting of interest rates in 1997.

- Central banks control the money supply primarily through the refinancing rate and the associated open market operations. An increase in the refinancing rate means that it is more expensive for banks to borrow from the central bank on a short-term basis if they are short of reserves to cover their lending, and so they will tend to reduce their lending and the money supply will contract. Conversely, a reduction in the refinancing rate will tend to expand the money supply.

- The central bank can also use outright open market operations to affect the money supply: a purchase of government bonds and other assets from the banking sector increases the money supply, and the sale of assets decreases the money supply.

- When banks lend, they create money but when loans are paid back, this destroys money. Central banks adopted quantitative easing as a means of providing a stimulus after the Financial Crisis through buying assets from the banking sector and expanding the money supply.

- A bank run occurs when depositors suspect that a bank may become insolvent and, therefore, 'run' to the bank to withdraw their deposits. Many countries have a system of deposit insurance and central banks are lenders of last resort so bank runs can be managed more effectively.

QUESTIONS FOR REVIEW

1 What distinguishes money from other assets in the economy?

2 What is commodity money? What is fiat money? Which kind is in use in the country in which you are studying?

3 What are demand deposits, and why should they be included in the stock of money?

4 Who is responsible for setting monetary policy at the European Central Bank? How is this group chosen? Who is responsible for setting monetary policy at the Bank of England? How is this group chosen?

5 If the central bank wants to increase the money supply with outright open market operations, what does it do?

6 How do banks make profit and what considerations must banks give to the trade-off between security and profit?

7 What is the refinancing rate? What happens to the money supply when the European Central Bank raises its refinancing rate?

8 What is meant by macroprudential policy and why is it important in managing systemic risk?

9 What is quantitative easing and in what way does it help to counter slow economic growth in an economy?

10 What is the difference between credit risk and liquidity risk?

PROBLEMS AND APPLICATIONS

1 What characteristics of an asset make it useful as a medium of exchange? As a store of value?

2 Suppose that someone in one of the euro area countries discovered an easy way to counterfeit €100 banknotes. How would this development affect the monetary system of the euro area? Explain.

3 Should central banks place as much emphasis on financial stability as on price stability? Justify your answer.

4 To what extent is a policy of quantitative easing likely to be inflationary?

5 Should financial markets be subject to more or less regulation if we are to avoid another financial crisis of the scale of that witnessed between 2007 and 2009? Justify your answer.

6 A bank is under pressure from its shareholders to improve its profits. Explain the term 'spread' and how a bank must manage the trade-off between risk and security to provide shareholder value.

7 In what way can central banks attempt to control the broad money stock in an economy? What limitations does a central bank face in this task?

8 Why do banks have to have a portfolio of assets and liabilities on its balance sheet to enable them to manage risk? If banks commit to a large proportion of short-term lending, how might this affect its long-term security?

9 Does macroprudential policy place too many restrictions on banks to enable them to provide the intermediary function of channelling funds from savers to those who wish to borrow? Justify your reasoning.

10 News organizations often refer to quantitative easing as the central bank 'printing money' and giving it to banks. To what extent is this true? Is QE effectively 'free money' to banks? Explain.

28 MONEY GROWTH AND INFLATION

ata from the ONS for 1971 shows that a typical loaf of bread in the UK was priced at 9p (€0.11), a pint of milk at 5p (€0.06) and a dozen eggs at 23p (€0.29). In February 2016, the price of each of these goods were £1.40 (€1.77), £0.45 (€0.57) and £1.50 (€1.90) respectively. The increase in price of each is 1455 per cent for bread, 800 per cent for milk and 552.2 per cent for eggs. This may not come as a huge surprise; in advanced economies, most prices tend to rise over time.

Price rises over time can vary quite considerably. Post-First World War Germany experienced a spectacular example of a rise in the price level. The price of a newspaper rose from 0.3 marks in January 1921 to 70 000 000 marks less than two years later. Other prices rose by similar amounts. This period of significant price rises had such an adverse effect on the German economy that it is often viewed as one contributor to the rise to power of the National Socialists (Nazis) and, as a result, the Second World War.

In more recent times there have been episodes of significant rises in the price level in the former Yugoslavia and in Zimbabwe. Price rises in Yugoslavia ran at 5 quadrillion per cent (5 with 15 zeros after it) between October 1993 and January 1995. The Zimbabwean authorities announced that the CPI had reached 231 000 000 per cent in June 2008. However, the prices of some goods rose by considerably more. The Zimbabwean central bank reported that some goods on the black market had risen by 70 000 000 per cent. Laundry soap was one of the goods that had risen by this much, but cooking oil also rose by 60 000 000 per cent and sugar by 36 000 000 per cent. Unskilled workers earned around Z$200 000 000 000 a month – at the time, equivalent to about US$10 (€9.2, £6.80). In July 2008 the government issued a Z$100 billion note. If you had one, it would just about have bought you a loaf of bread. This chapter explores some theories of why prices rise over time and why one of the core functions of central banks is to target price stability.

WHAT IS INFLATION?

In Chapter 21, we looked at how measures of the cost are living are calculated. Many countries use the CPI as their measure of inflation. Recall that if the index is calculated at 100 in the base year, and 103 in the following year, each of these measures describes the price level. The price level is a snapshot of the weighted average of a basket of goods at a point in time. If in the subsequent year, the price level was also measured at 103, the price level would not have changed.

In our example, the price level changed from 100 to 103 from the base year to the following year. The rate of change in prices between these two years is 3 per cent. Inflation is an increase in the price level over a period. The rate of change in the price level reflects the speed at which prices are rising. If inflation is recorded as 3 per cent in one month, 3.5 per cent the next and 3.7 per cent the month after that, the rate at which prices are rising is getting faster or accelerating. If in the next month the inflation rate is 3.65 per cent and then 3.45 per cent the following month, prices are still rising but at a slower rate. Here inflation is not 'falling' but the rate of change is slowing or decelerating. Now assume that the inflation rate in the next four months is 3.45 per cent, again, prices are still rising but at a stable rate.

In the UK and parts of Europe in 2015, the price level actually fell. In our example, the price level might be recorded as 103 in one month and then 102 in the following month. In this case the rate of inflation would be negative at about −0.97 per cent. A negative rate of inflation is called **deflation**. Deflation is a fall in the price level over a period and occurs when the inflation rate is less than 0 per cent.

deflation a fall in the price level over a period occurring when the inflation rate is less than 0 per cent

THE CLASSICAL THEORY OF INFLATION

We begin our study of inflation with the quantity theory of money. This theory is often called 'classical' because it was developed by some of the earliest thinkers about economic issues as far back as the 16th century, when French lawyer philosopher, political theorist and economist Jean Bodin (c.1529–96), sought to explain price rises by the increase in supply of gold and silver. Like all theories, it can be used to predict or explain phenomena, in this case why prices rise over a period.

The Level of Prices and the Value of Money

One of the reasons why inflation is such an important issue is because it is related to the value of money (the goods and services any given amount of money can be exchanged for).

The price level can be seen as a measure of the value of money. A rise in the price level means a lower value of money because each unit of money now buys a smaller quantity of goods and services. Suppose P is the price level as measured by the CPI or the GDP deflator. P measures the number of euros needed to buy a basket of goods and services. Now turn this idea around: the quantity of goods and services that can be bought with €1 equals $\frac{1}{P}$. P is the price of goods and services measured in terms of money, and $\frac{1}{P}$ is the value of money measured in terms of goods and services. If P rises, the amount of goods and services €1 can buy falls. Thus when the overall price level rises, the value of money falls.

Money Supply, Money Demand and Monetary Equilibrium

In the preceding chapter we discussed how the central bank, together with the banking system, influences the supply of money. We are going to assume that the central bank has total control over the money supply and that it is fixed.

The demand for money reflects how much wealth people want to hold in liquid form. Many factors influence the quantity of money demanded. The amount of cash people carry round with them, for instance, depends on how much they rely on credit cards and on whether an automatic cash dispenser is easy to find. The quantity of money demanded is also assumed to depend on the interest rate that a person could earn by using the money to buy an interest-bearing asset such as a bond rather than having it in their pocket or low-interest bank account.

People hold money because it is the medium of exchange. Unlike other assets, such as bonds or stocks, cash is highly liquid in that it can be used to buy goods and services. How much they choose to hold for this purpose depends on the prices of those goods and services. The higher prices are, the more money the typical transaction requires, and the more money people will choose to hold in liquid form. A higher price level (a lower value of money) increases the quantity of money demanded.

Equilibrium in the market depends on the time horizon being considered. Later in this book we will examine the short run, and we will see that interest rates play a key role. In the long run, however, *the overall level of prices is assumed to adjust to the level at which the demand for money equals the supply.* Figure 28.1 illustrates this idea. The horizontal axis of this graph shows the quantity of money. The left-hand vertical axis shows the value of money $\frac{1}{P}$, and the right-hand vertical axis shows the price level P. Notice that the price level axis on the right is inverted: a low price level is shown near the top of this axis, and a high price level is shown near the bottom. This inverted axis illustrates that when the value of money is high (as shown near the top of the left axis), the price level is low (as shown near the top of the right axis).

The two curves in this figure are the supply and demand curves for money. The supply curve is vertical because of the assumption that the central bank can fix the money supply. The demand curve for money is downwards sloping, indicating that when the price level is high (and the value of money low), people demand a larger quantity of it to buy goods and services. At the equilibrium, shown in Panel A as point A, the quantity of money demanded balances the quantity of money supplied. This equilibrium of money supply and money demand determines the value of money and the price level.

If the price level is above the equilibrium level, for example at 4 in Panel B, people will want to hold M^D to pay for goods and services but the money supply is fixed at M^S resulting in an excess demand for money at this price level. The price level must fall to balance supply and demand. If the price level is below the equilibrium level at 1.33 in Panel B, people will want to hold M^D_1 but the supply of money is fixed at M^S, and the price level must rise to balance supply and demand. At the equilibrium price level, the quantity of money that people want to hold exactly balances the quantity of money supplied by the central bank.

FIGURE 28.1

How the Supply and Demand for Money Determine the Equilibrium Price Level
In Panel A, the horizontal axis shows the quantity of money. The left vertical axis shows the value of money, and the right vertical axis shows the price level. The supply curve for money is vertical because the quantity of money supplied is assumed to be fixed by the central bank. The demand curve for money is downward sloping because people want to hold a larger quantity of money when each euro buys less. At the equilibrium, point A, the value of money (on the left axis) and the price level (on the right axis) have adjusted to bring the quantity of money supplied and the quantity of money demanded into balance. In Panel B, if the price level is higher at 4, the demand for money exceeds the available supply and the price level will fall back to the equilibrium at point A.

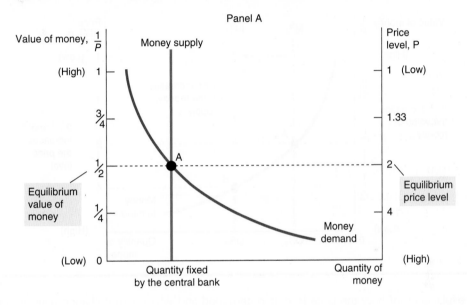

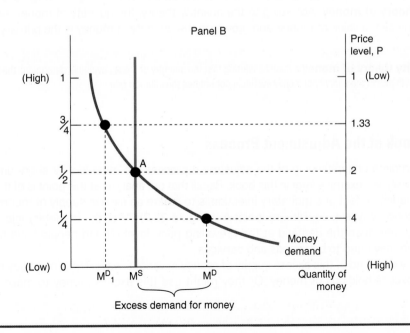

The Effects of a Monetary Injection

Starting with an assumption of equilibrium, now assume that the central bank doubles the supply of money through purchases of government bonds from the public in open-market operations.

Figure 28.2 shows that the monetary injection shifts the supply curve to the right from MS_1 to MS_2, and the equilibrium moves from point A to point B. As a result, the value of money (shown on the left axis) decreases from ½ to ¼, and the equilibrium price level (shown on the right axis) increases from 2 to 4. In other words, when an increase in the money supply makes euros more plentiful, the result is an increase in the price level that makes each euro less valuable.

FIGURE 28.2

An Increase in the Money Supply

When the central bank increases the supply of money, the money supply curve shifts from MS_1 to MS_2. The value of money (on the left axis) and the price level (on the right axis) adjust to bring supply and demand back into balance. The equilibrium moves from point A to point B. Thus, when an increase in the money supply makes euros more plentiful, the price level increases, making each euro less valuable.

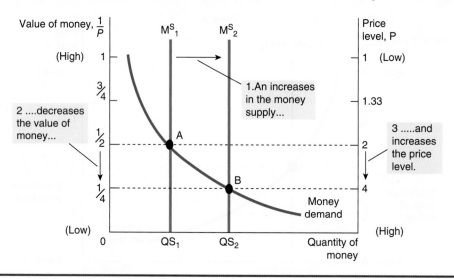

This explanation of how the price level is determined and why it might change over time is called the **quantity theory of money**. According to the quantity theory, the quantity of money available in the economy determines the value of money, and growth in the quantity of money is the primary cause of inflation.

> **quantity theory of money** a theory asserting that the quantity of money available determines the price level and that the growth rate in the quantity of money available determines the inflation rate

A Brief Look at the Adjustment Process

To get a complete understanding of the adjustment process we must look at short-run fluctuations in the economy, which we examine later in this book. Recall that our analysis at this point is of the long-run position.

The immediate effect of a monetary injection is to create an excess supply of money. Before the injection, the economy was in equilibrium (point A in Figure 28.2). After the monetary injection, the supply of money is greater than the demand at the prevailing price level (2) and people have more euros in their pockets than they need to buy goods and services.

People try to get rid of this excess supply of money in various ways. They might buy goods and services with their excess holdings of money. Or they might use this excess money to make loans to others by buying bonds or by depositing the money in a bank savings account. These loans allow other people to buy goods and services. In either case, the injection of money increases the demand for goods and services.

The economy's ability to supply goods and services, however, has not changed. As we saw in Chapter 22, the economy's output of goods and services is determined by the available labour, physical capital, human capital, natural resources and technological knowledge. None of these is altered by the injection of money.

Thus, the greater demand for goods and services causes the prices of goods and services to increase. The increase in the price level, in turn, increases the quantity of money demanded because people are using more euros for every transaction. Eventually, the economy reaches a new equilibrium (point B in Figure 28.2), at which the quantity of money demanded again equals the quantity of money supplied.

The Classical Dichotomy and Monetary Neutrality

The quantity theory predicts that changes in the money supply lead to changes in the average level of prices of goods and services. Whether changes in the money supply affect other important macroeconomic variables, such as production, employment, real wages and real interest rates is a question that has long intrigued economists. Indeed, the great classical economist and philosopher, David Hume, wrote about it in the 18th century.

Hume and his contemporaries suggested that all economic variables should be divided into two groups. The first group consists of **nominal variables** – variables measured in monetary units. The second group consists of **real variables** – variables measured in physical units. For example, the income of wheat farmers is a nominal variable because it is measured in euros, whereas the quantity of wheat they produce is a real variable because it is measured in kilos. Similarly, nominal GDP is a nominal variable because it measures the euro value of the economy's output of goods and services; real GDP is a real variable because it measures the total quantity of goods and services produced and is not influenced by the current prices of those goods and services. This separation of variables into these groups is now called the **classical dichotomy**. (A *dichotomy* is a division into two groups; *classical* refers to the earlier economic thinkers or classical economists.)

> **nominal variables** variables measured in monetary units
> **real variables** variables measured in physical units
> **classical dichotomy** the theoretical separation of nominal and real variables

Relative Prices Prices in the economy are normally quoted in terms of money and, therefore, are nominal variables. For instance, when we say that the price of wheat is €2 a kilo or that the price of barley is €1 a kilo, both prices are nominal variables because we are referring to the number of units of a currency which have to be given up to acquire the good or service. We could represent this in the following way:

$$P_{Wheat} = \frac{€2}{Wheat}$$

$$P_{Barley} = \frac{€1}{Barley}$$

The price of wheat equals €2 per unit of wheat and the price of barley equals €1 per unit of barley.

The **relative price** is defined in terms of the nominal price of one good divided by the nominal price of another. In our example, the relative price of wheat in terms of barley is given by:

$$Relative\ price\ of\ wheat = \frac{\dfrac{€2}{Wheat}}{\dfrac{€1}{Barley}}$$

This can be simplified as follows:

$$\text{Relative price of wheat} = \frac{\dfrac{\text{€2}}{Wheat}}{\dfrac{\text{€1}}{Barley}} \times \frac{\dfrac{Barley}{\text{€1}}}{\dfrac{Barley}{\text{€1}}}$$

Cancelling through results in:

$$\text{Relative price of wheat} = \frac{2_{Wheat}}{1_{Barley}}$$

The real value of a good is what other goods have been sacrificed in purchasing the good. This is the opportunity cost. In our example, to buy a kilo of wheat we have to sacrifice two kilos of barley. Similarly, the relative price of barley is given by $\dfrac{\text{€1}}{\text{€2}}$ which cancels through to give ½. To buy a kilo of barley, we must sacrifice half a kilo of wheat. Relative prices are not expressed in terms of money and so relative prices are real variables.

> **relative prices** price expressed in terms of how much of one good has to be given up in purchasing another

Real Wages The concept of relative prices has several important applications, and in particular for wages. Imagine that a consumer only ever buys bananas and that the price of a banana is €2. If the consumer's wage is €10 per hour, then the consumer can buy five bananas with their wage. Ten euros per hour is the nominal wage rate measured in money terms. The **real wage** rate is given by the ratio of the wage rate to the price of bananas, $\dfrac{W}{P}$. In this example the real wage rate is the number of bananas the consumer can buy with their wage, $\dfrac{10}{2} = 5$ bananas per hour. In order to be able to afford five bananas the consumer has to work for an hour. If the wage rate and prices change, then the real wage rate gives a more accurate reflection of how the consumer has been affected. If the wage rate increases to €12 per hour and the price of bananas rises to €3, the real wage is now $\dfrac{12}{3} = 4$ bananas per hour. We can say that the worker is now worse off since they can now only buy four bananas for every hour they work, rather than five. The real wage (the money wage adjusted for inflation) is a real variable because it measures the rate at which the economy exchanges goods and services for each unit of labour. Similarly, the real interest rate (the nominal interest rate adjusted for inflation) is a real variable because it measures the rate at which the economy exchanges goods and services produced today for goods and services produced in the future.

> **real wage** the money wage adjusted for inflation, measured by the ratio of the wage rate to price $\dfrac{W}{P}$

Monetary Neutrality Hume suggested that the classical dichotomy is useful in analyzing the economy because different forces influence real and nominal variables. In particular, he argued that nominal variables are heavily influenced by developments in the economy's monetary system, whereas the monetary system is largely irrelevant for understanding the determinants of important real variables.

Notice that Hume's idea was implicit in our earlier discussions of the real economy in the long run. In previous chapters we examined how real GDP, saving, investment, real interest rates and unemployment are determined without any mention of the existence of money. As explained in that analysis, the economy's production of goods and services depends on productivity and factor supplies, the real interest rate adjusts to balance the supply and demand for loanable funds, the real wage adjusts to balance the supply and demand for labour, and unemployment results when the real wage is for some reason kept above its equilibrium level. These important conclusions have nothing to do with the quantity of money supplied.

Changes in the supply of money, according to Hume, affect nominal variables but not real variables. When the central bank doubles the money supply, the price level doubles, the euro wage doubles, and all other euro values double. Real variables, such as production, employment, real wages and real interest rates, are unchanged. This irrelevance of monetary changes for real variables is called **monetary neutrality**.

> **monetary neutrality** the proposition that changes in the money supply do not affect real variables

An analogy sheds light on the meaning of monetary neutrality. Recall that, as the unit of account, money is the yardstick used to measure economic transactions. If the central bank doubles the money supply, all prices double, and the value of the unit of account falls by half. A similar change would occur if a European Union directive reduced the definition of the metre from 100 to 50 centimetres: as a result of the new unit of measurement, all *measured* distances (nominal variables) would double, but the *actual* distances (real variables) would remain the same. The euro, like the metre, is merely a unit of measurement, so a change in its value should not have important real effects.

Is this conclusion of monetary neutrality a realistic description of the world in which we live? The answer is, not completely. A change in the length of the metre from 100 to 50 centimetres would not matter much in the long run, but in the short run it would certainly lead to confusion and various mistakes. Similarly, most economists today believe that over short periods of time – within the span of a year or two – there is reason to think that monetary changes do have important effects on real variables. Hume himself doubted that monetary neutrality would apply in the short run.

Many economists accept Hume's conclusion as a description of the economy *in the long run*. Over the course of a decade or more, for instance, monetary changes have important effects on nominal variables (such as the price level) but only negligible effects on real variables (such as real GDP). When studying long-run changes in the economy, many economists believe that the neutrality of money offers a reasonable approximation of how the world works.

Velocity and the Quantity Equation

We can obtain another perspective on the quantity theory of money by considering the following question: how many times per year is the typical €1 coin used to pay for a newly produced good or service? The answer to this question is given by a variable called the **velocity of money**. The velocity of money refers to the rate at which money changes hands as it moves around the economy.

> **velocity of money** the rate at which money changes hands

To calculate the velocity of money, we divide the nominal value of output (nominal GDP) by the quantity of money. If P is the price level (the GDP deflator), Y the quantity of output (real GDP) and M the quantity of money, then velocity is:

$$V = \frac{(P \times Y)}{M}$$

To see why this makes sense, imagine a simple economy that produces only pizza. Suppose that the economy produces 100 pizzas in a year, that a pizza sells for €10, and that the quantity of money in the economy is €50, made up of fifty €1 coins. Then the velocity of money is:

$$V = \frac{(€10 \times 100)}{€50}$$

$$V = 20$$

In this economy, people spend a total of €1000 per year on pizza. For this €1000 of spending to take place with only €50 of money, each euro coin must be spent (i.e. change hands) on average 20 times per year.

With slight algebraic rearrangement, this equation can be rewritten as:

$$M \times V = P \times Y$$

This equation states that the quantity of money *(M)* times the velocity of money *(V)* equals the price of output *(P)* times the amount of output *(Y)*. It is called the **quantity equation** because it relates the quantity of money *(M)* to the nominal value of output *(P × Y)*. The quantity equation (which is an identity or a truism) shows that an increase in the quantity of money in an economy must be reflected in one of the other three variables: the price level must rise; the quantity of output must rise or the velocity of money must fall.

> **quantity equation** the equation *(M × V = P × Y)*, which relates the quantity of money, the velocity of money, and the currency value of the economy's output of goods and services

This equation is called the *equation of exchange* and was formulated by an American economist, Irving Fisher (1867–1947). The equation of exchange provides a means of linking changes in the money supply with the price level. It is assumed that the velocity of money is relatively stable over time. As a result, when the central bank changes the quantity of money *(M)*, it causes proportionate changes in the nominal value of output *(P × Y)*. The economy's output of goods and services *(Y)* is primarily determined by factor supplies (labour, physical capital, human capital and natural resources) and the available production technology. In particular, because money is neutral, money does not affect output. With output *(Y)* determined by factor supplies and technology, when the central bank alters the money supply *(M)* and induces proportional changes in the nominal value of output *(P × Y)*, these changes are reflected in changes in the price level *(P)*. Therefore, when the central bank increases the money supply rapidly, the result is a high rate of inflation.

CASE STUDY   The Austrian School on the Velocity of Circulation

The quantity theory of money makes an important assumption – that the velocity of circulation of money *(V)*, is stable over time. How accurate is such an assumption? One part of the answer might be to consider what is meant by 'stable' and over what time period we are looking. Stable does not mean constant but what degree of volatility is acceptable to describe *V* as 'stable'?

Is the argument about the stability of *V* actually relevant? Whilst many economists do place some value in the quantity theory, there are some who cast doubt on it and they do so because of the velocity of circulation, which they believe is a fallacy. The Austrian school cast doubt on the validity of *V*. Their argument is as follows.

When individuals make market transactions they pay through the value of the goods and services they produce themselves. A university lecturer, in reality, pays for the food they consume with the value of the lecture services they produce. Money is merely the means to facilitate the exchange. The number of times a €10 note changes hands, has nothing to do with the lecturer's ability to be able to fund their desired purchase of food; it is determined by the lecturer's ability to provide teaching services. What happens, so the argument goes, is that the lecturer is exchanging their services for money which then enables them to make transactions. The food retailer is exchanging the services they provide for money and use it to buy the goods and services they need. In making these transactions both parties are assigning a value to the transactions they make in relation to their own particular well-being. The Austrian school argues that it is individuals' actions that determine the prices of goods and services and not the speed at which money changes hands. *V* cannot, therefore, say anything about the average price level or the average purchasing power of money. *V* is simply the value of transactions, the price multiplied by output, divided by the money stock $V = P\left(\dfrac{Y}{M}\right)$, and as such is a truism which is not helpful. *V* cannot

How stable is the velocity of circulation?

be defined independently of the rest of the equation – it needs P, Y and M, and to give it any meaning and as such V in itself cannot be a causal factor of anything. This implies that if M is rising, then if V was declining it cannot offset the growth in the price level.

The Austrian school link V to the demand for money. If V is unstable does that also mean that the demand for money is unstable? This statement is seen as being absurd – if individuals change their decisions to hold more or less money over time as a result of changes in their personal circumstances, why would this be an issue? Their view would be that over time the demand for money changes – in the same way that over time the demand for any good or service changes. It would be absurd to expect the demand for fish to be stable over time so why should we treat the demand for money in any different way?

The Austrian school does not deny a link between the money supply and prices but questions the quantity theory (or the equation of exchange) as being an accurate way of looking at the economy. In doing so, they argue, false conclusions may be drawn.

The Inflation Tax

Government spending, for example, building roads, paying salaries to police officers, or giving transfer payments to the poor or elderly, necessitates raising funds. The majority of the funding will come through levying taxes, such as income and sales taxes, and the rest through borrowing from the public by selling government bonds. Governments can also pay for spending by simply 'printing' the money it needs.

When the government raises revenue by printing money, it is said to levy an **inflation tax**. When the government prints money, the price level rises, and the value of money falls (assuming wages are constant). If governments print money, it acts like a tax on everyone who holds money. It is even, roughly speaking, a progressive tax since the richer you are, the more money you are likely to hold and therefore the more the inflation tax will affect you.

inflation tax the revenue the government raises by creating money

The importance of the inflation tax can be seen in cases of extreme inflation termed **hyperinflation**. Hyperinflation is a period of extreme and accelerating increase in the price level. During the hyperinflations in Germany in the 1920s, various Latin American countries during the 1970s and 1980s, and in Yugoslavia and Zimbabwe more recently, the inflation tax would have been quite considerable.

hyperinflation a period of extreme and accelerating increase in the price level

Nearly all hyperinflations follow the same pattern: the government has high spending, limited ability to borrow, inadequate tax revenue (perhaps because the level of income in the economy is low, or there is widespread tax evasion or a poorly developed tax system, or a combination of all these factors) and, as a result, it turns to the printing press to pay for its spending. The massive increases in the quantity of money lead to accelerating inflation. The inflation ends when the government institutes fiscal reforms – such as cuts in government spending – that eliminate the need for the inflation tax or in some cases, abandons the currency completely and introduces a new currency.

As the economist John Maynard Keynes once pointed out, the temptation to just print money to pay for government spending through the inflation tax may be hard for a government to resist: 'The burden of the tax is well spread, cannot be evaded, costs nothing to collect, and falls, in a rough sort of way, in proportion to the wealth of the victim. No wonder its superficial advantages have attracted Ministers of Finance.' Of course, Keynes also recognized the great damage that high inflation can do to an economy, which is why he referred to the advantages of an inflation tax as 'superficial'.

The Fisher Effect

An important application of the principle of monetary neutrality concerns the effect of money on interest rates. Interest rates are important variables for macroeconomists to understand because they link the economy of the present and the economy of the future through their effects on saving and investment.

To understand the relationship between money, inflation and interest rates, recall the distinction between the nominal interest rate and the real interest rate given by the formula $r_t = i_t - \pi_t$. For example, if the bank posts a nominal interest rate of 7 per cent per year and the inflation rate is 3 per cent per year, then the real value of the deposits grows by 4 per cent per year. We can rewrite the equation to show that the nominal interest rate is the sum of the real interest rate and the inflation rate:

$$i_t = r_t + \pi_t$$

This way of looking at the nominal interest rate is useful because different economic forces determine each of the two terms on the right-hand side of this equation. As we discussed earlier in the book, the supply and demand for loanable funds determines the real interest rate. According to the quantity theory of money, growth in the money supply determines the inflation rate.

In the long run, over which money is neutral, a change in money growth should not affect the *real* interest rate. For the real interest rate not to be affected, the nominal interest rate must adjust one-for-one to changes in the inflation rate. Thus, when the central bank increases the rate of money growth, the result is both a higher inflation rate and a higher nominal interest rate. This adjustment of the nominal interest rate to the inflation rate is called the **Fisher effect**.

> **Fisher effect** the one-for-one adjustment of the nominal interest rate to the inflation rate

Keep in mind that our analysis of the Fisher effect has maintained a long-run perspective. The Fisher effect does not hold in the short run to the extent that inflation is unanticipated. A nominal interest rate is a payment on a loan, and it is typically set when the loan is first made. If inflation catches the borrower and lender by surprise, the nominal interest rate they set will fail to reflect the rise in prices. To be precise, the Fisher effect states that the nominal interest rate adjusts to expected inflation. Expected inflation moves with actual inflation in the long run but not necessarily in the short run.

The Fisher effect is crucial for understanding changes over time in the nominal interest rate. Figure 28.3 shows the nominal interest rate and the inflation rate in the UK economy since 1976. The nominal interest rate tends to rise when inflation rises and fall when inflation falls. This is true both in high-inflation periods, such as during the late 1970s and the late 1980s, as well as during low-inflation periods, such as the period between 1992 and 2002.

THE COSTS OF INFLATION

Inflation is closely watched and widely discussed because prices rising at too fast a rate can pose a number of problems.

A Fall in Purchasing Power? The Inflation Fallacy

We have seen that when prices rise, the value of money falls because people now need more money to buy any given set of goods and services. However, further investigation reveals that this is dependent on certain assumptions.

When prices rise, buyers of goods and services pay more for what they buy. At the same time, however, sellers of goods and services get more for what they sell. Because most people earn their incomes by selling their services, such as their labour, inflation in incomes has to be taken into account. *Inflation does not in itself reduce people's real purchasing power.* The reason behind the so-called inflation fallacy lies in the principle of monetary neutrality. A worker who receives an annual rise of 10 per cent in their salary tends to view that rise as a reward for their own talent and effort. When an inflation rate of 6 per cent reduces the real value of that pay rise to only 4 per cent, the worker might feel that they have been cheated of what is rightfully their due. In fact, as we discussed in Chapter 22, real incomes are determined by real variables, such as physical capital, human capital, natural resources and the available production technology. Nominal incomes are determined by those factors and the overall price level. If the central bank were to succeed in lowering the inflation rate from 6 per cent to zero, our worker's annual rise would fall from 10 per cent to 4 per cent. They might feel less robbed by inflation, but their real income would not rise more quickly. If nominal incomes do not keep pace with rising prices, as was the case for many people in the post-Crisis UK economy, then the cost of living does rise and people are worse off. Other costs of inflation show some way in which persistent growth in the money supply does, in fact, have some effect on real variables.

FIGURE 28.3

The UK Nominal Interest Rate and the Inflation Rate

This figure uses annual data since 1976 to show the nominal interest rate on 3-month UK Treasury bills (measured as the annual average rate of discount) and the inflation rate (as measured by the retail prices index). The close association between these two variables is evidence for the Fisher effect: when the inflation rate rises, so does the nominal interest rate.

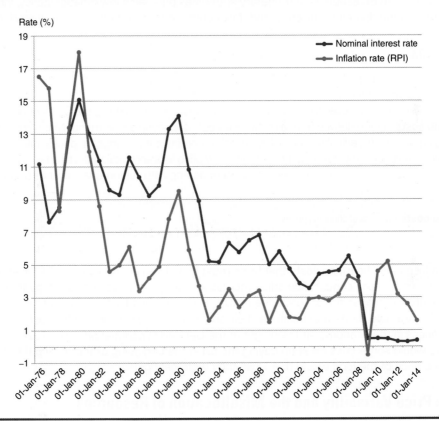

SELF TEST The government of a country increases the growth rate of the money supply from 5 per cent per year to 50 per cent per year. What happens to prices? What happens to nominal interest rates? Why might the government be doing this?

Shoeleather Costs

Because inflation erodes the real value of the money in your pocket, you can avoid the inflation tax by holding less money. One way to do this is to go to the bank more often. For example, rather than withdrawing €400 every four weeks, you might withdraw €100 once a week. By making more frequent trips to the bank, you can keep more of your wealth in your interest-bearing savings account and less in your pocket where inflation erodes its value.

The cost of reducing money holdings is called the **shoeleather cost** of inflation because making more frequent trips to the bank causes your shoes to wear out more quickly. Of course, this term is not to be taken literally: the actual cost of reducing your money holdings is not the wear and tear on your shoes but the time and convenience you must sacrifice to keep less money on hand than you would if there were no inflation – it is in effect a transaction cost, the opportunity cost of carrying out the trips to the bank.

 shoeleather cost the resources wasted when inflation encourages people to reduce their money holding

Shoeleather costs of inflation may seem trivial and they are in countries experiencing only moderate inflation. This cost is magnified in countries experiencing hyperinflation, however. With a very high and accelerating inflation rate, individuals do not have the luxury of holding the local money as a store of value. Instead, they are forced to convert the domestic currency quickly into goods or into another currency, which offer a more stable store of value. The time and effort that individuals expend to reduce their money holdings are a waste of resources. If monetary authorities pursued a low-inflation policy, individuals would be happy to hold the domestic currency, and they could put time and effort to more productive use.

Menu Costs

Most firms do not change the prices of their products every day. Instead, firms often announce prices and leave them unchanged for weeks, months or even years.

Firms change prices infrequently because there are costs involved in doing so. Costs of price adjustment are called **menu costs**, a term derived from a restaurant's cost of printing a new menu. Menu costs include the cost of deciding on new prices, adjusting internal systems to coordinate the changes in prices, the cost of printing new price lists and catalogues, the cost of sending these new price lists and catalogues to dealers and customers, the cost of advertising the new prices, and even the cost of dealing with customer annoyance over price changes.

menu costs the costs of changing prices

Inflation increases the menu costs that firms must bear. In an economy with low inflation of just a few percentage points a year, annual price adjustment is an appropriate business strategy for many firms. But when high inflation makes firms' costs rise rapidly, annual price adjustment is impractical. During hyper-inflations, for example, firms must change their prices daily or even more often just to keep up with all the other prices in the economy. At the height of the German hyperinflation in the 1920s, people eating in restaurants would sometimes insist on paying the bill at the beginning of the meal rather than at the end, because the price of the food would rise while they were eating!

Relative Price Variability and the Misallocation of Resources

Suppose that a fast food restaurant prints a new menu with new prices every January and then leaves its prices unchanged for the rest of the year. If there is no inflation, the restaurant's relative prices – the prices of its meals compared with other prices in the economy – would be constant over the course of the year. By contrast, if the inflation rate is 12 per cent per year, the restaurant's relative prices will automatically fall by 1 per cent each month. The restaurant's relative prices (that is, its prices compared with others in the economy) will be high in the early months of the year, just after it has printed a new menu, and low in the later months. The higher the inflation rate, the greater is this automatic variability. Thus, because prices change only once in a while, inflation causes relative prices to vary more than they otherwise would.

This matters because market economies rely on relative prices to allocate scarce resources. Consumers decide what to buy by comparing the quality and prices of various goods and services. Through these decisions, they determine how the scarce factors of production are allocated among industries and firms. When inflation distorts relative prices, consumer decisions are distorted, and markets are less able to allocate resources to their best use.

Inflation-Induced Tax Distortions

Almost all taxes change incentives and cause people to alter their behaviour. Many taxes, however, become more problematic in the presence of inflation. The reason is that politicians may fail to take inflation into account when writing the tax laws. Economists who have studied the tax system conclude that inflation tends to raise the tax burden on income earned from savings.

One example of how inflation discourages saving is the tax treatment of *capital gains* – the profits made by selling an asset for more than its purchase price. Suppose that in 2008 you used some of your savings to buy stock in Apple for €10 and that in 2018 you sold the stock for €50. According to the tax system, you have earned a capital gain of €40, which you must include in your income when computing how much income tax you owe. Suppose the overall price level doubled from 2008 to 2018. In this case, the €10 you invested in 2008 is equivalent (in terms of purchasing power) to €20 in 2018. When you sell your Apple shares for €50, you have a real gain (an increase in purchasing power) of only €30. The tax system, however, does not take account of inflation and assesses your tax liability on a gain of €40. Thus, inflation exaggerates the size of capital gains and inadvertently increases the tax burden on this type of income.

Another example is the tax treatment of interest income. Income tax treats the *nominal* interest earned on savings as income, even though part of the nominal interest rate merely compensates for inflation. To see the effects of this policy, consider the numerical example in Table 28.1. The table compares two economies, both of which tax interest income at a rate of 25 per cent. In economy A, inflation is zero, and the nominal and real interest rates are both 4 per cent. In this case, the 25 per cent tax on interest income reduces the real interest rate from 4 per cent to 3 per cent. In economy B, the real interest rate is again 4 per cent, but the inflation rate is 8 per cent. As a result of the Fisher effect, the nominal interest rate is 12 per cent. Because the income tax treats this entire 12 per cent interest as income, the government takes 25 per cent of it, leaving an after-tax nominal interest rate of only 9 per cent and an after-tax real interest rate of only 1 per cent. In this case, the 25 per cent tax on interest income reduces the real interest rate from 4 per cent to 1 per cent. Because the after-tax real interest rate provides the incentive to save, saving is much less attractive in the economy with inflation (economy B) than in the economy with stable prices (economy A).

TABLE 28.1	**How Inflation Raises the Tax Burden on Saving**

In the presence of zero inflation, a 25 per cent tax on interest income reduces the real interest rate from 4 per cent to 3 per cent. In the presence of 8 per cent inflation, the same tax reduces the real interest rate from 4 per cent to 1 per cent.

	Economy A (price stability) (%)	Economy B (inflation) (%)
Real interest rate	4	4
Inflation rate	0	8
Nominal interest rate (real interest rate + inflation rate)	4	12
Reduced interest due to 25 per cent tax (0.25 × nominal interest rate)	1	3
After-tax nominal interest rate (0.75 × nominal interest rate)	3	9
After-tax real interest rate (after-tax nominal interest rate – inflation rate)	3	1

The taxes on nominal capital gains and on nominal interest income are two examples of how the tax system interacts with inflation. There are many others. Because of these inflation-induced tax changes, higher inflation tends to discourage people from saving. Recall that the economy's saving provides the resources for investment, which in turn is a key ingredient to long-run economic growth. Thus, when inflation raises the tax burden on saving, it tends to depress the economy's long-run growth rate. There is, however, no consensus among economists about the size of this effect.

One solution to this problem, other than eliminating inflation, is to index the tax system. That is, the tax laws could be rewritten to take account of the effects of inflation. In the case of capital gains for example, the tax code could adjust the purchase price using a price index and assess the tax only on the real gain. In the case of interest income, the government could tax only real interest income by excluding that portion of the interest income that merely compensates for inflation.

In an ideal world, tax laws would be written so that inflation would not alter anyone's real tax liability. In the world in which we live, however, tax laws are far from perfect. More complete indexation would probably be desirable, but it would further complicate a tax system that many people already consider too complex.

Confusion and Inconvenience

Money is the economy's unit of account, and is what we use to quote prices and record debts. The job of the central bank is a little like the job of the government department that deals with weights and measurements, i.e. to ensure the reliability of a commonly used unit of measurement. Inflation erodes the real value of the unit of account over time.

It is difficult to judge the costs of the confusion and inconvenience that arise from inflation. Earlier we discussed how the tax system incorrectly measures real incomes in the presence of inflation. Similarly, accountants incorrectly measure firms' earnings when prices are rising over time. Because inflation causes money at different times to have different real values, computing a firm's profit is more complicated in an economy with inflation. Therefore, to some extent, inflation makes investors less able to sort out successful from unsuccessful firms, which in turn impedes financial markets in their role of allocating the economy's saving to alternative types of investment.

A Special Cost of Unexpected Inflation: Arbitrary Redistributions of Wealth

So far, the costs of inflation we have discussed occur even if inflation is steady and predictable. Inflation has an additional cost, however, when it comes as a surprise. Unexpected inflation redistributes wealth among the population in a way that has nothing to do with either merit or need. These redistributions occur because many loans in the economy are specified in terms of the unit of account – money.

Consider an example. Suppose that Lars, a student, takes out a €20 000 loan at a 7 per cent interest rate from Bigbank to attend university. In ten years the loan will have to be repaid. After his debt has compounded for ten years at 7 per cent, Lars will owe Bigbank €40 000 (rounded). The real value of this debt will depend on inflation over the decade. If inflation has been relatively high over the period, wages and prices will have risen by a relatively large amount and Lars will be in a position to be able to pay the €40 000 debt easier. In contrast, if the economy goes through a major deflation, then wages and prices will fall, and Lars will find the €40 000 debt a greater burden than he anticipated.

This example shows that unexpected changes in prices redistribute wealth among debtors and creditors. A high rate of inflation enriches Lars at the expense of Bigbank because it diminishes the real value of the debt; Lars can repay the loan in less valuable euros than he anticipated. Deflation enriches Bigbank at Lars' expense because it increases the real value of the debt; in this case, Lars has to repay the loan in more valuable euros than he anticipated. If inflation were predictable, then Bigbank and Lars could take inflation into account when setting the nominal interest rate (recall the Fisher effect). If inflation is hard to predict, it imposes risk on Lars and Bigbank that both would prefer to avoid.

This cost of unexpected inflation is important to consider together with another fact: inflation is especially volatile and uncertain when the average rate of inflation is high. This is seen most simply by examining the experience of different countries. Countries with low average inflation, such as Germany, tend to have stable inflation. Countries with high average inflation, such as many countries in Latin America, tend also to have unstable inflation. There are no known examples of economies with high, stable inflation. This relationship between the level and volatility of inflation points to another cost of inflation. If a country pursues a high-inflation monetary policy, it will have to bear not only the costs of high expected inflation but also the arbitrary redistributions of wealth associated with unexpected inflation.

SELF TEST List and describe six costs of inflation. Do people on fixed incomes benefit or lose out from periods of relatively high inflation?

DEFLATION

The majority of this chapter has focused on inflation – a period of generally rising prices. Economists generally see some inflation in the economy as being desirable (provided it is stable and manageable). The opposite of inflation is deflation where the price level actually falls. It might sound intuitive that falling prices would be a good thing but that is not necessarily the case.

In 2014, there were concerns expressed that the UK and the Eurozone might face deflation – a fall in the price level. In such a scenario, the CPI would be negative suggesting that prices, on average, had fallen. The Eurozone actually experienced deflation of 0.3 per cent in the year to January 2015 and the UK CPI was –0.1 per cent in the year to April 2015 and then again in October 2015.

It is important to note the distinction between a *fall* in the price level and a *slowdown* in the rate of growth of prices. If the CPI reports inflation at 2.5 per cent in March and then 2.0 percent in April, the rate of growth of prices has slowed down, not fallen, but if the CPI is recorded as –0.75 per cent in May, then prices have, on average, fallen.

Deflation is a relatively rare phenomenon; most economies experience inflation at varying levels and indeed an inflation rate of around 2 per cent is seen as being beneficial to an economy as it encourages businesses to expand and helps create a more dynamic economy. Where deflation has occurred it has tended not to last for very long and indeed the German and UK authorities were predicting that the deflation experienced in early 2015 would be short-lived. When deflation persists for some time, as it has done in Japan, for example, problems can arise. Japan experienced deflation from the mid-1990s until the latter part of the first decade of the 2000s. It is argued that one of the problems of deflation is a reluctance of consumers to spend when the expectation is that prices will be lower in the future. This argument has some logic and may apply to particular types of goods such as high-priced consumer goods – furniture, TVs and electrical goods, fridges, washing machines, dishwashers and so on. For many everyday goods like food, the likelihood of consumers deferring purchasing in the expectation that prices will be lower is less relevant. The evidence that consumers would delay purchases and thus plunge the economy into recession as consumption spending falls is not clear, especially where deflation does not persist for any length of time.

Other potential problems with deflation are related to interest rates. Interest rates in the Eurozone and UK were at historically low levels for a number of years following the Financial Crisis. The option for central banks to cut rates further as a means of boosting the economy was limited. Cutting rates below zero would be an incentive for savers to withdraw their deposits to prevent the value of them falling (a negative interest rate would in effect mean banks taking money out of savers deposits). If enough savers did this, then there could be pressure on banks and reduce their capacity for lending.

A period of deflation further affects borrowers and lenders. Banks lending to business would find that the sum lent would purchase more in future when the debt is paid back if prices continued to fall, whereas firms borrowing funds would find that the burden of the debt would increase. In such a situation it might be that businesses would be more reluctant to borrow for investment resulting in a fall in aggregate demand.

One way in which businesses can reduce real wages in a period of inflation is to put a freeze on pay increases for workers. A pay freeze results in an increase in real wages which, in effect, increases the costs of businesses. If prices are falling, firms might press workers to accept a reduction in wages. If the reduction in wages was less than the rate at which prices are falling, workers would not be any worse off in real terms. However, it is extremely difficult for firms to push through pay cuts, so at the very least a pay freeze is the most likely option. If firms' costs rise, then it is possible that supply is cut or employees are laid off and if either of these outcomes occur throughout the economy it can trigger a slowdown in economic activity. Given that all these effects could be experienced together, one of the fears of a period of persistent deflation is that the economy suffers from a downward spiral which is difficult to break.

CONCLUSION

This chapter discussed the causes and costs of inflation *in the long run*. The primary cause of inflation in the long run is growth in the quantity of money. When the central bank creates money in large quantities, the value of money falls quickly. To maintain stable prices, the central bank must seek to monitor the money supply and use the tools it has at its disposal to conduct monetary policy consistent with stable prices.

The costs of inflation are subtler. They include shoeleather costs, menu costs, increased variability of relative prices, unintended changes in tax liabilities, confusion and inconvenience, and arbitrary redistributions of wealth. Are these costs, in total, large or small? All economists agree that they become huge during hyperinflation. Their size for moderate inflation – when prices rise by less than 10 per cent per year – is more open to debate.

Although this chapter presented many of the most important lessons about inflation, the discussion is incomplete. When the central bank reduces the rate of money growth, prices rise less rapidly, as the quantity theory suggests. Yet as the economy makes the transition to this lower inflation rate, the change in monetary policy will have disruptive effects on production and employment. That is, even though monetary policy is neutral in the long run, it has profound effects on real variables in the short run. Later in this book we will examine the reasons for short-run monetary non-neutrality in order to enhance our understanding of the causes and costs of inflation.

IN THE NEWS

Quantitative Easing and Inflation

It is often the case in economics that disagreements about policy options arise not because of whether a particular policy will work but what its consequences will be and the extent to which it will have a beneficial effect.

The Consequences of Quantitative Easing

The Financial Crisis saw interest rates in the UK and Europe at historically low levels. Low interest rates appeared to have a limited stimulus effect on economies, and central banks looked at other options to generate economic activity with quantitative easing (QE) being an important tool for both the Bank of England and later, the ECB.

One concern that has been raised with such a policy is the possible long-term effect on prices – if billions of euros and pounds are being pumped into the economy, then the money supply will surely rise and as the quantity theory suggests, will make it more likely that inflation will accelerate in the future. The Bank of England had, as of December 2015, financed £375 billion (€510 bn) through QE and the ECB had financed €1 trillion (£736bn). Some reports put the resulting increase in the balance sheets of the Bank of England and ECB at 300 per cent and 150 per cent respectively.

Whether the increase in the money supply will lead to inflation depends on how other elements of the Fisher identity change. It has been suggested that QE will lead to a reduction in the velocity of circulation, and the rate at which Y increases (which is very much dependent on capacity in the economy) might mean the impact on inflation might not be a great as some feared. One concern that has been raised is that QE might be used as a tool of monetary financing – in other words, the central bank 'giving' money to government to finance spending, which is inflationary because it increases the money supply.

The argument is that government bonds are issued to fund government deficits – the difference between tax receipts and government expenditure. If central banks buy debt from financial markets and takes it onto their balance sheets, this is, in effect, financing government spending, which would be akin to overt monetary financing (OMF). OMF is when central banks 'print money' to finance government spending. This approach might remove fiscal discipline and lead to inflationary pressures building. With many governments struggling to manage deficits, it is possible to propose an argument along the lines of the following: if the central bank buys government bonds, the interest rate on government bonds falls and as a result government borrowing costs are lower. In addition, if the central bank is buying government bonds, what happens to the interest on these bonds – should the interest be accounted for on the central bank's accounts or on the government's (since it has issued the bonds)? The ECB is forbidden under its charter to engage in monetary financing. Monetary financing is also frowned upon by many other countries but where is the tipping point? There is a fine line between central bank open market operations involving government bonds and monetary financing largely depending on how different transactions are defined.

The counterargument is that QE requires money to be 'printed' by central banks, not for handing to people to spend but for the purchase of securities in financial markets. In this way, what is happening is that assets are being transferred within the financial system – in some cases, private firms are transferring bonds to the central bank's accounts and receiving deposits in return which are recorded in its account. In other cases, it is a transfer of assets between the government and the central bank – the central bank is acquiring government bonds and cash is indirectly going to the government. This might be seen as being pretty much the same as monetary financing except that in the long run the monetary base need not rise and as a result inflation may not result – unlike overt monetary financing.

If inflationary pressures do start to increase, will the central bank be able to spot when it is starting and take action in sufficient time to choke off any acceleration in prices over and above target rates? One way might be to destroy money in the same way that it was created through reversing QE by selling back bonds, taking money out of the economy and thus reducing the money supply. The success of such a policy depends on whether the central bank can indeed spot inflationary pressures at the time and whether they can act sufficiently early to be able to have an impact. Politically, this might prove difficult because unwinding QE would send a message to the markets that inflationary pressures are rising and that the economy is about to be squeezed.

Critics of QE have argued that the billions spent by central banks have not found their way through to the real economy (to people who spend more money on consumption) but instead have just been absorbed by the financial system to correct balance sheets. In addition, one other effect of QE is to feed its way through to exchange rates, as wealth holders with more liquidity as a result of QE sell off pounds and euros which weakens currencies. A weaker pound or euro benefits exporters but means importers face higher costs which can further feed through to inflation.

Questions

1. What effect would an increase in the money supply of 10 per cent have on the price level? On what does your answer depend?

2. Why would government borrowing costs fall if the central bank buys government bonds as part of an asset purchasing programme (QE)?

3. What is 'monetary financing' and why it is considered to be a taboo?

4. Assume that the pound weakens as a result of QE. What will be the effects of this on the economy, and what would determine the relative size of the effects?

5. Assume that QE leads to a fall in the velocity of circulation. Use the equation of exchange to show what the effect on the price level would be under different scenarios (i.e. assume M, V and Y all change by different amounts).

The financial system is a vital channel in the flow of funds from investors to the real economy.

SUMMARY

- The overall level of prices in an economy adjusts to bring money supply and money demand into balance. Persistent growth in the quantity of money supplied leads to continuing inflation.

- The principle of monetary neutrality asserts that changes in the quantity of money influence nominal variables but not real variables. Many economists believe that monetary neutrality approximately describes the behaviour of the economy in the long run.

- A government can pay for some of its spending simply by printing money. When countries rely heavily on this 'inflation tax', the result is hyperinflation.

- One application of the principle of monetary neutrality is the Fisher effect. According to the Fisher effect, when the inflation rate rises, the nominal interest rate rises by the same amount, so that the real interest rate remains the same.

- Many people think that inflation makes them poorer because it raises the cost of what they buy. This view is a fallacy if inflation also raises nominal incomes.

- Economists have identified six costs of inflation: shoeleather costs associated with reduced money holdings; menu costs associated with more frequent adjustment of prices; increased variability of relative prices; unintended changes in tax liabilities due to non-indexation of the tax system; confusion and inconvenience resulting from a changing unit of account; and arbitrary redistributions of wealth between debtors and creditors. Many of these costs are large during hyperinflation, but the size of these costs for moderate inflation is less clear.

- Deflation occurs when prices actually fall and the effects on the economy and on incentives can be as damaging as when inflation is rising too quickly.

QUESTIONS FOR REVIEW

1 What is the difference between the price level and inflation?

2 Explain how an increase in the price level affects the real value of money.

3 In one month, the CPI is reported as being 5.5 per cent and in the following month is reported as 5.0 per cent. Does this mean prices have fallen? Explain.

4 According to the quantity theory of money, what is the effect of an increase in the quantity of money?

5 Explain the difference between nominal and real variables, and give two examples of each. According to the principle of monetary neutrality, which variables are affected by changes in the quantity of money?

6 What is meant by the velocity of money and what is its relevance to the Fisher equation?

7 According to the Fisher effect, how does an increase in the inflation rate affect the real interest rate and the nominal interest rate?

8 What are the costs of inflation? Which of these costs do you think are most important for the economy of the country in which you are studying?

9 If inflation is less than expected, who benefits – debtors or creditors? Explain.

10 Why is deflation a potentially damaging phenomenon?

PROBLEMS AND APPLICATIONS

1 Suppose that this year's money supply is €500 billion, nominal GDP is €10 trillion and real GDP is €5 trillion.

   a. What is the price level? What is the velocity of money?
   b. Suppose that velocity is constant and the economy's output of goods and services rises by 5 per cent each year. What will happen to nominal GDP and the price level next year if the central bank keeps the money supply constant?
   c. What money supply should the central bank set next year if it wants to keep the price level stable?
   d. What money supply should the central bank set next year if it wants inflation of 10 per cent?

2 Suppose that changes in bank regulations expand the availability of credit cards, so that people need to hold less cash.

   a. How does this event affect the demand for money?
   b. If the central bank does not respond to this event, what will happen to the price level?
   c. If the central bank wants to keep the price level stable, what should it do?

3 It is often suggested that central banks should try to achieve zero inflation. If we assume that velocity is constant, does this zero inflation goal require that the rate of money growth equal zero? If yes, explain why. If no, explain what the rate of money growth should equal.

4 The economist John Maynard Keynes wrote: 'Lenin is said to have declared that the best way to destroy the capitalist system was to debauch the currency. By a continuing process of inflation, governments can confiscate, secretly and unobserved, an important part of the wealth of their citizens.' Justify Lenin's assertion.

5 Suppose that a country's inflation rate increases sharply. What happens to the inflation tax on the holders of money? Why is wealth that is held in savings accounts not subject to a change in the inflation tax? Can you think of any way in which holders of savings accounts are hurt by the increase in the inflation rate?

6 Hyperinflations are extremely rare in countries whose central banks are independent of the rest of the government. Why might this be so?

7 Let's consider the effects of inflation in an economy composed only of two people: Michael, a bean farmer, and Dorothy, a rice farmer. Michael and Dorothy both always consume equal amounts of rice and beans. In year 2017, the price of beans was €1, and the price of rice was €3.

   a. Suppose that in 2018 the price of beans was €2 and the price of rice was €6. What was inflation? Was Michael better off, worse off or unaffected by the changes in prices? What about Dorothy?

   b. Now suppose that in 2018 the price of beans was €2 and the price of rice was €4. What was inflation? Was Michael better off, worse off or unaffected by the changes in prices? What about Dorothy?

   c. Finally, suppose that in 2018 the price of beans was €2 and the price of rice was €1.50. What was inflation? Was Michael better off, worse off or unaffected by the changes in prices? What about Dorothy?

   d. What matters more to Michael and Dorothy – the overall inflation rate or the relative price of rice and beans?

8 If the tax rate is 40 per cent, compute the before-tax real interest rate and the after-tax real interest rate in each of the following cases.

   a. The nominal interest rate is 10 per cent and the inflation rate is 5 per cent.
   b. The nominal interest rate is 6 per cent and the inflation rate is 2 per cent.
   c. The nominal interest rate is 4 per cent and the inflation rate is 1 per cent.

9 Suppose that people expect inflation to equal 3 per cent, but in fact prices rise by 5 per cent. Describe how this unexpectedly high inflation rate would help or hurt the following:

   a. the government
   b. a homeowner with a fixed-rate mortgage
   c. a union worker in the second year of a labour contract
   d. a retired person who has invested their savings in government bonds.

10 Explain whether the following statements are true, false or uncertain.

   a. 'Inflation hurts borrowers and helps lenders, because borrowers must pay a higher rate of interest.'
   b. 'If prices change in a way that leaves the overall price level unchanged, then no one is made better or worse off.'
   c. 'Inflation does not reduce the purchasing power of most workers.'

PART 13
THE MACROECONOMICS OF OPEN ECONOMIES

29 OPEN-ECONOMY MACROECONOMICS: BASIC CONCEPTS

It goes without saying that economic agents in Europe and the UK not only participate in their own domestic economies but have their interests intricately tied up with those of other economies. In Chapter 19, we outlined the benefits of international trade: trade allows people to specialise in what they produce best and to consume the great variety of goods and services produced around the world. The neo-classical argument is that international trade can raise living standards by allowing countries to specialize in producing those goods and services in which it has a comparative advantage.

So far in our development of macroeconomics, we have largely assumed a closed economy. This assumption allows us to explore unemployment and the causes of inflation without the added complexity of the effects of international trade. In an open economy, however, new macroeconomic issues arise. This chapter and the next provide an introduction to open-economy macroeconomics. We begin in this chapter by discussing the key macroeconomic variables that describe an open economy's interactions in world markets – exports, imports, the trade balance and exchange rates. In the next chapter we develop a model to explain how these variables are determined and how they are affected by various government policies.

THE INTERNATIONAL FLOWS OF GOODS AND CAPITAL

An open economy interacts with other economies in two ways: it buys and sells goods and services in world product markets, and it buys and sells capital assets such as stocks and bonds in world financial markets.

The Flow of Goods and Services: Exports, Imports and Net Exports

Exports are domestically produced goods and services that are sold abroad, and imports are foreign-produced goods and services that are purchased by the domestic economy. When Lloyd's of London insures a building in Munich, it is paid an insurance premium for this service by the owner of the building. The sale of the insurance service provided by Lloyd's is an export for the United Kingdom and an import for Germany. When Volvo, the Swedish car manufacturer, makes a car and sells it to a Swiss resident, the sale is an import for Switzerland and an export for Sweden.

The net exports (*NX*) of any country are the value of its exports (*X*) minus the value of its imports (*M*). This is written: $NX = X - M$. The sale of insurance services abroad by Lloyd's raises UK net exports, and the Volvo sale reduces Swiss net exports. Because net exports tell us whether a country is, in total, a seller or a buyer in world markets for goods and services, net exports are also called the **trade balance**. If net exports are positive, exports are greater than imports, indicating that the country sells more goods and services abroad than it buys from other countries. In this case, the country is said to run a **trade surplus**. If net exports are negative, exports are less than imports, indicating that the country sells fewer goods and services abroad than it buys from other countries. In this case, the country is said to run a **trade deficit**. If net exports are zero, its exports and imports are exactly equal, and the country is said to have **balanced trade**.

> **trade balance** the value of a nation's exports minus the value of its imports; also called net exports
> **trade surplus** an excess of exports over imports
> **trade deficit** an excess of imports over exports
> **balanced trade** a situation in which exports equal imports

There are many factors that might influence a country's exports, imports and net exports, including:

- The tastes of consumers for domestic and foreign goods.
- The prices of goods at home and abroad.
- The exchange rates at which people can use domestic currency to buy foreign currencies.
- The incomes of consumers at home and abroad.
- The cost of transporting goods from country to country.
- The policies of the government towards international trade.

As these variables change over time, so does the amount of international trade.

The Flow of Financial Resources: Net Capital Outflow

Economic agents buy and sell goods and services across international markets but also participate in world financial markets. A UK resident with £20 000, for example, could use this money to buy a car from BMW in the goods market, but could instead use the money to buy stock in the German BMW corporation. The first transaction would represent a flow of goods, whereas the second would represent a flow of capital.

The term **net capital outflow** refers to the purchase of foreign assets by domestic residents minus the purchase of domestic assets by foreigners. (It is sometimes called *net foreign investment*.)

> **net capital outflow** the purchase of foreign assets by domestic residents minus the purchase of domestic assets by foreigners

Net Capital Outflow = Purchase of foreign assets by domestic residents –
Purchase of domestic assets by foreigners

When a UK resident buys shares in BMW, the purchase raises UK net capital outflow. When a Japanese resident buys a bond issued by the UK government, the purchase reduces UK net capital outflow.

Recall that the flow of capital abroad takes two forms. If the French car manufacturer Renault opens up a factory in Romania, that is an example of *foreign direct investment*. Alternatively, if a French citizen buys shares in a Romanian company, this is an example of *foreign portfolio investment*. In the first case, the French owner is actively managing the investment, whereas in the second case the French owner has a more passive role. In both cases, French residents are buying assets located in another country, so both purchases increase French net capital outflow.

These are some of the more important variables that influence net capital outflow:

- The real interest rates being paid on foreign assets.
- The real interest rates being paid on domestic assets.
- The perceived economic and political risks of holding assets abroad.
- The government policies that affect foreign ownership of domestic assets.

For example, consider German investors deciding whether to buy Ukrainian government bonds or German government bonds. To make this decision, German investors compare the real interest rates offered on the two bonds. The higher a bond's real interest rate, the more attractive it is. While making this comparison, however, German investors must also take into account the risk that one of these governments might *default* on its debt, as well as any restrictions that the Ukrainian government has imposed, or might impose in the future, on foreign investors in Ukraine.

The Equality of Net Exports and Net Capital Outflow

Net exports and net capital outflow each measure a type of imbalance in the goods and financial markets. Net exports measure an imbalance between a country's exports and its imports in the goods market. Net capital outflow measures an imbalance between the amount of foreign assets bought by domestic residents and the amount of domestic assets bought by foreigners.

An important but subtle fact of accounting states that, for an economy as a whole, these two imbalances must offset each other. That is, net capital outflow (*NCO*) always equals net exports (*NX*):

$$NCO = NX$$

This equation is an identity in that every transaction that affects one side of this equation must also affect the other side by exactly the same amount. To see why, consider an example. Suppose that BP sells some aircraft fuel to a Japanese airline which represents an export for the UK. The UK company (BP) gives aircraft fuel to a Japanese company, and the Japanese company gives yen to a UK company. Two things have occurred simultaneously. The UK has sold to a foreigner some of its output in the goods market (the fuel), and this sale increases UK net exports. In addition, the UK has acquired some foreign assets (the yen), and this acquisition increases UK net capital outflow.

Although BP most probably will not hold on to the yen it has acquired in this sale, any subsequent transaction will preserve the equality of net exports and net capital outflow. For example, BP may exchange its yen for pounds with a UK investment fund that wants the yen to buy shares in Sony Corporation, the Japanese maker of consumer electronics. In this case, BP's net export of aircraft fuel equals the investment fund's net capital outflow in Sony shares. Hence, *NX* and *NCO* rise by an equal amount.

Alternatively, BP may exchange its yen for pounds with another UK company that wants to buy computers from Toshiba, the Japanese computer maker. In this case, UK imports (of computers) exactly offset UK exports (of aircraft fuel). The sales by BP and Toshiba together affect neither UK net exports nor UK net capital outflow. That is, *NX* and *NCO* are the same as they were before these transactions took place.

The equality of net exports and net capital outflow follows from the fact that every international transaction is an exchange. When a seller country transfers a good or service to a buyer country, the buyer country gives up some asset to pay for this good or service. The value of that asset equals the value of the good or service sold. When we add everything up, the net value of goods and services sold by a country (*NX*) must equal the net value of assets acquired (*NCO*). The international flow of goods and services and the international flow of capital are two sides of the same coin.

Saving and Investment, and their Relationship to the International Flows

A nation's saving and investment are crucial to its long-run economic growth. Let's therefore consider how these variables are related to the international flows of goods and capital as measured by net exports and net capital outflow. We can do this most easily with the help of some simple mathematics.

The economy's gross domestic product (Y) as measured by the expenditure method is divided among four components: consumption (C), investment (I), government purchases (G) and net exports (NX). We write this as:

$$Y = C + I + G + NX$$

National saving is the income of the nation that is left after paying for current consumption and government purchases. National saving (S) equals $Y - C - G$. If we rearrange the above equation to reflect this fact, we obtain:

$$Y - C - G = I + NX$$

$$S = I + NX$$

Because $NX = NCO$, we can write this equation as:

$$S = I + NCO$$

Saving = Domestic Investment + Net Capital Outflow

This equation shows that a nation's saving must equal its domestic investment plus its net capital outflow. In other words, when UK citizens, for example, save a pound of their income for the future, that pound can be used to finance accumulation of domestic capital or it can be used to finance the purchase of capital abroad. In a closed economy, net capital outflow is zero, so saving equals investment. In contrast, an open economy has two uses for its saving: domestic investment and net capital outflow.

We can view the financial system as standing between the two sides of this identity. For example, suppose the Singh family decides to save some of its income for retirement. This decision contributes to national saving, the left-hand side of our equation. If the Singh's deposit their saving in an investment fund, the fund may use some of the deposit to buy shares issued by BP, which uses the proceeds to build an oil refinery in Aberdeen. In addition, the investment fund may use some of the Singh's deposit to buy shares issued by Toyota, which uses the proceeds to build a factory in Osaka. These transactions show up on the right-hand side of the equation. From the standpoint of UK accounting, the BP expenditure on a new oil refinery is domestic investment, and the purchase of Toyota stock by a UK resident is net capital outflow. Thus, all saving in the UK economy shows up as investment in the UK economy or as UK net capital outflow.

Summing Up

Table 29.1 summarizes the three possibilities for an open economy: a country with a trade deficit, a country with balanced trade and a country with a trade surplus.

TABLE 29.1   **International Flows of Goods and Capital: Summary**

This table shows the three possible outcomes for an open economy.

Trade deficit	Balanced trade	Trade surplus
Exports < Imports	Exports = Imports	Exports > Imports
Net exports < 0	Net exports = 0	Net exports > 0
$Y < C + I + G$	$Y = C + I + G$	$Y > C + I + G$
Saving < Investment	Saving = Investment	Saving > Investment
Net capital outflow < 0	Net capital outflow = 0	Net capital outflow > 0

A Trade Surplus A trade surplus means that the value of exports exceeds the value of imports. Because net exports are exports minus imports, net exports are greater than zero. As a result, income must be greater than domestic spending. But if income is more than spending, then saving must be more than investment. Because the country is saving more than it is investing, it must be sending some of its saving abroad. That is, the net capital outflow must be greater than zero.

A Trade Deficit A trade deficit means that the value of exports is less than the value of imports. Because net exports are exports minus imports, net exports are negative. Thus, income must be less than domestic spending. If income is less than domestic spending, then saving must be less than investment. Net capital outflow must be negative.

A Trade Balance A country with balanced trade is between these cases. Exports equal imports, so net exports are zero. Income equals domestic spending, and saving equals investment. Net capital outflow equals zero.

> **SELF TEST** Define net exports and net capital outflow. Explain how they are related. A Swiss resident buys shares in a Singapore company and the company purchases plant and equipment from a German manufacturer. Explain the effects on the accounts of the countries involved.

THE PRICES FOR INTERNATIONAL TRANSACTIONS: REAL AND NOMINAL EXCHANGE RATES

Different countries use different currencies. In trading internationally, firms will need to acquire these different currencies in order to complete transactions. This creates a demand and supply of currencies traded on foreign exchange markets.

Nominal Exchange Rates

The **nominal exchange rate** or more simply, *the exchange rate,* is the rate at which one currency exchanges for that of another. This rate is determined by the interaction of the demand and supply of the currency on foreign exchange markets.

> **nominal exchange rate** the rate at which a person can trade the currency of one country for the currency of another

If you go to a bank, you might see a posted exchange rate of 125 yen per euro (¥125 = €1). If you give the bank one euro, it will give you 125 Japanese yen; and if you give the bank 125 Japanese yen, it will give you one euro. (In fact, the bank will post slightly different prices for buying and selling yen. The difference gives the bank some profit for offering this service. For our purposes here, we can ignore these differences.)

An exchange rate can always be expressed in two ways. If the exchange rate is 125 yen per euro, it is also $\frac{1}{125} = 0.008$ euro per yen. If a euro is worth £0.74, a pound is worth $\frac{1}{0.74} = €1.35$. This can be a source of confusion, and there is no real hard and fast convention that people use. For example, it is customary to quote the US dollar–pound exchange rate as dollars per pound, e.g. £1 = $1.50 if 1 pound exchanges for 1.50 dollars. On the other hand, the pound–euro exchange rate can be quoted either way, as pounds per euro or euros per pound. In this book we shall, for the most part, think of the exchange rate as being the quantity of foreign currency that exchanges for one unit of domestic currency, or the foreign price of a unit of domestic currency. For example, if we are thinking of the UK as the domestic economy and the USA as the foreign economy, then the exchange rate is $1.50 per pound. If we are thinking of, say, Germany as the domestic economy, then we could express the exchange rate as dollars per euro, e.g. $1.08 dollars per euro.

In summary, when converting currencies:
To convert £ into (e.g.) € – *multiply* the sterling amount by the € rate
To convert € into £ – *divide* the € amount by the £ rate

For example:
To convert £5.70 to € at a rate of £1 = €1.47, multiply 5.70 × 1.47 = €8.38
To convert €3.45 to £ at the same rate, divide 3.45 by 1.47 = £2.35

Appreciation and Depreciation of Currencies If the exchange rate changes so that a euro buys more of another currency, that change is called an **appreciation** of the euro. If the exchange rate changes so that a euro buys less of another currency, that change is called a **depreciation** of the euro. For example, when the exchange rate rises from 125 to 127 yen per euro, the euro is said to appreciate (a larger amount of yen is received in return for every euro). At the same time, because a Japanese yen now buys less of the European currency, the yen is said to depreciate (more yen has to be given up to buy one euro). When the exchange rate falls from 125 to 123 yen per euro, the euro is said to depreciate, and the yen is said to appreciate.

> **appreciation** an increase in the value of a currency as measured by the amount of foreign currency it can buy
> **depreciation** a decrease in the value of a currency as measured by the amount of foreign currency it can buy

At times you may have heard the media report that the pound or the euro is either 'strong' or 'weak'. These descriptions usually refer to recent changes in the nominal exchange rate. When a currency appreciates, it is said to *strengthen* because it can buy more foreign currency. Similarly, when a currency depreciates, it is said to *weaken*. If an individual gets more of the foreign currency in exchange for the same amount of the domestic currency, the domestic currency is stronger. If an individual has to give up more of the domestic currency to get the same amount of the foreign currency, then the domestic currency is weaker.

The movement of currencies is important because of the effect it has on imports and exports. For example, a rise in the value of the pound against the dollar means that each pound buys more dollars. For example, if the pound appreciated from £1 = $1.50 to £1 = $1.55, UK firms buying goods from the US would have to give up fewer pounds to get the same amount of dollars to buy the goods, which makes imports prices appear cheaper. The flip side is that US buyers of UK goods will have to give up more dollars to acquire the same amount of pounds and so UK exports will appear to be more expensive.

If the pound depreciates in value, each pound now buys less of the foreign currency. In this case, UK exports appear cheaper to foreign buyers as they now get more pounds for every unit of their currency, but importers will find their costs rising as they have to give up more pounds to get the same amount of the foreign currency.

In summary:

- A depreciation in a currency – import prices dearer, export prices cheaper
- An appreciation in a currency – import prices cheaper, exports dearer

Exchange Rate Indexes For any currency, there are many nominal exchange rates. The euro can be used to buy US dollars, Japanese yen, British pounds, Mexican pesos and so on. When economists study changes in the exchange rate, they often use indices that measure the average change in many exchange rates. Just as the CPI turns the many prices in the economy into a single measure of the price level, an exchange rate index turns these many exchange rates into a single measure of the international value of the currency. So when economists talk about the euro or the pound appreciating or depreciating, they often are referring to an exchange rate index that takes into account many individual exchange rates.

Real Exchange Rates

The **real exchange rate** is the rate at which a person can trade the goods and services of one country for the goods and services of another. For example, suppose that you go shopping and find that a kilo of Swiss cheese is twice as expensive as a kilo of English cheddar cheese. We would then say that the real exchange rate is a $\frac{1}{2}$ kilo of Swiss cheese per kilo of English cheese.

> **real exchange rate** the rate at which the goods and services of one country trade for the goods and services of another

Real and nominal exchange rates are closely related. To see how, consider an example. Suppose that a kilo of British wheat sells for £1 and a kilo of European wheat sells for €3. What is the real exchange rate between British and European wheat? To answer this question, we must first use the nominal exchange rate to convert the prices into a common currency. If the nominal exchange rate is €2 per pound, then a price for British wheat of £1 per kilo is equivalent to €2 per kilo. European wheat, however, sells for €3 a kilo, so British wheat is only $\frac{2}{3}$ as expensive as European wheat. The real exchange rate is $\frac{2}{3}$ of a kilo of European wheat per kilo of British wheat.

We can summarize this calculation for the real exchange rate with the following formula, where we are measuring the exchange rate as the amount of foreign currency needed to buy one unit of domestic currency:

$$Real\ exchange\ rate = \frac{(Nominal\ exchange\ rate \times Domestic\ price)}{(Foreign\ price)}$$

Using the numbers in our example, the formula applies as follows:

$$Real\ exchange\ rate = \frac{€2\ per\ pound \times €1\ per\ kilo\ of\ UK\ wheat}{€3\ per\ kilo\ of\ European\ wheat}$$

$$= \frac{€2\ per\ kilo\ of\ UK\ wheat}{€3\ per\ kilo\ of\ European\ wheat}$$

$$= \frac{2}{3}\ kilo\ of\ European\ wheat\ per\ kilo\ of\ UK\ wheat$$

Thus, the real exchange rate depends on the nominal exchange rate and on the prices of goods in the two countries measured in the local currencies.

The real exchange rate is a key determinant of how much a country exports and imports. For example, when a British bread company is deciding whether to buy British or European wheat to make into flour and use in making its bread, it will ask which wheat is cheaper. The real exchange rate gives the answer. As another example, imagine that you are deciding whether to take a holiday in the Dordogne, France, or in Cancun, Mexico. You might ask your travel agent the price of a hotel room in the Dordogne (measured in euros), the price of a hotel room in Cancun (measured in pesos) and the exchange rate between pesos and euros. If you decide where to go on holiday by comparing costs, you are basing your decision on the real exchange rate.

When studying an economy as a whole, macroeconomists focus on overall prices rather than the prices of individual items. That is, to measure the real exchange rate, they use price indices, such as the CPI. By using a price index for a UK or European basket (P), a price index for a foreign basket (P^*), and the nominal exchange rate between the UK pound or euro and foreign currencies (e = *foreign currency per pound or euro*), we can compute the overall real exchange rate between the United Kingdom or Europe and other countries as follows:

$$Real\ exchange\ rate = \frac{(e \times P)}{P^*}$$

This real exchange rate measures the price of a basket of goods and services available domestically relative to a basket of goods and services available abroad.

A country's real exchange rate is a key determinant of its net exports of goods and services. A depreciation (fall) in the real exchange rate of the euro means that EU goods have become cheaper relative to foreign goods. This change encourages consumers both at home and abroad to buy more EU goods and fewer goods from other countries. As a result, EU exports rise and EU imports fall, and both of these changes raise EU net exports. Conversely, an appreciation (rise) in the euro real exchange rate means that EU goods have become more expensive compared to foreign goods, so EU net exports fall. It is important to remember that whilst we are talking about the prices of exports and imports changing, the domestic price for these goods and services may not change. For example, a French wine producer may have wine for sale priced at €10 per bottle. If the exchange rate between the euro and the UK pound is £1 = €1.47 then a UK buyer of wine will have to give up $\frac{€10}{1.47}$ = £6.80 to buy a bottle of wine. If the UK exchange rate appreciates to £1 = €1.50, then the UK buyer now has to give up $\frac{€10}{1.5}$ = £6.66 to buy the bottle of wine. The euro price of the wine has not changed but to the UK buyer the price has fallen. Equally, if the pound exchange rate depreciated from £1 = €1.47 to £1 = €1.45, then the UK buyer would now have to give up $\frac{€10}{1.45}$ = £6.90 to buy the wine. Again, the euro price of the wine has not changed but the price to the UK buyer has risen because the exchange rate between the pound and the euro has changed.

SELF TEST Define the nominal exchange rate and the real exchange rate, and explain how they are related. If the nominal exchange rate goes from 100 to 120 yen per euro, has the euro appreciated or depreciated? How would this affect European importers of goods from Japan and European exporters of goods to Japan?

CASE STUDY   Exchange Rates and Economic Data

Traders on foreign exchange markets pay considerable attention to economic data coming out of different countries. Part of the reason is to take into account the likely effect of the information on future demand and supply of currencies and thus the direction of exchange rates in the future.

In early January 2016, for example, data on UK manufacturing, mortgage approvals, changes to consumer credit levels, and lending securities on dwellings were all published. All but the manufacturing data was better than expected and as a result, traders bought sterling on foreign exchanges leading to an appreciation of sterling at that time. This was in contrast to the end of 2015 when the pound weakened against other currencies. The reason was largely due to floods which had affected many parts of northern Britain in December of 2015. Why would floods cause the currency to weaken? Part of the reason would be due to traders forecasting that heavy flooding was likely to affect overall economic performance and economic growth might slow down as a result. Some forecasts at the time put the cost of the floods at around £3 billion (€3.8 billion). If the economy is not as strong then the incentive is to sell pounds and buy currencies in countries where economic news is better, in the expectation of getting a better return.

Around the same time, Germany published its December CPI figures. Expectations had been that the CPI would be around 0.6 per cent but in the event it came in at 0.3 per cent. This news suggests that the German economy was not as strong as expected, and this encouraged traders to sell euro reducing its value against other currencies.

A natural event such as flooding can have a wider impact on exchange rates.

A FIRST THEORY OF EXCHANGE RATE DETERMINATION: PURCHASING POWER PARITY

Exchange rates vary substantially over time. In 1970, one UK pound could buy $2.4 but in 1985 the pound was only worth about half this amount of dollars (the exchange rate was about $1.25). In March 2008 one pound could buy over $2 but by February 2016 the rate stood at around £1 = $1.38. Over this 40-year period, the pound first almost halved in value from $2.40 to $1.25, and then increased by over 50 per cent from $1.25 to over $2.00.

Economists have developed many models to explain how exchange rates are determined, each emphasizing just some of the many forces at work. Here we develop the simplest theory of exchange rates, called **purchasing power parity** (PPP). This theory states that a unit of any given currency should be able to buy the same quantity of goods in all countries. Some economists believe that purchasing power parity describes the forces that determine exchange rates *in the long run*.

> **purchasing power parity** a theory of exchange rates whereby a unit of any given currency should be able to buy the same quantity of goods in all countries

The Basic Logic of Purchasing Power Parity

The theory of purchasing power parity is based on a principle called the *law of one price*. This law asserts that a good must sell for the same price in all locations, otherwise there would be opportunities for profit left unexploited. For example, suppose that coffee beans sold for less in Munich than in Frankfurt. A person could buy coffee beans in Munich for, say, €4 a kilo and then sell them in Frankfurt for €5 a kilo, making a profit of €1 per kilo from the difference in price. The process of taking advantage of differences in prices in different markets is called arbitrage. In our example, as the coffee buyer took advantage of the arbitrage opportunity, it would increase the demand for coffee in Munich and increase the supply in Frankfurt. The price of coffee would rise in Munich (in response to greater demand) and fall in Frankfurt (in response to greater supply). This process would continue until, eventually, the prices were the same in the two markets.

Now consider how the law of one price applies to the international marketplace. If a euro (or any other currency) could buy more coffee beans in Germany than in Japan, international traders could profit by buying coffee beans in Germany and selling them in Japan. This export of coffee beans from Germany to Japan would drive up the German price and drive down the Japanese price. Conversely, if a euro could buy more coffee beans in Japan than in Germany, traders could buy beans in Japan and sell them in Germany. This import of coffee beans into Germany from Japan would drive down the German price and drive up the Japanese price. In the end, the law of one price suggests that a euro must buy the same amount of coffee beans in all countries.

This logic is behind the theory of purchasing power parity. According to this theory, a currency must have the same purchasing power in all countries. That is, a euro must buy the same quantity of goods in Germany and Japan, and a Japanese yen must buy the same quantity of goods in Japan as in Germany. Indeed, the name of this theory describes it well. *Parity* means equality, and *purchasing power* refers to the value of money. *Purchasing power parity* states that a unit of all currencies must have the same real value in every country.

Implications of Purchasing Power Parity

The theory of purchasing power parity tells us that the nominal exchange rate between the currencies of two countries depends on the price levels in those countries. If a euro buys the same quantity of goods in Germany (where prices are measured in euros) as in Japan (where prices are measured in yen), then the number of yen per euro must reflect the prices of goods in Germany and Japan. For example, if a kilo of coffee is priced at ¥500 in Japan and €5 in Germany, then the nominal exchange rate must be ¥100 yen per euro $\left(\dfrac{¥500}{€5} = ¥100 \text{ per } €\right)$, otherwise the purchasing power of the euro would not be the same in the two countries.

To see more fully how this works, it is helpful to use a little mathematics. Think of Germany as the home or domestic economy. Suppose that P is the price of a basket of goods in Germany (measured in euros), P^* is the price of a basket of goods in Japan (measured in yen) and e is the nominal exchange rate (the number of yen needed to buy one euro).

Now consider the quantity of goods a euro can buy at home (in Germany) and abroad. At home, the price level is P, so the purchasing power of €1 at home is $\dfrac{1}{P}$. Abroad, a euro can be exchanged into e units of foreign currency, which in turn have purchasing power $\dfrac{e}{P^*}$. For the purchasing power of a euro to be the same in the two countries, it must be the case that:

$$\frac{1}{P} = \frac{e}{P^*}$$

With rearrangement, this equation becomes:

$$1 = \frac{eP}{P^*}$$

Notice that the left-hand side of this equation is a constant, and the right-hand side is the real exchange rate. Thus, if the purchasing power of the euro is always the same at home and abroad, then the real exchange rate – the relative price of domestic and foreign goods – cannot change.

To see the implication of this analysis for the nominal exchange rate, we can rearrange the last equation to solve for the nominal exchange rate:

$$e = \frac{P^*}{P}$$

That is, the nominal exchange rate equals the ratio of the foreign price level (measured in units of the foreign currency) to the domestic price level (measured in units of the domestic currency). According to the theory of purchasing power parity, the nominal exchange rate between the currencies of two countries must reflect the different price levels in those countries.

A key implication of this theory is that nominal exchange rates change when price levels change. Because the nominal exchange rate depends on price levels, it also depends on the money supply and money demand in each country. When a central bank in any country increases the money supply and causes the price level to rise, it also causes that country's currency to depreciate relative to other currencies in the world. In other words, when the central bank 'prints' large quantities of money, that money loses value both in terms of the goods and services it can buy and in terms of the amount of other currencies it can buy.

Referring back to the beginning of this section, why did the UK pound lose value compared to the US dollar between 1970 and 1985? A good deal of the answer relates to differences in inflation between the two countries. Between 1970 and 1985, the USA pursued, on average, a less inflationary monetary policy than the United Kingdom. Average price inflation in the UK over these 15 years was very high – about 10.5 per cent a year, while in the United States it was only about 6.5 per cent a year on average. This meant that between 1970 and 1985 the UK price level rose an average of 4 per cent a year faster than the US price level. As UK prices rose relative to US prices, the value of the pound fell relative to the dollar.

Whether the UK pound or the US dollar buy more or fewer euros 20 years from now than they do today depends on whether the ECB oversees more or less inflation in Europe than the Bank of England does in the United Kingdom or the Federal Reserve does in the United States.

FYI

Purchasing Power Standard (PPS)

If you look at statistics produced by Eurostat, the EU's statistical office, you are likely to see data expressed in *purchasing power standard (PPS)*. This is an extension of the PPP idea but applied to the EU. PPS is an artificial currency which expresses the purchasing power of the EU 28 (27 once the UK has negotiated leaving the EU), against the euro. In theory, therefore, one PPS would buy the same amount of goods in each EU country and so 1 PPS = €1. In reality there will be price differences between European countries so different amounts of euro will be needed to buy the same goods and services in different countries. PPS takes account of these differences. The PPS is found by taking any national economic aggregate, such as GDP, for example, and dividing by its PPP. PPPs can be seen as the exchange rate of the PPS against the euro and allows for more accurate comparisons between data from different EU countries. The PPS for the EU as a whole would be 100. If GDP per capita was expressed in PPS, then any figure above 100 would show GDP per capita in that country above the EU average and any figure below 100 would indicate GDP per capita below the EU average.

Limitations of Purchasing Power Parity

Purchasing power parity provides a simple model of how exchange rates are determined. For understanding many economic phenomena, the theory works well. In particular, it can explain many long-term trends, such as the examples discussed earlier. It can also explain the major changes in exchange rates that occur during hyperinflations. Yet the theory of purchasing power parity is not completely accurate. Exchange rates do not always move to ensure that a euro has the same real value in all countries all the time. There are two reasons why the theory of purchasing power parity does not always hold in practice.

The first is that many goods are not easily traded. Imagine, for instance, that haircuts are more expensive in Paris than in New York. International travellers might avoid getting their haircuts in Paris, and some haircutters might move from New York to Paris. Yet such arbitrage would probably be too limited to eliminate the differences in prices. Thus, the deviation from purchasing power parity might persist, and a euro (or dollar) would continue to buy less of a haircut in Paris than in New York.

The second reason is that even tradable goods are not always perfect substitutes when they are produced in different countries. For example, some consumers prefer German cars, and others prefer Japanese cars. Moreover, consumer tastes can change over time. If German cars suddenly become more popular, the increase in demand will drive up the price of German cars compared to Japanese cars. Despite this difference in prices in the two markets, there might be no opportunity for profitable arbitrage because consumers do not view the two cars as equivalent.

Thus, both because some goods are not tradable and because some tradable goods are not perfect substitutes with their foreign counterparts, purchasing power parity is not a perfect theory of exchange rate determination. For these reasons, real exchange rates fluctuate over time. Nonetheless, the theory of purchasing power parity does provide a useful first step in understanding exchange rates. The basic logic is persuasive: as the real exchange rate drifts from the level predicted by purchasing power parity, people have greater incentive to move goods across national borders. Even if the forces of purchasing power parity do not completely fix the real exchange rate, they provide a reason to expect that changes in the real exchange rate are most often small or temporary. As a result, large and persistent movements in nominal exchange rates typically reflect changes in price levels at home and abroad.

SELF TEST Over the past 20 years, Venezuela has had high inflation and Japan has had low inflation. What do you predict has happened to the number of Venezuelan bolivars a person can buy with a Japanese yen?

CONCLUSION

The purpose of this chapter has been to develop some basic concepts that macroeconomists use to study open economies. You should now understand why a nation's net exports must equal its net capital outflow, and why national saving must equal domestic investment plus net capital outflow. You should also understand the meaning of nominal and real exchange rates, as well as the implications and limitations of purchasing power parity as a theory of how exchange rates are determined.

The macroeconomic variables defined here offer a starting point for analyzing an open economy's interactions with the rest of the world. In the next chapter we develop a model that can explain what determines these variables. We can then discuss how various events and policies affect a country's trade balance and the rate at which nations make exchanges in world markets.

IN THE NEWS

Exchange Rates

For a number of years, there have been accusations levelled at China that it manipulates its currency for its own benefit, and in the process creates unfair competition for other nations.

China and Currency Manipulation Accusations

China's success in export markets has helped the country to experience tremendous growth in the last 20 years. As Chinese products penetrate every corner of the globe, the competition has not been slow in crying foul. One of the main points of contention is the accusation that China has manipulated its currency to benefit its exporters and limit the chance of overseas businesses selling into China.

This accusation is interesting in that it comes from countries whose central banks have used extensive quantitative easing in order to boost their own economies. One of the effects of QE is to cause the exchange rate to weaken and provide a benefit to exporters and in turn stimulate export led growth. Is this also a form of currency manipulation?

For some time, China pegged its currency against the US dollar. What this means is that the Chinese authorities use reserves of foreign currencies to intervene in the market for its currency to maintain its level against another currency. Pegging a currency means the exchange rate does not float freely against other currencies in relation to the demand and supply of international trade.

In the latter part of 2015 there were indications that China was going to broaden the range of currencies against which the yuan (or renminbi) would be pegged. One of the reasons it was suggested that it was doing this was because the Federal Reserve in the US was going to increase the federal funds rate and this was expected to lead to an appreciation of the dollar. If the yuan was pegged to the dollar only, there was a danger it would also have to appreciate. This was not seen as being helpful for China given the slowdown in the economy which had been the news throughout 2015.

Is the pegging of the Chinese currency against the US dollar an example of currency manipulation?

(*Continued*)

Questions

1 **How does international trade lead to changes in the exchange rate for a currency? Use supply and demand diagrams to illustrate your answer.**
2 **How does QE lead to a weakening of a currency and how does this help exporters?**
3 **If a country decides to peg its exchange rate against that of another currency, what must it do to maintain the link with the pegged currency? Use supply and demand diagrams to help illustrate your answer.**
4 **Why might broadening the range of currencies against which the renminbi is pegged be beneficial to China?**
5 **Why would an appreciation of the dollar be bad news for China if the renminbi also rose in value against other currencies as a result of the pegging?**

SUMMARY

- Net exports are the value of domestic goods and services sold abroad minus the value of foreign goods and services sold domestically. Net capital outflow is the acquisition of foreign assets by domestic residents minus the acquisition of domestic assets by foreigners. Because every international transaction involves an exchange of an asset for a good or service, an economy's net capital outflow always equals its net exports.

- An economy's saving can be used either to finance investment at home or to buy assets abroad. Thus, national saving equals domestic investment plus net capital outflow.

- The nominal exchange rate is the relative price of the currency of two countries, and the real exchange rate is the relative price of the goods and services of two countries. When the nominal exchange rate changes so that each unit of domestic currency buys more foreign currency, the domestic currency is said to *appreciate* or *strengthen*. When the nominal exchange rate changes so that each unit of domestic currency buys less foreign currency, the domestic currency is said to *depreciate* or *weaken*.

- According to the theory of purchasing power parity, a unit of currency should be able to buy the same quantity of goods in all countries. This theory implies that the nominal exchange rate between the currencies of two countries should reflect the price levels in those countries. As a result, countries with relatively high inflation should have depreciating currencies, and countries with relatively low inflation should have appreciating currencies.

QUESTIONS FOR REVIEW

1 Why do economists sometimes conduct analysis under assumptions of a closed economy?

2 What do you understand by the term an 'open economy'?

3 If a British citizen visits the French Alps to go for a skiing holiday, is this an import for France or an export? Explain.

4 What is a trade deficit and why is it important?

5 Define net exports and net capital outflow. Explain how and why they are related.

6 Explain the relationship between saving, investment and net capital outflow.

7 If a Japanese car is priced at 500 000 yen, a similar German car is priced at €10 000, and a euro can buy ¥100, what are the nominal and real exchange rates?

8 Describe the economic logic behind the theory of purchasing power parity.

9 If the European Central Bank started printing large quantities of euros, what would happen to the number of Japanese yen a euro could buy?

10 Explain the effect of an appreciation of the euro on German exporters and German importers.

PROBLEMS AND APPLICATIONS

1 How would the following transactions affect UK exports, imports and net exports?

   a. A British art lecturer spends the summer touring museums in Italy.
   b. Students in Paris flock to see the latest Royal Shakespeare Company perform *King Lear* on tour.
   c. The British art lecturer buys a new Volvo.
   d. A student in Munich buys a Manchester United official team shirt (in Munich).
   e. A British citizen goes to Calais for the day to stock up on French wine.

2 International trade in each of the following products has increased over time. Suggest some reasons why this might be so:

   a. wheat
   b. banking services
   c. computer software
   d. cars.

3 Describe the difference between foreign direct investment and foreign portfolio investment. Who is more likely to engage in foreign direct investment – a corporation or an individual investor? Who is more likely to engage in foreign portfolio investment?

4 How would the following transactions affect UK net capital outflow? Also, state whether each involves direct investment or portfolio investment.

   a. A British mobile telephone company establishes an office in the Czech Republic.
   b. A US company's pension fund buys shares in BP.
   c. Toyota expands its factory in Derby, England.
   d. A London-based investment trust sells its Volkswagen shares to a French investor.

5 Holding national saving constant, does an increase in net capital outflow increase, decrease or have no effect on a country's accumulation of domestic capital?

6 The business section of most major newspapers contains a table showing exchange rates amongst many countries, as does *The Economist*. Find such a table and use it to answer the following questions.

   a. Does this table show nominal or real exchange rates? Explain.
   b. What are the exchange rates between the euro and the UK pound, and between the UK pound and the US dollar? Calculate the exchange rate between the euro and the dollar.
   c. If UK inflation exceeds European inflation over the next year, would you expect the UK pound to appreciate or depreciate relative to the euro?

7 Would each of the following groups be happy or unhappy if the euro appreciated? Explain.

   a. US pension funds holding French government bonds.
   b. German manufacturing industries.
   c. Australian tourists planning a trip to Europe.
   d. A British firm trying to purchase property overseas.

8 What is happening to the Swiss real exchange rate in each of the following situations? Explain.

   a. The Swiss nominal exchange rate is unchanged, but prices rise faster in Switzerland than abroad.
   b. The Swiss nominal exchange rate is unchanged, but prices rise faster abroad than in Switzerland.
   c. The Swiss nominal exchange rate declines, and prices are unchanged in Switzerland and abroad.
   d. The Swiss nominal exchange rate declines, and prices rise faster abroad than in Switzerland.

9 List three goods for which the law of one price is likely to hold, and three goods for which it is not. Justify your choices.

10 A can of lemonade is priced at €0.75 in Europe and 12 pesos in Mexico. What would the peso–euro exchange rate be if purchasing power parity holds? If a monetary expansion caused all prices in Mexico to double, so that lemonade rose to 24 pesos, what would happen to the peso–euro exchange rate?

A MACROECONOMIC THEORY OF THE OPEN ECONOMY

Some countries experience persistent trade deficits whilst others have trade surpluses. To understand what factors determine a country's trade balance and how government policies can affect it, we need a macroeconomic theory of the open economy. The preceding chapter introduced some of the key macroeconomic variables that describe an economy's relationship with other economies – including net exports, net capital outflow, and the real and nominal exchange rates. This chapter develops a model that identifies the forces that determine these variables and shows how they are related to one another.

To develop this macroeconomic model of an open economy, we take the economy's GDP as given. We assume that the economy's output of goods and services, as measured by real GDP, is determined by the supplies of the factors of production and by the available production technology that turns these inputs into output. Secondly, the model takes the economy's price level as given. We assume that the price level adjusts to bring the supply and demand for money into balance. The goal of the model in this chapter is to highlight the forces that determine the economy's trade balance and exchange rate. The model applies the tools of supply and demand to an open economy but involves looking simultaneously at two related markets – the market for loanable funds and the market for foreign currency exchange. After we develop this model of the open economy, we use it to examine how various events and policies affect the economy's trade balance and exchange rate. We shall then be able to determine the government policies that are most likely to reverse trade deficits.

SUPPLY AND DEMAND FOR LOANABLE FUNDS AND FOR FOREIGN CURRENCY EXCHANGE

The market for loanable funds coordinates the economy's saving, investment and the flow of loanable funds abroad (net capital outflow). The market for foreign currency exchange coordinates people who want to exchange a domestic currency for the currency of other countries. In this section we discuss supply and demand in each of these markets. In the next section we put these markets together to explain the overall equilibrium for an open economy.

The Market for Loanable Funds

When we first analyzed the role of the financial system in Chapter 23, we made the simplifying assumption that the financial system consists of only one market, called the *market for loanable funds*. All savers go to this market to deposit their saving and all borrowers go to this market to get their loans. In this market, there is one interest rate, which is both the return to saving and the cost of borrowing.

To understand the market for loanable funds in an open economy, the place to start is the identity discussed in the preceding chapter:

$$S \quad = \quad I \quad + \quad NCO$$
$$Saving = Domestic\ investment + Net\ capital\ outflow$$

Whenever a nation saves some of its income, it can use that money to finance the purchase of domestic capital or to finance the purchase of an asset abroad. The two sides of this identity represent the two sides of the market for loanable funds. The supply of loanable funds comes from national saving (S). The demand for loanable funds comes from domestic investment (I) and net capital outflow (NCO). Note that the purchase of a capital asset adds to the demand for loanable funds, regardless of whether that asset is located at home or abroad. Because net capital outflow can be either positive or negative, it can either add to or subtract from the demand for loanable funds that arises from domestic investment.

The quantity of loanable funds supplied and the quantity of loanable funds demanded depend on the real interest rate. A higher real interest rate encourages people to save and, therefore, raises the quantity of loanable funds supplied. A higher interest rate also makes borrowing to finance capital projects more costly; thus, it discourages investment and reduces the quantity of loanable funds demanded.

In addition to influencing national saving and domestic investment, the real interest rate in a country affects that country's net capital outflow. To see why, consider two investment funds – one in the United Kingdom and one in Germany – deciding whether to buy a UK government bond or a German government bond. The investment funds would make this decision in part by comparing the real interest rates in the United Kingdom and Germany. When the UK real interest rate rises, the UK bond becomes more attractive to both investment funds. Thus, an increase in the UK real interest rate discourages Brits from buying foreign assets and encourages people living in other countries to buy UK assets. For both reasons, a high UK real interest rate reduces UK net capital outflow.

We represent the market for loanable funds on the familiar supply-and-demand diagram in Figure 30.1. As in our earlier analysis of the financial system, the supply curve slopes upward because a higher interest rate increases the quantity of loanable funds supplied, and the demand curve slopes downward because a higher interest rate decreases the quantity of loanable funds demanded. In an open economy, the demand for loanable funds comes not only from those who want loanable funds to buy domestic capital goods but also from those who want loanable funds to buy foreign assets.

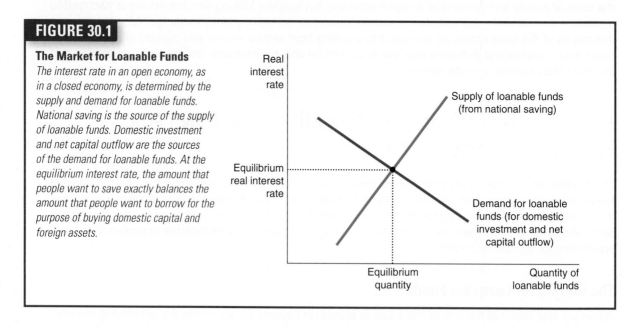

FIGURE 30.1

The Market for Loanable Funds
The interest rate in an open economy, as in a closed economy, is determined by the supply and demand for loanable funds. National saving is the source of the supply of loanable funds. Domestic investment and net capital outflow are the sources of the demand for loanable funds. At the equilibrium interest rate, the amount that people want to save exactly balances the amount that people want to borrow for the purpose of buying domestic capital and foreign assets.

The interest rate adjusts to bring the supply and demand for loanable funds into balance. If the interest rate were below the equilibrium level, the quantity of loanable funds supplied would be less than the quantity demanded. The resulting shortage of loanable funds would push the interest rate upward. Conversely, if the interest rate were above the equilibrium level, the quantity of loanable funds supplied would exceed the quantity demanded. The surplus of loanable funds would drive the interest rate downward. At the equilibrium interest rate, the amount that people want to save exactly balances the desired quantities of domestic investment and net capital outflow.

The Market for Foreign Currency Exchange

The second market in our model of the open economy is the market for foreign currency exchange. Let's think of the UK as the domestic economy. Participants in this market trade UK pounds in exchange for foreign currencies. To understand the market for foreign currency exchange, we begin with another identity from the last chapter:

$$NCO = NX$$
$$Net\ capital\ outflow = Net\ exports$$

This identity states that the imbalance between the purchase and sale of capital assets abroad (*NCO*) equals the imbalance between exports and imports of goods and services. For example, when the UK economy is running a trade surplus, foreigners are buying more UK goods and services than UK residents are buying foreign goods and services. What are Brits doing with the foreign currency they are getting from this net sale of goods and services abroad? They must be buying foreign assets, so UK capital is flowing abroad. Conversely, if the UK is running a trade deficit, Brits are spending more on foreign goods and services than they are earning from selling abroad. Some of this spending must be financed by selling UK assets abroad, so foreign capital is flowing into the UK.

Our model of the open economy treats the two sides of this identity as representing the two sides of the market for foreign currency exchange. Net capital outflow represents the quantity of pounds supplied for the purpose of buying foreign assets. For example, when a UK investment fund wants to buy a Japanese government bond, it needs to change pounds into yen, so it supplies pounds in the market for foreign currency exchange. Net exports represent the quantity of pounds demanded for the purpose of buying UK net exports of goods and services. For example, when a Japanese airline wants to buy aircraft fuel produced by BP, it needs to change its yen into pounds, so it demands pounds in the market for foreign currency exchange.

The real exchange rate is the relative price of domestic and foreign goods and, therefore, is a key determinant of net exports. When the UK real exchange rate appreciates, UK goods become more expensive relative to foreign goods, making UK goods less attractive to consumers abroad (exports would fall) and foreign goods more attractive to domestic consumers (imports would rise). For both reasons, net UK exports fall. Hence, an appreciation of the real exchange rate reduces the quantity of pounds demanded in the market for foreign currency exchange.

Figure 30.2 shows supply and demand in the market for foreign currency exchange. The demand curve slopes downward for the reason we just discussed: a higher real exchange rate makes UK goods more expensive and reduces the quantity of pounds demanded to buy those goods.

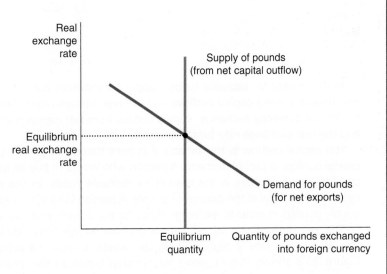

FIGURE 30.2

The Market for Foreign Currency Exchange
The real exchange rate is determined by the supply and demand for foreign currency exchange. The supply of pounds to be exchanged into foreign currency comes from net capital outflow. Because net capital outflow does not depend on the real exchange rate, the supply curve is vertical. The demand for pounds comes from net exports. Because a lower real exchange rate stimulates net exports (and thus increases the quantity of pounds demanded to pay for these net exports), the demand curve is downwards sloping. At the equilibrium real exchange rate, the number of pounds people supply to buy foreign assets exactly balances the number of pounds people demand to buy net exports.

The supply curve is vertical because the quantity of pounds supplied for net capital outflow does not depend on the real exchange rate. (As discussed earlier, net capital outflow depends on the real interest rate. When discussing the market for foreign currency exchange, we take the real interest rate and net capital outflow as given.)

The real exchange rate adjusts to balance the supply and demand for pounds just as the price of any good adjusts to balance supply and demand for that good. If the real exchange rate were below the equilibrium level, the quantity of pounds supplied would be less than the quantity demanded. The resulting shortage of pounds would push the value of the pound upwards. Conversely, if the real exchange rate were above the equilibrium level, the quantity of pounds supplied would exceed the quantity demanded. The surplus of pounds would drive the value of the pound downward. At the equilibrium real exchange rate, the demand for pounds by non-UK residents arising from the UK net exports of goods and services exactly balances the supply of pounds from UK residents arising from UK net capital outflow.

At this point, it is worth noting that the division of transactions between 'supply' and 'demand' in this model is somewhat artificial. In our model, net exports are the source of the demand for pounds, and net capital outflow is the source of the supply. Thus, when a UK resident imports a car made in Japan, our model treats that transaction as a decrease in the quantity of pounds demanded (because net exports fall) rather than an increase in the quantity of pounds supplied. Similarly, when a Japanese citizen buys a UK government bond, our model treats that transaction as a decrease in the quantity of pounds supplied (because net capital outflow falls) rather than an increase in the quantity of pounds demanded. This use of language may seem somewhat unnatural at first, but it will prove useful when analyzing the effects of various policies.

EQUILIBRIUM IN THE OPEN ECONOMY

Having considered the supply and demand in the market for loanable funds and the market for foreign currency exchange, let's now consider how these markets are related to each other.

Net Capital Outflow: The Link Between the Two Markets

We have discussed how the economy coordinates four important macroeconomic variables: national saving, domestic investment, net capital outflow (*NCO*) and net exports. Keep in mind the following identities:

$$S = I + NCO$$

and

$$NCO = NX$$

In the market for loanable funds, supply comes from national saving, demand comes from domestic investment and net capital outflow, and the real interest rate balances supply and demand. In the market for foreign currency exchange, supply comes from net capital outflow, demand comes from net exports, and the real exchange rate balances supply and demand.

Net capital outflow is the variable that links these two markets. In the market for loanable funds, net capital outflow is part of demand. A person who wants to buy an asset abroad must finance this purchase by obtaining resources in the market for loanable funds. In the market for foreign currency exchange, net capital outflow is the source of supply. A person who wants to buy an asset in another country must supply pounds in order to exchange them for the currency of that country.

The key determinant of net capital outflow, as we have discussed, is the real interest rate. When the UK interest rate is high, owning UK assets is more attractive, and UK net capital outflow is low. Figure 30.3 shows this negative relationship between the interest rate and net capital outflow. This net capital outflow curve is the link between the market for loanable funds and the market for foreign currency exchange.

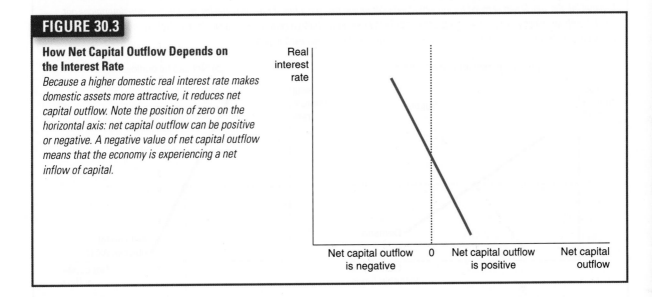

FIGURE 30.3

How Net Capital Outflow Depends on the Interest Rate
Because a higher domestic real interest rate makes domestic assets more attractive, it reduces net capital outflow. Note the position of zero on the horizontal axis: net capital outflow can be positive or negative. A negative value of net capital outflow means that the economy is experiencing a net inflow of capital.

Real interest rate

Net capital outflow is negative   0   Net capital outflow is positive   Net capital outflow

Simultaneous Equilibrium in Two Markets

We can now put all the pieces of our model together in Figure 30.4. This figure shows how the market for loanable funds and the market for foreign currency exchange jointly determine the important macroeconomic variables of an open economy.

Panel (a) of the figure shows the market for loanable funds (taken from Figure 30.1). As before, national saving is the source of the supply of loanable funds. Domestic investment and net capital outflow are the source of the demand for loanable funds. The equilibrium real interest rate brings the quantity of loanable funds supplied and the quantity of loanable funds demanded into balance.

Panel (b) of the figure shows net capital outflow (taken from Figure 30.3). It shows how the interest rate from panel (a) determines net capital outflow. A higher interest rate at home makes domestic assets more attractive, and this in turn reduces net capital outflow. Therefore, the net capital outflow curve in panel (b) slopes downward.

Panel (c) of the figure shows the market for foreign currency exchange (taken from Figure 30.2). Because foreign assets must be purchased with foreign currency, the quantity of net capital outflow from panel (b) determines the supply of pounds to be exchanged into foreign currencies. The real exchange rate does not affect net capital outflow, so the supply curve is vertical. The demand for pounds comes from net exports. Because a depreciation of the real exchange rate increases net exports, the demand curve for foreign currency exchange slopes downward. The equilibrium real exchange rate brings into balance the quantity of pounds supplied and the quantity of pounds demanded in the market for foreign currency exchange.

The two markets shown in Figure 30.4 determine two relative prices – the real interest rate and the real exchange rate. The real interest rate determined in panel (a) is the price of goods and services in the present relative to goods and services in the future. The real exchange rate determined in panel (c) is the price of domestic goods and services relative to foreign goods and services. These two relative prices adjust to balance supply and demand in these two markets. As they do so, they determine national saving, domestic investment, net capital outflow and net exports.

SELF TEST Describe the sources of supply and demand in the market for loanable funds and the market for foreign currency exchange. How are the two markets related?

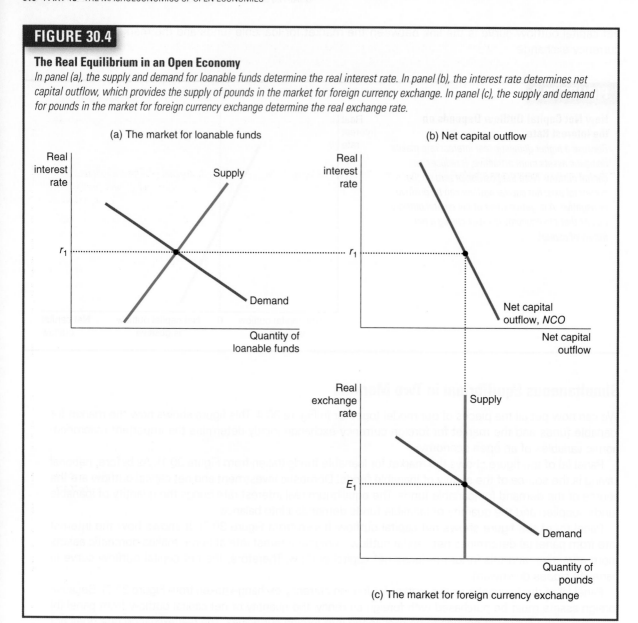

FIGURE 30.4

The Real Equilibrium in an Open Economy
In panel (a), the supply and demand for loanable funds determine the real interest rate. In panel (b), the interest rate determines net capital outflow, which provides the supply of pounds in the market for foreign currency exchange. In panel (c), the supply and demand for pounds in the market for foreign currency exchange determine the real exchange rate.

HOW POLICIES AND EVENTS AFFECT AN OPEN ECONOMY

Having developed a model to explain how key macroeconomic variables are determined in an open economy, we can now use the model to analyze how changes in policy and other events alter the economy's equilibrium. As we proceed, keep in mind that our model is just supply and demand in two markets – the market for loanable funds and the market for foreign currency exchange.

Government Budget Deficits

Assume the French government is running a budget deficit. A government budget deficit represents *negative* public saving, it reduces national saving (the sum of public and private saving). A government budget deficit, therefore, reduces the supply of loanable funds, drives up the interest rate and crowds out investment.

Because national saving is reduced, the supply curve for loanable funds shifts to the left. This is shown as the shift from S_1 to S_2 in panel (a) of Figure 30.5. The shift in the supply curve for loanable funds leads to a rise in the interest rate from to r_1 to r_2 to balance supply and demand. Faced with a higher interest rate, borrowers in the market for loanable funds choose to borrow less. This change is represented in the figure as the movement from point A to point B along the demand curve for loanable funds. In particular, households and firms reduce their purchases of capital goods. As in a closed economy, budget deficits crowd out domestic investment.

FIGURE 30.5

The Effects of a Government Budget Deficit

If the French government runs a budget deficit, it reduces the supply of loanable funds from S_1 to S_2 in panel (a). The interest rate rises from r_1 to r_2 to balance the supply and demand for loanable funds. In panel (b), the higher interest rate reduces net capital outflow. Reduced net capital outflow, in turn, reduces the supply of euros in the market for foreign currency exchange in panel (c). This fall in the supply of euros causes the real exchange rate to appreciate from E_1 to E_2. The appreciation of the exchange rate pushes the trade balance towards deficit.

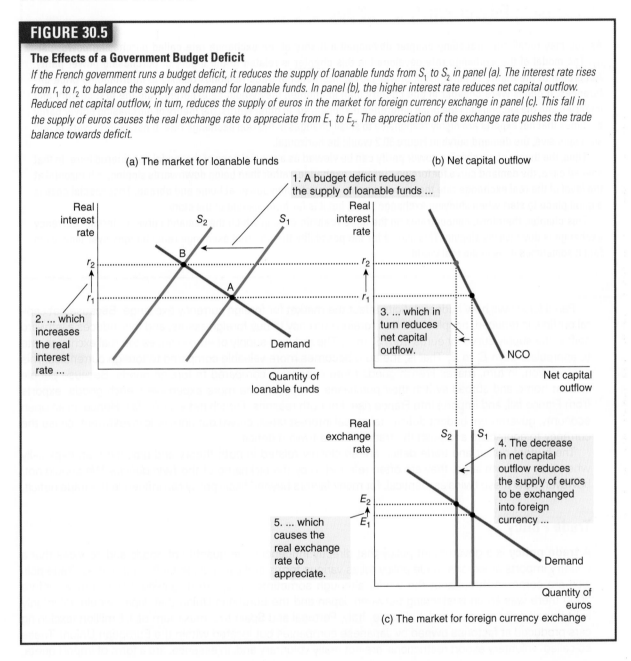

In an open economy, however, the reduced supply of loanable funds has additional effects. Panel (b) shows that the increase in the interest rate reduces net capital outflow. (This fall in net capital outflow is also part of the decrease in the quantity of loanable funds demanded in the movement from point A to point B in panel (a).) Because saving kept at home now earns higher rates of return, investing abroad is less attractive, and domestic residents buy fewer foreign assets. Higher interest rates also attract foreign investors, who want to earn the higher returns on French assets. Thus, when budget deficits raise interest rates, both domestic and foreign behaviour cause French net capital outflow to fall.

Purchasing Power Parity as a Special Case

As you may recall, the preceding chapter developed a theory of the exchange rate called purchasing power parity. The model of the exchange rate developed in this chapter is related to the theory of purchasing power parity. According to the theory of purchasing power parity, international trade responds quickly to international price differences. If goods were cheaper in one country than in another, they would be exported from the first country and imported into the second until the price difference disappeared. In other words, the theory of purchasing power parity assumes that net exports are highly responsive to small changes in the real exchange rate. If net exports were in fact so responsive, the demand curve in Figure 30.2 would be horizontal.

Thus, the theory of purchasing power parity can be viewed as a special case of the model considered here. In that special case, the demand curve for foreign currency exchange, rather than being downwards sloping, is horizontal at the level of the real exchange rate that ensures parity of purchasing power at home and abroad. That special case is a good place to start when studying exchange rates, but it is far from the end of the story.

This chapter, therefore, concentrates on the more realistic case in which the demand curve for foreign currency exchange is downwards sloping. This allows for the possibility that the real exchange rate changes over time, as in fact it sometimes does in the real world.

Panel (c) shows how budget deficits affect the market for foreign currency exchange. Because net capital outflow is reduced, people need less foreign currency to buy foreign assets, and this induces a leftward shift in the supply curve for euros from S_1 to S_2. The reduced supply of euros causes the real exchange rate to appreciate from E_1 to E_2. That is, the euro becomes more valuable compared to foreign currencies. This appreciation, in turn, makes French goods more expensive compared to foreign goods. Because people both at home and abroad switch their purchases away from the more expensive French goods, exports from France fall, and imports into France rise. For both reasons, French net exports fall. Hence, in an open economy, government budget deficits raise real interest rates, crowd out domestic investment, cause the currency to appreciate and push the trade balance toward deficit.

The budget deficit and trade deficit are so closely related in both theory and practice that, especially when they are both large, they are often referred to by the nickname of the *twin deficits*. We should not, however, view these twins as identical, for many factors beyond fiscal policy can influence the trade deficit.

Trade Policy

A **trade policy** is a government policy that directly influences the quantity of goods and services that a country imports or exports. Trade policy takes various forms and can include tariffs and quotas. Trade policies are common throughout the world, although sometimes they are disguised. For example, before 2000 there was an understanding between Japan and the European Union that Japan would voluntarily limit its sales of cars into the UK, France, Italy, Portugal and Spain to a maximum of 1.1 million (excluding cars produced at factories owned by Japanese companies but located within the European Union). These so-called 'voluntary export restrictions' are not really voluntary and, in essence, are a form of import quota.

 trade policy a government policy that directly influences the quantity of goods and services that a country imports or exports

Let's consider the macroeconomic impact of trade policy. Suppose that the European car industry, concerned about competition from Japanese car makers, convinces the EU to impose a quota on the number of cars that can be imported from Japan into the EU. In making their case, lobbyists for the car industry assert that the trade restriction would improve the overall EU trade balance. Are they right? Our model, as illustrated in Figure 30.6, offers an answer.

CASE STUDY   The Balance of Payments in Iceland

Iceland was badly affected by the Financial Crisis of 2007–9 with its three major banks all collapsing with large debts. Since 2008, negotiations had been ongoing to settle the outstanding issues from the collapse and in March 2016, the Central Bank of Iceland announced that an agreement had finally been reached. Under the agreement, 1.9 billion Iceland Krona (ISK) (€13.43 bn) was paid to banks' creditors and ISK7.134 billion (€50.32 billion) in debt will be written off. The settlement contributed to an improvement in Iceland's balance of payments position and build on the ISK8 billion balance of payments surplus in the final quarter of 2015.

Iceland's balance of payments is boosted by tourism, in particular the chance to see the northern lights.

The initial impact of the import restriction is, not surprisingly, on imports. Because net exports equal exports minus imports, the policy also affects net exports. Because net exports are the source of demand for euros in the market for foreign currency exchange, the policy affects the demand curve in this market.

As the quota restricts the number of Japanese cars sold in the EU, it reduces imports at any given real exchange rate. Net exports, which equal exports minus imports, will therefore *rise* for any given real exchange rate. Because non-Europeans need euros to buy EU net exports, there is an increased demand for euros in the market for foreign currency exchange. This increase in the demand for euros is shown in panel (c) of Figure 30.6 as the shift from D_1 to D_2.

Panel (c) shows that the increase in the demand for euros causes the real exchange rate to appreciate from E_1 to E_2. Because nothing has happened in the market for loanable funds in panel (a), there is no change in the real interest rate. Because there is no change in the real interest rate, there is also no change in net capital outflow, shown in panel (b). And because there is no change in net capital outflow, there can be no change in net exports, even though the import quota has reduced imports.

The reason why net exports can stay the same while imports fall is explained by the change in the real exchange rate: when the euro appreciates in value in the market for foreign currency exchange, European goods become more expensive relative to non-European goods. This appreciation encourages imports and discourages exports – and both of these changes work to offset the direct increase in net exports due to the import quota. In the end, an import quota reduces both imports and exports, but net exports (exports minus imports) are unchanged.

We have thus come to a surprising implication: trade policies do not affect the trade balance. That is, policies that directly influence exports or imports do not alter net exports. This conclusion seems less surprising if one recalls the accounting identity:

$$NX = NCO = S - I$$

Net exports equal net capital outflow, which equals national saving minus domestic investment. Trade policies do not alter the trade balance because they do not alter national saving or domestic investment. For given levels of national saving and domestic investment, the real exchange rate adjusts to keep the trade balance the same, regardless of the trade policies the government puts in place.

FIGURE 30.6

The Effects of an Import Quota

When the EU imposes a quota on the import of Japanese cars, nothing happens in the market for loanable funds in panel (a) or to net capital outflow in panel (b). The only effect is a rise in net exports (exports minus imports) for any given real exchange rate. As a result, the demand for euros in the market for foreign currency exchange rises, as shown by the shift from to D_1 to D_2 in panel (c). This increase in the demand for euros causes the value of the euro to appreciate from E_1 to E_2. This appreciation of the euro tends to reduce net exports, offsetting the direct effect of the import quota on the trade balance.

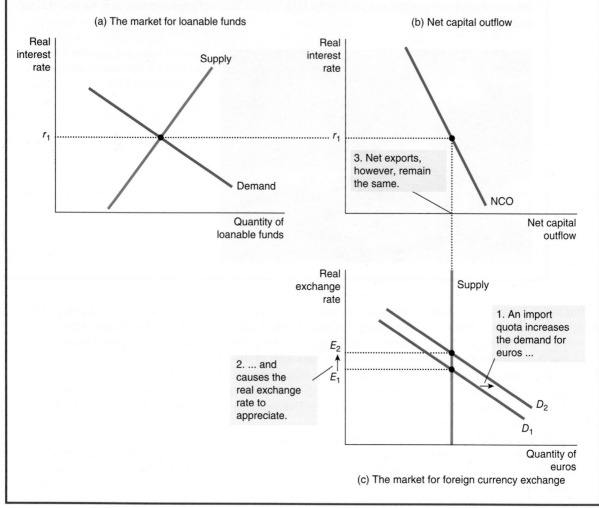

Although trade policies do not affect a country's overall trade balance, these policies do affect specific firms, industries and countries. When the EU imposes an import quota on Japanese cars, European car makers have less competition from abroad and will sell more cars. At the same time, because the euro has appreciated in value, Airbus, the European aircraft maker, for example, will find it harder to compete with Boeing, the US aircraft maker. European exports of aircraft will fall, and European imports of aircraft will rise. In this case, the import quota on Japanese cars will increase net exports of cars and decrease net exports of aeroplanes. In addition, it will increase net exports from the EU to Japan and decrease net exports from the EU to the United States. The overall trade balance of the EU economy, however, stays the same.

Capital Flight

Large and sudden movement of funds out of a country is called **capital flight**. To see the implications of capital flight for an economy, we again follow our three steps for analyzing a change in equilibrium.

capital flight a large and sudden reduction in the demand for assets located in a country

Consider first which curves in our model capital flight affects. We will use Nigeria as an example here because in early 2016 it was reported that the country had experienced a considerable outflow of funds. If investors around the world decide to sell some of their assets in Nigeria and use the proceeds to buy assets in other countries, this increases Nigerian net capital outflow and, therefore, affects both markets in our model. Most obviously, it affects the net capital outflow curve, and this in turn influences the supply of naira, the Nigerian currency, in the market for foreign currency exchange. In addition, because the demand for loanable funds comes from both domestic investment and net capital outflow, capital flight affects the demand curve in the market for loanable funds.

When net capital outflow increases, there is greater demand for loanable funds to finance these purchases of capital assets abroad. Thus, as panel (a) of Figure 30.7 shows, the demand curve for loanable funds shifts to the right from D_1 to D_2. In addition, because net capital outflow is higher for any interest rate, the net capital outflow curve also shifts to the right from NCO_1 to NCO_2, as in panel (b).

FIGURE 30.7

The Effects of Capital Flight

If people decide that Nigeria is a risky place to keep their savings, they will move their capital to safer havens, resulting in an increase in Nigerian net capital outflow. Consequently, the demand for loanable funds in Nigeria rises from D_1 to D_2, as shown in panel (a), and this drives up Nigerian real interest rate from r_1 to r_2. Because net capital outflow is higher for any interest rate, that curve also shifts to the right from NCO_1 to NCO_2 in panel (b). At the same time, in the market for foreign currency exchange, the supply of naira rises from S_1 to S_2, as shown in panel (c). This increase in the supply of naira causes the currency to depreciate from E_1 to E_2, so the naira becomes less valuable compared to other currencies.

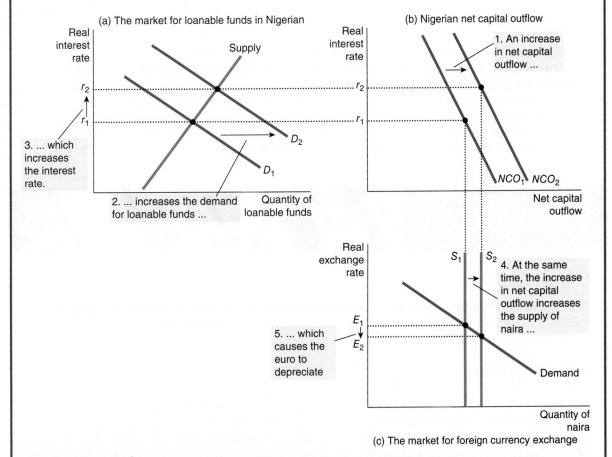

To see the effects of capital flight on the economy, we compare the old and new equilibria. Panel (a) of Figure 30.7 shows that the increased demand for loanable funds causes the interest rate in Nigeria to rise from r_1 to r_2. Panel (b) shows that Nigerian net capital outflow increases. (Although the rise in the interest rate does make Nigerian assets more attractive, this only partly offsets the impact of capital flight on net capital outflow.) Panel (c) shows that the increase in net capital outflow raises the supply of naira in the market for foreign currency exchange from S_1 to S_2. That is, as people try to get out of Nigerian assets, there is a large supply of naira to be converted into other currencies such as euros and pounds. This increase in supply causes the naira to depreciate from E_1 to E_2. Thus, capital flight from Nigeria increases Nigerian interest rates and decreases the value of the naira in the market for foreign currency exchange.

These price changes that result from capital flight influence some key macroeconomic quantities. The depreciation of the currency makes exports cheaper and imports more expensive, pushing the trade balance towards surplus. At the same time, the increase in the interest rate reduces domestic investment, which slows capital accumulation and economic growth.

Although capital flight has its largest impact on the country from which capital is fleeing, it also affects other countries. When capital flows out of Nigeria into the United States, for instance, it has the opposite effect on the US economy as it has on the Nigerian economy. In particular, the rise in Nigerian net capital outflow coincides with a fall in US net capital outflow. As the naira depreciates in value and Nigerian interest rates rise, the dollar appreciates in value and US interest rates fall. The size of this impact on the US economy is dependent on the relative size of the economy of the United States compared to that of Nigeria.

SELF TEST Suppose that Swedes decided to spend a smaller fraction of their incomes. What would be the effect on saving, investment, interest rates, the real exchange rate and the trade balance in Sweden?

CONCLUSION

Historically, international trade has always played a very important role in most European economies. In the past two centuries or so, international finance has also become increasingly important. The typical modern European country consumes a high proportion of goods produced abroad and exports a significant amount of its output to other European countries and to countries outside Europe. In addition, through investment funds and other financial institutions, Europeans borrow and lend in world financial markets, as indeed do the citizens of all advanced industrialized economies. This chapter has provided a basic model for thinking about the macroeconomics of open economies.

IN THE NEWS

Capital Flight

Capital flight can be caused by a lack of confidence in an economy or by political instability but it can also manifest itself in funds leaving a country illegally and possibly linked to criminal activity.

Capital Flight in Russia

Russia has experienced a number of political and economic challenges since the Financial Crisis, including the problems in Ukraine and the Crimea which have led to sanctions being imposed. Capital flight is also posing problems to the country's economy. The Russian central bank has estimated capital flight in 2014 as being €141 billion, and in 2015 estimates put the amount at around €64 billion. Since 1999, the Russian government says the amount is over

€503 billion but independent analysts put the figure at nearer €910 billion. Some of the difference may be the result of illegal capital flight. In early 2013 the governor of Russia's central bank, Sergei Ignatiev, said that some €44 billion had left the country illegally in 2012, consisting of income generated from criminal activities which include weapons smuggling, prostitution, people trafficking, drugs and corruption.

Money is also leaving Russia as a means of avoiding taxes, finding its way into offshore accounts outside Russian tax jurisdiction. The impact on tax revenue for the country runs into billions of euros every year. In addition, investment funds in Russia are reduced, which hampers the opportunities for economic development. It has been estimated that investment in 2015 was 20 per cent lower than in 2014 although government sources put the figure nearer to 10 per cent lower. Some observers suggest that Russia needs to do more to boost confidence in the economy not least addressing the problems of corruption which are alleged to be widespread, and moderating its political stance towards countries like Ukraine and Syria. The chances of such a change in policy in both areas seems unlikely in the short term.

Questions

1 Assuming the amount of money leaving Russia is greater than that coming in, what happens to the demand for loanable funds and the interest rate in Russia?
2 What effect would you expect capital flight of the size outlined in the article to have on the exchange rate between the Russian rouble and other currencies?
3 What effect is the capital flight likely to have on Russia's trading partners given the size of the sums quoted in the article?
4 Does the fact that some of the flows are illegal make any difference to your analysis in the previous questions?
5 Why is clamping down on illegal capital flight and corruption important to Russia's continued economic development?

Capital flight is seen as being an important issue for the Russian economy.

SUMMARY

● To analyze the macroeconomics of open economies we look at the market for loanable funds and the market for foreign currency exchange. In the market for loanable funds, the interest rate adjusts to balance the supply of loanable funds (from national saving) and the demand for loanable funds (from domestic investment, and net capital outflow). In the market for foreign currency exchange, the real exchange rate adjusts to balance the supply of domestic currency (for net capital outflow) and the demand for domestic currency (for net exports). Because net capital outflow is part of the demand for loanable funds and provides the supply of domestic currency for foreign currency exchange, it is the variable that connects these two markets.

- A policy that reduces national saving, such as a government budget deficit, reduces the supply of loanable funds and drives up the interest rate. The higher interest rate reduces net capital outflow, which reduces the supply of domestic currency in the market for foreign currency exchange. The domestic currency appreciates and net exports fall.

- Although restrictive trade policies, such as tariffs or quotas on imports, are sometimes advocated as a way to alter the trade balance, they do not necessarily have that effect. A trade restriction increases net exports for a given exchange rate and, therefore, increases the demand for the domestic currency in the market for foreign currency exchange. As a result, the domestic currency appreciates in value, making domestic goods more expensive relative to foreign goods. This appreciation offsets the initial impact of the trade restriction on net exports.

- When investors change their attitudes about holding assets of a country, the ramifications for the country's economy can be profound. In particular, political instability or a lack of confidence in an economy can lead to capital flight, which tends to increase interest rates and causes the currency to depreciate.

QUESTIONS FOR REVIEW

1 Why do we describe the formula $S = I + NCO$ as 'an identity'?

2 How is the interest rate in an open economy determined?

3 Describe supply and demand in the market for loanable funds and the market for foreign currency exchange. How are these markets linked?

4 What effect does a government budget deficit have on the interest rate? Draw a diagram to illustrate your answer.

5 What effect would you expect a government budget surplus to have on the exchange rate? Explain.

6 Why are budget deficits and trade deficits sometimes called the twin deficits?

7 What is 'trade policy'?

8 Suppose that a steel workers' union encourages economic actors to buy only European steel. What would this policy do to the European overall trade balance and the real exchange rate? What is the impact on the European steel industry? What is the impact on the European textile industry?

9 What effect would you expect a tariff to have on the real exchange rate? Explain using appropriate diagrams.

10 What is capital flight? When a country experiences capital flight, what is the effect on its interest rate and exchange rate?

PROBLEMS AND APPLICATIONS

1 Germany generally runs a trade surplus. Do you think this is most related to high foreign demand for German goods, low German demand for foreign goods, a high German saving rate relative to German investment, or structural barriers against imports into Germany? Explain your answer.

2 If the UK prime minister announces that the government are solidly on a course of deficit reduction, which should make the pound more attractive to investors, would such a deficit reduction in fact raise the value of the pound? Explain.

3 Suppose that the government passes an investment tax credit, which subsidizes domestic investment. How does this policy affect national saving, domestic investment, net capital outflow, the interest rate, the exchange rate and the trade balance?

4 Assume that there is a rise in the trade deficit of a country due largely to the rise in a government budget deficit. Assume also that some commentators in the popular press claim that the increased trade deficit resulted from a decline in the quality of the country's products relative to foreign products.

   a. Assume that the country's products did decline in relative quality during this period. How might this affect net exports *at any given exchange rate*?

   b. Use a three-panel diagram to show the effect of this shift in net exports on the country's real exchange rate and trade balance.

   c. Does a decline in the quality of the country's products have any effect on standards of living for its residents? (Hint: when a country's residents sell goods to non-country residents, what do they receive in return?)

5 Explain in words why European *export* industries would benefit from a reduction in restrictions on *imports* into the European Union.

6 Suppose the French suddenly develop a strong taste for British wine. Answer the following questions in words and using a diagram.

   a. What happens to the demand for pounds in the market for foreign currency exchange?
   b. What happens to the value of pounds in the market for foreign currency exchange?
   c. What happens to the quantity of UK net exports?

7 Suppose your country is running a trade deficit and you hear your trade minister on the radio, saying: 'The trade deficit must be reduced, but import quotas only annoy our trading partners. If we subsidize our exports instead, we can reduce the deficit by increasing our competitiveness.' Using a three-panel diagram, show the effect of an export subsidy on net exports and the real exchange rate. Do you agree with the trade minister?

8 Suppose that real interest rates increase across Europe. Explain how this development will affect UK net capital outflow. Then explain how it will affect UK net exports by using a formula from the chapter and by using a diagram. What will happen to the UK real interest rate and real exchange rate?

9 Suppose that Germans decide to increase their saving.

   a. If the elasticity of German net capital outflow with respect to the real interest rate is very high, will this increase in private saving have a large or small effect on German domestic investment?
   b. If the elasticity of German exports with respect to the real exchange rate is very low, will this increase in private saving have a large or small effect on the German real exchange rate?

10 Assume that saving in China has been used to finance investment into the EU. That is, the Chinese have been buying European capital assets.

   a. If the Chinese decided they no longer wanted to buy European assets, what would happen in the European market for loanable funds? In particular, what would happen to European interest rates, European saving and European investment?
   b. What would happen in the market for foreign currency exchange? In particular, what would happen to the value of the euro and the European trade balance?

PART 14
SHORT-RUN ECONOMIC FLUCTUATIONS

31   BUSINESS CYCLES

So far in the macroeconomics section of the book we have been considering long-run determinants of key economic variables. It is short-run fluctuations, however, which tend to be more obviously felt by most people. Over time, economies seem to fluctuate between periods of relative stability with economic growth, falling unemployment, and inflation at relatively low and stable levels, and periods where economic growth declines and unemployment rises. These periods of expansion and slowdown are referred to as the business cycle. Measuring business cycles was pioneered by Wesley C. Mitchell and Arthur F. Burns. Their book, *Measuring Business Cycles,* published in 1946, looked at how different economic variables change as economic growth changed. Burns and Mitchell wanted to investigate why economic variables moved together in times of economic slowdown; they defined a **recession** as characterized by a period of falling incomes and rising unemployment, which technically occurs after two successive quarters of negative growth. If such a contraction in growth continues and is more severe it might be described as a **depression**.

> **recession** a period of declining real incomes and rising unemployment. The technical definition gives recession occurring after two successive quarters of negative economic growth
> **depression** a severe recession

Business cycles can be analyzed through looking at periods of economic growth and identifying peaks and troughs in activity where each represent turning points. A **peak** occurs when output, employment, and other variables such as retail sales or manufacturing production, begin to decline together. A **trough** refers to the time when these economic variables begin to rise. Identifying when these events occur is difficult because of the complexity of the data involved and the way they are measured. In addition, some economic variables, such as employment, may not change at the same time as others and are regarded as 'lagged indicators'.

> **peak** a point where related economic variables begin to decline
> **trough** the point where related economic variables begin to rise

There are considerable disagreements about what causes short-run variations in economic activity. The term 'cycle' might imply that expansions and contractions are part of a regular pattern but that is not the case. There is no specific pattern to the periods between peaks and troughs, nor to the length of the upswing and downturn in economies. The UK recession of 1920–24, for example, saw GDP fall by about 9 per cent from its peak over the first 18 months, and then take a further 27 months to get back to its pre-recession peak; and in the next 12 months it rose to around 4 per cent above its pre-recession peak. In 1930–34, the length of time for the economy to recover to its pre-recession peak was around 48 months but the economy 'only' fell to around 7 per cent below its pre-recession peak. In the 1990–93 recession, the economy took around 32 months to recover but thereafter rose by over 8 per cent above its pre-recession peak and only fell to around 3 per cent below its pre-recession peak. The post-Financial Crisis of 2008 saw the economy falling to around 6 per cent below its pre-recession peak and it was not until around 2013/14 that the economy finally reached its pre-crisis level. The reasons why short-run fluctuations occur is part of business cycle theory. The fact that different models exist reflects the disagreement amongst economists about the causes of short-run fluctuations.

In theory, there is no reason why business cycles occur at all. If factor resources are being employed fully, investment is sufficient to cover depreciation, and labour productivity is stable then the economy could continue to grow. However, shocks to the economy through changes in consumption and government spending can cause full employment output to be disturbed. Rigidities in markets can exacerbate the problems and cause broader volatility in the economy. This view would be a demand side explanation to short-run fluctuations.

Other explanations include changes to productivity levels through changes in technology or the ability of workers to seek increases in real wages. Much debate on short-run fluctuations has centred on the role of monetary policy. As central banks increase and reduce interest rates and the money supply changes, short-run fluctuations tend to follow. Developing models which can help inform central banks' decision-making has been an important part of economic research in the last 30 years.

TREND GROWTH RATES

Most of the data we will be looking at in this chapter is classed as **time-series data**, observations on a variable over a time-period and which are ordered over time. Central to the analysis of business cycles is GDP over time. Figure 31.1 shows two graphs: panel (a) shows GDP in the UK from 1960–2014. The value of GDP is given on the vertical axis in current US dollars and the horizontal axis is the time period in years. Panel (b) shows GDP across the European Union over the same time period.

> **time-series data** observations on a variable over a time-period and which are ordered over time

Panel (a) shows that the value of the UK economy in 1960 was around $72 billion but by 2014 the UK economy was worth almost $3 trillion. Panel (b) shows the economy of the EU was worth around $365 billion in 1960 but has grown to some $18 trillion in 2014. A trend line has been added in both cases and this shows how, over time, the GDP of both the UK and the EU has risen. It also shows how actual GDP fluctuates around the trend.

The debate over what causes short-run fluctuations also focuses attention on policy response and welfare needs. Welfare issues arise if it is assumed that the economy is deviating in some way from its equilibrium; policy is put in place to address the welfare issues that arise. Some economists, however, believe that the economy may not be deviating from its equilibrium but instead moves from one equilibrium point to another. If this is the case, policy is not required because there are no welfare issues arising if the economy is in equilibrium. We shall explore these differences later in the chapter.

FIGURE 31.1

GDP in the UK and Europe, 1961–2014

Panel (a) shows UK GDP, measured in current US dollars, on the vertical axis over the period 1960–2014. Panel (b) shows GDP across the European Union (also in current US dollars) over the same time period. A trend line has been added in both panels.

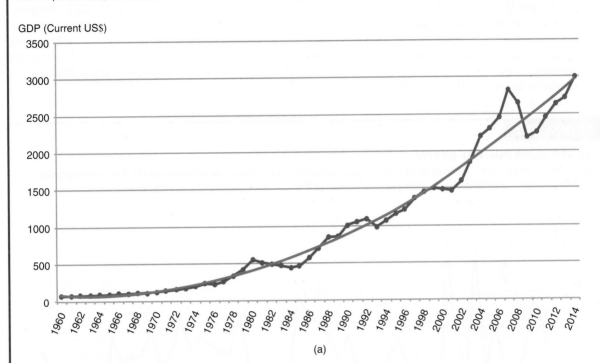

(a)

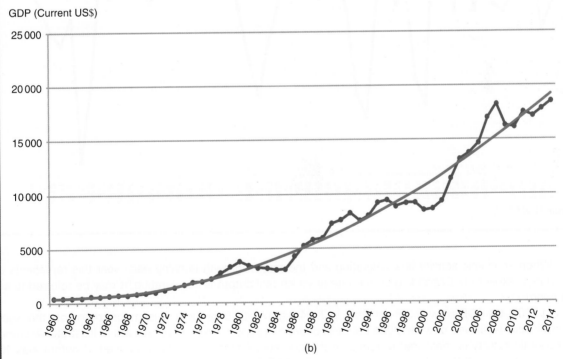

(b)

Source: *World Bank*

Data Concepts

When dealing with macroeconomic variables there are a number of concepts that we will utilize over the coming chapters which need to be understood. Figure 31.2 shows the rate of growth of UK GDP between 1960 and 2014. It is clear from this figure that the rate of growth fluctuates over the time period. From 1962, growth accelerated and reached 5 per cent in 1964 before slowing down up to 1968. Thereafter growth accelerated again reaching 7.3 per cent in 1973 before the economy slumped dramatically and economic activity actual shrank in 1974 and 1975. Further recessions occurred in the early 1980s and the early 1990s; and after a 15-year period of consistent growth there was a dramatic end in 2008, when the economy shrank. In 2009, the economy shrank by a further 4 per cent. Growth returned in 2010 but at a relatively low level before picking up in 2013.

FIGURE 31.2

UK GDP Growth Rate, 1961–2014 (%)

UK GDP fluctuates between various peaks and troughs over the period. In some cases, GDP growth is positive for a number of years and the economy is growing during that time, but in other years GDP growth is negative and the economy shrinks.

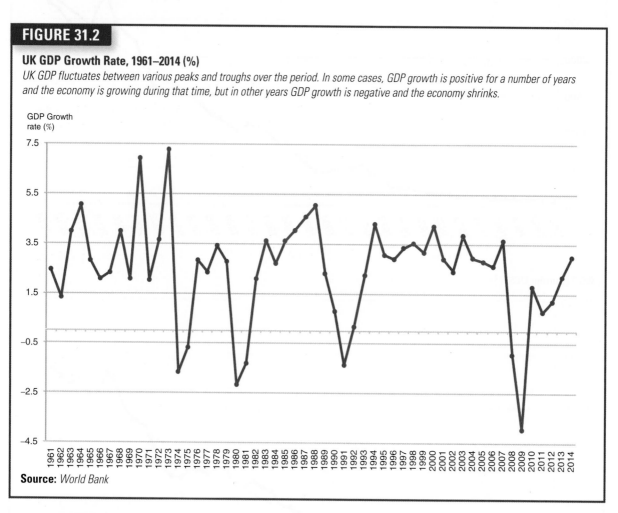

Source: *World Bank*

When economic activity is accelerating and the rate of growth is rising each year this represents a period of expansion. Depending on the rate at which real output is accelerating, it may be referred to as a *boom*.

In 2003, UK GDP grew at 3.8 per cent, in 2004 it grew at 2.9 per cent. It is important to note that economic activity slowed down in 2004 but still continued to grow. An example serves to illustrate: Assume economic activity is measured in terms of the number of tonnes of steel produced. If output was 10 million tonnes in 2015 and 12 million tonnes in 2016, then the growth rate is 2 per cent. If output is 13.5 million tonnes in 2017, the growth rate is now 1.25 per cent; growth has slowed compared to 2016 but the economy is still producing more steel than the year before. This is why we use the terms 'accelerating' and 'decelerating' to describe changes in the rate of growth of GDP when it is positive.

However, when real output actually shrinks then there is a **contraction** in the economy. If output of steel in 2018 was 13 million tonnes, the economy would have shrunk; less steel is being produced compared to 2017 and growth will be -3.8 per cent.

> **contraction** when real output is lower than the previous time period

The news media are keen to use emotive words such as 'boom', 'bust' and 'slump' when reporting growth data, but it is important to be aware of language when discussing economic growth. If expansion is considerably above trend, for example, then the term 'boom' might be appropriate but if growth is only just above trend then that term may not be applicable. For example, does a growth rate of 0.25 per cent for the year following a 2.0 per cent growth the year before, represent 'a slump'?

In Figure 31.2 we can find the mean of the data represented by adding the sum of the annual growth rates (130.3) and dividing by the number of years (54). The mean growth rate over this period is 2.4 per cent. In describing periods of accelerating and decelerating growth, therefore, we can compare the growth rate at a particular time period with the mean growth rate. The period from 1970 to 1973 might reasonably be called a period of 'boom' given that the rate of growth of GDP averaged almost 5 per cent during that time reaching a peak of 7.3 per cent in 1973. In 2008 and 2009, GDP growth was -0.1 and -0.4 per cent respectively, considerably below the mean growth rate for the whole period. The difference between a peak and a trough in the business cycle and trend output is called the **amplitude**. Figure 31.2 shows that this can vary considerably.

> **amplitude** the difference between peak and trough and trend output

> **SELF TEST** What are the main phases of the business cycle?

Trends

An important point of disagreement about economic time-series data is the existence of trends. A **trend** is the underlying long-term movement in a data series. The trend can be upwards over time, downwards or constant. Earlier we took the mean (average) of the growth rate in UK GDP between 1961 and 2014 as being 2.4 per cent. The mean of a set of time-series data can be used as the trend.

> **trend** the underlying long term movement in a data series

Figure 31.1 showed UK and EU GDP between 1961 and 2014 and a trend line was added to the data showing very clearly that the trend was upwards over the time period shown. Trends can demonstrate patterns over a period which can be described as *stationary* and *nonstationary*. **Stationary data** are time-series data that have a constant mean value over time, whereas **nonstationary data** are time-series data where the mean value can either rise or fall over time. The data in Figure 31.1 would suggest that GDP is nonstationary data rising over time. Other economic variables might exhibit the characteristic of stationary data; unemployment, for example, tends to be more characteristic of stationary data. In the period 1993 to 2003, UK unemployment averaged 1.92 million whereas in the period from 2004–15, unemployment averaged 2.012 million. As with any statistical analysis, care has to be taken to consider what data have been included, how the data have been constructed, what time period is involved and what test has been applied, and there is often disagreement about appropriate statistical tests and measurements used in economic analysis.

> **stationary data** time-series data that has a constant mean value over time
> **nonstationary data** time-series data where the mean value can either rise or fall over time

The disagreement about how statistical tests are used and applied is beyond the scope of this book, but disagreement between economists on vital issues, such as the path of business cycles and the policy options that might be applied, is derived in large part from different interpretations of the reliability and validity of different statistical methods. A trend over time has implications. For example, looking at Figure 31.1, would there be any reason to assume that the level of economic growth for the next 10 years will not continue to be positive and increasing in the UK and EU? Nonstationary data can be assumed to have what are called **deterministic trends** – trends that are constant, positive or negative, independent of time for the series being analyzed and which change by a constant amount each period. GDP might deviate from trend over short-term periods but when looked at over longer time periods will revert to the mean. In contrast, a **stochastic trend** is one where the trend variable changes by some random amount in each time period. If macroeconomic variables are analyzed assuming they exhibit a deterministic trend, for example that GDP will rise by 2.4 per cent on average, then the implication is that policy measures can be applied when GDP deviates from this average. What has caused GDP to deviate from the mean must be a transitory phenomenon (is temporary and only lasting for a short period of time) and this further implies that the cause of the deviation must also be temporary and can be influenced.

> **deterministic trends** trends that are constant, positive or negative, independent of time for the series being analyzed
> **stochastic trend** where trend variables change by some random amount in each time period

What if the deterministic trend is illusory and we have applied an inappropriate statistical test to the time-series data we are looking at? If the data exhibit a trend that is stochastic, then policy measures might be applied that are unnecessary and possibly distorting. If the deviations are removed the variable does not, unlike a deterministic trend, revert to the mean. Instead, the variable might move from its mean and stay away from that mean over the next time period. The law of large numbers states that, as the number of observations increases, the average of the observations is likely to be the mean of the whole population of observations. For example, if we toss a fair coin ten times, we might observe six instances of heads and four of tails. The mean of these observations in terms of the ratio heads to tails is 6:10 or 0.6. If we toss the coin a further 90 times we might observe 42 heads and 48 tails, a mean of 0.46. When we look at the mean of the population as a whole (100 observations) the mean is 0.48. If we toss the coin a further 10 000 times the chances are that the mean is likely to be close to 0.5. If we continued to toss the coin and observe the trend, it is likely that it would continue to be 0.5. Taking any selection of data from the total number of observations, the mean might be different as shown above but the greater the number of observations we observe the more likely it is that we will get the mean. It would not be unreasonable to assume that in future time periods the mean is going to continue to be 0.5.

If, however, something changes in the nature of the coin or the friction exerted by air, the surface on which the coin lands, etc., which affects the coin tossing outcomes, then the trends (mean) we observe might be completely random for every time period we observe and so when looking at the population as a whole, the consistency of the law of large numbers is destroyed.

This summary of statistical arguments is important to bear in mind as we look at short-run variations in macroeconomic variables. The study of time-series data is complex and it is important to take into account as we look at different schools of thought in economics, that many of the differences of opinion arise from different interpretations and use of statistics.

Procyclical and Countercyclical Movements in Macroeconomic Data

Let us assume that the GDP of a country exhibits a deterministic trend and that the trend growth over a 50-year period is 2.4 per cent. If GDP over an 18-month period is reported as 1.3 per cent, what might we expect to have happened to key macroeconomic variables? Given GDP has slowed from trend it might be expected that the number of people out of work would have risen, that inflation would have slowed, the money supply contracted and real wages would have also fallen. Observations over time do show that, when economic activity slows, unemployment rises and inflation decelerates. There is some intuitive common sense in this summary. If firms are cutting back production, as a slowing of GDP implies, then they might not need as many employees and so some might be let go and, at the same time, firms may think twice about increasing prices when economic activity is slowing for fear of losing sales. They may decide to keep prices constant or even lower them in an attempt to try and boost demand.

Economists often look at the movement of pairs of variables, which are called comovements. Typically, one of these variables is GDP. Economists will then compare another economic variable such as inflation or employment with GDP over time and see if any relationship can be determined.

Comovements may exhibit certain relationships. When a variable is above trend when GDP is above trend the variable is said to be **procyclical**. When GDP is above trend, inflation and employment also tend to be above trend and so are classed as procyclical. Real wages and nominal interest rates are also classed as procyclical. If a variable is below trend when GDP is above trend the variable is described as **countercyclical**. Unemployment can be classed as countercyclical because it tends to be below trend when GDP is above trend.

> **procyclical** a variable that is above trend when GDP is above trend
> **countercyclical** a variable that is below trend when GDP is above trend

> **SELF TEST** Would you expect inflation to be procyclical or countercyclical in a period when economic activity is declining?
> What would you expect real wages to be in a period of rising economic activity?

Variables as Indicators

Economists are not fortune tellers but, in trying to understand business cycles and whether it is possible to predict changes in economic activity, they have looked at the extent to which economic variables or collections of economic variables over time give any clue to deviations from trend. Research by Mitchell and Burns in the United States in the 1930s led to an index of cyclical indicators which is now utilized by the OECD to try and identify potential turning points in economic activity. Figure 31.3 shows the composite leading indicators index between 2003 and 2015 for the OECD area. The arrows show turning points. For example, it is clear that the index began to decline in the middle of 2007. The global recession followed. In early 2009, the index began to rise and this indicated a turning point to suggest economic activity would begin to improve.

Cyclical indicators can have three characteristics. They can be **leading indicators**, where the indicator tends to foretell future changes in economic activity, a **lagging indicator**, whose changes occur after changes in economic activity have occurred, and **coincident indicators** whose changes occur at the same time as changes in economic activity. The OECD's composite leading indicators (CLI) index is classed as a leading indicator.

> **leading indicator** an indicator which can be used to foretell future changes in economic activity
> **lagging indicator** an indicator whose changes occur after changes in economic activity have occurred
> **coincident indicator** an indicator whose changes occur at the same time as changes in economic activity

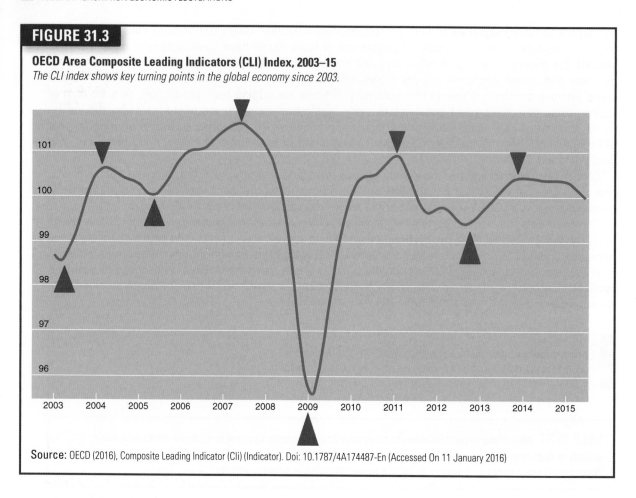

FIGURE 31.3

OECD Area Composite Leading Indicators (CLI) Index, 2003–15
The CLI index shows key turning points in the global economy since 2003.

Source: OECD (2016), Composite Leading Indicator (Cli) (Indicator). Doi: 10.1787/4A174487-En (Accessed On 11 January 2016)

CAUSES OF CHANGES IN THE BUSINESS CYCLE

We know that the economy is made up of households and firms so it is reasonable to expect that the behaviour of these two elements of the economy have a role to play in how economic activity changes.

Household Spending Decisions

Households make decisions on how much labour to supply. The amount of labour supplied depends in part on the real wage rate. The rate of growth of wages in relation to prices affects consumers' purchasing power. How consumers perceive changes in real wages is an important factor in decision-making. Households also make consumption decisions on everyday goods and services, leisure and entertainment and also on what are sometimes called 'big-ticket' items such as durable household goods (TVs, washing machines, cars, fridge freezers, etc.) not to mention decisions on purchasing houses or flats. Purchasing decisions on these items may in themselves be cyclical; if a newly-wed couple buys a house, for example, it may be that in the next year they spend considerable amounts on furniture, decorating and household goods. It then may be several years before goods begin to wear out and need replacing or the house needs decorating again.

Households will also make decisions based on changes in interest rates, house prices and taxation. Increases in interest rates may encourage a rise in saving and a reduction in consumption; changes in house prices affect people's wealth and the effect can lead to changes in spending, especially if people are able to borrow on the strength of the value of their property. Changes in tax rates affect different people in different ways and can have a considerable impact on behaviour.

Firms' Decision-Making

Firms make decisions about production levels – how much output to produce – based on what they think they can sell. If firms face strong demand they are likely to increase output, may have to take on more workers, and buy more raw materials and semi-finished goods in order to satisfy demand. Some firms may look to expand by investing in new equipment and machinery or by acquiring new premises or even other firms. Firms also make decisions about how many workers to hire (or release) based on the real wage rate and productivity levels. If the real wage rate falls then firms can afford to hire more workers; if productivity levels rise, then costs can be lowered and firms can be more competitive. Firms will also monitor stock levels (stock is often referred to as inventories). If stocks are building up then it may be that sales are slowing down, whereas if stocks are falling demand may be strong and sales rising. Firms will respond to changes in inventory levels by expanding or contracting output as necessary or investing in new plant and equipment or on mergers and acquisitions.

External Forces

In an open economy, movements in exchange rates affect the competitiveness of domestic and foreign firms through changes in import and export prices. Economic activity abroad can also have an impact on countries as consumption and investment decisions by firms and consumers abroad change. The problems faced by a number of countries in the Euro area since the Financial Crisis has slowed the pace of recovery.

We also have to take into account the effect of events which are often totally unpredictable such as drought, flood, tsunamis, hurricanes, extreme cold or earthquakes, through to events such as political upheaval, war, terrorism and conflict which can have far-reaching effects on individual countries and the global economy.

Government Policy

Governments have control over a considerable amount of economic activity. They make decisions about tax rates and have to try and consider the incentive effects of such changes. Decisions about major infrastructure investment can have ripple effects throughout an economy. Government agents can also have an effect on economic activity. Central banks are independent of most governments across Western Europe but in the UK, for example, the government sets the target for inflation. The Bank of England is responsible for setting monetary policy to meet the target the government has set. Changes in interest rates will affect both households and firms through policy decisions like quantitative easing and measures designed to help ease credit flows to business and households.

Confidence and Expectations

Households and firms not only make decisions based on current needs but also on the future. It is unlikely that an individual will make a decision to take out a loan for €15 000 to buy a car if that person believes the security of their job is in question. The news media provide information on the state of the economy, governments make pronouncements, senior finance ministers and banking officials are interviewed about their forecasts for the economy. Employees will get a sense of how the firms they work for are performing and those in the public sector may take close note of government policy decisions. Workers may look at current inflation rates and their wages and may make judgements about inflation in the future and, therefore, what sort of wage rise they need to maintain their standard of living. Firms may also consider inflation rates and make judgements about price rises to consumers based on what they expect inflation to be in the future and how inflation in raw materials might affect their costs.

Our expectations of the future shape our decisions, and confidence of firms and households to make decisions is something that is very difficult to quantify and equally difficult to know when it changes. At what point does any individual begin to believe that stock or house prices have reached a peak; at what point does a firm make the decision to make redundancies and why does confidence begin to decline or to pick up? These are all difficult questions to answer but confidence and expectations play a significant part in swings in economic activity.

> **SELF TEST** A country's finance minister presents the government's annual financial statement and advises that they expect GDP to contract sharply in the coming year because of adverse international economic conditions. How might such a speech influence confidence and expectations of households and firms?

BUSINESS CYCLE MODELS

Attempts to try and understand how business cycles occur have led to models which differ in the assumptions that are made. On the one hand there are models which assume that markets clear quickly and as a result the welfare of economic actors (firms and households) is maximized, and consequently, there are no reasons why economic actors should change their behaviour. On the other hand, there are models which assume that markets do not always clear quickly and that rigidities are present, particularly with regard to prices and wages which mean that for a time, economic actors will not be maximizing welfare.

We will provide an overview of some of the main business cycle models with perspectives that consider the supply side of the economy, the demand side of the economy and we will finish with dynamic stochastic general equilibrium (DSGE) models.

Supply Side – The New Classical Model

This model is based around analysis of the supply side of the economy and the operation of the labour market. It is assumed that the labour market clears but that workers have imperfect information. The model highlights the importance of anticipated and unanticipated price changes. If workers correctly anticipate price changes, they can change their behaviour such that real wages and the amount of labour they supply adjust to clear the market. For example, if the price level rises, real wages then fall, and therefore firms will be encouraged to hire more labour. Now if the price change is anticipated, workers will recognize that real wages will fall and therefore supply less labour. As a result, the demand for labour will be greater than the supply of labour so the nominal wage will rise. However, the real wage at the new equilibrium will be constant.

If workers do not anticipate the change in prices, the real wage will fall, firms demand more labour but workers continue to offer the same amount of labour hours, so the demand for labour will be in excess of the supply; this leads to a rise in nominal wages, but this rise will be less than the price rise. The result is that output will rise but the real wage will fall. The increase in output will be above trend GDP. In this model there has been a deviation from equilibrium output because workers have incomplete information and are not aware of the impact of changes in the price level.

Aggregate Supply Shocks A further aspect of the new classical model looks at how shocks to aggregate supply can cause deviations from trend output. These shocks affect the productivity of factors of production and can be temporary, such as the effect of natural disasters, or permanent as when new technologies are developed. The developments in computer technology over the last 30 years, for example, have had a permanent impact on productivity.

If supply shocks are temporary, such as the effect of an earthquake, productivity declines and demand for labour and other factors will fall which will also lead to a fall in output below trend GDP. It is possible to observe aspects of this argument in events which have occurred in the last ten years. An earthquake in Northern Japan in 2011 caused extensive damage and disruption to supply chains across the globe. Firms found that component parts were in short supply and some firms had to lay off workers and suspend production until the supply chains were re-established. The global nature of business means that such natural disasters can have far-reaching effects.

Supply Side – The Keynesian Model

In the next chapter we will look in more detail at the contribution of John Maynard Keynes to macroeconomics. One of the main propositions that Keynes put forward was that markets do not clear as quickly as classical economists believed. The assumption is that the ability of the goods and labour market to clear are impaired by the existence of *sticky prices* and *sticky wages,* which is associated with new Keynesian interpretations. In labour markets, firms enter into contractual agreements with workers and are also constrained by labour market legislation and regulation, which means that it is not always easy to adjust the labour force to changed economic circumstances. Excess demand or supply in the labour market will not be eliminated quickly by changes in wages because of these wage rigidities, and in particular wages tend to be sticky downwards. It becomes difficult for firms to adjust wages down when there is an excess supply of labour as a result of changing economic conditions, such as a change in the price level.

Sticky prices occur where there are costs to firms of changing prices. We introduced the idea of menu costs in Chapter 27. Changing economic conditions in the goods market may warrant a change in price to clear the market but because firms face costs in changing prices it may be that prices are changed infrequently. In addition to the internal costs to firms of diverting labour resources to changing prices, firms will have agreements with suppliers and retailers about prices built into contracts which may not be capable of being re-negotiated for some time. The existence of menu costs mean that prices will be sticky and prevent markets from clearing in the short run.

Demand Side – The New Classical Model

We have noted in earlier chapters that aggregate demand (AD) is composed of consumption spending, investment spending, government spending and net exports. Changes to any or all of the components of AD could cause a deviation of output from trend. Later in the book we will look at causes of shifts in AD but in this section we are going to trace through the effect of an assumed change in AD. An increase in AD, for example, will, *ceteris paribus,* lead to a rise in the price level. A rise in the price level reduces real wages and firms look to hire more workers with the result that the nominal wage will rise. The rise in AD will lead to an increase in output and the price level increases. The increase in the number of workers hired causes a fall in unemployment. The New Classical interpretation rests on workers misinterpreting a rise in nominal wages as a rise in real wages, in other words, they do not fully take into account the effect on wages of the price rise. We referred to this in Chapter 27 as the *inflation fallacy.*

The result of this is that the economy moves to a temporary equilibrium where the expectations of some economic actors are not fully incorporated because they are incorrect. However, over time, workers will begin to realize that real wages have changed and as a result begin to change their behaviour. As workers negotiate for wage rises that maintain their standard of living, firms' costs rise and some firms will cut back supply with the result that the economy returns to trend output but with a higher price level once expectations have fully adjusted.

If AD falls then the economy will enter a period of contraction with output and prices falling in the short run. The reverse process to the one outlined above will take place. Real wages rise and firms begin to cut back on output which increases unemployment. The demand for labour will be in excess of the supply of labour and nominal wage rates will fall. Workers see the fall in nominal wages as a fall in the standard of living but over time their expectations will adjust to take into account the fall in the price level and output will return to trend.

Cyclical Implications The analysis provided above has implications for the nature of the cyclicality of key macroeconomic variables. In the new classical model, when output is above trend, unemployment is countercyclical and employment will be above trend and so be procyclical. Inflation will be procyclical but real wages will be countercyclical because as output rises real wages fall.

Demand Side – The Keynesian Model

Remember that the Keynesian model assumes sticky prices and wages. If there is an increase in AD, then wages and prices will take time to adjust. The increase in demand will mean firms' stocks begin to decline and so they will take steps to increase output and in so doing increase employment. In the short run, therefore, output increases above trend but the price level does not change because of sticky prices.

Over time, however, the economy will return to trend because firms will eventually be able to raise prices and nominal wages will also increase. The rise in nominal wages affects firms' costs and some will begin to cut back output which returns to trend but with a higher price level. This is the same outcome as that given in the new classical model above but the way in which the economy has adjusted to the deviation from trend has differed. If AD is reduced, the reverse situation will apply and explains why recessions occur.

The speed with which the economy returns to trend after an AD shock will depend on the time it takes for prices and wages to adjust to the changed economic conditions. In this model, employment, real wages and inflation are procyclical and unemployment is countercyclical.

Real Business Cycles

At the heart of the model of real business cycles is the belief that changes in technology, both positive and negative technology shocks, affect productivity regardless of the real wage rate. The model assumes that there are no market imperfections, that firms and households are profit and utility maximizing and that markets clear. Against the background of these assumptions, if there is a negative technology shock then labour productivity falls and the demand for labour falls. Output will fall as a result and unemployment will increase. Output falls because aggregate supply (AS) falls, which creates excess demand in the economy. An excess of AD will lead to a rise in the price level. If the price level increases this affects the real interest rate. Recall that the real interest rate is the nominal interest rate minus inflation. If inflation rises and the nominal interest rate is constant, then the real interest rate will fall. A fall in the real interest rate would lead to a rise in investment by firms.

Real business cycle models suggest that technology shocks can be a major cause of short-run fluctuations in output. The causes of business cycles, therefore, are technology shocks that cause permanent shifts in AS, but when AS shifts the expectations of economic actors are still correct and so there is no reason for governments or central banks to intervene and apply policy prescriptions. The real business cycle model, therefore, does not see growth over time as being a deterministic trend but a stochastic one. In real business cycle models, employment, labour productivity and real wages are procyclical.

CASE STUDY   Kydland and Prescott and Real Business Cycles

Finn E. Kydland and Edward C. Prescott won the Nobel Prize for Economics in 2004 and their award was based on the work they had done on business cycles. Their work became associated with real business cycles because of the focus on real shocks to the economy as opposed to nominal shocks as the key driver of deviations in output. The question Kydland and Prescott were interested in was not measuring business cycles but focusing on the *pattern* of output and employment around the trend and asking why this seemed to happen in a repeated fashion over time.

Many textbooks explain the business cycle in terms of four phases – boom, slowdown, recession, upturn. The term 'cycle' implies a 'what goes around comes around' type of approach to an economy. Such a view of cycles implies an almost inevitable trend where growth turns into boom, which in turn leads to the start of decline that leads to recession before the process begins again. However, Kydland and Prescott used a generally agreed scientific definition of 'cycles' that makes reference to a point of departure – in this case the trend of economic growth. Kydland and Prescott refer to these recurrent departures as 'deviations'.

They argue that business cycles must be seen as periodic deviations from trend growth and that business cycles are neither inevitable nor evolutionary. As such the explanation for a downturn in economic activity cannot, in itself, be found in the reasons why growth occurred in the first place. Equally, the seeds of an expansion in growth are not to be found in a recession.

In analyzing the behaviour of these deviations from trend they sought to challenge some conventional wisdom that had grown up around business cycles. For example, in times of economic downturn the expectation would be that the price level would fall and in times of strong economic growth it would be anticipated that the price level would rise – in other words, inflation is procyclical. This implies that in a downturn firms seek to reduce prices to encourage sales and are prevented from increasing prices to improve margins because of the lack of demand. Similarly, in times of economic growth, firms experience rising demand and possibly wage and other costs. They are able to increase prices to improve margins without too much damage to business because of the strong growth in demand.

Kydland and Prescott argued that, in fact, price showed a countercyclical behaviour – when economic growth slowed down, prices rose and when economic growth was strong, prices fell. They further argued that real wages fall as growth increases and vice versa (or are not related to the business cycle) and that the money supply was an important factor in leading economic growth.

Price procyclicality is important because if we are looking for the causes of changes in economic activity as a whole, we would presume to be looking for something fairly major as being the cause – large price rises, for example, or shocks caused by changes in things like the money supply. If price procyclicality is a myth, then research into the causes of changes in cycles might be misguided. Think of it in terms of a thermometer in a room. The thermometer tells us what the temperature of the room is but is not a cause of the temperature. Looking at the properties of the thermometer to explain the temperature of the room would lead us down the wrong path.

Kydland and Prescott argued that an important factor in explaining business cycles is the decisions people make about how they devote their time between leisure (non-market activities) and income-earning activities. After analyzing the factors that may influence business cycles they come to the following conclusions:

- Aggregate hours worked (a measure of labour input) is strongly correlated with changes in GDP. The problem with this is that the contributions to GDP for all workers are considered the same. Kydland and Prescott point out that the contribution of the hours worked by a brain surgeon is not the same as that of a porter in a hospital. With some consideration of this, Kydland and Prescott conclude that real wages are more procyclical and something which traditional literature on business cycles would not suggest.

- The capital stock is largely unrelated to real GDP but is closely correlated if a time lag of about one year is included.

- With regard to the factors affecting AD, Kydland and Prescott report that consumption and investment are highly procyclical whereas government spending does not seem to be correlated with growth.

- They also comment that imports are procyclical, as are exports, but with a six-month to a one-year time lag.

- Labour and capital income is strongly procyclical.

- They find no evidence that narrow money (M1) leads the business cycle. In other words, they do not find evidence that a rise in M1 will lead to a spurt in growth.

- Credit arrangements are likely to play a significant role in future analysis of business cycle theory.

- The price level is countercyclical.

Kydland and Prescott's work has prompted considerable research not least the necessity to look at what might be happening in the macroeconomy. It might be necessary to look at factors other than those that simply describe the data. This emphasis

Finn E. Kydland; winner of the Nobel Prize for Economics in 2004

(Continued)

on the quantitative features rather than qualitative features (what it tells us rather than what we think it might signify) has been a feature of a re-assessment of statistical analysis in economics, particularly the analysis of time-series data. What do long-term time-series data tell us in relation to short-term series?

Real business cycle theory does not view a recession as a 'failure' in the economy nor might a boom also be seen as a failure. (A boom might be interpreted as a failure in economic management because it is unsustainable, which is why politicians often refer to the 'bad old days of boom and bust'.) Kydland and Prescott see business cycles as explanations of shock to the economy that are understandable reactions rather than failures. Their work tends to dismiss the 'sticky prices' explanation for a slowdown in growth and also the mismatch between investment and consumption and the monetarist argument of market failure in price signals. Instead they look at real shocks to the economy and the adjustment process to those shocks, which could last for some time after. Essentially, Kydland and Prescott argued that business cycles could occur perfectly naturally within a competitive environment despite the implication in traditional theory that, for example, perfect competition would not result in long periods of unemployment.

Real business cycle theory is not without its critics. In particular, the implication that shocks to supply tend to be permanent rather than transitory has been questioned as an explanation of recessions, and empirical studies have also questioned the extent to which the assumptions of the model and the predictions about the cyclicality of economic variables match the evidence.

MACROECONOMIC MODELS OF THE ECONOMY

Economists develop models in an attempt to help understand how the economy works. The economy is extremely complex and it is unlikely that any model will fully capture every element and interaction of the macroeconomy. However, models can be valuable in providing information to policymakers and analysts to provide perspectives about policy decisions, the effects of policy, and the anticipated effects of changes in key variables in the model. Since the 1970s, advances in statistical and econometric techniques have been significant. This has enabled economists to build ever more sophisticated models of the economy and the process continues as existing assumptions break down, observation reveals different behaviours and outcomes, and understanding develops. This has been the case for DSGE models.

Dynamic Stochastic General Equilibrium Models

DSGE models developed from the research spawned by real business cycle models. They are now increasingly used by central banks, including the ECB, as part of the toolbox in analyzing, forecasting and making policy decisions. They are highly complex and rely on a large number of equations each seeking to explain relationships between economic variables, many of which we have covered so far. They are subject to constant revision in an attempt to improve their rigour and predictive power. Policymakers can take these models and tweak coefficients and assumptions to explore different outcomes and match these outcomes to observed reality to assess the validity and reliability of the models.

DSGE models are called dynamic because they build in intertemporal choices. The decisions of economic actors are not only based on current circumstances but anticipated future situations. These models allow for interaction between policy and actors' behaviour. The term *stochastic* means 'random'. DSGE models include random shocks to the economy which can cause fluctuations in economic activity away from trend. The final element, general equilibrium, refers to the assumption that prices, wages and interest rates adjust to changes in supply and demand in markets.

The Building Blocks of DSGE Models

Whilst there are different DSGE models, most include three key elements, households, firms and a monetary authority (the central bank). Recent developments in DSGE models seek to include the financial sector and a government sector to help model the influence of fiscal policy. For the purposes of this introduction to DSGE models, we will focus on households, firms and the monetary authority.

Households Households represent the demand side of the economy which in turn determines GDP. The equations which define household relationships focus on the real interest rate and expectations of the future. Households are assumed to maximize their welfare subject to their budget constraint. It should be noted that the individual elements of the model are built on microeconomic foundations. The welfare maximising equations are increasingly being adapted to incorporate behavioural aspects of household behaviour, such as the effects of past consumption in decision-making.

We have looked at the role of interest rates in decision-making and the real interest rate plays a key role in these models. If interest rates fall, households have more of an incentive to consume rather than save, which in turn drives up demand. If interest rates rise the opposite effects are assumed. If expectations of the future are positive, then regardless of the interest rate, demand increases and vice versa. There is, thus, a negative relationship between real interest rates and desired spending. Demand influences inflation and expectations of future inflation.

Households are also the suppliers of labour. Consumption levels are influenced by the amount of hours worked which determines labour supply. Households trade-off work and leisure; if they want to increase consumption, then they may have to offer more hours. The wage received can either be spent or saved and the amount of goods consumers are able to purchase is affected by inflation. The amount saved is determined by the returns available given by the real interest rate.

Demand shocks can occur if, for example, households borrow extensively to finance consumption and then pull back on consumption to pay back debt or where widespread default hits households negatively.

Firms Firms are assumed to maximize profits and operate under a production function where output is dependent on technology, capital and labour. Labour is assumed a key element in firms' cost structures and the level of technology influences factor productivity. It is assumed that firms have some element of monopoly power and can set prices. Price is set on a mark-up basis over the marginal cost of production, which in turn is affected by labour costs. The extent of the mark-up is determined by the expected stream of profits that flow in the future and incorporates the importance of expectations in firms' decisions. It is further assumed that firms desire to change price is infrequent because of menu costs.

In times of economic growth, to increase output to meet demand, firms have to encourage workers to supply more labour. Workers will supply more labour if the wage rate increases but this increases firms' marginal costs and may result in an increase in price. There is a direct link, therefore, between real activity and inflationary pressures.

Supply shocks can arise in the form of changes in technology which affect productivity levels and real wages. The capital stock of firms is determined by the savings decisions of households but can also be affected by the efficiency of the financial sector. As noted earlier, the financial sector is being increasingly built into DSGE models. If the financial system is operating inefficiently, firms will find it harder to access the capital they need at the time they need it and, in addition, the price of accessing capital may increase.

Monetary Authorities The demand and supply in goods and labour markets feeds into monetary policy decisions by central banks who control short-term interest rates. Interest rates are set based on the central bank's analysis of current inflation, expected future inflation and GDP (or real activity). In making its decision, it is assumed central banks operate under what is called a *Taylor rule* (which we shall cover in more detail in a later chapter) linking interest rates to the target inflation rate the bank operates under, past interest rate setting, and the output gap. This is the difference between current output and trend. If inflationary pressures are building, the central bank increases interest rates which influences both household and firm decision-making. Equally, if the economy is suffering contraction (implying that inflation is decelerating), the central bank can reduce interest rates to help stimulate the economy to keep inflation at its target.

The Use and Value of DSGE Models

As noted, DSGE models can be used as part of the toolbox for monetary authorities. They can be used to help provide forecasts, to analyze the effect of different policy decisions, and to look at how outcomes can be affected by varying the policy parameters. It may even be the case the models can suggest that no policy action is needed. Research suggests that over a quarter (three months), DSGE models can be as reliable in forecasting output and inflation as purely statistical analysis but can be slightly more reliable over a year. This is not to say that policymakers rely solely on these models. They provide information which can be incorporated with statistical analyses, surveys carried out by business organizations and the expertise and judgements of central bankers in helping arrive at decisions. Where shocks occur, the models can help to identify the nature of the shock, and allocate weights to determine the magnitude and direction of the effects. In helping to provide a clearer picture of the symptoms, the use of these models can assist in determining the appropriate policy response.

Very few economists would claim that DSGE models are perfect and that there is not a lot more scope for improvement in developing the reliability and validity of these models. What many would say is that they are better than nothing and provide an aid to decision-making. Weaknesses which have been recognised include the assumption that consumption, wages, investment and output all tend to grow at the same rate in the long run, which is not always borne out by observation of the data. The Financial Crisis made it clear that the role of the financial sector needs to be more fully incorporated into future modelling designs as well as a greater recognition of the role and effect of fiscal policy on the economy. These are all works in progress and part of the way in which economics is evolving and developing its understanding of how the macroeconomy works.

CONCLUSION

In this chapter we have provided some background to the more extensive analysis of short-term economic fluctuations in the coming chapters. We have introduced a number of key concepts which need to be borne in mind as we tackle the next chapters, not least building a familiarity with the behaviour of key macroeconomic variables over time.

We have also learned that economists have different interpretations of business cycles based on different assumptions about how the economy works and the extent to which markets clear and how economic actors behave. Models of business cycles focus on both the supply side and demand side of the economy and it is likely that the answers to the questions surrounding policy decisions to help smooth out deviations in trend growth are to be found in a combination of these different models. The model of the real business cycle raises questions about whether the trends that we 'see' in time-series data, which form the basis of analysis, are actually present and if trends do not exist then policy measures designed to reduce deviations from trend are misguided.

IN THE NEWS

Business Cycles

Throughout this book, we have provided some different interpretations of economic issues and in this article we look at Austrian business cycle theory.

Austrian Business Cycle Theory (ABCT)

Expectations play a key role in modern macroeconomic modelling. Decisions are made not only with the past and present in mind but also in the future. People are aware that central banks control interest rates even if they are not fully conversant with the economics of central banks. Ask yourself a question, therefore: what do you think the next interest rate move will be in your country? Then consider where you think interest rates will be in two, three and five years' time. If you think interest rates are going to rise, how far will they increase and at what point do you think they will change direction?

ABCT puts a focus on the role of central banks in business cycles. Assume that the central bank decides to increase interest rates. Firms considering investment projects will now consider whether the project remains viable and, at the margin, some projects will be shelved. This leads to a slowdown in the economy. However, firms will also know that at some point in the future interest rates will fall and investment projects will then be undertaken helping to fuel growth. The increasing and lowering of interest rates by the central bank is seen as being 'artificial' in that it is not being changed because of imbalances in the demand and supply of loanable funds but because of perceptions of changes in inflation. The artificial changes in interest rates 'fool' firms and households into making decisions which generate expansions and contractions in the economy, and hence are a cause of business cycles.

Critics of the ABCT argue that firms and households are not so dumb as to be fooled by interest rate changes, at least not in the longer term having suffered repeated cycles. After all, few people expected interest rates to remain at historically low levels as they were following the Financial Crisis forever. However, many decisions are not made with the macroeconomy in mind. Individuals, for example, may have taken advantage of lower interest rates by rescheduling their mortgages or borrowing to fund high-end purchases such as cars. These individuals act in their own self-interest. Equally, firms will anticipate changes in demand when interest rates change. If rates are lowered, they expect demand to increase and put in place plans to be in a position to expand outpoint in preparation. Again, these firms are acting out of self-interest. Economic actors respond to short-term changes in economic circumstances not long-term. If a family can lower its mortgage payments by re-scheduling its mortgage it makes sense to do so. Equally, firms do not want to be caught out with no spare capacity when demand does increase and lose out to competitors who have prepared with more foresight.

Far from being 'fooled', economic actors are fully aware of the likely future direction of interest rates but that does not stop them from acting in a way which fuels cycles of expansion and contraction. According to some Austrian School economists, it is not economic actors that should shoulder the blame but central banks who intervene in financial markets.

Are households fooled by the future direction of interest rates?

Questions

1 **Why are expectations considered such an important element of macroeconomic analysis?**
2 **Critics of ABCT argue that economic actors cannot be 'fooled' repeatedly. To what extent are economic actors impeded by imperfect information?**
3 **When interest rates were reduced to almost zero across many developed economies, would you have foreseen that they would have stayed so low for so long? How might your view have affected your decision-making?**
4 **To what extent do you agree with the ABCT view that central banks are complicit in the creation of business cycles?**
5 **Of the theories presented in this chapter, which model do you think provides the best explanation of the causes of short-term economic fluctuations and why?**

SUMMARY

- Economies experience periods of changing levels of economic activity.
- Key macroeconomic data are often time-series data which can raise questions about the validity and reliability of statistical tests applied to data sets.
- Economic growth appears to follow a trend which rises over a period of time.
- Deviations from this trend are known as the business cycle.
- The business cycle has characteristic features which include peaks in economic activity, slowdown, troughs and upturns with key turning points.
- Trends can be stationary and nonstationary. Nonstationary data can exhibit deterministic trends which change by a constant amount independent of time, or be stochastic where the trend variable changes by a random amount.
- Macroeconomic data can be viewed in pairs with one of the pairs generally GDP. The variable compared may be either procyclical or countercyclical.
- Collecting macroeconomic data can allow economists to view certain indicators as leading, coincident or lagging.
- Changes in the business cycle can be caused by changes in decision-making by households and firms, by external shocks, government policy, and changes in confidence or expectations of the future.
- Business cycle models differ in the assumptions they make about the extent to which markets clear and the relationship between the supply side and demand side of the economy.
- Real business cycles emphasize the effects of changes in technology as causes of changes in economic activity.
- Central banks and policymakers have increasingly used sophisticated DSGE models of the economy to aid in decision-making.

QUESTIONS FOR REVIEW

1 What is time-series data? Give three examples of key macroeconomic variables that are examples of time-series data.
2 What are the main stages of a typical business cycle and how long do these stages last?
3 What is the difference between a deterministic trend and a stochastic trend?
4 Would you expect the following variables to be procyclical or countercyclical if GDP was above trend? Explain.

   a. inflation
   b. unemployment
   c. employment
   d. real wages
   e. nominal interest rates.

5 Unemployment is classified as a 'lagging indicator'. Explain what this means and why unemployment is classed as such.
6 Why might changes in household decision-making cause a deviation in GDP from trend?
7 What role does household and firms' confidence play in business cycles?
8 What is the role of unanticipated price changes in the new classical model of business cycles?
9 What is the key difference between real business cycle models and other business cycle models?
10 What are the principle features of DSGE models?

PROBLEMS AND APPLICATIONS

1 Look at Figure 31.1. For either the UK or the EU:

   a. estimate the amplitude of the deviations from trend over the period shown
   b. estimate the length of time between the beginning of the deviation from trend and the return to trend in each case.

2 In one time period, the growth rate of GDP of a country is recorded as 3.4 per cent against a trend growth rate of output of 2.8 per cent. In the next two time periods, the growth rate of GDP is recorded as 2.8 per cent and 2.0 per cent respectively. Is the country experiencing a recession? Explain.

3 Go to the national statistics office website for your country (this could be the ONS in the UK or Eurostat for the EU) and look up unemployment and inflation figures over the last 30 years. Plot the data on a spreadsheet, graph it and identify the trend. Is the trend stationary, nonstationary or indeterminate? Explain.

4 Is it always possible to discern a trend in any time-series data? What problems might arise if trends are apportioned to time-series data that are not really present?

5 Look up the following comovements for the country in which you are studying on an appropriate website. Explain whether the comovements are procyclical or countercyclical; GDP and:

   a. inflation
   b. employment
   c. unemployment
   d. the money supply (M1).

6 Firms experience a rise in stocks. Explain why this might have occurred and what you expect firms' response to this event might be and how this might affect output.

7 Why might household and firms' confidence and expectations change leading to deviations in output from trend? Is there any way in which changes in confidence can be measured to provide an indicator of changes in economic activity?

8 Critics of DSGE models argue that despite their complexity and sophistication, they failed to provide indications of the shock that was the Financial Crisis. Apart from the lack of a financial markets element built into the models, critics also claim that the neo-classical foundations and assumptions upon which the models are constructed are fundamentally flawed. Why do you think these critics level such accusations against these models and to what extent to do agree with their reservations of the value of these models in helping forecasting and policymaking?

9 To what extent do you think that workers are always fooled by the inflation fallacy?

10 Which business cycle model do you find the most compelling and why?

32 KEYNESIAN ECONOMICS AND IS-LM ANALYSIS

Neo classical orthodoxy had held that markets, including labour markets, cleared without government involvement in both the short run and the long run. The Great Depression of the 1930s across Europe and the US saw millions of people losing their jobs and unemployment remained at high levels throughout the decade.

In 1936, economist John Maynard Keynes published a book entitled *The General Theory of Employment, Interest and Money*, which attempted to explain short-run economic fluctuations in general and the Great Depression in particular. Macroeconomics as a separate path of economic research stemmed from the experiences of the Great Depression. Keynes was not the first to question classical paradigms; in the preceding chapter, we saw how Mitchell and Burns' work on business cycles was being carried out some 20 years before the Great Depression. Keynes picked up this tradition and helped create interest in the analysis of aggregate phenomena.

Keynes' primary message was that recessions and depressions can occur because of inadequate aggregate demand for goods and services. Keynes had long been a critic of classical economic theory because it could explain only the long-run effects of policies. A few years before *The General Theory*, Keynes had written the following about classical economics: 'The long run is a misleading guide to current affairs. In the long run we are all dead. Economists set themselves too easy, too useless a task if in tempestuous seasons they can only tell us that when the storm is long past, the ocean will be flat.'

Keynes' message was aimed at policymakers as well as economists. As the world's economies suffered with high unemployment, Keynes advocated policies to increase AD, including government spending on public works. Keynes argued for the necessity of short-run interventions in the economy. The focus on monetary and supply-side policy as the main ways of controlling the economy in most developed countries in Europe had largely consigned Keynesian demand management to the economic history books. However, the Financial Crisis and subsequent recession of 2007–9 reignited the debate about the role of Keynesian economics in macro policy. Keynes' contribution to economic thinking is widely acknowledged and it is valuable to have some insight into Keynesian economics. This chapter will begin this process.

THE KEYNESIAN CROSS

Classical economics placed a fundamental reliance on the efficiency of markets and the assumption that they would clear. At a macro level, this meant that if the economy was in disequilibrium and unemployment existed, wages and prices would adjust to bring the economy back into equilibrium at full employment. **Full employment** is defined as a point where those people who want to work at the going market wage level are able to find a job. Any unemployment that did exist would be classed as voluntary unemployment. The experience of the Great Depression of the 1930s brought the classical assumptions under closer scrutiny; the many millions suffering from unemployment could not all be volunteering to not take jobs at the going wage rates so some must, therefore, be involuntarily unemployed. We have also seen in the preceding chapter that prices can also be sticky, meaning markets may not always adjust to clear surpluses and shortages quickly.

 full employment a point where those people who want to work at the going market wage level are able to find a job

Planned and Actual Spending

Fundamental to Keynesian analysis is the distinction between *planned* and *actual* decisions by households and firms. **Planned spending, saving or investment** refers to the desired or intended actions of firms and households. A publisher, for example, may plan to sell 10 000 copies of a textbook in the first six months of the year; an individual may plan to go on holiday to Turkey in the summer and save up to finance the trip; a person may intend to save €1000 over the year to put towards paying for a wedding next year.

 planned spending, saving or investment the desired or intended actions of households and firms

Actual spending, saving or investment refers to the realized, *ex post* (after the event) outcome. The publisher may only sell 8000 copies in the first six months and so has a build-up of stock (inventories) of 2000 more than planned; the holidaymaker may fall ill and is unable to go on holiday and so their actual consumption is lower than planned (whereas actual saving is more than planned because they have not spent what they intended); and the plans for saving for the wedding may be compromised by the need to spend money on repairing a house damaged by a flood.

 actual spending, saving or investment the realized or *ex post* outcome resulting from actions of households and firms

Planned and actual outcomes, therefore, might be very different. Keynes suggested that there was no reason why equilibrium national income would coincide with full employment output. Wages and prices might not adjust in the short run because of sticky wages and prices, and so the economy could be at a position where the level of demand in the economy was insufficient to bring about full employment. The mass unemployment of the 1930s could be alleviated, he argued, by governments intervening in the economy to manage demand to achieve the desired level of employment.

The Equilibrium of the Economy

We have seen that a country's GDP (which we will refer to as national income), is divided among four components: consumption spending, investment spending, spending by government and net exports.

Imagine a situation where, at every point, total expenditure in the economy given by $C + I + G + NX$ was exactly the same as national income. We could represent this in diagrammatic form as a 45-degree line such as the ones in panels (a) and (b) Figure 32.1.

In panels (a) and (b), the 45-degree line connects all points where consumption spending (actual expenditure) would be equal to national income (planned expenditure). This line can be thought of as the equivalent of the capacity of the economy – the aggregate supply (AS) curve.

The $C + I + G + NX$ line is a function of income – in other words, spending depends on income. If income is higher, spending will also be higher and so the $C + I + G + NX$ line has a positive slope. The vertical intercept of the $C + I + G + NX$ line given as E_0, is termed **autonomous spending or**

autonomous expenditure. This is the component of expenditure which does not depend on income/output – government spending being a key element of this expenditure.

FIGURE 32.1

Deflationary and Inflationary Gaps

The 45-degree line shows all the points where consumption spending equals income. The vertical intercept of the expenditure line shows autonomous expenditure. The economy is in equilibrium where the expenditure line, $C + I + G + NX$, cuts the 45-degree line. In panel (a) this equilibrium is lower than full employment output (Y_f) at Y_1; there is insufficient demand to maintain full employment output. The government would need to shift the expenditure line up to $C + I + G + NX_1$ to eliminate the deflationary gap. In panel (b) the equilibrium is higher than full employment output – the economy does not have the capacity to meet demand. In this case the government needs to shift the $C + I + G + NX$ line down to $C + I + G + NX_2$ to eliminate the inflationary gap.

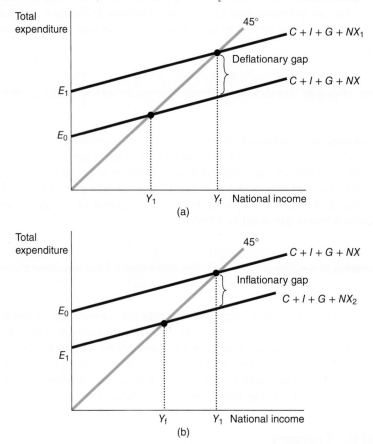

---

autonomous spending or autonomous expenditure spending which is not dependent on income/output

---

Where actual spending is equal to planned spending is the short-run equilibrium of the economy. Note that the use of the term 'equilibrium' in this context does not mean the 'best' or 'desired' equilibrium – it is simply a point where actual spending is equal to planned spending. The economy is in equilibrium where the $C + I + G + NX$ line cuts the 45-degree line. This is referred to as the *Keynesian cross*. In panel (a) the economy is in equilibrium at a national income of Y_1. However, full employment national income is at Y_f. Actual spending of $C + I + G + NX$ in panel (a) gives an equilibrium which is less than that required for full employment output (Y_f). At the equilibrium Y_1 there is spare capacity in the economy – some resources are not being used to their full extent, capital may be underused and unemployment will exist. This is the equivalent to an economy being at a point inside its production possibilities frontier which we looked at in Chapter 19. The difference between full employment output, and the expenditure required to meet it, is termed the **deflationary gap** (you may sometimes see this also referred to as the **output gap**). Expenditure needs to rise to $C + I + G + NX_1$ in order to eliminate the deflationary gap which is the vertical distance between actual spending and spending necessary to achieve full employment.

> **deflationary gap or output gap** the difference between full employment output and expenditure when expenditure is less than full employment output

In panel (b) the $C + I + G + NX$ line cuts the 45-degree line at an output level Y_1 which is higher than full employment output, Y_f. In this situation the economy does not have the capacity to meet actual spending. This will trigger inflationary pressures. The difference between full employment output and the expenditure line here is called the **inflationary gap**. Actual spending needs to be reduced to eradicate the inflationary gap and the $C + I + G + NX$ line needs to be reduced to $C + I + G + NX_2$ to bring the economy to an equilibrium where actual spending equals full employment output.

> **inflationary gap** the difference between full employment output and actual expenditure when actual expenditure is greater than full employment output

Demand Management The deviations in the business cycle in Keynesian analysis are primarily due to demand-side factors. The principle behind Keynesian economics is, at its heart, very simple and intuitive. Downturns in economic activity occur because firms fail to sell all the goods and services they planned to sell. If customers (and of course we are not only talking about final consumers, but also about other businesses as customers of firms) are not buying as many goods and services, firms will not need to produce as many and so cut back production as stocks rise. If production is cut back then firms do not need as many workers and either do not replace workers when they retire, make some workers redundant or lay off workers by reverting to shorter working weeks or even ceasing production temporarily for a time period. Unemployment rises and the cause is due to *demand deficiency*. The affected workers now see a fall in their incomes and so cut back on spending which exacerbates the problem.

The cause of a fall in consumption in the first place is often difficult to pinpoint as noted in the preceding chapter. It could be due to confidence and expectations; it could be due to the way in which the public respond to news items (the more the news media refer to the possibility of slowdown or recession, it might become a self-fulfilling prophecy); or it could be due to a change in patterns of consumption with some firms seeing a decline in demand for their goods whilst others see an increase, but the structural change causes a disruption in demand. Workers who are made redundant from the declining industries may not have the skills to move to jobs being created in the growth industries, and as a result, regardless of the wage rate, they remain unemployed.

Keynes argued that governments can use the tools of fiscal and monetary policy, and in particular fiscal policy, to influence demand in the economy and reduce deflationary and inflationary gaps. Taxation is a leakage from the circular flow of income but can be manipulated by the government. Equally, government can vary its own expenditure and the combinations of changes in tax and government spending can be used as levers to manage demand to bring the economy into equilibrium at a point nearer to full employment output. If the value of full employment output, the amount the economy is capable of producing if all existing resources are used fully (planned spending), is €1 trillion, for example, but actual spending is only €800 billion, the deflationary or output gap would be €200 billion. The government might introduce policy levers which lead to a cut in taxes and a boost to government spending to generate this additional €200 billion in spending. The use of these 'levers' has some interesting features which we will describe in the next section.

SELF TEST Why might actual spending differ from planned spending?
If planned spending in an economy is €500 billion but actual spending €400 billion, is there an inflationary gap or a deflationary gap? Explain.
What might the government do in this situation to bring spending more in line with full employment output?

THE MULTIPLIER EFFECT

The $C + I + G + NX$ line is referred to as the expenditure function. Planned expenditure is dependent on the level of consumption, plus investment, plus government spending plus net exports and can be written:

$$E = C + I + G + NX$$

Actual expenditure/output (remember that expenditure is one way of measuring output – these two things are the same) will be denoted as (Y). The economy will be in equilibrium when planned expenditure is equal to actual expenditure $(E = Y)$.

The positive slope of the expenditure function implies that planned spending rises as income rises. What determines the slope of the expenditure function has important policy implications. When a government makes a purchase, say it enters into a contract with a construction company for €10 billion to build a new nuclear power station, that purchase has repercussions. The immediate impact of the higher demand from the government is to raise employment and profits at the construction company (which we shall call Nucelec). Nucelec, in turn, has to buy resources from other contractors to carry out the job and so these suppliers also experience an increase in orders. Workers at these firms see higher earnings and the firms' owners see higher profits; they respond to this increase in income by raising their own spending on consumer goods. As a result, the government purchase from Nucelec, raises the demand for the products of many other firms in the economy. Because each euro spent by the government can raise the AD for goods and services by more than a euro, government purchases are said to have a **multiplier effect** on AD.

> **multiplier effect** the additional shifts in aggregate demand that result when expansionary fiscal policy increases income and thereby increases consumer spending

The multiplier effect continues even after this first round. When consumer spending rises, the firms that produce these consumer goods hire more people and experience higher profits. Higher earnings and profits stimulate consumer spending once again, and so on. Thus, there is positive feedback as higher demand leads to higher income, which in turn leads to even higher demand. Once all these effects are added together, the total impact on the quantity of goods and services demanded can be much larger than the initial impulse from higher government spending.

The multiplier effect arising from the response of consumer spending can be strengthened by the response of investment to higher levels of demand. For instance, Nucelec might respond to the higher demand for building services by buying more cranes and other mechanized building equipment. In this case, higher government demand spurs higher demand for investment goods. This positive feedback from demand to investment is sometimes called the *investment accelerator*.

CASE STUDY   The Accelerator Principle

The accelerator principle relates the *rate of change* of AD to the *rate of change* in investment. To produce goods, a firm needs equipment. Imagine that a machine is capable of producing 1000 tablet computers per week. Demand for computer tablets is currently 800. A rise in demand for computer tablets of up to 200 is capable of being met without any further investment in new machinery. However, if the rate of growth of demand continues to rise, it may be necessary to invest in a new machine.

Imagine that in year 1, demand for computer tablets rises by 10 per cent to 880. The business can meet this demand through existing equipment. In year 2, demand increases by 20 per cent and is now 1056. The existing capacity of the machine means that this demand cannot be met but the shortage is only 56 units so the firm decides that it might increase price rather than invest in a new machine. In year 3, demand rises by a further 25 per cent. Demand is now 1320 but the machine is only capable of producing a maximum of 1000 tablet computers. The firm decides to invest in a new machine. The manufacturers of the new machine will therefore see a rise in their order books as a result of the increase in demand. An

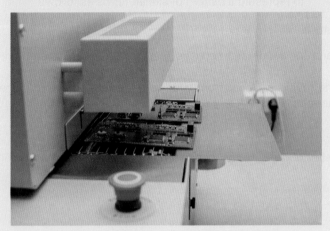

increase in demand of 25 per cent has led to an 'accelerated' rise in investment of 100 per cent. Investment is a component of AD and so economists are interested in the way investment adjusts to changes in demand in the economy. As this brief example shows, the relationship between an increase in demand and an increase in investment is not a simple one.

The relationship between changes in investment and changes in demand is not straightforward.

A Formula for the Spending Multiplier

A little algebra permits us to derive a formula for the size of the multiplier effect that arises from consumer spending. An important number in this formula is the **marginal propensity to consume** – the fraction of extra income that a household consumes rather than saves. For example, suppose that the marginal propensity to consume is $\frac{3}{4}$. This means that for every extra pound or euro that a household earns, the household spends $\frac{3}{4}$ of it and saves $\frac{1}{4}$. The **marginal propensity to save** (MPS) is the fraction of extra income that a household saves rather than consumes. With an MPC of $\frac{3}{4}$, when the workers and owners of Nucelec earn €10 billion from the government contract, they increase their consumer spending by $\frac{3}{4} \times$ €10 billion, or €7.5 billion. (You should see from the above that the $MPC + MPS = 1$. The formula below can also be expressed in terms of the MPS.)

> **marginal propensity to consume** the fraction of extra income that a household consumes rather than saves
> **marginal propensity to save** the fraction of extra income that a household saves rather than consumes

To gauge the impact on spending of a change in government purchases, we follow the effects step by step. The process begins when the government spends €10 billion, which implies that national income (earnings and profits) also rises by this amount. This increase in income in turn raises consumer spending by $MPC \times$ €10 billion, which in turn raises the income for the workers and owners of the firms that produce the consumption goods. This second increase in income again raises consumer spending, this time by $MPC \times (MPC \times €10$ billion). These feedback effects go on and on.

To find the total impact on the demand for goods and services, we add up all these effects:

Change in government purchases	$= €10$ billion
First change in consumption	$= MPC \times €10$ billion
Second change in consumption	$= (MPC)^2 \times €10$ billion
Third change in consumption	$= (MPC)^3 \times €10$ billion
⋮	⋮
Total change in demand	$= (1 + MPC + MPC^2 + MPC^3 = \ldots) \times €10$ billion

We can write the multiplier using '…' to represent a pattern of similar terms as follows:

$$\text{Multiplier} = (1 + MPC + MPC^2 + MPC^3 + \ldots)$$

This multiplier tells us the demand for goods and services that each euro of government purchases generates.

To simplify this equation for the multiplier, recall from your school algebra that this expression is an infinite geometric series. For x between -1 and 1:

$$1 + x + x^2 + x^3 + \ldots$$

The sum of this series as the number of terms tends to infinity, is given by:

$$\frac{1}{1-x}$$

In our case, $x = MPC$. Thus:

$$Multiplier(k) = \frac{1}{(1 - MPC)}$$

We have said that the $MPC + MPS = 1$ so the multiplier can also be expressed as:

$$Multiplier(k) = \frac{1}{MPS}$$

For example, if the MPC is $\frac{3}{4}$, the multiplier is $\dfrac{1}{\left(1 - \dfrac{3}{4}\right)} = 4$. In this case, the €10 billion of government spending generates €40 billion of demand for goods and services.

This formula for the multiplier shows an important conclusion: the size of the multiplier depends on the marginal propensity to consume. While an MPC of $\frac{3}{4}$ leads to a multiplier of 4, an MPC of $\frac{1}{2}$ leads to a multiplier of only 2. Thus, a larger MPC means a larger multiplier. To see why this is true, remember that the multiplier arises because higher income induces greater spending on consumption. The larger the MPC is, the greater is this induced effect on consumption, and the larger is the multiplier. The MPC determines the slope of the consumption element of the planned expenditure function.

Other Applications of the Multiplier Effect

Because of the multiplier effect, a euro of government purchases can generate more than a euro of AD. The logic of the multiplier effect, however, is not restricted to changes in government purchases. Instead, it applies to any event that alters spending on any component of planned expenditure – consumption, investment, government purchases or net exports.

For example, suppose that a recession overseas reduces the demand for Ireland's net exports by €1 billion. This reduced spending on Irish goods and services depresses Ireland's national income, which reduces spending by Irish consumers. If the MPC is $\frac{3}{4}$ and the multiplier is 4, then the €1 billion fall in net exports means a €4 billion contraction in output.

As another example, suppose that a stock market boom increases households' wealth and stimulates their spending on goods and services by €2 billion. This extra consumer spending increases national income, which in turn generates even more consumer spending. If the MPC is $\frac{3}{4}$ and the multiplier is 4, then the initial impulse of €2 billion in consumer spending translates into an €8 billion increase in AD.

The multiplier is an important concept in macroeconomics because it shows how the economy can amplify the impact of changes in spending. A small initial change in consumption, investment, government purchases or net exports can end up having a large effect on AD and, therefore, on the economy's production of goods and services.

Withdrawals from the Circular Flow The amount spent in each successive 'round' of spending is termed *induced expenditure*. The multiplier showed how the eventual change in income would be determined by the size of the MPC and the MPS. The higher the MPC the greater the multiplier effect.

However, in an open economy with government, any extra €1 is not simply either spent or saved, some of the extra income may be spent on imported goods and services or go to the government in taxation – withdrawals from the circular flow. Withdrawals (W) from the circular flow are classed as endogenous as they are directly related to changes in income. Withdrawals are saving (S), taxation (T) and imports (M).

We also have to take into consideration injections to the circular flow of income. Governments receive tax revenue (a withdrawal from the circular flow) but use it to spend on the goods and services they provide for citizens (an injection into the circular flow); firms earn revenue from selling goods abroad (exports) which are an injection into the circular flow; and firms, as we have seen in Chapter 22, use savings (a withdrawal) as a source of funds to borrow for investment (an injection). Injections into the circular flow are exogenous – they are not related to the level of output or income – and are investment (I), government spending (G) and export earnings (X).

The slope of the expenditure line as a whole, therefore, will be dependent on how much of each extra €1 is withdrawn. For each additional €1 of income, some will exit the circular flow of income in taxation, some through savings and some through spending on imports. The marginal propensity to taxation (MPT) is the proportion of each additional €1 of income taken in taxation by the government and the marginal propensity to import (MPM), the proportion of each additional €1 of income spent on goods from abroad. When we take into consideration the fact that each extra €1 in income is not disposable income, i.e. not all available for consumption, the multiplier effect when considering the *marginal propensity to withdraw* (MPW) will be much lower than if we were simply considering the MPC alone in any increase in income.

We can restate the formula for the multiplier (k) in an open economy with a government as:

$$k = \frac{1}{(MPS + MPT + MPM)}$$

Or:

$$k = \frac{1}{MPW}$$

The size of the MPW will determine the slope of the expenditure line: the steeper the slope of the expenditure line the greater the size of the multiplier, as shown in Figure 32.2.

FIGURE 32.2

The Slope of the Expenditure Line and Changes in Autonomous Expenditure

Panel (a) shows a relatively shallow expenditure line which would mean that the marginal propensity to withdraw would be high and the value of the multiplier was relatively low. Using the Greek letter delta (Δ) to mean 'change', the impact on national income (ΔY) of a change in government spending (ΔG) would be more limited in comparison to the effect as shown in panel (b) where the expenditure line is much steeper reflecting a higher value of the multiplier where the MPW was relatively low. In this case it takes a smaller rise in government spending to achieve the same increase in national income.

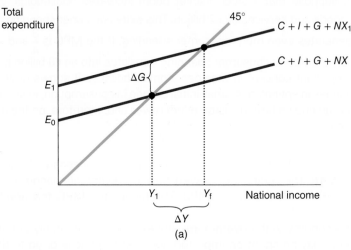

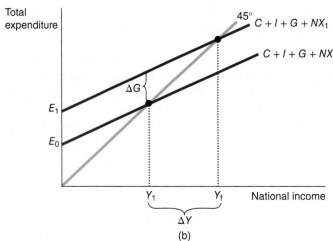

Equilibrium of Planned Withdrawals and Injections

Seeing the economy from the perspective of withdrawals and injections is helpful to understand how demand management might work. Let us start with the national income identity:

$$\text{Output} \equiv \text{Expenditure} \equiv \text{Income}$$

We know from Chapter 24 that in a closed economy $S = I$ with savings a withdrawal and investment an injection. We can extend this analysis to state that in equilibrium, in an open economy with a government, planned withdrawals would equal planned injections:

$$\text{Planned } S + T + M = \text{Planned } I + G + X$$

At this point all the output being produced by the economy would be 'bought' by households and firms. However, if actual withdrawals are greater than planned injections, then the economy would be experiencing a deficiency in demand. For example, assume that full employment output, (Y_f) is €120 billion. Withdrawals are a function of income; assume that S, T and M have the following values:

$$
\begin{aligned}
S &= 0.1Y \\
T &= 0.2Y \\
M &= 0.2Y
\end{aligned}
$$

Such that if income increased by €1, savings would change by 0.1 × 1 = 10 cents and so on. Now assume that investment is €20 billion, government spending also €20 billion and the value of exports is €10 billion. Given these figures the equilibrium level of national income would be:

$$
\begin{aligned}
\text{Planned } S + T + M &= \text{Planned } I + G + X \\
0.1Y + 0.2 + 0.2Y &= 20 + 20 + 10 \\
0.5Y &= 50 \text{ This implies that:} \\
Y &= 100
\end{aligned}
$$

This equilibrium is below the level of full employment output by €20 billion. The government could manage demand to achieve full employment output in different ways. It could increase its spending by €10 billion and through the multiplier effect see Y rise to €120 billion.

$$
\begin{aligned}
\text{Planned } S + T + M &= \text{Planned } I + G + X \\
0.1Y + 0.2Y + 0.2Y &= 20 + 30 + 10 \\
0.5Y &= 60 \text{ This implies that:} \\
Y &= 120
\end{aligned}
$$

In an open economy, the government might not simply target full employment but might wish to reduce net exports. For example, assume Y_f = €120 billion, the value of exports is given as €10 billion but the value of imports would be $0.2Y$ and so would be €24 billion (0.2 × 120). If the government wanted to reduce net exports to zero it might cut government spending but change tax rates so that the MPT increases. If government spending was cut to 5 and the marginal propensity to tax raised to 0.4 then the government could achieve zero net exports:

$$
\begin{aligned}
\text{Planned } S + T + M &= \text{Planned } I + G + X \\
0.1Y + 0.4Y + 0.2Y &= 20 + 5 + 10 \\
0.7Y &= 35 \text{ This implies that:} \\
Y &= 50
\end{aligned}
$$

It is clear that the policy to reduce net exports has had a severe effect on national income. One of the features of demand management is that it is possible for governments to use fiscal policy to achieve desired output levels but there will be consequences for other areas of the economy which may have more long-term effects.

If government sets policy to achieve a reduction in unemployment through boosting the economy, then net exports would fall and the country would be running a trade deficit $(NX < 0)$. We saw in Chapter 30 that trade influences net capital outflow and the exchange rate. Changes in the exchange rate affect the competitiveness of firms in the economy and so even though the government might reduce unemployment, its policy causes longer term effects which might cause it to have to alter policy to deal with these effects (such as a currency crisis) which in turn might reduce income and increase unemployment again.

THE IS AND LM CURVES

The Keynesian cross gives us a picture of the economy in short-run equilibrium. (Note, if you access a copy of Keynes' *General Theory* you might be surprised to see a complete absence of Keynesian cross diagrams. The use of these diagrams was developed by later economists to help portray Keynes' ideas.) In equilibrium, planned expenditure equals income ($E = Y$). This equilibrium is referred to as equilibrium in the *goods market*. We have also seen, in Chapter 28, how equilibrium in the money market is given by the intersection of the demand for money and the supply of money. At this point, we consider the concept of **real money balances** – what money can actually buy or the real value of money, given by the ratio of the money supply (M) to the price level P, $\dfrac{M}{P}$.

> **real money balances** what money can actually buy given the ratio of the money supply to the price level $\dfrac{M}{P}$.

The goods market and the money market are both interrelated with the linking factor being the interest rate. Following Keynes' analysis of the goods market and the money market (via the liquidity preference theory which we will look at in more detail in a later chapter), Nobel Prize-winning economist John Hicks, developed a theory that described the links between the two and showed how changes in both fiscal and monetary policy could be analyzed. The framework for this analysis is known as the IS–LM model.

IS–LM describes equilibrium in these two markets and together determines a *general equilibrium* in the economy. General equilibrium in the economy occurs at the point where the goods market and money market are both in equilibrium at a particular interest rate and level of income. The remainder of this chapter will provide an introduction to the IS–LM model. The model forms the basis of many intermediate courses in macroeconomics, although some have argued that it is now outdated and fails to represent how the modern economy works, particularly since the Financial Crisis. We will look at an alternative representation of the model that seeks to take into account some of these objections. Regardless of the debates about the validity of the model, it does represent a useful way of understanding how the goods and money markets interact and, as an exercise in analytical thinking, is helpful in seeing the effects of monetary and fiscal policy on the macroeconomy.

IS stands for investment and saving; LM stands for liquidity and money. The link between these two markets is the rate of interest (i).

The IS Curve

The IS curve shows the relationship between the interest rate and level of income (Y) in the goods market. In Figure 32.3, panel (a) shows the Keynesian cross diagram from Figure 32.2, with equilibrium point *a* where the expenditure line $C + I + G + NX$ crosses the 45-degree line. Panel (b) shows the IS curve. On the vertical axis is the rate of interest and on the horizontal axis is output (national income). The equilibrium point *a* in panel (a) is associated with a rate of interest i_1. This is plotted as point *a** on panel (b). If interest rates fall then the expenditure line shifts upwards to the left and there will be a new equilibrium point *b* where the expenditure line $C + I + G + NX_1$ crosses the 45-degree line. This is plotted as *b** on panel (b), showing the equilibrium of the goods market at a lower interest rate associated with a higher level of national income. If we connect these two points we get the IS curve. The curve connects all possible points of equilibrium in the goods market associated with a particular interest rate and level of national income.

The IS curve shows an inverse relationship between the interest rate and output – a fall in interest rates leads to a rise in income and vice versa. The rise in income will be dependent on the size of the interest rate change and the size of the multiplier. The slope of the IS curve is determined by the responsiveness of consumption and investment ($C + I$) to changes in interest rates. This is important because it leads to different outcomes; where economists tend to disagree is the *extent* to which $C + I$ are responsive to changes in interest rates rather than any disagreement about validity of the relationship of $C + I$ and the interest rate. The more responsive $C + I$ are, the flatter the IS curve.

FIGURE 32.3

The IS Curve

The IS curve is derived from the Keynesian cross diagram and shows all possible points of equilibrium in the goods market associated with a particular interest rate and level of income. In panel (a) initial equilibrium is where the C + I + G + NX line crosses the 45-degree line at point a. This point is plotted on the IS curve as point a*. An increase in C + I + G + NX to C + I + G + NX₁ shows a new equilibrium point in the goods market, b, which is plotted on the IS curve as b*. These two points are connected to form the IS curve.

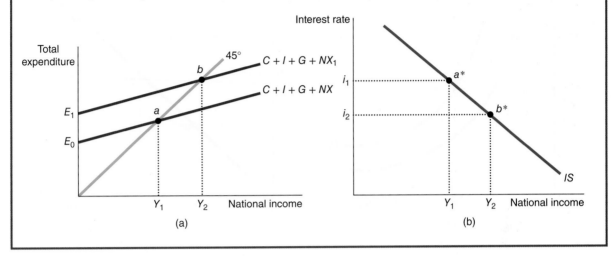

Shifts in the IS Curve Shifts in the IS curve come about as a result of changes in autonomous expenditure. If, for example, government spending rises, this occurs independent of any change in interest rates. A rise in autonomous spending would be associated with a shift in the IS curve to the right – the prevailing interest rate would now be associated with a higher level of income. Equally, if autonomous spending fell then the IS curve would shift to the left, showing a lower level of income at the prevailing interest rate.

The LM Curve

The LM curve shows all points where the money market is in equilibrium given a combination of the rate of interest and national income. In Figure 32.4, panel (a) shows the money market with the demand for money inversely related to the interest rate. The money supply is shown as a vertical line and it is assumed that the money supply is fixed by the central bank. Equilibrium in the money market is where the demand for money (D_m) curve intersects the money supply curve (M_s), at point a in panel (a) at interest rate i_1, and a quantity of real money balances M. Panel (b) shows the LM curve with the interest rate on the vertical axis and national income on the horizontal axis. The equilibrium point, a, in the money market is plotted as point a^* in panel (b). Increases in income will have an effect on the demand for money and assuming the money supply is fixed, will affect the equilibrium interest rate. Assume that national income rises; the demand for money curve in panel (a) would shift to the right to D_{m1}, indicating that the public wish to hold higher money balances at all interest rates. At the prevailing interest rate the demand for money is now higher than the supply of money and so the interest rate would rise. The new equilibrium in the money market is given as point b and this is plotted on the LM diagram as point b^*. If we connect the two points we get the LM curve. The LM curve plots all combinations of interest rates and national income where the money market is in equilibrium.

FIGURE 32.4

The LM Curve

The LM curve shows all points where the money market is in equilibrium given a combination of the rate of interest and national income. In panel (a), the money market is in equilibrium where the demand for money (D_m) equals the supply of money (M_s) at point a. This point is plotted on the LM curve in panel (b) as point a*. An increase in the demand for money causes a shift of the curve to the right to D_{m1} with a new equilibrium point of b. This is plotted on panel (b) as point b* and the points connected to form the LM curve.

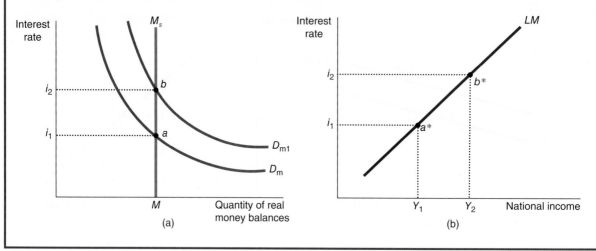

The LM curve has a positive slope showing that an increase in income is associated with an increase in the interest rate and vice versa. The slope of the LM curve will be dependent on the responsiveness of the demand for money to changes in interest rates. Again, the extent of this relationship is often a point of disagreement among economists.

Shifts in the LM Curve The LM curve can shift if the central bank expands or contracts the money supply (we will say more about how this might happen later in the chapter). Assuming income is held constant, a rise in the money supply (for example) will cause interest rates to fall and a new equilibrium will be reached at a given level of income. This would be associated with a shift of the LM curve downwards to the right showing a new combination of income and interest rate at which the money market is in equilibrium.

GENERAL EQUILIBRIUM USING THE IS–LM MODEL

Equilibrium is found where the IS curve intersects the LM curve. Remember that any point on either curve describes a point of equilibrium in the goods market and the money market at a rate of interest and level of national income. In Figure 32.5, the point where the IS curve intersects the LM curve gives a point where both markets are in equilibrium at an interest rate i_e and a level of national income Y_e. Hence, it follows that at this point planned expenditure equals actual expenditure ($E = Y$), and the demand for money equals the supply of money $D_m = M_s$.

Having established this general equilibrium, we can use the model to analyze the impact of fiscal and monetary policy changes in an attempt to stabilize the economy and how these two policies are interrelated. Further analysis of both policies will be covered in the next chapter but this uses our model of IS–LM. The detail of IS–LM analysis is beyond the scope of this book, being found in most intermediate courses in macroeconomics. However, the remainder of this chapter will introduce some of the key implications of the model.

FIGURE 32.5

General Equilibrium
Equilibrium in the economy is found where the IS curve intersects with the LM curve. At this point both the goods market and the money market are in equilibrium at a particular interest rate, i_e, and level of national income, Y_e.

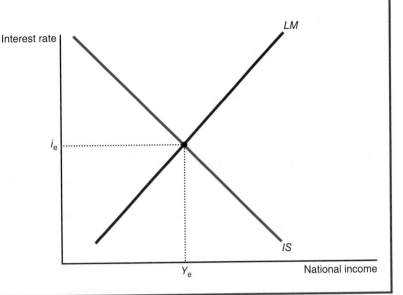

The Effect of a Change in Fiscal Policy

Assume that the government chooses to increase spending to boost economic activity. This increase in autonomous expenditure shifts the IS curve to the right as shown in panel (a) of Figure 32.6. The result is that national income will rise but there will also be an increase in interest rates. A similar outcome would occur if the government chose to cut taxes as the means of boosting the economy. The result of either policy would be dependent on the marginal propensity to withdraw and the size of the multiplier. The opposite would occur if the government chose to cut spending or increase taxes – national income and interest rates would both fall.

FIGURE 32.6

The Effects of Fiscal and Monetary Policy
In panel (a), a rise in government spending shifts the IS curve to the right resulting in a new equilibrium with a higher interest rate and level of national income. In panel (b), an increase in the money supply would shift the LM curve to the right and a new equilibrium would result in a lower interest rate and higher level of national income.

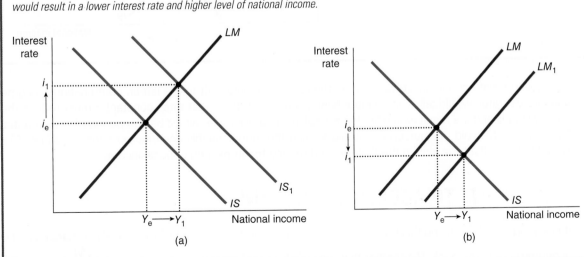

The Effect of a Change in Monetary Policy

If the central bank decided to expand the money supply the LM curve would shift to the right to LM_1 as shown in panel (b) of Figure 32.6. The new equilibrium would lead to a lower interest rate and a higher level of national income. The reverse outcome would occur if the central bank tightened monetary policy by reducing the money supply.

Fiscal and Monetary Policy Interactions In reality, central banks do not act totally in isolation of government even if they are independent. Central banks will be aware of what governments are doing as we will see when we look at the Case for an Active Stabilization Policy in Chapter 34. This presents a model to analyze the response of the central bank. The Bank of England and the ECB have a responsibility to maintain price stability and this may be presented in the form of a target for inflation. Central banks will be monitoring the effect of fiscal policy changes on the economy and how these changes might affect inflationary pressures. These inflationary pressures can be influenced by the central bank's control over short-term interest rates through the rate at which it lends to the financial system. Governments may wish to implement fiscal policy with the aim of influencing unemployment, for example. Such a policy may have effects on inflationary pressures which the central bank wants to nullify.

Let us assume that the government reduces taxation to encourage more people to take jobs in the economy or to increase spending through consumers having more disposable income. The IS curve would shift to the right as shown in Figure 32.7 and national income and interest rates would rise. If the central bank wants to keep interest rates constant it must expand the money supply. By doing so the LM curve shifts to the right to LM_1, national income would rise further than if the central bank had not acted, to Y_2, and the interest rate will remain at its initial level. If the bank had not altered the money supply, then the effects of the reduction in tax would have been partially offset by a rise in interest rates which would have curbed spending.

FIGURE 32.7

Maintaining Interest Rates Constant Following a Shift in the *IS* Curve
A shift in the IS curve to the right would, without central bank action, lead to a rise in the interest rate and in national income. If the central bank wants to maintain the interest rate it must increase the money supply and shift the LM curve to the right. The result would be to maintain the interest rate at i_e but the increase in national income would be greater than if the central bank had not acted.

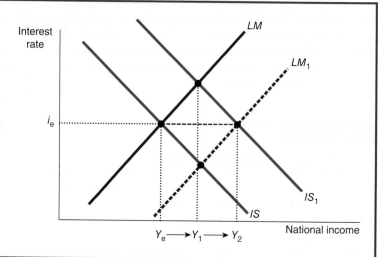

If government had increased taxes, then the IS curve would shift to the left and both national income and interest rates would fall. If the central bank wants to keep interest rates constant it must reduce the money supply and the result would be that the fall in national income would be compounded. If the central bank wanted to avoid this outcome, it could expand the money supply and interest rates would fall. This would help to offset the shift in the IS curve and reduce the impact on national income.

FROM IS–LM TO AGGREGATE DEMAND

It is a short step from using this model to the AD and AS model that we will use to analyze changes in the economy later in the book. Remember that the supply of real money balances is given by $\frac{M}{P}$. Assume the average price of a unit of output in the economy is €10 and the money supply is €100 billion. The supply of real money balances is $\frac{100}{10} = 10$; that is, at the current price level the supply of money in the economy can buy 10 units of output. If the average price of a unit of output in the economy rises to €20 and the money supply is constant, real money balances will fall to 5 units $\left(\frac{100}{20} = 5\right)$. This fall in the supply of real money balances shifts the LM curve to the left as shown in panel (a) of Figure 32.8. The result is that interest rates rise and national income falls. There is, therefore, an inverse relationship between the price level and national income. The AD curve is derived by plotting the relationship between national income and the price level as shown in panel (b) of Figure 32.8. The AD curve slopes downwards from left to right because of the inverse relationship between the price level and national income.

FIGURE 32.8

Deriving the Aggregate Demand Curve

In panel (a) a rise in the price level reduces real money balances and shifts the LM curve to the left to LM_1. This leads to a rise in the equilibrium interest rate to i_1 and a fall in national income from Y_0 to Y_1. The inverse relationship between the price level and national income is plotted in panel (b). A rise in the price level from P_0 to P_1, leads to a fall in national income from Y_0 to Y_1. The aggregate demand curve slopes downwards from left to right.

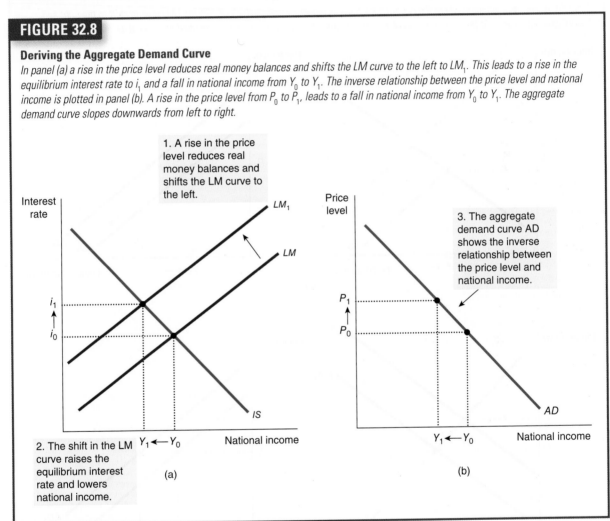

1. A rise in the price level reduces real money balances and shifts the LM curve to the left.

2. The shift in the LM curve raises the equilibrium interest rate and lowers national income.

(a)

3. The aggregate demand curve AD shows the inverse relationship between the price level and national income.

(b)

Shifts in the Aggregate Demand Curve If we assume the price level remains constant, a change in national income in the IS–LM model will result in a shift in the AD curve. Changes in both fiscal and monetary policy, assuming a given constant price level, will cause the AD curve to shift. If the government imposes an austerity package which seeks to cut government spending and raise taxes at a given price level, the IS curve will shift to the left and national income will fall. At the given price level, AD in the economy will now be less and the AD curve will shift to the left as shown in panel (a) of Figure 32.9.

If the central bank expands the money supply (possibly through a programme of asset purchasing or quantitative easing) the LM curve will shift to the right and national income will rise. At the given price level, the AD curve will shift to the right showing a higher level of national income at the given price level as shown in panel (b) of Figure 32.9.

A loosening of fiscal policy (increased government spending and/or lower taxes) and a reduction in the money supply (a tightening of monetary policy) will have the opposite effect to that described in Figure 32.9 respectively.

FIGURE 32.9

Shifts in the Aggregate Demand Curve as a Result of Monetary and Fiscal Policy
Panel (a) represents a situation where the government tightens fiscal policy which shifts the IS curve to the left and reduces national income. At a given price level, the AD curve shifts to the left and a lower level of national income is associated with the given price level.
Panel (b) represents a situation where the central bank loosens monetary policy which causes the LM curve to shift to the right and lowers national income. At the given price level, the AD curve shifts to the right with a higher level of national income.

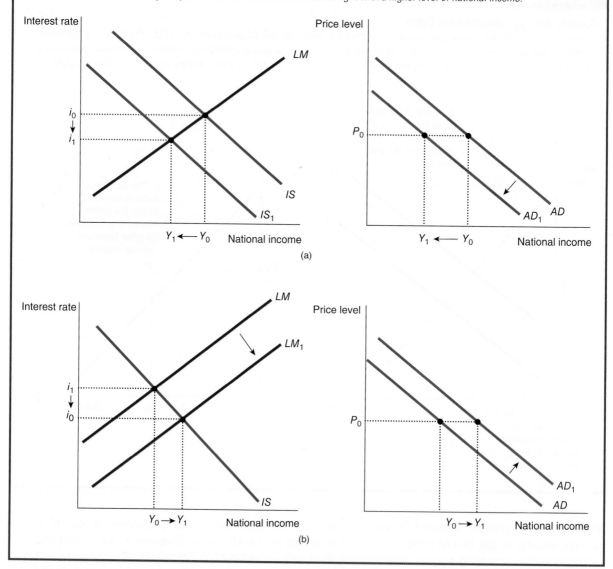

Criticisms of IS–LM and the Romer Model

This short introduction to IS–LM analysis and the effect of changes in fiscal and monetary policy helps to highlight a number of important issues that you may start to consider as your study of economics moves to the next level. The effects of changes in fiscal and monetary policy are dependent on a number of factors related to the slope of the IS and LM curves, their relative position and how far each shifts in response to changes in policy. It is entirely possible that a change in fiscal policy can be countered by a change in monetary policy that leaves national income unchanged. The potential outcomes are many and economists try to pinpoint more accurately what changes in policy will mean for the economy as a whole. This means conducting research to quantify such changes. The outcome of such research will be dependent on the value of variables that economists input into their models and on the relative strength of factors affecting the variables in the model.

One example of how the model has developed is the role which microeconomic analysis plays in understanding the macroeconomy. Some economists argue that microeconomic principles cannot be divorced from the macroeconomy. We have seen in Chapter 31 how changing economic conditions may lead to wages and prices adjusting at different rates and markets being slow to clear as a result. If national income falls, for example, the assumption might be that prices and wages in the economy would also fall to help bring markets back into equilibrium. As we will see in the next chapter, these sticky wages and prices may lag behind the reduction in economic activity as firms may be forced into trying to maintain cash flow rather than seeking to expand market share. As prices are sticky, sales fall and firms cut back output which further impacts on economic activity.

Professor Mankiw was one of the economists who helped to reconcile the idea of sticky prices and menu costs with rational behaviour in his paper, 'Small menu costs and large business cycles: A macroeconomic model of monopoly', published in *The Quarterly Journal of Economics* in 1985. The debate over IS–LM has continued and has generated large amounts of valuable and interesting research which has helped build our understanding of the economy as a whole. It still has its critics, however.

Indeed, one such disagreement focuses on a central assumption of the model itself. Some higher education institutions have questioned the value of teaching IS–LM at all because they argue that the world is now a very different place to the one Hicks knew back in the 1930s when he first developed Keynes' ideas. One of the major criticisms is that central banks no longer control the money supply but instead set interest rates. Attempts to control the money supply have proved to be difficult and so targeting the interest rate is seen as being a more viable option to achieve policy objectives.

In Chapter 27 we looked at how central banks set interest rates through open market operations. If the central bank wishes to reduce interest rates, its traders will be instructed to buy bonds. Banks and financial institutions who sell these bonds will receive funds in return which will effectively expand the money supply. This in turn shifts the LM curve to the right and interest rates fall. If the central bank increases interest rates the opposite occurs; traders will be instructed to sell bonds and thus take funds out of the banking system, reducing the money supply. The LM curve shifts to the left and interest rates rise.

The IS–MP Model One of Professor Mankiw's close colleagues, David Romer (indeed they are more than simply colleagues given that each was best man at the other's wedding), has suggested an approach termed the IS–MP model, which attempts to build on the IS–LM model to reflect how central banks and the economy work today. The assumption in the model is that central banks adjust the money supply as outlined above to generate the interest rate that they want. The interest rate is adjusted in accordance with the inflation target that the central bank is working with or, as is the case with the Bank of England, has been set by the government. In the IS–LM model the money supply is assumed to be exogenous (determined by factors outside the model). In the IS–MP model, the monetary policy reaction function is exogenous. Romer assumes that when output rises, the central bank increases interest rates to dampen inflationary pressures; and it reduces interest rates when output falls in order to maintain the price level at its target. National income is a positive function of the interest rate, therefore. Romer plots this upward sloping relationship as the MP curve. The MP function is assumed to be exogenous but in reality both the money supply and the MP function can and do change in response to economic activity and events.

The MP function takes into account the fact that central banks now target inflation and set interest rates to achieve this goal rather than simply assuming government (or a central bank) sets the money supply and that interest rates adjust to balance this supply of money with the demand for money. Crucially, Romer suggests that changes in inflation can cause a shift of the MP curve. If the central bank increases interest rates the money supply will fall which will affect the price level and expectations on inflation.

Equally, if the central bank cuts interest rates the money supply will rise and expectations on inflation will also change as a result.

It is at this point where the microeconomic element of the analysis takes on some importance. Expectations of price changes may not match the reality because of the extent of price stickiness. If we assume that prices are completely sticky (i.e. the price level is fixed) they will not change when the money supply changes. Expectations on inflation will, therefore, be zero. If the money supply rises then the supply of real money balances, $\frac{M}{P}$, also rises and is greater than the demand for real money balances. As the money market is now out of equilibrium we might expect the interest rate to fall but it could also be that the level of income could rise, or a combination of the two might occur. There will be a movement along the IS curve and a fall in interest rates will be accompanied by a rise in national income. This implies that the central bank can directly control the real interest rate by adjusting money supply appropriately to achieve the interest rate it desires.

If prices adjusted instantaneously then a change in the money supply would not affect the supply of real money balances because the ratio $\frac{M}{P}$ would hold as before at the rate of interest and level of income; in other words the money market would remain in equilibrium. There would be no movement along the IS curve and the central bank would not be able to affect the real interest rate.

In reality prices are not fixed, but the speed with which prices adjust to changes in economic conditions will vary – some will adjust relatively quickly, others will take much longer and will be sticky. These sticky prices will influence the ratio of the money supply to the price level (the supply of real money balances) and so there may be some expectations of inflation which will exist in the economy because M will rise by a greater proportion than P. An increase in the money supply will raise expected inflation and vice versa. If prices are sticky then an increase in the nominal money supply will cause the money market to move out of equilibrium but expected inflation will affect the real interest rate. The nominal interest rate may have to be higher as a result.

The extent to which prices are sticky, therefore, has an important influence on the way in which a central bank can influence the interest rate to achieve its inflation targets. Such an analysis raises interesting questions when interest rates are reduced as was the case in response to the Financial Crisis and the global recession in 2008–9. The UK, Europe and the US saw their central banks reducing interest rates to historically low levels. To reduce interest rates the central bank instructs its traders to buy bonds and the money supply will rise. Increases in the money supply may be associated with an increase in the price level; indeed, some economists have expressed alarm at the scale of quantitative easing conducted by central banks and have predicted accelerating inflation. In times where economic activity is restrained, however, expectations of inflation may remain subdued and the money market may remain out of equilibrium as a result. The reason is that at these low interest rates people are willing to hold a greater amount of real money balances without any change in interest rate or output – after all, the interest rate cannot fall much further. This is the *liquidity trap* which is covered in the next chapter and may imply that monetary policy can have little effect on stimulating economic growth.

SELF TEST Draw diagrams to show the effect on interest rates and the level of national income of: (a) a decision by the government to raise taxes to cut a public deficit; and (b) a decision by a central bank to increase interest rates.

A Return to Keynesianism?

The Financial Crisis of 2007–9 reignited the debate about the value of Keynesian demand management policies. A number of countries introduced fiscal stimulus packages in the wake of the Financial Crisis. This led to questions about the benefits of such packages and even whether they amount to a stimulus. In late 2008 the EU announced a fiscal stimulus package of €200 billion. In the UK the Chancellor of the Exchequer had to admit that government borrowing might reach £175 billion, and be 79 per cent of GDP in 2013–14 (in the latter part of 2012 it stood at 73 per cent of GDP). In the US the package was reported to be $800 billion; meanwhile, China was reported to be injecting $585 billion and Japan $275 billion. Critics argued that such packages were not enough to bridge the output gap that had widened in most economies. In the US, for example, the gap between potential and actual GDP was estimated by some economists at around $2 trillion. Other criticisms of fiscal stimulus packages suggested that they were not really what they seemed to be and if they were, then they would not bring the benefits that were claimed for them because of crowding out.

For example, in a study of the EU stimulus package in February 2009, David Saha and Jakob von Weizsäcker said, 'It should be recognized that the likely real impact on aggregate demand in the near future may well be more limited than suggested by the headline figures' (http://aei.pitt.edu/10549/1/UPDATED-SIZE-OF-STIMULUS-FINAL.pdf). In their analysis of the fiscal stimulus in Italy, announced as €80 billion, Saha and Weizsäcker conclude that the stimulus was not a stimulus at all but a fiscal tightening amounting to €0.3 billion. In parts of Europe there were concerns that any major fiscal stimulus package would put pressure on the public debt and affect the stability of the euro, around which so much of the future prosperity of the EU lies.

One of the concerns about any fiscal stimulus is the extent to which it creates 'real wealth'. Governments may spend more money but on what? If the money is spent on public works – the building of new schools, hospitals, roads and so on, then surely this would boost AD? To an extent it would, but how is this additional spending to be financed? To raise the money governments will either have to tax their citizens more or increase borrowing. Additional spending on the construction of a new road may put money into the pockets of construction companies and its workers, but to fund this the government has to tax other wealth producers, thus offsetting some of the benefits of the stimulus. If the spending goes on additional benefits for those who become unemployed then critics argue that the government is not contributing to wealth creation; these individuals may be supported in times of hardship and may spend their benefits on food and other goods but they are not actually generating any wealth in return for the benefits they receive. Indeed, Keynes himself acknowledged that there were limitations to stimulus packages. In an article in *The Times* newspaper in the UK in 1937, a year after the *General Theory* was published, he wrote:

> But I believe that we are approaching, or have reached, the point where there is not much advantage in applying a further general stimulus at the centre … It follows that the later stages of recovery require a different technique. To remedy the condition of the distressed areas ad hoc measures are necessary. The Jarrow marchers were, so to speak, theoretically correct … We are in more need today of a rightly distributed demand than of a greater aggregate demand.

Structural changes in the economy might require more long-term investment if improvements in unemployment prospects and growth are to be achieved.

If governments have to borrow more then crowding out may emerge. In this scenario, the government is competing with the private sector for funds. Since the supply of loanable funds is finite, if governments take more of these funds it is argued that there will be less available for the private sector. If it is also assumed that the private sector uses such investment funds more efficiently than the public sector, then not only do fiscal stimulus packages crowd out private investment they divert investment funds to less productive uses.

Krugman and Crowding In Whilst this view is accepted by some economists, there are those that suggest that extraordinary times call for extraordinary action. One such proponent of this view is Paul Krugman. Krugman has consistently argued that the depth of the Financial Crisis and global recession was such that a fiscal stimulus was necessary to get out of a liquidity trap and far from crowding out, fiscal stimuli would lead to 'crowding in'. A liquidity trap occurs when monetary policy is insufficient to generate the economic stimulus necessary to get out of recession. In the US and UK, for example, interest rates were lowered by the Fed and the Bank of England to near zero, the Bank of Japan's key interest rate stood at 0.1 per cent in August 2009 whilst the ECB had rates at 1 per cent.

Krugman argues that private investment is a function of the state of the economy and, given the depth of the global recession, investment has plummeted. Investment, therefore, in this situation is more responsive to product demand than to the rate of interest. If governments applied appropriate fiscal stimuli, this would improve the state of the economy and thus encourage private sector investment. As private sector investment increases, this improves productive potential and helps bring economies out of recession. Far from crowding out, Krugman argues, the fiscal stimulus would lead to crowding in.

Critics of this view suggest that increased government spending will crowd out private investment to an extent and so any fiscal stimulus has to take into account the loss of the benefits of that private investment in assessing the success of such a policy. The success of a stimulus package in putting economies on a sounder footing and bringing benefits to future generations would be highly dependent on the type of spending carried out by governments worldwide. Spending on new schools and transport infrastructure may improve the future productive potential of the economy and tackle the structural problems that exist in some economies as referred to above.

However, the issues of rent seeking and logrolling have to be taken into consideration. Remember that rent seeking occurs where decisions are made leading to resource allocation that maximizes the benefit to the decision maker at the expense of another party or parties, and log rolling is where decisions may be made on resource allocation to projects that have less importance, in return for the support of the interested party in other decision-making areas. In both cases, it is argued that resource allocation is not as efficient as that carried out by the private sector and this has to be taken into consideration in assessing the benefits of public sector spending as a result of any stimulus package.

CONCLUSION

There is still much debate on Keynesian approaches in macroeconomics in addition to the debate on the value and relevance of the IS–LM model. What is not in much doubt is that an understanding of the relationship between the goods market and the money market is a useful way of developing a broader understanding of analyzing the economy as a whole. This short introduction to such analysis provides some pointers to the IS–LM model and to some of the issues that economists are debating. Depending on the university that you attend, a greater or lesser emphasis may be placed on the IS–LM model. Having some awareness of the model does help to develop a focus on the important connections between the money supply, interest rates and economic activity.

IN THE NEWS

Austerity and Growth

The Financial Crisis led to renewed interest in Keynesian economics. In many countries, however, high levels of borrowing and debt were problems which had to be tackled. Austerity policies including cuts to public spending and tax increases, were introduced to help deal with these problems.

Expansionary Austerity or Keynesian Intervention?

Professor Lord Robert Skidelsky is professor of political economy at the University of Warwick in the UK and a renowned admirer of Keynes. He has written extensively about the wisdom of austerity policies, which many countries introduced in the aftermath of the Financial Crisis. The UK has attempted to cut the budget deficit by raising taxes and cutting public spending but despite many people suffering a great deal of hardship as a result of these policies, the deficit has not shrunk to the level initially forecast by the then-Chancellor, George Osborne.

In early January 2016, Osborne noted 'economic headwinds' which would impact on the recovery in the UK. These headwinds included the slowdown in growth in China, problems in the so-called BRIC countries, low oil prices, weak economic growth in Europe and the political problems across the Middle East. Skidelsky acknowledged these problems but suggested that austerity had left the UK in a weaker position to meet these challenges. He noted that the interest in Keynes in the immediate aftermath of the Crisis had been short-lived and after some initial fiscal impetus, Keynesian policies had been eclipsed by a move to austerity. Austerity, he claimed, had led to a fragile and weak recovery. The government is not pursuing expansionary fiscal policies because of a fear that the financial markets will react against further increases in the deficit, pushing yields down as fear of default increases.

Economic growth in the UK had been relatively strong throughout 2014 and 2015 at over 2 per cent and the output gap, according to the OECD, was at -0.017 per cent. This might suggest that the UK economy was in a strong position to manage the 'headwinds' but Skidelsky disagreed. He noted that productivity has remained well below pre-Crisis levels and anything up to 15 per cent below where it might have been expected to be, according to historical trends. If the output gap is small, then the capacity of the UK economy must have shrunk, according to Skidelsky; in other words, AS has shifted to the left.

Skidelsky attributes this to the length of the recession which led to a lack of investment, a dysfunctional banking system and high levels of unemployment. These hangover effects of recession have, he argues, led to a fall in the productive capacity of the UK. The remedy for this problem, according to Skidelsky, is for government to invest more in capital spending projects which boost future productive capacity. There is no reason, he argues, that such spending should not be covered by borrowing. The focus on balancing the budget and austerity obscures the true state of the economy and prolongs the fragility of the recovery.

Questions

1 Use the concept of the multiplier to explain how cuts in government spending and higher taxes are likely to lead to a fall in national income.

2 Some 'Keynesian' impetus had been used by several governments in the wake of the Financial Crisis. Use diagrams to show how such impetus is designed to affect the economy.

3 Outline why governments such as that in the UK believe that there is no viable alternative to austerity if longer term sustainable growth is to be achieved.

4 Why does a shrinking output gap and lower productivity suggest a reduction in the UK's capacity to produce?

5 Why would borrowing for spending on capital investment be seen as a better way of boosting economic growth than continuing to focus on reducing the deficit?

Professor Lord Robert Skidelsky is an acknowledged expert on Keynes.

SUMMARY

● Keynes developed The General Theory as a response to the mass unemployment which existed in the 1930s.

● He advocated governments intervene to boost demand through influencing aggregate demand.

● The Keynesian cross diagram shows how the economy can be in equilibrium when $E = Y$.

● This equilibrium may not be sufficient to deliver full employment output and so the government can attempt to boost demand to help achieve full employment.

● John Hicks developed Keynes' ideas in the form of the IS–LM model which shows general equilibrium in the economy.

● The IS (investment–saving) curve shows all points of equilibrium in the goods market at a particular interest rate and level of national income.

● The LM (liquidity–money supply) curve shows points where the money market is in equilibrium at particular rates of interest and level of national income.

- General equilibrium occurs where the IS curve intersects the LM curve. At this interest rate and level of national income, both the goods market and money market are in equilibrium.

- Fiscal policy and monetary policy can cause shifts in the IS and LM curves bringing about new equilibrium positions. The outcome will depend on a variety of factors including the response of consumption and investment to changes in interest rates and the public's response to holding monetary balances as a result of a change in interest rates.

- There have been criticisms that the IS–LM model does not represent the way monetary policy is conducted in modern economies.

- Economists have developed new models to incorporate the changes in policy.

QUESTIONS FOR REVIEW

1 Distinguish between planned expenditure and actual expenditure.

2 Draw a Keynesian cross diagram to show the effects of a rise in autonomous expenditure on an economy operating below full employment output.

3 What is meant by the terms: *inflationary gap* and *deflationary gap*?

4 What is the marginal propensity to consume?

5 Why does the $MPC + MPS = 1$?

6 What is the multiplier? Can the multiplier be negative as well as positive? Explain.

7 Explain how the marginal propensity to withdraw affects the outcome of a rise in autonomous expenditure.

8 Use diagrams to describe how the IS and LM curves are derived.

9 Using the IS–LM model, explain the effect on the economy of a reduction in autonomous expenditure resulting from a cut in public spending by the government.

10 A central bank wishes to reduce inflationary expectations by increasing interest rates. Use the IS–MP model to analyze the effect on the economy of such a move.

PROBLEMS AND APPLICATIONS

1 What, according to Keynes, was the main reason why recessions and depressions occurred? As a result of identifying this key reason, what did Keynes suggest was an appropriate policy repose?

2 Explain, using an appropriate diagram, how a deflationary gap can occur and how this gap can be eliminated.

3 Suppose economists observe that an increase in government spending of €10 billion raises the total demand for goods and services by €30 billion.

    a. If these economists ignore the possibility of crowding out, what would they estimate the MPC to be?

    b. Now suppose economists allow for crowding out. Would their new estimate of the MPC be larger or smaller than their initial one? Explain your answer.

4 Suppose the government reduces taxes by €2 billion, that there is no crowding out and that the MPC is 0.75.

    a. What is the initial effect of the tax reduction on AD?

    b. What additional effects follow this initial effect? What is the total effect of the tax cut on AD?

    c. How does the total effect of this €2 billion tax cut compare to the total effect of a €2 billion increase in government purchases? Why?

5 Assume the economy is in equilibrium. Analyze the effect of a cut in autonomous expenditure on economic activity and the level of unemployment. You should use a diagram to help illustrate your answer.

6 What does the IS curve show? What does the LM curve show?

7 What determines the slope of the IS curve? What determines the slope of the LM curve? In relation to your answer to these questions, explain why these determinants can be a source of disagreement amongst economists?

8 Use the IS–LM model to explain the following:

   a. The government institutes significant cuts in public expenditure.

   b. The central bank institutes an asset purchasing facility (quantitative easing) which expands the money supply by €300 billion.

   c. The central bank fears that inflationary pressures are rising and increases interest rates.

   d. The government increases taxation to try and reduce a large budget deficit.

9 Assume that a period of deflation leads to a rise in the supply of real money balances. Explain the effect of this change on the economy using the IS–LM model and then what effect it would have on AD and why.

10 Do you think that Keynes' ideas still have some relevance today? Explain.

33 AGGREGATE DEMAND AND AGGREGATE SUPPLY

Although there remains some debate among economists about how to analyze short-run fluctuations, in this chapter we will look at the *model of aggregate demand (AD) and aggregate supply (AS)*, which is widely used among economists to analyze the short-run effects of various events and policies.

THREE KEY FACTS ABOUT ECONOMIC FLUCTUATIONS

Short-run fluctuations in economic activity occur in all countries and at numerous times throughout history. As a starting point for understanding these year-to-year fluctuations, let's remind ourselves of some of their most important properties.

Fact 1: Economic Fluctuations are Irregular and Unpredictable

Economic fluctuations correspond to changes in business conditions. When real GDP grows rapidly, business is good. During such periods of economic expansion, firms find that customers are plentiful and that profits are growing. On the other hand, when real GDP falls, many firms experience declining sales and dwindling profits. We saw in Chapter 31 that economic fluctuations are not at all regular, and they are almost impossible to predict with much accuracy.

Fact 2: Most Macroeconomic Quantities Fluctuate Together

Real GDP is the variable that is most commonly used to monitor short-run changes in the economy. Real GDP measures the value of all final goods and services produced within a given period of time. It also measures the total income (adjusted for inflation) of everyone in the economy.

It turns out, however, that for monitoring short-run fluctuations, it does not really matter which measure of economic activity one looks at. Most macroeconomic variables that measure some type of income, spending or production, fluctuate closely together. When real GDP falls in a recession, so do personal income, corporate profits, consumer spending, investment spending, industrial production, retail sales, home sales, car sales and so on. Because recessions are economy-wide phenomena, they show up in many sources of macroeconomic data.

Although many macroeconomic variables fluctuate together, they fluctuate by different amounts. In particular, investment spending varies greatly over the business cycle. When economic conditions deteriorate, much of the decline is attributable to reductions in spending on new factories, housing and inventories. Investment in the UK, for example, fell by 5.1 per cent in 2008, by 11.4 per cent in 2009, and was just positive at 0.1 per cent in 2010 before another fall of 2.9 per cent in 2011.

Fact 3: As Output Falls, Unemployment Rises

Changes in the economy's output of goods and services are strongly correlated with changes in the economy's utilization of its labour force. In other words, when real GDP declines the rate of unemployment rises. The negative relationship between unemployment and real GDP is referred to as **Okun's law** after the Yale economist who published his observations in the 1960s. Okun noted that in order to keep the unemployment rate steady, real GDP needs to grow at or close to its potential. If the unemployment rate is to be reduced, real GDP must grow above potential. Being more specific, to reduce the unemployment rate by 1 per cent in a year, real GDP must rise by around 2 per cent more than potential GDP over the year.

> **Okun's law** a 'law' which is based on observations that in order to keep the unemployment rate steady, real GDP needs to grow at or close to its potential

Okun's findings are hardly surprising: when firms choose to produce a smaller quantity of goods and services, they lay off workers, expanding the pool of unemployed. However, there is generally a time-lag between any downturn in economic activity and a rise in unemployment and vice versa. Even when positive growth resumes, therefore, unemployment is likely to continue to rise for some time afterwards. As we noted in Chapter 31, unemployment is referred to as a 'lagged indicator'.

EXPLAINING SHORT-RUN ECONOMIC FLUCTUATIONS

Describing the patterns that economies experience as they fluctuate over time is easy. Explaining what causes these fluctuations is more difficult; the theory of economic fluctuations remains controversial. In this chapter and the next two chapters, we develop a model used to explain short-run fluctuations in economic activity.

How the Short Run Differs from the Long Run

In previous chapters we developed theories to explain what determines most important macroeconomic variables in the long run. We have looked at the level and growth of productivity and real GDP; explained how the financial system works and how the real interest rate adjusts to balance saving and investment; why there is always some unemployment in the economy; explained the monetary system and how changes in the money supply affect the price level, the inflation rate and the nominal interest rate; and then extended this analysis to open economies in order to explain the trade balance and the exchange rate.

All of this previous analysis was based on two related ideas – the *classical dichotomy* and *monetary neutrality*. Recall that the classical dichotomy is the separation of variables into real variables (those that measure quantities or relative prices) and nominal variables (those measured in terms of money). According to classical macroeconomic theory, changes in the money supply affect nominal variables but not real variables. As a result of this monetary neutrality, we were able to examine the determinants of real variables (real GDP, the real interest rate and unemployment) without introducing nominal variables (the money supply and the price level).

Do these assumptions of classical macroeconomic theory apply to the world in which we live? The answer to this question is of central importance to understanding how the economy works: many economists believe that classical theory describes the world in the long run but not in the short run. Beyond a period of several years, changes in the money supply affect prices and other nominal variables but do not affect real GDP, unemployment or other real variables. When studying year-to-year changes in the economy, however, the assumption of monetary neutrality is no longer appropriate. Many economists believe that, in the short run, real and nominal variables are highly intertwined. In particular, changes in the money supply can temporarily push output away from its long-run trend.

To understand the economy in the short run, therefore, we need a new model. To build this new model, we rely on many of the tools we have developed in previous chapters, but we have to abandon the classical dichotomy and the neutrality of money.

The Basic Model of Economic Fluctuations

Our model of short-run economic fluctuations focuses on the behaviour of two variables. The first variable is the economy's output of goods and services, as measured by real GDP. The second variable is the overall price level, an average of prices of all goods and services in an economy as measured by the CPI or the GDP deflator. Output is a real variable, whereas the price level is a nominal variable. Hence, by focusing on the relationship between these two variables, we are highlighting the breakdown of the classical dichotomy.

We analyze fluctuations in the economy as a whole with the **model of aggregate demand and aggregate supply**, which is illustrated in Figure 33.1. On the vertical axis is the overall price level in the economy. On the horizontal axis is the overall quantity of goods and services. The **aggregate demand curve** shows the quantity of goods and services that households, firms and the government want to buy at each price level. The **aggregate supply curve** shows the quantity of goods and services that firms produce and sell at each price level. According to this model, the price level and the quantity of output adjust to bring AD and AS into balance.

> **model of aggregate demand and aggregate supply** the model that many economists use to explain short-run fluctuations in economic activity around its long-run trend
>
> **aggregate demand curve** a curve that shows the quantity of goods and services that households, firms and the government want to buy at each price level
>
> **aggregate supply curve** a curve that shows the quantity of goods and services that firms choose to produce and sell at each price level

FIGURE 33.1

Aggregate Demand and Aggregate Supply

Economists use the model of AD and AS to analyze economic fluctuations. On the vertical axis is the overall level of prices. On the horizontal axis is the economy's total output of goods and services. Output and the price level adjust to the point at which the AS and AD curves intersect.

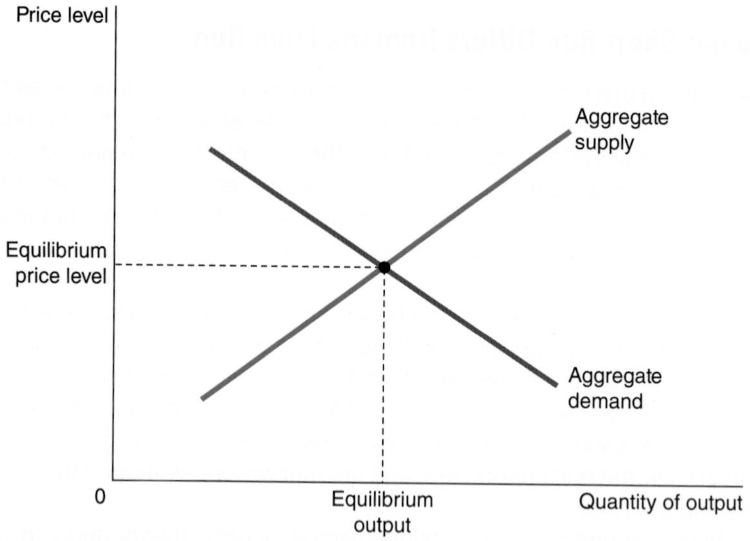

It may be tempting to view the model of AD and AS as nothing more than a large version of the model of market demand and market supply, which we introduced in Chapter 3; in fact, this model is quite different. When we consider demand and supply in a particular market for a good, such as tablet computers, the behaviour of buyers and sellers depends on the ability of resources to move from one market to another. When the price of tablet computers rises, the quantity demanded falls because buyers will use their incomes to buy products other than tablets. Similarly, a higher price of tablets raises the quantity supplied because firms that produce these gadgets can increase production by hiring workers away from other parts of the economy. This *microeconomic* substitution from one market to another is impossible when we are analyzing the economy as a whole. After all, the quantity that our model is trying to explain – real GDP – measures the <u>total</u> quantity produced in all of the economy's markets. To understand why the AD curve is downwards sloping and why the AS curve is upwards sloping, we need a *macroeconomic* theory. Developing such a theory is our next task.

SELF TEST How does the economy's behaviour in the short run differ from its behaviour in the long run? Draw the model of AD and AS. What variables are on the two axes?

THE AGGREGATE DEMAND CURVE

The AD curve tells us the quantity of all goods and services demanded in the economy at any given price level. As Figure 33.2 illustrates, the AD curve is downwards sloping reflecting the inverse relationship between the price level and national income we outlined in Chapter 32. This means that, *ceteris paribus*, a fall in the economy's overall level of prices (from, say, P_1 to P_2) tends to raise the quantity of goods and services demanded (from Y_1 to Y_2).

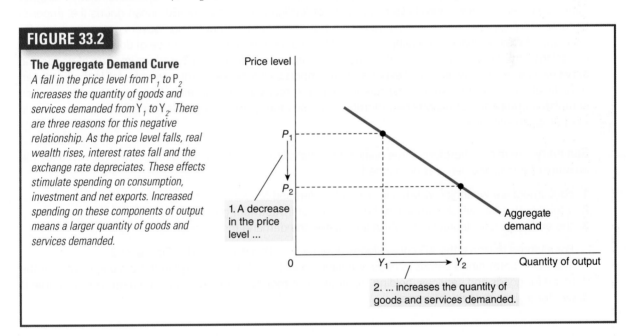

FIGURE 33.2

The Aggregate Demand Curve
A fall in the price level from P_1 to P_2 increases the quantity of goods and services demanded from Y_1 to Y_2. There are three reasons for this negative relationship. As the price level falls, real wealth rises, interest rates fall and the exchange rate depreciates. These effects stimulate spending on consumption, investment and net exports. Increased spending on these components of output means a larger quantity of goods and services demanded.

1. A decrease in the price level ...

2. ... increases the quantity of goods and services demanded.

Why the Aggregate Demand Curve Slopes Downwards

The level of AD is determined by the sum of consumption (C), investment (I), government purchases (G) and net exports (NX). For now, we assume that government spending is fixed by policy. The other three components of spending depend on economic conditions and, in particular, on the price level. To understand the downwards slope of the AD curve, we must examine how the price level affects the quantity of goods and services demanded for consumption, investment and net exports.

The Price Level and Consumption: The Wealth Effect Consider the money that you hold as cash, and your bank account. The nominal value of this money is fixed, but its real value is not. When prices fall, this money is more valuable because then it can be used to buy more goods and services. Thus, a decrease in the price level makes consumers wealthier, which in turn encourages them to spend more. The increase in consumer spending means a larger quantity of goods and services demanded.

The Price Level and Investment: The Interest Rate Effect The price level is one determinant of the quantity of money demanded. The lower the price level, the less money households need to hold to buy the goods and services they want. When the price level falls, therefore, households try to reduce their holdings of money by lending some of it out, which in turn increases the supply of real money balances. For instance, a household might use its excess money to buy interest-bearing bonds. Or it might deposit its excess money in an interest-bearing savings account, and the bank would use these funds to make more loans. In either case, as households try to convert some of their money into interest-bearing assets, they drive down interest rates. Lower interest rates, in turn, encourage borrowing by firms that want to invest in new factories and equipment and by households who want to invest in new housing. Thus, a lower price level reduces the interest rate, encourages greater spending on investment goods, and thereby increases the quantity of goods and services demanded.

The Price Level and Net Exports: The Exchange Rate Effect As we have just discussed, a lower price level lowers the interest rate. In response, some investors will seek higher returns by investing abroad. For instance, as the interest rate on European government bonds falls, an investment fund might sell European government bonds in order to buy US government bonds. As the investment fund tries to convert its euros into dollars in order to buy the US bonds, it increases the supply of euros in the market for foreign currency exchange. The increased supply of euros causes the euro to depreciate relative to other currencies. Because each euro buys fewer units of foreign currencies, non-European goods (i.e. imports) become more expensive to European residents but exporters find that foreign buyers get more euros for each unit of their currency. This change in the real exchange rate (the relative price of domestic and foreign goods) increases European exports of goods and services, and decreases European imports of goods and services. Net exports, which equal exports minus imports, also increase. Thus, when a fall in the European price level causes European interest rates to fall, the real value of the euro falls, and this depreciation stimulates European net exports and thereby increases the quantity of goods and services demanded in the European economy.

Summary There are, therefore, three distinct but related reasons why a fall in the price level increases the quantity of goods and services demanded:

1. consumers are wealthier, which stimulates the demand for consumption goods
2. interest rates fall, which stimulates the demand for investment goods
3. the exchange rate depreciates, which stimulates the demand for net exports.

For all three reasons, the AD curve slopes downwards. This is reflected in Figure 33.2.

The AD is determined *ceteris paribus*; we have considered how a change in the price level affects the demand for goods and services, holding the amount of money in the economy constant. The AD curve is drawn for a given quantity of money.

Why the Aggregate Demand Curve Might Shift

In Chapter 32, we noted how changes in monetary and fiscal policy can cause a shift in the LM and IS curves and, at a given price level, a shift in AD. We are going to explore shifts in the AD curve in more detail here. The downwards slope of the AD curve shows that a fall in the price level raises the overall quantity of goods and services demanded. Many other factors, however, affect the quantity of goods and services demanded at a given price level. When one of these other factors changes, the AD curve shifts.

Shifts Arising from Consumption Suppose people suddenly become more concerned about saving for retirement and, as a result, reduce their current consumption. Because the quantity of goods and services demanded at any price level is lower, the AD curve shifts to the left. Conversely, imagine that a stock market boom makes people wealthier and less concerned about saving. The resulting increase in consumer spending means a greater quantity of goods and services demanded at any given price level, so the AD curve shifts to the right.

Thus, any event that changes how much people want to consume at a given price level shifts the AD curve. One policy variable that has this effect is the level of taxation. When the government cuts taxes, it encourages people to spend more, so the AD curve shifts to the right. When the government raises taxes, people cut back on their spending and the AD curve shifts to the left.

Shifts Arising from Investment Any event that changes how much firms want to invest at a given price level also shifts the AD curve. For instance, imagine that the computer industry introduces a faster line of computers, and many firms decide to invest in new computer systems. Because the quantity of goods and services demanded at any price level is higher, the AD curve shifts to the right. Conversely, if firms become pessimistic about future business conditions, they may cut back on investment spending, shifting the AD curve to the left.

Tax policy can also influence AD through investment. An investment tax credit (a tax rebate tied to a firm's investment spending) increases the quantity of investment goods that firms demand at any given interest rate. It therefore shifts the AD curve to the right. The repeal of an investment tax credit reduces investment and shifts the AD curve to the left.

Another policy variable that can influence investment and AD is the money supply. As we discuss more fully in the next chapter, an increase in the money supply lowers the interest rate in the short run (the LM curve shifts to the right). This makes borrowing less costly, which stimulates investment spending and thereby shifts the AD curve to the right at a given price level. Conversely, a decrease in the money supply shifts the LM curve to the left and raises the interest rate, discourages investment spending, and thereby shifts the AD curve to the left at the given price level. Many economists believe that changes in monetary policy have been an important source of shifts in AD in most developed economies at some points in their history.

Shifts Arising from Government Purchases The most direct way that policymakers shift the AD curve is through government purchases. For example, suppose the government decides to reduce purchases of new weapons systems. Because the quantity of goods and services demanded at any price level is lower, the AD curve shifts to the left. Conversely, if the government starts building more motorways, the result is a greater quantity of goods and services demanded at any price level, and the AD curve shifts to the right.

Shifts Arising from Net Exports Any event that changes net exports for a given price level also shifts AD. For instance, when the US experiences a recession, it buys fewer goods from Europe. This reduces European net exports and shifts the AD curve for the European economy to the left. When the US recovers from its recession, it starts buying European goods again, shifting the AD curve to the right.

Net exports sometimes change because of movements in the exchange rate. Suppose, for instance, that international speculators bid up the value of the euro in the market for foreign currency exchange. This appreciation of the euro would make goods produced in the euro area more expensive compared to foreign goods, which would depress net exports and shift the AD curve to the left. Conversely, a depreciation of the euro stimulates net exports and shifts the euro area AD curve to the right.

Summary In the next chapter we analyze the AD curve in more detail in relation to the tools of monetary and fiscal policy which can shift AD and whether policymakers should use these tools for that purpose. At this point, however, you should have some idea about why the AD curve slopes downwards and what kinds of events and policies can shift this curve.

SELF TEST Explain the three reasons why the AD curve slopes downwards. Give an example of an event that would shift the AD curve. Which way would this event shift the curve?

THE AGGREGATE SUPPLY CURVE

The AS curve tells us the total quantity of goods and services that firms produce and sell at any given price level. Unlike the AD curve, which is always downwards sloping, the AS curve shows a relationship that depends crucially on the time horizon being examined. In the long run, the AS curve is vertical, whereas in the short run the AS curve is upwards sloping. To understand short-run economic fluctuations, and how the short-run behaviour of the economy deviates from its long-run behaviour, we need to examine both the long-run AS curve and the short-run AS curve.

Why the Aggregate Supply Curve is Vertical in the Long Run

In the long run, an economy's production of goods and services (its real GDP) depends on its supplies of labour, capital and natural resources, and on the available technology used to turn these factors of production into goods and services. Because the price level does not affect these long-run determinants of real GDP, the long-run AS curve is vertical, as in Figure 33.3. In other words, in the long run, the economy's labour, capital, natural resources and technology determine the total quantity of goods and services supplied, and this quantity supplied is the same regardless of what the price level happens to be.

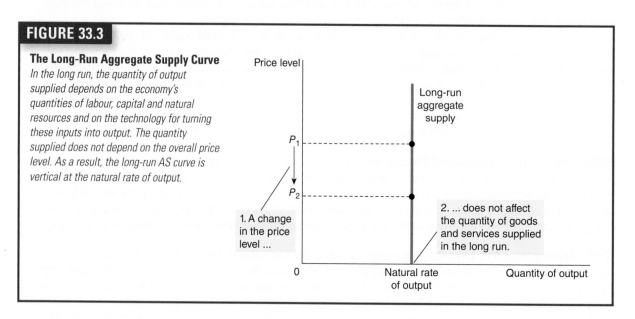

FIGURE 33.3

The Long-Run Aggregate Supply Curve
In the long run, the quantity of output supplied depends on the economy's quantities of labour, capital and natural resources and on the technology for turning these inputs into output. The quantity supplied does not depend on the overall price level. As a result, the long-run AS curve is vertical at the natural rate of output.

The vertical long-run AS curve is, in essence, just an application of the classical dichotomy and monetary neutrality. As we have already discussed, classical macroeconomic theory is based on the assumption that real variables do not depend on nominal variables. The long-run AS curve is consistent with this idea because it implies that the quantity of output (a real variable) does not depend on the level of prices (a nominal variable). As noted earlier, many economists believe that this principle works well when studying the economy over a period of many years, but not when studying year-to-year changes. Thus, the AS curve is vertical only in the long run.

One might wonder why supply curves for specific goods and services can be upwards sloping if the long-run AS curve is vertical. The reason is that the supply of specific goods and services depends on *relative prices* – the prices of those goods and services compared to other prices in the economy. For example, when the price of tablet computers rises, holding other prices in the economy constant, there is an incentive for suppliers of tablets to increase their production by taking labour, silicon, plastic and other inputs away from the production of other goods, such as mobile phones or laptop computers. By contrast, the economy's overall production of goods and services is limited by its labour, capital, natural resources and technology. Thus, when all prices in the economy rise together, there is no change in the overall quantity of goods and services supplied because relative prices and thus incentives have not changed.

Why the Long-Run AS Curve Might Shift

The position of the long-run AS (LRAS) curve shows the quantity of goods and services predicted by classical macroeconomic theory. This level of production is sometimes called *potential output* or *full-employment output.* To be more accurate, we call it the **natural rate of output** because it shows what the economy produces when unemployment is at its natural, or normal, rate. The natural rate of output is the level of production towards which the economy gravitates in the long run.

> **natural rate of output** the output level in an economy when all existing factors of production (land, labour, capital and technology resources) are fully utilized and where unemployment is at its natural rate

Any change in the economy that alters the natural rate of output shifts the LRAS curve. Because output in the classical model depends on labour, capital, natural resources and technological knowledge, we can categorize shifts in the LRAS curve as arising from these sources.

Shifts Arising from Labour Imagine that an economy experiences an increase in immigration from abroad and that these people found work. Because there is a greater number of workers, the quantity of goods and services supplied would increase. As a result, the LRAS curve would shift to the right. Conversely, if many workers left the economy to go abroad, the LRAS curve will shift to the left.

The position of the LRAS curve also depends on the natural rate of unemployment; any change in the natural rate of unemployment shifts the LRAS curve. For example, if a government were to raise the minimum wage substantially, the natural rate of unemployment would rise, and the economy would produce a smaller quantity of goods and services. As a result, the LRAS curve would shift to the left. Conversely, if a reform of the unemployment insurance system were to encourage unemployed workers to search harder for new jobs, the natural rate of unemployment would fall and the LRAS curve would shift to the right.

Shifts Arising from Capital An increase in the economy's capital stock increases productivity and, thereby, the quantity of goods and services supplied. As a result, the LRAS curve shifts to the right. Conversely, a decrease in the economy's capital stock decreases productivity and the quantity of goods and services supplied, shifting the LRAS curve to the left.

Notice that the same logic applies regardless of whether we are discussing physical capital or human capital. An increase either in the number of machines or in the number of university degrees will raise the economy's ability to produce goods and services. Thus, either would shift the LRAS curve to the right.

Shifts Arising from Natural Resources An economy's production depends on its natural resources, including its land, minerals and weather. A discovery of a new mineral deposit shifts the LRAS curve to the right. A change in weather patterns that makes farming more difficult shifts the LRAS curve to the left.

In many countries, important natural resources are imported from abroad. A change in the availability of these resources can also shift the AS curve. Events occurring in the world oil market, in particular, have historically been an important source of shifts in AS.

Shifts Arising from Technological Knowledge Perhaps the most important reason that the economy today produces more than it did a generation ago is that our technological knowledge has advanced. The invention of the computer, for instance, has allowed us to produce more goods and services from any given amounts of labour, capital and natural resources. As a result, it has shifted the LRAS curve to the right.

Although not literally technological, there are many other events that act like changes in technology. The opening up of international trade has effects similar to inventing new production processes, so it also shifts the LRAS curve to the right. Conversely, if the government passed new regulations preventing firms from using some production methods, perhaps because they were too dangerous for workers, the result would be a leftwards shift in the LRAS curve.

Summary The LRAS curve reflects the classical model of the economy we developed in previous chapters. Any policy or event that raised real GDP in previous chapters can now be viewed as increasing the quantity of goods and services supplied and shifting the LRAS curve to the right. Any policy or event that lowered real GDP in previous chapters can now be viewed as decreasing the quantity of goods and services supplied and shifting the LRAS curve to the left.

A New Way to Depict Long-Run Growth and Inflation

Having introduced the economy's AD curve and the LRAS curve, we now have a new way to describe the economy's long-run trends. Figure 33.4 illustrates the changes that occur in the economy from decade to decade. Notice that both curves are shifting. Although there are many forces that govern the economy in the long run and can, in principle, cause such shifts, the two most important in practice are technology and monetary policy. Technological progress enhances the economy's ability to produce goods and services, and this continually shifts the LRAS curve to the right. At the same time, because the central bank increases the money supply over time, the AD curve also shifts to the right. As the figure illustrates, the result is trend growth in output (as shown by increasing Y) and continuing inflation (as shown by increasing P). This is just another way of representing the classical analysis of growth and inflation we conducted earlier in the book.

FIGURE 33.4

Long-Run Growth and Inflation in the Model of Aggregate Demand and Aggregate Supply

As the economy becomes better able to produce goods and services over time, primarily because of technological progress, the LRAS curve shifts to the right. At the same time, as the central bank increases the money supply, the AD curve also shifts to the right. In this figure, output grows from Y_{1997} to Y_{2007} and then to Y_{2017}, and the price level rises from P_{1997} to P_{2007} and then to P_{2017}. Thus, the model of AD and AS offers a new way to describe the classical analysis of growth and inflation.

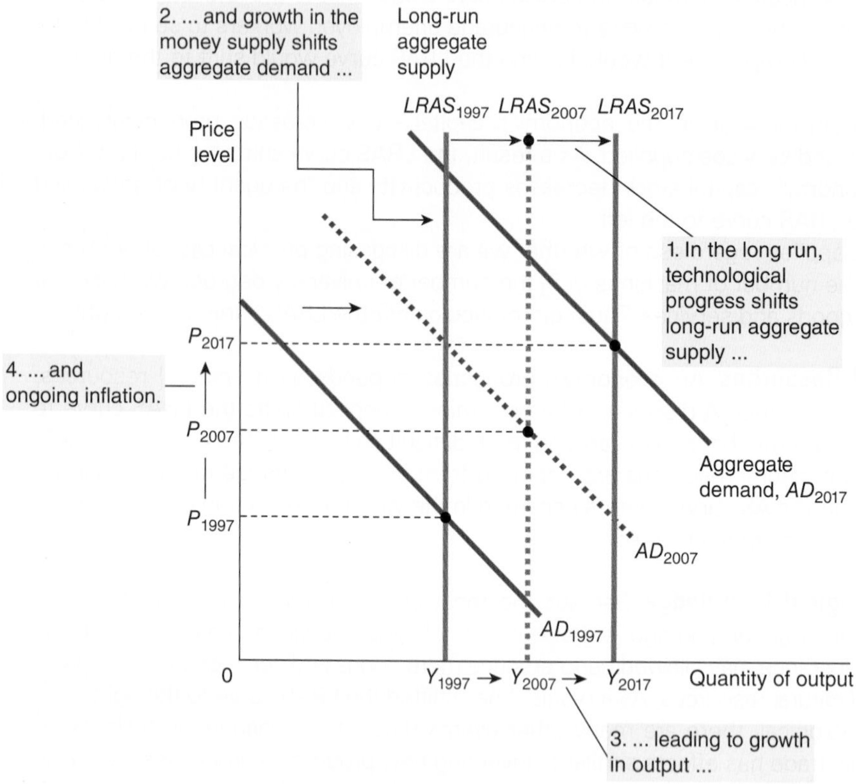

The purpose of developing the model of AD and AS, however, is not to dress our long-run conclusions in new clothing. Instead, it is to provide a framework for short-run analysis, as we will see in a moment. As we develop the short-run model, we keep the analysis simple by not showing the continuing growth and inflation depicted in Figure 33.4. It is worth remembering that long-run trends provide the background for short-run fluctuations. Short-run fluctuations in output and the price level should be viewed as deviations from the continuing long-run trends.

Why the AS Curve Slopes Upward in the Short Run

We now come to the key difference between the economy in the short run and in the long run: the behaviour of AS. As we have already discussed, the LRAS curve is vertical. By contrast, in the short run, the AS curve is upwards sloping, as shown in Figure 33.5. That is, over a period of a year or two, an increase in the overall level of prices in the economy tends to raise the quantity of goods and services supplied, and a decrease in the level of prices tends to reduce the quantity of goods and services supplied.

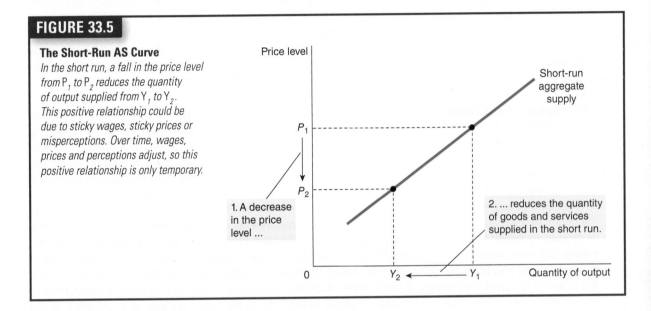

FIGURE 33.5

The Short-Run AS Curve
In the short run, a fall in the price level from P_1 to P_2 reduces the quantity of output supplied from Y_1 to Y_2. This positive relationship could be due to sticky wages, sticky prices or misperceptions. Over time, wages, prices and perceptions adjust, so this positive relationship is only temporary.

Macroeconomists have proposed three theories for the upward slope of the short-run AS (SRAS) curve. In each theory, a specific market imperfection causes the supply side of the economy to behave differently in the short run than it does in the long run. Although each of the following theories will differ in detail, they share a common theme: the quantity of output supplied deviates from its long-run or 'natural' level when the price level deviates from the price level that people *expected* to prevail. When the price level rises above the expected level, output rises above its natural rate, and when the price level falls below the expected level, output falls below its natural rate.

The Sticky Wage Theory The first and simplest explanation of the upwards slope of the SRAS curve is the sticky wage theory which we initially encountered in Chapter 23. According to this theory, the SRAS curve slopes upwards because nominal wages are slow to adjust, or are 'sticky', in the short run. To some extent, the slow adjustment of nominal wages is attributable to long-term contracts between workers and firms that fix nominal wages for a period. In addition, this slow adjustment may be attributable to social norms and notions of fairness that influence wage setting and change only slowly over time.

To see what sticky nominal wages mean for AS, imagine that a firm has agreed in advance to pay its workers a certain nominal wage based on what it expected the price level to be. If the price level P falls below the level that was expected and the nominal wage remains stuck at W, then the real wage, $\frac{W}{P}$, rises above the level the firm planned to pay. Because wages are a large part of a firm's production costs, a higher real wage means that the firm's real costs have risen. The firm responds to these higher costs by hiring less labour and producing a smaller quantity of goods and services. In other words, because wages do not adjust immediately to the price level, a lower price level makes employment and production less profitable, so firms reduce the quantity of goods and services they supply.

The Sticky Price Theory The sticky price theory emphasizes that the prices of some goods and services also adjust sluggishly in response to changing economic conditions. This slow adjustment of prices occurs in part because of the *menu costs* to adjusting prices. These menu costs include the cost of printing and distributing price lists or mail-order catalogues and the time required to change price tags. As a result of these costs, prices as well as wages may be sticky in the short run.

To see the implications of sticky prices for AS, suppose that each firm in the economy announces its prices in advance based on the economic conditions it expects to prevail. Then, after prices are announced, the economy experiences an unexpected contraction in the money supply, which (as we have learned) will reduce the overall price level in the long run. Although some firms reduce their prices immediately in response to changing economic conditions, other firms may not want to incur additional menu costs and, therefore, may temporarily lag behind. Because these lagging firms have prices that are too high, their sales decline. Declining sales, in turn, cause these firms to cut back on production and employment. In other words, because not all prices adjust instantly to changing conditions, an unexpected fall in the price level leaves some firms with higher-than-desired prices, and these higher-than-desired prices depress sales and induce firms to reduce the quantity of goods and services they produce.

The Misperceptions Theory A third approach to the SRAS curve is the misperceptions theory. According to this theory, changes in the overall price level can temporarily mislead suppliers about what is happening in the individual markets in which they sell their output. As a result of these short-run misperceptions, suppliers respond to changes in the level of prices, and this response leads to an upwards sloping AS curve.

To see how this might work, suppose the overall price level falls below the level that people expected. When suppliers see the prices of their products fall, they may mistakenly believe that their *relative* prices have fallen. For example, wheat farmers may notice a fall in the price of wheat before they notice a fall in the prices of the many items they buy as consumers. They may infer from this observation that the reward to producing wheat is temporarily low, and they may respond by reducing the quantity of wheat they supply. Similarly, workers may notice a fall in their nominal wages before they notice a fall in the prices of the goods they buy. They may infer that the reward to working is temporarily low and respond by reducing the quantity of labour they supply. In both cases, a lower price level causes misperceptions about relative prices, and these misperceptions induce suppliers to respond to the lower price level by decreasing the quantity of goods and services supplied.

Summary There are three alternative explanations for the upwards slope of the SRAS curve:

1. sticky wages
2. sticky prices
3. misperceptions.

Economists debate which of these theories is correct, and it is very possible each contains an element of truth. For our purposes in this book, the similarities of the theories are more important than the differences. All three theories suggest that output deviates from its natural rate when the price level deviates from the price level that people expected. We can express this mathematically as follows:

$$Q = NRQ + a(APL - EPL)$$

Where Q = Quantity of output supplied, NRQ = Natural rate of output, APL = Actual price level, EPL = Expected price level and a is a number that determines how much output responds to unexpected changes in the price level.

Notice that each of the three theories of SRAS emphasizes a problem that is likely to be only temporary. Whether the upwards slope of the AS curve is attributable to sticky wages, sticky prices or misperceptions, these conditions will not persist forever. Eventually, as people adjust their expectations, nominal wages adjust, prices become unstuck and misperceptions are corrected. In other words, the expected and actual price levels are equal in the long run, and the AS curve is vertical rather than upwards sloping.

Why the SRAS Curve Might Shift

The SRAS curve tells us the quantity of goods and services supplied in the short run for any given level of prices. We can think of this curve as similar to the LRAS curve but made upwards sloping by the presence of sticky wages, sticky prices and misperceptions. Thus, when thinking about what shifts the SRAS curve, we have to consider all those variables that shift the LRAS curve plus a new variable – the expected price level – that influences sticky wages, sticky prices and misperceptions.

As we discussed earlier, shifts in the LRAS curve normally arise from changes in labour, capital, natural resources or technological knowledge. These same variables shift the SRAS curve. For example, when an increase in the economy's capital stock increases productivity, both the LRAS and SRAS curves shift to the right. When an increase in the minimum wage raises the natural rate of unemployment, both the LRAS and SRAS curves shift to the left.

The important new variable that affects the position of the SRAS curve is people's expectation of the price level. As we have discussed, the quantity of goods and services supplied depends, in the short run, on sticky wages, sticky prices and misperceptions. Yet wages, prices and perceptions are set on the basis of expectations of the price level. So when expectations change, the SRAS curve shifts.

To make this idea more concrete, let's consider a specific theory of AS – the sticky wage theory. According to this theory, when workers and firms expect the price level to be high, they are more likely to negotiate high nominal wages. High wages raise firms' costs and, for any given actual price level, reduce the quantity of goods and services that firms supply. Thus, when the expected price level rises, wages are higher, costs increase, and firms supply a smaller quantity of goods and services at any given actual price level. Thus, the SRAS curve shifts to the left. Conversely, when the expected price level falls, wages are lower, costs decline, firms increase production at any given price level, and the SRAS curve shifts to the right.

A similar logic applies in each theory of AS. The general lesson is the following:

- An increase in the expected price level reduces the quantity of goods and services supplied and shifts the SRAS curve to the left.
- A decrease in the expected price level raises the quantity of goods and services supplied and shifts the SRAS curve to the right.

As we will see in the next section, this influence of expectations on the position of the SRAS curve plays a key role in reconciling the economy's behaviour in the short run with its behaviour in the long run. In the short run, expectations are fixed, and the economy finds itself at the intersection of the AD curve and the SRAS curve. In the long run, expectations adjust, and the SRAS curve shifts. This shift ensures that the economy eventually finds itself at the intersection of the AD curve and the LRAS curve.

SELF TEST Explain why the LRAS curve is vertical. Explain three theories for why the SRAS curve is upwards sloping. How believable do you find each of these three theories?

TWO CAUSES OF ECONOMIC FLUCTUATIONS

Our model of AD and AS provides the basic tools to analyze two basic causes of short-run fluctuations. To keep things simple, we assume the economy begins in long-run equilibrium, as shown in Figure 33.6. Equilibrium output and the price level are determined by the intersection of the AD curve and the LRAS curve, shown as point A in the figure. At this point, output is at its natural rate. The SRAS curve passes through this point as well, indicating that wages, prices and perceptions have fully adjusted to this long-run equilibrium. That is, when an economy is in its long-run equilibrium, wages, prices and perceptions must have adjusted so that the intersection of AD with SRAS is the same as the intersection of AD with LRAS.

The Effects of a Shift in Aggregate Demand

Suppose that for some reason a wave of pessimism suddenly overtakes the economy. The cause might be a government scandal, a crash on the stock market or the outbreak of conflict in an important economic region. Because of this event, many economic agents lose confidence in the future and alter their plans.

FIGURE 33.6

The Long-Run Equilibrium
The long-run equilibrium of the economy is found where the AD curve crosses the LRAS curve (point A). When the economy reaches this long-run equilibrium, wages, prices and perceptions will have adjusted so that the SRAS curve crosses this point as well.

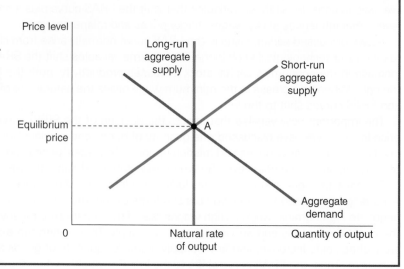

Households cut back on their spending and delay major purchases, and firms put off buying new equipment. This reduces the AD for goods and services. That is, for any given price level, households and firms now want to buy a smaller quantity of goods and services. As Figure 33.7 shows, the AD curve shifts to the left from AD_1 to AD_2.

In the short run, the economy moves along the initial SRAS curve AS_1, going from point A to point B. As the economy moves from point A to point B, output falls from Y_1 to Y_2, and the price level falls from P_1 to P_2. The falling level of output indicates that the economy is in a recession. Although not shown in the figure, firms respond to lower sales and production by reducing employment. Thus, the pessimism that caused the shift in AD is, to some extent, self-fulfilling: pessimism about the future leads to falling incomes and rising unemployment.

FIGURE 33.7

A Contraction in Aggregate Demand
A fall in AD, which might be due to a wave of pessimism in the economy, is represented with a leftward shift in the AD curve from AD_1 to AD_2. The economy moves from point A to point B. Output falls from Y_1 to Y_2, and the price level falls from P_1 to P_2. Over time, as wages, prices and perceptions adjust, the SRAS curve shifts to the right from AS_1 to AS_2 and the economy reaches point C, where the new AD curve crosses the LRAS curve. The price level falls to P_3 and output returns to its natural rate, Y_1.

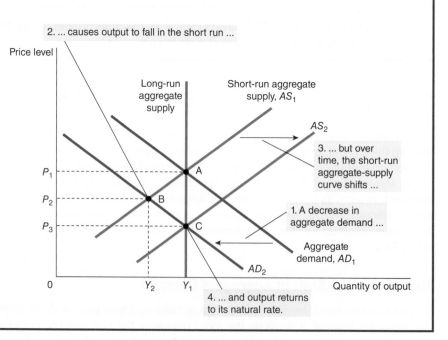

The short-run problem of recession prompts policymakers to take action and one option is to increase AD. As we noted earlier, an increase in government spending or an increase in the money supply would increase the quantity of goods and services demanded at any price and shift the AD curve to the right. If policymakers can act with sufficient speed and precision, they can offset the initial shift in AD, return the AD curve back to AD_1 and bring the economy back to point A. (The next chapter discusses in more detail the ways in which monetary and fiscal policy influence AD, as well as some of the practical difficulties in using these policy instruments.)

Even without action by policymakers, the recession will remedy itself over a period of time. Because of the reduction in AD, the price level falls. Eventually, expectations catch up with this new reality, and the expected price level falls as well. Because the fall in the expected price level alters wages, prices and perceptions, it shifts the SRAS curve to the right from AS_1 to AS_2 in Figure 33.7. This adjustment of expectations allows the economy over time to approach point C, where the new AD curve (AD_2) crosses the LRAS curve.

In the new long-run equilibrium, point C, output is back to its natural rate. Even though the wave of pessimism has reduced AD, the price level has fallen sufficiently (to P_3) to offset the shift in the AD curve. Thus, in the long run, the shift in AD is reflected fully in the price level and not at all in the level of output. In other words, the long-run effect of a shift in AD is a nominal change (the price level is lower) but not a real change (output is the same).

To sum up, this story about shifts in AD has two important lessons:

- In the short run, shifts in AD cause fluctuations in the economy's output of goods and services.
- In the long run, shifts in AD affect the overall price level but do not affect output.

The Effects of a Shift in Aggregate Supply

Imagine once again an economy in its long-run equilibrium. Now suppose that suddenly some firms experience an increase in their costs of production. For example, strong demand from Asia might drive up commodity prices which are used in the production of a wide variety of goods.

For any given price level, firms now want to supply a smaller quantity of goods and services. Thus, as Figure 33.8 shows, the SRAS curve shifts to the left from AS_1 to AS_2. (Depending on the event, the LRAS curve might also shift. To keep things simple, however, we will assume that it does not.)

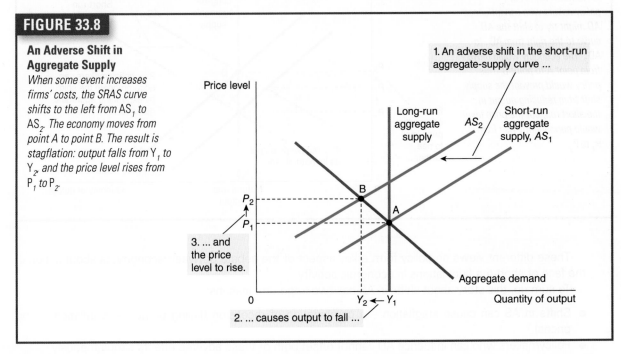

FIGURE 33.8

An Adverse Shift in Aggregate Supply

When some event increases firms' costs, the SRAS curve shifts to the left from AS_1 to AS_2. The economy moves from point A to point B. The result is stagflation: output falls from Y_1 to Y_2 and the price level rises from P_1 to P_2.

1. An adverse shift in the short-run aggregate-supply curve ...

Price level

Long-run aggregate supply

AS_2

Short-run aggregate supply, AS_1

B

P_2

P_1

A

3. ... and the price level to rise.

Aggregate demand

0

$Y_2 \leftarrow Y_1$

Quantity of output

2. ... causes output to fall ...

In the short run, the economy moves along the existing AD curve, going from point A to point B. The output of the economy falls from Y_1 to Y_2 and the price level rises from P_1 to P_2. Because the economy is experiencing both *stagnation* (falling output) and *inflation* (rising prices), such an event is sometimes called **stagflation**.

> **stagflation** a period of falling output and rising prices

Faced with stagflation there are no easy choices for policymakers. One possibility is to do nothing. In this case, the output of goods and services remains depressed at Y_2 for a while. Eventually, however, the recession will remedy itself as wages, prices and perceptions adjust to raise production costs. A period of low output and high unemployment, for instance, puts downwards pressure on workers' wages. Lower wages, in turn, increase the quantity of output supplied. Over time, as the SRAS curve shifts back towards AS_1, the price level falls, and the quantity of output approaches its natural rate. In the long run, the economy returns to point A, where the AD curve crosses the LRAS curve. This is the view that believers of free markets might adopt.

Alternatively, policymakers who control monetary and fiscal policy might attempt to offset some of the effects of the shift in the SRAS curve by shifting the AD curve. This possibility is shown in Figure 33.9. In this case, changes in policy shift the AD curve to the right from AD_1 to AD_2 – exactly enough to prevent the shift in AS from affecting output. The economy moves directly from point A to point B. Output remains at its natural rate, and the price level rises from P_1 to P_3. In this case, policymakers are said to *accommodate* the shift in AS because they allow the increase in costs to permanently affect the level of prices. This intervention by policymakers would be seen as being desirable by supporters of Keynes.

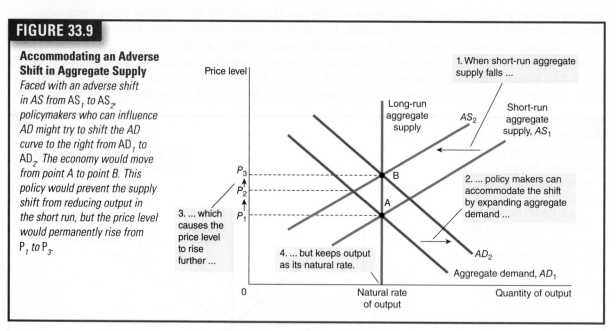

FIGURE 33.9

Accommodating an Adverse Shift in Aggregate Supply
Faced with an adverse shift in AS from AS_1 to AS_2, policymakers who can influence AD might try to shift the AD curve to the right from AD_1 to AD_2. The economy would move from point A to point B. This policy would prevent the supply shift from reducing output in the short run, but the price level would permanently rise from P_1 to P_3.

These different views on policy form a key aspect of the debate between economists about action in the face of short-run fluctuations in economic activity.

To sum up, this story about shifts in AS has two important lessons:

- Shifts in AS can cause stagflation – a combination of recession (falling output) and inflation (rising prices).
- Policymakers who can influence AD cannot offset both of these adverse effects simultaneously.

Stagflation In Brazil

Brazil is one of the so-called BRIC countries, those emerging countries which have seen high levels of growth and have been catching up with developed economies quickly. Brazil, however, has faced a number of problems in sustaining its development. One problem has been the fall in oil prices which began in 2014 and continued into the first part of 2016. In 2013, inflation stood at around 7 per cent, and in early 2016 it had accelerated to over 14 per cent. Economic growth meanwhile had slowed from around 7 per cent in 2010 to barely zero in 2014, and shrunk by over 3 per cent in 2015. Expectations were that the economy would further contract by over 2 per cent in 2016.

Brazil's economy has run into some challenges after a period of strong growth.

In the face of such stagflation, the Brazilian central bank held interest rates at 14.25 per cent in early 2016. Many economists had expected rates to be increased to try and curb inflation and when the central bank decided not to do so, expectations of inflation increased. The central bank in Brazil faced a difficult choice. Should it increase interest rates in an attempt to slow down inflation but in doing so risk damaging growth or should it cut rates to boost growth but risk inflation rising even faster?

Monetary policy is one policy aspect, the other is fiscal policy. The budget deficit has widened and given the fragile state of the economy, the option to increase taxes and cut public spending is limited. The decision by Standard & Poors to reduce the rating on Brazil's debt in the latter part of 2015, further compounded the problems the country faces. It means that Brazil will find it far more expensive to raise money on the international financial markets and increases the risk of capital flight from the country.

SELF TEST Suppose that the election of a popular prime minister suddenly increases people's confidence in the future. Use the model of AD and AS to analyze the effect on the economy.

NEW KEYNESIAN ECONOMICS

We introduced Keynesian economics and the IS–LM model in Chapter 32. Recall that Keynesian economics developed in response to the depression of the 1930s, when the assumptions of classical economics that markets would clear appeared to be failing. Keynesian ideas were the mainstay for economic policy across the developed world in the post-war era and there was something of a consensus amongst economists that our understanding of the macroeconomy was considerable. The latter part of the 1960s began to reveal some flaws in that assumption as global conditions changed. The breakdown of fixed exchange rates in the late 1960s and the oil crisis in the early 1970s presented macroeconomists with significant challenges in explaining the economic conditions that existed in some countries – stagflation in particular.

Economics came to be classified as a debate between Keynesians on the one hand, who pointed to markets not clearing quickly, and the neo or new classicists on the other hand, who re-emphasized the efficiency of markets and argued that microeconomics provided a foundation for understanding macroeconomics.

Out of this debate emerged a group referred to as 'New Keynesians'. New Keynesian economics placed an emphasis on providing sound microeconomic principles to underpin Keynesian macroeconomics. Specifically, New Keynesians sought to explain how price and wage stickiness had its foundation in the microeconomic analysis of labour markets and price setting by firms.

Features of New Keynesian Economics

New Keynesians would argue that short-run fluctuations in economic output violate the classical dichotomy, as outlined earlier in this chapter. Changes in nominal variables like the money supply do have an influence on output and employment – real variables – in the short run. In addition, they would argue that to develop an understanding of changes in economic activity, an understanding of the imperfections in the economy is necessary – that firms operate under imperfect competition, that consumers and firms are subject to imperfect information and that there are built-in rigidities in the economy which hinder the movement of prices and wages as we have noted.

Can we conclude from this that the economists classed as New Keynesians are supporters of demand management but with some reservations? The answer to this is 'no'. The splitting of economics into different schools of thought has been convenient for the mass media to present disagreements between economists in relatively simple terms. The reality is that there is probably more agreement in economics than most members of the public would imagine. A difference in some base assumptions and a difference in the relative size of parameters in models is largely the reason why economists disagree. Many economists would subscribe to the view that changes in the money supply affect AD (a so-called 'monetarist' view) but also agree that price rigidities in the macroeconomy exist because of imperfections in the microeconomy. Some New Keynesian economists would, equally, not be in support of policy intervention to correct short-term fluctuations in the economy by attempting to manipulate AD. The main reason being that they would argue that the effects of such policy interventions take time to work through the economy by which time economic conditions have changed and so the policy will not be as effective as anticipated. Changes in interest rates, for example, are estimated to take around 18 months to work through the economy; tax changes might be received in different ways by different people and it is never certain enough to predict how people will react to a tax cut or a tax increase in any precise quantifiable way to make such a policy option a clear-cut choice. Equally, policies to increase government spending, on infrastructure projects for example, often take many years to have any effect even if such projects are 'shovel ready' – able to be put in operation quickly.

New Keynesian economics reminds us that the complexities of the economy perhaps deserve a more discerning look at the detail behind what economists are actually saying and how much they agree and why they agree, as much as why they might disagree and the extent of such disagreements.

CONCLUSION

This chapter has achieved two goals. First, we have discussed some of the important facts about short-run fluctuations in economic activity. Second, we have introduced a basic model to explain those fluctuations, called the model of AD and AS. We continue our study of this model in the next chapter in order to understand more fully what causes fluctuations in the economy and how policymakers might respond to these fluctuations.

IN THE NEWS

Expectations

One of the key tasks of policymakers is to set the tone for expectations in the economy – such expectations have to be realistic and also believed by the population if the policy is to have any credence.

Expectations in the Eurozone

In the aftermath of the Financial Crisis, a number of economies faced a long, slow road to recovery but when that recovery came, inflation has stayed relatively low. In the UK, for example, growth was 2.2 per cent in 2013, 2.9 per cent in 2014 and over 2.0 per cent in 2015. Throughout this period, inflation hovered at or below zero per cent. In the Euro Area, growth has been slower at around 0.5 per cent throughout the period but inflation has also been subdued with some deflation in December 2014 and inflation at around 0.2 per cent in December 2015.

In the face of some growth and subdued inflation, economists and policymakers are reassessing their understanding of this phenom-

The Eurozone faces many economic challenges. Will these challenges be met by more QE?

enon. In the Euro Area, the different situations in different countries makes things more complex but this is what policymakers have to manage. In early 2016, the president of the ECB, Mario Draghi, speaking after the meeting of the monetary policy committee in January 2016, suggested that quantitative easing could be extended further when it next met in March. Euro Area interest rates were at 0.05 per cent. With inflation way below the target rate of 2.0 per cent, more quantitative easing would look to provide a further stimulus to the Euro Area. Part of the basis for any such decision would be forecasts of macroeconomic variables for 2018, which Draghi said would be available for the March meeting. Expectations on inflation were low and many professional economists were predicting that not only would there be a new round of QE but that the ECB's deposit rate (the rate on overnight deposits made by banks within the Eurosystem), might also be cut to 0.4 or 0.45 per cent.

Questions

1 **Using your understanding of the model of AD and AS, what factors might explain a growth rate of over 2.0 per cent and an inflation rate of near zero in the UK?**

2 **What might be a contributory factor to the slower growth rate being experienced by the Euro Area compared to that of the UK?**

3 **Use the AD and AS model and assume that initial equilibrium in the Euro area is at a price level indicated by an inflation rate at 0.2 per cent and an output level reflecting growth of 0.5 per cent. Use the model to help analyze the effect of an increase in QE and a reduction in interest rates by the ECB.**

4 **If expectations of lower inflation exist throughout the Euro Area, what would you expect to happen to the SRAS curve? Explain.**

5 **One possible explanation for the subdued inflation in the UK and the Euro Area since the Financial Crisis is a shift in the LRAS curve. Explain what might have caused such a shift and in which direction you expect it to have shifted. What would such a shift imply for policymakers?**

SUMMARY

- All societies experience short-run economic fluctuations around long-run trends. These fluctuations are irregular and largely unpredictable. When recessions do occur, real GDP and other measures of income, spending and production fall, and unemployment rises.

- We can analyze short-run economic fluctuations using the model of AD and AS. According to this model, the output of goods and services and the overall level of prices adjust to balance AD and AS.

- The AD curve slopes downwards for three reasons. First, a lower price level raises the real value of households' money holdings, which stimulates consumer spending. Second, a lower price level reduces the quantity of money households' demand; as households try to convert money into interest-bearing assets, interest rates fall, which stimulates investment spending. Third, as a lower price level reduces interest rates, the local currency depreciates in the market for foreign currency exchange, stimulating net exports.

- Any event or policy that raises consumption, investment, government purchases or net exports at a given price level increases AD. Any event or policy that reduces consumption, investment, government purchases or net exports at a given price level decreases AD.

- The LRAS curve is vertical. In the long run, the quantity of goods and services supplied depends on the economy's labour, capital, natural resources and technology, but not on the overall level of prices.

- Three theories have been proposed to explain the upwards slope of the SRAS curve. According to the sticky wage theory, an unexpected fall in the price level temporarily raises real wages, which induces firms to reduce employment and production. According to the sticky price theory, an unexpected fall in the price level leaves some firms with prices that are temporarily too high, which reduces their sales and causes them to cut back production. According to the misperceptions theory, an unexpected fall in the price level leads suppliers to mistakenly believe that their relative prices have fallen, which induces them to reduce production. All three theories imply that output deviates from its natural rate when the price level deviates from the price level that people expected.

- Events that alter the economy's ability to produce output, such as changes in labour, capital, natural resources or technology, shift the SRAS curve (and may shift the LRAS curve as well). In addition, the position of the SRAS curve depends on the expected price level.

- One possible cause of economic fluctuations is a shift in AD. When the AD curve shifts to the left, for instance, output and prices fall in the short run. Over time, as a change in the expected price level causes wages, prices and perceptions to adjust, the SRAS curve shifts to the right, and the economy returns to its natural rate of output at a new, lower price level.

- A second possible cause of economic fluctuations is a shift in AS. When the AS curve shifts to the left, the short-run effect is falling output and rising prices – a combination called stagflation. Over time, as wages, prices and perceptions adjust, the price level falls back to its original level, and output recovers.

- New Keynesian economics represents a research tradition that questions the classical dichotomy and recognizes imperfections in the economy as key elements in explaining short run deviations from trend.

QUESTIONS FOR REVIEW

1 What do you understand by the term 'economic activity'?

2 What is the official definition of a recession?

3 Name two macroeconomic variables that decline when the economy goes into a recession. Name one macroeconomic variable that rises during a recession.

4 Draw a diagram with AD, SRAS and LRAS. Be careful to label the axes correctly.

5 List and explain the three reasons why the AD curve is downwards sloping.

6 Explain why the LRAS curve is vertical.

7 List and explain the three theories for why the SRAS curve is upwards sloping.

8 What might shift the AD curve to the left? Use the model of AD and AS to trace through the effects of such a shift.

9 What might shift the AS curve to the left? Use the model of AD and AS to trace through the effects of such a shift.

10 What outcomes are possible if both AD and AS are both shifting? Use the model of AD and AS to outline some of these possible outcomes.

PROBLEMS AND APPLICATIONS

1 Why do you think that investment is more variable over the business cycle than consumer spending? Which category of consumer spending do you think would be most volatile: durable goods (such as furniture and car purchases), non-durable goods (such as food and clothing) or services (such as haircuts and medical care)? Why?

2 Suppose that the economy is in a long-run equilibrium.
Use a diagram to illustrate the state of the economy. Be sure to show AD, SRAS and LRAS.

  a. Now suppose that commodity prices are falling which suggest a downturn in the economy and a fall in AD. Use your diagram to show what happens to output and the price level in the short run. What happens to the unemployment rate?

  b. Use the sticky wage theory of AS to explain what will happen to output and the price level in the long run (assuming there is no change in policy). What role does the expected price level play in this adjustment? Be sure to illustrate your analysis with a graph.

3 Explain whether each of the following events will increase, decrease or have no effect on LRAS.

  a. A country experiences a wave of immigration.
  b. A government raises the minimum wage above the national average wage level.
  c. A war leads to the destruction of a large number of factories.

4 In Figure 33.7, how does the unemployment rate at points B and C compare to the unemployment rate at point A? Under the sticky wage explanation of the SRAS curve, how does the real wage at points B and C compare to the real wage at point A?

5 Explain why the following statements are false.

  a. 'The AD curve slopes downwards because it is the horizontal sum of the demand curves for individual goods.'
  b. 'The LRAS curve is vertical because economic forces do not affect LRAS.'
  c. 'If firms adjusted their prices every day, then the SRAS curve would be horizontal.'
  d. 'Whenever the economy enters a recession, its LRAS curve shifts to the left.'

6 For each of the three theories for the upwards slope of the SRAS curve, carefully explain the following.

  a. How the economy recovers from a recession and returns to its long-run equilibrium without any policy intervention.
  b. What determines the speed of the recovery?

7 Suppose the central bank expands QE and as a result, expectations of a rise in the price level increase. What will happen to output and the price level in the short run? Compare this result to the outcome if the central bank expanded QE but the public didn't change its expectation of the price level.

8 Suppose workers and firms suddenly believe that inflation will be quite high over the coming year. Suppose also that the economy begins in long-run equilibrium, and the AD curve does not shift.

  a. What happens to nominal wages? What happens to real wages?
  b. Using an AD/AS diagram, show the effect of the change in expectations on both the short-run and long-run levels of prices and output.
  c. Were the expectations of high inflation accurate? Explain.

9 Explain whether each of the following events shifts the SRAS curve, the AD curve, both, or neither. For each event that does shift a curve, use a diagram to illustrate the effect on the economy.

a. Households decide to save a larger share of their income.
b. Cattle farmers suffer a prolonged period of foot-and-mouth disease which cuts average cattle herd sizes by 80 per cent.
c. Increased job opportunities overseas cause many people to leave the country.

10 Suppose that firms become very optimistic about future business conditions and invest heavily in new capital equipment.

a. Use an AD/AS diagram to show the short-run effect of this optimism on the economy. Label the new levels of prices and real output. Explain, in words, why the aggregate quantity of output supplied changes.
b. Now use the diagram from part (a) to show the new long-run equilibrium of the economy. (For now, assume there is no change in the LRAS curve.) Explain, in words, why the aggregate quantity of output demanded changes between the short run and the long run.
c. How might the investment boom affect the LRAS curve? Explain.

34 THE INFLUENCE OF MONETARY AND FISCAL POLICY ON AGGREGATE DEMAND

In this chapter we examine in more detail how the tools of monetary and fiscal policy influence the position of the aggregate demand (AD) curve. We have previously discussed the long-run effects of these policies. In Chapters 22 and 23 we saw how fiscal policy affects saving, investment and long-run economic growth. In Chapters 27 and 28 we saw how central bank activity influences the money supply and how the money supply affects the price level in the long run. We now see how these policy tools can shift the AD curve and, in doing so, affect short-run economic fluctuations.

As we have already learned, many factors influence AD besides monetary and fiscal policy. In particular, desired spending by households and firms determines the overall demand for goods and services. When desired spending changes, AD shifts. If policymakers do not respond, such shifts in AD cause short-run fluctuations in output and employment. As a result, monetary and fiscal policymakers sometimes use the policy levers at their disposal to try to offset these shifts in AD and thereby stabilize the economy. Here we discuss the theory behind these policy actions and some of the difficulties that arise in using this theory in practice.

HOW MONETARY POLICY INFLUENCES AGGREGATE DEMAND

The AD curve shows the total quantity of goods and services demanded in the economy for any price level. As you may recall from the preceding chapter, the AD curve slopes downwards for three reasons:

- *The wealth effect.* A lower price level raises the real value of households' money holdings, and higher real wealth stimulates consumer spending.
- *The interest rate effect.* A lower price level lowers the interest rate as people try to lend out their excess money holdings, and the lower interest rate stimulates investment spending.
- *The exchange rate effect.* When a lower price level lowers the interest rate, investors move some of their funds overseas and cause the domestic currency to depreciate relative to foreign currencies. This depreciation makes domestic goods cheaper compared to foreign goods and, therefore, stimulates spending on net exports.

These three effects should not be viewed as alternative theories. Instead, they occur simultaneously to increase the quantity of goods and services demanded when the price level falls and to decrease it when the price level rises.

Although all three effects work together in explaining the downwards slope of the AD curve, they are not of equal importance. Because money holdings are a small part of household wealth, the wealth effect is the least important of the three. Whether or not the exchange rate effect is important depends upon the degree of openness of the economy. The UK and most other European economies have relatively open economies in the sense that imports and exports represent a much larger fraction of total GDP, so that the exchange rate effect can be significant. However, the exchange rate effect is probably secondary to the interest rate effect even in relatively open economies, for two reasons. First, the interest rate effect impacts immediately upon the whole economy, affecting consumers, homebuyers and firms across the board, while the loss of competitiveness that is part of the exchange rate effect impacts only upon traded goods, and affects mainly firms producing tradable goods and consumers buying tradable goods. Secondly, many of the countries of Europe have a common currency – the euro – which they share with many of their major trading partners, so that the exchange rate effect is muted.

To understand how policy influences AD, therefore, we shall examine the interest rate effect in more detail. Here we develop a theory of how the interest rate is determined, called the **theory of liquidity preference**, which was originally developed by John Maynard Keynes in the 1930s. After we develop this theory, we use it to understand the downward slope of the AD curve and how monetary policy shifts this curve. By shedding new light on the AD curve, the theory of liquidity preference expands our understanding of short-run economic fluctuations.

> **theory of liquidity preference** Keynes' theory that the interest rate adjusts to bring money supply and money demand into balance

The Theory of Liquidity Preference

In his classic book, *The General Theory of Employment, Interest and Money*, John Maynard Keynes proposed the theory of liquidity preference to explain what factors determine the economy's interest rate. The theory is, in essence, just an application of supply and demand. According to Keynes, the interest rate adjusts to balance the supply and demand for money. We introduced some elements of the theories covered here in Chapter 32 as part of the IS–LM model.

Recall the distinction between the *nominal interest rate* (the interest rate as usually reported), and the *real interest rate*, the interest rate corrected for the effects of inflation. Which interest rate are we now trying to explain? The answer is both. In the analysis that follows, we hold constant the expected rate of inflation. (This assumption is reasonable for studying the economy in the short run, as we are now doing.) Thus, when the nominal interest rate rises or falls, the real interest rate that people expect to earn rises or falls as well. For the rest of this chapter, when we refer to changes in the interest rate, you should envision the real and nominal interest rates moving in the same direction.

Let's now develop the theory of liquidity preference by considering the supply and demand for money and how each depends on the interest rate.

Money Supply The first element of the theory of liquidity preference is the supply of money. As we have previously noted, the money supply is assumed to be controlled by the central bank, such as the Bank of England, the European Central Bank or the US Federal Reserve. The central bank can alter the money supply through the purchase and sale of government bonds in outright open-market operations. When the central bank buys government bonds, the money it pays for the bonds is typically deposited in banks, and this money is added to bank reserves. When the central bank sells government bonds, the money it receives for the bonds is withdrawn from the banking system, and bank reserves fall. In addition to these open-market operations, the central bank can alter the money supply by changing the refinancing rate (the interest rate at which banks can borrow reserves from the central bank).

These details of monetary control are important for the implementation of central bank policy, and we discussed them in detail in Chapter 27, but they are not crucial in this chapter. Our goal here is to examine how changes in the money supply affect the AD for goods and services. For this purpose, we can ignore the details of how central bank policy is implemented and assume that the central bank controls the money supply directly. In other words, the quantity of money supplied in the economy is fixed at whatever level the central bank decides to set it.

Because the quantity of money supplied is fixed by central bank policy, it does not depend on other economic variables. In particular, it does not depend on the interest rate. Once the central bank has made its policy decision, the quantity of money supplied is the same, regardless of the prevailing interest rate. We represent a fixed money supply with a vertical supply curve in Figure 34.1.

What is important to keep in mind as we discuss the liquidity preference theory is that central banks interact with the banking system through setting overnight rates as we noted in Chapter 27. This sets the tone for the structure of interest rates throughout the economy but the spread of interest rates between the overnight rate and other interest rates is not directly controlled by central banks. It is these interest rates that are influenced by liquidity preference.

FIGURE 34.1

Equilibrium in the Money Market

According to the theory of liquidity preference, the interest rate adjusts to bring the quantity of money supplied and the quantity of money demanded into balance. If the interest rate is above the equilibrium level (such as at r_1), the quantity of money people want to hold (M_1^d) is less than the quantity the central bank has created, and this surplus of money puts downward pressure on the interest rate. Conversely, if the interest rate is below the equilibrium level (such as at r_2), the quantity of money people want to hold (M_2^d) is greater than the quantity the central bank has created, and this shortage of money puts upward pressure on the interest rate. Thus, the forces of supply and demand in the market for money push the interest rate towards the equilibrium interest rate, at which people are content holding the quantity of money the central bank has created.

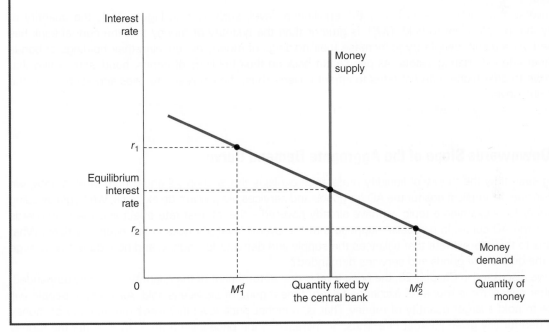

Money Demand The second element of the theory of liquidity preference is the demand for money. As a starting point for understanding money demand, recall that any asset's *liquidity* refers to the ease with which that asset is converted into the economy's medium of exchange. Money is the economy's medium of exchange, so it is by definition the most liquid asset available. The liquidity of money explains the demand for it: people choose to hold money instead of other assets that offer higher rates of return because money can be used to buy goods and services.

Although many factors determine the quantity of money demanded, the one emphasized by the theory of liquidity preference is the interest rate. The reason is that the interest rate is the opportunity cost of holding money. That is, when you hold wealth as cash in your pocket, instead of as an interest-bearing bond or bank account, you forgo the benefits of the interest you could have earned (the opportunity cost). An increase in the interest rate raises the opportunity cost of holding money. There is an incentive, therefore, for people to exchange cash holdings for interest-bearing deposits and this, as a result, reduces the quantity of money demanded. A decrease in the interest rate reduces the opportunity cost of holding money. The cost of the benefits forgone are not as high so there is more incentive to hold money as cash and as a result the quantity demanded increases. Thus, as shown in Figure 34.1, the money demand curve slopes downwards.

Equilibrium in the Money Market According to the theory of liquidity preference, the interest rate adjusts to balance the supply and demand for money. There is one interest rate, called the *equilibrium interest rate*, at which the quantity of money demanded exactly balances the quantity of money supplied. If the interest rate is at any other level, people will try to adjust their portfolios of assets and, as a result, drive the interest rate towards the equilibrium.

For example, suppose that the interest rate is above the equilibrium level, such as r_1 in Figure 34.1. In this case, the quantity of money that people want to hold, (M_1^d), is less than the quantity of money that the central bank has supplied. Those people who are holding the surplus of money will try to get rid of it by buying interest-bearing bonds or by depositing it in an interest-bearing bank account. Because bond issuers and banks prefer to pay lower interest rates, they respond to this surplus of money by lowering the interest rates they offer. As the interest rate falls, people become more willing to hold money until, at the equilibrium interest rate, people are happy to hold exactly the amount of money the central bank has supplied.

Conversely, at interest rates below the equilibrium level, such as r_2 in Figure 34.1, the quantity of money that people want to hold, (M_2^d), is greater than the quantity of money that the central bank has supplied. As a result, people try to increase their holdings of money by reducing their holdings of bonds and other interest-bearing assets. As people cut back on their holdings of bonds, bond issuers find that they have to offer higher interest rates to attract buyers. Thus, the interest rate rises and approaches the equilibrium level.

The Downwards Slope of the Aggregate Demand Curve

Having seen how the theory of liquidity preference explains the economy's equilibrium interest rate, we now consider its implications for the AD for goods and services. As a warm-up exercise, we begin by using the theory to re-examine a topic we have already covered – the interest rate effect and the downwards slope of the AD curve. In particular, suppose that the overall level of prices in the economy rises. What happens to the interest rate that balances the supply and demand for money, and how does that change affect the quantity of goods and services demanded?

As we discussed in Chapter 28, the price level is one determinant of the quantity of money demanded. At higher prices, more money is exchanged every time a good or service is sold. As a result, people will choose to hold a larger quantity of money. That is, a higher price level increases the quantity of money demanded for any given interest rate. Thus, an increase in the price level from P_1 to P_2 shifts the money demand curve to the right from MD_1 to MD_2, as shown in panel (a) of Figure 34.2.

Notice how this shift in money demand affects the equilibrium in the money market. For a fixed money supply, the interest rate must rise to balance money supply and money demand. The higher price level has increased the amount of money people want to hold and has shifted the money demand curve to the right. Yet the quantity of money supplied is unchanged, so the interest rate must rise from r_1 to r_2 to discourage the additional demand.

This increase in the interest rate has ramifications not only for the money market but also for the quantity of goods and services demanded, as shown in panel (b). At a higher interest rate, the cost of borrowing and the return to saving are greater. Fewer households choose to borrow to buy a new house, and those who do, buy smaller houses, so the demand for residential investment falls. Fewer firms choose to borrow to build new factories and buy new equipment, so business investment falls. Thus, when the price level rises from P_1 to P_2, increasing money demand from MD_1 to MD_2 and raising the interest rate from r_1 to r_2, the quantity of goods and services demanded falls from Y_1 to Y_2.

FIGURE 34.2

The Money Market and the Slope of the Aggregate Demand Curve

An increase in the price level from P_1 to P_2 shifts the money demand curve to the right, as in panel (a). This increase in money demand causes the interest rate to rise from r_1 to r_2. Because the interest rate is the cost of borrowing, the increase in the interest rate reduces the quantity of goods and services demanded from Y_1 to Y_2. This negative relationship between the price level and quantity demanded is represented with a downwards sloping AD curve, as in panel (b).

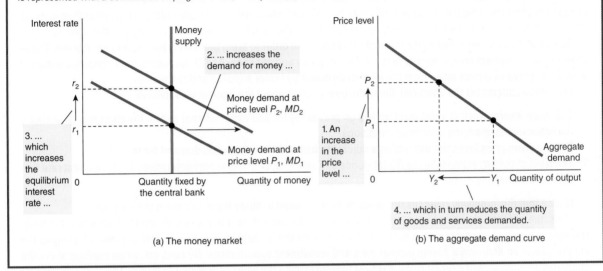

(a) The money market

(b) The aggregate demand curve

This analysis of the interest rate effect can be summarized in three steps:

1. A higher price level raises money demand.
2. Higher money demand leads to a higher interest rate.
3. A higher interest rate reduces the quantity of goods and services demanded.

Of course, the same logic works in reverse as well: a lower price level reduces money demand, which leads to a lower interest rate, and this in turn increases the quantity of goods and services demanded. The end result of this analysis is a negative relationship between the price level and the quantity of goods and services demanded, which is illustrated with a downwards sloping AD curve. This is the same conclusion we reached when looking at the effect of a shift in the LM curve in Chapter 32.

FYI

Interest Rates in the Long Run and the Short Run

At this point, we should pause and reflect on a seemingly awkward embarrassment of riches. It might appear as if we now have two theories for how interest rates are determined. One states that the interest rate adjusts to balance the supply of and demand for loanable funds (that is, national saving and desired investment). By contrast, we just established here that the interest rate adjusts to balance the supply and demand for money.

To reconcile these two theories, we must again consider the differences between the long-run and short-run behaviour of the economy. Three macroeconomic variables are of central importance: the economy's output of goods and services; the interest rate; and the price level. According to the classical macroeconomic theory we developed in Chapters 22, 23 and 24, these variables are determined as follows:

1. *Output* is determined by the supplies of capital and labour and the available production technology for turning capital and labour into output (the natural rate of output).
2. For any given level of output, the *interest rate* adjusts to balance the supply and demand for loanable funds.

(*Continued*)

3. The *price* level adjusts to balance the supply and demand for money. Changes in the supply of money lead to proportionate changes in the price level.

These are three of the essential propositions of classical economic theory. Many economists believe that these propositions do a good job of describing how the economy works *in the long run*.

Yet these propositions do not hold in the short run. As we discussed in the preceding chapter, many prices are slow to adjust to changes in the money supply; this is reflected in a SRAS curve that is upwards sloping rather than vertical. As a result, the overall price level cannot, by itself, balance the supply and demand for money in the short run. This stickiness of the price level forces the interest rate to move in order to bring the money market into equilibrium. These changes in the interest rate, in turn, affect the AD for goods and services. As AD fluctuates, the economy's output of goods and services moves away from the level determined by factor supplies and technology.

For issues concerning the short run, then, it is best to think about the economy as follows:

1. The *price level* is stuck at some level (based on previously formed expectations) and, in the short run, is relatively unresponsive to changing economic conditions.
2. For any given price level, the *interest rate* adjusts to balance the supply and demand for money.
3. The level of *output* responds to the AD for goods and services, which is in part determined by the interest rate that balances the money market.

Notice that this precisely reverses the order of analysis used to study the economy in the long run.

Thus, the different theories of the interest rate are useful for different purposes. When thinking about the long-run determinants of interest rates, it is best to keep in mind the loanable funds theory. This approach highlights the importance of an economy's saving propensities and investment opportunities. By contrast, when thinking about the short-run determinants of interest rates, it is best to keep in mind the liquidity preference theory. This theory highlights the importance of monetary policy.

Changes in the Money Supply

So far we have used the theory of liquidity preference to explain more fully how the total quantity demanded of goods and services in the economy changes as the price level changes. That is, we have examined movements along the downwards sloping AD curve. The theory also sheds light, however, on some of the other events that alter the quantity of goods and services demanded. Whenever the quantity of goods and services demanded changes *for a given price level*, the AD curve shifts.

One important variable that shifts the AD curve is monetary policy. To see how monetary policy affects the economy in the short run, suppose that the central bank increases the money supply by buying government bonds in open-market operations. (Why the central bank might do this will become clear later after we understand the effects of such a move.)

As panel (a) of Figure 34.3 shows, an increase in the money supply shifts the money-supply curve to the right from MS_1 to MS_2. Because the money demand curve has not changed, the interest rate falls from r_1 to r_2 to balance money supply and money demand. That is, the interest rate must fall to induce people to hold the additional money that the central bank has created.

Once again, the interest rate influences the quantity of goods and services demanded, as shown in panel (b) of Figure 34.3. The lower interest rate reduces the cost of borrowing and the return to saving. Households buy more and larger houses, stimulating the demand for residential investment. Firms spend more on new factories and new equipment, stimulating business investment. As a result, the quantity of goods and services demanded at a given price level $\overline{P}$ rises from Y_1 to Y_2. Of course, there is nothing special about $\overline{P}$: the monetary injection raises the quantity of goods and services demanded at every price level. Thus, the entire AD curve shifts to the right.

To sum up: when the central bank increases the money supply, it leads to a fall in the interest rate and increases the quantity of goods and services demanded for any given price level, shifting the AD curve to the right. Conversely, when the central bank contracts the money supply, the interest rate rises to bring the money market into equilibrium and reduces the quantity of goods and services demanded for any given price level, shifting the AD curve to the left.

We explored the same principle in Chapter 32 as part of the introduction to the IS–LM model. In that case a loosening of monetary policy causes the LM curve to shift to the right and at the given price level the AD curve shifts to the right (and vice versa).

The Role of Interest Rates

Our discussion so far in this chapter has treated the money supply as the central bank's policy instrument. When the central bank buys government bonds in open-market operations, it increases the money supply and expands AD. When the central bank sells government bonds in open-market operations, it decreases the money supply and contracts AD.

More reflective of current central bank policy is to treat the interest rate, rather than the money supply, as its policy instrument. The Bank of England, the European Central Bank and the US Federal Reserve, conduct policy by setting the interest rate at which they will lend to the banking sector – the refinancing rate for the European Central Bank, the repurchase or 'repo' rate for the Bank of England, and the discount rate for the Federal Reserve.

The central bank's decision to set interest rates rather than target a certain level (or rate of growth) of the money supply does not fundamentally alter our analysis of monetary policy. The theory of liquidity preference illustrates an important principle: monetary policy can be described either in terms of the money supply or in terms of the interest rate. When the central bank sets a target for the refinancing rate of, say, x per cent, the central bank's bond traders are told: 'Conduct whatever open-market operations are necessary to ensure that the equilibrium interest rate equals x per cent.' In other words, when the central bank sets a target for the interest rate, it commits itself to adjusting the money supply in order to make the equilibrium in the money market hit that target.

As a result, changes in monetary policy can be viewed either in terms of a changing target for the interest rate or in terms of a change in the money supply. As noted in Chapter 27, when you read in the newspaper that the central bank has lowered interest rates, you should understand that this occurs only because the central bank's bond traders are doing what it takes to make it happen. If interest rates have been lowered, then the central bank's bond traders will have bought government bonds, and this purchase increases the money supply and lowers the equilibrium interest rate (just as in Figure 34.3).

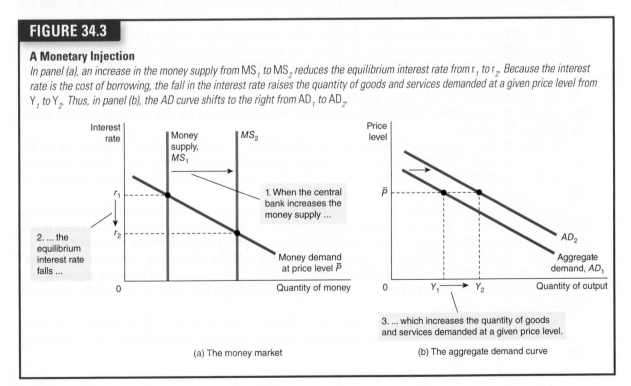

FIGURE 34.3

A Monetary Injection

In panel (a), an increase in the money supply from MS_1 to MS_2 reduces the equilibrium interest rate from r_1 to r_2. Because the interest rate is the cost of borrowing, the fall in the interest rate raises the quantity of goods and services demanded at a given price level from Y_1 to Y_2. Thus, in panel (b), the AD curve shifts to the right from AD_1 to AD_2.

(a) The money market

(b) The aggregate demand curve

The lessons from all this are: changes in monetary policy that aim to expand AD can be described either as increasing the money supply or as lowering the interest rate. Changes in monetary policy that aim to contract AD can be described either as decreasing the money supply or as raising the interest rate.

SELF TEST Use the theory of liquidity preference to explain how a decrease in the money supply affects the equilibrium interest rate. How does this change in monetary policy affect the AD curve?

HOW FISCAL POLICY INFLUENCES AGGREGATE DEMAND

The government can influence the behaviour of the economy not only with monetary policy but also with fiscal policy. Fiscal policy refers to the government's choices regarding the overall level of government purchases or taxes. Earlier in the book we examined how fiscal policy influences saving, investment and growth in the long run. In the short run, however, the primary effect of fiscal policy is on the AD for goods and services.

Changes in Government Purchases

We saw in Chapter 32 that changes in autonomous spending can have an effect on the level of spending in the economy which is greater than the initial injection. The multiplier effect means that AD will shift by a larger amount than the increase in government spending. However, the crowding-out effect, which we introduced in Chapter 24, suggests that the shift in AD could be *smaller* than the initial injection. While an increase in government purchases stimulates the AD for goods and services, it also causes the interest rate to rise, and a higher interest rate reduces investment spending and chokes off AD. The reduction in AD that results when a fiscal expansion raises the interest rate is called the crowding-out effect.

To see why the crowding-out effect occurs, let's consider what happens in the money market using an example we used in Chapter 32 when the government invests in nuclear power stations from Nucelec. As we discussed, this increase in demand raises the incomes of the workers and owners of this firm (and, because of the multiplier effect, of other firms as well). As incomes rise, households plan to buy more goods and services and, as a result, choose to hold more of their wealth in liquid form. That is, the increase in income caused by the fiscal expansion raises the demand for money.

The effect of the increase in money demand is shown in panel (a) of Figure 34.4. Because the central bank has not changed the money supply, the vertical supply curve remains the same. When the higher level of income shifts the money demand curve to the right from MD_1 to MD_2, the interest rate must rise from r_1 to r_2 to keep supply and demand in balance.

The increase in the interest rate, in turn, reduces the quantity of goods and services demanded. In particular, because borrowing is more expensive, the demand for residential and business investment goods declines. That is, as the increase in government purchases increases the demand for goods and services, it may also crowd out investment. This crowding-out effect partially offsets the impact of government purchases on AD, as illustrated in panel (b) of Figure 34.4. The initial impact of the increase in government purchases is to shift the AD curve from AD_1 to AD_2, but once crowding out takes place, the AD curve drops back to AD_3.

To sum up: when the government increases its purchases by €10 billion, the AD for goods and services could rise by more or less than €10 billion, depending on whether the multiplier effect or the crowding-out effect is larger.

FIGURE 34.4

The Crowding-Out Effect

Panel (a) shows the money market. When the government increases its purchases of goods and services, the resulting increase in income raises the demand for money from MD_1 to MD_2, and this causes the equilibrium interest rate to rise from r_1 to r_2. Panel (b) shows the effects on AD. The initial impact of the increase in government purchases shifts the AD curve from AD_1 to AD_2. Yet, because the interest rate is the cost of borrowing, the increase in the interest rate tends to reduce the quantity of goods and services demanded, particularly for investment goods. This crowding out of investment partially offsets the impact of the fiscal expansion on AD. In the end, the AD curve shifts only to AD_3.

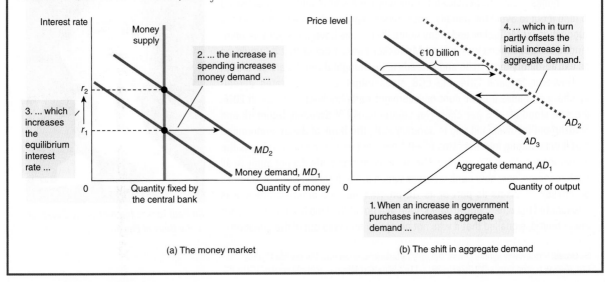

(a) The money market

(b) The shift in aggregate demand

Negative Interest Rates and 'Crank' Ideas

In the wake of the Financial Crisis, the central banks of many developed economies have interest rates at historically low levels. Some central banks have also used quantitative easing (QE) and other methods to try and trigger consumption and investment. There is some evidence to suggest that in many countries monetary policy proved impotent in countering the fiscal austerity programmes some governments have adopted, and as a result, economic growth remained sluggish. Some argue that the Bank of England's QE programme had simply led to banks building up their balance sheets but not extending their lending to businesses and consumers. With interest rates at very low levels in many countries, the idea of the *zero lower bound* has come to the fore, which basically says that interest rates should not fall below zero. Could the lower bound be below zero?

In 2009, Professor Mankiw wrote an article in the *New York Times* suggesting negative interest rates. Borrow €1000 today and pay back a smaller amount at some point in the future. If the interest rate was −4 per cent and you had borrowed the €1000 for a period of a year, you would pay back €960 in a year's time. In that same article, Professor Mankiw recounted a discussion with one of his graduate students at Harvard about a scheme, put forward by the student, whereby the central bank announces that in one year's time it would pick a digit from one to nine out of a hat and any currency ending in that number would cease to be legal tender. People would thus know that in one year's time 10 per cent of the cash would cease to be legal tender; what would they do? The logic is to spend it. The additional spending would increase AD and act as a boost to the economy. Such a policy might enable central banks to set negative interest rates provided the rate was less than 10 per cent because there would then be an incentive to lend at (say) −4 per cent rather than potentially losing 10 per cent.

(Continued)

Mankiw noted that the basic idea of a negative interest rate was not new – a late 19th-century economist, Silvio Gesell, had mooted this and Gesell's idea was picked up by Keynes. Keynes noted that initially he saw Gesell's ideas as being those of a 'crank' but changed his opinion and even referred to Gesell as an 'unduly neglected prophet'.

In 2013, the idea of negative interest rates was raised by the Bank of England deputy governor, Paul Tucker, who outlined the possibility, albeit in very cautious terms, when giving evidence to the Treasury Select Committee. If the Bank of England reduced its lending rate to the banking system to negative rates, banks would be penalized for holding cash and would be incentivized to lend it out to avoid the penalty. Economists expressed some surprise at the suggestion by Mr Tucker and many noted that it may have considerable unintended consequences and indeed Mr Tucker himself noted that it 'would be an extraordinary thing to do and it needs to be thought through very carefully'.

However, in June 2014, the ECB made negative interest rates a reality charging banks 0.1 per cent on overnight cash holdings. By March 2016, the rate stood at −0.3 per cent. The central banks of Sweden, Denmark and Switzerland followed suit and in January 2016, the Bank of Japan announced that it was cutting interest rates to −0.1 per cent as it attempted to break the deflationary cycle in the country. The negative interest rate did not apply to all bank reserves, only new bank reserves which arose from the Bank of Japan's purchases of assets as part of its QE programme. The announcement was unexpected but other central banks, who had not at the time breached the zero lower bound, signalled that it was not an option that was out of the question.

Sir Paul Tucker, former Deputy Governor of the Bank of England.

Sources: http://www.nytimes.com/ 2009/04/19/business/economy/19view.html?_r=0; http://www.ft.com/cms/s/0/978247fe-8013-11e2-96ba-00144feabdc0.html#axzz46ArQQwPK

Changes in Taxes

The other important instrument of fiscal policy, besides the level of government purchases, is the level of taxation. When the government cuts personal income taxes, for instance, it increases households' take-home pay. Households will save some of this additional income, but they will also spend some of it on consumer goods. Because it increases consumer spending, the tax cut shifts the AD curve to the right. Similarly, a tax increase depresses consumer spending and shifts the AD curve to the left.

The size of the shift in AD resulting from a tax change is also affected by the multiplier and crowding-out effects. When the government cuts taxes and stimulates consumer spending, earnings and profits rise, which further stimulates consumer spending. This is the multiplier effect. At the same time, higher income leads to higher money demand, which tends to raise interest rates. Higher interest rates make borrowing more costly, which reduces investment spending. This is the crowding-out effect. Depending on the size of the multiplier and crowding-out effects, the shift in AD could be larger or smaller than the tax change that causes it.

In addition to the multiplier and crowding-out effects, there is another important determinant of the size of the shift in AD that results from a tax change: households' perceptions about whether the tax change is permanent or temporary. For example, suppose that the government announces a tax cut of €1000 per household. In deciding how much of this €1000 to spend, households must ask themselves how long this extra income will last. If households expect the tax cut to be permanent, they may view it as adding substantially to their financial resources and, therefore, increase their spending by a large amount. In this case, the tax cut will have a large impact on AD. By contrast, if households expect the tax change to be temporary, they may view it as adding only slightly to their financial resources and, therefore, increase their spending by only a small amount. In this case, the tax cut will have a small impact on AD.

It should be noted that fiscal policy can also affect the AS curve and we will look at this in more detail in Chapter 36.

SELF TEST Suppose that the government reduces spending on motorway construction by €1 billion. Which way does the AD curve shift? Explain why the shift might be larger than €1 billion. Explain why the shift might be smaller than €1 billion.

USING POLICY TO STABILIZE THE ECONOMY

We have seen how monetary and fiscal policy can affect the economy's AD for goods and services. These theoretical insights raise some important policy questions: should policymakers use these instruments to control AD and stabilize the economy? If so, when? If not, why not?

The Case for an Active Stabilization Policy

Government spending is one determinant of the position of the AD curve. When the government cuts spending, AD will fall, this will depress production and employment in the short run. If the central bank wants to prevent this adverse effect of the fiscal policy, it can act to expand AD by increasing the money supply. A monetary expansion would reduce interest rates, stimulate investment spending and expand AD. If monetary policy responds appropriately, the combined changes in monetary and fiscal policy could leave the AD for goods and services unaffected.

This analysis is exactly the sort followed by the members of the policy-setting committees of central banks like the Bank of England and the European Central Bank. They know that monetary policy is an important determinant of AD. They also know that there are other important determinants as well, including fiscal policy set by the government, and so they will watch debates over fiscal policy with a keen eye.

This response of monetary policy to the change in fiscal policy is an example of a more general phenomenon: the use of policy instruments to stabilize AD and, as a result, production and employment. We have seen in Chapter 32 how the Great Depression in the 1930s spawned a belief that governments should act to manage AD in the wake of the research which followed Keynes' *General Theory*. As a result, economic stabilization has been seen as an explicit or implicit goal of government macroeconomic policy in European and North American economies following the Second World War. In the UK, for example, this view was embodied in a government White Paper, published in 1944, which explicitly stated: 'The Government accepts as one of its primary aims and responsibilities the maintenance of a high and stable level of employment after the War.' In the USA, similar sentiments were embodied in the Employment Act of 1946. This explicit recognition by governments of a responsibility to stabilize the economy has two implications. The first, more modest, implication is that the government should avoid being a cause of economic fluctuations itself. Thus, many economists advise against large and sudden changes in monetary and fiscal policy, for such changes are likely to cause fluctuations in AD. Moreover, when large changes do occur, it is important that monetary and fiscal policymakers be aware of, and respond to, the other's actions.

The second, more ambitious, implication of this explicit admission of responsibility – and one that was especially dominant in the first 30 years after the end of the Second World War – was that the government should respond to changes in the private economy in order to stabilize AD. To put the reasons for the pursuit of active stabilization policies into context, it is important to note that politicians remembered the problems of the Great Depression before the war, and were keen to avoid a recurrence, not only because of the misery involved for millions of people, but also because of the political effects of economic depression which were associated with a rise in extremism. Poverty was directly linked with the rise of extremism and political instability. As the war ended, therefore, they wanted to look forward to a better world in which governments could help avoid these problems. The adoption of Keynesian demand management policies seemed to offer some promise that full employment could be achieved.

Keynes (and his many followers) argued that AD fluctuates because of largely irrational waves of pessimism and optimism. He used the term 'animal spirits' to refer to these arbitrary changes in attitude.

When pessimism reigns, households reduce consumption spending, and firms reduce investment spending. The result is reduced AD, lower production and higher unemployment. Conversely, when optimism reigns, households and firms increase spending. The result is higher AD, higher production and inflationary pressure. Notice that these changes in attitude are, to some extent, self-fulfilling.

In principle, the government can adjust its monetary and fiscal policy in response to these waves of optimism and pessimism and, thereby, stabilize the economy. For example, when people are excessively pessimistic, the central bank can expand the money supply to lower interest rates and expand AD. When they are excessively optimistic, it can contract the money supply to raise interest rates and dampen AD.

The Case Against an Active Stabilization Policy

Some economists argue that the government should avoid active use of monetary and fiscal policy to try to stabilize the economy. They claim that these policy instruments should be set to achieve long-run goals, such as rapid economic growth and low inflation, and that the economy should be left to deal with short-run fluctuations on its own. Although these economists may admit that monetary and fiscal policy can stabilize the economy in theory, they doubt whether it can do so in practice.

The primary argument against active monetary and fiscal policy is that the effects of these policies may be, to a large extent, uncertain both in terms of magnitude and timing. As we have seen, monetary policy works by changing interest rates. This can have strong and rapid effects on consumer spending if (as in the United Kingdom) a large number of people are buying their house with a mortgage loan on which the interest rate can vary according to market interest rates: quite simply, if interest rates go up, then mortgage payments go up and people have less money to spend. Yet, if people have mortgages on which the interest rate is fixed for one or more years ahead, then the interest rate change will only affect mortgage payments with a very long lag. If most people live in rented accommodation (as is the case in many of the countries of continental Europe), then a rise in interest rates will have no strong effects through this channel at all. In all cases, however, the interest rate rise will still clearly affect consumer spending because buying goods on credit (e.g. with a credit card) will be more expensive. The net effect on consumer spending may, therefore, be hard to predict, especially in terms of its timing.

Monetary policy can also affect AD through its influence on investment spending. Many firms make investment plans far in advance. Thus, most economists believe that it takes at least six months for changes in monetary policy to have much effect on output and employment. Most central banks readily admit that changes in interest rates can take up to 18 months to work their way through the economy. Moreover, once these effects occur, they can last for several years.

Critics of stabilization policy argue that because of these uncertain lags, the central bank should not try to fine-tune the economy. They claim that the central bank often reacts too late to changing economic conditions and, as a result, ends up being a cause of, rather than a cure for, economic fluctuations. These critics advocate a passive monetary policy, such as slow and steady growth in the money supply.

Fiscal policy may also work with a lag. Of course, the impact of a change in government spending is felt as soon as the change takes place and cuts in direct and indirect taxation can feed through into the economy quickly. However, considerable time may pass between the decision to adopt a government spending programme and its implementation. In the UK, for example, the government has often tended to undershoot on its planned spending, partly because of problems in attracting sufficient extra staff into key public services such as transport, education and health. At the same time, announcements about changes to income taxes (both personal and corporate) tend to occur months (and sometimes years) before implementation. In the intervening time period, households and businesses factor in the impending changes into their behaviour and so the effects are uncertain.

These lags in monetary and fiscal policy are a problem in part because economic forecasting is so imprecise. If forecasters could accurately predict the condition of the economy a year in advance, then monetary and fiscal policymakers could look ahead when making policy decisions. In this case, policymakers could stabilize the economy despite the lags they face. Decisions are made, in part, on the basis of existing statistical data which are fed into models. That data can be inaccurate and subject to revision as we have seen. Without accurate and up-to-date information, the outcome from modelling can vary considerably. In practice, however, major recessions and depressions arrive without much advance warning. The best policymakers can do at any time is to respond to economic changes as they occur.

Automatic Stabilizers

All economists – both advocates and critics of stabilization policy – agree that the lags in implementation render policy less useful as a tool for short-run stabilization. The economy would be more stable, therefore, if policymakers could find a way to avoid some of these lags. In fact they have **automatic stabilizers**, changes in fiscal policy that stimulate AD when the economy goes into a recession without policymakers having to take any deliberate action.

> **automatic stabilizers** changes in fiscal policy that stimulate AD when the economy goes into a recession, without policymakers having to take any deliberate action

The most important automatic stabilizer is the tax system. When the economy goes into a recession, the amount of taxes collected by the government falls automatically because almost all taxes are closely tied to economic activity and because in many countries income taxes are progressive. This means that as economic activity increases an increasing proportion of income is paid in tax and vice versa. Income tax depends on households' incomes and corporation tax depends on firms' profits. Because incomes and profits both fall in a recession, the government's tax revenue falls as well. Taxes are a withdrawal from the circular flow which has the effect of dampening the level of AD. If tax revenues are lower, it means that consumers have more disposable income to spend on consumption and businesses on investment. If economic activity increases, then tax revenues will rise. These automatic tax changes either stimulate or dampen AD and, thereby, reduce the magnitude of economic fluctuations.

Government spending also acts as an automatic stabilizer. In particular, when the economy goes into a recession and workers are laid off, more people apply for state unemployment benefits, welfare benefits and other forms of income support. Extra spending on benefits and the welfare system helps to provide a cushion against too large a fall in economic activity. This increase in government spending stimulates AD at exactly the time when it is insufficient to maintain full employment. However, it must be taken into consideration that in order to finance this additional spending (at a time when tax revenue is falling) governments may have to borrow. This additional borrowing can put upward pressure on interest rates and dampen the overall effect.

Automatic stabilizers are generally not sufficiently strong to prevent recessions completely. Nevertheless, without these automatic stabilizers, output and employment would probably be more volatile than they are. For this reason, many economists would not favour a policy of always running a balanced budget, as some politicians have proposed. When the economy goes into a recession, taxes fall, government spending rises, and the government's budget moves toward deficit. If the government faced a strict balanced-budget rule, it would be forced to look for ways to raise taxes or cut spending in a recession. In other words, a strict **balanced budget** rule would eliminate the automatic stabilizers inherent in our current system of taxes and government spending and would, in effect, be an 'automatic destabilizer'.

> **balanced budget** where the total sum of money received by a government in tax revenue and interest is equal to the amount it spends, including on any debt interest owing

---

SELF TEST Suppose a wave of negative 'animal spirits' overruns the economy, and people become pessimistic about the future. What happens to AD? If the central bank wants to stabilize AD, how should it alter the money supply? If it does this, what happens to the interest rate? Why might the central bank choose not to respond in this way?

CONCLUSION

Before policymakers make any change in policy, they need to consider all the effects of their decisions. Earlier in the book we examined classical models of the economy, which describe the long-run effects of monetary and fiscal policy. There we saw how fiscal policy influences saving, investment and long-run growth, and how monetary policy influences the price level and the inflation rate.

In this chapter we examined the short-run effects of monetary and fiscal policy. We saw how these policy instruments can change the AD for goods and services and, thereby, alter the economy's production and employment in the short run. When the government reduces spending in order to balance the budget, it needs to consider both the long-run effects on saving and growth and the short-run effects on AD and employment. When the central bank reduces the growth rate of the money supply, it must take into account the long-run effect on inflation as well as the short-run effect on production. In the next chapter we discuss the transition between the short run and the long run more fully, and we see that policymakers often face a trade-off between long-run and short-run goals.

IN THE NEWS

The Multiplier and Fiscal Policy

In Chapter 32 and in this chapter we have spoken of fiscal policy being used as a tool to boost the economy. Part of the justification for using government spending and taxation in this way is the role of the multiplier.

Fiscal Multipliers

The theory seems intuitive enough – if government spends money on a major infrastructure project it is logical that the income received will be spent and feed through to other parts of the economy and as a result lead to a rise in national income that is a multiple of the initial injection. Most economists would not disagree with this base analysis, but where they do disagree is on the size of the multiplier effect and therefore whether this is the best way to smooth out short-term fluctuations in economic activity. There has been a considerable amount of research into the size of fiscal or government expenditure multipliers – the change in output that arises as a result of a change in government expenditure.

Does the size of the fiscal multiplier matter? The difference in the estimates of the size of the fiscal multiplier according to two leading macroeconomists, is revealing. Robert Barro, a Harvard professor, wrote in 2009 that the size of the fiscal multiplier in peacetime was close to zero; Christine Romer, a professor of economics at the University of California, Berkeley and a former Chair of Economic Advisors to President Obama, suggested that the multiplier was nearer to 1.6. When the US government passed a stimulus package of $787 billion (€721 billion) in 2009, the difference in the number of jobs created of these two estimates of the multiplier effects would be around 3.75 million according to three economists, Mendoza, Vegh and Ilzetzki, in an IMF working paper.

What the research does seem to show is that the size of the fiscal multiplier is dependent on a wide range of factors. The fiscal multiplier might be different in developed and less-developed countries, whether the government spending 'shock' is anticipated or unanticipated, how open the economy is, the exchange rate regime used by the country (whether exchange rates are fixed against other currencies, managed or allowed to float freely in response to market conditions), whether the economy is experiencing a financial or debt crisis and the time preferences of the population of a country. Time preferences refer to how people react to the fiscal stimulus; if a government cut taxes or increased spending, what proportion of the increase in income would be spent and what proportion saved, and to what extent would people build into their decision-making the expectation that a 'windfall' now, will 'inevitably' lead to tax rises in the future? The idea that people will save most of any increase in government spending because they expect to have to pay higher taxes in the future is called *Ricardian Equivalence* and was initially developed by

(Continued)

David Ricardo in the 19th century but has been refined somewhat by Robert Barro. The size of the fiscal multiplier will depend in part, therefore, on the extent to which consumers are Ricardian in their response.

A discussion paper written by Gilberto Marcheggiano and David Miles (Bank of England External MPC Discussion Paper no. 39, January 2013) noted that 'Empirical studies … face great challenges in measuring multipliers because of the difficulties of identifying exogenous fiscal shocks and controlling for other factors that might affect output responses'. They further note that studies on the size of fiscal multipliers include estimates between 1.2 and 1.8 and in other cases, 0.8 to 1.5.

Questions

1 How do you think the size of the fiscal multiplier would vary when a government announced an increase in spending of €50 billion to be spent on infrastructure projects compared to a cut in income taxes which would put an equivalent amount into people's pockets?

2 Why do you think that Barro and Romer have such a different view of the size of the fiscal multiplier?

3 Why might the size of the fiscal multiplier depend on whether it is anticipated or unanticipated?

4 The size of the fiscal multiplier will depend on Ricardian Equivalence. To what extent do you think people adjust their spending decisions in response to expectations of future tax changes?

5 If it is difficult to empirically arrive at a reliable and accurate measure of the size of fiscal multipliers, does this mean that policymakers should avoid resorting to the use of fiscal policy as a means of stimulating an economy? Justify your answer.

Source: https://www.imf.org/external/pubs/ft/wp/2011/wp1152.pdf

The size of the multiplier effect of increased investment and demand differs.

SUMMARY

- In developing a theory of short-run economic fluctuations, Keynes proposed the theory of liquidity preference to explain the determinants of the interest rate. According to this theory, the interest rate adjusts to balance the supply and demand for money.

- An increase in the price level raises money demand and increases the interest rate that brings the money market into equilibrium. Because the interest rate represents the cost of borrowing, a higher interest rate reduces investment and, thereby, the quantity of goods and services demanded. The downwards sloping AD curve expresses this negative relationship between the price level and the quantity demanded.

- Policymakers can influence AD with monetary policy. An increase in the money supply reduces the equilibrium interest rate for any given price level. Because a lower interest rate stimulates investment spending, the AD curve shifts to the right. Conversely, a decrease in the money supply raises the equilibrium interest rate for any given price level and shifts the AD curve to the left.

● Policymakers can also influence AD with fiscal policy. An increase in government purchases or a cut in taxes shifts the AD curve to the right. A decrease in government purchases or an increase in taxes shifts the AD curve to the left.

● When the government alters spending or taxes, the resulting shift in AD can be larger or smaller than the fiscal change. The multiplier effect tends to amplify the effects of fiscal policy on AD. The crowding-out effect tends to dampen the effects of fiscal policy on AD.

● Because monetary and fiscal policy can influence AD, the government sometimes uses these policy instruments in an attempt to stabilize the economy. Economists disagree about how active the government should be in this effort. According to advocates of active stabilization policy, changes in attitudes by households and firms shift AD; if the government does not respond, the result is undesirable and unnecessary fluctuations in output and employment. According to critics of an active stabilization policy, monetary and fiscal policy work with such long lags that attempts at stabilizing the economy often end up being destabilizing.

QUESTIONS FOR REVIEW

1 What are the three ways in which monetary policy affects AD?

2 What is the theory of liquidity preference?

3 How does the theory of liquidity preference help explain the downwards slope of the AD curve?

4 Use the theory of liquidity preference to explain how a decrease in the money supply affects the AD curve.

5 The government spends €500 million improving canals for trade and leisure use. Explain why AD might increase by more than €500 million. Explain why AD might increase by less than €500 million.

6 If governments commit to demand management policies in an attempt to maintain the economy as near to full employment output as possible, what effect do you think this may have on expectations and economic actors' responses to government policy initiatives?

7 Suppose that survey measures of consumer confidence indicate a wave of pessimism is sweeping the country. If policymakers do nothing, what will happen to aggregate AD? What should the government do if it wants to stabilize AD? If the government does nothing, should the central bank stabilize AD? If so, how?

8 How might a government use taxation as a tool in expansionary fiscal policy?

9 Outline the arguments for and against an active stabilization policy.

10 Give an example of a government policy that acts as an automatic stabilizer. Explain why this policy has this effect.

PROBLEMS AND APPLICATIONS

1 Explain how each of the following developments would affect the supply of money, the demand for money and the interest rate. Illustrate your answers with diagrams.

  a. The central bank's bond traders buy bonds in open market operations.
  b. An increase in credit card availability reduces the cash people hold.
  c. The central bank reduces banks' reserve requirements.
  d. Households decide to hold more money to use for holiday shopping.
  e. A wave of optimism boosts business investment and expands AD.
  f. A significant fall in oil prices shifts the SRAS curve to the right.

2 Suppose banks install automatic teller machines on every street corner and, by making cash readily available, reduce the amount of money people want to hold.

  a. Assume the central bank does not change the money supply. According to the theory of liquidity preference, what happens to the interest rate? What happens to AD?
  b. If the central bank wants to stabilize AD, how should it respond?

3 The economy is in a recession with high unemployment and low output.

    a. Use a graph of AD and AS to illustrate the current situation. Be sure to include the AD curve, the SRAS curve and the LRAS curve.

    b. Identify an open-market operation that would restore the economy to its natural rate.

    c. Use a graph of the money market to illustrate the effect of this open-market operation. Show the resulting change in the interest rate.

    d. Use a graph similar to the one in part (a) to show the effect of the open-market operation on output and the price level. Explain in words why the policy has the effect that you have shown in the graph.

4 This chapter explains that expansionary monetary policy reduces the interest rate and thus stimulates demand for investment goods. Explain how such a policy also stimulates the demand for net exports.

5 Suppose government spending increases. Would the effect on AD be larger if the central bank took no action in response, or if the central bank were committed to maintaining a fixed interest rate? Explain.

6 In which of the following circumstances is expansionary fiscal policy more likely to lead to a short-run increase in investment? Explain.

    a. When the investment accelerator is large, or when it is small?

    b. When the interest sensitivity of investment is large, or when it is small?

7 Assume the economy is in a recession. Explain how each of the following policies would affect consumption and investment. In each case, indicate any direct effects, any effects resulting from changes in total output, any effects resulting from changes in the interest rate and the overall effect. If there are conflicting effects making the answer ambiguous, say so.

    a. An increase in government spending.

    b. A reduction in taxes.

    c. An expansion of the money supply.

8 For various reasons, fiscal policy changes automatically when output and employment fluctuate.

    a. Explain why tax revenue changes when the economy goes into a recession.

    b. Explain why government spending changes when the economy goes into a recession.

    c. If the government was to operate under a strict balanced-budget rule, what would it have to do in a recession? Would this make the recession more or less severe?

9 Assume that a law has been proposed that would make price stability the sole goal of monetary policy. Suppose such a law were passed.

    a. How would the central bank respond to an event that contracted AD?

    b. How would the central bank respond to an event that caused an adverse shift in SRAS?

    c. In each case, is there another monetary policy option that would lead to greater stability in output?

10 An economy is operating with a negative output gap of €400 billion. The government of this economy wants to close this output gap. The central bank agrees to adjust the money supply to hold the interest rate constant so there is no crowding out. The MPC is 0.8, and the price level is fixed in the short run. In what direction and by how much would government spending need to change to close the output gap? Explain your thinking.

35 THE SHORT-RUN TRADE-OFF BETWEEN INFLATION AND UNEMPLOYMENT

Earlier in the book we discussed the long-run determinants of unemployment and inflation. We saw that the natural rate of unemployment depends on various features of the labour market, such as minimum wage laws, the market power of unions, the role of efficiency wages and the effectiveness of job search. By contrast, the inflation rate depends primarily on growth in the money supply, which a nation's central bank controls. In the long run, therefore, inflation and unemployment are largely unrelated problems. In the short-run the situation is very different. The relationship between inflation and unemployment is a topic that has attracted the attention of some of the most important economists of the last half century. The best way to understand this relationship is to see how thinking about it has evolved over time.

David Hume Studies on the relationship between unemployment and inflation is not a new phenomenon. In the early part of the 19th century, the convertibility of currency into gold was suspended during the Napoleonic Wars and the period was marred by accelerating inflation. At the same time, many small banks collapsed which resulted in a reduction in the money supply. The consequence was a serious economic decline which caused considerable hardship on the poor as unemployment rose. The Scottish philosopher, historian and economist, David Hume, wrote on the issue in 1752. In an essay entitled '*Of Money*', Hume suggested that if the money supply is increased when an economy is below full employment, spending will increase, which in turn creates economic expansion. Firms take on more workers as a result and unemployment falls. However, the demand for labour pushes up wage costs and firms pass on these additional costs onto consumers in the form of higher prices. Hume established a link between changes in the money supply and output and hinted at an inverse link between inflation and unemployment.

Tinbergen and Klein The first Nobel Prize in Economics winner, Jan Tinbergen, carried out econometric studies of links between inflation and unemployment in the late 1930s, which focused on the demand for labour, wage rates and prices. The resulting model implied a trade-off between wage increases and disequilibrium in the labour market. Tinbergen's work was followed up by the 1980 Nobel Prize winner, Lawrence Klein, in work at the Cowles Commission for Research in Economics at the University of Chicago in the 1940s and 50s. Klein's work was part of an intellectual tradition carried on by Friedman and Phelps who we will come to later. In building a model of the US economy, Klein suggested that workers' wage demands would be informed in part by inflation and expected inflation but that these demands would also take into account prevailing unemployment. The work of the Cowles Commission established a relationship between wage inflation and output gaps.

Arthur Brown The links between the rate of increase in wages and inflation is part of a short-run cause of inflation referred to as **cost-push inflation**. Cost-push inflation occurs where firms face higher costs and pass these on in the form of higher prices. Wages are one of the most important costs facing firms. Workers may demand higher wages, fuelled in part either by a recognition that there is excess demand in the labour market and/or because of expected higher inflation. If firms accommodate higher wages, they may pass them on to consumers as higher prices. This is particularly likely if firms believe that demand is likely to continue to be strong. As inflation accelerates, workers demand higher wages in the next round and a *wage–price spiral* develops.

cost-push inflation a short-run cause of accelerating inflation due to higher input costs of firms which are passed on as higher consumer prices.

We have noted that the long-run cause of inflation can be explained by the quantity theory of money but short-run causes may go deeper than simply a rise in the money supply. Arthur Brown was one such economist who wanted to understand the causes of inflation in more detail. Brown had spent the war years as a civil servant and then joined James Meade, the 1977 Nobel Prize winner, in the economic section of the Cabinet Office before becoming Professor of Economics at the University of Leeds. In 1955, he published a book entitled *The Great Inflation, 1939–51*. The book contained charts showing changes in wage rates on the vertical axis and unemployment on the horizontal axis. In an obituary published in *The Guardian* in 2003, one of Brown's students, Professor Tony Thirlwall (from the University of Kent), noted that: 'He precisely anticipated the Phillips curve, which plots the inverse relation between wage and price inflation and the rate of unemployment.' (Source: http://www.theguardian.com/news/2003/mar/12/guardianobituaries.obituaries)

Indeed, there are some who argue that the Phillips curve should more accurately be referred to as the 'Brown curve'.

THE PHILLIPS CURVE

In 1958, a New Zealand economist working at the London School of Economics, A.W. Phillips, published an article in the British journal *Economica* that would make him famous. The article was entitled '*The Relationship between Unemployment and the Rate of Change of Money Wages in the United Kingdom, 1861–1957*'. In it, Phillips showed a negative correlation between the rate of unemployment and the rate of inflation. That is, Phillips showed that years with low unemployment tend to have high inflation, and years with high unemployment tend to have low inflation. (It should be noted that Phillips examined inflation in nominal wages rather than inflation in prices, but for our purposes that distinction is not important. These two measures of inflation usually move together because of the relationship between wage inflation and the excess demand for labour.) George Akerlof, in his Nobel Prize lecture in 2001, referred to the Phillips curve as: 'Probably the single most important macroeconomic relationship'.

Origins of the Phillips Curve

The circumstances surrounding the publication of the paper which made Phillips famous are interesting. In 1957, Phillips was being supported as a candidate for the Tooke Chair of Economic Theory at the London School of Economics (LSE) but at that time he had only a limited publication record. Despite this, those that knew him, including James Meade, regarded him highly and there has been a suggestion that the paper published in *Economica* was 'a rushed job'. Indeed, Phillips himself said as much and noted that his analysis of the data from 1861–1913 was 'a good weekend's work'. Allan G. Sleeman, in a paper published in the *Journal of Economic Perspectives* in 2011, argues that the paper was pushed for publication as a means of providing support for the position at the LSE and not necessarily submitted by Phillips himself but by his supporters. Regardless of the circumstances surrounding the publication, the paper investigated the relationship between the rate of change in money wages and unemployment in the UK. The paper looks at two time periods, data between 1861 and 1913, and from 1913 to 1957. The first set of data seemed to imply a relationship between the rate of change of money wages (in per cent per year) which was drawn on the vertical axis, and unemployment (as a percentage) on the horizontal axis. The second period was one characterized by a great deal of upheaval, both economic and political. It seems that Phillips was not as satisfied that the relationship was as strong in the second period as the first; indeed, he did not make any claim that he had discovered a stable relationship. He referred to the paper as a 'crude attempt', and whilst other economists became fascinated with the seed which Phillips had planted, he himself moved on to other topics.

The paper did, however, spawn much further research with economists such as Richard Lipsey, Paul Samuelson and Robert Solow replicating Phillips' model and applying different techniques to assess its validity. The Phillips curve was introduced to the wider public after being included in Paul Samuelson's fifth edition of his undergraduate textbook *Economics* in the early 1960s, and in Lipsey's *An Introduction to Positive Economics,* published in 1963; both books were used widely in undergraduate teaching on both sides of the Atlantic.

Samuelson and Solow Although Phillips's discovery was based on data for the United Kingdom, researchers quickly extended his finding to other countries. Two years after Phillips published his article, Samuelson and Robert Solow published an article in the *American Economic Review* called '*Analytics of Anti-inflation Policy*' in which they showed a similar negative correlation between inflation and unemployment in data for the United States. They reasoned that this correlation arose because low unemployment was associated with high AD, which in turn puts upwards pressure on wages and prices throughout the economy. In other words, an inflationary gap, where AD is greater than trend output, leads to an increase in prices in the short-run. Samuelson and Solow dubbed the negative association between inflation and unemployment the **Phillips curve**. Figure 35.1 shows an example of a Phillips curve like the one found by Samuelson and Solow.

Phillips curve a curve that shows the short-run trade-off between inflation and unemployment

---

FIGURE 35.1

The Phillips Curve

The Phillips curve illustrates a negative association between the inflation rate and the unemployment rate. At point A, inflation is low and unemployment is high. At point B, inflation is high and unemployment is low.

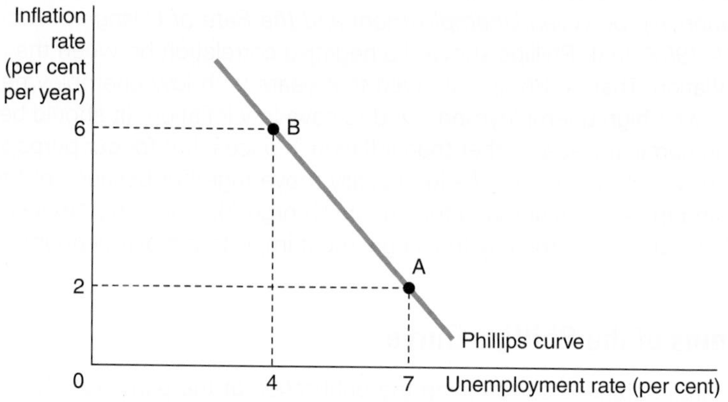

Samuelson and Solow were interested in the Phillips curve because they believed that it held important lessons for policymakers. In particular, they suggested that the Phillips curve offers policymakers a menu of possible economic outcomes. By altering monetary and fiscal policy to influence AD, policymakers could choose any point on this curve. Point A offers high unemployment and low inflation. Point B offers low unemployment and high inflation. Policymakers might prefer both low inflation and low unemployment, but the historical data as summarized by the Phillips curve indicate that this combination is not possible. According to Samuelson and Solow, policymakers face a trade-off between inflation and unemployment, and the Phillips curve illustrates that trade-off.

Aggregate Demand, Aggregate Supply and the Phillips Curve

The model of AD and AS provides an easy explanation for the menu of possible outcomes described by the Phillips curve. The Phillips curve simply shows the combinations of inflation and unemployment that arise in the short run as shifts in the AD curve move the economy along the SRAS. As we saw in Chapter 33, an increase in the AD for goods and services leads, in the short run, to a larger output of goods and services and a higher price level. Larger output means greater employment and, thus, a lower rate of unemployment. In addition, whatever the previous year's price level happens to be, the higher the price level in the current year, the higher the rate of inflation. Thus, shifts in AD push inflation and unemployment in opposite directions in the short run.

To see more fully how this works, let's consider an example. To keep the numbers simple, imagine that the price level (as measured, for instance, by the consumer prices index) equals 100 in the year 2017. Figure 35.2 shows two possible outcomes that might occur in 2018. Panel (a) shows the two outcomes using the model of AD and AS. Panel (b) illustrates the same two outcomes using the Phillips curve.

FIGURE 35.2

How the Phillips Curve is Related to the Model of Aggregate Demand and Aggregate Supply
Panel (a) shows the model of AD and AS. If AD is low, the economy is at point A; output is low (7500), and the price level is low (102). If AD is high, the economy is at point B; output is high (8000), and the price level is high (106). Panel (b) shows the implications for the Phillips curve. Point A, which arises when AD is low, has high unemployment (7 per cent) and low inflation (2 per cent). Point B, which arises when AD is high, has low unemployment (4 per cent) and high inflation (6 per cent).

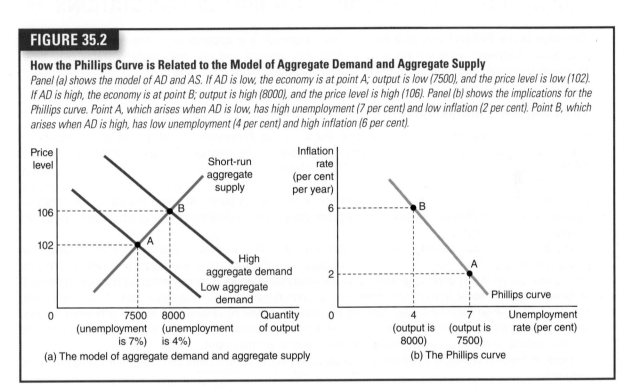

(a) The model of aggregate demand and aggregate supply

(b) The Phillips curve

In panel (a) of the figure, we can see the implications for output and the price level in 2018. If the AD for goods and services is relatively low, the economy experiences outcome A. The economy produces output of 7500, and the price level is 102. By contrast, if AD is relatively high, the economy experiences outcome B with output at 8000, and the price level 106. Thus, higher AD moves the economy to an equilibrium with higher output and a higher price level.

In panel (b) of the figure, we can see what these two possible outcomes mean for unemployment and inflation. Because firms need more workers when they produce a greater output of goods and services, unemployment is lower in outcome B than in outcome A. In this example, when output rises from 7500 to 8000, unemployment falls from 7 per cent to 4 per cent. Moreover, because the price level is higher at outcome B than at outcome A, the inflation rate (the percentage change in the price level from the previous year) is also higher. In particular, since the price level was 100 in year 2017, outcome A has an inflation rate of 2 per cent, and outcome B has an inflation rate of 6 per cent. Thus, we can compare the two possible outcomes for the economy either in terms of output and the price level (using the model of AD and AS) or in terms of unemployment and inflation (using the Phillips curve).

As we saw in the preceding chapter, monetary and fiscal policy can shift the AD curve. Therefore, monetary and fiscal policy can move the economy along the Phillips curve. Increases in the money supply, increases in government spending, or cuts in taxes expand AD and move the economy to a point on the Phillips curve with lower unemployment and higher inflation. Decreases in the money supply, cuts in government spending, or increases in taxes contract AD, and move the economy to a point on the Phillips curve with lower inflation and higher unemployment. In this sense, the Phillips curve offers policymakers a trade-off between combinations of inflation and unemployment.

SELF TEST Draw the Phillips curve. Use the model of AD and AS to show how policy can move the economy from a point on this curve with high inflation to a point with low inflation.

SHIFTS IN THE PHILLIPS CURVE: THE ROLE OF EXPECTATIONS

The value of the Phillips curve as a basis for policy decisions is dependent on the extent to which the relationship between wage growth and by extension, inflation and unemployment is stable over time. Research continued into the Phillips curve relationship throughout the 1960s.

The Long-Run Phillips Curve

In 1968, Milton Friedman published a paper in the *American Economic Review,* based on an address he had recently given as president of the American Economic Association. The paper, entitled '*The Role of Monetary Policy*', contained sections on 'What Monetary Policy Can Do' and 'What Monetary Policy Cannot Do'. Friedman argued that one thing monetary policy cannot do, other than for only a short time, is pick a combination of inflation and unemployment on the Phillips curve. At about the same time, another economist, Edmund Phelps, also published a paper denying the existence of a long-run trade-off between inflation and unemployment.

Friedman and Phelps based their conclusions on classical principles of macroeconomics. Recall that classical theory points to growth in the money supply as the primary determinant of inflation. Classical theory also states that monetary growth does not have real effects – it merely alters all prices and nominal incomes proportionately. In particular, monetary growth does not influence those factors that determine the economy's unemployment rate, such as the market power of unions, the role of efficiency wages, or the process of job search. Friedman and Phelps concluded that there is no reason to think the rate of inflation would, *in the long run*, be related to the rate of unemployment.

Here, in his own words, is Friedman's view about what the central bank can hope to accomplish in the long run:

> The monetary authority controls nominal quantities – directly, the quantity of its own liabilities [currency plus bank reserves]. In principle, it can use this control to peg a nominal quantity – an exchange rate, the price level, the nominal level of national income, the quantity of money by one definition or another – or to peg the change in a nominal quantity – the rate of inflation or deflation, the rate of growth or decline in nominal national income, the rate of growth of the quantity of money. It cannot use its control over nominal quantities to peg a real quantity – the real rate of interest, the rate of unemployment, the level of real national income, the real quantity of money, the rate of growth of real national income, or the rate of growth of the real quantity of money.

These views have important implications for the Phillips curve. In particular, they imply that monetary policymakers face a long-run Phillips curve that is vertical, as in Figure 35.3. If the central bank increases the money supply slowly, the inflation rate is low, and the economy finds itself at point A. If the central bank increases the money supply quickly, the inflation rate is high, and the economy finds itself at point B. In either case, the unemployment rate tends towards its natural rate. The vertical long-run Phillips curve illustrates the conclusion that unemployment does not depend on money growth and inflation in the long run.

The vertical long-run Phillips curve is, in essence, one expression of the classical idea of monetary neutrality. As you may recall, we expressed this idea in Chapter 33 with a vertical LRAS curve. Indeed, as Figure 35.4 illustrates, the vertical long-run Phillips curve and the vertical LRAS curve are two sides of the same coin. In panel (a) of this figure, an increase in the money supply shifts the AD curve to the right from AD_1 to AD_2. As a result of this shift, the long-run equilibrium moves from point A to point B.

FIGURE 35.3

The Long-Run Phillips Curve

Friedman and Phelps argued that there is no trade-off between inflation and unemployment in the long run. Growth in the money supply determines the inflation rate. Regardless of the inflation rate, the unemployment rate gravitates towards its natural rate. As a result, the long-run Phillips curve is vertical.

FIGURE 35.4

How the Long-Run Phillips Curve Is Related to the Model of Aggregate Demand and Aggregate Supply

Panel (a) shows the model of AD and AS with a vertical AS curve. When expansionary monetary policy shifts the AD curve to the right from AD₁ to AD₂, the equilibrium moves from point A to point B. The price level rises from P₁ to P₂, while output remains the same. Panel (b) shows the long-run Phillips curve, which is vertical at the natural rate of unemployment. Expansionary monetary policy moves the economy from lower inflation (point A) to higher inflation (point B) without changing the rate of unemployment.

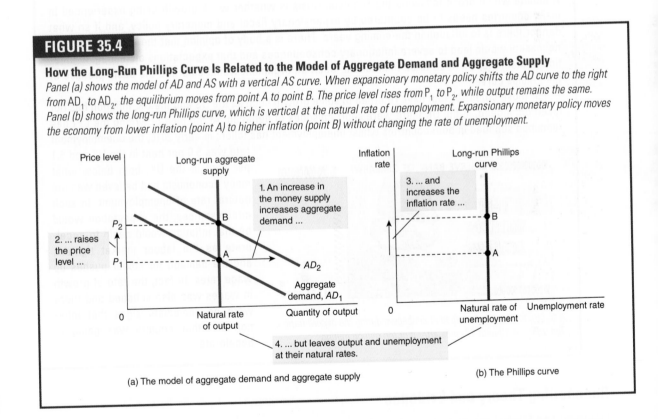

The price level rises from P_1 to P_2, but because the AS curve is vertical, output remains the same. In panel (b), more rapid growth in the money supply raises the inflation rate by moving the economy from point A to point B. Because the Phillips curve is vertical, the rate of unemployment is the same at these two points. Thus, the vertical LRAS curve and the vertical long-run Phillips curve both imply that monetary policy influences nominal variables (the price level and the inflation rate) but not real variables (output and unemployment). Regardless of the monetary policy pursued by the central bank, output and unemployment are, in the long run, at their natural rates.

The Natural Rate of Unemployment Friedman and Phelps used the adjective 'natural' to describe the unemployment rate towards which the economy tends to gravitate in the long run. As we have seen in Chapter 23, the natural rate of unemployment is not necessarily the socially desirable rate of unemployment. Nor is the natural rate of unemployment constant over time. This unemployment is 'natural' because it is beyond the influence of monetary policy.

Although the conclusion of Friedman and Phelps was that monetary policy cannot influence the natural rate of unemployment, other types of policy can. To reduce the natural rate of unemployment, policymakers could look to policies that improve the functioning of the labour market. In Chapter 23, we discussed how various labour market policies, such as minimum wage laws, collective bargaining laws, unemployment insurance and job-training schemes, affect the natural rate of unemployment. A policy change that reduced the natural rate of unemployment would shift the long-run Phillips curve to the left. In addition, because lower unemployment means more workers are producing goods and services, the quantity of goods and services supplied would be larger at any given price level, and the LRAS would shift to the right. The economy could then enjoy lower unemployment and higher output for any given rate of money growth and inflation. We will look at some of these policies designed to affect the supply side of the economy in the next chapter.

CASE STUDY   **A Fear of Inflation**

A debate which arose following the Financial Crisis is whether weak growth being experienced in many countries needs to be countered by expansionary fiscal and monetary policy, and if so what danger there is to inflation in the coming years. There is a body of opinion that the sort of expansion necessary would lead to severe inflationary consequences and that expectations on managing inflation at stable levels need to be maintained. Such an argument would embrace the basic premise of the Phillips curve.

For those countries that have returned to some growth such as the US and the UK, inflation has not taken off; indeed, in the UK there were short episodes of deflation. At the time of writing the CPI has remained subdued in both countries whilst unemployment has fallen; in early 2016, the unemployment rate was 5.0 per cent in the US and 5.1 per cent in the UK, both below what many economists had believed was the natural rate of unemployment. In such circumstances, the expectation would be that inflation would begin to accelerate as the labour market tightens and the demand for labour pushes up wage rates. In fact, the rate of growth in wages was also subdued and there were no immediate signs that inflation in either country was going to accelerate.

A ten trillion bank note issued in Zimbabwe during the hyperinflation. Ten trillion is 10 with 12 zeros after it or ten million million.

Reconciling Theory and Evidence

Friedman and Phelps' conclusion was based on an appeal to *theory*. In contrast, the negative correlation between inflation and unemployment documented by Phillips, Samuelson and Solow was based on *data*. Why should anyone believe that policymakers faced a vertical Phillips curve when the world seemed to offer a downwards sloping one? Shouldn't the findings of Phillips, Samuelson and Solow lead us to reject the classical conclusion of monetary neutrality?

Friedman and Phelps were well aware of these questions, and they offered a way to reconcile classical macroeconomic theory with the finding of a downwards sloping Phillips curve in data from the United Kingdom and the United States. They argued that policymakers can pursue expansionary monetary policy to achieve lower unemployment for a while (i.e. in the short-run), but eventually unemployment returns to its natural rate, and more expansionary monetary policy leads only to higher inflation.

Friedman and Phelps reasoned that the SRAS curve is upwards sloping, indicating that an increase in the price level raises the quantity of goods and services that firms' supply. In contrast, the LRAS curve is vertical, indicating that the price level does not influence quantity supplied in the long run. Chapter 33 presented three theories to explain the upwards slope of the SRAS curve: sticky wages, sticky prices and misperceptions about relative prices. Because wages, prices and perceptions adjust to changing economic conditions over time, the positive relationship between the price level and quantity supplied applies in the short run but not in the long run. Friedman and Phelps applied this same logic to the Phillips curve. Just as the AS curve slopes upwards only in the short run, the trade-off between inflation and unemployment holds only in the short run. Just as the LRAS curve is vertical, the long-run Phillips curve is also vertical.

To help explain the short-run and long-run relationship between inflation and unemployment, Friedman and Phelps focused on *expected inflation*. Expected inflation measures how much people expect the overall price level to change. As we discussed in Chapter 33, the expected price level affects the wages and prices that people set and the perceptions of relative prices that they form. As a result, expected inflation is one factor that determines the position of the SRAS curve. In the short run, the central bank can take expected inflation (and thus the SRAS curve) as already determined. When the money supply changes, the AD curve shifts and the economy moves along a given SRAS curve. In the short run, therefore, monetary changes lead to unexpected fluctuations in output, prices, unemployment and inflation. In this way, Friedman and Phelps explained the Phillips curve that Phillips, Samuelson and Solow had documented.

Yet the central bank's ability to create unexpected inflation by increasing the money supply exists only in the short run. In the long run, people come to expect whatever inflation rate the central bank chooses to produce. Because wages, prices and perceptions will eventually adjust to the inflation rate, the LRAS curve is vertical. In this case, changes in AD, such as those due to changes in the money supply, do not affect the economy's output of goods and services. Thus, Friedman and Phelps concluded that unemployment returns to its natural rate in the long run.

The Short-Run Phillips Curve

The analysis of Friedman and Phelps can be summarized in the following equation (which is, in essence, another expression of the AS equation we saw in Chapter 33):

$$Unemployment\ rate\ =\ NRU - a(Actual\ Inflation - Expected\ inflation)$$

This equation relates the unemployment rate to the natural rate of unemployment (NRU), actual inflation and expected inflation. In the short run, expected inflation is given. As a result, higher actual inflation is associated with lower unemployment. (How much unemployment responds to unexpected inflation is determined by the size of a, a number that in turn depends on the slope of the SRAS curve.) In the long run, however, people come to expect whatever inflation the central bank produces (or specifies as the target rate). Thus, actual inflation equals expected inflation, and unemployment is at its natural rate.

This equation implies there is no stable short-run Phillips curve. Each short-run Phillips curve reflects a particular expected rate of inflation. (To be precise, if you graph the equation, you'll find that the short-run Phillips curve intersects the long-run Phillips curve at the expected rate of inflation.) Whenever expected inflation changes, the short-run Phillips curve shifts.

According to Friedman and Phelps, it is dangerous to view the Phillips curve as a menu of options available to policymakers. To see why, imagine an economy at its natural rate of unemployment with low inflation and low expected inflation, shown in Figure 35.5 as point A. Now suppose that policymakers try to take advantage of the trade-off between inflation and unemployment by using monetary or fiscal policy to expand AD. In the short run when expected inflation is given, the economy goes from point A to point B. Unemployment falls below its natural rate, and inflation rises above expected inflation. Over time, people get used to this higher inflation rate, and they raise their expectations of inflation. When expected inflation rises, firms and workers start taking higher inflation into account when setting wages and prices. The short-run Phillips curve then shifts to the right, as shown in the figure. The economy ends up at point C, with higher inflation than at point A but with the same level of unemployment.

FIGURE 35.5

How Expected Inflation Shifts the Short-Run Phillips Curve

The higher the expected rate of inflation, the higher the short-run trade-off between inflation and unemployment. At point A, expected inflation and actual inflation are both low, and unemployment is at its natural rate. If the central bank pursues an expansionary monetary policy, the economy moves from point A to point B in the short run. At point B, expected inflation is still low, but actual inflation is high. Unemployment is below its natural rate. In the long run, expected inflation rises, and the economy moves to point C. At point C, expected inflation and actual inflation are both high, and unemployment is back to its natural rate.

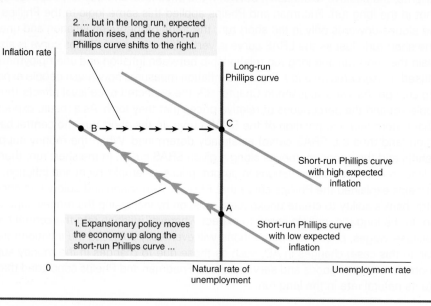

Thus, Friedman and Phelps concluded that policymakers do face a trade-off between inflation and unemployment, but only a temporary one. If policymakers use this trade-off, they lose it.

The Unemployment–Inflation Trade-Off

Friedman and Phelps had made a bold prediction in 1968: if policymakers try to take advantage of the Phillips curve by choosing higher inflation in order to reduce unemployment, they will succeed at reducing unemployment only temporarily. This view, that unemployment eventually returns to its natural rate regardless of the rate of inflation, is called the **natural-rate hypothesis**.

> **natural-rate hypothesis** the claim that unemployment eventually returns to its normal, or natural, rate, regardless of the rate of inflation

To some economists at the time, it seemed ridiculous to claim that the Phillips curve would break down once policymakers tried to use it. Research suggested, however, that this was exactly what happened in both the UK and the United States. Beginning in the late 1960s, the UK government, for example, followed policies that expanded the AD for goods and services. On top of this, the UK and many other developed economies in the late 1960s and early 1970s, experienced an increase in AD due to American involvement in the Vietnam War. This increased US government spending (on the military), boosted US AD and so boosted net exports from other countries to the USA. In addition, in 1971, as a result of the relaxation of certain controls on bank lending, the UK experienced a major expansion in the money supply. In the following year, the government announced an extraordinarily expansionary fiscal policy, in terms of extra spending and tax reduction, and the economy began seriously to overheat and inflation started to rise. But, as Friedman and Phelps had predicted, unemployment did not stay low.

As we have seen, many governments in the Western world adopted Keynesian policies as the basis for managing the economy. In the 20 years after the war, fiscal policy was dominant; in times of rising unemployment fiscal policy was loosened and tightened when inflation began to speed up. The government could pull its fiscal levers of tax and public spending to 'fine tune' the economy. The unusual circumstances of post-war reconstruction across Europe and the US meant that inflation did not seem to present a major problem.

Some economists argued that the focus on fiscal policy meant that not only did households form expectations about inflation but also about government policy. In the UK, many large industries were in public ownership including the railways, coal, electricity, airports and airlines, telecommunications and steel. In addition, trade unions enjoyed considerable power in many industries. Workers came to expect, it was argued, increases in real wages each year and that this would be accommodated by monetary expansion. In addition, the government would respond by loosening fiscal policy if the economy slowed down. This, it was argued, led to a fall in productivity and increased inflationary pressures as the government and industry accommodated wage increases. In the aggregate, UK industry became sluggish, lacked flexibility and lost competitiveness.

These conditions led to rising inflation and an inability of the government to reduce unemployment below the natural rate. After the oil crisis and miners' strike of the early 1970s and the fiscal boom produced by the government, stagflation took hold and the UK seemed to lurch from 'boom to bust'. Eventually the government was forced to borrow money from the IMF in 1976. In a famous speech to the Labour Party Conference in the same year, the then Prime Minister, James Callaghan, echoed Friedman and Phelps' theory to the nation when he said:

We used to think that you could spend your way out of a recession and increase employment by cutting taxes and boosting government spending. I tell you in all candour that that option no longer exists, and in so far as it ever did exist, it only worked on each occasion since the war by injecting a bigger dose of inflation into the economy. And each time that happened, the average level of unemployment has risen. Higher inflation followed by higher unemployment. That is the history of the last 20 years.

This effectively led to a move away from Keynesian policies and a shift in emphasis on monetary policy in the UK, while in the US a similar focus on the money supply was also pursued. The focus of policy on the use of monetary and supply-side policies was seen as the way of keeping inflation under control and lowering the natural rate of unemployment. Throughout the 1980s, the UK and US governments trumpeted the benefits of supply-side policies. These looked at ways of expanding the productive capacity of the economy to shift the AS curve to the right (we will look at these policies in the next chapter). Such policies stressed the importance of enterprise, reducing business regulation, improving incentives through cutting taxes and benefits, reducing trade union power and investing in education and training to improve the workings and flexibility of the labour market in the long run.

Supply-side policies take some time to have an effect but structural economic reforms by the UK government throughout the 1990s led to a leftward shift in the Phillips curve. What caused this favourable shift in the short-run Phillips curve? Part of the answer lies in a low level of expected inflation. The policy of inflation targeting since 1992, combined with the independence of the Bank of England in 1997, created a credible policy framework in which workers and firms knew that interest rates would be raised if the economy began to overheat, and they tended to moderate their wage claims and price setting accordingly. Since the Bank of England now sets interest rates independently, people also know that there is no way in which politicians can use expansionary monetary policy for political reasons, such as to gain popularity before an election. This led to a period of relatively stable economic conditions in the UK with economic growth, low inflation and relatively low levels of unemployment right up until around 2008 when the Financial Crisis began to unravel.

In contrast, many European countries suffered relatively high levels of unemployment despite the European Central Bank having independence in the setting of monetary policy. Why was this? One argument that has been put forward to explain high European unemployment in the 21st century, and which seems to have some credibility, centres on the level of labour market regulation. As we pointed out above, the 1980s in the UK were characterized both by a weakening of the power of the trades unions and by a reduction in business regulation in general, and in labour market regulation in particular. Whilst, for example, this had the effect of reducing job security for many people by making it easier for employers to terminate contracts, it also had the effect of making labour markets much more flexible. Thus, somewhat paradoxically perhaps, if it is harder to fire someone, firms will think hard before taking on new labour and unemployment may actually rise. Similarly, the minimum wage is typically set at a much higher level (relative to the average wage) in European countries like France and Germany, which again is a reason why the natural rate of unemployment might be higher in those countries.

Data on the history of UK inflation and unemployment from the early 1970s, shows very little evidence of the simple negative relationship between these two variables that Phillips had originally observed. In particular, as inflation remained high in the early 1970s, people's expectations of inflation caught up with reality, and the unemployment rate rose along with inflation. By the mid-1970s, policymakers had concluded that Friedman and Phelps had appeared to have been correct: There is no trade-off between inflation and unemployment in the long run.

SELF TEST Draw the short-run Phillips curve and the long-run Phillips curve. Explain why they are different.

THE LONG-RUN VERTICAL PHILLIPS CURVE AS AN ARGUMENT FOR CENTRAL BANK INDEPENDENCE

The question over whether monetary policy should be in the hands of an elected government or an unelected central banker rests in part on accountability. Most developed economies have opted to give central banks operational independence over monetary policy.

To see why, suppose the economy is at a point with the natural rate of unemployment and a low level of inflation. If a government is in charge of monetary policy, it can direct the central bank to change interest rates or the money supply. Now imagine that this government was facing a general election in a year's time. There is every temptation to provide a short-term stimulus by reducing interest rates and expanding the money supply so that the economy moves along the short-run Phillips curve. This stimulus might be a vote winner, but once the election has been fought people's expectations of inflation catch up with actual inflation, the short-run Phillips curve will shift up and the economy will return to its natural rate of unemployment but now with a higher level of inflation. In the long run the economy is in a worse state than if monetary policy had remained neutral.

This story implies a cynical view of politics, and most governments would strenuously deny that they would carry out such policies just to get re-elected. More importantly, however, the story also implies that people (workers and managers of firms) are easily duped. Why? Because everyone will know that the government has a strong incentive to pursue an expansionary monetary policy just before an election. In fact, firms and workers may begin raising prices and wages before the election in anticipation of the expansionary monetary policy. This is an interesting result, and one worth stressing: if people believe that the government is about to pursue an expansionary monetary policy, then inflationary expectations will increase and inflation will rise but unemployment will not fall. In essence, the economy jumps immediately to the new long-run equilibrium.

Credibility of policy is a crucial factor in macroeconomics. The importance of expectations is such that if control of monetary policy is given to the central bank and a clear mandate is given about its role, expectations adjust to the policy and it is more likely that inflation will be stable. The central bank's incentives are different from those of an elected government and provided its actions are credible, the economy ends up with unemployment no different from that if a government was in control of monetary policy, but with a lower level of inflation.

There are also potential benefits to governments of having an independent central bank in charge of monetary policy. If the government controlled monetary policy it might reason that firms and workers may factor the government's temptation into their price and wage setting, so that in fact the economy will jump to the long-run equilibrium just before the election.

This situation is an example of a *Nash equilibrium*. Remember that a Nash equilibrium is a situation in which economic actors interacting with one another each choose their best strategy given the strategies that all the other actors have chosen. Here, firms and workers know that if they don't raise inflationary expectations before an election, the government will most likely pursue an expansionary monetary policy and they will lose out because their prices and wages will be lower in real terms. As a result they raise inflationary expectations and the short-run Phillips curve shifts up, moving the economy to a long run equilibrium with higher inflation and the natural rate of unemployment. But doesn't the government still have the same temptation to inflate at this new equilibrium? Possibly, but there will certainly be some point on the vertical, long-run Phillips curve where inflation is already so high that the government will not want to risk pushing it higher, even if it means a short-run reduction in unemployment. If firms and workers can guess roughly what this level of inflation is, they will set their wages and prices so that the economy will jump straight to that point. If, at this point, the government has no temptation to inflate the economy in order to gain popularity, and if firms and workers know this so that they have no incentive to change their price and wage setting behaviour, then we will have reached the Nash equilibrium.

Another way of thinking about this is to say that the Nash equilibrium represents the *time-consistent policy*. A time-consistent policy is simply one which a government does not have a temptation to renege on at some point in time and will usually represent a Nash equilibrium.

This new point may represent time-consistency in economic policy, but it is actually worse than the original position for the government's electoral chances, since inflation is higher and unemployment is still at the natural rate. Hence, the best thing to do in order to maximize the chances of re-election is for the government to make the central bank independent in the sense of handing over control of monetary policy – providing of course that the central bank sees its role as the guardian of price stability; in other words, providing that the central bank is 'conservative' with respect to price stability.

It is a testimony to the power of macroeconomic theory that this argument has persuaded many governments around the world to grant independence to their central bank in the conduct of monetary policy. The European Central Bank, for example, has been independent since its inception in 1998, and the Bank of England was granted independence in 1997. The ECB both designs its monetary policy (e.g. decides what level of inflation in the Euro Area to aim for) and implements it. The Bank of England, on the other hand, has independence in the implementation of monetary policy but its inflation target is set by the UK Chancellor of the Exchequer.

SHIFTS IN THE PHILLIPS CURVE: THE ROLE OF SUPPLY SHOCKS

Friedman and Phelps had suggested in 1968 that changes in expected inflation shift the short-run Phillips curve, and the experience of the early 1970s convinced many economists that Friedman and Phelps were right. Within a few years, however, the economics profession would turn its attention to a different source of shifts in the short-run Phillips curve: shocks to AS.

Conflict between Israel and its Arab neighbours triggered a series of oil price shocks as Arab oil producers used their market power to exert political pressure on Western governments who supported Israel. In 1974, the Organization of Petroleum Exporting Countries (OPEC) also began to exert its power as a cartel in order to increase its members' profits. The countries of OPEC, such as Saudi Arabia, Kuwait and Iraq, restricted the amount of crude oil they pumped and sold on world markets. This reduction in supply caused the price of oil to almost double over a few years in the 1970s.

A large increase in the world price of oil is an example of a supply shock. A **supply shock** is an event that directly affects firms' costs of production and thus the prices they charge; it shifts the economy's AS curve and, as a result, the Phillips curve. Oil is a constituent part of so many production processes that increases in its price have far-reaching effects. For example, when an oil price increase raises the cost of producing petrol, heating oil, tyres, plastic products, distribution and many other products, it reduces the quantity of goods and services supplied at any given price level. As panel (a) of Figure 35.6 shows, this reduction in supply is represented by the leftward shift in the AS curve from AS_1 to AS_2. The price level rises from P_1 to P_2, and output falls from Y_1 to Y_2 and the economy experiences stagflation.

> **supply shock** an event that directly alters firms' costs and prices, shifting the economy's AS curve and thus the Phillips curve

FIGURE 35.6

An Adverse Shock to Aggregate Supply

Panel (a) shows the model of AD and AS. When the AS curve shifts to the left from AS_1 to AS_2, the equilibrium moves from point A to point B. Output falls from Y_1 to Y_2, and the price level rises from P_1 to P_2. Panel (b) shows the short-run trade-off between inflation and unemployment. The adverse shift in AS moves the economy from a point with lower unemployment and lower inflation (point A) to a point with higher unemployment and higher inflation (point B). The short-run Phillips curve shifts to the right from PC_1 to PC_2. Policymakers now face a worse trade-off between inflation and unemployment.

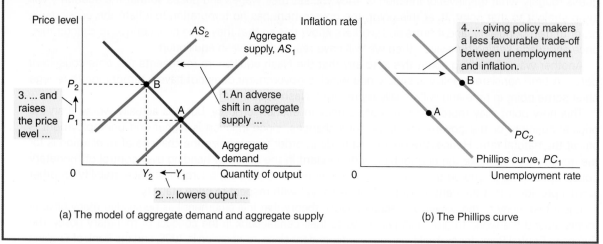

(a) The model of aggregate demand and aggregate supply

(b) The Phillips curve

This shift in AS is associated with a similar shift in the short-run Phillips curve, shown in panel (b). Because firms need fewer workers to produce the smaller output, employment falls and unemployment rises. Because the price level is higher, the inflation rate – the percentage change in the price level from the previous year – is also higher. Thus, the shift in AS leads to higher unemployment and higher inflation. The short-run trade-off between inflation and unemployment shifts to the right from PC_1 to PC_2.

Confronted with an adverse shift in AS, policymakers face a difficult choice between fighting inflation and fighting unemployment. If they contract AD to fight inflation, they will raise unemployment further. If they expand AD to fight unemployment, they will raise inflation further. In other words, policymakers face a less favourable trade-off between inflation and unemployment than they did before the shift in AS: they have to live with a higher rate of inflation for a given rate of unemployment, a higher rate of unemployment for a given rate of inflation, or some combination of higher unemployment and higher inflation.

An important question is whether this adverse shift in the Phillips curve is temporary or permanent. The answer depends on how people adjust their expectations of inflation. If people view the rise in inflation due to the supply shock as a temporary aberration, expected inflation does not change, and the Phillips curve will soon revert to its former position. But if people believe the shock will lead to a new era of higher inflation, then expected inflation rises, and the Phillips curve remains at its new, less desirable position.

SELF TEST Give an example of a favourable shock to AS. Use the model of AD and AS to explain the effects of such a shock. How does it affect the Phillips curve?

THE COST OF REDUCING INFLATION

At the time of writing, there are a number of governments facing the challenge of high inflation. In Brazil, for example, inflation was over 10 per cent, in Russia it was almost 15 per cent and in Turkey, over 8 per cent. If the Phillips curve trade-off holds, then government's seeking to reduce inflation must accept higher rates of unemployment because economic growth will be reduced. Economists have attempted to quantify the effects of **disinflation**, the reduction in the rate of inflation.

> **disinflation** the reduction in the rate of inflation

The Sacrifice Ratio

To reduce the inflation rate, the central bank has to pursue contractionary monetary policy. Figure 35.7 shows some of the effects of such a decision. When the central bank slows the rate at which the money supply is growing, it contracts AD. The fall in AD, in turn, reduces the quantity of goods and services that firms produce, and this fall in production leads to a fall in employment. The economy begins at point A in the figure and moves along the short-run Phillips curve to point B, which has lower inflation and higher unemployment. Over time, as people come to understand that prices are rising more slowly, expected inflation falls, and the short-run Phillips curve shifts downward. The economy moves from point B to point C. Inflation is lower, and unemployment is back at its natural rate.

FIGURE 35.7

Disinflationary Monetary Policy in the Short Run and Long Run
When the central bank pursues contractionary monetary policy to reduce inflation, the economy moves along a short-run Phillips curve from point A to point B. Over time, expected inflation falls, and the short-run Phillips curve shifts downwards. When the economy reaches point C, unemployment is back at its natural rate.

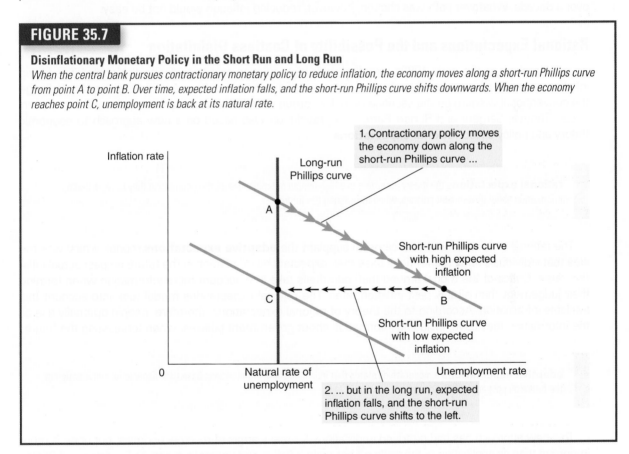

Thus, if a nation wants to reduce inflation, it must endure a period of high unemployment and low output. In Figure 35.7, this cost is represented by the movement of the economy through point B as it travels from point A to point C. The size of this cost depends on the slope of the Phillips curve and how quickly expectations of inflation adjust to the new monetary policy.

Many studies have examined the data on inflation and unemployment in order to estimate the cost of reducing inflation. The findings of these studies are often summarized in a statistic called the **sacrifice ratio**. The sacrifice ratio is the number of percentage points of annual output lost in the process of reducing inflation by 1 percentage point given by the formula:

$$Sacrifice\ Ratio = \frac{Euro\ cost\ of\ loss\ of\ production}{Percentage\ change\ in\ inflation}$$

A typical estimate of the sacrifice ratio is around three to five. That is, for each percentage point that inflation is reduced, 3 to 5 per cent of annual output must be sacrificed in the transition.

> **sacrifice ratio** the number of percentage points of annual output lost in the process of reducing inflation by 1 percentage point

According to studies of the Phillips curve and the cost of disinflation, this sacrifice could be paid in various ways. Assume that inflation was running at 10 per cent and a government wanted to reduce it to 5 per cent. If each percentage point reduction in inflation would cost 3 per cent of annual output, then the cost would be 15 per cent of annual output lost in a year. Such an outcome would be extremely harsh. Another option would be to spread out the cost over several years. If the reduction in inflation took place over five years, for instance, then output would have to average only 3 per cent below trend during that period to add up to a sacrifice of 15 per cent. An even more gradual approach would be to reduce inflation slowly over a decade. Whatever path was chosen, however, reducing inflation would not be easy.

Rational Expectations and the Possibility of Costless Disinflation

As policymakers in the early 1980s wrestled with high inflation and considering the costs of reducing inflation, a group of economics professors were leading an intellectual revolution that would challenge the conventional wisdom on the sacrifice ratio. This group included such prominent economists as Robert Lucas, Thomas Sargent and Robert Barro. Their revolution was based on a new approach to economic theory and policy called **rational expectations**.

> **rational expectations** the theory according to which people optimally use all the information they have, including information about government policies, when forecasting the future

The rational expectations model came to supplant the **adaptive expectations** model, which was the idea that individuals and organizations base their expectations of inflation in the future on past actual inflation rates. Critics of the model argued that individuals take into account more information when forming their judgement than simply past inflation rates. The rational expectations model took into account this available information. According to the theory of rational expectations, therefore, people optimally use all the information they have, including information about government policies, when forecasting the future.

> **adaptive expectations** a model which states that individuals and organizations base their expectations of inflation in the future on past actual inflation rates

This new approach has had profound implications for many areas of macroeconomics, but none is more important than its application to the trade-off between inflation and unemployment. As Friedman and Phelps had emphasized, expected inflation is an important variable that explains why there is a trade-off between inflation and unemployment in the short run but not in the long run. How quickly the short-run trade-off disappears depends on how quickly expectations adjust. Proponents of rational expectations built on the Friedman–Phelps analysis argue that when economic policies change, people adjust their expectations of inflation accordingly. Studies of inflation and unemployment that tried to estimate the sacrifice ratio had failed to take account of the direct effect of the policy regime on expectations. As a result, estimates of the sacrifice ratio were, according to the rational expectations theorists, unreliable guides for policy.

In a 1982 paper entitled *'The End of Four Big Inflations'* (one of which was the UK inflation of the late 1970s and early 1980s), Thomas Sargent described this new view as follows:

An alternative 'rational expectations' view denies that there is any inherent momentum to the present process of inflation. This view maintains that firms and workers have now come to expect high rates of inflation in the future and that they strike inflationary bargains in light of these expectations. However, it is held that people expect high rates of inflation in the future precisely because the government's current and prospective monetary and fiscal policies warrant those expectations… An implication of this view is that inflation can be stopped much more quickly than advocates of the 'momentum' view have indicated, and that their estimates of the length of time and the costs of stopping inflation in terms of forgone output are erroneous. This is not to say that it would be easy to eradicate inflation. On the contrary, it would require more than a few temporary restrictive fiscal and monetary actions. It would require a change in the policy regime… How costly such a move would be in terms of forgone output and how long it would be in taking effect would depend partly on how resolute and evident the government's commitment was.

According to Sargent, the sacrifice ratio could be much smaller than suggested by previous estimates. Indeed, in the most extreme case, it could be zero. If the government made a credible commitment to a policy of low inflation, people would be rational enough to lower their expectations of inflation immediately. The short-run Phillips curve would shift downward, and the economy would reach low inflation quickly without the cost of temporarily high unemployment and low output. The credibility of government policy is thus of prime importance.

SELF TEST What is the sacrifice ratio? How might a government improve credibility of its commitment to reduce inflation affect the sacrifice ratio?

FYI

Wage Curve Theory

We have said that Phillips's research looked at the relationship between the rate of growth of wages and unemployment. The relationship of the wage rate to unemployment takes us a small step towards linking the level of inflation with unemployment. The rate of growth in wages is a factor that influences the overall level of prices in the economy. Wages represent a cost to employers; other things being equal, if they rise then employers might well seek to raise prices to cover the increased cost. If this happens throughout the economy on an aggregate level, wage growth leads to inflation. If the rate of growth of wages slows down, we might expect the labour market to be looser; in other words, the demand for labour in relation to the supply of labour is falling. Under normal market conditions, we would expect the wage rate to start to fall. In reality, this translates to the slowing down in the rate of growth of wages.

We then saw how further research into the Phillips curve led to the development of the so-called expectations augmented Phillips curve, captured in the following formula:

$$\Delta p_t = E_t \Delta p_t + 1 + (NR_t - RU_t)$$

This says that the change in the inflation rate in a time period (Δp_t) is equal to expected inflation in a time period $(E_t \Delta p_t + 1)$ and the natural rate of unemployment minus the national unemployment rate. This helped to explain what seemed to be happening in many Western economies in the 1970s. Households were *anticipating* inflation in the future and basing their behaviour and decision-making on those expectations: therefore, the Phillips curve was shifting. This helped to explain how higher inflation might also be experienced at the same time as higher unemployment – so-called 'stagflation'.

There have, however, been a number of economists who have questioned the existence of the Phillips curve. One economist did pose that very question. David Blanchflower has worked at a number of institutions, including the University of Surrey and Warwick University, in the UK. He is a former member of the Bank of England's Monetary Policy Committee and works at Dartmouth College in New Hampshire, in the United States.

(Continued)

Remember that the assumption of the Phillips curve is that there is a relationship between the rate of growth of wages and unemployment. When unemployment rises, the *rate of growth of wages* falls and vice versa. This makes intuitive sense since if there is a large pool of unemployed workers; employed workers will be hesitant to push for higher wage claims for fear of joining the rank of unemployed.

Blanchflower has been quoted as suggesting that as a result of his work, 'the Phillips curve is wrong, it's as fundamental as that'. The following is a summary of his analysis in support of this view.

The traditional Phillips curve relates the rate of growth of wages with the level of unemployment. Within this relationship, a higher level of unemployment is associated with a lower level of the rate of growth of wages. Conversely, if unemployment rates were low, the rate of growth of wages would be higher. Such a relationship is given as a macroeconomic one rather than microeconomic, i.e. it holds for the economy as a whole. If the level of unemployment increases, therefore, it suggests there will be excess supply in the labour market. In such cases, the labour market will adjust and the rate of growth of wages will fall to eliminate the excess supply.

Blanchflower and his colleague, Andrew Oswald, spent time researching links between unemployment and wage rates at a *microeconomic level* and found that the relationship between unemployment and wages might be different depending on the region that was being investigated. Their research looked at the *level of pay* rather than the rate of growth of wages. They argued that the *level* of pay was negatively related to the level of unemployment rather than the rate of growth in pay.

According to this argument, a worker in region A, which has a high level of unemployment, would earn lower wages than an equivalent worker in region B with lower levels of unemployment. Blanchard and Oswald's research casts doubt upon the standard explanation, in both regional economics and labour economics, that the wage rate in an area is positively linked to the level of unemployment in an area. In other words, the higher the level of unemployment, the higher the wage level needed to persuade someone to work in that area and vice versa.

Their work would tend to call into question some of the basic 'laws' of economics, particularly those related to something like the minimum wage. The conventional wisdom might be that if the minimum wage was introduced into an economy, the higher wage levels would be associated with a rise in unemployment. Blanchflower and Oswald's analysis suggests that this may not be the case and that in some areas there might even be a rise in the level of employment associated with a rise in wage levels.

Figure 35.8 highlights the traditional view of the effect of the imposition of a minimum wage (*MW*) set above the market wage level (W_1) on the level of unemployment. The minimum wage causes a fall in the quantity of labour demanded and an increase in the quantity supplied of labour (a movement along the *D* and *S* curves for labour). The result is an increase in the amount of unemployment, shown by the distance $Q3 - Q2$.

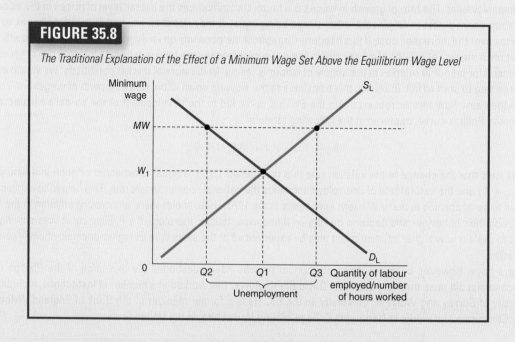

FIGURE 35.8

The Traditional Explanation of the Effect of a Minimum Wage Set Above the Equilibrium Wage Level

(Continued)

To understand this, it is important to refer back to the basic model of the labour market shown in Figure 35.9. If the demand for labour, for example, rose as indicated by a shift in the demand for labour curve to the right (D_L to D_{L1}), then there would be an excess demand for labour shown by the distance $Q2 - Q1$. Wage rates would rise in response to this shortage of labour and as the shortage is competed away, more people would end up being employed ($Q3$) at higher wage rates (W_2). A rise in wage rates, therefore, is positively correlated with a fall in unemployment and vice versa.

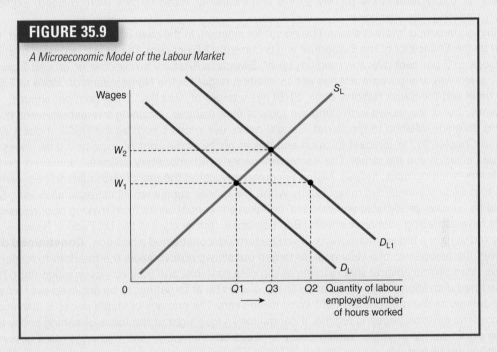

FIGURE 35.9

A Microeconomic Model of the Labour Market

Blanchflower and Oswald's research was based around millions of observations. They identified the existence of wage curves in 16 countries and since the publication of their research in 1994, a number of other researchers have confirmed their findings. Blanchflower and Oswald suggested that their wage curve would have an elasticity of -0.1. What this refers to is the responsiveness of rates of pay to changes in unemployment. An elasticity of -0.1, therefore, would suggest that if we took two regions within an economy, region A and region B, and if unemployment was 2 per cent in region B but 4 per cent in region A, we would expect wages to be around 10 per cent lower in region A than B. This suggests some sort of causal relationship stemming from the level of unemployment in an area feeding through to the level of wages in that area, rather than the other way round.

The suggestion that there is a relationship between the rate of growth of wages (and by implication, inflation) and unemployment, as we saw in the early part of this chapter, has implications for policymakers. This is based in part on the idea that controlling the rate of growth in wages (and hence inflation) is an important step in controlling unemployment. If, however, Blanchflower and Oswald's research on wage curves is correct, it changes the emphasis of policymaking both at a macro and at a micro level.

Let us assume that the government are looking at reducing unemployment. If they refer to traditional macroeconomic models of the labour market, they might look at wages as being one way of reducing unemployment in that area – in other words, a fall in wages would help to bring about a reduction in unemployment.

If a wage curve does exist, then attempts to reduce unemployment in this way could backfire, since falling wages would be associated with higher unemployment. In addition, it might be believed that high unemployment might affect most dramatically the high unemployment groups in that area – those with low levels of education, for example. It might be expected that these groups of people will be most likely to take on jobs that are created at lower wages and as such, policies to reduce unemployment could be achieved without a major impact on inflation. Again, the existence of a wage curve would tend to provide an argument against doing this. This is partly because it is the *level* of wages that are important rather than the rate of growth of wages.

INFLATION TARGETING

In many countries of the world today, including the UK and the Euro Area, the framework of monetary policy involves setting targets for inflation to be achieved over the medium term of two years or so, and then adjusting interest rates in order to achieve this objective. Inflation targeting arose partly because attempts to control the money supply in the 1980s proved extremely difficult. Governments announced targets for the growth in the money supply and invariably, these targets were missed. Explicit money supply targeting was abandoned.

Inflation targeting involves a target being set for inflation. In the case of the Bank of England, the target is set by the Chancellor of the Exchequer and is currently 2.0 per cent. The ECB's target is 'inflation below, but close to 2 per cent over the medium term', Sweden's Riksbank's objective is 'around 2 per cent per year', in Norway, the government has set an inflation target for the Norges Bank of 'close to 2.5 per cent over time' and the Swiss National Bank (SNB) has a target of 'less than 2 per cent per annum'.

Central banks are tasked with using the tools at their disposal, including interest rates and quantitative easing, to guide inflation to the target. Central banks use models such as the DSGE models we considered in Chapter 31, to forecast inflation and adjust policy in the light of expected differences between forecast inflation and the target. The framework under which monetary policy is conducted, could be carried out by applying rules. Indeed, Milton Friedman advocated the use of such rules to help central banks stick to publically announced measures by which the money supply would increase each year. Such rules would be 'simple, predictable and credible' and prevent central banks from making poor decisions which might have damaging economic effects. Ben Bernanke, former chair of the US Federal Reserve, however, preferred to have a broader framework which he termed 'constrained discretion'. **Constrained discretion** involves the recognition of a clear goal (or target) but allows policymakers the freedom to respond to economic, financial and political shocks using all the data available, and their collective judgement. The use of constrained discretion allows for inflation to not always be at target but to be achieved over a period, typically defined as the medium-term of two to three years. The primacy of stable prices is also important in a successful inflation targeting regime; if central banks lose sight of the focus of setting policy to achieve stable prices by, for example, setting policy to focus on unemployment, exchange rates or wages, then credibility will be lost.

> **constrained discretion** a monetary policy framework which acknowledges a clear goal (or target) but allows policymakers the freedom to respond to economic, financial and political shocks using all the data available and their collective judgement

Types of Targeting

The level of the money supply and the exchange rate can be thought of as intermediate targets of monetary policy. That is to say, they may be targeted in order to achieve certain other, policy targets, such as real GDP growth, employment and inflation. An important principle that we have learnt in our study of monetary policy is that many economists believe that, in the long run, monetary policy cannot affect the real side of the economy – i.e. real GDP and employment. In the long run, the only final target of monetary policy can be the inflation rate. Therefore, targeting the money supply or the exchange rate as a framework for monetary policy means that we are targeting those variables because it is felt that they will ultimately affect the rate of price inflation. Also, since neither the money supply nor the exchange rate is directly controllable, they cannot be instruments of monetary policy. In other words, the central bank cannot just set the level of the money supply it wants, it must attempt to bring about that level by open market operations and other means; similarly, it cannot just set the level of the exchange rate it wants, it must try to bring about that level by setting interest rates and by other means. Hence, the money supply and the exchange rate should really be viewed as intermediate targets that the central bank may aim for because it is believed that they will ultimately affect the final target of inflation. So why not just target the inflation rate? Interest rates (or at least some interest rates) are under the control of central banks, so they are definitely an instrument of monetary policy. We know that raising interest rates reduces AD and so dampens inflation. Monetary authorities could just raise interest rates whenever inflation rose above a level that was considered desirable – say 2 per cent. This would be a crude form of inflation targeting.

There are two problems with this crude inflation targeting. First, changing (or not changing) interest rates today will not affect inflation today, it will only affect inflation in the future, since it takes time for the policy to have an effect on the economy. Second, there may be other factors that would affect inflation in the future. Suppose, for example, that inflation was at its target of 2 per cent per year. The central bank, therefore, decides not to change interest rates, since it is achieving its inflation target. However, suppose there was, at the same time, a wave of very high wage settlements in the economy, above any increases in labour productivity. Over the next six months to a year, this is expected to lead to a rise in price inflation in the economy as workers spend more and as firms pass on some of the wage increases in the form of higher prices. Should the central bank wait for the inflation to arrive, or should it act now by raising interest rates in anticipation of the inflationary pressures coming from higher wages? Clearly, the better policy is to target not today's inflation, which it is already too late to have any effect on, but future inflation. Of course, no one knows with certainty what future inflation is going to be, therefore a policy of inflation targeting generally involves targeting the forecast rate of inflation.

The success of the central bank in achieving its target over the medium term is dependent in large part on its ability to accurately forecast inflation up to two years ahead. In the interests of transparency and credibility, the Bank of England publishes detailed analyzes of its forecasts and these are closely scrutinized. In the case of the Bank of England, if actual inflation does fall outside a range of plus or minus 1 per cent of the target, the Governor of the Bank of England is required to write a formal, public letter to the Chancellor of the Exchequer, explaining why inflation is out of the target range, what measures are being taken to get it back on course, and when it is expected to be back on target.

The Taylor Rule

Constrained discretion allows policymakers some leeway in making policy in response to economic, financial and political shocks to the economy. In addition to models, survey data and judgement, there may be some use of 'rules' in deciding monetary policy. In 1993 John Taylor, an economist at Stanford University in the United States, spent some time observing the behaviour of the Federal Reserve's Federal Open Market Committee (FOMC). Taylor's observations led him to put forward what has become known as the *Taylor rule* which has been an influential idea since it was published. For many economists, interest has centred on the extent to which the rule is followed in interest rate decision-making around the world, if at all. John Taylor was observing the US economy and the work of the FOMC. Inflation in the US had come under a far greater degree of control in the 1980s when the FOMC was headed by Paul Volcker. Part of Taylor's conclusion was that the FOMC had reacted more aggressively to inflation than had occurred before 1979. His observations led to the notion of the interest rate-setting body 'leaning into the wind' when it comes to inflation. By this he meant being willing to raise rates more significantly in response to an inflation threat (when the economy was deemed to be overheating, for example), and reducing interest rates if there was a slowdown in the economy along with a threat of recession, than had been the case prior to 1979.

Taylor suggested that the pattern of FOMC behaviour with regard to interest rates during the period 1979–92 could be expressed as a formula – the 'rule'. This formula, given below, has been simplified but in essence captures the main flavour of his original work.

$$r = p + 0.5y + 0.5(p - 2) + 2$$

In this formula, the following variables are expressed:
r = the short-term interest rate in percentage terms per annum
p = the rate of inflation over the previous four quarters measured as the GDP deflator
y = the difference between real GDP and potential output (the 'output gap').

Taylor made a number of assumptions about the US economy in this formula. He assumed that there was a target level of inflation, which he put at 2 per cent. He also made an assumption that the equilibrium real interest rate was also 2 per cent. The formula offers a rule or guide to policymakers about what the level of interest rates should be if there is a target for inflation of 2 per cent. In effect, interest rates can be set in response to the deviation of inflation from the target and the deviation of real output from potential output. It suggests that the response to inflation or output being off-target should be met with a more aggressive response to monetary policy – this is the so-called 'leaning into the wind'.

Suppose, for example, that the output gap was zero – that actual GDP was at its potential level – but that inflation was currently 5 per cent, 3 per cent above the assumed target level of 2 per cent. Then the *Taylor rule* would suggest that the central bank should aim to set the short-term interest rate at 8.5 per cent, corresponding to a real rate of interest of 8.5 – 5 = 3.5 per cent. If, however, GDP was, say, 2 per cent below its potential level, so that there was an output gap of -2 per cent, then the Taylor rule would suggest setting the nominal interest rate a little lower, at 7.5 per cent.

Studies have shown that a number of countries seem to have patterns of interest rates that follow the Taylor rule relatively closely. In reality, Taylor and other researchers appreciated that decision makers could not stick rigidly to such a rule because sometimes circumstances might dictate the need to apply discretion. Taylor argued that whilst a rule gave a guideline to policymakers, it also implied that any deviation from the rule had to be explained through a coherent and well-argued case and that such a discipline was helpful to overall monetary policy decisions.

Nominal GDP Targeting

Inflation targeting has been the target of some debate and criticism in the aftermath of the Financial Crisis. The typical expectation of post-recession macroeconomic variables is for a gradual recovery, growth beginning to pick up and as it does, inflationary pressures slowly build. As the output gap narrows, the labour market becomes tighter as demand for labour rises, unemployment falls and wage growth begins to accelerate. Central banks following an inflation target will monitor these developments and adjust monetary policy as appropriate to guide inflation to target. As unemployment falls and inflation accelerates (the expected Phillips curve relationship), interest rates will be gradually increased moderating the expansion in output and keeping the economy relatively stable.

The experience of some countries, notably the UK and US, has been somewhat different. In the five years to the beginning of 2016, the unemployment rate has fallen from over 8 per cent in 2011 to just over 5 per cent at the beginning of 2016. At the same time, GDP at market prices averaged 2.1 per cent each year and inflation as measured by the CPI slowed from over 5 per cent in 2011 and has hovered around zero for much of 2015. Right through this period, the Bank of England's repo rate has remained at 0.5 per cent. In 2011, the Bank of England increased its asset purchasing facility (QE) by £75 billion and in February 2012 by a further £50 billion. The Bank of England itself states that 'The objective of quantitative easing is to boost the money supply through large-scale asset purchases and, in so doing, to bring about a level of nominal demand consistent with meeting the inflation target in the medium term.'[1]

Given this economic situation, critics have argued that the Bank of England has 'unofficially' departed from inflation targeting. Some economists argue that the relationship between inflation and unemployment has broken down with inflation and unemployment moving in the same direction over the 5-year period observed. The Bank of England points out that its primary remit from the UK Chancellor is to maintain price stability but note that it is also expected to support the government's policy for growth and employment. Critics argue that the two targets are compromised if inflation targeting is used.

---

[1] *The Bank of England's Sterling Monetary Framework.* June 2015.
http://www.bankofengland.co.uk/markets/Documents/money/publications/redbook.pdf#page=11

Nominal GDP Targeting Another option which has been suggested by some economists as a preferable way to conduct monetary policy would be to target nominal GDP (NGDP). NGDP is the total expenditure in the economy calculated by multiplying output by the price at which that output is sold. If NGDP rises, this will be due to a rise in prices, a rise in output or a combination of the two. If prices rise by 2 per cent and output increases by 1 per cent, NGDP rises by 3 per cent.

NGDP targeting would mean that a central bank would use the tools at its disposal to target a particular growth rate of NGDP. If NGDP fell below trend, as happened in the recession following the Financial Crisis, the central bank would expand the money supply through a combination of interest rate changes and open market operations. The consequence of this might be inflation accelerating beyond any notional target for a period but the benefit would be that unemployment would not fall as much as would be the case under inflation targeting. If NGDP accelerated beyond trend, the central bank would tighten monetary policy and as a result inflation might be under 'target' for a period.

Proponents of NGDP targeting claim that it would not mitigate against all external shocks (such as the rapid fall in oil prices experienced in 2014–15) but would result in a more stable economy without the swings in unemployment, which can be so damaging to people and the economy as a whole. Part of the reason for this claim is that the decision to make people redundant in the midst of a recession tends to be delayed (unemployment, remember is a lagging indicator) and an assumption that wages are sticky. If spending in the economy falls, wages do not adjust downwards and firms find themselves having to pay wages to workers whose skills are not being exploited to the full. If wages do not fall, then the ultimate option facing firms is to let workers go. Under NGDP targeting, when spending falls, the central bank would expand the money supply to stimulate the economy, even if this meant that inflation gathered pace. Such a policy implies that the perceived costs of inflation in the short to medium term is less than the costs of higher unemployment which may be experienced under an inflation targeting policy.

Given the experience of the UK and the US in the five years to early 2016, inflation targeting does not make much sense. The Bank of England, for example, might be expected to have to reduce interest rates further and expand QE on order to stimulate inflation to target level, given that the CPI is well below 2.0 per cent. With the repo rate at 0.5 per cent, there seems limited flexibility to change interest rates, which leaves open market operations as the option but this has remained stable since 2012 until the Bank of England reduced rates to 0.25 per cent in August 2016. Economists are asking what policy the Bank is actually working to and what might explain the change in the relationship between inflation and unemployment since the Financial Crisis. Without a clear understanding of central bank policy, markets find it difficult to forecast, plan and make decisions, which in itself can lead to instability.

NGDP targeting is not a new idea. The 1977 Nobel Prize winner, James Meade (who supported Phillips' promotion at the LSE in the 1950s) made reference to the idea in his Prize lecture, and other economists, including Martin Weale, one of the members of the MPC, and Charles Bean, Deputy Governor of the Bank of England, have both explored the idea at different times in their career.

Whether NGDP would have been a better policy option in the wake of the Financial Crisis is, like much in economics, open to debate. Much depends on the period of time over which one considers economic variables such as growth, inflation and unemployment. Supporters of inflation targeting would argue that the policy in most developed countries is not so rigid as to ignore the wider economic environment and that inflation above or below target can be accommodated by inflation targeting provided the target is maintained in the medium-term. The CPI in the UK, for example, has fluctuated over the ten-year period from 2005 to 2015 as highlighted in Figure 35.10 but the average over this period has been 2.5 per cent. If the 'medium term' is defined as a period of three to four years, then between 2005 and 2009, the CPI averaged 2.6 per cent; between 2010 and 2014, the average was 2.9 per cent; and from 2013 to 2015 it was 1.35 per cent.

In a speech to the Institute for Economic Affairs (IEA) in February 2013, Charles Bean defended current policy by arguing that the Bank had sufficient flexibility to accommodate shocks and to allow inflation to deviate from target, and that given the availability and reliability of data on which to make decisions, the risk inherent in inflation targeting was lower than that of NGDP targeting.

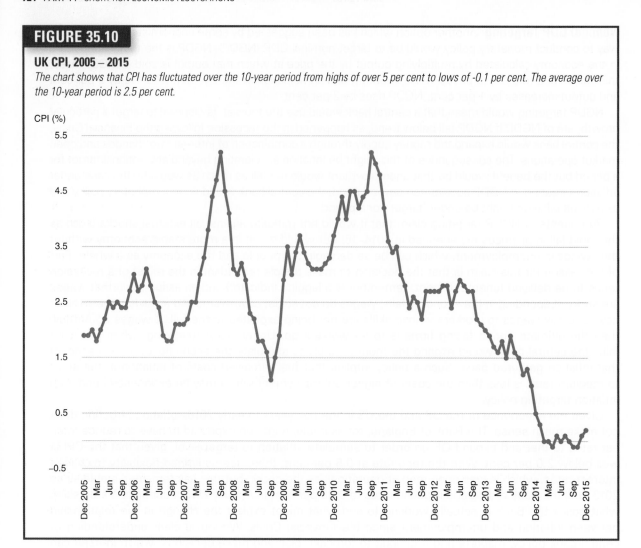

FIGURE 35.10

UK CPI, 2005 – 2015

The chart shows that CPI has fluctuated over the 10-year period from highs of over 5 per cent to lows of -0.1 per cent. The average over the 10-year period is 2.5 per cent.

REFLECTING ON THE PHILLIPS CURVE

It is not easy to fully appreciate the extent to which Phillips' 'weekend work' influenced macroeconomic thinking over the past 50 years. Some of the best minds in economics have debated the fundamental notion behind the Phillips curve – that there is a short-run trade-off between inflation and unemployment. In the early years after the Samuelson–Solow paper, then Federal Reserve chair, William McChesney Martin cast doubt on the suggestion that policymakers had at their disposal a 'menu' of options. One of Martin's criticisms was that focusing just on either an inflation or an unemployment target missed what he described as 'collateral, and perhaps deleterious, side effects on other objectives'. (Speech to the Joint Economic Committee of the US Congress, February 1963.)

The 1970s witnessed high and accelerating rates of inflation triggered by supply-side shocks which seemed to confirm what some economists and policymakers had thought, that there was no trade-off between inflation and unemployment. Economists turned their attention to other areas of research, notably the money supply and monetary policy. In the 1990s, however, interest in the Phillips curve was revived and the development of DSGE models incorporated Phillips curve like relationships. In particular, New Keynesians sought to incorporate the role of expectations in a New Keynesian Phillips curve which not only took into account expectations of current inflation but also future inflation and how this would impact on firms' marginal cost. As we saw in Chapter 33, this has implications for mark-up pricing which in turn affects inflation.

The focus on providing a regime which targets inflation and maintains credibility stemmed in part from the success of countries like Switzerland and Germany in maintaining stable, low rates of inflation. By the noughties, the majority of developed countries had moved to inflation targeting. What this did was herald a shift away from targeting monetary aggregates and focussed attention on the role of central banks in the economy. Central banks will act to change interest rates when it is forecast that inflation will begin to deviate from target. In so doing, there is an element of monetary discipline built into the actions of the monetary authorities which renders a focus on monetary aggregates redundant. This is one reason why there is criticism in some quarters of the retention of the teaching of the IS–LM model in some undergraduate programmes; central banks do not 'control' the money supply directly in 'modern' economies.

The New Keynesian Phillips curve links the output gap and inflationary pressures in the economy. Models can provide some estimation of the expected size of the output gap and this in turn helps form expectations of future inflation. There is debate over cause and effect; is inflation a symptom of an overheating economy or does an overheating economy cause inflation? If central banks take steps to moderate inflation by changing interest rates, the impact on other areas of the economy are not costless, in other words, costless disinflation is a fallacy. The New Keynesian Phillips curve assumes that inflation leads measures of the output gap but critics argue that the evidence suggests this is not the case. One of the challenges facing economists in understanding the cause and effect is the role of lags in models. Policy actions do not lead to instantaneous changes in inflation, unemployment or growth; each of these may be subject to different time lags and this has implications for the outcomes of models used, and for the importance of monetary aggregates. If growth in the money supply precedes inflation rather than the other way round, this implies money aggregates may be important in forecasting future inflation. Central banks have a difficult task in juggling the many different variables involved in complex models and getting the direction of cause and effect as well as the length and importance of time lags in making policy.

The Financial Crisis provided further evidence of the difficulties in identifying cause and effect. One of the agreed causes of the Crisis was the extent to which credit had ballooned in many economies – economic actors were borrowing extensively as we have seen. Was such a demand for credit borne out of the fear that interest rates were about to rise and thus borrowing rose substantially in advance or was it due to confidence that economies were perceived as strong and would continue to grow in the foreseeable future? The policy response of central banks would need to be different in each case. This is one of the reasons why financial markets are being incorporated into DSGE models as a way of making the models more robust and reflective of the workings of modern economies.

Ultimately, it can be concluded that the Phillips curve as originally developed was not sophisticated enough, and certainly not reflective of what could be argued as being an even more complex global economy, to provide policymakers today with a simple trade-off. What it did, however, was spawn research into areas of macroeconomics that continues today, and which has enriched our understanding. Few economists would argue that understanding is anywhere near complete and there is still much to do.

CONCLUSION

This chapter has examined how economists' thinking about inflation and unemployment has evolved over time. We have discussed the ideas of many of the best economists of the 20th century: from the Phillips curve of Phillips, Samuelson and Solow, to the natural-rate hypothesis of Friedman and Phelps, to the rational expectations theory of Lucas, Sargent and Barro. Six of this group have already won Nobel prizes for their work in economics, and more are likely to be so honoured in the years to come. Our discussion has been based around the UK economy but the principles apply across other economies too – the UK is a convenient case study in the changing interpretation and application of economic theory.

Although the trade-off between inflation and unemployment has generated much intellectual turmoil over the past 50 years, certain principles have developed that many economists would agree command consensus. Milton Friedman, perhaps, sums up this consensus in an *American Economic Review* paper entitled 'The Role of Monetary Policy' in 1968:

There is always a temporary trade-off between inflation and unemployment; there is no permanent trade-off. The temporary trade-off comes not from inflation per se, but from unanticipated inflation, which generally means, from a rising rate of inflation. The widespread belief that there is a permanent trade-off is a sophisticated version of the confusion between 'high' and 'rising' that we all recognize in simpler forms. A rising rate of inflation may reduce unemployment, a high rate will not.

But how long, you will say, is 'temporary'? ...We can at most venture a personal judgment, based on some examination of the historical evidence that the initial effects of a higher and unanticipated rate of inflation last for something like two to five years.

IN THE NEWS

Inflation Targeting

Having a target for inflation has been a mainstay of central bank policy over the last 20 years in many countries. Since the Financial Crisis, however, inflation has rarely been at, or even around target, in countries like the UK. Has this meant that inflation targeting has been abandoned, and if not should it be?

An Austrian Argument Against Inflation Targeting?

The initial years after the Financial Crisis saw inflation in the UK stubbornly hovering well above the 2.0 per cent target before slowing considerably and languishing around zero throughout 2015 and into 2016. Having a target is meant to send out a signal to everyone that the central bank will act to bring inflation as close to target as possible. Interest rates in the UK remained at 0.5 per cent into 2016 until being reduced to 0.25 per cent in August of that year. The fall in oil prices in 2015 suggested that inflation would remain well below target.

In July 2013, the Bank of England got a new governor, Mark Carney. Giving evidence before a Treasury Select Committee in February 2013, Carney noted that under his watch, the Bank of England would follow in the footsteps for the US Federal Reserve in keeping interest rates low to ensure economic recovery was firmly underway and if that meant higher inflation in the process then that would be a price worth paying. Was this a sign that inflation targeting had been abandoned in favour of NGDP targeting? The Bank claimed that inflation targeting had not been abandoned but as inflation remained subdued and unemployment fell, some economists suggested that the Phillips curve relationship had broken down.

In early 2016, Professor Anthony J. Evans, of ESCP Europe Business School, published a paper entitled *Sound Money: An Austrian proposal for free banking, NGDP targets, and OMO reforms*. In the paper, Evans suggests that the use of QE was in effect a means by which central banks expanded the money supply through open market operations whilst setting interest rates affects the price of money. This could be argued to be compromising the policy of inflation targeting since central banks cannot control both the money supply and interest rates at the same time.

Thomas goes on to argue that the MPC of the Bank of England should be disbanded, and that the Bank should shift to targeting not inflation but NGDP through the use of QE. This, Evans argues, would contribute to a more stable economy over time. However, Evans proposes even more radical reforms which he accepts are not likely in the foreseeable future but worth debating nevertheless. These reforms include abolishing the Bank of England and creating 'free banks'. The idea of free banking is not new – it has been a feature of Austrian economics for some time. Essentially, banks would be free to print their own money and set their own interest rates without any intervention by government or monetary authorities. The absence of a 'lender of last resort' (i.e. a central bank) would provide the necessary discipline for free banks in that if imprudent practices were followed, bankruptcy would be a possibility and moral hazard would be reduced.

Mark Carney, Governor of the Bank of England.

Questions

1 Explain how monetary policy can be used to target inflation.
2 How successful do you think central banks, such as the Bank of England, have been in achieving their inflation targets in the last 10 years? Justify your view.
3 How would a central bank go about setting policies designed to target nominal GDP at a growth rate of (say) 6 per cent?
4 Given falling unemployment, reasonable growth and inflation well below 2.0 per cent targets, do you think the Phillips curve relationship is now well and truly 'broken'? Explain.
5 Comment on the idea of 'free banking'. To what extent do you think that free banking would result in a more stable economic environment in comparison to an economy in which central banks intervene to set monetary policy, have a monopoly on printing money and act as a lender of last resort?

Source: http://www.adamsmith.org/wp-content/uploads/2016/01/Sound-Money-AJE4.pdf

SUMMARY

- The Phillips curve describes a negative relationship between inflation and unemployment. By expanding AD, policymakers can choose a point on the Phillips curve with higher inflation and lower unemployment. By contracting AD, policymakers can choose a point on the Phillips curve with lower inflation and higher unemployment.

- Many economists now subscribe to the view that the trade-off between inflation and unemployment described by the Phillips curve holds only in the short run. In the long run, expected inflation adjusts to changes in actual inflation, and the short-run Phillips curve shifts. As a result, the long-run Phillips curve is vertical at the natural rate of unemployment.

- The short-run Phillips curve also shifts because of shocks to AS. An adverse supply shock, such as the increase in world oil prices during the 1970s, gives policymakers a less favourable trade-off between inflation and unemployment. That is, after an adverse supply shock, policymakers have to accept a higher rate of inflation for any given rate of unemployment, or a higher rate of unemployment for any given rate of inflation.

- When the central bank contracts growth in the money supply to reduce inflation, it moves the economy along the short-run Phillips curve, which results in temporarily high unemployment. The cost of disinflation depends on how quickly expectations of inflation fall. Some economists argue that a credible commitment to low inflation can reduce the cost of disinflation by inducing a quick adjustment of expectations.

- Credibility in maintaining low inflation has been a driver behind many countries granting independence to central banks to conduct monetary policy with the primary aim of maintaining price stability.

- An alternative to inflation targeting is NGDP targeting which would allow for monetary policy to expand and contract in response to changes in nominal GDP. This might mean that inflation is higher or lower that a desired 'target' as monetary policy responds to shocks in the economy but would lead to a more stable economy.

QUESTIONS FOR REVIEW

1 Phillips originally looked at the rate of change in money wages rather than inflation but the Phillips curve has come to be associated with the trade-off between inflation and unemployment. What is the relationship between the rate of change of money wages and inflation?

2 Explain why, in the short run, there might be a trade-off between inflation and unemployment.

3 Draw the short-run trade-off between inflation and unemployment. How might the central bank move the economy from one point on this curve to another?

4 Draw the long-run trade-off between inflation and unemployment. Explain how the short-run and long-run trade-offs are related.

5 Why do economists place such importance on the role of expectations in macroeconomic policy?

6 What is so 'natural' about the natural rate of unemployment? Why might the natural rate of unemployment differ across countries?

7 Explain how expected inflation might cause a shift in the short-run Phillips curve.

8 Suppose a drought destroys farm crops and drives up the price of food. What is the effect on the short-run trade-off between inflation and unemployment?

9 What reasons are put forward for keeping central banks independent in setting monetary policy?

10 What are the main differences between inflation targeting and NGDP targeting?

PROBLEMS AND APPLICATIONS

1 Suppose the natural rate of unemployment is 6 per cent. On one graph, draw two Phillips curves that can be used to describe the four situations listed here. Label the point that shows the position of the economy in each case.

 a. Actual inflation is 5 per cent and expected inflation is 3 per cent.
 b. Actual inflation is 3 per cent and expected inflation is 5 per cent.
 c. Actual inflation is 5 per cent and expected inflation is 5 per cent.
 d. Actual inflation is 3 per cent and expected inflation is 3 per cent.

2 Illustrate the effects of the following developments on both the short-run and long-run Phillips curves. Give the economic reasoning underlying your answers:

 a. a rise in the natural rate of unemployment
 b. a decline in the price of imported oil
 c. a rise in government spending
 d. a decline in expected inflation.

3 Suppose that a fall in consumer spending causes a recession.

 a. Illustrate the changes in the economy using both an AD/AS diagram and a Phillips curve diagram. What happens to inflation and unemployment in the short run?
 b. Now suppose that over time expected inflation changes in the same direction that actual inflation changes. What happens to the position of the short run Phillips curve? After the recession is over, does the economy face a better or worse set of inflation–unemployment combinations?

4 Suppose the economy is in a long-run equilibrium.

 a. Draw the economy's short-run and long-run Phillips curves.
 b. Suppose a wave of business pessimism reduces AD. Show the effect of this shock on your diagram from part (a). If the central bank undertakes expansionary monetary policy, can it return the economy to its original inflation rate and original unemployment rate?
 c. Now suppose the economy is back in long-run equilibrium, and then the price of imported oil rises. Show the effect of this shock with a new diagram like that in part (a). If the central bank undertakes expansionary monetary policy, can it return the economy to its original inflation rate and original unemployment rate? If the central bank undertakes contractionary monetary policy, can it return the economy to its original inflation rate and original unemployment rate? Explain why this situation differs from that in part (b).

5 Suppose the central bank believed that the natural rate of unemployment was 6 per cent when the actual natural rate was 5.5 per cent. If the central bank based its policy decisions on its belief, what would happen to the economy?

6 Suppose the central bank announced that it would pursue contractionary monetary policy in order to reduce the inflation rate. Would the following conditions make the ensuing recession more or less severe? Explain.

a. Wage contracts have short durations.
b. There is little confidence in the central bank's determination to reduce inflation.
c. Expectations of inflation adjust quickly to actual inflation.

7 Some economists believe that the short-run Phillips curve is relatively steep and shifts quickly in response to changes in the economy. Would these economists be more or less likely to favour contractionary policy in order to reduce inflation than economists who had the opposite views?

8 Imagine an economy in which all wages are set in three-year contracts. In this world, the central bank announces a disinflationary change in monetary policy to begin immediately. Everyone in the economy believes the central bank's announcement. Would this disinflation be costless? Why or why not? What might the central bank do to reduce the cost of disinflation?

9 Given the unpopularity of inflation, why don't elected leaders always support efforts to reduce inflation? Economists believe that countries can reduce the cost of disinflation by letting their central banks make decisions about monetary policy without interference from politicians. Why might this be so?

10 Some economists have proposed that central banks should use the following rule for choosing their target interest rate (r):

$$r = 2 + p + \frac{1}{2}\frac{(y - y^*)}{y^*} + \frac{1}{2}(p - p^*),$$ where: p is the average of the inflation rate over the past year, y is real GDP as recently measured, y^* is an estimate of the natural rate of output and p^* is the central bank's target rate of inflation which is given as 2 per cent.

a. Explain the logic that might lie behind this rule for setting interest rates. Would you support the use of this rule?
b. Some economists advocate such a rule for monetary policy but believe p and y should be the forecasts of future values of inflation and output. What are the advantages of using forecasts instead of actual values? What are the disadvantages?

36 SUPPLY-SIDE POLICIES

The focus of policy in the post-war era was firmly on managing aggregate demand. In the late 1960s and into the 1970s demand management came to be questioned and some economists began looking at the capacity of the economy – aggregate supply. In particular, economists began looking at the effects of (often) frequent changes in taxes which was a feature of demand management on the supply-side of the economy.

We have seen that in the long run, the AS curve is vertical but in the short run it slopes upwards from left to right. Shifting the AS curve to the right would increase the capacity of the economy and increase national income (and thus lower unemployment) but reduce pressure on prices. A concentration on the supply-side of the economy could, therefore, help to bring about sustainable economic growth; higher growth, lower unemployment and stable or even lower inflation. Supply-side policies, therefore, focused on ways of influencing the factors which affect AS. If AS represents the quantity of goods and services that firms choose to produce at different price levels then looking at what influences firms' behaviour is an important starting point.

SHIFTS IN THE AGGREGATE SUPPLY CURVE

There is a range of factors which can cause the AS curve to shift, as we saw in Chapter 33. We summarized these as changes in labour, physical or human capital, the availability of natural resources, changes in technology, and expectations of the price level. This summary provides us with the bare bones on which to explore in more detail how shifts in the AS curve might arise.

So far we have looked at the AS curve in the short run as being upwards sloping and in the long run as vertical. The vertical long-run AS curve makes intuitive sense if you think about AS in terms of the capacity of the economy. Imagine that every individual in an economy who wanted to work at the going wage rate could find work (i.e. there was full employment), that every firm was producing at its maximum capacity and there were no machines lying idle, then the economy would be producing at its maximum capacity which we will refer to as full employment output (Y_f).

We have explored the analysis that in the short run the AS curve can shift causing temporary deviations from this full employment output but eventually, once changes in prices, wages and misperceptions work through the economy, output returns to its long-run equilibrium. Changes in AD can cause fluctuations in economic activity and fiscal and monetary policy can be implemented to manage demand and attempt to stabilize fluctuations. However, if policies are put in place to boost AD, for example, the effects might depend on the extent of the output gap that exists and the flexibility of the economy to respond to the increase in AD. The extent to which unemployment is reduced and how far the price level changes, will be affected by the flexibility of the economy.

Figure 36.1 shows a different shaped AS curve to those we have looked at so far. At the full employment level of output, the AS curve is vertical but between Y_1 and Y_f the AS curve becomes increasingly steep, whereas between Y_2 and Y_1 the AS curve is almost horizontal. This is referred to as the new Keynesian AS curve.

FIGURE 36.1

The New Keynesian Aggregate Supply Curve

The new Keynesian aggregate supply curve is vertical at full employment output Y_f. At low levels of national income, the AS curve is virtually horizontal reflecting the fact that there is considerable spare capacity in the economy but, as national income rises, the ability of firms to expand output becomes more difficult and so the AS curve becomes gradually steeper until it becomes vertical at full employment output.

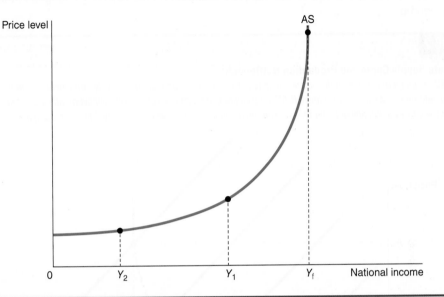

Between the origin and Y_2, there is a considerable amount of spare capacity in the economy but that spare capacity begins to diminish the closer to full employment output at Y_f. This has implications for the effect on national income and the price level if AD shifts as shown in Figure 36.2. If the economy starts out at Y_1 with the price level P_1, there is considerable spare capacity in the economy and the output gap is large. If fiscal and/ or monetary policy shifts the AD curve to the right, the increase in national income rises by a relatively large amount from Y_1 to Y_2. The increase in the price level is only small, suggesting that the Phillips curve is relatively shallow and the trade-off between the reduction in unemployment and the rise in the price level is favourable. If policy continues to push AD to the right, the trade-off changes and the increase in national income begins to get smaller the nearer to full employment output, whilst the rise in the price level increases at a faster rate.

Why does the trade-off become less favourable over time? The reason is that as AD increases, the pressure on society's scarce resources becomes greater. If AD increased from AD_3 to AD_4, for example, firms would be looking to expand output to meet the increased demand and would look to buy more factor inputs. As the demand for these factor inputs rises, the price of them increases. Certain types of labour might become scarce more quickly than others and wage rates in these industries might rise sharply as a result. The demand for skilled labour in the construction industry, for example, might rise but the supply of people with these skills tends to be inelastic in the short run. It takes time to train skilled bricklayers, plumbers, plasterers and electricians. Those who have these skills will find they are in demand and they can sell their labour for higher wages as a result. Firms that pay the higher wages see their costs increase but with demand rising they feel they can pass on these higher costs to the consumer in the form of higher prices and so inflation begins to accelerate. The closer the economy comes to full employment output the greater will be the production bottlenecks that arise as resources become scarcer, so the effect on prices will be greater but the ability of the economy to grow further will decline.

The Importance of the Output Gap

The supply-side focus arises because of the difficulty of policymakers knowing what the size of the output gap is at any particular moment in time; that is, where the economy is on the AS curve. The output gap can be calculated in two ways. The first is to subtract actual output from potential output where potential output is based on the assumption that markets are perfectly competitive. The second is to subtract actual output from natural output where natural output assumes imperfect competition and rigidities in prices and wages. We have seen how monetary and fiscal policy operate side-by-side and even if governments are not deliberately trying to influence AD, changes in tax rates, allowances and government spending decisions will have effects on the level of AD, whilst changes in monetary policy affect investment decisions and the exchange rate, and, as a result, net exports. If the net effect of monetary and fiscal policy is to boost AD, the size of the output gap will have an effect on the resulting changes in the price level and national income.

FIGURE 36.2

The Aggregate Supply Curve and Production Bottlenecks
Increases in AD, when there is considerable spare capacity in the economy, can lead to relatively large increases in national income with only relatively small rises in the price level. If AD keeps increasing resource constraints will eventually mean that national income will only rise by relatively small amounts but the pressure on resources will cause the price level to rise more quickly.

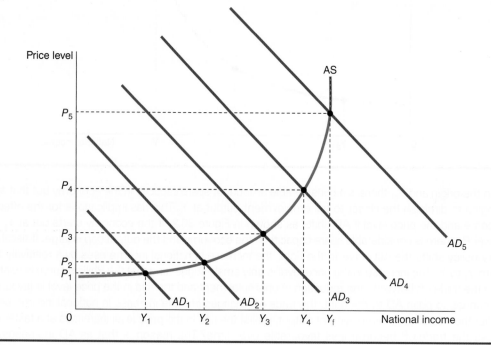

This is illustrated in Figure 36.3. Assume the economy in panel (a) is in equilibrium at Y_1. The output gap is given by the distance between full employment output and actual output $Y_f - Y_1$. An increase in AD to AD_2 would lead to a rise in national income to Y_2, and a rise in the price level to P_2. The output gap narrows but the economy is beginning to experience some bottlenecks in production and as a result the increase in national income has come at a price of accelerating inflation. Any further increases in AD would mean the economy is in danger of overheating – where supply-side constraints mean that the pressure on prices increases.

In panel (b), the initial equilibrium is given by Y_1 but the output gap, again given by $Y_f - Y_1$, is much smaller. The economy is already nearing the vertical section of the AS curve and an increase in AD means that the increase in national income is very small but the effect on the price level is much stronger. The economy is overheating and does not have the capacity to be able to cope with the rise in AD and so the main effect feeds through to prices.

The size of the output gap is simple in practice but much more difficult in reality to estimate. The models used vary and the size of the various parameters that modellers input into the equations can lead to widely differing results. If policymakers base decisions on an estimated output gap that is incorrect, the effects of policy can be different to those anticipated. It is for this reason that supply-siders argue that a focus on increasing the productive capacity of the economy needs to be an important element of the policy mix.

FIGURE 36.3

The Effect of the Size of the Output Gap
Panel (a) shows the effect on national income and the price level of a rise in aggregate demand where the output gap is relatively large. In contrast, if the economy is in an initial equilibrium when the output gap is small as in panel (b), then a rise in AD will have a much larger effect on the price level.

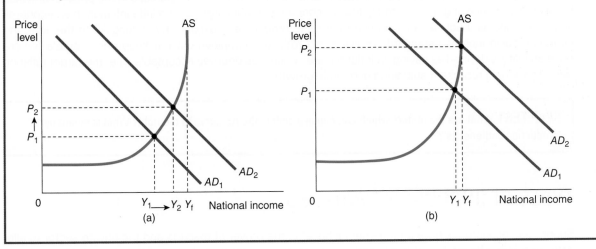

Sustainable Growth

Supply-side economists suggest that if policy is concentrated on increasing the capacity of the economy then in the long run it is possible to increase national income but keep the price level more stable. This is illustrated in Figure 36.4.

FIGURE 36.4

Sustained Economic Growth
If supply-side policies are successful in shifting the AS curve from AS_1 to AS_2, an increase in AD from AD_1 to AD_2 results in a relatively large increase in national income from Y_1 to Y_2 but with only a modest increase in the price level from P_1 to P_2. The new AS curve is associated with an increased capacity of the economy shown by the increase in full employment output from Y_{f1} to Y_{f2}.

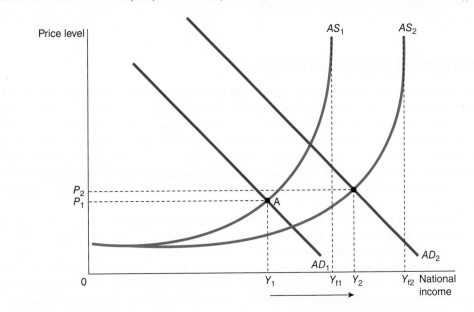

Assume society faces an initial AS curve, AS_1, and AD curve, AD_1. The initial equilibrium is at point A with a price level of P_1 and national income at Y_1. An increase in AD to AD_2 would, given the initial AS curve, see the economy begin to experience more significant production bottlenecks and as a result the price level would start to accelerate. If supply-side policies succeeded in shifting the AS curve to the right to AS_2, this would give a new full employment output capacity at Y_{f2} compared to Y_{f1}. The increase in AD to AD_2 would now result in a rise in national income to Y_2 from Y_1 but the increase in the price level would be relatively small rising from P_1 to P_2. Many economists would argue that a little inflation in an economy is a good thing as it acts as an incentive to firms to produce and expand. By shifting AS to the right, the economy could increase standards of living and reduce unemployment but keep prices stable (where price stability is defined as having an inflation rate which was deemed acceptable – i.e. the target inflation rate). This would represent sustained economic growth.

> **SELF TEST** What are the factors which can cause a shift in the AS curve to the right? What is meant by 'production bottlenecks'?

TYPES OF SUPPLY-SIDE POLICIES

Supply-side economists have a fundamental belief in the power of markets and the private sector to allocate resources efficiently – at least more efficiently than might be the case with public sector provision. Give these assumptions, policies addressing the extent to which the working of markets can be improved will ensure more efficient allocation of resources. These policies are classed as **market-orientated supply-side policies**. If governments are going to intervene in the economy then supply-siders believe that the focus should be on investing in resources that improve the working of the economy such as developing infrastructure, improving research and development and investing in education. These policies are referred to as **interventionist policies**. We will now look at the policies which come under these broad classifications in more detail.

> **market-orientated supply-side policies** policies designed to free up markets to improve resource allocation through more effective price signals
>
> **interventionist supply-side policies** policies focused on improving the working of markets through investing in infrastructure, education and research and development

Market Orientated Supply-Side Policies

The intention of market orientated supply-side policies is to help markets work more effectively by improving the effectiveness of price signals so that resources are allocated more efficiently. Underpinning these policies is a philosophical belief that markets are the most effective way of allocating resources. The use of Keynesian demand management policies had led to government becoming more and more involved in the economy, with a number of industries or firms run by the state on behalf of the people as a whole. Many governments increasingly built up the welfare state to support those in need and, of course, all this government spending meant taxes had to be raised to pay for the increase in the services provided by the state.

Supply-side policies came to the fore in the 1980s when governments in the developed world were trying to cope with stagflation. This section is not intended to be a history lesson but there will be references to policies put in place by the governments in the United States and the UK to highlight key issues arising in supply-side policies. A core of what was referred to as the 'supply-side revolution' was on rolling back the influence of the state in the economy, cutting government spending, reforming the tax and benefit system to improve incentives, freeing up the labour market to make it more flexible and encouraging a more entrepreneurial culture in society. Many of the policies implemented were designed to improve incentives.

Reform of Tax and Welfare Policy We have seen that taxes have an effect on incentives and can lead to distortions in market outcomes. Welfare payments can be viewed as negative taxes giving people support when they fall on hard times. Few would disagree with the necessity of taxing firms, products, and individuals to generate tax revenue for government and also to influence behaviour in desired directions, such as reducing smoking or encouraging reductions in waste. If we acknowledge the fact that taxes – positive and negative – distort market outcomes, then the debate shifts to the level of taxation.

In many countries in Europe and in the US, income and corporate taxes were relatively high in the 1970s and 1980s. In the UK, for example, the basic rate of income tax was 33 per cent in 1978, there were also other higher rates associated with higher levels of income, with the top tax rate being 98 per cent on unearned income and 83 per cent on earned income. Corporation tax in the UK in 1978 was 53 per cent for larger companies and 42 per cent for small companies. In the US, income tax rates ranged from 14 per cent to 70 per cent and corporate tax rates were near 50 per cent. Corporate taxes in Germany in 1981 were around 56 per cent, in Norway just over 50 per cent, 48 per cent in the Netherlands and in Sweden almost 58 per cent. Table 36.1 shows the top rates of income tax in a selection of nine European countries for 1979, 1995 and 2015.

TABLE 36.1 **Top Rates of Income Tax in Nine European Counties, 1979–2015**

Country	Top Income tax rate 1979 (%)	Top Income tax rate 1995 (%)	Top Income tax rate 2015 (%)
Belgium	76.3	55.0	70.0
Denmark	66.0	63.5	55.6
Germany	56.0	53.0	45.0
Ireland	60.0	48.0	41.0
Netherlands	72.0	60.0	52.0
Norway	75.4	13.7	47.2
Portugal	80.0	40.0	46.5
Sweden	86.5	30.0	56.6
UK	83.0	40.0	45.0

Source: OECD

Supply-siders argued that high rates of income and corporate taxes were acting as a disincentive to individuals and to businesses. We need here to remind ourselves of the distinction between average and marginal tax rates. Remember that marginal tax rates refer to the amount of tax taken on every extra euro or pound of earnings. In the UK, some people faced a marginal tax rate of 83 per cent – the government would leave the individual with just 17 pence from every extra pound earned. Supply-siders argued that such high rates of tax acted as a significant disincentive to work and be entrepreneurial, if the rewards from hard work were subject to such rates.

Cutting both income and corporate taxes, therefore, could lead to the incentive for people to take work and work harder (more hours) if the rewards were greater. Income tax rates, it was argued, altered the trade-off between work and leisure. Higher tax rates reduce the opportunity cost of leisure and so people will opt to reduce work and take more leisure. If tax rates are lowered and people get to keep more of the income they earn, the effect is like an increase in wages. The substitution effect is reinforced by the income effect, and labour supply increases.

High corporate and income taxes also act as an incentive for firms and individuals to engage in tax avoidance (which is legal) or tax evasion (which is illegal). Higher tax rates, it is argued, do encourage firms and individuals to find ways in which their tax liability can be reduced, which may include putting money into offshore 'tax havens', firms spending money on tax-deductible assets which may not have any major impact on productivity (like investing in plusher office suites, buying luxury company cars, locating conferences at more luxurious venues and so on), or on channelling income into offshore companies which then return the money in the form of 'loans' on which there is no income tax. Such schemes are not illegal but some would claim that they are morally wrong. Tax evasion is illegal and refers to attempts by firms and individuals to avoid declaring income which is subject to taxation. This might be in the form of traders accepting cash for work carried out which is then not declared as income, through to more sophisticated money laundering schemes. Estimates in the UK, for example, put the cost of tax evasion at around £14 billion a year and some research by the Tax Justice Network in 2011 put the cost of tax avoidance across 145 countries at $3.1 trillion (€2.86 trillion or £2.18 trillion).

Reducing tax rates can change incentives to work and also incentives to avoid or evade paying taxes. Cutting tax rates can, therefore, mean that tax revenues actually increase. An example serves to illustrate. Assume that the top rate of income tax in a country is 80 per cent and that this rate applies to the whole of an individual's income (in reality most income tax regimes in country's are progressive and stepped so that those on lower incomes pay a lower rate compared to those on higher rates). An individual earning €500 000 would have to pay €400 000 in tax and gets to keep the remaining €100 000. If the government reduced the tax rate to 60 per cent, the individual faces the incentive that they get to keep more of every €1 of earnings which acts as a powerful incentive to work harder. The individual works harder in the next year and earns €750 000, on which they pay tax of €450 000 and keeps €300 000. The individual has more of an incentive to work harder because they get to keep more of their earnings and the government generates more in overall tax revenue.

Income and corporate tax rates fell in many countries across Europe in the 1980s and into the 1990s. In addition to reducing actual tax rates, governments can also change tax allowances relating to the amount of income earned before having to pay tax. In the UK, for example, in 2010, the amount earned before paying tax stood at £6500 but in 2016 had increased to £10 600. Changing tax rates also has an effect on those who are looking for work. If tax rates are high or tax allowances are low, it can be the case that the incentive for people to go into work and come off benefits is also low. Assume, for example, an individual was receiving €10 000 a year in various benefits but pays no income tax. A job becomes available which pays €12 000. If the worker takes the job but then becomes liable for tax at a rate of (say) 25 per cent on all their earnings, then they will receive an after-tax income of €9000. There is no incentive for the person to take the job, to come off benefits and pay income tax. If the tax rate were reduced to (say) 10 per cent, the person would receive an after tax income €10 800 and so there would be more of an incentive to take the job and come off benefits. Not only would the government be better off by not having to pay this individual benefits, it would be receiving €1200 in tax revenue – a net benefit to the government of €11 200. In addition, by getting a job the individual is now not subject to the same issues and problems we outlined as the costs of unemployment to individuals in Chapter 23, which reduces the social externalities associated with unemployment.

This approach is also linked with reform of the welfare system to provide incentives to individuals to get off benefits and into work. By making access to benefits subject to more rigorous tests and/or reducing welfare payments, individuals are forced to reassess their position, not become so reliant on the welfare state and look to find ways to support themselves. This means they might have to be more flexible in taking jobs which they may otherwise have shunned because they did not match to their expectations, wage demands or qualifications.

The combined effects of these policies mean that the labour market is more efficient with fewer people being voluntarily unemployed, with those in work prepared to work harder and be more productive and for enterprise and initiative to be rewarded.

The analysis so far is fairly intuitive but the reality depends on a number of factors not least the elasticity of supply of labour. If the elasticity of supply of labour is relatively low then any increase in wages through tax cuts or changes in allowances will only have a limited effect on the increase in the supply of labour (often measured in labour hours). If the elasticity of supply of labour was 0.1, for example, a rise in the wage rate of 5 per cent would only lead to an increase in labour supply of 0.5 per cent. The long run elasticity of supply of labour, however, might be larger than those in the short run because workers have time to adjust their behaviour. Research by Nobel Prize-winning economist, Edward Prescott, in 2002 suggested that there was a considerable difference between the elasticities of labour supply in France and the US which were largely due to differences in tax systems between the two countries.

CASE STUDY The Laffer Curve and Supply-Side Economics

One day in 1974, rumour has it that the American economist, Arthur Laffer, sat in a Washington restaurant with some prominent journalists and politicians. He took out a napkin and drew a figure on it to show how tax rates affect tax revenue. The illustration looked like that shown in panel (b) of Figure 9.6, reproduced earlier in the book. Laffer suggested that the United States was on the downwards sloping side of this curve. Tax rates were so high, he argued, that reducing them would actually raise tax revenue.

Most economists were sceptical of Laffer's suggestion. The idea that a cut in tax rates could raise tax revenue was correct as a matter of economic theory, but there was more doubt about whether it would do so in practice. There was little evidence for Laffer's view that tax rates – in the United States or elsewhere – had in fact reached such extreme levels.

Nevertheless, the thinking underlying the **Laffer curve** (as it became known) became very influential in policy circles during the 1980s, particularly in the USA during the years of President Ronald Reagan's administration and in the UK during Prime Minister Margaret Thatcher's government. Tax rates – particularly income tax rates – were cut aggressively in both countries during the 1980s.

Laffer curve the relationship between tax rates and tax revenue

In the UK, for example, under Prime Minister Thatcher the top rate of income tax was cut from 83 per cent to 60 per cent in 1980 and then again to 40 per cent in 1988. Economists have, however, found it hard to trace any strong incentive effects of these tax cuts leading to increases in total tax revenue as the Laffer curve would suggest. A study by the UK's IFS, for example, concluded that at most about 3 per cent of the increase in tax revenue between 1980 and 1986 could be attributed to the 1980 income tax cut.

In the USA, President Reagan also cut taxes aggressively, but the result

Art Laffer, the man behind the Laffer curve.

was less tax revenue, not more. Revenue from personal income taxes in the United States (per person, adjusted for inflation) fell by 9 per cent from 1980 to 1984, even though average income (per person, adjusted for inflation) grew by 4 per cent over this period. The tax cut, together with policymakers' unwillingness to restrain spending, began a long period during which the US government spent more than it collected in taxes. Throughout Reagan's two terms in office, and for many years thereafter, the US government ran large budget deficits.

Laffer's argument is not completely without merit. Although an overall cut in tax rates normally reduces revenue, some taxpayers, at some times, may be on the wrong side of the Laffer curve. The idea that cutting taxes can raise revenue may be correct if applied to those taxpayers facing the highest tax rates, but most people face lower marginal rates. Where the *typical* worker is on the top end of the Laffer curve, it may be more appropriate. In Sweden in the early 1980s, for instance, the typical worker faced a marginal tax rate of about 80 per cent. Such a high tax rate provides a substantial disincentive to work. Studies have suggested that Sweden would indeed have raised more tax revenue if it had lowered its tax rates.

Policymakers disagree about these issues in part because they disagree about the size of the relevant elasticities. The more elastic that supply and demand are in any market, the more taxes in that market distort behaviour, and the more likely it is that a tax cut will raise tax revenue. There is no debate, however, about the general lesson: how much revenue the government gains or loses from a tax change cannot be computed just by looking at tax rates. It also depends on how the tax change affects people's behaviour.

> **SELF TEST** Consider the respective size of the income and substitution effects on the supply of labour curve as a result of a cut in higher rate taxes. Under what circumstances would a cut in tax rates actually lead to a backwards bending supply curve of labour?

Flexible Labour Markets In addition to changing the tax and benefits system, supply-siders argue for more flexibility in labour markets. There are different aspects to this policy which include reducing the power of trade unions and improving market signals to both employers and workers. We saw in Chapter 17 how trade unions can raise wages above market rates. The more powerful are trades unions the higher they can push wages above market rates. In the 1970s and into the 1980s, the power of trade unions in the UK was substantial; days lost to strikes averaged 12.8 million per year in the 1970s. The UK government, in the early 1980s, argued that trade unions exercised too much power and passed a series of new laws which reduced their power considerably. The result has been that trade unions had to adapt and evolve and the number of people belonging to trade unions and the number of days lost to strikes fell sharply in the latter part of the 1980s and beyond. Many more people now negotiate pay levels with employers individually or at local level rather than through unions, and supply-siders would argue that wage rates more accurately reflect market conditions as a result.

More flexible labour markets also relate to the ease with which employers can respond to market conditions by adjusting the labour force. This is sometimes referred to as the ability to 'hire and fire'. The more flexible the labour market, the fewer rigidities that would exist.

Flexible labour markets might include the use of short-term contracts with workers, having more flexible working arrangements so that workers with the right skills are attracted to work, and being able to shed workers more easily when the economy is contracting. Critics argue that flexible labour markets can put the interests of employers before those of workers and a balance does have to be struck between the rights of both parties.

Labour markets can also be made more flexible by improving market information for both employers and employees, such that those people looking for work can be matched with those seeking employment. Many governments provide so-called 'job centres' through which employers can advertise jobs and those looking for work can attend to get advice, be put in touch with prospective employers and given help with improving their CVs, interview skills, job application techniques and so on.

Reducing Government Spending The more money government spends the more it has to raise in tax revenue and also to borrow. We have seen in Chapter 34 how any fiscal expansion can be moderated by the crowding-out effect. It follows that if governments were able to reduce spending and borrow less, the opposite effect would occur – sometimes referred to as 'crowding-in'. Cutting back the amount that governments borrow has been a feature of the post-Financial Crisis austerity programmes which many countries have had to implement. If borrowing can be scaled back, interest rates will fall and this has an effect on firms' decisions to invest.

In addition to the crowding-in argument, there is a fundamental belief among supply-siders that government spending is not likely to be as efficient as the equivalent spending by the private sector. If government, therefore, steps back from its involvement in the economy and leaves resource allocation more to the private sector, the funds will be used more productively and more efficiently which will improve the productive capacity of the economy.

In practice, many governments find it extremely difficult to cut back spending. The effects on government services and those who use them can be considerable and the sort of people who are most affected are often the poor and the most vulnerable in society such as the elderly, the mentally ill, children, and those who require social and/or health care. The political decisions which have to be made when government spending is cut back are extremely difficult – few governments can be so sure of the mandate they receive from the electorate to make the sorts of decisions which would lead to a substantial fall in government spending when so many people are likely to be affected in an adverse way. Closing hospitals, schools, social care programmes, homes for the elderly and mentally ill might save considerable sums of money but represent electoral suicide.

Privatization and Deregulation One of the major changes in the economy of the UK in the last 30 years has been **privatization**, the move to transfer public ownership of assets to the private sector and the increase in the role of private sector firms in providing government services. Privatization has also been a feature of other European countries including Austria, Denmark, Finland, France, Germany, Ireland, Italy, the Netherlands and Spain.

> **privatization** the transfer of public ownership of assets to the private sector

In the post-war era in the UK, many industries were state owned – coal, the railways, the utilities (water, gas and electricity), steel, and telecommunications being key examples and in addition a number of firms were taken into state ownership including some in the motor, aviation and engineering industries. During the 1980s and 1990s, many of these industries and firms were sold and became private sector entities. In addition, other services such as refuse collection, cleaning and catering services were opened up to provision by private sector organizations.

Once again, the philosophical underpinning of privatization in all its forms is the belief that the private sector, driven by providing high quality services and the profit motive, is more likely to provide the services required by the public at lower cost, at higher productivity levels and more efficiently than if provision was in the public sector. It was also argued that transferring assets to the private sector would help increase competition with the resulting benefits of lower prices and increased choice.

It is the subject of much debate as to the extent to which the benefits which were at the heart of the justification for privatization have been realized. The privatization of natural monopolies such as water, gas and electricity has created a complex system which many consumers find difficulty in understanding and despite regulatory bodies being set up to monitor the activities of these now private monopolies, there is some suspicion that the existence of monopoly power has reduced consumer surplus and led to deadweight losses. There are some studies that have suggested that privatization has delivered better services, improved products, lower prices and more choice, more efficiently for the public.

In addition to privatization programmes, many governments looked to pass legislation which cut back on the regulations that were argued to impede the efficient working of financial and goods markets. Deregulation has succeeded in removing some of these imperfections in the market. For example, in transport, local bus routes have been deregulated to prevent local monopolies which have resulted in more choice and lower prices for consumers. In financial markets, there has been an explosion of new products and much greater freedom for individuals and firms to be able to access credit. Whilst this did have some impact on the global economy in the 1990s and into the 2000s, many have argued that deregulation went too far and that appropriate checks and balances were not in place to prevent the Financial Crisis in 2007–9.

SELF TEST Why do policies to improve the flexibility of labour markets have to balance the rights of employers and employees?

Interventionist Supply-Side Policies

In Chapter 10 we noted that the creation of knowledge is a public good, that firms free ride on knowledge created by others and as a result devote too few resources to creating new knowledge. In addition, the investment in infrastructure such as communications networks, roads, rail, ports and airports is vital to the effectiveness of an economy but the sort of sums needed to invest in this sort of infrastructure and the risk involved is often extremely high and the exploitation of the assets for profit by private firms not always easy, obvious or in some cases desirable. For example, the development of new motorway systems raises concerns among local people who are affected by the negative externalities, and of environmentalists. The planning process can often take many years and be extremely expensive in addition to the actual cost of construction. The result is that governments often take the lead in the provision of such infrastructure, albeit using private firms as noted above. Interventionist supply-side policies refer to the ways in which governments seek to encourage investment in education, training, research and development and infrastructure and location of firms in order to help the economy work more effectively and efficiently.

Infrastructure Investment Governments will often take the lead in providing funds for infrastructure projects which have been identified as having long-term beneficial effects on the economy and will help to improve capacity. The sort of projects that governments support are invariably identified as being important in helping businesses to be more efficient, cutting costs and waste, and improving supply chains. Improvements to roads, rail, ports and airports help firms to distribute goods more efficiently; improvements to communications networks help to make service industries more efficient; and developments to energy and water supplies through the building of new power stations or improvements to supply networks can also help firms secure their energy needs and reduce costs if these networks operate more efficiently.

Investment in Education and Training The school and higher education system in an economy is a source of improvements in the quality of future human capital. Whilst many would not see education as purely a means of producing future workers, the sort of skills which school and university leavers have influence their ability to secure work and their productivity levels. As we have seen, productivity is a key factor in improving economic growth and standards of living.

The sort of education system that a country has will, therefore, be important and a number of countries have invested in trying to improve standards. The difficulty comes in defining what appropriate standards are for individuals and for wider society. Some countries place a heavy emphasis on improving maths and science skills because these are crucial in helping to create new knowledge and innovation in industry. Governments might provide grants or allowances to help boost interest in maths, science and engineering degrees; maths and physics graduates may be given incentives to put their skills to use in teaching in schools where there tends to be a paucity of highly qualified individuals in these subject areas.

Governments may also help to support training; firms may be reluctant to invest too many resources into training workers because of the lack of control they have over what workers do with the training they receive. On the one hand, a better trained workforce is beneficial to a firm because it makes workers more productive. It also makes workers more marketable and there is a risk that the worker moves on to a better job and another firm will benefit from the investment in training made by the initial firm. By providing help and support for training, governments may help to overcome this free-rider problem.

Research and Development R&D is essential to the long-term improvement of knowledge creation, the development of new products and new processes. R&D is, however, expensive and unless the results can be protected in some way, the knowledge created becomes a public good. This is one of the reasons why many governments invest in supporting and funding R&D. Research bodies can be set up which receive requests for funding from firms and higher education institutions, sometimes in partnership, who then decide on the allocation of funds based on the perceived value and importance of the research being proposed. Governments may also provide tax credits, tax relief, or grants to help support R&D in smaller firms.

Regional or Industrial Policies In a number of European countries, economies are unevenly balanced – there are regions which are poorer than others. Firms will often gravitate to locate where the markets are biggest or where there are natural advantages such as ports, good infrastructure links and so on. Some regions are poor because they used to be the centre of industries that have declined. The decline of industries such as shipbuilding, iron and steel, the motor industry and the coal industry, for example, has not been matched by new industries springing up to absorb the jobs lost and as a result a negative multiplier process can take hold which means the region may stay economically undeveloped for long periods. Governments may seek to reverse such economic imbalance by locating some of its own activities in these regions, providing investment grants, premises at reduced rents, employment subsidies and other measures to encourage firms to locate in these areas and develop jobs. The intention is that, in encouraging investment in these areas, a positive regional multiplier effect will take hold.

SELF TEST Why is investing in the right sort of education and training considered important to the success of interventionist policies?

CONCLUSION

Supply-side policies have an intuitive feel to them; one of the main problems, however, is that shifting the AS curve to the right is a long-term process. Investing in education, training and R&D, for example, can boost the quality of human capital but the benefits to the economy may not be felt for many years. Market-orientated policies may sound impressive and laudable but the evidence to support the effectiveness of such policies is not overwhelming. It is perhaps safe to say that policies to improve the efficiency of markets and the capacity of the economy have to be carried out hand-in-hand with other policies and not be seen as being an either/or policy option to fiscal and monetary policy. Indeed, the differences between fiscal, monetary and supply-side policies are sometimes difficult to disentangle. If a government announces it is investing billions in a high-speed rail network does this represent a fiscal boost or is it purely focused on improving the supply-side of the economy?

IN THE NEWS

Supply-Side Policies in China

In 2015, stock markets fluctuated wildly partly in response to continued falls in oil prices and partly because of fears that growth in the Chinese economy was slowing, which would have knock-on effects across many other economies. How did the Chinese government respond to its changing economic situation?

Supply-side Reforms in China?

Throughout 2015, one of the major economic stories was the volatility on Chinese stock markets. Reports that economic growth in China had slowed to under 7 per cent for the first time in many years set alarm bells ringing not only in China but across other parts of the world given the importance of China's economy to global growth.

The Chinese government, led by President Xi Jinping, presided over policy approaches to the problems China faced. It has to be remembered that growth of 6 per cent was still impressive but as the economy begins to mature, different reforms will be needed, in particular structural reforms. It appeared that some of these reforms were supply-side in nature. In 2013, President Xi set up the China Academy of New Supply-side Economics to develop and analyze policy options for the country. In May 2015, there was an announcement that a programme of deregulation would be introduced and taxes on small businesses would be cut. Both of these could be described as being supply-side in nature.

One of the economic issues that the Academy may well have to think through is how to make investment more profitable and how to tackle the overproduction which exists in some industries. Investment funds invariably come from government and in some cases, the justification for the

Rising wages in China may be a factor in a move to more supply-side reforms in the country.

spending could be tighter so that what is spent contributes to improving productivity. Many economists think that productivity has to be at the forefront of policy in the coming years given that wages have risen in China and cheap labour is no longer one of the country's sources of economic power.

Questions

1 China's growth rate is reported to have slowed below 7 per cent. Why is this a cause for concern for China and the global economy?

2 What is meant by 'structural reforms' in an economy?

3 Explain how deregulation and tax reforms for smaller businesses might help the supply-side of the economy in China.

4 Given that supply-side policies aim to shift the AS curve to the right, why might the Chinese government be focusing on supply-side reforms if the country suffers from overproduction?

5 How do supply-side policies improve productivity and why is this such an important feature for the continued development of the Chinese economy?

SUMMARY

- Supply-side policies became a focus of many governments in the 1980s and into the 1990s.
- Supply-side policies are designed to shift the AS curve to the right.
- Shifting the AS curve to the right can lead to sustained economic growth which increases national income but keeps prices stable countering the production bottlenecks that can occur if the focus is on increasing AD through fiscal or monetary policy.
- Supply-side policies can take two main forms – market-orientated policies or interventionist policies.
- Market-orientated policies are designed to free up markets so that they allocate resources more effectively and efficiently.
- Interventionist policies are designed to improve the working of the market and which require government intervention to overcome the public good element of the investment in infrastructure education, training and research and development.

QUESTIONS FOR REVIEW

1 What is meant by 'sustainable economic growth'?

2 Explain the shape of the new Keynesian AS curve.

3 What are the two ways in which the output gap can be calculated and what is the difference between them?

4 What is the relevance of the size of the output gap in policy making?

5 Using an AS/AD diagram, show how a rise in AD could lead to a rise in national income but with no change in the price level.

6 What are the two main types of supply-side policy and what is the difference between them?

7 Why do supply-siders emphasize the importance of marginal tax rates in relation to incentives?

8 What is the Laffer curve?

9 Why do flexible labour markets improve the efficiency and capacity of the economy?

10 Why is it necessary for governments to invest in education, training and research and development?

PROBLEMS AND APPLICATIONS

1 Using the new Keynesian AS curve, explain why, when the output gap is very large, the AS curve has an almost horizontal slope.

2 Why might governments find it difficult to accurately measure the size of the output gap?

3 Assume that a government is successful in shifting the AS curve to the right. Show what happens to the Phillips curve in such a situation.

4 What sort of trade-offs do governments face if a decision was being considered to reduce the level of welfare benefits as part of a market-orientated supply-side policy?

5 Governments who have implemented major cuts in higher rates of income tax have been accused of giving more money to the rich at the expense of the poor. Construct an argument to counter such an accusation.

6 What sort of assumptions underlie the policy that cuts in income taxes would increase the supply of labour hours offered in an economy?

7 What are the potential costs and benefits of policies designed to improve the flexibility of labour markets?

8 Why do governments find it difficult to reduce spending?

9 A government announces a decision to increase investment in spending on higher education with the intention of increasing the participation rate in higher education by young people, to 45 per cent (i.e. that 45 per cent of school leavers choose to go to university).

   a. Does it matter what sort of degrees these young people do at university?
   b. To what extent is the proportion of young people going on to university an important factor in improving the quality of human capital?
   c. What else might the government need to put in place to ensure that the policy is a longer-term success (hint: will there be appropriate jobs for young people when they graduate)?

10 How would a government be able to tell whether a policy of increasing private sector involvement in public sector services provision actually lead to a more efficient outcome compared to having those same services provided by the public sector?

PART 15 INTERNATIONAL MACROECONOMICS

37 COMMON CURRENCY AREAS AND EUROPEAN MONETARY UNION

During the 1990s, a number of European nations decided to give up their national currencies and use a common currency called the *euro* by joining European Economic and Monetary Union (EMU).

A **common currency area** is a geographical area throughout which a single currency circulates as the medium of exchange. Another term for a common currency area is a *currency union*, and a closely related phenomenon is a *monetary union*: a monetary union is, strictly speaking, a group of countries that have adopted permanently and irrevocably fixed exchange rates among their various currencies. Nevertheless, the terms common currency area, currency union and monetary union are often used more or less interchangeably, and in this chapter we'll follow this practice.

 common currency area a geographical area throughout which a single currency circulates as the medium of exchange

Usually we speak of common currency areas when the people of a number of economies, generally corresponding to different nation states, have taken a decision to adopt a common currency as their medium of exchange, as was the case with European Monetary Union.

THE EURO

At the time of writing there are 19 countries that have joined **European Economic and Monetary Union**, or EMU. (Note that 'EMU' stands for 'Economic and Monetary Union', not European Monetary Union, as is often supposed.) The countries that currently form the euro area are Austria, Belgium, Cyprus, Estonia, Finland, France, Germany, Greece, Ireland, Italy, Latvia, Lithuania, Luxembourg, Malta, the Netherlands, Portugal, Slovakia, Slovenia and Spain. The move towards a single European currency has a very long history. The main landmarks in its formation, started in 1992 with the Maastricht Treaty (formally known as the Treaty on European Union), which laid down (among other things) various criteria for being eligible to join the proposed currency union. In order to participate in the new currency, member states had to meet strict criteria such as a government budget deficit of less than 3 per cent of GDP, a government debt-to-GDP ratio of less than 60 per cent, combined with low inflation and interest rates close to the EU average. The Maastricht Treaty also laid down a timetable for the introduction of the new single currency and rules concerning the setting up of an ECB. The ECB actually came into existence in June 1998 and forms, together with the national central banks of the countries making up the common currency area, the European System of Central Banks (ESCB), which is given responsibility for ensuring price stability and implementing the single European monetary policy.

> **European Economic and Monetary Union** the European currency union that has adopted the euro as its common currency

The single European currency – the euro – officially came into existence on 1 January 1999 when 12 countries adopted it (although Greece did not join the EMU until 1 January 2001). On this date, exchange rates between the old national currencies of euro area countries were irrevocably locked and a few days later the financial markets began to trade the euro against other currencies such as the US dollar, as well as to trade securities denominated in euros.

The period from the beginning of 1999 until the beginning of 2002 was a transitional phase, with national currencies still circulating within the euro area countries and prices in shops displayed in both euros and local currency. On 1 January 2002 the first euro notes and coins came into circulation and, within a few months, the switch to the euro as the single medium of exchange was complete throughout the euro area.

The formation of EMU was an enormously bold step for the 12 countries initially involved. Most of the national currencies that have been replaced by the euro had been in circulation for hundreds of years. There were political reasons for the impetus towards a single currency but perceived economic benefits as well. In particular, there was a belief that having a common European currency would help 'complete the single market' for European goods, services and factors of production that had been an on-going project for much of the post-war period.

THE SINGLE EUROPEAN MARKET AND THE EURO

Following the devastation of two World Wars in the first half of the 20th century, each of which had initially centred on European conflicts, some of the major European countries (in particular France and Germany) expressed a desire to make further wars impossible between them through a process of strong economic integration that, it was hoped, would lead to greater social and political harmony. This led to the development of the European Economic Community (EEC) – now referred to as the **European Union**, or EU. The official website of the European Union defines the EU as 'a family of democratic European countries, committed to working together for peace and prosperity'.

> **European Union** a family of democratic European countries committed to working together for peace and prosperity

Initially the EU consisted of just six countries: Belgium, Germany, France, Italy, Luxembourg and the Netherlands. In 1973, Denmark, Ireland and the United Kingdom joined. Greece joined in 1981, Spain and Portugal in 1986, and Austria, Finland and Sweden in 1995. In 2004 the biggest ever enlargement took place with ten new countries joining. Croatia became a member state in July 2013 and at the time of writing there are five 'candidate countries' seeking membership. These are Albania, the Former Yugoslav Republic of Macedonia, Montenegro, Serbia and Turkey. Bosnia and Herzegovina and Kosovo are classed as 'potential candidates'.

The Single European Market

The creation of the **Single European Market** has been a major political and economic development. In the Single European Market, labour, capital, goods and services can move freely. It was argued that as member states got rid of obstacles to trade between themselves, companies would start to enjoy economies of scale as they expanded their market across Europe. At the same time, inefficient firms would be exposed to more cross-border competition, either forcing them out of business or forcing them to improve efficiency. The aim was to provide businesses with an environment of fair competition in which economies of scale could be reaped and a strong consumer base developed to enable expansion into global markets. Households, on the other hand, would benefit from lower prices, greater choice of goods and services, and work opportunities across a wide area, while the economy in general would benefit from the enhanced economic growth that would result.

> **Single European Market** a (still not complete) EU-wide market throughout which labour, capital, goods and services can move freely

Early steps towards the creation of the Single European Market included the abolition of internal EU tariff and quota barriers in 1968 and a movement towards greater harmonization in areas such as indirect taxation, industrial regulation, and EU-wide policies towards agriculture and fisheries.

Nevertheless, it proved difficult to make progress on the more intangible barriers to free movement of goods, services, capital and labour. For example, even though internal tariffs and quotas had been abolished in the EU, local tax systems and technical regulations on goods and services still differed from country to country so that it was in practice often difficult to export from one country to another. Thus, a car produced in the UK might have to satisfy a certain set of emission and safety requirements in one European country and another set of requirements in another EU country. Or a qualified engineer might find that their qualifications, obtained in Italy, were not recognized in Germany. The result was that during the 1970s and early 1980s, growth in the EU member states began to lag seriously behind that of international competitors – especially the United States and Japan. Therefore, in 1985 a discussion document was produced by the European Commission that subsequently led to a European Act of Parliament – the 1986 Single European Act. This identified some 300 measures that would have to be addressed in order to complete the Single European Market and set 31 December 1992 as the deadline for completion. The creation of the Single European Market was to be brought about by EU Directives telling the governments of member states what changes needed to be put into effect in order to achieve four goals:

● The free movement of goods, services, labour and capital between EU member states.
● The approximation of relevant laws, regulations and administrative provisions between member states.
● A common, EU-wide competition policy, administered by the European Commission.
● A system of common external tariffs implemented against countries who are not members of the EU.

The Single European Market is still far from complete. In particular, there still exist between EU members strong differences in national fiscal systems, while academic and professional qualifications are not easily transferable and labour mobility across EU countries is generally low. Some of the reasons for this are hard to overcome; language barriers and relative levels of economic development hamper the movement of factors and member states continue to compete with one another economically, at times seeking their own national interest rather than the greater good of the EU.

Nevertheless, the years between 1985 and 1992 did see some important steps in the development of the Single European Market and the resulting achievements of the Single European Market project were not negligible: the European Commission estimates that the Single European Market helped create 2.5 million new jobs and generated €800 billion in additional wealth in the ten years or so following 1993.

In the context of the Single European Market project, therefore, the creation of a single European currency was seen as a final step towards 'completing the market', by which was meant two things: (a) getting rid of the transaction costs from intra-EU trade that result from different national currencies (and which act much as a tariff) and (b) removing the uncertainty and swings in national competitiveness among members that result from exchange rate movements. Before EMU, most EU countries participated in the

Exchange Rate Mechanism (ERM), which was a system designed to limit the variability of exchange rates between members' currencies. However, the ERM turned out not to be a viable way of reducing volatility in the exchange rate and, in any case, had no effect on the transaction costs arising from bank charges associated with changing currencies when engaging in intra-EU trade.

THE BENEFITS AND COSTS OF A COMMON CURRENCY

Benefits of a Single Currency

Elimination of Transaction Costs One obvious and direct benefit of a common currency is that it makes trade easier between members and, in particular, there is a reduction in the transaction costs involved in trade between members of the common currency area. When a German company imports French wine, it no longer has to pay a charge to a bank for converting German marks into French francs with which to pay the wine producer, it can just pay in euros. Of course, the banking sector loses out on the commission it used to charge for converting currencies, but this does not affect the fact that the reduction in transaction costs is a net gain. This is because paying a cost to convert currencies is in fact a deadweight loss in the sense that companies pay the transaction cost but get nothing tangible in return.

Reduction in Price Discrimination It is sometimes argued that a second albeit indirect gain to the members of a common currency area results from the reduction in price discrimination that should ensue when there is a single currency. If goods are priced in a single currency it should be much harder to disguise price differences across countries. As we have discussed, price discrimination involves a dead-weight loss to society, so this is a further gain from a single currency. This argument assumes that the transparency in prices that results from a common currency will lead to arbitrage in goods across the common currency area: people will buy goods where they are cheaper (tending to raise their price in that location) and reduce their demand for goods where they are more expensive (tending to reduce the price in that location).

Overall, however, EMU seems unlikely to bring an end to price discrimination across euro area countries. For items like groceries, having a single currency is unlikely to be much of an impetus to price convergence across the common currency area because of the large transaction costs (mainly related to travelling) involved in arbitrage, relative to the prices of the goods themselves. To take advantage of price differences, cross-border shopping can take place – if it is relatively easy and convenient – but doing so across the whole of the EU means that the effects are necessarily more limited. Big ticket items like household appliances and electronic goods, where the transaction costs may be lower as a percentage of the price of the good in question, are also unlikely to be arbitraged heavily across national borders by consumers because of their durable nature and the need for confidence in after-sales service. In addition, the fact that different countries in the EU still have different plugs and power systems, which are difficult to harmonize, also reduces the overall impact.

Reduction in Foreign Exchange Rate Variability A third argument in favour of a common currency relates to the reduction in exchange rate variability and the consequent reduction in uncertainty that results from having a single currency. Exchange rates can fluctuate substantially on a day-to-day basis. Before EMU, when a German supermarket imported wine from France to be delivered, say, three months later, it had to worry about how much a French franc would be worth in terms of German marks in three months' time and therefore what the total cost of the wine would be in marks. This uncertainty might deter the supermarket company from importing wine at all, and instead lead it to concentrate on selling German wines, thereby foregoing the gains from trade and reducing economic welfare. The supermarket could have eliminated the uncertainty by getting a bank to agree to sell the francs at an agreed rate against marks to be delivered three months later (an example of a forward foreign exchange contract). But the bank would charge for this service, and this charge would be equivalent to a tariff on imported wine and this again would represent a deadweight loss to society.

The reduction in uncertainty arising from the removal of exchange rate fluctuations may also have a positive effect on investment in the economy. This would clearly be the case for companies that export a large amount of their output to other euro area countries, since less uncertainty concerning the receipts from its exports means that it is able to plan for the future with less risk, so that investment projects such as building new factories appear less risky. An increase in investment will benefit the whole economy because it is likely to lead to higher economic growth.

Costs of a Single Currency

The major cost to an economy in joining a common currency area relates to the fact that it gives up its national currency and thereby gives up its freedom to set its own monetary policy and the possibility of macroeconomic adjustment coming about through movements in the external value of its currency. Monetary policy is decided by the ECB. This is a potential problem. Suppose, for example, that there is a shift in consumer preferences across the common currency area away from goods and services produced in one country (Germany, say) and towards goods and services produced in another country (France, say).

This situation is depicted in Figure 37.1, which shows a leftwards shift in the German AD curve and a rightwards shift in the French AD curve. What should policymakers in France and Germany do about this? One answer to this is, nothing: in the long run, each economy will return to its natural rate of output. In Germany, this will occur as the price level falls and wages, prices and perceptions adjust. In particular, as unemployment rises in Germany, wages eventually begin to fall. Lower wages reduce firms' costs and so, for any given price level, the amount supplied will be higher. In other words, the German SRAS curve will shift to the right, until eventually it intersects with the AD curve at the natural rate of output. The opposite happens in France, with the SRAS curve shifting to the left. The adjustment to the new equilibrium levels of output is also shown in Figure 37.1.

FIGURE 37.1

A Shift in Consumer Preferences Away from German Goods Towards French Goods

The German fall in AD leads to a fall in output from Y_1^G to Y_2^G, and a fall in the price level from P_1^G to P_2^G. The increase in French AD raises output from Y_1^F to Y_2^F. Over time, however, wages and prices will adjust, so that German and French output return to their natural levels, Y_1^G and Y_1^F, with lower prices in Germany, at P_3^G, and higher prices in France, at P_3^F.

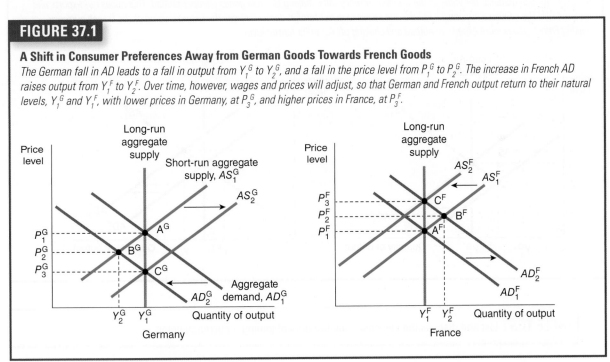

Note that, if Germany and France had maintained their own currencies and a flexible foreign exchange rate, then the short-term fluctuations in AD would be alleviated by a movement in the exchange rate: as the demand for French goods rises and for German goods falls, this would increase the demand for French francs and depress the demand for German marks, making the value of francs rise in terms of marks in the foreign currency exchange market. This would make French goods more expensive to German residents since they now have to pay more marks for a given number of French francs. Similarly, German goods become less expensive to French residents. Therefore, French net exports would fall, leading to a fall in AD. This is shown in Figure 37.2, where the French AD curve shifts back to the left until equilibrium is again established at the natural rate of output. Conversely – and also shown in Figure 37.2 – German net exports rise and the German AD curve shifts to the right until equilibrium is again achieved in Germany.

In a currency union, however, this automatic adjustment mechanism is not available, since, of course, France and Germany have the same currency (the euro). The best that can be done is to wait for wages and prices to adjust in France and Germany so that AS shifts in each country, as in Figure 37.1. The resulting fluctuations in output and unemployment in each country will tend to create tensions within the monetary union, as unemployment rises in Germany and inflation rises in France. German policymakers, dismayed at the rise in unemployment, will favour a cut in interest rates in order to boost AD in their country, while their French counterparts, worried about rising inflation, will be calling for an increase in interest rates in order to curtail French AD. The ECB will not be able to keep both countries happy. Most likely, it will set interest rates higher than the German desired level and lower than the French desired level.

The ECB pursues an inflation targeting strategy, and the inflation rate it targets is based upon a CPI constructed as an average across the euro area. If a country's inflation rate (or expected inflation rate) is below the euro area average, the ECB's monetary policy will be too tight for that country; if it is above the average, the ECB's monetary policy will be too loose for it. All that is possible is a 'one size fits all' monetary policy. It is for this reason that entry to the euro area is restricted to those countries that can meet the criteria outlined above where inflation and interest rates are close to the EU average.

FIGURE 37.2

A Shift in Consumer Preferences with Flexible Exchange Rates

Until prices have had time to adjust, the fall in German AD leads to a fall in output from Y_1^G to Y_3^G. However, because this is due to a fall in net foreign demand, the value of the German currency falls, making German goods cheaper abroad. This raises net exports and restores AD. The converse happens in France: the increase in net foreign demand raises the external value of the French currency, making French goods more expensive abroad and choking off AD to its former level.

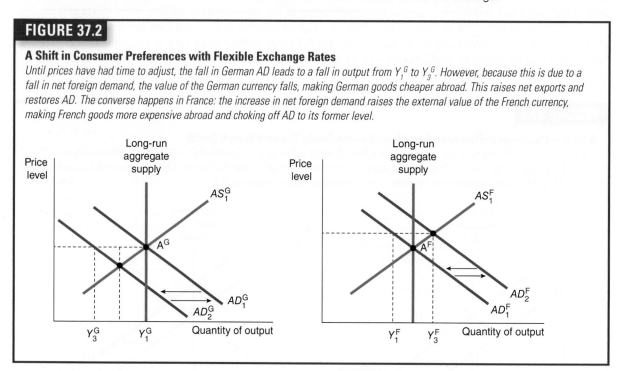

SELF TEST List and discuss the key costs and benefits of joining a currency union.

THE THEORY OF OPTIMUM CURRENCY AREAS

Optimum currency area (OCA) theory attempts to set down a set of criteria for a group of countries such that, if the criteria were satisfied, then it would in some sense be 'optimal' for the countries to adopt a common currency. The qualifier 'optimal' here refers to the ability of each of the countries to limit the costs of monetary union and enhance the benefits. It is generally used loosely, since there is no way for certain of ensuring whether it is indeed optimal for a group of countries to form a currency union and, more often than not, countries will fulfil some but not all of the OCA criteria.

> **optimum currency area** a group of countries for which it is optimal to adopt a common currency and form a currency union

Characteristics that Reduce the Costs of a Single Currency

Consider first the characteristics of a group of countries that would reduce the costs of adopting a common currency. As we have discussed, the main cost to participating in a monetary union is the loss of monetary policy autonomy for the individual countries concerned, as well as ruling out the possibility of macroeconomic adjustment through exchange rate movements. One way in which the economic (and political) tensions arising from the loss of the exchange rate instrument and the imposition of a 'one-size-fits-all' monetary policy will be alleviated, is if the economies in question move rapidly to long-run equilibrium following a macroeconomic shock: given the assumption of a short-run trade-off between inflation and unemployment, the faster the economies concerned can get to the long run – in other words, return to their natural rates of output and unemployment – the better. This speed of adjustment to long-run equilibrium will be high if there is a high degree of wage flexibility in the common currency area, and/or if there is a high degree of labour mobility.

Another way in which tensions across the common currency area would be alleviated would be if all countries in the currency union were prone to the same kind of demand shocks (e.g. if AD fell in all countries simultaneously), since then each would favour similar macroeconomic policy decisions (e.g. a reduction in interest rates).

We consider each of these types of characteristics in turn.

Real Wage Flexibility Suppose there is a high degree of wage flexibility in each of the member countries, so that wages respond strongly to rises and falls in unemployment. This means that the adjustment to long-run equilibrium, as shown in Figure 37.1, occurs very quickly. In our example, the shift in AD in Germany leads to falling wages, so that firms make more profit for any given level of prices, the AS curve shifts to the right and Germany returns to the natural rate of output. If wages are very flexible, this adjustment may be very rapid, so that the short run is very short indeed. Similarly for France: the rightwards shift in AD leads to rapidly rising wages and firms find it less profitable to produce any given level of output, so that the supply curve shifts leftwards and a new long-run equilibrium is established at the natural rate of output. Hence, by compressing the short run, tensions across the monetary union are ironed out very quickly.

Note that it is the real wage that is of importance here: it is real wages that must adjust in order to affect the AS curve by making it more (or less) profitable for firms to produce a given level of output at any given level of prices.

Labour Mobility Alternatively, suppose that labour is highly mobile between the member countries of the currency union: unemployed workers in Germany simply migrate to France and find a job. Again, the macroeconomic imbalance is alleviated, since unemployment in Germany will fall as many of the unemployed have left the country, and inflationary wage pressures in France decline as the labour force expands with the migrants from France. Therefore, it is clear that labour mobility may in some measure cushion a currency union from **asymmetric shocks**, a situation where changes in AD and/or supply differ from one country to another.

> **asymmetric shocks** a situation where changes in aggregate demand and/or supply differ from one country to another

Capital Mobility Sometimes economists argue that capital mobility can also compensate for the loss of monetary autonomy and the absence of exchange rate adjustment among the members of a common currency area. A distinction should be made here between physical capital (plant and machinery) and financial capital (bonds, company shares and bank loans). In terms of cushioning a currency union from asymmetric shocks, movements in physical capital can help by expanding productive capacity in countries experiencing a boom, as firms in other member countries build factories there. However, given the long lags involved in the installation of plant and equipment, physical capital mobility is likely to be helpful mainly for narrowing persistent regional disparities rather than offsetting short-term shocks.

The mobility of *financial* capital may be more useful in cushioning economies from short-term output shocks. For example, residents of a country experiencing a recession may wish to borrow money from the residents of a country experiencing a boom in order to overcome their short-term difficulties. In our two-country example, German residents would effectively borrow money from French residents in order to make up for their temporary fall in income. Clearly, this would require that German residents can easily borrow from French residents through the capital markets, so that financial capital mobility will be highest between countries whose capital markets are highly integrated with one another. For example, if a bank has branches in more than one country of a currency union, then borrowing and lending between growth and recession countries will be more or less automatic, as residents in the growth country increase the money they are holding in the bank as their income goes up and residents of the country in recession increase their overdrafts (or reduce their money holdings) as their income goes down.

We can relate this discussion back to the notion of permanent income, and to the market for loanable funds. Recall that a family's ability to buy goods and services depends largely on its permanent income, which is its normal, or average income, since people tend to borrow and lend to smooth out transitory variations in income. Now, when an AD shock adversely affects the German economy, a large amount of German households will see their transitory income fall and will want to borrow in order to increase income back up to the permanent or normal level. Since many German households are now doing this at the same time, if borrowing is restricted to German financial markets, this will tend to raise interest rates and generally make borrowing more difficult. If the market for loanable funds is restricted to the domestic market, then we might expect the supply of loanable funds to decrease in a recession and the demand to increase, raising interest rates. The resulting rise in interest rates may even make the recession worse by reducing investment.

On the other hand, in France, the economic boom means that many households are experiencing income levels above their permanent or average level, and so will tend to increase their saving. Now, if the German households can borrow from the French households – if the market for loanable funds covers both France and Germany – they can both consume at a level consistent with their normal or average levels of income with less of an effect on interest rates. There will be an increase in the supply of loanable funds because French residents are saving more and this will partly or even wholly offset the increase in the demand for loanable funds arising from German residents who want to borrow more. When the German economy comes out of recession and goes into recovery, German households can then repay the loans.

Of course, although we have discussed only bank loans, there are other forms of financial capital, such as bonds and company shares, but the principle of the recessionary economy being able to obtain funds from the booming economy remains the same. In effect, therefore, financial capital market integration across countries allows households to insure one another against asymmetric shocks so that the variability of consumption over the economic cycle can be reduced.

Symmetric Macroeconomic Shocks Note that, in describing the costs of belonging to a monetary union, we have used the example of a positive demand shock in one country and a simultaneous negative demand shock in another. A similar analysis would have followed if we had simply allowed either a positive or a negative demand shock in one country and no shock at all in the other country. The central point was that the demand shock was asymmetric in the sense that it impacted differently on different members of the currency union, requiring different short-run policy responses. Clearly, if the shock were symmetric there would be no problem. If, for example, AD rose simultaneously in all member countries, increasing expected future inflation, then a policy of raising interest rates would be welcomed by all members of the monetary union. This would be the case if the economic cycles of each of the countries making up the currency were synchronized in the sense that the various economies tended to enter recession at the same time and enter the recovery phase of the cycle at the same time, so that disagreements about the best interest rate policy are less likely to occur.

Characteristics that Increase the Benefits of a Single Currency

High Degree of Trade Integration The greater the amount of trade that takes place between a group of countries – i.e. the greater the degree of trade integration – the more they will benefit from adopting a common currency. One of the principal benefits of a currency union, and the most direct benefit, is the reduction in transaction costs that are incurred in trade transactions between the various countries when there is a constant need to switch one national currency into another on the foreign currency exchange market. Clearly, therefore, the greater the amount of international trade that is carried out between member countries – and therefore the greater the amount of foreign currency transactions – the greater the reduction in transaction costs that having a common currency entails.

The reduction in exchange rate volatility – another benefit of a currency union – will also clearly be greater, the greater is the degree of intra-union trade, since more firms will benefit from knowing with certainty exactly the revenue generated from their sales to other currency union members, rather than having to bear the uncertainty associated with exchange rate fluctuations.

SELF TEST What is meant by an optimum currency area? List and discuss the key characteristics of an optimum currency area.

IS EUROPE AN OPTIMUM CURRENCY AREA?

Having determined what characteristics of a group of countries would make the benefits of a single currency stronger and the costs weaker, we can take a closer look to see whether Europe – and in particular the group of 19 countries that comprise the euro area – forms an optimum currency area.

Trade Integration

The degree of trade integration can be assessed by looking at imports from and exports to other EU countries expressed as a percentage of GDP. The degree of trade integration across Europe is quite variable, but nevertheless on average quite high – with the notable exception of Greece. The degree of European trade integration has been rising over time, in nearly every country in the EU, but the integration has been more marked in some countries such as Austria than others such as Italy.

This has led some economists to argue that some of the criteria for an optimum currency area – such as a high degree of trade integration – may actually be endogenous: actually being a member of a currency union may enhance the degree of trade done between members of the union, precisely because of the decline in transaction costs in carrying out such trade.

Overall, many – if not all – European countries have gained a great deal from the reduction in transaction costs in international trade as a result of the single currency. Indeed, these gains have been estimated at about one quarter to one half of one per cent of euro area GDP. This may not sound massive, but remember that transaction costs are a deadweight loss. Moreover, the gains are not one-off: they accrue continuously as long as the single currency persists, since they would have to be paid in the absence of the currency union. They therefore become cumulative. In addition, if the degree of euro area trade integration tends to rise over time as a result of the single currency, as some economists have suggested, then the implicit gain from not having to pay transaction costs also rises over time.

The other, indirect benefit of a single currency when there is a high degree of trade integration, follows from the reduction in uncertainty associated with doing away with the volatility in the exchange rates between members' national currencies (since those currencies are replaced with a common currency). These gains are hard to quantify, but it is not incorrect to suggest that they are not negligible for the euro area.

Real Wage Flexibility

A great deal of research has been done on real wage flexibility in Europe and virtually all of it concludes that continental European labour markets are among the most rigid in the world. In contrast, the UK labour market, at least since the 1980s, has become one of the most flexible. One reason for this is the fact that all European Union countries have minimum wage laws, although this is not the whole story since the UK also has a minimum wage. Perhaps a more important reason is the high degree of collective wage bargaining that is common in continental Europe – i.e. wage agreements that cover a large number of workers. Figures on the degree of unionization of the labour force are quite deceptive in this sense: for example, in the early 2000s, in the UK, Italy and Germany about 30 per cent of the workforce belonged to a trade union, while in France the figure was around 10 per cent (this has since fallen to around 8 per cent). Continental European unions, however, often have collective bargaining and other workplace rights that UK trade unionists can only envy. The power of unions and the inflexibility of the labour market is something that has been a concern in France for some time and in 2013, an agreement was reached between the government and unions on reforms to the country's complex and strict labour laws. The agreement was greeted with mixed responses with some saying it did not go far enough and others suggesting the agreement marked the end of workers' rights in France.

The introduction of the single European currency may also have had a negative effect on European wage flexibility, since many European collective wage agreements between workers and a firm in one country will also often extend to the firm's workforce in other European countries, and a single currency brings transparency in wage differences across countries, as well as price transparency. To return again to our example of a negative demand shock in Germany and a positive shock in France, a company with employees in both countries would find it hard to reduce real wages in Germany while raising them in France.

Furthermore, European labour law is generally very much more restrictive in many continental European countries than it is in the UK or the USA, as is the level of payroll taxes, so that a firm's costs of either reducing the workforce or increasing it can be very high. This means that, even if there were movements in the real wage, firms would be slow to expand or contract their output in response, so that shifts in AS will be slow to come about.

On the whole, therefore, adjustment to asymmetric shocks through real wage movements is unlikely to be significant in the euro area.

Labour Mobility

Labour is notoriously immobile across European countries, at least if one rules out migration from the newer eastern European members of the EU such as Poland, Romania and Bulgaria, and considers just the 19 euro area countries or these plus Denmark and Sweden. In part this may perhaps be attributed to differences in language, culture and other social institutions across Europe that make it difficult for workers to migrate. However, it seems that European workers are also very loath to move location even within their own countries. Indeed, the degree of labour mobility as measured by the percentage of the workforce that moves geographical location over any given period, is much lower within any particular European country than it is within the United States, and is even lower between the euro area countries. Europe therefore scores very low on this optimum currency area criterion.

Financial Capital Mobility

In discussing financial capital mobility, a distinction must be made between the wholesale and the retail capital markets. The wholesale financial markets are the capital markets in which only financial institutions such as banks and investment funds operate, as well as very large corporations, while the retail financial markets (such as high street banks) are those open to individual households and to small and medium-sized corporations. Prior to the introduction of the euro, financial integration among euro area countries was probably quite low, in both the wholesale and retail sectors. However, following the introduction of the euro, integration of the wholesale financial markets has increased dramatically. In particular, a liquid euro money market with single interbank market interest rates was established so that a bank in, say, Luxembourg can now borrow euros just as easily and at the same rate of interest from another bank in Frankfurt as it can from a bank located in the same street in Luxembourg. In the government bond market, the degree of market integration is also high, and this is shown by the fact that the interest rates on government bonds of the different euro area countries are very close to one another and tend to move very closely together. On the other hand, the integration of retail market products, such as loans to households and small and medium-sized enterprises, is lagging behind compared with the wholesale market products. This becomes evident from persistent cross-country differences in bank lending rates and the rather limited cross-border retail banking activity. Indeed, national banking sectors have remained largely segregated with only marginal cross-border penetration.

Symmetric Demand Shocks

The economic cycle across the countries of the euro area does appear to be positively correlated, in the sense that the timing of strong growth and downturns appear to be very close. The problem is not so much that the turning points do not coincide, but that certain countries' growth rate, for example Ireland's and Greece's, outstripped the performance of the euro area as a whole between 2005 and 2007 but then they both saw considerable problems as a result of the Financial Crisis. Whilst Ireland has seen a recovery and is performing at a rate higher than the euro area as a whole, Greece has seen its growth shrinking. Whilst the euro area as a whole saw some weak recovery from 2010, Greece did not share in that recovery. It can be argued that monetary policy between 2008 and 2014 for the euro area as a whole has not been matched to the needs of the Greek and Irish economies over that same period.

Overall, therefore, the evidence is a little mixed, although on the whole it suggests that the problem of asymmetric demand shocks is not a great one for the current member countries of EMU. The fact that there is not strong evidence of asymmetric demand shocks at the aggregate level, however, does not rule out the possibility that there may be asymmetric shocks at other levels in the economy. In fact, researchers have found that many of the shocks that impact upon European countries asymmetrically tend to be specific to a region or to an industry rather than to a country as a whole. This is not a problem made worse by joining a monetary union, however, since a country that experienced, say, a negative shock to one of its industries or regions would not in any case be able to deal with this using monetary or exchange rate policy without generating imbalances in its other regions or industries. The idea of a two-speed EU to cater for the countries that have experienced debt crisis problems since the financial crisis – Portugal, Ireland, Italy, Greece and Spain – has highlighted that there are some countries that seem better able to weather economic storms than others. Germany, France, the Netherlands, Denmark and Sweden have all recovered from the Financial Crisis more quickly, albeit that the strength of their recovery has been muted. Economists have noted that the degree of integration of the euro area and the EU as a whole does impact on the ability of countries to recover from economic shocks. If EU countries rely on each other for export-led growth, then if a group of these countries face considerable fiscal difficulties and have to implement austerity measures, then the level of demand in these economies falls and this affects demand in the other economies, thus dragging down growth in all the euro area countries and the EU as a whole.

Summary: Is Europe an Optimum Currency Area?

As in many policy debates in economics, there is no clear-cut answer to this question. Certainly, many European countries have a high degree of intra-union trade and have economic cycles that are more or less synchronized. However, labour mobility and wage flexibility (and labour market flexibility in general) are low in Europe, and while the euro has increased financial market integration in the euro area's wholesale financial markets, the retail markets remain highly segregated at the national level.

Overall, therefore, if very strong differences in the economic cycle were to emerge across the euro area, the lack of independent monetary and exchange rate policy would be acutely felt. This could be a case argued in relation to the situations in Ireland and Greece. For that reason, many economists argue that Europe – meaning the current euro area – is not an optimum currency area. Nevertheless, as we have noted in our discussion, it is possible that some of the optimum currency area criteria may be endogenous.

In particular, the single currency is likely to generate even greater trade among EMU members. Given this, it is likely that the economic cycles of member currencies will become even more closely synchronized as AD shifts in one country have stronger spillover effects in other euro area countries; this may, however, take some time to synchronize and the problems the EU has faced since the Financial Crisis have exposed the differences in the relative strength of the economies of the countries, in the euro area in particular, which has pushed EMU to its limits.

Over time, the single currency, if it survives, may also raise labour mobility across Europe in the long run, since being paid in the same currency as in one's home country is one less issue to come to terms with when moving location to find a job. Also, with time, one would expect financial market integration to spread to the retail capital markets. In 2014, for example, the Single Euro Payments Area (SEPA) became operational in all euro area countries. SEPA has been designed to facilitate euro transfers, direct debits and payments between member states.

Perhaps the only true test of whether the euro area is an optimum currency area (or can become one) is to see whether EMU survives in the long run. The challenges faced by the euro area since the Financial Crisis have put the long-term survival of the whole euro project in doubt. Significant changes to the structure of the euro, in particular financial regulation and fiscal reform, are the subject of on-going discussion and fiscal policy is the subject of our next section.

FISCAL POLICY AND COMMON CURRENCY AREAS

Our discussion so far has tended to centre on the loss of autonomy in monetary policy that is entailed in adopting a single currency among a group of countries. However, it is obvious that there is nothing in the adoption of a common currency that implies that members of the currency union should not still retain independence in fiscal policy. For instance, in our example of an asymmetric demand shock that expands demand in France and contracts AD in Germany, the French government could reduce government spending in order to offset the demand shock, while the German government could expand government spending. In fact, even if France and Germany did not make up an optimal currency, because wages were sticky and labour mobility low between the countries, national fiscal policy could, in principle, still be used to ameliorate the loss of monetary policy autonomy.

Fiscal Federalism

Suppose that a currency union had a common fiscal policy in the sense of having a single, common fiscal budget covering tax and spending decisions across the common currency area. This means that fiscal policy in the currency union would work much as fiscal policy in a single national economy works, with a surplus of government tax revenue over government spending in one region used to pay for a budget deficit in another region. Return again to our example of an asymmetric demand shock that expands AD in France and contracts AD in Germany, as in Figure 37.1. Remember that there are automatic stabilizers built into the fiscal policy of an economy that automatically stimulate AD when the economy goes into recession without policymakers having to take any deliberate action. In particular, since almost all taxes are closely related to the level of economic activity in the economy, tax revenue will automatically decline in Germany as a result of the AD shock that shifts it into recession. At the same time, transfer payments in the form of unemployment benefit and other social security benefits will also rise in Germany. The opposite will be true in France, where the automatic stabilizers will be operating in reverse as transfer payments fall and tax receipts rise with the level of economic activity. These changes will tend to expand AD in Germany and contract it in France, to some extent offsetting the asymmetric demand shock.

If the governments of France and Germany have a common budget, then the increased net government revenue in France can be used to offset the reduction in net government revenue in Germany. If the resulting movements in aggregate are not enough to offset the demand shock, then the French and German governments may even go further and decide to increase government expenditure further in Germany and pay for it by reducing spending, and perhaps raising taxes in France.

This kind of arrangement – a fiscal system for a group of countries involving a common fiscal budget and a system of taxes and fiscal transfers across countries – is known as **fiscal federalism**. The problem with it is that the taxpayers of one country (here France) may not be happy in paying for government spending and transfer payments in another country (in this example, Germany).

> **fiscal federalism** a fiscal system for a group of countries involving a common fiscal budget and a system of taxes and fiscal transfers across countries

National Fiscal Policies in a Currency Union: The Free-rider Problem

Assuming that, for political reasons, fiscal federalism is not an option open to the currency union, we still need to explore the possibility of individual members of the union using fiscal policy in order to offset asymmetric macroeconomic shocks that cannot be dealt with by a common monetary policy. In particular, in our example, what is wrong with Germany running a big government budget deficit in order to counteract the fall in AD and borrowing heavily in order to finance the deficit? One answer may lie in the effect on other members of the currency union of a rise in the debt of a member country.

Whenever a government raises its levels of debt to very high levels, there is always the possibility that the government may default on the debt. In general, this can be done in one of two ways. Where a country is not a member of a currency union and controls its own monetary policy, it can engineer a surprise inflation by a sudden increase in the money supply, so that the real value of the debt shrinks. In addition, when there is a sharp rise in the price level, this will usually be accompanied by a sharp fall in the foreign currency value of the domestic currency. This means that, valued in foreign currency, the stock of government debt will now be worth far less. Thus, the government has in effect defaulted on a large portion of its debt by reducing its value both internally and externally.

If this is not possible – for example because, as in a currency union, the country no longer enjoys monetary policy autonomy and is not able to devalue the external value of its currency (since it uses the common currency) – then the only other way of reneging on the debt is through an outright default (e.g. stopping interest payments or failing to honour capital repayments when they fall due). Generally, the financial markets are good at disciplining governments that run up large debts, by charging them high rates of interest on the debt that the government issues – after all, if you thought there was even a slight possibility that you might not get your money back if you lent it, you would want to be paid a higher rate of interest in order to compensate for that risk. For example, the interest rate on ten-year government debt in Greece rose from 8.42 per cent in December 2014 to 12 per cent in April 2015, reflecting the concerns over the prospects of the country defaulting on its debt. In comparison, interest rates on equivalent German debt was 0.59 and 0.12 per cent respectively, over the same time period. It is rarely impossible for a country to borrow money on international markets but if interest rates are higher than about 7 per cent then the cost of servicing the debt becomes unsustainable in the longer term, particularly if economic growth is weak as it has been in Greece. If the cost of borrowing is consistently above 7 per cent, then it is likely that governments will be in even more trouble and become more likely to default.

In the case of a monetary union, therefore, this means that excessive debt issuance by one member country will tend to force up interest rates throughout the whole of the common currency area. Although the ECB controls very short-term interest rates in the euro area through its refinancing operations, it does not control longer-term interest rates such as those paid on 10- or 20-year government bonds. Hence, fiscal profligacy by a government in the euro area will tend to push up the cost of borrowing for all members of the currency union.

However interest rates may not be raised enough to discipline properly the high-borrowing government. This is because the markets feel that the other members of the monetary union would not allow the country concerned actually to default, and that if it threatened to do so the other members would probably rush in and buy up its government debt and 'bailout' the country concerned. If the markets believe in this possibility then the debt will not be seen as risky as it otherwise would be and so the interest rates charged to the debtor country on its debt will not be as high as they otherwise might be. The intervention by the ECB, EU finance ministers and the IMF to bailout the economies of Ireland, Greece and other countries since the Financial Crisis has been a case in point as ministers struggled to keep EMU together.

The net effect is for a government to pay interest rates on its large stock of debt that are lower because of the implicit belief that it will be bailed out if it has problems servicing the debt, and for all other members of the currency union to pay higher interest rates on their government debt, because the government has flooded the financial markets with euro-denominated government bonds. In essence, this is an example of the free-rider problem: the government is enjoying the benefits of a fiscal expansion without paying the full costs.

In addition, if that government is using the proceeds of its borrowing to fund a strong fiscal expansion, this may undo or work against the anti-inflationary monetary policy of the ECB by stoking up AD throughout the whole of the euro area.

In order to circumvent some of these problems, the currency union members can enter into a 'no bailout' agreement that states that member countries cannot expect other members to come to their rescue if their debt levels become unsustainable, as an attempt to convince the markets to charge profligate spend-and-borrow countries higher interest rates on their debt. In fact, exactly such a no bailout agreement exists among members of EMU. Unfortunately, however, it seems clear that the no bailout clause was not credible: the attempts by members to support profligate countries throughout the sovereign debt crisis have confirmed this. If an EMU member were to default on its debt, this would have strong repercussions throughout the euro area as it would lead to the financial markets losing confidence in debt issued by other members and to strong selling of the euro in the foreign currency exchange market. In order to avoid this, EMU members have acted to bailout member countries threatening to default on their debt.

For these reasons, the members of the currency union may wish to impose rules on one another concerning the conduct of national fiscal policies in order to avoid fiscal profligacy by any one member. At the outset of EMU, a set of fiscal rules was indeed drawn up and agreed to by EMU members. This set of rules was known as the Stability and Growth Pact (SGP) (see Case Study below).

CASE STUDY   The Stability and Growth Pact: A Ferocious Dog with No Teeth

The Stability and Growth Pact was a set of formal rules by which members of EMU were supposed to be bound in their conduct of national fiscal policy. Its main components were as follows:

- Members should aim to achieve balanced budgets.
- Members with a budget deficit of more than 3 per cent of GDP will be subject to fines that may reach as high as 0.5 per cent of GDP unless the country experiences exceptional circumstances (such as a natural disaster) or a very sharp recession in which GDP declines by 2 per cent or more in a single year.

If EMU members adhered to the SGP, then it would rule out any free-rider problems associated with excessive spending and borrowing in any one member country by forcing members to put a limit on the national government budget. The choice of a maximum budget deficit of no more than 3 per cent of GDP was related to a clause in the 1992 Maastricht Treaty that suggested that a 'prudent' debt-to-GDP ratio should be no more than 60 per cent. This was perhaps somewhat arbitrary – although it was very close to the actual debt-to-GDP ratio of Germany in 1992. To see, however, that a 60 per cent ratio of debt to GDP could entail 'prudent' budget deficits of no more than 3 per cent a year, let's do some simple budgetary arithmetic. Suppose a country is enjoying real GDP growth of 3 per cent a year and inflation of 2 per cent a year, so that nominal GDP is growing at the rate of 5 per cent a year. This means that the nominal value of its government debt can grow at a rate of 5 per cent a year and still be sustainable. If the debt-to-GDP ratio is 60 per cent, this means that debt can increase by 5 per cent of 60 per cent, or 3 per cent of GDP a year while keeping the debt-to-GDP ratio constant. In other, words, it can run a budget deficit of 3 per cent of GDP a year.

While, however, there was some logic in setting a maximum budget deficit of 3 per cent a year (given a maximum prudent debt-to-GDP ratio of 60 per cent), it is not clear why the SGP suggested that members should aim for a balanced budget. It should be clear from the budgetary arithmetic just discussed that it is not imprudent for countries to run small budget deficits as long as they are enjoying sustained long-term growth in GDP. The effective straitjacketing of national fiscal policy that the SGP implied, may have reflected a desire among the architects of EMU for the ECB to maintain an effective monopoly on demand management, so that its polices could not be countered by national fiscal policies.

The crucial question for the SGP, however, was whether or not the maximum allowable budget deficit would be enough for a country to let its automatic fiscal stabilizers come into play when it goes into recession. This is crucial in a monetary union because member countries will have already given up their right to pursue an independent monetary policy and they cannot use the exchange rate as an instrument of policy.

In practice, the SGP proved to be something of a toothless watchdog. As the euro area experienced slug-gish growth in the early years of EMU, several member countries – and in particular France and Germany, two of the largest member countries – found themselves in breach of the SGP excessive deficit criteria. However, both France and Germany managed to persuade other EMU members not to impose fines and, in 2004, the European Commission drew up guidelines for softening the SGP. These guidelines included consid-ering more widely the sustainability of countries' public finances on an individual basis, paying more atten-tion to overall debt burdens and to long-term liabilities such as pensions, rather than to a single year's deficit. The consequences of the Financial Crisis have made the limitation of the SGP even more clear.

The Stability and Growth Pact – a ferocious dog with no teeth?

SELF TEST What is fiscal federalism? How may it aid in the functioning of a common currency area?

The Fiscal Compact

The problems with the debt crisis faced by a number of European countries in the wake of the Financial Crisis and the attempts to keep the euro area together led to the negotiation of a treaty which came in to force on 1 January 2013. This has become known as the fiscal compact but its full title is the *Treaty on Stability, Coordination and Governance in the Economic and Monetary Union.* The intention of the fiscal compact is to:

> strengthen the economic pillar of the Economic and Monetary Union by adopting a set of rules intended to foster budgetary discipline through a fiscal compact, to strengthen the coordination of economic policies and to improve the governance of the euro area, thereby supporting the achievement of the European Union's objectives for sustainable growth, employment, competitiveness and social cohesion.

The treaty echoes some of the features of the SGP in that it requires the budgets of participating member states to be in balance or in surplus and that the structural deficit does not exceed 0.5 per cent of the country's nominal GDP. A **structural deficit** refers to a situation where the deficit is not dependent on movements in the economic cycle but indicate that a government is 'living beyond its means' – spending what it has not got and contrasts with a **cyclical deficit** where government spending and income is disrupted by deviations in the 'normal' economic cycle.

> **structural deficit** a situation where a government's deficit is not dependent on movements in the economic cycle
> **cyclical deficit** a situation when government spending and income is disrupted by the deviations in the 'normal' economic cycle

Each member country will have a minimum benchmark figure for long-term sustainability which will be reviewed annually. Deviation from the balanced budget rule will be allowed in exceptional circumstances, such as a severe economic downturn, but if the member state deviates from the rule, an automatic correction mechanism which has to be built into the country's legal system will be triggered. Participant countries were expected to have this legal mechanism enshrined in law by 1 January 2014. Member states will be subject to a budgetary and economic partnership programme which will outline detailed structural reforms that will have to be put into place if the deficit rules are breached which will detail how the country intends to remedy its deficit problems. The rules apply to all 26 countries which signed the agreement. The Czech Republic and the UK both opted out of the agreement.

Imposing greater fiscal discipline might sound sensible to prevent governments from profligacy and reducing the free-rider problem but the consequences are essentially simple – if debt is too high the government concerned must cut spending and raise taxes. If governments are seeking to balance budgets, account must be taken of the effect on the other aspects of the economy. This is why the fiscal compact has been referred to as 'institutionalized austerity'.

Recall that savings of households and firms is denoted as S and that in equilibrium, savings equals investment ($S = I$) in a closed economy. If governments have a balanced budget, then tax receipts (T) equal government spending (G): $T = G$. The external current account is given by net exports, (NX). If there is an imbalance in private savings and/or government budgets, this shows up in net capital outflow as we saw in Chapter 29. In Chapter 30, we noted the link between the market for loanable funds and the market for foreign currency exchange as $S = I + NX$. This can be rearranged to give $S - I = NX$ and rearranging the national accounting formula gives $(S - I) + (T - G) = NX$ where $T - G$ is the government deficit. If the government is to balance its budget then the sum of the other elements of the economy must also balance. Bringing these other aspects into balance is not easy.

If the government is forced to cut spending and increase taxes to bring the budget into balance, national income will fall, *ceteris paribus*. An increase in taxes will have the effect of reducing private saving; if saving falls then interest rates rise, investment may decline and the net result is a rise in unemployment. In addition, the reduced investment leads over time to a lower stock of capital. A lower capital stock reduces labour productivity, real wages, and the economy's production of goods and services. The political ramifications of bringing the budget into balance could be severe for governments and lead to political instability which further undermines market confidence.

CONCLUSION

This chapter has developed some of the main issues around common currency areas, focusing in particular on European Monetary Union. Where there is a high degree of trade among a group of countries, there are benefits to be had from forming a currency union, largely arising from the reduction of transaction costs in international trade and reductions in exchange rate uncertainty. However, there are also costs associated with joining a monetary union, largely associated with the loss of monetary autonomy (member countries are no longer free to set their own interest rates) and the loss of exchange rate movements as a means of achieving macroeconomic adjustment. Any decision to form a currency union must weigh these costs and benefits against one another to see if there is an overall net benefit. Although, in the long run, the loss of exchange rate adjustment and monetary autonomy may have little effect on the equilibrium levels of output and unemployment in the economies involved, there may be substantial short-term economic fluctuations in these macroeconomic variables as a result of joining the currency union. This is particularly the case if there are asymmetric demand shocks impacting on the currency union so that it is impossible to design a 'one-size-fits-all' monetary policy to suit every country. Short-run adjustment will also be long and painful when wages do not adjust very quickly, although this problem may be overcome by labour mobility across the member countries.

A group of countries for which the benefits of monetary union are high and the costs are relatively low is termed an optimum currency area. Even though there is quite a high degree of trade integration among the member countries of the current European Monetary Union and their economic cycles do seem more or less synchronized and of a similar amplitude (with some exceptions), labour mobility and wage flexibility in Europe are both notoriously low, and integration of euro area financial markets, although high in the wholesale sector, has so far been slower in the retail financial markets. Overall, therefore, the euro area is probably not an optimum currency area. Nevertheless, it is possible that some of these criteria may be endogenous: EMU may lead to increasing economic integration in the euro area that will in turn significantly raise the benefits and reduce the costs to each country of remaining in the monetary union.

IN THE NEWS

The UK and Europe

In the general election campaign of 2014, David Cameron, the leader of the Conservative party, promised to re-negotiate the UK's membership of the EU and put the proposals to the electorate on an 'in or out' referendum.

Brexit

The EU may define itself as a 'family' but even in the closest families, there can be disagreements and break-ups. The UK Prime Minister, David Cameron, faced a large section of his party being disgruntled with the terms of UK membership of the EU. By promising a referendum on UK membership of the EU, Cameron set in motion a period of uncertainty and tough negotiations with EU partners to provide a framework under which he could go to the electorate and get support for the continuation of UK membership. The election held in June 2016 provided, what many saw as a surprise result, as the UK voted to leave the EU.

The period up to the election was one of uncertainty for the UK and for Europe as a whole. In early 2016, the Governor of the Bank of England, Mark Carney, was appearing before the Treasury Select Committee and alluded to the potential dangers of the consequences of a vote to leave the EU. Markets and businesses were well aware of the plans for the referendum and, as with any uncertainty, calculations will have been made about the potential risks involved, regardless of how the vote went.

Carney noted that one problem area the government did need to consider was its trade deficit, which in early 2016 amounted to around 3.7 per cent of GDP; this is considered relatively high. A trade deficit has to be funded and that relies on foreigners being willing to purchase UK assets. If the UK were to leave the EU then it might be more difficult to encourage such funding. Carney said 'The global general environment has become much more febrile, much more volatile, and relying on the kindness of strangers is not optimal in that kind of environment'. In order to attract the funding necessary, the returns on investment would need to be higher – in other words, UK interest rates would need to rise.

A briefing paper published by the London School of Economics (LSE) Centre for Economic Performance (CEP) in 2015 (http://cep.lse.ac.uk/pubs/download/EA022.pdf) suggested that if the UK left the EU, trade with the EU would be likely to fall because trade costs would rise and whilst the contribution to the EU budget would offset these

(*Continued*)

costs, it estimated that an optimistic scenario would see Brexit costing the UK just over 1 per cent of GDP, but in a more pessimistic scenario the cost could be as much as 3.1 per cent of GDP or £50 billion (€65.7 bn). At the time of writing, the UK is yet to engage in formal negotiations to leave the EU. The initial effect of the vote was to see sterling weaken on foreign currency markets, stock prices initially falling (but then recovering) and in August 2016, the Bank of England reduced interest rates to 0.25 per cent. The full effect of the UK's decision to leave the EU is yet to be felt, whether this turns out to be positive as leave campaigners claimed or negative as supporters of the remain campaign argued.

Questions

1 Given that the UK is not part of the euro area, is leaving the EU less of a problem as a result?
2 Why does uncertainty over an issue of importance like a member state leaving the EU potentially damaging to the short- and medium-term prospects for an economy like the UK?
3 Why might the UK find it more difficult to attract inward funds to finance a trade deficit outside the EU?
4 With the UK leaving the EU, why would 'trade costs' rise?
5 To what extent do you think the economic argument for Brexit is eclipsed by the political arguments?

Brexit – a crucial decision for the UK economy and for Europe.

SUMMARY

- A common currency area (a.k.a. currency union or monetary union) is a geographical area through which one currency circulates and is accepted as the medium of exchange.

- The formation of a common currency area can bring significant benefits to the members of the currency union, particularly if there is already a high degree of international trade among them (i.e. a high level of trade integration). This is primarily because of the reductions in transaction costs in trade and the reduction in exchange rate uncertainty.

- There are, however, costs of joining a currency union, namely the loss of independent monetary policy and also of the exchange rate as a means of macroeconomic adjustment. Given a long-run vertical supply curve, the loss of monetary policy and the lack of exchange rate adjustment affect mainly short-run macroeconomic adjustment.

- These adjustment costs will be lower the greater is the degree of real wage flexibility, labour mobility and capital market integration across the currency union, and also the less the members of the currency union suffer from asymmetric demand shocks.

- A group of countries with a high level of trade integration, high labour mobility and real wage flexibility, a high level of capital market integration that does not suffer asymmetric demand shocks across the different members of the group, is termed an optimum currency area. An OCA is most likely to benefit from currency union.

- It is possible that a group of countries may become an OCA after forming a currency union, as having a common currency may enhance further trade integration, thereby helping to synchronize members' economic cycles, and having a single currency may also help foster increased labour mobility and capital market integration.

- While the current euro area displays, overall, a high degree of trade integration and does not appear to be plagued by asymmetric demand shocks, real wage flexibility and labour mobility both appear to be low. And while the introduction of the euro has led to a high degree of euro area financial market integration at the wholesale level, retail financial markets remain nationally segregated. Overall, therefore, the euro area is probably not at present an optimum currency area, although it may eventually become one.

● The problems of adjustment within a currency union that is not an OCA may be alleviated by fiscal federalism – a common fiscal budget and a system of taxes and fiscal transfers across member countries. In practice, however, fiscal federalism may be difficult to implement for political reasons.

● The national fiscal policies of the countries making up a currency union may be subject to a free-rider problem, whereby one country issues a large amount of government debt and pays a lower interest rate on it than it might otherwise have paid, but also leads to other member countries having to pay higher interest rates. It is for this reason that a currency union may wish to impose rules on the national fiscal policies of its members.

QUESTIONS FOR REVIEW

1 What are the main advantages of forming a currency union? What are the main disadvantages?

2 Are the advantages and disadvantages you have listed in answer to question 1 long-run or short-run in nature?

3 Is a reduction in price discrimination across countries likely to be an important benefit of forming a currency union? Explain.

4 What are the main characteristics that reduce the costs of a common currency?

5 How would an asymmetric supply-side shock to a country that was a member of a currency union affect the country and the other members of the currency union?

6 What is an optimum currency area? List the criteria that an OCA must satisfy.

7 Is EMU an optimum currency area?

8 What is fiscal federalism? How might the problems of macroeconomic adjustment in a currency union be alleviated by fiscal federalism?

9 Why might the members of a currency union wish to impose rules on the conduct of national fiscal policies?

10 What are the main features of the fiscal pact?

PROBLEMS AND APPLICATIONS

1 Consider two countries that trade heavily with one another – Cornsylvania and Techoland. The national currency of Cornsylvania is the cob, while the Techoland national currency is the byte. The output of Cornsylvania is mainly agricultural, while the output of Techoland is mainly high-technology electronic goods. Suppose that each economy is in a long-run macroeconomic equilibrium.

  a. Use diagrams to illustrate the state of each economy. Be sure to show AD, SRAS and LRAS.

  b. Now suppose that there is an increase in demand for electronic goods in both countries, and a simultaneous decline in demand for agricultural goods. Use your diagrams to show what happens to output and the price level in the short run in each country. What happens to the unemployment rate in each country?

  c. Show, using your diagrams, how each country could use monetary policy to reduce the short-run fluctuation in output.

  d. Show, using your diagrams, how movements in the cob–byte exchange rate could reduce short-run fluctuations in output in each country.

2 Suppose Techoland and Cornsylvania form a currency union and adopt the electrocarrot as their common currency. Now suppose again that there is an increase in demand for electronic goods in both countries, and a simultaneous decline in demand for agricultural goods. As president of the central bank for the currency union, would you raise or lower the electrocarrot interest rate, or keep it the same? Explain. (Hint: you are charged with maintaining low and stable inflation across the electrocarrot area.)

3 Suppose that Techoland and Cornsylvania decide to engage in fiscal federalism and adopt a common fiscal budget.

  a. Show, again using the AD/AS model, how fiscal policy can be used to alleviate the short-run fluctuations generated by the asymmetric demand shock.

  b. Given the typical lags in the implementation of fiscal policy, would you advise the use of federal fiscal policy to alleviate short-run macroeconomic fluctuations? (Hint: distinguish between automatic stabilizers and discretionary fiscal policy.)

4 The United States can be thought of as a non-trivial currency union since, although it is a single country, it encompasses many states that have economies comparable in size to those of some European countries. Given that the USA has had a single currency for 200 years, it may be thought of as a successful currency union. Yet many of the American states produce very different products and services, so that they are likely to be impacted by different kinds of macroeconomic shocks (expansionary and recessionary) over time. For example, Texas produces oil, while Kansas produces agricultural goods. How do you explain the long-term success of the US currency union given this diversity? Are there any lessons or predictions for Europe that can be drawn from the US experience?

5 Explain, giving reasons, whether the following statements are true or false.

   a. 'A high degree of trade among a group of countries implies that there would be benefits from them adopting a common currency and forming a currency union.'

   b. 'A high degree of trade among a group of countries implies that they should definitely adopt a common currency and form a currency union.'

6 Do you think that the free-rider problem associated with national fiscal policies in a currency union, as we discussed in the text, is likely to be a problem in actual practice? Justify your answer.

7 What is the function of the European Commission? What are the other five main institutions of the European Union and what are their respective roles? What are the other important EU bodies and what are their respective roles? (Hint: go to the European Union website: www.europa.eu.int.)

8 If the interest rate on Spanish government debt is rising whilst that of Germany is falling:

   a. What does this tell you about the view of the markets on the two countries?

   b. If the interest rate is rising, what is happening to the price of bonds for the two countries? Explain.

9 In order for a common currency area to work effectively it is argued that on joining, member states need to be at a similar stage in the economic cycle. Why do you think this is the case?

10 The fiscal pact would be fine if all countries in the euro area were at the same stage in the economic cycle and it was designed to act as a deterrent for profligacy in the future. As a means of solving the debt crisis in Europe it is doomed to fail. To what extent would you agree with this statement?

38 THE FINANCIAL CRISIS AND SOVEREIGN DEBT

INTRODUCTION

In Chapter 26, we presented a narrative of the Financial Crisis. In this chapter, we will look in a little more detail at some of the theoretical explanations for the Financial Crisis and then at its aftermath.

Recall that deregulation of financial markets had led to an increase in the number of financial institutions competing for customers, in particular, in the housing market. Access to borrowing, not only for the purchase of houses but for other consumption goods, became easier for millions of people. This was set against the background of relatively benign economic conditions in which unemployment had fallen, growth had been positive and relatively stable in a number of countries for some years, and inflation had slowed considerably from the high rates experienced in many developed economies in the 1970s and 1980s. Some of the credit for the control of inflation was attributed to inflation targeting. Such was the 'success' of macroeconomic policy that the period was referred to as The Great Moderation.

Two Related Cycles

As we also saw in Chapter 26, Hyman Minsky suggested that the seeds of future instability can be sowed in periods of benign economic conditions. In order to analyze the Financial Crisis, we distinguish between two related cycles, the business cycle and the financial cycle. In Chapter 31 we saw how early DSGE models had largely ignored the financial sector. This was primarily because it was assumed that the financial sector would work efficiently and even if there were shocks affecting the real economy, the financial sector would continue to function. The **real economy** refers to that part of the economy which is concerned with the production of goods and services. In contrast, the **financial economy** is that part of the economy associated with the buying and selling of assets on financial markets. The financial economy can be thought of as the lubrication for the real economy but the exchange of assets itself does not lead to anything being produced. The innovation in financial markets in the wake of deregulation had been extensive and some of the financial instruments developed were extremely complex and increasingly based on derivatives, so called because their value derived from other assets. In August 2009, Lord Turner, the head of the then regulator, the Financial Services Authority (FSA) in the UK, referred to some of these instruments in an interview as representing 'socially useless activity'.

> **real economy** that part of the economy which is concerned with the production of goods and services
> **financial economy** that part of the economy associated with the buying and selling of assets on financial markets

An economy can be subject to a business cycle and a financial cycle and, importantly, these cycles do not have to coincide. Business cycles, as we have seen, can be caused by shocks to either demand or supply (or both) through such things as war, changing commodity prices, significant natural disasters such as earthquakes, or changes in technology, amongst other things. These shocks tend to affect the real economy but as noted above, the financial sector may continue to operate relatively efficiently regardless of the impact on employment, output and productivity in the real economy.

The amplitudes of a financial cycle may be much longer than those in a business cycle. The upswing of a financial cycle may be characterized by increased profits in banks, an increase in borrowing or leverage and increases in asset prices. In the downswing the opposite occurs. The financial cycle can have effects on the real economy, both as the cycle develops and when the downswing occurs. When the downswing is severe and sufficient to be referred to as a crisis, the resulting impact on the real economy can be significant and the resulting recession severe and long lasting. Typically, recessions resulting from a Financial Crisis last longer and the growth which eventually follows is weaker in comparison to a recession caused by a shock to the real economy. The increase in both household and financial institution debt in a financial cycle upswing can be significant, and in the downswing, attempts are made by both to pay off debt and repair balance sheets. The effect on the real economy of households cutting back consumption to pay off debt reduces AD. The time taken to pay off debt and repair balance sheets can be lengthy and in part explains why the effects of a Financial Crisis can be so long lasting.

The Financial Accelerator

A paper published in 1994 by Bernanke, Gertler and Gilchrist[1] put forward the theory of the *financial accelerator*. The financial accelerator theory states that problems in financial markets can amplify shocks to the real economy and creates a feedback loop, which exacerbates economic problems. The financial accelerator can begin to operate if a positive price shock in one period leads to economic actors believing that prices in the next period will continue to increase. The process reflects much of what was witnessed in the lead up to the Financial Crisis.

One assumption underlying the theory is that households face limits to the amount they are able to borrow to finance consumption and to purchase housing. An increase in the demand for housing, *ceteris paribus*, leads to a rise in prices. The extent to which house prices rise is dependent on the speed with which demand can be satisfied, on the rate at which new housing can be built, and how many people wish to move house. As prices rise, house owners experience an increase in wealth, and given deregulation and financial innovation, they are able to exploit the positive equity in their homes to borrow further to spend not only on more housing but on wider consumption. This was particularly the case in the UK and US but not so much in Germany, Italy and France where house ownership tends not to be as widespread.

The fundamentals of supply and demand may mean that house prices continue to rise. Panel (a) in Figure 38.1 shows UK house prices from 1983–2008. It can be clearly seen that the average house price rose dramatically from the late 1990s to 2007. Panel (b) of Figure 38.1 shows an index of house prices in the US between 2000 and 2008, during which house prices in the US had risen by around 80 per cent.

A rise in asset prices such as that highlighted in Figure 38.1 does not necessarily mean that an asset bubble is forming; the rise in prices could be due to market fundamentals. Separating the two can be extremely difficult. The expectations of buyers, and those in the financial markets who are providing mortgage funding, about how the market will develop is crucial. The Great Moderation provided the conditions under which perceptions of risk are altered; if expectations are that house prices will continue to rise and economic conditions continue to be stable, decisions may be made in the expectation that risk is lower.

As house prices rise, the difference between the principal borrowed and the value of the house increases creates positive equity for house owners, which can be exploited as we saw in Chapter 26. Mortgage borrowing and borrowing on credit cards expanded. In the UK, for example, total personal debt, which includes credit card debt and mortgages, rose from around £400 billion in 1993 to a peak of over £1.45 trillion in 2008 (source: The Money Charity). To put this figure into context, UK GDP in 2008 was almost £1.66 trillion. Borrowing on credit cards tends to be used primarily for everyday consumption as well as larger ticket items such as household electrical items and holidays, and so feeds through to AD.

---

[1] Bernanke, B.S, Gertler, M and Gilchrist, S. (1994) The Financial Accelerator and the Flight to Quality, *NBER Working Paper No. 4789*

FIGURE 38.1

The Rise in House Prices

Panel (a) shows the rise in the average house price in the UK between 1983 and 2008. The average house price in 1983 was around £30 000 but by 2007 had peaked at around £190 000. Panel (b) shows the Standard & Poors (S&P)/Case–Schiller US National Home Price Index between 2000 and 2009 indicating the sharp increase in house prices in the first years of the noughties.

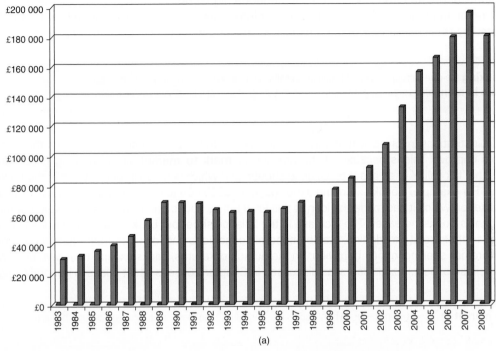

(a)

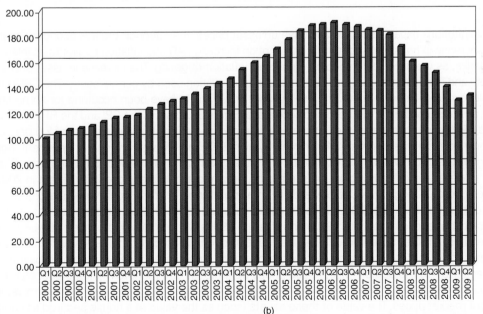

(b)

Source: Halifax House Price Index; S&P/Case-Shiller U.S. National Home Price Index are proprietary to and are calculated, distributed and marketed by S&P Opco, LLC (a subsidiary of S&P Dow Jones Indices LLC), its affiliates and/or its licensors and has been licensed for use. S&P® is a registered trademark of Standard & Poor's Financial Services LLC; Dow Jones® is a registered trademark of Dow Jones Trademark Holdings LLC and Case-Shiller® is a registered trademark of CoreLogic Case-Shiller, LLC. © 2009 S&P Dow Jones Indices LLC, its affiliates and/or its licensors. All rights reserved.

For financial institutions, the stable economic conditions, increased demand for credit, and a less stringent regulatory framework, means that they are in a position to generate higher returns for shareholders. The expansion of global banking led to retail and wholesale banks being less obviously separated. **Retail banking** refers to the core banking services of taking in deposits and making loans to households and businesses whereas **wholesale banking** is associated more with corporate finance and investment banking. The wholesale banking sector does not have a deposit taking function, instead it uses the returns generated from investments to generate higher returns. However, when the distinction between retail and wholesale banking becomes blurred, investment banks may utilize the funds being generated by retail banks to invest in financial assets and in particular, securitized assets.

> **retail banking** the core banking service of taking in deposits and making loans to households and businesses
>
> **wholesale banking** that part of banking dealing with corporate finance and investment in financial instruments

For financial institutions involved with extending mortgages, the rise in house prices means that their balance sheets improve. This is because of the practice of **mark to market**, an accounting procedure which records the 'fair value' of an asset on balance sheets, and which plays an important role in the financial accelerator. For example, a bank extending a mortgage for £250 000 to a couple may initially record the value of the asset on which it has made the loan at this level but as house prices increase, the value of this asset on the bank's books increases. The increase in the balance sheet put banks in a stronger position to seek to extend further credit. In addition, stable economic conditions and lower interest rates encourage banks to be more risk seeking in their behaviour. In the pursuit of returns, banks expand their own borrowing and the purchase of securitized assets, as discussed in Chapter 26, sees asset prices in general rising.

> **mark to market** an accounting procedure which records the 'fair value' of an asset on financial institutions' balance sheets

As financial institutions expand leverage and drive up asset prices, the effect on the real economy begins to amplify. The increase in household debt and consumption increases AD and inflation begins to accelerate. Many central banks, as we have seen, adopted a policy of inflation targeting. The increase in asset prices in financial markets and in housing do not feature in measures of inflation used by central banks. The CPI in the UK, for example, excludes housing costs. The rise in asset prices might have been occurring for some time before inflation as measured by the CPI begins to accelerate. Figure 38.2 shows the CPI and the RPI in the UK from 1997 to 2009. It can be seen that the CPI remained below the Bank of England's target of 2.0 per cent until 2005 when it edged above target to 2.1 per cent; even in 2007, the CPI was still only 2.5 per cent, not a sufficient variance in target to warrant an open letter from the governor of the Bank of England to the Chancellor. The RPI, however, which does include housing costs, began to accelerate above 2.0 per cent in 2002.

Interest rates in the UK began to edge upwards in small quarter point steps from November 2003 only reaching 5.0 per cent in November 2006. These were considered relatively low rates of interest in comparison to those experienced in the late 1980s and into the 1990s, when rates had peaked at 14.875 per cent in October 1989 and remained around 6–7 per cent throughout much of the 1990s. When interest rates edged upwards from 2003, marginal borrowers began to face challenges in maintaining payments and defaults began to rise. As defaults rise, house prices begin to fall and mark-to-market practices mean that banks' balance sheets begin to shrink. Mark-to-market is an accounting practice where a firm values assets at current market prices. The value of these assets (such as the value of a house secured as capital on a loan) can change over time and this method is designed to represent a 'fair value' of assets. Loans are called in and new loans cut back. As banks make efforts to repair their balance sheets, assets are sold and this causes their price to fall. Some financial institutions with high leverage and exposure to bad debts face insolvency. For retail banks facing this situation, there is a danger that this can lead to a run on the bank as depositors rush to withdraw their money. In the same way that the upswing in the financial cycle affects the real economy, so does a downswing.

FIGURE 38.2

UK CPI and RPI, 1997 – 2009

The figure shows that the CPI, which does not include housing costs, remained below the target of 2.0 per cent until 2005 and for the two years after, was only just above the target level. In contrast, the RPI, which does include housing costs, began to accelerate above 2.0 per cent in 2002 and by 2007 had reached 4.3 per cent.

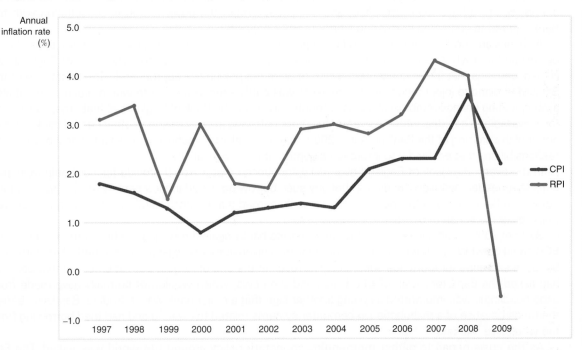

The Role of Central Banks

As the Financial Crisis unravelled, focus centred on the response of central banks around the world. The role of monetary policy in helping to alleviate the worst effects of the Crisis and the resulting recession is seen as important and came under scrutiny with regard to the effectiveness of the action of key poli-cymakers. The markets were looking for three aspects of policy response from central banks: speed of intervention, innovation and coordination. There were elements of each of these that occurred but there are also important differences in the degree to which each of the main central banks responded, partly because of the different levels of flexibility that each enjoyed.

The early signs of crisis emerged in 2007 when rumours of rising levels of default from sub-prime mortgages began to increase. In July of that year, Standard & Poors and Moody's downgraded ratings on bonds backed by sub-prime mortgages. In late July a German bank, IKB, said that it was in financial trouble as a result of its exposure to sub-prime and was swiftly taken over by German government-owned bank, KfW (Kreditanstalt für Wiederaufbau). By early August 2007, the ramifications of the downgrading of funds related to sub-prime were starting to unravel and, on 3 August, Bear Stearns had to contact its sharehold-ers following the collapse of two hedge funds that it managed and the subsequent fall in its share price. On 9 August, French bank BNP Paribas announced that it was ceasing trading three of its funds and with that credit markets effectively froze. Interbank lending ground to a halt as banks began to recognize that their exposure to sub-prime could be extensive.

The freezing of credit markets effectively marked the start of intervention by central banks around the world. The ECB was one of the first to react on 9 August with the then President, Jean-Claude Trichet, authorizing an injection of €95 billion into the financial markets to help ease overnight liquidity problems. On the following day a further €61 billion was authorized. Soon after the ECB move, the US Federal

Reserve announced that it would inject €38 billion to help ease liquidity; the Bank of England, however, did not follow suit. On 10 August, the Bank of England was involved in growing problems at Northern Rock, which had expanded rapidly in previous years but now found its expansion based on leverage unsustainable and, as credit markets froze, it was struggling to continue. In the coming weeks the extent of the problems at Northern Rock became public and a run on the bank ensued. Queues formed outside Northern Rock branches as worried account holders looked to withdraw their money. Moves to calm the situation did not seem to have too much effect and on 17 September the government, in consultation with the Bank, agreed to guarantee all existing Northern Rock deposits.

As banks around the world began to falter over the coming months; the question of which bank should be rescued and which left to fail had to be considered by central bank heads. The Bank of England had issued warnings that it was concerned investors were not pricing risk appropriately. The reluctance of the Bank of England to inject funds into the markets was partly seen as a concern with moral hazard but also as subjugating financial stability to a lesser priority. However, the Bank of England, at that time, had limited tools available to it to deal with the events that were unfolding in comparison to other central banks. It was not until the passing of the Banking Act in 2009, that the Bank of England was given additional powers and responsibilities that enabled it to improve its control of financial stability.

In the event, the Bank of England eventually announced that it would provide financial help to institutions that needed overnight funds but that any such borrowing would incur a penalty rate. It was not long before the Bank removed this penalty rate, since it seemed that far from calming nerves it merely served to increase the sense of panic.

By April 2008 it had gained the authority to lend to banks against mortgage debt – something that the ECB could do which the Bank could not. The Bank was given authority to issue short-dated UK government bonds in exchange for mortgage securities. However, at the end of August 2007 it emerged that Barclays had asked the Bank for a loan of £1.6 billion and the news, which would not normally have made front page headlines, was interpreted as being another sign that a major bank was in trouble. Barclays needed the funds because of a malfunction in computer systems related to clearing and had tried borrowing from the wholesale markets.

As the crisis began to gather momentum, monetary policy around the world was eased. The Fed cut the repo rate by 0.75 per cent in January 2008; the ECB held its rate at 4.0 per cent. The Bank of England had cut rates by a quarter point in February and April 2008 but by May that year the Fed had cut rates seven times in eight months with the fed funds rate standing at 2.0 per cent. As 2008 progressed the financial situation did show clear signs that it was 'spilling over' to the real economy and output levels began to contract in economies across the globe. The problems were such that, in October, seven major economies, the UK, US, China, the EU, Canada, United Arab Emirates (UAE) and Sweden, announced a coordinated 0.5 per cent cut in interest rates. By then end of October the Fed cut again, to 1 per cent.

In the US, discussions were taking place to set up the Troubled Asset Relief Plan (TARP), a $700 billion plan to support the banking system. In November the Fed announced a further $800 billion support fund. In that same month the Bank of England reduced rates by 1.5 per cent – the largest single change in rates since it was given independence in 1997. By March 2009 the MPC had cut interest rates in the UK to 0.5 per cent, the lowest since the Bank of England was established in 1694. The Fed cut its rates to a target of between 0 and 0.25 per cent and the ECB had cut rates to 1 per cent.

The scale of the intervention by central banks and the various fiscal stimulus programmes announced by governments made it clear that the crisis was serious. The 'contagion' from the sub-prime fall-out and the collapse of banks around the world accompanied by the alarming declines in output meant that global recession was now the real threat rather than the prospects for inflation, which, despite the economic downturn, remained stubbornly high in countries like the UK.

There are those who believe that, given the circumstances, central banks acted according to the three key aspects of policy response outlined above. The speed with which central banks intervened and the extent of these interventions did differ, largely because of technical as well as ideological differences, but most central bank heads argued that their responses were decisive in exceptional circumstances.

Central banks have had to be flexible and innovative in dealing with problems that were unusual. As with the Bank of England, central banks have expanded their roles and assumed new powers and responsibilities, and introduced new tools and instruments. Two such examples have been the growth of bilateral swap agreements between central banks of different countries, where local currencies can be swapped against the US dollar to enable trade to be financed and liquidity to be eased, and the use of quantitative easing.

Lessons Learned?

The OECD traces the development of the Financial Crisis through a series of four main stages.

1. A drive on the part of politicians to widen access to home ownership to the poor. Changes to regulations to facilitate this drive led to a growth in lending that was not prudent. This political impetus was evident through successive US Presidents from Clinton onwards and in the UK via New Labour. As a result, the expansion of sub-prime lending in the US and cases of banks in the UK lending at 125 per cent of the value of homes, wider access to credit cards and the build-up of debt and limited background checks for credit worthiness, were not acted upon by regulators with sufficient vigour.
2. Changes in regulatory structures, particularly in the US, which allowed entry of new businesses into the mortgage market.
3. Basel II regulations which created incentives and the conditions for banks to develop off-balance sheet entities. (Basel II refers to a framework of regulations developed through discussions at the Bank for International Settlements (BIS).)
4. Changes in policy by national regulatory authorities such as the Securities and Exchange Commission (SEC) in the US and the FSA in the UK, which allowed banks to change leverage ratios from around 15:1 to 40:1. (Leverage ratios, such as debt-to-equity ratios, measure the proportion of debt to equity.)

The OECD was critical of national regulatory bodies, suggesting that there were weaknesses in the way banks were regulated and that regulatory frameworks had not only failed to prevent the Financial Crisis but had been culpable in contributing to it. It identified a number of key causes which include:

- the bonus culture
- credit ratings agencies
- failures in corporate governance
- poor risk management strategies and understanding.

The IMF has broadly concurred with the OECD in its analysis of the key issues. It suggests that financial institutions and investors were both too bullish on asset prices and risk. The low interest rate environment and the extent of financial innovation (encouraged by changes in regulation) allowed excessive leverage, which increased the web of interconnectedness of financial products but at the same time rendered the inherent risks more opaque. It highlighted the lack of coordination between regulatory bodies and the legal constraints which prevented information sharing to be more widespread, thus helping authorities to be able to understand what was going on.

This meant that there were differences in the way in which national regulatory bodies dealt with bank failures and insolvency. In many cases these banks had a global presence not reflected by a global coordinated response by the regulators. The actions that were taken were described as being 'piecemeal' and 'uncoordinated', which not only led to a weakening of the impact of the policy response but also to market distortion. It also pointed to the lack of appropriate tools available to some central banks to provide the necessary liquidity support in times of crisis.

Other criticisms of the regulatory regimes in place throughout the world highlight the fact that the rules that are in place may not be appropriate to deal with the pace of change in financial markets, that regulators spend too much time 'ticking boxes' rather than identifying poor practice and intervening. There have been accusations that the existence of rules means regulators are able to hide behind them and shift blame. For example, there were a number of subsidiaries of three Icelandic banks which failed (Kaupthing, Glitnir and Landsbanki) operating in the UK but the FSA argued that these were, technically, outside its jurisdiction. In the US it has been estimated that the total assets of entities which were outside the banking system and the scope of regulation (referred to as the **shadow banking system**), but which act like banks, is as big as the 'official' banking system itself – a value estimated at around $10 trillion in late 2007.

shadow banking system financial intermediaries acting like banks but which are outside the scope of regulation

Part of the reason for these failures stems from internal problems of the regulators themselves. To have a high level of understanding of the financial system to be able to regulate it effectively, employees of the regulators have to be highly experienced and knowledgeable about the system itself. Over-regulation, it has been argued, was partly responsible for creating the incentives for financial innovation to generate improved returns. These new products were complex and highly interconnected to the extent that regulators and government financial departments had insufficient understanding of them. It has been argued that a number of senior executives in the banks themselves did not fully understand the complexity of securitization models, lacked the skills in asset valuation techniques and risk models, and were unaware of the extent to which 'tail losses' (the extremes of the normal distribution) could impact on operations. One reason for this was that such models were based on statistics from the 'good times' and had not been 'tested' by a downturn. If those at the forefront of such operations did not understand what they were dealing with, is it possible to expect those working for regulators to do so?

Recruitment of the expertize and skills necessary to staff regulatory bodies effectively is a further issue. Why work for the FSA, for example, for a salary of £116 000 when the skills possessed by individuals of the calibre to work in the FSA could be sold to other sectors of the industry for many millions? Without the resources to do the job properly therefore, regulators will always be hampered.

THE SOVEREIGN DEBT CRISIS

Sovereign debt refers to the bonds issued by national governments to finance expenditure. One of the consequences of the Financial Crisis has been the focus on the problems faced by a number of countries in Europe in managing debt. Recall that budget deficits are the difference between the amount of tax revenue and government spending. Deficits are financed by government borrowing and as borrowing increases the overall debt rises. Governments have to manage this debt by ensuring that they have enough funds to be able to pay back government bonds when they reach maturity and also to pay the interest on the bonds which are outstanding. Lending to governments has invariably been seen as relatively risk-free; in the wake of the Financial Crisis it became clear that for some governments, this was not the case.

sovereign debt the bonds issued by national governments to finance expenditure

The macroeconomic shock created by the Financial Crisis led to a global slowdown in economic activity. When countries experience a prolonged period of economic slowdown, tax revenues decline but spending on welfare support increases. Whilst automatic stabilizers moderate the effects, as we have seen, in a severe recessionary period these automatic stabilizers can be diluted. In this environment, governments need to increase borrowing but the confidence of markets in their ability to meet debt obligations means that some countries can be brought to the verge of bankruptcy. In other words, they cannot raise enough funds to be able to meet debt and everyday public spending obligations.

The Greek Debt Crisis

The country which has come to epitomize the sovereign debt crisis is Greece. The problems faced in Greece have been replicated to some extent in Ireland, Spain, Italy and Portugal. In 2009, Greece announced that its deficit would reach almost 13 per cent of GDP, double the amount it forecasted a year previously. In early 2010 the country's debt was reported as €300 billion, more than the value of its GDP. In fact its debt was 115.1 per cent of its GDP (remember that the original Stability and Growth Pact rules laid down that debt should not exceed 60 per cent of GDP). The budget deficit rose to nearly 14 per cent – well beyond the 3 per cent required as the terms of membership of EMU. Other members of the EU, notably Germany, accused Greece of being 'profligate' and living beyond its means on the back of its membership of the euro area.

Greece had to raise around €50 billion in 2010 to meet its debt obligations. On 19 May 2010, it needed to pay €8.5 billion to bondholders. On 25 January 2010, the Greek government went to the markets to borrow money in the form of its first bond issue of the year. In the event, the issue was oversubscribed as investors sought to pick up the bonds primarily because the interest on the bonds had to be high to persuade investors to take the risk. It was reported that the issue was valued at around €5 billion with a coupon of 6.12 per cent. Given that interest rates around the world at that time were at record low levels, this was high. The spread between the interest Greece had to pay to borrow compared with the Germans was almost 4.0 per cent. The wider the spread on different financial instruments (the difference in the coupon of similar bonds in this instance), the more the market is factoring in the risk of default on the bonds – Greek bonds in this case.

In February and March of 2010, the Greek government had tried to take a stance on public spending, proposing major cuts in jobs, pensions, wages and services. Greek workers took to the streets in protest. It seemed as though the government would find it difficult to implement the sort of fiscal cuts necessary to build confidence with the markets. On the back of the announcements about the increasing size of its debt and the deficit, it seemed that by April it would find it difficult to raise further money to meet its obligations. Agencies steadily cut the country's ratings until by late April, Greek debt was officially classed as 'junk'.

The spread between Greek and German bonds continued to rise into April reaching 19 per cent on 2-year bonds and 11.3 per cent on 1-year bonds. The nervousness on the financial markets over Greece's debt problems began to spread to other European countries. It became a real possibility that Greece would default and be forced to leave the euro. This fear led to a sharp drop in the value of the euro – if there is an expectation that the price of something is going to fall then there is a possibility of making some money and that is exactly what happened in February 2010. Data from the Chicago Mercantile Exchange (CME) showed that short positions against the euro from hedge funds and traders rose sharply. Traders took positions on the expectation that the euro would fall in value. Traders taking out contracts that the price of the euro would fall could exercise these contracts and make a profit if and when the euro fell in value. Data from the CME showed that over 40 000 contracts had been taken out against the euro with a total value of around €8 billion.

The crisis began to gather momentum and the markets looked to other EU governments to organize a bailout. On 10 April 2010, the finance ministers of the euro area announced an agreement on a package of loans to Greece totalling €30 billion. Greece said that it did not intend to use the loans and instead rely on its 'austerity measures'. The extent to which Greece could deliver on these measures was something the financial markets were not convinced about.

A week later the Greek Prime Minister, George Papandreou, finally bowed to what many thought was the inevitable and announced that Greece would take advantage of the emergency loans. Negotiations took place with the EU and the IMF on the structure of these loans, which were predicted to rise to €100 billion.

Whilst it was generally accepted that Greece needed the financial support there were questions raised about the terms under which the loans were to be given. The German government was financing a proportion of the loans with €8.4 billion being spoken of as a possible figure. In order to appease German taxpayers who were not supportive of bailing out the 'profligate Greeks', Chancellor Angela Merkel, under pressure from German taxpayers to take a strong line, insisted on very strict terms and a condition that the Greek government make significant cuts to public spending. The argument that Greece has exploited the free-rider problem within a common currency area, as we outlined in Chapter 37, seemed to be strong. For many Greeks, there was a feeling that their future was being dictated by outsiders, most notably the Germans. The Germans argued that it was unfair that its taxpayers should have to suffer to bailout a country which had clearly not played by the euro rules. On May Day, traditional worker protests in Greece had a new focus and the extent and severity of the violence which broke out shocked many. Austerity was clearly not going to be easy to implement and the strength of feeling against the Germans was clear. The Greek government was being squeezed from all sides. The financial markets were nervous that the problems in Greece would spread to other high-debt countries (so-called 'contagion effect') and there were fears that the crisis could tip Europe back into recession.

SHORT SELLING

On the morning of the 19 September 2008, newspaper headlines in the UK were plastered with the sort of invective normally reserved for rapists, murderers and child molesters! This time, the anger of headline writers was directed at mostly highly educated and highly skilled people. The target for the anger was traders on the financial markets. 'Share sharks', 'rogue traders', 'spivs' and 'dodgy dealing' were all terms or phrases which appeared in the press as the fallout of the £12 billion merger between HBOS and Lloyds TSB started to unravel. It was not only short-selling of stock that was seen to be problematic and exacerbating the Crisis, but short-selling of other financial instruments, such as currencies and sovereign debt, was equally damaging. Without such a 'heinous practice' HBOS would have survived intact and thousands of jobs across the country would have been saved. The whole practice of short-selling was questioned and it seems that the conclusion was that it was 'immoral'.

Short-selling is basically the practice of betting that an asset price is going to fall. Here is how it works using shares as an example: an investor expects the price of shares (for example, in HBOS) to fall; they are currently priced at 250p. They contact a broker and arrange to 'borrow' 3 million shares; the investor sells the shares at 250p, therefore receiving a credit of £7 500 000. At some point in the future, the investor will close the deal by buying 3 million shares to pay back the broker. Let us assume that the buy-back price is now 200p. The investor has therefore made a profit of £1 500 000.

Many short traders pursue this option as a means of hedging against long positions – a sort of insurance against losses they make elsewhere. If the price had not fallen by as much as hoped, however, the profit would have been less, and if the price had risen during that time the investor would have made a loss. The broker meanwhile gets interest on the value of the shares 'loaned' and if any changes occur during the period of the deal (for example if the company paid a dividend) or if the company announces some new share issue like a bonus issue (basically a two-for-one type issue), the investor must pay back the requisite number of shares – this could be 6 million shares at half the original value.

The argument put forward at the time was that short-selling was the reason for the dramatic fall in the share price of HBOS which prompted the merger talks with Lloyds. There was also concern that short-selling was behind other share price falls in banking companies and that further activities of this sort would lead to more instability in the financial markets. As a result, the FSA announced a ban on short-selling until 16 January 2009. The unprecedented move was greeted with mixed views by analysts and City insiders. Some believed that the action was a few days too late and others believed that the move was a knee-jerk reaction that did not take into account the widespread lack of confidence amongst investors – not just hedge funds – who were taking much of the blame for the uncertainty. In New York, the SEC considered similar moves and the US government and the Federal Reserve were working on plans to provide support for banks to help build confidence. The plan would see the US government take on billions of dollars of bad debt to enable the banks to begin functioning normally again and rebuild confidence.

Short selling – a legitimate practice or something to be banned?

The Development of the Crisis

Greece and Italy had never achieved the 60 per cent debt to GDP ratio required of membership for the euro – both countries had persistently run ratios over 90 per cent since the 1990s. Ireland, Spain and Portugal had managed to reduce their debt ratios just below the 60 per cent mark by 2007. At this time, the spread of interest rates across euro area sovereign debt was relatively small suggesting that markets did not anticipate the sort of problems that beset some governments post-Crisis. Underlying this apparently benign macroeconomic environment, however, was a sharp rise in borrowing from the private sector in Portugal, Spain, Ireland and Greece. In Greece, domestic credit as a proportion of GDP rose from around 32 per cent in 1998 to 84 per cent in 2007; in Ireland the increase was from around 81 per cent to 184 per cent; in Portugal, from 92 per cent to almost 160 per cent; and in Spain from almost 81 per cent to 168.5 per cent. One of the reasons given for this domestic credit boom was that banks could borrow euros on international markets. Prior to the euro, these banks would have had to borrow in other currencies and fluctuations in exchange rates would have made the borrowing more risky. Borrowing was made much easier by the relatively low interest rates which existed throughout much of the early years of the noughties.

This borrowing was used to help finance the boom in housing and construction which took place in each of these countries and helped to drive economic growth. When the Financial Crisis hit, credit dried up, the housing market collapsed and construction was badly hit. The banking systems across Europe were trying to identify the extent of the exposure that they faced, the potential size of the losses they were likely to make, and the possibility of having to borrow to overcome short-term financing problems. The reliance of countries like Greece, Ireland, Spain and Portugal on the ability to borrow internationally meant that they were hit hard by the credit crunch as credit dried up or became expensive. As banks in these countries teetered on the brink of collapse, they looked to national governments for support. If governments allowed these banks to fail then the effect on the population as a whole was likely to be significant, not to mention the wider banking sector in Europe. In order to help support their banking systems, governments had to borrow money – but few of these governments had the fiscal flexibility to do so without increasing borrowing.

In addition, the extent of the post-Crisis recession had started to affect tax revenues and government spending. In countries like Spain and Ireland, tax revenues decreased as a result of the contraction in the construction industry, which had been fuelling pre-Crisis growth. This, in turn, increased budget deficits, and with GDP shrinking, the size of the deficit to GDP ratio grew. As it became clearer that these governments were likely to breach EU fiscal rules, and with the need to support banking systems growing in intensity, the financial markets' confidence fell and interest rates on the sovereign debt of these countries rose. Europe had always had countries which were economically sound such as Germany, the Netherlands, Sweden and France alongside a group of weaker countries. Increasingly, Portugal, Spain, Ireland and Greece came to be referred to as 'the periphery'.

Greek Bailout The first part of the Greek bailout was negotiated in late April into May of 2010. In November 2010, Ireland's government also had to seek support and in May 2011, Portugal followed suit. In June 2011, Greece needed a second bailout, which was eventually agreed in March 2012. As part of the agreement, private sector creditors had to accept a 'haircut', losing 50 per cent of the value of their investments. The background of an increasing number of countries being dragged into the crisis and the somewhat chaotic response of the EU to the situation, merely increased nervousness on the financial markets and spreads widened further between the periphery and the core EU countries. The accusation that the response to the crisis had been chaotic led to self-fulfilling speculative attacks from financial markets. High risk countries are more likely to default so investors require higher yields to take on the debt of these countries. If countries have to borrow at higher rates of interest, this in itself increases the risk of default.

Why was the response so chaotic? One reason was the clear divide between those countries that had maintained some degree of fiscal restraint and the periphery which had been seen to free ride on their membership of the EU. Another reason was the realization that political pressures on domestic governments were huge. Domestic political pressures forced donor countries such as Germany, to insist that any terms of bailout packages include the implementation of significant cuts in public spending and tax rises. On the one hand, some element of fiscal consolidation was vital to show financial markets that some discipline would be exerted, and on the other that the countries seeking support were serious in their willingness to abide by the fiscal rules of the euro.

At the same time, governments knew that implementing austerity packages would be extremely unpopular and impose considerable hardship on citizens. Politically, this represented suicide; few governments could be confident of re-election under such circumstances. Opposition parties might promise to stand up to the 'bullies' in the EU who were imposing these policies, and to abandon austerity. Such a manifesto might be alluring to people suffering cuts in wages, loss of jobs, cuts to public services, cuts in pensions and increases in taxes, but the reality was that even if these opposition groups did find themselves in power, as was the case when the anti-austerity party Syriza in Greece came to power in January 2015, the reality of the situation does not go away. If countries become bankrupt, the potential damage to the country could be even worse than the effects of austerity packages.

Crisis in Cyprus In June 2012, Spain had to seek help and in March 2013, the banking system in Cyprus was on the verge of collapse. With banks closed for almost two weeks whilst the Cypriot government negotiated with the EU and IMF, the debate over the extent to which depositors in Cypriot banks should have to accept losses was a key focus. An initial bailout deal imposed a tax on all depositors in an attempt to raise €5.8 billion as part of a bailout deal. The tax was rejected and subsequent negotiations led to an agreement where those with deposits of over €100 000 would be taxed to raise the €5.8 billion contribution to the overall €10 billion bailout. It could be argued that those who have such large deposits ought to be the ones shouldering the biggest burden, and the amount of deposits from so-called Russian oligarchs in the Cypriot banking system was a feature of the news reporting at the time. However, it was not just wealthy Russians who, for whatever reason, deposited money in Cypriot banks who suffered a 'haircut' – businesses were also hit.

Cypriot banks were also subject to considerable restructuring and when banks re-opened in March 2013, there were significant limitations on the amount of money that could be withdrawn, and capital controls on money leaving Cyprus were also imposed. After reforms, the IMF approved a further instalment of the bailout fund of €280 million in June 2015 and in 2016 it was expected that there would be an end to the IMF funding, reflecting the progress the country made post-crisis.

Syriza and the Third Bailout in Greece Progress in Greece has been less successful. The election of the left-wing Syriza party in January 2015, heralded a period of intense negotiations between Greece and its creditors, the ECB, Germany and the IMF (referred to as the 'troika'). Deadlines came and went and there were several instances where Greek exit from the euro area was a distinct possibility. Syriza and its leader, Alexis Tsipras, battled against demands for further austerity measures in return for a third bailout. As talks continued, Tsipras called a referendum on the talks. This prompted the freezing of cash support for Greek banks, capital controls, and limits on the amount of cash which could be withdrawn from banks. The referendum on the 5 July backed Tsipras' stance rejecting the demand for further reforms and cuts by the troika. On the 9 July, Tsipras went back to the negotiating table with further proposals which, curiously, included some of the troika demanded reforms which had been rejected in the referendum. On 13 July an agreement was reached on a third bailout. Tsipras called fresh elections in September 2015 amidst much rancour in the country over the terms of the agreement. Syriza itself suffered a split as those who felt that Greece had been humiliated by the terms of the agreement formed a rival party.

The EU commissioner, Jean-Claude Juncker, noted that there were 'no winners or losers' in the agreement; but the challenges facing the country and the realisation that bankruptcy and exit from the euro would be potentially far more damaging to the country and its people in the long run left Greek government negotiators with little choice. The future of the country is far from settled and it is acknowledged by many economists that it will be many years before growth and stability return.

The European Financial Stability Fund (EFSF) and the European Stability Mechanism (ESM) The discussions over the first Greek bailout led European finance ministers to establish the European Financial Stability Fund (EFSF) in May 2010 to provide support for countries that faced default. The EFSF raised funds by issuing bonds and other financial instruments through capital markets. The money raised was lent to countries seeking assistance on the understanding that reforms are put in place. The sum of €750 billion was initially identified as needing to be raised. The initial bailout of Greece accounted for €110 billion of these funds; Ireland's €85 billion and Portugal's around €80 billion. The establishment of the EFSF was designed to be a temporary measure pending the establishment of a more permanent means of supporting countries in financial difficulties. The EFSF effectively ceased its operations in June 2015 but still exists to receive loan repayments and administer bond holdings.

The permanent replacement for the EFSF began operations in October 2012, as the European Stability Mechanism. Based in Luxembourg, the ESM is classed as an intergovernmental organization with a subscribed capital of €704.8 billion. The 19 members of the euro area are the shareholders and its lending capacity is around €500 billion. Like the EFSF, the ESM raises funds on the capital markets and will work with the IMF in dealing with member states who request assistance. The ESM is expected to be part of the solution to member states' problems in the future and will operate in conjunction with the fiscal compact in addressing the fiscal and structural problems facing member states. The ESM will only provide support if the member state seeking help agrees to implement fiscal adjustment and structural reform. Structural reform refers to changes in the labour and capital markets which are designed to help improve the efficiency of the economy. One of the elements of ESM support is a consideration of the situation of the member country and the overall stability of the euro area. If it is considered that the financial stability of the euro area is under threat then the ESM can provide support.

AUSTERITY POLICIES – TOO FAR TOO QUICKLY?

A feature of the sovereign debt crisis has been the adoption by a number of countries of austerity programmes – significant cuts in public spending, tax rises and structural reforms. In principle, it is easy to say that if a country is borrowing too much and has debt problems that it must cut its spending and raise more revenue. The practical implications of this policy are more complex. Not only are the people of the country where austerity programmes are implemented likely to be severely affected, if such policies are adopted during a period of weak economic activity, the effects are likely to be that national income will decline and unemployment rise. A deep and lasting recession in Greece, for example, means that the prospects for any growth-led recovery looked bleak; if a country like Greece is experiencing weak or negative GDP growth rates, then the chances of generating tax revenue to pay off debt and invest in improving the economy are slim. Firms are more likely to fail in such an environment and so corporate borrowing comes under pressure as the risk of default is higher. If corporate bond rates rise then firms will not be able to afford to borrow which further hampers the productive capacity of the economy. The periphery countries find themselves in a very difficult situation.

Austerity in the UK The UK also experienced a debt problem which the Coalition Government, elected in 2010, pledged to cut. Cuts in public spending and tax increases led to weak economic growth and the economy going back into recession in 2011 but from 2012, growth returned at around 2.0 per cent. There are many economists who agree that sorting out the UK's debt and deficit problem is important but there are also those that argue that the extent of the austerity measures introduced at a time of weak global economic growth was too much too quickly; they argued that policies focusing on growth ought to have taken priority, and would have resulted in a speedier return to growth and less damage to the economy.

Structural and Cyclical Deficits

The focus on public sector deficits raises questions about the difference between cyclical and structural deficits. A cyclical deficit occurs when government spending and income is disrupted by the 'normal' economic cycle. In times of strong economic growth government revenue from taxes will rise and spending on welfare and benefits will fall, resulting in public finances moving into surplus (or the deficit shrinks appreciably). In times of economic slowdown the opposite occurs and the size of the budget deficit will rise (or the surplus shrinks). A structural deficit refers to a situation where the deficit is not dependent on movements in the economic cycle but indicate that a government is 'living beyond its means' – spending what it has not got.

Economists are divided in their views about the nature and importance of structural deficits. What follows is a summary of the arguments on both sides.

Argument 1: Policymakers Need to Eradicate Structural Deficits The existence of a structural deficit implies that the public finances will be even worse when entering a recession, necessitating increasing levels of borrowing which is unsustainable in the long term. This was seen in examples of European government deficits in 2010 – some of the largest deficits in peacetime history created in part by governments committing to spending too much in the 'good times'.

As a result of the size of these deficits, the risk of default by governments on their debt is greater; increasingly they will find it difficult to service their debt and the cost of so doing will rise. This also creates uncertainty in financial markets and threatens the survival of the euro. As a result, fiscal consolidation is essential to reduce long-term interest rates and currency instability and help to promote economic growth. This fiscal consolidation should primarily be in the form of cuts in public spending rather than increases in taxes which may damage employment and investment.

Argument 2: The Idea of a Structural Deficit is a Myth The idea that government deficits are structural is unhelpful. The assumption is that governments have to borrow more because of the gap between income and expenditure, but how certain can we be that the only reason governments are borrowing money is simply due to the changes to public finances wrought by the recession? The whole notion of a structural deficit assumes that it is the amount governments borrow when the economy is operating at its trend level. This implies that to measure it we need to know how far the economy is operating below trend – the output gap.

The problem is that there is considerable disagreement on the size of the output gap. It is accepted that the recession will have destroyed some potential output but how much is open to some interpretation. There have been a number of studies attempting to quantify the impact of economic downturns on the output gap and the outcomes vary significantly. In the UK, the IFS estimated that the output loss of the economic downturn from 2008 was as much as 7.5 per cent whereas the Treasury estimates 5 per cent and other estimates put the gap as low as 2 per cent.

The size of the output gap is important because it has a direct effect on the cyclical component of the deficit – the larger the output gap the larger will be the cyclical component and the smaller the structural. This in turn affects any estimates of the size of borrowing when the economy does return to trend – in other words, the size of the structural deficit. Any calculations on the deficit would also be subject to assumptions about the sensitivity of taxes and spending to changes in GDP. How does tax revenue rise in relation to changes in GDP? This will depend in part on assumptions about the number of people who are able to find work as the economy expands but also on the extent to which potential output has been destroyed. How do changes in government spending vary in relation to changes in GDP? How many people will get off benefits and what effect will short-term fiscal stimulus measures have on spending?

As an increasing number of assumptions are made, calculations of the size of the structural deficit could be very different; which one should be used as the basis for policy decisions? In the light of this analysis is it useful to think of the idea of a structural deficit at all?

SELF TEST Explain why inaccurate information might affect forecasts of economic growth and thus the size of government budget deficits.

Fiscal Consolidation

The extent to which budget deficits should be a cause for concern is a persistent macroeconomic debate. Austerity measures imply that governments should consolidate fiscal policy to reduce deficits and 'balance the books'. In the UK, for example, the Chancellor of the Exchequer of the Conservative Government elected in 2015, George Osborne, repeatedly referred to 'balancing the budget' and in June 2015, suggested that the government should pass a law which would require future governments to maintain a budget surplus when the economy is growing. Whether a government should seek to balance budgets is a source of debate amongst economists. Our study of financial markets showed how budget deficits affect saving, investment and interest rates. But how big a problem are budget deficits?

Argument 1: The Government Should Balance its Budget When a government fails to balance its budget, it has to borrow money by issuing bonds in order to make up the shortfall. The most direct effect of high and rising government debt is to place a burden on future generations of taxpayers. When these debts and accumulated interest come due, future taxpayers will face a difficult choice. They can pay higher taxes, enjoy less government spending, or both, in order to make resources available to pay off the debt and accumulated interest. Or they can delay the day of reckoning and put the government into even deeper debt by borrowing once again to pay off the old debt and interest. In essence, when the government runs a budget deficit and issues government debt, it allows current taxpayers to pass the bill for some of their government spending on to future taxpayers. Inheriting such a large debt may lower the living standard of future generations.

In addition to this direct effect, budget deficits also have various macroeconomic effects. Because budget deficits represent *negative* public saving, they lower national saving (the sum of private and public saving). Reduced national saving causes real interest rates to rise and investment to fall. Reduced investment leads over time to a smaller stock of capital. A lower capital stock reduces labour productivity, real wages, and the economy's production of goods and services. Thus, when the government increases its debt, future generations are born into an economy with lower incomes as well as higher taxes.

There are, nevertheless, situations in which running a budget deficit is justifiable. Throughout history, the most common cause of increased government debt is war. When a military conflict raises government spending temporarily, it is reasonable to finance this extra spending by borrowing. Otherwise, taxes during wartime would have to rise precipitously. Such high tax rates would greatly distort the incentives faced by those who are taxed, leading to large deadweight losses. In addition, such high tax rates would be unfair to current generations of taxpayers, who already have to make the sacrifice of fighting the war.

Similarly, it is reasonable to allow a budget deficit during a temporary downturn in economic activity. When the economy goes into a recession, tax revenue falls automatically because income tax and payroll taxes are levied on measures of income, and transfer payments such as unemployment benefit increase. People also spend less so that government income from indirect taxes also falls. If the government tried to balance its budget during a recession, it would have to raise taxes or cut spending at a time of high unemployment. Such a policy would tend to depress AD at precisely the time it needed to be stimulated and, therefore, would tend to increase the magnitude of economic fluctuations. When the economy goes into recovery, however, the opposite is true: tax receipts grow as the level of economic activity rises and transfer payments tend to fall. The government should therefore be able to run a budget surplus and use the money to pay off the debt incurred by the budget deficit it ran during the recession; 'fixing the roof when the sun is shining' is how Mr Osborne referred to this in 2015.

Wars aside, therefore, over the course of the business cycle, there is no excuse for not balancing the budget. If the government runs a deficit when the economy is in a recession, it should run a comparable surplus when the economy recovers, so that on average the budget balances. Compared to the alternative of on-going budget deficits, a balanced budget – or, at least, a budget that is balanced over the economic cycle – means greater national saving, investment and economic growth. It means that future university graduates will enter a more prosperous economy.

Argument 2: The Government Should Not Balance its Budget The problem of government debt is often exaggerated. Although government debt does represent a tax burden on younger generations, it is often not large compared with the average person's lifetime income. The case for balancing the government budget is made by confusing the economics of a single person or household with that of a whole economy. Most of us would want to leave some kind of bequest to friends or relatives or a favourite charity when we die – or at least not leave behind large debts. Economies, unlike people, do not have finite lives – in some sense, they live forever, so there is never any reason to clear the debt completely.

Critics of budget deficits sometimes assert that government debt cannot continue to rise forever, but in fact it can have consequences. Just as a bank evaluating a loan application would compare a person's debts to their income, we should judge the burden of the government debt relative to the size of the nation's income. Population growth and technological progress cause the total income of the economy to grow over time. As a result, the nation's ability to pay interest on government debt grows over time as well. The focus should not be on looking at the total amount of debt but at the ratio of debt to income. As long as this is not increasing, then the level of debt is sustainable. In other words, as long as the level of government debt grows more slowly than the nation's income, there is nothing to prevent government debt from growing forever. Some numbers can put this into perspective. Suppose the output of the economy grows on average about 3 per cent per year. If the inflation rate averages around 2 per cent per year, then nominal income grows at a rate of 5 per cent per year. Government debt, therefore, can rise by 5 per cent per year without increasing the ratio of debt to income.

Moreover, it is misleading to view the effects of budget deficits in isolation. The budget deficit is just one piece of a large picture of how the government chooses to raise and spend money. In making these decisions over fiscal policy, policymakers affect different generations of taxpayers in many ways. The government's budget deficit or surplus should be considered together with these other policies. For example, suppose the government reduces the budget deficit by cutting spending on public investments, such as education. Does this policy make younger generations better off? The government debt will be smaller when they enter the labour force, which means a smaller tax burden. Yet if they are less well educated than they could be, their productivity and incomes will be lower. Many estimates of the return on schooling (the increase in a worker's wage that results from an additional year in school) find that it is quite large. Reducing the budget deficit rather than funding more education spending could, all things considered, make future generations worse off. A distinction has to be made between borrowing to finance investment, which helps boost the future productive capacity of the economy, and borrowing to finance current government expenditure (on things such as wages for public sector workers).

The qualification that the government budget on current expenditure will be balanced on average over the economic cycle allows for the effect of automatic stabilizers such as the increase in welfare expenditure and reduction in tax revenue that automatically occur in a recession (the opposite in a boom), and so help flatten out economic fluctuations. Allowing a budget deficit on investment expenditure is sensible because, although it leads to rising public debt, it also leads to further growth opportunities through spending on education, roads and so on. Just asserting that the government should balance its budget, irrespective of the economic cycle and irrespective of what kind of expenditures it is making, is overly simplistic.

SELF TEST Why might we wish to distinguish between government current expenditure and government investment expenditure, and take account of the economic cycle when judging whether the government should balance its budget?

Austerity or Growth?

The arguments outlined above crystallize the debate over the importance of austerity policies. Whilst there might be general agreement that countries do need to get more control over debt and their deficits, the current policies being adopted are, some argue, counterproductive.

In the UK, annual borrowing has fallen since 2010 and in the period April to December 2015, borrowing was £74.2 billion, £11.0 billion lower than the equivalent period in 2014. These figures compare favourably to the £153 billion borrowed in 2009–10. However, the Chancellor faces a challenge to move the government's finances into surplus by 2020, as promised in the election campaign of 2015 (which has since been 'dropped' following Brexit). Opposition politicians argued that the Coalition Government and the subsequent Conservative Government have gone too far too quickly with austerity, that the economy has been weakened as a result, and that the debt and deficit has not come down as planned. Why the difference of opinion?

One reason is the assumptions that underpin models used in calculating the effects of austerity. In the UK, the independent Office for Budget Responsibility (OBR) bases its calculations on the assumption of a fiscal multiplier of 0.5. In other words, every £1 of cuts in public spending would reduce economic output in the economy by 50p. The IMF have estimated the size of these fiscal multipliers to be much higher, at somewhere between 0.9 and 1.7. At the upper end of these estimates of the fiscal multiplier, the effect on the economy is considerable. Analysis has put the effect of the government's cuts at around 8 per cent of GDP over five years if the fiscal multiplier is assumed to be 1.3, about the middle of the IMF's range. The government of the UK would argue that even if the size of the fiscal multiplier was at this level, some of the effects would be offset by the level of quantitative easing by the Bank of England.

The Argument for Austerity Countries must take steps to get public finances under control. If attempts are made to increase borrowing to spend out of recession the effect will be increased inflation, higher borrowing costs across the whole of the EU and further uncertainty which threatens the whole of the euro area. There is also a moral dimension to the necessity for austerity – it is not fair to expect the taxpayers of countries which have maintained a sound fiscal stance, and abided by the rules of the euro area, to pay for the lax behaviour of governments in other countries.

In the short to medium term, the effects of austerity are considerable but the long-term benefits of sounder finances, improved structural reforms and a stronger banking sector will mean that all countries in Europe will be more competitive and in a position to benefit from stronger and more sustained economic growth in the future.

The Argument for Growth The main cause of the problems facing Europe stem from the financial system not from government debt. Austerity at a time of economic slowdown will affect economies considerably, and will be further exacerbated by the lack of credit in economies caused by banks seeking to recapitalize and rebuild their balance sheets. Without an adequate supply of credit, consumer spending and business investment will decline and lead to a prolonged and damaging period of economic depression. If output declines, tax revenues will fall and government spending on benefits will rise, and far from alleviating the debt crisis, will merely mean governments are forced to borrow more. The only way to solve the debt crisis is to get economies growing again. Governments need to adopt Keynesian style stimulus spending; stronger economic growth will lead to increased tax revenues; and if unemployment falls, government spending on welfare support drops, reducing the need to borrow.

A Resolution?

The debate over austerity and growth is far from resolved and indeed it is probably unfair to suggest that the argument is a simple split between those pushing to maintain austerity at all costs and those who want to abandon austerity and go for growth. The EU Commission issued a statement in the Spring of 2013 refuting suggestions that austerity policies lacked flexibility and that the necessity for growth was being ignored.

The Commission argued that the extent of the spreads on sovereign debt did indicate that there were legitimate concerns over the threat of default by some countries but acknowledged that there were also some speculative reasons for the extent of the spreads. It also points to the policy adopted by the ECB of outright monetary transactions (OMT) where the ECB buys the bonds of Europe's indebted countries to help push up the price and lower yields. This will not only help reduce the cost of servicing debt but also signals to the markets that the euro will be protected. To make such a policy credible, structural reforms and fiscal consolidation is necessary. Structural reforms, such as improving the flexibility of labour and product markets, will help to reduce wage and price rigidities, and take time to yield benefits but are essential if Europe is to be competitive in a global economy.

IN THE NEWS

Ireland

Ireland was one of the countries which suffered significantly as a consequence of the Financial Crisis. It sought a bailout and imposed harsh austerity policies. Have austerity policies been the driver to a successful recovery in the country?

Ireland and Economic Recovery

In the wake of the housing market collapse and the Financial Crisis, Ireland was one of the countries which was affected to a large extent. The Irish government had to seek a €64 billion bailout from the EU and IMF, and between 2007 and 2009, the economy shrunk by over 11 per cent. The austerity policies introduced by the government hit many people in Ireland hard; unemployment rose from around 4.5 per cent in 2007 to just over 15 per cent in 2010 and 2011, before beginning to

(*Continued*)

ease to around 8.6 per cent in early 2016. Ireland exited from the bailout in 2013 and public debt was expected to fall below 100 per cent of GDP in 2016, after reaching a high of 120 per cent of GDP in 2012–13. The improvements in the Irish economy have been partly put down to the acceptance of austerity measures by the government, and the country's attractiveness to global corporate giants such as Apple, Facebook, Google and Pfizer. A corporate tax rate of 12.5 per cent might help explain this attraction but there are other benefits to these firms too; the workforce is well educated and plentiful in supply and the relative weakness of the euro has helped exports. In early 2016, one of the credit ratings agencies, Fitch, upgraded Irish sovereign debt from A- to A. The accompanying report noted that strong growth in GDP of around 4 per cent was expected in 2016 and debt was expected to continue to fall to around 70 per cent of GDP by 2024. The Irish Taoiseach, Enda Kenny, at the time of the early stage in the austerity programme, noted that 'it's absolutely critical for governments to be able to bring people with them and to explain both the nature of the problem, the scale of that problem, the plan and the strategy to deal with it'. The way the Irish economy has emerged from the Financial Crisis has been observed with envy by other countries that were similarly affected but have not managed to grow and reduce debt in the way in which Ireland managed.

Questions

1 Why do you think that the Irish Taoiseach placed an emphasis on it being 'absolutely critical for governments to be able to bring people with them and to explain both the nature of the problem, the scale of that problem, the plan and the strategy to deal with it' in managing an orderly exit from an EU bailout?

2 To what extent do governments like Ireland and Greece have little option but to impose austerity measures if they are to sort out their public finances and restore confidence in banking systems?

3 Why is reducing public debt seen as being important in managing the sovereign debt of a nation?

4 Why is a low corporate tax rate appealing to large corporate entities like Apple and Google and to what extent is this a major reason for such companies locating in Ireland?

5 What do you think has been the most important reason for the improvement in the Irish economy from the problems it suffered as a result of the Financial Crisis?

Is there a brighter future for Ireland following the problems it faced after the Financial Crisis?

SUMMARY

- In addition to business cycles, economies can also experience financial cycles which tend to have longer amplitudes.

- The financial accelerator theory states that problems in financial markets can amplify shocks to the real economy. Benign economic conditions can lead to an increase in risk taking by banks and households, and debt levels increase. Whilst asset prices are rising, the financial sector and the real economy benefits from the expansion of debt.

- Ultimately, when asset prices fall, the effect on the banking sector and households can be extensive and emergence from financial crises tend to take much longer than downturns in business cycles due to real economy shocks.

- Inflation rate targeting may have been one factor contributing to the Financial Crisis given central banks' focus on inflation rather than debt or rising asset prices.

- Both central banks and regulators have come in for criticism about their role in the crisis and their response after, and reforms to banking systems and regulation continue to be discussed.

- The sovereign debt crisis developed as a result of the Financial Crisis. Countries experiencing economic slowdown were forced to borrow more and the extent of their debt created nervousness of the prospect of default.

- The spreads on sovereign debt widened into 2010 and 2011 and a number of countries had to seek financial assistance from the EU and IMF. The ESM represents a permanent mechanism to help support countries in financial difficulties.

- Part of the conditions for receiving assistance has been the implementation of austerity programmes which have further impacted on economic growth across the EU.

- A debate between the benefits of austerity and the need to promote growth has developed which is ongoing.

QUESTIONS FOR REVIEW

1 What is the difference between the 'financial economy' and the 'real economy'?

2 What is the difference between a financial cycle and a business cycle?

3 Why does a recovery from a Financial Crisis tend to take much longer than from a downswing caused by shocks to the real economy?

4 Briefly describe the theory of the 'financial accelerator'.

5 Why can mark-to-market accounting methods contribute to persistent increases in asset prices?

6 How did central banks respond to the Financial Crisis?

7 Why did governments such as those in Greece, Spain, Ireland, Portugal and Italy experience such a rise in deficits and debt in the wake of the Financial Crisis?

8 What is meant by the term 'contagion' in the context of the sovereign debt crisis?

9 What are the main arguments for the continuation of austerity programmes in countries which have experienced sovereign debt problems?

10 What are the main arguments against austerity programmes as a solution to the sovereign debt crisis?

PROBLEMS AND APPLICATIONS

1 To what extent do you think innovation in the financial sector is an indication of increased risk seeking? Justify your answer

2 In the face of a Financial Crisis such as that created by the dot.com collapse and the 9/11 terrorist attacks in the United States, why would a central bank have responded by lowering interest rates and flooding the markets with liquidity?

3 Why is it assumed that financial markets will continue to function normally in the event of a demand or supply side shock to the real economy, which causes a recession. What does 'function normally' mean in this context?

4 To what extent do you think that Minsky's Financial Instability Hypothesis (Chapter 26) is the most accurate theory to explain the Financial Crisis of 2007–9?

5 To what extent do you think that the response by central banks to the Financial Crisis was 'fragmented'?

6 Why have some critics argued that the cause of the sovereign debt crisis lies in the poor design of the euro system and the ability of countries within the euro area to free ride?

7 What is the role of the European Stability Mechanism in managing sovereign debt problems of member countries?

8 Governments across Europe have instituted austerity measures in an attempt to cut budget deficits which ballooned after the Financial Crisis. Are they right to do this if economic recovery is weak?

9 Suppose the government cuts taxes and increases spending, raising the budget deficit to 12 per cent of GDP. If nominal GDP is rising 7 per cent per year, are such budget deficits sustainable forever? Explain. If budget deficits of this size are maintained for 20 years, what is likely to happen to your taxes and your children's taxes in the future? Can you do something today to offset this future effect?

10 The chapter says that budget deficits reduce the income of future generations, but can boost output and income during a recession. Explain how both of these statements can be true.

GLOSSARY

ability-to-pay principle the idea that taxes should be levied on a person according to how well that person can shoulder the burden

abnormal profit the profit over and above normal profit

absolute advantage exists where a producer can produce a good using fewer factor inputs than another

absolute poverty a level of poverty where an individual does not have access to the basics of life – food, clothing and shelter

accounting profit total revenue minus total explicit cost

actual spending, saving or investment the realized or *ex post* outcome resulting from actions of households and firms

ad valorem tax a tax levied as a percentage of the price of a good

adaptive expectations a model which states that individuals and organizations base their expectations of inflation in the future on past actual inflation rates

adverse selection where a principal knows more about their situation than the agent, leading to the agent preferring not to do business with the principal

agent a person who is performing an act for another person, called the principal

aggregate demand curve a curve that shows the quantity of goods and services that households, firms and the government want to buy at each price level

aggregate risk risk that affects all economic actors at once

aggregate supply curve a curve that shows the quantity of goods and services that firms choose to produce and sell at each price level

allocative efficiency a resource allocation where the value of the output by sellers matches the value placed on that output by buyers

amplitude the difference between peak and trough and trend output

annual chain-linking a method of calculating GDP volume measures based on prices in the previous year

appreciation an increase in the value of a currency as measured by the amount of foreign currency it can buy

arbitrage the process of buying a good in one market at a low price and selling it in another market at a higher price in order to profit from the price difference

asymmetric information where two parties have access to different information

asymmetric shocks a situation where changes in aggregate demand and/or supply differ from one country to another

automatic stabilizers changes in fiscal policy that stimulate AD when the economy goes into a recession, without policymakers having to take any deliberate action

autonomous spending or autonomous expenditure spending which is not dependent on income/output

average fixed cost fixed costs divided by the quantity of output

average revenue total revenue divided by the quantity sold

average tax rate total taxes paid divided by total income

average total cost total cost divided by the quantity of output

average variable cost variable costs divided by the quantity of output

balanced budget where the total sum of money received by a government in tax revenue and interest is equal to the amount it spends, including on any debt interest owing

balanced trade a situation in which exports equal imports

bargaining process an agreed outcome between two interested and competing economic agents

barriers to entry anything which prevents a firm from entering a market or industry

barter the exchange of one good or service for another

benefits principle the idea that people should pay taxes based on the benefits they receive from government services

birth rate the number of people born per thousand of the population

bond a certificate of indebtedness

bounded rationality the idea that humans make decisions under the constraints of limited, and sometimes unreliable, information

brain drain the emigration of many of the most highly educated workers to rich countries

brand proliferation a strategy designed to deter entry to a market by producing a number of products within a product line as different brands

branding the means by which a business creates an identity for itself and highlights the way in which it differs from its rivals

budget constraint the limit on the consumption bundles that a consumer can afford

budget deficit where government tax revenue is less than spending and the government has to borrow to finance spending

budget surplus where government tax revenue is greater than spending because it receives more money than it spends

business cycle fluctuations in economic activity such as employment and production

capital flight a large and sudden reduction in the demand for assets located in a country

capital the equipment and structures used to produce goods and services

capitalist economic system a system which relies on the private ownership of factors of production to produce goods and services which are exchanged through a price mechanism and where production is operated primarily for profit

cartel a group of firms acting in unison

catch-up effect the property whereby countries that start off poor tend to grow more rapidly than countries that start off rich

central bank an institution designed to regulate the quantity of money in the economy

choice set the set of alternatives available to the consumer

classical dichotomy the theoretical separation of nominal and real variables

club goods goods that are excludable but non-rival in consumption

Coase theorem the proposition that if private parties can bargain without cost over the allocation of resources, they can solve the problem of externalities on their own

coincident indicator an indicator whose changes occur at the same time as changes in economic activity

collective bargaining the process by which unions and firms agree on the terms of employment

collusion an agreement among firms in a market about quantities to produce or prices to charge

commodity money money that takes the form of a commodity with intrinsic value

common currency area a geographical area throughout which a single currency circulates as the medium of exchange

common resources goods that are rival but not excludable

comparative advantage the comparison among producers of a good according to their opportunity cost. A producer is said to have a comparative advantage in the production of a good if the opportunity cost is lower than that of another producer

comparative statics the comparison of one initial static equilibrium with another

compensating differential a difference in wages that arises to offset the non-monetary characteristics of different jobs

competitive advantage the advantages a firm has over rivals which are both distinctive and defensible

competitive market a market in which there are many buyers and sellers so that each has a negligible impact on the market price

complements two goods for which an increase in the price of one leads to a decrease in the demand for the other

compounding the accumulation of a sum of money in, say, a bank account, where the interest earned remains in the account to earn additional interest in the future

concentration ratio the proportion of total market share accounted for by a particular number of firms

constant returns to scale the property whereby long-run average total cost stays the same as the quantity of output changes

constrained discretion a monetary policy framework which acknowledges a clear goal (or target) but allows policymakers the freedom to respond to economic, financial and political shocks using all the data available and their collective judgement

Consumer Prices Index a measure of the overall prices of the goods and services bought by a typical consumer

consumer surplus a buyer's willingness to pay minus the amount the buyer actually pays

consumption spending by households on goods and services, with the exception of purchases of new housing

contraction when real output is lower than the previous time period

copyright the right of an individual or organization to own things they create in the same way as a physical object, to prevent others from copying or reproducing the creation

cost of living how much money people need to maintain standards of living in terms of the goods and services they can afford to buy

cost the value of everything a seller must give up to produce a good

cost-benefit analysis a study that compares the costs and benefits to society of providing a public good

cost-push inflation a short-run cause of accelerating inflation due to higher input costs of firms which are passed on as higher consumer prices

countercyclical a variable that is below trend when GDP is above trend

cream-skimming a situation where a firm identifies parts of a market that are high in value added and seeks to exploit those markets

creative destruction the process where new technologies replace old ones and new skills are needed which render existing skills obsolete

credit default swap a means by which a bondholder can insure against the risk of default

credit risk the risk a bank faces in defaults on loans

cronyism a situation where the allocation of resources in the market is determined in part by political decision-making and favours rather than by economic forces

cross-price elasticity of demand a measure of how much the quantity demanded of one good responds to a change in the price of another good, computed as the percentage change in quantity demanded of the first good divided by the percentage change in the price of the second good

crowding out a decrease in investment that results from government borrowing

currency the paper banknotes and coins in the hands of the public

cyclical deficit a situation when government spending and income is disrupted by the deviations in the 'normal' economic cycle

cyclical unemployment the deviation of unemployment from its natural rate

de-merit goods goods that are over-consumed if left to the market mechanism and which generate both private and social costs which are not taken into account by the decision maker

dead labour labour used in the past to produce capital goods and raw materials used in the production of a good

deadweight loss the fall in total surplus that results from a market distortion, such as a tax

death rate the number of deaths per thousand of the population

deflation a fall in the price level over a period occurring when the inflation rate is less than 0 per cent

deflationary gap or output gap the difference between full employment output and expenditure when expenditure is less than full employment output

demand curve a graph of the relationship between the price of a good and the quantity demanded

demand deposits balances in bank accounts that depositors can access on demand by using a debit card

demand schedule a table that shows the relationship between the price of a good and the quantity demanded

depreciation a decrease in the value of a currency as measured by the amount of foreign currency it can buy

depression a severe recession

derived demand a situation where demand is determined by the supply in another market

deterministic trends trends that are constant, positive or negative, independent of time for the series being analyzed

diminishing marginal product the property whereby the marginal product of an input declines as the quantity of the input increases

diminishing marginal utility the tendency for the additional satisfaction from consuming extra units of a good to fall

direct taxes a tax levied on income and wealth

discount rate the interest rate at which the Federal Reserve lends on a short-term basis to the US banking sector

discrimination the offering of different opportunities to similar individuals who differ only by race, ethnic group, gender, age or other personal characteristics

diseconomies of scale the property whereby long-run average total cost rises as the quantity of output increases

disinflation the reduction in the rate of inflation

diversification the reduction of risk achieved by replacing a single risk with a large number of smaller unrelated risks

dominant strategy a strategy that is best for a player in a game regardless of the strategies chosen by the other players

double coincidence of wants a situation in exchange where two parties each have a good or service that the other wants and can thus enter into an exchange

economic activity how much buying and selling goes on in the economy over a period of time

economic agents an individual, firm or organization that has an impact in some way on an economy

economic growth the increase in the amount of goods and services in an economy over a period of time

economic mobility the movement of people among income classes

economic profit total revenue minus total cost, including both explicit and implicit costs

economic rent the amount a factor of production earns over and above its transfer earnings

economic system the way in which resources are organized and allocated to provide for the needs of an economy's citizens

economically inactive people who are not in employment or unemployed due to reasons such as being in full-time education, being full-time carers and raising families

economics the study of how society manages its scarce resources

economy all the production and exchange activities that take place

economies of scale the property whereby long-run average total cost falls as the quantity of output increases

effective demand the amount that people are not only willing to buy at different prices but what they can and do actually purchase

efficiency wages above-equilibrium wages paid by firms in order to increase worker productivity

efficiency the property of a resource allocation of maximizing the total surplus received by all members of society

efficient markets hypothesis (EMH) the theory that asset prices reflect all publicly available information about the value of an asset

efficient scale the quantity of output that minimizes average total cost

elasticity a measure of the responsiveness of quantity demanded or quantity supplied to one of its determinants

endogenous growth theory a theory that the rate of economic growth in the long-run, is determined by the rate of growth in total factor productivity and this total factor productivity is dependent on the rate at which technology progresses

endogenous variable a variable whose value is determined within the model

endowment effect where the value placed on something owned is greater than on an identical item not owned

Engel curve a line showing the relationship between demand and levels of income

entry limit pricing a situation where a firm will keep prices lower than they could be in order to deter new entrants

equilibrium or market price the price where the quantity demanded is the same as the quantity supplied

equilibrium quantity the quantity bought and sold at the equilibrium price

equity the property of distributing economic prosperity fairly among the members of society

European Central Bank the overall central bank of the 19 countries comprising the European Monetary Union

European Economic and Monetary Union the European currency union that has adopted the euro as its common currency

European Union a family of democratic European countries committed to working together for peace and prosperity

Eurosystem the system made up of the ECB plus the national central banks of each of the 19 countries comprising the European Monetary Union

excludable the property of a good whereby a person can be prevented from using it when they do not pay for it

exogenous variable a variable whose value is determined outside the model

expected utility theory the idea that preferences can and will be ranked by buyers

explicit costs input costs that require an outlay of money by the firm

exports goods produced domestically and sold abroad leading to an inflow of funds into a country

externality the cost or benefit of one person's decision on the well-being of a bystander (a third party) which the decision maker does not take into account when making the decision

falsifiability the possibility of a theory being rejected as a result of the new observations or new data

finance the field of economics that studies how people make decisions regarding the allocation of resources over time and the handling of risk

financial economy that part of the economy associated with the buying and selling of assets on financial markets

financial intermediaries financial institutions through which savers can indirectly provide funds to borrowers

financial markets financial institutions through which savers can directly provide funds to borrowers

financial system the group of institutions in the economy that help to match one person's saving with another person's investment

fiscal federalism a fiscal system for a group of countries involving a common fiscal budget and a system of taxes and fiscal transfers across countries

Fisher effect the one-for-one adjustment of the nominal interest rate to the inflation rate

fixed costs costs that are not determined by the quantity of output produced

fiat money money without intrinsic value that is used as money because of government decree

foreign direct investment capital investment that is owned and operated by a foreign entity

foreign portfolio investment investment that is financed with foreign money but operated by domestic residents

framing effect the differing response to choices dependent on the way in which choices are presented

free rider a person who receives the benefit of a good but avoids paying for it

frictional unemployment unemployment that results because it takes time for workers to search for the jobs that best suit their tastes and skills

full employment a point where those people who want to work at the going market wage level are able to find a job

fundamental analysis the study of a company's accounting statements and future prospects to determine its value

future value the amount of money in the future that an amount of money today will yield, given prevailing interest rates

game theory the study of how people behave in strategic situations

GDP at constant prices gross domestic product calculated using prices that existed at a particular base year which takes into account changes in inflation over time

GDP at current or market prices gross domestic product calculated by multiplying the output of goods and services by the price of those goods and services in the reporting year

GDP deflator a measure of the price level calculated as the ratio of nominal GDP to real GDP times 100

geographical immobility where people are unable to take work because of the difficulties associated with moving to different regions

Giffen good a good for which an increase in the price raises the quantity demanded

Gini coefficient a measure of the degree of inequality of income in a country

gold standard a system in which the currency is based on the value of gold and where the currency can be converted to gold on demand

government deficit a situation where a government spends more than it generates in tax revenue over a period

government failure a situation where political power and incentives distort decision-making so that decisions are made which conflict with economic efficiency

government spending spending on goods and services by local, state and national governments

Great Moderation the period of economic stability characterised by relatively low inflation, high employment, low unemployment and stable and persistent growth

gross domestic product (GDP) the market value of all final goods and services produced within a country in a given period of time

gross domestic product per capita the market value of all goods and services produced within a country in a given period of time divided by the population of a country to give a per capita figure

gross value added the contribution of domestic producers, industries and sectors to an economy

heuristics short cuts or rules of thumb that people use in decision-making

horizontal equity the idea that taxpayers with similar abilities to pay taxes should pay the same amount

human capital the accumulation of investments in people, such as education and on-the-job training

hyperinflation a period of extreme and accelerating increase in the price level

hysteresis the lagging effects of past economic events on future ones

idiosyncratic risk risk that affects only a single economic actor

imperfect competition exists where firms are able to differentiate their product in some way and so can have some influence over price

implicit costs input costs that do not require an outlay of money by the firm

import quota a limit on the quantity of a good that can be produced abroad and sold domestically

imports goods produced abroad and purchased for use in the domestic economy leading to an outflow of funds from a country

in-kind transfers transfers to the poor given in the form of goods and services rather than cash

income effect the change in consumption that results when a price change moves the consumer to a higher or lower indifference curve

income elasticity of demand a measure of how much quantity demanded of a good responds to a change in consumers' income, computed as the percentage change in quantity demanded divided by the percentage change in income

indexed the automatic correction of a money amount for the effects of inflation by law or contract

indifference curve a curve that shows consumption bundles that give the consumer the same level of satisfaction

indirect tax a tax levied on the sale of goods and services

inferior good a good for which, ceteris paribus, an increase in income leads to a decrease in demand (and vice versa)

inflation rate the percentage change in the price index from the preceding period

inflation tax the revenue the government raises by creating money

inflation an increase in the overall level of prices in the economy

inflationary gap the difference between full employment output and actual expenditure when actual expenditure is greater than full employment output

informationally efficient reflecting all available information in a rational way

interest elasticity of demand and supply the responsiveness of the demand and supply of loanable funds to changes in the interest rate

internalizing an externality altering incentives so that people take account of the external effects of their actions

intertemporal choice where decisions made today can affect choices facing individuals in the future

intertemporal substitution effect the response of economic actors to changes in the interest rate by changing consumption and savings decisions

interventionist supply-side policies policies focused on improving the working of markets through investing in infrastructure, education and research and development

investment or mutual fund an institution that sells shares to the public and uses the proceeds to buy a portfolio of stocks and bonds

investment spending on capital equipment, inventories and structures, including household purchases of new housing

involuntary unemployment where people want work at going market wage rates but cannot find employment

isocost line a line showing the different combination of factor inputs which can be purchased with a given budget

job search the process by which workers find appropriate jobs given their tastes and skills

labour force participation rate (or economic activity rate) the percentage of the adult population that is in the labour force

labour force labour force the total number of workers, including both the employed and the unemployed

labour the human effort both mental and physical that goes in to production

Laffer curve the relationship between tax rates and tax revenue

lagging indicator an indicator whose changes occur after changes in economic activity have occurred

land all the natural resources of the earth

law of demand the claim that, other things equal (*ceteris paribus*) the quantity demanded of a good falls when the price of the good rises

law of supply and demand the claim that the price of any good adjusts to bring the quantity supplied and the quantity demanded for that good into balance

law of supply the claim that, ceteris paribus, the quantity supplied of a good rises when the price of a good rises

leading indicator an indicator which can be used to foretell future changes in economic activity

leveraging borrowing funds for investment in the expectation of a return

liberalism the political philosophy according to which the government should choose policies deemed to be just, as evaluated by an impartial observer behind a 'veil of ignorance'

libertarianism the political philosophy according to which the government should punish crimes and enforce voluntary agreements but not redistribute income

life cycle the regular pattern of income variation over a person's life

liquidity risk the risk that a bank may not be able to fund demand for withdrawals

liquidity the ease with which an asset can be converted into the economy's medium of exchange

living labour labour utilised in the production of the good itself

living wage an hourly rate set independently, based on an estimation of minimum household needs which provide an 'acceptable' standard of living in the UK

logrolling the agreement between politicians to exchange support on an issue

long run the period of time in which all factors of production can be altered

Lorenz curve the relationship between the cumulative percentage of households and the cumulative percentage of income

lump-sum tax a tax that is the same amount for every person

macroeconomics the study of economy-wide phenomena, including inflation, unemployment and economic growth

macroprudential policy policies designed to limit the risk across the financial sector by focusing on improving 'prudential' standards of operation that enhance stability and reduce risk

marginal abatement cost the cost expressed in terms of the last unit of pollution not emitted (abated)

marginal changes small incremental adjustments to a plan of action

marginal cost the increase in total cost that arises from an extra unit of production

marginal product of labour the increase in the amount of output from an additional unit of labour

marginal product the increase in output that arises from an additional unit of input

marginal propensity to consume the fraction of extra income that a household consumes rather than saves

marginal propensity to save the fraction of extra income that a household saves rather than consumes

marginal rate of substitution the rate at which a consumer is willing to trade one good for another

marginal rate of technical substitution the rate at which one factor input can be substituted for another at a given level of output

marginal revenue product the extra revenue a firm gets from hiring an additional unit of a factor of production

marginal revenue the change in total revenue from an additional unit sold

marginal tax rate the extra taxes paid on an additional unit of income

marginal utility the addition to total utility as a result of consuming one extra unit of a good

mark to market an accounting procedure which records the 'fair value' of an asset on financial institutions' balance sheets

market a group of buyers and sellers of a particular good or service

market economy an economy that addresses the three key questions of the economic problem by allocating resources through the decentralized decisions of many firms and households as they interact in markets for goods and services

market failure a situation where scarce resources are not allocated to their most efficient use

market for loanable funds the market in which those who want to save supply funds, and those who want to borrow to invest demand funds

market power the ability of a single economic agent (or small group of agents) to have a substantial influence on market prices or output

market segments the breaking down of customers into groups with similar buying habits or characteristics

market share the proportion of total sales in a market accounted for by a particular firm

market-orientated supply-side policies policies designed to free up markets to improve resource allocation through more effective price signals

maximin criterion the claim that the government should aim to maximize the well-being of the worst-off person in society

medium of exchange an item that buyers give to sellers when they want to purchase goods and services

menu costs the costs of changing prices

merit goods goods which can be provided by the market but may be under-consumed as a result of imperfect information about the benefits

microeconomics the study of how households and firms make decisions and how they interact in markets

migration rate the difference between the number of people entering a country from abroad and the number leaving

minimum wage the lowest price an employer may legally pay to a worker

model of aggregate demand and aggregate supply the model that many economists use to explain short-run fluctuations in economic activity around its long-run trend

monetary neutrality the proposition that changes in the money supply do not affect real variables

monetary policy the set of actions taken by the central bank in order to affect the money supply

money market the market in which the commercial banks lend money to one another on a short-term basis

money stock the quantity of money circulating in the economy

money supply the quantity of money available in the economy

money the set of assets in an economy that people regularly use to buy goods and services from other people

monopolistic competition a market structure in which many firms sell products that are similar but not identical

monopoly a firm that is the sole seller of a product without close substitutes

monopsony a market in which there is a single (or dominant) buyer

moral hazard the tendency of a person who is imperfectly monitored to engage in dishonest or otherwise undesirable behaviour

multiplier effect the additional shifts in aggregate demand that result when expansionary fiscal policy increases income and thereby increases consumer spending

negative externality the costs imposed on a third party of a decision

negative income tax a tax system that collects revenue from high-income households and gives transfers to low-income households

Nash equilibrium a situation in which economic actors interacting with one another each choose their best strategy given the strategies that all the other actors have chosen

national debt the accumulation of the total debt owed by a government

national saving (saving) the total income in the economy that remains after paying for consumption and government purchases

natural monopoly a monopoly that arises because a single firm can supply a good or service to an entire market at a smaller cost than could two or more firms

natural rate of output the output level in an economy when all existing factors of production (land, labour, capital and technology resources) are fully utilized and where unemployment is at its natural rate

natural rate of unemployment the normal rate of unemployment around which the unemployment rate fluctuates

natural resources the inputs into the production of goods and services that are provided by nature, such as land, rivers and mineral deposits

natural-rate hypothesis the claim that unemployment eventually returns to its normal, or natural, rate, regardless of the rate of inflation

neoclassical synthesis the idea that markets can be slow to adjust in the short run due to sticky prices and sticky wages but revert to long-run classical principles which could be aided by appropriate use of fiscal and monetary policies

net capital outflow the purchase of foreign assets by domestic residents minus the purchase of domestic assets by foreigners

net exports spending on domestically produced goods and services by foreigners (exports) minus spending on foreign goods by domestic residents (imports)

nominal exchange rate the rate at which a person can trade the currency of one country for the currency of another

nominal GDP the production of goods and services valued at current prices

nominal interest rate the interest rate as usually reported without a correction for the effects of inflation

nominal variables variables measured in monetary units

non-price competition a situation where two or more firms seek to increase demand and market share by methods other than through changing price

nonstationary data time-series data where the mean value can either rise or fall over time

normal good a good for which, ceteris paribus, an increase in income leads to an increase in demand (and vice versa)

normal profit the minimum amount required to keep factors of production in their current use

normative statements claims that attempt to prescribe how the world should be

objective well-being measures of the quality of life using specified indicators.

occupational immobility where workers are unable to easily move from one occupation to another

Okun's law a 'law' which is based on observations that in order to keep the unemployment rate steady, real GDP needs to grow at or close to its potential

oligopoly competition amongst the few – a market structure in which only a few sellers offer similar or identical products and dominate the market

open market operations the purchase and sale of non-monetary assets from and to the banking sector by the central bank

opportunity cost whatever must be given up to obtain some item; the value of the benefits foregone (sacrificed)

optimum currency area a group of countries for which it is optimal to adopt a common currency and form a currency union

originator a bank or financial institution that securitizes assets

outright open market operations the outright sale or purchase of non-monetary assets to or from the banking sector by the central bank without a corresponding agreement to reverse the transaction at a later date

Pareto improvement when an action makes at least one economic agent better off without harming another economic agent

participation rate (or economic activity rate) the percentage of the adult population that is in the labour force

patent the right conferred on the owner to prevent anyone else making or using an invention or manufacturing process without permission

payoff matrix a table showing the possible combination of outcomes (payoffs) depending on the strategy chosen by each player

peak a point where related economic variables begin to decline

perfect complements two goods with right-angle indifference curves

perfect price discrimination a situation in which the monopolist knows exactly the willingness to pay of each customer and can charge each customer a different price

perfect substitutes two goods with straight line indifference curves

permanent income a person's normal income

Phillips curve a curve that shows the short run trade-off between inflation and unemployment

Pigovian tax a tax enacted to correct the effects of a negative externality

planned economic systems economic activity organized by central planners who decided on the answers to the fundamental economic questions

planned spending, saving or investment the desired or intended actions of households and firms

positional arms race a situation where individuals invest in a series of measures designed to gain them an advantage but which simply offset each other

positional externality purchases or decisions which alter the context of the evaluation by an individual of the positional good

positive equity the positive difference between the principal borrowed on a house and its value

positive externality the benefits to a third party of a decision

positive statements claims that attempt to describe the world as it is

poverty line an absolute level of income set by the government below which a family is deemed to be in poverty. In the UK and Europe this is measured by earnings less than 60 per cent of median income

poverty rate the percentage of the population whose family income falls below an absolute level called the poverty line

Prebisch–Singer hypothesis a hypothesis suggesting that the rate at which primary products exchange for manufactured goods declines over time meaning that countries specialising in primary good production become poorer

predatory or destroyer pricing a situation where firms hold price below average cost for a period to try and force out competitors or prevent new firms from entering the market

present value the amount of money today that would be needed to produce, using prevailing interest rates, a given future amount of money

price ceiling a legal maximum on the price at which a good can be sold

price discrimination the business practice of selling the same good at different prices to different customers

price elasticity of demand a measure of how much the quantity demanded of a good responds to a change in the price of that good, computed as the percentage change in quantity demanded divided by the percentage change in price

price elasticity of supply a measure of how much the quantity supplied of a good responds to a change in the price of that good, computed as the percentage change in quantity supplied divided by the percentage change in price

price floor a legal minimum on the price at which a good can be sold

price level a snapshot of the prices of goods and services in an economy at a particular period of time

price–consumption curve a line showing the consumer optimum for two goods as the price of one of the goods changes, assuming incomes and the price of the good are held constant

principal a person for whom another person, called the agent, is performing some act

prisoners' dilemma a particular 'game' between two captured prisoners that illustrates why cooperation is difficult to maintain even when it is mutually beneficial

private goods goods that are both excludable and rival

private saving the income that households have left after paying for taxes and consumption

private sector that part of the economy where business activity is owned, financed and controlled by private individuals

privatization the transfer of public ownership of assets to the private sector

privatization the transfer of publicly owned assets to private sector ownership

procyclical a variable that is above trend when GDP is above trend

producer prices index a measure of the prices of a basket of goods and services bought by firms

producer surplus the amount a seller is paid for a good minus the seller's cost

production function the relationship between the quantity of inputs used to make a good and the quantity of output of that good

production isoquant a function representing all possible combinations of factor inputs that can be used to produce a given level of output

production possibilities frontier a graph that shows the combinations of output that the economy can possibly produce given the available factors of production and technology

productivity the quantity of goods and services produced from each hour of a worker or factor of production's time

progressive tax a tax for which high-income taxpayers pay a larger fraction of their income than do low-income taxpayers

property rights the exclusive right of an individual, group or organization to determine how a resource is used

proportional tax (or **flat tax**) a tax for which high-income and low-income taxpayers pay the same fraction of income

prospect theory a theory that suggests people attach different values to gains and losses and do so in relation to some reference point

public choice theory the analysis of governmental behaviour, and the behaviour of individuals who interact with government

public goods goods that are neither excludable nor rival

public interest making decisions based on a principle where the maximum benefit is gained by the largest number of people at minimum cost

public saving the tax revenue that the government has left after paying for its spending

public sector that part of the economy where business activity is owned, financed and controlled by the state, and goods and services are provided by the state on behalf of the population as a whole

purchasing power parity a theory of exchange rates whereby a unit of any given currency should be able to buy the same quantity of goods in all countries

quantity demanded the amount of a good that buyers are willing and able to purchase at different prices

quantity equation the equation ($M \times V = P \times Y$), which relates the quantity of money, the velocity of money, and the currency value of the economy's output of goods and services

quantity supplied the amount of a good that sellers are willing and able to sell at different prices

quantity theory of money a theory asserting that the quantity of money available determines the price level and that the growth rate in the quantity of money available determines the inflation rate

random walk the path of a variable whose changes are impossible to predict

rational expectations the theory according to which people optimally use all the information they have, including information about government policies, when forecasting the future

rational ignorance effect the tendency of a voter to not seek out information to make an informed choice in elections

real economy that part of the economy which is concerned with the production of goods and services

real exchange rate the rate at which the goods and services of one country trade for the goods and services of another

real GDP the measure of the value of output in the economy which takes into account changes in prices over time

real interest rate the interest rate corrected for the effects of inflation

real money balances what money can actually buy given the ratio of the money supply to the price level $\frac{M}{P}$

real variables variables measured in physical units

real wage the money wage adjusted for inflation, measured by the ratio of the wage rate to price $\frac{W}{P}$

recession a period of declining real incomes and rising unemployment. The technical definition gives recession occurring after two successive quarters of negative economic growth

refinancing rate the interest rate at which the European Central Bank lends on a short-term basis to the euro area banking sector

regressive tax a tax for which high-income taxpayers pay a smaller fraction of their income than do low-income taxpayers

regulatory capture a situation where regulatory agencies become unduly influenced and dominated by the industries they are supposed to be regulating

relative position the idea that humans view their own position against a reference point which provides a means of comparison on feelings of well-being

relative poverty a situation where an individual is not able to access what would be considered acceptable standards of living in society

relative prices price expressed in terms of how much of one good has to be given up in purchasing another

rent seeking where individuals or groups take actions to redirect resources to generate income (rents) for themselves or the group

repo rate the interest rate at which the Bank of England lends on a short-term basis to the UK banking sector

repurchase agreement the sale of a non-monetary asset together with an agreement to repurchase it at a set price at a specified future date

retail banking the core banking service of taking in deposits and making loans to households and businesses

risk averse exhibiting a dislike of uncertainty

risk the probability of something happening which results in a loss or some degree of hazard or damage

rival the property of a good whereby one person's use diminishes other people's use

sacrifice ratio the number of percentage points of annual output lost in the process of reducing inflation by 1 percentage point

satisficers those who make decisions based on securing a satisfactory rather than optimal outcome

sovereign debt the bonds issued by national governments to finance expenditure

saving or investment the realized or ex post outcome resulting from actions of households and firms

Say's law an argument that production or supply is a source of demand, that supply creates its own demand

scarcity the limited nature of society's resources

screening an action taken by an uninformed party to induce an informed party to reveal information

securitization the packaging of mortgage-backed securities into pools of debt and selling them on

shadow banking system financial intermediaries acting like banks but which are outside the scope of regulation

shoeleather cost the resources wasted when inflation encourages people to reduce their money holdings

shortage a situation in which quantity demanded is greater than quantity supplied at the going market price

short run the period of time in which some factors of production cannot be changed

signalling an action taken by an informed party to reveal private information to an uninformed party

Single European Market a (still not complete) EU-wide market throughout which labour, capital, goods and services can move freely

social security government benefits that supplement the incomes of the needy

social welfare function the collective utility of society which is reflected by consumer and producer surplus

socially necessary time the quantity of labour necessary under average conditions of labour productivity to produce a given commodity

special purpose vehicle an entity set up to issue bonds to investors to raise finance to buy collections of assets

special-interest effect where benefits to a minority special-interest group are outweighed by the costs imposed on the majority

specific tax a fixed rate tax levied on goods and services expressed as a sum per unit

spread the difference between the average interest banks earn on assets and the average interest rate paid on liabilities

stagflation a period of falling output and rising prices

standard of living refers to the amount of goods and services that can be purchased by the population of a country. Usually measured by the inflation-adjusted (real) income per head of the population

stationary data time-series data that has a constant mean value over time

steady-state equilibrium the point in a growing economy where investment spending is the same as spending on depreciation and the capital–output ratio remains constant

stochastic trend where trend variables change by some random amount in each time period

stock (or share or equity) a claim to partial ownership and the future profits in a firm

store of value an item that people can use to transfer purchasing power from the present to the future

strike the organized withdrawal of labour from a firm by a union

structural deficit a situation where a government's deficit is not dependent on movements in the economic cycle

structural unemployment unemployment that results because the number of jobs available in some labour markets is insufficient to provide a job for everyone who wants one

sub-prime market individuals not traditionally seen as being part of the financial markets because of their high credit risk

subjective well-being the way in which people evaluate their own happiness

subsidy payment to buyers and sellers to supplement income or lower costs and which thus encourages consumption or provides an advantage to the recipient

substitutes two goods for which an increase in the price of one leads to an increase in the demand for the other (and vice versa)

substitution effect the change in consumption that results when a price change moves the consumer along a given indifference curve to a point with a new marginal rate of substitution

sunk cost a cost that has already been committed and cannot be recovered

supply curve a graph of the relationship between the price of a good and the quantity supplied

supply schedule a table that shows the relationship between the price of a good and the quantity supplied

supply shock an event that directly alters firms' costs and prices, shifting the economy's AS curve and thus the Phillips curve

surplus a situation in which the quantity supplied is greater than the quantity demanded at the going market price

synergies where the perceived benefits of the combined operations of a merged organization are greater than those which would arise if the firms stayed separate

systemic risk the risk of failure across the whole of the financial sector

tacit collusion when firm behaviour results in a market outcome that appears to be anti-competitive but has arisen because firms acknowledge that they are interdependent

tariff a tax on goods produced abroad and sold domestically

tax incidence the manner in which the burden of a tax is shared among participants in a market

technological knowledge society's understanding of the best ways to produce goods and services

theory of liquidity preference Keynes' theory that the interest rate adjusts to bring money supply and money demand into balance

time-series data observations on a variable over a time-period and which are ordered over time

total expenditure the amount paid by buyers, computed as the price of the good times the quantity purchased

total revenue the amount received by sellers of a good, computed as the price of the good times the quantity sold

total surplus the total value to buyers of the goods, as measured by their willingness to pay, minus the cost to sellers of providing those goods

total utility the satisfaction gained from the consumption of a good

trade balance the value of a nation's exports minus the value of its imports; also called net exports

trade deficit an excess of imports over exports

trade policy a government policy that directly influences the quantity of goods and services that a country imports or exports

trade surplus an excess of exports over imports

tragedy of the commons a parable that illustrates why common resources get used more than is desirable from the standpoint of society as a whole

tranching the splitting up bundles of debt into different levels of risk

transactions costs the costs that parties incur in the process of agreeing and following through on a bargain

transfer earnings the minimum payment required to keep a factor of production in its current use

transfer payment a payment for which no good or service is exchanged

trend the underlying long term movement in a data series

trough the point where related economic variables begin to rise

utilitarianism the political philosophy according to which the government should choose policies to maximize the total utility of everyone in society

unemployment insurance a government programme that partially protects workers' incomes when they become unemployed

unemployment rate the percentage of the labour force that is unemployed

union density a measure of the proportion of the workforce that is unionized

union a worker association that bargains with employers over wages and working conditions

unit of account the yardstick people use to post prices and record debts

utility the satisfaction derived from the consumption of a certain quantity of a product

value of the marginal product the marginal product of an input times the price of the output

variable costs costs that are dependent on the quantity of output produced

velocity of money the rate at which money changes hands

vertical equity the idea that taxpayers with a greater ability to pay taxes should pay larger amounts

voluntary unemployment where people choose to remain unemployed rather than take jobs which are available

wealth the total of all stores of value, including both money and non-monetary assets

welfare economics the study of how the allocation of resources affects economic well-being

wholesale banking that part of banking dealing with corporate finance and investment in financial instruments

willingness to pay the maximum amount that a buyer will pay for a good

world price the price of a good that prevails in the world market for that good

INDEX

CREDITS

IMAGES

The following images have been reproduced with the kind permission of the copyright holders:

Image 1.1 Incentives are a powerful influence ... p. 12. *Source*: © Lightspring/Shutterstock

Image 2.1 Discussions over the relative costs ... p. 26. *Source*: © Hakan Kiziltan/Shutterstock

Image 2.2 Understanding the implications ... p. 28. *Source*: © Sam72/Shutterstock

Image 3.1 The market for wheat has a number of characteristics of a perfect ... p. 45. *Source*: © Xen0phile/Thinkstock

Image 3.2 The demand for ... p. 52. *Source*: © maciek905/Thinkstock

Image 4.1 Copy piracy is ... p. 72. *Source*: © alexskopje/Thinkstock

Image 4.2 Tax relief is one ... p. 75. *Source*: © Chris Howes/Wild Places Photography/Alamy Stock Photo

Image 5.1 The supermarket may tell ... p. 93. *Source*: © webking/Thinkstock

Image 5.2 Improvements in technology ... p. 108. *Source*: © wenht/Thinkstock

Image 6.1 As the size ... p. 126. *Source*: © tcly/Thinkstock

Image 6.2 Will Bitcoin ever become a widely used ... p. 141. *Source*: © 3DSculptor/Thinkstock

Image 7.1 What are the real ... p. 151. *Source*: © Milenko Bokan/Thinkstock

Image 7.2 Healthy lifestyle choices can improve overall well ... p. 160. *Source*: © Purestock/Thinkstock

Image 8.1 The design of policies in towns and cities can lead ... p. 167. *Source*: © akiyoko/Thinkstock

Image 8.2 Coal-fired power like ... p. 176. *Source*: © pumpapictures/Thinkstock

Image 9.1 Taxes on income ... p. 189. *Source*: © ShaunWilkinson/Thinkstock

Image 9.2 Scandinavian countries often top happiness surveysp. 194. *Source*: © Cn0ra/Thinkstock

Image 10.1 Common land doesn't always result in tragedy!p. 205. *Source*: © marinzolich/Thinkstock

Image 10.2 Reform of fisheries ... p. 208. *Source*: © Stockbyte/Thinkstock

Image 11.1 The pressure to reduce ... p. 225. *Source*: © Stocktrek Images/Thinkstock

Image 11.2 Fracking remains a highly ... p. 233. *Source*: © doranjclark/Thinkstock

Image 12.1 Giving gifts can ... p. 242. *Source*: © sam74100/Thinkstock

Image 12.2 Behavioural economics ... p. 247. *Source*: © hroe/Thinkstock

Image 13.1 How do businessess ... p. 258. *Source*: © Felipe Dupouy/Thinkstock

Image 13.2 Reional support can ... p. 259. *Source*: © Top Photo Corporation/Thinkstock

Image 14.1 Would the merger of ... p. 267. *Source*: © nata-lunata/Shutterstock

Image 14.2 Barriers to entry in the ... p. 283. *Source*: © Amar and Isabelle Guillen - Guillen Photo LLC/Alamy Stock Photo

Image 15.1 Advertising is all ... p. 294. *Source*: © Purestock/Thinkstock

Image 15.2 The fast food company ... p. 298. *Source*: © Stars and Stripes/Alamy Stock Photo

Image 16.1 Game theory provides an ... p. 315. *Source*: © BananaStock/Thinkstock

Image 16.2 The brewing industry ... p. 320. *Source*: © Rodolfo Arpia/Alamy Stock Photo

Image 17.1 Would you continue ... p. 332. *Source*: © Martynasfoto/Thinkstock

Image 17.2 Are the benefits ... p. 352. *Source*: © Wolfilser/Shutterstock

Image 18.1 Inequality remains high ... p. 363. *Source*: © dabldy/Thinkstock

Image 18.2 A key thrust of ... p. 374. *Source*: © Nathan King/Alamy Stock Photo

Image 19.1 Indian workers face ... p. 401. *Source*: © Purestock/Thinkstock

Image 19.2 The closure of steel ... p. 405. *Source*: © Dermot Blackburn/Alamy Stock Photo

Image 20.1 The complexity of ... p. 423. *Source*: © Stockbyte/Thinkstock

Image 20.2 There are many factors that ... p. 431. *Source*: © Purestock/Thinkstock

Image 21.1 Gone with the Wind ... p. 444. *Source*: © robertharding/Alamy Stock Photo

Image 21.2 Double-digit Uruguayan ... p. 446. *Source*: © W101/Thinkstock

Image 22.1 Does the development of a ... p. 460. *Source*: © Nenadpress/Thinkstock

Image 22.2 Growth of China may ... p. 473. *Source*: © silkwayrain/Thinkstock

Image 23.1 Long-term unemployment ... p. 488. *Source*: © Nikolas Georgiou/Alamy Stock Photo

Image 23.2 Unemployment rates in UK ... p. 495. *Source*: © Roger Bamber/Alamy Stock Photo

Image 24.1 Understanding the difference ... p. 509. *Source*: © Wavebreakmedia Ltd/Thinkstock

Image 24.2 Road construction may be ... p. 516. *Source*: © wabeno/Thinkstock

Image 25.1 David Li was referred to ... p. 528. *Source*: © Ken Tam/Alamy Stock Photo

Image 25.2 Could present value ... p. 530. *Source*: © nito100/Thinkstock

LIST OF FORMULAS

Average Fixed Cost:

$$AFC = \frac{FC}{Q}$$

Average Revenue:

$$AR = \frac{Total\ Revenue}{Output}$$

Average Tax Liability:

$$ATR = \frac{Tax\ liability}{Taxable\ income}$$

Average Total Cost:

$$ATC = \frac{TC}{Q}$$

Average Variable Cost:

$$AVC = \frac{VC}{Q}$$

Chain-Weighted GDP Deflator:

$Chain\text{-}weighted\ GDP\ deflator\ in\ Year\ X =$

$$\frac{Nominal\ GDP_{Year\ X}}{Real\ GDP\ at\ average\ prices} \times 100$$

Classical Quantity Theory of Money:

$MV = PY$
$M_d = kPY$

Comparing Inflation Over Time:

$$\frac{Amount\ in}{today's\ curency} = \frac{amount\ in\ year}{t\ currency} \times \frac{Price\ level\ today}{Price\ level\ in\ year\ t}$$

Consumer Optimum in the Standard Economic Model:

$$\frac{MUx}{Px} = \frac{MUy}{Py}$$

Consumer Prices Index:

$$CPI_{year\ t} = \frac{Cost\ of\ basket\ of\ goods\ in\ year\ t\ prices}{Cost\ of\ basket\ of\ goods\ in\ base\ year\ prices}$$

Cross-Price Elasticity of Demand:

$$\frac{Cross\text{-}price\ elasticity}{of\ demand} = \frac{Percentage\ change\ in\ quantity\ demanded\ of\ good\ 1}{Percentage\ change\ in\ the\ price\ of\ good\ 2}$$

Deviation of Output from the Natural Rate:

$Q = NRQ + a\ (APL - EPL)$

Entry Point:

Enter if $P > ATC$

Exit Point:

Exit if $P < ATC$

Expectations Augmented Phillips Curve:

$\Delta\pi_t = E_t\Delta\pi_t + 1 + (NP_t - PY_t)$

Gini Coefficient:

$$Gini\ coefficient = \frac{Area\ between\ the\ line\ of\ perfect\ income\ equality\ and\ Lorenz\ curve}{Area\ under\ the\ line\ of\ perfect\ income\ equality}$$

Gross Domestic Product (Expenditure Method):

$GDP\ (Y) = C + I + G + NX$

GDP Deflator:

$$GDP\ Deflator = \left(\frac{Nominal\ GDP}{Real\ GDP}\right) \times 100$$

Growth Rate of Real GDP:

$$Growth\ rate\ of\ real\ GDP\ in\ year\ t = \frac{(GDP_t - GDP_{t-1})}{GDP_{t-1} - 1}$$

Income Elasticity of Demand:

$$Income\ elasticity\ of\ demand = \frac{Percentage\ change\ in\ quantity\ demanded}{Percentage\ change\ in\ income}$$

Inflation rate between consecutive years:

$$Inflation_{year\ t} = \frac{(Price\ index_{year\ t}) - (Price\ index_{year\ t-1})}{(Price\ index_{year\ t-1})} \times 100$$

Implicit GDP Deflator

$$Implicit\ GDP\ Deflator = \frac{Nominal\ GDP}{Real\ GDP} \times 100$$

Labour Force Participation Rate:

$$Labour\ force\ participation\ rate = \left(\frac{Labour\ force}{Adult\ population}\right) \times 100$$

Marginal Cost:

$$MC = \frac{\Delta TC}{\Delta Q}$$

$$MC = \frac{dTC}{dQ}$$

Marginal Propensity to Consume:

$$MPC = \frac{\Delta C}{\Delta Y}$$

Marginal Product of Capital

$$MP_K = \frac{change\ in\ the\ quantity\ of\ output\,(\Delta Q)}{change\ in\ the\ quantity\ of\ capital\,(\Delta K)}$$

Marginal Product of a Factor:

$$MP_F = \frac{change\ in\ total\ product}{change\ in\ quantity\ of\ the\ factor}$$

Marginal Product of Labour

$$MP_L = \frac{change\ in\ the\ quantity\ of\ output\ (\Delta Q)}{change\ in\ the\ quantity\ of\ labour\ (\Delta L)}$$

Marginal Propensity to Save:

$$MPS = \frac{\Delta S}{\Delta Y}$$

Marginal Rate of Substitution:

$$MRS = \left(\frac{MUx}{MUy}\right)$$

Marginal Rate of Technical Substitution

$$MRTS = \frac{MP_L}{MP_K}$$

Marginal Revenue:

$$MR = \frac{\Delta TR}{\Delta Q}$$

Marginal Tax Rate

$$MTR = \frac{Change\ in\ tax\ liability}{Change\ in\ the\ taxable\ income}$$

Market Equilibrium:

Market Equilibrium occurs where $Qd = Qs$

Multiplier (k):

$$Multiplier = \frac{1}{(1 - MPC)}$$

$$Multiplier = \frac{1}{MPS}$$

$$k = \frac{1}{MPS + MPT + MPM}$$

$$k = \frac{1}{MPW}$$

Net Capital Outflow:

Net Capital Outflow = Purchase of foreign assets by domestic residents – Purchase of domestic assets by foreigners

$$NCO = NX$$
Net capital outflow = Net exports

Net Exports:

$$NX = X - M$$

Nominal Exchange Rate:

$$e = \frac{P*}{P}$$

Opportunity Cost:

$$Opportunity\ cost\ of\ good\ y = \frac{Sacrifice\ of\ good\ x}{Gain\ in\ good\ y}$$

Price Elasticity of Demand:

$$Price\ elasticity\ of\ demand = \frac{Percentage\ change\ in\ quantity\ demanded}{Percentage\ change\ in\ price}$$

Mid-Point Method:

$$Price\ elasticity\ of\ demand = \frac{(Q_2 - Q_1)/[(Q_2 + Q_1)/2]}{(P_2 - P_1)/[(P_2 + P_1)/2]}$$

$$Price\ elasticity\ of\ demand = \frac{P}{Qd} \times \frac{1}{\frac{\Delta P}{\Delta Qd}}$$

$$Price\ elasticity\ of\ demand = \frac{P}{Qd} \times \frac{dQd}{dP}$$

Price Elasticity of Supply:

$$Price\ elasticity\ of\ supply = \frac{Percentage\ change\ in\ quantity\ supplied}{Percentage\ change\ in\ price}$$

Mid-Point Method:

$$Price\ elasticity\ of\ supply = \frac{(Q_2 - Q_1)/[(Q_2 + Q_1)/2]}{(P_2 - P_1)/[(P_2 + P_1)/2]}$$

$$Price\ elasticity\ of\ supply = \frac{P}{Qs} \times \frac{1}{\frac{\Delta P}{\Delta Qs}}$$

$$Price\ elasticity\ of\ supply = \frac{P}{Qs} \times \frac{dQs}{dP}$$

Production Function (Assuming Two Factor Inputs, Land and Capital):

$Q = f(K,L)$

Productivity:

$$Productivity = \frac{Total\ output}{Units\ of\ the\ factor}$$

Profit:

$Profit = Total\ revenue - Total\ cost\ (\pi = TR - TC)$

$Profit = (P - ATC) \times Q$

Profit Maximizing Output:

where $MC = MR$

Real Exchange Rate:

$$Real\ exchange\ rate = \frac{(Nominal\ exchange\ rate \times Domestic\ price)}{Foreign\ price}$$

$$Real\ exchange\ rate = \left(\frac{e \times P}{P^*}\right)$$

Real GDP:

$$Real\ GDP = \frac{Nominal\ GDP}{GDP\ Deflator}$$

Real Interest Rate:

$Real\ interest\ rate = Nominal\ interest\ rate - Inflation\ rate$

$r_t = i_t - \pi_t$

Real Money Balances:

$$Real\ Money\ Balances = \frac{M}{P}$$

Relative Price:

$$Relative\ price = \frac{Nominal\ Price\ X}{Nominal\ Price\ Y}$$

Real Wage:

$$Real\ Wage = \frac{W}{P}$$

Returns to Scale:

$$Returns\ to\ scale = \frac{\%\Delta\ in\ quantity\ of\ output}{\%\Delta\ in\ quantity\ of\ all\ factor\ inputs}$$

Sacrifice Ratio:

$$Sacrifice\ Ratio = \frac{Euro\ cost\ of\ loss\ of\ production}{Percentage\ change\ in\ inflation}$$

Saving:

$$S = I + NCO$$
$$Saving = Domestic\ investment + Net\ capital\ outflow$$

Shut Down Point:

Shut down if $P < AVC$

Slope of a Demand Curve:

$$Slope = \frac{\Delta P}{\Delta Qd}$$

Taylor Rule:

$r = p + 0.5y + 0.5(p - 2) + 2$

The Demand Function:

$D = f(P_n, P_n \ldots P_{n-1}, Y, T, P, A, E)$

Where:

- P_n = Price
- $P_n \ldots P_{n-1}$ = Prices of other goods (substitutes and complements)
- Y = Incomes (the level and distribution of income)
- T = Tastes and fashions
- P = The level and structure of the population
- A = Advertising
- E = Expectations of consumers

The Equilibrium of the Economy:

$Planned\ S + T + M = Planned\ I + G + X$

The Supply Function:

$S = f(P_n, P_n \ldots P_{n-1}, H, N, F_1 \ldots F_m, E, S_t)$

Where:

- P_n = Price
- $P_n \ldots P_{n-1}$ = Profitability of other goods in production and prices of goods in joint supply
- H = Technology
- N = Natural shocks
- $F_1 \ldots F_m$ = Costs of production
- E = Expectations of producers
- S_f = Social factors

The Least Cost-input Combination:

$$\frac{MP_L}{P_K} = \frac{MP_K}{P_L}$$

The Marginal rate of Substitution:

$$MRS = \frac{Px}{Py}$$

Total Cost:

$Total\ cost = Fixed\ costs + Variable\ cost\ (TC = FC + VC)$

$TC(Q) = VC(Q) + FC$

Total Revenue:

$TR = P \times Q$

Total Surplus:

$Total\ surplus = Value\ to\ buyers - Cost\ to\ sellers$

Unemployment Rate:

$$Unemployment\ rate = \left(\frac{Number\ of\ unemployed}{Labour\ force} \right) \times 100$$

$$Unemployment\ rate = NRU - \alpha(Actual\ Inflation - Expected\ inflation)$$

Value of Marginal Product of Labour:

$VMP_L = P \times MP_L$

Velocity of Circulation:

$$V = \frac{(P \times Y)}{M}$$